# THE WONDERFUL WORLD OF
# TOYS, GAMES & DOLLS
## 1860··1930

Edited by Joseph J. Schroeder, Jr.

Associate Editor, Barbara C. Cohen

DIGEST BOOKS, INC., NORTHFIELD, ILLINOIS

ISBN: 0-695-80219-4     Library of Congress Catalogue Card Number: 77-148521

# Foreword

Toys, games and dolls have occupied an important portion of children's lives since the dawn of humanity. It is the advent of the industrial age and mass production, however, that created children's playthings in sufficient profusion to require their documentation in print. This documentation, in the form of catalogues and ads and illustrations in periodicals, is, like the articles it represents, progressively more difficult to find with increasing age. Prior to the Civil War, it was to all practical purposes non-existant.

*The Wonderful World of Toys, Games and Dolls* is, then, a representative sampling of catalogue pages, advertising and illustration that display the toys, games and dolls of the period from the 1860s through 1930. The materials used have been selected with a two-fold purpose: first, to illustrate the broad evolutionary picture of children's playthings to the casual viewer; and second, to retain sufficient coverage of each period and each type of plaything to be of value to the serious student or collector.

# Introduction

Childhood's playthings never totally lose their fascination, as there are remnants of the child in all of us. There is something about a world in miniature, whether it is in the exquisite artisanship of a "real-as-life" doll, the faultless functioning of a tiny mechanism, or even the caricature of life provided by a paper-maché puppet or cast iron horse, that never quite relinquishes its hold on the human imagination.

The following pages illustrate the evolution of toys in America through reproductions of rare and unusual original catalogues and ads. Insofar as possible these appear in their original form, though some of them have of necessity been slightly reduced in size and/or somewhat edited to conform to our format. Because of the much broader product coverage offered by distributors, most of the book consists of their catalogue pages; in a few cases, notably the early years of the electric train and of the ubiquitous Tootsietoy, we have included some very rare manufacturer's catalogue pages, or ads from periodicals.

With few exceptions the material is presented in chronological order, and each page is identified as to year as well as source. This affords a unique opportunity to examine the diverse ways in which the *Wonderful World of Toys, Games and Dolls* echoes the realities of the full size world around us.

Joseph J. Schroeder Jr.
Glenview, Illinois

*Joseph J. Schroeder, Jr. is the editor of the 1894 Montgomery Ward & Company, 1896 Marshall Field & Company, and 1900 and 1908 Sears, Roebuck & Company replica catalogues. He has authored a number of articles for electronics technical journals and firearms periodicals, and is co-author of the book,* System Mauser, *a history of the Mauser 1896 pistol.*

# Acknowledgements

The success of a book of this type rests largely on the quality of the material from which it is assembled. The following individuals and organizations, through their assistance and through the use of rare materials from their personal collections or from company archives, have all made substantial contributions to *The Wonderful World of Toys, Games and Dolls.*

Mr. and Mrs. William Anderson
George Burke
Loren Godwin
Don La Spaluto
Raymond Melzer
Ken Meyer
Richard Shure
Warren Tingley
Bassett-Lowke (Railways) Ltd.
City Products Corporation (formerly Butler Brothers)
D'Arcy Advertising Company
Montgomery Ward & Company
F.A.O. Schwarz
Tootsietoy (Strombecker)

# Contents

# THE WONDERFUL WORLD OF·

# TOYS, GAMES & DOLLS

# Toys, Games & Dolls

Toys, games and dolls are all of ancient origin. In one form or another all are shown or discussed in the earliest surviving records of all civilized societies, and evidence of their existence is not uncommon in archeologists' digs of pre-historic civilizations. In all societies and in all ages playthings have served a valuable dual function, first as a means of entertainment but more importantly (and perhaps less obviously) that of introducing the child to the realities of the world into which he was growing.

Until fairly recent times the vast majority of children's playthings were home made. At the most elementary level, the child created (and, in fact, still creates) his own playthings out of sticks, pebbles and cast-offs from his elders. Mothers, fathers and grandparents were (and are) another fertile source for original play materials. The existence of a toy making industry as such is a comparatively recent phenomenon, apparently originating in Germany in the 16th Century. Prior to that time the little commercial toy making there was existed solely as a sideline of various artisans, done only by special order for a wealthy parent. Such custom-made playthings were well known to the aristocracies of Egypt, Greece and Rome.

By the late 16th Century the products of the Toymakers Guild of Nuremburg were being distributed across Germany. The individual playthings themselves were still the hand-made products of skilled craftsmen, however, and only the landed and the titled were in a position to buy them. It was not until the coming of the industrial revolution in the early 19th Century, which brought manufactured goods down in price while increasing the living standards of large

numbers of people, that the toy industry as we know it today came into being.

In the United States most of the early toy production was in the larger, wooden outdoor toys—wagons, sleds and the like. It wasn't until the 1860s that commercially manufactured indoor toys began to be widely distributed in this country, and even then these were for the most part European imports. Distributors devoted to the marketing of playthings came into existence at this time and the earliest, F.A.O. Schwarz in New York City (1862), is still probably the largest retail toy-only outlet in the country.

Aiding the growth of the burgeoning toy industry in the latter half of the 19th Century was the introduction of the great mail order houses. Founded in 1872, by 1878 Montgomery Ward & Company was including a few sleds, velocipedes, wagons and hobby horses in its catalogue to tempt the younger set. Each succeeding year saw the addition of another page or two of toys, games and dolls, bringing the Ward's catalogue toy section to over a dozen pages by the end of the next decade. Sears, Roebuck arrived on the mail order scene in the early 1890s, and quickly followed suit.

The wholesale suppliers, those who served the general stores of the frontiers and the small merchants of the rural Midwest, also pushed playthings as a fast moving, high profit product area for their customer's shelves. Butler Brothers, then as now (City Products Corporation) one of the largest "wholesale only" outlets, devoted a good portion of their monthly catalogue *Our Drummer* to an extraordinarily comprehensive array of items designed to gladden boys' and girls' hearts. It should be noted in passing that Butler Brothers, along with their mail order competitors, found it expedient to put their emphasis on toys in the Christmas-oriented fall and early winter catalogues—spring and summer editions carry only a fraction as many listings in this area. Marshall Field & Company was another important wholesale outlet during that period, and their 1892 "Holiday Goods" wholesale catalogue contains what is probably the most attractive toy, game and doll display of its time.

Not all playthings were—or are—designed for children. Some of the most elaborate and beautifully fashioned "toys" that survive from the middle ages are the dolls and doll houses created by the master toymakers of Nuremburg for the collections of wealthy noblemen and merchants. Men share children's enthusiasm for anything mechanical, as evidenced by the number of electric trains "received" by babies, regardless of sex, for their first Christmas.

Before electricity was used to power toy trains, toy steam locomotives were actually *steam powered,* as were a variety of motor launches, steam rollers, cranes and shovels. Some of these were true toys, but many were not. Early Bassett-Lowke catalogues show steam locomotives ranging from a few inches to several feet in length, the latter nearly equalling in complexity the full size prototype and obviously not designed to cope with the instinctive destructive abilities of childhood.

Steam engines as toys date from about 1870, and it appears that the earliest steam-powered toy locomotive was marketed about 10 years later. There is some evidence that doll heads made of ceramic were being made in Philadelphia as early as 1830, and wooden outdoor toys were being produced commercially in this country even earlier. Cast iron became popular as a toy material in the mid 1860s, initially for mechanical banks, though toy banks made of tin were produced here in the 1820s. Visual games and toys have long fascinated children, as demonstrated by the full page of shadow caricatures from *Der Bazar* of 1860 and the great popularity of the magic lantern and similar-type devices following their introduction into the American market at about that same time. Although playing cards, checkers, dominoes and other adult games were of much earlier origin, in the early 1880s Milton Bradley Company achieved rapid success with their introduction of simple, colorful games specifically designed for children. It is remarkable to see how long so many of these have survived with little or no change.

The period covered in the following pages was truly the evolutionary period of the great American toy industry. Despite the rapid increase in number and size of domestic toy manufacturers in the last half of the 19th Century, the market seemed to grow even faster. At mid-century most playthings available domestically were imports, and by 1900 imports still accounted for about 75 cents of every toy dollar spent. The drastic reduction in toy flow from Europe resulting from World War I permitted American manufacturers to catch up with demand and finally achieve domination of the domestic market.

F.A.O. Schwarz

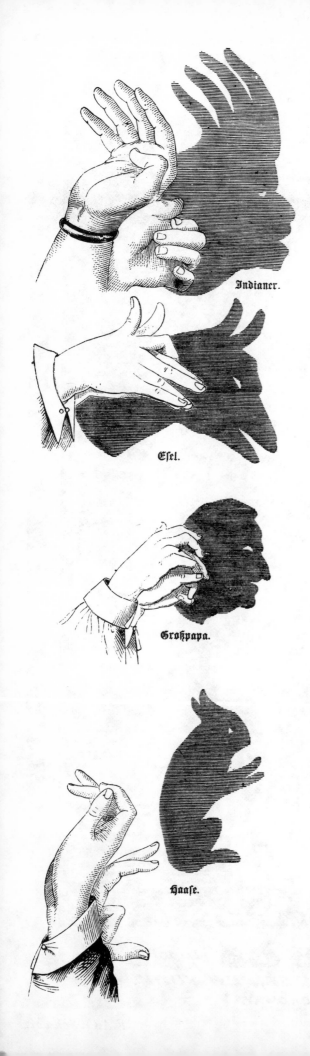

Indianer.

Esel.

Großpapa.

Haase.

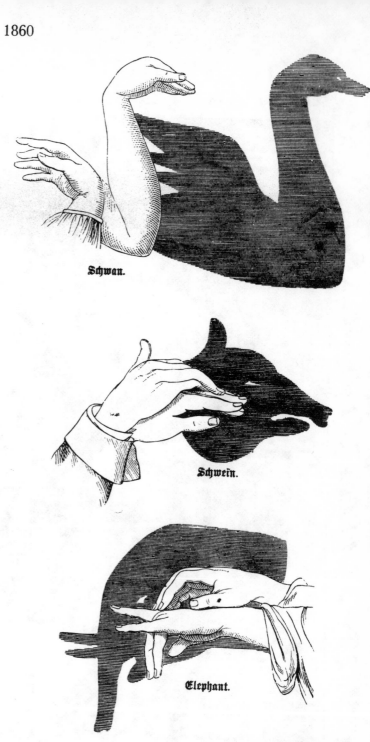

Schwan.

Schwein.

Elephant.

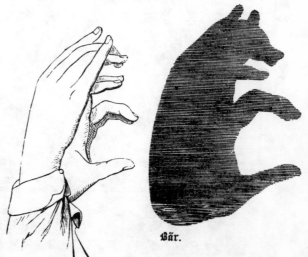

Bär.

**BABY CARRIAGES.**

WITH ALL THE LATEST IMPROVEMENTS AND MADE BY THE
MOST EXPERIENCED WORKMEN. A VARIETY OF
MORE THAN 50 KINDS.

Round top, plain, iron axles, carpet and dash rail, ....... $10 00
Stuffed and lined top, side curtains, carpet and dash rail,. 12 00
Superior finished, plated double joints, ................ 15 00
Rep or Velvet lining, fluted back, ...................... 18 50
Damask or Silk lining, silver-plated double joints,........ 20 00
    with metal front top,...... ...... 22 00
Silk Damask or Satin, best upholstered and trimmed,...... 25 00
    Silk top-lining and Lamps, extra fine,.. ...... 30 00
    CARRIAGE WOOL MATS, AFGHANS, LAMPS, ETC., IN GREAT
VARIETY.

**BOYS' FOOT VELOCIPEDE.**

No. 1. For Boys from 4 to 8 years,.................... $ 7 50
   2.    "    8 " 12   " .................... 9 00
   3    "   12 " 19   " .................... 11 00

**BOYS' WAGON.**

Extra strong with Iron Axles, in 5 sizes,... from $4 50 to $8 00
    Shafts and Poles for Goats, $1 50 extra.
CARTS AND WHEEL-BARROWS, all sizes.
GARDEN TOOLS,..................... from $0 75 to $2 75 @ set

**DOLL CARRIAGE.**

WOOD BODY, finished like Baby Carriages above, 10 kinds,
    from $1 00 to $10 00
WILLOW BODY,............... " 1 00 " 3 50

**Combination NURSERY or BABY CHAIR.**

ROCKING, WALKING AND NECESSARY CHAIR combined,
    at $10 00 and $12 00

**NEW PATENT BABY TENDER.**

Nursery, Walking and Parlor Playing Sledge combined,
    at $8 00 and $10 00

N. B.—NO FAMILY SHOULD BE WITHOUT IT. IT MAKES MOTHERS
AND THEIR BABIES HAPPY.

**SPRING HORSES.**

WOOD PAINTED,.. ..... small, $10 00. medium, $13 00. large, $18 00
SKIN COVERED,......... " 13 50. " 18 00. " 24 00

**LEAPING HORSES.**

In 4 sizes,... ............ ..... $10 00, $13 00, $15 00 and $22 00

**ROCKING HORSES.**

WOOD PAINTED, in 8 sizes,................ from $2 00 to $10 00
SKIN COVERED, in 4 sizes... .. ...........from $10 00 to $16 00

# SPRING CIRCULAR

OF

# F. A. O. SCHWARZ,

## 765 Broadway,

Between 8th and 9th Sts.,

## NEW YORK,

### IMPORTER OF

# TOYS,

## Fancy Goods

AND

# NOVELTIES.

DEPOT FOR BABY CARRIAGES, VELOCIPEDES,
LAWN GAMES AND HOME AMUSEMENTS
IN ENDLESS VARIETY.

**Particular Attention is Called to the Following :**

FIELD CROQUETS, with 4 balls, 4 mallets, etc., a set,  $1 00
   "      full set, 8  "  8   " from $2 50 to 15 00
CARPET AND TABLE CROQUETS, a set,.from $1 00 to $7 50
CHIVALRIE, a new favorite Lawn Game.
BASE BALLS and BATS, FOOT BALLS, PARLOR BALLS.
MAGIC HOOPS, RING TOSS and GRACE HOOPS.
WOOD and STEEL BOWS, ARROWS and STRAW TARGETS.
PARLOR AIR GUNS, best, $5 00.
            PARLOR AIR PISTOLS, $1 75
FISHING TACKLE, HORSE REINS, WHIPS and CANES.
BALLOONS, KITES, and FLYING TOPS.
BATTLEDOORS, JUMPING ROPES, TOPS and MARBLES.
CHIME HOOPS, WITH HANDLE,........from $0 65 to $1 25
STEAMBOATS, propelled by Steam,... from $2 00 to $10 00
STEAM LOCOMOTIVES, with circular track, 4 wheels, $6 00
    "       "     8 wheels, $10 00
STEAM ENGINES,..................from $1 00 to $5 00
SAIL BOATS, in 10 sizes,............. " $0 40 to $5 50
MECHANICAL OARSMAN, to run in water or on floor.
   "    HORSE TRAINER, CHIME BELLS, RACER,
   "    VELOCIPEDE, SWING, SEE-SAW, RIDER,
   "    WALKING DOLL, etc.
   "    DANCER, new and very comical, 1 figure, $2 00
   "    "    improved, 2 " 3 00
NOVELTY CASHIER BANKS, WEATHER HOUSES.
METALLOPHONS and METAL PIANOS, new, from $1 to $20
HOME GYMNASIUM, very complete, in sets or single.
BEEHIVE GAME, new and very amusing. AVILUDE PAR-
CHEESI, CRISPINO, CHANCERY, BAMBOOZLE,
RAILROAD GAME, and many others.

☞ NEW ARTICLES ADDED ALMOST EVERY DAY.

**NOVELTY CARRIAGE.**

CRADLE AND CARRIAGE COMBINED.

No. 1. Willow Body, rep. lined, plain canopy, ........ $18 00
   2.    "    superior work, fringed canopy,.. 20 00
   3.    "    side lining, plated springs and rod, 25 00
   5. Walnut Body, carved, plain canopy, ......... 20 00
   6.    "    side lining, fringed canopy,...... 25 00
   7.    "    plated springs and rod, silk canopy, 30 00

**PORTABLE FOLDING CARRIAGE.**

VERY DESIRABLE FOR TRAVELING, FOR THE COUNTRY OR
LIMITED SPACE.

No. 1. Ash painted, upholstered in enameled cloth,..... $10 00
   2.    "    superior, better ornamented,........ 13 00
   3.    "    upholstered in reps,...... ...... 16 00
   4.    "    "    extra finish. ............ 18 00
   5.    "    extra upholstered in coteline, ... ... 23 00

N. B.—Close Black Tops can be furnished for above at $2 00 extra.

**BOYS' AND GIRLS' HAND PROPELLER."**

WITH FOUR WHEELS, VERY STRONG.

No. 1. For Children, 4 to 8 years, .................... $ 8 50
   2.    "    6 " 10   " .................... 9 00
   3.    "    8 " 12   " .................... 10 00
   4.    "   12 " 18   " .................... 12 00

**BOYS' THREE WHEEL PROPELLERS,**

WITH HORSEHEAD, at $4.00, $4.50, $5.00.

**CHAIR ROCKER.**

A DELIGHTFUL ARTICLE FOR CHILDREN FROM 1 TO 4 YEARS.

No. 1. Plain single Horsehead, ................$2 00
   2. Round rim, single Horsehead, ................ 2 75
   3. Uphol. in Enameled Cloth, front strap, double head, 4 00
   4. Upholstered in Rep,    "    "    4 50

**SHOO-FLY ROCKERS WITH TABLE TRAY,**

at $3 50 and $4 00.

**COLDWELL'S PATENT BABY JUMPER.**

Oakwood, $4 50. Walnut, $5 00.

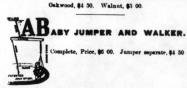

**ABABY JUMPER AND WALKER.**

Complete, Price, $6 00. Jumper separate, $4 50

**DOORWAY SWINGS with safe enclosure.**

Very strong Walnut, $2 50.

**PATENT SELF-OPERATING SWINGS.**

Plain, $3 00. Chair Seat, $3 50.

## Rifle Air Pistol.

This "air gun," or as it is called, "Rifle Air Pistol," is simple in construction, can be easily taken apart, is made entirely of metal, and therefore not liable to get out of order. As its name indicates, *air* and not *powder* is the projecting force; the air is compressed in the tube very simply and easily It takes but the fraction of a second to do it. By this compressed air a steel dart is projected with such force as to carry it a distance of fifty feet with perfect accuracy. No loud explosion follows, and the instrument is therefore as pleasant and gratifying for ladies to use as for gentlemen.

This pistol can be lengthened into a rifle, simply by attaching a skeleton stock, that accompanies it. As a parlor game or amusement, it has proved very popular and attractive. There is no expense of ammunition or of caps in its use. It shoots with perfect accuracy, and is as free from anything that will soil hands or garments, as the games of parlor croquet, or ring toss.

This Air gun is handsomely finished; the air chamber and a portion of the breach is black enameled, and the skeleton stock and barrel silver plated. It is put up in a neat box, with three darts, three targets, and full directions.

## A Pocket Telescope.

We will not guarantee that the sun will condescend to show his spots through this little Telescope, but after dropping its high sounding name, and calling it a boy's **Spy Glass**, we *will* guarantee that it will show a good many spots that a boy's eye could not clearly see without it. The cylinder is of brass, neatly painted, and so is its bright extension tube. Its length when fully extended, is seven inches — when closed, four. A quiet and very pleasant pocket companion, and a much more respectable "eye-opener" than some we could name!

## The Toy Cannon.

This pretty toy is made of wood well finished, and mounted on wheels. The projecting force is a strong spring within the centre of the gun. The Cannon is about eight inches in length. Several wooden balls and a set of "Nine Pins," accompany it. These balls can be thrown twenty-five or thirty feet, and with a little practice the "Pins" can be quite successfully "bombarded" at that distance.

## Our Family Jig Saw.

Among the thousands interested in Bracket or Jig Sawing, there are many inquiring for a foot-power machine, low priced yet practical. We have aimed to meet this want, and we feel quite sure this new Saw will do it. It is made entirely of iron, handsomely finished, and runs with great rapidity and ease. It swings fifteen inches, and is capable of doing large and heavy work. With it you can saw through a two-inch plank. In almost any town there can be bought for a dollar or two, cast-off sewing machine tables with wheel and treadle attached. This Jig Saw placed upon such a table is equal to any $15 machine. They can also be used upon any sewing machine without doing it injury. Boys can, without much difficulty, make a good foot power themselves with which to run the Saw.

## Parlor Air Pistol.

This Air Pistol works on the same principle as the Air Rifle, which we offered last year. It is about six inches long, is made of the best material, and shoots with great accuracy a distance of many yards. It is just the thing for pistol practice, as there is no danger, and no expense for ammunition.

## Two Steam Engines.

We offer two Miniature Steam Engines, for one new subscriber. They are perfect machines, — *bona fide* Engines. Each one is carefully made, its parts nicely adjusted, and so constructed that they can be taken apart for examination, and put together again by almost any lad of nine years. There is not the slightest danger in using them, as they cannot burst.

## A Two Dollar Steam Engine, No. 2.

This is a double cylinder, double acting Steam Engine. It has four times the power, and runs four times longer than the dollar Engine that we offer in another column.

## The Horizontal Steam Engine, No. 3.

This is acknowledged the prettiest toy of the kind yet invented. It has a heavy brass boiler, a safety valve, a steam chest, one inch stroke, and makes more than 1,000 revolutions a minute. A perfect machine.

## A Massasoit Steel Bow.

An article published in the COMPANION, (April 29,) entitled the "Bow and Arrow Club" has excited enthusiasm among some of our readers on the subject of *Archery*. Good results, we trust, may come from it, for the practice of Archery cannot be too highly recommended, as it combines healthy, invigorating exercise with amusement. It is also a sport in which the girls can successfully compete with their brothers for the championship. By a special arrangement we are able to offer for only one new name this beautiful STEEL BOW. It is about three feet long, handsomely finished, and durable. It will send an arrow a long distance with great accuracy.

## A Toy Swing and Doll.

This Premium is designed for the little folks, and we are quite sure it will please them, too. The frame is 8x10½ inches, made of Black Walnut, and nicely finished. The seat of the swing is so constructed that when Miss Dolly (who is dressed in her best gown) is placed on her little throne and gently started, she will swing some moments, very much to the delight of all little people who may see her graceful movements.

## Wax Doll.

We think the eyes of a good many little girls will sparkle when they see this charming Wax Doll among our Premiums. It is about 12 inches in length, has *movable* eyes, which close when put in its "little bed." It has also a fine head of hair, of which it may well be proud. We do not send the Doll dressed.

## A Three Dollar Microscope.

This instrument is in itself a wonder of mechanical skill, and shows the wonders of nature in such an admirable and satisfactory manner, that we wish it might be owned by every boy and girl who takes an interest in natural history, and by every person who is to spend a summer vacation in the country.

The body of the instrument is of brass, beautifully finished. Its height, when not extended, is three inches. Its parts are adjusted as in all ordinary microscopes, and its mechanism is perfect. No one can fail to be delighted with it. It is sufficiently small to be carried in the pocket, and yet its magnifying power is not far from 100 diameters, so that an object less in size than the head of the smallest pin is made to appear through its lens nearly an inch and a half in diameter. It shows the finest points, as well as the colors and shadings of an object, with remarkable perfectness and distinctness. By it a drop of stagnant water is made to reveal the strange creatures that inhabit it, and the leaf of a plant becomes an insect world.

The beauty and simplicity of this instrument adapt it to general use. It is packed in a small mahogany case. One mounted object is given with it, also two glass slips and a pair of brass forceps. The case is fitted to serve as the standard of the instrument.

## Our Dragon Kite.

We have recently invented a kite, which we shall call the Dragon Kite. Its size when ready for flying is 40x25 inches. It is made adjustable, so that it can be taken apart and put together in a short time. The paper with which it is covered is red, and is ornamented with the picture of a Dragon, similar to those found on many of the Japanese kites. With the Kite we send several hundred feet of strong twine; also a quantity of tissue paper (assorted colors) with which to make the Bobs and Tassels. We also send several large sheets of *Red Dragon* Paper, so that in case you tear one you will have others with which to replace it. We send also directions for putting the Kite together. It will be safely packed in a strong box.

## Package for School Use.

This contains a Box of Crayon Pencils, in which are six Pencils of different colors; a Cushman's Magic Ink Extractor and Lead Eraser, three inches in length, the Extractor being in one end, and the Eraser in the other. Its use is to remove ink stains from the fingers, or from linen or other fabric if desired — a very useful article; a neat Enameled Penholder, two Lead Pencils, one a tablet pencil, the other plain; a patent Pencil Point Protector; a metallic Book Mark; a Sponge; six golden colored Pens; six nice Falcon Pens and six Common Pens, also a Box of Paints.

## Package for School Use, No. 2.

This useful Package consists of a beautiful Cocoa-wood Pocket Ink-stand, which can when filled be carried with perfect safety. A Box-wood 8-inch School Ruler, a Writing-Book, a Drawing-Book, and a fine Composition or Exercise-Book.

## An Amusing Game.

This is a box of **Wooden Jack-Straws**, and consists of plain sticks or straws, with a large number of other pieces of various shapes, such as guns, lances, arrows, &c. It is said that light wood Jack-Straws are superior to any others made. Directions for playing are sent with the game. Also, in the box will be enclosed the curious Magnetic Fish, a Metallic Book-Mark, and a Pretty Ivory Photograph Charm.

## Chivalrie.

This beautiful Lawn Game is regarded by all who have learned to play it as being one of the most desirable and fascinating Lawn Games ever invented. By a special arrangement we can offer it as a Premium to our subscribers. Send a 3-cent stamp for an illustrated catalogue, containing description of the set, with rules, &c.

## A Box of Wooden Puzzles.

This contains three Wooden Puzzles, all of them ingenious and difficult. They are the White Wood Block Puzzle, — the Star Puzzle, of black wall nut, — the Carrol Puzzle. For boys, or persons who enjoy trying to solve the mysteries of block puzzles, this box should have great attractions.

## The "Florence Spring Skate."

These beautiful "Spring Skates" have highly polished, forged steel runners, with blued steel plates and clamp. The sole clamps are entirely sufficient of themselves to hold the Skate firmly to the sole of the boot, the strap being added to brace the foot closely to both the boot and the Skate. Sizes from 8 to 11½ inches.

## Bradley's Patent Croquet Set.

We again offer, as a Premium, this favorite Croquet Set, which gave such universal satisfaction last year. We have received scores of letters from the hundreds who obtained it, and in every case they speak of it in the highest praise. Its advantages over other Croquet Sets consist chiefly in the patent socket bridges (see cut) and the improved mallets and balls. The sockets are wooden pins, pointed at one one end, so that they may be easily driven into the ground. Into these the ends of the bridges are placed. The bridges are thus held firmly, and can be readily taken from the ground and replaced at pleasure. When in position they cannot be knocked out of place, as when simply the points are inserted in the ground. The mallets and balls are made of the best Northern rock maple, and contain eight of each. Each set is packed in a neat chestnut box, and is accompanied by Prof. Rover's Croquet Manual.

FIG. 1.   FIG. 2.

FIG. 1 represents the usual appearance of the socket bridge when in use in whatever soil it may be placed. FIG. 2 will be recognized by all as the general condition of the ordinary bridge in a soft or sandy soil.

The price of this Croquet Set is $5.

## The Caxton Self-Inking Printing Press.

This Press is thoroughly built, simple and strong. It has four screws in the back of the bed for adjustment of impression. Two rollers pass entirely over the form twice at each impression, and a revolving disc insures good distribution; and for printing cards, tags, circulars, &c., it has no equal. Size inside of chase 4x6 inches.

## A Powerful Magnet.

Every boy and girl, we think, would be pleased to become the owner of this beautiful Magnet. It is six inches in length, finely finished, and is a source of great "attraction."

# Schwarz' Toy Bazaars,

## 765 Broadway, bet. 8th & 9th St.,
## 1159 Broadway, cor. 27th St., NEW-YORK.

Merry Christmas!!

Happy New-Year!!

# The Grand Christmas Exhibition

AT

# SANTA-CLAUS HEAD-QUARTERS,

### NOW OPEN.

COMPRISING ALL THE LATEST AND RAREST NOVELTIES IN

## Fancy Goods, TOYS, DOLLS and Games,

Personally selected in Europe by our Mr. F. A. O. Schwarz.

At no previous time have we imported SO LARGE and ATTRACTIVE a variety of DESIRABLE GOODS at

## *EXCEEDINGLY LOW PRICES.*

The **DOLL DEPARTMENT** this season is unexceptionally large and handsome, and particular attention is invited to the many beautiful **Dressed Dolls and Dolls with complete Trousseaux** designed by our special Modiste in Paris, **Model Wax Dolls** with natural hair, **Crying Baby Dolls, Walking and Talking Dolls**, and the so much favored **Indestructible Jointed Dolls**.

To avoid the usual inconvenience at Christmas time, we advise all

 TO MAKE THEIR PURCHASES EARLY

## Selected Goods can be laid aside until Christmas, if desired.

Very Respectfully,

|  |  |
|---|---|
| **Stores:** { NEW YORK:—765 Broadway. <br> " 1159 Broadway. <br> PHILADELPHIA:—1006 Chestnut St. <br> BALTIMORE:—211 W. Baltimore St. <br> BOSTON:—497 & 499 Washington St. | **F. A. O. SCHWARZ,** <br> *MANUFACTURER AND IMPORTER,* <br> **765 Broadway, bet. 8th & 9th Street,** <br> **1159 Broadway, cor. 27th Street.** |

*F.A.O. Schwarz*

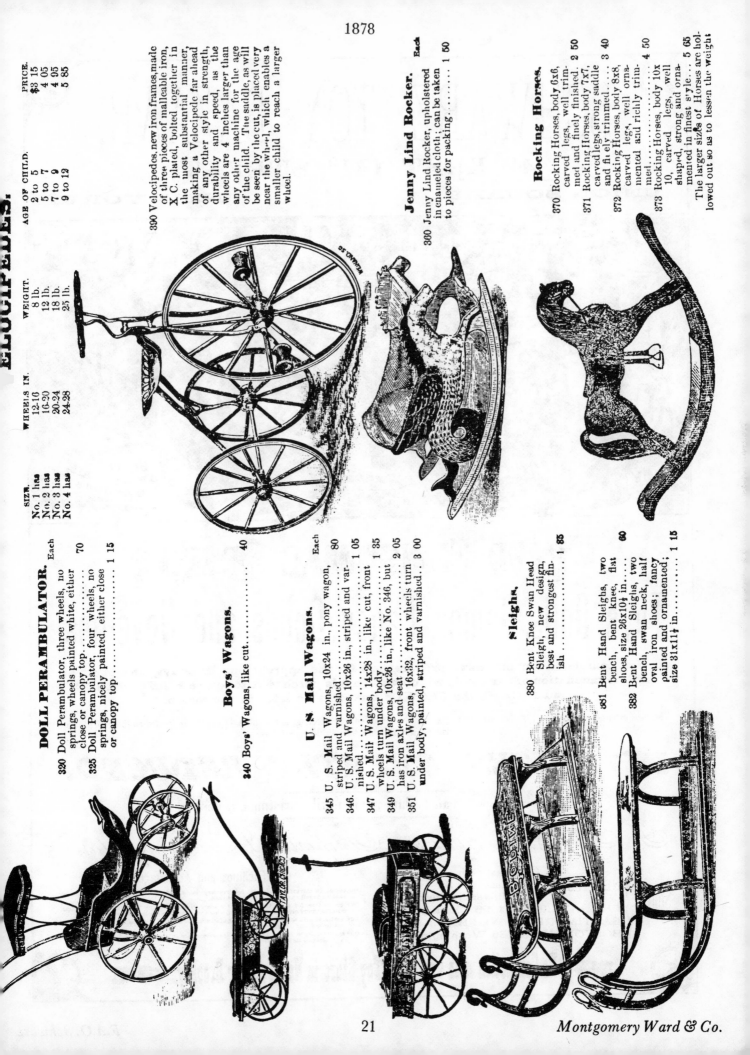

# VELOCIPEDES.

| AGE OF CHILD. | PRICE. |
| --- | --- |
| 2 to 5 | $3 15 |
| 5 to 7 | 4 05 |
| 7 to 9 | 4 95 |
| 9 to 12 | 5 85 |

390 Velocipedes, new iron frames, made of three pieces of malleable iron, X. C. plated, bolted together in the most substantial manner, making a Velocipede far ahead of any other style in strength, durability and speed as the wheels are 4 inches larger than any other machine for the age of the child. The saddle, as will be seen by the cut, is placed very near the wheel, which enables a smaller child to reach a larger wheel.

| WEIGHT. | WHEELS IN. |
| --- | --- |
| 8 lb. | 12-16 |
| 12 lb. | 16-20 |
| 18 lb. | 20-24 |
| 25 lb. | 24-28 |

| SIZE. | |
| --- | --- |
| No. 1 has | 12-16 |
| No. 2 has | 16-20 |
| No. 3 has | 20-24 |
| No. 4 has | 24-28 |

## Jenny Lind Rocker. Each

360 Jenny Lind Rocker, upholstered in enameled cloth; can be taken to pieces for packing.......... 1 50

## Rocking Horses.

370 Rocking Horses, body 6x6, carved legs, well trimmed and finely finished. 2 50
371 Rocking Horses, body 7x7, carved legs, strong saddle and finely trimmed... 3 40
372 Rocking Horses, body 8x8, carved legs, well ornamented and richly trimmed... 4 50
373 Rocking Horses, body 10x10, carved legs, well shaped, strong and ornamented in finest style... 5 65
The larger sizes of Horses are hollowed out so as to lessen the weight

## DOLL PERAMBULATOR. Each

320 Doll Perambulator, three wheels, no springs, wheels painted white, either close or canopy top...... 70
325 Doll Perambulator, four wheels, no springs, nicely painted, either close or canopy top........ 1 15

## Boys' Wagons.

340 Boys' Wagons, like cut......... 40

## U. S. Mail Wagons. Each

345 U. S. Mail Wagons, 10x24 in., pony wagon, striped and varnished........ 80
346 U. S. Mail Wagons, 10x26 in., striped and varnished... 1 05
347 U. S. Mail Wagons, 14x28 in., like cut, front wheels turn under body... 1 35
349 U. S. Mail Wagons, 10x26 in., like No. 346, but has iron axles and seat... 2 05
351 U. S. Mail Wagons, 16x32, front wheels turn under body, painted, striped and varnished.. 3 00

## Sleighs.

380 Bent Knee Swan Head Sleigh, new design, best and strongest finish... 1 85
381 Bent Hand Sleighs, two bench, bent knee, flat shoes, size 26x10½ in.... 60
382 Bent Hand Sleighs, two bench, swan neck, half oval iron shoes; fancy painted and ornamented; size 31x11½ in........ 1 15

# SCHWARZ' TOY BAZAAR,

## 42 EAST 14TH STREET,

UNION SQUARE,

NEW YORK.

FROM SCHWARZ'S TOY BAZAAR, Santa Claus Headquarters.

# GRAND CHRISTMAS OPENING

OF

# Toys, Dolls, Games, Fancy Goods and Novelties.

**Having completed our extensive preparations for the approaching Holidays, we suggest an early examination of our Stock, which will enable purchasers to secure FIRST CHOICE and ESCAPE the CROWDS unavoidable later in the season.**

The new extension through to 13th St., will greatly add to the convenience in selecting, as the entire display is now located on the ground floor, covering a space of more than 8000 square feet.

☞ *PRICES GREATLY REDUCED!*

Selected Goods can be laid aside until Christmas, if desired.

*F. A. O. Schwarz, Importer & Manufacturer,*

Stores:
NEW YORK, { 42 East 14th St.
43 East 13th St.
77 University Place.
PHILADELPHIA, 1006 Chestnut St.
BALTIMORE, 211 West Baltimore St.
BOSTON, 484 & 486 Washington St.

**Our Facilities and Advantages:**

Importing in extensive quantities for *four large stores*, and purchasing for *cash* only, we are enabled to sell our goods at the *lowest rates*.

Our connection for more than *twenty-five years* with the leading European and American manufacturers gives us *great facilities*, which we devote to the *benefit of our customers*.

Our contracts with some of the best manufacturers in Europe procure for us many *novelties* not to be found elsewhere.

Our agents in Paris, Berlin, Vienna and Nüremberg, are instructed to send us by every steamer *the latest novelties*.

 ☞ **No Connection with any other Toy Store in New York or Brooklyn.** ☜

*F.A.O. Schwarz*

# TOYS AND NOVELTIES

## Toy Steam Engines.

### "THE HERO."

New design, brass boiler, complete with lamp, etc., and can be run by a child, with no possibility of danger. Great speed can be attained with this engine, which is the largest yet made for anything like the price we ask. Similar to cut. Price each 40c.; per dozen, $4.30. Extra by mail, 5c.

13745 THE HERO.

### THE "AJAX.'

Each engine carefully packed in a wood box complete with lamp, etc. A sensible, practical, instructive toy. Warranted to work perfectly. Absolutely safe. Brass boiler, with copper band, iron stand, etc. Price each, 90c. Per dozen, $9.70. Extra by mail, 16c.

13747 THE "AJAX" STEAM ENGINE.

## The "Empire" Walking Beam Steam Engine.

13748 A Horizontal Engine, boiler and stand similar to the "Ajax," except is better finished, with vertical cylinder, walking beam and fly wheel. An entirely new model, perfect in operation and capable of running at a high rate of speed. Every engine tested before leaving factory and warranted to work. Price each $2 00 Extra by mail, 20c.

## Toy Machinery.

Can be operated by either our Empire, Ajax or Hero steam engines.

| | | Each. |
|---|---|---|
| 13752 | Circular Saw and Table | $0 45 |
| 13753 | Turning Lathe | 55 |
| 13754 | Grindstone | 35 |
| 13755 | Cone Pulley to connect with lathe | 20 |
| 13756 | Hangers for Shafting | 10 |
| 13757 | Pulleys, ½ to 2½ in. in diameter | 03 |

## Tin Trumpets.

Painted and striped, with porcelain mouth pieces. (Will not send Trumpets by mail.)

| | | | Each. | Per doz. |
|---|---|---|---|---|
| 13760 | 4 in. long | | 04 | 40 |
| 13761 | 6 " " | | 05 | 50 |
| 13762 | 8 " " | | 06 | 60 |
| 13763 | 10 " " | | 07 | 70 |
| 13764 | 12 " " | | 10 | 1 00 |
| 13765 | 14 " " | | 14 | 1 50 |

## Toy Iron Stoves.

Iron Stoves with tea and dish kettle and wash boiler.
(Will not send by mail, as they are liable to be damaged.)

| | Height. | Length. | Width. | Each. | Per doz. |
|---|---|---|---|---|---|
| 13769 | 3¾ in. | 4 in. | 2¾ in. | $0 60 | $6 50 |
| 13770 | 4 in. | 6 in. | 3¾ in. | 90 | 9 75 |
| 13771 | 6¼ in. | 7 in. | 4 in. | 1 25 | 14 00 |

## Marbles.

| | | Per sack. |
|---|---|---|
| 13775 | Common (Mibs), 1000 in sack | $0 90 |
| | (Do not sell less than a sack.) | |

| | | Per box. |
|---|---|---|
| 13777 | Painted China, (100 in box)— | |
| | No. 00 | $0 10 |
| | No. 0 | 12 |
| | No. 1 | 15 |
| | No. 2 | 20 |
| | Per dozen, assorted | 5 |
| 13778 | Imitation Agate, (100 in box)— | |
| | No. 0 | 30 |
| | No. 1 | 35 |
| | No. 2 | 50 |
| | No. 3 | 65 |
| | Per dozen, assorted | 8 |
| 13779 | Glass, A1 quality, (100 in box)— | |
| | No. 1 | 30 |
| | No. 2 | 35 |
| | No. 3 | 40 |
| | No. 4 | 85 |
| | Per dozen, assorted | 8 |
| 13780 | Polished Japan, or Cloudies, (100 in box)— | |
| | No. 0 | 25 |
| | No. 1 | 35 |
| | No. 2 | 45 |
| | No. 3 | 65 |
| | Per dozen, assorted | 8 |
| 13781 | Brandies, (100 in box)— | |
| | No. 0 | 30 |
| | No. 1 | 35 |
| | No. 2 | 45 |
| | No. 3 | 60 |
| | Per dozen, assorted | 8 |

## Tin Toys--Miscellaneous.

### (Not illustrated.)

Our Tin Toys are all strongly made and finely painted.
(Will not send by mail, as they are liable to be damaged.)

| 13789 | Tin Dust Pans, 6½ in. wide, with covers, each 12c., per doz | $1 10 |
|---|---|---|
| 13791 | Tin Horses on Wheels, 6½ in. long, each 15c., per doz | 1 50 |
| 13792 | Tin Horses on Wheels, 5½ in. long, with rider, each 19c., per doz | 2 00 |
| 13794 | Tin Express Wagons, with 1 horse, entire length, 13 in., each 25c., per doz | 2 50 |
| 13795 | Tin Dump Carts, 1 horse, length 12½ in., each 25c., per doz | 2 50 |
| 13796 | Tin Milk Wagons, 1 horse and gong, length 12 in., each 30c., per doz | 3 20 |

## Magnets.

13798 Horse Shoe Magnets, superior quality.
Length—
2 in. 2½in. 3 in. 4 in. 5 in. 8in. 10 in.
Price each—
14c. 18c. 22c. 40c. 60c. $1.35 $2.75.
13799 Loadstone or Natural Magnet 50c., 75c. and $1.00, according to size of piece.

## Metallophones.

This Musical Instrument is of superior quality in tone and finish. Frame is glued together, and keys are finished in gold bronze and tacked to frame. One in a box with mallets ready for use.

| | | Each. | Per doz. |
|---|---|---|---|
| 13800 | Metallophones, 12 notes | $0 25 | $2 70 |
| 13801 | Metallophones, 22 notes | 52 | 5 60 |

## Turtle Sleeve Buttons.

13803 The latest novelty. Useful and ornamental. Neatly made, mounted in white metal, and heavily silver plated. The turtle always "on the move."

| Per pair | $0 40 |
|---|---|
| Per dozen pairs | 4 30 |

## Kaleidoscopes.

Object tubes filled with Aniline colors, superior in finish and brilliancy to those formerly manufactured.
13804 Kaleidoscopes, round, 8 in. high, each 15c., per doz. $1 60

## Rattles and Whistles.

| 13805 | Common | $0 02 |
|---|---|---|
| 15806 | Fancy | 03 |

## Tin Boats.

(Not safe to send by mail.)

The very best made; all sharp corners avoided.
13808 Row Boats, will float in water, 12 in. long, each 12c., per doz. $1 25
13809 Tin Steamboats, patented, will float or to draw, 17 in. long, each 48c., per doz. 4 75
13810 Tin Steamboat, patented, 20½ in. long, will float or to draw, "Jumbo" large and fine, each $1.00; per doz. 10 50

## Toy Steamboats

(Mailable.)

13811 The smallest and most wonderful little steamer ever made, run by a real engine, only 9 inches long. Hull, boiler, smoke-stack and lamp of bright brass. Engine ¼ in. bore by 5-16 stroke. Will run about 15 minutes. Price, each in neat wooden box $1 25
13812 Same, 13 in. long, will run about 20 minutes, in neat wooden box, each 2 60
Extra, by mail, each 20c.

## Universal Pocket Puzzle.

13608 Each, 8 cents.
Per doz., 75 cents.
Postpaid, each 10c.

### A, B, C, Jack Straws.

13610 The old game improved, furnishing pastime for both parent and child. A very interesting game. Each 23 cents. Per dozen, $2.30.

13608.

## Calendar Match Safes.

PATENTED.

13347.

13347 Nickel Match Safe, a convenient pocket case, combining a perpetual calendar and 3-inch rule; the rule is marked off into eighths, sixteenths and thirty-seconds, as per cut, each 16c.; per dozen, $1.70.

## Iron Banks.

13475 Log Cabin Bank (C T E); size, 2 in. high, 3½ inches long, and 3 in. wide, finished in assorted rustic colors; weight, 15 oz.; each, 11c.; per dozen _____ $1 20

13477 Iron Bank Safes (C H) with key, painted in solid colors, panels and doors decorated in contrasting colors; size, 3 inches high, 2¼ wide and 2½ deep; weight, 10 oz.; each, 9c.; per dozen _____ 1 00

13480 Guarantee Bank Safe (H C) with lock and key, new design and construction, and is beautif'ly painted in colors and decorated with pictures; size, 4 in. high, 2¾ in. wide, 3½ inches deep; weight, 20 ounces. Each, 30c.; per doz__ $3 25

13480.

13482 Iron Safe, with lock and key, same style as No. 13480; size 4¼ inches high, 3½ inches wide, and 3½ in. deep; weight, 31 ounces. Each, 45c.; per dozen _____ 4 90

## Combination Safe.

13484 This is something new, and is hardly a toy. Impossible to open it unless you have the combination. A good, large, substantial bank in every particular. Similar in shape to No. 13480, but better finished. Each _____ $0 75

### Combination Safe—continued.

13490 Pavilion Iron Bank (CX C); size, 3½ in. high, 3½ wide, 2¼ deep; painted in fancy colors; weight 6 oz. Each, 10c.; per doz., $1.10.

13492 Ornamental Iron Bank (CXT) similar to cut 13490, finished in solid colors, relieved with bronze or fancy colors; size, 3 inches high, 3 wide, 2 deep; weight, 5¼ ounces. Each, 8c.; per doz _____ $0 88

13495

13495 Uncle Tom Iron Bank (CXP). This is a comical and amusing bank; by pressing a button at back of neck the eyes roll up and the tongue is thrust out for coin, which placed upon it, is drawn in and deposited in the vault; size, 5¼ in. high, 4 wide and 3¼ deep; each, 45c.; per doz., $4.87.

13498

13498 Confectionery Bank (CXR) size, 8 in. high, 4 wide and 4½ deep; weight, 64 ozs. New mechanical, novel and interesting toy. Deposit coin in the slot and press the knob in front of the counter and the saleswoman will give you the equivalent in candy. Beautifully decorated in colors, each 75c.; per dozen, $8.55.

13501

### Combination Safe—continued.

13501 Iron Organ Bank (CXO) elegantly finished, large chime of bells, dancing figures revolve when the handle is turned, the monkey deposits the coin in the vault and politely raises his hat; size 8½ inches high, 5¼ wide, and 3¼ deep; each, $1.00; per dozen _____ $10 50

## Chimes.

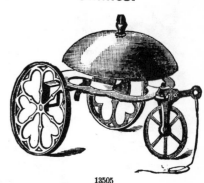

13505

13505 Size 5¼ in. long, 4 high, 3¼ wide; gong, 3 in. in diameter; the gong gives a very musical sound, (HB) each, 23c.; per dozen _____ $2 50

13508 Monkey Chimes' Chariot, well made of iron. This is a new and highly amusing toy for children. When the carriage is drawn along by a string, the monkey beats upon the gong with his hands alternately. Beautifully decorated, size, 5 inches high, 6½ inches long, 3¼ inches wide; weight, 24 ounces. Each, 50c.; per dozen _____ $5 50 This is not a bank.

13508

13511 Liberty Chime (CEX,) size 7¼ in. long, 5¼ wide, 6¼ high. This toy is elegantly painted and bronzed in colors; when the chariot is drawn along by the string, the gong is struck, giving forth a musical sound, and the figure waves the flag of our nation. Each, $1.00; per dozen _____ $10 50

*₊* In ordering goods from our Catalogue, be sure ALWAYS to give the name of article wanted and price. Catalogue number alone is not always sufficient.

*₊* All our goods are sold in any quantity to suit the purchaser, unless we distinctly state otherwise.

Montgomery Ward & Co.

## A New Game of Marbles. "TIVOLI."

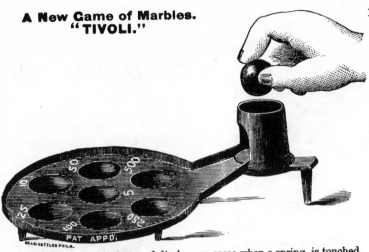

HELE&SATTLER PHILA.
PAT APP'D.

balances marble on his feet, and discharges same when a spring is touched. and better finished than No. 13515. Price each, 18c.; per dozen, $1.85.

## Toy Scales.

13517.

inches high, 2½ inches wide. Delicately adjusted, with a set of correct weights accompanying each scale. Nicely finished; one in a box. Each, 20c.; per dozen, $2.00.

## All-Iron Penny Toys.

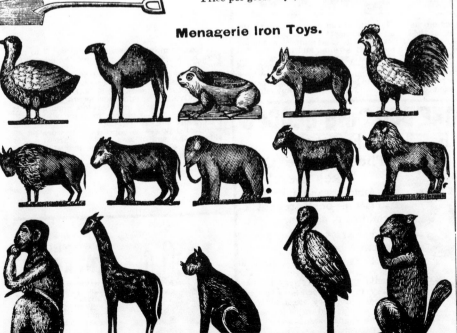

13518½ Three pieces to a set. Size, 4¾ inches long, coppered.
Price per set of 3 ----------------------------------- $0 03
Price per dozen sets----------------------------- 25
Price per gross toys, assorted---------------- 80

## Menagerie Iron Toys.

13519 Menagerie Coppered Iron Toys. Sizes, 1 to 2¾ inches. An endless fund of amusement for children. 24 pieces to the set, all different, brightly coppered. Weight, 19 ounces per set, assorted. Per set of 24 pieces, 16c.; per gross----------------$0 80

13515 Size, 5½ inches long, 3 inches wide and 1¾ inches high. This is a simple and amusing game for children, and can be played either in or out of doors. It is handsomely bronzed, with the hollows painted in assorted colors. Price each, with marble, 10c.; per doz., $1.00.
13516 Tivoli Game. Same as 13515, but has acrobat who balances marble on his feet, and discharges same when a spring is touched. This toy is larger

13517 Size, without scoop, 4½ inches long, 1½ inches high, 2 inches wide. Scoop, 3¼x2 inches. Nicely painted and bronzed, and has 3 coppered weights. Price each, 10c.; per dozen, $1.00.
13518 The "Gem" Toy Scales, 4½ inches long, 3

## Toy Hatchets.

13525 Small Hatchets, all iron, 8 inches long. Japanned and polished; weight, 5¼ oz.; each, 5c.; per doz., 55c.

## Child's Sad Irons.

13550 Stands, coppered irons, japanned and polished; size of irons 1⅜ inch, stand 3 inches, weight 3 ounces; per set of two pieces, 4c.; per dozen sets, 40c.

13552.

13552 Same as 13550; size iron 2¼ in., stand 3½ in., weight 4½ oz. Per set of two pieces, 5c.; per dozen sets, 50c.
13553 Same as 13550; size iron, 2¾, stand 5 in.; weight 8 ounces; iron and stand, 7c.; per dozen sets, 75c.
13555 Same style as 13550; size iron, 3½ in., stands 5¼ in.; weight 13 oz.; iron and stand 11c.; per dozen sets, $1.20.

13558 Sad Irons and Stand: two irons, with japanned and polished copper stand; per set of 3 pieces, weight 5 oz., 6c.; per dozen sets, 65c.

13560 Sad Irons and Stand, larger, w't, 9 oz.; per set of three pieces, 9c.; per dozen sets, 96c.

## The Duplex Spring Roller Spring.

**Always mention size of shoe worn.**

Nearly a pound lighter than any skate in the market.

No rubber. No breakage of parts. No troublesome keys. The wheels are always in track.

All the parts of this skate are interchangeable. This is the latest thing out in Roller Skates, and we claim it to be the simplest, cheapest and most reliable of any skate offered to the public.

Can turn a shorter circle than any skate made.

If not satisfactory, send them back, and we will refund your money.

13655.

13654 RINK SKATE.—Has *toe and heel straps*, foot board and frame, bright tinned finish; springs nicely nickeled. Price per pair only $2.40; per dozen pairs $26.50.
13655 RINK CLUB SKATE (see cut), same as Rink Skate, with toe clamp in place of toe strap, in all other respects the same. The toe clamps are perfect, working by a thumb screw, positive in action, no troublesome keys. Price per pair $3.00. Per dozen pairs $32.00.
Special rates to rinks.

*Montgomery Ward & Co.*

# Child's Decorated China Tea Set.

Given for only 20 trial subscribers at 10 cents each; or, for only 10 trial subscriptions and 50 cents extra in cash.

The handsomest toy set we have ever given, consists of 23 pieces handsomely decorated in gold, **Tea Pot, Sugar Bowl, Cream Pitcher, 6 Plates and 6 Cups and Saucers.** Plates are 2¾ inches in diameter, other pieces in proportion. Size of set can be judged accordingly. The shape is new and unique, made in Germany for us and imported expressly for the LADIES' HOME JOURNAL little ones. By having them made in large quantities we can afford to sell them at a low price, only $1.00, carefully packed in a strong wooden box and can be sent to any address with safety.

Should be sent by express, which will be but a trifle to any point east of Rocky Mountains, **can** be sent by mail to distant points for 50 cents extra.

## A REAL STEAMBOAT
### A SPLENDID PREMIUM FOR THE BOYS.

This is a real steamboat, 11 inches long, having a brass boiler, and steam engine to work the screw. Steam is made by placing a small lamp under the boiler, and filling the boiler with water. Will run half an hour without refilling. Perfectly safe; will not explode. Directions accompany each boat. The hull is of metal, handsomely painted. Has a nice cloth awning, and gaily painted flag floating at the stern. A fine model, sharp bows, a fast sailer. Great fun in playing ocean steamer. It will sail across the pond without any string to keep it from going astray. Your friend on the other side will turn it back again. You can call it a "mail" steamer by writing notes back and forth and sending them by the steamer safely tucked away in the hold. Will take light freight such as a pen-knife, or marble. We will sell this boat for $1.50, and send it postpaid to any address.

## "ANCHOR" STONE BUILDING BLOCKS.
### REAL STONE.   THREE COLORS.

## The Best Toy Out.

A. CLEVER TOY FOR EVERY CHILD.

A price-curling mode of amusement.

A SPLENDID PRESENT.

The Blocks will Make CASTLES, PALACES, CHURCHES, TOWERS, BRIDGES, STREETS, FORTRESSES, and Buildings of all kinds.

### The Toy the Child Likes Best!

Amusing and instructive, in fact the **best present** for children of all ages.

For $1.75 or $2.00 a good average box.

Mr. CHAS. P. KRAPP, M. D. at Wyoming, Pa., writes: "The building stones are very satisfactory, *in fact the best toy I have ever bought*, and they are a source of amusement and education for the children and parents alike."

Descriptive Catalogue post free on application to

## F. AD. RICHTER & CO.,
### 310 BROADWAY NEW YORK

---

## A Steam Engine Free!
### Show This to Your Boys.

---

## The Weeden Upright Steam Engine

A real, complete, working machine. You can blow the whistle or start and stop the engine by opening and closing the throttle valve as in a large engine. It is a scientific toy, nearer in appearance and operation to a large engine than any heretofore made. It is both amusing and instructive. It is safe and easy to operate. It will run small toys, and develop ingenuity. It is a simple and complete machine which will practically illustrate to the youthful mind that wonderful power so constantly at work on all sides in this age of steam. There are 41 pieces and over 400 operations in the manufacture of this engine. Every engine is tested and warranted to be in every respect as described.

## THE TOY KNITTER

It charms the Girls and quiets the noisy boys.

Who does not remember the pleasure derived from knitting with a spool? The knitter is an improvement on the spool, and is a source of endless pleasure to children. A good rainy day amusement. Full directions accompany each knitter, which we send, postage paid, for only one new subscriber.

# BOYS' TOOL CHESTS.

**28250** Boys' Tool Chest, "The Little Buttercup" (AX). Not illustrated. Size, 9½ inches long, 4½ inches wide, 2½ inches deep, with slide cover to box, contains 13 assorted tools and articles, suitable for little ones only.
Each, 12c; Per dozen.....................$1 25

**28251** Boys' Tool Chest, "The Daisy" (CHX), size of chest, 9½ inches long, 4½ inches wide, 2½ inches deep, with slide cover, contains 10 assorted tools, including hand saw This box is for small children. Each, 25c; per dozen.........$2 20

**28252** Boys' Tool Chest, "The Companion" (MX). Size of box, 8½ inches long, 4½ inches wide, 2½ inches deep, with hinge cover, with walnut bands and base, nicely varnished, contains the following articles: Hammer, rule, hand saw, lead pencil, drawing square, crayon, try square, mallet, triangle, plumb bob, nails and tacks. This is a good chest for the money. Each 35c; per doz. $3 6 ).

**28253** Youth's Tool Chest. Not illustrated (A). Size of chest, 1 foot 10½ inches long, 11½ inches wide, 9½ inches deep. Made of superior quality of black walnut and chestnut woods, nicely dovetailed, beautifully finished in oil and varnish, with heavy base and bands, folding handles, brass and bronze trimmings, and large till with partitions and chest lock. Containing 70 superior quality assorted tools: Cast steel panel saw, cast steel iron smoothing plane, cast steel iron jack plane, 4 cast steel firmer chisels, with polished hickory handles, assorted sizes; 2 cast steel firmer gauges, carpenters' brace bit stock, cast steel brace bits, saw file and handle, steel bracket saw frame, 12 cast steel bracket saws, assorted; cast steel shingling hatchet, hickory mallet, cast steel screw driver, appletree brad-awl set, containing 20 assorted cast steel tools and wrench, file and handle, oil stone, oil can, beechwood marking gauge, two-foot boxwood rule, cast steel brad-awls, handled, assorted; pair compasses, 4 cast steel nail gimlets, cast steel regulator, cast steel nail hammer, slitting gauge, cast steel nail punch. The tools in chest are of good quality, and a young man so disposed can perfect himself in the use of tools so as to be able to do a man's work in the carpenter line.
Price, each ............................ 14 00

**28254** Boys' Tool Chest (Etx), 11 inches long, 5½ inches wide, 3½ inches deep, well made, with end till, contains 10 assorted tools for boys' use.
Price, complete................... 50

**28255** Boys' Tool Chest (atx), 13½ inches long, 6½ inches wide, 5 inches deep, well made, with movable till and partitions; contains 10 assorted tools; better quality for boys' use.
Price, complete...................$0 75

## Boys' Tool Chests—continued.

**28256** Handy Tool Chest (CHEt) chest, 25 inches long, 7 inches wide, 3¾ inches deep; neatly made, well varnished, has large end till; contains 17 good tools, as follows: 1 panel saw, 14 inches; 1 bit brace, 1 cast steel auger bit, 3 cast steel gimlet bits, assorted, 1 cast steel firmer chisel, 1 scratch awl, 1 brad awl, 1 saw file, 1 screw driver, 1 hammer 2 gimlets, 1 two-foot boxwood rule, 1 screw wrench, 1 nail set.
Price, complete.................... $3 25

**28258** The Universal Tool Chest, hard oil finish, size of box, 19½x10½x11 inches; made of chestnut wood, trimmed with heavy bands and bases, japanned lifting handles, and fitted with secure tumbler locks. Contents.—C. S. hand saw, adze-eye nail hammer, chisel, gouge, wood bench vice, hand screw, try square, iron plumb bob, cold chisel, nail set, counter sink, ball brace, auger bit, gimlet, reamer, flat plyers, smooth plane, square, mallet, screw driver, two-foot rule, combination tool, flat file, iron pocket level.
Price, complete................... 8 00

## Iron Banks.

**28260** Roller Bank Safe (cxt), with lock and key; new design and construction, and is beautifully painted in colors and decorated with pictures of roller skaters; 3¼ inches high, 2¾ inches wide, 2¾ inches deep; weight, 20 ounces.
Each........ $0 15
Per dozen.... 1 62

## Combination Safe.

**28261** This is something new, and is hardly a toy. Impossible to open it unless you have the combination A good, large, substantial bank in every particular.
Each......... $0 75

**28262** The same bank in principle as 28261, but a much finer get up. Elegantly finished in nickel.
Price, each ... ......... 95

**28263** Security Safe, same principle as the preceding, but larger, finished in nickel. Double combination.
Each.... .................. 1 45

**28264** Santa Claus Bank. This is the bank for the little ones.
Price, each...........$0 40

**28265** Jolly Nigger Bank. Similar to the Uncle Tom bank, but larger and more perfectly finished. Weighs 4½ pounds. Stands nearly 7 inches high.
Each.....$0 60

## Toys—continued.

**28266** The Speaking Dog Bank. This is an ingenious mechanical bank, weighing 4½ pounds, length, 7 in.; width, 2½ in.; height, 7 inches. Handsomely painted in seven different colors. The coin is placed on the plate, which the girl holds, and upon pressing the lever it is deposited in the seat at the girl's side, at the same time the dog opens its mouth and wags its tail in an amusing manner.
Price, each.....................$0 80

**28267** Uncle Sam Bank. This is a comical bank that well deserves its popularity. It is well made and handsomely finished in colors. Price, each. $0 75

**28267½** The Trick Dog Savings Bank. This is an interesting fancy bank, the base of which measures 8½ inches in length by 2½ inches in width. The bank represents a clown dressed in full circus colors, holding a hoop; the coin is placed in the dog's mouth, and by touching the lever the dog jumps through the hoop and deposits the coin in the barrel.
Price, each.....................$0 85

**28268** The Pug. This is an interesting toy bank for a small child. This is one of the cheapest novelties in the market.
Price, each......$0 10

## Puzzle Locomotive Savings Bank.

*Cannot be opened until filled with coin.*

**28269** Made entirely of iron, finely finished in full nickel plate. The weight of the money dropped in the slot on top of cab will, after the bank is full (and not before), loosen the smokestack, which can then be lifted out and the money poured from the opening. As it is a perfect imitation of a locomotive, and the wheels turn, it is a toy that will please the children.
Price, each....................... $0 35
Per dozen....................... 3 40

**8269½** Uncle Tom Iron Bank (CXP). This is a comical and amusing bank; by pressing a button at back of neck the eyes roll up and the tongue is thrust out for coin, which, placed upon it, is drawn in and deposited in the vault; size, 5½ in. high, 4 wide and 3½ deep.
Each........ $0 45
Per dozen ........ 4 87

*Montgomery Ward & Co.*

**Savings Banks—continued.**

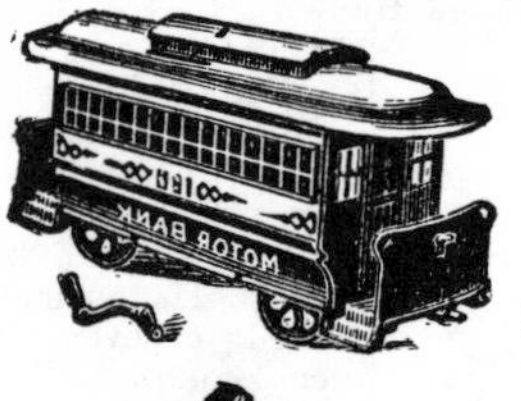


28270 The Motor Bank is an interesting mechanical toy. Drop a coin in the slot and the car is set in motion.
Price, each...$0 90

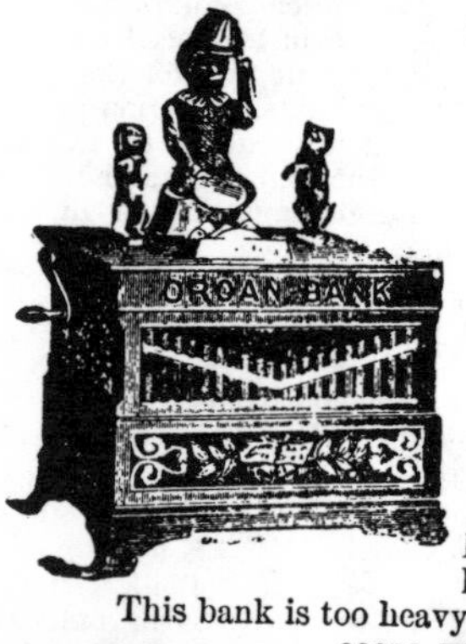


28271 Iron Organ Bank (CXO), elegantly finished, large chime of bells, dancing figures revolve when the handle is turned; the monkey deposits the coin in the vault and politely raises his hat; size, 8½ in. high; 5½ wide, and 3¾ deep.
Each....... $0 85
Per dozen... 9 25
This bank is too heavy to go by mail.

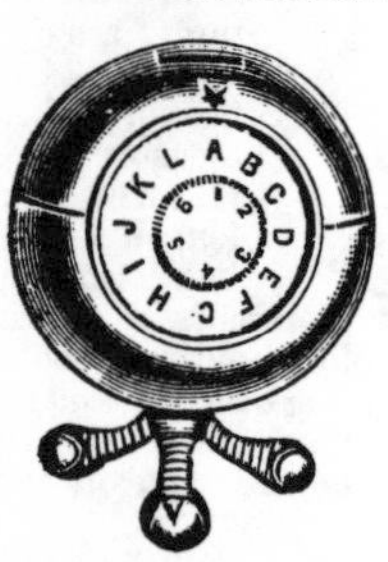

28272 The Globe Combination Bank. This is an ingeniously constructed ornamental bank, mounted on a pedestal as shown in cut. This bank has a double combination lock, which when removed gives access to the bank. The body of the bank is elegantly finished in japan, with colored decorations; size, 12½ in. in circumference.
Price, each.......................... $0 50
28273 Same bank as 28272, but in nickel finish. Price, each............... 70
28274 Same as 28272, larger, the circumference being 15 inches. Price, each. 75
28275 Same as 28274, nickel finish.
Price, each.......................... 1 0?

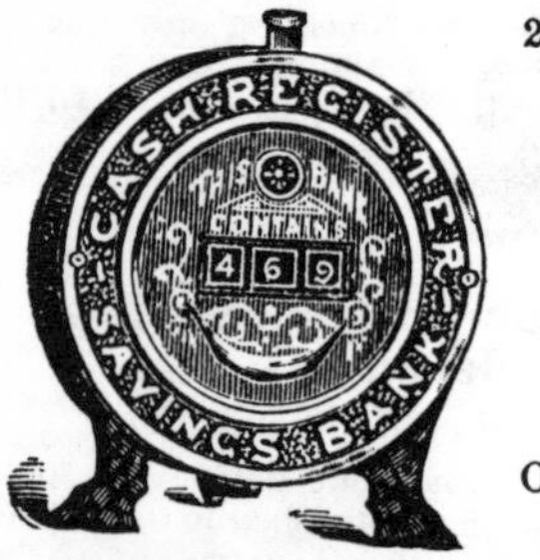


28276 Cash Register Savings Bank, accurately registers amount deposited from 1 cent to $10. Diameter, 4¾ in.; height, 6 in. Has handsomely ornamented brass front. This is a $1.00 article.
Our price....$0 8?

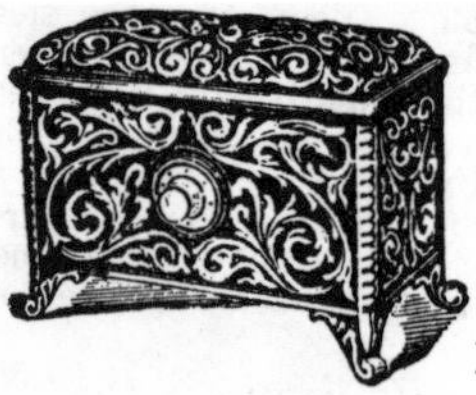

28277 The Treasure Box. This is a beautifully designed toy bank or treasure casket; 5½ in. long, 3 in. wide, stands 4½ in. high. Finished in antique brass.
Price, each.....$0 75

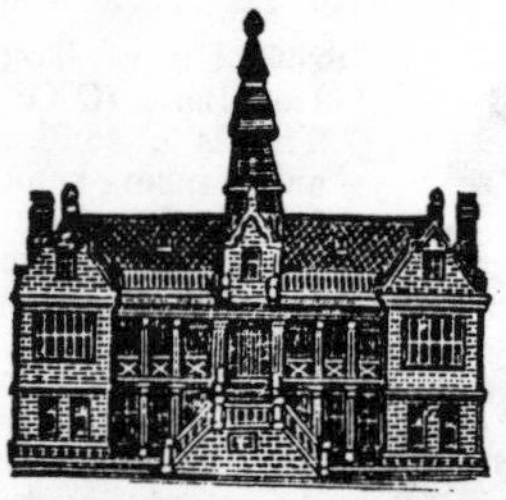

28278 Palace Bank. A popular and standard toy bank with lock and key. Japan body with gilt trimmings. Length, 7½ inches; width, 4½ inches; height to top of cupola, 7 inches.
Each.........$ 80

*** It will be a favor to us (and perhaps to your friends) if you will place where th y will do the most good, any duplicate catalogues or adv.rtising matter which you may receive f.om us.*

**Savings Banks—continued.**

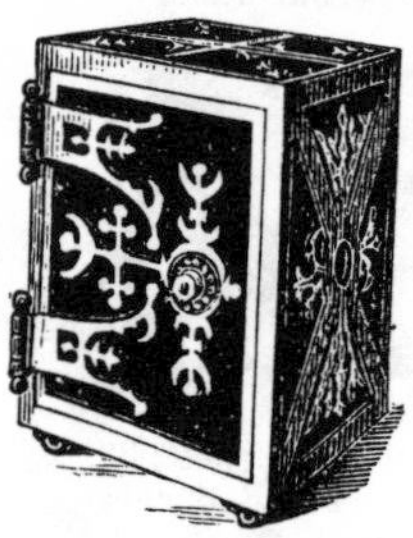

28279 The Boudoir Combination Lock Safe, with divisions and drawer. A practical article for every household, for the safe keeping of valuables, such as money, jewels, etc.
rice, each.......$5 00

## MISCELLANEOUS TOYS AND NOVELTIES.

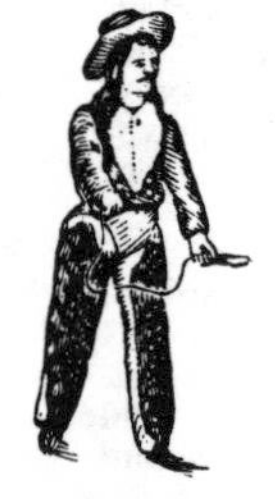

28284 Cowboy Dolls, as natural as life, 8 inches long, made of papier mache, with jointed arms and legs. Handsomely painted representing the cowboy in full costume. Assorted designs
Price, each........... $ 25
Per dozen............ 2 50

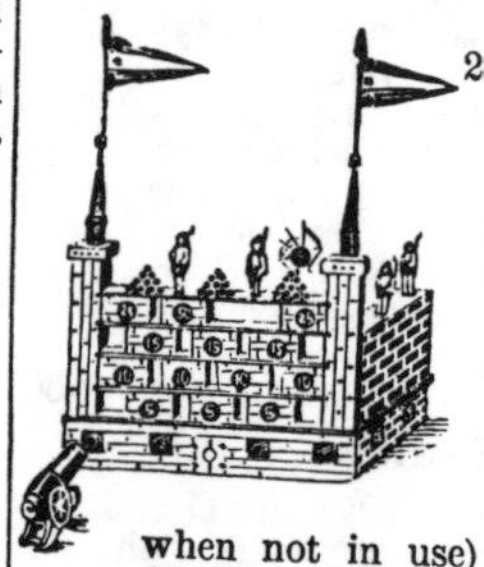

28628 Boy's Wooden Forts, something entirely new. Complete with sentinels and cannon. One of the most amusing and durable toy forts made The sides and corners are dowelled together and to the box (in which the whole outfit is packed for shipment or put into when not in use) The other parts are filled in, giving a natural appearance Full directions are given with each game.
Price, each.......................$0 75
Weight of above, complete, 5 lbs.

### Chimes.

28294 Drummer Boy Chimes, size, 3x8x10 inches; one in a neat wooden box, large and showy, durable and a pretty toy; best $1.00 chime in the market.
Price, each........................ $0 80
28296 Telephone Chime, two bells, quick and sharp rings, size, 3½x4x9 inches; one in pasteboard box; has monkey on rear seat. The best 50c. chime of the season.
Price, each.......................... 40

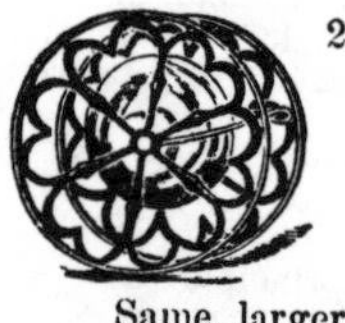

28298 White Metal Revolving Bell Chime, gives a very musical sound; silver white chime, small.
Each.............. 12
Per dozen.......... 1 25
Same, larger size.
Each........................ 23
Per dozen.................. 2 50

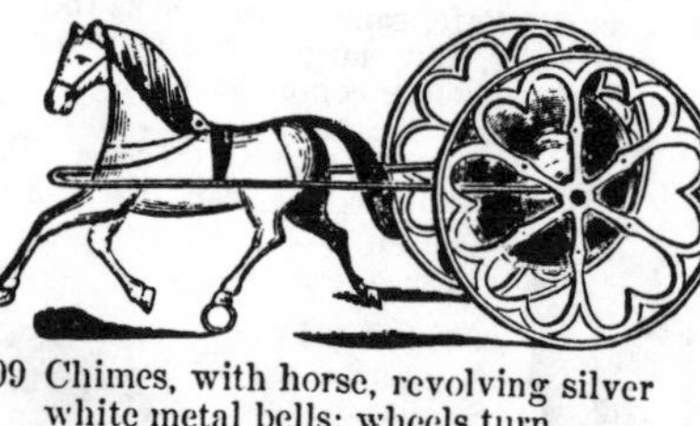

28299 Chimes, with horse, revolving silver white metal bells; wheels turn.
Each............................ $0 20
Per dozen......................... 2 00

*** Always give name and price when ordering from us. Catalogue number alone is not always sufficient.*

### Toy Stoves.

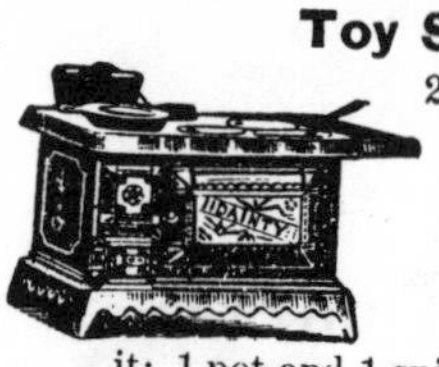

28302 Sunshine Toy Cook Stove, exact miniature of a large stove; over 5½x5½x3¼ inches. Fire can be built in this stove and cooking on a small scale may be done with it; 1 pot and 1 spider furnished.
Price, each.......................... $2 50

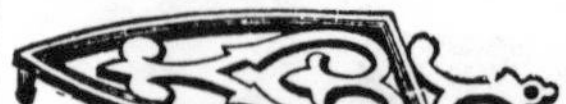

### Child's Sad Irons.

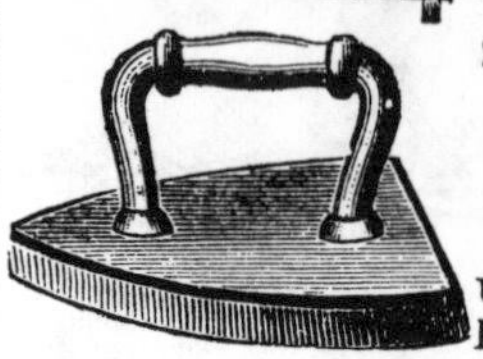

28304 Stands, coppered irons, japanned and polished, size of irons, 1⅞ inch; stand, 3 inches; weight, 3 ounces.
Per set of 2 pieces $0 04
Per dozen sets.... 40

### Marbles.

Diameters as follows: 0—⅝ inch; 1—¾ inch; 2—⅞ inch; 3—1 inch; 4—1⅛ inch. We do not sell marbles in less quantities than quoted.

28308 Common "Mibs," 1,000 in a sack.
Per sack........................ $0 55
28310 Polished "Mibs," 1,000 in a sack.
Per sack ...................... 65
28311 Unglazed Painted Chinas (100 in box). No. 0, 12c.; No. 1, 15c.; No. 2, 20c.; No. 3, 30c. per box.
28312 Glazed Painted Chinas (100 in a box). No. 0, 25c.; No. 1, 35c.; No. 2, 45c.; No. 3, 60c. per box.
28313 Imitation Agates (Falsies) (100 in a box). No. 0, 30c.; No. 1, 35c.; No. 2, 45c.; No. 3, 60c. per box.
28314 Glass, A 1 quality, threaded (100 in a box). No. 0, 25c.; No. 1, 30c.; No. 2, 35c.; No. 3, 50c. per box.
28315 Glass, threaded, large (1 dozen in a box). No. 6, 25c.; No. 8, 35c.; No. 10, 75c.; No. 12, $1.25. per box.
28316 Glass Opals (assorted colors) (100 in a box). No. 0, 35c.; No. 1, 45c.; No. 2, 60c.; No. 3, 90c. per box.
28317 Glass Opals, threaded (new) (100 in a box). No. 0, 40c.; No. 1, 50c.; No. 2, 65c.; No. 3, $1.00. per box.
28318 Threaded Glass Opals, large (1 dozen in a box). No. 8, 50c.; No. 10, 85c. per box.
28319 Brandies (assorted colors) (100 in a box). No. 0, 30c.; No. 1, 35c.; No. 2, 45c.; No. 3, 60c. per box.
28320 Jaspers, glazed (Polished Cloudies) (100 in a box). No. 0, 25c.; No. 1, 30c.; No. 2, 40c.; No. 3, 60c. per box.
28321 Genuine Carnelian Agates (Blood Agates) (25 in a box). Price per box: No. 3, 95c.; No. 4, $1.70; No. 5, $2.90.
28322 Ballot Marbles, white or black (100 in a box). No. 0, 40c. per box.
28323 Glass Figured—

| | Each. | Per doz. |
|---|---|---|
| No. 5 | $0 04 | $0 35 |
| No. 7 | 5 | 50 |
| No. 9 | 6 | 65 |
| No. 11 | 15 | 1 75 |

### Tops.

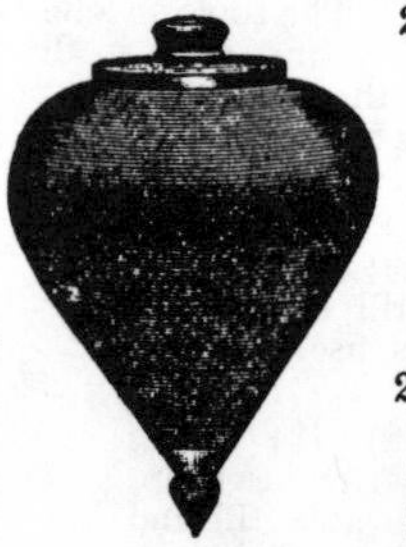

28325 Hardwood, extra quality, peg all the way through, cannot come out; brass button rivet on top; selected hardwood, malleable iron pegs, points hardened; assorted colors; cut ½ size. Each, 4c.; 40c. per dozen.
28326 Stained Wood Peg Tops, boxwood shape, assorted colors, and in four sizes.
Price, each, 1c., 2c., 3c. and 4c. Per dozen, 10c., 20c., 30c. and 40c.

## Boxwood Tops.

| | | Price, each. | Per dozen. |
|---|---|---|---|
| 28328 | No. 0 size ....... | 2c. | 20c. |
| | No. 1 size ....... | 4c. | 40c. |
| | No. 2 size ....... | 6c. | 55c. |
| | No. 3 size ....... | 8c. | 75c. |

28330 Top Strings, with wooden button. Each, 1c. Per dozen, 10c.

## The Celebrated Gyroscope Top.

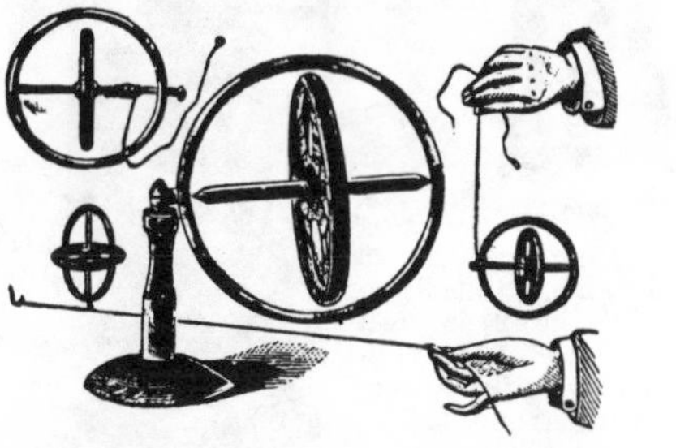

28331 The above cut shows our new Gyroscope Top in some of the positions in which it can be spun. It is made of metal, neatly finished, and ornamented in bright colors. It will spin in almost any position. Scientists are unable to explain why it will spin when suspended.
Price, each ........................ $0 09
Per dozen ........................ 90

## French Choral or Musical Tops.

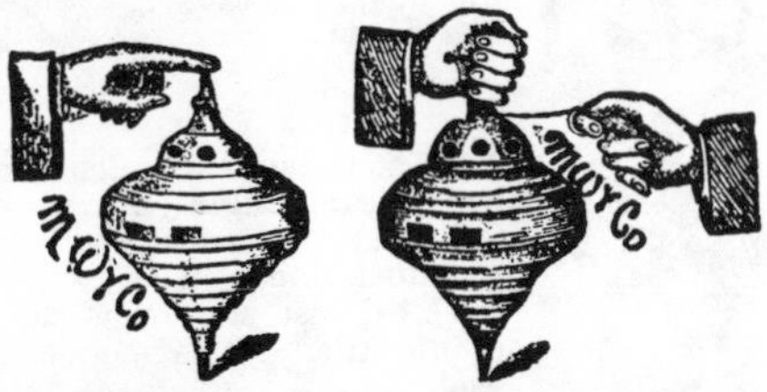

Changing Tune. Starting to Spin.

28332 Humming Top, made of tin, striped in bright colors; stands 3½ inches high; not changeable.
Price, each ........................ $0 05
Per dozen ........................ 50

28333 French Musical Top, like cut with handle; produces a beautiful melody while spinning. Made of tin in variegated co ors. Height, 5¼ inches; not changeable
Price, each ........................ 10
Per dozen ........................ 1 00
By mail, extra, each, 8c.

28334 French Choral Changeable Tops (see cut); changes tunes while spinning by touching on top; simple and wonderful. The melody is as finely blended and the chords are as perfect as those of a church organ. Strong, and not liable to get out of order. A mammoth toy. Height, with handle, 7½ inches. Striped in variegated colors. Retail price, 50 cents.
Our price, each ........................ 25
Per dozen ........................ 2 70
By mail, extra, each, 11c.

## Return Balls.

28336 No 2 size, gilt striped return balls.
Each ........................ $0 03
Per dozen ........................ 30
No. 5 size, gilt striped return balls.
Each. ........................ 5
Per dozen ........................ 50

**** Nearly all the FURNITURE sold by us is made to order, thus insuring bright, clean goods, and enabling us to figure close margins, as we never have old stock on hand, and do not devote valuable space in our store to carrying a large stock, to say nothing of the cost of handling each piece two or three times.*

## The Roaming Turtle.

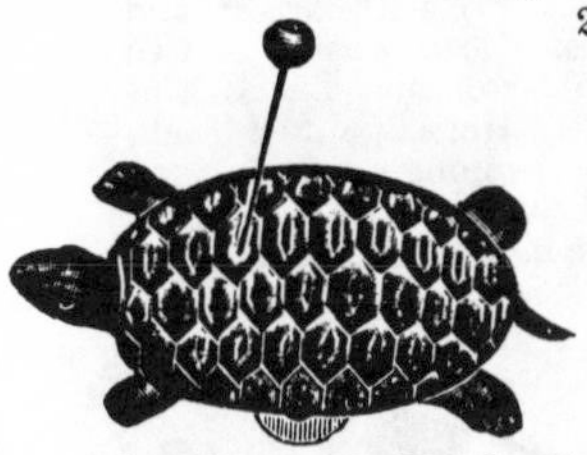

28338 Another of the world's surprises in popular toys. Made of metal, and colored in gold, green and blue. Length, 7 inches. Led by a string. Lead it about 10 feet by the string, when it will go 10 feet by itself and lead you. Lots of fun for children under 12 years of age.
Price, each ........................ $0 09
Per dozen ........................ 95

We also have the Roaming Parrot, which is of similar construction and equally popular, and which we sell at same price as the Turtle.

## Automatic Butterfly.

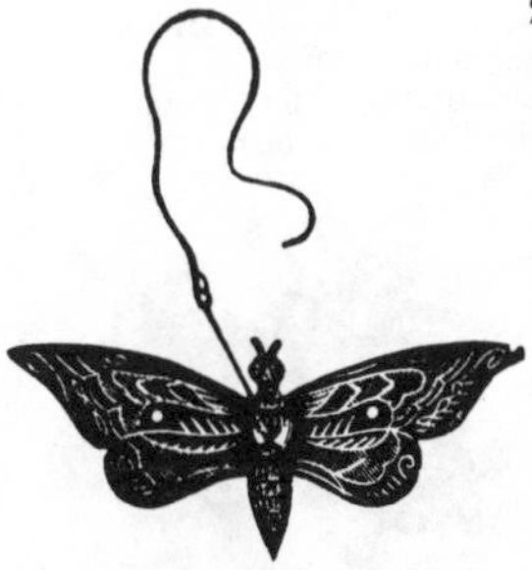

28339 The Butterfly, an amusing toy for the little ones, and will interest the older people as well; at the same time may be used as an ornament. Is handsomely decorated, perfectly made, automatic movable wings. When raised up and down in the air the wings move as though it were flying.
Each ........................ $0 09
Per dozen ........................ 95

## "Tivoli."

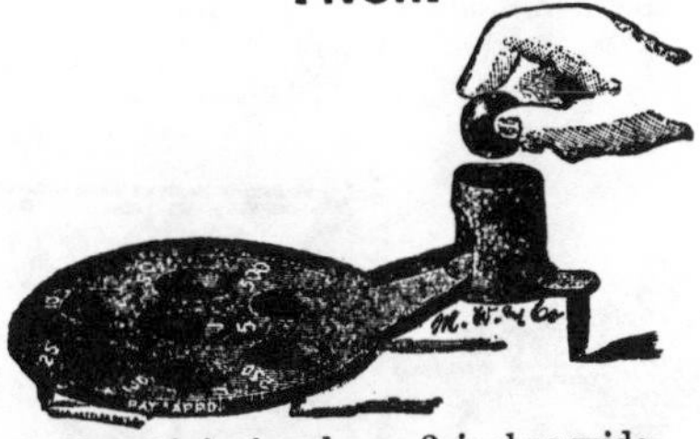

28340 Size, 5¼ inches long, 3 inches wide, and 1¾ inches high. A simple and amusing game for children. It is handsomely bronzed, with the hollows painted in assorted colors.
Price, each, with marble........ $0 10
Per dozen ........................ 1 00

28341 Tivoli Game. Same as 28340, but has acrobat who balances marble on his feet, and discharges same when spring is touched. This toy is larger and better finished than No. 28340.
Price, each ........................ 18
Per dozen ........................ 1 85

## Toy Scales.

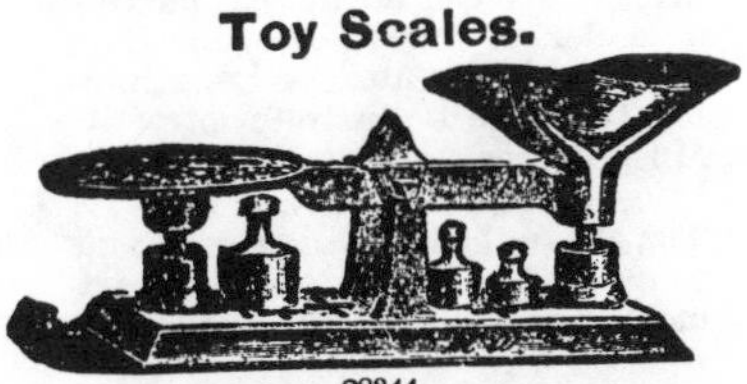

28344.

28344 Size, without scoop, 4½ inches long, 1¾ inches high, 2 inches wide. Scoop, 3½x2 inches. Nicely painted and bronzed, and has three coppered weights.
Price, each ........................ $0 10
Per dozen ........................ 1 00

28346 The "Gem" Toy Scales, 4¾ inches long, 3 inches high, 2½ inches wide. Delicately adjusted, with a set of correct weights accompanying each scale. Nice y finished; one in a box.
Each ........................ 20

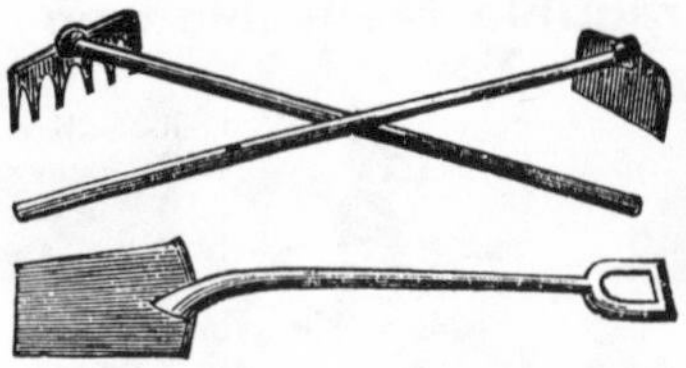

## All Iro[n] Penn Toys

28347 Three pieces to a set. Size, 4¾ inches long, coppered.
Price, per set of three ............ $0
Price, per dozen sets ............
Price, per gross toys, assorted......

## Coppered Iron Toys.

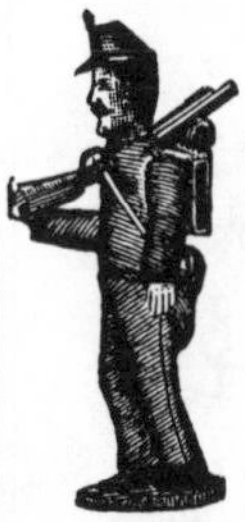

28348 Coppered Iron Toy Soldiers These toys are about 2 inches i[n] length and made of iron coppered and represent a full company o[f] soldiers.
Price, per set ............ $0 1

## Toy Iron Trains.

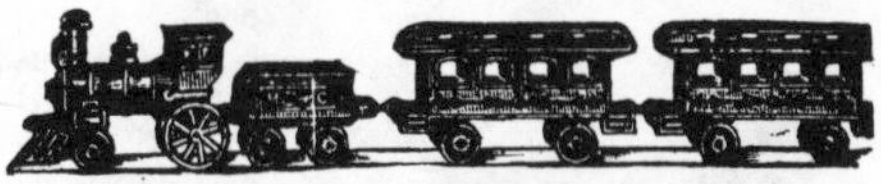

28349 The "Hero" passenger train, locomotive, tender and two passenger cars. Handsomely finished, new design. Each train in a box. Length of train, 14 inches (186 .
Each ........................ $0 40
Per dozen ........................ 4 00

28350 Freight Train, iron. Length, 19 inches (185). Locomotive, tender and one flat car. Nicely painted and neatly put up; one train in a wooden box.
Each ........................ 50
Per dozen ........................ 5 50

28351 Freight Train, iron. Length, 26 inches. Locomotive, tender and two freight cars; a brakeman in each car; painted in light colors, strong and durable; decidedly the best train in the market for the price (187); one train in a box.
Each ........................ 90
Per dozen ........................ 9 50

28352 Mechanical Iron Locomotive, new model and finish, guaranteed to work perfectly. Length, 7 inches. Each one in a wood box (19-9).
Price, each ........................ 90
Price, per dozen ........................ 9 50

28353 Same, with tender. Length, 10 inches (19-10).
Price, each ........................ 1 10
Price, per dozen ........................ 12 00

28354 Large Size Engine and Tender, to pull with a string (1). This engine and tender are the finest finished and most perfectly made of anything on the market. Put up in a neat box.
Price ........................ 2 00

28355 Iron Train, including engine and tender, as above, with a combination car (1 and 2).
Price for train complete, each...... 3 50

28356 Extra Freight Car (4), to be attached to engine and tender No. 28354.
Each ........................ 1 00

28357 Extra Passenger Car (3), to be attached to engine and tender No. 28354.
Each ........................ 1 00

28358 Extra Oil Tank Car (5), to be attached to engine and tender No. 28354.
Each ........................ 85

**WALL PAPER. PRICES AND QUALITIES GUARANTEED. ALL NEW STYLES.**

## Indestructible Malleable Iron Toys.

28360 Sulky, with jockey (A) and horse, as represented in cut, nicely painted and well made, to be drawn with string; these are packed one in a box. Length, 8 in.; width, 3 in.; height, 4 in.
Price, each................... $0 50

361 Dray (B), as represented in cut, with driver and box; length of toy, 10½ in.; one in a box.
Each ...................... $0 50

28362 Dog Cart (C), as represented in cut, elegantly japanned, with driver in livery costume; length, 12 in. One in a box.
Each......................... $0 75

28363 Hansom Cab (D) and Driver, as represented in cut Horse and hansom gilt trimmed and finely decorated. Length, about 12 in. Each in a box.
Price ...................... $0 75

28364 Railroad Train, (G) engine, tender and two flat cars, two brakemen. Painted in bright colors, engine gilt trimmed. Total length of train, 34 inches. Price of train complete, one in a box......................... $0 85

28365 Single Truck (I) with driver and load of merchandise as represented in cut; length, 13 in., handsomely painted in colors. Each, complete... $0 80

## Toys—continued.

28366 Double Truck (J) with driver and two horses. Load consists of two boxes, two barrels and one sack of merchandise. Horses painted black, harness and running gear of truck painted a bright red, black striped. Packed one in a box, complete.
Each ...................... $1 75

28367 Barouche (K), with driver in coachman's livery. Cream colored horses, with fancy colored hip blankets. Running gear maroon, gold striped; body black. Both horses trotting when toy is in motion. A particularly handsome article. Packed one in a box.
Each........................ $1 85

28368 Fire Engine (R), with driver and engineer in full regulation uniform. When in motion the horses gallop and the gong rings. A complete miniature fire engine, with nickel-plated boiler and valves. Length, 18 in., packed one in a box.
Each........................ $2 00

28369 Hose Cart (S), with driver and fireman in full uniform, with two Pompier Corps ladders as shown in cut. Cream colored horses with red running gear to cart and alarm gong, which rings while in motion. Whole finely painted in bright colors. A companion piece to 28368. Length, 18 inches.
Each........................ $2 00

28370 Hook and Ladder Truck (T), with driver and steerman in full uniform. Four red extension ladders, which can be united, making a ladder 51 in. in length. Two axes, gaily painted. Length, 24 in. Too large to illustrate correctly. Must be seen to be appreciated.
Price, each, complete............ $2 00
The above three numbers making a complete miniature fire department................ $5 50

28371 Single Truck, with galloping horse and driver (402-1), without load. Length, 15 inches; height to top of seat, 6 inches. Packed one in a wooden box. Price, each ..... $0 75

## Toy Steam Engines.

28375 The "Hero" Improved Steam Engine. The cheapest perfect running steam engine made.
Price, each................ $0 20

"Hero"

28376 Vertical Steam Engine, stands 9½ in. high, has 2¾-in. steel fly wheel, ⅜-in. cylinder and ¾-in. stroke, good, strong boiler, with smoke stack and steam whistle; mounted on strong wooden base and finished in red, gilt and bronze; furnished with lamp, funnel, water cup and directions for use. Nothing equals it at the price.
Each......................... $0 80

28377 The "Hero" Horizontal Steam Engine. Best engine made for the money. Every one perfect. Good size, clean and easy to handle,
Each................. $0 45
Per dozen............ 4 40

28378 The Genuine Weeden Upright Steam Engine, American manufacture, with whistle. weighted safety valve, smoke stack exhaust, starts and stops by throttle. This engine is well known all over the country.
Retail price............. $1 50
Our price............... 1 00

28379 The Clipper Steam Engine (303). This is a model engine, perfect in its operations and absolutely safe; 3¾-inch brass boiler, iron furnace, cover painted in imitation of brick. Packed in a wooden box.
Each............. $1 50

28380 Horizontal Engine, 7 inches long, 4 inches high, 4½-inch fly wheel, weight, 4 lbs., heavy copper boiler, riveted, has safety valve. Packed in box with lamp, funnel, etc. A fine model and perfect specimen of mechanics.
Price, each ................ $3 25

28381 The Gem Horizontal (7) Engine, with single cylinder, ⅓-inch bore, ½-inch stroke, smooth flue boiler The Gem engines are 10 inches long and 10 inches high. The furnace and engine rests on solid iron frame.
Price, each................ $2 50
28382 Gem Horizontal Engine (9), same description as above, but fitted with double cylinder, ½-in. bore, ½-in. stroke, steam and smoke flue boiler. Each.................. $3 00

## Toys—continued.

28383 The Walking Beam Engine 7 in. long, 7 in. high, 4-in. fly wheel, 4½-in. walking beam, heavy riveted brass boiler, with safety valve. Put up in a neat paper box complete. Price.......$4 50

28384 The Peerless Horizontal Steam Engine, 7-inch copper boiler, covered with sheet iron jacket. Has stationary cylinder 2 inches long, and a 5-inch fly wheel. This is one of the most powerful and practical toy engines in the market. Has steam chest and automatic cut off. Price, each.........$5 00

28385 The Diamond "C" Stationary Steam Engine (style A), large and powerful, made on strictly scientific principles. Length, 10 in., width, 9 in., height, 8½ in. Price, each $10.00

28386 The Diamond "C" Upright Engine (style B), 9 inches long, 5½ inches wide, 12 in. high. This engine is fitted with water gauge safety valve, etc. The boiler, and in fact every portion of this engine, is made from the very best material. The lamp is filled with asbestos, which absorbs the alcohol, avoiding waste and danger. Packed one in wooden box. The retail price of this engine is.......$15 00
Our price.........................  11 00

28387 The Model Steam Fire Engine (3½). This is a beautiful scientific toy and one that the boys will appreciate This has copper boiler, has japanned gearing and red striped painting. Single oscillating cylinder and pump. Will throw a stream of water quite a distance. Price, each...........................$4 25

28388 Complete Steam Train, good model of a large locomotive, made in the most perfect and careful manner. Guaranteed to run perfectly. Run by steam on a circular track, for about 20 minutes, with each filling of the lamp and boiler. Brass Locomotive (90-1), track and two cars complete....................$8 00

## Toys—continued.

Nickel Locomotive (90-3) track and two cars complete................... $10 00

28389 Weeden New Steam Locomotive Tender and Passenger Car with jointed track on wood sleepers. Diameter of track 3½ feet. Locomotive 8 inches long, car and tender in proportion, it is the best tin train ever made, put up in wooden box, price for train complete... $3 00

28390 The New Weeden Beam Engine, tin boiler, fly-wheel and working parts made of well finished cast metal. Dimensions, 6½-in. base, 3½ in. wide, 5½-in. high. Price, each................$1 50

28391 The Weeden "Favorite" is a new model this season, is complete and perfect in all its parts, has tin boiler and lamp, measures 6 in. high and 4½ in. at base. Price, each........... $0 50

28392 The Weeden New Side Wheel Steamboat. The steamer is new this season, and is modeled after the modern side wheel excursion boats. Is made of tin, and weighs about one pound with ballast. Will steam in a tub or tank of water or on a still water pond. Dimensions, 12 inches long, 3½-inch beam, 5 inches high. Price, complete, packed in a wooden box $2 00

## Attachments for Steam Engines.

28395 Steam Engine Attachments, moving figures, etc., all comical and ingenious. Well made, with pulleys and belt, ready to run. A large number of figures can be attached to one engine.
Small size, single figures, each..... $0 20
Medium size, large, single or medium size double figures, each........  35
28396 The Village Blacksmith Steam Engine Attachment. Very novel and interesting. Pleases old and young alike. Each...................  40
28397 The Machine Shop Engine Attachment, length, 15 inches, height, 10 inches. Each...................  85

## Patent Hot Air Toys.

28398 Hot Air Attachments, single and double figures, made with the patented air wheel. Each, complete......$0 25

## Toy Machinery.

Can be operated by any of our toy steam engines.
28399 Circular Saw and Table ... ... $0 45
28400 Turning Lathe....................  55
28401 Grindstone (wood wheel)..........  35
28402 Cone Pulley to connect with lathe..  20
28403 Hangers for shafting..............  10
28404 Pulleys, ¼ to 2½ in. diameter.......  03

## Boys' Whips.

28403½.

8403 Boy's Whip, with loop fancy. Each..$0 05
Per dozen ....................  50
28403½ With whistle in handle, braided lash, as per cut. Each............  10
Per dozen...................  1 00

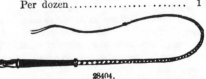

28404.

28404 A splendid one, good length, with braided leather lash, fancy colored braided stock, whistle in end of handle. Each...................  15
Per dozen...................  1 50

## A Big Leader.

28405 Toy Police Lantern, 1½-inch bull's eye, burns candle, changeable light. A great favorite with the boys. Throws a strong light.
Each...................$ 0 12
Per dozen.................  1 30

## The New Calliope Whistle.

26406 Made of wood, finished in bright colors. All of the notes can be sounded by pulling out the stopper. A good whistle, plenty of fun for the boys and girls.
Each...................$ 0 05
Per dozen.................  50

## The Double Pop Gun.

28407 Two corks, two reports, new pattern, strong metal rod, greatly improved in construction, makes lots of noise.
Price, each...............$ 0 08
Per dozen .................  85
28407½ Double Pop Guns, made with brass tube.
Each...................  12
Per dozen.................  1 25

## Automatic Toy Cart Wagon.

28408 Automatic Toy Cart Wagon, made of tin, nicely painted with canvas covered top. Lady driver. This toy is very simple to handle, and when set in motion will run 10 or 15 feet on level surface.
Each.........  .................$0 50

## Wooden Soldiers.

28409 Wooden Soldiers. Movable, each made to stand alone. In box, per set.... $0 20
Per doz. 2 10
28409½ Same, larger and better quality
Per set .....................$ 0 40
Per dozen ...................  4 50

## Toy Swords.

28410 Toy Swords with strap, belt and guarded handle, in sheath, length, 25 inches.
Each.....................$ 0 50
28411 Toy sword, similar to above, though not as well made, no guard, in sheath 24 inches long.
Each...................  25

## Toy Guns.

28412 Toy Gun with bayonet and strap, measures 41 inches in length without bayonet. Shoots paper cap and stick.
Price, each .................$ 0 90

**Toy Guns—continued.**

28413 Same style and finish, only smaller, 36 inches long.
Price, each ........................ 60

28414 Toy Gun 24½ inches long, shoots a cork, has strong spring, and will shoot peas or beans.
Each........................ 35

28415 Toy Gun, regular style, 24-inch, shoots a stick.
Each........................ 12

18415½ The Echo Toy Pistol. A harmless, novel and ingenious toy. No caps to endanger the eyes of the little ones, but a loud report to please the boys. It will throw a pea or bean 40 feet with remarkable accuracy.
Price, each........................ 10

## Trumpets.

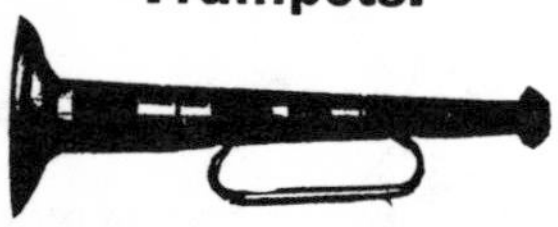

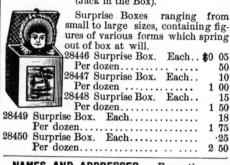

28416 Tin Toy Trumpets, nicely striped and painted, about 9 inches long.
Each ........................ $0 05
Per dozen........................ 50

28417 Tin Toy Trumpets, length about 12 inches, better quality.
Each........................ 12
Per dozen ........................ 1 20

28418 Horn Toy Bugles, about 6½ inches long.
Each ........................ 05
Per dozen........................ 50

28419 Toy Horn Bugles, about 9 inches long, with porcelain mouthpiece.
Each ........................ 12
Per dozen........................ 1 20

28420 Toy Horn Bugles, with horn mouth piece, length about 10 inches, extra quality.
Each........................ 20
Per dozen ........................ 2 25

28421 Heavy Tin Bugles, with tassels; double note.
Each........................ 16
Per dozen ........................ 1 20

## Metallophones.

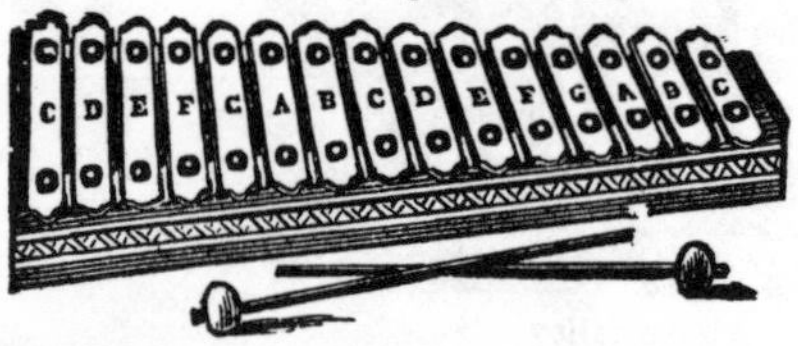


28425 Metallophones, nickel, 12 key, in box with two hammers.
Each........................ $0 23
Per dozen ........................ 2 40

28426 Metallophones, 18 keys, each with two hammers. Put up in neat box.
Each........................ 45
Per dozen........................ 4 70

## Toy Drums.

For larger and better quality drums, see Musical Goods Department.

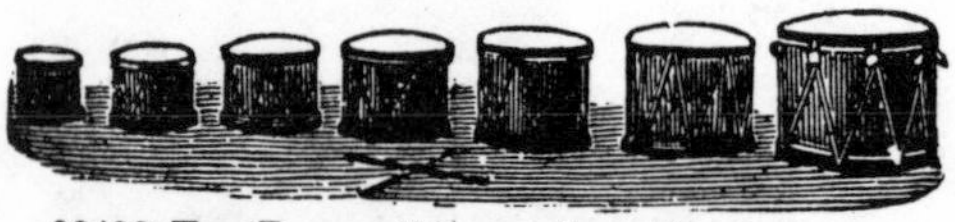

28428 Toy Drums (0½), good quality, brass body, corded with sticks, height, 5¾ inches, diameter, 6½ inches.
Each ........................ $0 25
Per dozen........................ 2 75

28429 Same (1), height, 6¾ inches, diameter, 8 inches.
Each........................ 38
Per dozen ........................ 4 15

28430 Same (2), height, 7¼ inches, diameter, 9 inches.
Each........................ 44
Per dozen ........................ 4 75

**Toy Drums—continued.**

28431 Same (3), height, 7½ inches, diameter, 10 inches.
Each........................ 50
Per dozen ........................ 5 40

28432 Same (4), height, 8 inches, diameter, 11 inches.
Each........................ 75
Per dozen ........................ 7 75

28433 Same (5), height, 9 inches, diameter, 12 inches.
Each........................ 90
Per dozen........................ 9 00

28434 Calf Head, imitation mahogany body, 1 -inch head.
Each........................ 1 00

28435 Same, 12-inch head.
Each........................ 1 50

28436 Same, 14-inch head.
Each ........................ 2 00

*For Metallophones, Music Boxes, Jews Harps, Mouth Harmonicas, etc., etc., see Musical Goods Department,*

## Magnets.

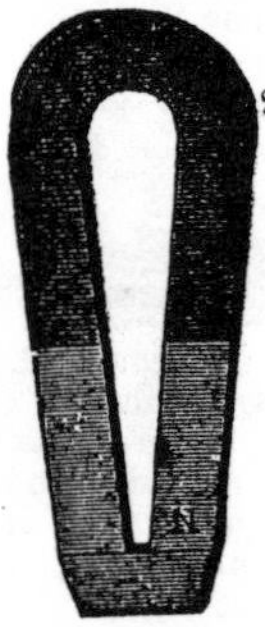

28438 Horseshoe Magnets, superior quality. Note reduction in prices.

| Length. | Each. | Price per doz. |
|---|---|---|
| 2 inches.. | $0 06 | $0 60 |
| 2½ " .. | 10 | 95 |
| 3 " .. | 15 | 1 50 |
| 4 " .. | 20 | 2 10 |
| 6 " .. | 45 | 5 00 |
| 8 " .. | 85 | 9 25 |
| 10 " .. | 1 50 | 16 00 |
| 12 " .. | 2 00 | 20 00 |

## Surprise Boxes.

(Jack in the Box).

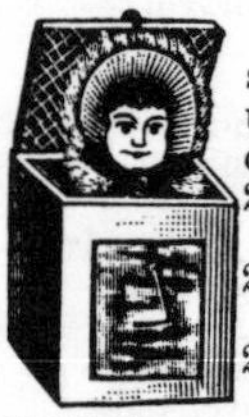

Surprise Boxes ranging from small to large sizes, containing figures of various forms which spring out of box at will.

28446 Surprise Box. Each.. $0 05
Per dozen........................ 50

28447 Surprise Box. Each.. 10
Per dozen ........................ 1 00

28448 Surprise Box. Each.. 15
Per dozen........................ 1 50

28449 Surprise Box. Each........................ 18
Per dozen........................ 1 75

28450 Surprise Box. Each........................ ·25
Per dozen........................ 2 50

**NAMES AND ADDRESSES.**—*Every time you write us, no matter how often, sign your name and give your full address. Married ladies should always give the same name, as we have no way of knowing that Mrs. Wm. Hope and Mrs. Maria Hope are the same person. If Mr., Miss or Mrs. is not given, we are liable to call a gentleman madame, or a lady sir. It is a good business rule to always sign your name the same way. J. Low, and Jas. H. Low, are two different persons to us.*

**SAMPLES.**—*We make no charge for samples, and for that reason we request you, when writing for them, to be very explicit in stating exactly what is wanted, giving Catalogue Number when possible, if not, the width, price, quality, color, etc., so that we can send you just what you need, instead of a great lot of samples that are of no use to you and cost us considerable money.*

⁂ *Chairs. Nothing so handy to have about the house. Nothing makes a home more attractive than pretty, serviceable and comfortable CHAIRS. You can now buy them at reasonable prices. Peruse our quotations.*

⁂ *It will be a favor to us (and perhaps to your friends) if you will place where they will do the most good, any duplicate catalogues or advertising matter which you may receive from us.*

## Japanese Lanterns.

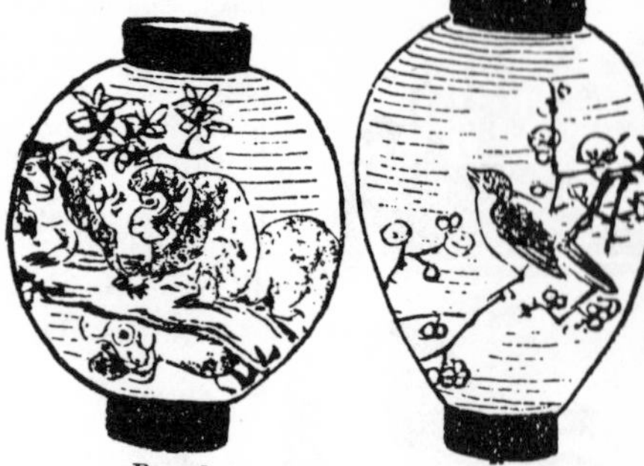

Round. Oval.

We are extensive importers of Japanese goods of all kinds. Our Japanese lanterns are all bright colors, and are the best possible decoration for lawn parties, Fourth of July celebrations, church, hall and parlor entertainments. They come in red, green, yellow and blue, with assorted flowers, birds, figures, landscapes, etc.

| | | Per doz. | Per 100. |
|---|---|---|---|
| 28451 | 5½x 8, oval shape ........ | $0 60 | $4 00 |
| 28452 | 6 x 7, round........ | 60 | 4 40 |
| 28453 | 7 x11, oval shape ........ | 75 | 6 00 |
| 28454 | 8 x 9, round shape........ | 75 | 6 00 |
| 28455 | 10 x10, round shape........ | 1 00 | 8 00 |
| 28456 | 10 x12, oval shape........ | 1 25 | 10 00 |
| 28457 | 12 x12, round shape........ | 1 50 | 12 00 |

Special prices furnished on case lots of 500, one size. Fancy shapes—men, birds, fish, houses, etc.; price furnished upon application.

## Alphabet and Building Blocks.

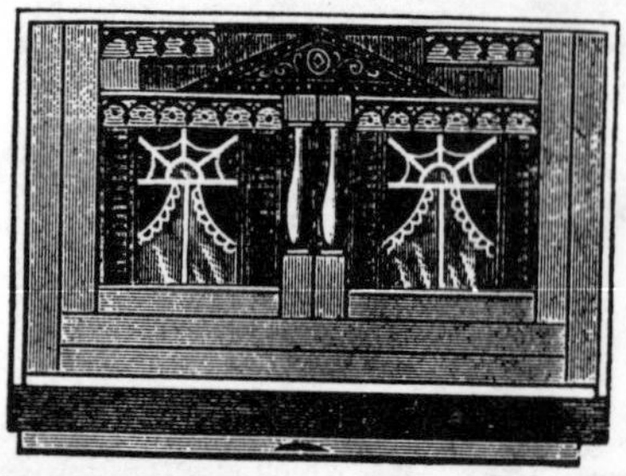

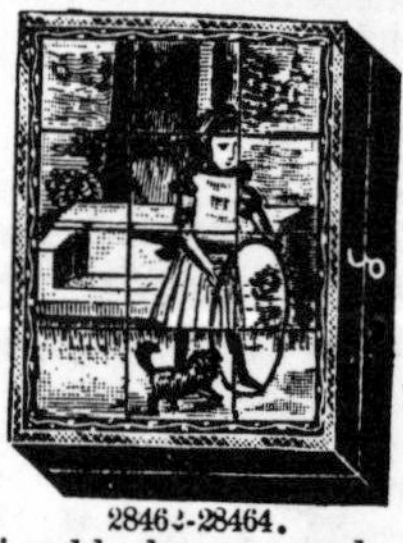

2846?-28464.

28460 Swiss Building Blocks in sliding cover wood box. Per box..... $0 25
Per dozen........ 2 60

28461 Swiss Building Blocks larger and better assorted than 28460, in wooden box. Per box..... $0 45
Per dozen........ 4 50

28462 Tower's Log Cabin Building Blocks; one of the most interesting and instructive sets of building blocks ever made. When fitted together, as per instructions, which accompany the blocks, a perfect log cabin, fence and well is constructed.
Price per set........................ $0 60

28463 Crandall's Building Blocks. This old and well-known style of dovetailed building blocks is still one of the most economical and popular blocks in the market. Per set........ 20

28464 Picture Blocks, put up in fancy folding box, containing twelve cubes, making six puzzle pictures. Sample pictures with each box; very fine for children, extra quality for the price.
Per box........................ 22
Per dozen........................ 2 10

28465 Same, large size. Per box........ 40

28466 Alphabetical Blocks (87), containing letters and figures; also six pictures, 1½x1½ inches, flat, put up in a neat box. Per box........................ 5
Per dozen........................ 54
Extra by mail, each, 3c.

**When you buy from a house that sells for CASH only, you do not have to pay the losses occasioned by a "credit system."**

## Magnetic Toys.

Each box of magnetic toys has a magnetized wand, and when the various figures, boats, fish, etc., are thrown into a basin of water, they will follow this wand, though several inches away all the time. Lots of fun for the children, and will keep them out of mischief.

28550 Magnetic Toys, in glass covered box, set of 3 pieces, 5c. per set. Per dozen, 53c.

28551 Same, larger, set of 5 pieces, 10c. per set. Per dozen, $1.05.

2 552 Same Box, 5x8½ inches (like cut), set of 7 pieces, 25c. per set......... $2 60

28553 Same Box, larger than 28552, 14 pieces, price, per set, 50c.

## Jointed Snakes.

28554 Jointed Snakes, made of wood, fancy painted, length, 16½ inches. Each.....$0 05 Per dozen.......$0 50

28555 Jointed Snakes, larger, length, 29 inches. Each.....$0 10 Per dozen.......$1 00

## Bagatelle Boards.

28557 Bagatelle Boards, 16 inches long, with spring cue, each, 50c.

28558 Bagatelle Boards, 26 inches long, well made, each, 90c.

## Toy Violins.

28560 Toy Violin, 16 inches long, one in a box, with bow. Each, 25c. Per doz., $2 75. All complete, and good enough to learn the rudiments on.

## MISCELLANEOUS TOYS AND NOVELTIES.
### Rattles and Whistles.

| | Each | Per doz. |
|---|---|---|
| 28561 Common Tin | $ 0 02 | $0 20 |
| 28562 Fancy Tin | 3 | 30 |
| 28563 Globe Bell Tin Rattle, wooden handle | 5 | 50 |

28564 Chime Bell Rattle, wood handle. Each, 8c. Per dozen .$0 75

28·64

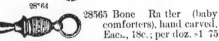

28565 Bone Rattler (baby comforters), hand carved, Each, 18c.; per doz. $1 75

28566 Globe Bell, iron rattles, sleigh bell pattern, japanned wood handles; each $0 06 Per dozen 65

28567 Same, with ribbon in handle. Each. 8 Per dozen 85

### Toy Dinner Bells.

28570 Brass, wood handle, height, 2¼ inches Each.....$0 04 Per dozen....$0 40

28571 Iron, galvanized wood, handle, length, 3 in. Each.....$0 05 Per dozen.....$0 50

28572 Call Bell, 2¼ inch, japanned iron base, iron hammer, silvered bell, brass push or tongue. The neatest toy call bell made.
Each.............. $0 15
Per dozen........ 1 50

## Toy Balloons.

28573 Red Rubber Balloons with trumpet ends. One of the all-the-year-around sellers. A good loud one. Each, $0 04 Per doz., $0 40

## Jumping Ropes.

28574 Jute Rope, ¼ in., length, 6½ ft., stained handles. Each $0 04 Per dozen..$0 40

28575 Jute Rope, ¼ in., length, 8 ft., japanned handles. Each $0 06 Per dozen..$0 60

28576 Jute Rope, ¼ in., length, 7 ft., japanned or polished handles. Each .... $0 05 Per dozen...................... 50

## Jack Stones.

28577 Nicely coppered, good sizes. Per dozen....$0 04 Per gross.....$0 30

## Toy Reins.

28578 Toy Horse Reins, with bells. Price governs quality. Each, 5, 10, 20, 50, 75c., and $1.35

## Clown on Stick.

28579 Always in demand, sells all the year around. Assorted clowns and monkeys, the same kind as you had when a boy. They never change. Price governs size. Price, each, 4, 8, and 12c. Per dozen, 40c., 80c., $1.20.

## Big Chief Bow and Arrow.

28580 A large bow and arrow new pattern, strong and accurate. The largest and best toy of the kind for the price in the market. Each, $0 03 Per doz., $0 60 We do not furnish extra arrows for this bow.

## The Jester.

28581 The Jester, a small bladder fastened by a string to the end of a stick. Hit your friend on the head as hard as you can; it may make him jump, but it won't hurt him a bit. Lots of fun for the boys. Each. $0 20 Per doz..$2 00

## Noah's Arks.

This toy has been a seller ever since the flood, and probably will be as long as the world stands.

28585 Noah's Ark filled with neatly painted animals, flat ark, small. Each..$0 05 Per dozen..$0 50
Noah's Ark, same as above, larger. Each.. 10
Per dozen.... 1 00
Noah's Ark, same as above, larger. Each.. 20
Noah's Ark, same as above, larger. Each.. 40

28586 Noah's Ark, boat shape, fancy. Each ..$0 20
Per dozen .. 2 00
Noah's Ark, same style as 28586, but larger and better assorted. Each......$0 35
Per dozen.......... 4 20
Noah's Ark, same style, but larger and better. Each.................$0 60

## Animal Sets.

28587 Animal Set, in wooden box, 3½x6½ inches, per box, 5c.; per dozen, 50c. Same as 28587, but larger, each, 10c.

28588 German Animal Set, in wooden box, 7½x12, well made, and complete, per box, 50c.; per dozen, $5.00.

## Noah's Arks—continued.

28589 Swiss Animal Set, extra well made, house and out buildings, in strong wooden box, size, 7x12 inches, sliding cover, per box, 25c.

The number of animals, as well as the quality and assortment of trees, houses, figures, etc., are regulated by the price.
Swiss Animal Set, larger than 28589, each, 40c.
Swiss Animal Set, still larger and more complete than preceding ones, each, 80c.

28590 Villages, put up in a wooden box, complete with houses, out buildings, etc., each, 25c.
Villages, same as above, but larger, 40c.
Villages, same as above, but much finer and larger; a superior article, 75c.

## Games, Puzzles, Etc.

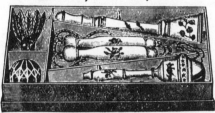

28592 Game Box, consisting of jumping rope, shuttlecock, cup and two balls, as illustrated. Finely finished in white and gold enamel. A fine present for a girl.
Price........................$0 75

## Game of Fish Pond.

28593 Westcott's Game of Fish Pond; complete with full directions. A most popular and interesting home game. Price, each.$0 25

28593½ Westcott's Game of Fish Pond; similar to 28582, but larger and better finished. Elegantly put up. Each.... ......... $0 50

## GAMES, PUZZLES, ETC.
### Toy Panorama.

28591 Alphabetical Toy Panorama, just out. A happy invention for the children. Will be treasured after more expensive toys have lost their attractions. By turning the crank the letters with their interesting object lessons and illustrations appear and disappear in and out of the barrel, every two letters making a simple rhyme that will delight the little ones. The barrel is made of strong wood, elegantly colored and polished, length 3 inches. The 26 illustrations are printed on a strip of glazed holland cloth, 2 inches wide and 53 inches long. Almost impossible to break this toy. It is undoubtedly destined to be the most popular toy of this season from the reports of the manufacturers. Retail price, 25 to 30c.

Our price, each.................. $0 15
Per dozen...................... 1 50
Per gross...................... 15 00
By mail, extra, each, 4c

28594 The new game of Moneta or money makes money, is a deservedly popular game. Consists of fifty illustrated, well finished cards, each representing a coin of United States money. Is instructive and interesting Full directions accompany each game.
Regular price, 50c, our price......$0 38
Per dozen...................... 3 85

## Jack Straws.

**28595** This is an old-fashioned game, but its popularity increases yearly.
Price, per box, with directions......$ 0 08
Per dozen .................. 83

**28596** Jack Straws, consisting of carved wooden implements such as rakes, hoes, forks, poles, hooks, etc., put up in a neat wood box. The latest forms and the most difficult game, all made of carved wood.
Per box............. ......... 10
Per dozen ............. 1 00

**28596¼** Jack Straws, same, finely finished and hardwood, in sliding cover wood box, nicely varnished.
Per box ......... 35
Per dozen..................... 3 50

## Loto.

This famous German game has become very popular in America. It is easily learned and may be played by the youngest children. Directions in each box.

| | Each. | Per doz. |
|---|---|---|
| **28597** In paper box, ordinary quality, | $0 08 | $0 85 |
| **28598** In neat wooden box, good quality (25c. size) .......... | 15 | 1 60 |
| **28599** In nice wood box, extra fine quality (50c. grade)....... | 30 | 2 10 |

## The Game of "Authors," Etc.

| | Each. | Per doz |
|---|---|---|
| **28600** **This interesting little game,** giving titles and works of the best authors, contains classified and lettered books, and is interesting to old and young alike. Directions in each box | $0 16 | $1 70 |
| **28601** **Authors,** same as above, extra fine quality, 50c. grade............. | 35 | |

**28603** **Peter Coddle.** This humorous game consists of about 200 cards, containing amusing sentences together with a 16-page book, describing in a spicy manner the adventures of Peter Coddle in New York. Parts of the story are omitted and blanks left to be supplied by the cards. One of the most amusing and comical games published. Directions in each box.... 16   1 70

**28605** **Old Maid.** This is an exceedingly funny popular game, contains 35 comical cards put up in sliding box, with directions for playing.. 08 85

**28605¼** **Old Maid, better quality,** full assortment, superior finish cards...... 16 70

## Cut-Up Jumbo Puzzles.

**28606** Cut-Up Jumbo Puzzles consists of a large colored picture of the celebrated elephant "Jumbo," 12x15 inches, mounted on heavy board, and cut up into irregular pieces of a small size, put up in a handsome box. Each box also contains a complete picture showing how pieces look when put together.
Each ..................$ 0 19
Per dozen................... 2 00

**28607** Blown Up Steam Boat Puzzle, same as No. 28606, only the picture is that of a steamboat.
Each ..................... 19
Per dozen ................... 2 00

**28608** Bird Slips, or puzzle picture games, for the little folks, put up in fancy colored box.
Each ..................... 20

**28609** Animal Slips, same as above, only animals. Each ................. 25

## Hardwood Ten Pins.

Polished and striped, complete with balls. In strong wood boxes. Well made and finished.

| No | Size. | Per set. | Per doz. |
|---|---|---|---|
| 28610 | 6 in. | 25c. | $2 40 |
| 28611 | 8 in. | 50c. | 5 50 |
| 28612 | 12 in. | 85c. | 9 60 |

**28615** **Drawing Teacher** a neat box containing 20 different designs; perforated on heavy paper with full instructions. Each, 25c.

**28616** **Lawson's Base Ball Game,** with cards. This is the only perfect base ball game with cards in the market. Price, per pack, with full instructions, 15c.

---

**28620** Spelling Boards. These boards are 13½ inches long, by 9 inches wide, and have 56 lettered hardwood blocks, neatly made and highly ornamented. Instructive and amusing; letters cannot come out or be placed in a position upside down.
Price, each.....................$0 75

**28621** The Spelling Puzzle, 3¾x6¼ inches in size, a new puzzle, interesting to old and young alike. Put up in a neat box.
Price....... $0 20

**28622** **Pigs in Clover** This popular puzzle is too well known to need a description. Put up in a neat box. Each.........$0 10

**28623** **The Scientific Planchette Board.** made on the same principle as the old and popular planchette boards of 1860. Style (No. 2), fine polished board, cherry finish, nickel-plated castors, with swivel joint, boxwood wheels, lead pencil with rubber tip. Put up in paper box, with full directions and full account of its workings.
Price, each...................... $1 25

**28624** Planchette (No. 3) Hardwood Board, varnished, brass castors, maple wheels and pencil. Put up in neat paper box with full directions.............$0 75

**28625** **The Gilt Edge Building Blocks,** These are an extra large and finely finished block, made in three different designs and sizes.
Price for smallest, per set..........$0 25
Medium, per set............. 50
Large, per set.................... 75

**28626** **The World's Educator.** This is a new and interesting folding game.
Price .................... $0 75

**28627** **The Fortune Telling and Base Ball Game** complete, with full directions.
Price, each................. $0 75

**28628** **The Fort.** This is another interesting home game for the little ones which well deserves its popularity; well put up.
Price....................$0 75

**28629** **Church and Sunday School Building Blocks.** Good value, and a set of blocks that we can recommend.
Price, per set.............. $0 75

## Dolls' Extension Cradles.

**28635** Dolls' Extension Cradle, a novelty in a doll's cradle, made of plain, smooth finish wood and may be folded or extended to full size without taking apart. Size when open, 7x9.
Each.......$0 20
Per dozen... 2 20

**28636** Dolls' Cradle, plain finish, light wood, well made. Price, each...........$0 25

**28637** Dolls' Crib, light wood, neatly finished. Each.....................$0 20

**28638** Furniture Set, strongly made and well finished. Price, complete, per set.. $0 75

**28639** The Girls' Favorite Combination Set.
Price ..................... $0 85

**28640** Toy Extension Tables, small...... 25

**28641** Toy Extension Tables, larger size and stronger made.... ...............$0 50

**28642** Dolls' Folding Chairs, plain wood, smooth finish, each ...................$0 20

**28643** Dolls' Chairs, straight back, each.... 15

**28644** Dolls' Rocking Chairs, plain wood, nicely finished. Each.............. $0 20
Same, larger size, each ............. 30

**28645** Dolls' High Chairs, each ......... 20

**28645½** Dolls' High Chairs, with dishes .. 30

---

## Kitchen and Wash Sets.

**28646** Kitchen and Wash Set, nicely packed in wooden box, about 22 wooden utensils, all neatly made, such as tubs, pails, ladles, spoons, roller, masher, wash board, stand, churn and many other articles.
Per box..$0 85   Per dozen boxes...$9 00

**28647** Kitchen and Dairy Sets, packed in wooden box containing nicely made wooden utensils, small size. Each.........$0 20

**28648** Same as 28647, medium size ... ... 40

**28649** Same, large size and more complete.. 75

## Toy Parlor and Bedroom Sets.

28650.

**28650** Parlor Sets, 9 pieces, put up in pasteboard boxes. Per set.....................$0 25
Per dozen sets................. 2 50

**28651** Parlor Sets of 11 pieces, upholstered in sateen; a well-made set. Per set....$0 50
Per dozen sets................. 5 00

**28652** Parlor Set of 8 pieces, satin upholstered, has long pier glass; turned legs on table, chairs and sofa. Per set.........$0 95
Per dozen sets................. 9 50

**28653** Bed Room Set of 8 pieces, as represented in cut. Each....$0 45 Per doz....$4 75

## Clapping Figures.

**28655** Cymbal Clapping Figures, gaily dressed and decorated.
Each........$0 10

**28656** Cymbal Clapping Figures, better got up than preceding.
Each.:........$0 15

**28657** Double Face Clapping Cymbal Figures.
Each........$0 20

**28658** Clapping Cymbal Figure, with hair and cap.
Each........$0 35

**28659** Clapping Cymbal Figure, gilt trimmed and bisque head.
Each........$0 75

## Table Croquet.

28660 Table Croquet, with arches, mallets and balls, complete; highly polished and painted. Per set........................$0 50
28661 Table Croquet, complete, as above, but larger, with 8 balls and mallets, elegantly striped. Per set....................$0 85
28662 Parlor Croquet, suitable for playing on the floor, finely varnished and painted. Price, per set, complete............$0 85
28663 Ring Toss, with 5 silvered wire hoops, handsomely painted base, with sliding cover. This game is suitable for parlor or lawn, complete, with full directions. Per set...........................$0 50

## Rubber Toys.

28665 Rubber Mouse, fancy painted, with whist e. Each....................$0 20
28666 Rubber Doves, life size, natural color. Each...........................$0 75

28667 Rubber Bird, life size. Each.......$0 20

28668 Rubber Horse and Rider; size, 6x6 inches; nicely painted. Each...........$0 35

28669 Rubber Elephant and Rider. Measures 6x7 inches, very neat. Each.........$0 50

28670 Rubber Young Chick, natural as life Each.......$0 15

28671 Rubber Young Goslin. Each...............$0 15

28672 Rubber Boy, toy doll, 10¼ inches long, represented as dressed, with complete suit. Each.............$0 65.

## Children's Table Sets.

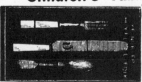

28675 Children's Memento Sets, knife, fork and spoon, on card. Per set.. $0 10
Per dozen sets.... 1 00

### Mementos.

28676 Set of Knife, Fork and Spoon, in neat box, steel knife and fork, with bone handle, and good nickeled spoon. Per set................... 30
Per dozen sets.................... 3 25

*₊* Goods delivered to depots free of charge. We make no charge for cartage.

---

### Table Sets—continued.

28677 Toy "Britannia" Sets, consisting of knife, fork, spoon, napkin and ring and knife rest, in neat box.

Price, per set....................$0 21
Price, per dozen sets ........... 2 10
28678 Same as above, but put up in box containing three sets.
Per box............................ 45
Per dozen boxes.................. 4 25

## Toy Tea Sets.

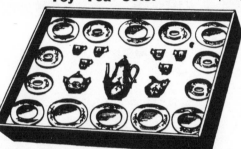

Our large trade in toy tea sets last year has warranted us in placing one of the largest import orders ever given for these goods. Our order was placed last spring with one of the most celebrated makers in Germany, and we think the prices we offer them at include some of the best value in the country.

| | Per set. | Per doz. sets. |
|---|---|---|
| 28680 Decorated China Tea Set, containing tea pot, sugar bowl, milk pitcher, bowl and cups and saucers, for a small child; securely packed in box ................. | $0 10 | $1 10 |
| 28681 Decorated China Tea Set, containing covered tea pot, sugar bowl, cream pitcher, 4 cups and 4 saucers, in pasteboard box............ | 15 | 1 50 |
| 28682 Decorated China Tea Set of 15 pieces and 6 spoons, has 6 each cups and saucers, a sugar bowl, cream pitcher and tea pot, in pasteboard box................... | 20 | 2 00 |
| 28683 Decorated China Tea Set (Champion), same assortment, but larger dishes.... | 35 | 3 50 |
| 28684 Decorated China Tea Set, good size, well-made dishes, set consisting of 6 cups, 6 saucers, 6 plates, 2 cake plates, a tea pot, sugar bowl and pitcher............... | 50 | 5 00 |
| 28685 China Tea Set, handsomely decorated, bright colors, set consisting of 6 cups, 6 saucers, 6 plates, 3¼-inch diameter, tea pot, pitcher and sugar bowl, nicely packed in box............. | 75 | 8 00 |
| 28686 Plain White Tea Sets, consisting of 6 saucers, 4 inches diameter; 6 cups, large tea pot, pitcher and sugar bowl, packed in box............ | 1 00 | 11 00 |
| 28687 Handsomely Painted China Tea Set, extra size, a splendid set, consisting of 6 cups, 6 saucers, 6 plates, 2 fruit or cake plates, sugar bowl, cream pitcher and tea pot.. | 1 50 | 16 00 |
| 28688 Decorated China Dinner Set of a dozen pieces, consisting of 6 plates, 1 extra large plate, a platter, sauce boat, soup tureen, vegetable dish and pickle dish........... | 75 | 8 00 |

*₊* Always give name and price when ordering from us. Catalogue number alone is not always sufficient.

---

## White Stone China Toy Tea Sets.

The pieces in this set are larger than usually sold in toy sets; the cups stand about 2½ inches high and the plates measure about 5 inches across.

Toy Tea Pot.　　Toy Slop Bowl.　　Toy Sugar Bowl.

Toy Creamer.　Toy Cup and Saucer.　　Toy Plate.

28689 White Stone China Tea Set of 24 pieces, as follows: 6 plates, 6 cups, 6 saucers, 1 sugar bowl and cover, 1 tea pot and cover, 1 creamer, 1 slop bowl. This set is large enough for a miss of from 8 to 14 years of age. (Not safe to send by mail.)
Price, per set....................$1 25
28690 Gilt-Lined Tea Set, same assortment as 28690; elegant and complete. Per set............... 1 75

## Decorated China Toy Toilet Sets.

28691 Small Toilet or Wash Set, packed in pasteboard box.
Per set....$0 20
Per doz.sets 2 10
28692 Decorated Toilet or Wash Set, good size, 5 pieces and 2 perforated covers.
Per set........................... $0 40
Per dozen sets.................... 4 50
28693 Extra Size Wash or Toilet Set, gilt lined and brilliantly decorated; a handsome set. Packed in strong box.
Per set ........................... 90
Per dozen sets.................... 8 50

## Toy Watches.

Postage on toy watches, each, 3c.

All our toy watches have movable hands and are stem winding.

28694 Toy Watch, with chain; best for the price ever offered. Each.............$0 04
Per dozen........ 40
28695 Toy Watch; a beautiful little fancy gilt watch, 1¼-inch diameter, with ¾-inch open face dial; has long gilt chain, and is just the thing for little girls.
Each............................. $0 05
Per dozen.......................... 40
28696 Toy Watch, new style Swiss dial and front; very pretty and durable.
Each.............................. 12
Per dozen......................... 1 25
28696½ Toy Watch, fancy gilt, with heavy gilt chain and whistle charm; has bell attachment; open face. Each.. 15
Per dozen......................... 1 50
28697 Toy Watch, enameled face, good size and shape, with vest chain; for boys. Each ..................... 16
Per dozen......................... 1 75
28698 Toy Watch, same as 28703, with neck chain; for girls. Each...... 17
Per dozen......................... 1 85

*₊* INLAID SILVER SPOONS AND FORKS.—Stronger than Solid Silver, at one-third the price. Warranted for forty years.

---

**$2.50 Buys a genuine REED ROCKER, good style, ladies' size. This is a leader. For page, see index.**

## Toy Watches—continued.

28698½ Toy Watch, figured gilt, open face, fancy gilt chain, as illustrated. Each..$0 20
Per dozen... 2 00

28699 Toy Watch, has automatic tick movement, stem winding. Turn stem a few times, when the hands will make several revolutions automatically, accompanied with a loud ticking. Very interesting.
Each...... $0 22
Per dozen.. 2 20

## Paper Dolls.

28710 Dolls, made of heavy cardboard, printed in colors, showing both front and back; furnished with four complete costumes, with bonnets to match, all fashionable styles. Three designs, each in separate envelopes, 4x7 inches. Price, each .........$0 04
Per dozen, assorted, 3 kinds...... 40
28712 Same; size, 6x10 inches. Each.... 10
Per dozen, assorted, 3 kinds....... 1 10

## Dolls in Great Variety.

*N. B.—We do not handle any dolls outside of those quoted below. Please do not order any except as quoted.*

28701 China Dolls. Each 4c., 5c., 6c., 8c. and 10c. Per dozen, 40c., 50c., 60c., 75c. and $1.00.

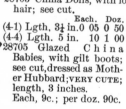

28703 China Dolls, with long flowing hair; see cut.

| | Each. | Doz. |
|---|---|---|
| (4-1) Lgth. 3½ in. | 0 05 | 0 50 |
| (4-4) Lgth. 5 in. | 10 | 1 00 |

28705 Glazed China Babies, with gilt boots; see cut, dressed as Mother Hubbard; VERY CUTE; length, 3 inches.
Each, 9c.; per doz. 90c.

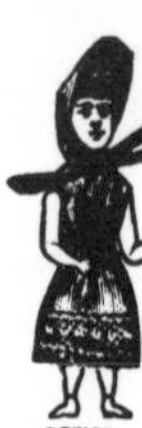

28703.     28705.

28706 Glazed China Babies, with gilt boots, (1882) dressed as Red Riding Hood, 3¼ inches long.
Each, 9c.; per dozen, 90c.
28708 Dolls with China heads, arms and feet, nankeen bodies, not dressed.

| | Each. | Doz. |
|---|---|---|
| Length, 7 inches | $0 05 | $0 55 |
| Length, 13½ inches | 18 | 1 95 |
| Length, 14½ inches | 25 | 2 70 |

28710 China Dressed Dolls, nicely assorted.

| | Each. | Doz. |
|---|---|---|
| Length, 5 inches | $0 05 | $0 50 |
| Length, 8 inches | 10 | 1 00 |
| Length, 11 inches | 19 | 2 00 |
| Length, 12 inches | 22 | 2 40 |
| Length, 14 inches | 42 | 4 50 |

28711 Patent Indestructible Heads on cloth bodies dressed as servants, with aprons and dusting caps; length, 11 in. (566).
Each, 22c ; per dozen, $2.40.
28712 Patent Indestructible Dolls' Heads, on cloth bodies, painted hair (551), dressed, assorted colors, 12¼ inches long.
Each........... $0 25
Per dozen. ..... 2 70
28713 Patent Indestructible Heads, on cloth bodies, painted hair (551½), dressed, trimmed with satin and lace; length, 16½ inches.
Each .... .....$0 45
Per dozen....... 4 80

28710-13.

## Dolls—continued.

28714 Indestructible Dressed Dolls, bisque finish, washable head; large size, 25 in. long.
Each.............$0 90
28715 Indestructible Dressed Dolls, bisque finish; washable head; extra size, 27 in. long.
Each.............$1 10

28714-15.

28719 Patent Dolls, boys and girls to match, dressed in red, white and blue flannel toboggan suits, trimmed with same in contrasting colors, 16 inches (852-62), painted hair.
Each...........$0 40
Per dozen........... 4 30
28721 Patent Dolls, sailor boy and girl to match, dressed in blue flannel suits, trimmed in white, 18 inches; one in box; girl has flowing hair with jaunty sailor cap; boy has white woolly hair and sailor cap.
Each..............$1 00

28726 Patent Heads, on cloth corset bodies, with shoes and stockings, chemise and adjustable corset; 12¼ inches long. Until sold,
Each....................$0 25
Per dozen.................... 2 70

28734 Dolls' Bodies (no head), made of fine white muslin, with seat, stitched red, white kid arms. Until sold,

| | Each. | Doz. |
|---|---|---|
| Length, 11½ in. | $0 20 | $2 15 |
| Length, 14½ in. | 25 | 2 70 |
| Length, 17 in. | 40 | 4 25 |

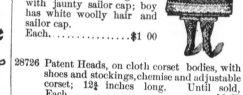

28734.

28736 Patent Corset Bodies (no head), with seat, kid arms, colored stockings, shoes with tassels (105).

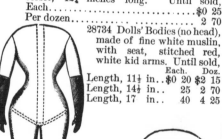

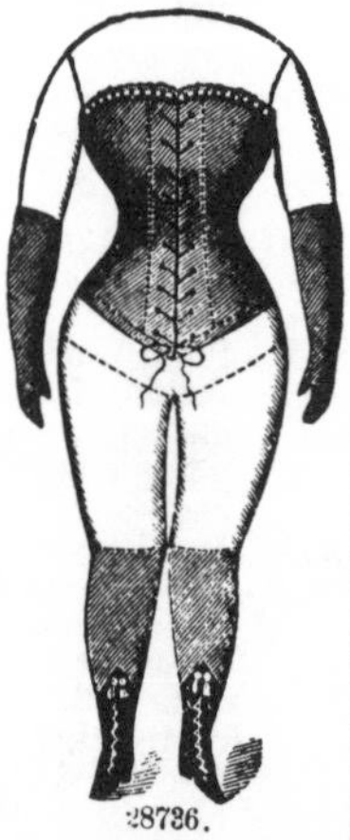

28726.

| | Each. | Doz. |
|---|---|---|
| Length, 10 inches | $0 20 | $2 15 |
| Length, 12¼ inches | 24 | 2 60 |
| Length, 15 inches | 32 | 3 45 |
| Length, 17 inches | 48 | 5 20 |
| Length, 20 inches | 60 | 6 00 |

28737 Patent Dolls' Heads, painted hair. Each, 10c., 20c. and 25c.

## Dolls—continued.

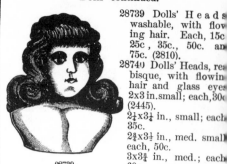

28739 Dolls' Heads washable, with flowing hair. Each, 15c. 25c., 35c., 50c. and 75c. (2810).
28740 Dolls' Heads, real bisque, with flowing hair and glass eyes 2x3 in. small; each, 30c (2445).
2¼x3½ in., small; each 35c.
2¾x3½ in., med. small each, 50c.
3x3¾ in., med.; each 60c.

28739.

| 3x4 in., med.; each | $0 6 |
|---|---|
| Larger | 7 |

This line of bisque heads are small and medium size. Do not order expecting them to fit large doll bodies.

28741 Dolls, not dressed, muslin bodies, patent heads painted hair, 16 in.
Each....................$0 2
Per dozen ...... ... 2 1
28741½ Dolls, not dressed, fine muslin bodies, fancy stitched and hair stuffed, patent heads, painted hair, with shoes and stockings.
Each................ $0 2
Per dozen........... 2 70
28742 Patent Indestructible Dolls, flowing hair, cloth body. hair stuffed, patent leather laced boots, similar to cut; length, 13 inches.
Each.................$0 25
Per dozen........... 2 70
28743 Dolls, same description as 28742, but large size, length, 18 in. Each.........$0 35

28741 to 28748.

## Undressed Real Bisque Dolls.

28745 Real Bisque Dolls, all kid body and hair stuffed, long flowing hair, teeth and moving eyes, stockings and slippers......................... $0 75
28746 Real Bisque Dolls, with teeth, all kid body and hair stuffed, long flowing hair, see cut (2625), length, 19 in., similar to cut............... 1 25
28747 Real Bisque Dolls, with moving eyes, all kid body, hair stuffed, lace stockings and leather slippers, similar to cut (2650)................. 1 25
28748 Real Bisque Dolls, all kid body, hair stuffed, lace stockings and leather slippers; length, 18 inches, similar to cut (2645).............. 1 25

## Bisque Dolls Dressed.

28750 Bisque Dolls, jointed, moving head, hair and chemise, painted boots.
Each....................$0 13
Per dozen.................... 1 35

28751 Bisque Dolls, with hair, jointed and movable heads, can be put in striking attitudes; nicely dressed, see cut; length, 11 in. (3905).
Each................. $0 30
Per dozen........... 3 10
28752 Bisque Dolls, with hair, jointed and movable heads, assorted sailor boys and girls dressed in flannel suits trimmed with white and sailor turbans. These are very cute; length, 8¼ in. (No cut) (3930).
Each................. $0 25
Per dozen............ 2 50
28753 Bisque Dolls, with hair, long skirt, kid and cloth body, 11 in. (2545).
Each....................$0 25
Per dozen.................... 2 50

28751.

**ALL our buggies are warranted for one year. Write for price delivered at your station.**

*Montgomery Ward & Co.*

## Bisque Dolls—continued.

28754 Bisque Jointed Dolls, with teeth, long plaited chemise, with moving head and eyes, flowing hair.
Each.... .......... $0 45
Per dozen............ 4 40

28755 Bisque Dolls, with flowing hair, long chemise with lace, shoes and stockings, movable head and eyes; length, 16 in., similar to cut (2565), all kid body.
Each ................$1 25

28756 Bisque Doll's, with flowing hair, long chemise, trimmed with lace, shoes and stockings, all kid body, large size, 17 inches long, similar to cut.
Each.................$1 20

28757 Bisque Dolls, with flowing hair, long chemise, plaited and trimmed with lace, double ball jointed movable head; length, 17 in., (3705-5) similar to cut.

28754 to 28757.

Each.................$1 25

28758 Bisque Dolls, with flowing hair, long chemise, plaited and trimmed with lace, double ball jointed movable head, extra size; length, 20 in. (3705-7).
Each.................$2 10

28760 Bisque Dolls, with flowing hair, dressed complete in satin, velvet and lace, shoes and stockings, jointed and moving head.
Each.... .......$0 60
Also sailor boy complete in full sailor dress, companion to girl.

28761 Bisque Dolls, with flowing hair, shoes and stockings, dressed complete in elaborate combination costume of satin, lace, etc., bonnet and all complete; jointed, movable head (5320); length, 15 inches.
Each.................$1 25

28762 Bisque Dolls, with flowing hair, shoes and stockings, dressed complete in elaborate combination costumes of satin, lace tinsel, braid, etc., lace mitts and lace trimmed bonnet and underwear. Extra large, 21 inches (5324).

28760 to 28762.

Each.................$2 10

The above line of bisque dolls are all imported and we cannot duplicate any style when sold out, and so shall take the liberty of substituting the next nearest style, unless ordered not to.
This line of bisque dolls have beautiful French faces, and must be seen to be appreciated. The cuts do not do them justice. They are packed one in a box and are not safe to be sent by mail.

28765 Fine Jointed Bisque Japanese Doll, dressed in native costume, full length, 10½ inches. See cut (5520-4-0).
Each... ..... $0 85

28765.

## Bisque Dolls—continued.

28767 Washable Dolls, with long chemise, embroidered yoke. It can say papa, mamma, when the strings are pulled. This is a very pretty pink-cheeked doll, 15 inches long, similar to cut, but with bonnet and embroidered chemise.
Each ............ $0 50
Per dozen . ..... 5 50

28768 Baby Doll, with flowing hair, long chemise, with lace collar and bib, knitted hood, eyes open and close automatically; length, 11 in (2535-0).
Each .... ........$ 0 55
Per doze.........  6 00

25767.

### Wax Dolls with Flowing Hair.

At about one-half price to close.

| | Each. | Per doz. |
|---|---|---|
| 28770 Wax Dolls, long chemise braided and trimmed with tinsel, painted boots and stockings; length, 16 inches. | $0 22 | $2 10 |
| 28771 Wax Dolls, long chemise trimmed with tinsel braid and lace, painted boots and stockings; length, 24 inches. | 45 | |
| 28772 Wax Dolls, same as 28771, 30 inches long............ | 85 | |
| 28773 Wax Dolls, same as 28771, 34 inches...... ...... | 1 00 | |

### Indestructible Wool Dolls.

28775 Worsted Dolls, assorted boys and girls, 9½ inches (1175).
Each.............. $0 20
Per dozen..........  2 15

28776 Worsted Dolls, assorted boys and girls, 14 inches (1176).
Each.... ......... $0 40
Per dozen.........  4 30

28778 Worsted Dressed Girl Dolls, assorted, similar to cut; length, 10 inches.
Each ..$0 22
Per doz. 2 30

28775-6.

28779 Worsted Dolls, girls, larger and much handsomer dresses than 28778; six in box. No two dresses alike.
Each .................$ 0 45
Per dozen..............  4 60

28778-9.

28780 Worsted Dolls (girls), large size, fine dresses, assorted, 15 inches.
Each............ $0 85
Per dozen.......  8 50

28782 Worsted Knit Clown, in fancy dress, with gilt rattle buttons. Boys and girls, assorted; length, 12 inches. See cut (1186).
Each..$0 45
Per doz. 3 85

28785.

## Rubber Dolls.

28785 Rubber Doll, musical, worsted hat and dress. See cut (8 inches).
Each ................. $0 25
Per dozen ................  2 50

28786 Rubber Dolls, musical, worsted dress and hat. Much larger than 28785; 9½ inches.
Each.................. $0 35
Per dozen ...............  3 50

28787 Rubber Dolls, musical, worsted hat and dress; 10½ inches.
Each......................$0 40
Per dozen...................  4 10

28785-6-7

## Miscellaneous.

28790 White Woolly Elephant, with blanket. Unbreakable. See cut.
Each........ $0 25
Per dozen...  2 70

28791 White Woolly Dog, with red ribbon. Unbreakable. See cut.
Each.... $0 25
Per doz..  2 70

28792 Woolly Cats, with ribbon and bell; three colors. Maltese, white and golden brown. See cut.
Each.... $0 25
Per doz.  2 70

28793 Canton Flannel Dogs, on castors, in three colors, red, white or gold. See cut.
Each........ $0 25
Per dozen....  2 70

28793.

28794 Arabian Horse on castors, made of Canton flannel. See cut. Colors: White, mouse or gold.
Each...... $0 25
Per dozen.  2 70

28795 Our Celebrated Plush Pug Dog. Special attention is called to our dog. It is the best toy for a young child ever placed on the market.
Each ........ $0 50
Per dozen.......  5 40

28796 Plush Pug Dog, on castors, smaller
Each ...... .......  40
Per dozen .................  4 30

## Toy Musical Instruments.

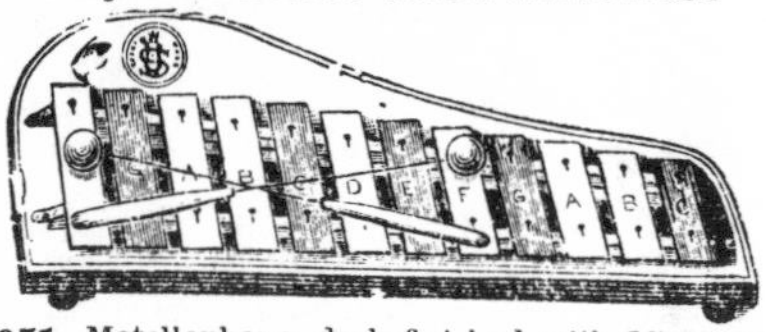

**H 9951** Metallophone, dark finished, with fifteen notes, bronzed keys, neatly finished and put up in pasteboard box. Shipping weight, 2 lb. Each..................**45c.**

**H 9956** Special Size High Grade Metallophone or Parlor Bells, has twenty-two notes and is a high grade instrument with bronzed metal keys, accurately tuned for use with piano or stringed instruments. Shipping weight, 7 lb. Each..................**$1.25**

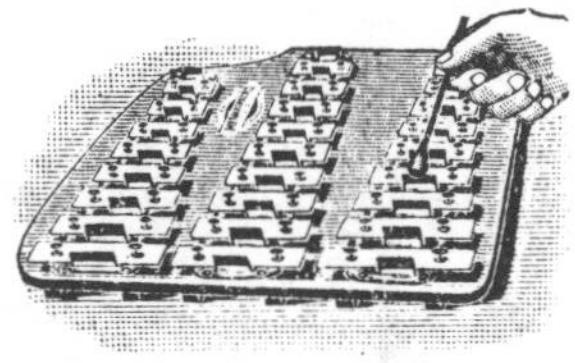

**H 9960** Metallochord. The Twentieth Century Toy Musical Instrument Novelty, always in tune. Discords impossible, easy to play from numbered music. It is played with one hand. One stroke plays the harmony accompaniment in addition to the air. An excellent instrument for a beginner in music. Packed in box with striker and six pieces of music with directions for playing. Shipping weight, 4½ lb. Each..................**95c.**

## Toy Pianos.

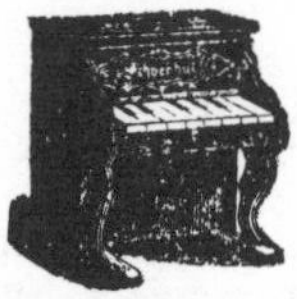

Accurately tuned. Best quality made.

**H 9968** Upright Toy Piano, with 15 keys, and case is finished in neat style as cut represents. Size, 16⅛x 11½x8½ in. Shipping weight, 5 lb. Each..................**89c.**

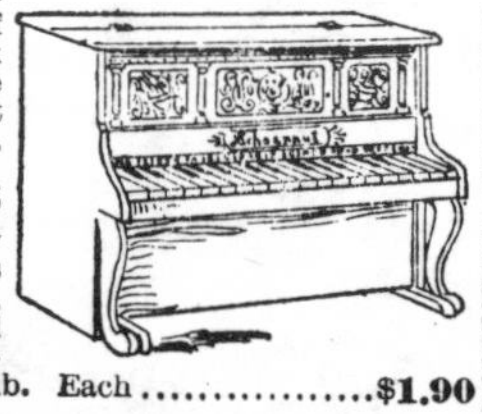

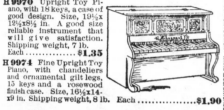

**H 9970** Upright Toy Piano, with 18 keys, a case of good design. Size, 19½x 12¼x8½ in. A good size reliable instrument that will give satisfaction. Shipping weight, 7 lb. Each..................**$1.35**

**H 9974** Fine Upright Toy Piano, with chandeliers and ornamental gilt legs, 15 keys and a rosewood finish case. Size, 16½x14-x9 in. Shipping weight, 8 lb. Each..................**$1.90**

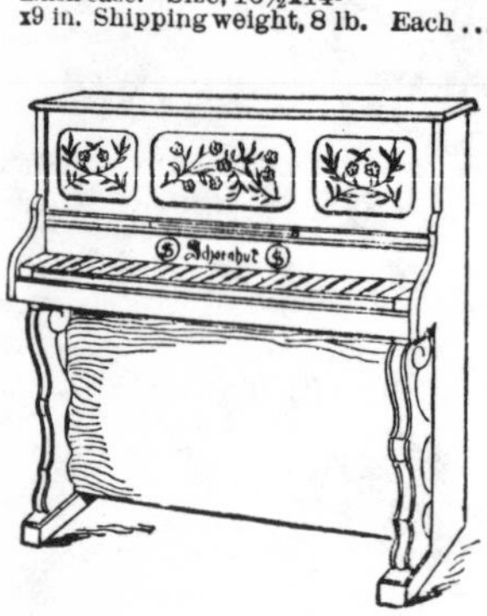

**H 9977** Extra Large Fine Toy Piano, upright style, with 22 keys; a well-finished case; size, 23x24x11 in.; suitable for a child to sit up to on stool or small chair. Shipping weight, 48 lb. Each.......**$5.00**

**H 9981** Toy Upright Piano, rosewood finish, 23x 24x12 in.; 37 keys, 3 octaves including half-notes. Shipping weight, 54 lb. Each.......**$8.75**

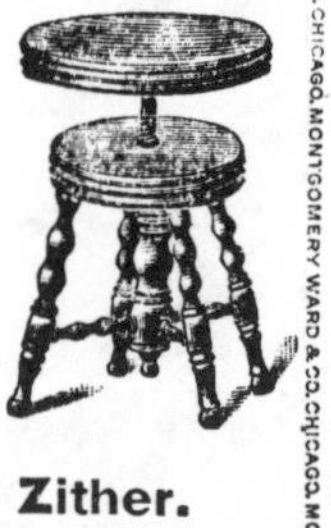

**H 9989** Toy Piano Stool with revolving seat which is fitted with steel screw for raising or lowering, nicely made in mahogany finish. Shipping weight, 2¾ lb. Each..................**50c.**

## Toy Zither.

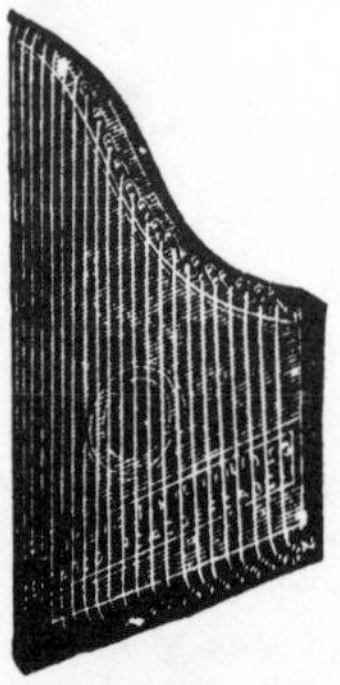

An attractive toy musical instrument on which the chords may be learned with ease; instructive and interesting to all. These goods are handsomely made and finished and are appreciated and enjoyed by young people of all ages, as they are all tuned to concert pitch.

**H 10015** American Zither, harp shaped, with 22 strings. It can be tuned like a piano by means of a key. Can be played by notes or figures. Any person can play on it in less than 5 minutes. Put up in a neat case with key, instructions and music sheet. Shipping weight, 4 lb. Each..................**75c.**

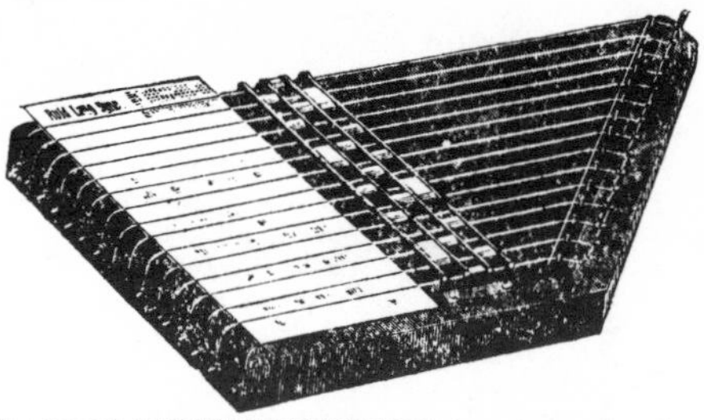

**H 10022 MUSICAL PHONOHARP** is not merely a toy, but a musical instrument with 15 strings and hollow sounding board, and having three bars, by the use of which cords are produced to harmonize with sounds obtained by picking the strings as a common zither; sheet music with each instrument, which can readily be played by a child. Shipping weight, 3¼ lb. Each..................**$1.00**

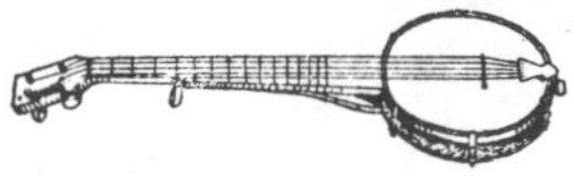

**H 10031** Toy Banjo, with 8 in. calf head, nickel-plated metal rim with nickeled brackets; full length, 27 in. Shipping weight, 2¾ lb. Each.....**$1.00**

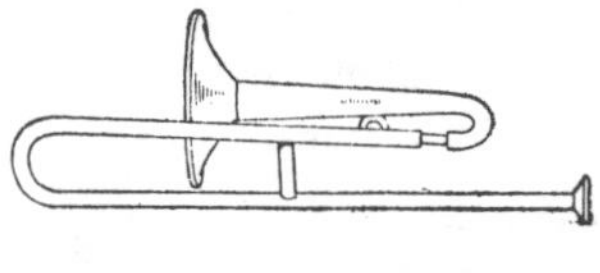

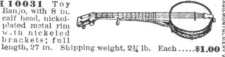

**H 10034** Toy Trombone, made of brass, gilt finish, large size. Shipping weight, 12 oz. Each.....**49c.**

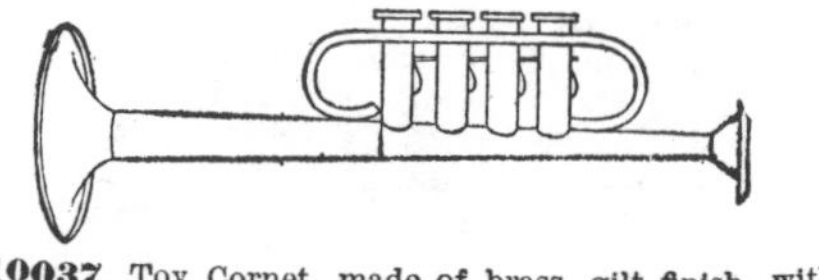

**H 10037** Toy Cornet, made of brass, gilt finish with four notes; large size. Shipping weight, 11 oz. Each..................**48c.**

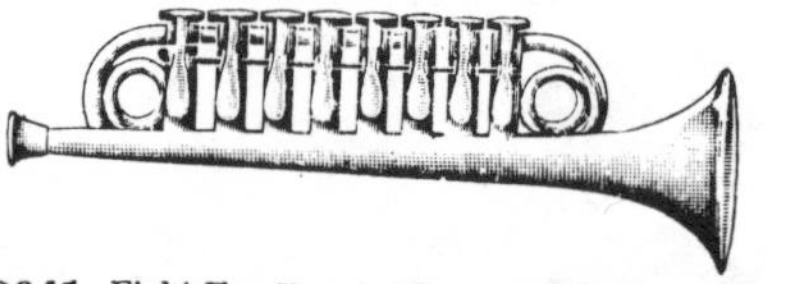

**H 10041** Eight-Key Toy Cornet, made of metal nickel plated. Full length, 13 inches. Shipping weight, 16 oz. Each..................**85c.**

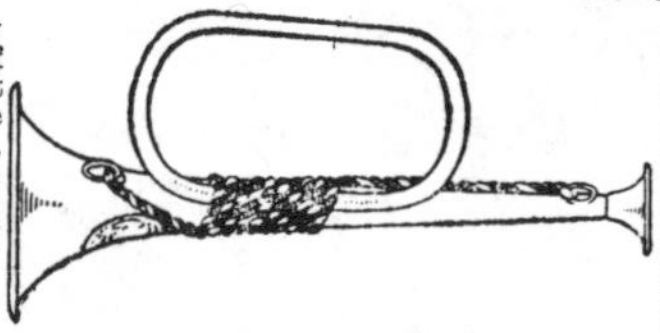

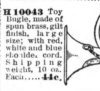

**H 10043** Toy Bugle, made of spun brass, gilt finish, large size; with red, white and blue shoulder cord. Shipping weight, 10 oz. Each.....**44c.**

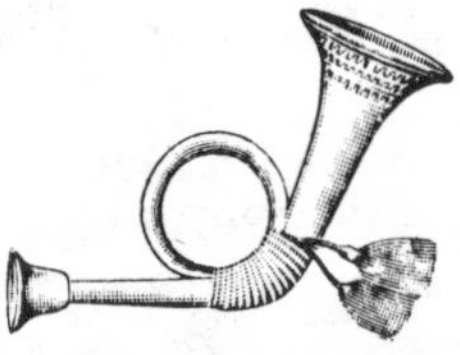

**H 10047** "Fox Horn," made of spun brass nickel plated. Full length 6¾ inches. Shipping weight, 5 ounces. Each..................**25c.**

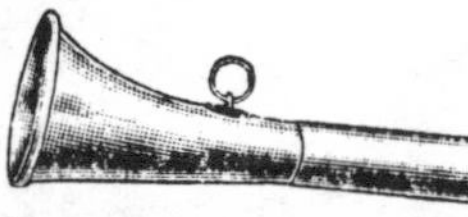

**H 10055** Nickel Plated Hunting Horn, length 5½ in., made of spun brass with ring for hanging on belt or shoulder. Shipping weight, 5 oz. Each..................**19c.**

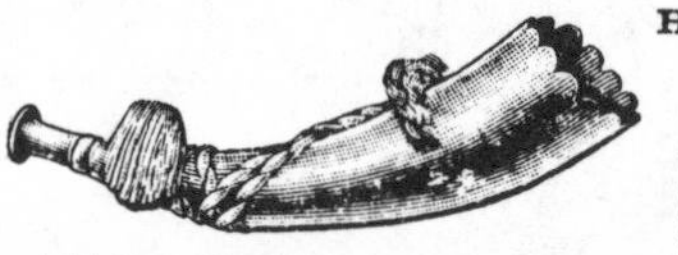

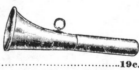

**H 10056** "Hunting Horn" made of genuine Beef Horn with real horn mouthpiece. Full length 9 in. Shipping weight, 8 oz. Each..................**20c.**

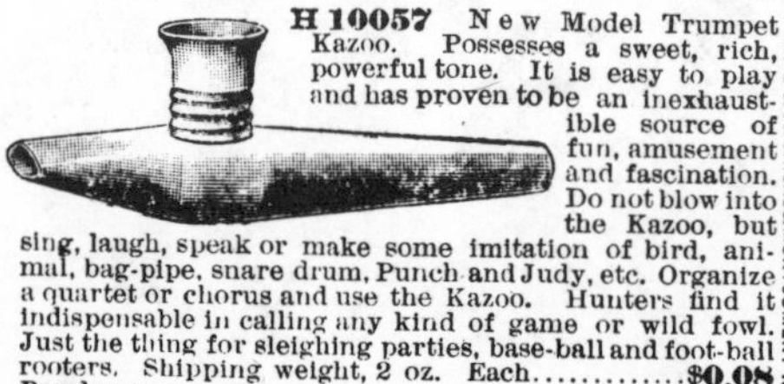

**H 10057** New Model Trumpet Kazoo. Possesses a sweet, rich, powerful tone. It is easy to play and has proven to be an inexhaustible source of fun, amusement and fascination. Do not blow into the Kazoo, but sing, laugh, speak or make some imitation of bird, animal, bag-pipe, snare drum, Punch and Judy, etc. Organize a quartet or chorus and use the Kazoo. Hunters find it indispensable in calling any kind of game or wild fowl. Just the thing for sleighing parties, base-ball and foot-ball rooters. Shipping weight, 2 oz. Each..................**$0.08**

Per dozen.................. .70

Per gross.................. 7.70

**H 10058** Vibrators for the Kazoo. Per doz....... **.10**

## Alphabet and Spelling Blocks.

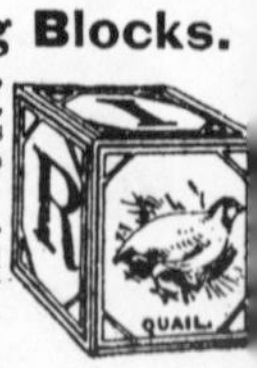

**H 10059** Thirty-five pieces, 1-in. cubes, natural wood, embossed ends, making a whole lot of small size blocks that the little hands can hold and help pile up. Shipping weight, 16 oz. Per set..................**20c.**

**H 10061** Twenty-five pieces, painted and embossed, 1⅜ in. cubes, profusely illustrated, also the alphabet and numerals. Shipping weight, 18 oz. Per set..**22c.**

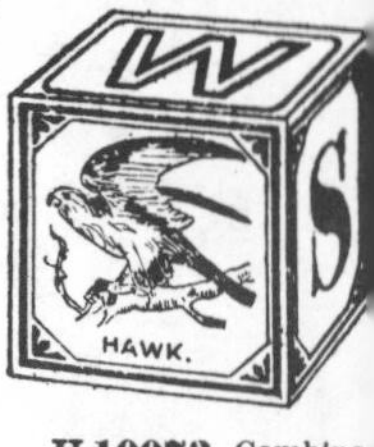

**H 10070** Sixteen pieces, painted and varnished 1¾-in. cubes, natural wood, embossed ends, printed in colors; letters, figures and illustrations. Shipping weight, 2 lb. Per set..................**25c.**

**H 10072** Twenty pieces, 1¾-in. cubes, natural wood, embossed ends, printed in colors; profusely illustrated; numerous impressions of each letter and the numerals. Shipping weight, 2¼ lb. Per set..................**35c.**

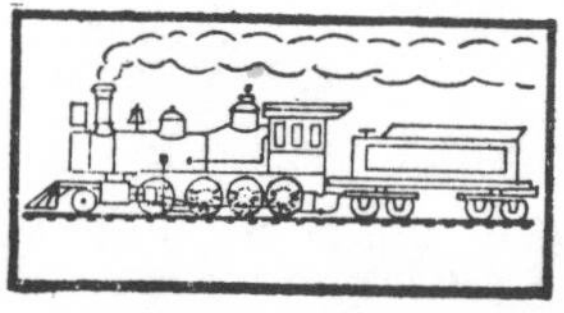

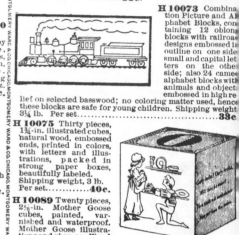

**H 10073** Combination Picture and Alphabet Blocks, containing 12 oblong blocks with railroad designs embossed in outline on one side small and capital letters on the other side; also 24 cameo alphabet blocks with animals and objects embossed in high relief on selected basswood; no coloring matter used, hence these blocks are safe for young children. Shipping weight 3¼ lb. Per set..................**33c**

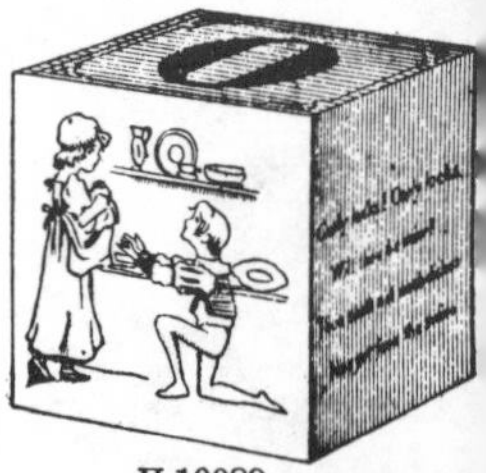

**H 10075** Thirty pieces, 1¾-in. illustrated cubes, natural wood, embossed ends, printed in colors, with letters and illustrations, packed in strong paper boxes, beautifully labeled. Shipping weight, 3 lb. Per set............**40c.**

**H 10089** Twenty pieces, 2⅛-in. Mother Goose cubes, painted, varnished and waterproof. Mother Goose illustrations and rhymes. Wood frame boxes. Shipping weight, 3 lb. Per set..................**65c.**

H 10089

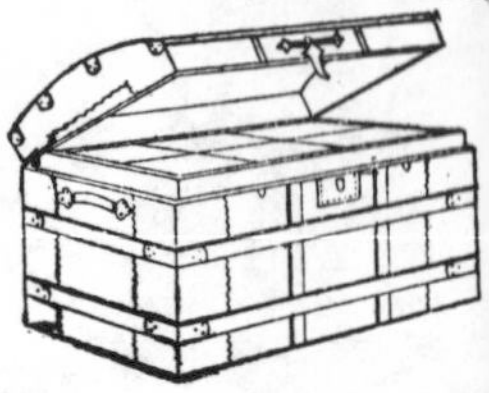

**H 10102** Doll's Trunk with Blocks, clever imitation of a Saratoga Trunk, 7 in. long, 5 in. wide, and 5 in. high, containing a tray filled with a set of lithographed blocks, showing the alphabet and six different pictures. Sure to please and instruct the children, and provides a place to keep the doll's clothing. Shipping weight, 15 oz. Each..................**20c.**

## Building Blocks.

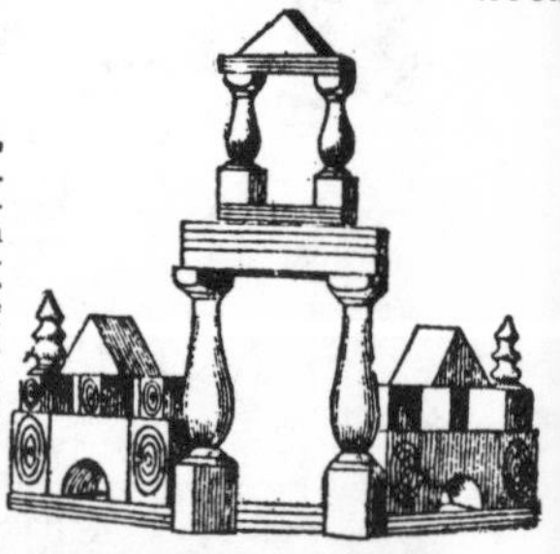

**H 10115 ARCHITECTURAL BUILDING BLOCKS** in wooden box comprising eighty-four assorted blocks of different colors, and sheet of designs. Special value at the price. Shipping weight, 4½ lb. Per set........**25c.**

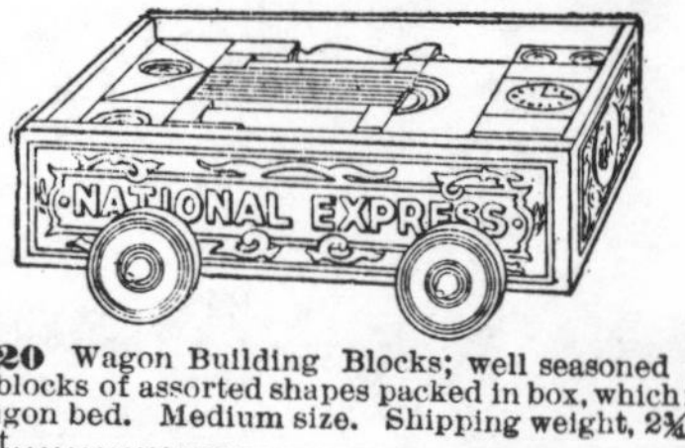


**H 10120** Wagon Building Blocks; well seasoned hard-wood blocks of assorted shapes packed in box, which forms the wagon bed. Medium size. Shipping weight, 2¾ lb. Per set..................**20c.**

**H 10124** Large Size Wagon Building Blocks. Shipping weight, 4½ lb. Per set..................**40c.**

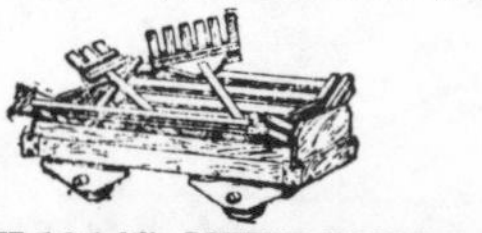

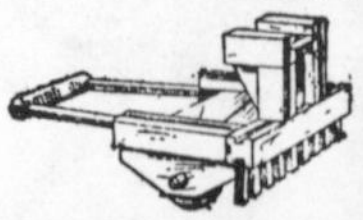

**H 10147 LITTLE FARMER SET** consists of 88 separate and interchangeable blocks, fitting into each other in such manner as to make almost any number of different articles or designs, taxing the ingenuity of the young people. These blocks are great mechanical educators and will make farm wagons, sleighs, seeder, wheel rake, forks, hoes, shovels, plow and numerous other things, and afford

### Toy Blocks—continued.

28467 Alphabet Blocks (000), square, colored letters, 1½x1½ in., flat, put up in neat box.
Per box ...... ..$0 09
Per dozen ...... 96
Extra by mail, per box............ 8

28468 Alphabet Blocks (0) better quality, same shape as 28466, colored letters, flat, put up in box.
Per box........................ 12
Per dozen.... ........... 1 30
Extra by mail, per box............ 9

28469 Alphabet Blocks (1), 25 pieces, flat, embossed blocks, 1½ inches square, handsomely colored, with letters on both sides, put up in box.
Per box.... .......... 18
Extra by mail.... ....... 14

28470 Alphabet Blocks (25), colored embossed letters 2 inches square, flat, in a box.
Per box.................... 20
Per dozen.................. 2 16
Extra by mail, per box......... .. 15

28471 Alphabet Blocks (70a), illustrated cubes with letters and figures, 1¼x1¼ inches, in colors, put up in a box.
Per box.....$0 25
Per dozen... 2 70
Extra by mail, per box..... 10

(Cut one-half full size).

28472 Alphabet Blocks (12), wood, embossed and printed, 16 blocks in a box.
Per box.................... 30
Extra by mail....... ...... 12

28473 Alphabet Blocks (48), natural wood cubes embossed and printed; 48 blocks, put up in a box.
Per box.... ......... 40
Extra by mail, per box.... ... 23

28474 Alphabet Blocks (86), natural wood, printed in colors with 144 letters and illustrations, 24 pieces or cubes, packed in a beautifully labeled wood frame box.
Per box.................... 45
Extra by mail, per box........... 40

28475 Alphabet Blocks (60), illustrated and carved cubes, like cut, 2x2 inches, in colors, put up in a box.
Per box.................... 60
Per dozen ................. 6 48
Extra by mail, per box....... 33

28476 Alphabet Blocks (45), illustrated in colors and gilt, half cubes, having figures and words; very fine quality.
Per box.................... 75
Per dozen ................. 8 10
Extra by mail per box..... 35

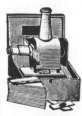

28478 Westcott's Spelling Blocks, put up as shown in cut. This makes one of the best value, and most instructive spelling blocks in the market.
Per box, 15c.

### Toy Blocks—continued.

28479 Westcott's Combination Building and Spelling Blocks, with dove-tailed edges, as shown in cut; a new and novel block. Per set .............$0 22

28480 Westcott's Combination Blocks, different style and larger set than preceding. Per set .............. 38

28381 Westcott's Solid Cubes Combination Building, Spelling and Picture Blocks. Per box................. 50

### Imported Toy Magic Lanterns.
*Our own importation.*
Price governs quality and size.

Each.

28495 Toy Magic Lanterns, metal body, neatly japanned, uses 1¼-inch slides, magnifies pictures 2 feet in diameter, 12 slides packed with lantern..$ 0 40

28496 Toy Magic Lanterns, same as 28495, but larger; uses 1½-inch slides, magnifies pictures 2 to 2½ feet in diameter ................ 90

28498 Toy Magic Lanterns, larger, will show pictures from 2½ to 3 feet in diameter, uses 1¾ inch slides........ 1 40

28500 Toy Magic Lantern, larger, will show 3½ to 4 feet pictures, uses 2⅜ inch slides..................... 2 20

### The Young America Outfit.

28505 Young America Magic Lantern Outfit, contains japanned metal lantern, 12 1½-inch colored slides containing from 36 to 48 pictures; also the following set of 6 slides (about 16 subjects), with lectures:

1 Singing Lessons.    4 Four American Poets.
2 Four Presidents.    5 Welcome.
3 Mother Goose Tales  6 Good Night.

With show bill and 24 admission tickets. This is the most popular small boy's outfit ever placed on the market.
Complete outfit....................$1 50

### Our Amateur Magic Lantern Outfit.

28507 M. W. & Co.'s "Amateur" Magic Lantern Outfit, contains lantern, new design; height, 10½ inches, condenser, 1½-inch diameter, japanned metal body, kerosene lamp, glass chimney and nickel-plated reflector. Brass lens tube and chimney Lantern is mounted on wooden base, and packed in handsome wooden box with hinged top; twelve imported colored slides 1¼ inch, one revolving chromatrope, one comic movable slide, and full directions for operating; will show pictures about 3 feet in diameter (3517).

28507.

Price, complete.............$ 2 75

28509 Boys' Lantern Outfit, same contents as No. 285 7, with new design, lantern, gilt facings, with slide on double glass; height of lantern, 10½ inches; with full directions.
Price, complete .......... 4 00

### The Home Magic Lantern.

28515 The Home Magic Lantern, metal body, red japanned-gilt decorations, three finely ground lenses in each lantern; kerosene lamp, 12 slides (36 to 48 views) with each lantern, magnifies to about 4 feet in diameter (using slides No. 28529 or any 3½-inch slide). Each ......$4 50

28516 The Home Magic Lantern, same as 28515, magnifies views to about 5 feet in diameter (using slides No. 28530 or any 4-inch slide); 12 slides with lantern.
Each................. ....$ 5 50

### The Polyopticon or Wonder Camera.

28519 Produces views on screen or wall from cuts from newspapers, magazines, portraits, comic cuts, chromo cards, photographs, flowers, etc , in all their colors, enlarged about 400 times; over a hundred different pictures are given with each polyopticon, covering almost every conceivable subject; with reflector, lamp and burner, chimney, lens and door, with 3-inch picture window. Price, complete......$4 40

### Imported Toy Magic Lantern Slides.

28525 Slides for use in lantern No. 28495, 1¼ inches wide nursery tales, Mother Goose fables, humorous, etc.. assorted. Each...$0 04
Per dozen.. ...................... 35

| | | | Each. | Per doz |
|---|---|---|---|---|
| 28526 | Same as 28525, | 1⅜ in. wide...| $0 06 | $0 60 |
| 28527 | " | " 1½ " | 5 | 45 |
| 28528 | " | " 2⅜ " | 10 | 1 00 |
| 28529 | " | " 3⅓ " | 16 | 1 75 |
| 28530 | " | " 4 " | 25 | 2 50 |

28533 Comic Movable Lantern Slides, colored, for amateurs.

| Width..... | 1¼ in. | 1¾ in. | 2⅜ in. | 3⅓ in. | 4 in. |
|---|---|---|---|---|---|
| Each...... | $0 10 | $0 15 | $0 18 | $0 23 | $0 36 |
| Per dozen.. | 1 00 | 1 60 | 1 90 | 2 45 | 4 25 |

28535 Movable Landscapes, etc., colored, assorted designs, all desirable, for amateurs.

| Width.... | 1¾ in. | 2⅜ in. | 3⅓ in. | 4 in. |
|---|---|---|---|---|
| Each .... | $0 15 | $0 18 | $0 90 | $1 35 |
| Per dozen. | 1 60 | 1 90 | 9 72 | 16 50 |

28536 Geometrical Chromatrope Slides, consists of two varied colored wheels, revolving in opposite directions by means of a crank and belt, producing a brilliant effect.

| Width.... | 2 in. | 2⅜ in. | 3⅓ in. | 4 in. |
|---|---|---|---|---|
| Each..... | $0 45 | $0 60 | $0 75 | $1 00 |

### Magic Lanterns and Sciopticons.
**For Sunday Schools, Societies, Army Posts, Home and Public Entertainments.**

We carry a full stock of high grade magic lanterns, sciopticons, slides, screens and accessories at all times. Special list of these goods sent by mail, free upon application. We do the largest business in this line west of Philadelphia, and our prices are usually low for first quality goods.

Montgomery Ward & Co.'s "American Exhibitor," No. 2400; ten to 12 feet pictures.
Price.........................$28 50

Montgomery Ward & Co.'s Triplex Sciopticon, No. 525, will show a 10 to 12 foot picture.
Price... ......................... $32 00

Montgomery Ward & Co.'s "Royal" Sciopticon, will enlarge a 3-inch view up to 14 or more feet in diameter. Price ..................$45 00

No. 540, New Improved Duplex Magic Lanterns, the most popular lantern in America.
Price........................... $ 9 50

Outfits, $16.00, $17.50, $21.00, $30.00, $35.00, $60.00 and upwards.

If you are at all interested in the subject of magic lanterns or views do not neglect to send for our special list of magic lanterns and slides, No. 244. Free upon application.

# DOLLS.

No. 800 to 802.

No. 0

No. 804 to 806.

## ENGLISH RAG DOLLS.

Best quality indestructible dolls, linen faces, glass eyes, fancy dresses, soft arms and limbs, dressed in costumes, "Little Red Riding Hood," "Bo Peep," "Blue Eyes," "Dew Drop."

| No. 00. | 13½ inches long, | ⅓ dozen in package | per doz., | $4 00 |
|---|---|---|---|---|
| 0. | 15 " " | ⅓ " " " | " " | 6 00 |
| 1. | 17 " " | | " " | 8 00 |
| 2. | 19 " " | | " " | 12 00 |

## WASHABLE DOLLS.

Extra size heads, with teeth, glass eyes, lace trimmed chemise, imitation shoes and stockings, soft limbs. The popular line.

| No. 800. | 18 inches. | 1 dozen in packages | per doz., | $2 00 |
|---|---|---|---|---|
| 801. | 22 " | ½ " " " | " " | 3 50 |
| 802. | 29½ " | ⅓ " " " | " " | 8 00 |

## WASHABLE DOLLS, EXTRA QUALITY.

Washable heads, glass eyes, mohair hair dressings, fancy chemises, bare feet.

| No. 803. | 17½ inches, | 1 dozen in package | per doz., | $2 00 |
|---|---|---|---|---|
| 804. | 23½ " | ½ " " " | " " | 3 50 |
| 805. | 27½ " | ⅓ " " " | " " | 6 50 |
| 806. | 30 " | ⅙ " " " | " " | 9 00 |

## FINE WASHABLE DOLLS.

Fine washable heads, fine waved hairdressing, full lace chemise, trimmed with bows, fine double stitched body, glazed limbs and arms.

No. 766.  23½ inches,  ⅓ dozen in package............per doz., $8 50

## WASHABLE DOLLS.

**"Papa and Mama."**

No. 808.  14 inches,  1 dozen in package..............per doz., $2 00

**"Fat Baby."**

No. 807.  13 inches,  1 dozen in package..............per doz., $2 00

## BOY WASHABLE DOLLS.

Washable heads, glass eyes, boy hair dressings, fancy shirts, bare feet.

| No. 809. | 17½ inches, | 1 dozen in package | per doz., | $2 00 |
|---|---|---|---|---|
| 541. | 16 " | ½ " " " | " " | 4 00 |

## BOY WASHABLE DOLLS.

Fine washable heads, glass eyes, new side-parted hairdressing, bosom front shirt with bow, bare feet.

| No. 797. | 16 inches, | ½ dozen in package | per doz., | $3 75 |
|---|---|---|---|---|
| 798. | 20½ " | ⅓ " " " | " " | 6 00 |

Fine grade wig, natural lamb's wool, fine body and shirt.

No. 799.  16 inches,  ½ dozen in package..............per doz., $3 75

No. 809.

No. 803.

No. 6.

"Jumeau.

No. 4.

No. 727.

## BEBE JUMEAU.

Bisque head, paper body, jointed, chemise in rose and blue.

Original Standard Numbers.

| | | | |
|---|---|---|---|
| No. 1. | Per dozen | | $18 00 |
| " 2. | " " | | 22 50 |
| " 3. | " " | | 27 00 |
| " 4. | " " | | 33 00 |
| " 5. | " " | | 39 00 |
| " 6. | " " | | 42 00 |
| " 7. | " " | | 48 00 |
| " 8. | " " | | 54 00 |

## FINEST QUALITY JOINTED DOLL, EXTRA LARGE SIZES.

Can be used as models, ball jointed, paper body, latest model bisque head, showing teeth, with moving eyes, new wave hair dressing, fine chemise.

| | | |
|---|---|---|
| No. 726. | 26 inches | per dozen, $ 78 00 |
| " 727. | 35 " | " 180 00 |

## EXTRA QUALITY FINE JOINTED DOLLS.

Latest model French head, long, flowing hair, waving bangs, fine lace trimmed chemise, shoes and stockings.

| | | | |
|---|---|---|---|
| No. 2. | Length 13 inches | | per dozen, $16 00 |
| " 3. | " 15 " | | " 21 00 |
| " 4. | " 17 " | | " 27 00 |
| " 6. | " 20½ " | | " 36 00 |

## JOINTED DOLLS.

Bisque head, teeth, fancy chemise, full jointed.

| | | | | |
|---|---|---|---|---|
| No. 550. | Length 10¾ inches; 1 dozen in box | | | per dozen, $ 2 00 |
| " 551. | " 12¼ " ⅛ " | | | " 2 25 |
| " 552. | " 14¾ " ¼ " | | | " 3 25 |
| " 553. | " 15 " ⅜ " | | | " 4 50 |
| " 554. | " 16½ " ⅜ " shoes and stockings | | | " 6 75 |
| " 555. | " 18½ " | | | " 8 50 |
| " 556. | " 20 " | | | " 10 50 |
| " 557. | " 20 " special doll | | | " 13 50 |

## NEGRO JOINTED DOLLS—FANCY SHIRTS.

| | |
|---|---|
| No. 542. | Length 6 inches; 1 dozen in box | per dozen, $4 75 |

## NURSING DOLLS.

Jointed Doll in chair, with nursing bottle, emptying the same.

| | |
|---|---|
| No. O. Length 11 inches | per dozen, $16 50 |

No. 659.

## DRESSED DOLLS—TAILOR MADE COSTUMES.

Jointed body and wrists, moving eyes, teeth, latest model head, tailor-made dresses in the latest American fashion.

| | | | |
|---|---|---|---|
| No. 1. | 14 inches | | per dozen, $ 60 00 |
| " 2. | 15 " | | " 72 00 |
| " 3. | 16½ " | | " 90 00 |
| " 4. | 19 " | | " 126 00 |
| " 5. | 22 " | | " 180 00 |
| " 6. | 24 " | | " 216 00 |

## PREMIER DRESSED DOLL—BEBE STEINER.

No. 660. Papier mache body, double jointed, jointed wrists, human eyes, shoes and stockings, promenade costumes, length 14 inches. per dozen, $60 00

No. 659. Same as No. 660, but larger; length 18 inches. " 90 00

# DOLLS.

745

## INFANT DOLLS.

No. 587. Bisque head, teeth, lace hood, long dress, length 13½ inches, 1 doz. in package........................per doz., $2 00

No. 588. Bisque head, teeth, lace hood, long dress, length 14½ inches, ¼ doz. in package........................per doz., 4 50

No. 586. Patent head, teeth, fancy flannel dress, shoes and stockings, length 14½ inches.....................per doz., 9 00

No. 590. Fine quality bunting dress, moving eyes, with baby rattle, length 14½ inches.....................per doz., 12 00

No. 591. Same as No. 590, but larger size, length 19 inches; per doz................................................ 24 00

No. 745. Bisque heads with teeth, fancy dress ball costume, 8 inches, ½ doz. in package, per dozen ................................. $2 25

No. 744. Bisque head, fancy wool dresses, boys and girls, 8 inches, ½ doz. in box....per doz., 2 25

No. 743. Bisque heads, jointed body, shoes and stockings, toboggan suits, capes and hats in white cotton flannel, 9 inches, ½ doz. in box, per doz................................... 2 75

No. 782. Bisque heads, showing teeth, kid bodies, shoes and stockings, in fancy assorted costumes, 12 inches, ⅓ doz. in box......per doz 4 50

No. 754. Bisque head, soft body, shoes and stockings, fancy wool costume with Astrachan front, 12 inches.....................per doz., 6 00

767

## SMALL FINE DRESSED DOLLS.

No. 770. Bisque heads, in fancy costumes, satin trimmed, 3 styles, ½ doz. in package, 5 inches...........per doz., $2 00

### BISQUE JOINTED BODIES AND HEADS.

No. 767. Bisque heads, in bathing costumes, boys and girls, 3¾ inches, ½ doz. in package................per doz., $2 12

No. 771. Bisque heads, flowing hair, glass eyes, knit costumes, girls, 3¾ inches, ½ doz. in package....per doz., 2 25

No. 768. Bisque heads, promenade plush costumes, fancy trimmed, boys and girls, 3½ inches, ½ doz. in package; per doz....................................... 2 75

No. 769. Bisque heads, Lilliputians, in fancy costumes, 3½ inches, ½ doz. in package...................per doz., 2 75

761

### DRESSED DOLLS WITH CHINA HEADS.

No. 759. Silk skirts, fancy braid trimming, 4¾ inches, 1 doz. in package.........per doz., 75

No. 761. All china dolls, with silk dresses, lace trimmed, 3¾ inches, ½ doz. in package, per doz................................... 1 00

No. 762. All china dolls, lace bodice, fancy bows, 10 inches, ½ doz. in package..per doz., 2 25

No. 763. Fancy outing dresses, 13 inches, ½ doz. in package...................per doz., 3 75

### DRESSED DOLLS WITH WASHABLE HEADS.

No. 764. Assorted dresses, laced trimmed, poke bonnets, glass eyes,16 inches, ½ doz. in package...................................per doz., $2 25

No. 765. Satin fronts, felt hats, glass eyes, 18 inches, ⅓ doz. in package........per doz., 4 00

769

*Marshall Field & Co.*

# DRESSED DOLLS.

**All with bisque heads with teeth, jointed bodies, shoes and stockings.**

NO 776.

NO. 748.

No. 746.　Two boys and two girls in Scotch costume, 10½ inches, ⅓ doz. in package..................................per doz., $4 00

No. 776.　Winter costume with Astrachan trimmed jacket, cap and muff, 15 inches................................per doz., $12 00

No. 748.　Fine brocaded silk dress, satin trimmed straw hat to match, 19 inches................................per doz., $27 00

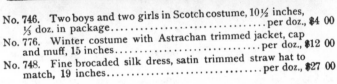

No. 752.　All satin dress, lace trimmed bonnet to match, 15 inches per doz..................................................$12 00

No. 572.　Scotch plaid costume, 15 inches, per doz.............$12 00

No. 756.　Fancy toboggan costume, hat to match Astrachan trimmed, 15 inches................................per doz., $12 00

No. 774.　Silk and velvet costume, 18 inches...........per doz., $12 00

No. 757.　Red Riding Hood costume, satin trimmed hat to match, 15 inches................................per doz., $13 50

No. 751.　Belgian costume, satin straw hat trimmed to match, 15 inches................................per doz., $13 50

No. 783.　Fancy dress with velvet cape, 13 inches.......per doz., $6 75

No. 775.　White dress, lace trimmed, with long bridal veil, 13 inches................................per doz., $9 00

No. 755.　Street costume in cashmere, velvet trimmed cape, 15 inches................................per doz., 13 50

No. 778.　Spanish costume, velvet trimmed, velvet trimmed straw hat, 18 inches................................per doz., 18 00

No. 749.　Light shade cashmere dresses with capes, feather trimmed hat, 18 inches................................per doz., 24 00

No. 777.　Infant, light colored cashmere dresses, fine trimmed poke bonnet, 18 inches................................per doz., 27 00

No. 780.　Satin, lace trimmed dress, satin bonnet, 24 inches, per doz................................................45 00

No. 753.　Long baby costume, 12 inches.................per doz., 6 00

No. 753.

No. 756.

No. 774.

No. 757.

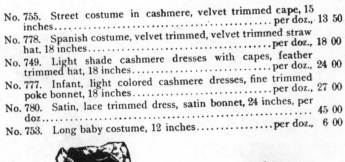

*Marshall Field & Co.*

# DOLLS SUNDRIES.

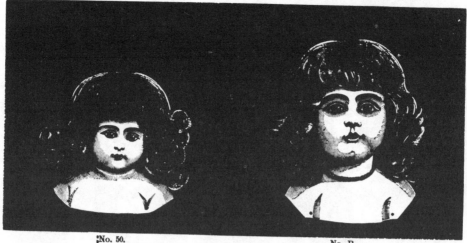

No. 50.            No. B.

## BISQUE DOLLS' HEADS.

**French model best Bisque, moving eyes, showing teeth, extra heavy hairdressing in curls.**

| No. 50. | 4. | 3¾ inches high | | per doz., | $5 25 |
|---|---|---|---|---|---|
| " " | 5. | 4 | " " | " | 6 00 |
| " " | 6. | 4½ | " " | " | 6 75 |
| " " | 7. | 4¾ | " " | " | 8 00 |
| " " | 8. | 5 | " " | " | 9 00 |
| " " | 9. | 5 | " " heavier | " | 10 50 |
| " " | 10. | 5½ | " " | " | 13 50 |
| " " | 11. | 6 | " " | " | 15 00 |
| " " | 12. | 6½ | " " | " | 16 75 |

**French model, turning head, necklace, wave curls, moving eyes. Best quality.**

| No. B 707. | 4¼ inches high | | per doz., | $ 8 50 |
|---|---|---|---|---|
| " B 708. | 4½ | " " | " | 10 50 |
| " B 709. | 5 | " " | " | 12 00 |
| " B 710. | 6 | " " | " | 13 50 |
| " B 711. | 6½ | " " | " | 19 50 |
| " B 712. | 8½ | " " | " | 33 00 |

## DOLL SLIPPERS.

Imitation patent Leather, ½ gross in package, assorted, sizes, sizes from 2 to 7 . . . . . . . . . . . . . . . . . . . . . per gross, $6 00

No. 1206. Bronzed Leather with rosettes, assorted sizes 1 to 9, 1 dozen assorted in package . . . . . . . . . . . . . . . per doz., 2 00

## DOLL STOCKINGS.

Cotton Stockings, assorted colors, Sizes 2, 4, 6, 8, 10, 12; 1 dozen of one Size in each bundle . . . . . . . . . . . . . per doz., $0 50

Silk Stockings, assorted colors, same Sizes and put up same as above . . . . . . . . . . . . . . . . . . . . . . . . per doz., 1 25

## DOLLS' HATS.

Assorted sizes felt, lace and straw hats, 1 doz. in package, per doz., $2 00

## IMPROVED DOLL STANDS.

**Made of Metal with Extension Clamp Slide. Nickel finished.**

No. 1.  Small.  2 inches, extends 3¼ inches.
Per doz . . . . . . . . . . . . . . . . . . . . . . . . $1 50

No. 2.  Medium.  4 inches, extends 6 inch.
Per doz . . . . . . . . . . . . . . . . . . . . 3 00

No. 3.  Large.  9 inches, extends 15 inches.
Per doz . . . . . . . . . . . . . . . . . . . 6 00

*Marshall Field & Co.*

# RUBBER TOYS.

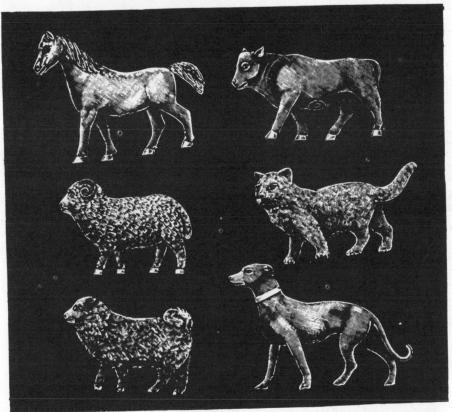

No. 102.

No. 102.  Animals, plain finish, with whistles.   2½ inches; assorted 6 kinds in package of 1 dozen..............................per doz., $1 25
" 100.   "   "   "   "   "   4   "   "   4 "   "   "   "   ...............................   "   2 00
" 103.   "   "   "   "   "   5½   "   "   4 "   "   "   " ½ "   ...............................   "   4 00

No. 108.

*Marshall Field & Co.*

# STEAM TOYS.

No. 128 B.  Steam Propeller, complete with engine, finished in brass, 11
inches long..................................................per doz., $15 00
No. 128.  Same as above, 13 inches long.....................  "   "   24 00

No. 403 L.  Steam Switch Locomotive with brass
boiler, complete...........................per doz., $18 00

No. 126 A.  Steam Switch Locomotive, with brass boiler,
tender and whistle.......................per doz., $48 00

No. 129.  Steam Propeller with awning, complete with engine, finished in
brass, 15¾ inches long.........................................per doz., $36 00
No. 191.  Same as above with cabin, 15¾ inches long............  "   "   72 00
No. 192.  Same as above with two masts, compass, 19¾ in. long .  "   "   150 00

# STEAM TRAINS WITH TRACKS.

No. 2.  Steam Locomotive, track 3½ feet in diameter, in 9 sections, each 14 inches long, on which rails and sleepers are securely mounted, hinge lock on each section forming a solid
track with a wooden base....................per doz., $42 00

No. 40.  Complete Train, consisting of brass locomotive with
tender, 2 passenger cars and track.................per doz., $42 00
No. 124 A.  Complete Train, consisting of locomotive with tender,
2 passenger cars and track......................per doz., $54 00

No. 26.  Complete Train, consisting of locomotive with tender,
2 passenger cars and track........................per doz., $90 00

# STEAM TOYS.

**Excellent Show Pieces.**

No. 411. Steam Engine, finished in brass, with whistle, per doz., $16 50

No. 421A. Steam Brewery, complete, with brass trimmed stationary engine.........per doz., $72 00

No. 107. Stationary Engine, extra fine, with double working cylinder, whistle and steam pipe, all complete, per doz................................$120 00

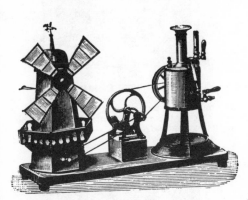

No. 116. Steam Windmill, with stationary engine, complete......per doz., $45 00

No. 423. Stationary Engine, with boiler, complete..................per doz., $45 00

No. 111. Steam Forge, with stationary steam engine, finished in brass, with whistle steam pipe........per doz., $27 00

No. 117. Steam Fountain, with stationary brass-finished engine........per doz., $45 00

No. 100. Stationary Engine, with polished brass boiler..per doz., $10 50

No. 121. Steam Dredge and Conveyor, with brass trimmed stationary engine, complete...........................per doz., $48 00

*Marshall Field & Co.*

# STEAM TOYS.

Steam Derrick, per dozen....$9 00     Steam Pile-driver, per dozen, $9 00     No. 1.  Upright Steam Engine, per dozen................$9 00     No. 3.   Steam Engine, per dozen...  ....    $12 00

## MECHANICAL ATTACHMENTS

For Toy Steam Engines, size 6x6 inches, per dozen, $4.00.

### ROMEO AND JULIET.

Romeo *plays vigorously*, while Juliet peeps from her window and throws him repeated kisses; the old man peeks out from the half open door, and on seeing Romeo, he makes the dark lover suddenly acquainted with the toe of his boot, while the black cat under the window gets his back up at the row.

### THE OLD MILL.

When the toy is in motion the Old Mill sails go round, and the old Miller beats his donkey, who, instead of going ahead, kicks up behind, thus making an interesting scene.

### VILLAGE PUMP.

When the scene is in motion, the youngster at the handle pumps hard, while the thirsty boy catches the running water from the spout in his hat and carries it to his lips and drinks, the three motions being extremely animated and natural.

### THE IRISH JIG.

When in motion the old man draws his bow to a lively tune, while Pat merrily steps out the Jig to the tune of the old man's playing, at the same time twirling his black thorn Shillalah, in true Irish style.

### THE ORGAN GRINDER.

When in motion, the Italian leisurely turns the crank, while Jocko takes off his hat, in thanks for the coin.

This is a well known and always pleasing scene for children.

### THE SMOKER.

When the toy is in motion, the flame and smoke of the fire go slowly up the chimney, while fat old Hans takes the pipe from his mouth, which he opens wide, letting great puffs of smoke roll upwards, the several motions making a very effective and realistic scene.

*Marshall Field & Co.*

# ELECTRIC TOYS.

## EXCELLENT SHOW PIECES.

No. 151.   Electro Motor with battery, complete . . . . . . . . . . . . . . . per doz., $24 00

No. 133.   Electro Motor with battery, complete . . . . . . . . . . . . . . . per doz., $30 00

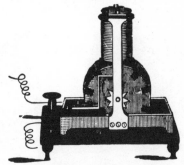

No. 152.   Electro Motor with brass drum, complete with battery, . . . . . per doz., $45 00

No. 136.   Electric Forge, complete with motor 151 and battery, in one piece, per doz. . . . . . . . . . . . . . . . . . . . . . . . . . . . $36 00

No. 161.   Dynamo, very powerful, complete with battery . . . . . . . . per doz., $36 00

No. 146.   Electric Dredge and Conveyor, complete with 151 motor and battery, per doz . . . . . . . . . . . . . . . . . . . . . . . . . . . . . $54 00

No. 140.   Electric "Merry go around" complete with 151 motor and battery, per doz . . . . . . . . . . . . . . . . . . . . . . $45 00

No. 139.   Electric Fountain, complete with 151 motor and battery, per doz . . . . . . . . . . . . . . . . . . . . . . . . . $60 00

No. 143.   Electric Wind Mill, complete with 151 motor and battery . per doz., $45 00

*Marshall Field & Co.*

# ELECTRICAL RAILROAD.

### EXCELLENT SHOWPIECES.

No. 156.   Electric Car, finely finished, with strong track, 21¾ inches in diameter and double battery, complete................per piece $10 50

## ELECTRIC EXPERIMENT BOXES.

**Instructive and entertaining experiments, suitable for older boys, being a means for the furtherance of instruction in physics.   Each piece has been tested before being sent out.**

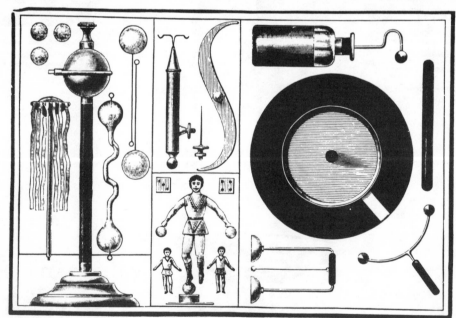

FREE ELECTRICITY OR ELECTROSTATIC INDUCTION.

Box of experiments B 1, contains 12 solidly constructed objects accompanied by book of correct illustrations and easy and clear instructions.

### CONTENTS.

1.  One Vulcanite Electrophorus.
2.  One brass Prime Conductor with Vulcanite handle.
3.  One piece of Flannel for exciting the Electrophorus.
4.  One Universal Stand, finely wrought in Brass.
5.  One Electrical Fly Wheel, complete.
6.  One Electrical Double-Pendulum, complete.
7.  One Electrical Harlequin.

8.  One Electrical Bellchimes.
9.  Pith Balls for executing the Ball Dance; Dice and small figures of Elder pith, for various Experiments.
10.  One Geissler Tube.
11.  One Electrical Hercules.
12.  One Leyden Jar, includiug Discharger.

Each $4 50

*Marshall Field & Co.*

# MAGIC LANTERNS.

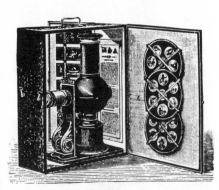

### CLIMAX.

Painted red, wood cabinet double doors, containing six slides and three rotary slides.

No. 1231C.  Size of lens 1 inch..per doz. $13 50
No. 1233C.    "    "   1½ "  ..    "      21 00

No. 1800.  Painted red, in wood case with handle, contains 12 slides, per doz.................................$12 00
No. 40.  Painted red, in wood case with handle, contains 12 slides, 2 changeable pictures, 1 chromotrope, lens 1½ inches..per doz., $24 00

### BALL SHAPED LANTERN.

Painted red, double door, wood case.

No. 532C.  Size of lens 1 inch, contains 10 slides, per doz...................................$12 00
No. 535C.  Size of lens 1¼ inch, contains 10 slides, per doz..................................... 16 50

### SQUARE SHAPED LANTERN.

Polished Russia Iron, Brass trimmings in double door, wood box.

No. 1757.  Contains 8 slides, 1 chromotrope, 1 changeable picture, 1 mechanical picture, size of lens 1⅝ inches........per doz., $42 00

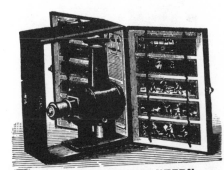

### OBLONG SHAPED LANTERN.

Painted body, in double door wood case, contains 10 slides.

No. 524C.  Size of lens 1 inch..........................per doz., $12 00
No. 529C.  Size of lens 1½ inch.........................   "      18 00

### BRASS CLIMAX.

Polished brass body, contains 4 slides, 6 circular pictures, 2 changeable pictures.

No. 648.  Size of lens 1⅜ inch..per doz., $24 00

### THE POPULAR LANTERN.

Painted body, neatly packed.

No. 523.  Contains 6 slides, size of lens 1 inch.....................per doz., $4 50
No. 524.  Contains 12 slides, size of lens 1 inch.....................per doz., $8 00
No. 527.  Contains 12 slides, size of lens 1⅛ inch.................per doz., $12 00

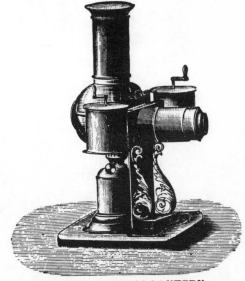

### ROTATING MAGIC LANTERN.

Contains 100 pictures on rollers.

No. 206..........................per doz., $42 00

*Marshall Field & Co.*

# MAGIC LANTERNS.

### HELIO LANTERNS.

Extra fine quality, body polished Russia iron, duplex burners, contains 12 slides, 1 changeable landscape, 1 changeable comic picture, 1 chromotrope.

| | | | | | |
|---|---|---|---|---|---|
| No. 782. | Size of lens | 1¾ | ......per doz., | $78 | 00 |
| " 784. | " " | 2⅛ | ...... " " | 120 | 00 |
| " 786. | " " | 2¾ | ...... " " | 162 | 00 |

### GLORIA LANTERNS.

Fine quality, body polished Russia iron, duplex burners, contains 12 slides, 1 chromotrope, 1 comic changeable picture, 1 changeable landscape.

| | | | | | |
|---|---|---|---|---|---|
| No. 4 01. | Lens | 2 inches | ......per doz., | $90 | 00 |
| " 4003. | " | 2⅜ " | ...... " " | 120 | 00 |
| " 4005. | " | 3 " | ...... " " | 180 | 00 |

### SCIOPTICON.

Finest magic lanterns, polished Russia iron, with a chromatic lens with thumbscrew, duplex burner, contains 24 slides, 1 chromotrope, 1 changeable comic picture, 1 changeable landscape.

No. 763. 4 inch lens.........per doz., $360 00

### THE IMPROVED.

No. 624. Enameled Russia iron body, stands 18½ inches high, contains 12 slides, 1 chromotrope, 2 changeable pictures, duplex burners.......................................per doz., $126 00
No. 625. Same as above, one size larger.............. " " 180 00

### THE IMPROVED.

No. 622. Enameled Russia iron, brass mounted-body, triplex burner, stands 24½ inches high, contains 12 slides, 6 changeable pictures, 2 chromotropes......................per doz., $300 00

## VIEWS FOR MAGIC LANTERNS.

Glass slides, hand painted colored pictures, will fit corresponding diameter of lenses.

| | | | | | | | |
|---|---|---|---|---|---|---|---|
| No. 3. | 1¼ inches diameter, | 1 doz. in package | ........per doz., | $ 60 |
| " 4. | 1½ " " | 1 " " | ........ " " | 60 |
| " 3½. | 1⅜ " " | 1 " " | ........ " " | 60 |
| " 4½. | 1¾ " " | 1 " " | ........ " " | 75 |
| " 5. | 2 " " | 1 " " | ........ " " | 1 00 |
| No. 6. | 2⅜ inches diameter, | 1 doz. in package | .........per doz., | $1 50 |
| " 7. | 2¾ " " | 1 " " | ......... " " | 2 00 |
| " 8. | 3⅛ " " | 1 " " | ......... " " | 2 65 |
| " 9. | 3½ " " | 1 " " | ......... " " | 3 00 |
| " 10. | 4 " " | 1 " " | ......... " " | 4 00 |

# MECHANICAL TOYS.

No. 11-2. Mechanical Monkey, by clockwork, per doz..................................$33 00

Mechanical Cake Walk................................................per doz.,$33 00

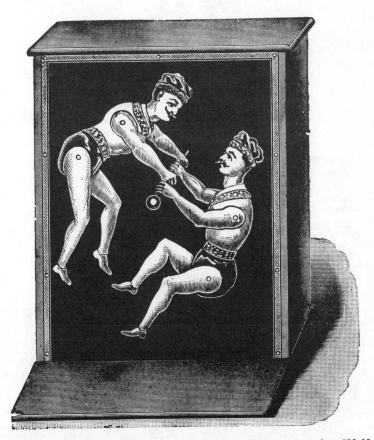

No. 32-9. Mechanical Clown Rider........per doz., $33 00

No. 49-16. Mechanical Acrobats, performing on bar........per doz., $36 00

# MECHANICAL TOYS.

No. 49–1.   Mechanical bear......................per doz., $33 00

Mechanical mule clowns.......................................per doz., $33 00

No. 22–2.   Mechanical dancer..................per doz., $24 00

Mechanical fire engine house with fire engine................per doz., $60 00

No. 49–7.   Mechanical nurse....................per doz., $24 00

*Marshall Field & Co.*

# MECHANICAL LOCOMOTIVES.

No. 19-12.   Locomotive, with tender, run by clock work; 14 in. long ............................................. per doz., $21 00

No. 19-9.   Iron locomotive, run by clock work; 7 inches long, per dozen ...................................................... $ 9 00

No. 19-10   Iron Locomotive and tender, run by clock work; 10½ inches long ................................... per doz., $12 00

No. 19-11.   Locomotive, run by clock work; 10 inches long, per dozen ..................................................... $16 00

## IRON TOYS.

No. 6.   Gondola Car, size to go with locomotive No. 1;  14 inches long, 3½ high ............................. per doz., $9 00

No. 1.   True model of a modern style extension front locomotive, finished in colors, 16 wheels, all turn, 21 inches long with tender included ...................................... per doz., $16 50

No. 3.   Passenger Car, size to go with locomotive No. 1; 17 inches long, 4¾ high ...................................... per doz., $12 00

No. 2.   Combination baggage, express and smoking car, size to go with locomotive No. 1; 17 inches long, 4¾ high .... per doz., $12 00

No. 7.   Caboose, finished in bright colors, to go with locomotive No 1; size, 7½x5½ inches ..................... per doz., $9 00

No. 4.   Model Freight Car, 8 turning wheels made to the same gauge as locomotive and tender No. 1; size, 17 inches long, 4¾ high ........................................... per doz., $12 00

# IRON TRAINS.

No. 47.  Railroad Train, locomotive, tender and passenger, 10 inches long, 2½ high.............................per doz., $2 00

No. 40.  Railroad Train, locomotive and tender, gondola car, brakemen on cars, length 18 inches................per doz., $4 00

No. 48.  Railroad Train, locomotive, tender and passenger car; 14 inches long, 2½ high......................................$2 75

No. H.  Railroad Train; locomotive—boiler, black, gilt bands; wheels, red; stack, red; tender—black, bronzed wheels; car, red, black striped; wheels, black; caboose—red; wheels, black; total length 25 inches.........................per doz,, 4 50

No. G.  Railroad Train; locomotive—boiler, black, gilt bands; wheels red; stack, red and black; brass bell; cab—maroon, gilt striped; tender—black, bronzed wheels, gold number; cars—red, black lettered; wheels, black; 34 inches long............................per doz. $9 00

No. 43½.  Locomotive and tender, two passenger cars, combination car, brakemen on cars, length 33 inches......................per doz., $9 00

No. 70.  Train, locomotive, tender, combination and passenger car; 38 inches long...............................................per doz., $13 50

No. F.  Passenger Train; locomotive—boiler, black; wheels, red; stack, red; bell, etc., gilt; cab—black, gilt striped; tender—black, gilt striped and lettered; car—red, black striped and lettered; 28½ inches long................................................per doz., $9 00.

No. F. F.  Railroad Train, locomotive, tender, combination and passenger car, finished in correct colors, 45 inches long.........per doz., $15 00

No. F. F. F.  Locomotive—boiler, black, gilt trimmed; wheels, red; stack and domes, red and gilt trimmed; brass bell and frame; cab—black, gilt striped; tender—black, gilt trimmed and lettered; wheels, red; buffet car—olive green, gilt trimmed and lettered; ventilators and wheels, red; vestibule coach—olive green, gilt trimmed and lettered, ventilators and wheels, red; 60 inches long.....per doz., $66 00

*Marshall Field & Co.*

# IRON TOYS.

No. 1000.   Fire Engine; painted in bright colors, horses black, driver in uniform, 16½ inches long and 6¾ inches high.
..............................................per doz., $8 50

## MODEL HOSE CART, No. 155.

Length 10½ inches, with rubber hose................per doz., $5 50

Fire Engine No. R.   Horses black, harness gilt trimmed, harness and housings red; engine gear red, black striped, nickel plated boiler and valves, body green and black, gilt striped, brass bell, gauge and whistle, engineer and driver in uniform; length 18¼ inches.................per doz., $20 00

Hose cart S S.   Horse white, harness black; hames and housings red, cart body green, gilt striped, gear red, black striped, panels, seat, footboard and inside of reel red, length 15¾ inches.....................................per doz., $13 50

## MODEL FIRE ENGINE No. 125.

Length 19 inches.............................................................................per doz., $18 00

No. 40–5.   Mechanical Fire Engine, extra large, 2 running horses, driver, fireman and sectional hose; when wound 2 small wheels and the pump work rapidly imitating an engine at work at a fire; size, 19x7x5.................................................per doz., $33 00

*Marshall Field & Co.*

# IRON TOYS.

No. 170.   Fire captain's wagon, 12½ inches long,
5½ inches high....................per doz., $7 50

No. 135.      Model Hose Cart, length 15 inches..........................per doz., $ 8 50
"  135½.   Same as No. 135, with rubber hose, length 15 inches...........  "      10 00

No. 0.   Fire Chief's Wagon.   Horse white, harness black, hames
and  housings red; body of wagon red, gear red, wheels red,
black striped; driver in uniform ....................per doz., $13 50

No. P.   Fire Patrol, horses white and black, 18 inches long, wagon
body light blue, gear white, driver and  three firemen in uniform ..............................................per doz., $20 00

No. 1010.   Hook and Ladder Truck; 2 ladders, horses
black, men in uniform, 24 inches long, 7⅓ inches
high..............................…...per doz., $9 00

Hook and Ladder No. T.   Horses white, harness black, hames and housings red, gear red, black striped, body black and green, with gilt
stripes and ornamentations, four red extension ladders, which can be
united,  making a ladder, 51 inches long, 2 axes with red handles,
men in uniform; length of toy, 29 inches.................per doz., $20 00

No. 130.   Hook and Ladder Truck, length, 32 inches....................................................................per doz., $18 00

# IRON TOYS.

Engine House V; size 26½x10x18; canvas roof, wood and malleable iron............................per doz., $39 00

No. M. Contractor's Wagon; horses, black; harness, gilt trimmed; hames and collar, red; wagon—box, blue, gilt letters; gear, red; wheels, red, black striped...............per doz., $20 00

Tally-Ho. Galloping horses, harness, metal figures; length, 18 inches; per dozen.................................. $54 00

No. D. Hansom, horse black, harness silver trimmed, hip blanket maroon, hansom black, panels yellow, with red stripes, driver in coachman's livery...................................per doz., $9 00

No. 190. Model Landau; length 16½ inches, finest iron horse toy ever made.................................per doz., $13 50

No. KK. Pony Phaeton; horse, white; harness, gilt trimmed; hip blanket, maroon; phaeton—body, black; seat, maroon; mat, orange; gear, red, black striped; wheels, red, black striped; lady driver................................per doz., $10 50

No. L. Express Wagon; 2 horses, driver and wagon, painted in bright colors; load, 2 boxes, 2 barrels, 1 sack; length 17½ inches.................................................per doz., $20 00

No. J. Double Truck; horses black, harness gilt trimmed, harness and collar red, truck gear red, black striped, side stakes green, gilt striped panels, seat and footboard red; load, 2 boxes, 2 barrels, 1 sack; length 17½ inches...........per doz., $18 00

*Marshall Field & Co.*

# IRON TOYS.

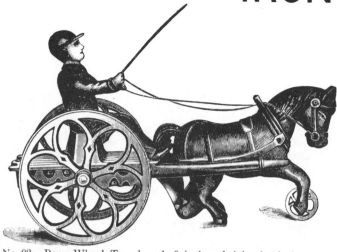

No. 93. Pony Wheel Toy; length, 9 inches; height, 5½ inches; width, 3¼ inches. As the toy is drawn, each revolution of the wheels causes the driver to strike the pony with the whip. Handsomely painted in fancy colors; ⅙ dozen in package, per dozen................................................$4 25

No. A. Sulky; horse black, harness gilt trimmed, sulky black, gilt striped, driver in jocky costume, length, 9½ inches, per dozen ................................................ $4 25

No. B. Dray; horse black, harness gilt trimmed, dray wheels red, sides and front green, gilt stripes, load one box; length, 11½ inches...........................................per doz., $4 25

No. CC. Dog Cart; horse black, harness gilt trimmed, cart yellow, wheels red and striped.......................per doz., $4 00

No. E. Surrey; horse brown, harness black, gilt trimmed, hip blanket buff, surrey body black, seats buff, gear black, red striped, driver in livery, length 15-inches...........per doz., $9 00

No. 175. Pony Express Wagon; length 14 inches.......per doz., $8 50

No. 185. Model Cart; length 13½ inches................per doz., $9 00

No. 1. Single Truck; horse black, harness silver trimmed, collar and housings red, truck gear red, black striped, side stakes green, panels and foot board red, gilt striped, load, 1 box, barrel and sack; lehgth 14 inches.................per doz., $9 00

*Marshall Field & Co.*

# TOYS.

No. 180.   Farm Wagon, length 16 inches................................................per doz., $9 00

## GATHMANN TORPEDO GUN.

A neat model of the most powerful weapon of war of the day.   It is entirely harmless as a toy, no explosives or powder being used; rubber bands are used to furnish the propelling power.   The torpedo is upheld in its flight by wings which guide and balance it, keeping it straight in the air. It will hit the mark.

No. 1.   Cannon 11 inches, nicely mounted.............................per doz., $ 8 00
"  2.      "     15   "   U. S. Navy pattern...........................   "      16 50

Two torpedos, four bullets and a ship target are with each cannon.

### PASTIME.

Toy base burner stove, transparent red windows, candle stick inside; base, top and urn nickel plated, one joint of pipe with each stove.   Size of base 5¾ inches in square.   Total height 12½ inches..........per doz., $9 00

No. W.   Extra large, heavy Artillery; horses mismatched in color, gun carriage and limber dark green, red striped, gun dead black, brass mounted, men in uniform, length of toy 34 inches................................................per doz., $48 00

No. 409.   Flying Artillery; brass cannon, 2 running horses, driver and odd rider; size 24x6½....................................per doz., $27 00

# TOY STOVES.

**No. 10. JEWEL TOY RANGE.**

**No. 15. JEWEL TOY RANGE.**

## JEWEL TOY RANGE—TWO STYLES.

Price.

No. 10. Square top............................................................................................each, $5 25

No. 15. With reservoir and high shelf..................................................................." 7 50

  The above cuts show the two styles. This is undoubtedly the best and most handsome toy range made. In its mechanical construction it embraces all the practical features found in the larger ranges, being complete in all its working parts. Nickel plated doors, panels and edges, nickel plated legs, frame and ornamental high shelf. Cooking can be done upon this range. Each stove packed in a box with kettle, spider and cake griddle.

**"THE O. K. No. 1" RANGE.**

Length, 6⅝ inches; height, 3⅞ inches; width, 5 inches; has 4 boiling holes, dumping grate, large fire box with door, oven with door, front door, draft damper openings; kettle, spider, baking pan, length of pipe and lifter included; each range is packed in a paper box, 1 dozen boxes in a large box, and 4 boxes in a crate.....................................per doz., $6 50

**THE "I. X. L." RANGE.**

Length, 8¼ inches; height, 5¼ inches; width, 5⅛ inches; has 4 boiling holes, reservoir, dumping grate, large fire box, oven with door, front door, damper openings; kettle, spider, baking pan, griddle, length of pipe and lifter included; each range is packed in a paper box, 1 dozen boxes in large box, and 4 boxes in a crate.........................................per doz., $9 00

**THE "PET" RANGE.**

Length, 11½ inches; height, 7 inches; width, 7 inches; har 4 boiling holes, reservoir, dumping grate. reservoir damper, large fire box with door, oven with door, front door with draft damper; large and small kettle, spider, baking pan, length of pipe and lifter included; each range is packed in a box, 1 dozen boxes in a crate....................................per doz., $18 00

**THE "BABY" RANGE.**

Length, 16 inches; height, 9¼ inches; width, 8¾ inches; has 6 boiling holes, reservoir, dumping grate, direct and reservoir dampers, large fire box with door, oven with door, front door with draft damper, and ash pit with door; kettle, spider, coffee pot, tea kettle, baking pan, length of pipe and lifter included; each range is packed in a box, ½ doz. boxes in a crate, per doz., $26 00

*Marshall Field & Co.*

# BELL TOYS.

No. 24.   Bellringers; half size cut......................per doz., $3 75

No. 4.   Chime, with horse; 6½ inches, ½ dozen in package, per dozen ....................................................... $1 75

No. 15.   Half size cut; ⅓ dozen in package.............per doz., $1 85

No. 39.   Half size cut; horse swings on pedestal and rings the bell.........................................................per doz., $4 00

No. 37.   Half size cut; girl with doll on sled, with chimes, per dozen ....................................................... $4 00

No. 23.   Half size cut; jumping horse and monkey rider, per doz., $3 75

*Marshall Field & Co.*

# TOY BANKS.

No. 8.  Half doz. in package, size 3¼ x 2½ x 2¼......per doz., $0 75

No. 15.   Height, 4¼ in., width, 3 in., depth 3 in.; quarter doz. in package .........per doz., $2 00

No. 35.   Watch Dog Safe, with combination lock.  Height, 6 in., width, 4¾ in., depth, 4½ in.   When deposits are made the watch dog barks.  Beautifully finished in gold bronze and colors......per doz., $8 50

No. 400.   Size, 6 inches high,  4¾ wide, 4¾ deep.   New and accurate combination lock, also has attached to the slot a patented money guard, which will make the abstraction of money an impossibility.   It is fitted up with a handsome oak cabinet, containing two drawers with nickel trimmings.   It is finished in black japan, relieved with different shades of bronze.  Packed one in a wooden box ............................................................per doz., $9 00

No. 150.   Security Safe Deposit.   Size 4¼ inches high, 3 wide, 3¾ deep.   With brass combination lock and patent money guard.   It has a different style of combination lock from regular safes, consisting of one movable dial only which is turned forward or backward to certain numbers.   Full particulars will be given on a tag accompanying each safe.   Beautifully finished in nickel only.   Packed three in a box. ............................................................per doz., $5 50

*Marshall Field & Co.*

# TOY BANKS.

No. 200. Nickel-plated security safe deposit, with brass combination lock and patent money guard. Size, 4¾ inches high, 3¾ wide, 3½ deep.. per doz., $7 50

No. 119. Home Savings bank. Height, 6 in.; width, 4½ in.; depth, 3½ in. ¼ doz. in package, per doz...$2 00

National safe deposit bank with coppered combination lock and patented burglar-proof attachment. Finished in black and copper bronze. Size 6 in. high, 4½ in. wide, ¼ doz. in package............per doz., $4 00

No. A. Full nickel-plated, burglar proof, combination lock capable of 900 changes, 6½ in. wide, 6 in. high and 4 in. deep..................per doz., $9 00

Junior safe deposit bank with coppered combination lock and patented burglar proof attachment. Finished in black and copper bronze. Size, 4⅝ in. high, 3⅜ in. wide. ½ doz. in package..........per doz., $2 00

# TOY BANKS.

Minstrel Bank. The body of the bank is divided into two parts, the lower being the coin safe, while the upper part contains the mechanism for giving motion to the performers. A charge of one penny by the owner of a bank to see the performance will soon pay its cost. Each bank is tested and is known to be in proper working order before being packed at the factory.....................................per doz., $9 00

No. 275. Cabin Bank; length 4¼ inches, height 3⅝ inches, width 3 inches. Place the coin upon the roof above the negro's head, move the handle of the white-wash brush, and the negro will be made to stand on his head and kick the coin into the bank, ¼ dozen in package.................per doz., $4 00

No. 1013. The Dairy; nickel finished, with brass bands, protected money slot, puzzle padlock; size 4 inches high, ½ dozen in package....................per doz., $4 50

No. 485. Presto Trick Bank, with lock and key opening; size 4½ inches high, 4 wide, 2½ deep. This bank contains the novel feature of a trick drawer. Press down the button over the front door, and the drawer will fly open. Put the coin in and close it. When the button is again pressed, the drawer will fly open, but the coin will have mysteriously disappeared. The money can be removed from the bottom of the bank by means of a lock and key. Handsomely decorated, and packed one-half dozen in a box...................................................per doz., $2 25

No. 60. 5¾ inches, nickel plated.....................per doz., $9 00    No. 65. 5 inches, nickel plated........................per doz., $8 00
The Bank of Columbia, constructed as near as possible on the plan of a real safe, with dials and handles on one side, Goddess of Liberty on the other, Uncle Sam with grip, marked "World's Fair." No. 75 same as No. 65 but in old copper finish.....................per doz., $8 00

# TOY BANKS.

No. 323. Bicycle Bank. Length, 11 in., height, 8 in., width 3½ in. As the crank is turned and the lever pressed, Prof. Pug Frog performs his great bicycle feat, and the coin placed on the bicycle is deposited in the bank. During the performance, Mother Goose gives attention to her melodies..................................................per doz., $8 50

No. 225. Organ Bank, with revolving figure. Size, 4 in. high, 3½ wide, 2½ deep. Place the coin in the recess before the figure, and when the handle is turned a chime of bells will ring and the monkey will revolve and deposit the money in the bank. Appropriately decorated in colors, and packed one half dozen in a box........................per doz., $2 00

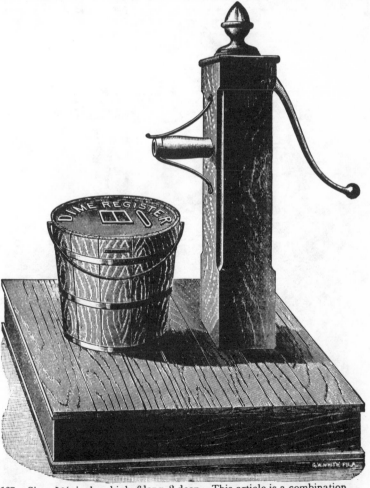

No. 116. Size, 6½ in. high, 4 wide, 3 deep. This bank is calculated to highly amuse children, as it is a musical toy as well as a savings bank. When the handle is turned a chime of bells will ring continuously, while at the same time the monkey will deposit in the bank any coins which may be placed on his tambourine, expressing his thanks by lifting his cap. Highly decorated, and packed one in a box...........................................per doz., $4 00

No. 127. Size, 5½ inches high, 6 long, 3 deep. This article is a combination of a mechanical and registering bank. It is a very attractive novelty and cannot fail to please. The bucket is designed for dimes, in ordinary use only, and not for mutilated or old-fashioned coin of approximately the same size. Put a dime in the slot and push the pump handle up and down, when the amount will be correctly registered. When $5 have been deposited the lid of the bucket can be taken off; when replaced it is ready for business. If the directions pasted on the bottom of each bank are complied with, it cannot fail to work properly. Handsomely finished in nickel and wood colors, and packed one in a wooden box.....................per doz., $8 50

*Marshall Field & Co.*

# TOY BANKS AND WHEELTOY.

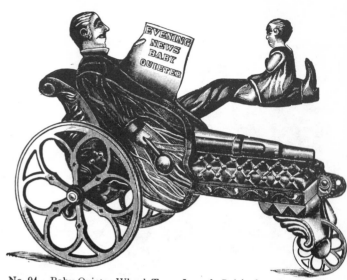

No. 300. Eagle Bank. Length, 8 inches; height, 6 inches; width, 4 inches. Place a coin in the Eagle's beak, press the lever, and the Eaglets rise from the nest crying for food. As the Eagle bends forward to feed them, the coin falls into the nest, and disappears in the receptacle below.............................................. per doz., $8 50

No. 94. Baby Quieter Wheel Toy. Length, 7½ inches; height, 6 inches; width, 3¾ inches. As the toy is drawn, each revolution of the wheels rings the bell and jumps the baby. Handsomely finished in fancy colors, ⅙ doz. in package... per doz., $4 25

No. 119. Organ Bank, with new dancing figures, complete with lock and key; size, 8½ inches high, 5½ wide, 3¾ deep. This handsomely finished bank has proven the most satisfactory article of the kind ever put on the market. It has very sweet chimes of bells, which sound when the handle is turned, and the monkey deposits all coin in the bank, and politely raises his cap, while the figures at his side revolve, producing a pleasing effect. Packed one in a wooden box......................... per doz., $8 00

No. 324. Cat and Mouse Bank. Height, 11½ inches; width, 5½ inches; depth, 4 inches. Place a coin in front of the mouse over the cat, press the lever, and as the coin disappears into the bank, the kitten, in fancy dress, appears, turning a somersault, holding the mouse and ball. Handsomely ornamented in fancy colors............................... per doz., $8 50

# DRUMS.

## ASSORTMENT NO. 10.   ONLY SOLD BY THE CASE.

Embossed metal drum, imitation brass shell, having embossed figures, red, white and blue cord, and metal hooks and hoops, belts with each drum, excepting the 6½ inch.  Case contains:

| | | | |
|---|---|---|---|
| Diameter 6½ inches | ..................................................... | 1 | dozen. |
| " 8 " | ..................................................... | ½ | " |
| " 10 " | ..................................................... | ½ | " |
| " 13 " | ..................................................... | ½ | " |
| Per case | ..................................................... | $12 00 | |

---

## TOY BOOKS.

No. 604.  16 pages, 6 kinds assorted, half bound.

---

### THE EXPANDING TOY AND PAINTING BOOK SERIES.

The pictures are so arranged that they stand out in relief of the background, giving the illustrations a panoramic, and hence, an interesting effect to children.   The backgrounds are printed in tone, and intended to be filled in with bright colors by aspiring little artists. These books contain 16 pages; are substantially bound in heavy board covers; illuminated and varnished; cloth back, and are among the most novel productions of the season.  "Robinson Crusoe," "Little Red Riding Hood," "Three Bears," "Three Kittens," "Fun at the Circus," "Our Friends at the Zoo."

Per doz....................................$2 00

No. 639.   8 pages, 4 kinds assorted colored pictures, size, 4x6, covers cut in shapes. "Hush-a-Bye-Baby," "Old Woman in Shoe," "Good Morning," "My Pet," ¼ gross, as'td in each package, per gross, $4 75

No. 591.   14 pages, 4 kinds assorted cut out covers, monochrome illustrations, size, 5¾x8.  "Puggies Stories," "Merry Winter Time," "Life's Sunny Hours," "Told by the Cat," 1 doz. assorted in each package..........................per doz., $1 20

No. 602.   16 pages, 2 kinds assorted colored pictures, size, 7¼x9.  "The night before Christmas," "Behind the bars at the Zoo," 1 dozen in each package, per doz....................................$2 00

No. 616.   14 pages, 2 kinds assorted monochrome illustrations, shape cover, size, 7¼x8¼.  "Hurrah for Christmas," "Seaside Toddlers," 1 dozen in each package, per doz....................................$2 00

No. 615.  "Only a Jap Dollee."  Book in shape of a "Jap Doll." 12 pages of artistic colored illustrations, with rhymes by Miss Burnside. Stiff board covers, printed in colors front and back.   Size, 5x11¼, 1 doz. in each package, per doz., $2 00

# PYRAMID AND A B C BLOCKS.

No. 579½. The "Baby Bunting" A B C and Picture Blocks. 5 Blocks, 3½ x 4 inches closed, 19 inches high when set up. ½ doz. package. Per doz.... $1 85

The set contains five blocks, the largest being 3½x3½x4 inches, and the smallest 2x2x4 inches. The sides are decorated with handsome lithographs of subjects especially attractive to children. Each subject has a descriptive title below it. Upon the tops of the set are the letters of the alphabet divided among the different blocks.

No. 579. Tom Thumb Blocks, per doz......... $4 00

HORSE.

No. 6.

No. 509½. Contains 6 blocks and is a very showy and handsome set of nested blocks. per doz.........$4 00

No. 6. Twelve pieces. Natural wood, printed in colors. Packed in paper boxes with fine label, ½ doz. in package. per doz......... $2 00

No. 509. The blocks nest together, forming a package 7 inches square, but when opened form a pyramid 41 in. high..per doz., $7 00

COCK

No. 35. Thirty-five pieces. Embossed ends. Numerous illustrations, together with all the letters and numerals. Natural wood and printed in colors. ¼ doz. in package...............per doz., $4 00

No. 000. Twelve pieces, Embossed hard wood, in glazed paper boxes, with label in four colors, glossed. This block is intended to retail for 10 cents, and is acknowledged to be the best ever offered for the price. ½ doz. in package ........................per doz., $0 65

No. 25. Sixteen pieces. Natural wood. In paper boxes, with fine labels. An excellent block to retail for 25 cents. ½ doz. in package...per doz., 1 85

No. 580. Little Bo-Peep Alphabet and Picture Blocks. New..............per doz., $8 00

# ALPHABET AND PICTURE BLOCKS.

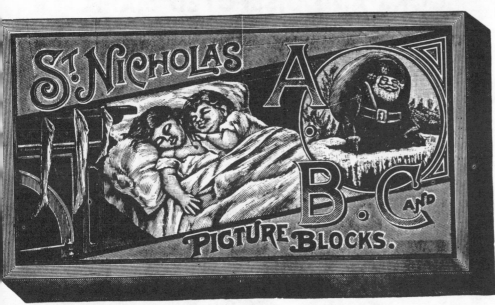

No. 664.

No. 664. St. Nicholas' A B C and Picture Blocks. 7½x12½ inches. This set is made up of twenty-four flat blocks. Each block is three-eighths by one and one-half by four inches. The pictures on one side are of children at play, and on the other a large picture to be put together as a puzzle. ½ doz. package......................per doz., $2 00

No. 92. Illustrated cubes. Mother Goose. Twenty pieces, Mother Goose illustrations and rhymes; with alphabet complete. Painted and varnished, and waterproof. Wood frame box.......per doz., $9 00

No. 3. Illustrated Cubes. Twenty pieces. Natural Wood. Special designs engraved for this line of blocks. Packed in wood frame boxes. Mother Goose pictures and rhymes. ¼ dozen package. ........................per doz., $4 00

No. 3.

No. 658. Railroad and Menagerie Blocks, ½ dozen package, per doz.,.....................$2 00

No. 92.

No. 520. Little Folks' Cubes. 8x11 inches. Series—Six kinds.

Cinderella.  Red Riding Hood.  Puss in Boots.
Jack and the Beanstalk.  Goody Two Shoes.  The Three Bears.

These sets of blocks contain twelve cubes, each two and a half inches square. Upon the cubes of each set are portions of six pictures, illustrative of the stories indicated by the titles. When the cubes are properly set up the complete pictures are formed. To form the pictures is the object of the play.............................per doz., $5 50

No. 674. Tommy Snooks' A B C. Improved. 7½x12½ inches. ½ doz. package....................per doz., $2 00

This is a set of twenty-four flat blocks, one and a half by five and a quarter by three-eighths inches. On one side are letters and animals, and on the other scenes from the circus.

No. 505. 1,000 Jolly Cats and Dogs. 8x8 inches. ¼ dozen in package.................................................per doz., $3 50

These blocks consist of nine cubes, two and a half inches square. They have heads bodies and feet of cats in grotesque attire and positions on the different blocks. These fit together and make innumerable comical combinations.

*Marshall Field & Co.*

# ALPHABET BLOCKS AND DISSECTED MAPS.

## No. 661.  Cats and Dogs.

Size 7½x12½ inches, 9 flat blocks with red ends, each block 4x2½x⅞ inches.  The illustrations are new, of an amusing character and illustrate the story of Dash's Holiday on one side and Miss Pussy Cat's School on the other.  The edges have a large and a small alphabet.

½ dozen in a package..................per doz., $2 00

---

## No. 663.  Rich Mrs. Duck Blocks.

Size 8x12½ inches, the set contains 9 flat blocks, each 4x2½x⅞ inches, the blocks having red ends.  The designs of the pictures are new and handsome and illustrate the stories of Rich Mrs. Duck and The House that Jack Built.  A large and small alphabet appears on the edges.

½ dozen in a package..................per doz., $2 00

---

## No. 666.  Joyful Tales Blocks.

Size 12x15 inches, this set contains 18 flat blocks with red ends, 4x2½x⅞ inches.  Cats and Dogs No. 661 and Rich Mrs. Duck Blocks No. 663 make up this set.

½ dozen in a package..................per doz., $4 00

---

## No. 568.  The World's Fair Building Blocks.

Size 8x10½ inches, these cubes are 2½ inches square, 12 in a set.  The pictures are of the Machinery Hall, the U. S. Government Building, the building of Mines and Mining, Agricultural Hall and the Transportation Building.

Per doz......................................$5 00

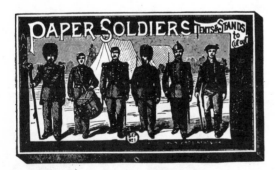

No. 548.  Army Tent and Soldiers, size 6x11½ inches.  Two kinds put up, assorted.  These boxes contain ninety of our new paper soldiers—nine kinds, ten of each kind—tin stands to make them all stand upright, and four tents.  The soldiers are intended to be cut out and put on their stands, after which they may be divided into two armies, set up at a couple of yards' distance, and bowled at by their respective commanders with marbles for cannon balls.  The one first bowling down all the opposition men win the battle.  ½ dozen in a package.............................................per doz., $2 00

---

## No. 678.  Blocks of Delight.  New.

Size 10x16 inches.  These blocks are 4x1¼x3¼ inches.  The illustrations are of birds, dressed up animals and alphabets.

¼ dozen in a package..................per doz., $4 00

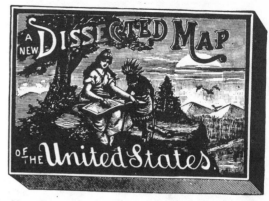

No. 596.  New dissected map U. S.  Size of map 9x14; ½ dozen in a package.......................................per doz., $2 00
No. 597.  New dissected map U. S.  Size of map 11x17..per doz.,  4 00

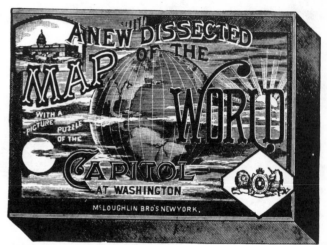

No. 598.  Dissected map of the U. S., new; we make this map in three sizes; No. 598 is the largest, and is dissected by state boundaries; large wood boxes and brilliant labels....per doz., $8 00
No. 599.  Dissected map of the world, new; the fine large map, 16½x21½ inches, is accurate in all particulars, and gives also supplemental maps of the United States and Great Britain, showing these two countries much larger than is practicable in the large map; upon the back of the map is a very fine picture of the United States' Capitol at Washington..per doz., $8 00

No. 547.  The Pretty Village.  This toy village is a set of ten cardboard houses, stores, churches, etc., printed to represent buildings, hinged together so that they fold up when the roofs are lifted off.  They are about 6x3 inches on the ground, and high in proportion.  When set up they make a pretty imitation of a village street.  Some figures of the villagers are put up with them, to be cut out, to inhabit the settlement........per doz., $8 00
No. 545.  Smaller size...............................  "   4 00

*Marshall Field & Co.*

# PUZZLES.

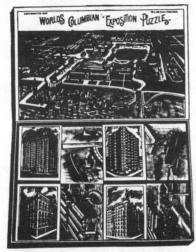

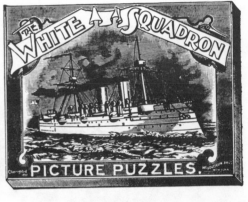

No. 524. Santa Claus Scroll Puzzles; new, 12 kinds. There are 12 different puzzles, as follows : Santa Claus in Africa, Santa Claus in Lapland, Santa Claus down the Chimney, Santa Claus in Russia, Santa Claus in Arabia, Santa Claus in North America, Santa Claus filling the Stockings, Santa Claus in Scandinavia, Santa Claus Opening his Pack, All Snug in Bed, Christmas Eve, Merry Christmas. Assorted 1 dozen in package..............per doz., $2 00

World's "Columbian Exposition" Puzzle consists of 49 squares which when matched form a perfect picture, 14x 22 inches, in beautiful colors, of a bird's eye view of the completed World's Fair, while on the reverse side is given 49 views (engraved) in Chicago. The puzzle is put in a handsome box 7x8 inches, with a highly colored label showing the bird's eye view on a reduced scale and giving valuable statistics concerning the size of grounds and buildings, cost of the latter, etc., together with a key to the buildings. The views on the back of each one of the 49 squares are separate and distinct engravings, so that, aside from the interest of the puzzle it forms a fascinating picture of the World's Fair, ½ dozen in a ackage, per doz., $2 00

No. 572. White Squadron Picture Puzzles. This is a scroll puzzle making a picture of one of the ships of the New Fleet about 12x22 inches when put together. The puzzle is put up in a wooden box 9x12 inches. Each box contains a pattern picture for a guide in putting the puzzle together and a full description of the ship. The ships are the

| | |
|---|---|
| Baltimore, | Boston, |
| Chicago, | Pirate, |
| Monterey, | Massachusetts. |

Each representative of a different type or style of modern fighting ships ½ dozen package..........per doz., $4 00

## No. 543. Young America— Scroll Puzzles.

Series, four kinds, put up assorted.

**Old Woman and her Pig.**
**Circus Picture Puzzle.**
**Wild West Picture Puzzle.**
**St. Nicholas Picture Puzzle.**

These puzzles are made from board about one-eighth of an inch thick, upon which a picture is mounted. The board is then sawed up into various fantastic shapes. The amusement is to restore the pieces to place, and hence the picture. These scrolls contain one picture, 12x20 inches. Size, 9x12 inches..........per doz., $4 00

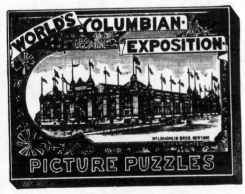

No. 574. World's Columbian Exposition Picture Puzzles. 6 kinds of Scroll Puzzles. They are put up in a wood box 10x12 inches. Each box contains one of the buildings for the Chicago World's Fair, mounted on thick card board and cut up into a scroll puzzle. Also a pattern of the building to put the puzzle together by and a description of the building. Each picture is about 12x22 inches when completed. The buildings shown are "Machinery Hall," "The United States Government Building," "Building for Mines and Mining," "Agricultural Hall" and "The Transportation Building," ½ dozen package..................per doz., $4 00

No. 515. Chopped Up Niggers. Scroll puzzles, three kinds, two puzzles in each box. As comical puzzles they will be found unequaled. Put up in our new style boxes; each one packed separately.................per doz., $4 00

## No 566. Young Shipbuilder's Cubes.

These Cubes are put up in a box 8x10½ inches, 12 2½ cubes in a set. They have pictures of the same ships as No. 546, but different views and smaller pictures. They have full descriptions of the ship and pattern designs to aid in putting the puzzle together................per doz., $5 00

## No. 519. Happy Hour Puzzle Cubes.

These sets are put up in boxes 5½x8 inches. There are four kinds, the cubes 2½ inches. The pictures are very fine lithographs, equal or superior to any imported goods. The stories illustrated, two on a set, are

**The Three Bears.**
**Old Mother Hubbard.**
**Bo Peep.**
**Puss in Boots.**
**Jack the Giant Killer.**
**Red Riding Hood.**

The fourth set is made up of pictures not illustrating any story but of a character to interest children generally and to attract all by their beauty of design and execution, ½ dozen in package......................per doz., $2 75

*Marshall Field & Co.*

# PUZZLES.

No. 592. Locomotive Puzzle. 9x12 inches. In this puzzle the subject, as the title indicates, is a locomotive. The details of construction are carefully brought out in the picture. The print is mounted and sawed up like other scroll puzzles for boys to fit together again. It is 18x24 inches in size. Per doz.............$6 00

No. 594. Circus Scroll Puzzle. Series, two kinds put up, assorted. The cut up pictures in these scrolls are scenes from the circus. Per doz., $6 00

No. 521. Santa Claus Cube Puzzles. 11x13 inches. Two kinds, put up assorted. Each puzzle contains twenty 2½ inch cubes. By their use six pictures, each 10x12½ inches in size, can be made. The pictures are from the experiences and travels of "Santa Claus," the beloved of all children. Per doz., $8 00

## No. 590. Fire Engine Puzzle.

9x12 inches. In this picture puzzle the subject is a fire engine going to a fire. The size of the picture is 18x24 inches. It is carefully and accurately drawn to show all the details of a modern steam fire engine. Per doz.............$6 00

No. 534. Artistic Puzzle Cubes. 2 kinds. Size 8x10½ inches. 12 cubes 2½ inches square. Two sets of the Happy Hour Cubes No. 519 are put together in a box with a new label. Per doz................................................. $5 00

## No. 542. Ideal Puzzle Cubes.

11x19 inch wood box containing 24 2½ inch cubes. All four of the Happy Hour Cubes, No. 519, are put together in this set with a new label. Per doz................................................$10 50

No. 546. White Squadron Naval Puzzle Blocks. These puzzle cubes are put up in a wooden box 11x21 inches with a very attractive label representing the new Fleet of United States Men-of-War at sea. There are 32 2½ inch cubes in the set with parts of six of the pictures of new naval vessels on each. When properly put together the Baltimore, (same as the U. S. S. Philadelphia,) the Pirate, the Boston, (same as the U.S.S. Atlanta), the New York, the torpedo boat Cushing, (named after the gallant officer who blew up the Confederate ram, Albemarle, from a little steam launch during the late war,) and the Chicago, (same as the U. S. S. Newark.) A full description of these ships accompanies each set of blocks as also a set of cuts to aid in putting the blocks together properly. The ships have been selected to show best the new types of vessels being built for Uncle Sam and cannot fail to post boys on Naval matters as well as amuse them. Per doz.........................$12 00

No. 549. The World's Columbian Exposition. This box of puzzle cubes contains 32 2½ inch blocks, the box itself being 11x21 inches. The pictures on these blocks are of the buildings in course of erection on the Fair Grounds at Chicago. They represent the Machinery Hall, the United States Government Building, the Building of Mines and Mining, Agricultural Hall and the Transportation Building. Per doz..................$12 00

# GAMES.

No. 522. Across the Continent. The most elaborate board game ever issued. It has utensils for six players, but can be played by any number. It is an exciting amusement, and the value of its educational features cannot be overestimated..................................................per doz., $33 00

No. 532. Presidential Election. This is the presidential year. This game therefore comes upon the market at a very opportune moment. The game is both simple and practical. It is elegant in appearance. It gives information concerning the electoral vote, and is played in such a manner as to combine instruction with lots of fun.........................per doz., $8 00

No. 525. Innocence Abroad. Comes in large, handsome box, enclosing large folding board superbly lithographed; it represents the journey of a party of people, who travel by various routes toward the same destination, and who meet with various experiences and occurrences; the detail work is very fine, showing roads running through a very picturesque country, past farms, forests, mountains and across rivers, whose course can be traced from their sources to the coast; in handsome box complete........................per doz., $10 00

No. 519. Knuckle Billiards. A peculiar new game. A very excellent one. It is simple and makes a great deal of fun, per dozen.......................................................$4 00

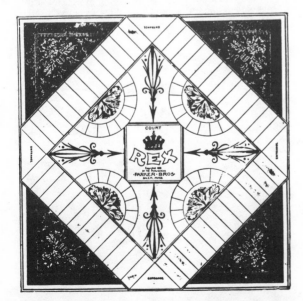

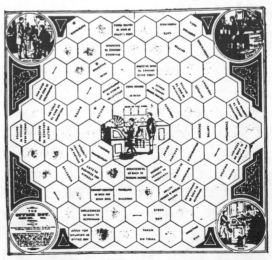

No. 526. Rex and the Kilkenny Cats. Combination. These games are now issued in a large flat box containing a heavy board with a game on each side. It makes quite a show for the money..............................................per doz., $8 00

No. 528. Office Boy. The game is very simple and affords great amusement; it shows the haps and mishaps in the career of a business man, from his start as office boy, gradually working his way up to the head of the firm; each game is accompanied with 4 metal office boys, making the game very attractive and realistic..............................per doz., $8 00

# GAMES.

No. 517. Game of American History. An educational game. This gives, in the form of an interesting game, the prominent facts of American history, from the time of Columbus to the present day. Consists of sixty handsome enameled cards on which are printed questions relating to the various subjects, these questions being selected for their general interest and importance .......................................... per doz., $4 00

No. 516. Wild Flower Game. In colors. A beautiful game. There are over sixty cards, all expensively lithographed with pictures of wild flowers. The game follows the course in botany prescribed by the Chautauqua course for the present year, and is especially recommended to students. It is simple in its playing qualities. ½ doz. in package........ per doz., $4 00

No. 518. The Literary Game of Quotations. This is a splendid high-class game, abounding in the celebrated quotations which have made authors famous. Consists of sixty finely finished round-cornered cards with fancy assorted backs, each devoted to a certain author or one of his works. A most enjoyable entertainment ..................... per doz., $4 00

No. 530. Crazy Traveler. It is the unexpected that happens in this game. It consists of a board arranged with circular pockets, combined with an apparatus which whirls a ball with great rapidity. Players count according to the numbers on the pockets in which they succeed in driving other balls with their large one, and also according to their success in making the ball knock over the tall wooden pins that rest upon the board. A lively game, and a good one. Pleases both children and adults................................ per doz., $8 00

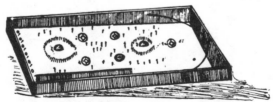

No. 523. Bagatelle. An elegant bagatelle board with shellacked wood frame furnished with brass mountings, and two nickeled bells. A thoroughly first-class article, per doz ...................................... $8 50

No. 531. A beautiful novelty. The game represents a tower with a princess appearing and disappearing at the upper casement. Also a dungeon cell, and a vine, by climbing upon which the knights endeavor to reach and rescue the princess. When the board is ready for play it is placed in an upright position, thereby giving a more realistic effect....... per doz., $8 00

No. 1. Popular edition, is bound in durable and handsome black paper (imitation cloth), with scarlet labels printed in best gold bronze. A box containing eight dice, sixteen brass-bound counters, four dice cups, and directions accompany the board; the whole forming the most complete and attractive dollar game in the market..................... per doz., $9 00

# GAMES.

No. 529. The Battle Game. Box contains one large army gorgeously arrayed, and fully officered, with toy pistol, etc., and full directions. A showy and desirable game.......per doz., $8 00

No. 509. Great Battlefields. The only game treating of this subject. Elegantly printed on fine cardboard. Exceedingly entertaining and giving instruction upon events interesting to people of all ages. It is well that all young people should know the great generals who have fought the famous battles of the world. Played on the book system with certain copyrighted improvements. In box with battle scene on the illuminated label. ½ doz. in ackage................per doz., $2 00

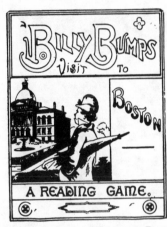

No. 506. Billy Bumps' Visit to Boston. This new humorous reading game has a very large sale; the book describes Billy's adventures and experiences in his journey to the "Hub," the accompanying cards fill in the blank spaces, in a manner calculated to make young people very merry, per doz..............................$2 00

No. 507. Johnny's Historical Game. One of the most pleasing and instructive games on our list, and one that should be played in every home, by young and old. The great events of national history are, by its use, firmly fixed in the mind, per doz...................................$2 00

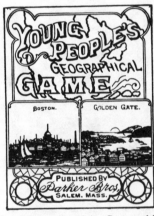

No. 513. Young People's Geographical Game New 1890. A carefully prepared and excellent game. A good geographical game always meets with a ready sale, both with the young folks themselves and with their parents, handsomely issued at a popular price.......per doz., $2 00

No. 500. The Game of Luck. A most interesting game of pure luck and chance, comes with spinner on top, counters and full directions. Very exciting...........................per doz., $2 00

No. 501. A simple, pleasing little game of skill. The game is to seize the ball and convey it safely to a goal by moves, each side moving alternately. ½ doz. in package.........per doz., $2.00

# GAMES.

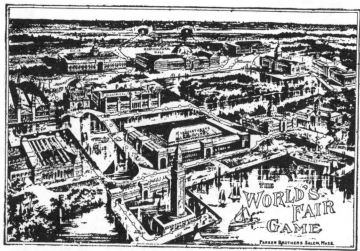

**No. 527.** The World's Fair Game. The game of the season. Everybody wants one this year. Brilliantly lithographed board, showing an exact reproduction of the Exposition grounds and buildings at Chicago. This is an excellent game to play. It is also a beautiful and showy article. Per doz ....................................................$8 00

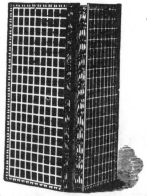

**No. 424.** Go-Bang, 8x16 closed. Go-Bang is one of the most remarkable games published. The object is simply to make a row of five men first, by putting pieces on the board one after the other. It is tit-tat-to improved. Yet with all its simplicity it fascinates the oldest game player as easily as it amuses the youngest child. It is a standard game for all. Per doz....................................................$8 00

**No. 430½.** The Improved Game of Steeple Chase. Steeple Chase is a mimic horse race. The horses are entered and moved over the spaces on the race track according to the throws of the dice. Obstructions, in the nature of hurdles, ditches and falls, are introduced. The winner is the player who can get his piece over the course first, dodging or overcoming obstructions as best he can. Six may play. It is a game for boys. Per doz., $8 00

**No. 464.** Game of Louisa, 9x16 inches. Board 16x17. Louisa is the best of a class of games combining chance with moderate skill. It is a game which will meet the approval of the great majority of players of all ages. Two, three, or four may play it. By means of the throws of two dice the four men of each player are entered, one at a time for each die, carried around the spaces at the margin of the board back to the place of beginning, and thence moved to the centre. The combination of a good throw, with skillful play, may enable a player to take up some of the adversaries' men and force them to start over again. The object is to get round and to the center of the board first with all a player's pieces. Per doz.................$8 00

**No. 499.** Improved Scripture Cards, 6x9 inches. This game contains over 200 cards, upon which are printed names from Scripture or questions on Scriptural subjects. With the names are printed statements concerning them. A Leader or Teacher reads these statements or asks the questions on the cards. The players or pupils give the name or answers in turn. A correct answer entitles a player to take the card as a counter for game. By discreetly selecting questions or subjects the leader can vary the difficulty of the exercise to suit the ability of various players. They are designed to give thorough home instruction in the Scriptures, and constitute one of the best possible Sunday amusements. ¼ dozen in package........per doz., $6 75

**No, 498.** Improved Geographical Cards. This game contains over 200 cards bearing geographical names, and facts concerning them. A Leader or Teacher gives the facts on a card, and the players or pupils give the name. The player who answers correctly receives the card as a counter for game. The game is designed to amuse a party of young people or children who desire to improve their knowledge of geography, or for school use. ¼ dozen in each package................................per doz., $6 75

*Marshall Field & Co.*

# GAMES.

No. 536½. Fish Pond Game, new and improved. The finest game of Fish Pond ever offered at a popular price. It contains patented features; is gotten up in the very best manner with very handsome labels and with the best of implements. ½ doz. package................per doz., $2 00

Our new and desirable Fish Pond Games. (Patented.)
No. 535. Improved Game of Fish Pond. Extra fine edition......per doz., $8 00
No. 536. Improved Fish Pond Game. Fine edition. ½ doz. package......per doz., 4 00

No. 328. Leatherette Lotto. Size of box 9¼x7¾ in. It is of wood, covered with imitation of alligator skin leatherette of the color and appearance of Russia Leather. The title and an ornamental design are stamped in gold on the lid. The box contains a large box of glass, a set of 90 well finished lotto men, and 24 lotto cards............per doz., $5 35

No. 521. Geographical. An educational game. An excellent edition, from which those who play it will find in condensed form most of the important facts concerning the geography of the world. An excellent amusement, especially adapted for the use of schools, as well as the home circle. ½ doz. in package.
................per doz., $4 00

No. 452. Golden Locks Series. Size, 10½x20 in. Three kinds, assorted, in quarter dozens. Little Golden Locks, Little Red Riding Hood, Jack the Giant Killer. The Golden Locks Games are the largest and handsomest ever offered at the price. The boards are laid flat and fastened in the bottoms of the boxes, and are, consequently, of the same size as the boxes. This is a form adopted last season for the first time. It has proved very satisfactory..........per doz., $4 00

No. 692. Diamond series. New. Three kinds put up, assorted, in quarter dozens. Cats and Mice and Tousel. Captive Princess and Ambuscades. Life's Mishaps and Bobbing around the Circle. This series is compiled from the old Favorite Series, revised, corrected and improved. The best of the old games have been selected, new and very handsome labels have been designed, and the boxes doubled in size. The series is designed for children; per doz., $4 00

Trunk Box Lotto—design patented. Lotto is one of the very few games which grows into popularity year after year. It is so simple and easily learned that very young children readily master it. It provides a fund of constant interest and amusement, and does not become the least bit monotonous.

No. 417. ½ doz. in package, per doz., $2 00
" 418. ½ " " " 4 00
" 419. ¼ " " " 6 75
No. 327½. "American" Lotto, Black Box, ¼ doz. in package, per doz., $4 00

*Marshall Field & Co.*

# GAMES.

No. 511. My Wife and I. A new reading game. The game consists of a small book with illustrated covers, with 100 blank spaces in it, to be filled out by the different players, with 100 cards bearing reading matter upon them. per doz., $2 00

No. 512. The Game of Letters. This old standard, reliable game is now issued in improved form, with nearly 300 letters and simplified directions, both for letters and anagrams. In good box with illuminated label.....per doz., $2 00

No. 508. Country Auction. The auctioneer knocks down the articles to the highest bidder, and after the auction is over the player having cleared the most profit by his shrewd bids is the winner. The game affords a chance for considerable ability and judgment, and is of unusual laughable excitement. Country Auction is suitable for people of all ages; in large box, attractively issued ........................per doz., $2 00

No. 504. The good old Game of Proverbs. Revised for 1892. An old standard game which we have taken great care in revising, and making suitable for the demands of the present day. There are 100 cards containing the best proverbs, and there are directions for playing the game in seven different ways, ½ dozen package ...........per doz., $2 00

No. 510. Forbidden Fruit. This excellent selling game is not at all instructive, but makes "quantities of fun." A new edition, nearly every card being handsomely illustrated, and printed on fine card board with tinted backs..........per doz., $2 00

No. 505. County Fair. New. This is another addition to the list of popular trading games, and will be found worthy to be placed beside Corner Grocery and others of the series. Contains cards bearing names of articles usually exhibited at "Cattle Shows," with tickets of admission, and money for premiums and various expenses, etc.....per doz., $2 00

No. 2. Jack Straws. New. Fine edition. Best imported pieces put up in a box with handsome label, equal to any set on the market...per doz., $4 00

No. 1. Jack Straws. Popular edition. New. Same as No. 2, only not so many pieces in the box.................................per doz., $2 00

No. 503. Corner Grocery. It is played with some forty illustrated grocery cards marked with the proper prices, and over one hundred pieces representing money. The cards are very attractive and have been improved since the first editions. ½ doz. package ....per doz., $2 00

## Toy Watches.

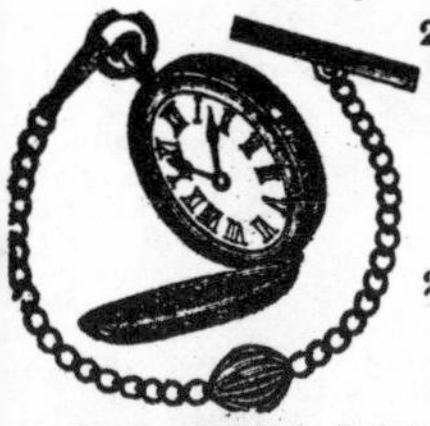

24960 Panoramic watches, open face, gilt chain and charm. As watch is wound the hands revolve and a succession of pictures of birds, animals, etc., are brought into view. Each.....$0.05
Per dozen............ .50
24961 Toy Watch, for girls, open face Swiss style, fancy gilt chain; has long neck chain. Each..........$0.08
Per dozen............ .90
24963 Toy Watch, figured hunting case, hour and minute hand, stem winder, steel vest chain. Each.......... .10
Per dozen.......... 1.00
24964 Toy Watch with bell. Wind watch up and bell will strike. Each.......... .15
Per dozen.......... 1.60
24965 Toy Watch, automatic tick movement, stem winding, hands move separately A good one. Each.......... .20
24966 Souvenir Watch, open face, 1¼ inch diameter, finely finished, hour and minute hands move separately: has fine neck chain. Each. .25
24967 Grandfather's Clock. A good imitation of the old timepiece. No doll house complete without one. Each.......... .25
Postage on toy watches.......... .03

## Noah's Arks.

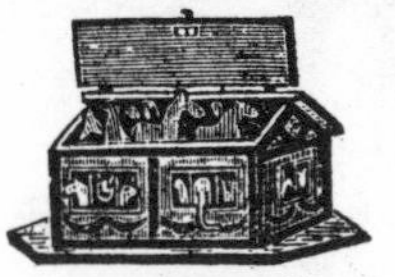

This toy has been a seller ever since the flood, and probably will be as long as the world stands.
24970 Noah's Ark, filled with neatly painted animals, flat ark. Each..........$0.10
Per dozen.......... 1.00
Weight, ½ lb.
24971 Noah's Ark, same as above, larger. Each, .25
Weight, 1 lb.

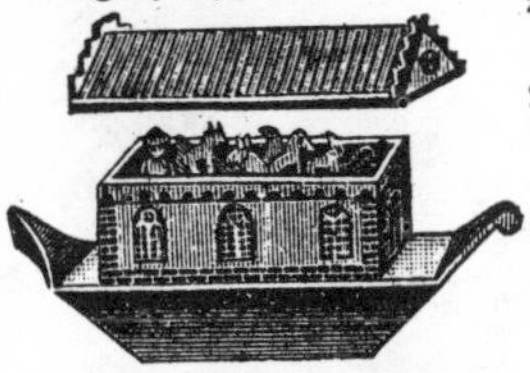

24972 Noah's Ark; boat shape, fancy; weight, 10 oz., 50c.
24973 Noah's Ark., same style as 24972. but larger and better. Each..........$0.75
Weight, 1¼lb.

## Surprise Boxes.

(Jack in the Box.)

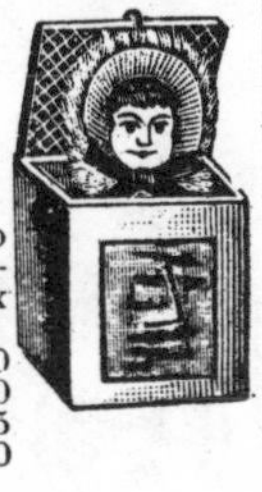

Surprise Boxes ranging from small to large sizes, containing figures of various forms which spring out of the box at will.
24975 Surprise Box. Each.......$0.10
Per dozen.......... 1.00
24976 Surprise Box. Each....... .25
Per dozen.......... 2.50

## WOODEN TOYS.

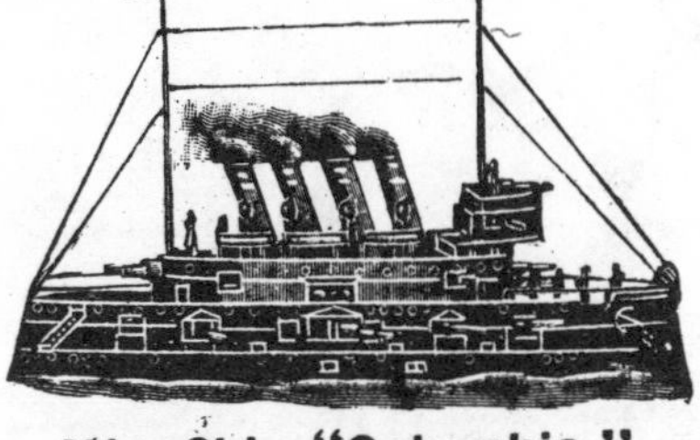

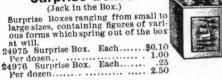

## War Ship "Columbia."

24978 A perfect reproduction of this powerful and fast war ship, a model of strength and beauty, and the largest and most complete toy cruiser ever made. A feature is the smoke, giving the cruiser the appearance of being under full steam, and moving at a high rate of speed. It is finely lithographed, thoroughly made, and rigged with two masts; has four smoke stacks, eight ventilators, wire railing, cord, six boats, cannons, etc., and has a crew of twelve officers and sailors. All parts pack inside of boat. Full directions for setting up accompany each boat. Length from stem to stern, 36 inches; 24 inches on top of mast. Price..........$0.90

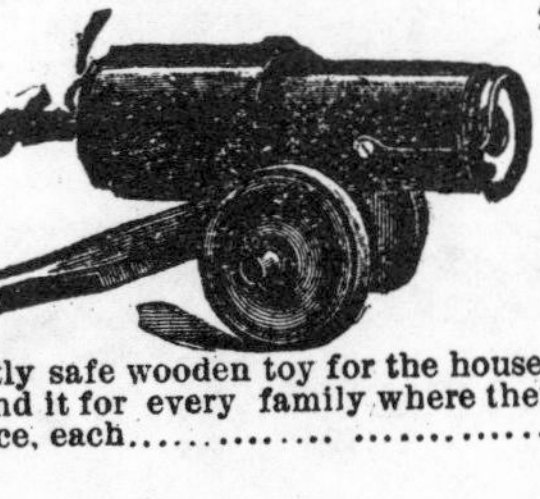

24980 Columbus Krupp Cannon, mounted in gun carriage; a large toy, weighing less than two pounds; a ten inch gun, makes a loud report, but can do no harm; a perfectly safe wooden toy for the house. We can recommend it for every family where there is a small boy. Price, each..........$0.40

## The Royal Guards.

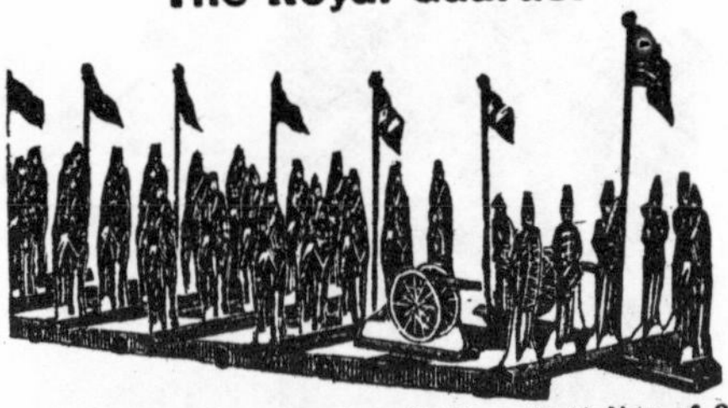

24981 A new and imposing Military Battalion of 33 men, arranged in 5 companies, with band, 2 cannon, 2 gunners, and commander, carrying 8 handsome flags; the whole mounted on wheels. The soldiers are made to march company front, or right and left oblique. The companies can be used separate or together as desired. The soldiers are 7½ inches high, wearing rich, brilliant uniforms. Full length of toy, 42 inches, width 12¼ inches. Very easy to set up. Packed in nice box with elegant label. Price...$0.90

## Military Parade.

24982 Same design as No. 24981. Has a force of 28 handsome soldiers arranged in 5 companies, commander and 2 aids, and carries 6 flags; all mounted on wheels. Can be made to march obliquely when desired. Height of soldiers 5¼ inches. Comes packed in nice box 20 inches long, 10 in. wide, with attractive label. Price..........$0.50

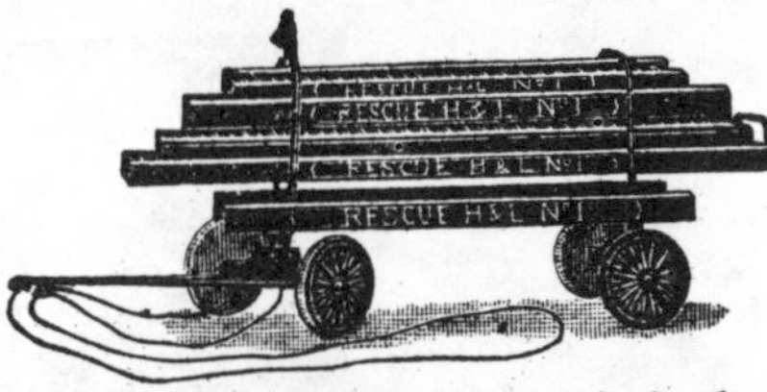

24983 Rescue Hook and Ladder Truck Co. 1, made wholly of wood. Has four handsomely painted ladders, which are so made that they can be joined together, forming one long ladder. An interesting toy for any boy. Price..........$0.50

## Buffalo Bill.

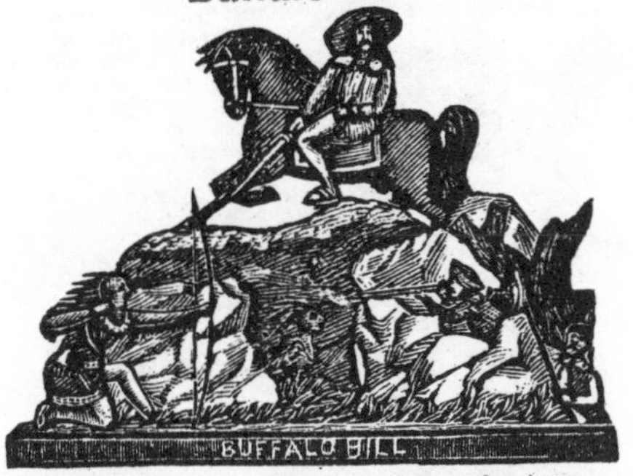


24985 This is a new departure in wooden toys and is decidedly novel in every respect. It illustrates vividly how Buffalo Bill and his scouts overcame a party of ambuscaded Indians. Best thing out. Price..........$0.75

## The Brownie Ladder.

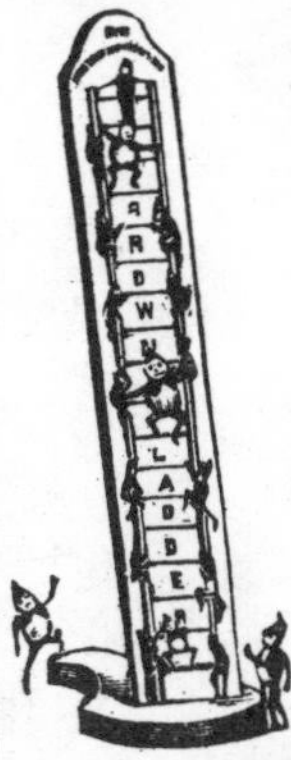

24986 A most pleasing and comical novelty. Finely lithographed in bright colors; representing a ladder with Brownies climbing up and down. Two Brownies are provided, made of hardwood, which, when placed between nails at top of ladder, come wriggling down to the bottom in a most laughable manner. The smallest child can operate the toy, while at the same time it is intensely amusing to older people. Height 32 in.
Price..........$0.25

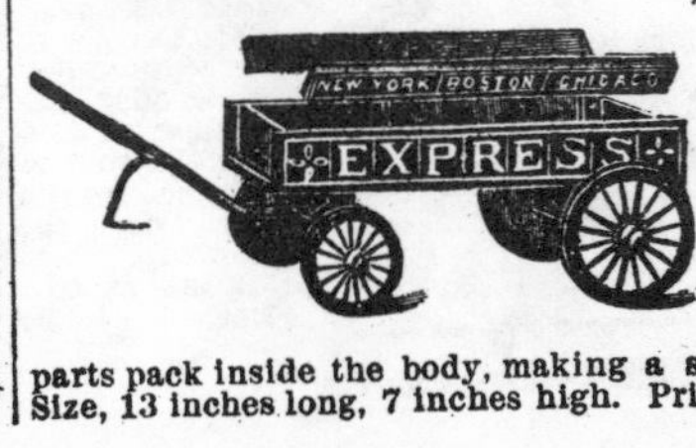


24987 Express Wagon. A new and attractive wagon, neatly ornamented and colored, very strongly made, has two wings and is easily set up. All parts pack inside the body, making a small package. Size, 13 inches long, 7 inches high. Price..........$0.20

## Wooden Soldiers.

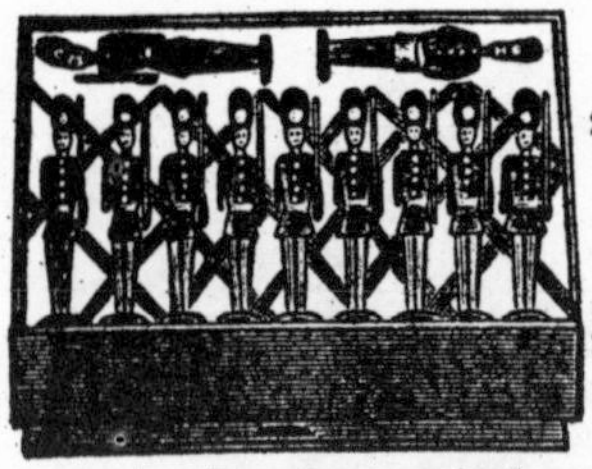

24988 Wooden Soldiers, Movable, each made to stand alone. In box.
Per set......$0.20
Per doz. .. 2.10
24989 Wooden Soldiers, large size.
Per set......$0.40

## Bows and Arrows.

(Unmailable.)

The practice of archery is rapidly coming into style again. To be "in the swim" and to please your boy or girl, get him or her one of our archery sets. We have them in all sizes; for the five year old or for the five year old's big brother.

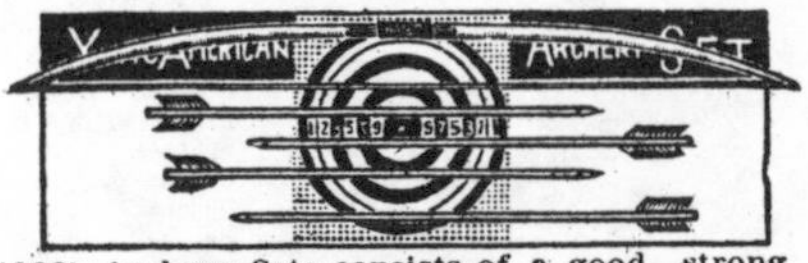


24990 Archery Set: consists of a good, strong bow, 30 inches long, two arrows and target. Bow is nicely finished and arrows striped, feathered and metal tipped. Price..........$0.19
24991 Archery Set: Contains bow, three arrows and target. The bow is made of polished wood, very strong and pliable, and is 33 inches long. Arrows are handsomely striped, feathered and metal tipped. Price.......... .40
24992 Archery Set: This handsome set consists of a strong 39-inch bow, made of very pliable wood, four nicely striped, feathered and metal tipped arrows and a target 9 inches in diameter. With this outfit a boy can become expert in the use of the bow and arrow. Price.......... .90

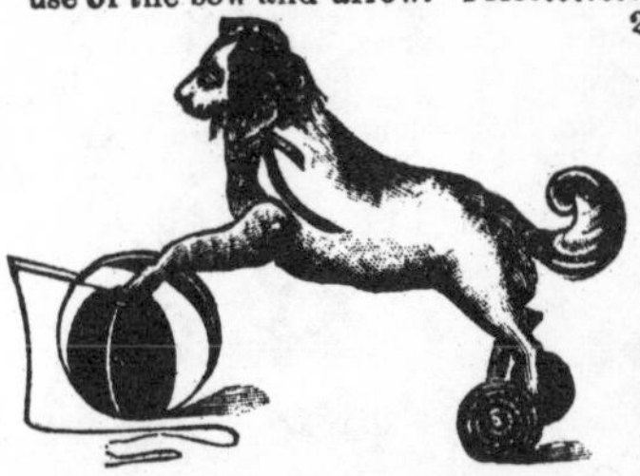

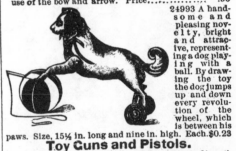

24993 A handsome and pleasing novelty, bright and attractive, representing a dog playing with a ball. By drawing the toy the dog jumps up and down every revolution of the wheel, which is between his paws. Size, 15¼ in. long and nine in. high. Each.$0.23

## Toy Guns and Pistols.

Toy Guns cannot be sent by mail on account of length and liability of breakage.

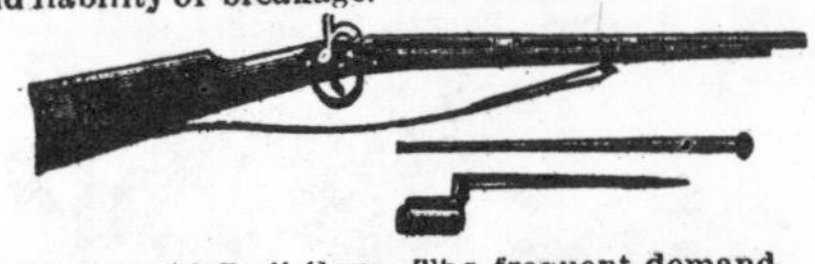

24994 School Drill Gun. The frequent demand for a large size boy's gun for drilling purposes in school or otherwise, has induced us to introduce this gun. It is made of hardwood, well finished, and has the percussion lock to fire off paper caps; it is in size large enough for boys from 12 to 16 years of age. Stock 42 in. long, with bayonet. Each..........$1.00
24995 Toy Gun, with bayonet and strap, measures 41 inches in length without bayonet; shoots paper cap and stick. Weight, 1¼ lbs. Each... .90
24996 The "Harmless" Gun. Price.......... .85
24998 The Swift and Sure gun. Price.......... .25

## Vacuum Tipped Arrows, Pistols and Rifles.

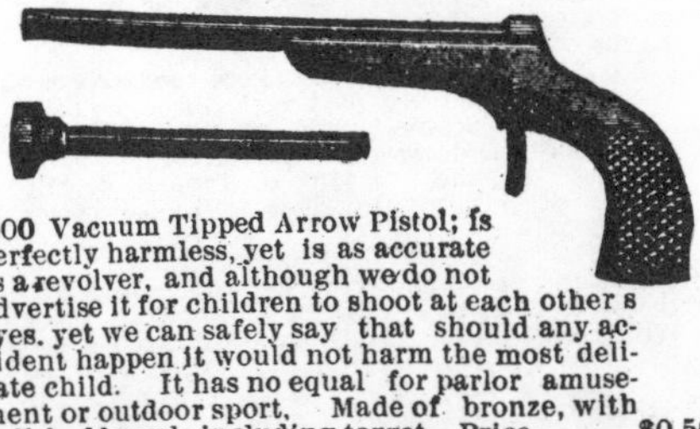

25000 Vacuum Tipped Arrow Pistol; is perfectly harmless, yet is as accurate as a revolver, and although we do not advertise it for children to shoot at each other s eyes, yet we can safely say that should any accident happen it would not harm the most delicate child. It has no equal for parlor amusement or outdoor sport. Made of bronze, with polished barrel; including target. Price........$0.50
25001 Same as above in full nickel, with target.. .75
25002 Vacuum Tipped Arrow Rifles, regulation pattern, wood stock and 16 in. bronze barrel. Price includes one arrow, Each.......... .95
25003 Same as 25002, but with nickel-plated barrel. Price.......... 1.40
25005 Extra arrows, each.......... .15
25006 The Echo Toy Pistol. A harmless, novel and ingenious toy. No caps to endanger the eyes of the little ones, but a loud report to please the boys. It will throw a pea or bean 40 feet with remarkable accuracy. Weight, 4 ounces. Price, each.......... .10

**24789** Double Truck, with driver and two horses. Load consists of two boxes, two barrels and one sack of merchandise. Horses painted black, harness and running gear of truck painted a bright red, black striped. Packed one in a box; complete. Each.........................$1.75

**24790** Express Wagon, with driver and two horses. Load consists of two boxes, and one sack. Horses painted cream color, harness black, hames red, collar black, wagon body red, black striped, gilt letters; gear yellow, black striped. Packed one in a box, complete. Each...$2.00

**24791** Barouche, with driver in coachman's livery. Cream colored horses, with fancy colored hip blankets, running gear, maroon, gold striped; body black. Both horses trotting when toy is in motion. A particularly handsome article. Packed one in a box. Each............$1.85

**24792** Fire Engine, with driver and engineer in full regulation uniform. When in motion the horses gallop and the gong rings. A complete miniature fire engine, with nickel plated boiler and valves. Length, 18 inches; packed one in a box. Each.....................$2.00

**24793** Hose cart, (S), with driver and fireman in full uniform, with two Pompier Corps ladders, as shown in cut. Cream colored horses with red running gear to cart and alarm gong, which rings while in motion. Whole finely painted in bright colors. A companion piece to 24792. Length, 18 in. Each...................$2.00

**24794** Hook and Ladder Truck, with driver and steersman in full uniform. Four red extension ladders, which can be united, making a ladder 51 inches in length. Two axles, gaily painted. Length, 24 inches. Too large to illustrate correctly. Must be seen to be appreciated. Each, complete....................... 2.00

**24795** The above three numbers make a complete miniature fire department. Price per set.. 5.50

**24796** Engine House, made of malleable iron and wood, handsomely painted in fancy colors, length 26¼ inches; width, 10 inches; height, 18 inches. Has swinging doors, with bell at top. Price, each................ 3.25

**24797** The "Brave Boy" fireman's complete outfit, consisting of helmet, trumpet and axe. Helmet is made of papier mache and painted black with gilt stripes and is ornamented with a gilt badge fastened to the front. Trumpet is of papier mache and axe of wood. Handsomely painted in bright colors; it is an outfit that will please any boy. Cannot be sent by mail. Price.. 2.50

**24798** Artillery, made of indestructible iron and steel, in a good, substantial manner, as per cut. Horses mismated in color, gun carriage and limber dark green, red stripes. Gun dead black, brass mounted. Men in uniform. Total length of toy, 84 inches. Price.......... .....$4.00

**24800** Donkey Cart and stable; a new, complete, well made and finished house toy, amusing for either boys or girls. Price, each...$1.75

## Mechanical Novelties.

**24801** Mechanical Walking Horse, made of iron and painted. Size 8½x7 inches. After winding up the concealed spring, place the horse on the floor or any smooth surface, and it will start off at a brisk walk, as natural as life. Weight, packed in pasteboard box, 2 lbs. Each.........$2.00

**24803** Mechanical Monkey; looks as much like a real monkey as it is possible to make it appear. Wind it up and it will vigorously ring a bell. Dressed in bright costumes. Packed one in a box. Price.........$2.50

**24805** Mechanical Performing Acrobats, representing two gymnasts in various feats of turning on a horizontal bar. A neat and novel toy, interesting to all. Size 8x6x6. Packed one in a heavy pasteboard box. Price.........$2.75 Weight, 3 pounds.

**24806** Mechanical Jumping Rabbit, covered with natural skin, white in color; it looks just like a real rabbit. Wind it up and it hops along in a most comical manner. Weight, 4 oz. Price.........$0.50 Size, 4½x7 in.

**24807** Mechanical Dog and Rider, similar in construction to the rabbit and a very amusing toy. Price. ...............$1.00 Postage.................. .06

## Natural Skin Animals.

**24808** Natural Skin Rabbits, with musical attachment. Amusing and interesting for a small child. Price, each............$0.22

**24809** Natural Skin Lamb, mounted on wooden base with wheels; to be drawn with a string. Price, each, .....$0.25

**24810** Natural Skin Lamb, musical attachment and with rider in fancy colored costume. Mounted on wooden base, with wheels. Price.. 1.25

**24812** Natural Skin Lambs, with musical attachment, mounted on wooden base, with wheels, 13x5 inches. Length of lamb, 12 inches, height to top of head, 9¼ inches. They bleat as natural as life by pressing on the nose. Price .......... 1.75

**24813** Natural Skin Cow, with voice, mounted on wooden base with wheels, 10x4½ inches. By pressing on the nose the cow will low as natural as life. Price, each.$0.95

**24814** Toy elephant on platform with wheels, with swinging head and fancy colored blanket. Size of platform, 8x3½ in. Length of figure, 8 in. Height 5 in. Price.........$0.30

**24815** Large Size Toy Elephant, with swinging head and fancy trimmed blanket; length of toy, 12 in.; height, 8½ in. Mounted on rollers concealed in each foot. Each....................90

**24816** Natural Skin Donkey, mounted on wooden base with wheels. Press on his nose and he will bray as earnestly as though alive. Size 6½x10 in. weight, 12 oz. Price.......$0.85

**24817** Natural Skin Horse, mounted on wooden base with wheels. Has leather saddle and bridle complete. Length, 5½ in.; height, 7½ to top of head. Price, each.........$0.65

**24818** Natural Skin Horse, mounted on wooden base with wheels. Has leather saddle and bridle complete. This is an extra large fine horse, and will please any child. Price.........$1.00

**24819** Natural Skin Horse and Cart, as shown in cut. Length of toy, 11 inches. Price...$0.75

**24820** Natural Skin Horse and Truck. See illustration of No. 24789 for style of wagon. A fine large toy 20 inches in length. Price..........$1.00

**24821**—Seed Wagon, and Team of natural skin horses. Wagon box 4x8 inches long. Horses 7½ inches high. Price.................$1.25

## Animals Mounted on Platforms.

**24822** Pressed Paper Horses, patent German process, very light and handsome, small size. Each............$0.10

**24823** Same description, large size. Each........ .20

**24824** Same Horse as No. 24822, but harnessed to cart. Body of cart is natural wood oiled, wheels of pressed paper. Each.............. .35

**24825** Saddle Horse, made of composition with handle. Size of horse, 10 inches high, 8 inches long. Price............ .50

**24826** Saddle Horse, same as No. 24825, but 12 inches high. 10 inches long and large in proportion. Price............ .96

**24827** Assorted Animals, small size, on platforms. Assortment consists of tigers, elephants, wildcats, lions, bears and dogs. State kind preferred, and they will be sent if in stock. If not, substitution will be made. Each............ .25

## Plush Animals.

**24830** New Plush Dogs, small size, well made. Price.$0.25

**24831** Our New Plush Pug Dog; nice size, and well made. Each.........$0.50 Per dozen.............. 5.40

**24833** Plush Cats, good size, well made and natural as life. Each ....... .. $0.20

## Toy Zithern.

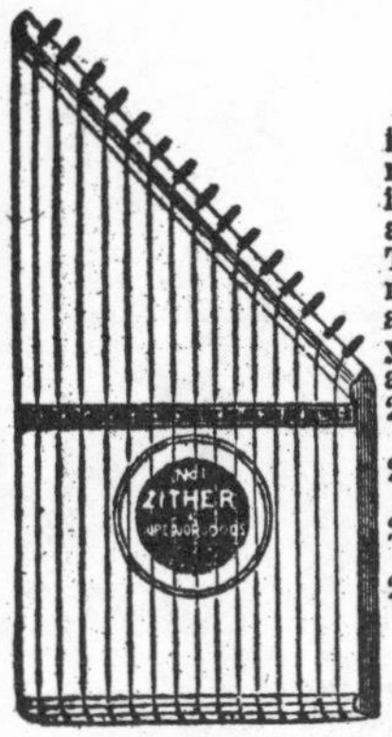

An attractive toy musical instrument, on which the cords may be learned with ease, both instructive and interesting to all. Made plain and harp shape. These goods are handsomely made and finished, and are appreciated and enjoyed by young people of all ages, as they are all tuned to concert pitch.

25084 Plain Shape, 10 strings. Each..................$0.50
25085 Plain Shape, 15 strings. Each..................$0.85
25086 Harp Shape, 15 strings. Each..................$1.00
25087 Harp Shape, 22 strings. Each..................$1.25

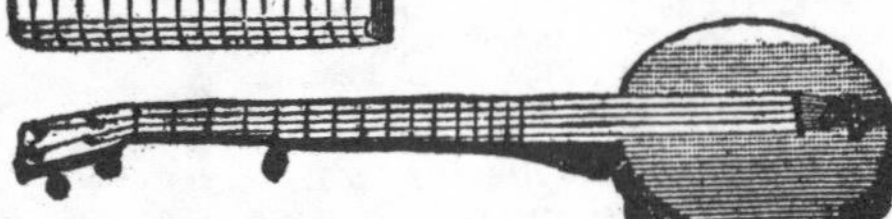

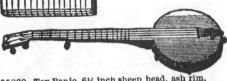

25090 Toy Banjo, 6¼ inch sheep head, ash rim, iron hoop, four brackets. Each..................$0.50
25091 Toy Banjo, 8½ inch calf head, embossed wood rim, brass hoop, six brackets. Each...... .90

## Toy Violins.

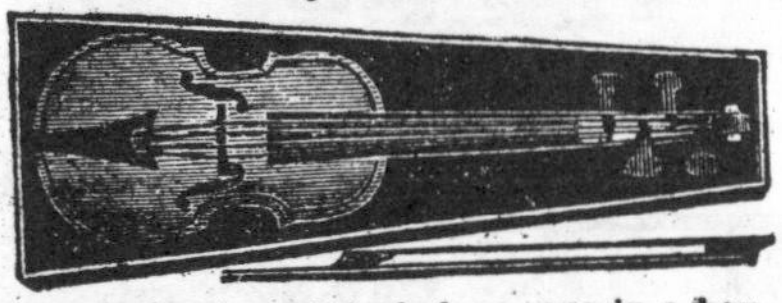

25092 Toy Violin, 16 inch long, one in a box with a bow. Each..................$0.25
Per dozen.................. 2.75
25093 Toy Violins, 18 inches long, one in a box, with bow. Each.................. .50
Per dozen.................. 5.00
25094 Toy Violins, 20 inches long, packed in a box with folding cover and handle for carrying, with bow. Price, each.................. .90

## Toy Pianos.

(Cannot be sent by mail.)

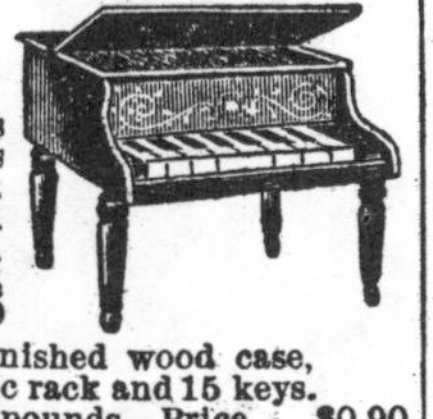

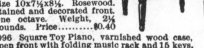

25095 Square Toy Piano, as shown in cut, with high legs and open front, single cover. Size 10x7½x8½. Rosewood. Stained and decorated front. One octave. Weight, 2½ pounds. Price.........$0.40
25096 Square Toy Piano, varnished wood case, open front with folding music rack and 15 keys. Size 6¼x10¼x9. Weight, 5 pounds. Price....$0.90

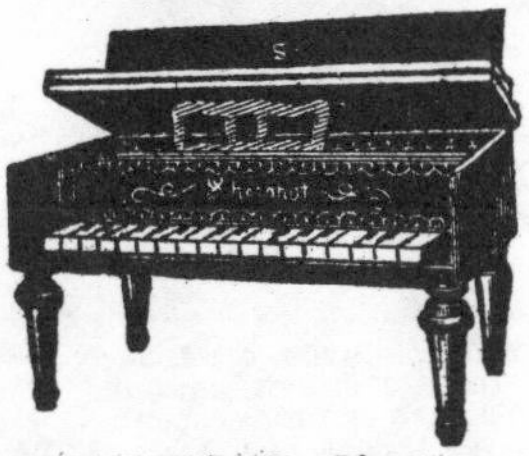

25097 Square Toy Pianos, with high turned legs and full-hinged cover to close. Has 13 keys and folding music rack. Size, 19½ x 10½ x 9½. Weight, 6 lbs. Price..........$1.50

25099 Upright Toy Piano, case varnished, open front and hinged cover, 15 keys. Size 16¼x11 x8. Weight, 5 pounds. Price.................. 1.25

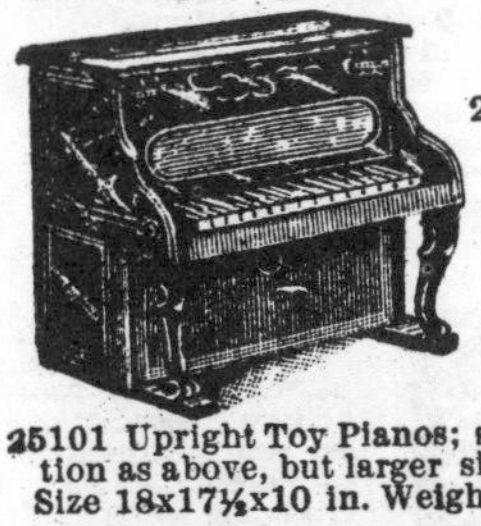

25100 Upright Toy Piano; case handsomely finished, ornamented legs and chandeliers, 15 keys. Packed one in a pasteboard box. Weight, 7¾ pounds. Price..........$2.25

25101 Upright Toy Pianos; same general description as above, but larger size and with 18 keys. Size 18x17¼x10 in. Weight, 11 lbs. Price..... 3.50

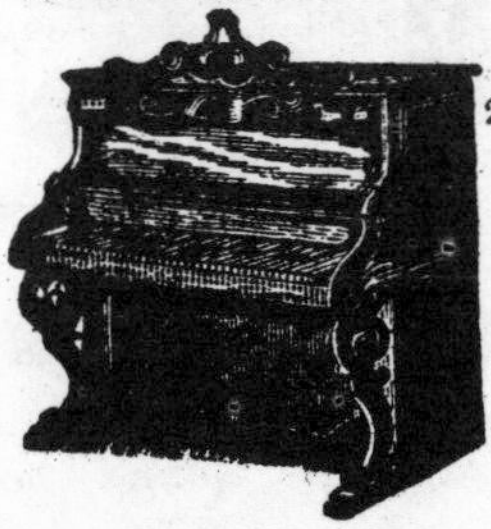

25102 Upright Toy Piano; extra quality, three octaves, tuned to a perfect concert pitch. Finely carved legs. 23x 24x11. Ornamented and has two gilded chandeliers. Weight, 11 pounds. Price....$5.00 Each packed in wooden case.

## Blocks.

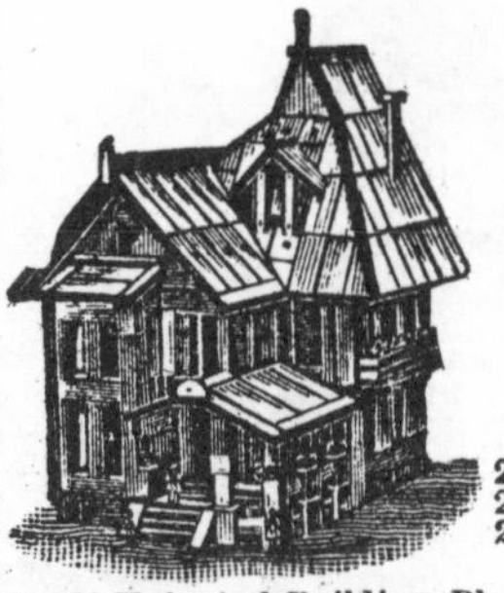

Gilt Edge Building Blocks, made of thoroughly seasoned hardwood, finely finished. The variety and quality of blocks are sufficient to build a large number of pleasing designs.

25105 No. 1 size...$0.20
25106 No. 2 size... .45
25107 No. 3 size... 1.00

25108 Universal Building Blocks, made of hard wood, smooth finished, with ball and joint connecting pins, the best and handsomest plain block on the market. Large size, containing 150 blocks and 206 ball joints. Weight, 11 lbs. Price.................. 2.00
25110 Browers' Building Blocks in *colors;* box contains 75 pieces common to all buildings, such as windows, arch door ways, floors, roofs, chimneys, turrets, etc., adaptable to be interchangeably used to form residences, churches, stores, etc. An intensely interesting toy. Price...... .50
25111 Same, but larger size. Box contains 120 pieces. Price.................. 1.00

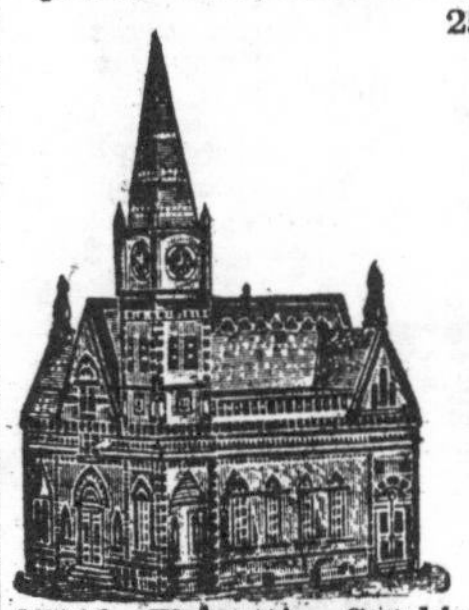

25112 New Cathedral Building Blocks. When put together the blocks form a beautiful cathedral, as shown in cut; 9¾x7¾ in. and 17 inches to top of steeple. It contains a set of blocks beautifully illustrating the story of Noah and the animals entering the ark, with appropriate text of Scripture, a Book of Prayer and one of the Ten Commandments, also the alphabet. Weight, complete, 5 lbs. Each..................$0.75

25113 Wescott's Combination Building and Spelling Blocks with dovetailed edges; a new and novel block. Per set.................. .38
Weight, 2¼ pounds.

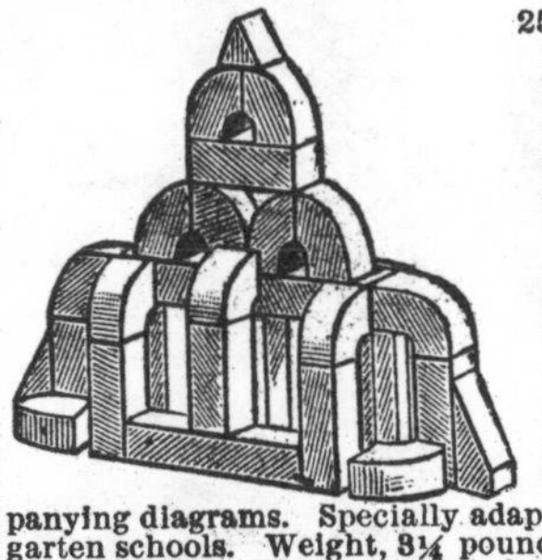

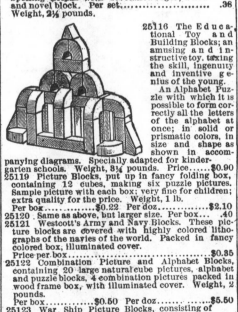

25116 The Educational Toy and Building Blocks; an amusing and instructive toy, taxing the skill, ingenuity and inventive genius of the young.
An Alphabet Puzzle with which it is possible to form correctly all the letters of the alphabet at once; in solid or prismatic colors, in size and shape as shown in accompanying diagrams. Specially adapted for kindergarten schools. Weight, 3¼ pounds. Price......$0.90
25119 Picture Blocks, put up in fancy folding box, containing 12 cubes, making six puzzle pictures. Sample picture with each box; very fine for children; extra quality for the price. Weight, 1 lb.
Per box..........$0.22 Per doz..........$2.10
25120 Same as above, but larger size. Per box... .40
25121 Westcott's Army and Navy Blocks. These picture blocks are covered with highly colored lithographs of the navies of the world. Packed in fancy colored box, illuminated cover.
Price per box.................. $0.35
25122 Combination Picture and Alphabet Blocks, containing 20 large natural cube pictures, alphabet and puzzle blocks, 4 combination pictures packed in wood frame box, with illuminated cover. Weight, 2 pounds.
Per box..........$0.50 Per doz..........$5.50
25123 War Ship Picture Blocks, consisting of twenty-four large size cubes, with which can be made pictures of six of the famous vessels of the White Navy. Pictures are 7¾x20½ inches. Packed in neat box, with pattern pictures.
Price.................. .90
25124 Capitol Picture Blocks, same description as above, but pictures are those of six prominent buildings at the National Capital. Price...... .90

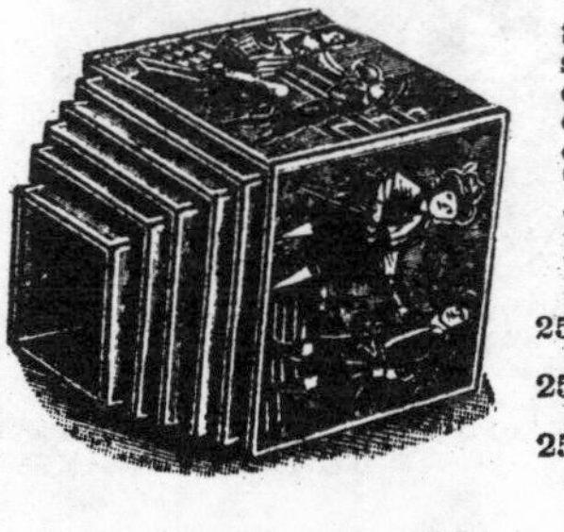

Telescopic Picture Blocks, consisting of hollow cube blocks, covered with fancy lithographed designs. These blocks pack one into another, thus affording endless amusement for the little ones.

25125 Per set of 7 blocks........$0.25
25126 Per set of 9 blocks........$0.40
25127 Per set of 12 blocks........$0.95

## Alphabet and Spelling Blocks—Flat.

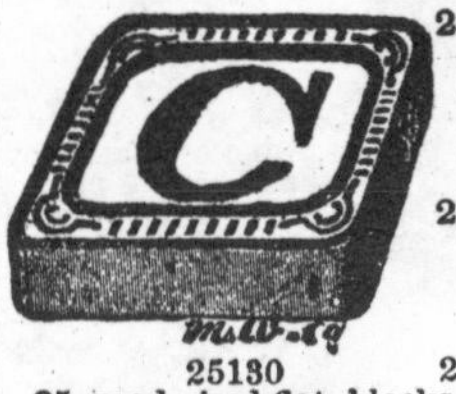

25130

25130 Embossed hardwood blocks, containing letters and numerals. Packed in metal box containing eighteen blocks.
Price..................$0.10
25131 Box contains 9 1¾ inch half cubes, natural wood stamped in colors with letters and pictures.
Price..................$0.12
25132 Box contains 25 good sized flat blocks, embossed in colors, with letters and numerals.................. .18
25133 Handsome box containing 20 2½ inch half cubes embossed in colors, with numerals, letters and words. Price.................. .25
25134 Spelling Blocks, 20 blocks, half cubes, printed in colors, pictures and numerals, packed in wood box, 6x6 inches, slide cover.
Price each.................. .35

## Alphabet Blocks, Cubes.

25139 Mother Goose Cube Blocks, being a combination of letter cubes with the Mother Goose pictures and rhymes oil-painted in a variety of shades and colors. The illustrations are from new and original designs. 12 blocks in a set, packed in a wooden box 7¾x6x2.
Weight, 1½ pounds. Price..................$0.25
25140 Mother Goose Cube Blocks. Better and larger kind; contains 16 blocks, large size, natural wood, printed in bright colors. Packed in paper box with the fine label on cover.
Weight, 2¼ pounds.................. .45
25141 Mother Goose Cube Blocks, still better and larger. Contains 20 2½ inch painted and varnished square blocks with letters, illustrations and rhymes; bright colors and superior finish.
Price.................. .85
Weight, 3¾ lbs.

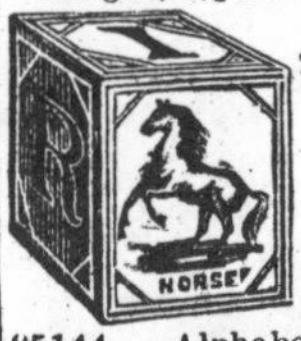

25142 Alphabetical Blocks, 12 illustrated cubes, embossed ends, medium size, with letters and figures, natural wood, printed in bright colors. Per box.................. .20
Postage.................. .15

25144 Alphabetical Blocks, consists of a set of 35 small size cubes, with embossed ends, containing letters, figures and illustrations of animals, printed in bright colors. Per box...... .34
25145 Alphabet Blocks, 12 medium size cubes, ornamented with letters and figures in bright colors; packed in neat box, Per box...... .20
25146 Alphabet Blocks, 12 large cubes, with illustrations, alphabet and numerals, printed in bright colors; packed in neat box. Per box ... .25
25147 Alphabet Blocks, 12 large fine cubes, with illustrations, figures and alphabet. The colors are bright and attractive, and workmanship the best. Per box.................. .50
25148 Alphabet Blocks. Same as above, but box contains 20 cubes. Per box.................. .75
25149 Hill's Alphabet Blocks, contains 24 plain cubes, ornamented with figures and alphabet. Per box.................. .40
25151 Hill's Spelling Blocks, full cubes, 30 blocks, printed in colors, pictures, letters, numerals and indicators, wood box, 9½x11½ inches, hinge cover. Price, per set.................. .90

## China Toy Tea Sets.

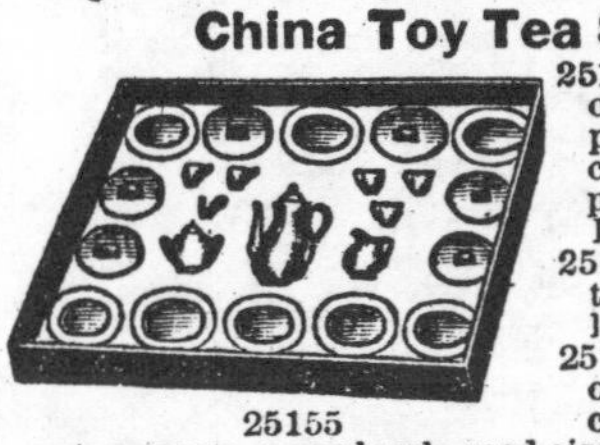

25155

25155 Set consists of cups, saucers, tea pot, sugar bowl and cream; small size; packed in paper box.
Price..........$0.10
25156 Same description as above but larger. Price.$0.25
25157 Set consists of decorated plates, cups, saucers, tea pot, creamer, sugar bowl; good sized dishes.
Price..................$0.50
25158 Same description but larger. Price....... .75
25159 Same, but larger size and assortment.
Price.................. 1.00
25163 White Stone China Tea set of 24 pieces, as follows: 6 plates, 6 cups, 6 saucers, 1 sugar bowl and cover, 1 tea pot and cover, 1 creamer, 1 slop bowl. This set is large enough for a miss from 8 to 14 years of age. (Not safe to send by mail.) Weighs 8½ lbs. Per set..................$1.25
The pieces in this set are larger than usually sold in toy sets; the cups stand 2 inches high, and the plates measure 4¼ inches across.

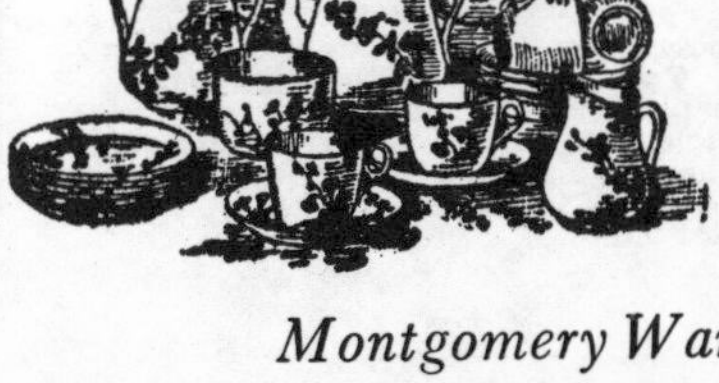

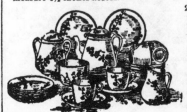

25164—Fancy Decorated Tea Set, same size and assortment as above; elegant patterns. Packed in wooden box, weight 8½ lbs. Price.$1.75

## Decorated China Toy Toilet Sets.

25170 Small Toilet or Wash Set packed in pasteboard box; weight ¼ lb.
Per set.......$0.20
Per doz. sets.. 2.00
25171 Decorated Toilet or Wash Set. good size, 5 pieces, and 2 perforated covers; weight, 1¼ lbs.

Per set.................$0.35
Per dozen sets.................3.75
25172 Extra Size Wash or Toilet set, gilt lined and brilliantly decorated; a handsome set. Packed in strong box: weight 3 lbs.
Per set.................. .65
Per dozen sets................. 7.00

## Britannia Tea Sets.

25175— Britannia Tea Sets silver finish, consisting of tea pot sugar bowls, sugar tongs, creamer, four plates and cups, Put up in neat pasteboard box; weight, 5 oz.................$0.09
25176 Britannia Tea Set silver finish, consisting of tea pot, sugar bowl, creamer, six plates, six cups. six spoons and sugar spoons. Embossed decorations; weight, 10 oz. Price................. .22
25177 Britannia Tea Set, silver finish, consisting of tea pot, sugar bowl, creamer, six plates, six cups and six spoons. A very handsome set; weight, 1¼ lbs..................45
25178 Britannia Tea Set, silver finish, consisting of tea pot, sugar bowl, creamer, spoon holder, six plates, six cups, six spoons and fancy filigree work sugar tongs. The entire set is handsomely decorated in bas-relief design, making a large showy set; weight, 3¾ lbs.
Price................. .85

## Superior Quality Toy Tin Kitchen Sets.

25180 Tin Kitchen Set, small size; consisting of about fifteen pieces tin kitchen utensils. See illustration. Weight, 6 ounces. Price.........$0.10
25181 Tin Kitchen Set, medium size; consisting of 25 or more pieces, tin and wooden utensils. Weight, 12 oz. Price.................. .20
25182 Tin Kitchen Set, large size, containing 30 pieces. Weight, 1¼ lbs. Price.................. .40
25183 Tin Kitchen Set, Large size. Has 42 or more utensils of good size; some of the pans in Nos. 25181 and 25182 are large enough for baking small loaves, cakes, etc. Weight, 1¾ lbs. Price.................. .65

## Superior Quality Embossed Tin Kitchens.

Painted in bright colors and very attractive to the little folks.

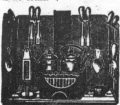

25185 Embossed Tin Kitchen, small size; contains 1-hole range and ten pieces kitchen tinware. Size 6½ in. high, 11 in. long, 2¼ in. deep. Postage.................$0.15
Price.............. .25
25186 Embossed Tin Kitchen, medium size. Has in addition a two-hole range, a water cooler and 12 utensils. Size 7x14x4 inches. Weight, 1¾ lbs. Price.................$0.45
25187 Embossed Tin Kitchen. One of the largest and best. Two-hole range with warming oven above, water cooler and twenty pieces tin and wooden kitchen utensils of large size. Size 8½ x19x5 inches. Weight, 2¾ lbs. Price.................. .75
All of the above kitchen and kitchen sets are packed in neat boxes

## Children's Table Sets.

25190 Children's memento sets; knife fork and spoon, on card.
Per set.................$0.10
Per dozen sets............. 1.00
Postage.................. .04
25191 Child's Set of three pieces, consisting of knife, fork and spoon, mounted on fancy picture card. 4½x7 inches. This set has cocobola handles, riveted with bolster and cap; blades made of good quality of steel, Per set .................$0.25

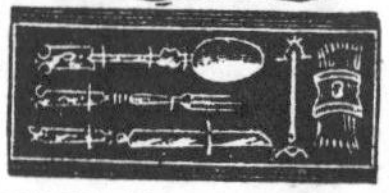

25192 Toy "Britannia" Sets, consisting of knife, fork. spoon, napkin and ring and knife rest in neat box, containing 3 sets.
Per set, .................$0.30
25193 Box containing knife, fork, spoon and napkin ring of doll size. Price............. .05
25194 Same, but larger size and provided in addition to above with knife rest. Price................. .10

25197 Folding Table. similar to cut. Legs fold under, making it convenient to handle. Nicely made and a new thing in a toy table; size, 21 x 13 x 14½ inches.
Price each.......$0.50
25198 Folding Table, larger than preceding, well made and useful size, 14x24x15½ in. Price each.................$0.75

25200 The "Triumph" Toy Wringer; frame made wholly of cast metal, smooth finished, white rubber rolls, ½ inch in diameter and 3 inches long. Can be fastened to side of tub by means of thumb screws. A perfect model of the regular Triumph wringer. Weight, 1 lb. Price, each..$0.40

## Unique Wash Sets.

25203 Entirely new and original in design, consisting of latest style Laundry Tub, Wringer, Washboard, Pail, Basket, and double line Clothes Reel with Clothes Pins. All parts pack inside of tub, Compact, attractive and strongly made. Size, 27in. long, 13 in. high, 9 in. wide. Reel 16 in. high. Price.................$0.90
25204 Similar in design to above. Consists of new style Laundry Tub, Wringer, Washboard, Basket, Clothes Reel and Pins. All parts pack inside of tub. Size, 18 in. long, 7 in. wide, 9½ in. high. Reel 11 in. high. Price.................. .50
23205 Toy Washing Machine. A complete practical toy for washing dolls' clothes. Modeled after pattern of a large washer. Is 6½ inches wide, 12½ inches long, stands 7½ inches high, and is nicely painted in bright colors. Price each ................. .95

## Kitchen and Wash Sets.

25206 Kitchen and Wash Sets, nicely packed in wooden box, about 22 utensils, all neatly made, such as tubs, pails, ladles, spoons, roller, masher, washboard, stand, churn, and many other articles. Per box.................$0.95
Per dozen boxes.................10.25

## Doll Beadsteads.

The Silver Queen Dolls' Wire Bedstead, with mattress and pillows. A most perfect dolls' bed; made in three sizes.

25207 18 inch. Price..................$0.75
25208 24 inch. Price.................. 1.00
25209 30 inch. Price.................. 1.25 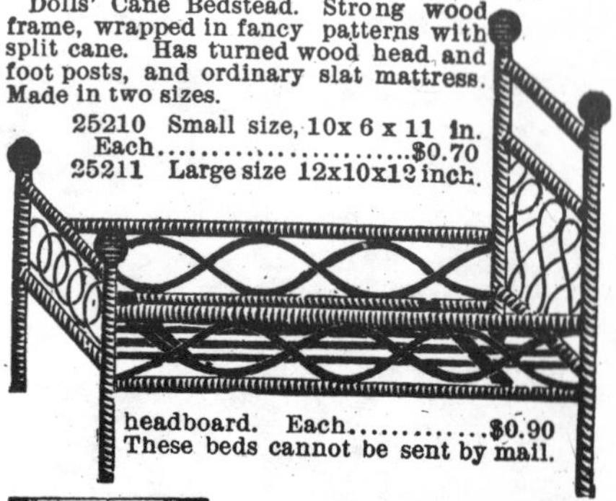
Dolls' Cane Bedstead. Strong wood frame, wrapped in fancy patterns with split cane. Has turned wood head and foot posts, and ordinary slat mattress. Made in two sizes.

25210 Small size, 10x 6 x 11 in. Each.................$0.70
25211 Large size 12x10x12 inch. headboard. Each.............$0.90
These beds cannot be sent by mail.

## Doll Swings.

25212 Dolls' swing; stands 20 inches high. Measures 12x12 inches at the base; the seat of the swing 7 inches across; knocks down flat. Each swing wrapped and tied in packages, 2x5x13.
Price, each.................$0.15
25213 A Doll's Swing, not illustrated. Different construction from the one quoted above, but a good swing.
Price ...... ............. $0.20

## Doll Hammocks.

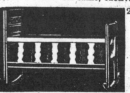

25162

25214 Toy Doll Hammocks. Made of fancy colored seine twine, hand woven, strong and durable. Metal rings in each end for suspending hammock. Length, 40 inches. Each......$0.15
Postage.................. .02
Stands for same. 2 ft. 6 in. long. Each.......25
25215 Toy Doll Hammocks. Fancy colors. Length, 50 inches. Designed to be used with a rack stand as illustrated. Price of hammock.................. .25
Stands for same, each.................. .25
25216 Toy Doll Hammocks. Fancy colors with pillow and spreaders. Corded edge of extra heavy braided twine, with variegated tassels. A very superior article. Price, each ........ .50
25217 Stands for same, each.................. .25

25219 Doll's Cradle, made of chestnut wood, with foot and head board paneled and painted in handsome design. Will hold a 20-inch doll. Extreme length, 22 inches; height, 16 inches; width, 11 inches. Packed knocked down for shipment. Weight, 3 lbs. Price.................$0.75
25220 Doll's Cradle, same style finish and wood as above, but designed to accommodate a 16-inch doll. Extreme length, 18 inches; width, 9 inches; height, 12 inches; weight, 2 lbs. Price.................. .45
25221 Doll's Cradle, same general construction, but smaller, extreme length being 15 inches; height, 8 inches; width, 7 inches; weight, 1 lb. Price.................. .25

## Kid Body Dolls, Ne Plus Ultra Patent Joints, Closing Eyes.

Will sit erect without support.

25257 Kid Body Doll, patent hip joint, jointed arms, fine bisque head, flowing hair on full woven wig, teeth, closing eyes, openwork stockings, and shoes. Length, 12 inches.
Price.........................$0.85

25257½ Same description, 14½ inches long....................1.00

25258 Same description, 17½ inches long..................1.35

25259 Same description, 21 inches long..................1.85

25260 Same description, 25 inches long................2.45

NOTE.—Above dolls are the finest we could buy, and anyone desiring a first-class doll with closing eyes will obtain it by purchasing one of this line.

Patent Indestructible Dolls; worthy of the name, as they cannot be broken by the rough usage to which a doll is usually subjected. Imitation bisque heads, flowing hair, solid eyes, teeth, stuffed cloth body, shoes, stockings, and chemise.
25262 12-inch, Price....$0.45

25263 14½-inch. Price.. .75

25264 18½-inch. Price.. 1.10

25265 22½-inch. Price.. 1.70

## Dressed Dolls, Patent Indestructible Heads.

25266 Indestructible Head, Dressed Dolls, cloth body, painted hair. Length 13 in. Price........................$0.20

25267 Indestructible Head, Dressed Doll, cloth body, hair stuffed, painted hair, cloth shoes. Length, 17 inches. Price.......................$0.40

25268 Indestructible Head, Dressed Doll. Same as above. 20 inches long. Price....$0.60

25269 Indestructible Head, Dressed Doll, largest size, 24 in. long. Price...............$0.80

## Dressed Dolls, American Bisque Heads.

25271 Dressed Dolls, American bisque heads, cloth body, painted hair. Length 10½ in. Price.....................$0.15

25272 Dressed Dolls, American bisque heads, same as above. Length, 14½ in. Price.....$0.25

25273 Dressed Dolls, American bisque heads, hair stuffed, cloth body, painted hair, cloth shoes. Length, 15 in. Price......$0.35

25274 Dressed Dolls, same description as No. 25273 but 18 in. in length. Price............$0.50

## Dressed Dolls, Cloth Bodies, with Kid Joints.

25275 Dressed Dolls, with kid joints, bisque heads and arms, teeth and flowing hair. Dressed in handsome costume; length, 13 inches.
Price....................$0.50

25276 Dressed Dolls, cloth body, kid joints, bisque heads and arms, flowing hair, teeth, shoes, stockings. Dressed in costume of handsome design and good material; length, 14½ inches.
Price.....................$0.85

25277 Dressed Dolls, cloth body, kid joints, bisque head and arms, flowing hair, teeth, solid eyes, shoes and stockings; dress is of the best *materials*, in fashionable colors and well made; length, 17 inches. Price.....................1.00

25278 Dressed Dolls, cloth body, kid joints, bisque heads, flowing hair, teeth, *solid eyes*, dressed in an elaborate costume of stockings, with large turned-up hat, length, 20 inches. Price.....................2.00

## Dressed Baby Dolls, Jointed.

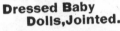
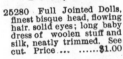

25280 Full Jointed Dolls, finest bisque head, flowing hair, solid eyes; long baby dress of woolen stuff and silk, neatly trimmed. See cut. Price... ......$1.00

25281 Same description but larger size, and more elaborate dress. Price ..$1.45

25282 Superior quality, superfine dolls; jointed, with bisque heads, flowing hair, teeth, shoes and stockings. Dressed in "Baby" costume of nun's veiling, with cap to match. Length, 12 inches.
Each ....................$0.65

25283 Same description as above, but larger. Each .........$0.90

25284 Large size "Baby" doll. Length, 16 inches. Price.....$1.50

## Jointed Dolls, Dressed.

25285 Finest bisque heads, solid eyes, flowing hair, teeth, shoes and stockings. Superior quality dolls. Dress made of cotton stuff, trimmed, silk bonnet. Price.....................$0.50

25286 Same description; dress of changeable silk, embroideries, straw hat. Price...........  .75

25287 Same desription; dress of muslin and lace, bonnet trimmed with ribbon. Price......1.00

25288 Same description; dress and bonnet of changeable silk trimmed with ribbons. Price..1.15

25289 Same description; dress, finest muslin, woven through with ribbons. Full silk bonnet with silk strings and balls. Price...............1.25

25290 Same dscription; dress of fine woolen goods, trimmed with silk ribbons or embroidered. Some hair lace hats, some bonnets. Price.....................2.00

25291 Same description; dress, fine cashmire trimmed with silk and lace. Full silk bonnet, lace trimmed. Price.....................2.25

25292 Same description; dress, full winter costume of fine woolen goods, trimmed with plush and ribbons. Bonnet to match. Price.........3.50

## Columbus Dolls.

These are the most beautifully dressed dolls now on the market. Each one in a full costume of a Spanish Cavalier of the XVth Century, consisting of "doublet and hose," cape, tunic, cap, and buckled shoes.

The costumes are works of art, made of the finest silk velvet and satin, in contrasting colors. Each Cavalier wears at his side a tiny sword. The broad cap is surmounted with an ostrich plume, while the inscription, "1493C. Columbus 1893" is emblazoned upon its front.

25293 Columbus Doll, jointed, bisque head, flowing hair, teeth, solid eyes. Length, 15 inches. Price.....................$1.80

25294 Columbus Doll, same description as above. Length, 18 inches. Price............$2.50

25295 Columbus Doll, large size. Length, 21 inches..................$3.25

## Indestructible Wool Dolls.

25296 Worsted, dressed girl dolls, assorted, similar to cut. 10 inches long.
Price....................$0.20

25297 Worsted, dressed dolls, 12½ inches long.
Price..................$0.35

25298 Worsted, dolls dressed to represent a clown. In full costume, cap and bells. Length, 12½ inches.
Price...................$0.50

25299 Worsted dolls, large size, with fine knitted wool dresses. Length, 15 inches.
Price...................$0.85

25300 Rubber Doll, musical, with knitted worsted hat and dress. Length, 7½ in. Price....................$0.25

25301 Rubber Doll, musical, with worsted hat and dress. Length, 9 in. Price.....................  .35

25302 Rubber Doll, musical, worsted hat and dress. Length about 11 in. Price.................  .50

25303 Rubber Jointed Boy Doll, musical. Will turn his head from side to side and raise his hands at will. Dressed in school costume. Length, 7 inches. Price............$0.25

25304 Same style as above, 9 in. length. Price...................  .40

## Clapping Figures.

25305 Various styles and costumes, bisque heads. We formerly catalogued these figures at from 25 to 75 cts. each, but to dispose of stock we offer them at the uniform price of each.....................$0.25

25306 Indestructible Soldiers, dressed in oilcloth suits in combination colors Length, 10½ in.
Each .................$0.10
Per doz.................  1.00

25307 Whistling Doll Figures, consists of a doll securely fastened upon a stick. The toy, upon being shaken produces a succession of shrill whistles.
Each............................$0.22

25308 Same as above, except that figure is that of a rabbit, covered with natural skin. Price.................$0.20

25309 The Musical Doll Figure is a doll head fastened upon a circular music box, secured to a stick handle. Upon being revolved, beautiful music is produced.. Price.................$0.40

25310 The Bird Musical Figure is the same style as above, but the figure is that of a bird, represented as standing over its nest. The music box is under the nest. See cut. Price.............$0.45

*Montgomery Ward & Co.*

## Toy Stoves.

24835 The Pastime Toy Heating Stove. A beautiful model of the modern base burner. Has transparent red windows: base, top and urn are nickel plated; place a candle in candle stick on inside of stove, and it diffuses a warm, brilliant glow; one joint of pipe with each stove. Size of base 5¾ inches; total height, 12½ in; weight, 6 lbs. Price................$0.90

24836 Toy Range, nickel-plated with polished edges and ornamentation. Useful and instructive toys. Size about 4x5x5 inches; packed one in a box with several utensils.
Price.................$0.50

24837 Same as above but larger and with more utensils. Price.................................... 1.00

24838 Large Size Toy Range: a perfect working stove, nickel plated and highly ornamented. Beautiful, useful and instructive. Price includes pipe and half dozen of the most needed utensils. Size about 8¾ inches wide, 8½ inches high, 15½ inches long. Price.................. 2.00

## Child's Sad Irons.

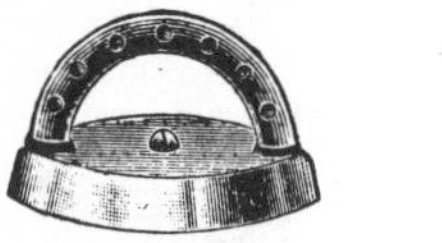

24840 Nickle plated Toy Sad Iron, half pound size, with stand.
Each.............. $0.15

24841 Nickel Plated Toy Sad Iron, one pound size, with stand Each..$0.20

24842 Same as No. 24841, but two pound size. A useful toy. Each..$0.24

24843

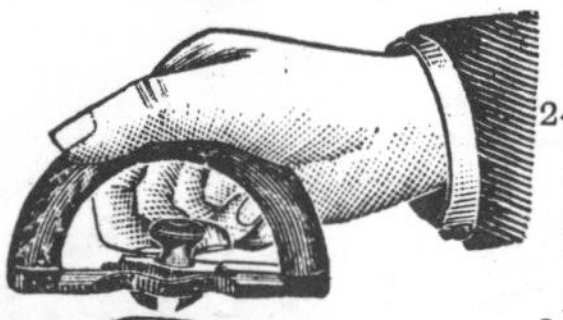

24843 Acme Toy Sad Iron, with solid handle, nickel plated, with stand; small size.
Each.........$0.10

24844 Mrs. Pott's Toy Sad Iron, with detachable nickle plated and with handle; medium size.
Each ........$0.25

24844-5.

24845 Mrs. Pott's Toy or Polishing Iron, nickel plated, with detachable walnut handle, about two pound size, large enough to be useful. Price with stand, each..................................$0.35

## Toy Scales.

24846 Size, without scoop, 4¼ inches long, 1¾ inches high, 2 inches wide; scoop, 3¼x2 inches. Nicely painted and bronzed, and has three coppered weights. Weight, ½ pound.
Price. each.........................................$0.10
Per dozen............................................. 1.00

24847 Toy Scales, 4¾ inches long, 3 inches high, 2¼ inches wide, with a set of weights accompanying each scale. Nicely finished; one in box. Weight, 1¼ pounds. Each.......................... .20

## Chime Toys.

24850 White Metal Revolving bell chime. Gives a very pleasant musical sound.
Small, each............$0.10
Weight, 3 oz. Per doz.. 1.00

24851 Same description as above, but larger size.
Weight, 4 oz Each....$0.20
Per dozen ........... 2.25

24852 White Metal Revolving bell chime, with horse attached.
Weight, 5 oz.
Each.......$0.22
Per doz.... 2.50

## The "Sea-Saw" Chimes.

24855 To be drawn with a string. As the wheels revolve, the figures at either end of the "teeter" rise and fall alternately, at same time vigorously ring a chime bell placed between them. Packed in a box. Price...........................$0.50

24856 The Young America Chime. A large, brightly painted iron chime, with large bell and flag. As toy is drawn the bell revolves and rings. Each............................................ .75

24858 The Roller chime is a handsome lithographed revolving drum with metal handles; as the drum revolves on being drawn over the floor, it produces a succession of musical sound. Weight, 1¼ lbs.
Each.......-......$0.25

## Magnetic and Electrical Toys.

24860 The Boston Motor and Battery Outfit. A new invention. A motor and battery combined. It is right in line with the advancement of the age and enables young people to keep up with the times in the studies of the problems of electricity. Its construction is complete and of the best materials, with all the parts of a large motor, including armature, commutator, magnets, brushes, and a pulley for transmitting power. It is especially adapted for running small mechanical figures, toy machinery, etc., and with a good charge of compound will run a four-inch fan. Packed with full directions in wooden box.
Weight, 2 pounds.
Price of outfit...........................................$1.00
Price, including fan...................................... 1.25

24862 The Novelty Medical Coil and Battery complete. This battery is especially designed for amusement purposes, but when required will serve the purposes of the best medical coils. It is provided with small hand regulator, and currents, thus produced range from the mildest to those that are quite enough for the strongest man. The outfit consists of medical coil and battery, one pair conducting cords, pair nickel plated handles and one dozen extra battery pads. Packed in wooden box. It weighs 2½ pounds. Price..........................$2.25

## Magnets.

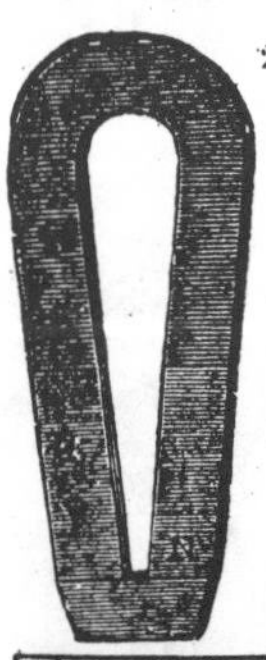

24865 Horseshoe Magnets, superior quality.

| Length. | Each. | Price Per doz. |
|---|---|---|
| 2 inches...... | $0.06 | $0.60 |
| Postage, each, 2c. | | |
| 2½ inches........... | .10 | .95 |
| Postage, each, 2c. | | |
| 3 inches.............. | .15 | 1.50 |
| Postage, each, 3c. | | |
| 4 inches.............. | .20 | 2.10 |
| Weight, each, 5 oz. | | |
| 6 inches.............. | .45 | 5.00 |
| Weight, each, ¾ lb. | | |
| 8 inches.............. | .85 | 9.25 |
| Weight, each, 1¼ lbs. | | |
| 10 inches.............. | 1.50 | 16.00 |
| Weight, each, 3¾ lbs. | | |
| 12 inches.............. | 2.00 | 20.00 |
| Weight, each, 4½ lbs. | | |

Magnetic Floating Toys. Place toys on water, attract them with the magnet and they will swim in a perfectly natural manner.

24867 Magnetic Toys, 8 pieces and magnet in tin sliding covered box, to be used as a tank.
Price........$0.35
Postage..... .10

24869 Magnet Toys, 9 large, fine pieces, and magnet in tin sliding covered box. Price.......... .50
Postage.............................................. .12

## Gray Rubber Toys.

24870 Rubber Mouse, black or white, with whistle. Each......................................$0.1

24871 Rubber Bird, life size
Each...................$0.2

24872 Rubber Doves, life size natural color. Each....$0.5

24873 Rubber Snakes, natural color and shape; you can have more fun with them than with a basket of monkeys. Large size, each...........$0.40
Small size, each..................................... .2

24874 Rubber Sheep, with whistle. Each...........$0.20

24875 Rubber Goat, with whistle
Each..........................$0.20

24876 Rubber Dogs, assorted kinds, poodle, mastiff, pointer, etc, Each..........$0.20

24877 Rubber Cat, with whistle...................$0.20

24878 Rubber Horse, with whistle. Each..........$0.20

24879 Rubber Donkey, with whistle......................$0.20

24881 Rubber Old Woman-in-shoe. Only this is not an old woman, but a beautiful little baby. Price...................$0.25

## Pure White Rubber Toys.

We wish to call special attention to this line of 50 cent toys. All are made of best pure white rubber, and each toy is a perfect model of the animal it represents.

24885 White Rubber Spitz Dog with whistle Each......$0.50
Size, 4½x7

24886 White Rubber Pug Dog, with whistle.
Each.............$0.50
Size, 4½x7 in.

24887 White Rubber Newfoundland Dog, with whistle. Each.......$0.50
Size, 4½x7 in.

24888 White Rubber Horse, large size, with whistle. Each.....$0.50
Size, 5½x8.

24889 Rubber Sheep, Cows, Donkey and Goats, assorted large size, with whistle. Not illustrated.
Each.............$0.50

24890 White Rubber Cat, with whistle. Each $0.50
Size, 4½x7 in.

24890

## RATTLES.

24895 Globe Bell Tin Rattle, wooden handle,
Each.........................................$0.05
Per dozen........................................ .50

24896 Globe Iron Rattles, sleigh bell pattern, japanned wood handles. Each......................... .06
Per dozen......................................... .65

24897 Same, better quality. Each.................. .09
Per dozen......................................... .85

24898 Bone Rattle, with teething ring and 4 metal bells. Each........................................ .20

24899 Chime Rattle, 4 chime bells on leather band, enameled handle. Each...................... .10

24900 Rattle and Teething Ring, one bell on enameled handle, rubber ring. Each.............. .12

# NICKELED IRON TOYS.

### BEST GOODS--BEST STYLES--and of Course LOWEST PRICES.

A few styles painted combinations, others with imitation oxidized portions. Neatest and best line made. Positively guaranteed not to rust and claimed to be the only line on the market that will not.

## 25-CENT IRON TOYS.

No. 121, $2.00 Doz.  No. 102, $2.05 Doz.

**Doz.**

**No. 121, Passenger Train**—Nickeled throughout, locomotive and two coaches, length over all 16¼ inches. Each in box...................(In lots of 4 doz. or more, $1.90) $2 00

**No. 102, Freight Train**—Large locomotive with tender, one large freight car, length over all 13½ inches.............. 2 05
Quantity price...............In lots of 4 doz. or more, $1.95

**No. 264, Street Car**—Nickeled throughout, prancing horses, total length 9¾ inches. Each in box..................... 2 15
No. 264, $2.15 Doz.  Quantity price...............In lots of 4 doz. or more, $2.05

## 50-CENT IRON TOYS.

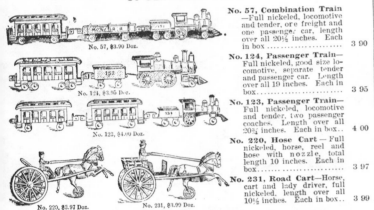

No. 57, $3.90 Doz.

No. 124, $3.95 Doz.

No. 123, $4.00 Doz.

**No. 57, Combination Train**—Full nickeled, locomotive and tender, one freight and one passenger car, length over all 20½ inches. Each in box..................... 3 90

**No. 124, Passenger Train**—Full nickeled, good size locomotive, separate tender and passenger car. Length over all 19 inches. Each in box..................... 3 95

**No. 123, Passenger Train**—Full nickeled, locomotive and tender, two passenger coaches. Length over all 20¾ inches. Each in box.. 4 00

**No. 220, Hose Cart**—Full nickeled, horse, reel and hose with nozzle, total length 10 inches. Each in box..................... 3 97

**No. 231, Road Cart**—Horse, cart and lady driver, full nickeled, length over all 10½ inches. Each in box.. 3 99

No. 220, $3.97 Doz.  No. 231, $3.99 Doz.

## "DOLLAR" IRON TOYS.

No. 62, Combination Freight and Passenger Train, $7.20 Doz.

**No. 62, Combination Train**—Thoroughly nickeled, good size locomotive, separate tender, two freight and one passenger car, 32½ inches long. Each in box..................... 7 20

No. 107, Four-Piece Freight Train, $8.15 Doz.

**No. 107, Freight Train**—Oxidized locomotive and tender and two nickeled freight cars, total length 34 inches. Each in box..................... 8 15

No. 128, Five-Piece Passenger Train, $8.25 Doz.

**No. 128 Passenger Train**—All nickeled, good size locomotive, separate tender and three passenger coaches, total length 35 inches. Each in box..................... 8 25

No. 205, Fire Chief, $7.85 Doz.  No. 200, Fire Engine, $8.65 Doz.

**No. 205, Fire Chief**—Nickeled top, painted running gear, horse and driver, total length 15¼ inches. Each in box..................... 7 85

**No. 200, Fire Engine**—Nickeled top, painted running gear, horses and driver, nickeled gong, spring attached to axles to prevent rattling. Length over all 15¼ inches. Each in box..................... 8 65

No. 225, Hose Cart, $8.65 Doz.

**No. 225, Hose Cart,** Nickeled carriage and reel, nickeled gong and driver, painted running gear and horses. Total length 14 inches. Each in box..................... 8 65

---

No. 126, Lightning Express Train, $8.25 Doz.

**Doz.**

**No. 126, Lightning Express Train**—Large oxidized engine and tender and one large nickeled passenger coach, total length 28¾ inches. Each in box..................... $ 8 25

No. 210, Hook and Ladder Truck, $8.70 Doz.

**No. 210, Hook and Ladder Truck**—Nickeled truck, painted running gear, horses and figures and nickel gong, painted removable ladders, total length 20¼ inches, spring attachment to axles. Each in box..................... 8 70

## EXTRA SIZE IRON TOYS.

No. 132, Three-Piece Pullman Train, $15.50 Doz.

*The biggest and best toys ever offered at these prices.*

**No. 132, "Pullman" Train**—Extra large oxidized locomotive and tender, large vestibule parlor coach (the latter nickeled), total length 35 inches. A big, fine toy. Each in box..................... 15 50

No. 252, Two-Horse City Truck, $17.50 Doz.

**No. 252, Two-Horse City Truck**—Nickeled throughout, two heavy draught horses, driver and load of merchandise. Total length about 17 inches. Makes a big show. Each in box..... 17 50

No. 256, Fire Patrol, $17.75 Doz.

**No. 256, Fire Patrol**—Full nickeled, two prancing horses, six removable firemen and driver, nickeled gong. Length over all 21 inches. Cheap at $2.50 retail. Each in box......... 17 75

No. 261, Police Patrol, $18.00 Doz.

**No. 261, Police Patrol**—Nickeled throughout, as above except manned with policemen instead of firemen. Each in box................. 18 00

*Any of these would readily retail from $2.25 to $3.00.*

---

## JAPANNED IRON SURREY.

**Doz.**

**Japanned Iron Surrey**—Well japanned, red wheels, patent axle so that you can revolve in any manner you wish. Size 6½x2¾. A great 25-cent toy. ½ doz. in package......... $1 98

## NICKELED TOY RANGES.

**You can build a fire in these.** Just what every girl, large or small, wants. Made exactly as a "full grown" range or stove in that doors swing, covers are removable, grates turn and best of all a fire can be made in them.

No. 1, $7.80 Doz.  No. 2, $17.50 Doz.

**Doz.**

**"O. K." Range**—Similar in style to No. 1. Full nickeled, burnished edges and legs, 5 inches square, 3½ high, complete with kettle, skillet, length of pipe and lifter in box........... $ 3 9

**No. 1 "Ideal" Range**—Length 7¾ inches, depth 5, height 4½, removable hearth, burnished ornamentations, removable edges, water tank, length of pipe, skillet, kettle and lifter complete in box..................... 7 8

**No. 2, "Ideal" Range**—Nickel plated, burnished edges and ornamentations, 11 inches long, 6¾ deep, 6 high, removable hearth, high shelf, water tank, tea kettle, skillet, kettle, saucepan, length of pipe and lifter complete in box..................... 17 5

**No. 3, "Ideal" Range**—Should retail for $5.00. Similar in style to No. 2. Nickel plated, burnished edges and ornamentations, removable hearth, high shelf, water tank, tea kettle, skillet, kettle, saucepan. length of pipe and lifter complete in box. Length 14¾ inches, depth 7⅜ inches, height 7⅜ inches. Price each........ 2 75

**Each**

**"Baby" Range**—Length 15½ inches, depth 8½, height 9, nickeled throughout, burnished edges and ornamentations, water tank, tea kettle, skillet, kettle, saucepan, length of pipe and lifter complete in box. Price each..... $1 9

*Butler Brothers (now City Products Corp.)*

# DOMESTIC TIN TOYS.

**IMPROVED LINE--All New Goods--Best Make, Painted in Brilliant Colors.**

We here offer what is certainly the best line of Tin Toys in America—honest make and painted in bright colors. New goods in all the latest designs. Packed in pasteboard boxes.

## DRIVING AND RAILROAD TOYS.

One Style No. 6, 45c Doz.

Doz.

**No. 6, Assorted Wagons with Horses**—4 Styles of wagons in assorted colors, regular goods. Size about 7 inches. 1 doz in box..............(In lots of 6 doz. or more, 43c) $0 45

**No. 7, Assorted Wagons with Horses**—6 styles in box of ½ doz., all painted in bright colors or made of embossed tin. Full length about 10 inches. Regular 15c goods. ½ doz. in package. (In lots of 6 doz. or more, 73c) 75

**No. 8, Extra Size Wagons with Horses**—6 styles in each box of ½ doz., each with driver. Decorated in bright colors. Full length about 14 inches...........(4 doz. or more, $1.75) 1 79

No. 9, Four-Piece Railroad Train, $1.92 Doz.

**No. 9, Four-Piece Railroad Train**—Comprising locomotive, tender and two passenger coaches, each with copper wheels. Full length about 21 inches, painted in attractive colors, each train in box...... 1 92
6 doz. or more, $1.87

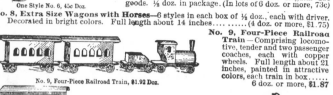

One Style No. 13, $1.94 Doz.

One Style No. 26, $2.00 Doz.

No. 25, Grocery Wagon, $2.10 Doz.

**No. 13, Covered Picture Wagon**—With two horses. Wagon on 4 wheels, large size chromo sides and extension platform front, full length about 14½ inches, handsomely painted. ⅓ doz. in box...................... 1 94
Quantity price........4 doz. or more, $1.89

**No. 26, Assorted Delivery Wagons**—Assortment comprises one brewery wagon with wood barrels, one milk wagon with tin cans, one express wagon with barrels, one covered grocery wagon. Each on wheels with horse and driver, attractively painted and lettered, full length about 13½ inches. 2 00
Quantity price........4 doz. or more, $1.95

**No. 25, Grocery Wagon**—With one horse, mounted on four wheels, canopy top and sides so that you can open at will, length about 14 inches, height 6¼. ⅓ doz. in box 2 15
Quantity price........4 doz. or more, $2.10

No. 27, Extra Size Express Wagon, $3.90 Doz.

**No. 27, Extra Size Express Wagon**—With two horses, canopy top and driver, painted in colors, wagon on four wheels, full length 17½ inches. "Express" lettered on each wagon. Goods that should retail at 75c. 1-6 doz. in box.... 3 90

**No. 14, Covered Picture Wagon**—Large 50c size, two horses, extension platform front, length about 18 inches, height 7¾, painted in bright colors. ½ doz. in box 3 95

No. 14, Covered Picture Wagon, $3.95 Doz.

## GONG AND BELL TOYS.

No. 17, 87c Doz.

No. 18, $1.83 Doz.

No. 20, Circus Toy, $4.18 Doz.

**No. 17, Assorted Bell Toys**—Big articles for 10c. Entirely new this season, 3 styles in box. When rolled across the floor the gong sounds. Handsomely painted, raised platform on four wheels, size about 6 inches. ½ doz. in box..(In lots of 6 doz. or more, 84c) 87

**No. 18, Assorted Bell Toys**—Animals with riders with striking gong. A big toy for little money. Raised platform on four wheels, length about 8½ inches. ⅓ doz. in box........ 1 83
Quantity price.........................................In lots of 4 doz. or more, $1.78

**No. 20, 50-Cent Circus Toy**—Large horse on raised platform, 4 large nickeled wheels, painted in bright colors, boy with whip on platform. Length about 14 inches, height 12½. Each in box. ⅓ doz. in package................................................ 4 18

## MECHANICAL TOYS.

No. 12, $2.00 Doz.

No. 11, $2.15 Doz.

No. 21, $4.00 Doz.

**No. 12, Assorted Mechanical Animals**—Size about 5½ inches. 6 styles in box of ½ doz. 2 00
Quantity price..................................................In lots of 4 doz. or more, $1.95

**No. 11, Mechanical Locomotive**—Good springs on four wheels. Size about 5¼ inches, with fender. ½ doz. in box.......................................(In lots of 4 doz. or more, $2.10) 2 15

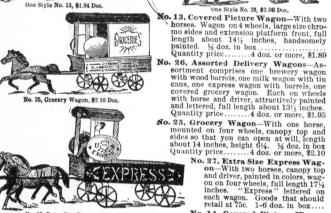

**No. 21, Mechanical Cable Car**—With driver and gong. A new toy this season. Size about 12 inches. Each in box.................................................................. 4 00

**No. 10, Mechanical Railroad Train**—The best half-dollar toy of '95. Comprising locomotive, tender and one car. Size about 18¼ inches. Each in box.......................... 4 17

## TIN ANIMALS ON PLATFORMS.

Specimen Animal.

No. 4, 78c Doz.

**No. 1, Assorted Animals**—6 horses and 6 other animals, average size about 4 inches. 1 doz. in box..........(6 doz. or more, 32c)

**No. 2, Assorted Animals**—*Our 5-cent leaders.* 3 kinds—horse, ram and goat. About 6 inches long. 1 doz. in box..(6 doz. or more, 42c)

**No. 3, Assorted Horses**—Good lively effects, assorted colors. Size about 7 inches. ½ doz. in box, assorted.....(6 doz. or more, 70c)

**No. 4, Assorted Animal Groups**—Each on 4-wheel raised platform. Length 7 inches, width nearly 2¼ inches. 6 styles assorted in box of ½ doz. Handsomely painted in bright colors ..........
Quantity price ......................In lots of 6 doz. or more, 75c

**No. 5, Assorted Animals**—*Regular 15-cent goods.* 6 styles in box of ½ doz. Size about 9 inches.......... .....(6 doz. or more, 88c)

## TIN KITCHENS.

**No. 5, Tin Kitchen**—Regular shape, embossed colored tin, complete with a number of kitchen utensils. 6 inches long and 4 high. 1 doz. in box...........(6 doz. or more, 40c)

**No. 10, Tin Kitchen**—As above, very much larger, about 9½ inches long and 5½ high. Complete with a number of kitchen utensils, with spaces for holding. 1 doz. in pkg..
Quantity price................In lots of 6 doz. or more, 75c

**No. 25, Tin Kitchen**—As above, only with larger fire place and pump on side for water. Length 13½ inches, about 8 high, with a large number of kitchen utensils. ½ doz. in pkg......................(In lots of 4 doz. or more, $1.95)

# PATENTED ROAMING TOYS.

**No Holiday Stock is Complete without These Quick Selling Novelties.**

Among the best and most life-like toys in the market. They are led by a string, always the move, no winding up, handsomely painted in natural colors and well made in every way.

Mouse, 30c Doz

Beetle, 35c Doz.

Alligator, 72c Doz.

Turtle, 72c Doz.

Parrot, 72c Doz.

Dog, 72c Doz.

Hippopotamus, 73c Doz.

Cat, 73c Doz.

Trolley Car, 73c Doz.

**Roaming Mouse**—With movable tail. So life-like that it will make any young lady scream. 2½-inch. 1 doz. in pkg......
Quantity price..................In lots of 6 doz. or more, 28c

**Roaming Beetle**—Entirely new this season and very life-like. Painted in bright colors, size about 3-inch. 1 doz. in pkg...
Quantity price..................In lots of 6 doz. or more, 33c

**Roaming Alligator**—Size 10-inch, hand painted in natural colors. 1 doz. in pkg.....(In lots of 6 doz. or more, 69c)

**Roaming Turtle**—The old stand-by. Painted in bright colors, length about 7 inches and 4¼ in width. 1 doz. in package..
Quantity price..................In lots of 6 doz. or more, 69c

**Roaming Parrot**—With spreading tail, painted in gay colors and well shaped, length about 7½ inches. 1 doz. in package
Quantity price..................In lots of 6 doz. or more, 69c

**Roaming Dog**—Brightly painted, good size, being about 7½ inches long. Sure to please. 1 doz. in pkg
In lots of 6 doz. or more, 69c

**Roaming Hippopotamus**—With moving tongue. Very life-like and as clumsy in motion as a real one. Size about 6½-inch. 1 doz. in pkg......(6 doz. or more, 70c)

**Roaming Cat**—Length about 6¼ inches. We could not get enough of them last season. 1 doz. in pkg
In lots of 6 doz. or more, 70c

**Roaming Trolley Car**—Painted in good bright colors, four styles, back and front platform, length about 6 inches. 1 doz. in pkg....
In lots of 6 doz. or more, 70c

25-Cent Trolley Car, $1.79 Doz.

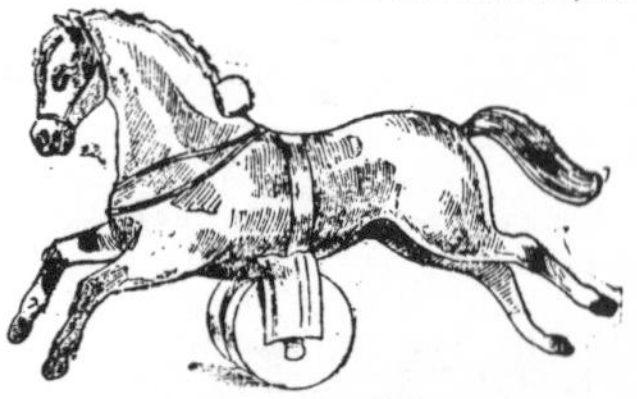

Roaming Horse, $1.80 Doz.

**25-Cent Roaming Trolley Car**—Entirely new this season. Painted in attractive colors, four copper wheels, back and front platform, size 8½x3. A big toy to retail at a quarter. ½ doz. in pkg.......................................................(In lots of 4 doz. or more, $1.75) 1

**Roaming Horse**—Entirely new. When going has a fine motion, same as a trotting horse. Good size, length about 9½ inches and height 6½. ½ doz. in pkg..(4 doz. or more, $1.75) 1

# SOLID STEEL TOYS.

**Very light, yet the most destructive youngster can't break them. We could not keep up with the demand on these last year, but this season placed orders far enough ahead to insure plenty for all.**

No. 1, $2.10 Doz.

One of the Toys at $8.90 Doz.

Do

**No. 1, Steel Dump Cart**—Every part made of steel except the axle, which is wood, one-piece body, 10¼ inches long, 7-inch wheels fastened by bolts, 27-inch spear handle. Finished in 3 colors. 2 doz. in crate, sold only by crate.............(4 doz. or more, $2.04) $2

**Assortment of Solid Steel Toys**—Comprising 3 styles as follows: city coal wagon, length of body 18 inches; city dray wagon, length of body 18 inches, and milk wagon with milk cans, All complete with spears and finished in bright attractive colors. Put up ½ doz. in crate, 2 each of above styles, sold only by crate.... ... ........................ 8

# MISCELLANEOUS IMPORTED TOYS

## PLUSH AND WOOLY ANIMALS.

No. 912, 80c Doz.

No. 861, 88c Doz.

No. 913, $2.08 Doz.

Doz.

**No. 912, Wooly Dog**—Covered with long black hair. 7¼x7¼, each on 4-wood-wheeled platform. 1 doz. in box................................ $0 80
Quantity price........................In lots of 6 doz. or more, 76c

**No. 861, Assorted Wooly Animals**—Not large, but well shaped, felt cotton stuffed, each with ribbon around neck and elastic cord, size about 4-inch. Assorted animals in flat box of ½ doz. 88
Quantity price........................In lots of 6 doz. or more, 84c

## SHAKING-HEAD ANIMALS.

No. 899, Assorted Horses and Donkeys, 81c Doz.

No. 900, Assorted Animals, $2.10 Doz.

**No. 899, 10-Cent Assortment**—Natural finish, each with saddle and on a 4-wheeled platform, size about 5¼x6. Horses, donkeys and cows assorted in each box of 1 doz........ 81
Quantity price........................In lots of 6 doz. or more, 78c

**No. 900, 25-Cent Assortment**—Comprising cow, donkey, and horse with bridle. Length 9 inches, height 6½. Made of papier mache, covered with a preparation like cloth, each with shaking head and on platform. ½ doz. in box......(In lots of 4 doz. or more, $2.00) 2 10

## ASSORTMENTS OF GERMAN TOYS.

Our German Toy assortments will average worth ten per cent more than most.

No. 873, Two Styles 5-Cent German Toys, 34c Doz.

**No. 873, 5-Cent German Toys, Assorted**—*Best lot of 5-cent goods ever imported.* 12 styles in each box: 9-inch dressed clapping figure, wood horse on platform, 10-inch double jumping jack, shaking head donkey on platform, horse drawing wood cart, length 9 inches; two sheep on platform drawing hay wagon, 6-inch darkey on platform, butterflies on wired frame, 9-inch sail boat, 5-inch wooly lamb on platform, 10-inch whistling darkey and surprise box with voice.. 34
Quantity price........................6 doz. or more, 32c

No. 874, Two Styles 10-Cent German Toys, 75c Doz.

**No. 874, 10-Cent German Toys, Assorted**—Extra size, being *regular 15-cent goods.* Each box contains 15-inch double sided jumping jack, shaking head donkey on 7-inch platform, horse with mane on 7-inch platform, 11-inch full rigged sail boat, 9-inch wagon with wooly sheep, Punch and Judy, soldier boy in chair with clappers, 11-inch fancy clapping figure, stable with two horses, surprise box with voice, automatic gymnast on chair. 1 doz. in box............(In lots of 6 doz. or more, 72c) 75

## TOY HORSES.

No. 904, 37c Doz.

No. 906, $2.08 Doz.

No. 907, $4.10 Doz.

**No. 904, 5-Cent Horse**—On wood platform, body made of pasteboard with wood legs and wooly mane and tail, height 5½ inches, length 5 inches. Painted in natural gray. 1 doz. in box........................(In lots of 6 doz. or more, 35c) 37

**No. 905, 10-Cent Horse**—As above, only 7¼x6¼. 1 doz. in box ....(6 doz. or more, 75c) 78

**No. 906, 25-Cent Horse**—As above, only 10 inches high and 10 inches long. An immense toy for a quarter. ½ doz. in box........................(In lots of 4 doz. or more, $2.00) 2 08

**No. 907, Plush Horse**—Height 10-inch, well made, natural appearance, mane and tail, complete with saddle and harness with stirrups, saddle, blanket and bridle, all on 4-iron-wheel axle platform. ¼ doz. in pkg. 4 10

**No. 908, Plush Horse**—Size 12-inch, as above, only with plush seat on saddle and surcingle. 1-6 doz. in pkg. 6 00

## LARGE PLUSH HORSES.

Big fellows for show window use as well as easily salable at a good profit.

Each.

**No. 909, Large Plush Horse**—*A big one for a dollar.* Size 12¾x12¾, well made, natural appearance, mane and tail complete with saddle and harness, all on 4-iron-wheel axle platform. Length of platform, 13¼ inches. Each in box............ $0 67

**No. 910, Large Plush Horse**—As above only much larger, 17x14½, size of platform 4⅜x15. Each in pkg. Each............ 1 12

**No. 911, Extra Size Plush Horse**—As above, only very much larger, measuring 21x19, all leather saddle. Length of platform 20¾ inches. Makes a staving good window advertiser. Each in pkg. Each............ 1 62

Large Plush Horse (Nos. 909 to 911).

# DRESSED PERFORMING ANIMALS.

No more comical or better toys are made

Two Styles No. 902, $1.92 Doz.

Two Styles No. 903, $3.85 Doz.

Doz.

**No. 902, Dressed Performing Animals**—Each on platform. When spring is touched in back the bellows makes a noise and works the head and arms. The rooster plays a violin, the rabbit shines shoes, etc. Height 8 inches. 6 styles in each box of ½ doz............ $1 92
Quantity price........................In lots of 4 doz. or more, $1.87

**No. 903, Dressed Performing Animals**—As above, only two figures on each platform. 4 styles in box. A big 50-cent toy. ⅙ doz. in box............ 3 85

## TIN ENGINES AND TRAINS.

**No. 826, 5-Cent Toy Engine**—Well made of bright decorated tin on four wheels. Operates with rubber motion. 1 doz. in box............(6 doz. or more, 31c) 33

No. 826, 33c Doz.

No. 827, 10-Cent Toy Train, 84c Doz.

**No. 827, 10-Cent Toy Train**—*A rattling dime seller.* Engine, tender and passenger car, each on four wheels. Brightly decorated, length 8¼ inches. Each in box, 1 doz. in pkg. (6 doz. or more, 80c) 84

No. 828, 25-Cent Toy Train, $2.12 Doz.

**No. 828, 25-Cent Toy Train**—As above, only four cars, engine and tender, each having painted pictures on sides. Each train in box. ½ doz. in pkg............ 2 12

No. 829, 50-Cent Toy Train, $4.20 Doz.

**No. 829, 50-Cent Toy Train**—As above, 6 pieces, one very fancy engine, tender, 2 passenger cars, 1 express car and one open freight car. Total length 22 inches. Each in box... 4 20

## MISCELLANEOUS IMPORTED TIN TOYS.

One Style No. 832, $1.95 Doz.

One Style No. 833, $1.98 Doz.

**No. 832, Assorted Tin Toys**—Two styles—hook and ladder, size 14-inch, and 11-inch hose cart with hose and tin engine that will throw water, size 12-inch. Each with 2 horses and driver, painted in bright colors. ¼ doz. assorted in box............ 1 95

**No. 833, Assorted Tin Toys**—Comprising open carriage, closed carriage with doors, and horse car. Each with driver and two horses, all made of bright tin and good sizes. ¼ doz. in box ............ 1 98

## IMPORTED TIN STOVES.

No. 992, 42c Doz.

No. 993, 82c Doz.

No. 994, $1.75 Doz.

**No. 992, Decorated Tin Stove**—*Our big 5-center.* 4 feet, size 3¾x2¾, 5-inch back, 2 dishes, covered pan and fire dish with 2 hooks for hanging utensils on. Each with oven. ⅔ red and ⅓ assorted colors in box of 1 doz............(In lots of 6 doz. or more, 40c) 42

**No. 993, Decorated Tin Stove**—As above, size 5½x3¾, 6½-inch back. Each with 7 kitchen articles—3 covered stew pans, 3 miscellaneous dishes and 1 handled stew pan, with 3 hangers on back of stove. Regular 15-cent goods. ⅔ red and ⅓ assorted in box of 1 doz............ 82
Quantity price......6 doz. or more, 79c

**No. 994, Decorated Tin Stove**—As above, only larger and with 2 ovens, 4 covered stew pans, 1 covered tea kettle, 5 assorted dishes and 1 long handled stew pan, 5 hangers. Size 6½x4½, back 7¼-inch. ⅔ red and ⅓ assorted colors. ½ doz. in box............ 1 75
Quantity price......4 doz. or more, $1.68

**No. 995, Decorated Tin Stove**—As above, 2 ovens and 7 kitchen utensils with hooks, 3 covered stew pans, 1 extra size handled and covered tea kettle, 1 round brass stew pan and 2 long handled pans. Size 9x6, 10-inch back. ½ doz. in pkg. ............ 3 65

No. 995, $3.65 Doz.

*Butler Brothers (now City Products Corp.)*

## MISCELLANEOUS IMPORTED TOYS—Continued.

No. 840, $1.75 Doz.

### PATENT AUTOMATIC TOYS.

Wound by a key on the side, which starts the wheels and springs in motion. Nicely made of decorated tin. **Good action**—not the unsatisfactory toys sometimes sold.

Doz.

**No. 840, Mechanical Walking Monkey**—Length about 6 inches. As natural as life in looks and action. Each in box. ½ doz. in pkg. .... $1 75

No. 830, $1.88 Doz.

**No. 830, Mechanical Cable Car**—Winding with key attached to side, good coil spring, 4 wheels, man on front platform, made of decorated tin, full length 6 inches. ½ doz. in box .... 1 88

**No. 831, Mechanical Swiching Engine**—Mechanical, so will move forward and then backward without touching. Good size, fancy tin, winding with attached key, length 6¾ inches. ¼ doz. in box .... 1 92

No. 831, $1.92 Doz.

No. 841, $3.98 Doz.

**No. 841, Mechanical Sulky with Jockey Driver**—A good big toy to retail at a half dollar. Comprises sulky, with jockey driver and horse, all mechanical, with spring. Painted in colors, size about 7½-inch. **Each in box** .... 3 98

### IMPORTED STEAM ENGINES.

Complete with alcohol or kerosene lamp. Interesting and instructive toys.

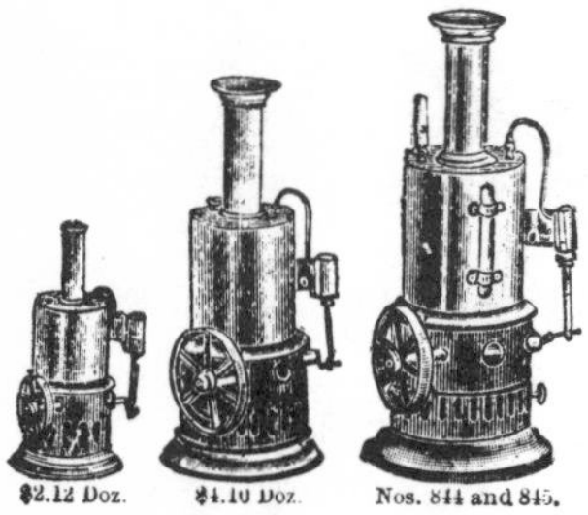
$2.12 Doz. $4.10 Doz. Nos. 844 and 845.

**No. 842, Upright Engine**—Nickeled and japanned driving rod and wheel, alcohol lamp, height about 5½ inches. Each in box with full instructions. ½ doz. in pkg. .... 2 12

**No. 843, Upright Engine**—Same as No. 842 above, 8¾ inches high, brass bound, fancy smoke stack. Each in box. ½ doz. in pkg.... 4 10

**No. 844, Upright Engine**—With kerosene lamp which fits bottom of engine. Height about 10½ inches, glass water gauge on side and steam whistle. Each in box with measure and funnel for filling and full directions. A regular two-dollar article. ¼ doz. in pkg. .... 8 15

**No. 845, Upright Engine**—Same as above, only very much larger, combining all the special features, height 11½ inches. Retails from $2.00 to $2.50. Each in box .... 16 50

### MISCELLANEOUS IMPORTED TOYS.

33c Doz.

**No. 931, Deception Wine Glass**—Regular blown wine glass, filled with red liquor with thin glass top. One naturally starts to drink before he finds that he is sold. Height 3 inches. Each in box. 1 doz. in pkg. .... 33
Quantity price. ....6 doz. or more, 31c

No. 863, High Flyer, 35c Doz.

**No. 863, High Flyer**—With 3 flyers, full length 11 inches, size of flyers, 2¾-inch. An old toy, but a good one and better than ever.........(6 doz. or more, 33c) 35

**No. 862, Clown Target**—A double clown target, well made, ball attachment, when you strike the bull's eye with the ball the rear clown jumps up on the other's shoulder. Full size when open 10¼-inch, painted in attractive colors. 1 doz. in box......(6 doz. or more, 75c) 78

No. 862, 73c Doz.

No. 936, Tennis Racket, 79c Doz

**No. 936, Tennis Racket and Ball**—The latest popular toy. Comprises cat-gut racket with wood handle and frame, size 13¼x4¼, and wool covered elastic return ball with 2 brass bells. Ball can be used separately as in tennis, or tied to racket, making a great combination game. 1 doz. in pkg .... 79
Quantity price..6 doz. or more, 75c

No. 1138, 82c Doz.

**No. 1138, Little Painter Set**—A good drawing teacher. Comprises 4 good size embossed sheets for coloring, 4 perforated sheets (different subjects) with tracing paper for each, artist's pallette and 6 colored paint tablets. Put up in 9-inch fancy labeled box with brush....(6 doz. or more, 79c) 82

No. 849, $2.00 Doz.

**The Monkey Drummer**—One of the best novelties of the season. Works easily, and will drum any tune the operator knows. Natural motion, painted in bright colors. A good toy and can't help being a seller. ½ doz. in box..(4 doz. or more, $1.75) 1 80

**No. 849, Tin Stable**—With cab and horse on wheels. Size of stable 4⅞x5⅛, all painted in bright colors. ½ doz. in box..(4 doz. or more, $1.95) 2 00

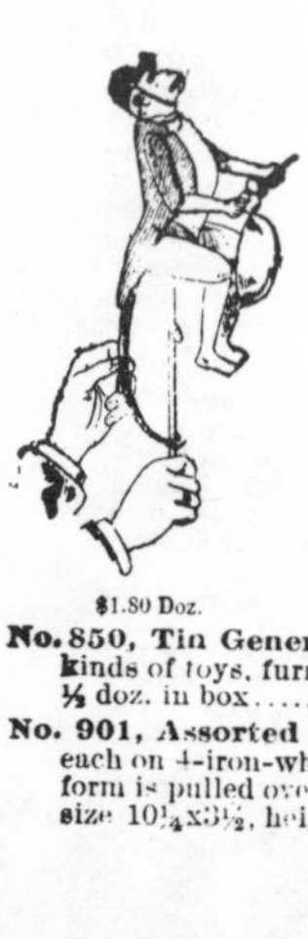
$1.80 Doz.

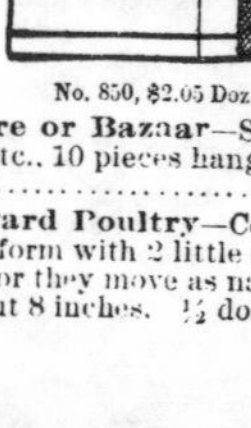
No. 850, $2.05 Doz.

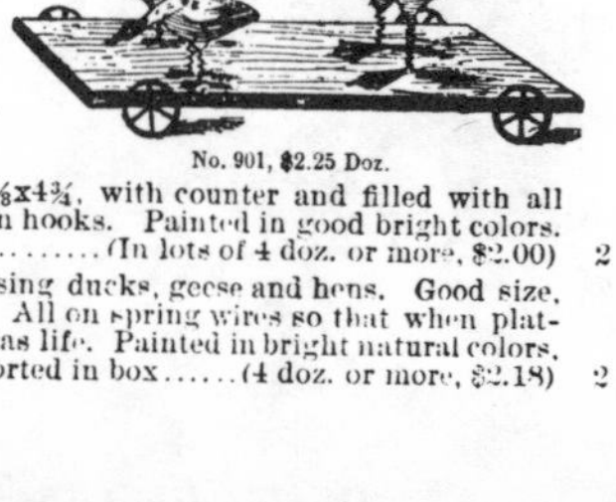
No. 901, $2.25 Doz.

**No. 850, Tin General Store or Bazaar**—Size 6½x4¾, with counter and filled with all kinds of toys, furniture, etc., 10 pieces hanging on hooks. Painted in good bright colors. ½ doz. in box....(In lots of 4 doz. or more, $2.00) 2 05

**No. 901, Assorted Farmyard Poultry**—Comprising ducks, geese and hens. Good size, each on 4-iron-wheel platform with 2 little ones. All on spring wires so that when platform is pulled over the floor they move as natural as life. Painted in bright natural colors, size 10¼x3½, height about 8 inches. ½ doz. assorted in box......(4 doz. or more, $2.18) 2 25

### FRICTION TOYS.

Operated by pulling a string, causing the friction wheel to play on the rest of the toy and start it in motion. All first-class toys and big sellers.

No. 834, Two of the Styles at 27c Doz.

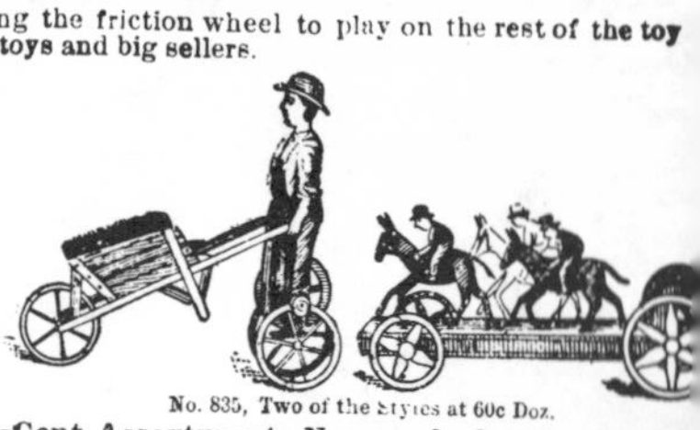
No. 835, Two of the Styles at 60c Doz.

**No. 834, 5-Cent Assortment**—New goods, 6 styles, larger than last year's, each on 4 wheeled platform. 1 doz. in box........(In lots of 6 doz. or more, 25c)

**No. 835, 10-Cent Assortment**—As above, 6 styles, larger and better than last year s. 1 doz. in box....
Quantity price..........In lots of 6 doz. or more, 58c

No. 836, Express Wagon, 87c Doz.

**No. 836, Express Wagon**—On two wheels, man with moving feet in shafts. When in motion the wheels turn and the man walks. Decorated tin. ½ doz. in box....
Quantity price..............In lots of 6 doz. or more, 87c

**No. 837, African Letter Carrier**—When in motion the ostrich moves head and feet and the driver his arms. Length 7 inches. Each in box, ½ doz. in pkg ....
Quantity price............In lots of 4 doz. or more, $1.30

No. 837, African Letter Carrier, $1.33 Doz.

No. 838, $1.50 Doz.

No. 839, $1.80 Doz.

**No. 838, The "Midway" Coach**—When in motion the gentleman salutes and the umbrella revolves, size 5x5½, made of tin, brightly painted. Each in box, ½ doz. in pkg........
Quantity price.......................In lots of 4 doz. or more, $1.45

**No. 839, Dog Cart Friction Toy**—Entirely new. A dog cart with driver and horse. When in motion the horse balks and the driver waves his whip. Made of decorated tin, size about 8½-inch. Each in box, ½ doz. in pkg........(In lots of 4 doz. or more, $1.75)

### MECHANICAL EATING TOYS.

No. 896, Two of the Mechanical Eating Animals at $1.92 Doz.

**No. 896, 25-Cent Mechanical Eating Animals**—Each on 4-wheeled platform and with side crank which when turned opens the mouth and passes food in. The faster you turn the faster it eats. Height about 5½ inches. Assortment comprises 2 elephants, 1 rabbit, 1 bear, 1 cat and 1 tiger. The elephant moves his trunk and the rabbit his ears. ½ in box. In lots of 4 doz. or more, $1.89

No. 897, $1.95 Doz.

No. 898, $3.75 Doz.

**No. 897, 25-Cent "All-Nations" Eating Figures**—As above, men of different nationalities, painted in bright colors. Size about 5x6 inches. Faces are very funny, and combined with the eating effect make one of the best 25-cent toys we ever offered. ½ doz. in box, 6 nationalities..
Quantity price....In lots of 4 doz. or more, $1.90

**No. 898, 50-Cent "All-Nations" Eating Figures**—As above, only much larger, and with jaws working on a spring, so that the mouth opens every time a bite passes in. 6 nations in each box of ½ doz. Size about 6x7 inches............ 3

### MECHANICAL RACE GAMES.

These "parlor race games" are getting more and more popular every season. **They are just the thing for parties.**

No. 890, Bicycle Race Game, $1.15 Each.

No. 888, Double Horse Race Game, $1.25 Each.

**No. 887, Single Horse Race Game**—*You can sell it for a dollar.* A circular course, 10 inches in diameter with track and 6 horses with jockeys. So constructed that by turning the pivot the horses race for a considerable time. Which will win no one can tell until the wire is crossed. Made of tin and pewter with green center, starting post and flag staff, decorated in colors. Each in box.... 80

**No. 890, Bicycle Race Game**—Latest racing game. Made as above only winding with attached key in center. 3 riders on correct shape bicycles, dressed in different costumes, all attached to key in center, starting flag on side. Diameter 9½-inch. Each in box 1

**No. 888, Double Horse Race Game**—Same as No. 887, only double track and with four horses in each track, diameter 12¼ inches. The regular $3.00 article .... 1

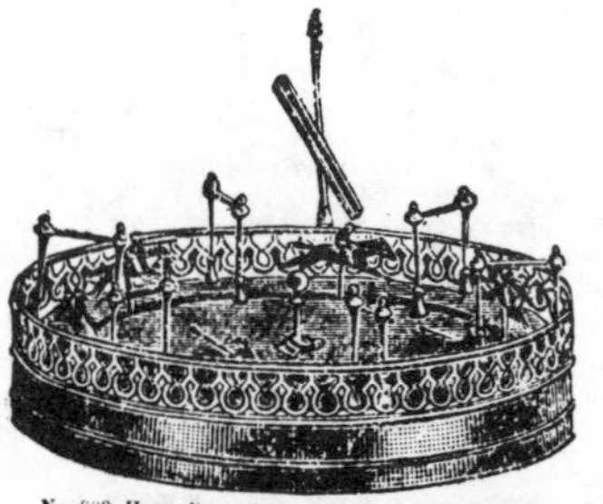
No. 889, Horse Race Game with Rings, $1.72 Each.

**No. 889, Horse Race Game with Rings**—Similar to above, single track, 14⅜ inches in diameter, 6 horses. Has chute attachment and set of rings. While the horses are going at full speed the rings slide through the chute and are caught on the spears of the horsemen, each of whom carries a spear for that purpose. This introduces a new element of chance and therefore doubles the fun .... 1

# MUSICAL AND NOISY TOYS.

**Couldn't Make a Mistake by Ordering "a Dozen All Around" of These Sure Selling Toys.**

## DECORATED MUSICAL TRUMPETS.

Doz.

No. 789, 25c Doz.

**No. 789, 3-Cent Assortment**—9½-inch, made of bright decorated tin with porcelain mouthpiece, handle and cord. 1 doz. in box, assorted ........... $0 25
Quantity price.... ....In lots of 6 doz. or more, 23c

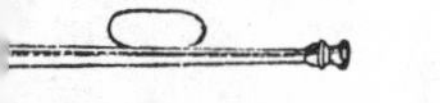
No. 792, 36c Doz.

**No. 792, 5-Cent Assortment**—Silvered and brass assorted, porcelain mouthpiece and double reed—a new feature in a 5-cent trumpet—9¾-inch, good handle, wound with cord. 1 doz. in box........... 36
Quantity price.... ....In lots of 6 doz. or more, 34c

No. 790, 37c Doz.

**No. 790, Banner 5-Cent Assortment**—Fancy decorated tin, 12½-inch, wide cup-shaped porcelain mouthpiece, handle and cord. 1 doz. in box, assorted 37
Quantity price.........In lots of 6 doz. or more, 35c

No. 791, 38c Doz.

**No. 791, Trumpet Horn**—Handsomely made of decorated tin, 12 inches long, porcelain mouthpiece. Nice goods, clean value. 1 doz. in box ............ 38
Quantity price ........In lots of 6 doz. or more, 36c

**No. 793, Leader 5-Cent Assortment**—Regular dime goods. Wide cup-shape porcelain mouthpiece, decorated tin, size 14½-inch, handle and cord. 1 doz. in box, assorted......(In lots of 6 doz. or more, 41c) 43

No. 793, 43c Doz.

No. 794, 78c Doz.

**No. 794, Dime Assortment**—Double reed, porcelain mouthpiece, 17½ inches long, handle and cord. 1 doz. in box, assorted ..................... 78
Quantity price......In lots of 6 doz. or more, 75c

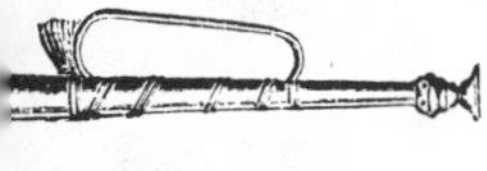
No. 795, 79c Doz.

**No. 795, Double Reed Trumpets**—13-inch, painted funnel, metal cup mouthpiece, ⅔ nickel and ⅓ brass finished, tassel and cord. 1 doz. in box..................(In lots of 6 doz. or more, 75c) 79

**No. 796, Bugle Horn Trumpets**—Double reed, metal cup mouthpiece, ⅔ nickel and ⅓ brass, polished funnel and fancy cord. 1 doz. in box.. 81
Quantity price.....In lots of 6 doz. or more, 79c

No. 796, 81c Doz.

**No. 797, 15-Cent Assortment**—Large double reed, ⅔ nickel and ⅓ brass, cup-shape mouthpiece, large handle with tassel and painted funnel, size 17½-inch. A good trumpet. 1 doz. in box.............(In lots of 6 doz. or more, $1.10) 1 17

No. 801, $1.75 Doz.

No. 797, $1.17 Doz.

**No. 801, Natural Trumpet Horn**—Nickel bound, double reed, tassel attachment with cord for hanging around the neck, made from the genuine horn. ½ doz. in box......(4 doz. or more, $1.68) 1 75

**No. 798, Odd-Shape Assortment**—Large fancy handles with cords, double reed, cup metal mouthpieces, 4 shapes. A1 25-cent goods. 1 doz. in box, assorted......(4 doz. or more, $1.75) 1 79

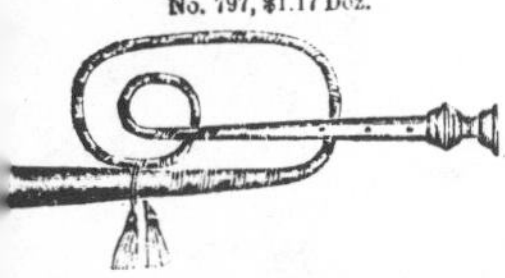
No. 798, $1.79 Doz.

**No. 800, Round Horn Shape Trumpets**—⅔ nickel and ⅓ brass, extra size, well made, double reed, wound with fancy cord and tassel, 23 inches around. Really 35-cent goods. ½ doz. in box... 2 00
Quantity price....In lots of 4 doz. or more, $1.95

**No. 799, Firemen's Shape Trumpet**—Heavy solid trumpet, double reed, regular oval metal mouthpiece, heavily nickeled, size 10½-inch and very stout, heavy cord to hang around the neck, good reeds. 1 doz. in box.................. 2 10
Quantity price....In lots of 4 doz. or more, $2.00

No. 799, $2.10 Doz.

## DECORATED TIN RATTLES.

No. 820, 24c Doz.

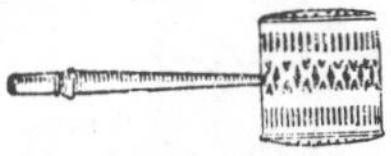
No. 821, 31c Doz.

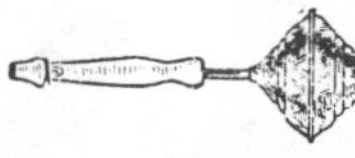
No. 822, 38c Doz.

**820, 3-Cent Assortment**—*Regular 5-cent goods.* Hammer shape, assorted open-work designs, decorated tin with porcelain mouthpieces, trumpet sound, size about 6½-inch. 1 doz. in box..................(In lots of 6 doz. or more, 23c) 24

**No. 821, Nickeled Tin Rattles**—Hammer shape, assorted open-work designs, porcelain mouthpieces, trumpet sound, size about 6½-inch. 1 doz. in box... 31
Quantity price..........In lots of 6 doz. or more, 29c

No. 823, 39c Doz.

**No. 822, Big 5-Cent Assortment**—Fancy combination rattles, copper colored, wood handles, whistle ends, with bead and tassel attachments. 1 doz. in box, assorted..............(In lots of 6 doz. or more, 36c) 38

**No. 823, Rattle Trumpet**—Good goods, porcelain mouthpiece, size 6½-inch, good handle, made of decorated tin. Formerly in the dime business........... 39
Quantity price..........In lots of 6 doz. or more, 37c

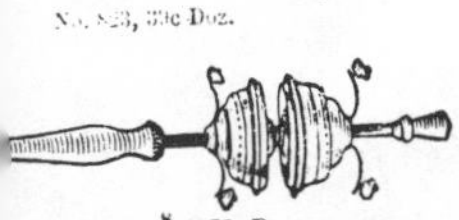
No. 824, 72c Doz.

**No. 824, Combination Assortment**—Fancy double rattles with brass bells, varnished handles, whistle ends, size about 9-inch. 1 doz. in box, assorted...... 72
Quantity price ........6 doz. or more, 69c

No. 825, 85c Doz.

**No. 825, Extra Value Dime Assortment**—Fancy combination rattles, with about a dozen bells on each with bead tongues, painted handles, whistle ends, decorated tin, size about 11½-inch. 1 doz. in box, assorted.....(In lots of 6 doz. or more, 82c) 85

## BOYS' TOY VIOLINS.

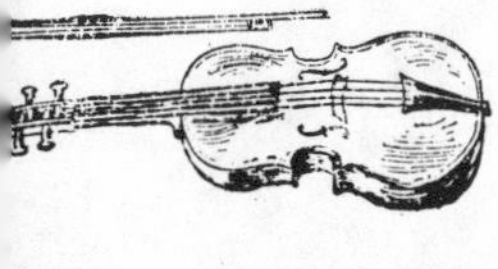

**No. 869, Toy Violin**—Fairly well made, regular shape, bridge and 4 strings, 17½ inches long. Each in box with bow. ½ doz. in pkg ........................ 2 10
Quantity price.....In lots of 4 doz. or more, $2.00

**No. 870, Toy Violin**—Better than above, raised back and front, 18 inches long, screw bow. Each in box. ½ doz. in pkg ....................................... 4 05

## ZYLONITE RATTLES.

Pretty goods and splendid sellers.

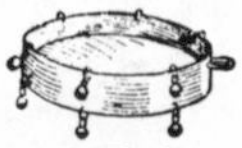
No. 986, 79c Doz.

**No. 986, Tambourine Rattle**—Assorted colors, 10 bells with bone ring on each rattle, 2⅜ inches in diameter. 1 doz. in box.................. 79
Quantity price............................In lots of 6 doz. or more, 75c

**No. 987, Ball Rattle with Bone Handle**—Whistle end and bone ring, assorted colors, 4⅝ inches long. Regular quarter goods. 1 doz. in box.... 81
Quantity price......In lots of 6 doz. or more, 77c

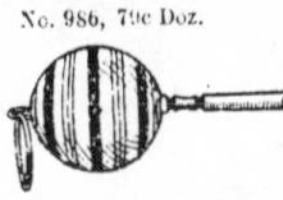
No. 987, 81c Doz.

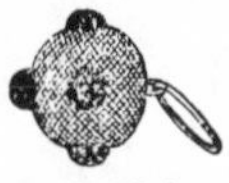
No. 988, 96c Doz.

**No. 988, Fancy Perforated Rattle**—Fine perforated ball shape with small half-ball decorations and bone ring. You can retail this at a dime as a "leader"..............(6 doz. or more, 94c) 96

## IMPORTED METALAPHONES.

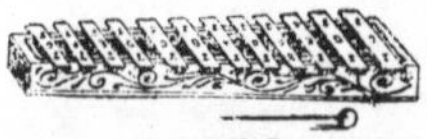
No. 814, 79c Doz.

**No. 813, 5-Cent Metalaphone**—6-key, 2 hammers, high shape. Each in box, 1 doz in pkg.......... 36
Quantity price........In lots of 6 doz. or more, 34c

**No. 814, 10-Cent Metalaphone**—As above, only very much larger. 1 doz. in pkg...... ...... 79
Quantity price ........In lots of 6 doz. or more, 76c

No. 815, $2.18 Doz.

**No. 815, Heart-Shape Metalaphone**—Extra quality, wide keys, fastened with nickeled-head nails, well made, 10-key. Each in box, ½ doz. in pkg.... 2 18

**No. 816, Heart-Shape Metalaphone**—As above, only very much larger. Each in box. ¼ doz. in pkg. 3 80

## PATENTED MUSICAL CRANK TOYS.

**No. 808, "Echo" Crank Toy**—The "Echo Revotina." Has 6 reeds and plays a tune when crank is turned, wood handle, made of very handsome bright colored tin. 1 doz. in box. .....(In lots of 6 doz. or more, 37) 39

39c Doz. 77c Doz. $1.79 Doz.

**No. 809, "Echo" Crank Toy**—As above, only larger in every way and 8 reeds. 1 doz. in box........... 77
Quantity price...........In lots of 6 doz. or more, 75c

**No. 810, "Echo" Crank Toy**—As above, still larger and 18 reeds. ½ doz. in box........................ 1 79
Quantity price........In lots of 4 doz. or more, $1.74

## CHIME TOYS.

Nos. 811 and 812.

**No. 811, "Revotina" Chime Toy**—Made of decorated tin on wheels, 4 reeds. When pulled along the floor will play. Size 3x3. ½ doz. in box...............................(In lots of 6 doz. or more, 80c) 84

**No. 812, "Revotina" Chime Toy**—As above, only larger and 8 reeds, size 4½x3½. ½ doz. in box. (In lots of 4 doz. or more, $1.80) 1 86

## WOOD TRUMPETS, FLUTES AND CLARIONETS.

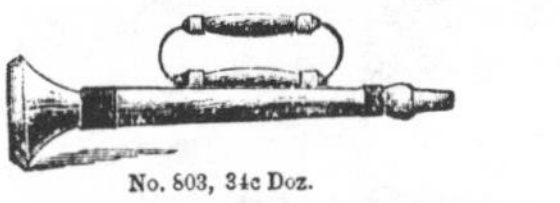
No. 803, 34c Doz.

**No. 803, Wood Trumpet**—*Extra size for a nickel.* 9 inches long, movable handle, painted in fancy colors, harmonica sound. 1 doz. in pkg. 34
Quantity price......In lots of 6 doz. or more, 32c

No. 804, 40c Doz.

**No. 804, Wood Flute**—With 6 holes and harmonica bottom, size 12-inch. Regular dime goods...... 40
Quantity price.....In lots of 6 doz. or more, 37c

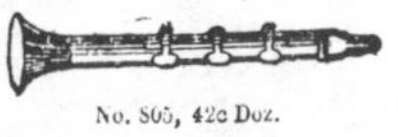
No. 805, 42c Doz.

**No. 805, Wood Clarionet**—Enameled wood, 3 keys, nickel plated, 7 inches long. 1 doz. in pkg. 42
Quantity price.....In lots of 6 doz. or more, 40c

**No. 806, Trumpet Clarionet**—Polished wood, 9½ inches long, 4 nickel keys with tuned reeds. Specially good value. 1 doz. in box ......... 79
Quantity price .....In lots of 6 doz. or more, 76c

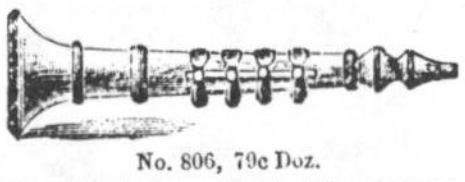
No. 806, 79c Doz.

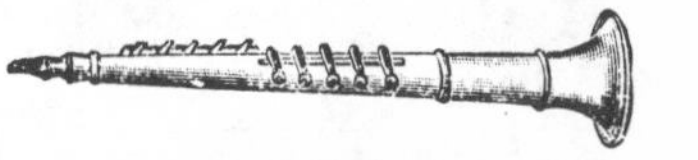
No. 807, $1.92 Doz.

**No. 807, Trumpet Clarionet**—Polished wood, 15 inches long, 10 keys. Nearly good enough for a musician. ½ doz. in box...................(In lots of 4 doz. or more, $1.87) 1 92

## TOY PIANOS—Genuine "Schoenhut."

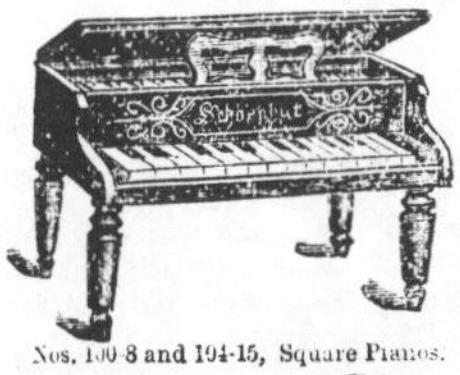
Nos. 100-8 and 104-15, Square Pianos.

**Instructive as well as entertaining.** Just the thing for children to use in taking their first drill in music. Made of wood, rightly proportioned and handsomely finished. Instruction book free with each.

Each.

**No. 114-6, 25-Cent Upright Piano**—Entirely new this season and one key larger than the one heretofore retailed at 25 cents. 6 keys. Size 7½x6½x5, varnished all over. 4 in pkg........................................ $0 16

**No. 100-8, Eight-Key Square Piano**—Size 7½x10, height 8½ inches. Mounted on 4 legs, attractively varnished all over. 2 in pkg........................ 30

**No. 114-8, Eight-Key Upright Piano**—A regular 75-cent one. Size 10x9½x7½, varnished and well made, as above........................................ 35

**No. 104-15, "Champion" Dollar Square Piano**—As above, size 10½x16½, 9 inches high, 15 keys. A very good instrument for the money.................. ....... 60

No. 113-15, Joseffy Piano.

**No. 114-15, "Hoffman" Upright Piano**—Wood frame stained and varnished in imitation rosewood. 16½ inches long, 11¾ high, 15 keys (2 octave), each properly lettered. Neat scroll design over keyboard....... 72

**No. 102-18, "Sterling" Square Piano**—Imitation rosewood, triple hinged lid opening in full, music rack, scroll design in gold and colors over keyboard, fancy turned legs, 18 keys. Size 19½x10½x9½. Each in box........................................ 1 05

**No. 114-18, Extra Size Upright Piano**—With 18 keys, well made in every particular, size 19½x12½x8½..... 1 12

**No. 113-15, "Joseffy" Upright Piano**—Stained and polished imitation rosewood frame, 13¾ inches high, 16½ long, gilded iron legs upholding keyboard, ornamental design on front. 15 keys, properly tuned..... 1 38

No. 109-22, Rubenstein Piano.

**No. 112-18, "Lambert" Concert Upright Piano**—Larger than above being 19½ inches long, and 17½ high. 18 keys, properly tuned. Imitation rosewood cover, unusually well finished. Each in box........ 2 20

**No. 109-22, "Rubenstein" Square Piano**—Richly finished imitation rosewood with raised moulding running entirely around at top and bottom. Size 24x14x11 inches. 22 keys, splendidly tuned. Carved legs and fancy design over keyboard. Each in box... ..... 3 50

**No. 112-22, "Blind Tom" Upright Piano**—One of the finest miniature pianos made. Elegant rosewood finish, size 25x24x11 inches, gilt and colored ornamentation, stationary music rack, 3 octaves, 22 keys, tuned to perfect concert pitch.......................... 4 00

# DOLL DEPARTMENT.

### A Line in Which We Are "EASILY FIRST"—Both in Extent of Sales and in Average Bigness of Value.

We offer a magnificent line—ranging from cute "penny goods" up to sumptuously gowned dolls for young aristocrats—all of best quality possible at the price and all prices figured down to hard pan.

No. 754, $7.75 Each.

## TWO FINELY DRESSED BISQUE DOLLS.

**Continued from page 107.** The following are the finest goods of the world's best doll maker. Finest bisque turning heads, full jointed bodies, natural human eyes, and all the other good points of the best dolls. Each dressed in full costume of costly material and stylish make.

Each.

**No. 754, "Annie Laurie"**—29-inch and sumptuously gowned. Pale blue moire silk and plush, skirt trimmed with band of plush edged with corded trimming, gathered to yoke of cream silk full combination plush and moire sleeves and plush bretelles. Yoke made of cream silk with clusters of three tiny tucks, trimmed with blue silk beaded feather stitching. Combination baby bonnet of blue silk trimmed with blue satin ribbon and lace ruching, large satin edge ribbon ties. Patent leather shoes, real stockings, full suit of flounce and lace trimmed muslin underwear, 3 skirts. Each.................................. $7 75

**No. 755, "Prima Donna"**—Very rich costume, after one of Worth's triumphs, charming in style and make and of costly material. Size 29-inch. Pink satin dress, skirt trimmed with two rows of fancy jet spangles and shirred to yoke of cream silk with straps of pleated pink satin over shoulder. Leg-o' mutton sleeves, elaborately jet spangled shoulder pieces, handsomely trimmed bretelles. Artistic hat to match, trimmed with cream ribbon. Patent leather shoes, real stockings, full suit of lace and flounce trimmed muslin underwear, 3 skirts. Each.......... ....... 8 25

No. 755, $8.25 Each.

---

## SOLID CHINA DOLLS.

Better finished goods and better sizes than ever before.

### "Penny" Solid China Goods.

Gross.

**No. 550, Big Penny Doll**—Unglazed, painted shoes, large size, being 2⅜-inch. ½ gross in box ....... $0 75

**No. 551, Glazed Nigger Baby**—Open arms and legs, size 1¼-inch. 1 gross in box ........ 78

**No. 552, Glazed China Doll**—Size 1½-inch. 1 gross in box......................... 79

**No. 553, Bisque Doll with Hair**—Size 2-inch with braid of hair down back. 1 gross in box....... 80

**No. 554, Glazed Doll with Gold Feet**—Size 1⅝-inch. A good penny item. 1 gross in box ....... 82

**No. 555, Bisque Doll with Jointed Arms**—Size 2⅜-inch, jointed arms. 1 gross in box........... 83

**No. 556, Dressed China Doll**—Jointed arms, worsted dress and hood. 1 doz. on card, 1 gross in box 84

No. 551. No. 552.
No. 550.
No. 553.
No. 554. No. 555. No. 556.

### Glazed Solid China Dolls.

All with gilt boots and other good points.

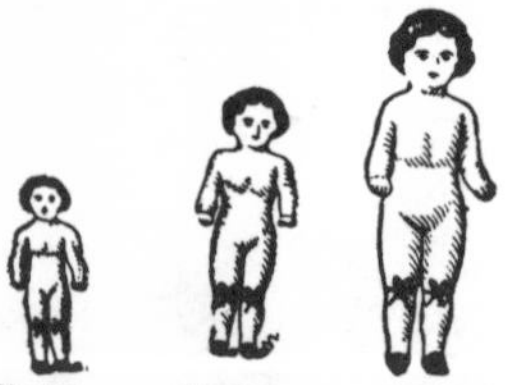

Doz.

**No. 557, Glazed China**—*Special 3-center.* Gold shoes, free arms and legs, painted features and garters, size 3-inch, good quality. 1 doz. in box...... $0 24
Quantity price.......In lots of 6 doz. or more, 23c

**No. 558, Glazed China**—As above, 4-inch. 1 doz. in box....... .......(In lots of 6 doz. or more, 37c) 39

**No. 559, Glazed China**—As above, 5¼-inch. 1 doz. in box............. (In lots of 6 doz. or more, 73c) 75

No. 557. No. 558. No. 559.

### Glazed Nigger Dolls.

**No. 560, Glazed Nigger Doll**—Free arms and legs, size 3¼-inch. 1 doz. in box..(6 doz. or more, 22c) 24

**No. 561, Glazed Nigger Doll**—As above, 4⅝-inch. A leader at 5c. 1 doz. in box....(6 doz. or more, 38c) 40

### Tam O'Shanter Dolls.

**No. 562, Tam O'Shanter Doll**—4¼-inch, white china, painted features, hair and feet, jointed arms and fancy painted Tam O'Shanter hat. 1 doz. in box.. 33
Quantity price.......In lots of 6 doz. or more, 31c

**No. 563, Tam O'Shanter Doll**—7-inch, as above. 1 doz. in box........(In lots of 6 doz. or more, 74c) 77

Nos. 560 & 561. No. 562. No. 563.

### Glazed China Dolls with Hair.

**No. 564, Glazed China Doll with Hair**—Painted features, free arms and legs, painted feet, braid of hair down back. Size 3¼-inch. 1 doz. in box. .. 42
Quantity price.......In lots of 6 doz. or more, 40c

**No. 565, Glazed China Doll with Hair**—As above, 4⅜-inch. 1 doz. in box.......(6 doz. or more, 75c) 78

### Dressed Solid China Dolls.

**No. 568, Dressed China Doll**—3-inch, jointed arms, painted shoes and stockings, summer dress, Tam O'Shanter hat. 1 doz. in box, sewed in............ 24
Quantity price........In lots of 6 doz. or more, 23c

**No. 569, Dressed China Doll**—4¼-inch, jointed arms, with hood, painted feet. ½ doz. on card, 1 doz. in box.........(In lots of 6 doz. or more, 34c) 36

**No. 570, Dressed China Doll**—*Special 5c quality.* Glazed china, gold feet, free arms and legs, colored dress, size 3½-inch. Sewed in box of 1 doz...... 37
Quantity price........In lots of 6 doz. or more, 35c

**No. 571, Dressed China Doll**—4¼-inch, as above. Sewed in box of ½ doz.......(6 doz. or more, 67c) 70

No. 568. No. 570. No. 571.

### Dolls' Memento.

**No. 1439, Doll Memento**—Small box containing knife, fork, spoon, knife rest, napkin ring, napkin, made of pewter. 10-cent goods last year and worth it now. 1 doz. in pkg. ....................... 48

No. 1439, 48c Doz.

---

## CHINA LIMB DOLLS.

**The best line in America,** embracing all the old standbys and the best of the new ones as well.

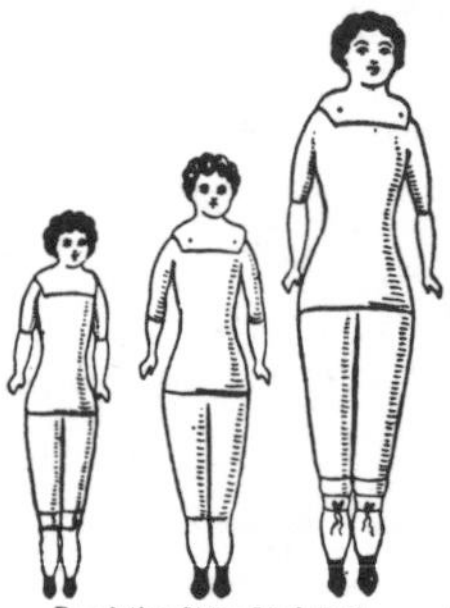

### "Regulation" China Limb Dolls.

Our "Regulation" line of China Limb Dolls have full-size heads, arms and legs, and are not to be classed with those with stingy heads and scant limbs. All bodies in this line are *well-proportioned* and are not stretched out or lengthened. Two-thirds black hair and one-third brown in each box.

**No. 575, Regulation**—7¾-inch, good body, painted eyes, face, hair and feet. Well worth 5 cents. 1 doz. in box..
Quantity price..............In lots of 6 doz. or more, 29c

**No. 576, Regulation**—9¼-inch, as above. 1 doz. in box..
Quantity price .............In lots of 6 doz. or more, 41c

**No. 577, Regulation**—10-inch, larger head than above. Good leader at 5c for "bargain day." 1 doz. in box.....
Quantity price...........In lots of 6 doz. or more, 46c

**No. 578, Regulation**—11¼-inch, as above, body well proportioned. 1 doz. in box..(In lots of 6 doz. or more, 69c)

**No. 579, Regulation**—12¼-inch, as above. 1 doz. in box.
Quantity price....In lots of 6 doz. or more, 79c

**No. 580, Regulation**—12¾-inch, head and body much larger in proportion. A 15-cent doll in size and value. 1 doz. in box.(6 doz. or more, 96c)

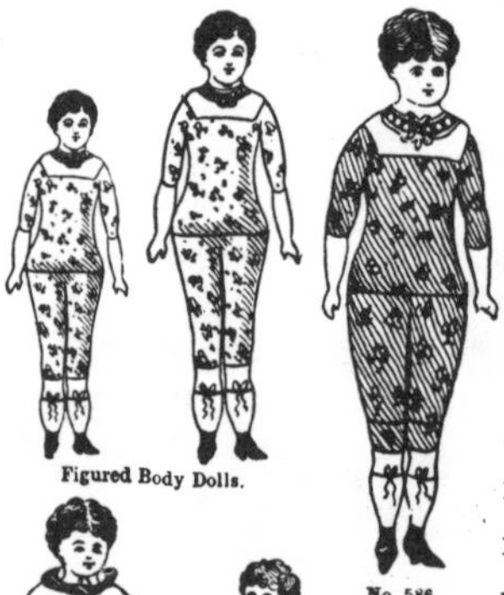

Regulation China Limb Dolls.

### "Our Own" Line China Limbs.

**Made specially for us.** The best value and the novelty of the season, as the best features of several dolls are combined in this line. Fine glazed china heads with gold collars, imitation ruching at neck, ornamented in gold with imitation gold studs. China hands and painted feet. Bodies are extra plump, well proportioned as to length, and figured in pleasing subjects for children. Assorted colored bodies in each box.

**No. 581, Figured Body**—7½-inch. 1 doz. in box.
Quantity price....In lots of 6 doz. or more, 41c

**No. 582, Figured Body**—10¼-inch. 1 doz. in box.
Quantity price....In lots of 6 doz. or more, 79c

**No. 583, Figured Body**—11-inch. 1 doz. in box.
Quantity price....In lots of 6 doz. or more, 89c

**No. 584, Figured Body**—13-inch. ½ doz. in box.
Quantity price....In lots of 4 doz. or more, $1.20

**No. 585, Figured Body**—16-inch. ¼ doz. in box.
Quantity price....In lots of 4 doz. or more, $1.75

**No. 586, Figured Body**—16½-inch. ¼ doz. in box...........(In lots of 4 doz. or more, $2.05)

**No. 587, Figured Body**—17¼-inch. ¼ doz. in box ...........(In lots of 4 doz. or more, $2.20)

**No. 588, Figured Body**—19¾-inch. ¼ doz. in box

Figured Body Dolls.
No. 586.

Turning Head China Limb Dolls.

### "Hooded" China Limb Dolls.

**Entirely new shape,** insertion front, white and tinted china heads, pretty hoods with bow tie strings in contrasting colors, gold dots in front, handsome features, china hands and feet. Very pretty goods.

**No. 590, Hooded Doll**—8¼-inch. 1 doz. in box 40
Quantity price...In lots of 6 doz. or more, 39c

**No. 591, Hooded Doll**—10⅝-inch. 1 doz. in box 81
Quantity price...In lots of 6 doz. or more, 79c

**No. 592, Hooded Doll**—13⅜-inch. ¼ doz. in box 1 30
Quantity price..In lots of 4 doz. or more, $1.25

**No. 593, Hooded Doll**—16¼-inch. ¼ doz. in box 2 15
Quantity price..In lots of 4 doz. or more, $2.10

Hooded China Limb Dolls.

*Butler Brothers (now City Products Corp.)*

# FINELY DRESSED BISQUE DOLLS—Continued.

**Each.**

**o. 743, "Empress"**—As No. 742, size 21-in. Salmon color walking costume with front footing of fur, in beautiful contrasting color and lined skirt. Zouave jacket with white reveres edged with fur, pale blue shirred front with rosette at girdle, puffed sleeves edged with fur. Large hat to match, latest Newport style, trimmed with silk cord and ostrich feathers. Patent leather slippers with fancy buckles and rosettes, stockings and full suit of underwear. Each in box. Each ...... $2 75

**No. 744, "Parisian"**—Finer than above and more elaborately dressed. 22½-inch. Crepon costume in delicate shades, beaded band on bottom of skirt, yoke of lace over satin, double puffed sleeves with lace cuffs over satin, bow and streamers of delicate shade ribbon to match satin, bead trimmed bretelles. Hat to match costume, trimmed with ostrich feathers and ribbon bows. Patent leather slippers with buckles and rosettes, stockings and lace trimmed muslin underwear. Beautiful, natural curly hair, with wavy bangs. Each in box...... ...... 2 92

No. 743, $2.75 Each.  No. 744, $2.92 Each.

- No. 745, $3.35 Each.  No. 746, $3.50 Each.

**5, "Carnival"**—As above, only different costume, 22¼-inch. Cerese or cherry r skating costume, with Zouave jacket, edged with white swan's-down, fancy pleated t and belt, large puffed sleeves. Large hat to match, with ribbon rosette. Patent her slippers with buckles and rosettes, stockings and full suit of lace-trimmed muslin erwear, with 2 skirts. Each in box.............. 3 35

No. 747, $3.75 Each.  No. 748, $3.90 Each.  No. 749, $4.25 Each.

For illustrations of Nos. 747, 748 and 749 see bottom of preceding column. **Each.**

**No. 747, "Beatrice"**—As No. 746, more costly costume, size 22-inch. Tan serge Autumn costume, imitation feather-trimmed throughout, double pointed detachable cape, so dress can be worn either without or with cape, and pink edged muff attached to silk cord. Large felt hat to match, feather and ribbon trimmed. Patent leather pointed slippers with buckles and rosettes, real stockings, and full suit of muslin underwear, with 2 skirts..... $3 75

**No. 748, "American Countess"**—Finer dress than above and finer features, wrist joint. Size 22-inch. Sherry's reception costume of satin and plush, skirt with one row feather stitching, double scalloped bertha of plush, satin edged, with pearl beads. Large puffed sleeves of silk and plush. Tasty fluted bonnet, beaded edge with large bow of satin ribbon and inner row of white lace, shirred. Patent leather slippers with buckles and rosettes, stockings, and full suit of lace and ruffle trimmed underwear, 2 skirts.......... 3 90

**No. 749, "Society Belle"**—Smaller than above, but very much finer and more costly dress. Size 20-inch. Pink and green mixed satin costume with over-dress of rich striped gauze, in same colors, with 3 rows of narrow green ribbon, pink silk stitched. Shirred yoke of shaded green and pink satin, large puffed sleeves of same material, ribbon girdle, brought to front in artistic bow, with flowing ends. Large fluted Saratoga hat of pink satin, trimmed with pink stitched narrow green ribbon and rosettes of narrow ribbon and tiny pink feathers and large pink bow on crown. Patent leather shoes, real stockings, full suit of embroidery trimmed underwear. No living belle of to-day can excel her in beauty and elegance................. 4 25

No. 750, $4.50 Each.  No. 751, $5.25 Each.

**No. 750, "Trilby"**—Worthy her name. 23½-inch, and richly gowned. Fancy blue-silk-striped white challie, full skirt, wide hem, gathered to yoke of pale blue satin, with steel beaded trimming. Blue satin bertha, cut from Worth's own pattern, edged with steel beads and deep frill of fine point lace across front. Fluted hat of challie, trimmed with picot-edge ribbon and ostrich tips, exact match to dress. Patent leather slippers, real stockings, full suit of lace-trimmed underwear, with 2 skirts .... ......................... 4 50

**No. 751, "Lily Langtry"**—Size 23-inch. Rich costume of yellow satin, full skirt gathered to yoke of plush in contrasting color, headed with a row of pleated ribbon, feather-stitched near bottom of skirt, forming deep hem. Large puffed sleeves edged with silk fancy stitching. Exquisite bertha of silk chiffon lace, which falls overfull sleeves, giving very beautiful effect. Large hat of satin to match dress, daintily trimmed with bows of satin and feathers. Patent leather shoes and real stockings, full suit of muslin underwear, lace and ruffled trimmed, with 2 skirts..,................................... 5 25

No. 752, $5.50 Each.  No. 753, $6.55 Each.

**No. 752, "Sweet Alice"**—Size 27-inch, costly and stylish dress. Lavender costume, skirt gathered to yoke of cream satin, laid in clusters of tiny tucks, with insertion of narrow lavender ribbon, large puffed sleeves, cuffs trimmed with two rows of narrow lace, double bertha of white lace and satin. Large poke hat, satin crown, trimmed with large fancy edge satin bow; entire brim of lace, shirred to wire frame, trimmed with very full ribbon rosettes. Patent leather shoes, black stockings, full suit of muslin underwear, lace and ruffle trimmed, with 3 skirts............................... 5 50

*Butler Brothers (now City Products Corp.)*

## MISCELLANEOUS DOLLS.

No. 598. No. 718 (Double Head), $2.05 Doz. Three Styles No. 719, Fritz Brownie Dolls, $4.20 Doz.

Doz.

**No. 598, Special 5c Patent Doll**—Painted eyes, features and hair, papier mache hands and feet, cheesecloth slip. Size 9½-inch 1 doz. in box.... (In lots of 6 doz. or more, 39c) $0 40

**No. 718, Double Head Dolls**—Natural glass eyes, 2 styles of dress, one darkey head and the other a bisque head with pretty baby face and lace cap. Appropriate dresses. Full length, including dress, 14-inch. 1 doz. in box...... In lots of 4 doz. or more, $2.00 2 05

Three Styles No. 720, Wild West Dolls, $8.35 Doz.

**No. 719, Assorted "Fritz" Brownie Dolls**—Cotton stuffed, Jersey faces, painted soft bodies, very stout, 3 characters, Uncle Sam, Dutchman and policeman, all with hats. Size 11½-inch. The funniest dolls in the trade. ⅓ doz. in box.............. 4 20

**No. 720, Assorted "Wild West" Dolls**—Comprising Indian, squaw and Mexican cowboy, all dressed in appropriate costumes, size 13¾-inch. All with bisque heads, natural eyes, open mouth exposing teeth, characteristic hair. French jointed bodies with hip, knee, elbow, arm and wrist joints, and turning heads. Each in box, ¼ doz. in pkg. These are very fine and attractive goods.. 8 35

## "EXHIBITION" BABY DOLLS.

**Magnetic show window attractions.** Very lifelike in modeling, tint and features. They are the best "show window" dolls we can import. The quality is splendid. Each in strong box.

*No other "show window dolls" are as good.*

Each.

**No. 618, 20-Inch**—Patent washable material, cotton stuffed, modeled in the exact proportions of a live baby, perfect features, fine hair, lace baby cap tied under chin with silk ribbons, large natural expression eyes, painted teeth, sitting body, being jointed at hip, natural modeled limbs, flesh tinted throughout, length 20 inches. Dressed in extra good slip with knife pleating on the bottom, edged with lace, lace yoke ruffled and trimmed with satin ribbon. Each in strong paper box.......................................... $0 69

**No. 619, 22½-Inch**—Same fine quality as above, 22½ inches long. Each in strong paper box.......................... 1 25

**No. 620, 25½-Inch**—As above, 25½-inch and larger in proportion. Each in wood box........................ .... 1 92

**No. 376, 27-Inch**—As above, naturally proportioned in every way. Each in wood box.................................. 2 40

**No. 375, 31-Inch**—Just the size for show window use. Put one in a cradle and display it in your window and you'll make a sensation Each in wood box................................ 3 45

## FRENCH-JOINTED BISQUE DOLLS.

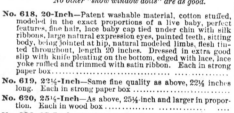

No. 663. No. 664. No. 665.

No. 666, $1.15 Doz. No. 667, $1.72 Doz.

Each with bisque head and patent jointed body.

Doz.

**No. 663, Jointed Bisque Doll**—6-inch, hip and shoulder joints, Rembrandt hair, glass eyes, bisque turning head, cotton slip night dress. 1 doz. in box. Quantity price.........In lots of 6 doz. or more, 37c $0 39

**No. 664, Jointed Bisque Doll**—*Big 10-center.* As above, 9¼-inch, open mouth, showing teeth 1 doz. in box................(In lots of 6 doz. or more, 75c) 77

**No. 665, Jointed Bisque Doll**—Finer features than above, natural eyes, better slip, painted shoes and stockings, 7¾-inch, stout body with turning head, open mouth showing teeth, Rembrandt hair. 1 doz. in box.. ..........(In lots of 6 doz. or more, 85c) 88

**No. 666, Jointed Bisque Doll**—As above, 9¾-inch. 1 doz. in box..............(In lots of 6 doz. or more, $1.10) 1 15

**No. 667, Jointed Bisque Doll**—Same as No. 664, only 12-inch and with hip, knee, shoulder and elbow joints. 1 doz. in box........................... Quantity price........In lots of 4 doz. or more, $1.69 1 72

**No. 668, Jointed Bisque Doll**—14½-inch, as above. Special value for 25 cents. ½ doz. in box... .. .... Quantity price........In lots of 4 doz. or more, $1.87 1 92

**No. 669, Jointed Bisque Doll**—As above, 15¾-inch, wrist joints, nice slip with lace lapel front tied with ribbon, full jointed in every way. ⅓ doz. in box .... 3 65

Two Styles No. 727, $2.25 Doz.

**No. 726, Large 25-Cent Assortment**—11-inch, as above, soft limbs, real shoes and stockings, 6 fancy dresses with assorted hats, caps and bonnets. Regular 35-cent goods. ½ doz. in flat box, sewed in.........(In lots of 4 doz. or more, $2.08) 2 15

**No. 727, Novelty Assortment**—*Best 25c novelty goods of '96*, 8¼-inch, bisque turning heads, natural eyes, open mouths showing teeth, jointed bodies. Each box of ½ doz. contains 1 Indian, 2 squaws and 3 Chinese women, all in characteristic national costumes, ½ doz. in flat box...... 2 25

## FRENCH-JOINTED BISQUE SLEEPING DOLLS.

**The best goods of the world's best doll maker.** It is not possible to make better grade of goods than these.

No. 672, $4.10 Doz.

No. 673, $6.33 Doz.

No. 674, $8.25 Doz.

No. 675, $11.40

No. 678, $40.00 Doz.

Doz.

**No. 672, 11¼-Inch**—Fine bisque head, delicately chiseled features, natural moving eyes, curly hair, open mouth, nice even teeth, sewed mohair wig, arms jointed at shoulder, elbow and wrist, legs jointed at hip and knee, open fingers, real shoes and stockings. Each doll dressed in tastefully designed night-robe, with fancy open work at neck tied with bow of ribbon and lace collar. Each in box.....$ 4 10

**No. 673, 14½-Inch**—As above. Each in box 6 33

**No. 674, 16-Inch**—As above. Each in box.. 8 25

**No. 675, 19-Inch**—As above. Each in box.. 11 40

**No. 676, 21¼-Inch**—As above. Each in box 19 75

**No. 677, 25½-Inch**—As above. Each in box 28 00

**No. 678, 28½-Inch**—As above. Each in box 40 00

No. 677, $28.00 Doz.

No. 721, 78c Doz. Two Styles No. 722, $1.60 Doz.

Two Styles No. 723, $1.65 Doz. No. 724, $1.98 Doz.

## DRESSED FRENCH-JOINT BISQUE DOLLS.

Each doll dressed in fancy costume and jo These are all new, fresh goods and the best the has produced.

**No. 721, 10-Cent Assortment**—Bisque turning heads, flowing hair, natural eyes, open mouths showing teeth, painted shoes and stockings, underwear, fancy hats and lace trimmed dresses, shoulder and hip joints, size 7-inch. ⅓ doz. assorted in flat box.... Quantity price, in lots of 6 doz. or more, 75c

**No. 722, 25-Cent Assortment**—Pretty goods, 8¼-inch, as above, real shoes and stockings and assorted dresses in colors, flowing hair. Each in box, ½ doz. in pkg. sewed in..... Quantity price, lots of 4 doz. or more, $1.55

**No. 723, Boy and Girl Assortment**—Lads and lassies in assorted fancy costumes, real shoes and stockings, fancy caps to match, size 7½-inch, otherwise as above. ½ doz. in box, sewed in.....(4 doz. or more, $1.60)

**No. 724, Baby Assortment**—As above, baby bonnets and long dresses, fancy baby caps, ribbon trimmed, full size 11-inch. ½ doz. in box. .. (In lots of 4 doz. or more, $1.92

Two Styles No. 725. $2.05 Doz.

Two Styles No. 726, $2.15 Doz.

**No. 725, Dressed Bisque Dolls**—2 styles of dress in 6 colors, fancy calico and ribbed trimmed, all with bonnets, large size, being 9½-inch, otherwise as above. Customers to get a full assortment should order several dozen. ½ doz. in box, sewed in and 2 boxes in each pkg .......... ..... Quantity price ...In lots of 4 doz. or more, $2.00

# TOY SAD IRONS.

A line that can't be matched in America at the prices. — Doz.

**No. 5, Toy Sad and Stand**—*Best 5-center we ever offered.* 3 inches long, solid iron, double pointed, polished sides and bottom. 1 doz. in box with stands....(In lots of 6 doz. or more, 39c) $0 41

$2.00 Doz.

**No. 10, Toy Sad and Stand**—3⅝ inches long, double ender, nickeled sides and bottom, gilt on top and handles. ½ doz. in box with stands....(6 doz. lots or more, 72c) 76

**No. 200, Toy Sad and Stand**—Detachable handle, 4⅜ inches long, nickeled sides and bottom, gilt top, double pointed. Extra large and extra good 25-cent toy. Each in box with stand....(In lots of 4 doz. or more, $1.90) 2 00

### Potts' Pattern Sad Irons.

**No. 1, Potts' Pattern Sad Iron**—Exact model of the regular full size Potts' iron, nickel plated sides and bottom, walnut handle, each with stand, size 2½-inch. Good as many 10-centers. 1 doz. in box..(6 doz. or more, 46c) 48

**No. 2, Potts' Pattern Sad Iron**—Same as No. 1 above, only 3¾ inches long. Too good for 10 cents except as a "leader." ½ doz. in box.... 92
Quantity price....In lots of 6 doz. or more, 90c

**No. 25, Miniature Potts' Sad Iron**—*Neatest of 25-cent toys.* 3⅝ inches long, detachable black walnut handle, nickel plated sides and bottom. Used by ladies for doing fine laces. Each in box with stand.... 1 70
Quantity price....In lots of 4 doz. or more, $1.60

# PEWTER TOYS.

We have the best goods made in this quick-selling line.

### Sundry Pewter Toys.

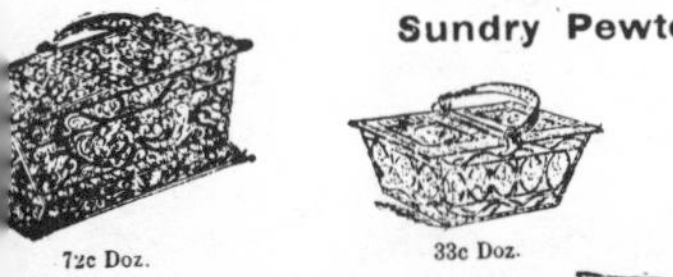

72c Doz. 33c Doz.

Doz.

**Openwork Handled Basket**—Very bright pretty goods with covers. Size 3¼x2. 1 doz. in box.... $0 33
Quantity price..6 doz. or more, 31c

**Openwork Handled Basket**—As above only larger, being 4x2 with foot and decorated. 1 doz. in box.. 72
Quantity price..6 doz. or more, 69c

4-Piece Parlor Suite, $1.80 Doz. Sets.

**4-Piece Parlor Suite**—Comprising arm sofa with back, 2 arm chairs and rocking chair. Size of chairs about 2x2, height 3½, sofa 4x2, height 3½. Each set in box. Very handsome ware. Regular 50-cent goods....(4 doz. or more, $1.75) 1 80

### Pewter Casters.

79c Doz. $1.92 Doz.

**Two-Bottle Caster**—Pewter frame, regular finish, 2 glass bottles, height about 4⅝ inches. A great toy. Each in box....(In lots of 6 doz. or more, 75c) 79

**Four-Bottle Caster**—Round shape, height about 7¼ inches. Each in box....(In lots of 4 doz. or more, $1.87) 1 92

### Pewter Tea Sets.

a Set, $1.95 Doz. Sets. 50c Tea Set, $3.90 Doz. Sets.

ent Tea Set—Made of good metal, 23 pieces packed in spaced box, size 7x5. 1 doz. ts in package. Per doz. sets....(In lots of 6 doz. or more, 72c) 75

ent Tea Set—As above only much larger, 24 good size pieces nicely packed in spaced x, size 10x8¼. Per doz. sets....(In lots of 4 doz. or more, $1.88) 1 95

ent Tea Set—24 good size pieces, fancifully ornamented, all packed in spaced box, ze 13¼x8¾. A very showy set and special value.... 3 90

r Tea Set—Comprising 24 very large pieces, all pieces except spoons being ornaented with landscapes. Nicely packed in strong spaced box, size 16½x10¾.... 7 20

ar Leader" Tea Set—Really $1.25 goods. Much larger pieces than above, handmely ornamented and packed in strong spaced box, size 16¼x12½.... 8 75

# DRUM ASSORTMENTS.

The best Drums made and the latest styles, put up in assortments so small that any merchant e safely. Not only can we name lower prices when selling in original cases, but goods carry better than when repacked.

### Our $7.07 "Metal" Assortment.

All of the following, with the exception of the 7-inch, have whistle stick and Nicely packed in case. No charge for case. Total, 1½ doz.

| | Doz. | Total. |
|---|---|---|
| ½ doz. **7-Inch Plain Brass Drums**—Good hoop, with cord and ears.... | $2 10 | $1 05 |
| ½ " **9-Inch Plain Brass Drums**—As above.... | 4 20 | 2 10 |
| ¼ " **11-Inch Fancy Brass Drums**—Red and blue metal shell, embossed stars, fancy cord and metal hoops.... | 6 90 | 1 73 |
| ¼ " **13-Inch Fancy Brass Drums**—Brass lithographed shell, fancy cord and metal ears.. | 8 75 | 2 19 |

**Price per Case, $7.07.**

### Our $5.35 "Combination" Assortment.

Natural wood shells, high shape, fancy cords, metal hooks, whistle stick to each pair. One-half lithographed, the balance embossed in handsome designs. Three big drums for the money, to retail at 50c, 75c and $1.00. 1 doz. nicely packed in case, no charge for case.

| | | |
|---|---|---|
| ½ doz. **8-Inch Drums**.... | 3 75 | 1 88 |
| ⅓ " **10-Inch Drums**.... | 6 25 | 2 08 |
| 1-6 " **13-Inch Drums**.... | 8 35 | 1 39 |

**Price per Case, $5.35.**

# TOY MONEY BANKS.

### We Have Picked the "CREAM SELLERS" and Offer them at Right Prices.

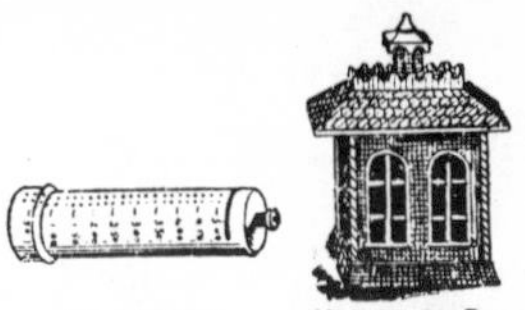

No. 3, 55c Doz. No. 2000, 35c Doz.

Jewel Bank. White Metal Combination Bank.

Doz.

**No. 3, Gem Pocket Savings Bank**—For dimes only, of which it holds $5.00. Nickel plated, opened by screw at top. 1 doz. in box.... $0 55

**No. 2000, 5-Cent Bank**—Bronzed iron, nicely decorated, size 2x1⅝, 3 inches high. 1 doz. in box.... 38
Quantity price....In lots of 6 doz. or more, 35c

**No. 2250, 10-Cent Bank**—As above, size 2⅝x2, 4⅛ high. ½ doz. in box....(6 doz. or more 66c) 69

**"Jewel" White Metal Bank**—Nickel plated corners, bronze window trimmings, fine nickel plated dome, height 4¼ inches, width 3¾, lock and key. ½ doz. in box....(In lots of 6 doz. or more 82c) 85

**No. 2650, 25-Cent Bank**—Same as No. 2250 above, size 4x2⅞, 5¾ high. ½ doz. in box.... 1 98
Quantity price....(In lots of 6 doz. or more, $1.90)

**White Metal Combination Bank**—Best 25-cent bank of '95. 4¼ inches high by 2¾ square, all nickel plated edges and all raised ornaments on nickel plate. ½ doz. in box.(4 doz. or more, $1.95) 2 00

**White Metal Combination Bank**—As above, 5 inches high by 3¾ square. ½ doz. in box.... 3 15

**White Metal Combination Bank**—As above, 5½ inches high by 4¼ square. A big 50-cent bank and a good one. ½ doz. in box.... 4 00

# IMPORTED SHELL BOXES.

The best English goods and large sizes for the money. We do not handle the inferior shell boxes. They cost but little less and are risky stuff to touch.

No. 1036, 35c Doz. No. 1037, 38c Doz. No. 1038, 75c Doz. No. 1039, 77c Doz.

Doz.

**No. 1036, Round Shell Box**—Made of wicker with row of shells on each end and with cord handle, open end, size 3¾-inch. 1 doz. in box....(In lots of 6 doz. or more, 33c) $0 35

No. 1041, $3.60 Doz. No. 1040, $1.89 Doz.

**No. 1037, Assorted Shell Boxes**—3 styles, sizes 3x4, 4x6 and 3½x3½. Larger and better than any former 5-cent goods. 2 doz. in box....(In lots of 6 doz. or more, 36c) 38

**No. 1038, Silk Cushion Shell Boxes**—In assorted shapes and colors. Extra well made. 1 doz. assorted in box.... 75
Quantity price....In lots of 6 doz. or more, 72c

**No. 1039, Assorted Shell Boxes**—Nice 10c goods. Size 4¼x4½ hinged covers trimmed with handsome shells. 1 doz. in box, 3 specially good styles....(In lots of 6 doz. or more, 74c) 77

**No. 1040, Assorted Shell Boxes**—6 new styles in each lot, all covered with fine pearl shells. Trunk, book case, ottoman, basket, slipper, etc. Very nicely packed. 1 doz. in box....(4 doz. or more, $1.85) 1 89

**No. 1041, Assorted Shell Boxes**—6 styles, all covered with fancy pearl shells. Thoroughly nice goods and large 50c size. ½ doz. in box.... 3 60

# COMMON AND FANCY MARBLES.

### Buy at These Prices and Capture the Trade of Your Town.

| | | |
|---|---|---|
| **Common Gray Marbles**—American. Put up 1,000 in a bag. Sold only by thousand. | Per M | $0 37 |
| **Common Painted Marbles**—American. Assorted fancy colors. Put up as above... | Per M | 45 |
| **No. 0, Painted China Alleys**—Beautiful goods. Put up 500 in a box.... | Per M | 38 |
| **No. 1, Painted China Alleys**—.... | Per 100 | 07 |
| **No. 2, Painted China Alleys**—Medium large size.... | Per 100 | 10 |
| **No. 4, Painted China Alleys**—Large size.... | Per 100 | 20 |
| **No. 0, Glazed China Marbles**—.... | Per 100 | 10 |
| **No. 1, Glazed China Marbles**—.... | Per 100 | 14 |
| **No. 2, Glazed China Marbles**—.... | Per 100 | 18 |
| **No. 4, Glazed China Marbles**—.... | Per 100 | 37 |
| **No. 1, Bull's Eye Glazed Chinas**—100 in box.... | Per 100 | 15 |
| **No. 2, Bull's Eye Glazed Chinas**—.... | Per 100 | 22 |
| **No. 0, Imitation Agates**—Assorted in box.... | Per 100 | 07 |
| **No. 1, Imitation Agates**— " " .... | Per 100 | 11 |
| **No. 2, Imitation Agates**— " " .... | Per 100 | 16 |
| **No. 1, Patent Agates**—Assorted in box of 100.... | Per 100 | 15 |
| **No. 2, Patent Agates**—.... | Per 100 | 20 |
| **No. 3, Patent Agates**—.... | Per 100 | 28 |
| **No. 1, Glass Tigers**—Assorted in box of 100.... | Per 100 | 25 |
| **No. 2, Glass Tigers**—.... | Per 100 | 39 |
| **No. 3, Glass Tigers**—.... | Per 100 | 47 |
| **No. 0, Glass Brandies**—4 colors in each box.... | Per 100 | 23 |
| **No. 1, Glass Brandies**—4 " " " .... | Per 100 | 28 |
| **No. 2, Glass Brandies**—4 " " " .... | Per 100 | 37 |
| **No. 0, Fine Glass Marbles**—Extra quality. 100 in box.... | Per 100 | 18 |
| **No. 1, Fine Glass Marbles**—.... | Per 100 | 22 |
| **No. 2, Fine Glass Marbles**—Medium large size.... | Per 100 | 29 |
| **No. 4, Fine Glass Marbles**—Large size.... | Per 100 | 46 |
| **No. 6, Fine Glass Marbles**—24 in box.... | Per box | 33 |
| **No. 8, Spangles**—Large size, solid glass, spangled; beautiful ornaments or playthings; retail like hot cakes at 5 cents. 1 doz. in wood box... | Per doz. | 25 |
| **No. 10, Extra Large Spangles**—As above, but big as a hen's egg. 1 doz. in box.... | Per doz. | 60 |

Spangle.

### Fancy Colored Glass Marbles.

Silver birds, animals, etc.

| | | |
|---|---|---|
| **No. 5, Fancy Colored Glass Marbles**—.... | Per doz. | 27 |
| **No. 7 Fancy Colored Glass Marbles**—.... | Per doz. | 39 |
| **No. 9, Fancy Colored Glass Marbles**—.... | Per doz. | 62 |
| **Nos. 14 to 18, Assorted**—Selected goods, 25 in a box.... | Per box | 79 |
| **Nos. 18 to 21, Assorted**— " " 25 " .... | Per box | 1 15 |

### Marbles in Draw String Bags.

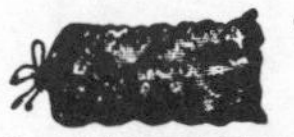

Doz.

**Our 5-Cent Bag**—Bag is made of strong calico with a "draw-string." Contains the following: 1 large spangled knocker, 5 painted china alleys, 2 glass marbles (fancy), 7 polished painted marbles, 10 "common marbles." *Boys buy it quick*.... $0 35

**Our 10-Cent Bag**—Containing a fine assortment of all glass "alleys" as follows: 3 extra large No. 4 glass marbles, 3 large No. 2 glass marbles, 10 medium No. 0 glass marbles. 65

95 Butler Brothers (now City Products Corp.)

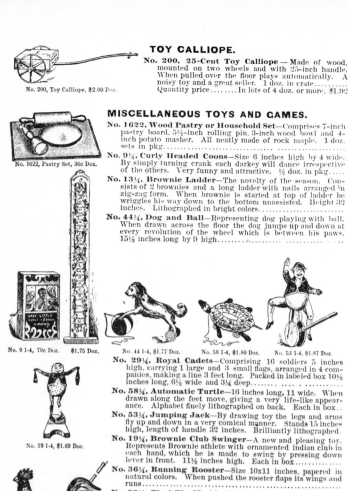

## TOY CALLIOPE.

No. 200, 25-Cent Toy Calliope—Made of wood, mounted on two wheels and with 25-inch handle. When pulled over the floor plays automatically. A noisy toy and a great seller. 1 doz. in crate............ Doz. $2 00
Quantity price........In lots of 4 doz. or more. $1.92

No. 200, Toy Calliope, $2.00 Doz.

## MISCELLANEOUS TOYS AND GAMES.

No. 1622, Wood Pastry or Household Set—Comprises 7-inch pastry board, 5½-inch rolling pin, 3-inch wood bowl and 4-inch potato masher. All neatly made of rock maple. 1 doz. sets in pkg.............................. 36

No. 1622, Pastry Set, 36c Doz.

No. 9¼, Curly Headed Coons—Size 6 inches high by 4 wide. By simply turning crank each darkey will dance irrespective of the others. Very funny and attractive. ½ doz. in pkg...... 79

No. 13¼, Brownie Ladder—The novelty of the season. Consists of 2 brownies and a long ladder with nails arranged in zig-zag form. When brownie is started at top of ladder he wriggles his way down to the bottom unassisted. Height 32 inches. Lithographed in bright colors. 1 75

No. 44¼, Dog and Ball—Representing dog playing with ball. When drawn across the floor the dog jumps up and down at every revolution of the wheel which is between his paws. 15½ inches long by 9 high.......................... 1 77

No. 9 1-4, 79c Doz.    $1.75 Doz.    No. 44 1-4, $1.77 Doz.    No. 58 1-4, $1.80 Doz.    No. 53 1-4, $1.87 Doz.

No. 29¼, Royal Cadets—Comprising 16 soldiers 5 inches high, carrying 1 large and 3 small flags, arranged in 4 companies, making a line 3 feet long. Packed in labeled box 10½ inches long, 6½ wide and 3¾ deep................... 1 80

No. 58¼, Automatic Turtle—16 inches long, 11 wide. When drawn along the feet move, giving a very life-like appearance. Alphabet finely lithographed on back. Each in box.. 1 80

No. 53¼, Jumping Jack—By drawing toy the legs and arms fly up and down in a very comical manner. Stands 15 inches high, length of handle 32 inches. Brilliantly lithographed. 1 87

No. 19 1-4, $1.89 Doz.

No. 19¼, Brownie Club Swinger—A new and pleasing toy. Represents Brownie athlete with ornamented indian club in each hand, which he is made to swing by pressing down lever in front. 11½ inches high. Each in box............ 1 89

No. 36¼, Running Rooster—Size 10x11 inches, papered in natural colors. When pushed the rooster flaps its wings and runs.................................................. 1 90

No. 39½, Tip-i-Tip Marble Game—Very interesting game. The marbles are put in at top and pass automatically from one cup to the other until they roll on the board and are counted. Size when set up 16 inches long by 17 high, lithographed in attractive colors............................. 3 95

No. 36 1-4, $1.90 Doz.

No. 58, Tom Stout Marble Game—Very amusing and entertaining. The marbles are dropped into hat of top man, come out of his mouth, roll over star and cause it to revolve, then into hat of next man and so on down. After passing the last man they strike a bell, roll on the board and are counted. Size when set up 18½x8¾, 21 high....................... 8 25

No. 39 1-2, $3.95 Doz.    No. 58, $8.25 Doz.     No. 97, $8.25 Doz.

No. 97, Puss-in-Boots Target—Represents puss dressed in fantastic suite with boots, and set in base. When a ball is rolled against the bull's eye it releases a spring and causes puss quickly to place another face in front of her own. 32 inches high. Handsomely lithographed, each in box............................................. 8 25

No. 15, Brownie Ten Pins—Latest novelty in Brownie goods. Comprises 10 turned figures of different shapes 6 to 7½ inches high, all painted in bright colors and making a very laughable group. Securely packed in handsome box, containing two rubber balls. Size of box 12x15, 3 inches deep................................ 8 25

No. 55, Sunbeam Alphabet Tower—52 inches high, handsomely lithographed in colors, pictures, A B C's and spelling lessons. Tower is surmounted by Japanese lady holding wheel which revolves when crank is turned. At base is an opening showing comical picture which, by use of a ball with rubber attached, can be knocked away, when another one instantly appears. 8 30

No. 15, $8.25 Doz.

No. 87, Woodbine Farm—Standard and popular toy. Comprises model barn. 30 animals and people, cupola and substantial fence consisting of 14 sections each 4 inches long, making largest and most complete toy farm made. All lithographed in appropriate colors and showing a farm scene during the busy season. Size set up 19¾ inches long, 9½ high, 15½ to top of cupola....... 8 35

No. 87, $8.35 Doz.    No. 55, $8.30 Doz.

## SHOO FLY ROCKING HORSES.

No. 29, $6.45 Doz.    No. 50, $8.90 Doz.

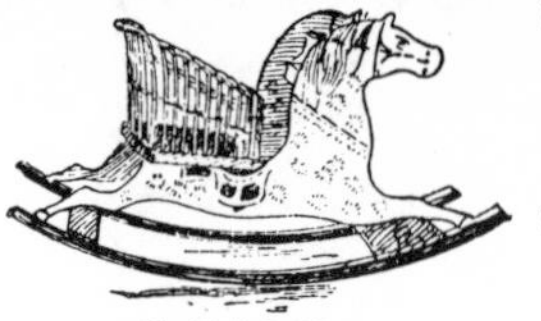

No. 10, Rocking Horse: 40 inches long, 12 wide, painted and dappled, painted seat and mane,hair tail. ½ doz. in crate....

No. 20, Upholstered Rocking Horse: As above with seat and back upholstered in cretonne.

No. 50, Upholstered Rocking Horse: 12 inches wide and 44 long, wood seat, plush-covered, willow back, hardwood bent rockers, reins and box in front. ½ doz. in crate, finished in white and dappled, 3 in light brown.

## IMPROVED CRADLES.

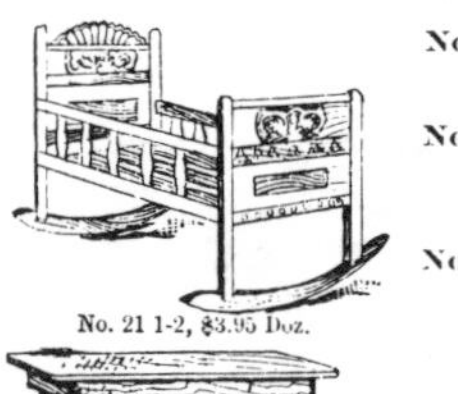

No. 47¼, Improved Cradle—New design. 16 inches long, 7¼ wide, 10 high. High rounded headboard, fancy sides and posts.

No. 21¼, Improved Cradle—Finely lithographed in rich patterns. High rounded serpentine headboard, artistic sides, fluted rails and posts. Size 9¼x19, 13 inches high. First-class in every particular.

No. 21 1-2, $3.95 Doz.

No. 42, Improved Cradle—Handsomely lithographed to represent a high-grade of carving and spindle work. Size 12x23½, 17½ inches high. Has high rounded headboard with serpentine finish, fancy sawed sides, fluted rails and posts. Strongly made and well finished.

## HARDWOOD TABLES.

No. 41¼, Hardwood Table—The largest and best 25-cent table ever made. Lock-corner frame, highly finished, new design carved legs. Size 18 inches long, 12 wide and 13½ high....

No. 41½, Hardwood Table—Similar to above, round corners, top ½-inch thick. Size 24 inches long, 14 wide, 18 high. Large enough for a child to set at. Strong and durable.......

No. 4. 1-2, $3.65 Doz.

## NINE AND TEN PINS.

Best value we have ever been able to offer in this staple line.

10-Cent Set of Nine Pins—6-inch size, each set in box with 2 balls....
Quantity price. .......... ...... ..... In lots of 6 doz. or more, 75c

25-Cent Set of Ten Pins—Striped and polished, size 7-inch. Each set in box with 3 balls....
Quantity price....... ..........In lots of 4 doz. or more, $1.60

25-Cent Leader Set of Ten Pins—As above, only 8-inch.
Quantity price........ .........In lots of 4 doz. or more, $2.12

35-Cent Set of Ten Pins—As above, only 9-inch....

50-Cent Set of Ten Pins—As above, only 10-inch....

50-Cent Bargain Set of Ten Pins—As above, only 11-inch....

75-Cent Set of Ten Pins—As above, only 14-inch....

Dollar Set of Ten Pins—As above, only 16-inch.....

## BOYS' TOOL CHESTS.

*The best items in America to retail at 25c, 50c and a dollar.*

No. 45A, 25-Cent Tool Chest—Wood box, size 9½x4x2¼, with cover and lock, well finished. Contains about 9 tools.
Quantity price....4 doz. or more, $1.75

No. 60A, 50-Cent Tool Chest—As above, only much larger and with till. Size of box 11x5x3¼ inches. Contains about 10 tools....

No. 700A, Dollar Tool Chest—With tray. Size about 7x15. Heavy black mouldings and bronze handles. Contains about 22 tools....

## CHILDREN'S TOY "RED CHAIRS."

**Best Made and Best Finished Goods in the Market.**

### Bow-Back Red Chairs.

No. 101, Doll's Chair: Seat 5½x5½, height of back 12 inches. Beats all other 10-cent chairs. 2 doz. in crate.

No. 1120, Bow-Back Chair: Three-spindle back, seat 9½x9½, height of back 19 inches. ½ doz. in crate....

No. 1080, $2.90 Doz.

No. 1080, Bow-Back Chair: Seat 11x11, height of back 21 inches. ½ doz. in crate.

No. 900, Kindergarten Chair: Seat 12x12, height of back 26 inches. ½ doz. in crate....

### Square-Top Toy Rockers.

No. 630, Square-Top Rocker: Seat 9x9, height 18½ inches. ½ doz. in crate....

No. 680, Square-Top Rocker: As above, 3 spindles, seat 11x11, height 21 inches. ½ doz. in crate......

### Bow-Back Toy Rockers.

No. 1130, Bow-Back Rocker: 3-spindle back, seat 9½x9½, height of back 19 inches. ½ doz. in crate....

No. 1090, Bow-Back Rocker: Seat 11x11, height of back 21 inches. ½ doz. in crate....

No. 1070, Bow-Back Arm Rocker: Seat 12½x12½, height of back 24 inches, arm above seat 6 inches. ½ doz. in crate.

No. 1090, $3.40 Doz.    No. 1070, $4.20 Doz.

## OUR $5.60 ASSORTMENT OF TOY TRUNKS.

Small quantities of the three popular styles, packed in good case.

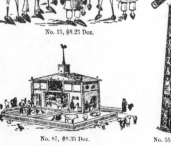

Doz.

½ doz. Children's—12-inch, round top, paper covered, set-up top, leather handles with brass holders, brass hinges, lock and key. Lock is Yale pattern with flat key..... $4 10

⅓ doz. Misses' Saratoga—14-inch, barrel-stave top, 2-compartment set-up tray, 3-slat top, slatted sides and bottom, full brass trimmed, including corners, leather handles, lock and catch.... 6 55

1-6 doz. Misses' Saratoga, Large—16-inch, set-up tray with covered bonnet box, trimmed with brass head nails, fancy slat-end strengthening bands, lock and key and two spring snap fastenings.... 8 25

Total 1 doz.    Price for Complete Assortment, $5 60

*Butler Brothers (now City Products Corp.)*

# TOY WAGONS AND WHEELBARROWS.

**A Line That Cannot Be Matched In America.**

All these goods are sold by crate only. No charge for crate.

## Boys' Wheelbarrows.

No. 1, $2.25 Doz.

No. 3, $3.75 Doz.

Doz.

**1, Boys' Wheelbarrow:** *Did you ever before see a 30-inch barrow to retail at 25 cents?* pecial bargain. Length over all 30 inches, 6-inch wood wheel, well put together and eatly finished. ½ doz. in crate .......... $2 25

**, Boys' Wheelbarrow:** Full length 24 inches, 6-inch spoke wheels with tin tires, varished and stenciled. ½ doz. in crate .......... 2 20

**, Boys' Wheelbarrow:** Same as above only 35 inches long, 8-inch spoke wheels and on tires. ½ doz. in crate .......... 3 75

**, Boys' Wheelbarrow:** As above, full length 40 inches, 11-inch wheels, thoroughly raced throughout. ½ doz. in crate .......... 4 75

## Boys' Wood Body Wagon.

Dollar Express Wagon, $6.90 Doz.

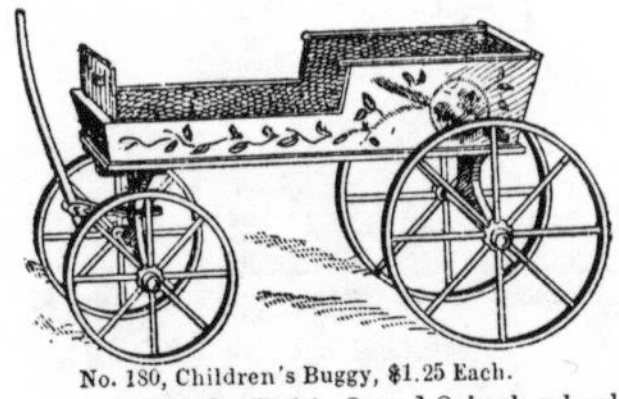

No. 180, Children's Buggy, $1.25 Each.

**ny" Express Wagon:** *Dandy quarter seller.* Size of body 7x14, 6 and 8-inch wheels with tin tires. Body painted red. Front wheels turn under body. 1 doz. in crate .......... 2 25

**s' Half-Dollar Express:** Full maple finish. Edges trimmed in red. Size of box 8x16. olid tail-board; 6-inch front and 8-inch hind wheels; metal tires. Front wheels turn under ox. ½ doz. in crate .......... 3 10

**s' 75-Cent Express:** 8-inch front and 12-inch hind wheels, metal tires. Size of box 0x20, tail-board and fastening pins. Front wheels turn under box. Edge of box ainted red. Maple finish throughout. ½ doz. in crate .......... 3 90

**lar Express Wagon:** Size of box 12x25, wheels 11 and 14 inches. Iron box in hub, ron axles, right and left hand nuts. Handsomely painted in red with attractive trimmings. ½ doz. in crate .......... 6 90

**ung America" Express Wagon:** Hardwood body, size 13x28, 11x14-inch wheels. Heavy iron axles in iron thimble skeins, wooden braces, malleable iron tongue fastening and fifth wheel. ⅓ doz. in crate .......... 8 25

No. 100, Junior Express Wagon, $1 40 Each.

Each.

**No. 100, "Junior" Express Wagon:** Size of body 14x28 inches, new style hardwood paneled body, landscape painting, high seat and dashboard, wheels 12 and 16-inch, iron axles in iron thimble skeins, malleable iron tongue fastening and fifth wheel, hub caps and bent handle. 2 in crate. Each .......... $1 40

**No. 180, Children's Buggy:** Size of body 13x26 inches at base, flaring top, wheels 12 and 16-inch, heavy iron axles in iron thimble skeins, malleable iron tongue fastening and fifth wheel, hub caps and seat, whip and whip socket. Body nicely ornamented and varnished. 2 in crate. Each .......... 1 25

## Boys' Iron Body Wagons.

Boys' Iron Body Wagon

Each.

**No. 240, Boys' Iron Wagon:** Sides made of sheet steel, heavy iron wired top, solid iron axles and body. Size of body about 9x8, handsomely painted and varnished. Patent fifth wheel connection and metal tongue attachment, 6 and 8-inch metal wheels, right and left hand bolts. 4 in crate. Each .......... $0 67

**No. 250, Boys' Iron Wagon:** As above, only 10x20 body, wheels 8 and 12-inch. 3 in crate. Each .......... 85

**No. 270, Boys' Iron Wagon:** As above, only larger, body being 12x24, wheels 10 and 14-inch. 2 in crate. Each .......... 1 10

**280, Boys' Iron Wagon:** As above only larger, body being 14x28, wheels 12 and 16-inch. 2 in crate. Each .......... 1 45

# WILLOW DOLL CARRIAGES.

No. 1, $2.10 Doz

We have not handled these for several years because we thought prices were higher than they ought to be. This season, however, we have got them where we want them.

Doz.

**No. 1, Willow Doll Carriage:** *Our 25-cent leader.* 16 inches long. 6-inch wheels, well put together. 1 doz. in crate .......... $ 2 10

**No. 2, Willow Doll Carriage:** 20 inches long, 8-inch wheels, bent handles. ½ doz. in crate .......... 3 75

**No. 3, Willow Doll Carriage:** 24 inches long, 10-inch wheels, wood springs and bent handles. ½ doz. in crate .......... 7 20

**No. 4, Willow Doll Carriage:** Same as above only with silesia parasol. Too good—almost—to retail at a dollar. ½ doz. in crate .......... 8 35

No. 3, $7.20 Doz.

No. 5, $10.50 Doz.

**. 5, Willow Doll Carriage:** 26 inches long and extra wide, 10-inch wheels, wood springs, square back with seat, lined in silesia and trimmed with lace, 8-inch silesia parasol. ½ doz. in crate .......... 10 50

# SPECIALTIES IN FRENCH GLASS.

All in the beautiful mosaic mottled effect. Forty-nine buyers out of fifty would take the first two items below to be 25-cent goods, and *any* buyer would call the pitcher cheap at $4.50.

No. P102, $3.60 Doz.

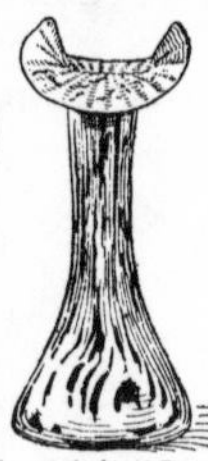

No. P101, $1.25 Doz.

No. P100, $1.20 Doz.

Doz.

**No. P100, Blown Glass Rose Bowl**—French blown glass in mosaic mottled effect. Crimped top, 14½ inches in circumference. ½ doz. in package, assorted .......... $1 20

**No. 101, Mosaic Glass Vase**—8-inch, scalloped tops, good thick glass, four shapes and patterns in package of ⅓ doz .......... 1 25

**No. P102, Mosaic Glass Pitcher**—Three pint, very handsome combination of colored glass. Average height about 9 inches, good handles. Two fancy shapes in pkg. of ⅙ dozen. Certainly the most beautiful 50-cent pitcher we ever saw .......... 3 60

# THREE JEWELRY SPECIALTIES FROM FRANCE.

**Three special bargains** in the now-so-popular cloissonne work. Imported direct from Paris and received only a few days before issuing this catalogue, so that styles are the same as are selling in Paris to day.

No. P156, $1.80 Doz.

No. P157, 3 Styles, $2.10 Doz.

No. P153, $2.25 Doz.

Doz.

**No. P156, Real Enameled Lace Pins**—Best gilt, blue, pink and torquois colors in handsome armorial designs (center ornaments in designs similar to the three shown on No. P157 scarf pin). Combination brooch, waist or skirt pins. Latest design and look like high priced goods. Each on card and in box .......... $1 80

**No. P157, Enameled Stick or Scarf Pins**—As above, elegantly put up in satin-lined leatherette box with spring catch. Fine grade of real enamel work and tasty designs. 12 styles in handsome display box .......... 2 10

**No. P153, Medallion Brooch**—Exact imitation of goods worth from $5 to $10 a *piece*. Handsomely made, each with historical French miniature portrait, assorted in package, such as Marie Louise, Josephine, etc. Half gilt and half silver. Each in box, ½ doz. in carton .......... 2 25

# RUSTIC BASKETS AND VASES.

Ornamental and lasting. Made of white wood with gilt decorations in rustic designs, filled with natural grasses and flowers dyed in assorted bright colors.

35c Doz.

67c Doz.

68c Doz.

Doz.

**No. 0, Rustic Basket**—4¾ inches high. 1 doz. in box .......... (In lots of 6 doz. or more, 33c) $0 35

**No. 1, Rustic Vase**—About 8¼ inches high. ½ doz. in box ..... (In lots of 6 doz. or more, 64c) 67

**No. 1, Rustic Basket**—Oblong shape, size 2⅞x4. 6¼ inches high. ½ doz. in box .......... Quantity price. ..In lots of 6 doz. or more, 65c 68

**No. 3, Rustic Vase**—Same style as No. 1 vase. About 13½ inches high. ⅓ doz. in box .......... Quantity price..In lots of 4 doz. or more, $1.70 1 75

**No. 3, Rustic Basket**—Same style as No. 1 basket. Size 3¾x5¾, 10 inches high. ⅓ doz. in box .......... (In lots of 4 doz. or more, $1.70) 1 75

# HIGH GRADE MICROSCOPES.

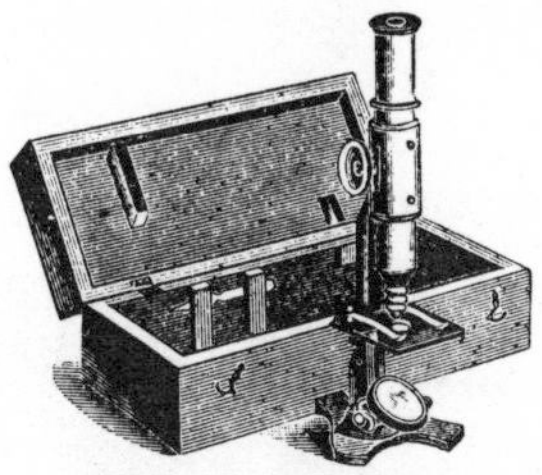

Students' Compound Microscope.

Each.

**No. 1219, Students' Microscope**—The style used by scientists. Magnifies many times. Made of brass and highly burnished. 6 inches high. Focused by draw to suit any sight. Reflecting mirror in base for throwing light on the object. Each in polished mahogany hinged box with tweezers, one prepared object glass and two extra glasses for mounting transparent specimens. Price each .......... $1 40

**No. 1220, Students' Compound Microscope**—7¼ inches high, hinged to heavy base so can be adjusted to convenient angle. 3 plano-convex lenses and universal mirror for illuminating transparent objects. Magnifies 90 times. Finely polished brass body. Each in polished hinged cover mahogany box with tweezers, 2 object glasses, 1 prepared object. Each .......... 3 60

**No. 1221, Students' Compound Microscope**—As above, 8⅜ inches high, magnifying 110 times. Each in box. As above. Each .......... 4 25

# STAPLE LOW PRICED TELESCOPES.

Doz.

**No. 710, Brass Telescope:** 3-draw, 3 inches long when closed, 6 inches long when open. A popular 25-cent seller. ½ doz. in box .......... $1 95

Each.

**No. 711, Imitation Leather Covered Telescope:** 3-draw, a good magnifier, object glass 1-inch in diameter. 7¾ inches long when closed, 21½ long when open. Each in case .... $0 75

# STEREOSCOPES AND GRAPHOSCOPES.

Not the common goods—made to sell—but very best quality.

$2.20 Each.

Nos. 10 and 20, Stereoscope.

Stereo-Graphoscope, $3.25 Doz.

Doz.

**No. 10, Stereoscope**—Neat wood frame and imitation rosewood head, with sliding bar and spring set; full size; good lens. An excellent offering for a quarter. ½ doz. in box .......... $1 45

**No. 20, Stereoscope**—*Till now a 50-center.* A genuine fine quality instrument, polished hard wood hood, hinged handle, sliding bar. ½ doz. in box .......... 2 10

**Patent Stereo-Graphoscope**—One of the new wonders. Extra heavy double lens, full cherry wood frame, fine polished veneered hood, sliding focus bar with folding metal rests. Can be used as a stereoscope, and by a simple arrangement turned instantly into a graphoscope for the magnifying of cabinet photos. Each in box .......... 3 25

**Combination Stereoscope and Graphoscope**—Beautifully polished stand and frame. The graphoscope has a highly magnifying 4-inch lens, making a cabinet photo appear life-size. Below this are the lenses of the stereoscope, nickeled eye tube. Each in box. **Each, $2.20.**

# DOMESTIC WOOD TOYS.

**Best Made and Best Finished Goods to be Found in the Market. Quality Considered Our Prices Are Much Under Value on These Quick-Selling Goods.**

## ASSORTMENTS OF TOY FURNITURE.

**Best American goods.** Not the common stuff—made to sell—but every piece well finished. Good large sizes for the money.

Three Styles No. 1618, 38c Doz.

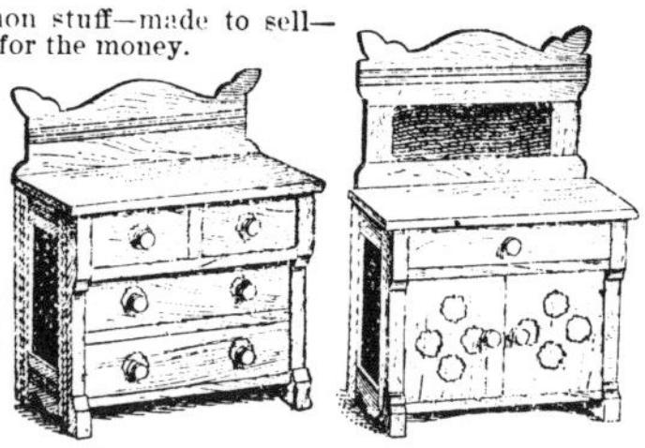

Two Pieces in Assortment No. 1619, 75c Doz.

**No. 1618, 5-Cent Assortment**—Good size and painted in attractive colors. Each box of ½ doz. comprises 2 sideboards, 2 bureaus, and 2 buffets........ (6 doz. or more, 36c) Doz. $0 38

**No. 1619, 10-Cent Assortment**—*Every piece a 10-cent leader.* Comprising 3 pieces still larger than above. ½ doz. in pkg...... 75
Quantity price.......................In lots of 6 doz. or more, 72c

Two Pieces in Assortment No. 1620, $1.87 Doz.

**No. 1620, 25-Cent Assortment**—Comprising 4 pieces as follows: Combination sideboard, about 7½x12: combination bureau with 5 drawers, 8½x8½: combination cheffonier, 7½x10, and combination desk, 8¼x8½. 1 each of above in box of ⅓ doz.................. 1 87
Quantity price, 4 doz. or more, $1.80

**No. 1621B, 50-Cent Assortment**—Extra large and finely finished. Comprising combination desk and folding bed. Size of desk 5⅞x11, 10¾ inches high, made with drop front, lock and key, 6 spaces, lower closet and drawer. Bed made with wardrobe front and drawer, the back lets down making a regular bed with foot board, height 11⅞ inches, width 7⅛, full length when open 14⅛. Both pieces in antique oak finish. 1-6 doz. in box........ 3 95

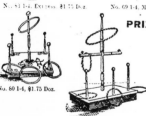

S. Sideboard in Asst. No. 1621A, $3.95 Doz.

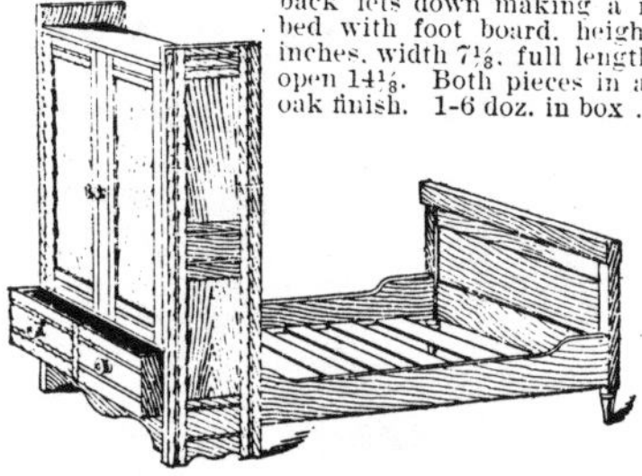

Folding Bed in Assortment No. 1621B, $3.95 Doz.

**No. 1621A, 50-Cent Assortment**—As above only different variety of pieces: One combination sideboard, 9x13½; and one fancy 6-drawer bureau, 9⅛x10. Antique oak finish, immense 50-cent pieces. 1-6 doz. in box. .... .... 3 95

## WOOD TOYS ON WHEELS.

No. 83 1-4, Express, $1.75 Doz.

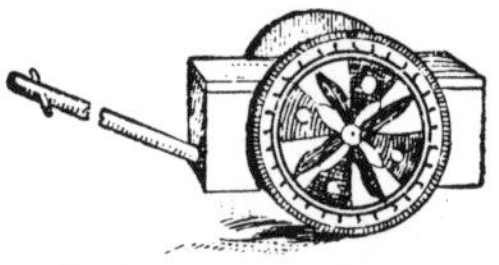

No. 69 1-4, Musical Cart, $1.79 Doz.

No. 28 1-4, Coal Cart, $1.85 Doz.

## PRIZE RING TOSS.

No. 80 1-4, $1.75 Doz.

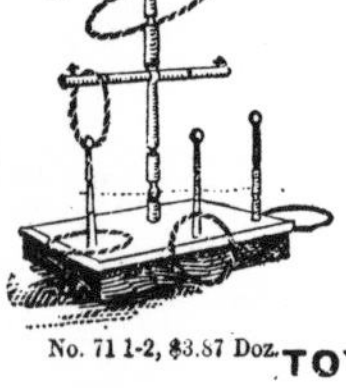

No. 71 1-2, $3.87 Doz.

**No. 80¼, Prize Ring Toss**—Comprises 5 well finished posts and 4 colored rings, 10½ high, 8 long and 8 wide. Top of box nicely lithographed............ 1 75

**No. 71½, Prize Ring Toss**—19 inches high, 13 long, 8 wide. Has 5 rattan rings, wound with fancy colored tape, posts striped and varnished, box lithographed.......... 3 87

## TOY CHAIRS.

No. 56 1-4, $1.75 Doz.

No. 52 1-4, $1.78 Doz.

No. 57 1-4, $1.79 Doz.

No. 61 1-4, $1.80 Doz.

**No. 56¼, Alphabet High Chair**—Full alphabet lithographed in pretty colors on back of seat. Something new in a doll's high chair. Each in box.......... 1 75

**No. 52¼, Spelling Rocker**—List of common words spelled out on back. Decidedly novel and instructive. Height 14 inches. Each wrapped.......... 1 78

**No. 57¼, Baby High Chair**—Height 20½ inches, ornamented and lithographed to represent baby sitting in chair. Very attractive.......... 1 79

**No. 61¼, Story Rocker**—Lithographed in upholstery pattern, reversible back and story on one side. Height 13½ inches.......... 1 80

## TOY FURNITURE.

No. 24 1-4, $1.87 Doz.

**No. 24¼, Folding Bed**—20 inches long, 11 wide and 10½ high. Very neat and attractive and substantially put together..........

No. 81, Doll's Bed-Room Suite, $8.33 Doz.

No. 44 1-2, Folding Bed, $3.90 Doz.

**No. 44½, Folding Bed**—25 inches long, 13 wide and 15 high. Richly carved and handsome panels. A fine 50-cent toy..

**No. 81, Doll's Bedroom Suite**—Consisting of 8x15-inch bedstead with mattress, chiffonier with mirror, 2 chairs and rocker covered with plush in assorted colors, center table, small table, 2 scarfs and lamp. Nicely finished and lithographed. Each set in 16½x12½ box with elegant label..........

No. 79, Dining-Room Suite, $8.34 Doz.

**No. 79, Doll's Dining-Room Suite**—Size 16½x12¼ inches. Set comprises lithographed sideboard with mirror, dining table, 4 dining chairs and 2 arm chairs covered with rich plush in assorted colors, side table scarf and lamp. Each in handsome box..........

No. 77, Doll's Parlor Suite, $8.35 Doz.

**No. 77, Doll's Parlor Suite**—Superior finished set of parlor furniture, covered with plush in assorted colors. Consists of piano with piano stool, 2 arm chairs, rocker, center table, sofa, foot-rest, easel, picture, lamp and table scarf. Each in elaborate box, size 16½x12½..

## EASEL BLACK BOARDS.

No. 60, $8.30 Doz.

No. 60 1-2, $3.85 Doz.

**No. 25¼, Easel Black Board**—Stands 32 inches high, size of board 15½x12½, alphabet and pictures printed on both sides of frame and extention. Well made and neat design..........

**No. 60½, Easel Black Board**—Alphabet and pictures lithographed on frame and extension as above, strongly made. 38 inches high, size of board 18½x12½. Can be used either in desk or easel form..........

**No. 60, Large Easel Black Board**—Height 50 inches, size of board 21x17, frame and desk richly lithographed in colors. Board is made of new material and drops forward to form desk. ½ doz. in crate..........

## NAUTICAL TOYS.

No. 68 1-4, Tugboat and Barge, $1.80 Doz.

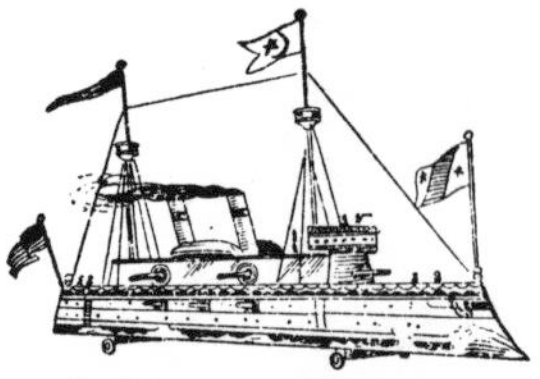

No. 42 1-4, Cruiser Boston, $1.92 Doz.

**No. 68¼, Tugboat and Barge**—Comprising 10-inch tugboat, 12½-inch barge, officers and men. Total length 25 inches. Strongly made and beautifully lithographed..........

**No. 42¼, War Cruiser "Boston"**—Complete miniature warship and fully equipped. Has six cannon, 8 officers and sailors and 2 boats. 19 inches long and 16¼ high to top of masts..........

No. 42 1-2, Tugboat and Barge, $3.95 Doz.

**No. 42½, Tugboat and Barge**—Most attractive and interesting toy in the market for the money. Comprises 18-inch tugboat, 18½-inch barge, fitted out for dredging, officers and men. Total length 40 inches. Can be used single or double. Finely lithographed....

No. 38 1-2, Cruiser New York, $4.00 Doz.

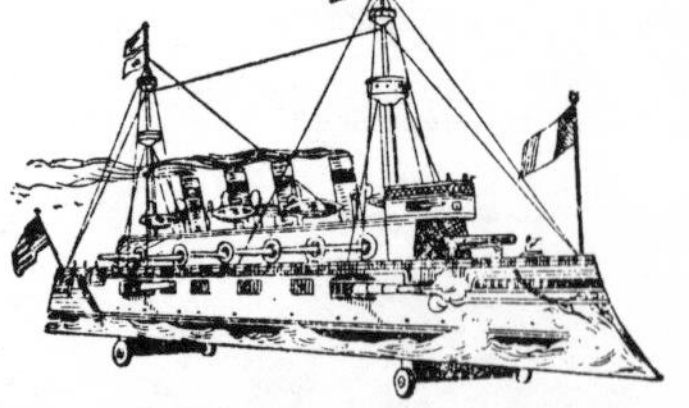

No. 26, Cruiser Minneapolis, $8.35 Doz.

**No. 38½, War Cruiser "New York"**—Patterned after the mammoth original cruiser. 29 inches long and 20 high to top of masts. 12 officers and sailors, 2 masts, 3 smokestacks and smoke, 8 ventilators, 6 boats and cannon. Well made and equipped.......... 4

**No. 26, War Cruiser "Minneapolis"**—The largest and most complete toy vessel made, patterned after the most powerful and swiftest warship in the world. 4 smokestacks and smoke, 6 boats, 10 ventilators, 2 masts, each having 2 turrets, 4 flagstaffs with flags, 14 cannon, decks, 16 officers and sailors. Length from stem to stern 38 inches, height to top of mast 25½. Elegantly lighographed.......... 8

# POPULAR GAMES.

**ffer the Leading Popular Sellers in These Well Known Goods at Prices Such That Any Merchant Can Safely Handle Them.**

78c Doz.

$1.75 Doz.

## ASSORTED CARD GAMES. Doz.

**Assorted Card Games:** Made specially for us and the largest 5c games on the market. 1 doz. in pkg..(6 doz or more, 37c) $0 39

**Assorted Card Games:** Uniform with above. 6 different styles in pkg. of ½ doz., as follows: Peter Coddle, Shopping, Trades, Famous, Ivanhoe and 'Round the World..(6 doz. or more, 72c) 75

**Assorted Card Games:** All in bright colors. Assorted Robinson Crusoe, Cinderella, Cock Robin, Bo-Peep and Apple Pie in box of ½ doz..................(In lots of 6 doz. or more, 74c) 78

**Assorted Card Games:** Special value at 25 cents. Put up 6 different styles in pkg., such as Corner Grocery, County Fair, Wife and I, Proverbs, Fortune Telling and Great Battlefields.. 1 75

**Assorted Card Games:** Comprising the most popular 25-cent games of the day. Put up ½ doz. in pkg. assorted as follows: Uncle Sam's Farm, Mother Goose, K K Cards, National Flower, Wonderland and Zoo........................ 1 80

Authors, 73c Doz.

## AUTHORS.

**Game of Authors:** Superior edition for the price. Consists of 30 cards, 10 of which contain portraits of distinguished authors. ½ doz. in pkg...........(In lots of 6 doz. or more, 70c) 73

**Game of Authors:** Similar to above, only printed on fine glazed cards. Very handsome. ½ doz. in pkg...................... 1 65

Old Maid, 72c Doz.

## OLD MAID.

**Game of Old Maid:** The best and greatest variety of colored pictures ever produced. Artistic representations in tastefully lithographed colors. ½ doz. in pkg..(6 doz. lots or more, 70c) 72

**Game of Old Maid:** As above, only better grade of cardboard and highly polished. ½ doz. in pkg........................ 1 72

No. 121, $1.67 Doz.

## MISCELLANEOUS CARD GAMES.

**No. 121, The Brownies and Other Queer Folks:** A new and comical game, played similar to Old Maid. Illustrated in colors........................ 1 67

**No. 122, Doctor Busby:** Oldest American game and the only authorized edition. Illustrated humorously in bright colors.. 1 69

**Game of Auction:** No more amusing card game can be bought. Full of excitement. ½ doz. in pkg........................ 1 90

. 2, 79c Doz.

## ASSORTED CARDBOARD GAMES.

**No. 2, Assorted Cardboard Games:** Size 7½x7½. Assorted as follows in pkg. of ½ doz.: House that Jack Built, News Boy and Puss in the corner. Best 10-cent games to be found.. Quantity price...................In lots of 6 doz. or more, 76c 79

No. 1, 80c Doz.

**No. 1, Assorted Cardboard Games:** Extra large 10-cent games, being 6½x9½. Formerly retailed at 25 cents. ½ doz. in pkg., assorted as follows: Red Riding Hood, Steeplechase, Jack and the Bean Stalk..(In lots of 6 doz. or more,78c) 80

**No. 1173, Assorted Cardboard Games:** Yacht Race and Steeplechase, assorted. Put up in very pretty boxes, size 10¾x5½, with full drawings of game, fancy chance pin, and six metal stand figures with each. 1 doz. assorted in package ............ In lots of 6 doz. or more, 79c 81

3, $1.79 Doz.

No. 4, $2.00 Doz.

**No. 3, Assorted Cardboard Games:** Size 8½x8½. 6 styles in pkg., such as Base Ball, Foot Ball and Luck. Particularly interesting for boys..... 1 79

**No. 4, Assorted Cardboard Games:** The most popular games of the day. Assorted Alphabet, Crossing the Ocean and Robin Hood in pkg. of ½ doz............................ 2 00

## MISCELLANEOUS CARDBOARD GAMES.

, **Cut-up Map of the United States:** The particular feature of this map is that each tate is cut out on the exact state line. Size of map 7¼x11 inches, all states in colors. 1 doz. in box .................. (In lots of 6 doz. or more, 85c) 88

No. 1, 88c Doz.

Tiddledy Winks.

**Tiddledy Winks:** A standard well known game, as well as a quick seller. Pieces are made of wood, and will accommodate 4 players. 1 doz. in pkg ..... (6 doz. or more, 68c) 70

**Tiddledy Winks:** Same size as above, only pieces are made of bone. ½ doz. in pkg...... 1 00

**ke's Peak or Bust" Puzzle:** Consists of board 8 inches square, bearing picture of Pike's Peak. 75 brass pegs dot the precipitate sides of the mountain, over which a ittle traveler of twisted wire climbs. The greatest puzzle game since the introduction of Pigs in Clover........................ 1 70

**119, Hare and Hounds:** Size of board 12x12, covered with various paths over which hare runs to escape the hunters. If the hare reaches its hole safely it wins, otherwise the hunter scores........................ 2 10

**14, Hop Scotch Tiddledy Winks:** Suitable for 6 players and also an excellent solitaire game. Has thick felt mat, marked to represent Hop Scotch court and cup to take the place of "Pudding." Players pop their pieces from space to space, finally getting them into the cup........................ 3 60

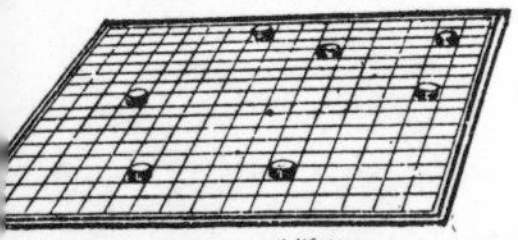

No. 52, Go-Bang, $3.95 Doz.

**No. 31, Steeple Chase:** Large board, showing spirited pictures of the race, in box with brilliant label. Metal pieces for horses and riders, dice cups, etc........................ 3 90

**No. 52, Game of Go-Bang:** The popular edition. Large folding board with gold squares and a variety of wooden pieces for playing. Each player endeavors to get five pieces in a row, his opponents trying to block him and get five of their own in a row........................ 3 95

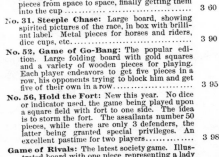

No. 56, Hold the Fort, $3.98 Doz.

**No. 56, Hold the Fort:** New this year. No dice or indicator used, the game being played upon a square field with fort to one side. The idea is to storm the fort. The assailants number 50 pieces, while there are only 3 defenders, the latter being granted special privileges. An excellent pastime for two players........................ 3 98

**Game of Rivals:** The latest society game. Illustrated board with one piece representing a lady and the other players gentlemen, all of whom intend to carry her through the various features of courtship, in hopes to gain her affections. The player succeeding wins the game.......... 4 00

## CARDBOARD GAMES—Continued.

**No. 48, Knuckle Billiards:** Improved edition. Modeled on the idea of billiards and can be played with the knuckles or cue, using checkers in place of balls. A very amusing game. $ 4 05

No. 27, Menagerie, $7.75 Doz.

**No. 71, Bicycle Game:** Played upon a picture map with pieces representing bicycles, route cards and spinning indicator. The riders start their wheels from different points and journey by various routes, all meeting again at a certain destination. Size 12½x12½. A very enjoyable novelty. 4 10

**No. 27, Menagerie:** New 1895 game, representing a visit to the menagerie. Particularly adapted for little folks. Board is illustrated in colors with pictures of various animals. Each player takes a trip through the grounds, stopping at the different cages. Played with a spinning indicator........................ 7 75

No. 26, Yankee Doodle, $7.80 Doz.

**No. 26, Yankee Doodle:** Handsome and instructive novelty. Similar to the new game Napoleon. The spaces upon which the game is played are a series of pictures in colors, illustrating the events in the history of our country. Each player receives counters when they reach a glorious event, otherwise pay counters........................ 7 80

**No. 36, Game of Travel:** A pleasing and interesting journey through Europe. Consists of different colored steamships and railroad trains. The game is played with route tickets (a new and patented system), the idea being to travel to Europe as far as Constantinople and then to return to America. New style patent game-board, size 14x21 inches, with drawer........................ 8 10

No. 36, Game of Travel, $8.10 Doz.

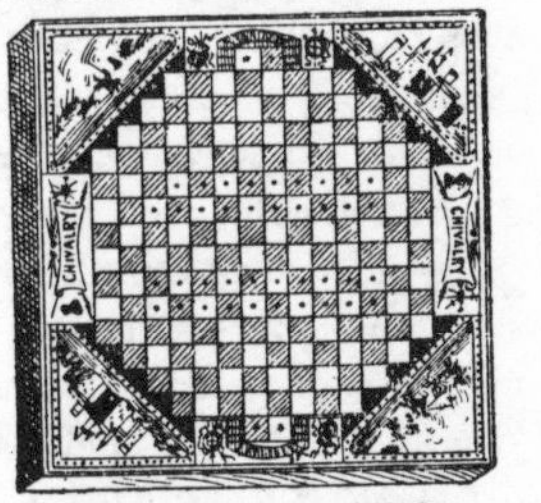

No. 19, Game of Chivalry, $8.20 Doz.

**No. 19, Game of Chivalry:** Popular game of skill and granted to be the most noteworthy modern invention. Comprises speial design checkered board, 16 inches square, each player having 20 pieces (8 of which are knights), his object being to force two of his pieces past the ranks of his opponent to the starred squares........................ 8 20

**No. 11, Battle Game:** Good table game and an A1 amusement for boys. Each box contains 1 army with commander-in-chief and other officers, 2 toy pistols, also ammunition. Soldiers are made of heavy material, handsomely lithographed and mounted on wood bases. Pistols make a loud report and discharge missiles........................ 8 25

**No. 20, Game of Soldier Boy:** Large showy folding board, about 2 feet square, with 4 metal soldiers and spinning indicator for playing. The game relates the stirring story of the battlefield and illustrates the promotions gained. The one who first attains the position of commander-in-chief wins. Very attractively boxed and a captivating game for boys........................ 8 40

No. 11, Game of Battle, $8.25 Doz.

**No. 13, Innocence Abroad:** Put up in very handsome box with folding board very finely illustrated, showing roads, farms, forests, mountains, rivers, mills, waterfalls, etc., through which the various people travel by many routes toward the same point, meeting with varied occurrences and expenses. A very funny and catchy game........ 8 75

**No. 39, Game of Waterloo:** A novel game, and one which promises an enormous sale. Can be played in two ways, to suit young and old. 21x14-inch board with illustrations of Paris and Versailles at one end, Brussels and Namur at the other, connected by numerous roads and dotted with hills. Each player has 10 pieces for attack and defense. Players throw three dice and play 1 piece for each dice, the object being to capture the enemy's city by occupying it with 3 pieces........................ 8 90

No. 13, Innocence Abroad, $8.75 Doz.

**No. 2, Game of Napoleon:** Latest 1895 novelty, both handsome and instructive. Comprises a series of colored pictures showing events in the life of Napoleon, with a variety of counters, part of which are given to the players, the remainder forming the pool. If a player stops upon a space illustrating a victory, he receives counters, if not he pays to the pool. The one having the most counters on arrival in St. Helena, wins 9 00

**No. 204, Battledore and Shuttlecock:** This old and well known English game is a fascinating sport both in and outdoors. Put up in substantial box with elegant lithographed label, containing 2 battledores and 2 shuttlecocks. Specially healthful amusement........................ 9 25

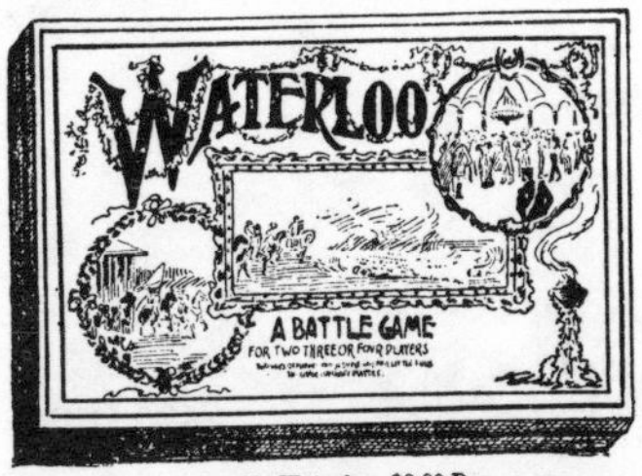

No. 39, Waterloo, $8.90 Doz.

**No. 25, Barnum's Greatest Show on Earth:** With real toy tent 2 feet in diameter and 20 inches high, 5 poles and guy ropes, nicely embossed standing animals, several circus groups (to be cut out), circus poster, sheet of tickets, flag and 3 paper rings. Size of box 13¼x21 inches. A very realistic toy show, from which the children can have additional sport with by charging one or two cents admission........ 9 40

No. 1, Across the Continent, $11.80 Doz.

**No. 1, Across the Continent:** Suitable for players of all ages. Extra large folding board, measuring 3½ feet when open, covered with colored bird's-eye-view of the U. S., showing principal cities, railway lines, etc. Railway tickets with each. Box enclosing outfit is 22x11, with label as shown in illustration. New style drawer game board 14x21, with utensils for 6 players, but can be played by any number of people........................ 11 80

## ELECTRIC LOCOMOTIVE.

### (Catalogue No. 100.)

### (Actual size, 12 inches long.)

This is a faithful reproduction of the 1,800 horse power electric locomotives used by the B. & O. R. R. for hauling trains through the tunnels of Baltimore. Every line is carried out to the proper proportions. The trucks, buffers and couplers are cast iron, perfectly constructed and reinforced to withstand more than the ordinary amount of usage. The cab is constructed of sheet steel. All parts are japanned and lettered in harmonious colors.

A full description of the other parts follows:

The CONTROLLER in front, which starts, stops and reverses the car is an exact reproduction of those ordinarily used on large cars. It is cast and nicely finished.

The MOTOR is designed to attain high speed and hauling power, and at the same time consume a minimum amount of current. The armature is laminated and drum wound. To those conversant with electricity the merits of this will be readily appreciated.

The COMMUTATOR AND BRUSHES are scientifically designed, both as to wearing quality and simple adjustment. (Refer to directions on car.)

The WHEELS are two inches in diameter.

The SPRING BEARINGS are one of the principal features of the trucks. They take up any variations in the track, which prevents the car leaving the rails, no matter at what speed it may be going.

The GEARS in this outfit are all machine cut; they will not break or wear out. They are perfectly adjusted, and work noiselessly. Friction is reduced to a minimum.

The SIDE and CROSS BRACES which hold the mechanism in place are cast iron. They are very rigid, and will withstand more than the ordinary amount of wear and tear.

The Rails are made of 3-8 inch steel, and are cut in sections, so that any shaped track may be formed.

The Ties are grooved to admit the insertion of the rails. The guage of track is 2 7-8 inches.

The Axles are made of 3-16-inch steel rod.

This outfit consists of the car, 30 feet of rail and 60 ties, which will make a rigid track.

Price complete, boxed ................ **$6.00**

## ELECTRIC EXPRESS.

### (Catalogue No. 200.)

### (Actual size, 12 inches long.)

This car has the same mechanism in every respect as the car described before. It will afford the user great pleasure, as it may be loaded and unloaded.

The car body is constructed of sheet steel. It is perfectly japanned and lettered, and is fitted with steps and hand rails.

Price of outfit complete, with 30 feet of rail and 60 ties ..................... **$6.00**

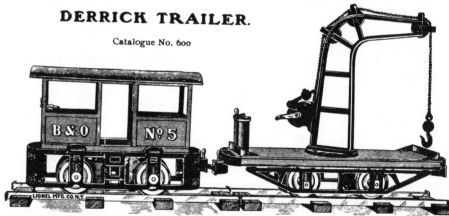

## ELECTRIC TROLLEY CAR.

### (Catalogue No. 300.)

### (Actual size, 16 1-2 inches.)

By reference to the above cut, it will be noticed that this car is built on the lines of the regular electric trolley cars. Every feature is carried out to the minutest detail.

The car body is built of cold rolled steel. It has 6 seats, all of which are reversible, as are the signs at the top. It is finely enameled and lettered.

The mechanism is similar to that of other cars described.

Price of car with 30 feet of rail and 60 ties ................................. **$7.00**

# DERRICK TRAILER.

### Catalogue No. 600

This illustration shows the derrick car described on the preceeding page used as a trailer. This outfit should easily commend itself.

**Price of Derrick Trailer .................. $3.25**

## SWITCH AND SIGNAL.

### (Catalogue No. 320.)

### (Actual size, 17 1-2 x 8 x 4 1-2 inches.)

This auxiliary to the road is very desirable. Its mechanical construction is perfect. All parts work on spring bearings. The lever which shifts the track changes the signal at the same time. The signal discs are red and white enameled. The switch is 17 1-2 inches long, 8 inches wide and 4 1-2 inches high. It is put in connection with the track the same as any of the sections. All electrical contacts are permanent. The signal is cast iron and neatly finished.

Price, boxed ......................... **$1.50**

**1902/1903**

## W. J. Bassett-Lowke & Co., Northampton.

# Model Steam Locomotives.

No. 8969.—Best quality Locomotive, Turned Brass Flanged Wheels, two Oscillating Cylinders, Oxydized Brass Boiler, Whistle, Safety Valve, all Fittings and Bedplate Polished Brass, complete with Spirit Lamp. Loco. 7in. long, 1¼in. Gauge, ... 6/-

No. 8969.

No. 8969/1.—Similar to No. 8969, and fitted with Cab, as illustration. 8in. long, 1¼in. Gauge, 8/-

No. 8971.—As above, with loose Tender, 16in. long over all, 1¼in. Gauge, 9/6

No. 8972.—Ditto.

No. 8969/1.

16in. long over all, 2in. Gauge, 12/-

No. 8373.—Superior quality Locomotive and Tender, fitted with Oxydized Brass Boiler, Oscillating Cylinder, nickel plated Brass Flanged Wheels, Brass Handrail, Bell, Whistle, Safety Valve, and enamelled in best style. 1¼in. long (including tender). 1¼in. Gauge, 10/6

No. 8373.

No. 8373/1.—Ditto ... ... 15in. long, 1¼in. Gauge, 12/6
No. 8373/2.—Ditto, with Water Gauge and Head Lamp. 17in. long, 2in. Gauge, 17/-
No. 8373/3.—Ditto, ... ... 18in. long, 2¼in. Gauge, 27/-
No. 8373/4.—Ditto, double-action Oscillating Cylinders, with 4-wheel Bogie, Starting Tap, and three Head Lights. ... 20in. long, 3in. Gauge, 34/-

## PRUSSIAN STATE RAILWAY EXPRESS LOCOMOTIVE AND TENDER.

No. 198.—This Loco. is exact to illustration, and is fitted with a pair of powerful Double Action Slide Valve Cylinders, Oxydized Brass Boiler, 14in. long, 2¾in. diameter, Bogie Carriage with four 2in. Brass Wheels, Driving Wheels 3¾in. diameter, Steam taken from Dome and Starting Lever worked from Cab. Reversing Motion, Water Gauge, Whistle Safety Valve. All bright parts plated. Tender, Cab, and Bedplate enamelled green and picked out with black and gold. Length over all with 6-wheel Tender, 2ft. 8in. Height to top of Cab, 7½in., Width, 5½in. **3in. Gauge.** Price, complete with Tender, £6 17s. 6d.

No. 198.

No. 197.—This Loco. is similar to the above, and is fitted with Double Action Cylinders, 1¼in. stroke, ⅝in. bore, Whistle, Safety Valve, Starting Tap, Bogie Carriage, and all bright parts nickel plated. Length over all, including Tender, 26in. **3in. Gauge.** £3 18s. 6d.

No. 197.

For Special Points, Rails, and Coaches for these Locos, see page 53.

## LOCOMOTIVES WITH REVERSING MOTION.

No. 9642.

THE above Locomotives, which were introduced to meet the demand for a first-class Loco. with reversing motion, have given every satisfaction. They are fitted with a pair of Double Action Slide Valve Cylinders, the steam exhausts into funnel, and the reversing motion is worked from cab, which also acts as a stop valve when lever is in mid position. The Loco. can also be reversed automatically by using our reversing switches (see Rail section, page 56) which consists of an ordinary rail with lever which works a small brass block, this catches the reversing mechanism and reverses the Loco.

THESE LOCOS. ARE MADE IN FOUR GAUGES, AS FOLLOWS:—

No. 1.—15in. long, including Tender. **1¼in. Gauge.** 19/6
No. 2.—17in. ,, ,, ,, **2in. ,,** 24/6
No. 3.—19in. ,, ,, ,, **2¼in. ,,** 34/6
No. 4.—21in. long, including Tender, Water Gauge, and six Wheels. **3in. Gauge.** 46/-

No. 504.

No. 1.—This is a similar Locomotive to No. 503, and is fitted with two powerful Oscillating Cylinders, Whistle, Safety Valve, and Steam Dome, REVERSING MOTION worked from cab by lever, as illustrated, and EXHAUSTS INTO THE FUNNEL, is in every respect a first-class Loco. 16in. long. **1¼in. Gauge.** 12/6

No. 2.—Ditto, 17in. long. **2in. Gauge.** 16/6

## NEW PATTERN LOCOMOTIVES.

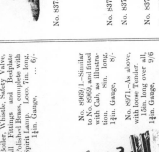

No. 505.

No. 1.—Best Quality Locomotive with Oxydized Brass Boiler, turned Brass Wheels, pair of Double Action Slide Valve Cylinders (Patent), Whistle, Safety Valve, Dome and Starting tap. 16in. long. **1¼in. Gauge.** 14/6

No. 2.—Ditto, 17in. long. **2in. Gauge.** 20/6
No. 3.—Ditto, 24in. long. **2¼in. Gauge.** 47/6

No. 503.

No. 0.—Best Quality Locomotive, with Tender, fitted with long Oxydized Brass Boiler, Turned Brass Wheels, Oscillating Cylinders, Steam Whistle, Safety Valve and Dome. 12in. long, including Tender. **1¼in. Gauge.** 8/3

No. 1.—Ditto, 16in. long. **1¼in. Gauge.** 10/6
No. 2.—Ditto, 17in. long. **2in. Gauge.** 14/6

Bassett-Lowke Ltd.

## SCALE MODEL OF THE CELEBRATED G. N. R. 8-FT SINGLE EXPRESS LOCOMOTIVE, NO. 776.

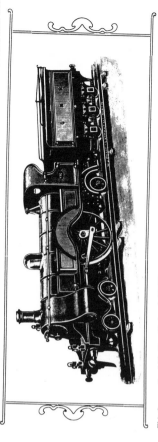

This Locomotive is built entirely of CASTINGS throughout, and is fitted with a strong Brass Boiler, Double Action Slide-Valve Cylinders, fitted with Link Motion Reversing Gear worked by a lever in cab, 4in. turned Brass Driving Wheels, exhaust steam into funnel, Steam Dome, Safety Valve, Whistle in cab, turned Brass Hand Rails, Three Headlights, loose 4-wheel Bogie Carriage. *The Tender is fitted with a Spirit Tank with Cock and Rubber Tube for supplying Spirit Lamp.* The whole Locomotive, including the Boiler, is enamelled and finished in best style and in correct G. N. R. colours, and in every small detail has had our careful attention. We can safely say it is the finest Model of its kind on the market. This Locomotive is very powerful and will run for half-an-hour without stopping. Length over all 24in. Height, 7½in. **2⅜in. Gauge.** Price complete, **£6 6s. 0d.**

Steam Gauge and Syphon, 7/6 extra.

---

## SCALE MODEL OF L. & N. W. R. EXPRESS LOCOMOTIVE "BLACK PRINCE."

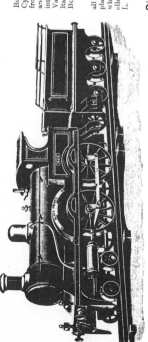

This Locomotive is fitted with a strong Brass Boiler, two double-action fixed Cylinders, with Reversing Motion worked from cab; four Coupled Driving Wheels and Loose Bogie Carriage, exhausts steam into funnel, Water Gauge, Whistle, Safety Valve, Steam Gauge, Steam Dome, Hand Rail, Name Plates, Head Lights, SPRING BUFFERS, etc.

The Boiler, Dome, etc., are Oxydized, all Wheels, including Tender, have plated rims and wide flange, and the whole of the Engine and Tender is enamelled and lined in best style, exact to L. & N. W. R. pattern.

Length over all, 23½in., 7in. high, **2⅜in. Gauge.** **£3 15s. 6d.**

If fitted with Spirit Tank in Tender, Union Cock, and Connections, 4/6 extra.

Price Complete, with Tender, Steam Gauge, and Syphon ... ... ... ... ...

*The Model Engineer and Amateur Electrician* for February 1st, says:—

"Owners of model railways who think of adding to their motive or rolling stock departments, will be well advised in communicating with Messrs. W. J. Bassett-Lowke & Co., 18-20, Kingswell Street, Northampton, with respect to some very interesting new models they are placing before the public. The most important of these is a really creditable representation of the 'Black Prince,' L. & N. W. R. locomotive and tender, with slide-valve cylinders and reversing motion, which is deserving of great praise as a genuine step in the direction of more realistic model locos. than have often been supplied by professional model makers. Our remarks, however, may well go a little farther than this, as, after a practical trial of a sample engine, we were able to commend its good running ability. In this respect we can endorse the opinion of one of the happy purchasers of a similar engine who writes:—' The appearance is most realistic, and it works splendidly. With only four burners going, and running light with tender only, it ran without a stop for 40 minutes, and covered over 3,000 yards. The way in which it keeps the steam up is surprising. The above was on a track with many curves and points; on a straight track it would doubtless do far better.'"

---

## CONTINENTAL PATTERN LOCOMOTIVE.

This Locomotive possesses extra strong Clockwork arrangement, will not derail when running alone, has Reversing Gear, Brake, Fast and Slow movement. It has turned Wheels, and other fittings as illustration. Length, including Tender, 17in. **1¾in. Gauge.** **£1 6s. 0d.**

Ditto, 20in. including Tender. **2in. Gauge.** **£1 18s. 6d.**

## ENGLISH PATTERN LOCOMOTIVE.

This Locomotive is fitted with extra strong Clockwork, will not derail when the Engine is running alone, has Reversing Gear, Brake, and Fast and Slow Movement. It has turned Wheels and other fittings as illustration. Length, including Tender, 18in. **1¾in. Gauge.** **£1 10s. 6d.**

Ditto, 21in. long, including Tender. **2in. Gauge.** **£2 5s. 0d.**

---

# Clockwork Locomotives.

AS WE ARE CONSTANTLY RECEIVING ENQUIRIES FOR CLOCKWORK LOCOMOTIVES, WE HAVE DECIDED TO HOLD A LARGE STOCK OF THESE, AND HAVE SELECTED THE FOLLOWING AS BEING THE BEST ON THE MARKET, AS REGARDS MECHANICAL CONSTRUCTION AND FINISH.

## AMERICAN PATTERN LOCOMOTIVE.

The above Locomotive is fitted with extra strong Clockwork, and will not derail when the Engine is running, alone, has Reversing Gear, Brake, and Fast and Slow Movement. It has turned Wheels, Cowcatcher, Bell, and other fittings as illustration. Length, including Tender, 18in. **1¾in. Gauge.** **£1 12s. 6d.**

Ditto, ditto, 22in. long. **2in. Gauge.** **£2 5s. 0d.**

Bassett-Lowke Ltd.

## Powerful Horizontal Hot Air Engine.

Extra Large Hot Air Engine, of accurate and elegant construction, it will run continuously for four or five hours; and makes a splendid shop window show piece, and can be used for driving a number of small Models. 13in. high, and mounted on base 20in. by 9in. ... ... ... ... Price 50/-

## MODEL SUBMARINE BOAT.

This Submarine Boat is as Illustration, and imitates in a surprising manner the movements of its large prototypes It first swims for a short time on the surface of the water, then suddenly dives and disappears from view, appearing again at a spot which even the most attentive onlooker hardly expected, then again glides along to dis appear again for a short time.

On the exterior are the Look-out Tower, Telescope, and Flags. It is fitted with a powerful Clockwork, and dives and rises alternately until the clockwork has run down.

No. 1—13½in. long, 8/-. No. 2—18in. long, 14/6.

No. 3—27in. long, 38/6.

✦ A ✦ NOVELTY, ✦ ORIGINAL, ✦ INTERESTING, ✦ INSTRUCTIVE, ✦ ENTERTAINING. ✦

### THE PLUNGING PIKE.

This is a most amusing novelty and it rises and dives alternately, similarly to Submarine Boat.

15in. long ... ... ... ... 9/6

It is impossible for either the Submarine Boat or Plunging Pike to sink, as they rise to the surface and float when the clock- work is run down.

## FIRE ESCAPES, ETC.

### METROPOLITAN FIRE ESCAPES.

Strongly made of metal, complete with raising and lowering gear. Enamelled bright red, and lined.

| | | |
|---|---|---|
| No. 1—23in. when at full height... ... ... ... | 5/6 |
| No. 2—31in. ,, ,, ... ... ... ... | 7/- |

### SALVAGE CORPS WAGGONS.

Complete with shafts, ladders, tool boxes, lanterns, bell, etc. Finely finished; enamelled red.

| | |
|---|---|
| No. 1—With four ladders, two hooks, 9½in. long without shaft, 6½in. high... | 7/- |
| No. 1A—With two ladders, two buckets, two hooks, etc., 10in. long without shaft, 4½in. wide, 7in. high | 9/6 |
| No. 2—With one Mechanical Fire Escape, three ladders, one hand pump, two hooks, etc., 12in. long without shaft, 6in. wide, 15in. high ... ... | 15/6 |

## MODEL STEAM FIRE ENGINES.

The above Steam Fire Engine is from a design by Mr. W. J. Bassett-Lowke, and is a vast improvement upon the usual run of those on the market. It is fitted with a powerful double-action slide valve cylinder, with exhaust into chimney; turned solid fly wheel, powerful pump, with air chamber and two deliveries. The boiler is made of brass, and highly polished, and is fitted with large size spirit lamp.

The Engine is mounted on a proper designed carriage, with shafts. The wheels are cast iron, and nickel-plated rims and imitation springs, suction pipe and rose; also, delivery pipes and branches are sent out with the model. This is certainly one of the most novel introductions of the season, and is sure to give every satisfaction.

12in. long without shafts, 5in. wide, 8in. high ... ... ... ... ... 47/6

Bassett-Lowke Ltd.

## CRANE & DONKEY ENGINE COMBINED.

The above is fitted with a powerful Reversing Cylinder, Geared Windlass and Jib, Brass Flywheel 3¼in. diam., Bright Brass Boiler with Funnel, Water Tap, Safety Valve, special Reversing Cock, Lamp, &c. ... ... Price 11/6

If mounted on Polished Wood, Revolving Base, and four Turned Brass Wheels ... ... Price 15/6

N.B.—This Model will lift 1 lb. in weight, and by throwing the Windlass out of gear, can be used as a Donkey Engine.

## MODEL CRANE.

This is a useful and instructive Model, having all movements the same as the largest cranes now in use. Strongly made ... ... ... ... ... 2/6

Cheaper quality, ingeniously designed ... ... ... 1/-

## MODEL STEAM ROLLER.

The above steam oxydised Roller is fitted with a strong brass boiler, safety valve, whistle, and oscillating cylinder, with reversing motion.

Length over all 10½in., 8¼in. high ... ... 17/6

Cheaper pattern, with polished brass boiler, 8in. over all, 7in high ... ... ... 10/6

## MODEL GAS ENGINE.

Powerful Horizontal Gas Engine. Cylinder, 1in. bore, 2in. stroke. Mounted on strong cast iron bed plate.

Highly finished all over, complete with Indiarubber Tubes for connecting to gas bracket. Fly wheel, 5½in. diameter.

Base, 6in. by 3¼in. ... ... ... £1 5s. 0d.

# Model Motor Cars (Clockwork.)

No. 518.

No. 517.—Tonneau Body Motor Car, fitted with strong Clockwork, Adjustable Steering Gear for straight or circular run, Wheels fitted with Pneumatic Indiarubber Tyres, One Lamp, and the whole Car finely enamelled and lined. 10in. long, 5in. wide, 6in. high. 11/6

No. 518.—Ditto, extra strong Clockwork, with Two Lamps as per illustration. 11in. long, 6in. wide, 6¼in. high ... 15/-

No. 516.

No. 516.—Phaeton Pattern Motor Car, fitted with extra strong Clockwork, the Car running in an original zig-zag track, with Horn sounding Pip! Pip! nickel-plated Wheels with Double Spokes, Pneumatic Indiarubber Tyres, Two Lamps, and Cushioned Leather Seats, high-class finish, finely enamelled and lined as illustrated. 13¾in. long, 7¼in. wide, 8in. high... 29/6

# Model Motor Cars (Steam.)

No. 515.

No. 514.—Model Steam Motor Car, with Adjustable Steering Gear for straight or circular run, Double Spoke Wheels, fitted with Pneumatic Tyres, Two Lamps, Leather Cushion Seat. Car fitted with a strong Boiler, a Safety Valve, and Spirit Lamp complete.

This Car can also be supplied with Clockwork, instead of Steam, for 13/6.

No. 515.—Steam Motor Car, Dog Cart Style, with adjustable Steering Gear for straight or circular run, Double Spoke Wheels, fitted with Pneumatic Tyres, Two Lamps, Leather Cushion Seats. Car fitted with a strong Boiler, Safety Valve, and Spirit Lamp, complete. 9½in. long, 5in. wide, 7in. high ... ... 14/6

No. 514.

9½in. long, 5in. wide, 6¼in. high, 13/-

*Bassett-Lowke Ltd.*

## NEW SCALE MODEL STEAM CRANE.

No. 93. Actual Working Model of Steam Crane, No. 3 - Gauge, 3 Cylinders, 8 Gearing Wheels.

**Will run by steam, raise and lower by steam, revolve and reverse by steam.**

Specification—Frame on Four Wheels. Total length 10in. height 9in. without jib, with 2 oscillating cylinders, steam starting lever.

Revolving frame with geared windlass, reversing tap, throw off lever controlling revolving mechanism, double action Cylinder, heavy fly wheel.

Jib of correct pattern, with pulley wheel and supporting chains.

Boiler of Brass, with valve, water gauge, funnel, etc.

The whole painted and lined correctly, wheels, pinions, etc. of brass.

Guaranteed to lift a weight of 2½ lbs.

No. 93. The most practical and perfect reproduction made, £3 18s. 6d. each.

## MODEL PAPER WEIGHTS.

The accompanying Illustrations show our series of Model Paper Weights (illustrations half full size). They are made with movable parts, and are finely finished and mounted on marble base.

No. 1.—Vertical Engine, with Cigar Cutter in Chimney ... 3/6
   Cheaper pattern ... 1/3
No. 2.—Horizontal Engine, with Cigar Cutter in Chimney, Boiler Barrel forming a Matchbox ... 7/6
   Cheaper pattern ... 2/-
No. 3.—Model Motor Car, Body forming Box for Postage Stamps ... 9/-
No. 4.—Dynamo, complete in all details ... 5/6

The MODEL ENGINEER, August 15th, 1902, says:—
"A Novelty in Paper Weights.—Messrs. W. J. Bassett-Lowke & Co., of Kingswell Street, Northampton, have produced quite a novel paper weight in the shape of a MODEL of a working model vertical engine and boiler, such as they supply in the ordinary way. The paper weight or ornament, for it can serve the purpose admirably, is about 3½ inches high, about quarter full size of the working engine, and is very well made and finished. In the moving parts are not altogether "dummy," the flywheel and axle with crank, connecting-rod, eccentric sheave and strap, handles of whistles and taps, all are capable of movement.

## MODEL STEAM CRANE.

As will be seen by illustration, this magnificent Model, is an exact reproduction of the Steam Cranes in use in Dockyards, Shipping Ports, &c. It is fitted with a powerful Steam Engine and Boiler, with Double Action Slide Valve Cylinder, and Exhaust into Chimney.

The Engine can be thrown in or out of gear, and can be reversed. The Boiler has bell whistle, water gauge, and safety-valve, and the Engine is supplied with a reliable steam lubricator.

The Crane house is made to represent corrugated galvanised iron, with glass windows, and three sides to open, and revolves on imitation brickwork base, the whole is complete in every way. Size with arm and without chimney 22in. long, 9in. wide, 12in. high. ... £3 5s. 0d.

## CRANE & DONKEY ENGINE COMBINED.

The above is fitted with a powerful Reversing Cylinder, Geared Windlass and Jib, Brass Flywheel 3½in. diam., Bright Brass Boiler with Funnel, Water Tap, Safety Valve, special Reversing Cock, Lamp, &c. ... ... ... Price 12/6

If mounted on Polished Wood, Revolving Base, and four Turned Brass Wheels, as illustration ... ... Price 17/-

N.B.—This Model will lift 1 lb. in weight and by throwing the Windlass out of gear, can be used as a Donkey Engine.

## HORIZONTAL DONKEY ENGINE.

Brass Horizontal Engine, with powerful cast Oscillating Cylinder, Bright Brass or Copper Dome Top, Boiler, Starting Tap, Blow-off Tap, and mounted on heavy Cast Iron Stand complete, with Spirit Lamp ... ... ... ... ... 6/6

*Bassett-Lowke Ltd.*

## MODEL MOTOR CARS (*Clockwork.*)

**MODERN DESIGNS.**

**STYLISH COLOURS.**

13659

These Motor Cars are fitted with extra strong Clockwork, Pneumatic Tyres, Cushioned Seats, Brass Engine Hood, Front Axle adjustable to run either straight or circular, with three Lamps.

No. 7. 10in. long, 4½in. wide 4in. high ... ... ... ... ... ... ... ... 9/-

No. 8. 11½in „ 5in „ 5in. „ ... ... ... ... ... ... ... ... ... 14/-

No. 9. 13¾in. „ 6¼in. „ 6¼in. „ with nickel-plated Headlight, for burning oil ... ... ... ... ... ... ... ... ... ... ... 40/-

## MODEL RACING MOTOR CARS (*Clockwork.*)

### UP-TO-DATE DESIGNS.

13661

These Motor Cars are fitted with extra strong Clockwork, Pneumatic Tyres, Cushioned Seats Brass Engine Hood, Front Axle adjustable to run either straight or circular, with spare Tyres.

No. 60. 11½in. long, 4½in. wide, 4¾in. high ... ... ... ... ... ... ... 10/6

No. 61. 15½in. „ 5½in. „ 6¼in. „ as illustration ... ... ... ... ... 17/6

13662/3

## MODEL HOUSE BOATS.

This new and original novelty is made after a Model of the well-known Henley House Boats, the interior is richly furnished and the exterior is complete with palms, chinese lanterns, flower pots, hammocks, flags and pennants, embossed windows, small boats, ladders, life-buoys, etc., as illustration. The Model is enamelled in attractive colours.

No. 1.—Plainly furnished, 13½in. long, 6in. wide, 11½in. high ... ... 15/6

No. 2.—Richly furnished, tables and chairs on deck, 19½in. long, 8½in. wide, 16¼in. high ... ... ... ... ... 33/6

No. 3.—Exquisitely furnished, as illustration, 26in. long, 11in. wide, 20in, high 53/6

## *A FEW OF OUR MODEL STEAMBOATS.*

11

4

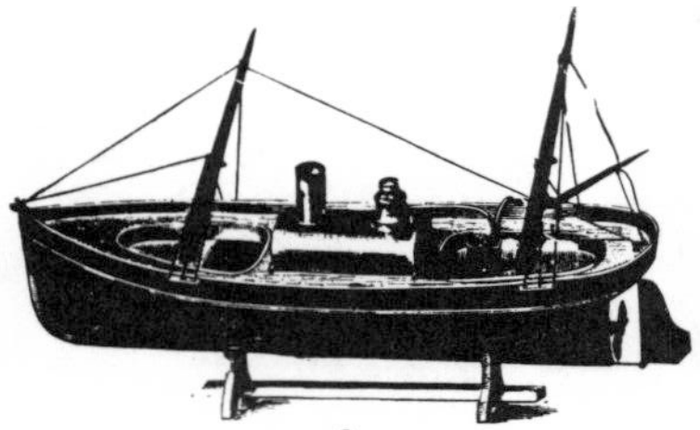

3

No. 11—**Model Torpedo Boat Destroyer,** with Ram, Polished Brass Boiler, Double-action Oscillating Cylinder, Steam Dome, Funnel, Whistle, Safety Valve, Starting Tap, Polished Brass Barbette with large Gun Metal Cannon, 3¼in. long, Polished Mahogany Deck, Fancy Figurehead, Anchors, Handrail with Turned Brass Staunchions, Length 22in., beam 4½in. Price 42/-

No. 3—**Model Screw Steam Boat,** fitted with Polished Brass Boiler, Steam Dome, Funnel, Double-action Oscillating Cylinder, 2 Masts and Rigging, Silk Flags. The whole Boat finished in Black and Bronze. Length 15in., beam 4in. ... ... ... ... Price 18/6

No. 4—**Model Screw Gun Boat,** with Ram, Polished Brass Boiler, Handrail, Steam Dome, Funnel, Double-action Oscillating Cylinder, fitted with turned Gun Metal Cannon on Stand, and Brass Shield. Boat finished in Black and Bronze, and Polished Mahogany Deck. Length 17in., beam 3½in. ... ... ... Price 19/6

## Model
# L. & S.W. Railway Express Locomotive, No. 370.

THIS Locomotive is fitted with a strong Brass Boiler, 11½ in. long by 2¼ in. diameter, one pair of Double-action Slide-Valve Cylinders 1½ in. stroke, fitted with Slide Bars and Lubricators, Reversing Motion worked from Cab, exhaust steam into Funnel, Bell Whistle, Two-cock Water Gauge, best quality Steam Gauge with Gun-metal Syphon. The Boiler Filler is out of sight, being in the Chimney. The Loco. is very substantially made. The Driving Wheels, which are 3½ in. diameter, are of correct design, and are suitable for our Model Permanent Way. The enamelling and lining are exact in every detail as in the real Loco., including the Coat of Arms. Imitation Headlights and Vacuum Brake Pipes are included. The Dome, Safety Valve, Whistle, Chimney Cap, and Handrails are of Polished Brass. The Tender is a splendid Model, with correct shape Axle-boxes and Dummy Springs, and six Turned Wheels 2⅛ in. diameter. The Loco. is very powerful, and will run for about three-quarters of an hour without re-filling.

3 in. gauge, length over all 2 ft. 5 in., height to top of funnel 8 in. ... ... ... ... Price **£7 7 0**

# Scale Model G.E.R. Locomotive.
## No. 1870.

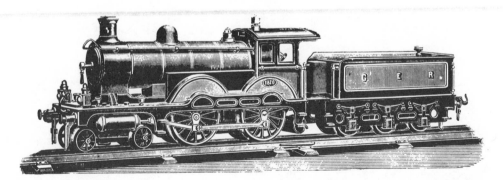

THE above Locomotive, which is a perfect scale Model in external appearance (with the exception of the Cylinders) is built of Castings throughout. It has Double-action Slide-valve Cylinders with packing glands, and exhausts into Funnel, **Reversing Motion worked from Cab,** Tubular Brass Boiler with **internal firing**, Spirit Tank in Tender with **visible drip feed,** Spring Buffers, Bell Whistle in Cab, Water Gauge, Stop-cock and all details, as illustrated. Enamelled and lined in correct G.E.R. Colours.

This Locomotive is of very solid construction, and is the best Model we supply for this gauge.

| | £ s. d. |
|---|---|
| No. 1.—1¾ in. gauge, 23 in. long, including Tender ... ... ... ... ... Price | 4 10 0 |
| 2½ in. „ 29 in. „ „ ... ... ... ... ... ... | 6 10 0 |

Owing to length of wheel base, this Loco. will **not** negotiate the small radii curves in the tin-plate rails.

*Bassett-Lowke Ltd.*

## THE LATEST NOVELTY!

A WORKING MODEL OF George Stephenson's "Rocket," 1829.

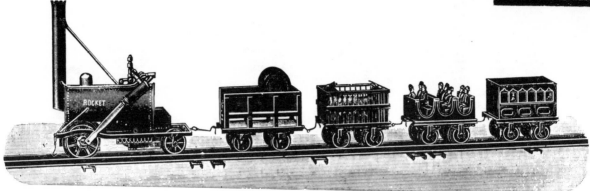

AS the above illustration shows, we are able this season to provide a very unique working Model Locomotive, viz.: of George Stephenson's famous "Rocket," the first locomotive intended for passenger service, and which, by attaining a speed of thirty-six miles an hour at the Rainhill trials in 1829, showed the world that the steam locomotive was a practical success.

The Model is a very close replica of the original, and has a strong Brass Boiler, patent Spirit Lamp, Double-action Slide Valve Cylinders, Whistle, and Safety Valve. · The Model has a Tender of the proper pattern with water barrel. The train is a copy of those originally used in the early days of railway travel, and comprises one Cattle Truck and two Passenger Cars.

1¾ in. gauge, length of train, 32 in.  ...  ...  ...  Price complete, **19/6**

## Clockwork "New York Central" Express Locomotive.

No. 2350 C.

THIS excellent model is one of the best replicas of a typical American Vauclain compound Locomotive ever produced, and is quite as accurate as the first quality scale models of English Clockwork Locomotives described in these pages. It has coupled Driving Wheels, Cylinders, Coupling and Connecting Rods, four-wheeled Bogie Truck, and eight-wheeled Tender. Every detail is as illustration, including Cow-catcher, which is removable. The Clockwork is very strongly made, and has Regulator, Brake and Reversing Gear.

|  |  |  |  |  |  |  |  |  |
|---|---|---|---|---|---|---|---|---|
| No. 0.—1¼ in. gauge, 17 in. long | ... | ... | ... | ... | ... | Price £1 | 13 | 0 |
| ,, 1.—1¾ in. ,, 22 in. ,, | ... | ... | ... | ... | ... | 2 | 8 | 0 |
| ,, 2.—2 in. ,, 24½ in. ,, | ... | ... | ... | ... | ... | 2 | 17 | 6 |

*These Locomotives will run on the small Radii Curves, but the large Radii should be used to obtain the best results.*

*Bassett-Lowke Ltd.*

## No. 2. Electric Railway, with Double Truck Car.

### PRICE, $7.90.

8 VOLTS.                    ½ AMPERE.

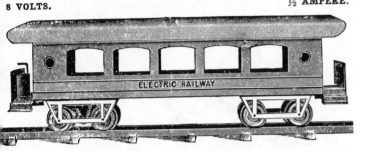

This is an entirely new design and is made to meet the demand for a larger and more elaborate equipment than our small four-wheel car. It has 18 feet of steel track, 2 inch gauge, which may be arranged in any shape to suit purchaser. The car is 19 inches long 6 inches high, and 4 inches wide. It has handsomely finished body and has brass wheels, 1¼ inches in diameter.

It is powerful enough to climb considerable grades. Speed of car about 150 feet per minute.

Only one motor is used and this is mounted on the forward truck near the reversing switch. The motor is geared to one axle and is very powerful and of the highest efficiency.

The car is strong and thoroughly well made throughout.

**The entire equipment consists of car, 18 feet of strip steel track and 5 dry batteries.**

Weight, complete, in box, 17 pounds.

**Motor Car only, $3.75.**

Track and Ties (strip steel) in 9 ft. lengths, 35 cents. By mail, 50 cents.

Dry Batteries, 25 cents each.

1¼ in. brass wheels with axles and insulating bushings, 50 cents per set of four. By mail, 55 cents.

## No. 3. Coal Mining Locomotive and Train.

### PRICE, $5.75.

5 to 6 VOLTS.                    ¾ AMPERE

This represents a modern hauling plant as used in our large coal mines. The motor is self-starting, and on top of locomotive is a lever connecting with a reversing switch, by means of which the train may be run backward or forward.

Connection is made from the motor to the wheels by means of double reduction spur gearing with accurately cut teeth. The wheels are spoked, two inches in diameter, and made of iron.

The locomotive is very powerful. It will climb grades and haul the three cars heavily loaded. It will haul 10 to 12 empty cars on a straight, level track. The speed is somewhat less than that of the railways Nos. 1 and 2.

**The equipment consists of locomotive, three coal cars, 18 feet of 2 inch gauge strip steel track, and four dry batteries.**

Coal cars are iron, with brass wheels. They will stand hard usage. The track may be arranged in any shape. It is better to see that it is level, as the locomotive will run easier and be easier on the battery when track is in this condition. Oil all moving parts of locomotive and train frequently.

Length of train, 18 inches.

Weight, complete, boxed, 13½ pounds.

Coal cars, 25 cents each. By mail, 35 cents.

Track and Ties (strip steel) in 9 ft lengths, 35 cents. By mail 50 cts.

Extra dry batteries, per cell, 25 cents.

## No. 42. Electric Railway.

### Price, $4.70.

4 to 5 VOLTS.                    ½ AMPERE.

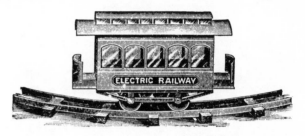

This model is an entirely new and improved design and is without doubt the most perfect and complete car that has ever been sold in the way of a toy. It has trucks the same as a large trolley car. The motor is connected to the axle by means of brass spur gearing—machine cut. The motor is reversible and has strong and substantial bearings, brushes and commutator. It is provided with a 3-pole self-starting armature.

A reversing switch enables the operator to run the car backwards or forwards, or start and stop it at will.

The car is 8 inches long, 5 inches high; has brass wheels 1¼ inch in diameter. It will fit our standard 2 inch gauge track.

Speed of car, 150 to 200 feet per minute.

**The complete equipment consists of car, 9 feet of strip steel track and 4 cells of dry battery.**

Weight, boxed, 12½ lbs.

**Motor car only, $3.35.**

Track and ties strip steel in 9 ft. lengths, 35 cents. By mail 50 cents.

Extra dry batteries, per cell, 25 cents.

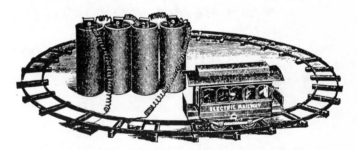

This illustration shows the complete No. 42 Railway with battery.

St. Louis, Mo.

Gentlemen:

I bought one of your No. 2 motor cars a month or two ago and it goes so fast that I cannot run it at full speed on a curve unless it is very gradual. I have had lots of fun with it. Please tell me when your next catalogue is out and please send me one.

Yours very truly,
L. BENTON PRINCE,
3846 Lindell Ave.

## No. 3. Coal Mining Locomotive Only.

### PRICE, $3.50.

5 to 6 VOLTS.                    ¾ AMPERE.

This is the locomotive which is used with our No. 3 train. It is sold separately so that customers wishing to add to their equipment can obtain extra locomotives without having to buy the complete No. 3 outfit.

No track or battery is furnished, but the locomotive only.

Length, 7½ inches. Height 3¼ inches. Weight, 2½ lbs, boxed.

*Carlisle & Fitch*

## No. 4.  Electric Locomotive and Freight Train.

### PRICE $12.35.

**8 to 10 VOLTS.**              **¾ AMPERE.**

A complete and perfect model of a modern freight train. The locomotive has headlight, cylinders, connecting rods, pilot, bell, steam dome, etc. The locomotive is operated by an electric motor concealed in the boiler. The power is transmitted to the wheels by means of double reduction spur gearing with accurately cut teeth.

The locomotive runs at a high speed, about 150 to 200 feet per minute, and is of such power that it will haul ten or twelve cars.

The locomotive will haul the three cars up considerable grades, but it is best to have the track as nearly level as possible. Wheels of locomotive are of iron, 2 inches in diameter, while those of the tender and cars are 1 inch in diameter.

In the cab of the locomotive is placed a reversing switch, and a lever projects outside of the cab, by means of which the locomotive may be started, stopped and reversed.

The motor is a self-starting one, and has no dead center.

The complete equipment consists of locomotive, tender, flat car, box car, and caboose, 18 feet of 2 inch gauge strip steel track and six dry batteries. These dry batteries are connected together and mounted in the packing box with terminal wires ready for use.

Length of complete Train, 49 inches.
Length of Locomotive and Tender, 19 inches.
Weight of complete outfit, boxed, 22 pounds.
**Locomotive with tender, $6.50.**

Flat Cars, 60 cents each.  By mail, 80 cents.
Box Cars, $1.20 each.  By mail, $1.55.
Dry Batteries, per single cell, 25 cents

## No. 11. Gondola Flat Car.

PRICE, 60c.                    BY MAIL, 80c.

Made of heavy tin; brass wheels 1 inch in diameter. Very strong and substantial. Can be loaded with coal, sand, gravel, etc. Designed for use with our No. 4, No. 20 and No. 34 locomotives.
Length, 10 inches.  Height above rails, 2⅝ inches.  Width, 3 inches.
Weight, boxed, 1¼ lbs.

## No. 47. Coal Car.
### PRICE, $1.50.

Made of heavy tin, 1-inch brass wheels, windlass and trap doors in bottom for dumping coal, etc. An exact imitation of the large B. & O. coal cars. For use with No. 4, No. 20 and No. 34 locomotives.
Length, 10 inches.  Height above rails, 4 inches.  Width, 3 inches.
Weight, boxed, 2 lbs.

## No. 49. Oil Car.

PRICE, $1.35.                    BY MAIL, $1.70.

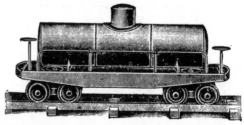

A tank line car with tank, hand rails, etc. Makes a nice addition to any railway. Painted and well finished.
Will fit our standard 2-inch gauge track. For use with No. 4, No. 20 and No. 34 locomotives.
Length, 10 inches.  Height, 4¾ inches.  Width, 3 inches.
Weight, boxed, 2 lbs.

## No. 12.  Box Car.

PRICE, $1.20.              BY MAIL, $1.55.

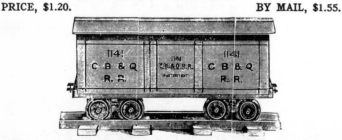

Made of heavy tin, 1 inch brass wheels, sliding doors, etc. Strong and durable.
Designed for use with our No. 4, No. 20 and No. 34 locomotives.
Length, 10 inches.  Height above rails, 4¾ inches.  Width, 3 inches.
Weight, boxed, 2 lbs.

## No. 46.  Caboose.

PRICE, $1.20.              BY MAIL, $1.55.

Made of heavy tin; 1 inch brass wheels. Strong and durable.
Designed for use with our No. 4, No. 20 and No. 34 locomotives.
Length 10 inches.  Height, 5½ inches.  Width, 3 inches.  Weight, boxed, 2 lbs.

*Carlisle & Fitch*

## No. 61. Railway.

### PRICE, $20.00.

**10 TO 12 VOLTS.**      **¾ AMPERE.**

A complete model passenger train. Everything is correctly proportioned and well made. This train is new and is just being put on the market.

The complete outfit consists of our No. 34 locomotive and tender, one No. 59 baggage car and two No. 60 passenger cars, 36 feet of strip steel track and 8 dry batteries all connected up ready to run. Great care should be used in setting up track for this train and we recommend that the curves be 24 inch radius or over.

Length of complete train, 70 inches.

Weight, boxed, 39 lbs.

———

Pittsburgh, Pa.

Gentlemen:

I believe I will tell you some of the things I have, and how nice I like them. I have one of your No. 42 cars, No. 19 summer car, No. 4 locomotive, No. 50 flat car, and 81 ft. of strip steel track, two switches. All of my cars run fine, and I like everything I have. I think the Carlisle & Finch Co. is the best electrical firm I know of. I like all of your cars, and I have seen most of them run; they run fine, especially your No. 45 locomotive.

Yours very truly,

JOHN F. SCOTT,

5617 Elgin Ave.

Ilion, N. Y.

Gentlemen:

I have one of your No. 16 water power dynamos, which I got from J. H. Bunnell & Co. It is satisfactory in every way. I had it running on thirty pounds water pressure, and it ran a ten volt motor so fast that I could scarcely stop it.

Yours truly,

JOSEPH J. RUSSELL.

———

## No. 60. Passenger Car.

### PRICE, $2.25.

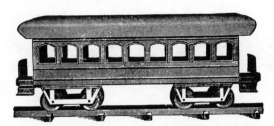

Suitable for the No. 34 locomotive. Made with polished brass sides and painted metal roof. Has platforms, etc., as shown. Trucks are made of a sheet stamping. Wheels, 1¼ inch, brass.

Length, 15½ inches. Height above rail, 6 inches. Width, 3½ inches.

Weight, boxed, 3¼ lbs

## No. 4. Electric Locomotive and Tender only.

### PRICE, $6.50.

**8 to 10 VOLTS.**      **¾ AMPERE**

Locomotive same as furnished with our No. 4 and No. 32. Strong and substantial and well made in every particular. Will haul long trains of cars at a good speed.

| | |
|---|---|
| Length of Locomotive and Tender | 19 inches. |
| Width | 4 inches. |
| Height | 5½ inches |
| Locomotive Wheels | 2 in. dia. |
| Weight, with Tender | 3 lbs. |

No track nor battery is furnished with the locomotive at above price.

## No. 20. Suburban Locomotive.

### PRICE, $6.00.

**8 to 10 VOLTS**      **¾ AMPERE**

A double ender locomotive for moving cars on sidings, doing switching and hauling suburban trains. Has the same mechanism as our No. 4 locomotive, but the tender is omitted and the boiler and cab are shorter. Well made, strong and substantial. Will haul long trains of cars.

| | |
|---|---|
| Length | 13 inches. |
| Width | 4 inches. |
| Height | 5½ inches. |
| Wheels | 2 in. dia. |
| Weight | 2 lbs. |

No battery nor track is included at above price.

## No. 59. Baggage Car.

### PRICE, $2.00.

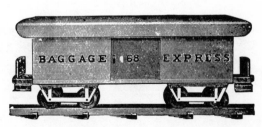

Suitable for the No. 34 locomotive, made of heavy tin, neatly painted. Has sliding doors, platforms and steps as shown. Trucks are made of a sheet stamping. Wheels, 1¼ inch, brass.

Length, 15½ inches. Height above rail, 6 inches. Width, 3½ inches.

Weight, boxed, 3¼ lbs.

# THE BING MINIATURE RAILWAY SYSTEM
## TRAIN COMBINATIONS.

Gauge 0 == $1^3/_8$ in.

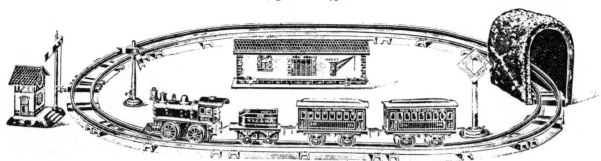

**510/902**

Train consisting of: cast iron locomotive with guaranteed clockwork and brake (train can be stopped by a brake section) tender, 2 passenger cars, japanned and lettered in the exact colors of New York Central R. R.; watchman's house with signal, crossing pole, 1 extra signal, freight station and tunnel. Track formation ⬭ 8 curved and 2 straight sections.

**510/904**

Train consisting of: cast iron locomotive with guaranteed clockwork and brake (train can be stopped by a brake section) tender, 3 passenger cars, japanned and lettered in the exact colors of New York Central R. R.; passenger station, tunnel, watchman's house with automatic bell, crossing pole, watchman's house with signal. Track formation ⬭ 8 curved and 4 straight sections.

## ELECTRICAL TRAIN SETS

### (Series VIII)

See pages 18—20 for reducers, switches, etc. — See pages 53—55 for electric accessories.

**523/141/0** Electric *New York Central* Train Set;

length 25 in., *cast iron New York Central* type locomotive with field magnet motor for use on *battery, direct or alternating current,* equipped for electric headlight. 2 eight wheel Pullman cars. Track formation ⬭ consisting of 8 curved and 4 straight sections including connecting rail with switch. Gauge 0 = $1^3/_8$ in. wide.

### (Series IX)

**524/12/0N** Electric *New York Central* Train Set;

length 60 in., 8 wheel *cast iron Express* locomotive, reversible with field magnet motor for use on *battery, direct or alternating current,* with electric headlight. Tender (loco and tender 18 in.), 2 eight wheel Pullman cars and 1 eight wheel combination car with 2 sliding doors. *Every car is fitted with light inside and electric tail lamp at the end of the train.* Track formation ⬭ consisting of 8 curved and 6 straight sections including connecting rail with switch. Gauge 1 = $1^7/_8$ in. wide.

# BING'S MODEL STEAM LOCOMOTIVES

**Suitable for Gauge 0 = 1³/₈ in. wide.**

*Our Steam Locomotives* are absolutely reliable in every direction and can be worked very easily. Every piece guaranteed to work. No special kind of trackage wanted; will run on any track for mechanical or electrical trains.

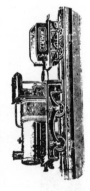

**30593/0**

*Steam Tender Loco* with oscillating brass cylinder, stamped frame, polished brass boiler and safety valve, 7¹/₂ in. long. Gauge 0 = 1³/₈ in. wide.

**31593/0**

*Steam Loco with Tender*, stamped frame, polished brass boiler, oscillating brass cylinder and safety valve, 10³/₄ in. long incl. tender. Gauge 0 = 1³/₈ in. wide.

**29593/0**

*Steam Loco with Tender*, stamped frame, polished brass boiler, oscillating brass cylinder, safety valve and steam whistle, 11³/₄ in. long incl. tender. Gauge 0 = 1³/₈ in. wide.

**67593/0**

*Steam Locomotive with Tender*, finest finish with 2 oscillating outside cylinders, steam dome, steam whistle, flame guard and safety valve, 11⁵/₈ in. long incl. tender. Gauge 0 = 1³/₈ in. wide.

**39593/0**

*Steam Locomotive and Tender*, exact working model with finely japanned brass boiler with 2 oscillating cylinders, steam dome, hand rails, steam whistle, flame guard, safety valve and japanned driving wheels. 13¹/₄ in. long incl. tender. Gauge 0 = 1³/₈ in. wide.

**60593/0**

*Fine Steam Locomotive with Tender*, with 2 fixed slide valve cylinders, with reversing gear, finely japanned brass boiler, nickeled wheels, steam dome, bell steam whistle, improved lubricating device built in the smoke box, safety valve, Loco with flame guard and alcohol lamp. 13⁵/₈ in. long incl. tender. Gauge 0 = 1³/₈ in. wide.

# BING'S MODEL STEAM RAILWAYS

**Gauge 0 = 1³/₈ in. wide.**

**160/20/00**

Steam Train; tender-locomotive with polished brass boiler, oscillating brass cylinder and safety valve; 1 Passenger car. Complete train 12 in. long. Track formation ◯ consisting of 4 curved sections. Gauge 0 = 1³/₈ in. wide.

**160/30/00**

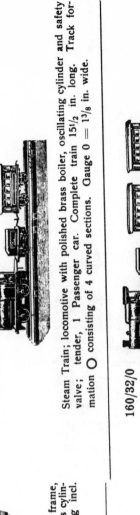

Steam Train; locomotive with polished brass boiler, oscillating cylinder and safety valve; tender, 1 Passenger car. Complete train 15¹/₂ in. long. Track formation ◯ consisting of 4 curved sections. Gauge 0 = 1³/₈ in. wide.

**160/32/0**

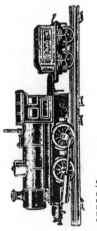

Steam Train; locomotive with polished brass boiler, oscillating brass cylinder and safety valve; tender, 2 Passenger cars. Complete train 20¹/₄ in. long. Track formation ◯ consisting of 2 straight and 4 curved sections. Gauge 0 = 1³/₈ in. wide.

**160/40/0**

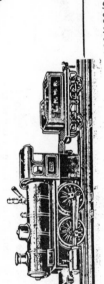

Steam Train; locomotive with polished brass boiler, oscillating cylinder, safety valve; tender, 2 Passenger cars, 1 Baggage car with doors to open. Complete train 29 in. long. Track formation ◯ consisting of 6 curved and 4 straight sections. Gauge 0 = 1³/₈ in. wide.

**160/169/0**

Steam Train; locomotive with 2 oscillating cylinders, blue oxydised brass boiler and steam whistle, safety valve; tender, 2 Passenger cars and 1 Baggage car with doors to open. Complete train 33¹/₂ in. long. Track formation ◯ consisting of 6 curved and 4 straight sections. Gauge 0 = 1³/₈ in. wide.

# SOME OF BING'S MODEL BOATS.

155/603

155/603 *U. S. Fire Boat,* exact model with guaranteed *clockwork,* actually pumping and throwing out water. Made in 4 sizes.

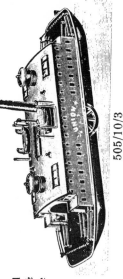

505/10/3

*Ferry Boat,* exact model with guaranteed *clockwork* and moved by 2 side wheels.

Made in 3 sizes.

## War Fleets.

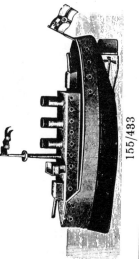

155/483

155/483 *Battle Ship,* perfect model with guaranteed *clockwork.* Made in 12 different sizes and shapes.

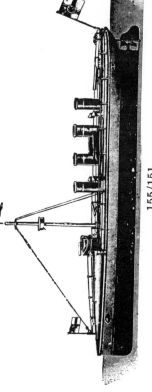

155/151

*Torpedo Boat,* exact model with guaranteed *clockwork* for quickest speed, long and narrow shaped body. Made in 7 different sizes.

---

# THE BING MINIATURE RAILWAY SYSTEM

## ELECTRIC TROLLEY CARS

See pages 18—20 for reducers, switches, etc. — See pages 53—55 for electr. accessories.

**179/50/00 Electric Trolley Car;**

length 6½ in., fitted with permanent magnet motor for *battery use* only. Track formation O consisting of 4 curved sections including connecting rail. Gauge 00 = 1⅛ in. wide.

**519/51/00 Electric Trolley Car;**

length 6½ in., fitted with field magnet motor for use on *battery, direct or alternating current,* equipped for electric headlight. Track formation O consisting of 4 curved sections including connecting rail. Gauge 00 = 1⅛ in. wide.

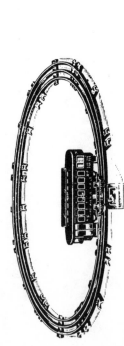

**520/45/0 Electric Trolley Car;**

length 7 in., "Pay as you enter" or "Broadway" model, fitted with field magnet motor for use on *battery, direct or alternating current.* Track formation O consisting of 8 curved sections including connecting rail with switch. Gauge 0 = 1⅜ in. wide.

**520/47/0 Electric Trolley Car;**

same as above, but equipped for electric headlight. Gauge 0 = 1⅜ in. wide.

# SOME OF BING'S MODEL BOATS.

1910

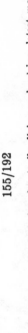

**Submarine** with guaranteed *clockwork* actually diving and raising, latest model. 5 different styles and sizes.

155/192

*River Boat* with guaranteed *clockwork* and 2 side wheels. Made in 3 different sizes.

155/363

11599

**Butterfly Game**, Revolver will shoot a propeller in shape of a Butterfly either horizontally or vertically. Very amusing. Made in 3 different styles.

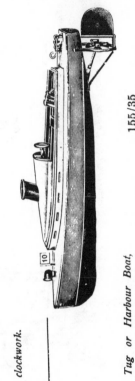

*Motor Lunche* with guaranteed clockwork. Made in 9 different sizes.

155/35

11612

**Flying Machine**, made out of steel spring wire and covered with silk material. No *clockwork*, will fly about 50 yards. Made in 5 different styles.

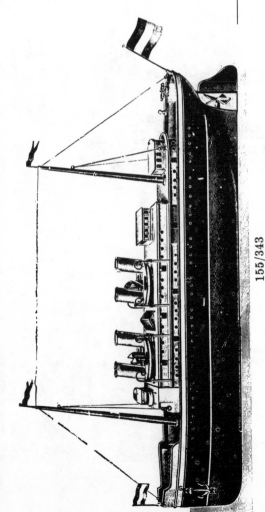

*Ocean Liner*, fine finish, guaranteed *clockwork*. Made in 8 different sizes.

155/343

*Tug or Harbour Boat*, exact model with guaranteed extra strong clockwork. Made in 3 sizes.

505/11/1

505/11/1

157/53

**Cannon**, fine finish; shoot India rubber shells by way of caps to regulate for different distances.

**Made in 8 different styles and sizes.**

157/53

115

*Bing*

# SOME OF BING'S MODEL STEAM ENGINES.

**130/742** *Model Street Roller* fitted with fine steam engine, reversible, steam whistle, blue oxydized brass boiler. Can be made to run forward, backward, straight and in circle.

Made in 2 different sizes.

130/742

130/732

*Steam Traction Engine,* Steam engine of very fine quality. Removing of the chain stops the engine from running on the floor. Engine can be used as an ordinary stationary engine.

Made in 3 different sizes.

10253

*Model Steam Derrick,* fitted with good quality steam engine, steam whistle, reversing gear for raising and lowering the whole derrick. Can revolve mechanically.

13⅝ in. long, 12⅝ in. high.

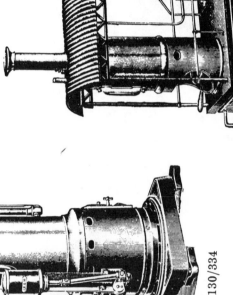

10253

**130/114** *Model Steam Engine,* new type oxydized brass boiler, fixed cylinder with tubular slide valve, feeding pump, steam whistle, water gauge, governor, lever safety valve, base and bearings of cast iron. Powerful alcohol lamp.

Made in 6 different sizes.

130/114

130/334

**130/334** *Model Steam Engine* with brass boiler fixed cylinders with tubular slide valve, base and bearings of cast iron, whistle, water gauge and extra powerful alcohol lamps.

Made in 4 different sizes

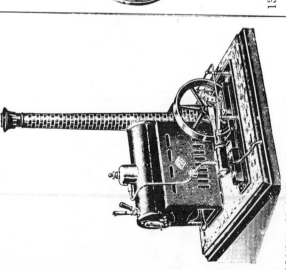

**130/234** *Model Steam Engine* with reversible gear horizontal type, oxydized boiler, fixed cylinder with slide valve, steam whistle, water gauge for the larger sizes. Finely finished. Made in 6 different sizes.

## SOME OF BING'S MODEL AUTOMOBILS.

## MECHANICAL FIRE DEPARTMENT.

156/162/1 *Motor Fire Engine* with extra strong clockwork with exchange gear to drive the car or pump water, signal bell which sounds while car is running; wheels with rubber tires and brake.
156/161/1, 10¼ in. long, 4⅛ in. wide, 5¼ in. high.
156/162/1, 12⅜ in. long, 4¾ in. wide, 6¼ in. high.

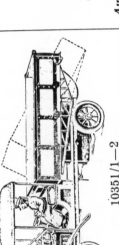

156/162/1

*Motor Hook and Ladder Car* with extra strong clockwork, ladder to extend and turn mechanically, signal bell which sounds while car is running. Extra fine finish, wheels with rubber tires and brake.
156/161/3, 30 in. long with ladder extended, 5¼ in. high.
156/162/3, 36 in. long with ladder extended, 6¼ in. high.

156/162/3

*Mechanical Street Roller* with extra strong clockwork, runs straight and in circle.
13639/0, 5 in. long, 4 in. high.
13639/1, 6½ in. long, 4¼ in. high.

13639/1

*Auto Truck* high class quality with guaranteed clockwork and brake, with tilting arrangement, rubber tires, can run straight and in circle. Made in 2 different sizes.
10351/1—2

10469
*Auto Coal Truck* up-to-date model, with guaranteed clockwork and brake, 2 doors at bottom to dump the load.
11½ in. long, 4¾ in. high.

10469

*Auto Bus* (model of 5th Ave Bus) high class quality with guaranteed clockwork and brake, can run straight and in circle. Made in 2 different sizes.
500/10/1 and 2

*Motor Patrolwagon* with extra strong clockwork signal bell which sounds while car is running. Finest finish, wheels with rubber tires and brake.
156/161/2, 10¼ in. long, 4¾ in. high.
156/162/2, 12 in. long, 6⅛ in. high.

156/162/2

14489/1
*Mechanical Floor Engine* with extra strong clockwork, 8 wheels.
8 in. long, 4½ in. high.

560/10 *Mechanical Street Roller* with extra strong clockwork. Fine reproduction of large rollers with steering wheel and movable pistons rods.
9 in. long, 5½ in. high.

560/10

## SOME OF BING'S FAMOUS WALKING DOGS.

*These dogs walk owing to a patented mechanism, no clockwork; simply can pull them along on a leash. Most lifelike movement. Very original.*

268/11/1—4 *Ceaser,* white silk plush with black spots. Made in 4 sizes.

255/11/1—2 *Dashhound* very original, brown felt. Made in 2 sizes.

260/11 *White Bull*
261/11 *White Bull*
262/11 *Brown Bull*
White and Brown. Made in 2 sizes.

256/11/1—3 *Bear,* brown silk plush. Made in 3 sizes.

299/11/1—4 *Poodel,* extra long hair of silk plush white. Made in 4 sizes.

264/11/1—4 *Spaniol,* white silk plush with brown spots. Made in 4 sizes.

**H 7918** IMPROVED GAME OF "PETER CODDLE" and his latest trip to New York, and what he saw there, A comical combination of curious circumstances for 100 evenings. This game is played with a large number of small cards and a book describing Peter's journey. Shipping weight, 10 oz.
Each .................. $0.19
Per dozen .................. 2.00

**H 7925** New Century Game of "Proverbs," is clean, wholesome, interesting and instructive, and makes a most delightful game for home and party play; also fitting and appropriate for church and social gatherings. Packed in a handsome leatherette case, resembling a book, and contains 60 round cornered cards to the set. Printed in two colors on superfine ivory board. Shipping weight, 5 oz. Each .................. $0.20
Per doz .................. 2.25

**H 7928** "Foxy Grandpa" Card Game, with 40 cards illustrating Foxy and the boys and all their doings; showing Foxy's home, his dog, cat and donkey, his pet pig and cow, all drawn by Bunny, the great cartoonist, in his very best style, and made up into a most amusing game, at which all can play, affording amusement for the entire family. Shipping weight, 8 oz. Each .................. $0.25
Per doz .................. 2.40

**H 7933** Buying and Selling Game, new edition. This outfit includes toy money for representing about $100 in coins, and 36 pictures of such things as a pound of coffee, ton of coal, etc., which are intended to be bought and sold. The box also contains a miniature cash carrier. Price, each .................. 25c. Postage, 15 cents extra.

**H 7953** Logomachy, or War of Words. The premium game. One of the best parlor card games published. This game contains seventy-two round cornered cards, heavy pictures printed in full lithographic colors. The card backs are in scarlet and gold. Full directions accompany each game; put up in handsome box. Shipping weight, 10 oz. Each .................. 40c.

**H 7968** Bible Authors. A Bible Game that is instructive, entertaining and impressive, entirely new and a work of art; shows faces of the leading Bible writers; eighteen different books, making 72 cards that are first-class and put up in a neat box. Shipping weight, 12 oz. Per box .................. 40c.

**H 7975** "Progressive Queries," a new game adapted for evening parties, ladies' clubs, church socials and all social gatherings where a game to entertain everybody at the same time is desired. The game is arranged for a company of twenty-four persons at six tables, each table being provided with a different subject, some in the form of conundrums and others, pictures of noted characters, etc., each table having something new and interesting. This game has become very popular, and takes the place of Progressive card games, being interesting, and something that everyone can play. Shipping weight, 14 oz. Each .................. 50c.

---

**H 7980** "Uncle Sam's Cabinets," an interesting card game for persons of all ages for fun, instruction and culture; any number from 2 to 20 persons can play. Consists of 104 cards, 2¼ x3½ in., with round corners, enameled finish, having fine halftone engravings of all presidents and their secretaries. This collection of portraits is alone worth any time the price of the game. Statesmen, teachers and authors recommend it for the young as a game which furnishes wholesome amusement and gives better acquaintance with the great men of American history than many books published. Shipping weight, 10 ounces. Each .................. 40c.

**H 7985** "Flinch," one of the most popular card games ever produced. More simple than Authors, more scientific than Whist. Played on the book plan with a pack of 150 cards, of 10 books each, numbered consecutively from 1 to 15. Any number from 2 to 8 persons may play the game. When more than 4 or 5 persons play it makes the game more interesting to use two packs. Shipping weight, 10 ounces.
Per pack .................. $0.38
Per doz. packs .................. 3.75
**H 7987** Gold-edged Flinch, otherwise same as H 7985. Shipping weight, 10 ounces. Per pack .................. 60c.

## Fireside Card Games.

Enameled Card Games, a highly finished card, and the games are selected carefully in regard to their special merit and contain an element of instruction and general information beyond the ordinary card game of Authors, although played in a similar manner.

**H 8008** Flags, showing the national flags of the principal countries of the world; the flags are reproduced in many colors; a most instructive and useful game. Shipping weight, 5 oz. Each .................. 20c.
**H 8011** In the White House, a new historical game. Halftone portraits of all the presidents of the United States, with principal events of each administration. Shipping weight, 5 oz. Each .................. 20c.

## PUZZLES.

**H 8072** Wire Puzzle Set. A collection of eight puzzles, every one good, and from simple to complicated designs. This set with instructions for working is the most complete and in every way the best collection of wire puzzles ever offered. Shipping weight, 8 oz. Per set .................. 60c.

**H 8083** DISSECTED MAP of the United States and World. Is engraved in outline, with only the more prominent features and localities, thereby presenting to the child no more than can be easily remembered; and is cut out on state lines. On the back is the map of the world, the whole forming a complete object lesson of the geography of the United States and the world. Size, when put together, 12x18. Packed in pasteboard box. Shipping weight, 1½ lb. Each .................. 44c.

## DOWN ON THE FARM.

**H 8087** "Down on the Farm," an interchangeable puzzle picture on wooden blocks, permitting of 300 combina-

---

tions and so arranged that where a change is made, joining pieces match, thus making a perfect picture after each change— for illustration, the barn can be placed where the house was and the house where the barn was. Each object can be placed in a different position. In the picture is shown every domestic animal and fowl usually found on a farm or in a barn yard. The picture is printed in colors. Size 12x18 inches. Put up in neat box. Shipping weight, 18 ounces. Price, complete .................. 40c.

**H 8091** "Sliced Animals," a popular dissected picture puzzle. Each section of the picture has a letter, which, when the puzzle is put together, spells the name of the picture. Shipping weight, 12 oz.
Per dozen .................. $2.00
Each .................. .20

**H 8094** Sectional Birds, extra fine edition. The pictures are reproduced in bright colors from sketches made from life by a prominent artist. The strips are lettered so that the child can learn the various names of the animals and birds. Shipping weight, 14 ounces. Each .................. 15c.

## The Conyne Chicago Kite.

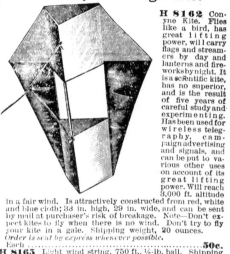

**H 8162** Conyne Kite. Flies like a bird, has great lifting power, will carry flags and streamers by day and lanterns and fireworks by night. It is a scientific kite, has no superior, and is the result of five years of careful study and experimenting. Has been used for wireless telegraphy, campaign advertising and signals, and can be put to various other uses on account of its great lifting power. Will reach 3,000 ft. altitude in a fair wind. Is attractively constructed from red, white and blue cloth; 33 in. high, 29 in. wide, and can be sent by mail at purchaser's risk of breakage. Note—Don't expect kites to fly when there is no wind. Don't try to fly your kite in a gale. Shipping weight, 20 ounces. *Order is sent by express whenever possible.*
Each .................. 50c.
**H 8165** Light wind string, 750 ft., ½-lb. ball. Shipping weight, 9 ounces .................. 25c.
**H 8168** Strong wind string, 460 ft., ½-lb. ball. Shipping weight, 9 ounces .................. 35c.

## TOYS.

In which we include an assortment of staple and new interesting toys, dolls and games, carefully selected as to quality, value and merit.

## PRINTING PRESSES.

**H 8531** "Marvel" Printing Press, operates with a wheel attachment, causing an even pressure and powerful leverage, thus offering a perfect device for perfect printing. It will print a form 2x 3½ inches. The outfit embraces a font of regular Printers' Type, put up in a Slide-Lid Cover Partitioned Type Tray, Ink Roller, pair of Tweezers, box of Gold Bronze, box of Silver Bronze, Bronzing Cotton, can of Printers' Ink, Cards and full directions for using, all packed in a strong wooden box. Weight of Press and outfit, 8 lbs. Price, complete .................. $1.75

## PHOTOGRAPH ALBUMS

Desirable styles, at prices within the reach of all buyers. See pages 461 to 464 for quotations.

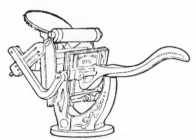

**H 8538** Baltimorean Self-Inker Outfit. Inside of chase, 2⅛x3¼ in. This size is especially adapted for printing small jobs, such as cards, envelopes, etc.; it carries one roller, has grippers, and is in every way a complete self-inking press. Press and card font of standard long type, 100 blank cards, ink, gold and silver bronze, tweezers and furniture..................$2.75
Shipping weight, 10 lb.

**H 8542** Baltimorean Self-Inker Outfit. Inside of chase, 2½x4 in. Press, with one roller and outfit of one card font of standard long type, 100 blank cards, ink, gold and silver bronze, tweezers and furniture. Shipping weight, 16 lb. Each.................$3.90

---

**YOU CANNOT BUY**
a more Instructive Toy than a Printing Press for a wide-awake Boy or Girl.

---

**H 8547** Baltimore Rotary Printing Press. Embodies the greatest improvements that have been effected in Amateur Printing Press construction in 25 years. By turning the crank the Press is set in motion, printing cards, envelopes, tags and other jobs. Inside of chase, 2⅛x3¼ in. Has a feed table. It is put up complete with one font of type, bronze, ink, tweezers, cards and instructions. Retail price, $6.00. Shipping weight, 10 lbs. Each......$4.00

**H 8551** Baltimorean Self-Inker Outfit. Inside of chase 4¼x6¼ in., has two rollers, and outfit of assorted card fonts of standard long type, set of quoins, oil can. shooting stick, composing stick, furniture, leads and ink. Complete..................$15.50
Shipping weight, 92 lb.

**H 8555** Baltimorean Self-Inker Outfit. Inside of chase, 5½x8 in., has two rollers, and outfit of assorted card fonts of standard long type, set of quoins, oil can, shooting stick, composing stick, furniture, leads and ink. The press has impression screws for regulating the form. The grippers are depressible. The press is well built and capable of fine impressions. Shipping weight, 140 lb.
Complete..................$21.50

---

**H 8559** Baltimorean Self-Inker Outfit. Inside of chase, 6x9 in., has two chases, two rollers, feed table, wrench, hand roller and outfit of assorted card fonts of standard long type; set of quoins, oil can, shooting stick, composing stick, planer, furniture, leads and ink. This is a powerful, well built press; rapid in its movement and finely finished. The grippers are depressible at will; impression screws regulate the platen and the revolving ink table is actuated by a pawl and cam in direct connection with the ink-motion and rocker-arm. The chase fastens to the bed by means of a latch. Shipping weight, 225 lb. Complete......$29.75

## Type.

Our type is put up in wood cases with division for each letter, and sliding cover. Quads, spaces and figures go with every font. This type is of standard make, and is full size. The following styles of type are small fonts, and are suitable for presses Nos. H 8531 to H 8559.

**H 8561**          5A    5½ Point          48c.
NEAT LETTER FOR NAMES AND OTHER USE. 1234567890
Shipping weight, 8 oz.

**H 8565**          5A.   10 Point          45c.
LETTER-WRITER PRINT. 12345
Shipping weight, 1½ lb.

**H 8569**          5A.   10 Point          60c.
ATTORNEY AND COUNSELLOR AT LAW. 93
Shipping weight, 13 oz.

**H 8573**                                  85c.
BALTIMOREAN SELF-INKERS
Are worthy of Imitation. 95     2A 5a
Shipping weight, 11 oz.

**H 8574**          2A 5a.   10 Point.       75c.
Descriptive MATTER 14850
Shipping weight, 11 oz.

**H 8575**          2A 5a.   8 Point.        80c.
A Contrast with Lighter Faces 12
Shipping weight, 8 oz.

**H 8579**          2A 5a.   22 Point.       $2.00
*Miss George Bush 123*
Shipping weight, 2¾ lb.

The above simply shows the style of type included in each font, also the number of letters in same, taking "a" as a basis, the other letters all being in proportion usually required.

## Printing Ink, Sizing and Varnish.

|  |  | Shipping Weight. | Each. |
|---|---|---|---|
| **H 8584** | 2-oz. cans, black | 5 oz. | $0.15 |
| H 8587 | 2-oz. cans, blue | 5 oz. | .20 |
| H 8590 | 2-oz. cans, Printers' Varnish | 5 oz. | .15 |

## Tool Chests.

**H 8703** Boys' Tool Chest; 11 in. long, 5¼ in. wide, 3½ in. deep, well made; with end till; contains 10 assorted tools for boys' use. Weight, 2½ lb. Complete..................50c.

**H 8707** Boys' Tool Chest; 13¼ in. long, 6¾ in. wide, 5 in. deep, well made, movable till and partitions, containing 12 assorted tools; better quality; for boys' use. Weight, 7½ lb. Complete..75c.

**H 8711** Boys' Tool Chest, 15½ in. long, 8¼ in. wide, 5¾ in. deep. Extra quality, made of chestnut wood with brown moldings, and all nicely varnished; has movable till with partitions, containing 18 assorted tools. Weight, 9 lb. Complete..................$1.25

**H 8715** Youths' Tool Chest; 15½ in. long, 8½ in. wide, 5¾ in. deep, made of chestnut and walnut woods, nicely varnished, heavy base and bands, with large till and compartments and bronzed handles, and chest lock; contains 22 assorted tools. Weight, 19 lb. Complete..................$4.50

---

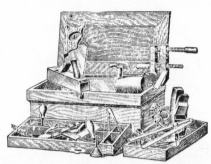

**H 8720** Youths' Tool Chest, made of selected chestnut and walnut woods, nicely varnished, heavy base and bands, with large till and partitions, japanned handles, and chest lock. Size, 1 ft. 9 in. long, 11¼ in. wide, 7½ in. deep. Contains 37 superior quality assorted tools. *Retail value, $12.00.* Weight, 35 lb. Our price, only..................$8.50

## Toy Scroll Saw Outfit.

**H 8751** EUREKA TOY SCROLL SAW OUTFIT. Any boy can earn money by making and selling brackets, card cases, handkerchief boxes, jewel cases, easels, photo frames, doll furniture and hundreds of other useful and ornamental articles. No experience or skill required. Any one can use it. A useful, instructive and interesting device. Outfit contains: 1 Eureka saw frame, 3 saw blades, 1 V strip with screws, 1 awl, 1 sheet impression paper, 6 patterns. Shipping weight, 15 oz. Per set..20c.

## Banner Scroll Saw Outfit.

**H 8754** Is a complete set of practical tools, suitable as well for an experienced mechanic as for an inexperienced boy or girl. The saw frame is made of best Bessemer steel, nickel plated and highly polished, and has stained hardwood handle. The other parts of the outfit are all made of the best of material, and warranted. Size of saw frame, 11 in. long. Each outfit put up in a neat box, with full directions for using, and contains the following: 1 saw frame, 1 V strip, 1 awl, 1 sheet impression paper, 6 saw blades, 2 screws, 1 sheet sand paper, 15 patterns. Shipping weight, 1 lb.
Price of outfit, complete..................38c.

## Iron Banks and Safes.

**H 8760** "MARY AND HER LAMB" BANK for cents, dimes and nickels; finished in hard white enamel with red and gilt bronze trimmings, 4¼x4¼ in. Shipping weight, 20 oz. Each..................20c.

**H 8769** "ST. BERNARD BANK." Body finished in hard black enamel; pack on back finished in aluminum bronze, and cross on breast in red. Will hold pennies, nickels, dimes and quarters. This is a beautiful ornament as well as toy and pleases everyone. 5x7¾. Shipping weight, 28 oz. Each..22c.

**H 8771** "INDIAN HEAD" Bank, is of neat design and has a perfect typical Indian face. It is finished in copper, gold and brown, and is a fine work of art that will attract attention anywhere. 4⅜ inches high, 3⅞ inches wide, 2¼ inches deep. Shipping weight, 1½ lb. Each..................21c.

**H 8775** "SKY-SCRAPER" Bank, with lock and key, finished with gold bronze roof and towers, green bronze door trimmings, and aluminum bronze base. Handsomest and most attractive 25c. bank on the market. Has over 500 open windows. Size, 6¾ inches high, 4⅝ inches deep, 3½ inches wide. Shipping weight, 3¼ lb. Each......25c.

**H 8786** "Grand Jewel Safe" Bank with double combination lock, 6¼x4½x4 inches, made of steel and iron in antique oxidized copper finish; has money guard which prevents coins from dropping out. Shipping weight, 2½ lbs.
Each......................**45c.**

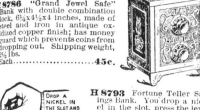

DROP A NICKEL IN THE SLOT AND HAVE YOUR FORTUNE TOLD

**H 8793** Fortune Teller Savings Bank. You drop a nickel in the slot, press the lever and it revolves the wheel that tells your fortune every time. Its mystery fascinates and no one can withstand the temptation of dropping another nickel into the slot. It simply coaxes the coin out of everybody's pocket into its capacious vault and enriches the owner of this Wonderful Savings Bank beyond expectation. It is made of cast iron, well enameled, highly decorated and a combination lock protects the contents. It is made to last and to look well. Nickeled finish. Shipping weight, 5¾ lbs.
Our price each, only....**90c.**

**H 8794** Home Safe Bank. An artistically designed and highly finished, nickel-plated, combination lock bank, with special patent security key, which prevents the door from being opened. Size, 6½x5x4½ in. Shipping weight, 5 lb.
Our price, each, only..**95c**

**H 8799** Security Safe Bank with double combination lock, made of steel and iron in antique oxidized copper finish; large size, 7½x5½x5 in., has money guard which prevents coins from dropping out. Weight, 5½ lbs.
Each.................**90c.**

## Mechanical Banks.

**H 8804** The Cabin Bank. Length, 4¼ in.; height, 3⅜ in.; width, 3 in. Place the coin upon the roof above the negro's head, move the handle of the whitewash brush and the negro will be made to stand on his head and kick the coin into the bank. Shipping weight, 2 lb.
Each.............**45c.**

**H 8812** The Educational Pig Bank. Place a coin on the tray and press the lever; the pig catches it in his mouth, moves his tongue and swallows it. Size, height, 6 in.; depth, 3¼ in.; width, 2⅞ in. Shipping weight, 2¼ lb.
Each.................**40c.**

**H 8815** "Trick Dog" Bank. Place the coin in proper position in the dog's mouth; press the lever and the dog drops the coin into the barrel. It is finished in fancy colors and in size measures 8¼x7½x3 in. Shipping weight 4½ lbs.
Each......**84c.**

**H 8821** "Funny Clown" Bank. When the globe is brought into position and the lever is released, the clown whirl around in a very amusing manner. By pressing the knob the clown will change position, standing on his head. Is painted in fancy colors. Shipping weight, 6 lbs.
Each.................**85c.**

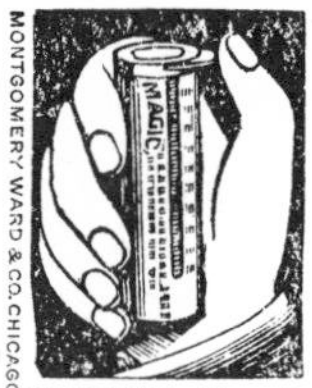

**H 8836** Little Gem Pocket Savings Bank, for dimes; locks itself and registers the amount deposited; opens automatically when $5 in dimes have been deposited, without the use of force; is handsomely nickel plated, and can be carried in the pocket without inconvenience.
Each.................**$0.06**
Per doz. .70
Postage, 2c. extra, each.

**H 8840** Gem Pocket Savings Bank for copper cents; will hold 50 cents. Otherwise same as No. H 8836.
Each.................**$0.06**
Per doz. .70

## Jack Stones.

**H 9020** Nicely finished, good sizes. Per doz.........**$0.04**
Per gross................. .50
Weight, per doz., 2 oz.

## Toy Reins.

**H 9023** Boy's Driving Reins, made of extra heavy red, white and blue webbing, having fancy colored yoke, with snap hooks; brass chime bells on yoke piece. This is an especially good set. Length, 54 in.
Per set..**$0.25**
Postage.... .08

## Child's Sad Irons.

**H 9031** "Sensible" Toy Sad Iron with removable handle, medium weight polished iron with stand; is the right size for the 4 to 6 year old. Shipping weight, 22 oz.
Each.................**15c.**

**H 9033** "Sensible" Toilet or Girl's Iron, double pointed; detachable handle, never becomes hot; excellent for laces, ribbons and small articles. Shipping weight, 3 lbs.
Each.................**25c.**

**H 9038** Misses' Toilet Sad or Polishing Irons of the Mrs Potts style, with detachable handle and highly polished surface; is provided with a rounded end for polishing, and is adapted for small, fine work that requires a small iron that is better than is usually sold as a toy. A miss can handle this iron nicely. Shipping weight 2¾ lb. Each.................**25c.**

## Toy Stoves.

**H 9039** "Pet" Toy Range, a handsome little model like illustration; polished and nickel-plated, with full set of utensils; large enough for the first stove and exceptional value; will please any little tot. Size, 10¼x5½x5 in. Shipping weight, 4 lb.
Each......**45c.**

**H 9042** "Grand Jewel" Toy Range; large and beautifully ornamented, handsomely full steel polished and high grade of nickel plating; all ornamented parts highly burnished. Complete set of utensils. Size, 10½x8x5¼ in. Shipping weight, 4½ lb. Each **95c.**

### Always Acceptable at Holiday Time:
### One of those nice
# POCKET BOOKS
Quoted on Pages 489 to 492.

**H 9045** "Prize" Toy Range. A handsome toy range, complete in all parts. Heavy castings, trimmings nickel plated. Each one packed in a box with kettles, spiders, etc. Height, 11¾ in.; length, 9¾ in.; width, 6¾ in. Shipping weight, 12 lb.
Price......**$1.75**

**H 9049** "Rival" Toy Range, with elevated warming oven and with kettles, spider, etc; is finely polished and nickel plated and is undoubtedly one of the handsomest toy ranges on the market. Height, 14½ in.; length, 16 in.; width, 8½ in.; shipping weight, 23 lb.
Each..**$2.85**

**H 9052** "Eclipse" Toy Range, extra large size, with elevated warming oven and with kettles, spider, etc., is finely polished and nickel plated and is undoubtedly one of the handsomest toy ranges on the market. Height, 15½ in.; length, 17 in.; width, 9¾ in.; shipping weight, 32 lb. Each..**$3.90**

**H 9053** "Baby" Hollow-ware Set for use with toy stove, 4 pieces; outside nickel plated; inside finished in white enamel, except tea kettle. Shipping weight, 2 lb.
Per set......**47c.**

## Nut Crackers.

**H 9054** "Old Dog Tray," a large toy dog and nut cracker. Bright red base, black body, colored eyes: cannot be broken; a child of six can crack the hardest nuts; meats come out whole: enjoyed by young and old. Size, 13 in. long, 7 in. high; can be used to stand on floor to hold a door when not wanted as a toy or nut cracker; weight, 5¾ lbs. Each...................**40c.**

**H 9057** Harper Nut Cracker, with holder for shells. Every housekeeper will appreciate this improvement, as it prevents littering the floor. The cracker is nicely nickel plated and very powerful. Shipping weight 12 oz.
Each...................**$0.19**
Per doz................. 1.95

*Montgomery Ward & Co.*

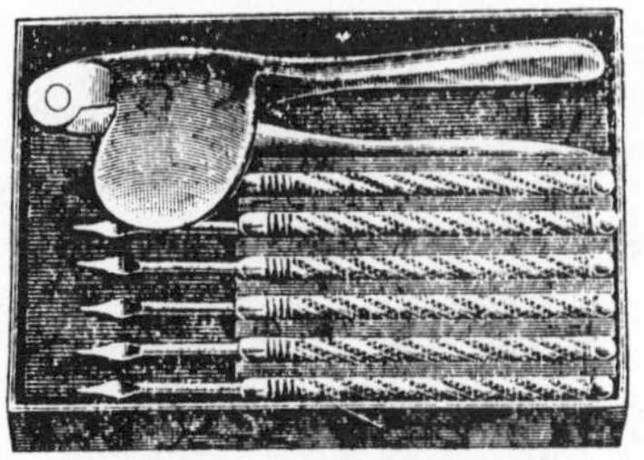

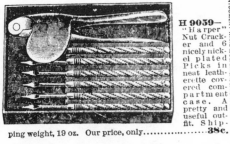

**H 9059**—"Harper" Nut Cracker and 6 nicely nickel plated Picks in neat leatherette covered compartment case. A pretty and useful outfit. Shipping weight, 19 oz. Our price, only.................**38c.**

## Edward's Adjustable Nut Crack.

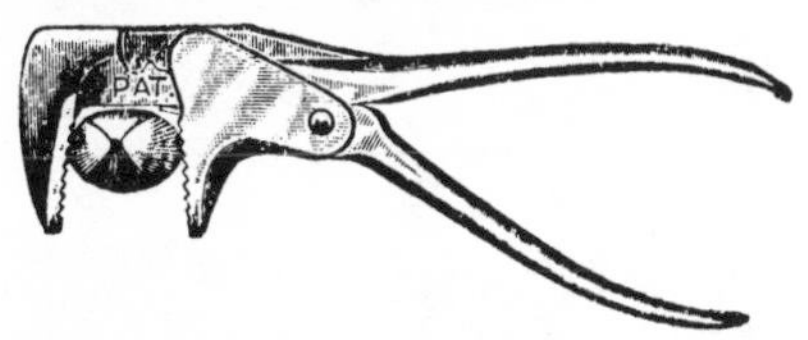


**H 9068** Edward's Adjustable Nut Crack, simple, powerful, cheap; can be adjusted to any size or variety of nuts, and is the smallest and most powerful ever manufactured. Leverage is always the same, no matter how adjusted. No danger of pinching your fingers or scattering shucks over your carpet or floor. Finely nickel plated and so simple that a child can operate it with ease. Shipping weight, 12 oz. Each.................**25c.**

## Bell Toys.

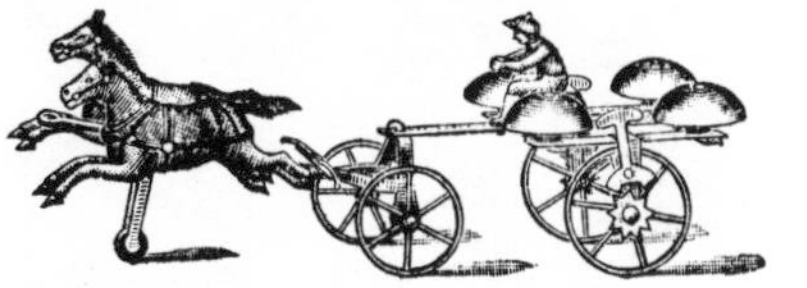

**H 9081** Bell Toy or Floor Chimes, having 2 horses and driver, and 4 1¾-in. gongs with ratchet movement. Shipping weight, 2¼ lb. Each.................**48c.**

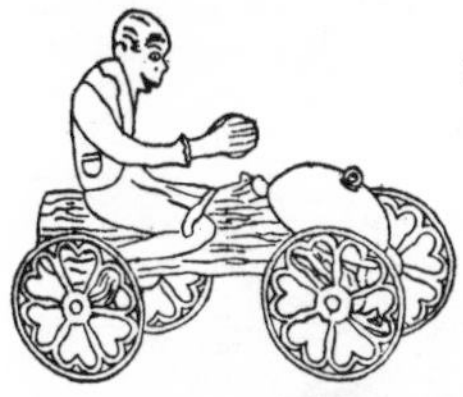

**H 9093** "Monkeymobile," a new automatic bell toy, painted in colors. 5¼x6½ in. When drawn along the floor the monkey rings the bell by striking the bell hammer with a cocoanut. Shipping weight, 1½ lb. Each.................**20c.**

## Toy Iron Trains.

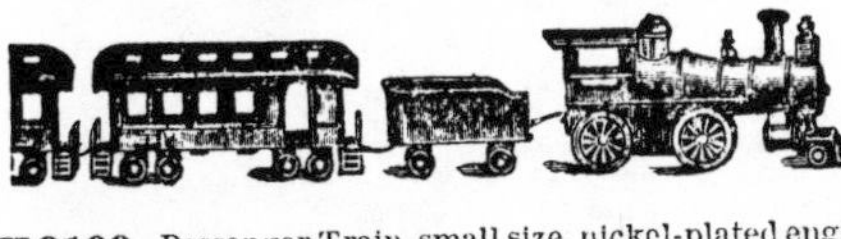

**H 9100** Passenger Train, small size, nickel-plated engine, tender and 3 coaches; length of train, 28 in. Packed one in a box. Shipping weight, 4¼ lb. Each.................**50c.**

**H 9103** Ideal Passenger Train, consisting of locomotive, tender and 3 passenger coaches. Made of iron, handsomely finished in nickel. All wheels revolve. Length of train, 42 in. Packed one in a box. Shipping Weight, 8¾ lb. Each.................**$1.00**

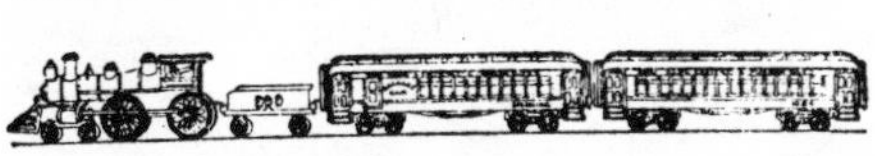

**H 9104** "Limited Express" Vestibuled Train, consisting of locomotive, tender, and 2 vestibuled coaches with moving passengers. A perfect model of a modern passenger train. Finished in oxidized nickel. Length, 51 in. Shipping weight, 17½ lb. Each.................**$2.20**

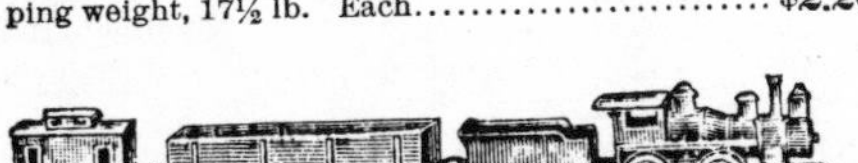

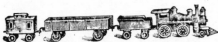

**H 9117** Freight Train. Medium size, engine, tender and 2 flat cars and caboose. Made of sheet-steel, finished in bright colors. Length, 33 in. Shipping weight, 4¾ lb. Each.................**50c.**

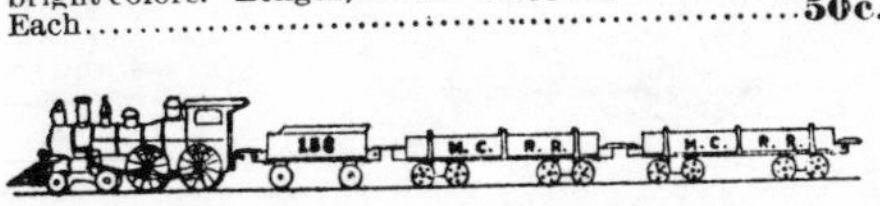

**H 9122** Freight Train, consisting of large size locomotive, with separate tender; flat car of large size and caboose, nickel plated. Drive wheels on engine have jointed connecting rod, and all wheels revolve. Length of train, 33 in. Packed in a box. Shipping weight, 5 lb. Each..**90c.**

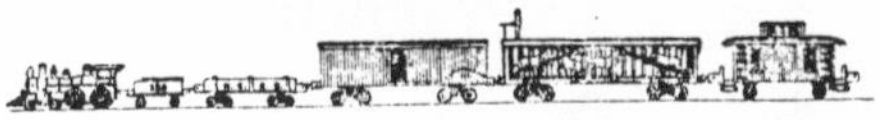

**H 9125** Large Combination Freight Train, complete with extra size locomotive and tender, with flat car, box car, stock car with moving horses and caboose. This makes the finest full freight train, with all parts as complete as possible to make in a toy. Length, 60½ in. Shipping weight, 20 lb.................**$2.25**

## Iron Toys.

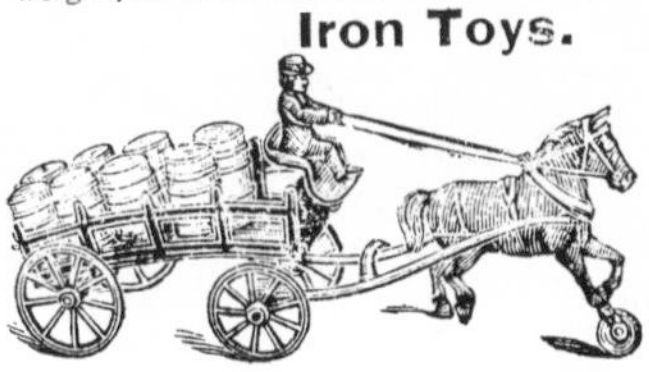

**H 9129** Toy Truck Wagon with horse and driver, made of iron and finished in colors; has six-barrel load. Full length, 11 in. Ship'ng weight, 1¾ lb. Each...**25c.**

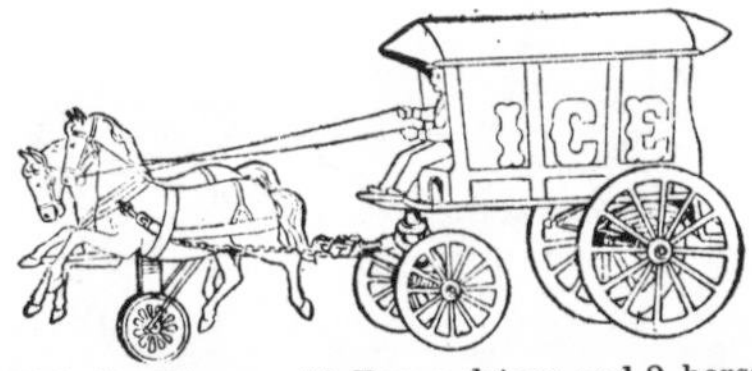


**H 9131** Ice Wagon with Top, a driver and 2 horses; 13 in. long; a fine toy in every way. The whole toy is brightly painted. Shipping weight, 3½ lb. Each.................**45c.**

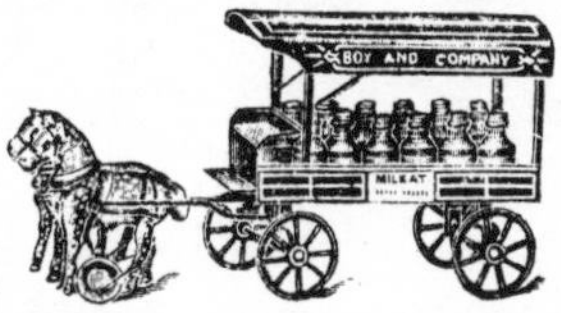


**H 9134** Boys' Wholesale Milk Wagon, made of steel, lithographed in bright colors, contains ten wooden milk cans and has a folding top which can be removed instantly, leaving a nice large express wagon. Has two horses with movable legs. Full length, 23 in. Shipping weight, 5 lbs. Each.................**85c.**

## Electrical Toys.

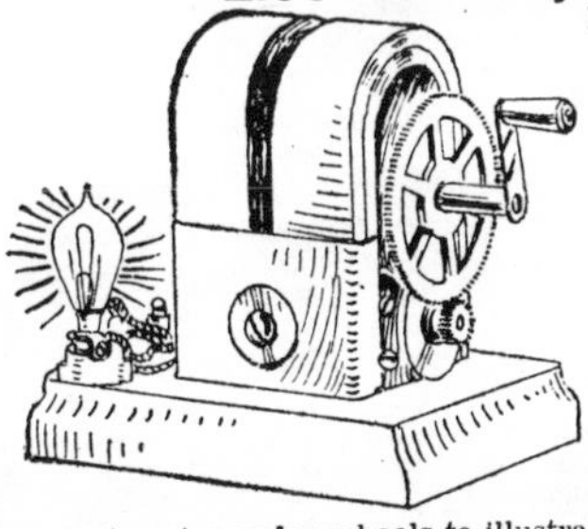

**H 9142 BUBIER HAND DYNAMO**, for schools, amateur electricians, etc. Stands 6 in. high, armature about 2½ in. long. This little generator is suitable for experimental work, such as giving shocks, will run two 1-c. p. incandescent lamps, ring magnetic bells, etc. Just the thing for the young experimenter or for schools to illustrate the principle of all dynamo machinery. Perfectly harmless, no danger, a child can use it. Shipping weight, 8½ lb.

Dynamo only, each.................**$2.25**

ATTACHMENTS FOR H 9142.

**H 9144** Lamp and receptacle................. .75

H 9146 Hand electrodes and cords................. .50

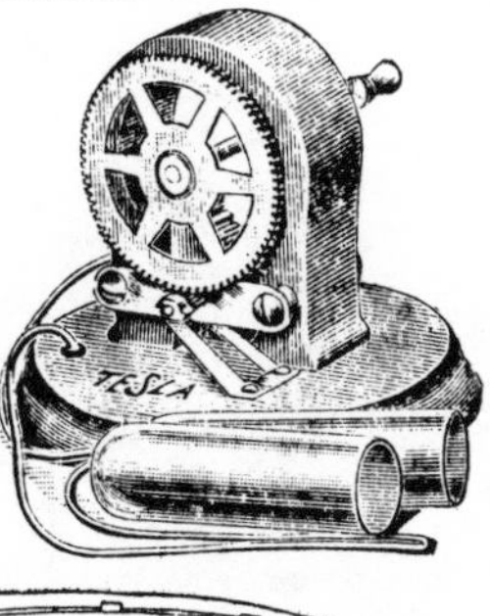


**H 9151** "Tesla" Magneto Electric Machine. Simple to operate, new in design, finished in red enamel, with nickel trimmings, and mounted on a polished wood stand. A very attractive, well made and finished machine. Electricity is produced from magnets by friction when turning the crank. Shipping weight, 1½ lbs. Each.................**75c.**

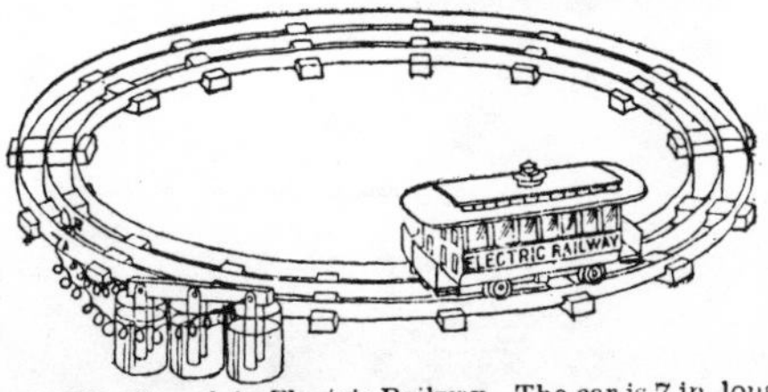


**H 9153** Complete Electric Railway. The car is 7 in. long, 4½ in. high. Is made of polished brass and has iron wheels that are set with axles parallel and are all of same diameter. The car may thus be run on straight or curved tracks. The track furnished is a circle, 3 ft. in diameter and 2-in. gauge, made of polished rolled steel. Speed about 150 ft. per minute. The electric current is conducted through the rails and thence by the wheels of car to the motor. Battery consists of 3 zinc-carbon elements and one 10-oz. can of chromite. Use any ordinary tumbler or jelly glass as a battery jar. The 10 oz. of chromite dissolved in 1 qt. water makes enough solution for two charges. Weight of entire equipment, packed in wooden box, 6 lb. Each.................**$3.00**

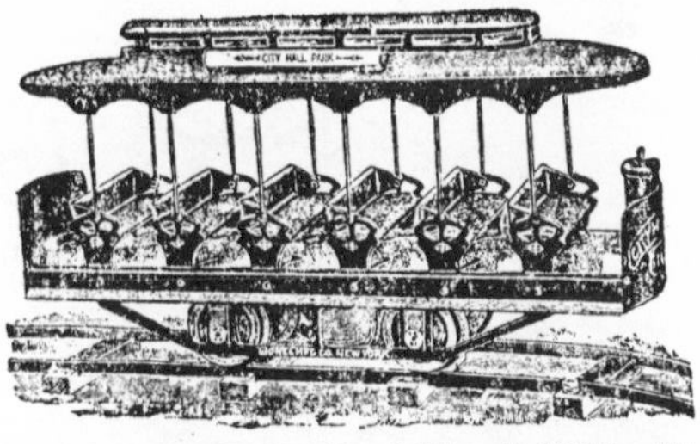


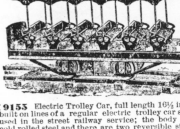

**H 9155** Electric Trolley Car, full length 16½ in. This is built on lines of a regular electric trolley car such as are used in the street railway service; the body is made of cold rolled steel and there are two reversible signs at top of car; controller in front starts, stops or reverses the car, and is an exact reproduction of those used on large cars. The motor is regulation style and of sufficient power to operate the car properly on any surface where a toy car may be used. Outfit includes 30 feet of ⅜-in. steel rails cut in sections so that any shaped track may be formed. The ties are grooved to admit insertion of rails which are 2⅞ in. apart. Outfit also includes dry cell batteries for operating the car. Shipping weight, 12 lb. Per set.................**$7.20**

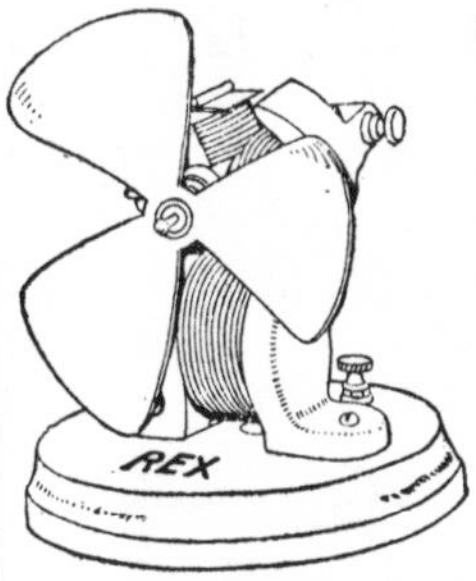


**H 9157** "Rex" Toy Motor and Fan Outfit, with 3½-in. nickel plated fan. Superior in every way to any motor manufactured for the price; made for durability, finished in black enamel, screws and bearings nickel-plated, mounted on a polished wood stand. This motor is a wonder for power and speed. It can be used for operating small mechanical toys and advertising devices; runs on a single cell dry battery. Shipping weight, 18 oz. Each.................**$1.00**

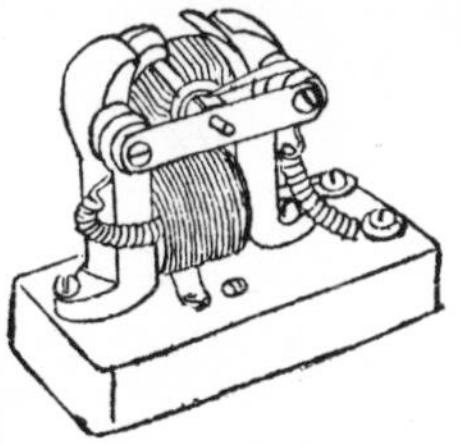

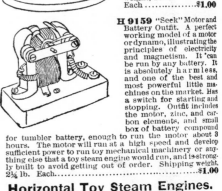

**H 9159** "Seek" Motor and Battery Outfit. A perfect working model of a motor or dynamo, illustrating the principles of electricity and magnetism. It can be run by any battery. It is absolutely harmless, and one of the best and most powerful little machines on the market. Has a switch for starting and stopping. Outfit includes the motor, zinc, and carbon elements, and small box of battery compound for tumbler battery, enough to run the motor about 3 hours. The motor will run at a high speed and develop sufficient power to run toy mechanical machinery or anything else that a toy steam engine would run, and is strongly built to avoid getting out of order. Shipping weight, 2¼ lb. Each.................**$1.00**

## Horizontal Toy Steam Engines.

*Will not operate machinery.*

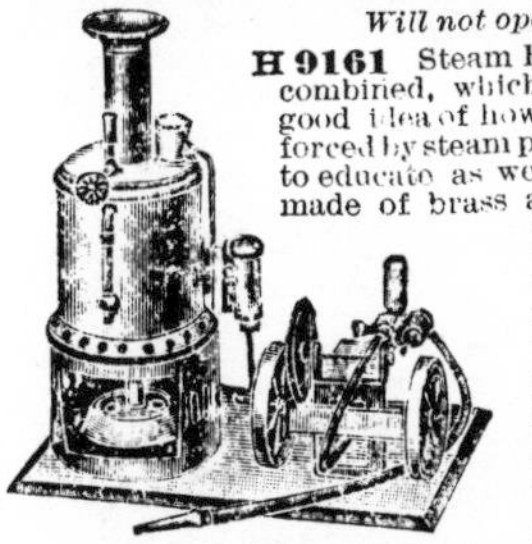

**H 9161** Steam Engine and Force Pump combined, which in operation gives a good idea of how water is pumped and forced by steam pressure, and is designed to educate as well as amuse. Boiler is made of brass and has a safety valve, whistle and water glass. The lamp is provided with a large wick to give a good sized flame and run the engine at high speed. The double balance wheel serves to regulate the speed and insure a steady flow of water from the nozzle. At ordinary speed it will throw a stream of water six feet. Suction hose, leading hose and nozzle are provided with each pump. Height, 8¾ inches, base, 6x8¼ inches. Directions for running accompany each outfit. Shipping weight, 30 ounces. Each.................**$1.40**

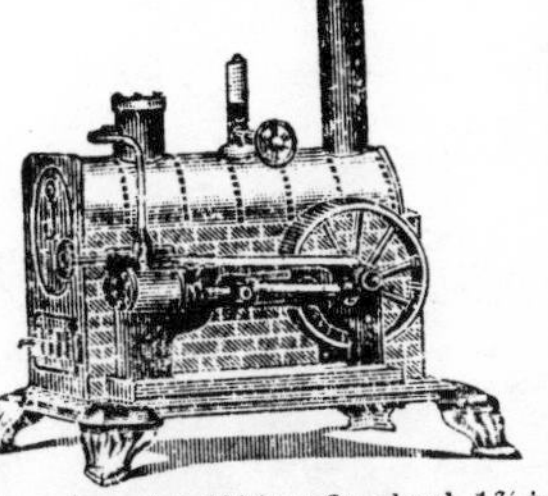

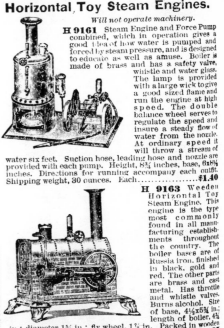

**H 9163** Weeden Horizontal Toy Steam Engine. This engine is the type most commonly found in all manufacturing establishments throughout the country. The boiler bases are of Russia iron, finished in black, gold and red. The other parts are brass and cast metal. Has throttle and whistle valves. Burns alcohol. Size of base, 4½x5¾ in.; length of boiler, 4½ in.; diameter 1⅝ in.; fly wheel, 1⅞ in. Packed in wooden box it weighs 24 oz. Each.................**$1.35**

## AN EVENING AT HOME

**Will be full of pleasure for the whole family, if one of our splendid Game Boards be included in your next order.** **See page 468 for quotations.**

**H 9165** Weeden Horizontal Toy steam Engine; has large polished brass boiler with steam dome, throttle, whistle and safety valve. The frame is cast malleable iron, to which the boiler and engine are firmly attached. The cylinder, steam chest and slide rest are cast in one piece and can not get out of order. The whole engine is in every way a strong and durable steam toy. Burns alcohol. Shipping weight, 5¼ lb. Each.......$2.25

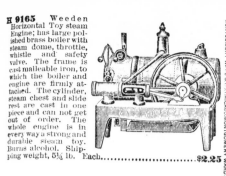

**H 9167—** Large Horizontal Toy Steam Engine; this is the largest and strongest engine we handle. It has a large brass boiler enveloped with a sheet iron jacket to prevent loss of heat. It starts and stops with a throttle. The boiler trimmings are safety

valve, whistle, steam dome and water gauge. The boiler frame and engine bed are made of malleable iron, well riveted and pinned together. The cylinder, steam chest and cross head slide rest are made in one piece of solid brass. The piston and rod, the crank and connecting rod, the eccentric and valve rod and slide valve are all made of brass. The balance wheel is made of brass with a polished face. All parts of the engine are securely put together, trimmings and frame are nickel plated, well finished and very durable. Burns alcohol. Each engine is carefully tested before packing. Full directions for operating engine will be found in each box. Weight, 8½ lb. Each.......$7.50

**H 9169** Weeden Double Upright Toy Steam Engine, size of base 7x 11; 11 in. high, has a large polished brass boiler, with steam dome, whistle, safety valve and water gauge, and is connected to steam chest by a brass steam pipe. The frame is malleable iron, to which engine is attached. Burns alcohol. Runs rapidly and easily; all parts are interchangeable. Each engine is thoroughly tested before packing, and is fully warranted. Shipping weight, 7 lb. Each.......$3.50

**H 9171** Weeden Reversible Upright Toy Steam Engine; brass boilers with whistle and safety valve locked on and steam tight; is provided with water glass; also with a reversing valve, so that engine can be run backward or forward with equal speed. Burns alcohol. Shipping weight, 3 lb. Each.......$1.50

**H 9174** Weeden Upright Toy Steam Engine. This is a large and attractive engine, 11 in. high and will run with kerosene in lamp. It has a finely fitted water gauge, made perfectly tight by means of adjustable nuts which can be easily adjusted with a little wrench, packed in box with each engine. It has a large balance wheel, and all the parts necessary to make it complete. The boiler is polished brass and the base and running parts are finished in colors. The lamp and draught arrangement in this engine is especially adapted for the use of petroleum oil as a fuel (with perfect safety), although we recommend the use of alcohol as it is much cleaner and more agreeable. Every engine is thoroughly tested before packing and fully warranted. Full directions for running the engine will be found in each box, with price of duplicate parts. Shipping weight, 2½ lb. Each.......80c.

## Toy Steamboats.

**H 9175** "Hudson" Toy Steamboat (torpedo type), with a nicely modeled hull, has a polished brass boiler firmly secured to the thwarts; steam chest mounted on an inclined frame to which the cylinder is adjusted. A small balance wheel is connected to the cylinder and propeller shaft, and on the latter is fixed a three blade brass propeller. The alcohol lamp is securely soldered in the bottom of the boat, which prevents its sliding about while boat is in motion. Length of hull 18 inches, of boiler 4 inches. This boat is neatly decorated in colors. Shipping weight, 3 lb. Each.......$1.25

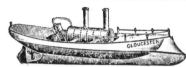

**H 9180** The "Gloucester" Steamboat has a nicely modeled hull (torpedo type); well put together and is very attractive in appearance. It has a polished brass boiler firmly secured to the thwarts; steam chest mounted on an inclined frame to which the cylinder is adjusted. Length of hull, 20 in.; of boiler, 4¾ in. A small balance wheel is connected to the cylinder and propeller shaft, and to the latter is fixed a three-bladed brass propeller. The lamp burns alcohol and is securely soldered in the bottom of the boat to prevent it sliding about while the boat is in motion and burns alcohol. The whole is finely decorated in colors, and each one is tested and guaranteed. Shipping weight, 4 lb. Each.......$1.85

## Toy Steam Trains.

**H 9182** Weeden Steam Locomotive, Tender and Passenger Car, with jointed track on wooden sleepers, mounted on wood base. Diameter of track, 3½ ft.; locomotive, 8 in. long; car and tender in proportion. Put up in wooden box. Weight, 4 lb. For train complete.......$3.50

**H 9187** Weeden Steam Train of special size and perfect construction, locomotive (has connecting-rods and exhausts through smoke stack) tender, and two passenger cars. Put up complete with track. The best toy steam train made. Diameter of track is 5 ft., mounted on wood base. Length of train, over all, 30 in. Shipping weight, 6 lb. Each.......$8.00

## Toy Hot Air Engine.

**H 9189** Buffalo Hot Air Engine, a novel and scientific engine; full of interest for the young people with mechanical ideas. No water is used and the engine is absolutely safe from explosion. The quantity of alcohol used is small. A ⅜-in. round wick being sufficient to run it at full speed and power. 18-in. long over all, fly-wheel, 6-in. diameter; cylinder, 2-in. bore, 1¼-in. stroke. Shipping weight, 12 lb. Each.......$4.50

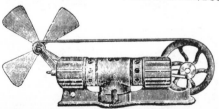

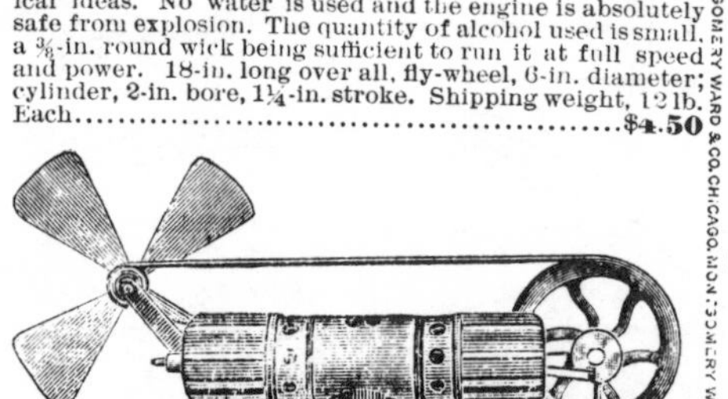

**H 9193** "Essex" Hot Air Engine, Model B, 18 in. long; with fly wheel 6 inches in diameter; cylinder 2 in. bore; 1¼ in. stroke; equipped with 4¼ in. fan and alcohol lamp. Operated by the expansive force of heated air with alcohol for fuel, and when once started will run continuously with little attention until flame is extinguished. No water used and explosion is impossible. Excellent for running fans, window advertising devices, model machinery and similar purposes. Full of interest for a boy and of material aid in developing engineering talent. Shipping weight, 15 lb. Each.......$7.50

## Lubricating Graphite.

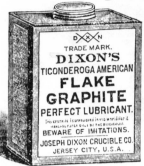

**H 9225** Dixon's Pure Flake Lubricating Graphite No. 1. A perfect lubricant for steam engine cylinders, valves, rods, gears, bearings, journals and other metallic surfaces.
1 lb. can, each.......$0.20
5 lb. screw top tin can, each.......85
10 lb. screw top tin can, each.......1.60
25 lb. box, each.......3.75

**H 9229** Dixon's Pure Flake Lubricating Graphite No. 2 or fine, for lubricating gas engine cylinder valves, air brakes, delicate parts of scientific instruments and other small close fitting bearings.
1 lb. can, each.......$0.25
5 lb. screw top tin can, each.......1.00
10 lb. screw top tin can. each.......2.00

**H 9233** Dixon's Graphite Pipe-Joint Compound, invaluable for all steam, gas and water piping and equally valuable for smearing gaskets or flange joints of meters, traps, etc., also for bolts, screws, etc. Makes a tighter joint than red lead and they can be opened with perfect ease after many years.
1 lb. package, each.......$0.20
5 lb. package, each.......90
10 lb. package, each.......1.50
25 lb. package, each.......3.50

## Attachments for Steam Engines, Toy Motors & Hot-Air Engines.

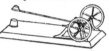

**H 9290** "Trip Hammer" Attachment for Toy Steam Engine, Electric Motor or Hot Air Engine; made of metal. Shipping weight, 6 oz. Each.......19c.

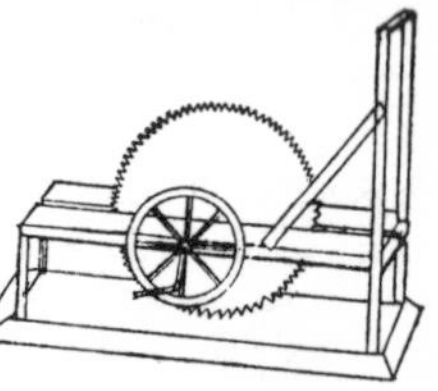

**H 9293** "Circular Saw" Attachment for Toy Steam Engine, Electric Motor or Hot Air Engine; made of metal. Shipping weight, 6 oz. Each.......20c.

**H 9294** Double Emery Wheel Attachment for Toy Steam Engine, Electric Motor or Hot Air Engine; wheels of stone, base of wood and upright of metal. Shipping weight, 9 oz. Each.......45c.

**H 9296** Toy Steam Engine Attachment combining a circular saw, drill and vise. Full length 6¼ inches, height 3 inches. Made of metal and mounted on wood base and finished in colors. Shipping weight, 14 ounces. Each.......43c.

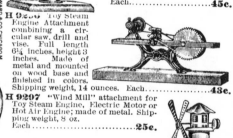

**H 9297** "Wind Mill" attachment for Toy Steam Engine, Electric Motor or Hot Air Engine; made of metal. Shipping weight, 8 oz. Each.......25c.

**H 9299** "Four Pulley Shafting" attachment for use with Toy Steam Engines, Electric Motor or Hot Air Engine and H 9290 to H 9297 attachments. Shipping weight, 8 oz. Each.......30c.

## Mechanical Toys.

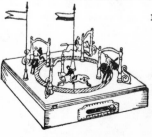

**H 9306** Mechanical Horse Race. You pull the spring lever and the horses go round and round the course until stopped by natural friction, and you know if you have guessed the winner. Shipping weight, 2 lb. Each.......$1.00

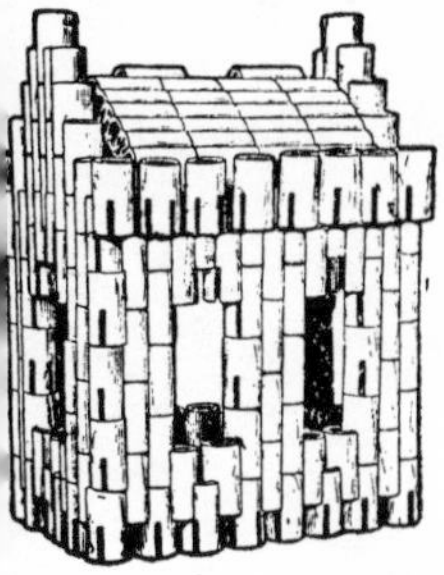

**H 10149** "Van" Building Blocks. A set of 60 tubular blocks, having four slots in one end, which enables the child to build a great variety of designs by interlocking blocks together in such a way that they will not easily fall down. There is no limit to the number of designs which may be made. Shipping weight, 2 lbs. Per set..............**45c.**

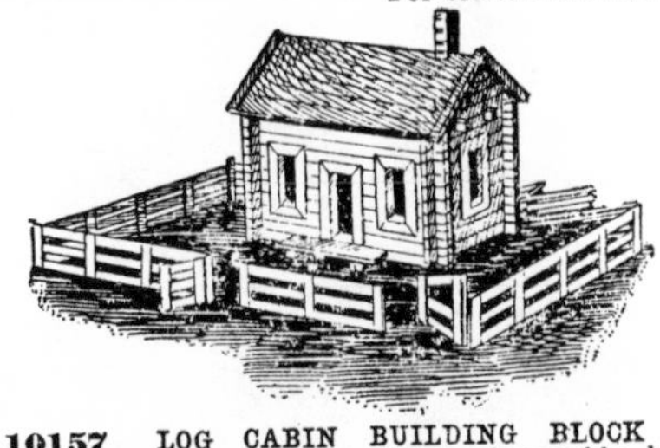

**H 10157 LOG CABIN BUILDING BLOCK SET.** Consists of 195 separate and interchangeable blocks, fitting into each other in such manner as to make log cabins in a variety of designs, taxing the ingenuity, not only of the young people, but of the older ones also. These detachable toy blocks are great mechanical educators and very amusing. This set will make cabin and fences, and are a continuous round of pleasure and instruction. RETAIL PRICE, ONE DOLLAR. Shipping weight, 2 lb. Our price, per set, only..............**85c.**

## China Toy Tea Sets.

*Fancy Color Decorations.*

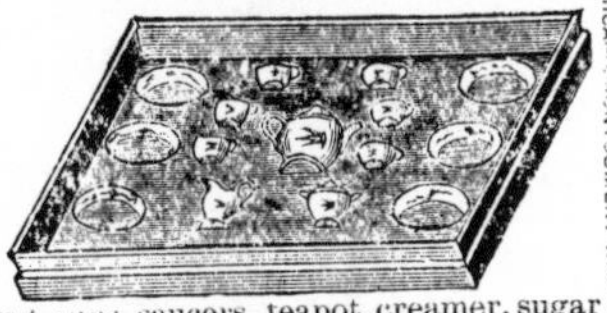

**H 10168** Set consists of cups, saucers, teapot, sugar bowl and creamer; medium sized pieces; packed in paper box; shipping weight, 24 oz. Per set....**25c.**

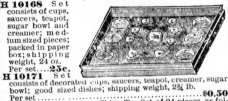

**H 10171** Set consists of decorated cups, saucers, teapot, creamer, sugar bowl; good sized dishes; shipping weight, 2¾ lb. Per set..............**$0.50**

**H 10180** White Stone China Tea Set of 24 pieces, as follows: 6 plates, 4¾ in. in diameter; 6 cups, 2 in. high; 6 saucers, 4¼ in. in diameter; 1 sugar bowl and cover, 1 teapot and cover, 1 creamer, 1 slop bowl. This set is large enough for a miss from 8 to 14 years of age. Weighs 8½ lb. Per set..............**$1.25**
The pieces in this set are larger than usually sold in toy sets.

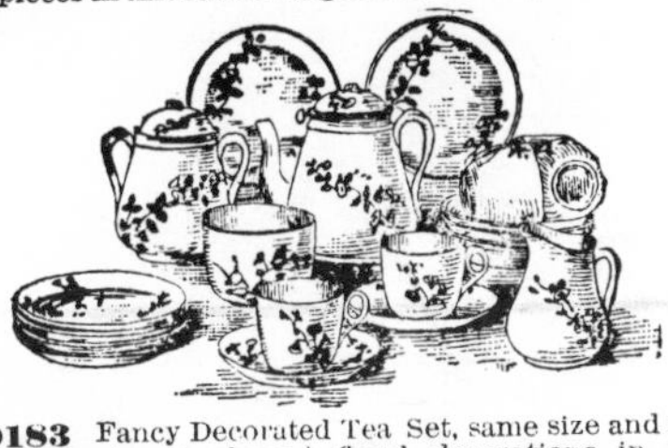

**H 10183** Fancy Decorated Tea Set, same size and assortment as above; elegant floral decorations in colors; packed in wooden box. Weight, 8½ lb. Per set,...**$1.75**

**H 10186** Extra Quality 24-Piece Decorated Toy Tea Set of special design and quality; beautiful floral decorations in colors and gold. The best toy tea set at the price ever produced and can be used at the young folks' tea parties. Shipping weight, 8½ lb. Per set..............**$2.50**

## Children's Aluminum Table Ware.

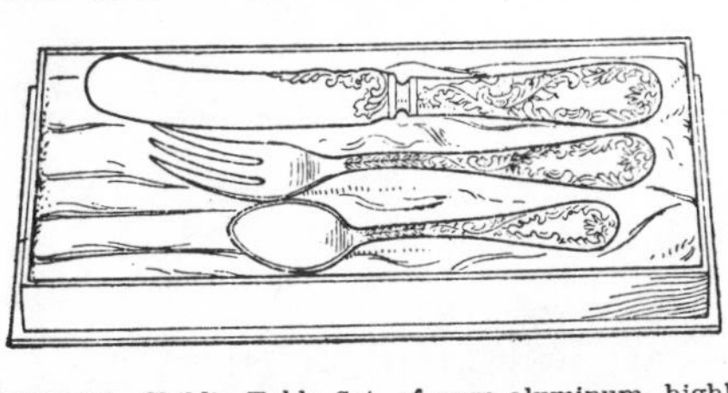

**H 10191** Child's Table Set, of pure aluminum, highly polished; consisting of knife, fork and spoon, in satin lined box. Shipping weight, 4 oz. Per set..............**25c.**

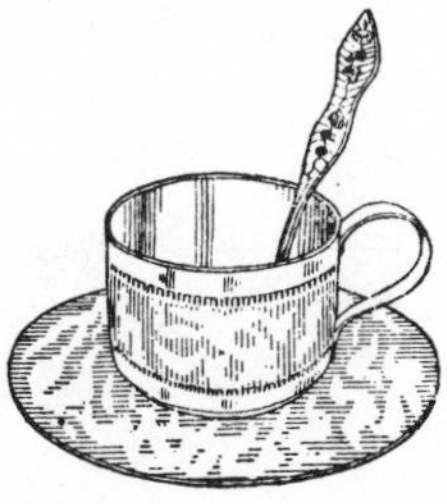

**H 10193** Child's Table Set, of pure aluminum in neat design, consisting of cup 1⅞x2⅞ in., saucer 4 in. in diameter, and tea spoon to match. Shipping weight, 6 oz. Our price per set only..............**29c.**

**H 10195**—Misses' Cup and Saucer, of pure aluminum of tasty design in matt finish: cup 1¾x3 in.; saucer 4½ in. in diameter. Excellent for use as "after-dinner coffee" cup and saucer. Shipping weight, 6 oz. Our price per set only..............**35c.**

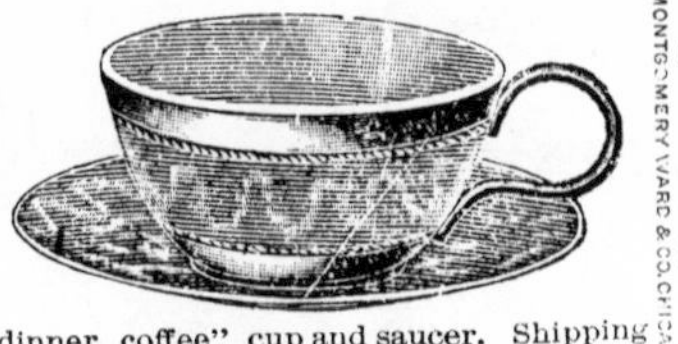

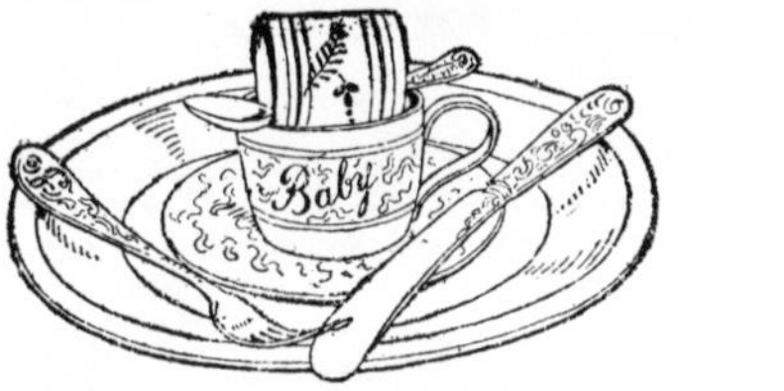



**H 10197** Child's Table Set, of pure aluminum; in handsome finish; consisting of plate 7 in. diameter, napkin-ring, cup, saucer, knife, fork and teaspoon. A very attractive set and excellent value at the price. Shipping weight, 9 oz. Per set..............**95c.**

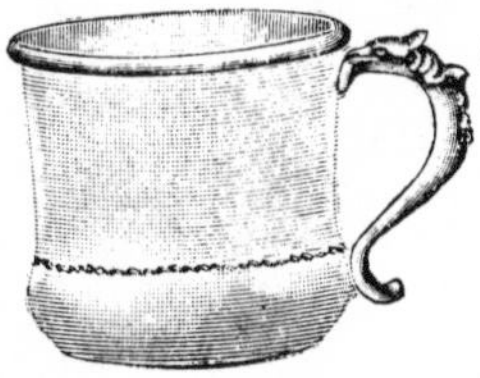

**H 10203** Child's Drinking Cup of pure aluminum, fancy shape, 2½ in. high, 2⅝ in. in diameter, highly polished, ornamented with mottled mat finish band and etched borders, fancy cast handle. Shipping weight 4 ounces. Each..............**33c.**

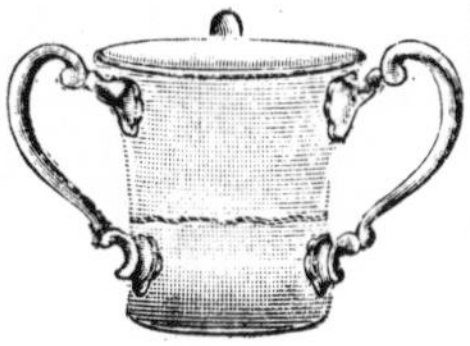

**H 10205** Child's Loving Cup of pure aluminum, highly polished and having fancy mottled designs also three fancy aluminum handles. 2¼ in. high, 2⅜ inches in diameter at top. Shipping weight 6 ounces. Each..............**40c.**

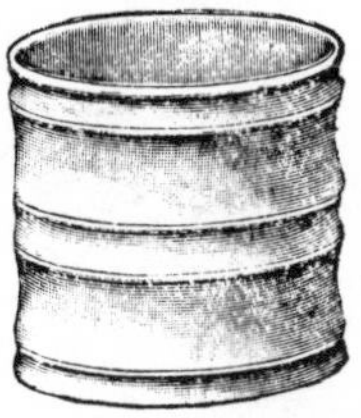

**H 10207** Ivory Finish Napkin Ring of "Pyralin" (same composition as celluloid,) length 1½ inches, diameter 1⅜ inches. Excellent for children's use. Shipping weight 3 ounces. Each..............**10c.** Per doz..............1.05

## Britannia Tea Sets.

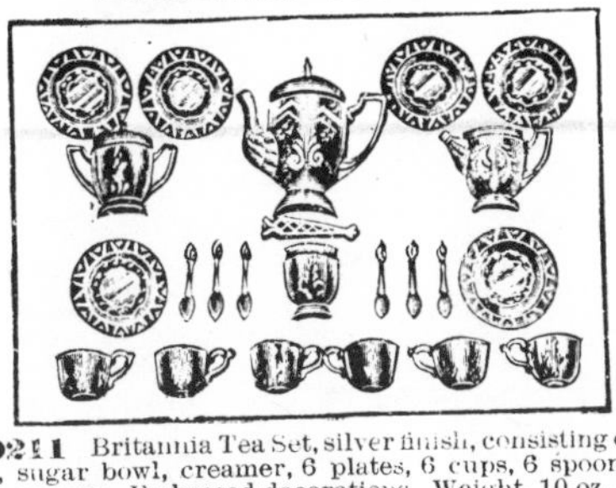

**H 10211** Britannia Tea Set, silver finish, consisting of teapot, sugar bowl, creamer, 6 plates, 6 cups, 6 spoons and sugar spoon. Embossed decorations. Weight, 10 oz...**22c.**

**H 10214** Britannia Tea Set, silver finish, consisting of teapot, sugar bowl, creamer, 6 plates, 6 cups and 6 spoons. A very handsome set. Weight, 1¼ lb. Per set..........**45c.**

**H 10217** Britannia Tea Set, silver finish, consisting of teapot, sugar bowl, creamer, spoon holder, 6 plates, 6 cups, 6 spoons and fancy filigree work sugar tongs. The entire set is handsomely decorated in bas-relief design, making a large, showy set. Weight, 3¾ lb. Per set..........**75c.**

## German Decorated Set.

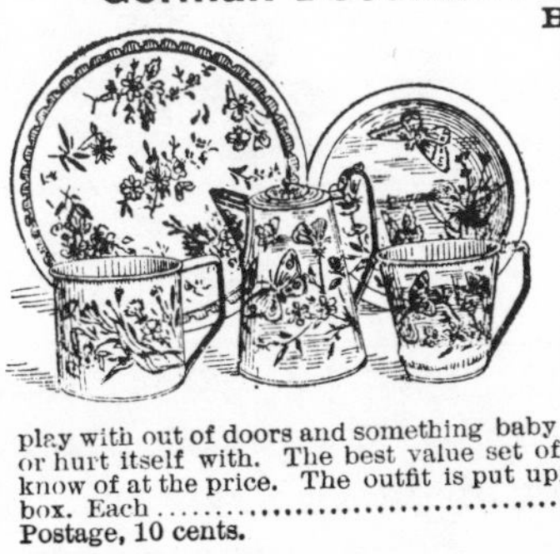

**H 10226** Tea Party Outfit of German Decorated Tin, nicely finished, consisting of plate, mug, coffee pot, cup and saucer. These utensils are light in weight and practically indestructible; just what the little folks like to play with out of doors and something baby will not smash or hurt itself with. The best value set of dishes that we know of at the price. The outfit is put up in a neat paper box. Each..............**25c.**
Postage, 10 cents.

## Jack in the Box.

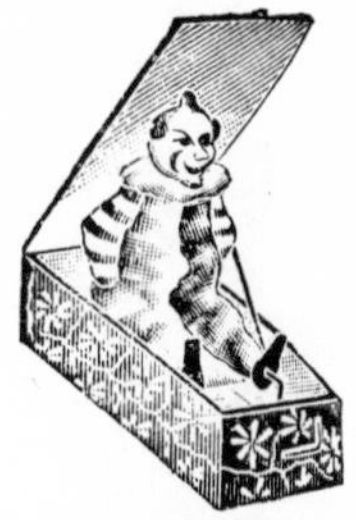

**H 10243** Jack in the Box, a late novelty. A comical clown springs out of the box in the same old way, but designs of box and figures are new. Shipping weight, 7 ounces. Each..............**20c.**

**H 10246** "Paradise" Surprise Box, from which a large-sized snake springs when the box is opened; certain to surprise all the onlookers. Shipping weight, 9 ounces. Each..............**25c.**

## Cloth Animals.

Stuffed and made up neat and strong, in as perfect designs as possible.

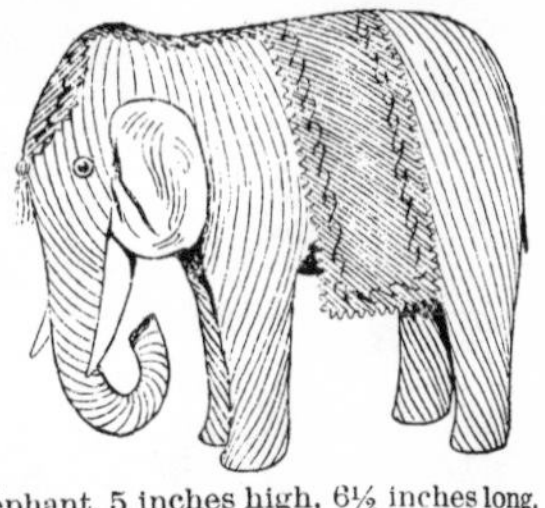

**H 10301** "Jumbo" Elephant, 10 inches high, 12 inches long, of gray felt stuffed with cork, making it very light in weight and easy for a small child to handle; has embroidered red felt blanket and head piece. Shipping weight, 23 ozs. Each..........**80c.**

**H 10305** Small Elephant, 5 inches high, 6½ inches long, of gray felt with red blanket. Shipping weight, 8 ounces. Each..............**22c.**

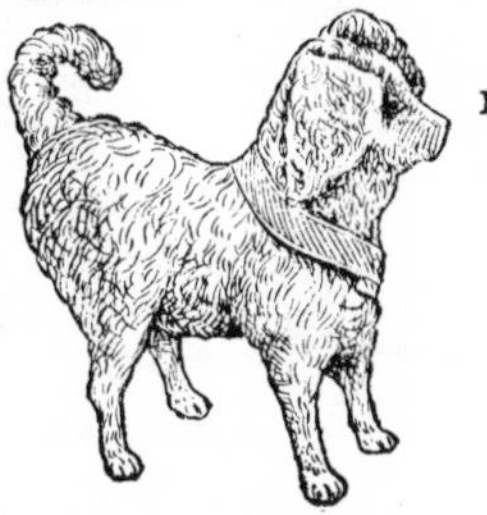

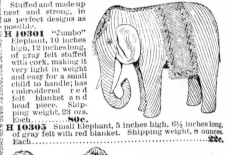

**H 10309** Astrakhan Poodle Dog, 6¾ inches high, 6¾ inches long, very light in weight and not easily broken. Shipping weight, 9 ounces. Each..............**28c.**

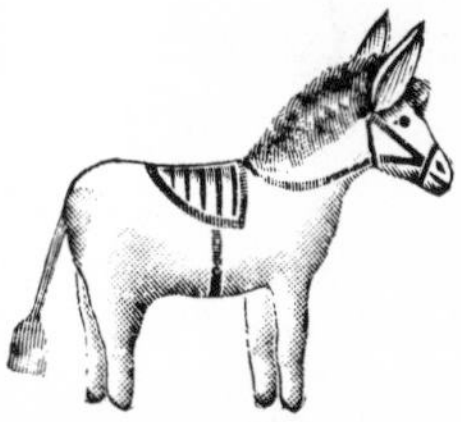

**H 10314** Flannel Donkey, 6½ inches high, 8 inches long; with hair, mane and fetlock, colored harness. Very light in weight and not easily broken. Shipping wt. 6 ounces. Each...**22c.**

## Dolls! Dolls!! Dolls!!!

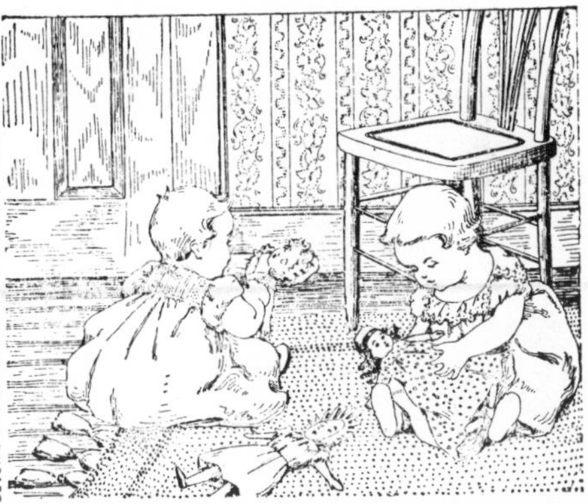

All kinds and sizes. Do not delay ordering Christmas dolls until December, as by sending us your order early you may be reasonably certain of receiving exactly what you select, and avoid receiving a substitute. We handle only such dolls as are quoted on this and on the following pages, and only the best make of each class. No cheap trash in the list. Remember that a 15-in. correctly formed and proportioned doll is better value than a drawn out doll that may measure 18 or 19 in. We give you value in *quality*, not in show of length.

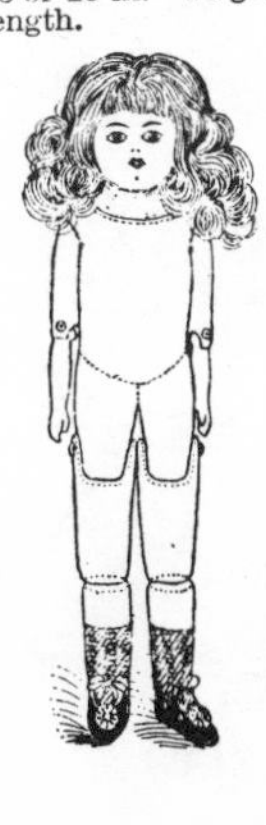

## Fixed Eye Kid Body Dolls.

With wavy hair wig, shoes and stockings and hip swivel joint; they will all sit up straight.

**H 10430** Kid Body Dolls, with bisque heads, flowing hair, teeth and full jointed body. Length, 12 in. Shipping weight, 16 oz. Each..........**25c.**

**H 10434** Kid Body Dolls, with bisque heads, woven wig, flowing hair, teeth and solid eyes. Length, 14 in. Shipping weight, 20 oz. Each..........**50c.**

**H 10438** Kid Body Dolls, bisque heads, woven wig, flowing hair, and teeth. Length, 16½ in. Shipping weight, 28 oz. Each..........**75c.**

**H 10441** Kid Body Dolls, bisque heads, woven wig, flowing hair, and with teeth. Length, 20 in. Shipping weight, 36 oz. Each..........**$1.00**

## Moving Eye, Patent Joint, Kid Body Dolls.

Can not be shipped by mail with safety.

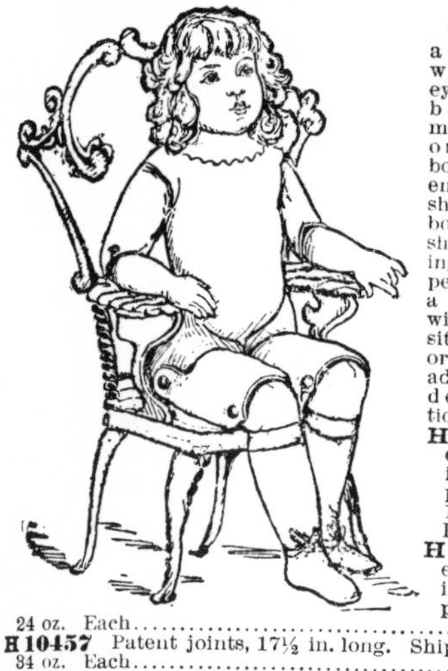

These dolls are made with closing eyes, sewed wig, beautifully modelled heads on best kid body, with patent hip, knee, shoulder and elbow joints, and shoes and stockings, making as perfect a doll as a child could wish for. Can sit up straight or otherwise be adjusted to any desired position.

**H 10452** Patent joints, 12 in. long. Shipping weight, 18 oz. Each....**75c.**

**H 10455** Patent joints, 15 in. long. Shipping weight, 24 oz. Each....**$1.00**

**H 10457** Patent joints, 17½ in. long. Shipping weight, 34 oz. Each....**$1.50**

**H 10462** Patent joints, 21 in. long. Shipping weight, 4 lb. Each....**$2.25**

**H 10465** Patent joints, 25 in. long. Shipping weight, 5 lb. Too heavy to ship by mail. Each....**$3.00**

WE DO NOT BELIEVE

**You can find anywhere else as fine an assortment of desirable toys for children and at such low prices as those carried in our big stock.**

"Kæstner" Patent Joint, Kid Body Dolls. Cannot be shipped by mail. These dolls are made with extra fine quality kid bodies, ½ cork stuffed, riveted hip and knee joints, composition arms with ball jointed shoulder, elbow and wrist; large fine quality bisque head with teeth, moving eyes and fine sewed wigs, fitted with shoes and stockings.

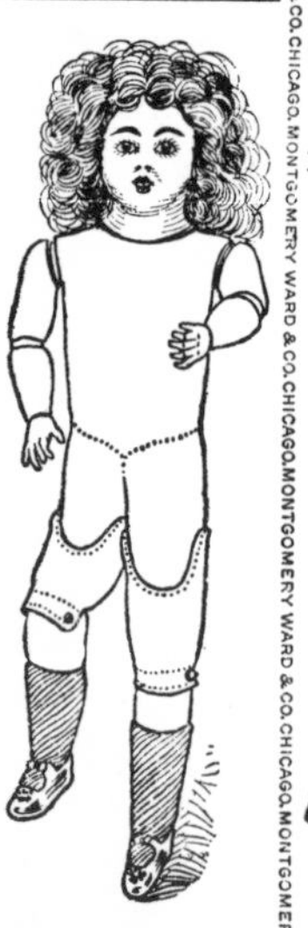

**H 10075** Length, 23 inches. Shipping weight 4½ lbs. Each....**$3.75**

**H 10477** Length 24½ inches. Shipping weight 5 lbs. Each....**$5.00**

**H 10478** Length, 28 inches. Shipping weight 6 lbs. ....**$5.75**

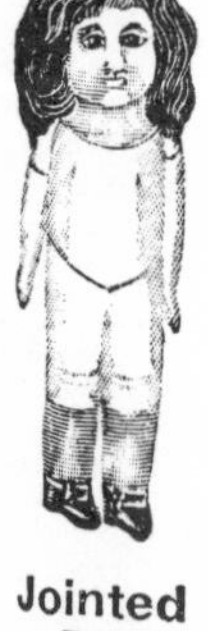

**H 10480** "Kæstner" Fat Baby Kid Doll. Length, 8½ inches; with flowing hair, bisque head, teeth, glass eyes, bisque arm, shoes and stockings. Shipping weight, 10 ounces. Each....**25c.**

## Jointed Dolls Dressed.

**H 10482** Finely dressed, bisque head, jointed body, 13-in. doll, well made throughout and of pleasing style. Shipping weight, 30 ounces. Each....**50c.**

**H 10486** Stylishly Dressed Doll, bisque head, solid eye, flowing hair, of good size; length, 15 in. Shipping weight, 38 ounces. Each....**$1.00**

**H 10489** Fine Dressed Doll, jointed body and bisque head with good wig; has shoes and stockings and very tastefully dressed; length, 16½ in. Shipping weight, 4 lb. Each **$1.50**

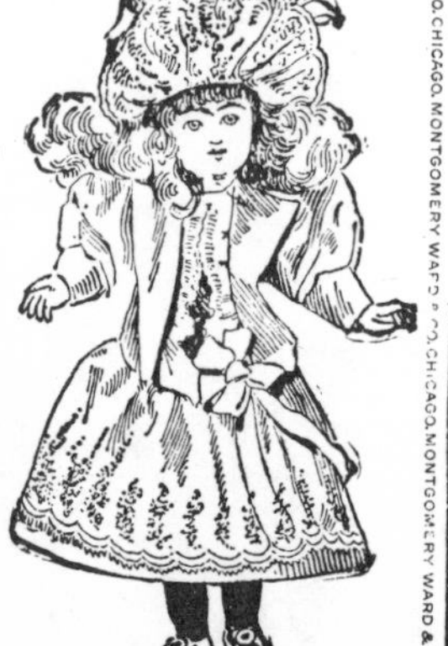

## Rag Dolls.

UNBREAKABLE—VERY POPULAR EXCELLENT FOR YOUNG CHILDREN.

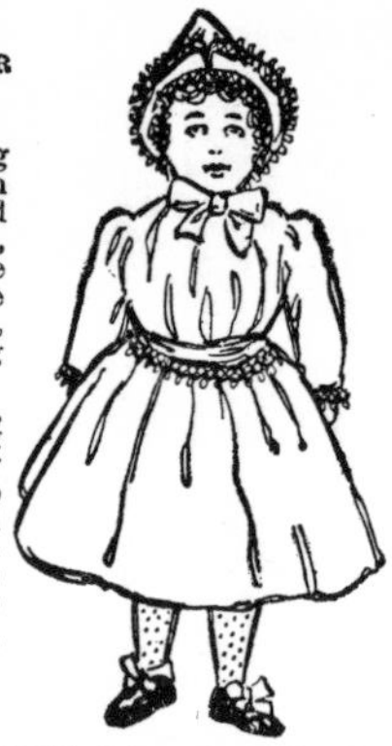

**H 10542** "Daisy" Girl Rag Dolls, 13 in. long, cotton stuffed, nicely lithographed faces; neatly made clothing, which may be removed; the thing for rough use by the baby, and is a real serviceable, well made rag doll. Shipping weight, 10 ounces. Each....**50c.**

**H 10544** "Sailor Boy" Rag Doll, 13 inches long, nicely lithographed face, neatly made clothing and sailor cap. A well made and serviceable doll suitable for use as a companion to H 10542. Shipping weight, 10 oz. Each....**49c.**

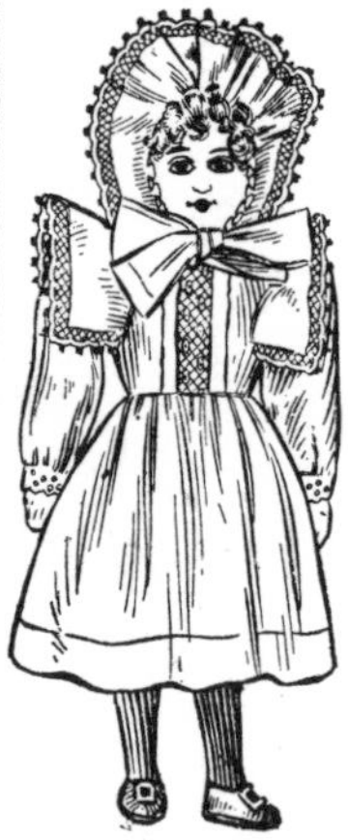

**H 10547** "American Lady" Dressed Rag Doll, length, 14 in., stuffed with cotton, lithographed washable face with hair bangs; jointed arms and limbs; has shoes and stockings and neatly made and trimmed underwear, clothing and sun bonnet; each garment takes off, and is excellent value at the price. Will certainly please you in style and durability. Shipping weight, 16 ounces. Each....**85c.**

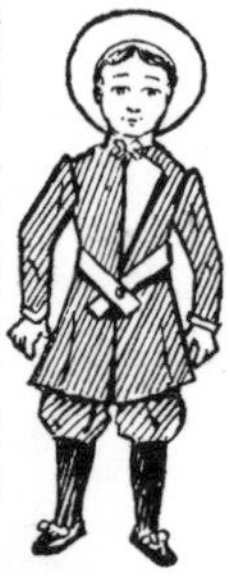

**H 10549** Boy Rag Doll, 15 in. long, dressed in Russian blouse suit with white trimmings and cap to match. A suitable companion for H 10547. Shipping weigth, 15 ounces. Each....**83c.**

**H 10552** "Darky" Nurse Rag Doll, a well made and appropriately dressed doll in bright colored clothing; length, 14 in. Sure to please little folks; also suitable for use as a favor or booby prize for card parties, etc. Ought to be in every collection of dolls. Shipping weight, 15 oz. Our price, each, only **50c.**

**H 10553** "Mammy" Rag Doll, 16 in. long, appropriately dressed in a fac-simile costume such as was worn by the real old Southern mammy, with bandana kerchief on head, white kerchief over shoulders, long colored dress and white apron. Shipping weight 18 ounces. Each....**75c.**

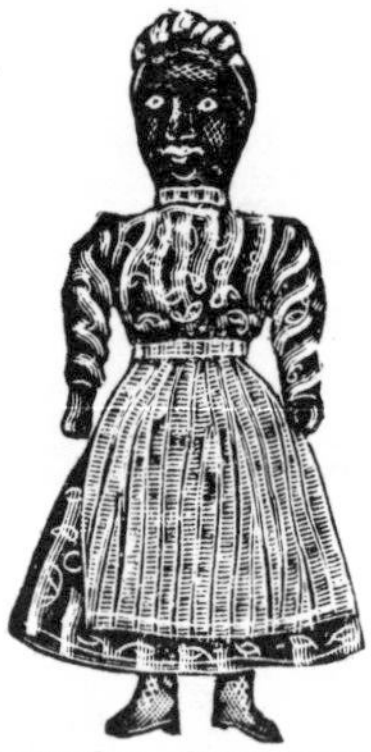

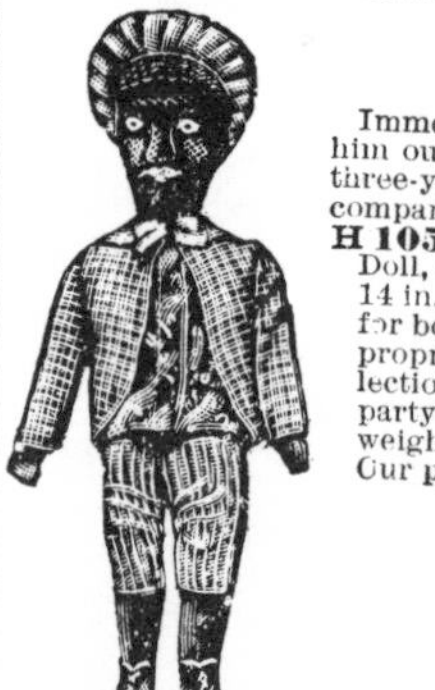

Immensely popular. Don't leave him out of your order. The two or three-year-old child will enjoy his company for months.

**H 10555** "Dusky Dude" Rag Doll, companion to H 10552; length 14 in. A novel and desirable doll for boy's use, and will make an appropriate addition to any doll collection. An excellent souvenir for party favor or prize. Shipping weight, 15 oz. Our price, each, only....**50c.**

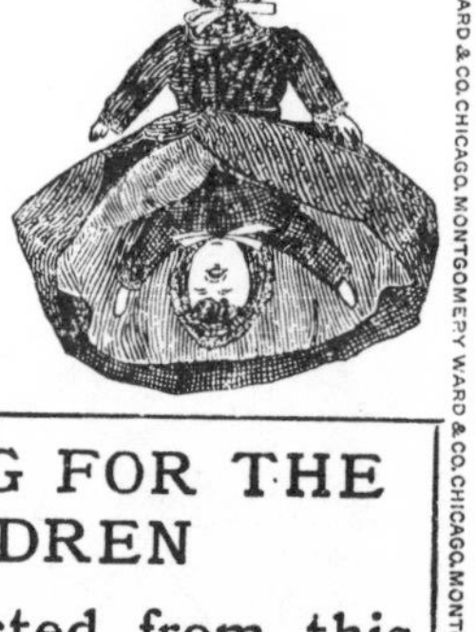

**H 10559** Reversible Rag Doll with laughing and crying lithographed faces with hair bangs, neatly made clothing and sun bonnets. Full length 12½ ins. Baby's friend and should be in every household. Shipping weight, 11 ounces. Each....**50c.**

CLOTHING FOR THE CHILDREN

**Can be selected from this book at ¼ to ½ the price you would pay elsewhere.**

## Minerva Knock-about Dolls.

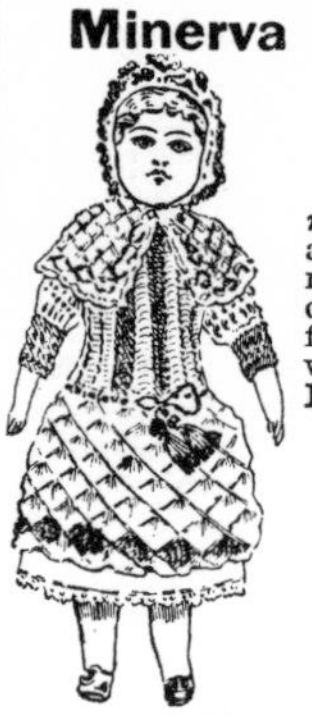

Fitted with the celebrated *Minerv metal doll heads.* Extra strong bodi and hands, especially constructed t match the durability of the heads. A dresses have buttons, hooks and ey for undressing. Underwear trimme with lace.

**H 10563** Minerva Knock-about Dol 11 in. long; dress, hood and cap crocheted by hand in two colors; a artistic sample of German needle work. *Regular one-dollar valu* Shipping weight, 11 oz. Each....**75c**

## Bisque Doll Arms.

Good shaped forearm and hand of bisque, with upper arr of kid.

H 10592 4 in. long. Shipping weight, 5 oz. Per pair..$0.1
H 10595 6 in. long. Shipping weight, 8 oz. Per pair.. .2
H 10596 8½ in. long. Shipping weight, 12 oz. Per pair. .3
H 10598 10 in. long. Shipping weight, 16 oz. Per pair .5

## Doll Heads.

NOTE.—The measurements on bisque doll heads are fron shoulder to shoulder and from front to back of bust.

"KAESTNER" BISQUE DOLL HEADS, with closing eyes, and fitted with selected sewed wigs; have teeth; model of face is excellent and will please the most critical.

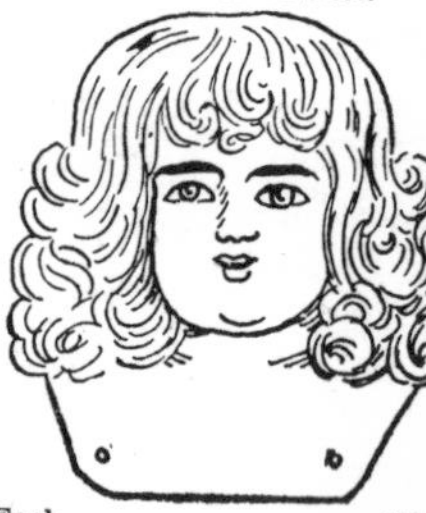

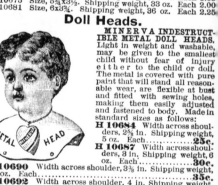

**H 10652** Size, 3x1¾. Shipping weight, 12 oz. Each....**45c.**

H 10654 Size, 3¼x2¼. Shipping weight, 18 oz. Each....$0.55

H 10657 Size, 3¼x2½. Shipping weight, 22 oz. Each....$0.75

H 10659 Size, 4x2¾. Shipping weight, 25 oz. Each....$0.90

H 10663 Size, 4¼x3. Shipping weight, 26 oz. Each 1.10
H 10668 Size, 4½x3¼. Shipping weight, 27 oz. Each 1.25
H 10669 Size, 4¾x3¼. Shipping weight, 28 oz. Each 1.40
H 10671 Size, 5¼x3½. Shipping weight, 30 oz. Each 1.65
H 10675 Size, 5¾x3½. Shipping weight, 33 oz. Each 2.00
H 10681 Size, 6x3¾. Shipping weight, 36 oz. Each 2.25

## Doll Heads.

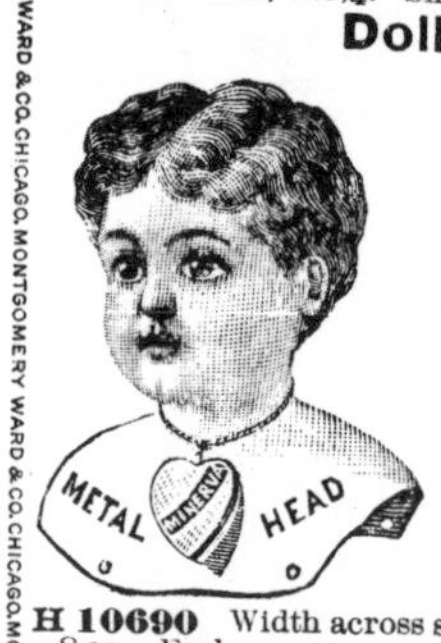


MINERVA INDESTRUCTIBLE METAL DOLL HEADS. Light in weight and washable, may be given to the smallest child without fear of injury either to the child or doll. The metal is covered with pure paint that will stand all reasonable wear, are flexible at bust and fitted with sewing holes, making them easily adjusted and fastened to body. Made in standard sizes as follows:

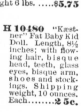

**H 10684** Width across shoulders, 2⅝ in. Shipping weight, 5 oz. Each....**25c.**

**H 10687** Width across shoulders, 3 in. Shipping weight, 6 oz. Each....**30c.**

**H 10690** Width across shoulder, 3⅜ in. Shipping weight, 8 oz. Each....**35c.**

**H 10692** Width across shoulder, 4 in. Shipping weight, 10 oz. Each....**45c.**

**H 10695** "MINERVA" METAL DOLL HEAD, with teeth and glass eyes. Width across shoulder, 4 in. Shipping weight, 10 oz. Each....**75c.**

MINERVA DOLL HEADS, made of metal, same as the all metal head, except these have a sewed wig and have closing glass eyes.

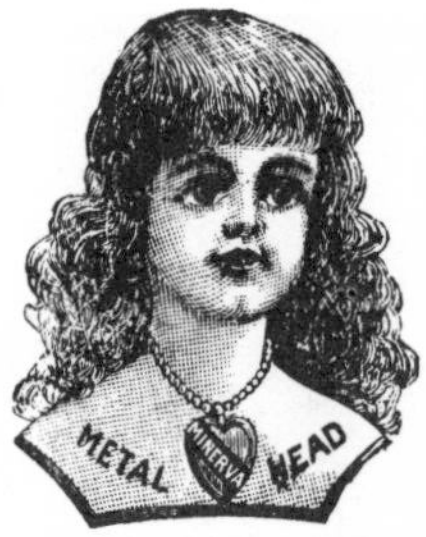


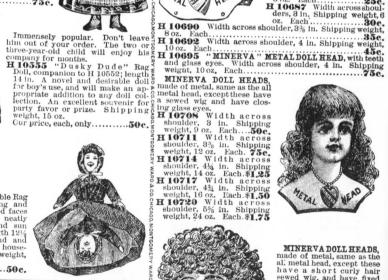

**H 10708** Width across shoulder, 3 in. Shipping weight, 9 oz. Each....**50c.**

**H 10711** Width across shoulder, 3⅜ in. Shipping weight, 12 oz. Each. **75c.**

**H 10714** Width across shoulder, 4¼ in. Shipping weight, 14 oz. Each. **$1.25**

**H 10717** Width across shoulder, 4¾ in. Shipping weight, 16 oz. Each. **$1.50**

**H 10720** Width across shoulder, 5⅝ in. Shipping weight, 24 oz. Each. **$1.75**

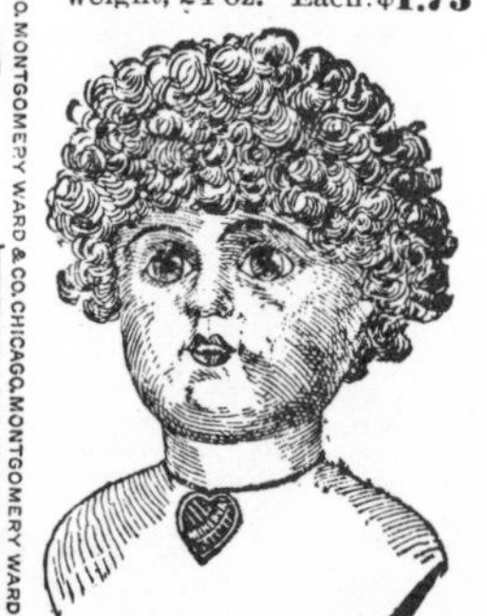

MINERVA DOLL HEADS, made of metal, same as the all metal head, except these have a short curly hair sewed wig, and have fixed glass eyes. Excellent for use in making up a "boy" doll for the collection.

**H 10728** Width across shoulder, 3 in. Height, from breast to top of head, 4¼ in. Shipping weight, 7 oz. Each..**50c.**

**H 10729** Width across shoulder, 3⅜ in. Height, from breast to top of head, 4½ in. Shipping weight, 8 oz. Each..**75c.**

MONTGOMERY WARD & CO. CHICAGO

## Fine Silesia Doll Bodies.

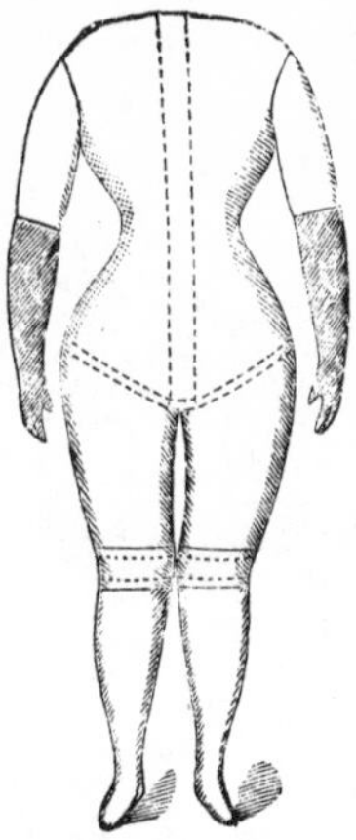

Fine Doll Bodies (no heads), made of extra heavy silesia, flesh colored, wool stuffed. Bisque forearms and hands, shoes and stockings. This body, used in conjunction with H 10652 to H 10729 heads, will make a superfine doll.

**H 10735** Length, 12¾ in. For head 3 to 3¼ in. across shoulders. Shipping weight, 12 oz.
Each....................**25c.**

**H 10744** Length, 16½ in. For head 3¾ to 4 in. across shoulders. Shipping weight, 19 oz.
Each....................**40c.**

**H 10747** Length, 19 in. For head 4½ in. across shoulders. Shipping weight, 22 oz.
Each....................**50c.**

**H 10750** Length 21¾ in. For head 5¼ in. across shoulders. Shipping weight, 26 oz.
Each....................**60c.**

**H 10753** Length, 23½ in. For head 5¾ in. across shoulders. Shipping weight, 30 oz.
Each....................**75c.**

**H 10756** Length 25 in. For head 6¼ in. across shoulders. Shipping weight, 36 oz.
Each....................**90c.**

## Wigs for Dolls.

**H 10765** Dolls' Wigs, made of selected human hair, sewed and parted, natural light or dark brown; in shoulder curls and in all regular doll's head sizes from No. 7, the smallest, to No. 15, the largest; make your choice as to color and size.

| Size. | | Size. | |
|---|---|---|---|
| 7 and 8 | $0.75 | 11 and 12 | $1.25 |
| 9 and 10 | 1.00 | 13, 14 and 15 | 1.50 |

Shipping weight, 5 oz.

## Doll's Sundries.

**H 10783** American Beauty Doll hat, stylish and trimmed in fine style and taste, good materials. Is specially a summer hat, but suitable for any season for the doll; they are well made and come in three sizes for the small, medium or large doll. Shipping weight, 8 oz. Each....................**25c.**

**H 10791** Dolls' Shoes, in sizes 2 to 7, ladies' lace-up low shoe style, and fine quality. Shipping weight, 4 oz.
Per pair....................**15c.**

**H 10795** Dolls' Stockings; full-fashioned, machine-knit; made in three sizes for small, medium and large dolls; put up assorted colors in each doz. Shipping weight, 2 oz.
Per pair....................**10c.**

## Doll's Knit Wear.

**H 10806** Doll's Knit-wear Set, consisting of hand-made sacque knit from Shetland floss, with hood, muff and bootees to match. *Regular 75c value.* Shipping weight, 10 ounces.
Per set....................**50c.**

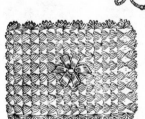

**H 10809** Doll's Carriage Robe, hand-made, knitted from Shetland floss in fancy pattern with double row of wide satin ribbon in center. Size, 14x18 in. *Regular 75c value.* Shipping weight, 10 oz.
Each....................**50c.**

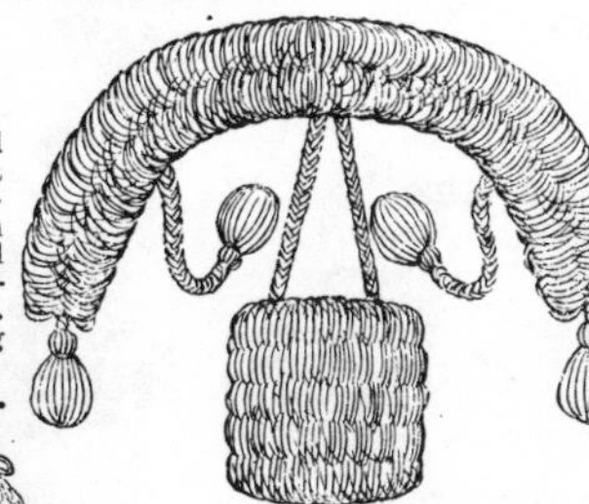

**H 10814—** Doll's Knitted Muff and Boa Set, hand-made, from fine Shetland floss. *Excellent 50c value.* Shipping weight, 5 oz.
Per set..**29c.**

**H 10820** Doll's Golf Cape, hand made, knit from fine white Shetland floss with colored floss around edge. Makes a dressy garment for doll. Shipping weight 2 ounces.
Each....................**38c.**

**H 10823** Doll's Sacque, hand made, knit from fine white Shetland floss with colored floss around edge. Made in three sizes, small, medium and large, for dolls from 14 to 21 inches in length. Shipping weight 3 ounces.
Each....................**33c.**

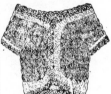

**H 10829** Doll's Sweater, hand made, knit from colored Shetland floss, with contrasting color around edges; draw string with tassel ends at neck. Made in three sizes, small, medium and large for dolls from 14 to 21 inches in length. Shipping weight 3 ounces.
Each....................**35c.**

**H 10831** Doll's White Tam O'Shanter, with colored silk floss mixture in pompon and in edge of tam. *Regular 25c. value.* Shipping weight, 2 oz.
Each....................**15c.**

**H 10837** Doll's Hand Knit Hood, made of Shetland floss; striped in contrasting colors; knitted ties with tassels, excellent value. Shipping weight, 2 oz. Each......**12c.**

**H 10840** Doll's Corded Pique Suit, consisting of hat, skirt and blouse trimmed with colored baby ribbon; also drawers and skirt of white lawn trimmed with valenciennes lace; all neatly made of good material, which can be laundered when necessary. Shipping weight, 10 oz.
Sizes suitable for dolls 15 to 21 in........**$1.00**
Sizes suitable for dolls 24 to 27 in........**$1.25**

**H 10842** Doll's Colored Dimity Suit, with lace trimmed bonnet; also white lawn drawers and skirt trimmed with valenciennes lace. Shipping weight, 10 oz.
For dolls 15 to 21 in........**$1.20**
For dolls 24 to 27 in........**$1.40**

**STANDARD DIARIES FOR 1904.**

A line of popular styles listed at popular prices on page 443.

**H 10827** Doll's Golf Vest, hand made, knit from fine white Shetland floss, with colored floss around edge. Made in three sizes, small, medium and large for dolls from 14 to 21 inches in length. Shipping weight, 3 ounces.
Each....................**25c.**

**H 10844** Doll's 5-Piece Colored Lawn Suit, consisting of dress and hat trimmed with lace; also white lawn drawers, skirt and corset cover trimmed with valenciennes lace. Shipping weight, 10 oz.
For dolls 15 to 21 in........**$2.00**
For dolls 24 to 27 in........**$2.45**

## Doll Comb Sets.

**H 10853** Doll Comb Set, consisting of cute little rubber combs. Contains Dressing, Toilet, Fine, Back and Round Comb, neatly arranged on card as shown in cut.
Per set....................**$0.12**
Per doz. sets....................1.20
Shipping weight, per set, 5 oz.
Per dozen sets, 10 oz.

**H 10855—** Doll's La Petite Nursing Bottle, 2¾ inches long, 1¼ inches wide, made of glass with rubber nipple. Shipping weight, 3 oz.
Each....................**10c.**

## American Theater.

**H 10861** Has a front in full colors and gold; size 15½x 12½ inches. The play is "Red Riding Hood." There are three scenes and a tableau, book of the play, cut out figures, roll-up curtain and slotted stage to hold scenery, all complete, and all to be taken apart and snugly packed. The scenery and figures are in full colors. Shipping weight, 5 lb. Each....................**85c.**

## New Pretty Village.

24 Figures and 8 Buildings in each set.
**H 10863** This toy is a set of folding cardboard houses, stores, churches, etc., made to set as a village or town. The buildings are jointed at the corners and have detachable roofs. They are printed in bright colors. Shipping weight, 2 lb. Each....................**50c.**

## Folding Doll Houses.

**H 10865** Dolly's Playhouse is 9½x12 inches on the ground and 17 inches to the peak of the roof when set up. It is two stories high, made of strawboard and wood, lined outside and in with paper printed to represent carpets, wall paper, brick walls and windows. This is a very fine residence for any family of small dolls. Shipping weight, 4¾ lb.
Each....................**75c.**

**H 10867—** Doll's Japanese Furniture Set made of bamboo, with imitation cane seats; consisting of table, 2 dining chairs, 2 arm chairs, and one davenport. Shipping weight. 6 oz. Per set..........**25c.**

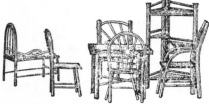

**H 10869** Doll's Bamboo Furniture Set in mottled green finish, consisting of table 3½ in. high; 2 dining chairs, seat, 2 inches high, back, 5 inches high; 2 arm chairs, seat, 2½ in. high, back, 5 inches high; and one davenport with seat 2 inches high and back 5 inches high; also four shelf corner bric-a-brac cabinet 7 inches high. Shipping weight, 18 ounces. Per set..........**60c.**

## For Ladies' Correspondence

the stylish note papers and envelopes quoted in our Stationery columns. Qualities suitable for all purposes. Prices right. See pages 437 to 440 for quotations.

## Toy Telescopes.

**H 10870** Toy Telescope Case, 12 in. long, 5¾ in. wide, made of canvas, riveted, with leather corner protectors, straps and handle. Shipping weight, 14 oz. Each..........**25c.**

**H 10875** Doll Case, telescope style, made of canvas, riveted, with leather corner protectors, straps and handles, length 16 in., width 5¾ in. Shipping weight, 18 oz. Each..........**42c.**
**H 10879** Doll case, 20 in. long and 6¾ in. wide, otherwise same as H 10875. Shipping weight, 27 oz. Each..........**65c.**
**H 10883** Doll Case, 22 in. long, 9¼ in. wide, otherwise same as H 10875. Shipping weight, 36 oz. Each..........**75c.**
**H 10887** Doll Case, 24 inches long, 9½ in. wide, otherwise same as H 10875. Shipping weight, 40 oz. Each..........**$0.87**
NOTE.—The above doll cases are intended for carrying "Dolly," her clothing, etc., when visiting or on a journey.

**H 10891** Toy Dress Suit Case for carrying "Dolly's" wardrobe when on a journey or visiting; made of gray duck, riveted, with leather corner protectors, straps and handle, cloth lined, length 12 in., width 7½ in. Shipping weight, 14 oz. Each..........**25c.**
**H 10895** Toy Dress Suit Case, 14 in. long, 8½ in. wide, otherwise same as H10891. Shipping weight, 15 oz. Each..........**38c.**
**H 10899** Toy Dress Suit Case, 16 in. long, 9 in. wide, otherwise same as H 10891. Shipping weight, 22 oz. Each..........**50c.**

## Toy Trunks.

**H 10912** Toy Trunk, imitation leather covered, set-up tray with two compartments; long slats on top and body with tinned clamps; leather handles, hasp lock, 14-in. size. Good value at price. Shipping weight, 5 lb. Each.**60c.**

---

**H 10915—** Crystal Eugenie Toy Trunk, covered with fancy metal, long strips with clamps, removable tray with two compartments, length 16 in. Shipping wt., 14 lb. Splendid value. Each...**$1.00**

**H 10918** Canvas Covered, Metal Bound, Flat Top Toy Trunk; has removable tray with two covered compartments; has good lock and key; strong and well made; length, 18 in. Excellent value at price. Shipping weight, 15 lb. Each......**$1.50**

## Doll Bedsteads.

These Doll Beds are modern, high-grade goods, the finest of their kind. Each bed comes knocked down, packed in strong paper box, and is easily put together.
**H 10925** Trimmed Wire Doll Bed, brass finish, 18 in. long, 11 in. wide, 15 in. high, lace-trimmed pillows and mattress, covered with fancy printed silkaline, and head-

piece trimmed with same material. Shipping weight, 4 lb. Each..........**75c.**
**H 10928** Trimmed Wire Doll Bed, brass finish, 24 in. long, 12½ in. wide, 16½ in. high; otherwise same as No. H 10925. Shipping weight, 6 lb. Each..........**98c.**

**H 10935—** Doll's Iron Bed, finished in colored enamel with gilt stripings; height at head, 13 inches; at foot, 11½ in.; length, 24 in.; fitted with woven wire mattress in silver steel finish. Shipping weight, 6 lbs. Each...**$1.00**

**H 10939** Doll's Iron Bed, finished in colored enamel with gilt stripings; height at head, 16 in., at foot, 13 in.; length, 24 in. Fitted with woven wire mattress in silver steel finish. Shipping weight, 2 lb. Each, **$1.25**

**Always Acceptable at Holiday Time:**
One of those nice
# POCKET BOOKS
Quoted on pages 489 to 492.

---

## Toy Sewing Machines.

**H 10953—** "Triumph" Sewing Machine, automatic tension, neat in design, elegantly enameled and finished in floral designs of different colors; fastens to a table with a clamp which accompanies each machine; makes Wilcox and Gibbs stitch and will do plain sewing after operator has learned to run it; has patent feed motion and perfect stitch regulator; uses Wilcox and Gibbs self-setting needle, which has a short blade and long shank not easily broken. A small light running sewing machine for the little housekeeper on which all kinds of plain sewing may be done. Especially adapted for kindergarten use. Extra clamp and needle sent with each machine, Shipping weight, 2 lbs. Each..........**$1.50**

**H 10957** "Tourist" Sewing Machine; 8 in. high, 8½ in. wide, made entirely of metal, and is a perfect hand power sewing machine within the reach of all; makes a desirable and useful present, and is superior in construction, finish and working qualities to any similar machine heretofore offered. Has a perfect feed motion, stitch regulator, automatic tension and uses the Wilcox & Gibbs needle. It is thoroughly tested and properly adjusted before leaving factory, and when used intelligently makes a practical machine for tourists and travelers as well as for household purposes for plain sewing. May be easily carried in a grip when traveling, as it weighs only 2⅛ lbs. Instructive and entertaining to the young members of the family, and excellent for use in kindergartens and primary schools. Shipping weight, 4 lbs. Each..........**$2.95**

## Wedding Stationery.

Write for samples before ordering elsewhere. Price and quality sure to please. See page 438 for quotations.

## Nursery Clock.

**H 10961** Nursery Clock, ships knocked down, all the different parts being attached to a card with full directions for putting the clock together and operating it properly. Simple in construction, and may be easily put together by any child or person having a little mechanical ability; runs accurately and keeps good time when properly set up. Consists of the following parts: Wooden case, motion wheel works, chain wheel, center wheel, escape wheel with pinion, weight, chain, escapement, cannon pinion, minute wheel, hour wheel, dial and hands. Shipping weight, 2 lbs. Excellent for school use in demonstrating the mechanism of a clock. Each..........**$1.25**

## Student's Blackboard.

**H 10993** Student's Blackboard. Neatly finished in natural hardwood, a combination blackboard and desk, with revolving copy sheet, fitted with cranks for changing the copy. These copies are composed of new and original designs, both instructive and amusing. The blackboard, 23x19½ in., when dropped forward, forms a convenient desk. The interior is furnished with pockets for holding stationery, etc. Height, 51 in. Excellent $2.00 value. Shipping weight, 25 lb. Each..........**$1.50**

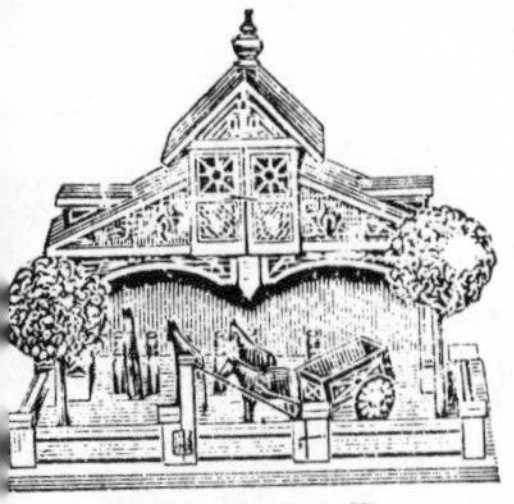

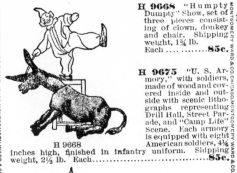

**H 9643** "Stock Farm" consisting of stable with six stalls, large yard, with fence, and swinging gate, imported horses, carts, trees, etc. Painted, stained and lithographed in bright colors. Size of stable, 12x11½x5 ins.; size of yard, 15½x12¼ ins. Shipping weight, 5 lbs. Each............**83c.**

## Humpty Dumpty Shows.

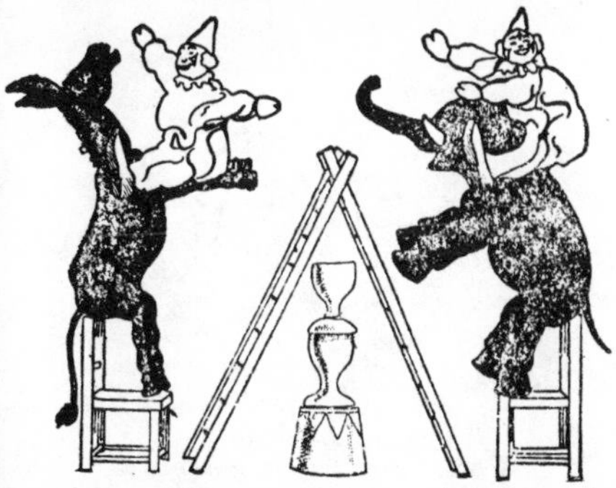

**H 9658** "Humpty Dumpty" Show, a set of eleven pieces including jointed wooden elephant, donkey, clowns with extra fancy dresses, two ladders, two chairs, two tumblers and one tub. Clowns and animals are jointed similar to dolls and have movable heads, arms and legs, so that the figures can be set in an endless variety of positions producing fascinating and grotesque results. These toys are educators as they teach children patience and perseverance, to think and create new ideas, etc. Entertaining and amusing for children and grown folks as well. Shipping weight, 4¼ lbs. Per set............................**$2.25**

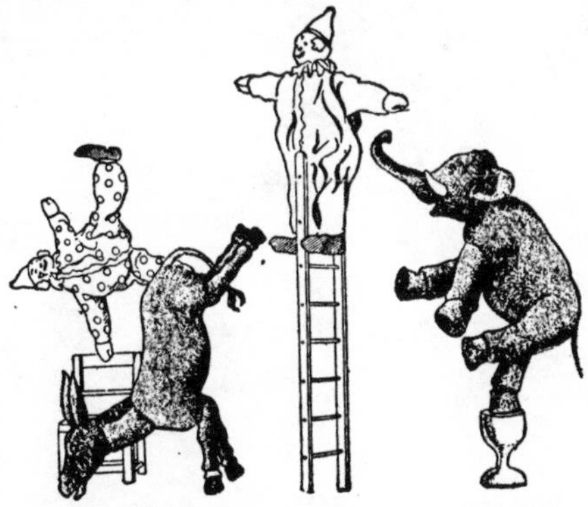

**H 9662** "Humpty Dumpty" Show, a set of seven pieces consisting of elephant, donkey, two clowns, chair, ladder and tumbler. Shipping weight, 3¾ lbs. Per set...**$1.75**

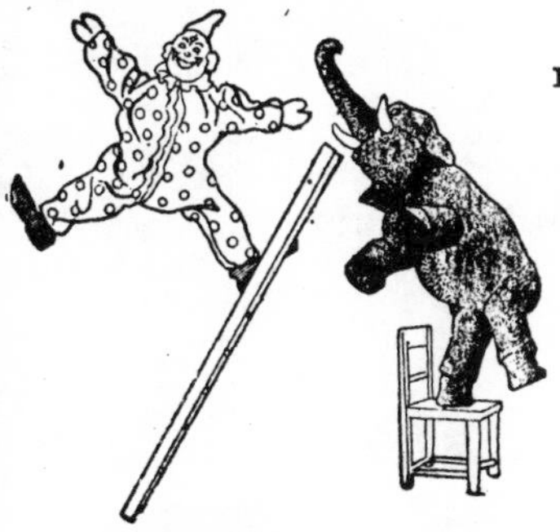

**H 9664** "Humpty Dumpty" Show, set of four pieces consisting of elephant, clown, ladder, chair. Shipping weight, 3 lb. Per set......**$1.00**

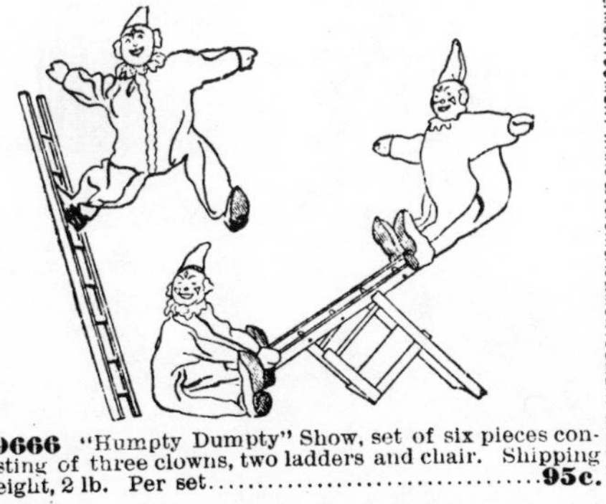

**H 9666** "Humpty Dumpty" Show, set of six pieces consisting of three clowns, two ladders and chair. Shipping weight, 2 lb. Per set............................**95c.**

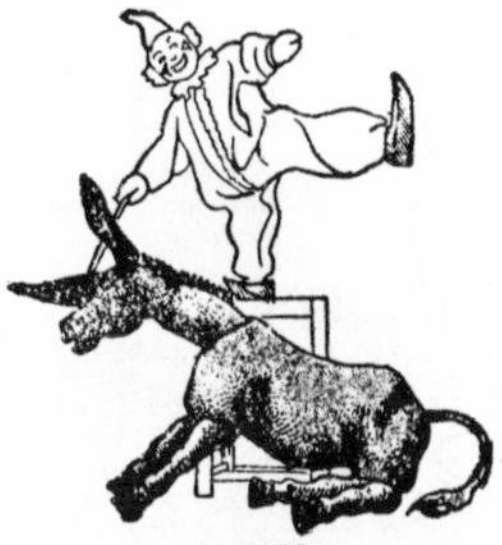

H 9668

**H 9668** "Humpty Dumpty" Show, set of three pieces consisting of clown, donkey and chair. Shipping weight, 1¾ lb. Each.............**85c.**

**H 9675** "U. S. Armory," with soldiers, made of wood and covered inside and outside with scenic lithographs representing Drill Hall, Street Parade, and "Camp Life" Scene. Each armory is equipped with eight American soldiers, 4¼ inches high, finished in infantry uniform. Shipping weight, 2½ lb. Each..............................**85c.**

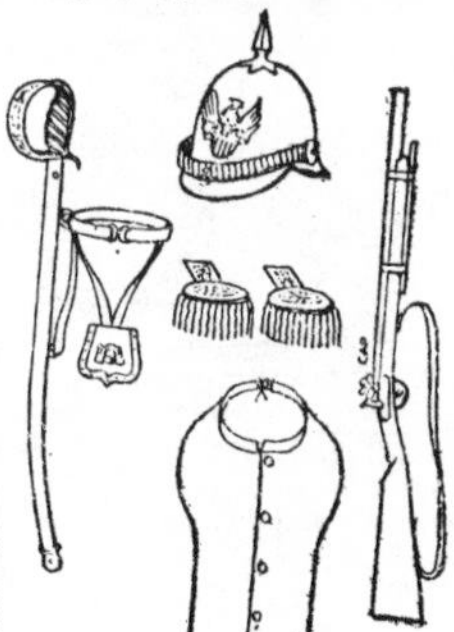

**H 9677** Toy Soldier Equipment Set, consisting of helmet, breast-plate, epaulets, sword with belt, and gun. Shipping weight, 42 oz. Each............**85c.**

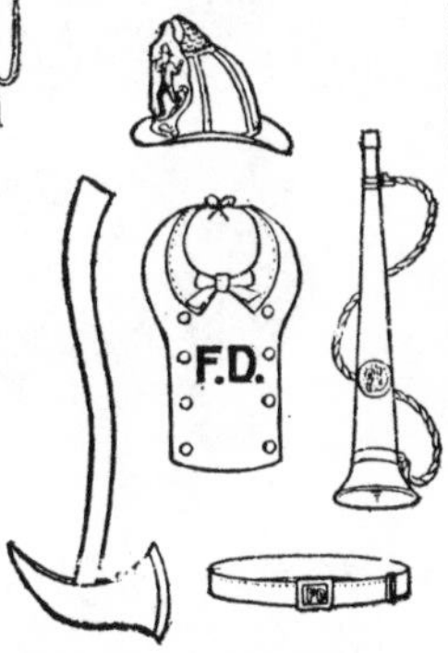


**H 9679** Toy Fireman's Equipment Set, consisting of helmet, breastplate, belt, speaking trumpet and axe. Shipping weight, 38 oz. Each..............**83c.**

## Rubber Ball Shooting Gallery.

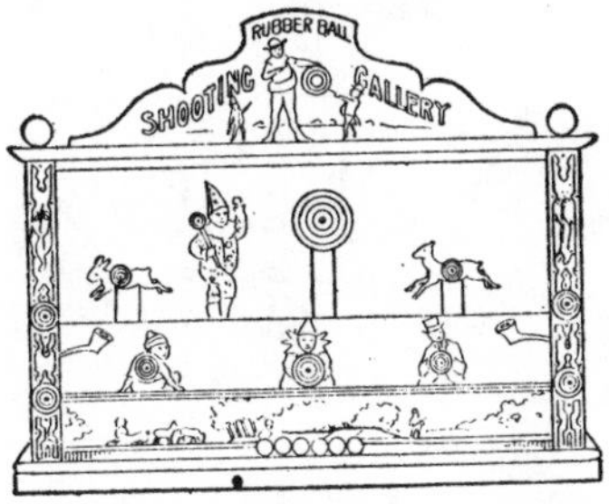


**H 9683** Rubber Ball Shooting Gallery, 18½x12x6¼ in. Latest and most attractive toy. Handsomely finished. Positively harmless. Immense indoor or outdoor amusement for all young sports. These galleries are handsomely finished in fancy colors, each accompanied with a fine rubber ball gun, shooting ⅝-inch hollow rubber balls, entirely harmless. Six balls and six corks go with each gun. Shipping weight, 5 lb. Each..............................**95c.**

## Harmless Rubber Tipped Arrow and Target Pistols.

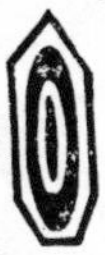

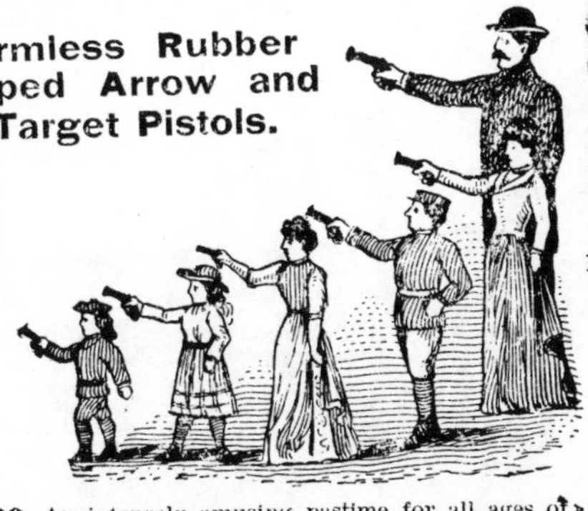

**H 9690** An intensely amusing pastime for all ages of the entire human family throughout the civilized world, at all seasons of the year. When first invented, it was thought its use would be confined to the requirements of sporting boys, but when brought home and hung up it was found that all members of the family took an equal interest in it—even parents took much pleasure with it. No amusement game has ever been received with such universal favor. Complete outfit, with Pistol, Arrow, Target, and Target Holder. Shipping weight, 1½ lb. Per set.......**42c.**

**H 9694** Harmless Rubber-Tipped Arrows. Each..**10c.**

## Liquid Pistol.

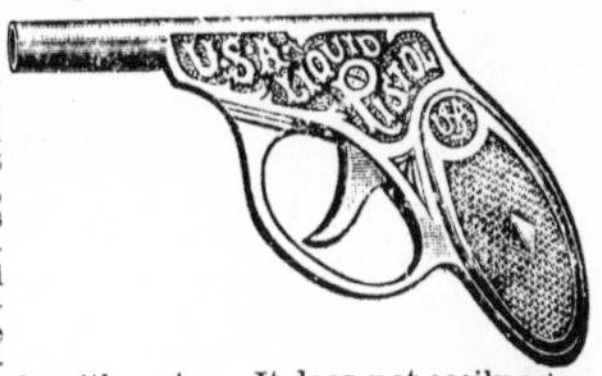


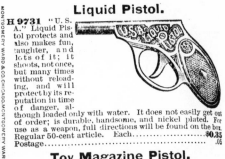

**H 9731** "U. S. A." Liquid Pistol protects and also makes fun, laughter, and lots of it; it shoots, not once, but many times without reloading, and will protect by its reputation in time of danger, although loaded only with water. It does not easily get out of order; is durable, handsome, and nickel plated. For use as a weapon, full directions will be found on the box. Regular 50-cent article. Each......................**$0.35**
Postage...............................................................................**.05**

## Toy Magazine Pistol.

NICKEL PLATED. 7¼ IN. LONG.

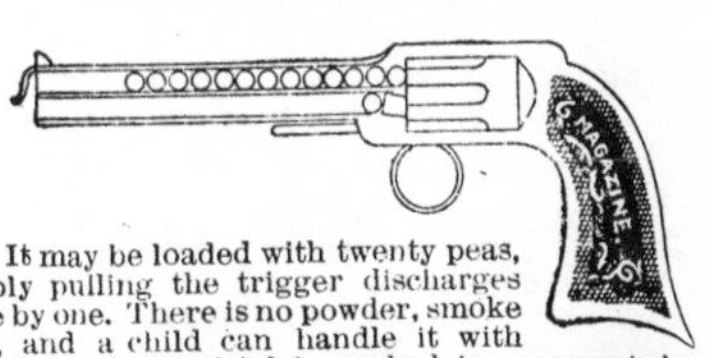


**H 9737** It may be loaded with twenty peas, and simply pulling the trigger discharges them one by one. There is no powder, smoke or noise, and a child can handle it with perfect safety. Each pistol is packed in a separate box, together with supply of ammunition. It has no equal for target shooting. Each...........................**$0.20**
Postage.................................................................................**.17**

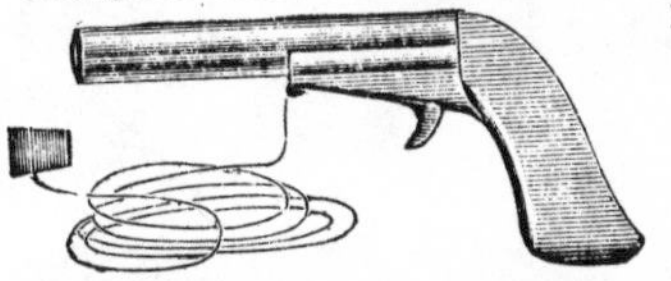

**H 9785** The King Pop Pistol. Made on same principle as the well known King Air Rifle. By means of compressed air a cork is fired from the gun with a loud report. Perfectly harmless. Weight, 6 ounces. Price, each..............**$0.20**
Per dozen..............................................................................**2.00**

## Boys' Brigade Guns.

Made of hardwood and well finished, resembling regular military guns.

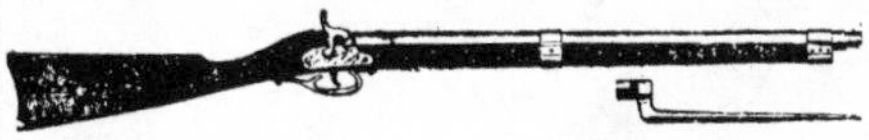

**H 9795** Boys' Brigade Gun; size, 42 in. long, bayonet 12 in. long, silver-bronzed finish; shoots small percussion caps; a good drill gun for boys. Shipping weight, 3 lb.
Per doz..................$9.00 Each........................**90c.**

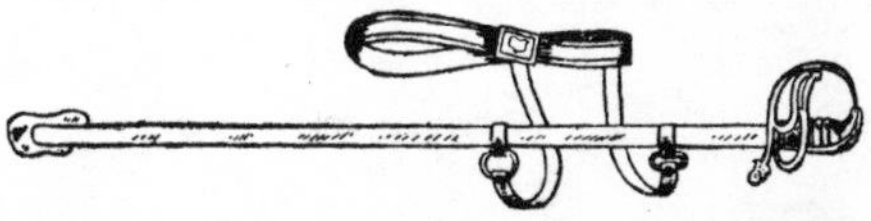

**H 9801** Boys' Brigade Captain's Sword, made of polished steel, brass trimmings, strong leather belt. Shipping weight, 1½ lb. Each.......................................**$1.50**

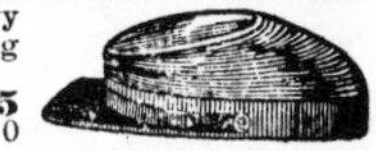

**H 9805** Boys' Brigade Cap, navy blue cloth, best make. Shipping weight, 10 ounces.
Each........................**$0.75**
Per doz.........................8.10

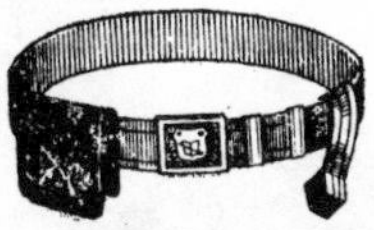

**H 9807** Boys' Brigade Belt, russet color, with bayonet holder and cartridge box, brass buckle. Shipping weight, 8 ounces.
Each............................**$0.50**
Per doz..................................5.00

## Toy Drums.

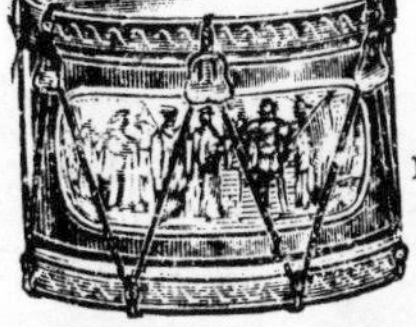

**H 9830** Toy Drum; good quality, metal body, with flags embossed in panels, imitation rosewood hoops, ornamented and varnished, corded; 9 in. in diameter. Shipping weight, 2 lb. Each.................**$0.65**

**H 9833** Same description as above, but larger size, 11 in. in diameter. Each.........**$0.75**
Per doz..................................7.50

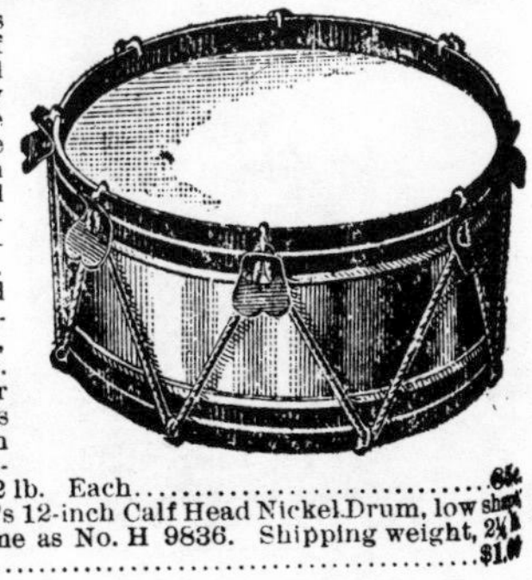

**H 9836** Boy's 11-inch Calf Head Nickel Drum, low shape. One calf and one sheepskin head, nickel shell, enameled hoops, ornamented. Red, white and blue cord, metal hooks, leather ears. A belt and pair of drumsticks with each drum. Shipping weight, 2 lb. Each...............................**65c.**

**H 9839** Boy's 12-inch Calf Head Nickel Drum, low shape; otherwise same as No. H 9836. Shipping weight, 2½ lb. Each...............................................**$1.00**

**H 9308** "Balky Mule." A Mechanical Action German Tin Toy that is really comical. The Funny Clown sitting upon a two-wheel cart endeavors to drive the Stubborn Donkey, which persists in backing up, then goes ahead again. The toy is wound up by attached thumbpiece; comes put up in pasteboard box. *Regular 50c value.* Shipping weight, 10 ounces.
Each .......................... **$0.25**
Per doz .......................... 3.00

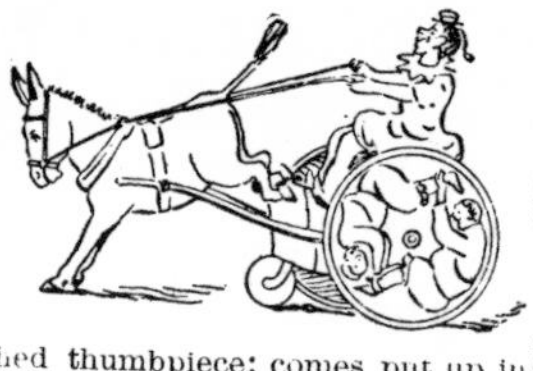

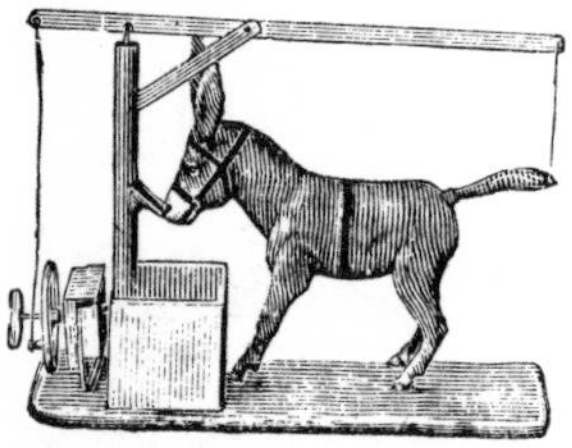

**H 9312** "Donkey at the Pump," mechanical toy which winds up with a key. Donkey works pump handle with his tail and moves his ears. Made of metal and finished in colors. Shipping weight, 10 oz.
Each ....... **25c.**

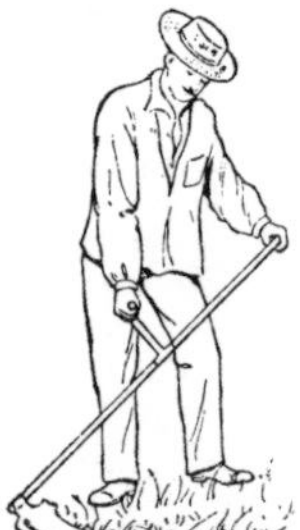

**H 9314** Mechanical Mower, a dressed figure 7 inches high, swings a scythe, which is 3½ inches long, (handle is 7 inches long); as he swings the scythe, figure moves along in very natural way. True to life. Shipping weight, 10 oz.
Each.......................... **25c.**

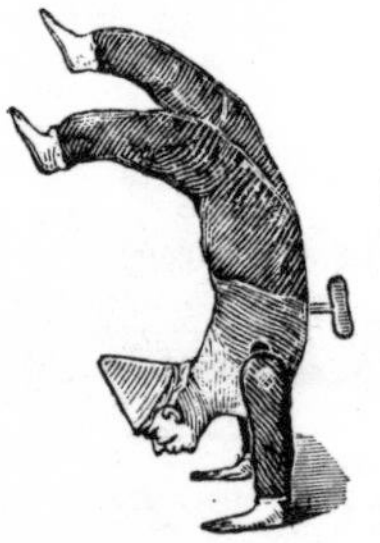

**H 9316** "Clown Hand Walker." A mechanical toy operated by clock movement, winds up with attached key, finished in bright colors, height 6¼-in. Shipping weight, 7 oz.
Each.......................... **20c.**

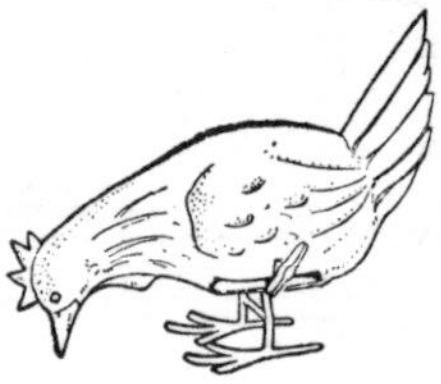

**H 9319** Mechanical Hen, 8 in. long; has very natural voice; pecks and moves around; finished in colors. Shipping weight, 9 oz.
Each.......................... **25c.**

## Hill Climber Friction Power Toys.

All Hill Climber Toys are now equipped with a new patent "Self Adjustable Friction Distributing Idler" which presses together the working parts and causes the power axle to bite and grip at every touch. The slightest touch starts the toy, and by pressing down and giving it two or three hard pushes, sufficient momentum will be given to the power to travel a long distance. It runs backward and forward, uphill or down hill over small obstructions with ease. It may be used outdoors as well as in and furnishes unlimited amusement to children of all ages.

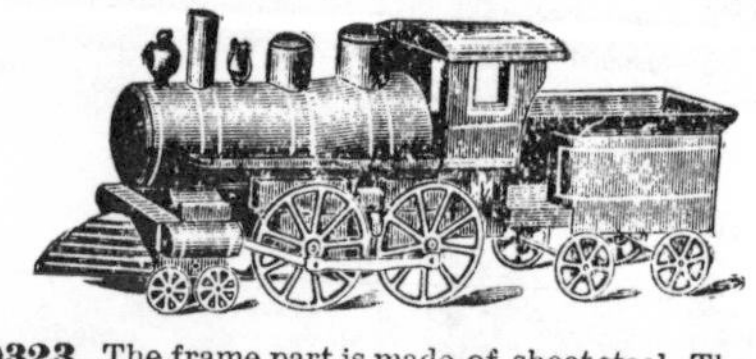

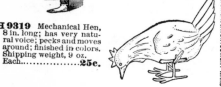

**H 9323** The frame part is made of sheet steel. The shaft of the power wheel is stationary and cannot become loose or clogged with the wheels. It is the most powerful toy locomotive ever built, 18x6½x4 in. It goes down and up hill, and runs over great obstructions with ease. It is a fine test of skill to try how far different persons can make it go with a given length of push. The secret is to start slowly and gradually increase the speed, like a railroad train. Shipping weight, 5 lb. Each.......................... **$1.00**

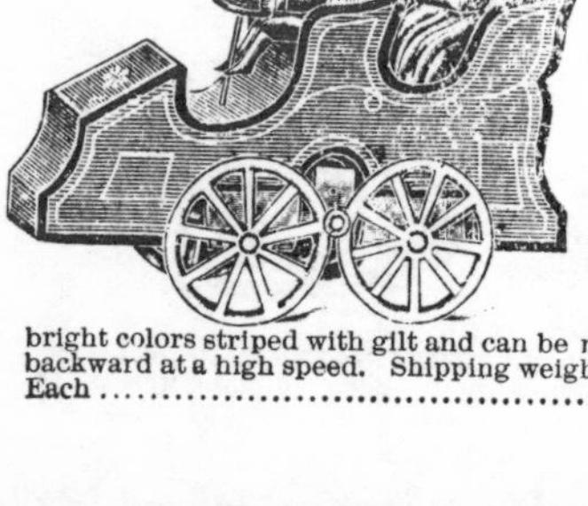

**H 9326** "Hill Climber Automobile," an entirely new model patterned after the latest and most fashionable styles of automobiles. Length, 10½ in.; width 4¼ in.; height, 8 in. Contains three neatly painted passengers; nicely finished in bright colors striped with gilt and can be run forward or backward at a high speed. Shipping weight, 5½ lbs.
Each.......................... **$1.00**

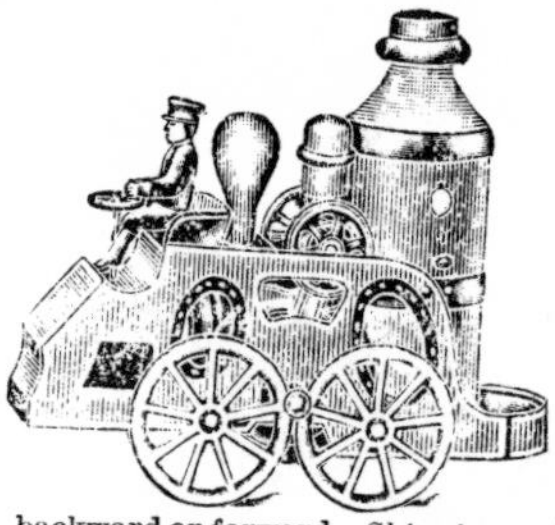

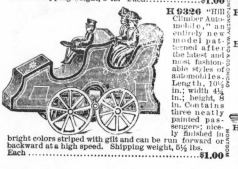

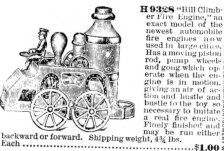

**H 9328** "Hill Climber Fire Engine," an exact model of the newest automobile fire engines now used in large cities. Has a moving piston rod, pump wheels and gong which operate when the engine is in motion, giving an air of action and hustle and bustle to the toy so necessary to imitate a real fire engine. Finely finished and may be run either backward or forward. Shipping weight, 4¾ lbs.
Each.......................... **$1.00**

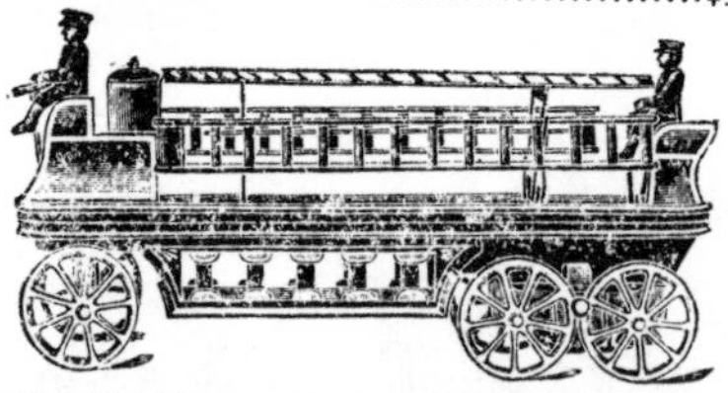

**H 9331** "Hill Climber Hook and Ladder Truck," a new model of the automobile hook and ladder truck such as is used in large cities. Equipped with an extension ladder which enables the child to run toy up to the supposed fire and by a clever arrangement extend the ladder up into it; equipped with an automatic gong which rings when the truck is run forward or backward. Length 19 in., width 4½ in., height 9 in. Shipping weight, 6½ lbs.
Each.......................... **$1.00**

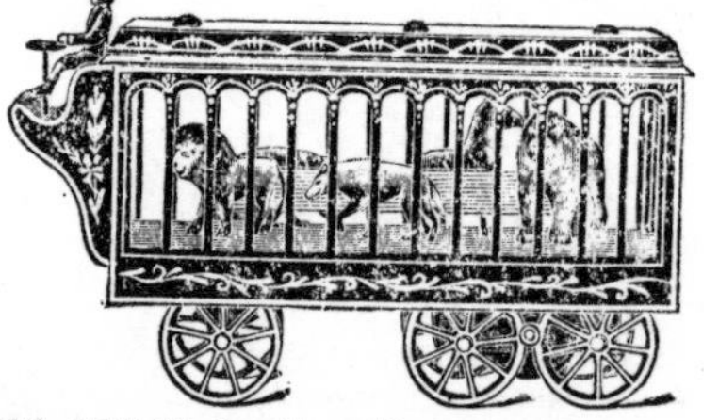

**H 9334** "Hill Climber Circus Menagerie Wagon" is a reproduction in miniature of the average gorgeous circus menagerie wagon, contains five animals, each of which moves cleverly around in the cage as it runs on the floor. It is well finished in bright colors and equipped with a full friction power movement which enables it to run forward or backward. Length 17¼ in., width 5 in., height 10¼ inches. Shipping weight, 8 lbs. Each.......... **$2.00**

**H 9337** Mechanical Auto-Truck, with clock work movement; 8 in. long, 5 in. wide; finished in bright color with gilt ornamentation; rubber tired wheels. Shipping weight, 26 oz. Each........ **67c.**

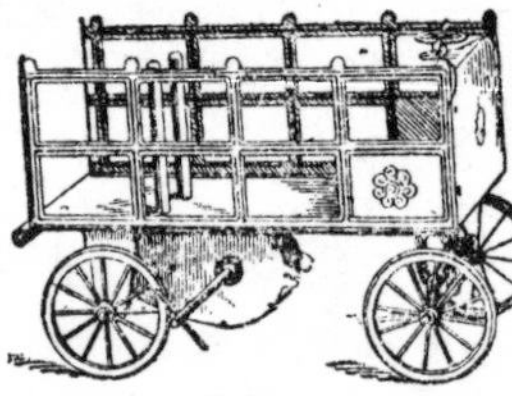

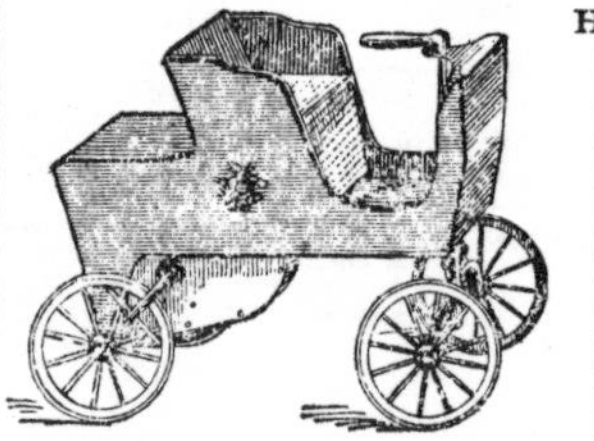

**H 9339** Mechanical Auto-Runabout, with clock-work movement; 8x5x5in. enameled in bright color with gilt ornamentation, plush seat-cushion and rubber-tired wheels, making it almost noiseless and an excellent toy for use in the house. Shipping weight, 26 oz.
Each.......... **68c.**

## Mechanical Railway Trains.

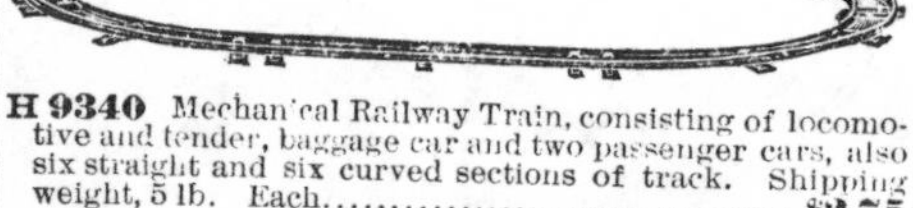

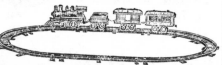

**H 9340** Mechanical Railway Train, consisting of locomotive and tender, baggage car and two passenger cars, also six straight and six curved sections of track. Shipping weight, 5 lb. Each.......................... **$2.75**

**H 9342** Mechanical Railway Train, consisting of iron locomotive with brake attachment, tender, one baggage car and two passenger cars, also three straight and nine curved sections of track, one curved section with brake lever, one straight section with brake lever, and one cross section. Shipping weight, 6 lb. Each.......... **$4.25**

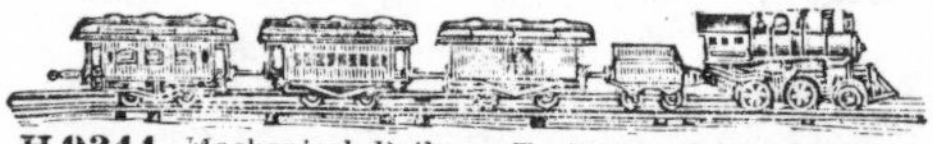

**H 9344** Mechanical Railway Train, consisting of large iron locomotive, with brake attachment, tender, one baggage car, two passenger cars, five straight and ten curved sections of track, and two brake sections. Shipping weight, 7 lb. Each.......................... **$7.25**

**H 9346** Mechanical Railway Train, consisting of larg iron locomotive, with brake attachment and speed reg lator, tender, one passenger car, one drawing-room ca six straight and nine curved sections of track, one each straight and curved brake sections and one pair right and left switch sections. Shipping weight, 8 lb.
Each.......................... **$9.5**

**H 9350** Curved track sections for use with mechanic trains, numbers 9640 to 9346. Each.......... **10**

**H 9353** Straight section of track for use with 9340 9346 trains. Each.......................... **10**

**H 9355** Brake sections of track for use with mechanic trains. Each.......................... **25**

**H 9357** Cross sections of track for use with mechanic trains. Each.......................... **45**

**H 9359** Right and left switch sections of track for us with mechanical trains. Per pair.......... **$1.7**

**H 9406 LAUGHING CAMERA.** See the passing show. Your friends grotesquely photographed; stout people look thin, thin people look stout. By getting a focus on passing pedestrians, horses, wagons, cars, etc., the most grotesque and ludicrous pictures are witnessed. The passer-by takes on the swing and stride of a daddy-long-legs, horses look like giraffes, and altogether there is more genuine and hearty fun crowded into the four cubic inches of this little instrument than theaters could show in centuries. Shipping weight, 3 oz.
Per doz.......... $1.50 Each.......... **13c**

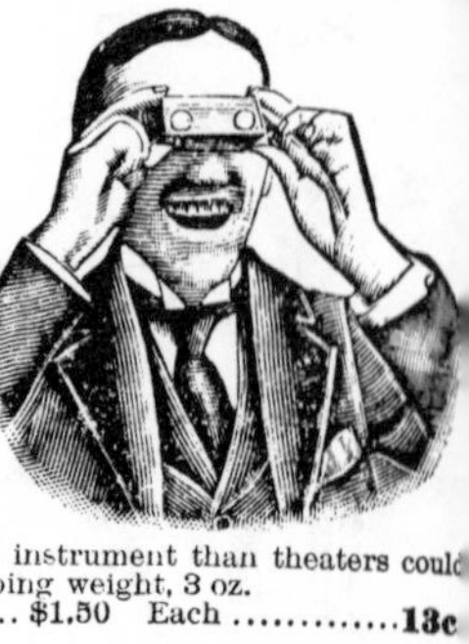

## Toy Magic Lanterns.

No other toy has been the source of more wonderment and delight to children than the magic lantern. The line quoted below are high grade toys, and one of them will be the means of providing many hours of entertainment to the little folks.

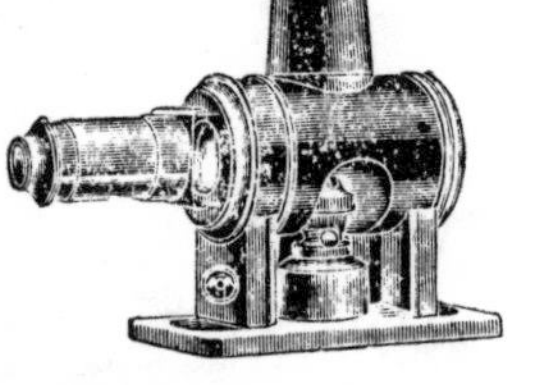

**H 9413** Toy Magic Lantern, barrel shape, painted bright and striped, contains 1 doz. 1⅜-in. slides, uses kerosene oil lamp, and is put up in wooden box, making a very complete magic lantern, and will give satisfactory results considering size of slide. Shipping weight, 4 lb.
Each.......... **85c.**

**H 9415** Toy Magic Lantern, neatly ornamented metal body, provided with good condensing and objective lenses and lamp, packed in neat box, with 1 doz. slides. Uses 1⅜-in. slides, and magnifies picture to 2½ or 3 ft. in diameter. Shipping weight, 4½ lb.
Each....... **$1.25**

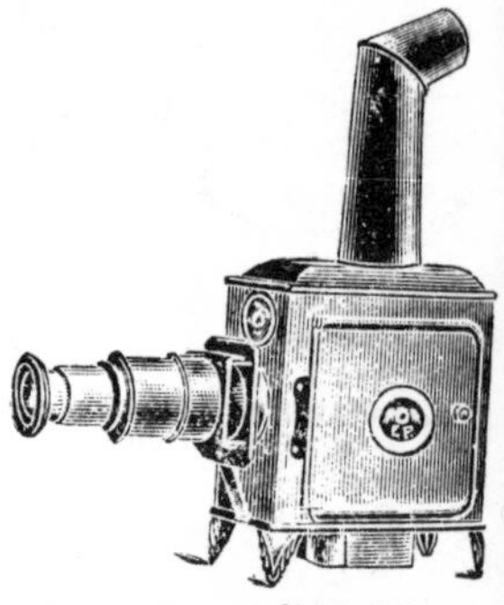

| | | Ship'g W't. | |
|---|---|---|---|
| H 9419 | Same description, for 1¾-in. slides... | 5 lb.... | $1.75 |
| H 9425 | Same description, for 2⅜-in. slides... | 6¼ lb.... | 2.75 |

## "Gloria" Magic Lanterns.

For parlor and amateur entertainments. These magic lanterns combine economy and superior brilliant effects over the ordinary juvenile magic lanterns, having a duplex lamp so constructed as to avoid the necessity of using glass chimneys; metal lacquered body, nickel-plated chimney and fronts, 1 crown glass condenser, 2 superior crown glass lenses in tubes, dark glass disc in door to avoid blinding vision when regulating flames; includes 12 long covered slides, having from 4 to 6 subjects on each slide. Complete, in neat carrying case.

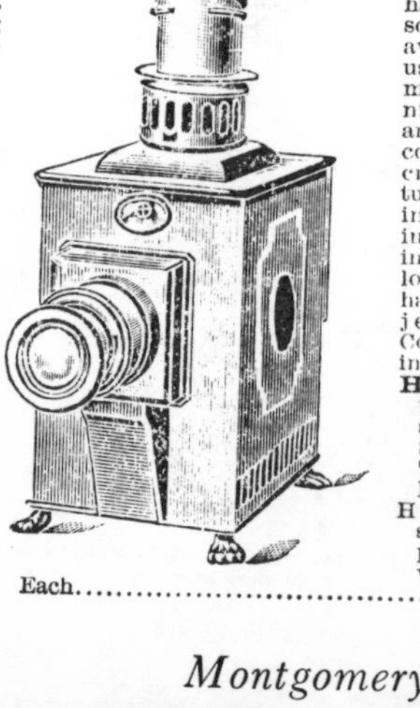

**H 9428** Gloria Lantern, with 2-in. slides, showing 2-ft. picture. Shipping weight, 7 lb.
Each.......... **$4.50**

H 9432 Same, 2¾-in. slide, showing 3¾-ft. picture. Shipping weight, 9 lb.
Each.......................... **$6.75**

## Toy Magic Lantern Slides.

NOTE.—We cannot fill orders for any SPECIAL SUBJECTS in toy lantern slides, except as indicated under numbers H 9455 to H 9469. These slides come to us from the manufacturers put up 1 doz. in a box, and in three to five assortments only.

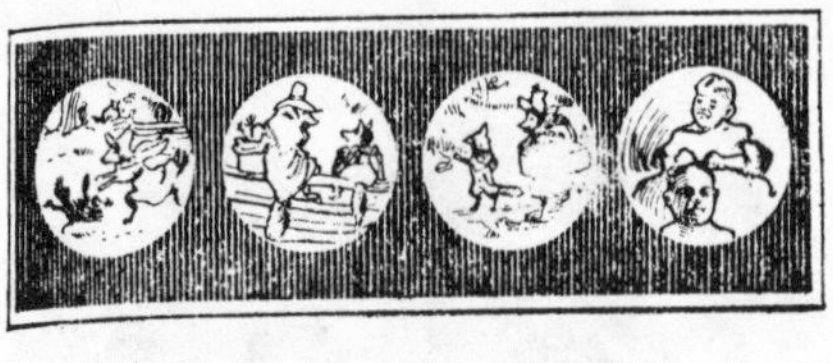

Plain Slides, highly colored, for amateurs.

**H 9441** Width, 1⅛ in.; weight, per doz., 7 oz. Per doz. **$0.25**
**H 9443** Width, 1⅜ in.; weight, per doz., 8 oz. Per doz. .35
**H 9445** Width, 1½ in.; weight, per doz., 16 oz. Per doz. .45
**H 9447** Width, 1¾ in.; weight, per doz., 17 oz. Per doz. .60
**H 9448** Width, 2 in.; weight, per doz., 1¼ lb. Per doz. .75
**H 9449** Width, 2⅜ in.; weight, per doz., 1½ lb. Per doz. .90
**H 9451** Width, 2¾ in.; weight, per doz., 2½ lb. Per doz. 1.25
**H 9455** Life in America Series, with program, 1¾ in. wide. Weight, per dozen, 17 oz. **70c.**
**H 9457** Same as H 9455, 2 in wide. Shipping weight, per dozen, 20 oz. **80c.**
**H 9459** Same as H 9455, 2¾ in. wide. Shipping weight, per dozen, 40 oz. **$1.15**
**H 9461** Round the World Series, with program, 1¾ in. wide. Shipping weight, per dozen, 17 oz. **70c.**
**H 9463** Same as H 9461, 2 in. wide. Shipping weight, per dozen, 20 oz. **80c**
**H 9464** Same as H 9461, 2¾ in. wide. Shipping weight, per dozen, 40 oz. **$1.15**
**H 9467** Soldiers of All Nations Series, with program, 1¾ in. wide. Shipping weight, per dozen, 17 oz. **70c.**
**H 9468** Same as H 9467, 2 in. wide. Shipping weight, per dozen, 20 oz. **80c.**
**H 9469** Same as H 9467, 2¾ in. wide. Shipping weight, per dozen, 40 oz. **$1.15**

## Polyopticon.

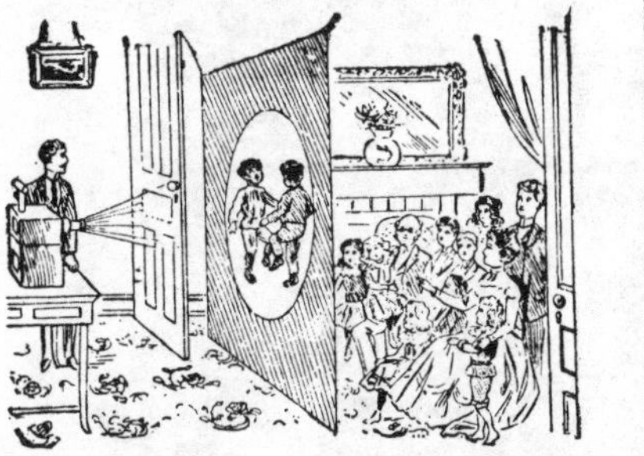

**H 9470** Polyopticon, an improved magic lantern for amateurs, which reproduces pictures without the use of slides, by the reflection process. You can find no end of nice and funny prints in the papers, chromo advertising cards, children's picture books, photographs of friends, kodak views, or any small pictures with sharp outlines; all of which will show up by the Polyopticon, enlarged many times, and in their original colors, too, and thus you get a variety of views at little or no cost. The clever or ingenious operator can make for himself moving pictures that roll the eyes, put out the tongue, or a dog that wags his tail. He can make plenty of fun out of tricks with his friends' portraits. Shipping weight, 5½ lb. Each **$5.00**

**H 9472** Polyopticon Picture Book. A set of pictures 2½ inches in diameter, lithographed in bright colors and combining popular subjects such as Robinson Crusoe, Old Mother Hubbard, Jack the Giant Killer, Red Riding Hood, Cinderella, Jack and the Bean Stalk, John Gilpin, Blue Beard, etc. Shipping weight, 10 ounces. Each **$0.50**

**H 9474** Polyopticon Picture Book No. 3. Comic subjects lithographed in bright colors. Shipping weight, 10 ounces. Each **$0.50**

## Miniature Cameras.

Not toys, but real Cameras, with which pictures can be made.

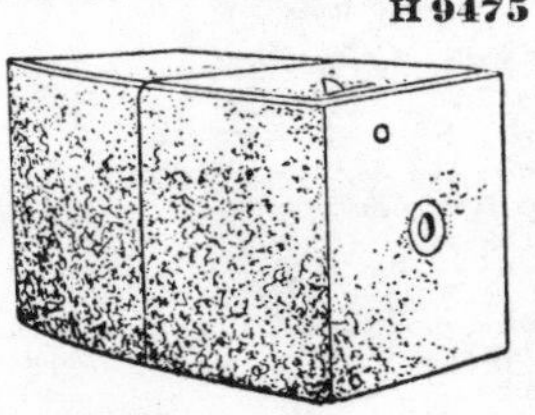

**H 9475** The Lakeside Camera Equipment uses glass plates only. While not as good work can be done with these as with larger, better and higher priced instruments, yet they make surprisingly good pictures and are a boon to those who do not care to invest much money in a camera, as well as to the amateur just beginning his photographic education. The Lakeside is a neat little instrument, covered with black cloth and measuring about 2¼x2¼x3½ inches. Fitted with an achromatic lens and practical shutter. Makes a picture 2x2 inches. The equipment includes, in addition to the camera, a package of dry plates and a complete miniature developing and printing outfit, trays, chemicals, full instructions, etc. A marvel of cheapness. Equipment complete **$0.35**
Postage .10
**H 9476** Extra Dry Plates, per doz. **.12**
Postage, 8 cents extra.

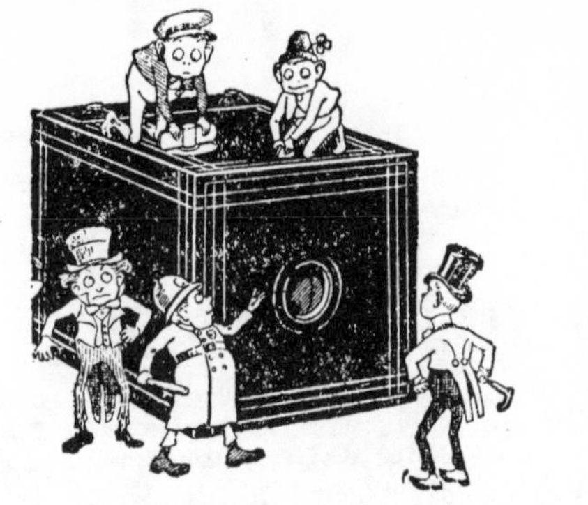

**H 9478** No. 1 Brownie Camera. A Genuine Eastman Camera that uses Film Cartridges, can be loaded and unloaded in daylight, and that does the best of work. The Brownie Cameras make pictures 2¼x2¼ inches, load in daylight for six exposures, have fine meniscus lenses, and the Eastman Rotary shutter. These instruments measure 3x3⅛x4⅞ inches and weigh 8 ounces. The Brownies are strongly made, are covered with imitation leather and have nickeled fittings. Forty-four page instruction book free with every instrument.

| | Price. |
|---|---|
| No. 1 Brownie Camera, for 2¼x2¼ pictures | **$1.00** |
| H 9483 Transparent Film Cartridge, 6 exposures, 2¼x2¼ | .15 |
| H 9485 No. 1 Brownie Carrying Case, holds camera and finder | .50 |
| H 9487 No. 1 Brownie Developing and Printing Outfit, including Dekko Paper for 24 prints | .75 |

If interested in larger and more complete Photographic Apparatus, send for a copy of our Special Photographic Catalogue K, free on request.

## Toy Stereoscopes.

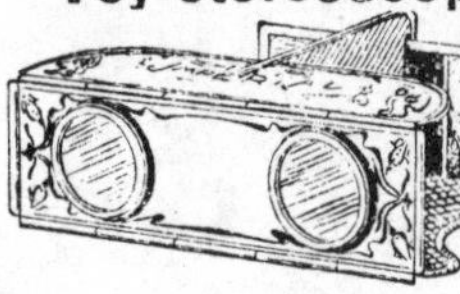

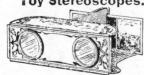

**H 9491** Imperial Portable Folding Stereoscope, pocket size; with 25 assorted views, size 2⅞x1⅛ inches; excellent amusement and entertainment for children can be had by using this scope. Shipping weight, 5 ounces. Each **$0.35**
**H 9493** Extra Views for H 9491. An assortment of 25 landscapes of various countries. Per set **$0.20**
**H 9495** Extra Views for H 9491. Assortment of 25 art pictures, Per set **$0.20**

## Horseshoe Magnets.

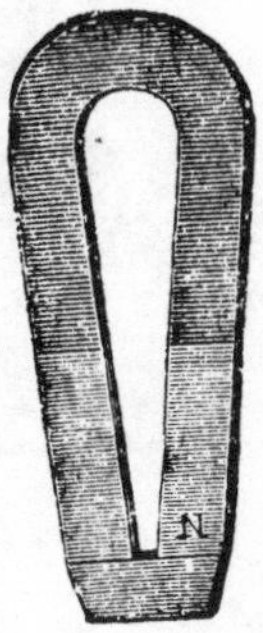

Horseshoe Magnets, superior quality. Suitable for scientific work, as well as for ordinary purposes.

| | Length. | Per doz. | Each. |
|---|---|---|---|
| **H 9501** | 2½ in. | $ 0.95 | **$0.10** |
| Postage, each, 2 cents. | | | |
| H 9503 | 3 in. | 1.50 | .15 |
| Postage, each, 3 cents. | | | |
| H9505 | 4 in. | 2.50 | .25 |
| Weight, each, 5 oz. | | | |
| H9507 | 6 in. | 5.00 | .50 |
| Weight, each, ¾ lb. | | | |
| H9509 | 8 in. | 10.00 | 1.00 |
| Weight, each, 1¼ lb. | | | |
| H 9511 | 10 in. | 18.00 | 1.75 |
| Weight, each, 3¼ lb. | | | |
| H 9513 | 12 in. | 25.00 | 2.50 |
| Weight, each, 4½ lb. | | | |

## Magnetic Toys.

**H 9517** Magnetic Floating Toys; set of 7 pieces, decorated in bright colors; also a metal pan for use with the toys. Place the toys in the water, attract them with a magnet and they will swim about in a natural manner. Shipping weight, 9 oz. Each **20c.**

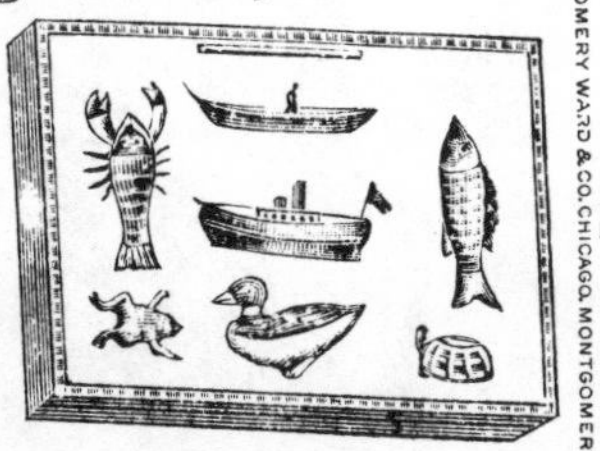

## Rattles.

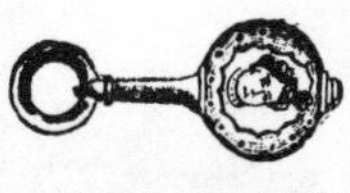

**H 9525** Musical Rubber Rattle, with teething ring. Each **$0.10**
Per doz 1.00
Shipping weight, 8 oz.

**H 9531** "Pyralin" Rattle (same composition as celluloid), having long twist colored handle with ring end. Full length 7¼ in. Shipping Weight, 6 oz. Each **10c.**

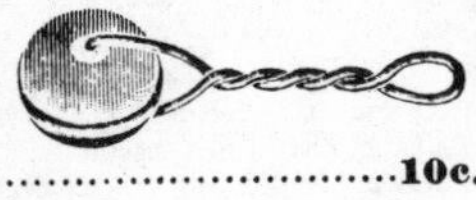

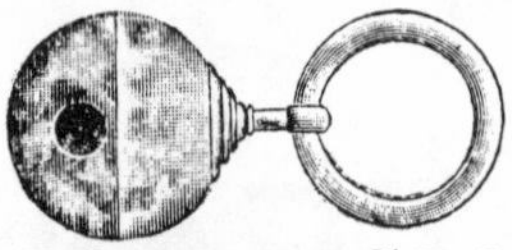

**H 9533** Combination Rattle and Teething Ring, made of "Pyralin" (same composition as celluloid), in four colors. Length 4¼ in. Shipping weight, 4 oz.
Per doz $1.95 Each **19c.**

## Rubber Balls.

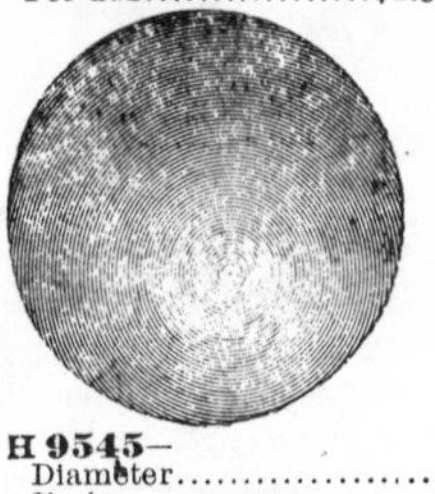

**H 9543**—*Solid Balls.*
Diameter in inches 2
Each **$0.10**
Per doz 1.10
Weight 4 oz.

## Light Inflated Balls.

The Children's Favorite.

| **H 9545**— | | | |
|---|---|---|---|
| Diameter | 2¾ in. | 3 in. | 4 in. |
| Each | **$0.10** | **$0.12** | **$0.21** |
| Per doz | 1.08 | 1.35 | 2.40 |

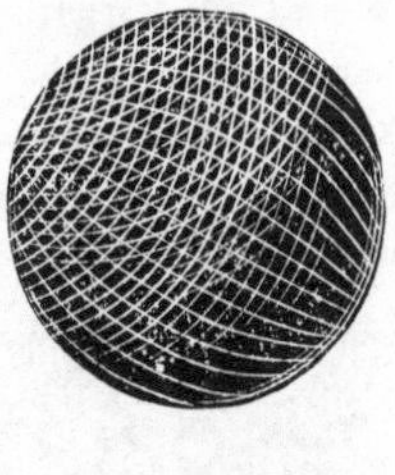

**H 9549** Net Covered Sponge Ball, large size covered with silk finish colored netting. Great bouncer, very light in weight and will not injure mirrors, etc. Shipping weight, 5 oz. Each **15c.**

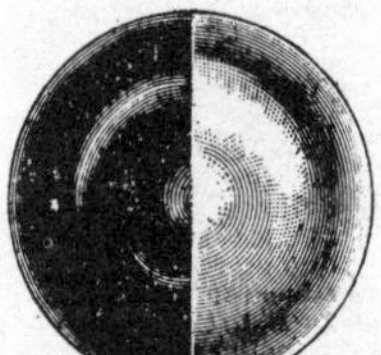

**H 9551** Finely Colored Celluloid Ball, 2½ in. in diameter. A lively bouncer; very light in weight. Shipping weight, 3 oz. Each **10c.**

## Marbles.

**H 9561** Carnelian (blood) genuine agates, medium size, each **10c.**
**H 9565** Large size, each **15c.**

## A Bag of Marbles.

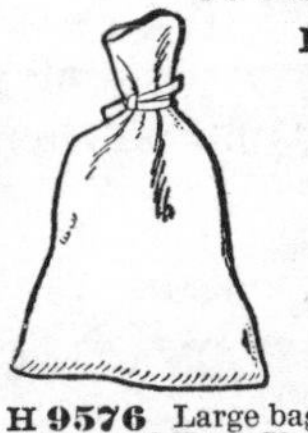

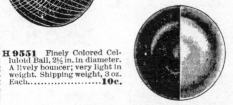

**H 9574** This bag of assorted marbles is what the average boy wants and must have; we aim to supply him in a satisfactory manner as possible: 10, No. 1 Chinas, 10 No. 2 Imitation Agates, 10 No. 1 Glazed Jaspers, 10 No. 2 Brandies, 5 No. 1 Opals, 5 No. 2 Glass Tipple and Threaded, making 50 assorted marbles of the right sizes for popular use, all in a bag that the boy can use and appreciate. Shipping weight, 19 oz. Per bag **10c.**

**H 9576** Large bag of assorted imported marbles containing: 10 No. 0 Glazed Chinas, 10 No. 1 Glazed Chinas, 10 No. 1 Imitation Agates, 10 No. 1 Glazed Bull-Eyes, 5 No. 2 Glazed Bull-Eyes, 10 No. 1 Threaded Glass, 5 No. 2 Threaded Glass, 10 No. 1 and 5 No. 2 Brandies, 10 No. 1 Opals, 10 No. 2 and 3 No. 6 Imitation Agates, 2 No. 8 Threaded Glass Bowlers. Shipping weight, 2½ lb. Per bag **25c.**

**H 9583** CANARY WHISTLE. Made of metal. All of the notes can be sounded. A good whistle, plenty of fun for boys and girls.
Each **$0.04**
Per doz .45
Postage .02

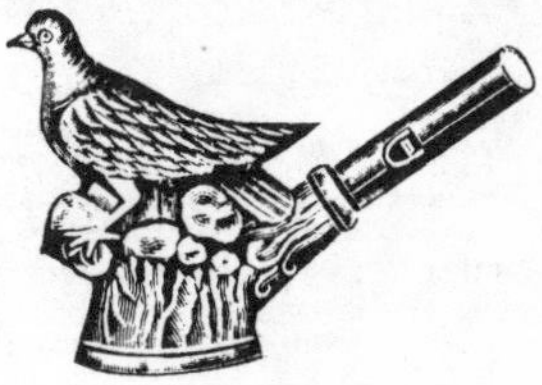

## "Practical" Wash Set.

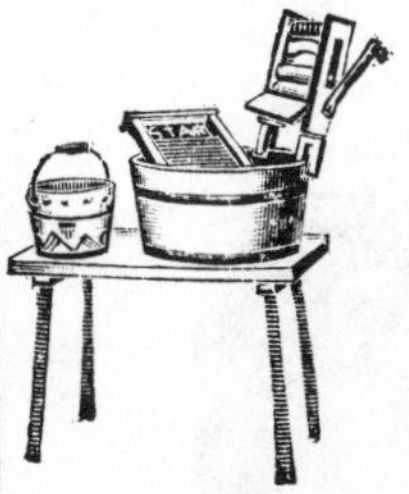

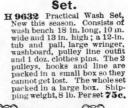

**H 9632** Practical Wash Set, New this season. Consists of wash bench 18 in. long, 10 in. wide and 13 in. high; a 12-in. tub and pail, large wringer, washboard, pulley line outfit and 1 doz. clothes pins. The 2 pulleys, hooks and line are packed in a small box so they cannot get lost. The whole set packed in a large box. Shipping weight, 8 lb. Per set **75c.**

## Toy Clothes Wringer.

**H 9636** "Gem" Toy Clothes Wringer, for the little "housekeeper." An exact reproduction of a first-class wringer in miniature. Has rubber rollers ¾ x4 in. Shipping weight, 2 lb. Each **45c.**

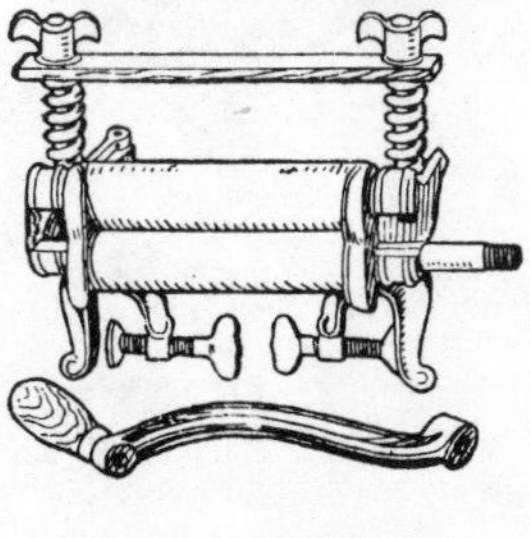

MONTGOMERY WARD & CO. CHICAGO.

129

*Montgomery Ward & Co.*

# THE "BIG GIANT" STEAM ENGINE.

## Ordinary Kerosene Used as Fuel.

THE YOUNG ENGINEER. Every boy ought to own one of these superb Engines. It will not only afford hours of pleasure, but in many cases will develop a taste for mechanical work and engineering. The Engine is designed for running toy machinery at a high rate of speed. These toys, such as machine shops, mills, forges, etc., can easily be made by the boys. They will thus enjoy both the making and the running of their "plant." Power can be transmitted to the machine shop or mill through an attached pulley wheel, with a cord for a belt.

## DESCRIPTION.

The illustration does not show the full size of the Engine. It stands eleven inches high, and the boiler, which is formed from heavy brass, is absolutely safe. It is an improvement over all former styles in that ordinary kerosene can be used as fuel instead of alcohol. It can be run full speed continuously for ten hours at a cost of less than one cent. It has a safety valve, steam whistle, and a finely fitted water gage which will always indicate the exact amount of water in the boiler. It has a large balance wheel and other necessary parts to make it the most powerful Steam Engine for toy machinery now on the market. It is finely finished, free from danger of explosion, and one of the most popular articles for boys offered in this List.

### RUNS TOY MACHINERY.

Boys, just think of the fun you can have running this Engine and making toy machinery for it! There will be no dull times, even on stormy days, if you have a "Big Giant" in the house. When steam is up the "Big Giant" will develop "horse power" sufficient to run any of the Motion Toys described on this page, as well as the toy machinery you can make. The Engine will also supply steam for a shrill blast of the whistle whenever the engineer so desires. Besides the fun you can have in this way, you will learn many things about steam power and machinery which may help you when you grow up.

---

### Weeden's Horizontal Steam Engine.

Given to any Companion subscriber for one new subscription and 40 cents extra. Price $1.50. Sent by express, charges in either case paid by receiver. Shipping weight 3 lbs.

Weeden's Horizontal Engine has a solid brass boiler and Russia iron casing, steam dome, safety valve, steam whistle, cylinder, steam chest, slide valve, eccentric, eccentric rod, piston, cross head, pitman, double-grooved pulley and fly wheel 2¼ inches in diameter. Height to top of stack 6½ inches, length of boiler 4¾ inches. This Engine is capable of operating the Motion Toys, and the models made from Kilbourn's Construction Strips. Alcohol only is used for fuel.

### Eight Motion Toys for the "Big Giant."

The Eight Motion Toys given, post-paid, to any Companion subscriber for one new subscription and 15 cents extra. See Conditions, page 546. Price $1.00, post-paid. The Toys sold separately at 20 cents each, post-paid.

The demand for our Motion Toys the past season was very large. The set consists of 1 Three-Pulley Shafting, 1 Pumping Station, 1 Buzz Saw, 1 Mill Tower, 1 Windmill, 1 Scissors Grinder, 1 Drop Forge, 1 Trip Hammer. Each made of metal, enameled in colors, and fitted with a pulley wheel by which power may be conveyed from the "Big Giant" Engine or Electric Motor. The Toys measure about 3 x 4 inches. We call special attention to the Three-Pulley Shafting offered this season for the second time. It is equally useful for connecting mechanical toys with electric power.

### Village Blacksmith Shop.

Given, post-paid, to any Companion subscriber for one new subscription and 15 cents extra. Price $1.00, post-paid.

This interesting toy is made of metal, and represents a small Village Blacksmith Shop, with the blacksmith and his assistant at work among the appurtenances of their trade. Upon connecting the pulley wheel with a small steam engine or electric motor, the blacksmith at the anvil will hammer away with all the strength of his brawny arm, while his assistant industriously works the bellows and heats an iron bar in the forge. The Blacksmith Shop measures 7½ x 4½ inches at the base and stands 6 inches high.

## Rhumkoff Induction Coil.

Given to any Companion subscriber for three new subscriptions; or for one new subscription and 90 cents extra. Price $2.25. Sent by express, charges paid by receiver.

This is designed for the study of electrical discharges through rarefied gas contained in a Geissler Tube. The effect of this experiment is very beautiful. With each Coil we include a dry battery and one Geissler Tube. Extra Tubes may be purchased for 35 cents each, postpaid.

**POCKET VOLT-AMMETER.** Given, post-paid, for one new subscription and $1.10 extra. Price $2.75, post-paid.

This combination meter will give an instantaneous reading of a battery up to 15 volts and 30 amperes. Will work perfectly, is not liable to get out of order, and can be highly recommended. Nickel-plated and easily carried in the pocket.

## Electric Railway.

Given, post-paid, to any Companion subscriber for one new subscription and 40 cents extra. Price $1.25, post-paid.

This Electric Railway is a natural result of the rapid development of electric science during recent years. Our Offer

includes an insulated Three-Track Service, nearly 14 inches in diameter, also a Motor Engine and one Passenger Car. Each made of metal and japanned in colors. Two batteries will develop sufficient power for running the train. These are not included in our Offer, but can be purchased at any electrical store near your home to save express charges.

## The Boy's Own Electric Plant.

Given to any Companion subscriber for one new subscription and $1.00 extra. Price $2.50. Sent by express, charges in either case paid by receiver, or by mail for 35 cents extra.

This is a complete set of apparatus for performing all kinds of experiments with electric motors. With this Outfit you can have lots of fun and at the same time learn a great deal about that wonderful and mysterious power—electricity. We describe briefly its contents:

**St. J. Motor.** This is well called "a Motor that can do things." It has four binding posts,—making it possible to energize the field or armature separately,—and can be used in circuits with reversers and rheostats. The speed can be varied and the direction of rotation changed at will. It will run toys and do all sorts of tricks and experiments.

**Two Rheostats.** The Outfit contains two Rheostats, a five speed and an eleven speed. These are used to regulate the speed of the Motor or the brilliancy of the Electric Lamp.

**Double Key Reverser.** A key, push-button, two-point switch, and a reverser combined. Very handy for experimenting with Motors, because it can be used in many different ways.

**Handy Current Detector.** A Current Detector; also shows the direction in which the current is flowing.

**Two-Point Switch.** Can be used to advantage in motor-experimenting. This Switch will turn the current from one purpose to another at the will of the operator.

**Strap Key.** Used to make and break electric current circuits where an intermittent current is desired.

**Miniature Electric Lamp and Socket.** A perfect little Electric Lamp and Socket with connections for wiring into the Motor circuit. An attractive feature of the Outfit.

In addition to the above the Outfit also contains Wires for connections, one Magnetic Needle, assorted Experimental Packages, and one copy of "The Study of Electric Motors by Experiment," an illustrated book of 106 pages containing sixty experiments.

## Electric Motor.

Given to any Companion subscriber for one new subscription and 10 cents extra. Price $1.00. Sent by express, charges in either case paid by receiver. Shipping weight 2 lbs.

This Motor may be belted to any light toy machinery. Speed from 300 to 2000 revolutions per minute. The armature and fields are both

laminated; the commutator is brass, properly insulated; the brushes are self-adjusting. All parts of the Motor, which are made from electrified steel and brass heavily nickeled, are interchangeable. It also has a steel shaft with a set screw and a grooved pulley. Size of base 6 x 4 inches, height 4½ inches, diameter of balance wheel 2½ inches. The Motor is wound for battery current only, and will run satisfactorily on a single cell dry battery.

## Reversing Motor.

Given, post-paid, to any Companion subscriber for one new subscription and 55 cents extra. Price $1.50, post-paid.

This attractive Motor, 5 inches high, and mounted on a metal base 7 x 4 inches, will give sufficient power to run any light toy machinery on a single cell dry battery. It is equipped with a four-pulley shafting and reversing lever, which enables the operator to run the toys at varying speeds in either direction. The Motor has an adjustable shafting and a two-field magnet.

## The Codegraph.

Given, post-paid, for one new subscription and $1.00 extra. Price $2.50, post-paid.

This new invention is designed for home instruction in telegraphy. The set consists of 2 miniature Dry Batteries, 1 each Key and Sounder mounted on a base, 1 Codegraph Plate, 1 Pen with attached insulated Cord, and 1 illustrated Booklet of Instructions. When the Pen is lightly drawn over any one of the raised character embossings on the plate, the Sounder responds, and shows exactly how that particular letter should sound. In this way a student can practise each letter until perfect, when a message can be sent over the wires.

## Electric Motor and Pump.

Given to any Companion subscriber for one new subscription and 50 cents extra. Price $1.50. Sent by express, charges in either case paid by receiver. Shipping weight 3 lbs.

The base of this toy, 6 x 8½ inches, is mounted with an Electric Motor and miniature Force Pump. It is supplied with a switch for throwing the current off or on. By connecting two batteries with the Motor and placing the suction hose in a dish of water, a tiny stream will be thrown out through the nozzle. Handsomely nickel-plated, with metal parts throughout. One of the most attractive toys offered on this page.

# GREAT WESTERN RAILROAD SYSTEM.

ONE of the most attractive toy combinations. Perfectly fascinating. The young people go into ecstasies over these toys, and the older ones can hardly keep their hands off. Here is a complete railroad system in miniature. Engine and tender, passenger cars, freight cars, straight and curved track in sections, sidings, switches, turn table, bumper, passenger station with

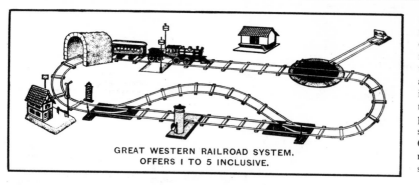

GREAT WESTERN RAILROAD SYSTEM.
OFFERS 1 TO 5 INCLUSIVE.

signal, crossing gates and announcement board, automatic crossing bell, freight station, tunnel, all really working just like the big railroads. Boys of to-day are certainly fortunate in having such interesting toys within reach. Offer No. 1 is the starting point in acquiring this railroad system. By adding the other Offers from time to time the railroad may be completed as shown in the smaller illustration.

### Offer No. 1. Mechanical Motor Train with Circular Track.

Given to any Companion subscriber for one new subscription and 10 cents extra. See Conditions, page 546. Price $1.00. Sent by express, charges in either case paid by receiver; or by mail for 40 cents extra. Shipping weight 3 lbs.

This consists of the Locomotive, Tender, Car, and a *Circular* Track. The Track is 62 inches in circumference. All the parts are of metal. The Train is painted in attractive colors. A concealed spring within the Locomotive supplies the force for driving the Train round the Track.

Mechanical Hand Car.

### Offer No. 2. Extra Track and Switch Outfits.

Given to any Companion subscriber for one new subscription. See Conditions, page 546. Price 85 cents. Sent by express, charges in either case paid by receiver; or by mail for 35 cents extra. Shipping weight 2 lbs.

Consists of Extra Track and Switches for enlarging the Circular Track to 140 inches in circumference. This is shown, complete, in the illustration. Each Outfit consists of 1 Pair Switches, 4 Straight Sections and 2 Curved Sections.

### Offer No. 3. Railroad Equipment.

Given to any Companion subscriber for one new subscription. See Conditions, page 546. Price 85 cents. Sent by express, charges in either case paid by receiver; or by mail for 30 cents extra. Shipping weight 2 lbs.

This Offer, an important feature of the System, comprises 1 Turn Table, 1 Bumper, and 1 Train Guide with 6 Destinations. Each piece is made of metal and painted in colors. By means of the Turn Table a freight or passenger car can be quickly transferred from the main line of the System.

### Offer No. 4. Railroad Equipment.

Given to any Companion subscriber for one new subscription. See Conditions, page 546. Price 85 cents. Sent by express, charges in either case paid by receiver; or by mail for 30 cents extra. Shipping weight 2 lbs.

This Equipment consists of 1 Passenger Station, 1 Freight Shed 6½ x 3½ inches, with sliding door, and 1 Railroad Crossing Signal. Each is made of metal and painted in colors. Small articles intended for future shipment may be stored in the Shed. This popular combination is a most important feature of the Great Western Railroad System.

Electric Semaphore.

### Offer No. 5. Railroad Equipment.

Given to any Companion subscriber for one new subscription. Price 90 cents. Sent by express, charges in either case paid by receiver; or by mail for 35 cents extra. Shipping weight 2 lbs.

This Equipment consists of a Tunnel, a Railroad Crossing with Gates, and an Automatic Crossing Signal. The Crossing Signal is operated by a lever located in the Track, which, when pressed by the wheels of the Engine, causes a bell to ring vigorously until the Train has passed that point. This Signal is shown in the miniature illustration.

### Offer No. 6. Freight Equipment.

Given to any Companion subscriber for one new subscription and 10 cents extra. Price $1.00. Sent by express, charges in either case paid by receiver; or by mail for 30 cents extra. When the Special Offer of the Great Western Railroad System is ordered we will include this Equipment for 85 cents extra.

This additional feature of the Great Western Railroad System will provide our subscribers with rolling stock for the transportation of freight. The Equipment consists of 1 Lumber Car, 1 Oil Tank, 1 Live Stock Car and 1 Caboose, a total length of 20 inches.

### Offer No. 7. Electric Semaphore Signal Tower.

Given to any Companion subscriber for one new subscription. Price 75 cents. Sent by express, charges in either case paid by receiver; or by mail for 20 cents extra. Dry Battery 30 cents extra, post-paid. When the Special Offer of the Great Western Railroad System is ordered we will include the Electric Semaphore Signal Tower with Dry Battery for 90 cents extra.

An Electric Semaphore Signal Tower will make a very attractive addition to the Great Western Railroad System. The Tower stands 13½ inches high, is supplied with a real electric lantern, and has adjustable red and green signals.

### Offer No. 8. Mechanical Hand-Car Equipment.

Given, post-paid, to any Companion subscriber for one new subscription. Price 75 cents, post-paid. When the Special Offer of the Great Western Railroad System is ordered we will include the Mechanical Hand-Car Equipment for 40 cents extra.

This is the latest addition to the Great Western Railroad System. It is made of metal and enameled in colors to represent the hand cars used by section men on the big railroads. The power is supplied by a spring coil motor which causes the two figures to send the Car round the Track at a rapid rate. The Car is 5 inches long, and with the figures is 5 inches high. It is designed for use only on the Track furnished in our Great Western Railway Outfits.

**SPECIAL OFFER.** All the articles named in the first five Offers of the Great Western Railroad System sold for only **$3.95.** Sent by express, charges to be paid by receiver. Shipping weight 10 lbs.

## The Three-Coin Register and Adding Bank.
### Every Man His Own Banker.

THIS is a most wonderful Bank; wonderful in the simplicity of its construction, and wonderful in the fact that it will receive a nickel, a dime, or a quarter, and automatically add it to the amount already deposited, showing the total amount in the Bank in plain figures at the front. Nothing is required of the depositor but to drop in the coin and pull down the lever. This Bank provides an interesting method of accumulating small savings, and fills a long-felt need.

**The Young Banker.** Every boy and girl, as well as the older members of the family, should have one of these Banks and keep a savings account of their own. One cannot begin too early to learn the value of money. This Registering Bank will show the young bankers how quickly the small amounts which they so often thoughtlessly spend will count up and make a large total if saved and deposited in this way. Habits of thrift and economy thus acquired will be of inestimable value in later business or household responsibilities.

**Description.** The Three-Coin Register and Adding Bank is stamped from sheet steel, handsomely finished and decorated, and guaranteed by the manufacturer to be mechanically perfect. It measures 4½ × 5½ inches, and stands 5 inches high. The coin chamber is entirely separate, so that the coins cannot get into the adding mechanism. The Bank receives nickels, dimes and quarters indiscriminately through the same slot, and adds and registers them as deposited. It remains locked until $10.00 have been deposited, and then opens automatically.

**OUR OFFER.** The Three-Coin Register and Adding Bank will be given, post-paid, to any Companion subscriber for one new subscription and 45 cents extra. See Conditions, page 546. Price $1.35, post-paid.

### Fun with Science.

Either of the following Outfits given, post-paid, to Companion subscribers for one new subscription, or both Outfits given, post-paid, for one new subscription and 25 cents extra. See Conditions, page 546. Price 65 cents each, post-paid.

Each Outfit contains Instructions, illustrated, also complete apparatus for performing many delightful experiments. Intelligent parents will appreciate this rare combination of fascinating amusement and science.

**Outfit No. 1. Electricity.** Here are a few of the experiments: An Electric Whirligig, The Baby Thunderstorm, A Race with Electricity, An Electric Frog Pond, The Magic Finger, Daddy Long-Legs, Jumping Sally, An Electric Kite, Very Shocking, Condensed Lightning, An Electric Fly-Trap, An Electric Ferry-Boat, A Joke on the Family Cat, Electricity Plays Leap-Frog, Lightning Goes Over a Bridge, Electricity Carries a Lantern, and 40 others.

**Outfit No. 2. Chemistry.** The Outfit affords the following captivating experiments: From White to Black, or the Phantom Ship, Yellow Tears, An Ocean of Smoke, A Tiny Whirlwind, A Smoke Cascade, A Gas Factory in a Test-Tube, Making Charcoal, Flame Goes Over a Bridge, A Smoke Toboggan Slide, Fountains of Flame, Making an Acid, A Chemical Fight, Through Walls of Flame, Steam from a Flame, The Flame that Committed Suicide, A Magic Milk Shake, The Wizard's Breath, and many other experiments.

### The Matador Building Blocks.

Given, post-paid, to any Companion subscriber for one new subscription and 25 cents extra. Price $1.15, post-paid.

This wonderful little box of building materials will develop mechanical tastes in the young, and afford them many hours of pleasure. With the set we give an illustrated Booklet, which shows how 138 models of different articles can be made with the pieces included in the outfit. There seems to be no limit to the number of these articles. One of the chief merits of the outfit consists in the opportunity for the exercise of a child's talent in original planning and construction.

### Harbutt's Plasticine Modeling Outfits.

**No. 1. THE BEGINNER'S BOX.** This contains Plasticine in five colors, together with a Modeling Board and Tool, a Sheet of Modeling Designs, with full Instructions. Given, post-paid, for one new subscription. Price 60 cents, post-paid.

**No. 2. THE COMPLETE MODELER.** This is like the Beginner's Box, but larger and with more fittings. Given for one new subscription and 35 cents extra. Price $1.25.

**No. 3. PLASTICINE BUILDER.** This is for the young architect and modeler. Contains Materials, Tools, Forms and Instructions for making bridges, houses, etc., in miniature. The real thing in the building line! Given for one new subscription and 70 cents extra. Price $2.00. Sent by express, charges in either case paid by receiver. Shipping weight 3 lbs.

Plasticine is a comparatively new modeling material, as pliable as moist clay but not as "mussy." It is clean and inexpensive, and can be used over and over again. Furthermore, it is absolutely antiseptic, and contains no animal matter to turn rancid and smell. All young people love to model. It is much easier than drawing, and is lots of fun besides. It develops the artistic sense and teaches accuracy of observation.

### The Flexible Flyer.

**No. 1.** Given for one new subscription and $1.00 extra. Price $2.50. 38 inches long. Weight 9 lbs.

**No. 2.** Given for one new subscription and $1.30 extra. Price $3.00. 40 inches long. Weight 11 lbs.

The Flexible Flyer is the famous "sled that steers." The turning of the steering bar as you would the handle of a bicycle curves the spring steel runners of the sled, enabling you to steer it easily and accurately. There is no retarding of the sled by dragging your feet in the snow. It saves its cost in shoe leather, and prevents wet feet and colds. We offer the two popular sizes and the latest improved models.

### Hessmobile Racer.

Given, post-paid, to any Companion subscriber for one new subscription and 15 cents extra. Price $1.00, post-paid.

This is a perfect imitation of a high-powered French racing motor car, with the driver and his assistant in position. The propelling power is supplied by a motor of the friction type, momentum being secured by turning the crank in front. This makes it an especially desirable and durable toy, as there is no spring motor to wear out. The car is 8 inches long, and is decorated with two small flags.

### Ideal Shooter and Targets.

The Complete Outfit given, post-paid, to any Companion subscriber for one new subscription. Price $1.00, post-paid.

While the Ideal Shooter is intended for indoor practise, it is equally suitable for lawn or piazza. The Outfit contains 1 Wall Target and Tray, 1 Pistol, 1 Rubber-Tipped Arrow, and 1 Swinging Target and Stand. When the Wall Target

is struck the arrows adhere by force of vacuum, showing the score made by each hit. The Swinging Target is separate from the rest of the Outfit. It consists of an Indian pony and rider mounted on an upright spring. A touch of the finger sets it in motion. When the Target is hit, the Indian and pony fall to the ground. The Ideal Shooter and Targets will furnish unlimited amusement for parties of young people and adults.

## Children's Play Suits.

THE Play Suits offered have been selected with special reference to their popularity as well as their durability. For a small boy no better holiday gift could be chosen.

**OUR OFFER.** Any One of the following Play Suits given, post-paid, to Companion subscribers for one new subscription and 30 cents extra. See Conditions, page 546. Price $1.10 each, post-paid.

### Cowboy Suit.

This Suit consists of 1 pair of Trousers, made of strong khaki cloth, with fringe down the outside seam; 1 Outing Shirt, of cotton and wool mixture, blue shade; also 1 khaki Hat. Sizes from 6 to 14 years of age. State size wanted.

## Boy's Rough Rider Suit.

A practical Play Suit. Strictly military cut. Ma of khaki, with straps of red in fast colors down sid of trousers. The coat has red facings on pockets a sleeves, red collar and epaulets. The brass butto are detachable. The fit of this Suit gives the b the soldierly appearance that he so much desire Sizes 6 to 14. State size wanted.

## Boy's Indian Suit.

This Suit consists of 1 Jacket, 1 pair Trousers ar 1 War Bonnet. The Jacket and Trousers are mac of strong khaki cloth, trimmed with yellow and re The War Bonnet has bright-colored feathers roun the crown, and is adjustable in size. Any size Su furnished, from 6 to 14 years of age inclusive. Whe you order be sure to state size wanted.

---

## Little Rosebud Doll.

Given, post-paid, to any Companion subscriber for one new subscription and 25 cents extra. See Conditions, page 546. Price $1.15, post-paid.

LITTLE ROSEBUD is just as sweet as her name. With her pink cheeks, bright, laughing eyes, pretty white teeth and curly locks, she will make a charming "daughter" for any little girl who wants to "mother" her. Little Rosebud is a travelled young lady, too. She has come all the way from Germany to America for you. She is 15 inches tall, has a jointed kid body, an unbreakable Minerva metal head, and lovely hair that you can really curl. When Little Rosebud goes to you she will take with her a Set of Paper Patterns and full Instructions for making a French Dress, Tam O'Shanter, Middy Suit with Military Cape and Cap. The illustration shows how she will look in a dress made according to one of these Patterns.

### Little Rosebud's Folding Bassinet.

Given to any Companion subscriber for one new subscription. Price 75 cents. Sent by express, charges in either case paid by receiver. Shipping weight 3 lbs.

This attractive accessory for the comfort of Little Rosebud is furnished with a mattress, pillow, canopy and drapery. These are made of silkolene, and match in material and design. The stand is of steel, brass-finished. It is 18 inches high, 18 inches long and 8 inches wide.

**CHILD'S 12-PIECE CHINA TEA SET.** Given for one new subscription. Price 75 cents. Sent by express, charges in either case paid by receiver. Shipping weight 5 lbs.

A Tea Set that will delight the heart of our younger girl readers. It consists of 4 Cups, 4 Saucers, 1 Covered Teapot, 1 Covered Sugar Bowl, 1 Cream Pitcher, and 1 Fancy Cake Plate. The pieces are all decorated to match in a pine cone pattern and edged with gold. They are sufficiently large for actual use. The Cups are 2 inches high, the Teapot 4½ inches high, the Fancy Plate 3½ inches in diameter, and the other pieces in proportion. The young hostess will take great pride in using this Set when entertaining her playmates in the house or outdoors on piazza or lawn.

## Kilbourn's Construction Outfit.

Given for one new subscriptio and 20 cents extra. Price $1.00 Sent by express, charges in eithe case paid by the receiver. Shippin weight 4 lbs.

This Outfit consists of a supply o link strips, wheels, posts, paddles dowels, pegs, split rings, bolts, etc. for making the following toys Windmill Tower, as shown in th cut, Machine Shop, Automobile Shoot the Chute, Car and Statio Performing Skeleton, Pantograph Grist Mill, Stage, Bridge, San Mill, Merry-go-Round. The num ber of other articles which can als be constructed is limited only b the skill of the young engineer Directions accompany each box.

## Chautauqua Wall Desk and Blackboard.

Given to Companion subscribers for one new subscription and 50 cents extra. Price $1.50 Sent by express, charges in either case paid by receiver. Shipping weight 20 lbs.

A clever combination Desk and Blackboard. Hangs on the wall. Just the thing fo boys and girls who like to draw and write. The front has a blackboard surface for copying the lessons from the roll chart at the top. The blackboard front is hinged, and will le down to make a desk, exposing to view the racks for note paper, pens, pencils, chalk eraser, etc. Size of combination Desk and Blackboard when closed 22 x 30 inches.

## Little Rosebud's Dressing Set.

Given, post-paid, to any Companion subscriber for one new subscription and 30 cents extra. See Conditions, page 546. Price $1.15, post-paid.

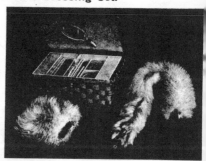

The Dressing Set consists of 1 Comb, 1 Powder Box, 1 Mirror, 1 Round Comb, 1 Tooth Brush, 1 fitted Sponge and 1 Fine Comb. These are enclosed in a handsome Basket, as shown in illustration. A Muff and Boa of soft white fur complete the outfit.

**Special.** With each Dressing Set we will include a miniature Hot Water Bottle, that can be used for warming Little Rosebud's feet.

### The Five-in-One Doll.

Given, post-paid, to any Companion subscriber for one new subscription and 40 cents extra. See Conditions, page 546. Price $1.25, post-paid.

This is one of the newest and cleverest ideas in dolls. It has five interchangeable heads: 1 Boy's Head, with "sandpapered" hair, 1 Girl's Head, with real hair, 1 Pussy Cat's Head, 1 Girl's Head, enameled hair, 1 Boy's Head, enameled hair. Each of the heads will fit into a socket in the neck of the Doll, and the change from one head to another can be made in an instant. The Doll is of the unbreakable type. It is 9½ inches tall, is made of celluloid, and has jointed arms and legs. The children will never tire of this plaything because of the number of different characters it represents. By changing the head, a different playmate is provided for almost every day in the week.

### The "Candy Kid."

Given, post-paid, for one new subscription and 40 cents extra. See Conditions, page 546. Price $1.25, post-paid.

This boy doll, modeled from life, is one of a new family of American-made character dolls which are taking the country by storm. The "Candy Kid" is 12 inches tall, has a practically unbreakable head, and is dressed in striped rompers, with red cuffs, yoke and belt. His feet are encased in cute little socks and sandals. He has jointed and movable arms and legs, a merry smile that positively "won't come off," and a name that is hard to beat.

# POPULAR GAMES OF ALL KINDS

## Popular Parchesi Game, 65c.

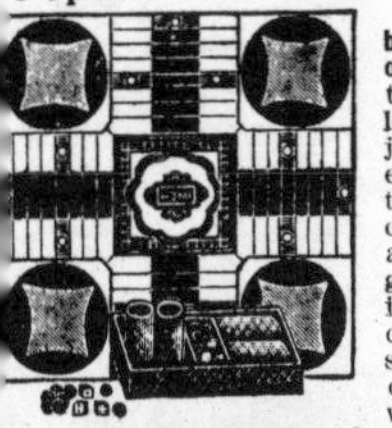

**It is the popular backgammon game of India,** as illustrated. Nevertheless, experience, judgment and skill enable the player to make every move count to the best advantage. The game consists of an imitation leather covered 18-inch square board, eight dice, four dice cups, various colored counters with directions for playing. Shipping weight, 28 ounces. Regular $1.00 value.
No. 49K100 Price.................. **65c**

## Fish Pond, 17 Cents.

**Fifteen colored cardboard fish,** two wooden fish poles with line and hook. Fine lithographed box, 9¾x19 inches. Very old game, yet most popular. High grade article. Shipping weight, 1½ lbs. 25-cent size.
No. 49K103 Price.................. **17c**

## Large Size Fish Pond, 10 Cents.

**Similar to above,** yet smaller pieces, but furnished complete with fish, poles, lines and hooks. Great amusement for children. Biggest value offered for 10 cents. Board, 9x18 inches. Shipping weight, 1 lb. 15-cent size.
No. 49K104 Price... **10c**

## Magnetic Fish Ponds, 39c and 19c.

**Colored cardboard aquarium and fish,** with hooks, lines and magnets. Angler cannot see the fish, but can feel the magnetic "bite." Each fish numbered to represent pounds. Packed in colored compartment picture box, 11½ inches square. Shipping weight, 25 ounces.
No. 49K189 Price.................. **39c**

**Same style as above, but smaller size.** Packed in colored compartment pretty picture box, 9⅞ inches square. Shipping weight, 16 oz.
No. 49K105 Price.................. **19c**

## Table Croquet, 98 Cents.

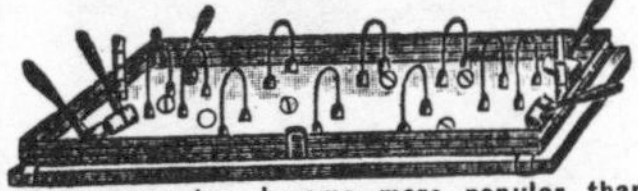

**This game has become more popular than ever** and we offer below exact duplicates of the larger sets, which are adapted to play on table or floor. Our best set consists of eight fancy turned and varnished 9½-inch mallets with eight balls 1½-inch size to match, with two fancy colored posts and complete set of arches and tape to prevent balls going off table. An exceptionally fine set. Size of box, 14¾x6x3¼ inches. Shipping wt., 3½ lbs.
No. 49K110 Price.................. **98c**

**A set similar to the above,** but containing eight unvarnished mallets and balls and wood tipped instead of heavy metal tipped arches. A very good set for the price. Packed in wood box, 13½x6¾ inches. Shipping wt., 2½ lbs.
No. 49K111 Price.................. **47c**

**Set similar to the above,** but consisting of four unvarnished mallets and balls, and wood tipped arches. A first class set at the price. Packed in wood box, 13x5¾x2¼ inches. Shipping weight, 2 pounds.
No. 49K121 Price.................. **21c**

## Floor Croquet, 95 Cents.

**An Exceptionally Fine Indoor Floor Croquet Set.** Consisting of four 25½-inch mallets and handles, four 2½-inch balls, two posts and complete set of arches. All nicely varnished. Good quality and practical. A fine set for indoor use. Packed in sliding cover box, 31¼x7x3½ inches. Shipping weight, 7 pounds.
No. 49K229 Price.................. **95c**

## Real Battle Game, 39 Cents.

**Consists of shooting a dummy soldier with a pistol and small wooden pins for ammunition.** Outfit consists of 8-inch patent trigger wooden pistol, thirteen 6-inch soldiers on foot, and one 7½-inch captain on horseback. Neat box, size 10x14½ inches. Shipping wt., 21 ounces.
No. 49K113 Price.................. **39c**

## Perfection Reversible Combination Game Board, $2.65.

100 GAMES CAN BE PLAYED ON THIS BOARD.

**The board is 28¼ inches square, reversible, with good net pockets.** Furnished complete with 109 pieces of equipment, including twenty-nine rings (four colors), two cues, fifteen number discs, ten pins, backstop, two dice boxes, four dice, thirty-eight pawns (four colors), direction book, two boxes for men, three removable legs and revolving stand. Only the very best basswood is used. No warping. Not like some boards, sold with two or three different colored woods on each face, making it more difficult to play and of bad appearance. All the squares, circles, diagrams, decorations, checker board and stencil work are in high polish, varnished and rubbed. Very artistic finish. Result of many years' experience. One hundred separate games can be played, including such popular games as Auto Race, Chuck-a-Luck, Chess, Checkers, Fortune Telling, Fox and Geese, Go-Bang, Nine Pins, Pool games, Backgammon, Shuffle Board, Crokinole. Twenty-five cue games can be played. Each board guaranteed perfect and complete. Separate parts can always be furnished at small nominal cost. Largely sold for progressive parties. After once seeing and trying it, you will thank us many times for urging you to buy this beautiful board. No other game board contains so many new and interesting games. Shipping weight, 14 pounds. Regular price, $3.50.

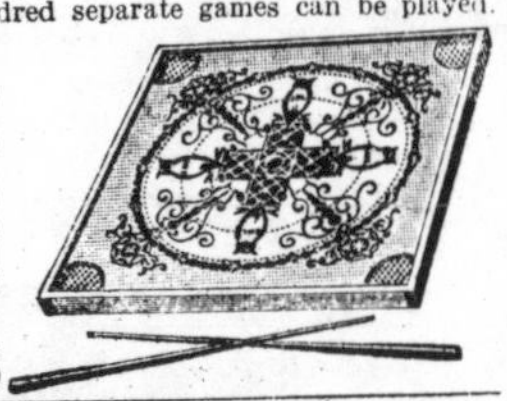

No. 49K3000¼ Price for board complete, 28¼ inches square, with the 109 pieces of equipment .................. **$2.65**

## Monarch Combination Game Board, $1.98.

**A very high class nicely finished game board, 28½ inches square.** Has revolving stand and all necessary equipment for playing seventy-five popular games. Without doubt the best board ever made that can be sold for a medium price. This board easily sells for $2.50, yet we sell it to you for only $1.98. A fine investment for the home and the source of many pleasant evenings. Thousands of satisfied purchasers of this board throughout the country. It is a board that we know will please you. Every board perfect and guaranteed not to split. Carefully crated for shipping. Shipping weight, 14 pounds.

No. 49K3001¼ Price, complete, including board, revolving stand, cases, rings, and full instructions.................. **$1.98**

## Donkey Party, 19c and 9c.

PUT THE TAIL ON THE DONKEY.

**Donkey Party consists of a sheet having a donkey without tail printed in bright colors upon it.** Tails are provided separately and numbered. The player is to be blindfolded and then hang the tail on the donkey at the first position touched. The player hanging nearest to the correct position wins. Amusement for old and young.

**Our Best Donkey Party.** Handsome painted donkey in bright colors on heavy muslin sheet, 36x30 inches, with twenty-three numbered tails. Twenty-five cents everywhere. Shipping weight, 8 ounces.
No. 49K135 Price.................. **19c**

**A Popular Size Donkey Party.** Sheet, 21x20 inches. Printed in three colors. Shipping weight, 6 ounces.
No. 49K185 Price.................. **9c**

## Jolly Tumblers, 89 Cents.

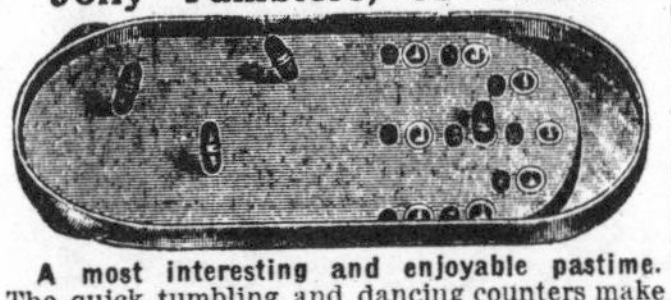

**A most interesting and enjoyable pastime.** The quick tumbling and dancing counters make it an exciting game for everyone. The board is 22x9 inches, soft felt covered, and four assorted colored celluloid weighted counters to tumble down the board and be caught in highest counting metal openings. Very enjoyable. Shipping weight, 3 pounds.
No. 49K106 Price.................. **89c**

## Clown Tenpins, 21 Cents.

**Six clown figures,** 6 in. high, painted in funny colors, and 2-in. net covered ball. A very amusing toy for indoor use. Shipping wt., 8 ounces.
No. 49K184 Price.................. **21c**

## "Lasso" or Jumping Ring Game.

**A new very showy game.** Inside game has comic face with various counting pegs. The object is to work the plunger to lasso pegs of the highest number with the small rings. Easy to learn and fascinating. 50 cents everywhere. Shipping weight, 25 oz.

No. 49K230 Price.................. **39c**

## Large Size Ouija or Egyptian Luck Board, 83 Cents.

**A most remarkable, interesting and mystifying game.** Its operations are always interesting and highly amusing, answering as it does questions concerning the past, present and future. One of the best selling games of today and exceedingly popular. Full directions for operating the Ouija Luck Board accompany each package. Size, 15x22 inches. Unmailable. Shipping weight, 10 pounds. Regular $1.00 size. Do not confuse this with the smaller size sold by others at 75 cents.
No. 49K112 Price.................. **83c**

## Progressive Parlor Baseball, 39c.

**The great national game for old and young.** Handsome lithographed color embossed pasteboard field. Furnished complete with wooden men, and large die with figures for "Home Run," "Out," Etc. Full directions. Very realistic. Shipping weight, 16 ounces.
No. 49K220 Price.................. **39c**

## Jolly Coon Race, 89 Cents.

**A new and very comical game for two or three people.** Metal figures of darkies with movable arms, racing along three poles. Their comical actions are very funny. All start at the same time and it is exceedingly amusing to see the race. Lithographed box, 22x8½ inches. Regular price, $1.00 to $1.25. Shipping weight, 16 ounces.
No. 49K159 Price.................. **89c**

## Ring My Nose, 19 Cents.

**Lithographed in lifelike colors.** Clown target with curved nose and eight assorted color rings, and assorted valuations on pegs on face. In neat box, 9x14 inches. Very popular and amusing game. Shipping weight, 6 oz.
No. 49K136 Price.................. **19c**

## Alabama Coon.

**One of the very best toys.** Object is to toss balls into mouth and they roll out of numbered holes at bottom, each hole counting differently. Six colored balls. Any number can play. In lithographed picture box, 14x9½x2 inches. Shipping weight, 19 ounces.
No. 49K192 Price.................. **39c**

**Same as above, but not so large,** and with but three balls. 11x7½x2 in. Shipping wt., 12 ounces.
No. 49K193 Price.................. **21c**

## Combination Game Board, 97c.

**The latest and most popular low priced combination game board ever offered.** Wood frame and extra heavy cardboard center. Strong and durable. Twenty-five games can be played, including such popular games as Checkers, Baseball, Ring a Peg, Carrom, Bang, Quoits, and many other new and interesting games. Size, 15½x15½ inches. Nicely lithographed in colors. Shpg. wt., 4 lbs.
No. 49K232 Price.................. **97c**

## Cloth Fishing Party, 19c.

**A lone fisherman with fish to be cut out.** Player must be blindfolded and try to pin the fish on the line. Good quality cloth sheet, 36x36 inches. Great fun and very popular. Shipping weight, 5 ounces.
No. 49K231 Price .......... **19c**

## Deck Ring Toss, 39 Cents.

**A very fascinating and popular game.** Can be used upon the lawn or in the house. Comprises four rings made of rope, handsome post with polished base and two colored ring holders. Size of box, 7½x12½ inches. Shipping weight, 2 pounds.
No. 49K130 Price.................. **39c**

## Blow Football, 39 Cents.

**A colored celluloid ball, very light in weight,** is driven by players blowing through good quality hollow reed pipes. Object is to blow the ball between the goal posts. From two to eight persons can play the game. Not a dull moment in this game. Shpg. wt., 16 oz.
No. 49K190 Price.................. **39c**

## Your Choice, 13 Cents.

**Large size boards, 10¼x19½ inches,** nicely lithographed. Comes in two subjects. Steeplechase or Fox and Hounds. **State which game is wanted.** Big values and easy games for children to play. Shipping wt., 1¼ pounds.
No. 49K107 Price, each.................. **13c**

## Battledore and Shuttlecock, 47c.

**An exceptionally well made set.** Consists of two 15-inch rackets, two finely feathered shuttles and two fancy celluloid balls with rattles. A great game for either in or out of doors. Very popular. Well made. Shipping weight, 16 ounces.
No. 49K228 Price.................. **47c**

## Soldier Tenpins, 10 Cents.

**Consists of five 4-inch soldier figure tenpins** nicely painted in colors and 2-inch net covered ball. A fine indoor game for the little ones. Good value. Shipping wt., 8 oz.
No. 49K183 Price.................. **10c**

# BEST AND MOST POPULAR MUSICAL TOYS

## Tin Violins and Bows.

**Our Best Toy Violin in Case.**

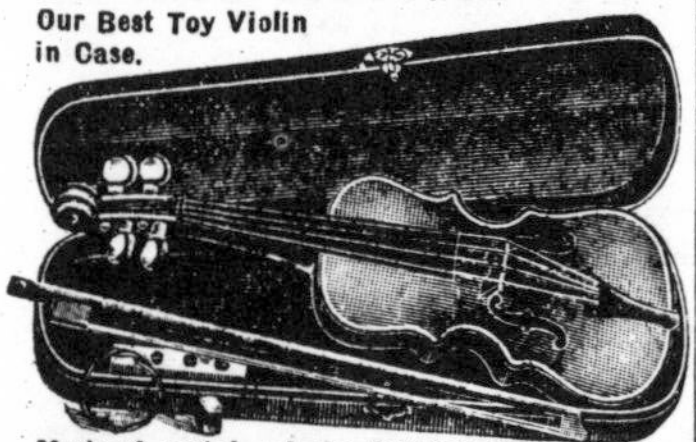

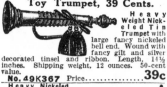

**Made of metal, nicely finished to resemble a real violin.** Four genuine violin strings, tightening pegs, extra strings, rosin and tuning instrument, enabling proper tuning. Size violin, 19x6 inches; bow, 17½ inches long; hinged cover painted case, 19½x6½ inches. One of the very best and most popular musical instruments. Shipping weight, 3½ pounds.
**No. 49K304** Price.............. **89c**

**Violin in Case. Same as above, but** slightly smaller size. Violin, 16½ inches long and furnished with bow, rosin and tuning fork. Shipping weight, 2½ pounds.
**No. 49K373** Price.............. **68c**

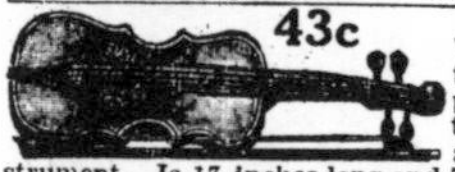

**43c** **A Very Nice Violin. Similar to above,** but packed in carton, extra strings and tuning instrument. Is 17 inches long and 5¼ inches wide. Four genuine bow strings and tightening pegs. Bow, 15¾ inches long. Shipping weight, 1½ pounds.
**No. 49K305** Price.............. **43c**

**A Good Value Violin. Similar to above, but** not so nicely finished. Packed in carton. Length, 12½ inches; width, 4 inches. Four violin strings and tightening rods. Shipping weight, 1 pound.
**No. 49K365** Price.............. **21c**

## Our Best Grade Toy Cornets.

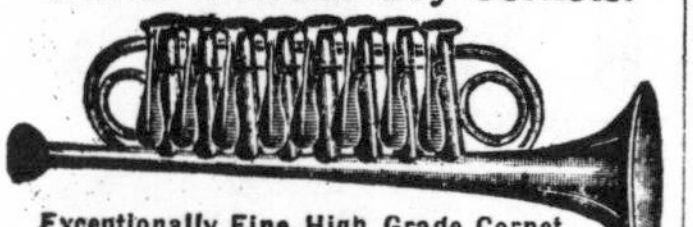

**Exceptionally Fine High Grade Cornet.** Best grade, full spun brass bells, heavy weight metal, well made and nicely finished. Notes are clear and well toned. A music sheet accompanies each cornet. Three sizes as follows:

**Eight-Key Cornet.** Easy movement, full octave. Length, 12½ inches. Shipping weight, 20 ounces.
**No. 49K379** Price.............. **$1.45**

**Six-Key Cornet. Same as above, but** slightly smaller size and having six keys. Length, 11½ inches. Shipping weight, 16 ounces.
**No. 49K380** Price.............. **$1.25**

**Four-Key Cornet. Same as above, but** slightly smaller size and having four keys. Length, 10 inches. Shipping wt., 12 oz.
**No. 49K381** Price.............. **98c**

## Our Best Grade Toy Slide Trombones.

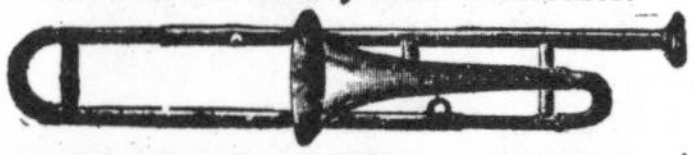

**An exceptionally well made horn with 3¾-inch bell of spun highly burnished brass.** Good quality tone. Full eight-note. Not to be compared with the cheap horns sold at this price. A child can easily learn to play, as music sheet accompanies each instrument. Full length, 25 inches. Shipping weight, 20 ounces.
**No. 49K376** Price.............. **$1.87**

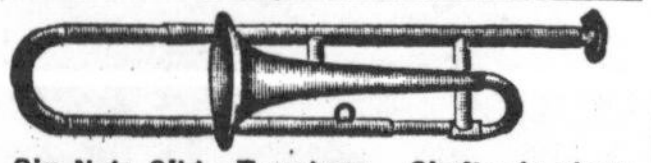

**Six-Note Slide Trombone. Similar to above,** but smaller in size, having six notes. Same handsome finish. Full length, 20½ inches. Shipping weight, 18 ounces.
**No. 49K377** Price.............. **$1.38**

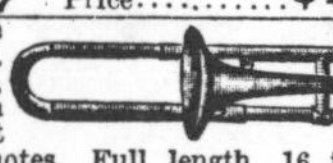

**Four-Note Slide Trombone. Similar to above,** same fine finish and quality, but has only four notes. Full length, 16 inches. Shipping weight, 16 ounces.
**No. 49K378** Price.............. **98c**

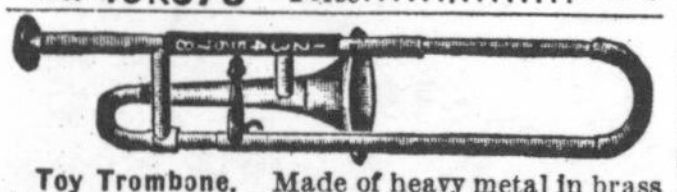

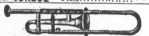

**Toy Trombone.** Made of heavy metal in brass finish. Has eight notes, easy to play. Numbered music sheet with each instrument. Entire length, 20 inches. Shipping weight, 15 ounces.
**No. 49K302** Price.............. **87c**

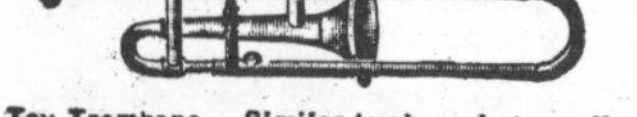

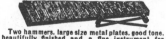

**Toy Trombone. Similar to above,** but smaller size. **Has six notes** with music sheet. Entire length, 20 inches. Shipping wt., 12 oz.
**No. 49K375** Price.............. **67c**

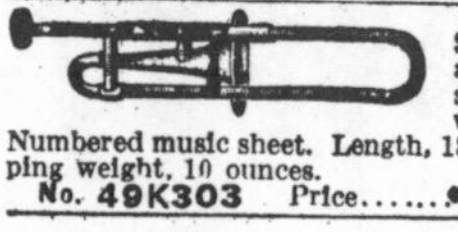

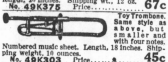

**Toy Trombone. Same style as above, but smaller and with four notes.** Numbered music sheet. Length, 18 inches. Shipping weight, 10 ounces.
**No. 49K303** Price.............. **45c**

## Toy Cornets, 45c, 67c and 89c.

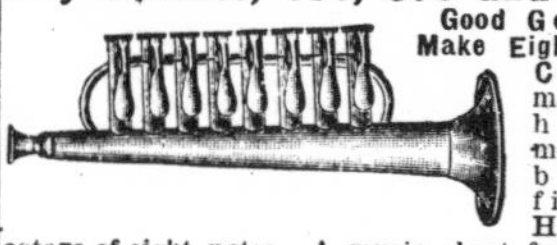

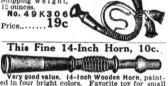

**Good German Make Eight-Note Cornet,** made of heavy metal in brass finish. Has full octave of eight notes. A music sheet furnished with each cornet. Length, 12½ inches. Shipping weight, 12 ounces.
**No. 49K300** Price.............. **89c**

**Six-Note Toy Cornet. Same style as above, but** with only six notes. Same high grade finish. Good tone. Music sheet with each cornet. Length, 11 inches. Shipping wt., 10 oz.
**No. 49K374** Price.............. **67c**

**Four-Note Toy Cornet. Same style, quality and finish as above,** but with only four notes. Music sheet with each instrument. Length, 12 inches. Shipping weight, 6 ounces.
**No. 49K301** Price.............. **45c**

## Our Best Grade Toy Accordion.

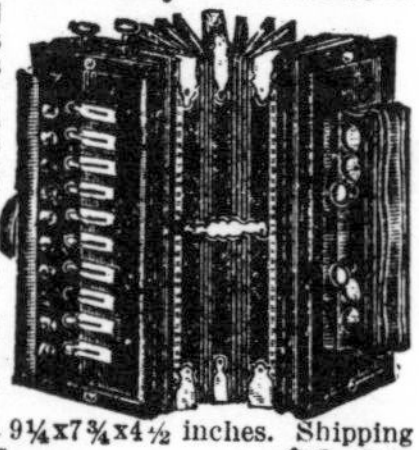

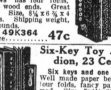

**An exceptional instrument at this price.** Frame is stained ebony color with fluted molding. Has double style six folds, with kid and metal corner protectors, two sets of reeds, ten keys with nickel buttons, two bass notes. All trimmings are full nickel plated. Great value. Size, 9¼x7¾x4½ inches. Shipping weight, 2¾ pounds.
**No. 49K371** Price.............. **$1.00**

## This Fine Toy Accordion, 69c.

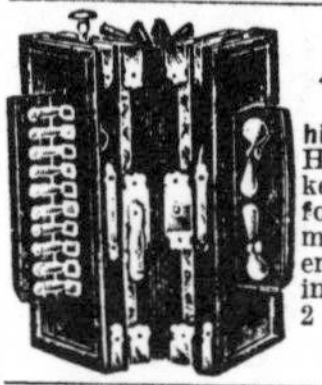

**A very handsome and high grade instrument.** Has ten notes, two bass keys. Bellows has four folds, nickel plated trimmings, ebony finish wood ends. Size, 8¾x6¼x6 inches. Shipping weight, 2 pounds.
**No. 49K370** Price.............. **69c**

## Eight-Key Toy Accordion, 47c

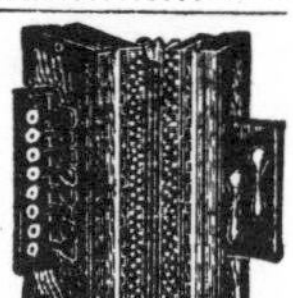

**Has eight bone tipped brass keys, two bass keys.** Bellows has four folds, fancy wood ends. Great value. Size, 8¼x6¾x4 inches. Shipping weight, 1½ pounds.
**No. 49K364** Price.............. **47c**

## Six-Key Toy Accordion, 23 Cents.

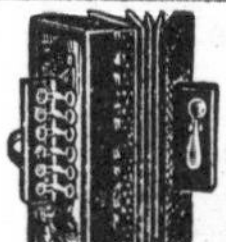

**Six keys and one bass key.** Well made paper bellows has four folds, fancy paper trimmed. Size, 7x4½x3¼ inches. Shipping weight, 16 ounces.
**No. 49K343** Price.............. **23c**

## Our Best Grade Toy Clarinet.

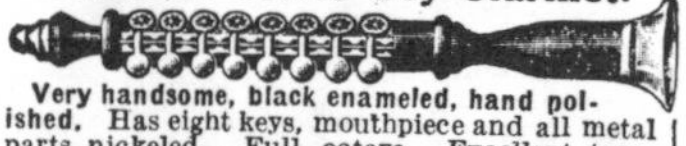

**Very handsome, black enameled, hand polished.** Has eight keys, mouthpiece and all metal parts nickeled. Full octave. Excellent tone. Exceptional value. Size, 14½ inches. Shipping weight, 10 ounces.
**No. 49K372** Price.............. **45c**

## Toy Clarinet, 21 Cents.

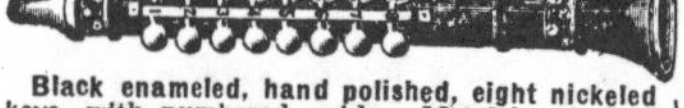

**Black enameled, hand polished, eight nickeled keys,** with numbered guide. Metal hands and music holder. Numbered music sheets with each clarinet. Easy to play. Real airs can be played on this instrument. Size, 13½ inches. Shipping weight, 8 ounces.
**No. 49K311** Price.............. **21c**

## Eight-Key Toy Clarinet, 10c.

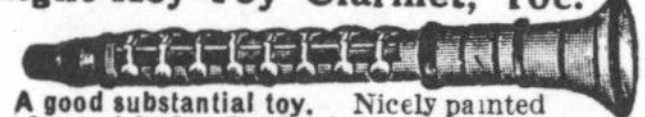

**A good substantial toy.** Nicely painted and varnished. Good value and tone. Length, 12 inches. Shipping weight, 6 ounces.
**No. 49K382** Price.............. **10c**

## Fourteen-Key Metalaphone, 19c.

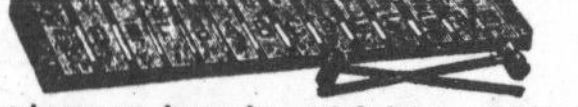

**Two hammers, large size metal plates, good tone, beautifully finished and a fine instrument for the price.** Packed in box. Keys have notes stamped on face, making it easy to learn to play. Size, instrument, 4x17⅛ inches. Shipping weight, 2 pounds.
**No. 49K309** Price.............. **19c**

## Our Twelve-Key Metalaphone.

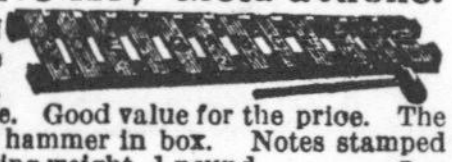

**A number of tunes can be played upon it.** Imported article. Good value for the price. The instrument and hammer in box. Notes stamped on keys. Shipping weight, 1 pound.
**No. 49K310** Price.............. **8c**

## Toy Trumpet, 39 Cents.

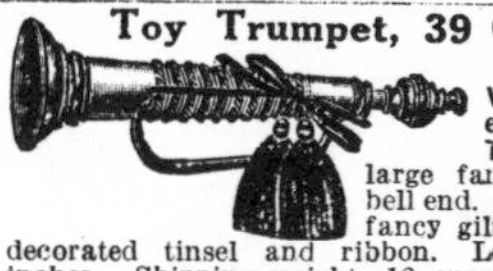

**Heavy Weight Nickeled Tin Trumpet** with large fancy nickeled bell end. Wound with fancy gilt and silver decorated tinsel and ribbon. Length, 14½ inches. Shipping weight, 12 ounces. 50-cent value.
**No. 49K367** Price.............. **39c**

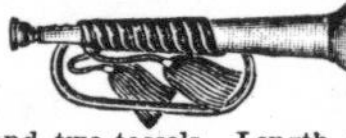

**Heavy Nickeled Trumpet, correct pattern, strongly made.** Has clear note and recall. Ornamented with red and gilt cord and two tassels. Length, 15 inches. Shipping weight, 10 ounces.
**No. 49K308** Price.............. **21c**

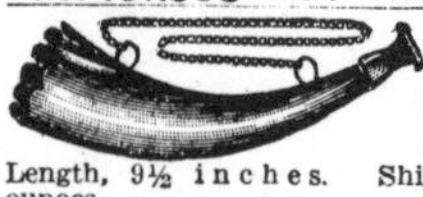

**Made of real cow horn with horn mouthpiece.** Metal chain for hanging. Has clear tone. Length, 9½ inches. Shipping weight, 10 ounces.
**No. 49K307** Price.............. **19c**

## Fancy Nickeled Tin Trumpet, 19c.

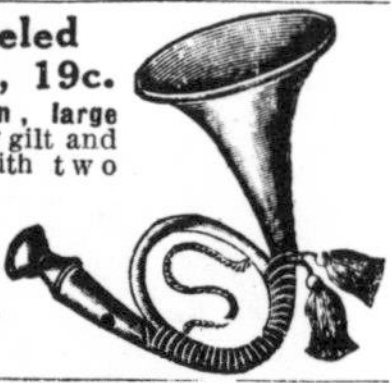

**Popular design, large mouthpiece.** Fancy gilt and green trimming, with two large fancy tassels. Shipping weight, 12 ounces.
**No. 49K306** Price.............. **19c**

## This Fine 14-Inch Horn, 10c.

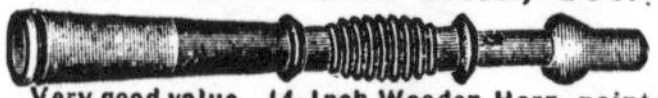

**Very good value. 14-Inch Wooden Horn,** painted in four bright colors. Favorite toy for small boys. Shipping weight, 10 ounces.
**No. 49K347** Price.............. **10c**

## Wonder Value Tin Horn, 10c.

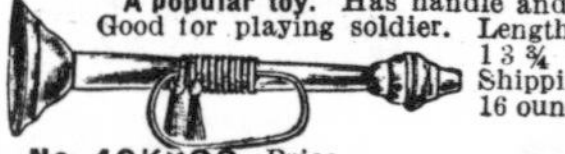

**A popular toy.** Has handle and tassel. Good for playing soldier. Length, about 13¾ inches. Shipping wt., 16 ounces.
**No. 49K328** Price.............. **10c**

## A Very Good Flute, 9 Cents.

**Nice Metal Flute at this low price.** Has six notes; 14 inches long. Shipping weight, 5 ounces.
**No. 49K346** Price.............. **9c**

## Genuine Swiss Music Boxes.

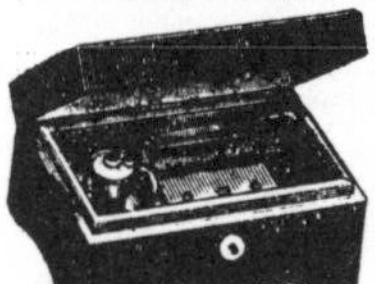

**Genuine mahogany box,** three tunes, patent spring for winding. Music can be turned on or off. Handsome finish. Size, 5¼x3½x2¾ inches. Shipping weight, 2 pounds.
**No. 49K323** Price.... **$2.83**

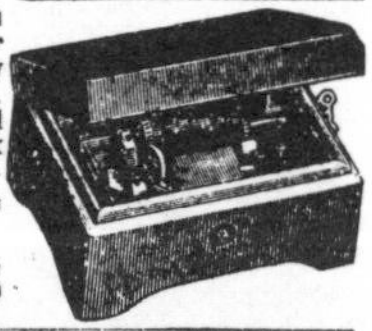

**Genuine Swiss, with patent spring for winding.** Fancy holly hinged cover box. Music can be turned on or off. Size, 4¾x3½x2½ inches. Shipping weight, 1½ pounds.
**No. 49K324** Price...... **$1.55**

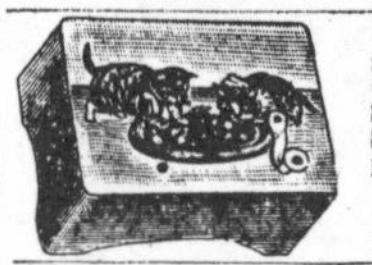

**Beautifully polished square hardwood box.** Crank attachment. Size, 4¾x3½x2¾ in. Shipping weight, 1 pound.
**No. 49K325** Price...... **$1.85**

## Two-Air Music Box, 87 Cents.

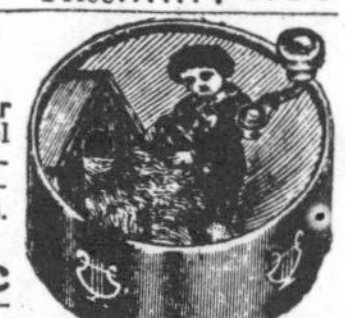

**Plays two popular tunes.** Beautifully nickel plated edge. Very popular instrument. Shipping weight, 8 ounces. Each in box.
**No. 49K326** Price........ **87c**

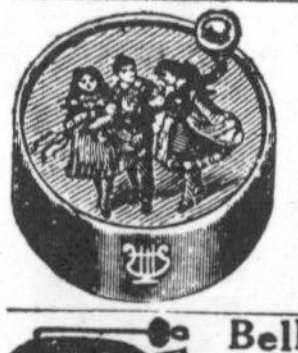

**Fine Imported Genuine Swiss Music Box,** playing popular and pleasing tune. Finely nickel plated edge. Diameter, 2¾ inches. Shipping weight, 6 ounces.
**No. 49K327** Price........ **49c**

## Bell Revotina.

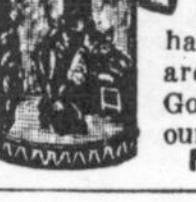

**Medium Priced Music Box.** Good handle and music box swings around it. Has bell attachment. Good grade. Shipping weight, 12 ounces.
**No. 49K369** Price.... **21c**

## Cheap Music Box, 19 Cents.

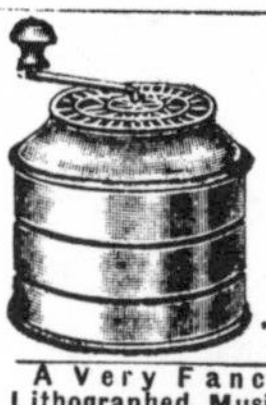

**Very pretty box,** crank attachment. Size, 3¼x3 inches. Shipping weight 7 ounces.
**No. 49K330** Price.............. **19c**

## Toy Music Box, 9c.

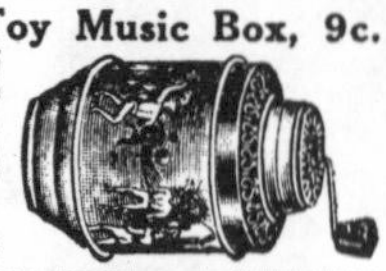

**A Very Fancy Lithographed Music Box in several colors.** Size, 5¼x2¾ inches. Shipping weight, 6 ounces.
**No. 49K331** Price.......... **9c**

## Musical Floor Chimes.

**Our Finest Value.** **$1.96**

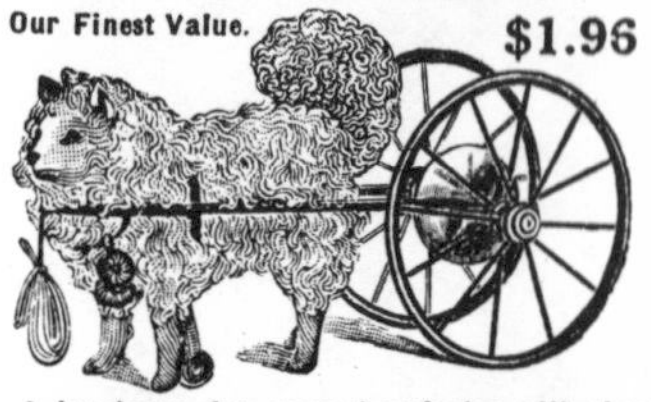

**A handsome fur covered curly dog with glass eyes and large bushy tail.** Dog, 8½x10 inches. Fancy tassels and drawing cord. Wheels painted red, 8½ inches in diameter, oval rims, securely fastened metal spokes and brass finish hubs. 3½-inch bell, heavy steel, good sounding chimes. Metal harness, gilt bronze finish. Total length, 19 in. Shipping wt., packed, 5 lbs.
**No. 49K340** Price.............. **$1.96**

## Horse and Bell Chimes.

**$1.45**

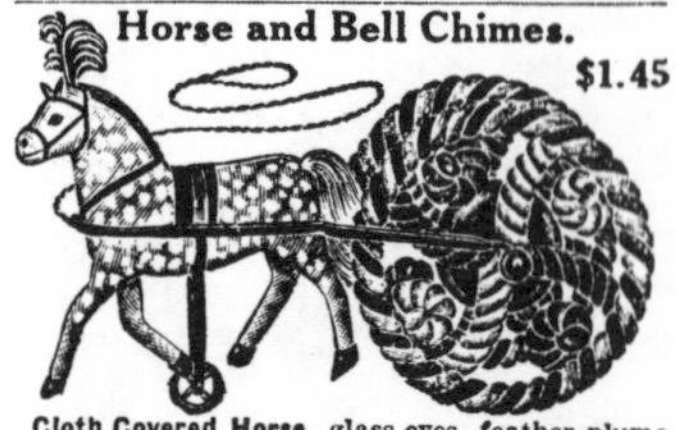

**Cloth Covered Horse,** glass eyes, feather plume on head. Steel chime bell, 2½ inches; drawing cord. Imitation leather harness, 7½-inch wool covered wheels. Good value. Total length, 15¾ inches. Shipping wt., packed, 3 lbs.
**No. 49K339** Price.............. **$1.45**

**98c**

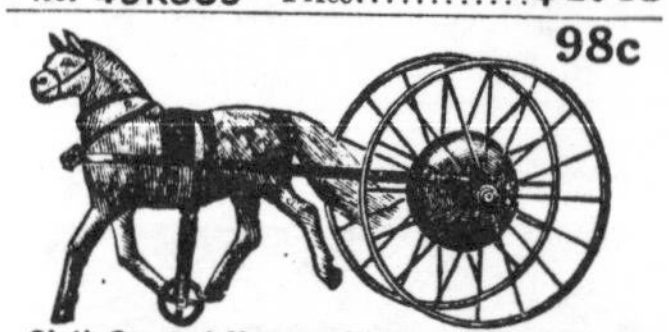

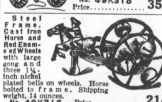

**Cloth Covered Horse, with fine mane and tail, glass eyes, metal gilt finish frame.** Large size nickel plated bell. Large 7-inch blue enamel finish gilt trimmed metal wheels. Size horse, 7½x7 inches. Genuine leather draw string with clasp. Size over all, 15x7⅛ inches. Shipping weight, 2 pounds. (Unmailable.)
**No. 49K314** Price.............. **98c**

**Same as above, but smaller size.** 4½-inch wheel, and horse in proportion. Shipping weight, 1 pound.
**No. 49K315** Price.............. **47c**

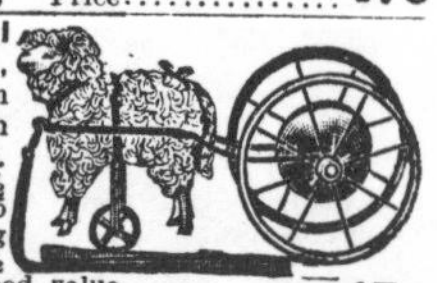

**Natural Wool Covered Sheep,** 4⅜-inch oval rim wheels; 2⅜-inch steel bell chime. Total length, 9½ inches; height, 5 inches. Shipping weight, 1½ pounds. Very good value.
**No. 49K338** Price.............. **47c**

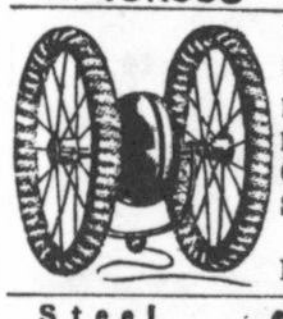

**Noiseless Wool Covered Metal Wheels.** Large nickel plated bell in center, with pulling attachment. Wheels 6 inches in diameter. Shipping weight, 1 pound.
**No. 49K318** Price.............. **35c**

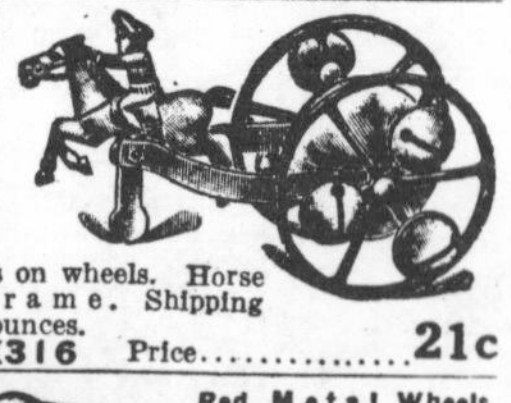

**Steel Frame, Cast Iron Horse and Red Enameled Wheels** with large gong and three 1¼-inch nickel plated bells on wheels. Horse bolted to frame. Shipping weight, 14 ounces.
**No. 49K316** Price.............. **21c**

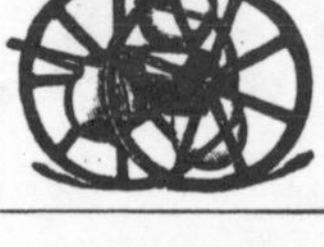

**Red Metal Wheels.** Three 1¼-inch nickel bells and drawing attachment. Big value. Shipping weight, 8 oz.
**No. 49K317** Price.............. **9c**

### Three Fine Whistles, 10 Cents.

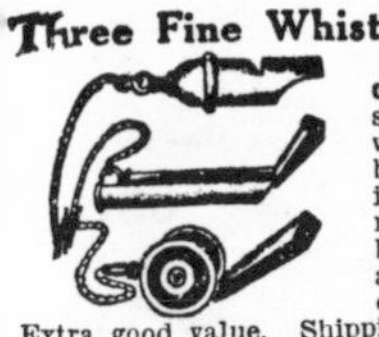

One policeman's call whistle, one odd shape warbling echo whistle, and one two-barrel bicycle shrieking whistle. All full nickel plated, with bright chains with attachment for fastening to pockets

Extra good value. Shipping weight, 3 ounces.
No. 49K1060 Price, 3 for........10c

### Bird Whistles, 3 for 10 Cents.

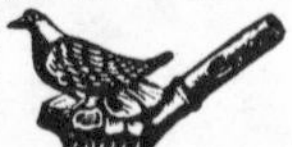

Colored Metal Bird Whistles. Can be made to resemble canary bird notes. Shipping weight, 4 ounces.
No. 49K329 Price, 3 for.... 10c

### Official Boy Scout Whistle, 10c.

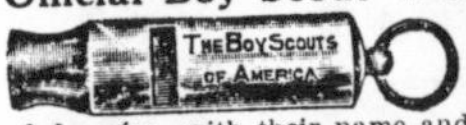


The only official whistle of the Boy Scouts' of America, with their name and seal stamped on whistle. Has ring for hanging. Fine gun-metal finish. Shipping weight, 2 oz.
No. 49K1096 Price............ 10c

### Bicycle Whistle, 21 Cents.

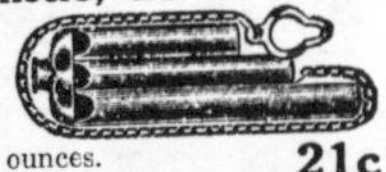

Three-barrel whistle, nicely plated, strong tone; chain and clasp; 5½ inches long. Shipping weight, 3 ounces.
No. 49K1097 Price............ 21c

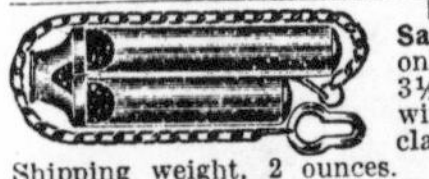

No. 49K1098 Same as above, but only two barrels; 3½ inches long, with chain and clasp.
Shipping weight, 2 ounces. Price..... 13c

### Our Finest Reins, 79c.

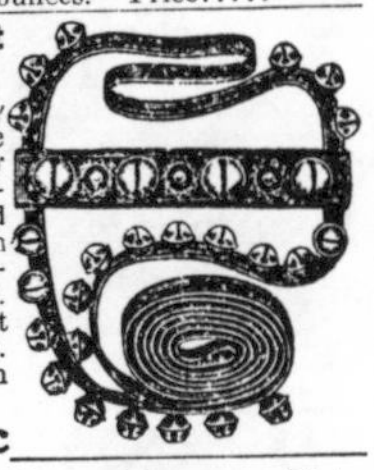

Exceptionally heavy soft fine grade orange color leather, with twenty-four nickel plated steel bells on reins, and four 1¼-inch bells on front. Not cheap, but finest reins made. Shipping weight, in box, 1½ pounds.
No. 49K319 Price 79c

### Our Twenty-Five Bell Toy Reins.

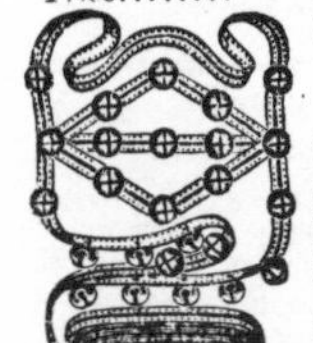

White oilcloth, securely sewed, with fancy front piece. Sixteen bells on reins and nine 1¼-inch bells on front. Bells nickel plated steel, not tin. Shipping weight, 1 pound.
No. 49K320 Price 39c

### Eleven-Bell Toy Reins.

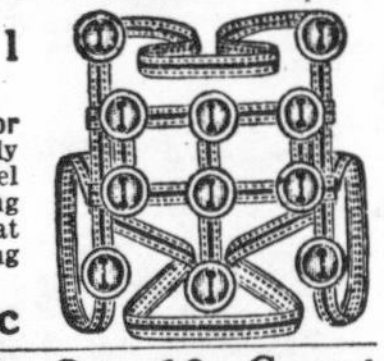

Fancy Two-Color Oilcloth Reins, nicely sewed, eleven nickel plated good sounding bells. Big value at this price. Shipping weight, 8 ounces.
No. 49K321 Price 19c

### Our 10-Cent Wonder Value.

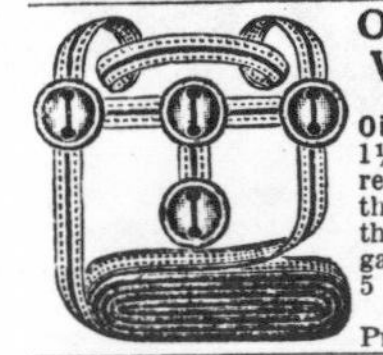

Fancy Two-Color Oilcloth Reins. Four 1¼-inch bells. These reins are far better than usually sold at this price. A big bargain. Shipping weight, 5 ounces.
No. 49K322 Price........ 10c

### Kirby's Musical Toy Gongs, 9 Cents.

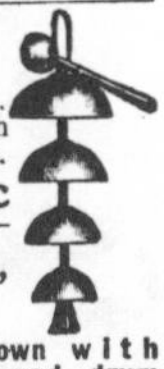

Four nickel plated steel gongs. 2¼, 1¾, 1½ and 1¼ inches, with mallet. Packed in box. Big favorite. Shipping weight, 10 ounces.
No. 49K341 Price........ 9c

### Musical Clown, 39 Cents.

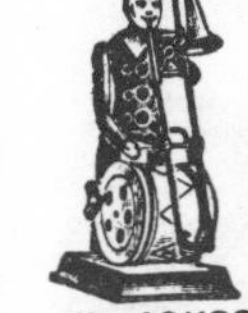

A Mechanical Clown with imitation trombone and drum and moving arms. By winding up the spring of the music box, the movable arms of the clown perform, playing in a very natural manner. Nicely finished. 3¼x3½x8½ inches. Shipping weight, 10 oz.
No. 49K334 Price 39c

### A Fine Musical Toy.

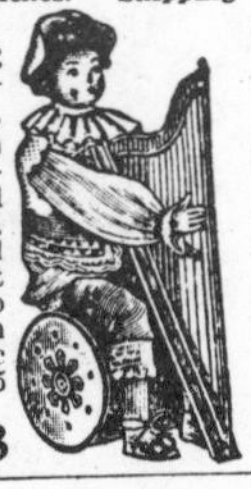

Figure is silk and plush dressed, lace trimmed stockings and slippers. Total height, 12 inches. Music box, 4 inches in diameter. Metal harp, 11 inches high, gilt decorated. Moves hands up and down and head from side to side while music plays. Shipping weight, 5 pounds.
No. 49K360 Price $1.98

### Orchestra Pipe Organ, 98 Cents.

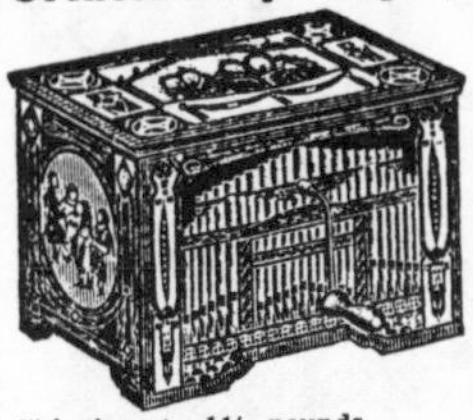

Handsomely decorated in colors to resemble pipe organ. Plays loud or soft notes, according to strength used in turning crank; very natural good tone. Size, 7¼x5x4⅝ inches.
Shipping wt., 1½ pounds.
No. 49K355 Price............ 98c

### Lifelike Piano Player, 89 Cents.

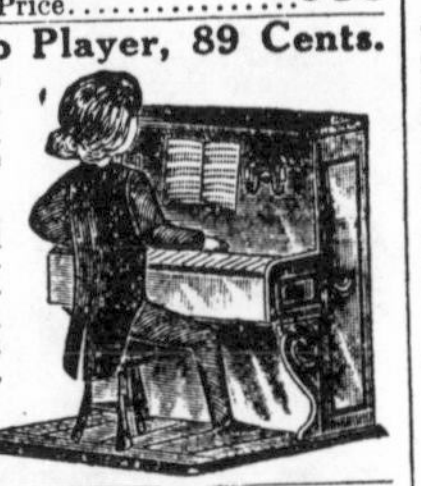

The popular Music Master. Moves head, body and hands over the keys as music plays. Fancy cloth dress, bushy hair. Metal piano nicely painted and very durable. Height, 6 in. Base, 4½x5 inches. Shipping weight, 25 ounces.
No. 49K459 Price....89c

### Musical Negroes, 98 Cents.

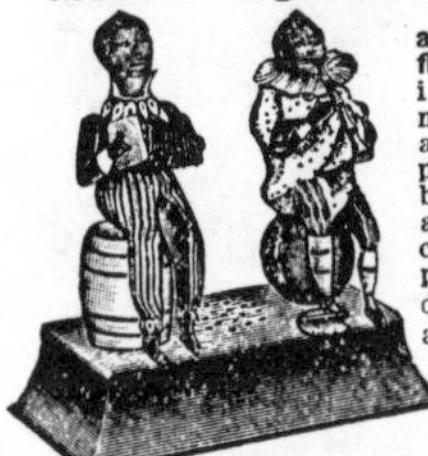

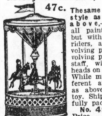

Darkies playing accordion and flute. One playing accordion moving head and arms, and flute player moving body and head, and beats foot cymbal. All painted and decorated. Size, about 9 inches long, 4½ in. wide, 9 inches high. Regular $1.25 to $1.50 value. Shipping weight, 2 pounds.
No. 49K359 Price............ 98c

### Merry-Go-Round, 89c.

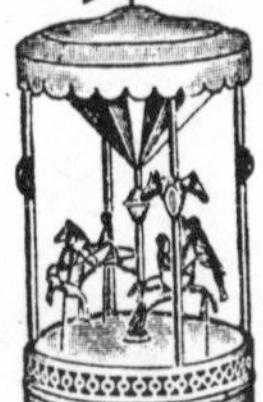

A handsomely decorated article. Large size, nicely painted, four galloping horses on revolving platform and music attachment which plays as merry-go-round revolves. Good spring and surprising value at the price. Size, 16 inches high, 7½ inches in diameter. Shipping weight, carefully packed, 4 pounds.
No. 49K354 Price 89c

### Merry-Go-Round, 47c.

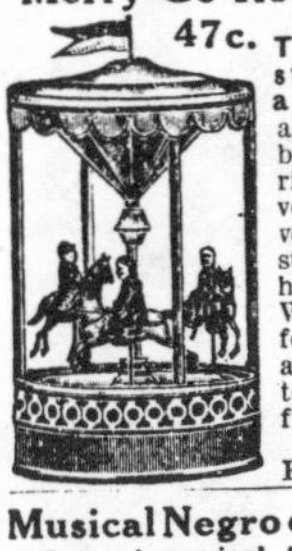

The same style as above, all painted and trimmed, but with three horses and riders, all in colors. Revolving platform, 4-inch revolving painted fan, flag on staff, without gilt horses' heads on posts. Good spring. While music plays the different attachments revolve as above. Very attractive toy. Shipping weight, carefully packed, 22 ounces.
No. 49K332 Price 47c

### Musical Negro on Chair.

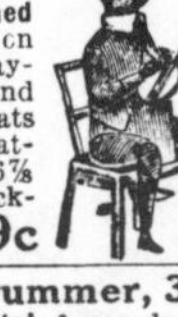

A most comical toy, finished in colors. Represents negro on chair dressed in uniform, playing banjo. Moves hand and head up and down, and beats time with his feet in most natural manner. Total height, 6⅞ inches. Shipping weight, packed, 14 ounces.
No. 49K333 Price 39c

### Clown Drummer, 39c.

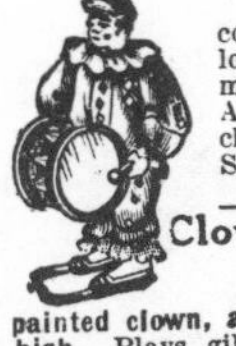

Made of metal, fancy dress in colors, with cap. Painted celluloid face. Beats a decorated metal drum in rapid fashion. A very catchy novel toy for children. Height, 9½ inches. Shipping weight, 16 oz.
No. 49K356 Price 39c

### Clown and Harp, 59c.

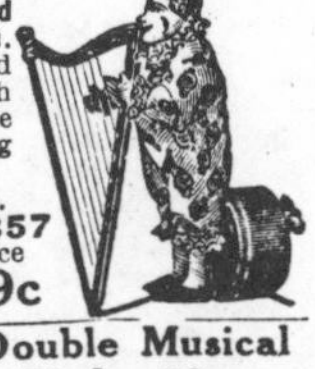

Fancy dressed painted clown, about 9 in. high. Plays gilt painted metal harp, moving both hands up and down while music plays. Shipping weight, packed, 20 oz.
No. 49K357 Price 59c

### Double Musical Birds, 79c.

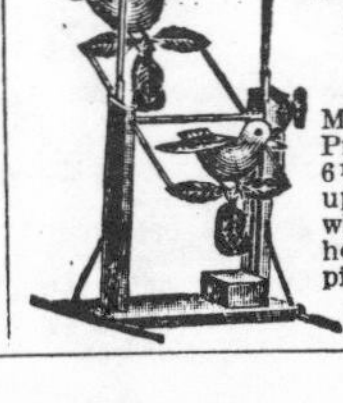

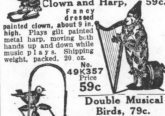

A very handsome toy. Made entirely of metal. Prettily colored birds, 6½ inches long. Swing up and down on bough while music plays. Total height, 16 inches. Shipping weight, 2 pounds.
No. 49K358 Price 79c

## BOYS' DRUMS.

### Our Best Drum, $2.45.

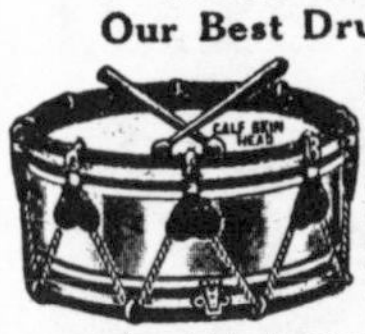


Boys' Highly Finished Drum, 12-inch nickel shell, genuine calfskin head, sheepskin bottom, with snare tightener. This is a very high class drum. Drumsticks furnished with each drum. Each carefully packed in box.
Shipping weight, 5 pounds.
No. 49K3005¼ Price........ $2.45

### A Fine Drum for $1.47.

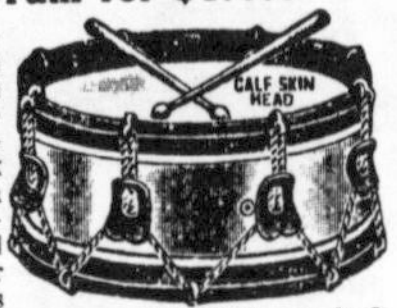


Sheepskin Bottom Drum, 12-inch genuine calfskin head, nickel plated sides. Furnished with black enamel finish hoops, cord tightener and metal hooks and leather ears. Drumsticks furnished with each drum. Carefully packed. Shipping weight, 5 pounds.
No. 49K3006¼ Price......... $1.47

### Only 85c for This Drum.

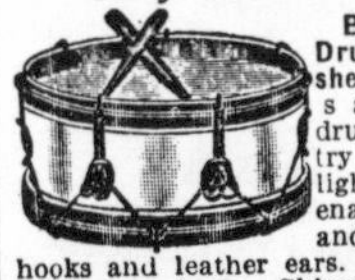

Boys' Fiber Bottom Drum, 11-inch nickel shell, sheepskin top. This is a good medium priced drum, known the country over as the Boy's Delight. Furnished with enamel hoops, red, white and blue cord, metal hooks and leather ears. Drumsticks furnished with each drum. Shipping wt., 40 oz.
No. 49K3007¼ Price........ 85c

### Our Great 59c Value.

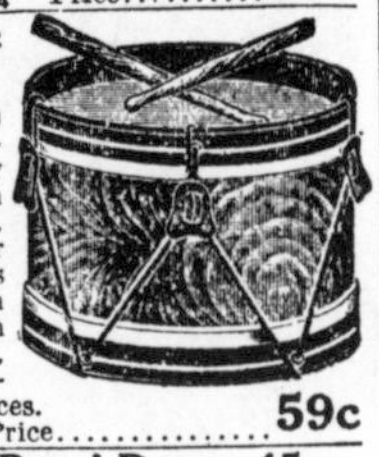

Boys' Sheepskin Head and Fiber Bottom Drum, nicely painted in imitation wood. Metal sides, adjustable leather cord fasteners, hoops painted black with red stripes; 9½-inch drum sticks. Size, 9x6½ inches. Shipping weight, 45 ounces.
No. 49K389 Price............ 59c

### The Popular Boys' Drum, 45c.

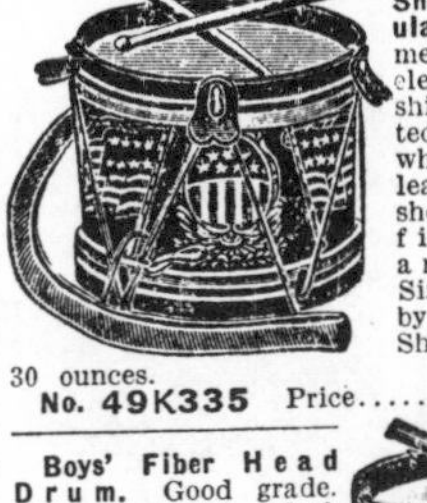

The Uncle Sam Snare Drum. Regulation pattern, metal shell, enameled U. S. flag and shield designs, fitted with hoops, white cord and leather braces. Has sheepskin head and fiber bottom and drumsticks. Size, 8 inches wide by 6¼ inches high. Shipping weight, 30 ounces.
No. 49K335 Price.............. 45c

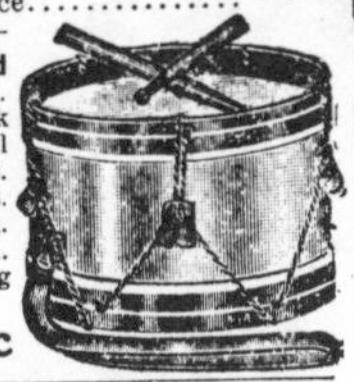

Boys' Fiber Head Drum. Good grade. Hoops painted black with red stripes. Nickel plated metal sides. Leather tighteners. Drum sticks, 9½ in. Size drum, 8x6¼ in. Great value. Shipping weight, 18 ounces.
No. 49K388 Price 39c

### Our High Grade Metal Drum, 25c.

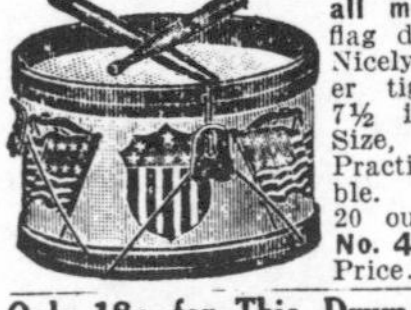

Handsomely painted all metal, with U. S. flag decoration on sides. Nicely varnished leather tighteners. Sticks, 7½ inches in length. Size, 9x5½ inches. Practically indestructible. Shipping weight, 20 ounces.
No. 49K387 Price 25c

### Only 18c for This Drum.

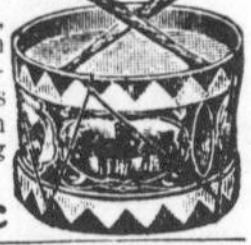

An all Metal 9-Inch Drum, fancy decorated sides. Can be taken apart and put together easily. A noisy boy's favorite. Furnished with sticks complete. Shipping weight, packed, 16 ounces.
No. 49K336 Price............ 18c

### Our Best Piano Stool, 49 Cents.

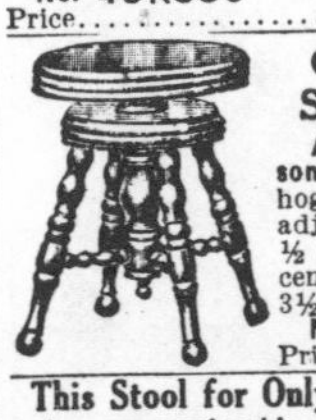

A strongly made handsome Stool, imitation mahogany finish, with 7-inch adjustable revolving top, ½-inch screw, 1⅜-inch center post. Shipping wt., 3½ pounds.
No. 49K1041 Price 49c

### This Stool for Only 23c.

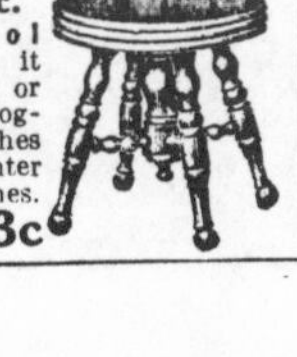

A very serviceable Stool without revolving top, so it can be used as play stool or for piano. Imitation mahogany finish. Top, 7½ inches in diameter. 1¼-inch center post. Height, 7½ inches. Shipping wt., 2 lbs.
No. 49K1042 Price. 23c

### Very Best Toy Piano, $8.98.

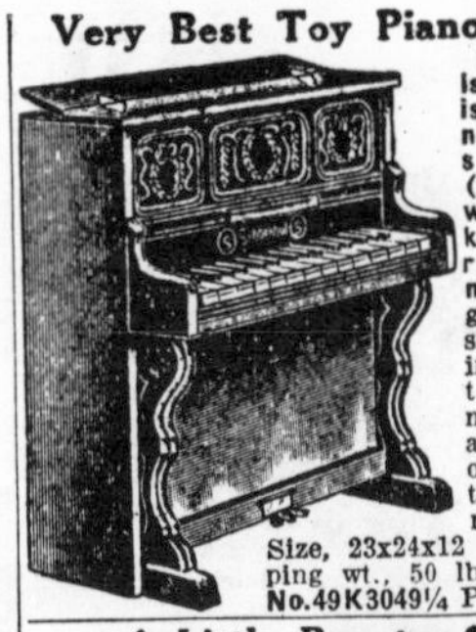

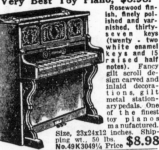

Rosewood finish, finely polished and varnished, thirty-seven keys (twenty-two white enamel keys and 15 raised half notes). Fancy gilt scroll design carved and inlaid decorations, gilt metal stationary pedals. One of the finest toy pianos manufactured. Size, 23x24x12 inches. Shipping wt., 50 lbs.
No. 49K3049¼ Price $8.98

### A Little Beauty, $5.69.

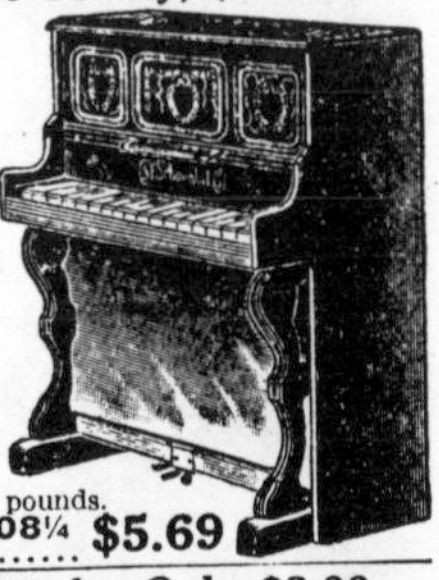

Upright style with twenty-two keys. A very well finished imitation rosewood case with fancy gilt scroll inlaid panels on front. Movable cover and imitation gilt pedals. Carved and decorated front with inlaid panels. Size, 11x24x24 in. Shipping wt., 50 pounds.
No. 49K3008¼ Price $5.69

### This Piano for Only $3.88.

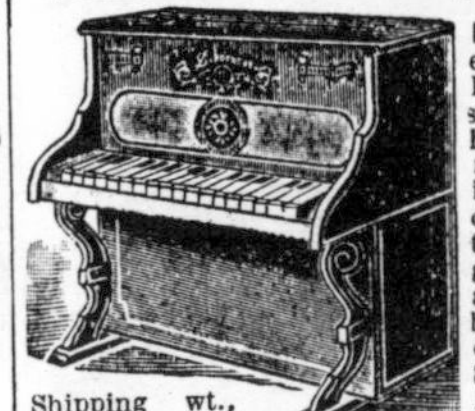

A high class Piano. Has eighteen regular piano shaped keys, handsome rosewood finish case with chandelier attachment and gilt legs. Movable cover and handsomely decorated. Size, 19x17½x10 inches. Shipping wt., 25 pounds.
No. 49K3009¼ Price........ $3.88

### Upright Toy Pianos at

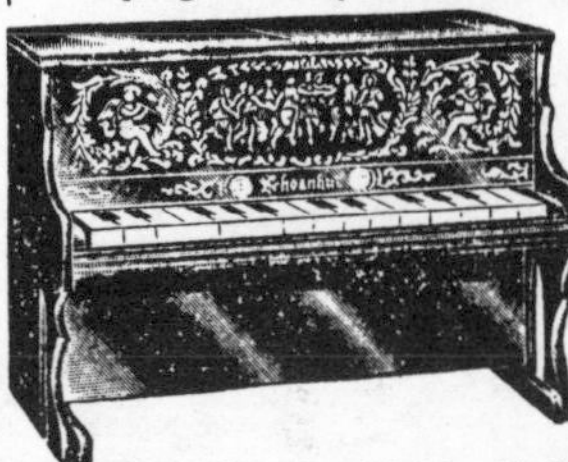


$2.55
$1.98
$1.29
98c
69c
50c
25c

All beautiful rosewood finish, gilt decorated. Very good tone and high quality. Sizes depending on number of keys as follows:

Twenty-Two-Key Piano. Size, 23x9½x13½ inches. Shipping wt., crated, 25 lbs.
No. 49K3010¼ Price........ $2.55

Eighteen-Key Piano. Size, 19¼x12½x8¼ inches. Shipping weight, 8¾ lbs.
No. 49K390 Price............ $1.98

Sixteen-Key Piano. Size, 16½x11x8¼ inches. Shipping weight, 6½ pounds.
No. 49K391 Price............ $1.29

Fifteen-Key Piano. Size, 15½ x 8 x 10¾ inches. Shipping weight, 6 pounds.
No. 49K392 Price............ 98c

Nine-Key Piano. Size, 10¼x8¼x7¼ inches. Shipping weight, 4½ pounds.
No. 49K393 Price............ 69c

Eight-Key Piano. Size, 9¼x8x6½ inches. Shipping weight, 3½ pounds.
No. 49K394 Price............ 50c

Six-Key Piano. Size, 7½x6¼x5 inches. Shipping weight, 2 pounds.
No. 49K395 Price............ 25c

### Wonderful Value Baby Grand Piano, $5.95.

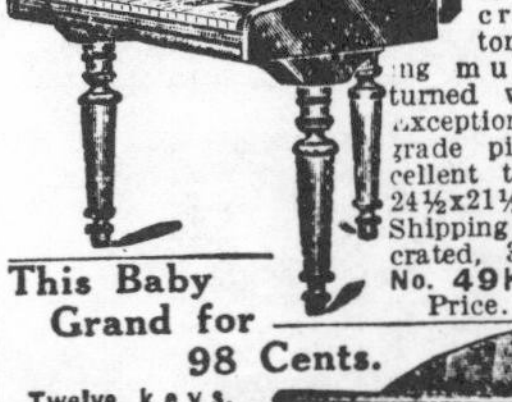

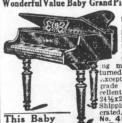

Twenty-two keys, fine rosewood finish, raised lid and back to allow increase of tone. Folding music rest, turned wood legs. Exceptional high grade piano. Excellent tone. Size, 24½x21½x18½ in. Shipping weight, crated, 36 pounds.
No. 49K3016¼ Price.... $5.95

### This Baby Grand for 98 Cents.

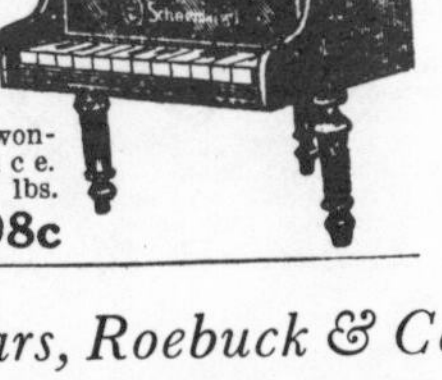


Twelve keys, rosewood finish, raised lid to allow increase in tone. High grade tone, exceptional value. Size, 13x13x9 inches. A wonder at the price. Shipping wt., 6 lbs.
No. 49K396 Price 98c

# HIGH GRADE TOY DISHES

## Our Finest China Tea Set.

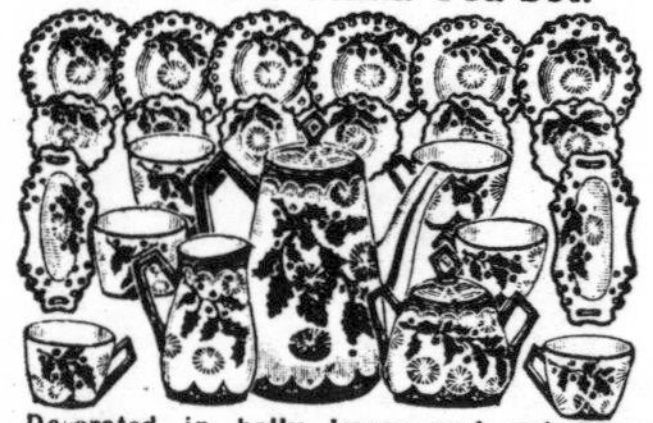

**Decorated in holly leaves and red berry design** with dainty gilt decorations. Twenty-five pieces, as follows: 5-inch teapot with cover, 2½-inch sugar bowl with cover, 2¼-inch creamer, two 4-inch open vegetable dishes, six 1⅝-inch cups, with six 2⅝-inch saucers and six 3¼-inch plates. Not the largest set made but for quality and daintiness of design cannot be equaled. Size, 18x14½ inches. Shipping weight, 5 pounds.
**No. 49K731** Price............ **$1.47**

## Our Large Set, 69 Cents.

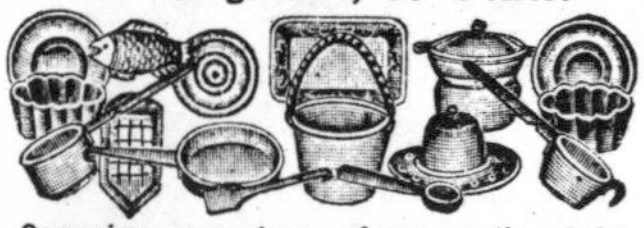

**Comprises seventeen pieces, satin finish, aluminum kitchen cooking utensils.** Lace trimmed box, 12½x13½ inches. Shipping weight, 22 ounces.
**No. 49K782** Price.............. **69c**

## Fourteen-Piece Set, 47 Cents.

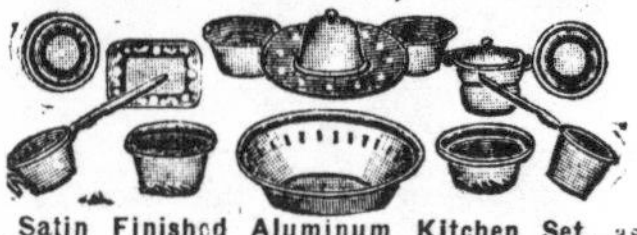

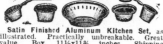

**Satin Finished Aluminum Kitchen Set,** as illustrated. Practically unbreakable. Great value. Box, 11½x11¾ inches. Shipping weight, 18 ounces.
**No. 49K716** Price.............. **47c**

## Our Finest Tea Set, $2.98.

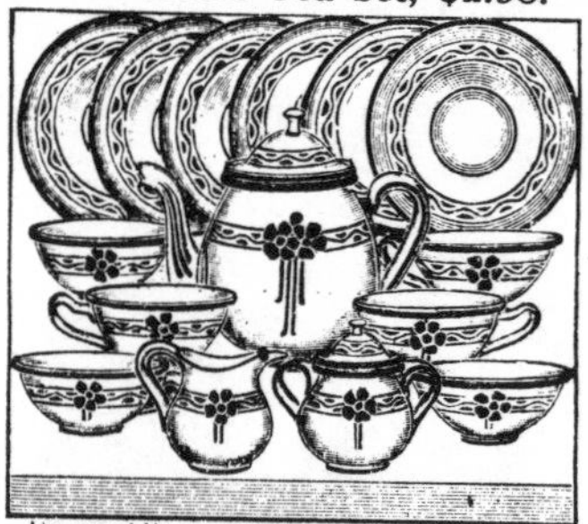

**Heavy white enameled,** beautiful colored raised flower decorations, gold trimmed. Six 4-inch saucers; six cups, 2⅝ inches in diameter, 1¼ inches high; cream pitcher, 2¼ inches high; sugar bowl, 2¾ inches high; teapot, 4¾ inches high and 6 inches wide over all. Resembles china, but far more durable, will not break. A very handsome and practical set. Will last for years. Size box, 12x13½x4 inches. Shipping weight, 4 pounds.
**No. 49K705** Price........... **$2.98**

## Britannia Tea Sets.

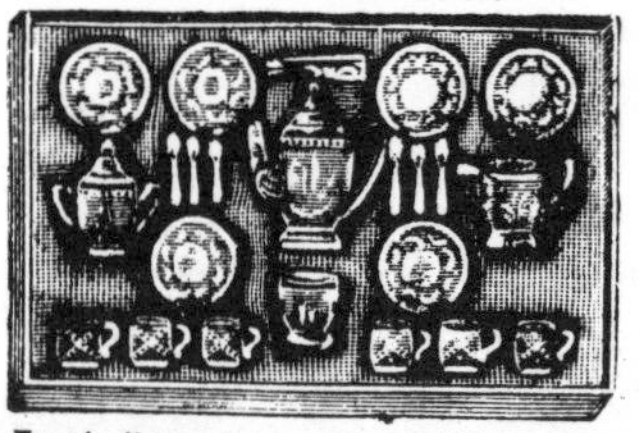

**Twenty-three pieces, silver finished.** Cups, saucers, teapot, sugar bowl and creamer and other articles. Box, 10½x16½ inches. Shipping weight, 40 ounces.
**No. 49K722** Price.............. **89c**

## Our Finest Grade Tin Tea Set.

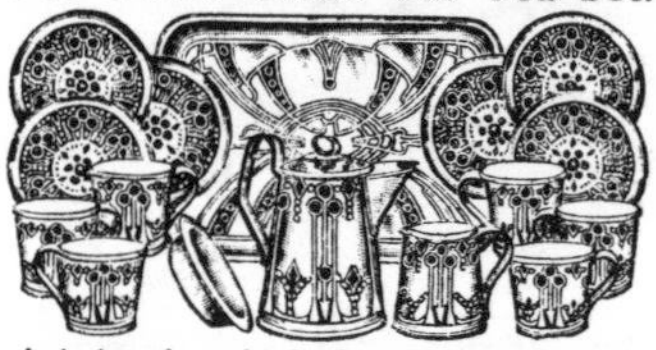

**Latest embossed raised pattern design painted decorations.** Seventeen pieces. Consists of 3½-inch teapot, creamer, six cups and saucers, sugar bowl, and 11¾x7½-inch tray. Nicely made. Shipping wt., 20 oz.
**No. 49K710** Price............ **45c**

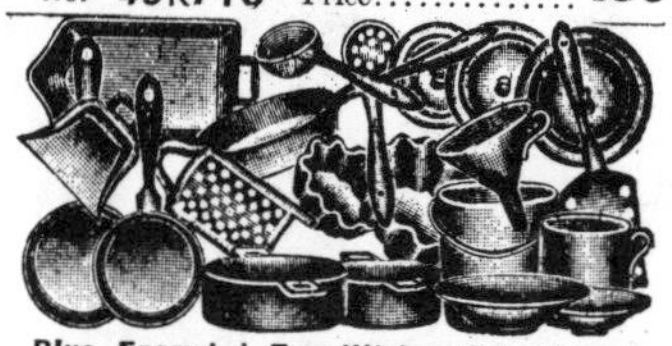

**Blue Enameled Toy Kitchen Set.** Twenty-one pieces, including such as pots, pans, spoons, ladles, covers, grater, cups, pails, etc. Absolutely unbreakable. Size of box, 12½x16 inches. Shipping weight, 3¼ pounds.
**No. 49K725** Price............ **97c**

**Kitchen Set, similar to the above,** but consisting of fourteen pieces high grade blue enameled ware, but smaller in size. A big value for our price. Size of box, 9½x13½ inches. Shipping weight, 2½ pounds.
**No. 49K727** Price.............. **47c**

**Kitchen Set, same make and style as above,** but consisting of only nine pieces. A very attractive set at the price. Size of box, 8x11 inches. Shipping weight, 20 ounces.
**No. 49K726** Price.............. **33c**

**An excellent set for the price.** Dark blue enameled tin. Well made. Unbreakable. Polished surface. Fine for small child. In box. Shipping weight, 5 ounces.

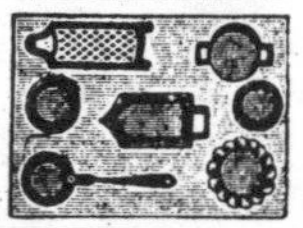

**No. 49K747** **19c**

## Children's Table Set.

**69c**

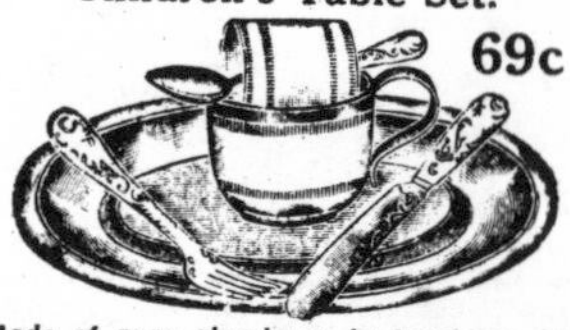

**Made of pure aluminum in handsome satin finish.** Good size cup and saucer, 7-inch plate, knife, fork, spoon and napkin ring. Of sufficient size for regular use. In strong box, 7½x7½x2½ inches. Makes fine birthday gift. Can be used without danger of breakage. Shipping weight, 9 ounces.
**No. 49K719** Price.............. **69c**

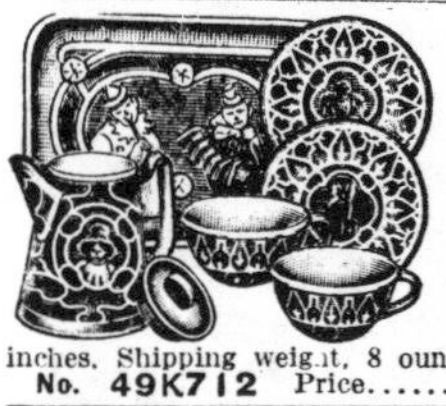

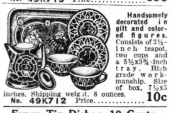

**Handsomely decorated in gilt and colored figures.** Consists of 2½-inch teapot, two cups and a 5½x3¾-inch tray. High grade workmanship. Size of box, 7½x5 inches. Shipping weight, 8 ounces.
**No. 49K712** Price.............. **10c**

## Fancy Tin Dishes, 19 Cents.

**About fifty-five pieces,** including enameled cups, saucers and plates, and other assorted plain and decorated pieces. Shipping weight, 1 pound.

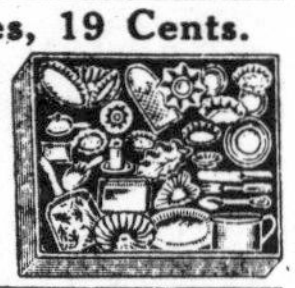

**No. 49K709** Price **19c**

## Tin Dish Set, 9 Cents.

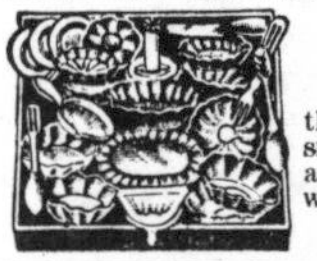

**Similar to above,** about thirty pieces, somewhat smaller, and two cups and saucers. Shipping weight, 8 ounces.
**No. 49K769** Price.............. **9c**

# STOCK FARMS, ARKS AND ANIMALS

## Our Highest Grade Stock Farm, $2.19.

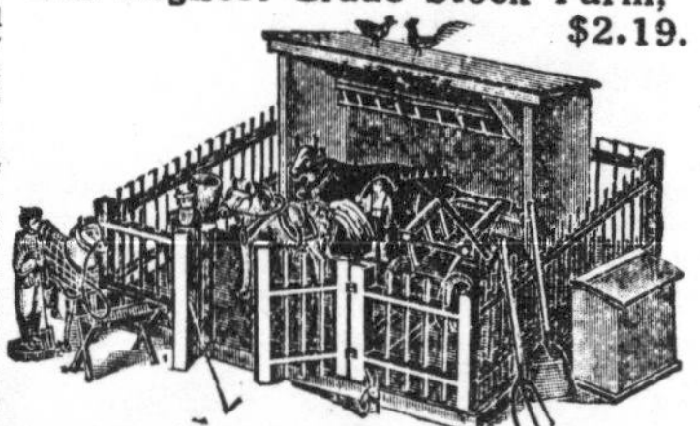

**A handsome and complete set of farm animals,** with wagon, stable, farming utensils and figures, farmer, milkmaid and boy. Without doubt the best value ever offered at the price. Includes two skin covered horses, one with cloth blanket and the other with riding saddle and bridle. Skin covered cow with bell; stable, 7¼x4¾ inches with feed boxes; strong wooden hay rack; two chickens with real feathers; farmer, 5 inches tall; milkmaid, 3¾ inches tall; 3¼-inch boy with whip. All handsomely colored in natural colors. Picket farm fence, 15x15x4 inches, with double swinging gate. A toy that will amuse as well as instruct. A very fine toy. Regular $3.50 value. Size of box, 16x16 inches. Shipping weight, 5 pounds.
**No. 49K1219** Price........ **$2.19**

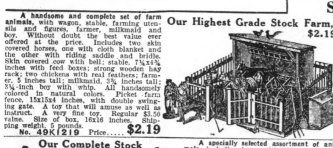

## Our Complete Stock Farm, $1.79.

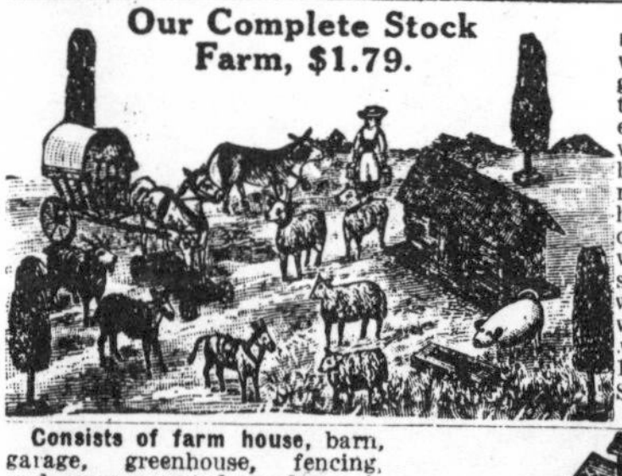

**A specially selected assortment of animals,** including horse with harness, donkey with bridle and saddle, cow, calf, sheep, goat, pig, milkmaid, wagon, log cabin and trees. The animals are skin and fur covered, nicely painted in natural colors and very realistic. The horse on platform can be attached to canvas covered wagon. The milkmaid is 4 inches tall. The log cabin has nicely painted green roof and base. A quantity of green paper moss is furnished with each set. The four trees are assorted sizes from 4 to 6 inches tall. A toy that will please the most particular. For those who desire quality not quantity. A set which is complete and accurate. In box 17½x12 inches. Regular $3.00 value. Shipping weight, 3 pounds.
**No. 49K1221** Price...... **$1.79**

## Sunnyside Stock Farm, 95c.

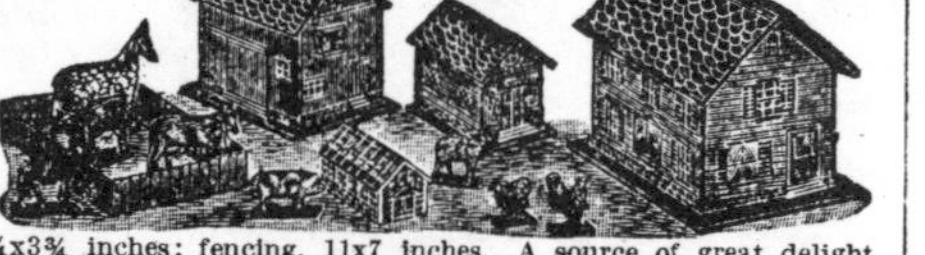

**Consists of farm house, barn,** garage, greenhouse, fencing, and seven assorted wooden animals, consisting of horse, cows, sheep, pig, donkey and chickens, all nicely embossed on wood. Animals have wooden stands. The buildings are stamped in colors and nicely painted to represent boarding, windows, doors, etc. Size of house, 11x8¾x10 inches; barn, 9x8x6½ inches; garage, 6½x5¼x4¾ inches; greenhouse, 4¾x3¾x3¾ inches; fencing, 11x7 inches. A source of great delight for children. Very popular and a big seller. Shipping weight, 7½ pounds.
**No. 49K1349** Price.............................. **95c**

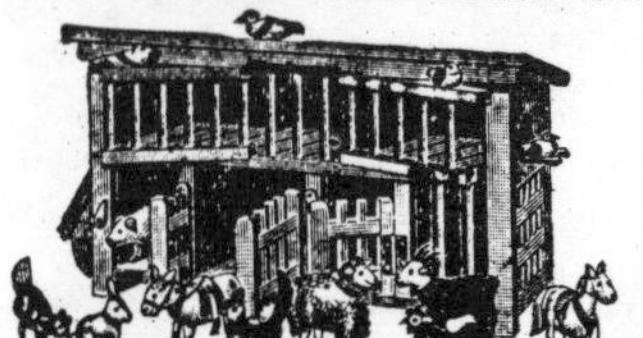

**A complete farm stable outfit,** consisting of well made wooden building with six swinging hinge doors, hog pen with trough; one skin covered horse and mule with saddles and harness; three chickens, with real feathers; wool covered sheep and goat, skin covered pig, four doves and two rabbits. Size of house, 10¾x5¼ inches. Shipping wt., 1½ lbs.
**No. 49K1220** Price........ **$1.15**

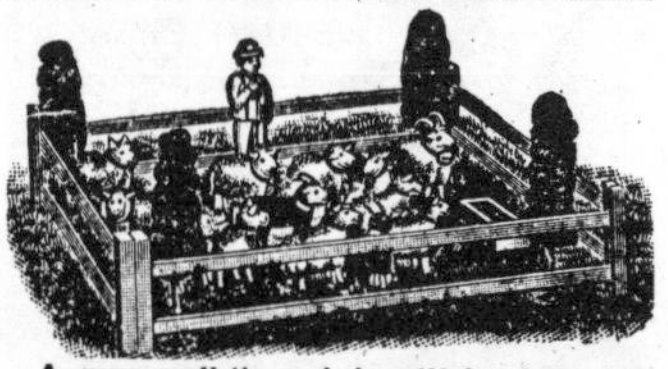

**A very realistic and beautiful set** of real fur covered goats, sheep and dog, with 5¼-inch shepherd, nicely painted in natural colors. Four artificial trees with metal base; 14½-inch square fencing, 3¼ inches high, artificial green paper moss and wood feed box. Large size ram with bell. Dog has real fur and bushy tail. Sells anywhere for $1.50. In box 13x15 inches. Shipping wt., 2½ lbs.
**No. 49K1222** Price........... **98c**

## Our Most Popular Toy—A Complete Stock Farm, 90 Cents.

**90c**

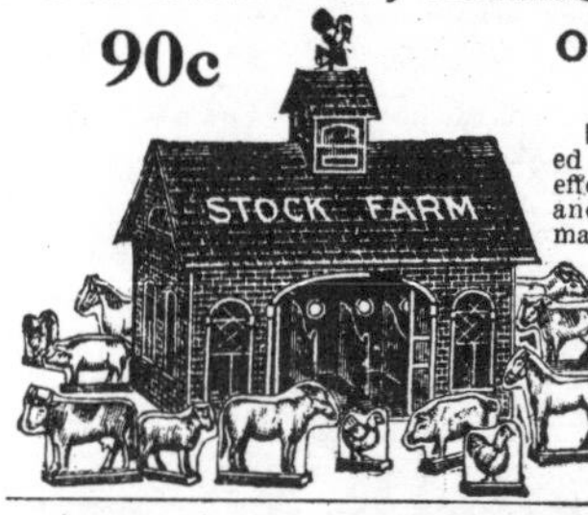

**Made throughout of good wood,** and the barn painted in colors to imitate a real brick barn with window effects. The barn has six stalls with mangers, stalls and cut out windows, and an assortment of farm animals and poultry. Six larger animals for the stalls, and sheep, pigs and chickens to place around the barn. All pieces finished in burnt wood effect. Front of the barn has two swinging doors and the cupola is equipped with a metal rooster weather vane. Height of barn, not including weather vane, 17¼ inches; 19½ inches long, 10 inches wide. This is one of the finest stock farms and a big favorite. Shipping weight, 12 pounds.
**No. 49K3045¼** Price........... **90c**

## Animals of the Ark, 39 Cents.

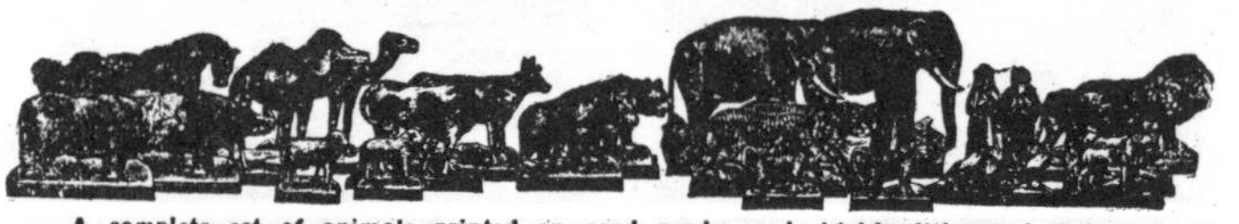

**A complete set of animals printed on good grade card,** highly lithographed in natural colors, with Noah and his wife. Consists of elephants, camels, rhinoceros, lions, tigers, horses, cows, bears, baboons, dogs, sheep, birds, etc. All on wooden stands. Educational and amusing. 75-cent value. Size of box, 9½x7½ inches. Shipping weight, 16 ounces.
**No. 49K1288** Price........................................................ **39c**

## Our Finest Noah's Arks and Stables at

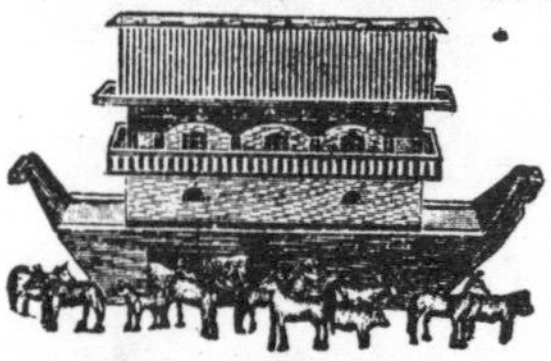

89c
67c
45c
21c

**Have stable in basement of ark,** sliding doors, stalls and hay rack. Fancy windows, removable roof and veneered wooden decorations on sides. Sizes as follows:

**Our 89-Cent Ark.** Contains thirty-six large hand carved animals with four men, all nicely painted. Size, 16¾x10x4¼ inches. Shipping weight, 3½ pounds.
**No. 49K1140** Price............ **89c**

**Our 67-Cent Ark. Same as above,** but smaller size ark and animals. Contains thirty-six animals and four men. Size, 14¼x8¾ inches. Shipping weight, 3 pounds.
**No. 49K1165** Price............ **67c**

**Our 45-Cent Ark. Same as above,** but smaller size. Contains thirty animals and four men. Size, 13x7½ inches. Shipping weight, 2 pounds.
**No. 49K1135** Price............ **45c**

**Our 21-Cent Ark. Same as above,** but smaller. Contains ten animals and sliding doors. Size, 9¾x6¼ inches. Shipping weight, 1½ pounds.
**No. 49K1284** Price............ **21c**

## Noah's Arks at 59c, 39c, 25c, 10c.

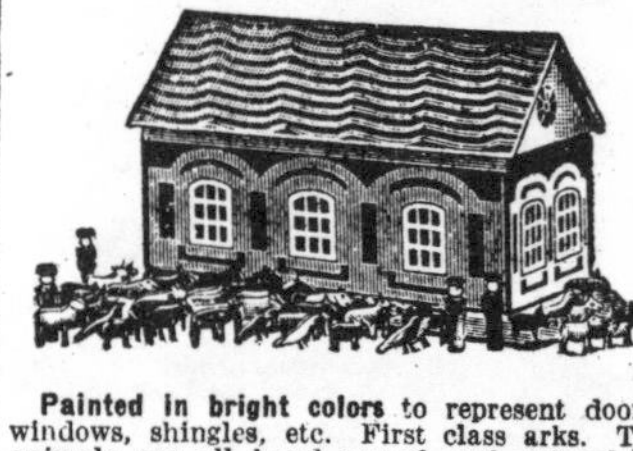

**Painted in bright colors** to represent doors, windows, shingles, etc. First class arks. The animals are all hand carved and painted in different colors. Sizes as follows:

**Our 59-Cent Ark.** Size, 21x6¼x8½ inches. Consists of eighty large varnished animals and five men. 75-cent value. Shipping weight, 2 pounds.
**No. 49K1285** Price.............. **59c**

**Our 39-Cent Ark.** Size, 17½x5¾x7½ inches. Consists of fifty-nine varnished animals and four men. 50-cent value. Shipping weight, 1½ pounds.
**No. 49K1286** Price.............. **39c**

**Our 25-Cent Ark.** Size, 14¾x4x6¼ inches. Consists of forty large varnished animals. Shipping weight, 1¼ pounds.
**No. 49K1136** Price.............. **25c**

**Our 10-Cent Ark.** Size, 11½x3¾x4½ inches. Consists of twenty painted animals. Shipping weight, 1 pound.
**No. 49K1287** Price.............. **10c**

# FINEST DOLL BEDS, TRUNKS AND DOLL FURNITURE

## Doll Beds With Canopy, 45 Cents to $1.27.

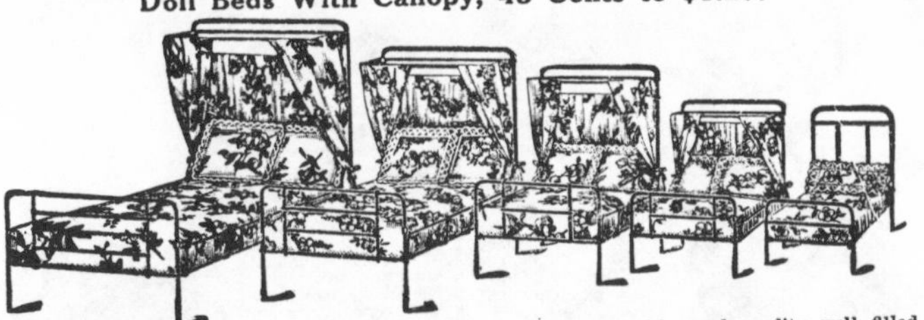

**Exceptional High Grade Doll Beds.** Heavy wire frame with good quality well filled mattress, with sheet and spread. Two pillows with ¾-inch lace trimmings, cloth panel in head board. Canopy has two curtains tied with bow. All made in the latest design nicely decorated flowered design silkoline. Every child who has a doll wants a doll bed, and we believe these to be the greatest bargains ever offered. The quality of material and excellence of workmanship cannot be beat. We furnish in five sizes, all the same high grade beds:

**Our Large 30-Inch Doll Bed.** Width, 14½ inches. With canopy. Shipping weight, 6½ lbs. **No. 49K3090¼** Price ...**$1.27**

**Our 24-Inch Doll Bed.** Width, 12 inches. With canopy. Shipping weight, 4½ lbs. **No. 49K776** Price ......**89c**

**Our 18-Inch Doll Bed.** Width, 10 inches. With canopy. Shipping weight, 3½ lbs. **No. 49K777** Price ......**67c**

**Our 14-Inch Doll Bed.** Width, 8 inches. With canopy. Shipping weight, 3 lbs. **No. 49K778** Price ......**45c**

**Our 12-Inch Doll Bed.** Width, 5¾ inches. Without canopy and only one pillow. Shipping weight, 2 pounds. **No. 49K779** Price ..........**21c**

## Fine Folding Doll Cradles, 95c and 45c.

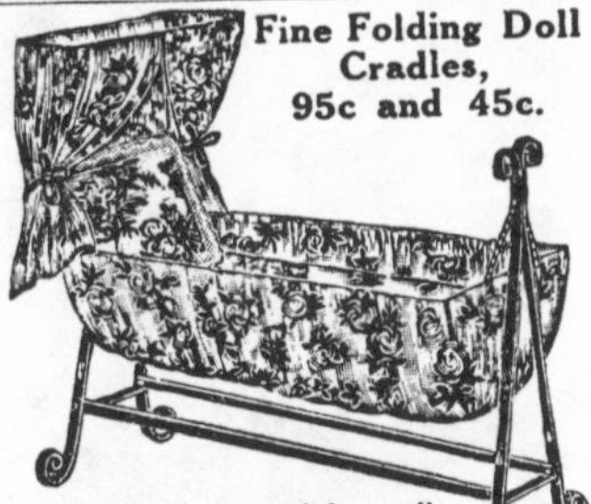

**Heavy metal, finished in scroll designs and beautiful gilt finish.** Excelsior stuffed mattress, large lace edge pillow and muslin sheet. Floral pattern silkoline spread and canopy. Length, 23 inches and 9 inches wide. Packed in nice carton. Shipping wt., 3 lbs.
**No. 49K738** Price.............. **95c**

**Doll Cradle, same style and material as above,** measuring 15x7½ inches. Shipping weight, 28 ounces.
**No. 49K739** Price.............. **45c**

## Enameled Wicker Doll Cradles.

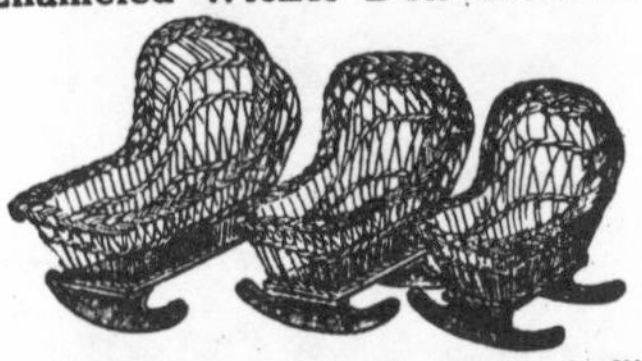

**Nicely painted with white enamel and gilt bronze.** Made from good strong willow in pretty design with canopy; 1½-inch woven edge painted with gilt bronze. A handsome and durable cradle. Good wooden rockers. Sure to please. Three sizes.

**Our 23-Inch Cradle.** 23 inches long, 18½ inches high, 11 inches wide. Shipping weight, 3 pounds.
**No. 49K790¼** Price............ **95c**

**Our 21-Inch Cradle.** 21 inches long, 16 inches high, 10 inches wide. Shipping weight, 2½ pounds.
**No. 49K791** Price.............. **69c**

**Our 18-Inch Cradle.** 18 inches long, 14½ inches high, 8½ inches wide. Shipping weight, 2 pounds.
**No. 49K792** Price.............. **45c**

## White Enameled Brass Trimmed Doll Bed.

### Something Out of the Ordinary.

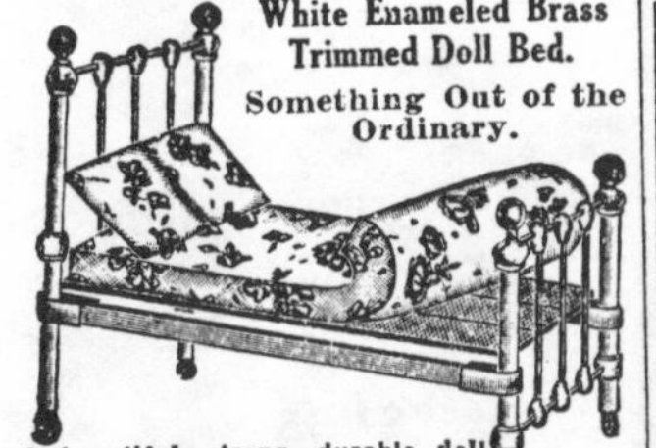

**A beautiful, strong, durable doll bed.** Steel tubing and good springs, white enamel finished and 4 brass knobs. Complete with good stuffed mattress and pillows. Size, 28x18 inches. Shipping weight, 28 pounds. Regular $4.50 to $5.00 value. Satisfaction guaranteed.
**No. 49K3096¼** Price.......... **$3.95**

## Folding Wire Mattress Bed.

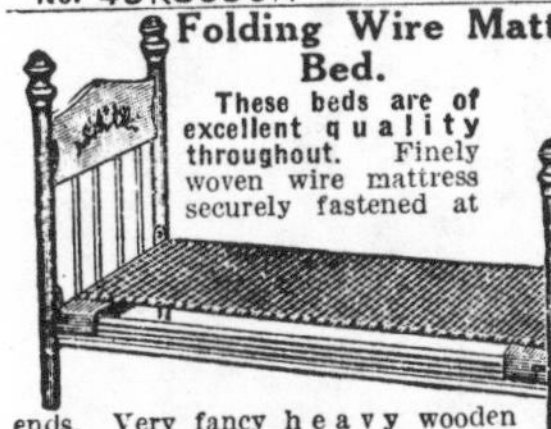

**These beds are of excellent quality throughout.** Finely woven wire mattress securely fastened at ends. Very fancy heavy wooden head and foot and all parts nicely finished in white enamel, decorated with gilt knobs and flowers in natural colors. Folds up completely. Size, 31x17 inches and 22½ inches high. Shipping wt., 5 lbs.
**No. 49K3028¼** Price......... **$1.47**

**Same high grade bed as above,** but smaller size. Length, 26 inches; width, 15 inches; height, 18¾ inches. Same beautiful finish and high quality. Shipping wt., 3 lbs.
**No. 49K775** Price.............. **$1.00**

## Our Colonial Style Brass Bed.

### The Handsomest and Most Substantial Solid Brass Bed Ever Sold.

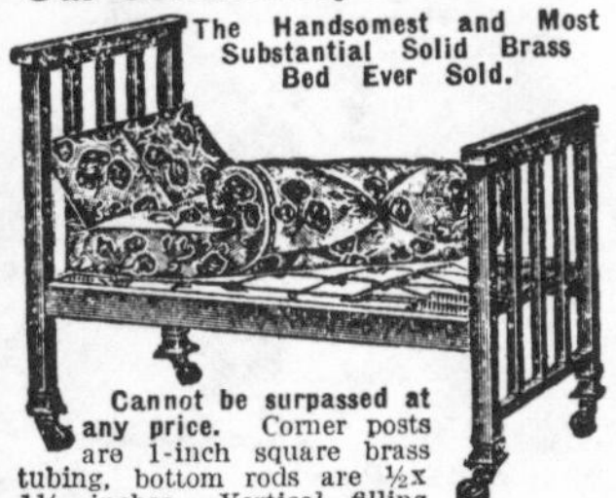

**Cannot be surpassed at any price.** Corner posts are 1-inch square brass tubing, bottom rods are ½x1½ inches. Vertical filling rods are ⅝-inch square, top rods are 1½x¾ inch; all highly polished and lacquered. Will not tarnish. Good quality steel springs with interlocking joints. An exact duplicate of a high priced regulation spring. The casters are regulation ball bearing. Especially made for us by a large manufacturer of brass beds and for style, beauty of finish and workmanship it cannot be surpassed. Retail price, $10.00 to $12.00. Size, 30x21x14 inches. Shipping weight, 25 pounds.
**No. 49K3091¼** Price...... **$8.75**

## Complete Trimmed Doll Bed, $4.95.

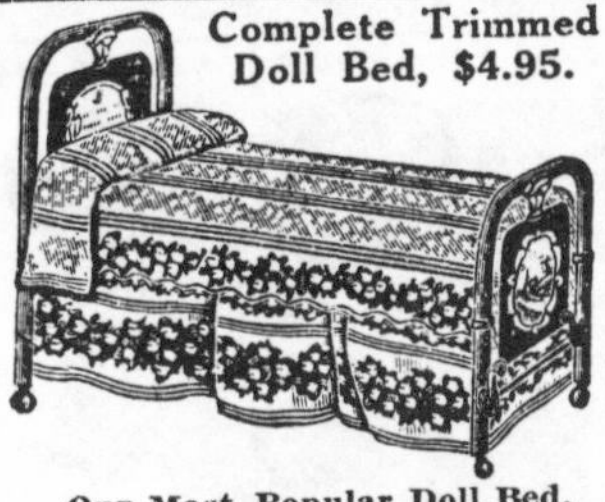

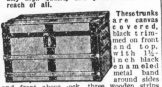

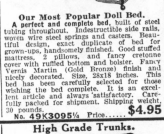

**Our Most Popular Doll Bed.**

**A perfect and complete bed,** built of steel tubing throughout. Indestructible side rails, woven wire steel springs and casters. Beautiful design, exact duplicate of bed for grown-ups, handsomely finished. Good stuffed mattress, 2 pillows, and fancy cretonne cover with ruffled bottom and bolster. Fancy Vernis Martin (Gold Bronze) finish and nicely decorated. Size, 28x18 inches. This bed has been carefully selected for those wishing the bed complete. It is an excellent article and always satisfactory. Carefully packed for shipment. Shipping weight, 30 pounds.
**No. 49K3095¼** Price...... **$4.95**

## Children's Folding Tables.

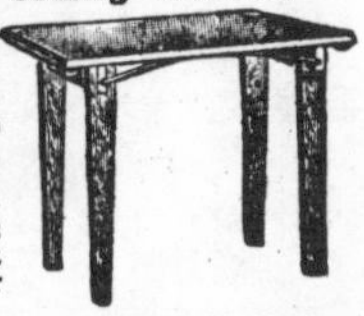

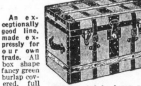

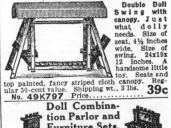

**These beautiful and handsomely finished birchwood tables are great favorites with children.** Each table folds up flat with enameled steel spring, well made, best materials and occupies little space when not in use. Come in four sizes.

**Folding Table.** Size top, 18x28 inches; height, 18½ inches. Shipping wt., 8 lbs.
**No. 49K3030¼** Price.......... **95c**

**Folding Table.** Size top, 16x24 inches; height, 15½ inches. Shipping wt., 7 lbs.
**No. 49K3073¼** Price.......... **67c**

**Folding Table.** Size top, 14x20 inches; height, 14½ inches. Shipping wt., 6 lbs.
**No. 49K768** Price.......... **39c**

**Folding Table.** Size top, 10x15 inches; height, 12 inches. Shipping wt., 5 lbs.
**No. 49K783** Price.......... **21c**

## Dolly's Swing, 39 Cents.

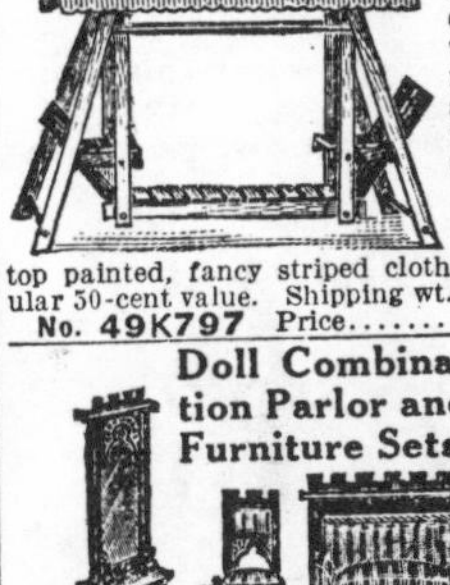

**Double Doll Swing with canopy. Just what dolly needs.** Size of seat, 4½ inches wide. Size of swing, 24x19x12 inches. A handsome little toy. Seats and top painted, fancy striped cloth canopy. Regular 50-cent value. Shipping wt., 3 lbs.
**No. 49K797** Price.......... **39c**

## Medium Grade Trunks.

**None better made at the price. Exceptionally high quality and priced within the reach of all.**

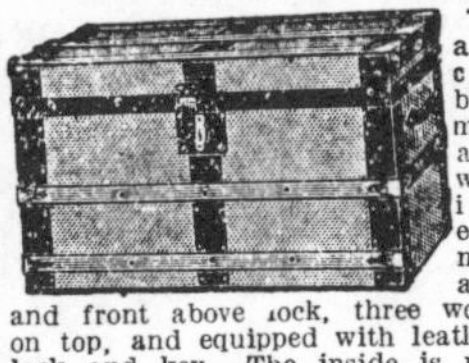

**These trunks are canvas covered, black trimmed on front and top, with 1½-inch black enameled metal band around sides** and front above lock, three wooden strips on top, and equipped with leather handles, lock and key. The inside is paper lined, with two compartment trays in body of trunk, one tray being covered. Exceptional values. Three sizes.

**No. 49K3058¼** 10½ inches high, 18 inches long, 10⅝ inches wide. Shipping weight, 10 pounds. Price........ **95c**

**No. 49K3060¼** 8 inches high, 14 inches long, 8 inches wide. Shipping weight, 9 pounds. Price........ **69c**

**No. 49K3059¼** 6¾ inches high, 12 inches long, 6½ inches wide. Shipping weight, 8 pounds. Price........ **45c**

## High Grade Trunks.

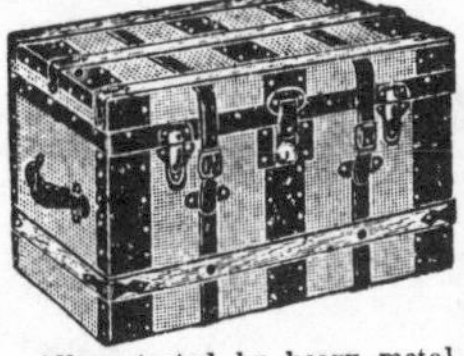

**An exceptionally good line, made expressly for our own trade.** All box shape fancy green burlap covered, full cloth lined. All protected by heavy metal, black enameled, wide binding and slats, with metal bumpers, genuine leather (colored to match burlap) straps, and brass buckles. Fine quality brass suit case lock, with brass snap lock on each side. Compartment tray with lid under top, and two compartment trays in body. Each trunk in crate.

**No. 49K3055¼** 13¾ inches long, 10½ inches high, 10¾ inches wide. Shipping weight, 8 pounds. Price.... **$1.98**

**No. 49K3056¼** 16¾ inches long, 9 inches high, 9 inches wide. Shipping weight, 7 pounds. Price.... **$1.75**

**No. 49K3057¼** 14¼ inches long, 8 inches high, 8 inches wide. Shipping weight, 6 pounds. Price.... **$1.50**

## Doll Combination Parlor and Furniture Sets.

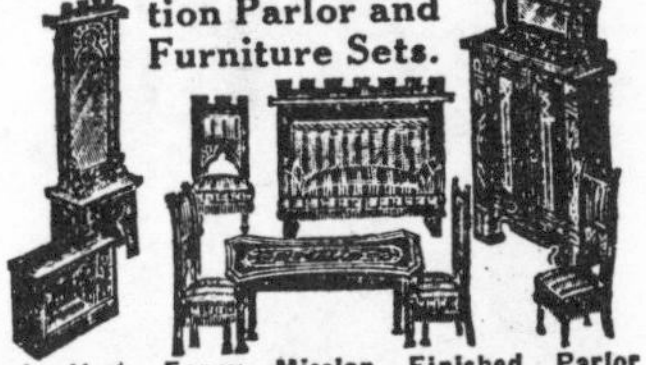

**A Very Fancy Mission Finished Parlor and Furniture Set.** Has silk striped heavy padded upholstering with fancy braided edge and fringe. A set we know will please you. Packed in lace trimmed box. Size, 12x18 inches. Shipping weight, 3 pounds.
**No. 49K766** Price.......... **95c**

**Doll Parlor and Furniture Set, similar to the above, but only containing eight pieces.** Packed in lace trimmed box. Size, 9½x15 inches. Shipping weight, 2 pounds.
**No. 49K767** Price.......... **43c**

## This Fine Brass Bed for $1.65.

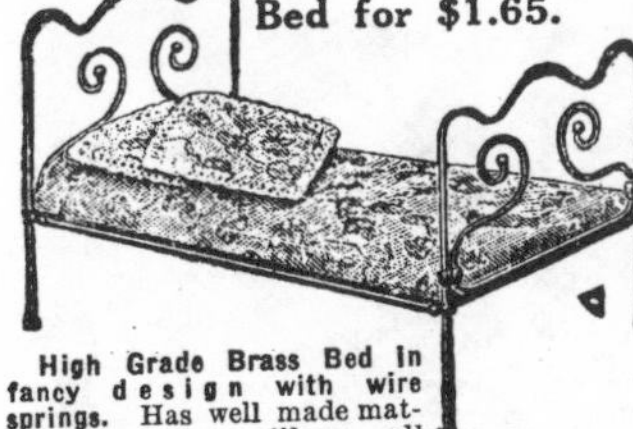

**High Grade Brass Bed in fancy design with wire springs.** Has well made mattress and two pillows, all covered with good grade fancy flowered design silkoline. Pillows are lace trimmed. An exceptionally well made and handsome bed. Regular $2.00 value. Size, 24x13¼x13½ inches. Shipping weight, 5½ pounds.
**No. 49K798** Price.......... **$1.65**

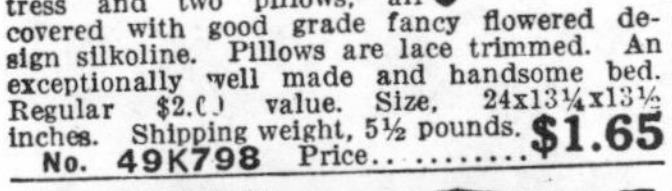

## CHILD'S TOY DOLL HAMMOCK.

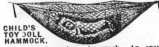

**Every doll needs a hammock.** An exceptionally nice hand made metal braced doll hammock. Length over all, about 36 inches; width, 11 inches; with metal rings. Just the thing to rock dolly to sleep and a little toy with which any child can spend hours of amusement. Shipping weight, 10 ounces.
**No. 49K737** Price.............. **23c**

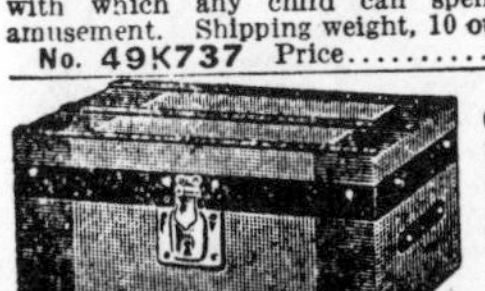

**Canvas Covered and Metal Trimmed Trunk.** Has three slats on top, leather handles and lock and key. Inside is paper lined and has removable tray. An exceptional bargain at the price. Size, 9¾x6x4¾ inches. Shipping weight, 2½ pounds.
**No. 49K732** Price.............. **21c**

# LAUNDRY SETS AT 95, 47, 39 AND 10 CENTS.

## Dolly's Wash Set, 95 Cents.

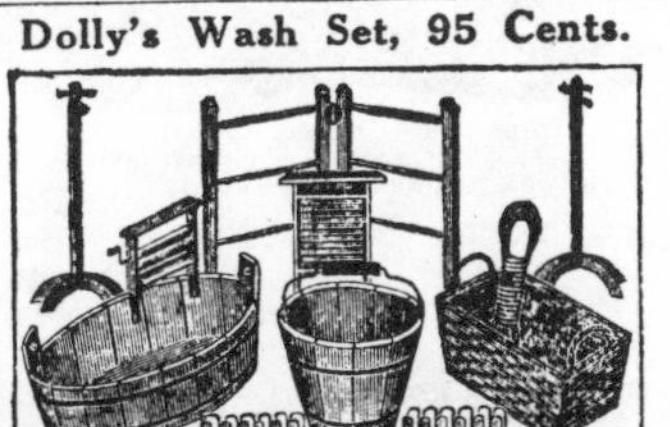

**A great seller.** Complete wash set, as per illustration. High class in every respect and a fine present for any girl. Packed in wood box. Shipping weight, 5 pounds.
**No. 49K748** Price.............. **95c**

## Big 10-Cent Value Wash Set.

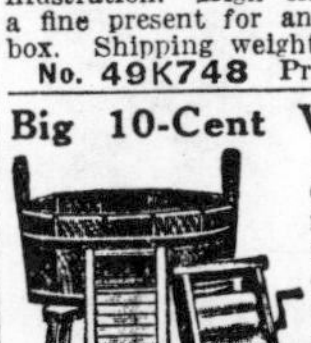

**Consists of tub, wringer, washboard,** all nicely made. Size of tub, 6x4 inches. No doll's outfit complete without this set. Great value. Shipping weight, 14 ounces.
**No. 49K714** Price.......... **10c**

## Rotary Washing Machine, 47c.

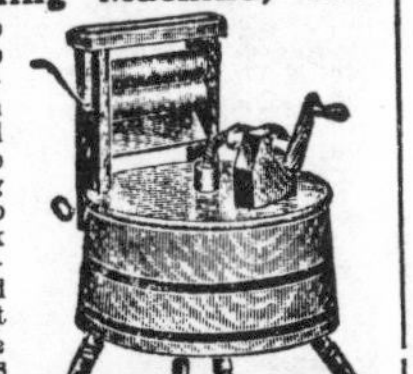

**Real Miniature Washing Machine and Wringer.** Really works. When handle is turned agitator inside tub revolves, cleansing the clothes. Tub painted red. Black iron hoops. Removable turned wooden legs. Height over all, 15½ inches; 7½ inches wide. A practical toy. Shipping weight, 3 pounds.
**No. 49K781** Price... **47c**

## Great Value Wash Set, 39 Cents.

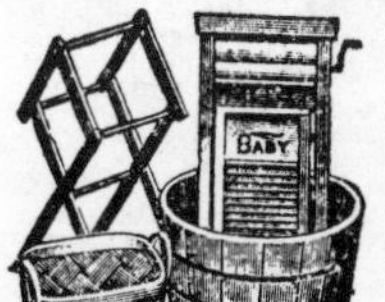

**Dolly's Wash Set,** consisting of 9-inch washtub, 8-inch washboard, 7-inch wringer, 6¼-inch basket, 10-inch rack, all well made. No dolly's outfit complete without a wash set. Regular 50-cent value. Shpg. wt., 2½ lbs.
**No. 49K794** Price.... **39c**

## Five-Piece Bedroom Set, $1.45.

**Consists of spring mattress,** wooden frame bed, 18x10½x12 inches; round table, 7½x7½x7½ inches; chair, 5½x5x13½ inches; rocker, 5½x5x13½ inches, and clothes rack, 11x11x24 inches. All mahogany finished and beautifully decorated. Shipping weight, 15 pounds.

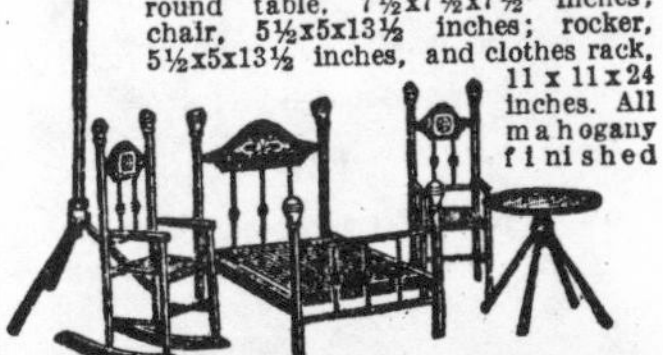

**No. 49K3018¼** Price........ **$1.45**

## Dolly Clothes Line Outfit, 8c.

**This outfit consists of about 5 yards of small best cotton rope, two galvanized pulleys, and one-half dozen clothes pins.** Endless amusement for children. Shipping weight, 5 oz.
**No. 49K773** Price.............. **8c**

# FINEST QUALITY PET ANIMAL TOYS

**Plush Covered Horses.**

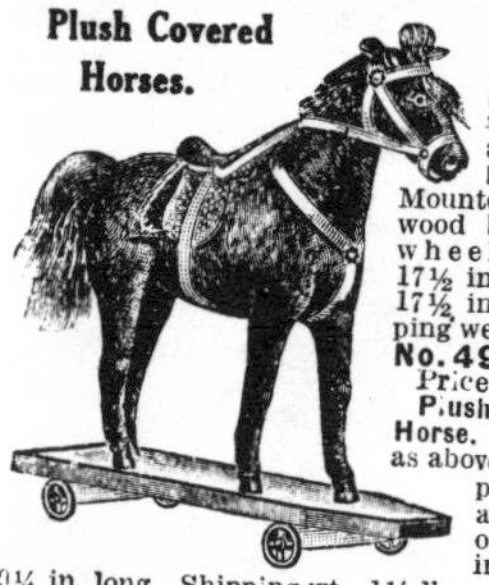

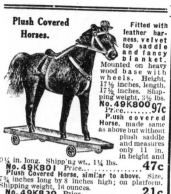

Fitted with leather harness, velvet top saddle and fancy blanket. Mounted on heavy wood base with wheels. Height, 17½ inches, length, 17½ inches. Shipping weight, 3½ lbs.
**No. 49K800** Price........**97c**

Plush covered Horse, made same as above but without plush saddle and measures only 11 in. in height and 9¼ in. long. Shipping wt., 1¼ lbs.
**No. 49K801** Price........**47c**

Plush Covered Horse, similar to above. Size, 7¾ inches long by 8 inches high; on platform. Shipping weight, 16 ounces.
**No. 49K820** Price........**21c**

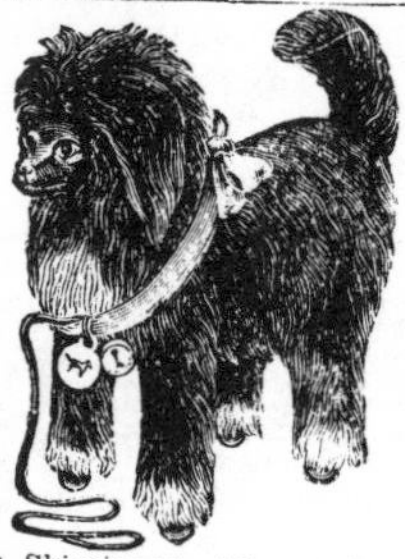

These are the famous Casper soft black fur dogs of Europe. They are the finest manufactured, well made in every detail, beautiful black, heavy and soft fur. Extra strong wood frame. They have metal rollers on feet and a pull string. Can be used either in the house or on sidewalk.

**OUR BEST DOG.** 10½ inches long by 11½ in. high, metal feet on rollers. Shipping wt., 3 lbs.
**No. 49K802** Price........**89c**

**THIS DOG FOR ONLY 39 CENTS.** 10 inches high, 9½ inches long, without metal feet, with rollers. Shipping wt., 2½ lbs.
**No. 49K803** Price........**39c**

**ONLY 21 CENTS FOR THIS DOG.** 8 inches high, 7 inches long, without metal feet, with rollers. Shipping weight, 2 pounds.
**No. 49K804** Price........**21c**

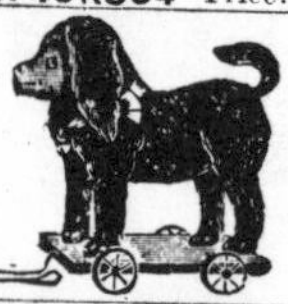

**THIS FUR DOG FOR 10 CENTS.** This fine black fur dog is 6½ inches high, 6 inches long, on wooden platform, with wheels. Shipping weight, 1½ pounds.
**No. 49K805** Price........**10c**

**Leather Covered Cow, 95 Cents.**

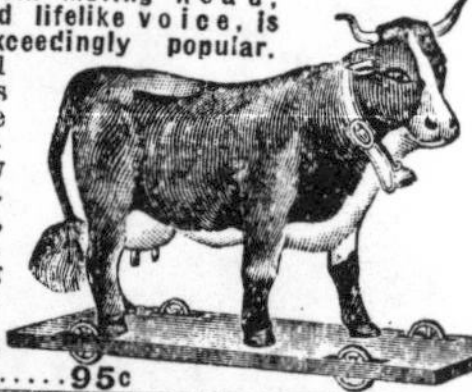

A cow with moving head, horns, and lifelike voice, is always exceedingly popular. Natural color glass eyes; fine reproduction. Cow on platform. Size, 11¾x9 in. Shipping wt., 2 lbs.
**No. 49K823** Price........**95c**

**Fur Covered Lion, 95 Cents.**

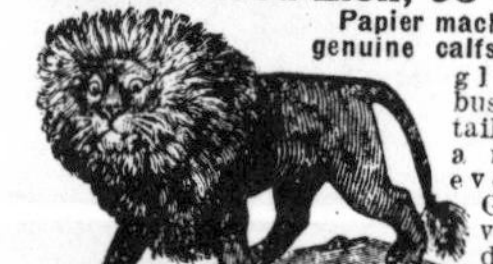

Papier mache lion in genuine calfskin cover, glass eyes, bushy mane and tail, resembling a real lion in every respect. Growling voice produced by pulling metal ring. Attached to wooden base on wheels. Length, 11½ inches. Shipping wt., 1½ lbs.
**No. 49K813** Price........**95c**

**Plush Dog, 44 Cents.**

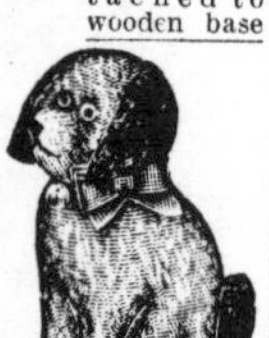

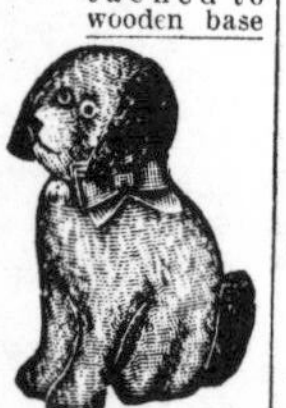

Well proportioned and lifelike. Ribbon collar. White plush with black ears and tail. Height, 9½ inches. Voice attachment. Shipping weight, 8 ounces.
**No. 49K832** Price........**44c**

**Fine White Plush Cat, 42 Cents.**

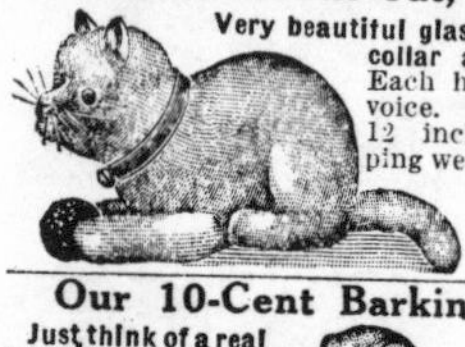

Very beautiful glass eyes, ribbon collar and brass bell. Each has natural voice. Entire length, 12 inches. Shipping weight, 8 ounces.
**No. 49K831** Price, **42c**

**Our 10-Cent Barking Dog.**

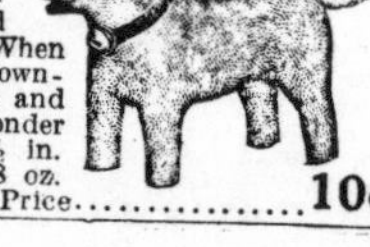

Just think of a real barking dog for 10 cents. Cloth covered, natural decorated, glass eyes and worth 25 cents. When head is pressed downward mouth opens and dog barks. A wonder seller. Size, 5x5¼ in. Shipping weight, 8 oz.
**No. 49K822** Price........**10c**

**FINEST QUALITY PLUSH TEDDY BEARS.**

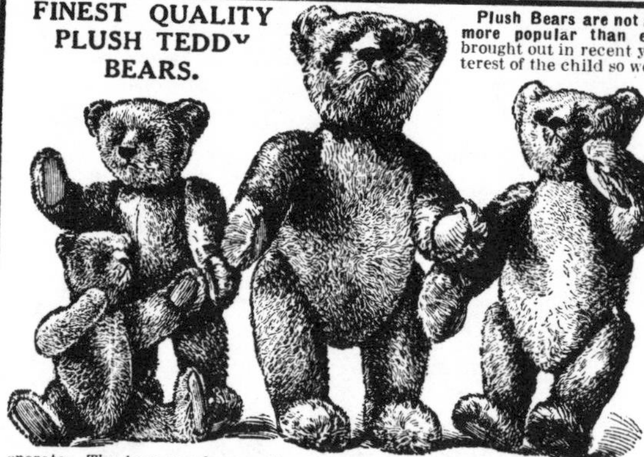

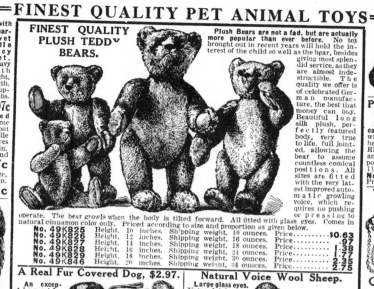

Plush Bears are not a fad, but are actually more popular than ever before. No toy brought out in recent years will hold the interest of the child so well as the bear, besides giving most splendid service, as they are almost indestructible. The quality we offer is of celebrated German manufacture, the best that money can buy. Beautiful long silk plush, perfectly featured body, very true to life, full jointed, allowing the bear to assume countless comical positions. All sizes are fitted with the very latest improved automatic growling voice, which requires no pushing or pressing to operate. The bear growls when the body is tilted forward. All fitted with glass eyes. Comes in natural cinnamon color only. Priced according to size and proportion as given below.

| | | | |
|---|---|---|---|
| No. 49K825 | Height, 10 inches. | Shipping weight, 10 ounces. | Price........$0.63 |
| No. 49K826 | Height, 12 inches. | Shipping weight, 16 ounces. | Price........ .97 |
| No. 49K827 | Height, 14 inches. | Shipping weight, 18 ounces. | Price........1.38 |
| No. 49K828 | Height, 16 inches. | Shipping weight, 24 ounces. | Price........1.77 |
| No. 49K829 | Height, 18 inches. | Shipping weight, 30 ounces. | Price........2.35 |
| No. 49K846 | Height, 20 inches. | Shipping weight, 34 ounces. | Price........2.75 |

**A Real Fur Covered Dog, $2.97.**

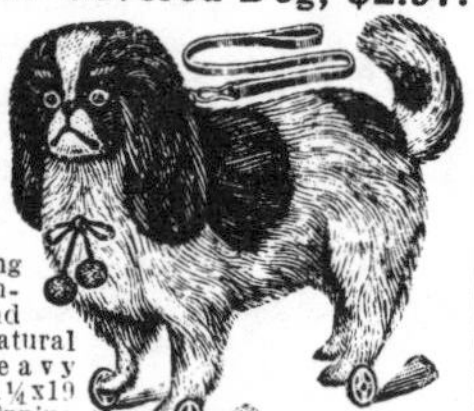

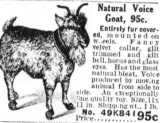

An exceptionally pretty dog, covered with real dogskin. A St. Charles Spaniel with white fur and black spots. Glass eyes, long silky ears, leather collar and drawstrap, natural face, long heavy tail. Size, 11¼x10 inches. Shipping weight, 3 pounds.
**No. 49K824** Price........**$2.97**

**Natural Voice Wool Sheep.**

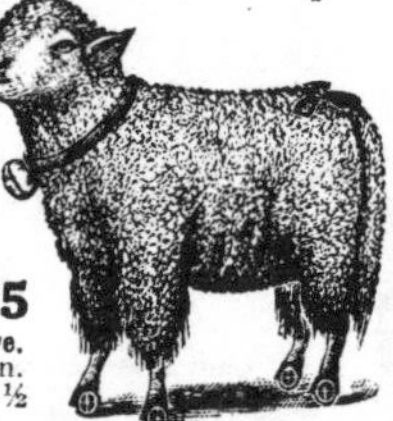

Large glass eyes. Natural bleat. Mounted on metal wheels. Has wide ribbon around neck with metal bell. Size, 13½x15 inches. Shipping weight, 2½ pounds.
**No. 49K842** Price........**$1.85**

Similar to above. Size, 10½x11½ in. Shipping weight, 1½ pounds.
**No. 49K850** Price........**$1.00**

**Natural Voice Goat, 95c.**

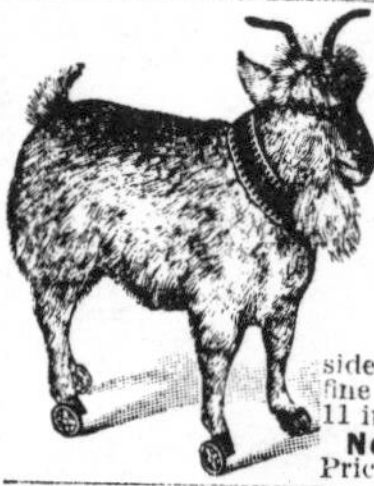

Entirely fur covered, mounted on wheels. Fancy velvet collar, gilt trimmed and gilt bell, horns and glass eyes. Has the most natural bleat. Voice produced by moving animal from side to side. An exceptionally fine quality toy. Size, 11x11 in. Shipping wt., 1 lb.
**No. 49K841** Price........**95c**

**Our German Bull Dog, 98 Cents.**

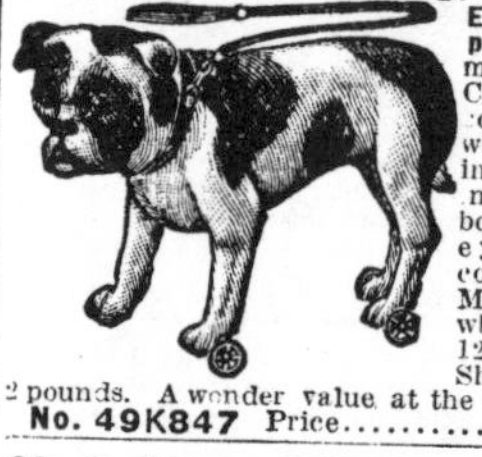

Extra good expression, papier mache body. Canton flannel covered. White with dark markings, even showing muscles in body. Glass eyes, leather collar and strap. Mounted on wheels. Size, 12x8 inches. Shipping wt., 2 pounds. A wonder value at the price.
**No. 49K847** Price........**98c**

**Fox Terrier, 97c.**

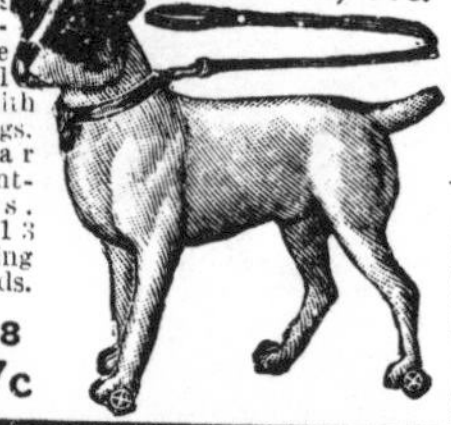

If you could only see this beautiful lifelike dog. White Canton flannel covered body with dark markings. Leather collar and strap. Mounted on wheels. Size, 10¼x13 inches. Shipping weight, 2 pounds.
**No. 49K848** Price........**97c**

**Cloth Covered Horse, 89 Cents.**

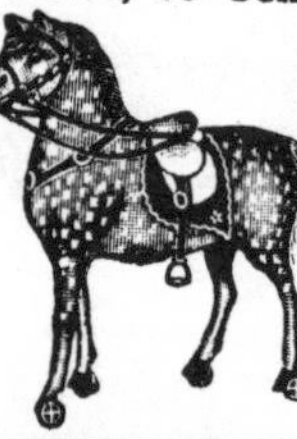

Fine expression; cloth covered body with markings; white kid saddle, leather bridle and reins, glass eyes, fancy blanket, hair tail. Horse mounted on rollers. Size, 12x12 inches. Shipping weight, 2 pounds.
**No. 49K849** Price........**89c**

**Red Rubber Animals.**

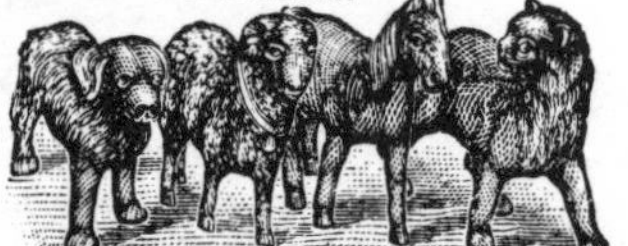

Made entirely of red rubber. Very practical and harmless toys for small children. Shipping weight, each, 5 ounces.

| | | | |
|---|---|---|---|
| No. 49K839 | Cat. | Length, 5 in. | Price, 29c |
| No. 49K821 | Dog. | Length, 5 in. | Price, 29c |
| No. 49K838 | Horse. | 5½ inches. | Price, 29c |
| No. 49K837 | Sheep. | 4¾ inches. | Price, 29c |

**White Poodle Dogs.**

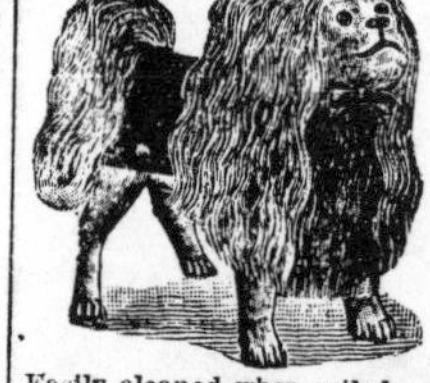

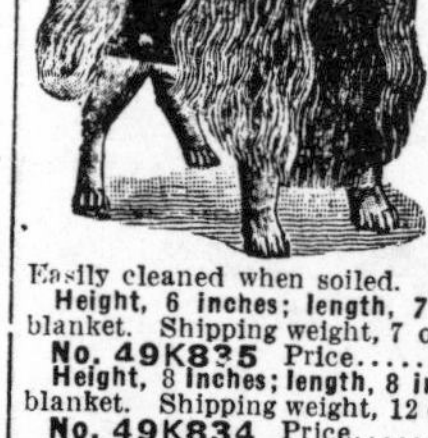

Exceptionally handsome, finely made, practical. Excellent stuffed flannel covered hand sewed very natural shape body and limbs, lifelike face, with brown glass eyes, pretty ribbon around the neck. Long silk angora hair on head, shoulders and tail. Easily cleaned when soiled.

Height, 6 inches; length, 7 inches. Without blanket. Shipping weight, 7 ounces.
**No. 49K835** Price........**21c**

Height, 8 inches; length, 8 inches. Made with blanket. Shipping weight, 12 ounces.
**No. 49K834** Price........**42c**

Height, 10 inches; length, 12½ inches. Made with blanket. Shipping wt., 1½ lbs.
**No. 49K833** Price........**95c**

**Real Wool Sheep.**

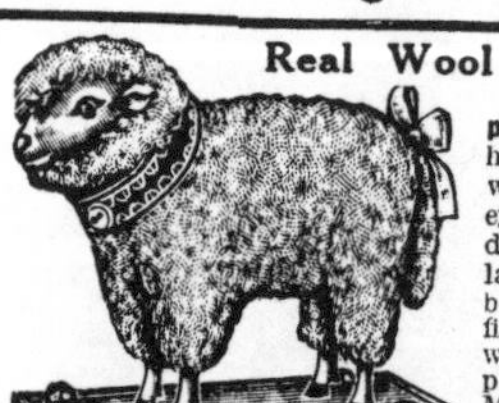

Well proportioned, heavy white wool, glass eyes, pretty decorated collar, ribbon on back, and feet firmly set on wooden wheel platform. Moving the head causes the sheep to bleat. Three sizes as follows:

**No. 49K814** Height, 11 inches; length, 13 inches. Shipping weight, 3½ pounds. Price........**89c**
**No. 49K815** Height, 8½ inches; length, 8½ inches. Shipping wt., 1½ lbs. Price........**39c**
**No. 49K816** Height, 6½ inches; length, 6¼ inches. Shipping wt., 1 lb. Price........**21c**

**The Bear Family, Only 19c.**

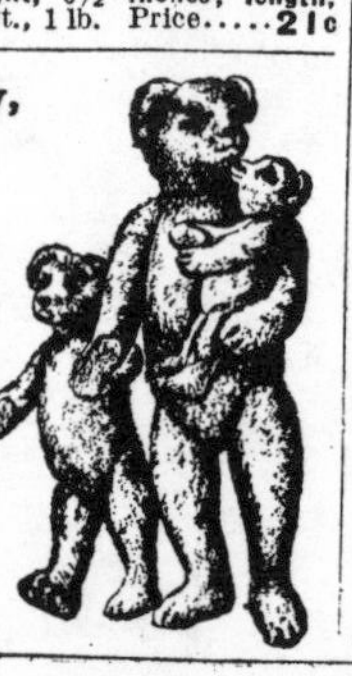

This Bear Family is one of the most popular toys ever produced. Consists of one bear, 7¾ inches high and two bears 4½ inches high. Bears are made of prepared cotton on strong wire; arms and legs are movable. Each set in neat box. Shipping weight, 6 ounces.
**No. 49K830** Price........**19c**

**Velvet Bunny, 33 Cents.**

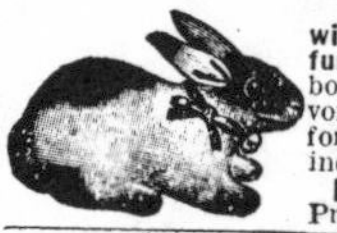

Made of soft white velvet with brown trimmings and fur tail. Has blue baby ribbon collar, brass bell and voice attachment. A fine toy for the baby. Length, 9½ inches. Shipping wt., 8 oz.
**No. 49K808** Price........**33c**

**Pussy Pippin, 98 Cents.**

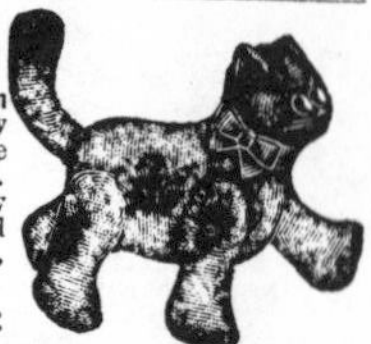

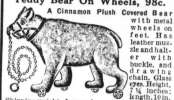

Something new in cats. Fine plush body with unbreakable head and moving legs. Ribbon on neck. New and very pretty and popular. Shipping wt., 1½ pounds.
**No. 49K844** Price........**98c**

**Teddy Bear On Wheels, 98c.**

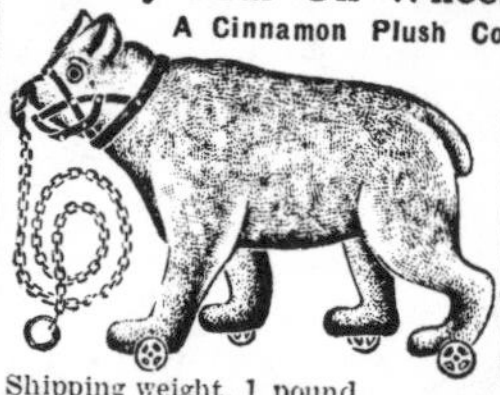

A Cinnamon Plush Covered Bear with metal wheels on feet. Has leather muzzle and halter with buckle, and drawing chain. Glass eyes. Height, 7¼ inches; length, 10 in. Shipping weight, 1 pound.
**No. 49K817** Price........**98c**

**White Poodle.**

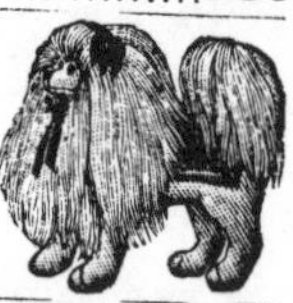

Large size, fine plush covered, glass eyes, well formed body. Has fancy blanket. An extra grade animal. Size, 15x13½ inches. Shipping weight, 2½ pounds.
**No. 49K836** Price **$1.95**

**Silk Mohair Dogs With Voices, 98c.**

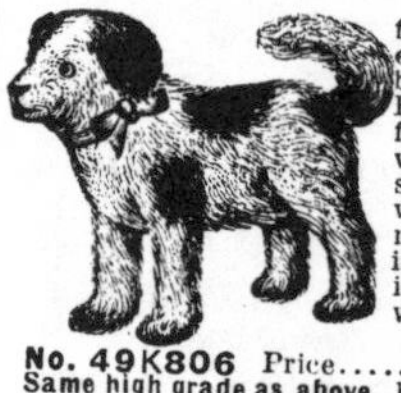

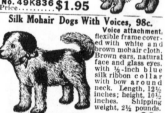

Voice attachment, flexible frame covered with white and brown mohair cloth. Brown ears, natural face and glass eyes, with ½-inch blue silk ribbon collar with bow around neck. Length, 12½ inches; height, 10½ inches. Shipping weight, 2½ pounds.
**No. 49K806** Price........**98c**

Same high grade as above, but of smaller size. Size, 10 inches long by 8½ inches high. Carefully packed in box. Shipping wt., 1½ lbs.
**No. 49K807** Price........**79c**

**Fur Cat With "Meow," 57 Cents.**

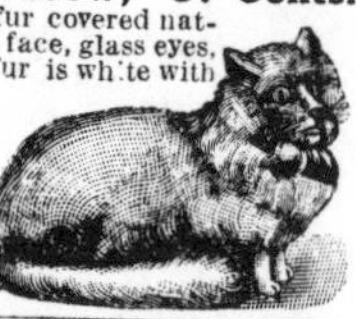

A very pretty kitty, fur covered natural appearance, good face, glass eyes, and well made. The fur is white with Maltese spots. Pressing hips causes it to open its mouth and "meow." Tail is 5 inches in length. Size, 12x5½ inches. Shipping wt., 11 oz.
**No. 49K818** Price **57c**

**My Bully Bull Doggy, 98 Cents.**

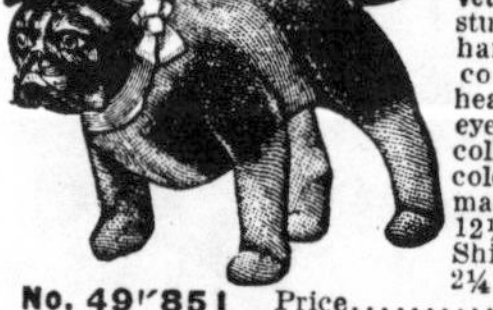

Made of velvet body cork stuffed, with hard to break composition head. Glass eyes, ribbon collar. Brown color with black markings. Size, 12½x7¾ in. Shipping wt., 2¼ lbs.
**No. 49K851** Price........**98c**

**Cat and Dog Cloth Animals, 15c.**

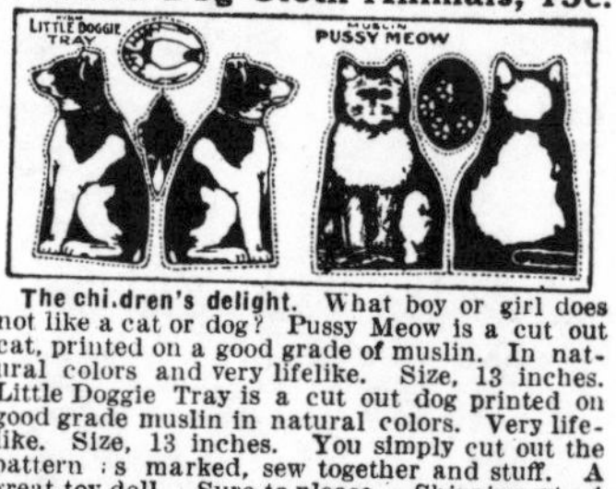


The children's delight. What boy or girl does not like a cat or dog? Pussy Meow is a cut out cat, printed on a good grade of muslin. In natural colors and very lifelike. Size, 13 inches. Little Doggie Tray is a cut out dog printed on good grade muslin in natural colors. Very lifelike. Size, 13 inches. You simply cut out the pattern as marked, sew together and stuff. A great toy doll. Sure to please. Shipping wt., 4 oz. packed one dog and one cat to envelope.
**No. 49K845** Price, per envelope........**15c**

**Six Cut Out Animals, 21 Cents.**

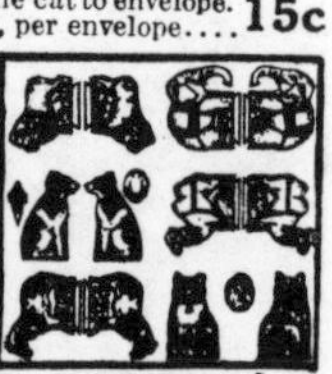

Printed on very heavy muslin, the piece measuring nearly 3 feet square. Animals average in height from 7 to over 9 inches. All printed in natural colors, very lifelike, with plain dotted lines for cutting, and simple complete directions. Shipping wt., 5 oz.
**No. 49K812** Price for the big sheet with 6 animals........**21c**

# RELIABLE MECHANICAL TOYS

### Ideal Patent Machine Rifle, 59c.

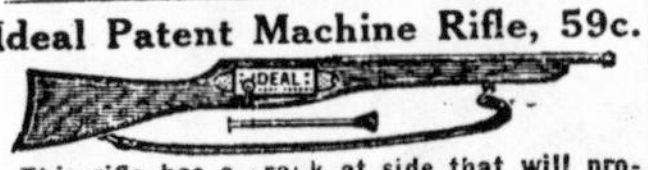

This rifle has a crank at side that will produce the effect of firing 500 shots per minute. The boys can have a sham battle, with real noise, but with absolutely no danger. This rifle also shoots vacuum darts. Leather band for carrying the gun across the shoulder. Length, 25 inches. Shipping wt., 32 oz.
No. 49K430 Price........................ 59c

### Ideal Machine Fire Gun, 37c.

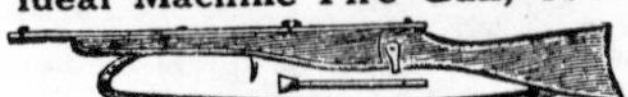

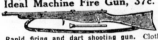

Rapid firing and dart shooting gun. Cloth shoulder strap and nicely finished gun. Beautifully colored target on cover of box. Length, 22 inches. Shipping wt., 24 ounces.
No. 49K431 Price........................ 37c

### Ideal Shooting Gallery, 97c.

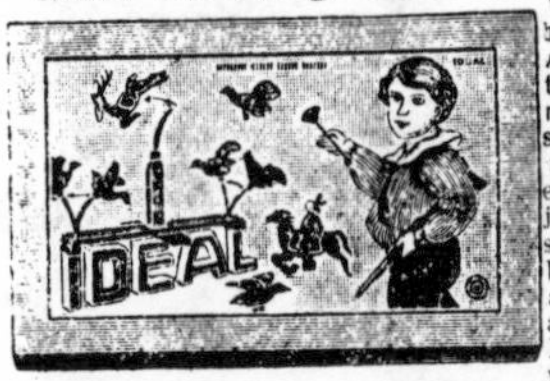

Wooden base, with three movable springs, and eight objects, such as birds, animals and an Indian, which move back and forth. 18-inch metal barrel gun, wood breech fitted with strong metal spring and trigger. Shoots rubber tipped arrows. Size of box, 11x19 inches. Shipping weight, 3 pounds.
No. 49K424 Price........................ 97c

### Ideal Gun and Pistol Set, 89c.

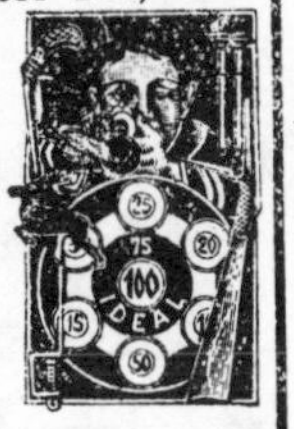

Comprises 18-inch metal barrel gun and 8-inch metal barred pistol with two rubber tipped arrows. Also large, beautifully colored decorated target. Size 13x20 inches. Has screw table attachment with flexible spring for outdoor shooting, with two figures, making a complete outfit, and for the price is an exceptionally fine toy. Packed in box. Shipping weight, 2½ pounds.
No. 49K425 Price. 89c

### Ideal Safety Target Pistol, 33c.

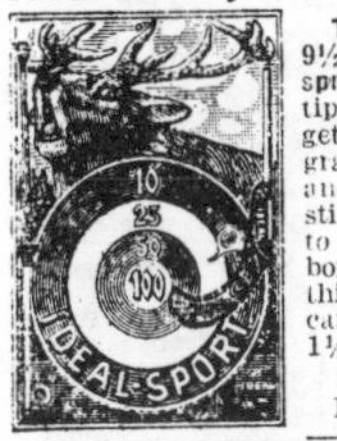

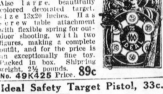

This set consists of 9½-inch good grade spring pistol, two rubber tipped suction darts, target 11¼x9¾ inches lithographed in high colors and box of colored paper stickers which are used to mark the shots. Every boy will want to own this set. Complete in carton. Shipping weight, 1½ pounds.
No. 49K426 Price, complete... 33c

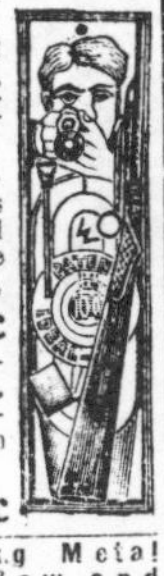

Smaller size than above, less expensive gun, one rubber tipped arrow and target 12½x7¾ inches. Complete on card. Shipping weight, 1 pound.
No. 49K427 Price...... 16c

### Ideal Safety Gun Sets.

Same principle as No. 49K426. Consists of good spring gun 23½ inches in length, rubber tipped dart and target, 5½x23½ inches. Complete in carton. Shipping weight, 1¾ pounds.
No. 49K428 Price....... 35c

Smaller size than above, 18½-inch length, less expensive gun, one rubber tipped arrow and target, 4¾x18¾ inches. Complete on card. Shipping wt., 1 lb.
No. 49K429 Price...... 16c

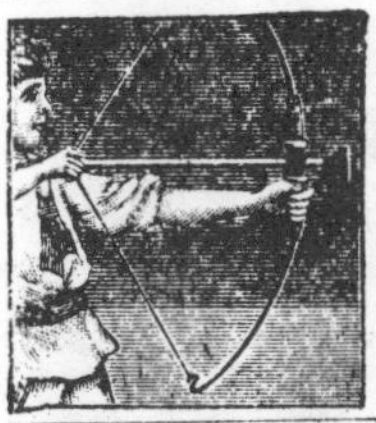

Folding Metal Steel Bow and long soft suction Rubber Tipped Arrow. With beautifully colored target on outside of cover. Size of bow, 20 inches. Size of box, 3¼x14 inches. Shipping weight, 1½ pounds. Regular price, 25 cents.
No. 49K432 Price...... 15c

### Our Special Pistol and Target, 9c.

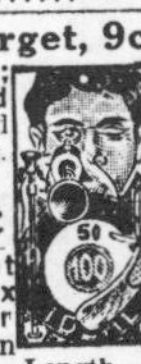

Painted target, 8½x4½ inches; 8¼-inch metal barrel pistol and rubber tipped wooden arrow. Good spring. A fine set for this low price. Shipping weight, 10 ounces.
No. 49K472 Price..... 9c

A set of six wooden arrows, with ¾-inch rubber suction tips. For use with above sets. Length, 6 inches. Shipping weight, 5 ounces.
No. 49K1195 Price for 6 arrows in box........ 19c

## HIGH GRADE POPGUNS FOR BOYS.

### Three Very Popular Sizes.

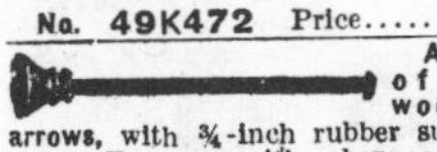

### The "Three-in-One," 59 Cents.

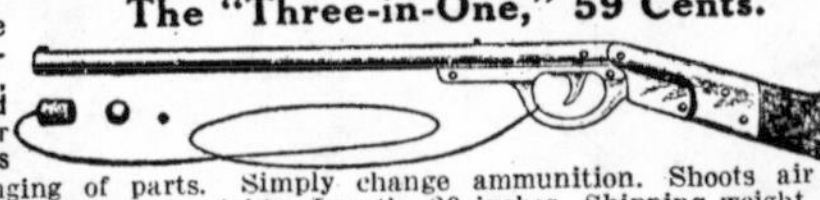

One of the finest combination air rifles, popguns and small rubber ball shooters made. No changing of parts. Simply change ammunition. Shoots air gun shot with accuracy. Neat sights. Length, 29 inches. Shipping weight, 3 pounds.
No. 49K474 Price........................ 59c

### Long Distance Popgun, 33 Cents.

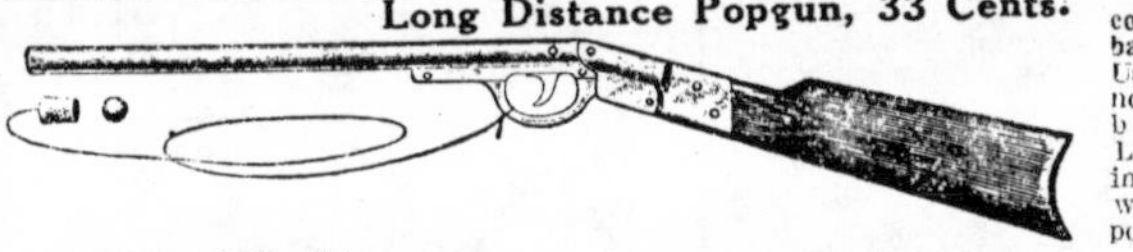

Shoots large cork and rubber ball. No danger. Use cork for noise and rubber ball for sport. Length, 21 inches. Shipping weight, 1½ pounds.
No. 49K422 Price........................ 33c

### Lever Action Popgun, 21c.

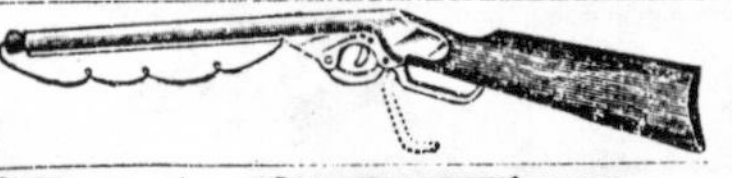

Has lever action like illustration. Length, 16½ inches. Shoots cork only. Loud report. Shipping weight, 10 ounces.
No. 49K423 Price............ 21c

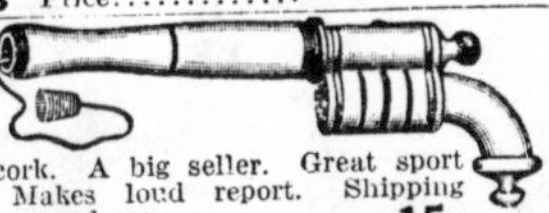

A fancy painted and decorated red, white and blue pistol popgun, 15 inches long, with good cork. A big seller. Great sport for small boy. Makes loud report. Shipping weight, packed, 1 pound.
No. 49K446 Price............ 15c

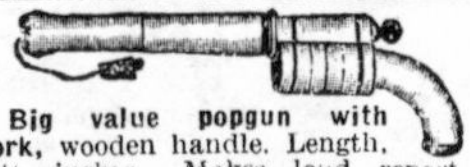

Big value popgun with cork, wooden handle. Length, 10½ inches. Makes loud report. Shipping weight, 12 ounces.
No. 49K447 Price...... 10c

## LEHMANN'S RELIABLE MECHANICAL TOYS.

### The Balking Mule, 35 Cents.

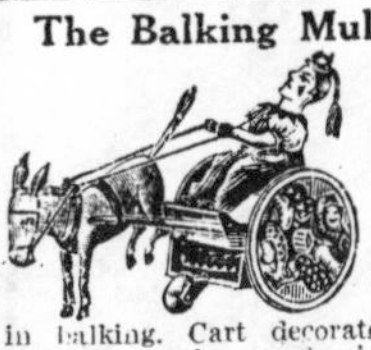

A really comical mechanical action toy. Clown in funny costume with movable head and jaw sits upon a two-wheeled cart and endeavors to drive the stubborn mule, who persists in balking. Cart decorated in comic colors. Wound up by mechanical spring. Length, 8 inches. Shipping weight, 10 ounces.
No. 49K413 Price........... 35c

### Walking Boy With Cart.

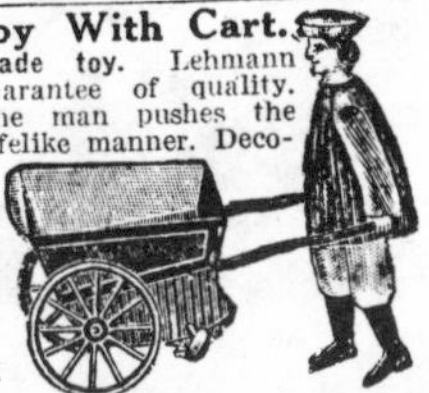

Very well made toy. Lehmann springs and guarantee of quality. When wound the man pushes the cart in a very lifelike manner. Decorated in fancy colors. Size, 5½ x 6¼ x 2¼ inches. Each in box. Shipping wt., 12 oz.
No. 49K452
Price.... 21c

### The Climbing Monkey.

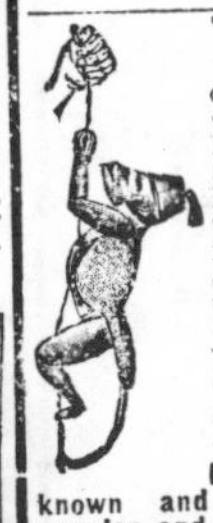

Distinctly a boy's toy. Mechanical monkey which moves at will up and down heavy cord. Movable arms and legs and can be made to stop in any position. Natural color finished. Cap with tassel, and felt covered coat. Full instructions with package. Size of monkey, 8 inches. Shipping weight, 10 ounces.
No. 49K414 Price.... 21c

### Naughty Boy, 21 Cents.

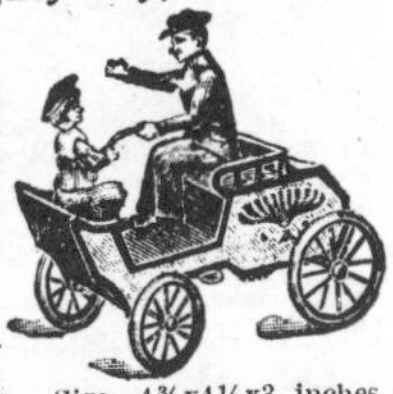

One of the best known and most popular and amusing toys. Boy and man in auto. Boy turns steering rod, causing auto to run in every possible direction. Lots of amusement. Strongly made and decorated in fancy colors. Size, 4¾x4½x3 inches. Shipping weight, 10 ounces.
No. 49K1270 Price........... 21c

### The Popular Autobus, 37c.

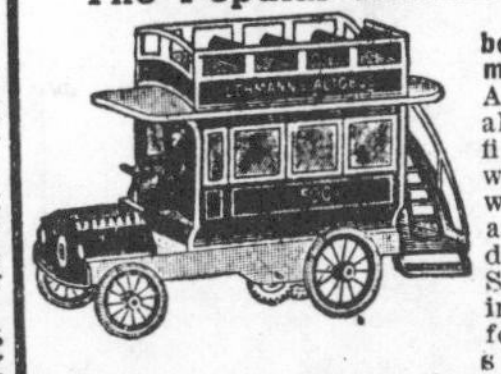

Made by the best German manufacturer. All sheet metal, attractively finished in white enamel, with yellow and brown decoration. Size, 8x3x5 inches. Platform at rear, seats inside and on top of bus reached by spiral stairway. Strong spring motor. Winds with key. Driver in front. Shipping weight, 13 ounces.
No. 49K416 Price........... 37c

### Mechanical Auto-Truck, 19c.

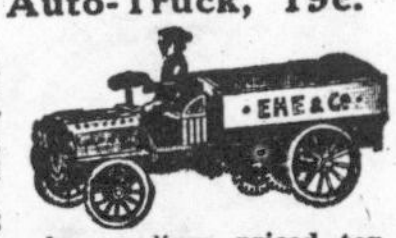

Well put together. Finished in red and white enamel with yellow trimmings. Winds up by spring and runs in a circle. Size, 7x3½x3 inches. A very popular medium priced toy. Shipping weight, 10 ounces.
No. 49K417 Price........... 19c

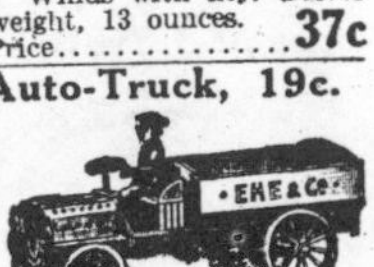

### One of Lehmann's Best Toys. Ziz-Zag, 39 Cents.

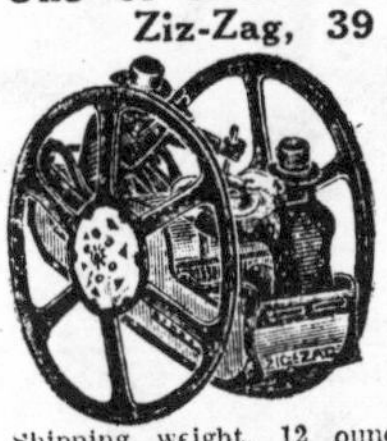

Two figures in box with steering device. When wound it runs in every possible direction, turning and twisting in a very comical manner. Lots of fun for the little ones. Nicely decorated in bright colors. Size, 5x4¾x3½ inches. 50-cent toy. Shipping weight, 12 ounces.
No. 49K1269 Price..... 39c

### Alabama Coon Jigger.

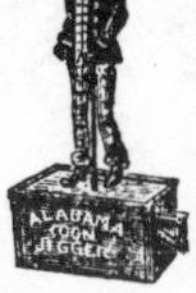

A realistic dancing Negro who goes through the movements of a Southern plantation dance. Very amusing and fascinating. Handsomely decorated in natural colors. A very lifelike and well made article. Stops or dances at will. One of the best selling toys. Height, 10½ inches. Shipping weight, 16 ounces.
No. 49K476 Price..... 39c

### Man on Motorcycle, 21c.

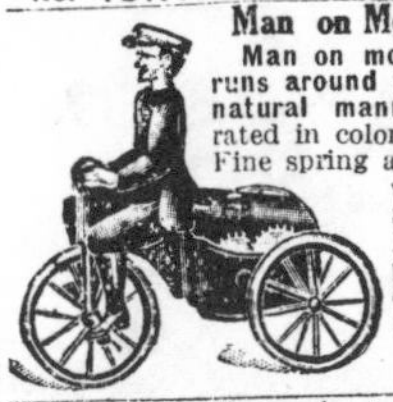

Man on motorcycle, which he runs around the room in a very natural manner. Nicely decorated in colors. Strongly made. Fine spring and mechanism. A very reliable toy. Size, 5x5 inches. Each in box. Shipping weight, 10 ounces.
No. 49K1273
Price..... 21c

### The Tut-Tut Automobile, 39c.

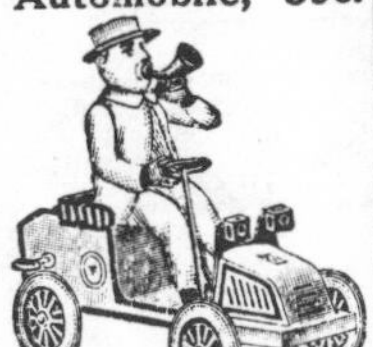

A most clever mechanical toy. Gives the familiar tut-tut when running along the floor. White enamel finish, red decorated, with imitation rubber tires. Size, 7x3½x6½ inches. Shipping wt., 10 oz.
No. 49K415
Price........ 39c

### Mechanical Battleship.

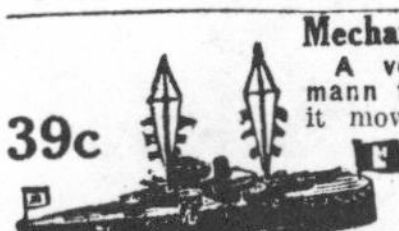

39c

A very popular Lehmann toy. When wound it moves over the floor. Good reproduction of a real battleship. Twelve movable guns in turrets, two boats, two masts, with decorated flags. Nicely painted in colors. Strong and durable. Lehmann guaranteed springs and workmanship. Size, 13½x6½ inches. Shipping wt., 16 oz.
No. 49K1272 Price........... 39c

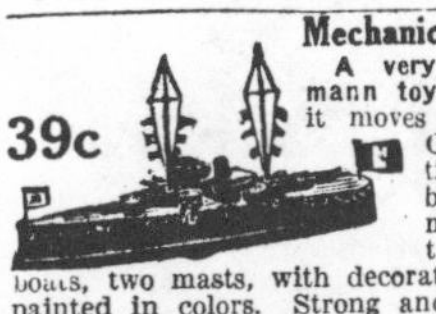

### Crawling Beetle, 19 Cents.

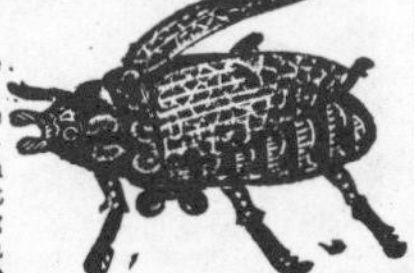

One of Lehmann's most popular toys. Mechanical beetle painted in natural colors. Fine spring and mechanism. When wound up it crawls, flapping its wings in a very realistic manner. Each in box. Size, 4¾x2¾ inches. Shipping weight, 8 ounces.
No. 49K1271 Price........... 19c

### Sioux Chief Bow and Arrow.

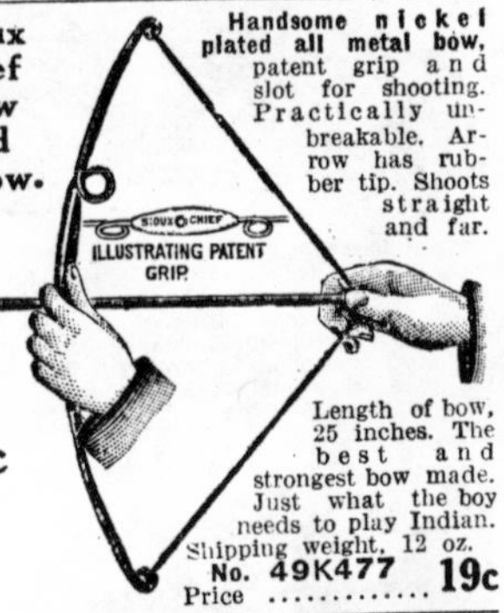


19c

Handsome nickel plated all metal bow, patent grip and slot for shooting. Practically unbreakable. Arrow has rubber tip. Shoots straight and far. Length of bow, 25 inches. The best and strongest bow made. Just what the boy needs to play Indian. Shipping weight, 12 oz.
No. 49K477
Price ........... 19c

### Moving Apple Man, 39c.

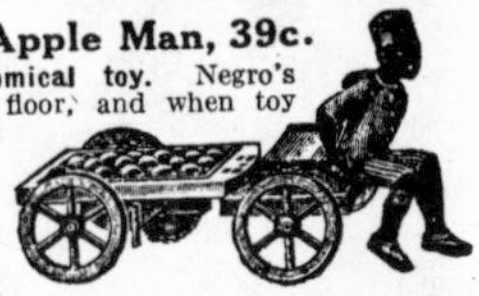

A very comical toy. Negro's feet rest on floor, and when toy is wound it runs backward in zigzag lines. Length, 7 inches. Shipping wt., 14 ounces.
No. 49K462 Price............... 39c

### Mechanical Dude, 39c.

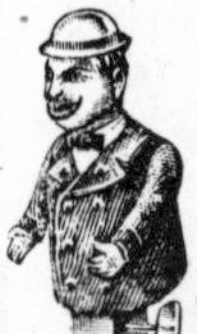

When wound up the man bows, moving his head and body. Very laughable. Height, 8½ inches. Shipping weight, 12 ounces.
No. 49K403 Price........... 39c

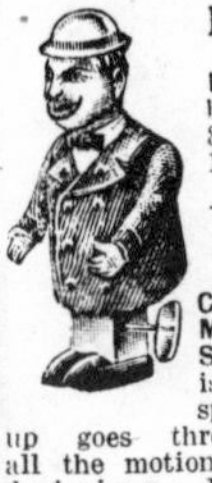

### Pig in Sulky, 37c.

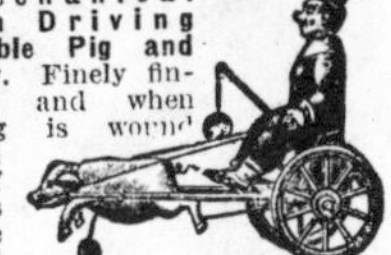

Mechanical Clown Driving Movable Pig and Sulky. Finely finished and when spring is wound up goes through all the motions of driving. Runs around in a circle in a most comical manner. Size, 7½x3x6 inches. Shipping weight, 6 ounces.
No. 49K404 Price........... 37c

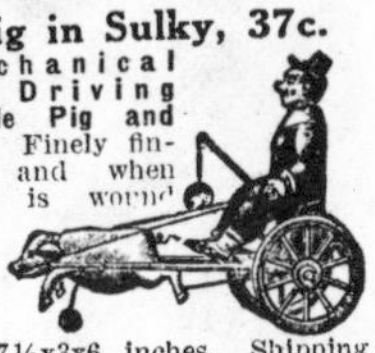

### The Fisherman, 39c

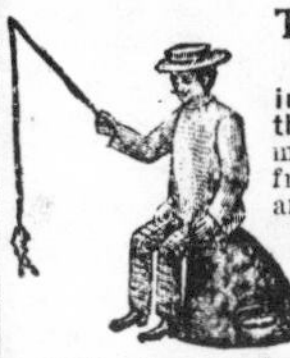

Imitates fisherman drawing fish through water and then "landing" it. Angler moves body line and head from side to side and up and down. Length, 8 inches. Shipping wt., 1 lb.
No. 49K461 Price 39c

### Messenger Boy, 39c.

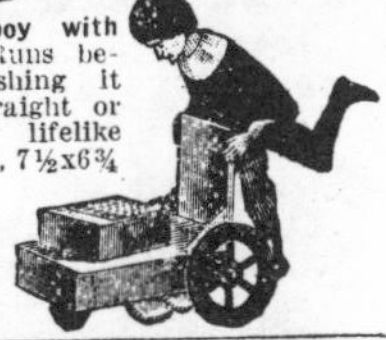

Cloth dressed boy with imitation hair. Runs behind cart, pushing it around. Runs straight or in circle. Very lifelike and comical. Size, 7½x6¾ inches. Shipping weight, 16 ounces.
No. 49K1265
Price.... 39c

### Squirrel in Cage, 47 Cents.

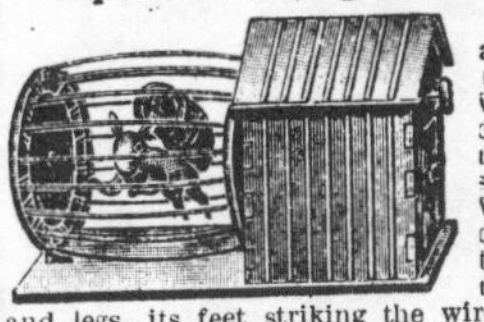

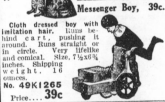

Runs for about ten minutes. Whirling wire cage, with mechanical squirrel. While the cage revolves the squirrel moves body and legs, its feet striking the wires in a very natural manner. Total length, 8½ inches; width, 3⅞ inches. Shipping weight, packed, 1½ pounds.
No. 49K458 Price.. 47c

### The Jolly Dancers, 47c

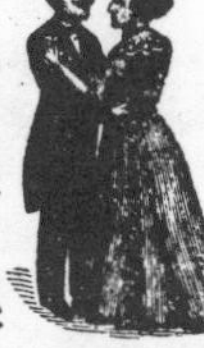

Full Cloth Dressed Figures.

One of the most amusing toys ever invented. When wound, the figures waltz over the floor, turning and waltzing in the most lifelike manner. Length about 7 inches. Shipping wt., 14 oz.
No. 49K460 Price 47c

### Monkey on the Bar, 39c

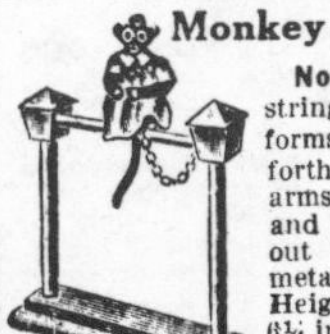

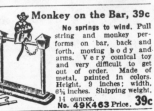

No springs to wind. Pull string and monkey performs on bar, back and forth, moving body and arms. Very comical toy and very difficult to get out of order. Made of metal, painted in colors. Height, 9 inches; width, 6¾ inches. Shipping weight, 14 ounces.
No. 49K463 Price. 39c

**Special at $1.79**

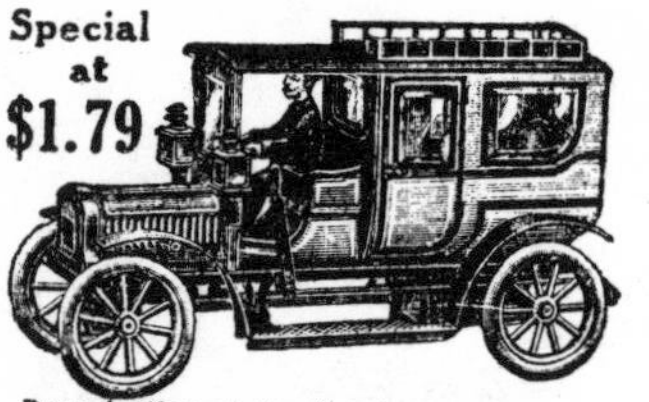

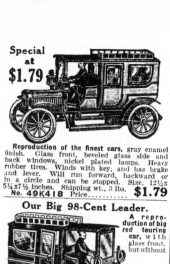

**Reproduction of the finest cars,** gray enamel finish. Glass front, beveled glass side and back windows, nickel plated lamps. Heavy rubber tires. Winds with key; and has brake and lever. Will run forward, backward or in a circle and can be stopped. Size, 12½x5¼x7½ inches. Shipping wt., 3 lbs.
No. 49K418 Price.......... **$1.79**

### Our Big 98-Cent Leader.

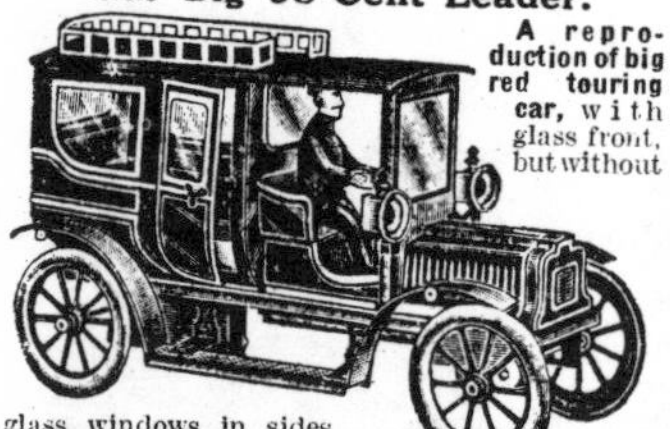

**A reproduction of big red touring car,** with glass front, but without glass windows in sides or ends. Tires of metal, painted to imitate rubber. Will run forward, backward or in a circle. Size, 12½x7¼ inches. Shipping weight, 2½ pounds.
No. 49K419 Price.......... **98c**

### Our Wonder 69-Cent Value.

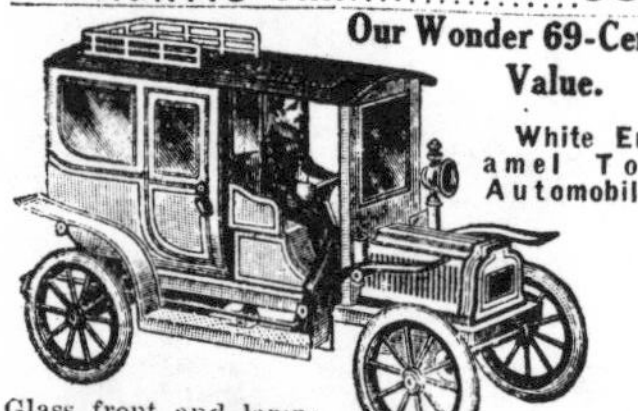

**White Enamel Toy Automobile.** Glass front and lamps. Winds by key, has brake and lever. Runs forward or backward. Rubber tires. Size, 8½x4x5½ inches. Shipping weight, 24 ounces.
No. 49K420 Price.......... **69c**

### Mechanical Trolley Car, 93c.

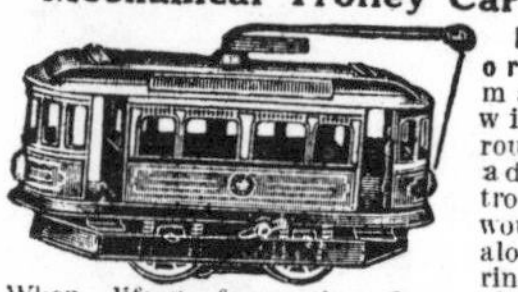

**Pretty colors,** motorman, glass windows, round ends, adjustable trolley. When wound runs along floor ringing bell. When lifted from the floor wheels stop. Will run on floor or carpet. Size, 10½x6 inches. Shipping weight, 32 ounces.
No. 49K926 Price.......... **93c**

### A Real Mechanical Steamboat.

No. 49K407 Price.......... **$1.37**

**A very handsome metal boat,** beautifully decorated. Runs in water. Good spring, real propeller. Size, 10½x7x2⅜ inches. Weight, 25 oz.

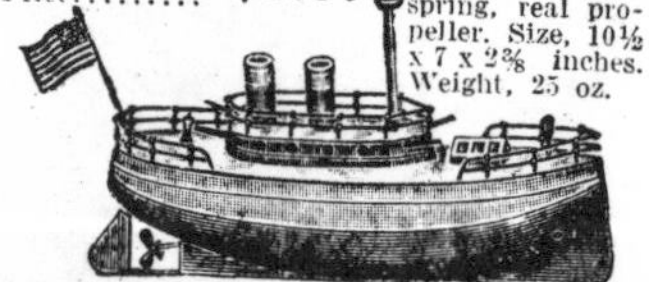

### This Fine Boat for 89c.

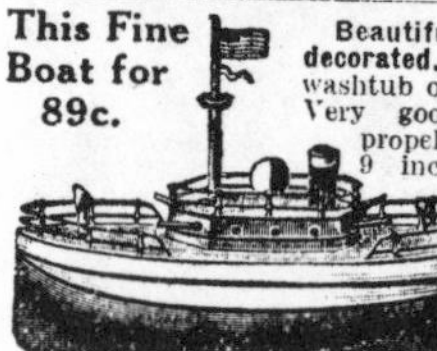

**Beautifully finished and decorated.** Can be used in washtub or body of water. Very good spring and propeller. Length, 9 inches. Shipping weight, 20 oz.
No. 49K401 Price, **89c**

### A Wonder Boat for Only 25c.

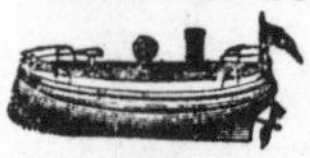

**Boat is very nicely enameled and gilt finished throughout.** Strong spring and propeller. Boat is nicely constructed. Length, 6 inches. Shipping weight, 15 ounces.
No. 49K402 Price.......... **25c**

### Flying Machine.

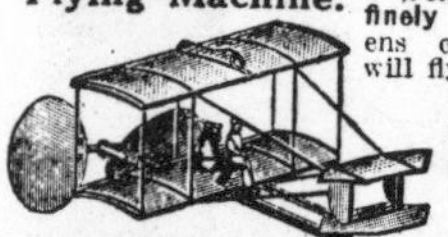

**Well made and finely finished.** Fastens on string and will fly around room. Size, 6x10 in. Shipping wt., 10 ounces.
No. 49K408 Price... **37c**

### Flying Airship.

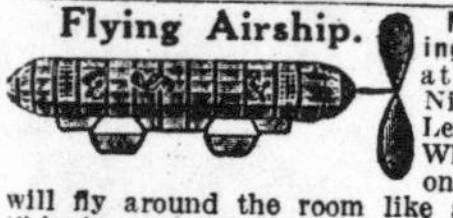

**Mechanical Flying Airship,** with attachments. Nicely finished. Length, 8 inches. When suspended on a string it will fly around the room like a real airship. Shipping weight, 8 ounces.
No. 49K451 Price.......... **15c**

## VERY GOOD TOY SEWING MACHINES.

**ALL THESE MACHINES ARE FURNISHED COMPLETE WITH NEEDLE AND THREAD.**

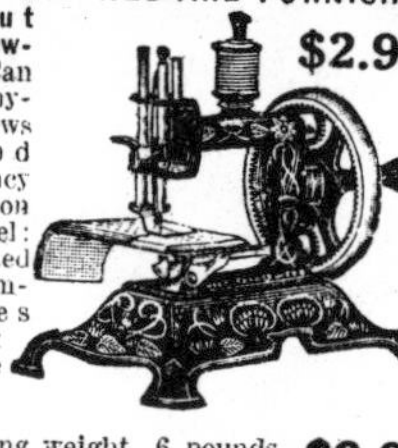

**$2.98**

**A small but practical Toy Sewing Machine.** Can be attached anywhere. Sews perfectly and smoothly. Fancy gilt decoration on black enamel: nickel plated wheel and trimmings. Makes four stitches at each turn of the driving wheel. Size, 8x5x7½ inches. Shipping weight, 6 pounds.
No. 49K437 Price.......... **$2.98**

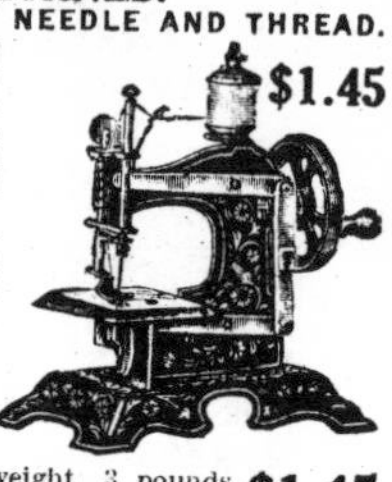

**$1.45**

**A perfectly working Toy Sewing Machine.** Simple in construction, no complicated parts. Worked easily by a child. Sews seam very rapid, regular, neat and tight. Beautifully finished, black enamel decorated with colored flowers and nickel trimming. Size, 7½x4x7 inches. Shipping weight, 3 pounds.
No. 49K438 Price.......... **$1.45**

**95c**

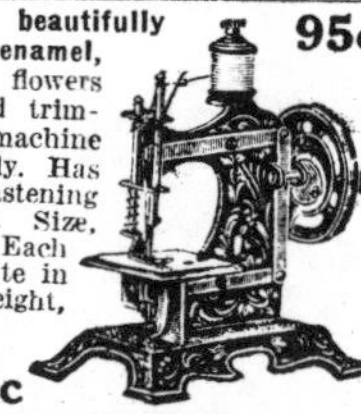

**Very practical, beautifully trimmed in black enamel,** decorated with flowers and nickel plated trimmings and a little machine that sews smoothly. Has attachment for fastening on table or chair. Size, 6x3¾x6½ inches. Each packed complete in box. Shipping weight, 2½ pounds.
No. 49K439 Price.......... **95c**

### Our Little Gem, 45c.

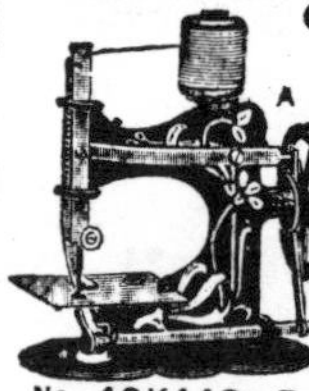

**A simply constructed machine,** very nicely finished in black enamel, gilt and nickel plated trimmings, attachment for fastening to table. Will sew cloth, chain stitch. Size, 4½x5 in. Shipping weight, 14 ounces.
No. 49K440 Price.......... **45c**

## FAMOUS HESS TOYS OF GERMANY.

### The Famous Hess Roller No Key Toys.

**These three mechanical rolling toys are late inventions of a reliable German manufacturer,** and while suitable for larger children, are especially made for little tots, who would have difficulty in winding up a spring. No keys are required. No winding. Simply take the toy in the hand and rub wheels over the floor and the friction will cause the patent device to revolve the wheels rapidly. The toys will run backward or forward. Can be operated equally well on boards, carpets or rugs. Can be used outdoors or in the home. Made entirely of metal, nicely painted in bright colors, difficult to get out of order, and are extra good value.

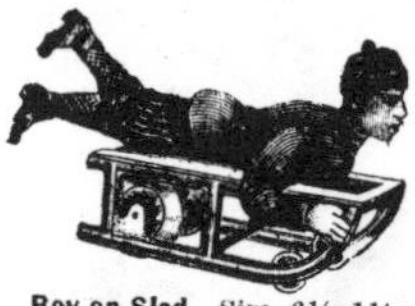

**Boy on Sled.** Size, 6½x1⅛x3¼ inches. Shipping weight, 8 ounces.
No. 49K469 Price.. **19c**

**Moving Duck.** Wabbles from side to side.

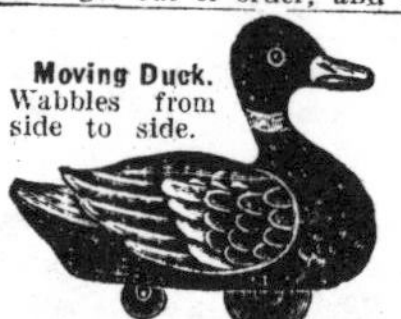

Bright colors. Size, 4x2x3 in. Shipping wt., 8 oz.
No. 49K468 Price. **17c**

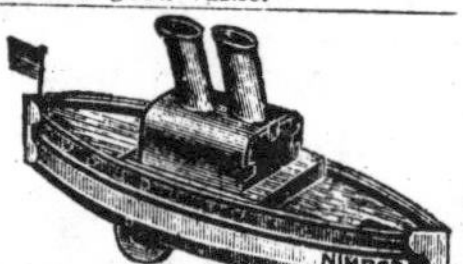

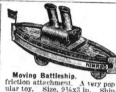

**Moving Battleship,** friction attachment. A very popular toy. Size, 9½x3 in. Shipping wt., 8 ounces.
No. 49K470 Price... **19c**

### Hess Friction Auto, 57c.

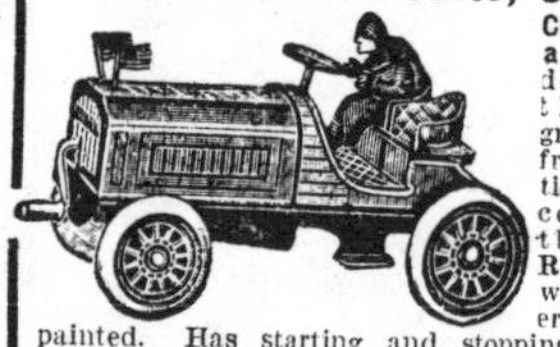

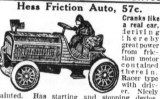

**Cranks like a real car,** deriving thereby great power from friction motor contained therein. Racer type with driver. Nicely painted. Has starting and stopping device. No spring to break. A practical and very popular high class toy. Size, 9x4½ inches. 75-cent size. Shipping weight, 20 oz.
No. 49K1267 Price.......... **57c**

### Columbia Battleship, 37c

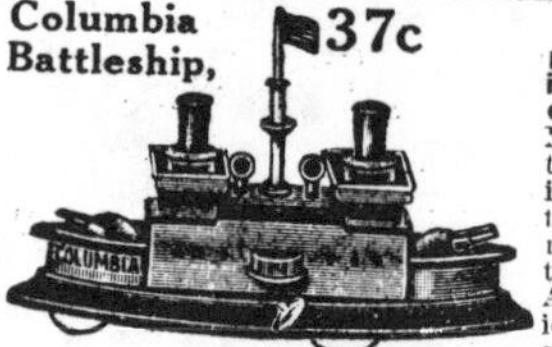

**Nicely painted in six colors.** Movable turrets, imitation of a real battleship. American flag on mast. Strong spring. Runs on floor with rocking motion as in water. Not easily broken. A great toy for a boy. Size, 8¼x5 inches. Shipping weight, 11 ounces.
No. 49K1266 Price.......... **37c**

### Hess-Mobile.

**THE PATENT FRICTION MOTOR. 37c**

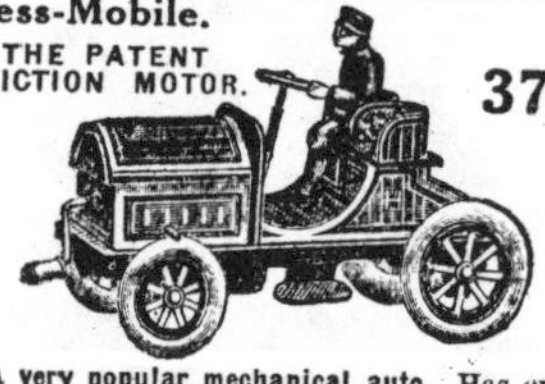

**A very popular mechanical auto.** Has crank attachment, which when wound up starts machine. By turning lever same can be made to go forward or stop at will. Nicely finished, very practical. Made by one of the best makers in Europe. Can be relied upon. Size, 7½x2¾x4½ inches. Full instructions for running with car. Shipping weight, 1 lb.
No. 49K412 Price.......... **37c**

### Dynomobile.

**89c**

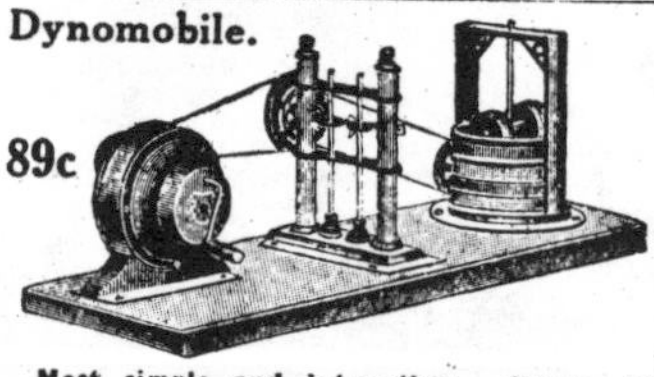

**Most simple and interesting.** Obtains its power through friction by simply turning the crank. Attached to this motor by means of pulley cords is a stamp mill and a grind mill. These three pieces are mounted on a wooden base, measuring 14x4½ inches. This toy is strongly made. All parts enameled in high colors. Shipping weight, 3 pounds.
No. 49K410 Price.......... **89c**

## TWO SPECIAL VALUES IN FLOOR ENGINES.

### Floor Locomotive and Tender, $1.89.

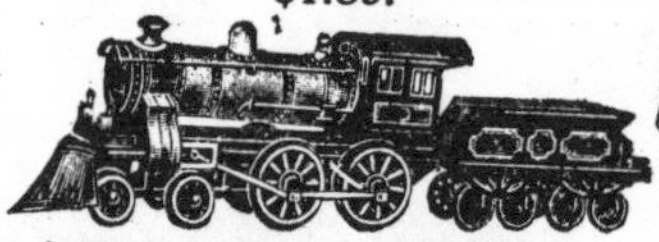

**A very high class toy.** Heavy metal. Decorated in gilt and bright colors, with brass railings. When wound runs on floor or carpet. Extra quality, strong and durable. Entire length, 24½ inches. Height, 6¾ inches. Good $2.50 value. Shipping wt., 3 lbs.
No. 49K917 Price.......... **$1.89**

### Mechanical Floor Engine and Tender, 97c.

**Good reproduction of large locomotive and tender,** all heavy metal, finely painted and decorated, bell and whistle painted gilt, and gilt trimmings on both engine and tender. Fourteen wheels in all. Good spring. Will run on floor or carpet. Total length, 20 inches; height, 5¼ inches. Extra good value. Weight, 2¼ pounds.
No. 49K912 Price.......... **97c**

## EXAMINE THESE TWO VALUES AT 10 CENTS EACH.

### Floor Engine, Tender and Car. 10c

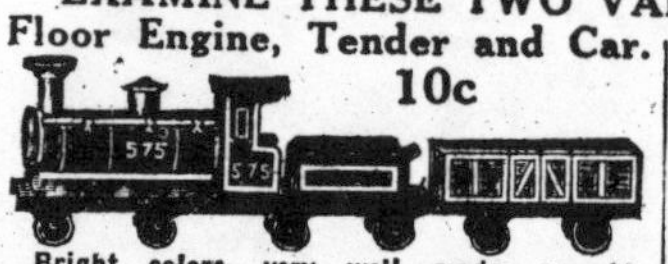

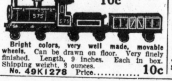

**Bright colors, very well made, movable wheels.** Can be drawn on floor. Very finely finished. Length, 9 inches. Each in box. Shipping weight, 8 ounces.
No. 49K1278 Price.......... **10c**

### Mechanical Trolley System, 10c.

**Curved six-section interlocking track,** making a circle 13 inches in diameter; 4-inch mechanical trolley car with spring. Wonder value. Complete in box. Shipping weight, 8 ounces.
No. 49K1279 Price.......... **10c**

### Jumping Rabbit.

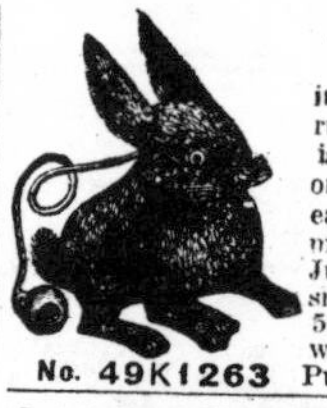

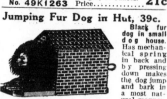

**Real fur covered jumping rabbit,** glass eyes and rubber bulb. When bulb is pressed it jumps around on the floor, flapping its ears in a very comical manner. Very popular. Just the thing for the small child. Size, 7x5¾ inches. Shipping weight, 10 ounces.
No. 49K1263 Price.......... **21c**

### Jumping Fur Dog in Hut, 39c.

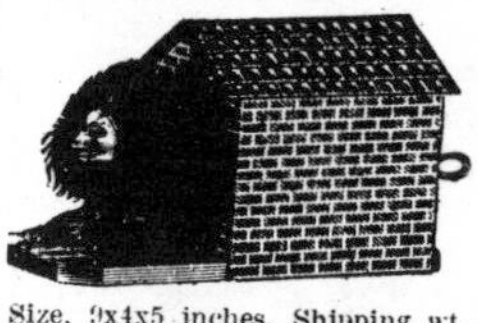

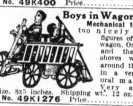

**Black fur dog in small dog house.** Has mechanical spring in back and by pressing down makes the dog jump and bark in a most natural manner. Size, 9x4x5 inches. Shipping wt., 16 oz.
No. 49K400 Price.......... **39c**

### Boys in Wagon, 39c.

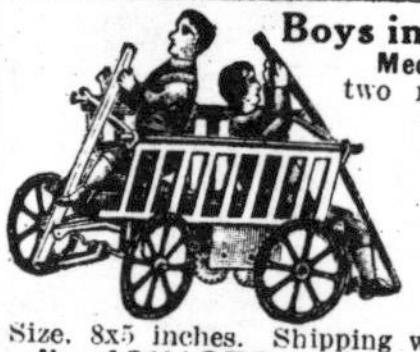

**Mechanical toy.** Has two nicely painted figures of boys in wagon. One steers and the other shoves wagon around the room in a very natural manner. Very amusing. Size, 8x5 inches. Shipping wt., 12 oz.
No. 49K1276 Price.......... **39c**

### Flying Acrobat, 19c.

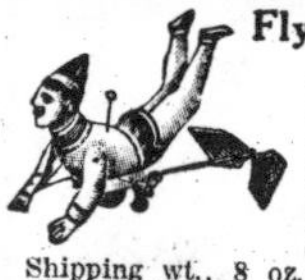

**This toy is fastened to the ceiling by means of a cord,** and when wound up flies around the room in the same manner as an aerial performer. Strongly made and finished in bright colors. Length, 7 inches. Shipping wt., 8 oz.
No. 49K455 Price.......... **19c**

### Tumbling Negro, Movable Jaw, 28c.

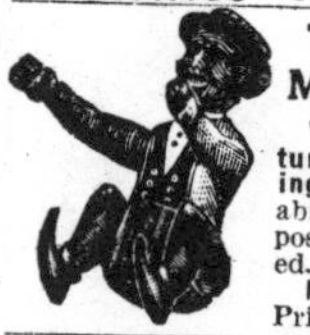

**Winds up by arms and tumbles around floor turning somersaults.** Has movable jaw. Assumes varied positions. Comically dressed. Shipping weight, 6 oz.
No. 49K442 **28c**

### "Punch" Tumbling Clown, 18c.

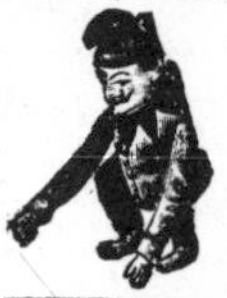

**All metal,** painted in different colors to resemble "Punch." Good spring. When wound, goes through antics like a clown. Shipping weight, 12 ounces.
No. 49K450 Price.......... **18c**

### Rocking Horse.

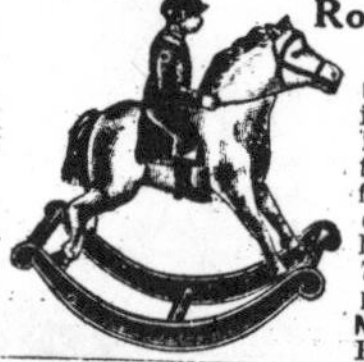

**Made entirely of metal,** nicely painted in colors. When spring is wound, the metal frame rocks back and forth and movable legs on horse give it a galloping motion. Size, 7x6¾ inches. Shipping wt., 14 oz.
No. 49K473 Price.......... **33c**

### Mechanical Dove, 37c.

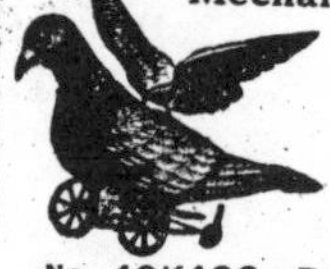

**Movable head and wings.** Natural color. When wound moves along in most natural manner, flapping its wings and moving its head at the same time. Length, 8 inches. Shipping wt., 10 oz.
No. 49K406 Price.......... **37c**

### Jumping Grasshopper, 37c.

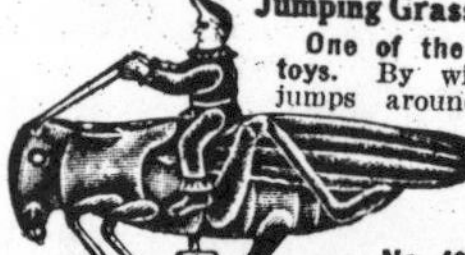

**One of the most popular toys.** By winding up, it jumps around in a very funny manner. Size, 8x6 inches. Shipping wt., 10 ounces.
No. 49K1274 Price.......... **37c**

### Mechanical Duck, 21c.

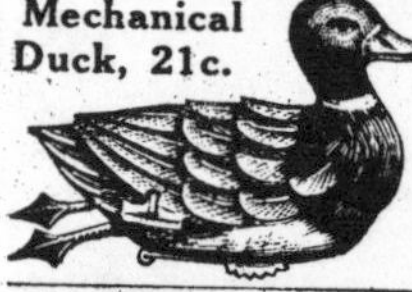

**Handsomely colored.** When wound runs over floor or carpet, wabbling from side to side. Size, 6¼x4½ inches. Sh'p'g wt., 6 oz.
No. 49K1275 Price.......... **21c**

### Mechanical Butterfly, 21c.

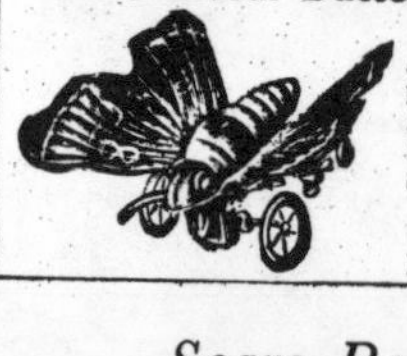

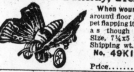

**When wound runs around floor or carpet flapping its wings as though flying.** Size, 7¼x5 inches. Shipping wt., 8 oz.
No. 49K1277 Price.......... **21c**

# BING'S CELEBRATED QUALITY MECHANICAL TOYS

## One of Bing's Best Toys.

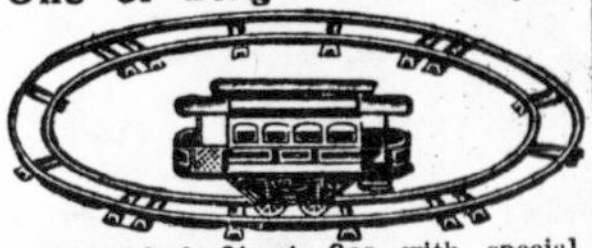

**Mechanical Street Car** with special strong clockwork and brake. Up to date model. Beautifully finished. All metal car, 6½ inches long and 3¼ inches high, with five feet of track. Great value at the price. Shipping weight, 20 ounces.
No. 49K454 Price.......... **42c**

## Most Clever Toy "Pay as You Enter" Car, 93 Cents.

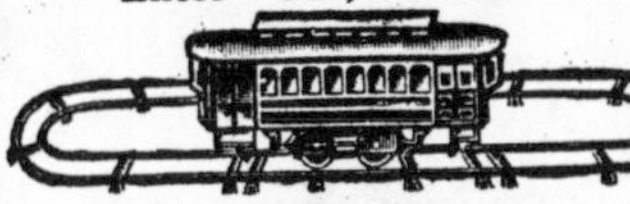

**Mechanical Street Car** with extra strong clockwork and brake. A copy of the modern "Pay as you enter" car. Designed from original model. Realistic coloring. Size of car, 8 inches long and 3¾ inches high, with 8 feet of track. Shipping weight, 2¾ pounds.
No. 49K453 Price.................... **93c**

## Our Latest Novelty, 89c.

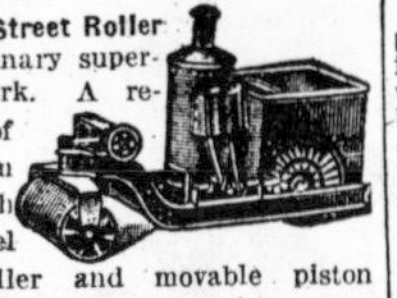

**Mechanical Street Roller** with extraordinary superforce clockwork. A reproduction of the large steam rollers, with steering wheel on front roller and movable piston rods. Finest finish in steel gray. Measures 9x5½x3 inches. Shipping weight, 1½ pounds.
No. 49K405 Price.......... **89c**

## "The Little Showman," $1.25.

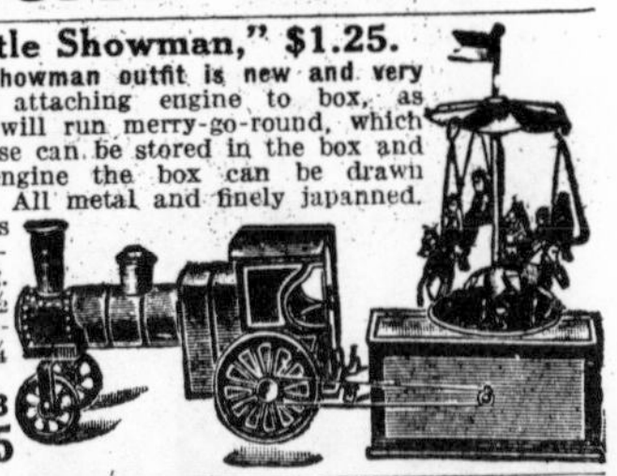

**This little showman outfit is new and very popular.** By attaching engine to box, as illustrated, it will run merry-go-round, which when not in use can be stored in the box and by winding engine the box can be drawn around room. All metal and finely japanned. Engine has strong clockwork spring. Size, 13x8½ inches. Shipping wt., 1¾ pounds.
No. 49K443
Price, **$1.25**

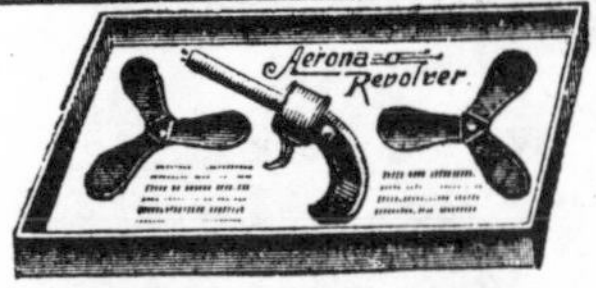

**Shoots a propeller either horizontally or vertically.** Fine mechanical revolver and two celluloid propellers. Size of box, 14x7½ inches. Shipping weight, 12 ounces.
No. 49K456 Price.......... **59c**

**Extra Propellers (celluloid) for Aerial Revolver.** Shipping weight, 2 ounces.
No. 49K0456 Price, per box of 3 propellers.................. **21c**

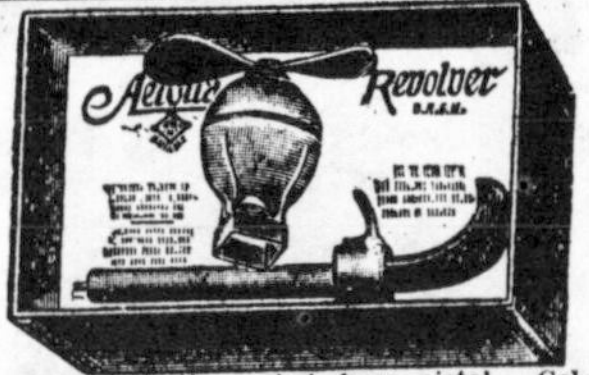

**Aerona Balloon shot from pistol.** Celluloid balloon in bright colors, equipped with celluloid basket. Balloon soars high in the air. Revolver is very easily handled and mechanism winds up by turning the barrel. Shipping weight, 16 ounces.
No. 49K475 Price.................... **89c**

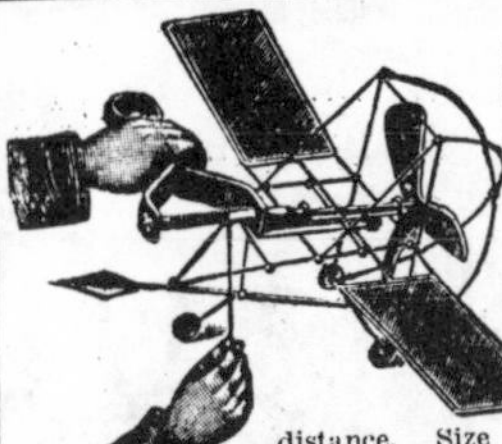

**Splendid copy of aeroplane,** made of flexible wire and silk. Well constructed. Very simple mechanism. Can be handled by any child. Full instructions with each aeroplane. Complete set in box, consisting of aeroplane, patent handle from which it flies and prepared cord to use with handle. Will fly a considerable distance. Size of aeroplane, 11x15x6 inches. Shipping wt., 16 oz.
No. 49K464 Price.................... **98c**

## Our Special Value, 43 Cents.

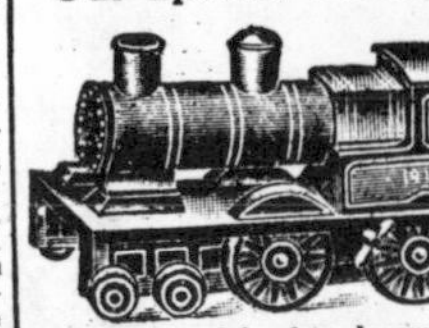

**Mechanical Floor Engine** with extra strong clockwork to run on carpet or any floor when wound up. A clever model of a locomotive. All metal with eight wheels. Beautifully japanned and decorated. Size, 8x4½ inches. Shipping wt., 12 ounces.
No. 49K411 Price.................... **43c**

## Submarine Boat, a Wonder Boat at $1.20.

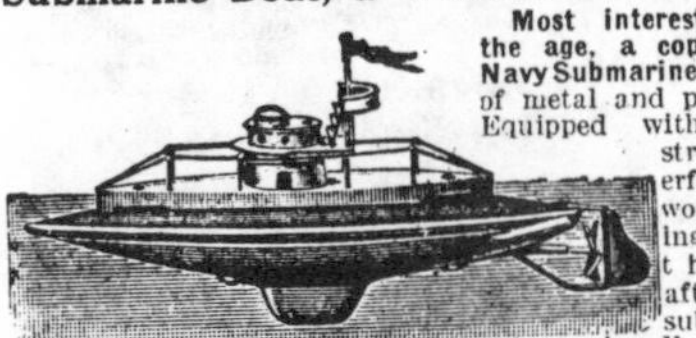

**Most interesting toy of the age, a copy of U. S. Navy Submarine Boat.** Made of metal and painted gray. Equipped with the very strongest superforce clockwork, propelling the boat to the surface after it has submerged itself under the water. Very simple to handle. The boat is wound up like every mechanical toy and after being put into the water it dives and reappears several times. Length, 10½ inches. Shipping weight, 14 ounces.
No. 49K1233 Price.................... **$1.20**

## Very Fine Racing Boat, 79c.

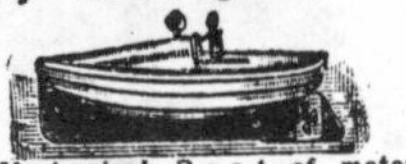

**Mechanical Boat of motor boat type,** made entirely of metal, equipped with extra strong clockwork. Regulated to run very fast, according to the type of the boat. Heavily enameled in beautiful colors. Comes with figure at wheel. Exceptional value. Length, 9¾ inches. Shipping weight, 1 pound.
No. 49K1239 Price.......... **79c**

## Torpedo Boats, $2.67 and $1.18.

Length, 16½ inches. Shipping weight, 28 oz.

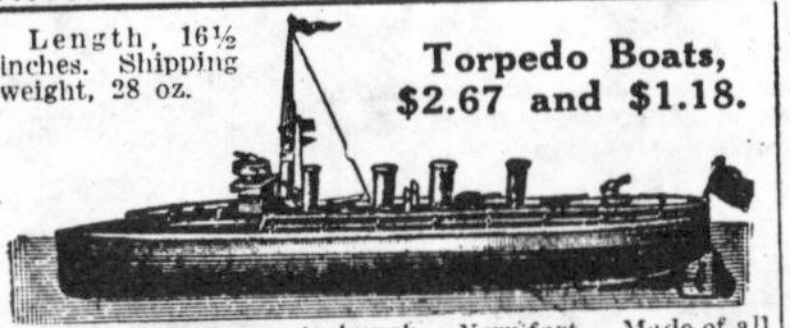

Strong superforce clockwork. Very fast. Made of all metal, painted in gray and black. Has four smoke stacks, flag mast with lookout basket, revolving gun turrets and cannon. Finish of boat and quality of springs the finest.
No. 49K1236 Price.................... **$2.67**

**Torpedo Boat, same as above,** only smaller. Length, 12 inches. Shipping weight, 20 ounces.
No. 49K1234 Price.................... **$1.18**

## Mechanical Fire Boat, $1.87.

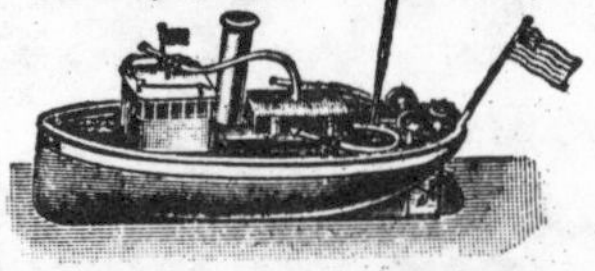

**Extraordinary strong clockwork.** Equipped with pumping apparatus and hose. When wound up and put into water the pump works automatically and throws water while the boat keeps on going. Length, 8 in. Shipping wt., 1 lb.
No. 49K1238 Price...... **$1.87**

## OCEAN LINERS. Real Mechanical Steamboats.

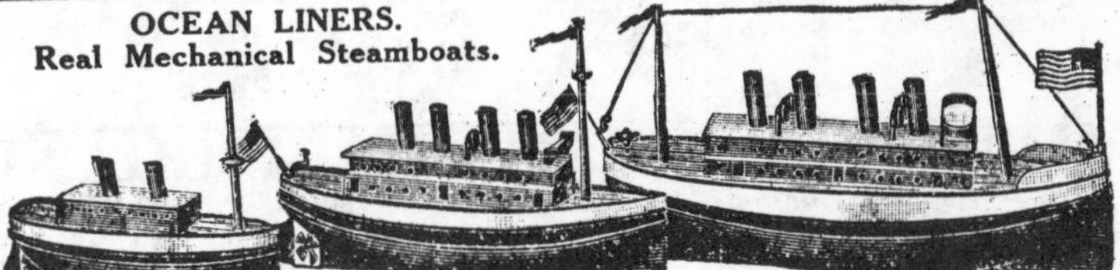

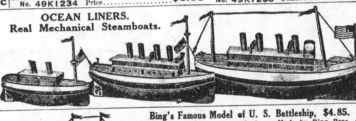

**Good reproduction of ocean steamer,** made entirely of metal, beautifully enameled in colors. Has smoke stacks, decks, ventilators and masts with American flags. An exceptionally handsome toy and one that will give plenty of amusement. The strong superforce clockwork, when wound, causes the screw to revolve, propelling the boat through the water at considerable speed. Movable rudder with which boat can be steered in any direction. No better or more handsome boat made, and being of metal will last for years. Sizes as follows:

13-Inch Boat. Four smoke stacks, double decks. Shipping weight, 2 lbs.
No. 49K1232 Price.................... **$1.96**

10-Inch Boat. Four smoke stacks, double decks. Shipping weight, 22 oz.
No. 49K1231 Price.................... **89c**

8-Inch Boat. Two smoke stacks, one mast. Shipping weight, 12 oz.
No. 49K1230 Price.................... **59c**

## Bing's Famous Model of U. S. Gunboat, $1.37.

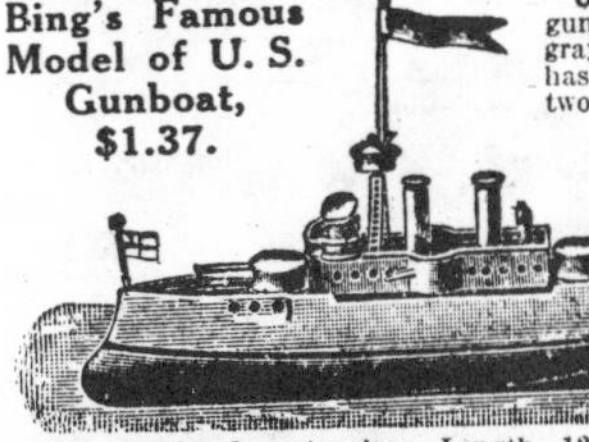

**U. S. Gunboat.** Beautiful model of an American gunboat, made entirely of metal. Enameled in gray and black like original from which same has been designed. Equipped with two funnels, two revolving gun towers, two cannon, flag mast with crow's nest. Equipped with famous Bing's clockwork spring mechanism. A toy that will delight any child and at the same time prove instructive regarding the American navy. When wound by means of key the screw will propel the boat through the water in a very natural manner and will be a source of great amusement for the child. Good value at price. Length, 12 inches. Shipping weight, 1½ lbs.
No. 49K1235 Price.................... **$1.37**

## Bing's Famous Model of U. S. Battleship, $4.85.

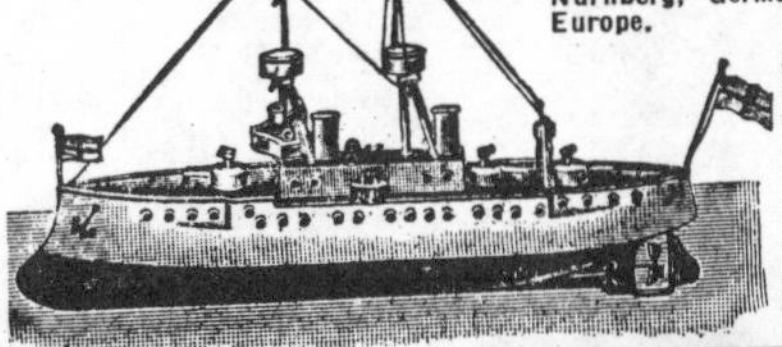

**One of our finest high grade toys. Made by Bing Bros. of Nurnberg, Germany, the best makers of high grade toys in Europe.**

**Splendid model, made of metal, painted in famous fighting gray.** Equipped with extraordinary strong superforce clockwork, regulated to run a very long time. Two masts, each having armored lookout basket, five revolving gun towers, cannon, three propellers, two anchors and all details pertaining to a war ship. Strong and well made; will last for years. Length, 20 inches. Shipping weight, 4 pounds.
No. 49K1237 Price.......... **$4.85**

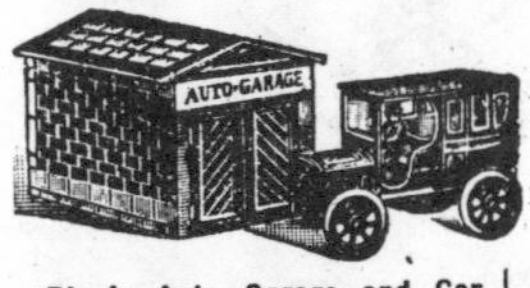


**Bing's Auto Garage and Car.** Heavy cardboard garage with high grade beautifully finished mechanical automobile of finest quality. Runs straight or in circle. With driver. Size, about 5½x3½x3¼ inches. Shipping weight, 10 ounces.
No. 49K1240 Price... **21c**

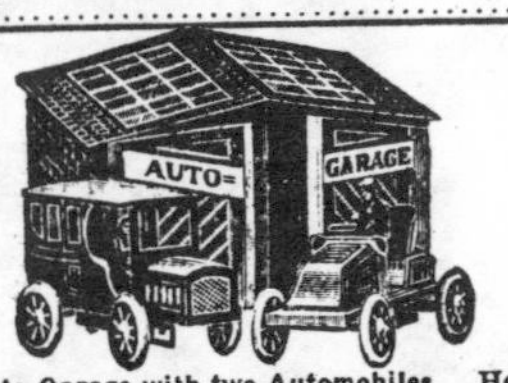


**Auto Garage with two Automobiles.** Heavy cardboard garage with double doors, two stalls, two finely finished touring and racing cars, with extra strong clockwork. Run straight or in circle; both with chauffeurs. Size of each auto, about 5½x3½x3¼ inches. Shipping weight, 1 pound.
No. 49K467 Price.................... **39c**

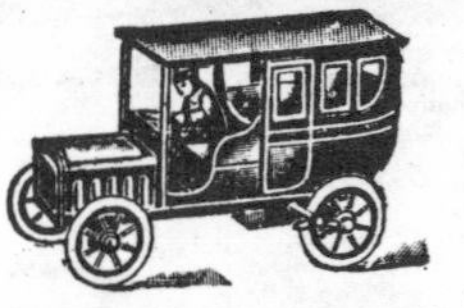

**Motor Car.** Very strong superforce clockwork. Beautifully enameled in bright colors. Doors that open. With driver. Flexible front wheels. Car runs straight or in circles. Size, 8x5x3½ inches. Shipping weight, 10 ounces.
No. 49K421 Price...... **43c**

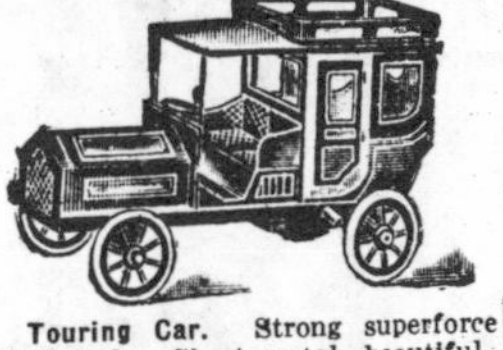

**Touring Car.** Strong superforce clockwork. Sheet metal, beautifully finished in bright colors, with driver. Runs straight or in circle. Brake on rear wheel. Exact reproduction of modern type touring car. Size, 8x5x3½ inches. Shipping weight, 14 ounces.
No. 49K1241 Price.... **73c**

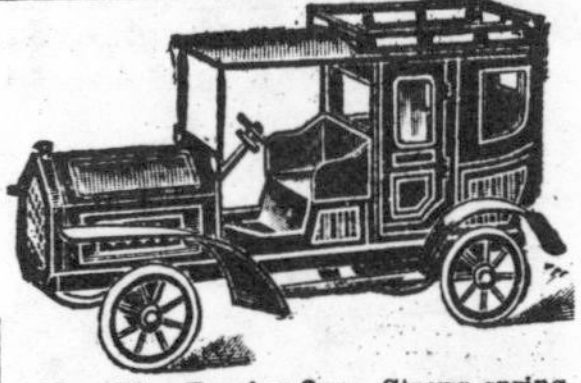

**Very Fine Touring Car.** Strong spring, rubber tires, steering gear, brake. Can run straight or in circle. Beautifully finished in bright colors. Size, 9½x5¾x4¾ inches. Shipping weight, 1½ pounds.
No. 49K1242 Price...... **98c**

## Bing's Fine Mechanical Limousine Car.

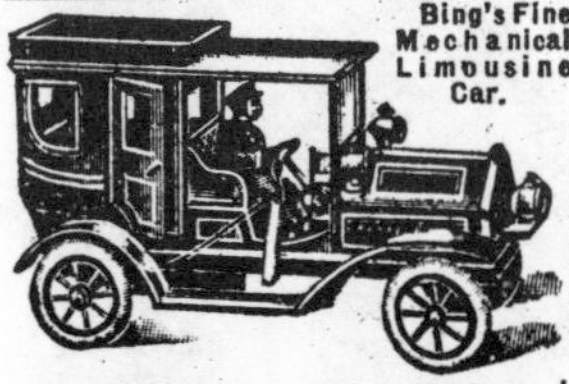

**With extra strong clockwork.** Beautifully finished in heavy enamel. Windows and wind shield of beveled glass, with two searchlights and lamps. Heavy rubber tires, mud guards, doors that open, cushioned seats. Brake and steering gear. Runs either straight or in circles. Taximeter registers automatically while the machine is running. Size, 12x7½x5½ inches. Shipping weight, 4½ pounds.
No. 49K1247 Price... **$4.95**

## Bing's Fine Toy Runabout.

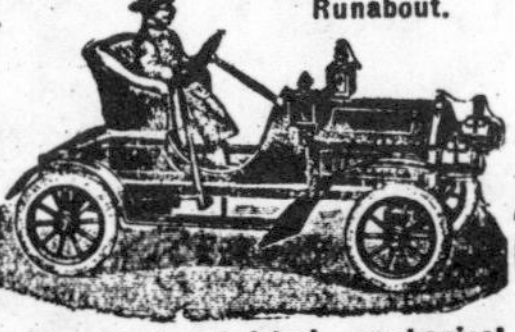

**Beautifully finished mechanical automobile.** High grade sheet metal, enameled in bright colors. Very fine superforce clockwork, extra strong. A splendid model with driver, steering gear on front wheels to allow auto to run straight or in circles. Brake on rear wheel. Equipped with mud guards, searchlight, lamps and rubber tires. Size, 9½x5x5 inches. Shipping weight, 2¾ pounds.
No. 49K1243 Price.. **$2.35**

## Bing's Finest Toy Runabout.

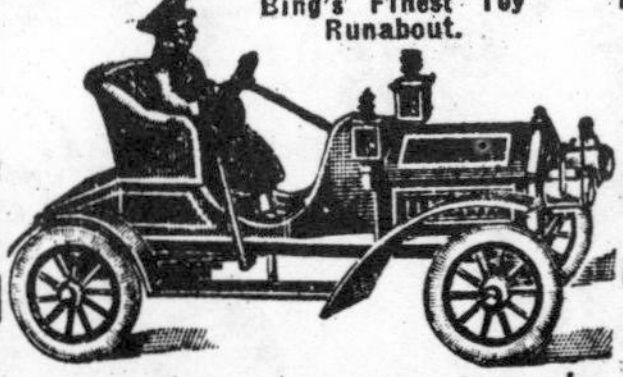

**Mechanical automobile.** Very best quality and finish, with extraordinarily strong superforce clockwork; practically indestructible. Equipped with two searchlights and lamps, heavy rubber tires, rear wheels with brake. Steering gear to either run straight or in circle, with mud guards and upholstered seats. Size, 11x5¾x5¼ in. Shipping weight, 3¼ pounds.
No. 49K1244 Price. **$3.25**

## Bing's Model Touring Car.

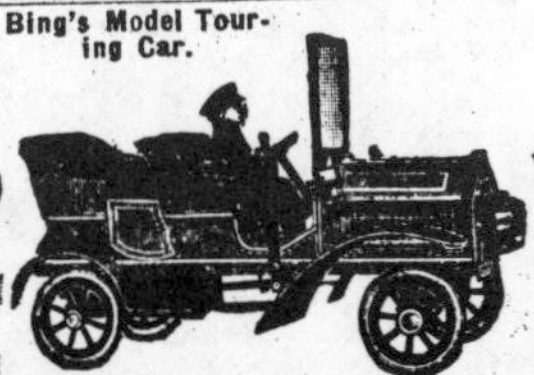

**Finest quality and finish,** with unusually strong clockwork. Finest sheet metal, in beautiful colors. Perfect in every detail with heavy rubber tires, mud guards, searchlight and lamps, glass wind shield and doors to open. Brake and steering gear to run straight or in circle. Size, 10½x6¼x5 inches. Shipping weight, 4 pounds.
No. 49K1246 Price. **$3.85**

## Packard Toy Automobile.

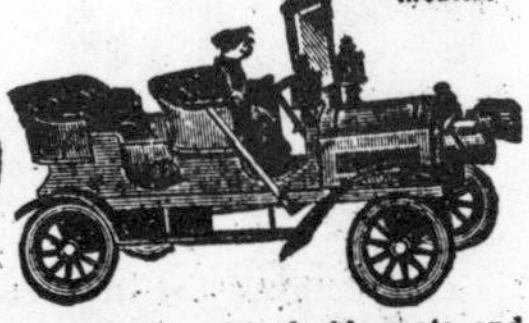

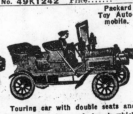

**Touring car with double seats** and equipped with heavy clockwork which allows fast and long running; two searchlights and four lamps, mud guards, doors that open. Brake and steering gear all heavily enameled in beautiful colors. Runs either straight or in circles. Size, 13x5¾x5¼ inches. Shipping weight, 4¾ pounds.
No. 49K1245 Price...... **$4.85**

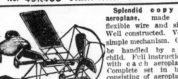

# BING'S FAMOUS WALKING ANIMALS AND TOYS

UNEXCELLED IN QUALITY OF LIFELIKE FURS, EXPRESSION AND MOVEMENT. SUBSTANTIALLY MADE AND WILL NOT EASILY BREAK.

### The Famous Caesar, $1.45.

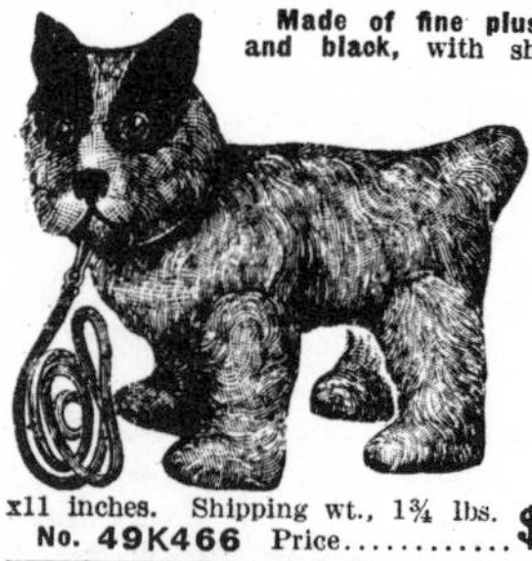

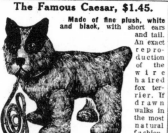

**Made of fine plush, white and black,** with short ears and tail. An exact reproduction of the wire haired fox terrier. If drawn walks in the most natural fashion. Size, 9½ x11 inches. Shipping wt., 1¾ lbs.
No. 49K466 Price **$1.45**

### The Funny Dachshund, 89c.

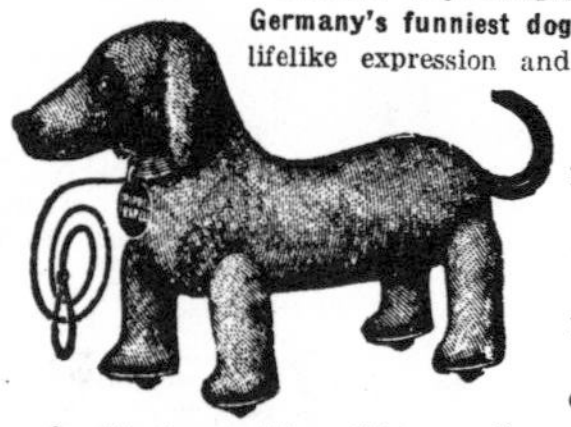

**Comical reproduction of Germany's funniest dog.** Most lifelike expression and when pulled moves like it were alive. Size, 15x7½ inches. Covered with brown felt. Ribbon collar, imitation eyes. Shipping wt., 1¾ lbs.
No. 49K1248 Price........... **89c**

### Our Bull Puppy, 89 Cents.

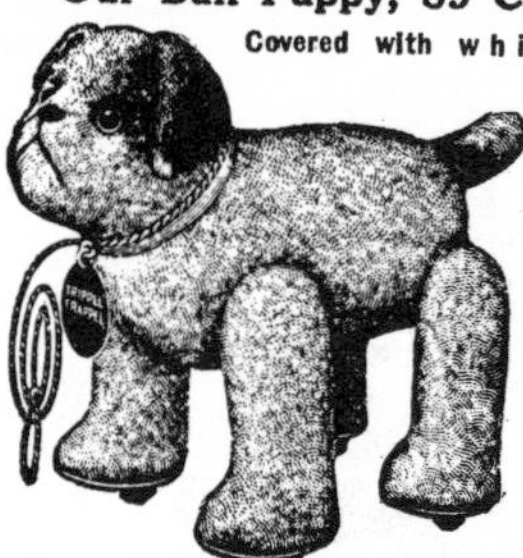

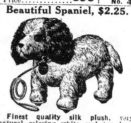

**Covered with white fuzzy cloth;** silk ribbon around neck. Walks in a lifelike way. Size, 8½ x 6¾ inches. Shipping weight, 22 oz.
No. 49K1250 Price............... **89c**

### Fine Bulldog, $1.25.

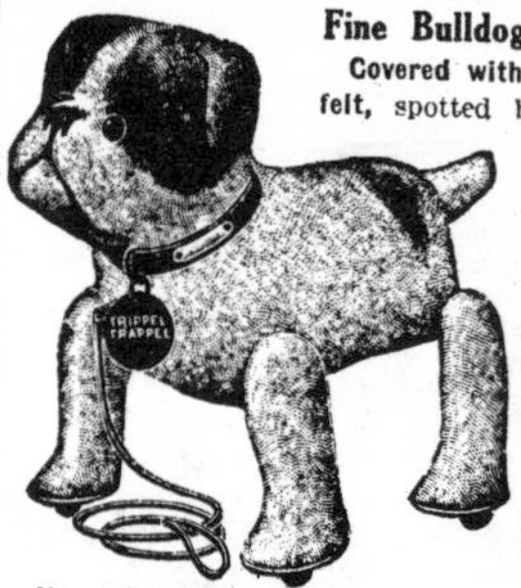

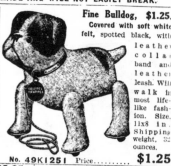

**Covered with soft white felt,** spotted black, with leather collar band and leather leash. Will walk in most lifelike fashion. Size, 11x8 in. Shipping weight, 32 ounces.
No. 49K1251 Price.......... **$1.25**

### Roller Skating Bear, 98c.

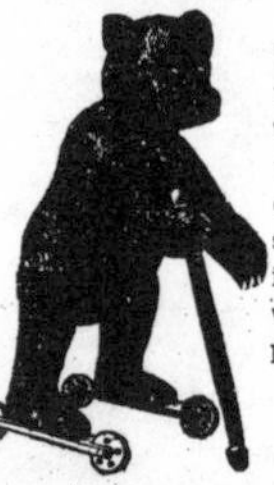

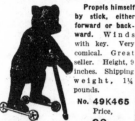

**Propels himself by stick, either forward or backward.** Winds with key. Very comical. Great seller. Height, 9 inches. Shipping weight, 1¼ pounds.
No. 49K465 Price, **98c**

### Teddy Bear, 89 Cents.

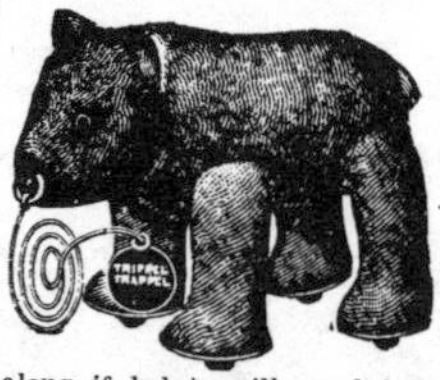

**Covered with fine quality of cinnamon brown silk plush.** Walks along if led by silk cord fastened to his nose. Very droll and fascinating movement. Size, 9x6½ inches. Shipping weight, 1½ pounds.
No. 49K1249 Price..... **89c**

### Walking Pussy Cat, $1.48.

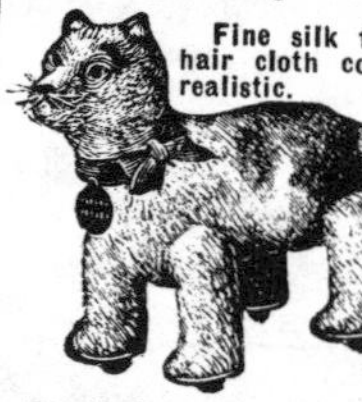

**Fine silk finished mohair cloth covered. Very realistic.**

**Practically unbreakable and will not easily get out of order.** Size, 14x8¾ inches. Shipping weight, 2¼ pounds.
No. 49K1252 Price.. **$1.48**

### Beautiful Spaniel, $2.25.

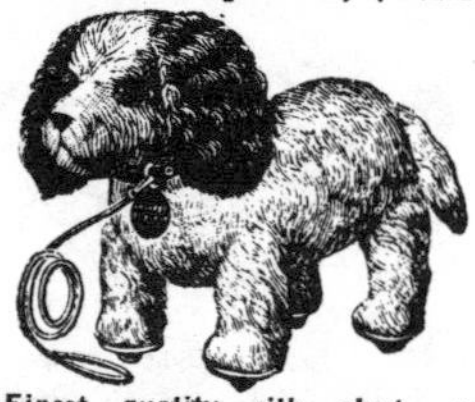

**Finest quality silk plush,** very natural coloring white and tan, long drooping ears and fine bushy tail. Leather collar and leash. Size, 15x9 inches. Shipping wt., 1½ lbs.
No. 49K1253 Price. **$2.25**

### Walking Poodle, $2.37.

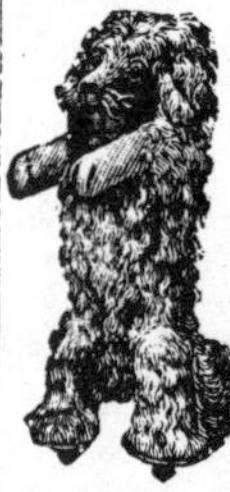

**Real lifelike imitation.** Covered with the finest long silk finished mohair cloth. Stands on his hind legs and when wound walks in the most comical manner. The clockwork is very strong and well regulated and stops when dog is raised from floor. Size, 11½ in. Shipping weight, 1¾ pounds.
No. 49K1259 Price.. **$2.37**

### Walking Duck, 89 Cents.

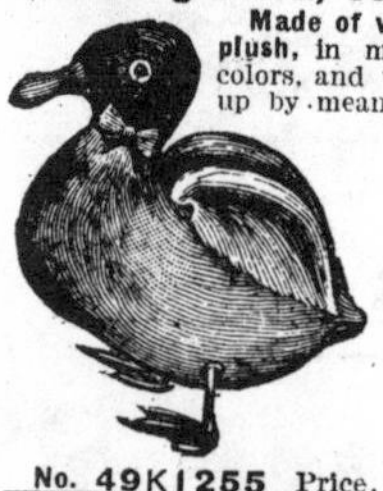

**Made of very fine silk plush,** in most natural colors, and when wound up by means of a key, the duck walks in the most lifelike manner. Size, 6x12 inches. Shipping weight, 1½ lbs.
No. 49K1255 Price..... **89c**

### Famous Luck Bird, 89c.

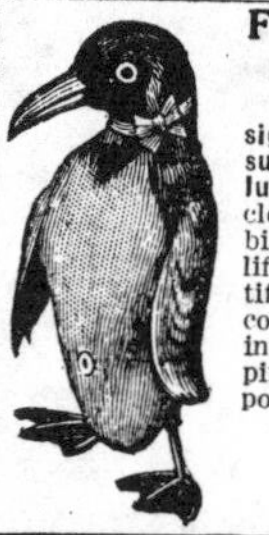

**Sailors believe the sight or possession of such a bird brings luck.** A very strong clockwork enables the bird to walk in most lifelike manner. Beautifully colored. Very comical. Size, 8¾ inches high. Shipping weight, 1¼ pounds.
No. 49K1254 Price..... **89c**

### Puss On Skates, $1.27.

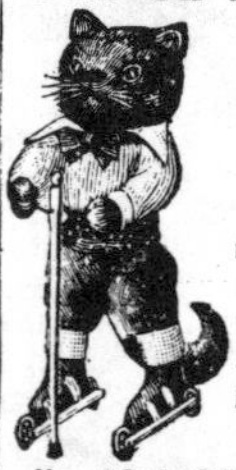

**Made of finest quality silk plush.** Fitted with a pair of roller skates. Winds with a key; moves forward and backward in the most lifelike manner. Size, 9¼ inches high. Shipping weight, 20 oz.
No. 49K1257 Price.. **$1.27**

### Jumping Monkey.

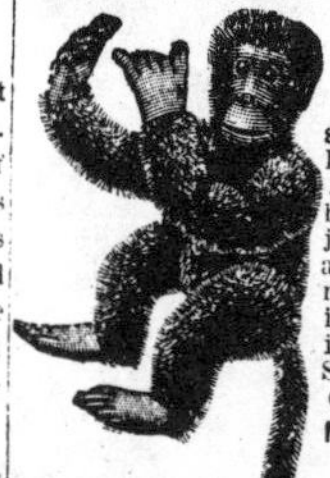

**Made of fine silk plush.** Most lifelike motion when wound up by key and jumps forward in a realistic manner. Very amusing. Size, 7 inches high. Shipping wt., 24 ounces.
No. 49K1256 Price...... **89c**

### The Expressman, $1.45.

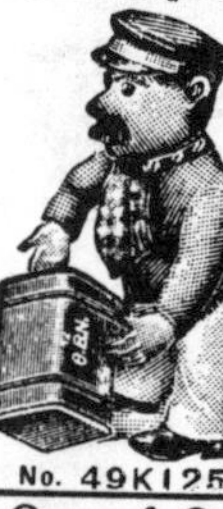

**Full cloth dressed man with trunk.** Equipped with very strong and durable clockwork and when wound walks along rolling the trunk before him. Size, 10 inches high. Shipping weight, 1½ pounds.
No. 49K1258 Price. **$1.45**

# MINIATURE STEAM AND MECHANICAL ENGINES

### A Popular Engine.

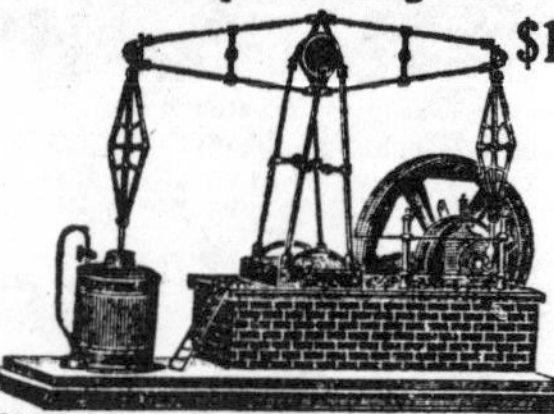

**$1.98**

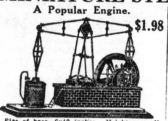

**Size of base, 6x18 inches.** Height over all, 12 inches. Finished in seven-color enamel and bronze decorated. Has easel clock spring and is one of the very best mechanical engines made. Shipping wt., 6 lbs.
No. 49K436 Price........ **$1.98**

### Our Little Hustler Engine, $1.47.

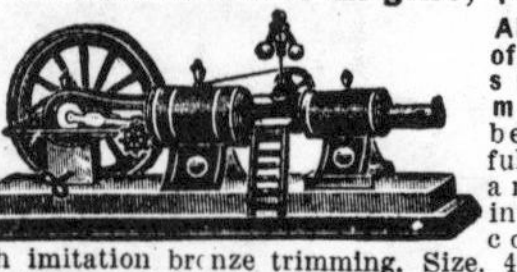

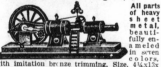

**All parts of heavy sheet metal,** beautifully enameled in seven colors, with imitation bronze trimming. Size, 4¼x13x5½ inches. Strong and well built. Shipping weight, 3 pounds.
No. 49K433 Price........... **$1.47**

### Our Big 89-Cent Value.

**89c**

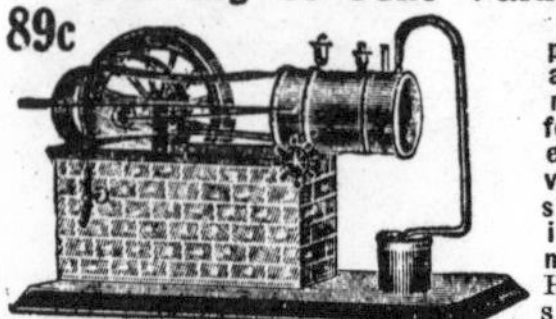

**Has pulley attachments for operating various small implements.** Heavy sheet metal, enameled in bright colors and imitation bronze fittings and trimmings. Size, 9¼x5x5 inches. Shipping weight, 3¼ pounds.
No. 49K434 Price........... **89c**

### This Engine for 39 Cents.

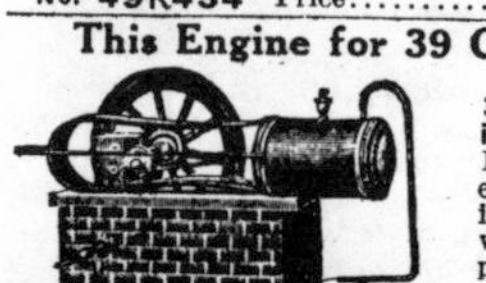

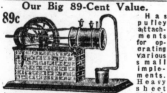

**Measures 3¾ x 6½x4¼ inches.** Beautiful enamel finish. Good value at the price. Shipping weight, 1¼ pounds.
No. 49K435 Price............ **39c**

## MINIATURE STEAM ENGINES.

EVERY ONE GUARANTEED PERFECT. EXCEPTIONAL VALUES.

### Wonderful Value at 89 Cents.

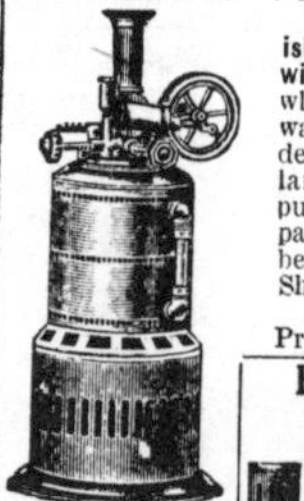

**Has well tempered polished sheet brass boiler with pop safety valve,** whistle and good glass water gauge. Heavy cylinder, rod, crank pin and large metal fly wheel with pulley attachments. All parts finely finished. Steams best with wood alcohol. Shipping wt., 1½ pounds.
No. 49K950 **89c**

### Horizontal Miniature Engine and Boiler.

**$4.98**

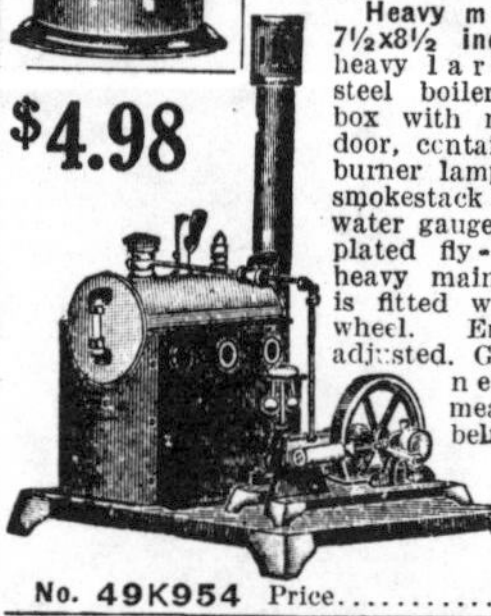

**Heavy metal base, 7½x8½ inches.** Extra heavy large nickeled steel boiler, steel fire box with nickeled fire door, containing double burner lamp, 10½-inch smokestack and a glass water gauge. Nickel plated fly-wheel on heavy main shaft and is fitted with pulley wheel. Engine finely adjusted. Governor connected by means of spring belt. Shipping weight, engine, 5 lbs.
No. 49K954 Price........... **$4.98**

### Our Best Value, $5.95.

**$5.95**

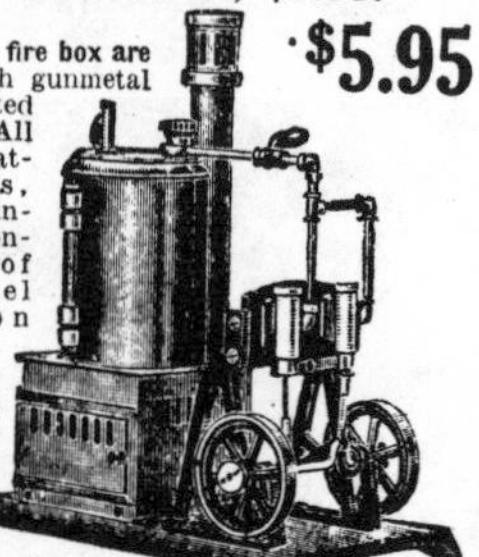

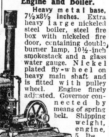

**Boiler and fire box are of brass with gunmetal nickel plated finish.** All necessary attachments, double cylinder. All connections of brass, nickel plated. Iron base, painted, polished nickeled feet. Size of base, 7x9¾ inches; height, 11 in. Shipping weight, 10 pounds.
No. 49K962 Price.......... **$5.95**

### A Very Fine Engine for Only $1.37.

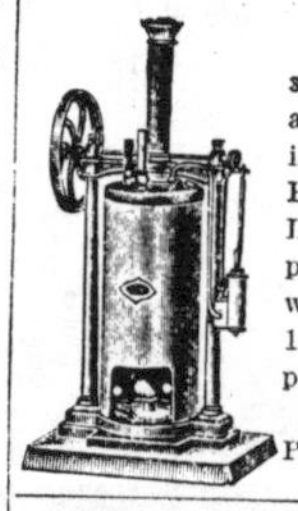

**Has heavy nickel plated steam boiler** mounted on enameled iron base, with sheet iron nickel end smokestack. Pop safety valve and whistle. Large metal fly wheel with pulley wheel. Will steam best with wood alcohol. Height, 10 inches. Shipping wt., 2½ pounds.
No. 49K952 Price.............. **$1.37**

### Horizontal Steam Engine and Boiler, $3.35.

**$3.35**

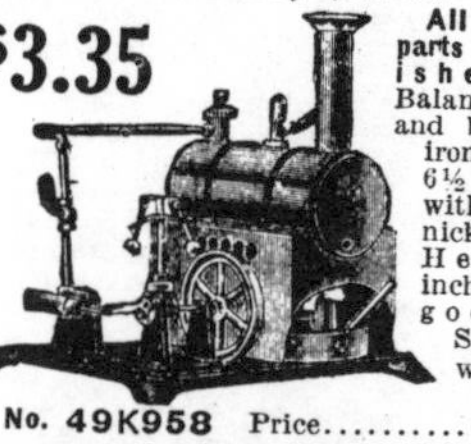

**All engine parts are polished nickel.** Balance wheel and base are of iron. Has 8½x6½-inch base with polished nickeled feet. Height, 8½ inches. Very good value. Shipping wt., 3½ lbs.
No. 49K958 Price............ **$3.35**

### A Very Popular Engine, $4.97.

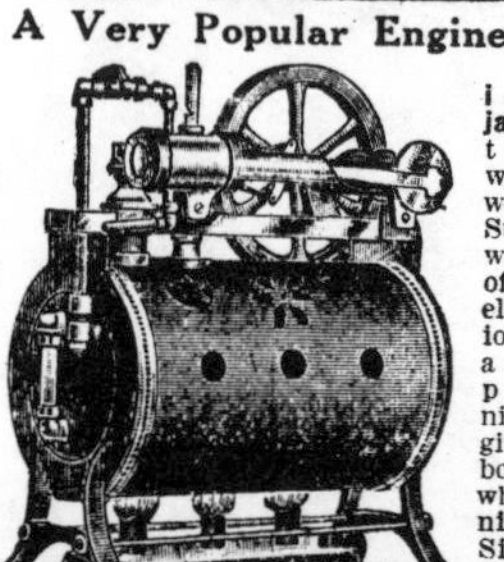

**Brass boiler in steel jacket.** Safety valve, whistle and water gauge. Steam and water pipes of brass and elbows, unions, pipes and valves polished nickel. Engine, frame, boiler and wheel iron, nickel plated. Size, 10x8 in. Shipping weight, 7 lbs.
No. 49K960 Price............ **$4.97**

### One of Our Best Toys.

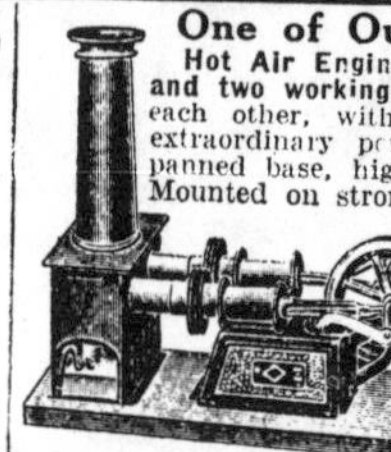

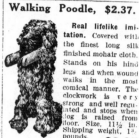

**Hot Air Engine with two deplacers and two working cylinders** fitted into each other, with cooling box. Has extraordinary power, with finely japanned base, highly nickeled fittings. Mounted on strong wood base. Size, 8¾ x 3¼ x 9½ inches. Shipping weight, 2¾ pounds.
No. 49K961 Price, **$2.43**

### Hot Air Engine, $1.35.

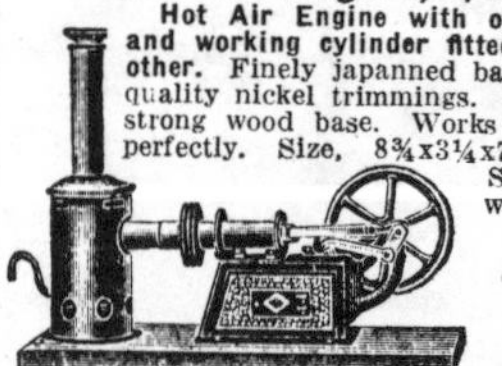

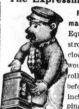

**Hot Air Engine with one deplacer and working cylinder fitted into each other.** Finely japanned base and high quality nickel trimmings. Mounted on strong wood base. Works easily and perfectly. Size, 8¾x3¼x7½ inches. Shipping wt., 2¼ lbs.
No. 49K959 Price, **$1.35**

### Traction Engine, $4.25.

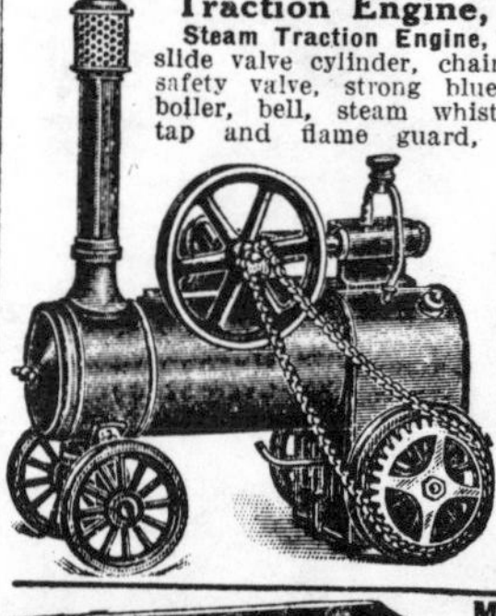

**Steam Traction Engine,** with fixed slide valve cylinder, chain gearing, safety valve, strong blue oxidized boiler, bell, steam whistle, outlet tap and flame guard. Excellent workmanship. Very instructive. Size, 7x9½ in. Shipping weight, 3¼ lbs.
No. 49K957 Price **$4.25**

### Machine Shop, 95c.

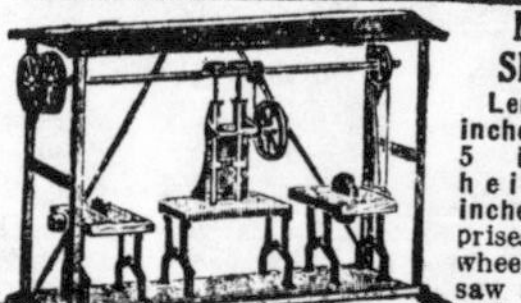

**Length, 11½ inches; width, 5 inches; height, 7½ inches.** Comprises emery wheel, slitting saw and stamp mill. Shipping weight, 3 lbs.
No. 49K965 Price.............. **95c**

# BING'S CELEBRATED MINIATURE RAILWAYS AND SUPPLIES

Manufactured by Bing Brothers, the celebrated toy makers of Nurnberg, Germany. Quality the very best, finish perfect, workmanship highest class, and for their respective prices the finest trains, everything considered, ever offered in America. **STUDY THIS PAGE CAREFULLY.**

**Examine This 47-Cent Value**

All metal Train, consisting of engine with extra strong superforce clockwork, speed regulator and brake, one tender and one finely japanned Pullman car. Train measures 16 inches long and comes with 5 feet of track to form circle. Shipping weight, 1½ pounds. No. 49K911 Price.... **47c**

**This Fine Train for Only $1.38.**

All metal Train, consisting of engine with extra strong clockwork, speed regulator and brake, one tender and three Pullman cars. Train 26 inches long and comes with 10 feet of track, including stop rail and crossover. Shipping weight, 3½ pounds. No. 49K902 Price.... **$1.38**

**A Wonder Value at 95 Cents.**

All metal Train, has engine with extra strong clockwork, speed regulator and brake, one tender and three finely japanned Pullman cars. Train 26 inches long and comes with 8 feet of track, including a stop rail. Shipping wt., 3½ lbs. No. 49K900 Price.... **95c**

## FINEST REPRODUCTIONS OF PASSENGER AND FREIGHT TRAINS

WITH CAST IRON LOCOMOTIVES. ALL CORRECT MODELS DESIGNED FROM THE LATEST TRAINS OF LEADING RAILROADS. ALL ENGINES WITH BRASS WORKS. EACH PIECE GUARANTEED.

**Please Examine This Value at $2.75.**

Passenger Train, has cast iron engine with superior clockwork made of brass with speed regulator and brake, absolutely guaranteed. Train 31 inches long and has 12 feet of track, including one stop rail. Shipping weight, 6 pounds. No. 49K903 Price.... **$2.75**

Freight Train, has cast iron engine with superior brass clockwork, with speed regulator and brake, each piece guaranteed; one tender and four freight cars, including caboose. Train 38 inches long and has 12 feet of track, including stop rail; $4.00 value. Shipping weight, 9 pounds. No. 49K905 Price.... **$3.47**

Freight Train, has cast iron engine with superior brass clockwork, with speed regulator and brake, absolutely guaranteed; one tender and three freight cars, including Dutch Cleanser car. Closed box car and caboose. Train 31 inches long and has 12 feet of track, including a stop rail; $3.50 value. No. 49K901 Price.... **$2.95**

**This Fine Train for Only $4.65.**

Passenger Train, high class cast iron engine, heavy type, with extraordinary superforce brass clockwork, with speed regulator and brake, each piece guaranteed; one tender and two beautifully finished Pullman and baggage cars with double trucks (eight wheels). Train 28 inches long and has 12 feet of track, including a stop rail. Shipping weight, 7½ pounds. No. 49K906 Price.... **$4.65**

**Our Finest Freight Train, $4.95.**

Freight Train, high class cast iron engine of the heavy type with extraordinary superforce brass clockwork, with speed regulator and outside piston rods and brake, absolutely guaranteed; one tender and three double truck freight cars. Train 34 inches long and comes with 14 feet of track, including a stop rail. Shipping weight, 7½ pounds. No. 49K908 Price.... **$4.95**

**A Wonder in Toy Railroading at $6.95.**

Passenger Express Train, consisting of extra fine cast iron engine of the express type with eight wheels, superior superforce clockwork, made of brass with speed regulator, brake and reverser to change the direction of the train; one coal fitted tender and three extra large and beautifully japanned Pullman and baggage cars designed after the latest models. Train measures 42 inches long and comes with 14 feet of track, including a stop rail. Shipping weight, 9¾ pounds. No. 49K909 Price.... **$6.95**

**The Best We Have to Offer—A Wonder Value at $8.95.**

Large Passenger Train, large high grade cast iron engine with eight wheels and unusual superforce brass clockwork, with speed regulator, outside piston rods, brake and automatic reverser, one tender and two unusually large modern type Pullman and baggage cars with double trucks. Train 48 inches long and comes with 14 feet of track in large gauge, including a stop rail to operate brake and reverser from. Shipping weight, packed, 16 pounds. No. 49K910 Price.... **$8.95**

## TO KEEP YOUR RAILROAD SYSTEM UP TO DATE,
SOME OF THE LATEST MODELS IN ENGINES, FREIGHT CARS AND PASSENGER CARS COPIED FROM THE LATEST MODELS OF OUR LEADING RAILROADS.

### SIGNALS AND STATIONS—DESIGNED FROM ORIGINAL MODELS IN REALISTIC FINISH

**Mechanical Cast Iron Engine With Tender.**
Has very strong superforce brass clockwork, with speed regulator and brake. Guaranteed. Size, 9½x3¾ inches. Shipping weight, 3 pounds. No. 49K945 Price.... **98c**

Fitted with an extraordinary brass clockwork with unusual pulling power and durability. The engine has outside piston rods and is equipped with a speed regulator and brake. Guaranteed. Size, 12x3¾ inches. Shipping weight, 3½ pounds. No. 49K946 Price.... **$2.75**

**Mechanical Cast Iron Express Engine With Tender, $4.65.**
Has eight wheels and outside piston rods, fitted with unusual superforce brass clockwork, with speed regulator, brake and automatic reverser, guaranteed. Size, 13x4 inches. Sh'p'g wt., 4½ lbs. No. 49K947 Price.... **$4.65**

**Pullman Cars, 45 and 21 Cents.**
Finished in natural colors. Two sizes.
No. 49K922 Eight-Wheel Car, 8 inches long. Shipping wt., 10 oz. Price.... 45c
No. 49K923 Four-Wheel Car, 7 inches long. Shipping wt., 8 oz. Price.... 21c

**Dutch Cleanser Refrigerator Cars.**
With inscription. Natural colors.
No. 49K928 Eight-Wheel Car, 8 inches long. Shipping wt., 10 oz. Price.... 45c
No. 49K929 Four-Wheel Car, 7 inches long. Shipping wt., 8 oz. Price.... 22c

**Box Cars at 43 and 22 Cents.**
Ill. Cent. Car, natural colors. Sliding doors. Two sizes.
No. 49K936 Eight-Wheel Car, 8 inches long. Shipping wt., 10 ounces. Price.... 43c
No. 49K937 Four-Wheel Car, 7 inches long. Shipping wt., 8 oz. Price.... 22c

**ASSORTED CABOOSE CARS.**
Finely enameled.
No. 49K940 Eight-Wheel Car, 8 inches long. Shipping wt., 10 ounces. Price.... 39c
No. 49K941 Four-Wheel Car, 7 inches long. Shipping wt., 8 ounces. Price.... 22c

**Oil Tank Car, 98 Cents.**
Beautifully finished. Assorted inscriptions. Eight-wheel car, 8 in. long. Shipping weight, 10 ounces. No. 49K942 Price.... **98c**

**Dump Coal Cars, 22 and 98 Cents.**
No. 49K943 Eight-Wheel Car, 8 inches long. Shipping weight, 13 ounces. Price.... 98c
No. 49K944 Four-Wheel Car, 7 inches long. Shipping weight, 8 ounces. Price.... 22c

**Lumber Cars at 47 Cents.**
Loaded with lumber. Eight-wheel car, 7 inches long. Shipping wt., 13 ounces. No. 49K939 Price.... **47c**

**Refrigerator Cars at 43 and 21 Cents.**
Natural colors. Two sizes.
No. 49K933 Eight-Wheel Car, 8 inches long. Shipping wt., 10 oz. Price.... 43c
No. 49K934 Four-Wheel Car, 7 inches long. Shipping wt., 8 ounces. Price.... 21c

**Coal Cars at 46 Cents.**
Hocking Valley Coal Co., with exact inscription and colors. Eight-wheel car, 10 inches long. Shipping wt., 12 ounces. No. 49K938 Price.... **46c**

**CROSSING POLES, 19c.**
Used by the railroads. Made of metal, finished in bright colors. Sizes, 6 and 8 inches high. Shipping wt., 4 ounces. No. 49K948 Price.... **19c**

**SEMAPHORE.**
Danger Signal with movable arm, all metal, nicely japanned. Size, 11¾ inches high. Shipping wt., 6 oz. No. 49K964 Price.... **21c**

**SEMAPHORE AND TELEGRAPH POLE.**
Latest design with movable arm, red and green glasses, other parts made of metal, beautifully japanned. Size, 12¼ inches high. Shipping wt., 8 ounces. No. 49K963 Price.... **39c**

**SEMAPHORE.**
New model, movable arms. Red and green glasses which can be set independently of each other. Made of all metal, finished in correct colors. Size, 13¾ in. high. Shipping wt., 10 ounces. No. 49K949 Price.... **67c**

**Switch House, 45c.**
Correct model, all metal, painted and beautifully finished with ladder and detachable roof. Size, 4¾ x 4¼ inches. Weight, 12 ounces. No. 49K966 Price.... **45c**

Finest Metal Railroad Station. Detachable roof and equipment for candle illumination. Size, 14¾x6¾ inches. Shipping weight, 3½ pounds. No. 49K918 Price.... **$1.85**

**Freight Station, Extraordinary Value, 39 Cents.**
Splendid imitation of Freight Station, all metal with sliding door and loading platform. Finely japanned. Size, 11½x3½ inches. Shipping weight, 13 ounces. No. 49K919 Price.... **39c**

**Modern Freight Station, 89c.**
Realistic painting, finest finish, with platform and sliding doors in front and rear, detachable roof. Designed after original model. Size, 10½x5½ inches. Shipping weight, 2 pounds. No. 49K920 Price.... **89c**

**RAILROAD TRACK.**
Straight, on ties, with joining pegs on both ends. Length, each, 12 inches. Packed half dozen pieces to box. Shipping weight, per box, 14 ounces. No. 49K914 Price.... **19c**

**RAILROAD TRACK.**
Curved, on ties, with joining pegs on both ends. Length, each, 12 inches. Packed half dozen pieces to box. Shipping weight, per box, 14 ounces. No. 49K913 Price.... **19c**

**RAILROAD CROSSOVER,** on ties, for track formation, with joining pegs on both sides. Length, 11 inches. Shipping weight, 8 ounces. No. 49K915 Price.... **37c**

**RAILROAD SWITCH,** on ties, for track formations, with joining pegs on both sides. Size, 11x7 inches. Shipping weight, 12 ounces. No. 49K916 Price.... **69c**

*Sears, Roebuck & Co.*

# PAINTED RUBBER BALLS.

## Painted Rubber Balls.

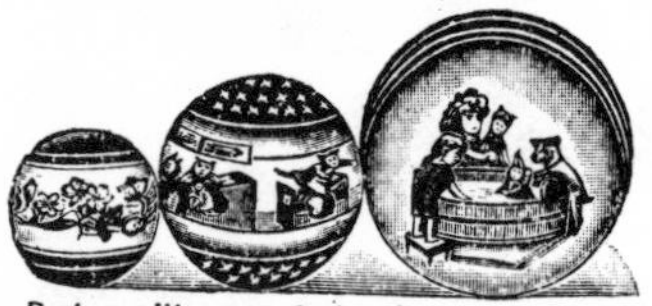

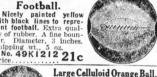

**Best quality manufactured,** beautiful colors and assorted decorations. Colors will not rub off. Harmless and great bouncers. All extra good value for the low prices. Assorted decorations.

No. 49K1205 4½ inches in diameter. Shipping weight, 7 ounces. Price........39c
No. 49K1204 3¾ inches in diameter. Shipping weight, 5 ounces. Price........21c
No. 49K1203 2¼ inches in diameter. Shipping weight, 4 ounces. Price........9c

## Inflated Rubber Football.

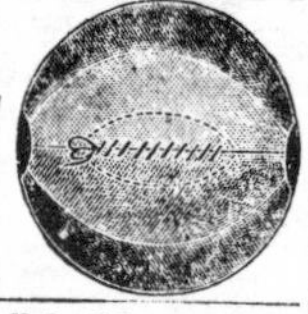

**Nicely painted yellow with black lines to represent football.** Extra quality of rubber. A fine bouncer. Diameter, 3 inches. Shipping wt., 5 oz.
No. 49K1212 Price.............21c

## Large Celluloid Orange Ball.

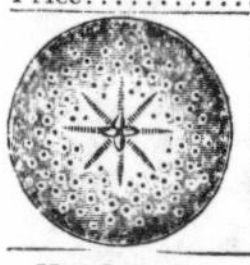

**Made of celluloid, colored to resemble orange.** Diameter, 3 inches. Very light. Has good bounce. Fine ball for indoor use and babies. Shipping weight, 4 ounces.
No. 49K1193 Price. 9c

## Hard Rubber Ball.

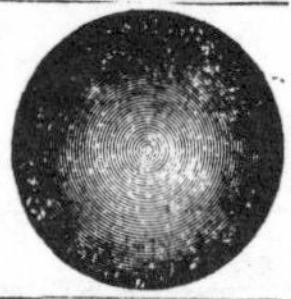

**Every child will enjoy this pretty 2⅛-inch diameter red enameled solid rubber ball.** A great bouncer. Shipping weight, 4 ounces.
No. 49K1400 Price.............9c

## Rugby Football, 39 Cents.

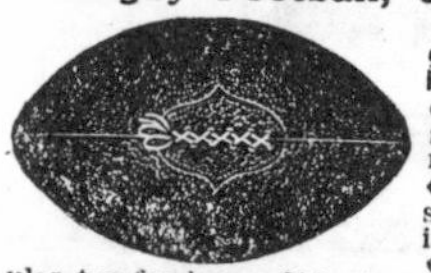

**Covered with good quality pebbled leather and containing good grade seamless** red rubber bladder. Lacing on side. Size, 22 inches circumference. A very popular toy for boys. Shipping wt., 10 oz.
No. 49K1401 Price.............39c

## Canvas Covered Football, 21c.

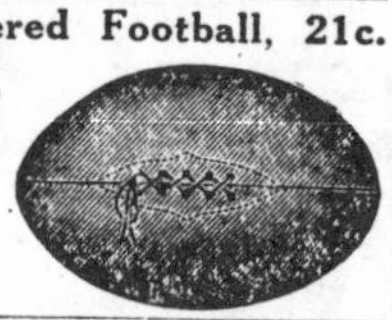

**Good grade canvas.** Laces at side and contains strong red rubber bladder. Full regulation size. Fine for small boys. Shipping wt., 8 oz.
No. 49K1402 Price.............21c

## Beauty House Balls.

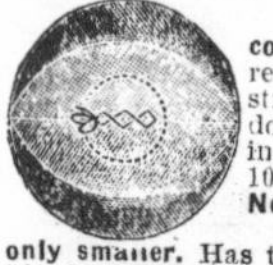

**Cover made of two assorted colored sateen.** Good, strong, red rubber bladder, light and strong. Just the thing for indoor play. Size, 7½ inches in diameter. Shipping wt., 10 ounces.
No. 49K1403 Price 39c
**House Ball.** Same as above only smaller. Has two-color sateen cover. Size, 5½ inches. Shipping wt., 8 oz.
No. 49K1404 Price.............21c

## Decorated Cloth Cut Out Balls.

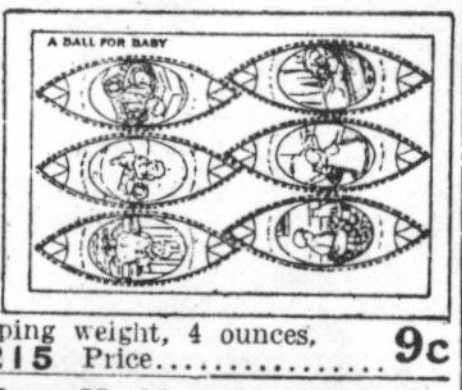


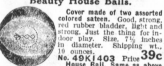

**A Beautifully Decorated Cut Out Ball to be stuffed, for home use.** Pretty colored kindergarten subjects printed on heavy muslin. Large size and very popular. Shipping weight, 4 ounces.
No. 49K1215 Price.............9c

## 100 Boys' Glass Marbles, for 33 Cents.

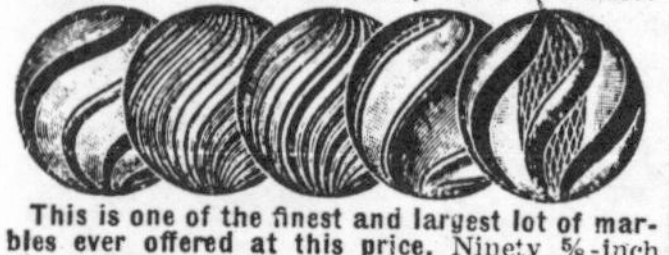

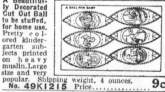

**This is one of the finest and largest lot of marbles ever offered at this price.** Ninety ⅝-inch size, handsomely colored, very pretty glass marbles and ten large shooters. Sh'p'g wt., 2 lbs.
No. 49K1148 Price, 100 for.....33c

22c

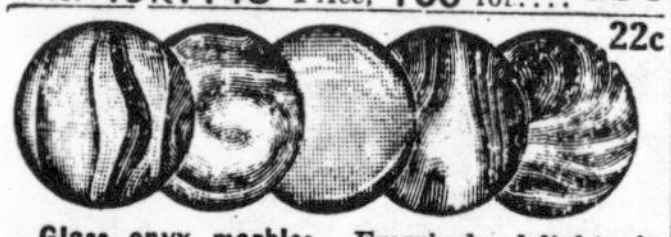

**Glass onyx marbles.** Everybody delights in them. The regulation ¾-inch shooters. The kind sold in many places as agates at 5 cents each. Shipping weight, 10 ounces.
No. 49K1147 Price, per box of 20 marbles.............22c

# GIBBS' CELEBRATED QUALITY TOYS.

**Strong, Beautiful Toys That Always Give Satisfaction.**

## Never Stop See-Saw Toy, 29c

**Very simple construction;** requires no winding. Figures "teeter-totter" up and down the pedestal then turn toy upside down and figures again assume upright position, and repeat the performance. Made entirely of metal, handsomely painted in ten bright colors. Height, 15 inches. Shipping weight, 12 ounces.

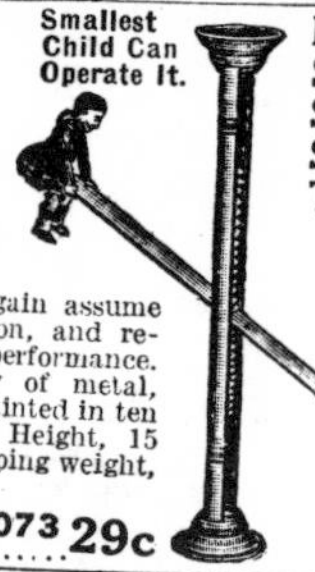


No. 49K1073 Price.............29c

## Pony Circus Wagon, 39 Cents.

**An exceptionally attractive toy.** Handsomely ornamented in bright artistic colors with circus scenes. The ponies walk when drawn along. Strongly constructed, with wheels, sides, legs and all moving parts made of metal. Size, 14x7 inches. Shipping wt., 30 oz.
No. 49K1065 Price.........39c

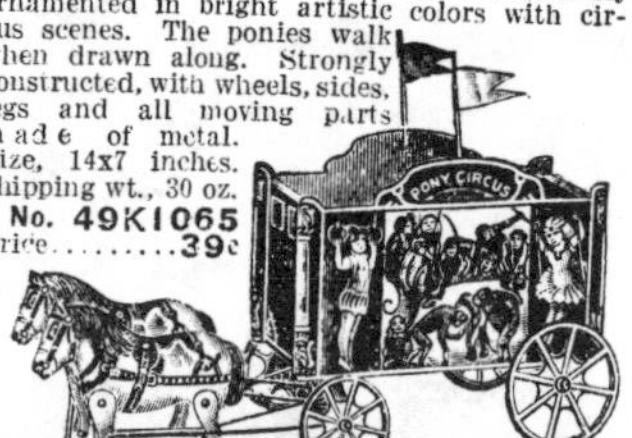


## The Gray Beauty Pacers, 39c.

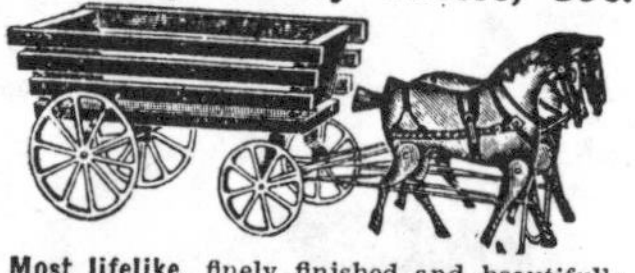

**Most lifelike,** finely finished and beautifully ornamented in seven colors. This toy will not upset, and when drawn along the horses step off with natural pacing gait. Strongly made and cannot get out of order. Wheels, legs and all moving parts are metal. Shipping weight, packed, 26 ounces. Size, 19x6½ inches.
No. 49K1066 Price.............39c

## "Pacing Bob," 19 Cents.

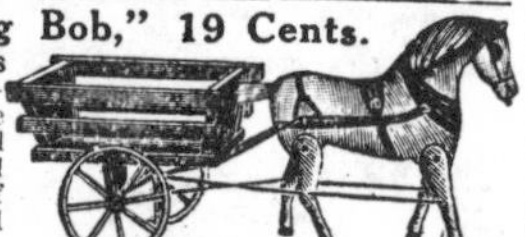

**Same as above,** except one horse, and two-wheel instead of four-wheel wagon. Size, 13½ inches long, 6½ inches high. Shipping weight, 20 ounces.
No. 49K1067 Price.............19c

## Two-Horse Gypsy Wagon, 39c.

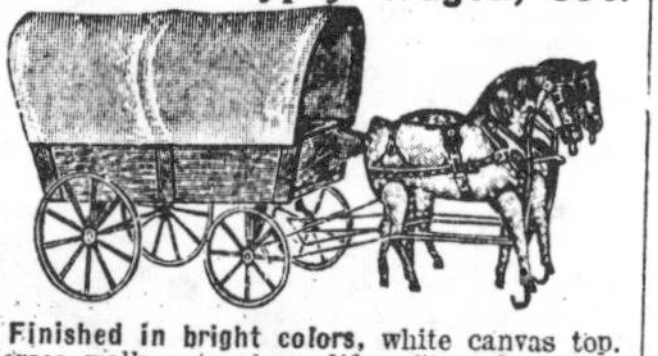

**Finished in bright colors,** white canvas top. Horses walk natural as life. Strongly made. Cannot upset. Wheels, legs and all moving parts made of metal. Length, 19 inches; height, 9 inches. Shipping weight, 30 ounces.
No. 49K1068 Price.............39c

## Single-Horse Gypsy Wagon, 19c.

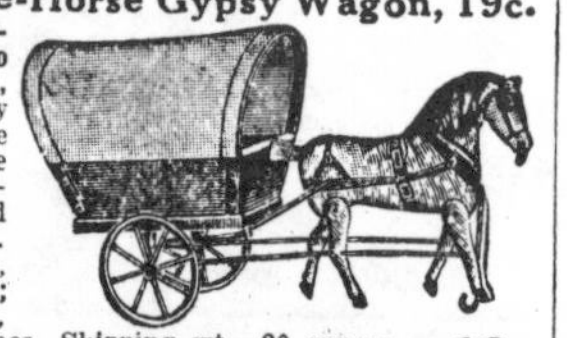

**Similar to above,** but only one horse and two-wheeled wagon. Length, 14 in.; height, 7½ inches. Shipping wt., 20 ounces.
No. 49K1069 Price.............19c

## Pony Pacer, Only 9 Cents.

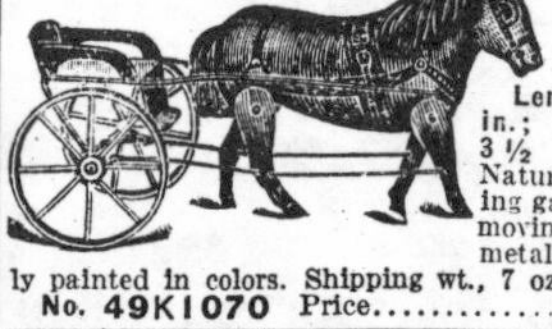

Length, 7 in.; height, 3½ inches. Natural pacing gait. All moving parts metal. Nicely painted in colors. Shipping wt., 7 oz.
No. 49K1070 Price.............9c

## Gibbs' Hobby Horse, 9 Cents.

**Well made and beautifully finished in bright colors.** Miniature hobby horse and so cute and attractive that children cannot resist it. Size, 6¼x3¾ inches. Shipping weight, 10 ounces.
No. 49K1071 Price.............9c

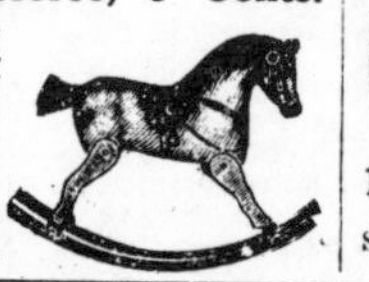

## Three 10-Cent Tops In One.

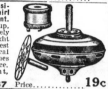

**Comprises the whirlabout, humming and rainbow colored disc tops in one.** Made for us exclusively. Any one of the three selling for 10 cents everywhere. The finest combination made. No matter what else you buy include one of these with your order. Beautifully decorated; 10 inches in circumference. Shipping weight, 6 ounces.

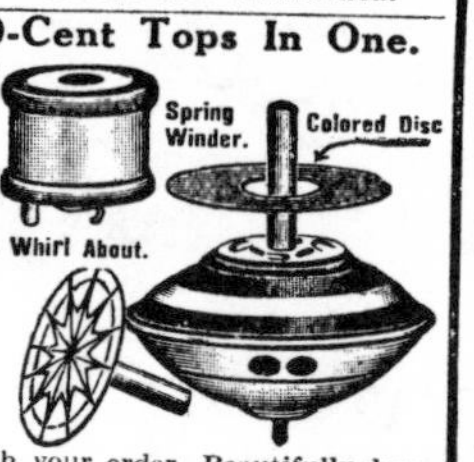


No. 49K1074 Price.............10c

## Dixie Dancing Top.

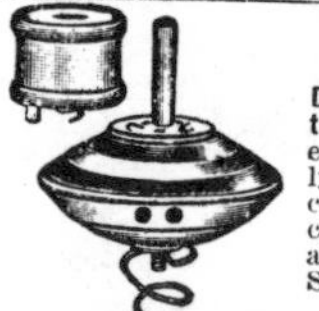

**This Humming and Dancing Top is a sensational seller.** Surprises everyone. Very attractively decorated in bright colors; 10 inches in circumference. Dances up and down while humming. Shipping weight, 6 oz.
No. 49K1168 Price.............8c

**Large size Musical Top with whirl about attachment.** Easily wound up, good tone, nicely decorated in light colors, and the best American musical top made; 13 inches in circumference. Shipping weight, 10 ounces.
No. 49K1167 Price.............19c

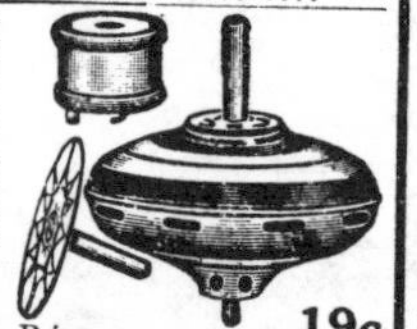

## Performing Bob, 9c.

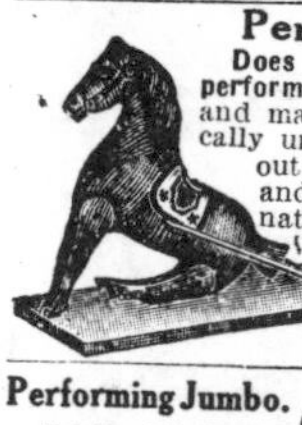

**Does all the tricks of the best performing horse you ever saw,** and many others besides. Practically unbreakable; nothing to get out of order. Nicely painted and finished in colors. Size, natural position, 7x8 inches. Very interesting toy. Shipping weight, 10 oz.
No. 49K1072 Price.........9c

## Performing Jumbo. 19c

**Trick Elephant.** On platform so it can be drawn around the room. Great fun. Size, 10x9 inches. Nicely painted and finished in seven bright colors. Children never tire of playing with it. Shipping weight, 24 oz.
No. 49K1077 Price.............19c

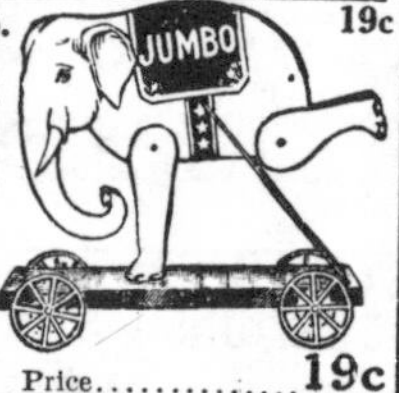


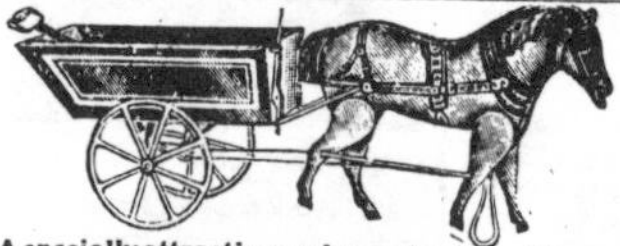

**A specially attractive and popular toy.** Strongly made and nicely decorated in bright colors. Horse has harness lithographed in natural colors. By pulling lever cart is dumped. The best dump cart on the market with the added feature of a horse. Heavy lifelike movements. Bronzed wheels, 4¼ inches in diameter. Size, 19x5x6½ inches. Shipping wt., 2 lbs.
No. 49K1076 Price.............39c

## Fairy Hay Wagon, 19 Cents.

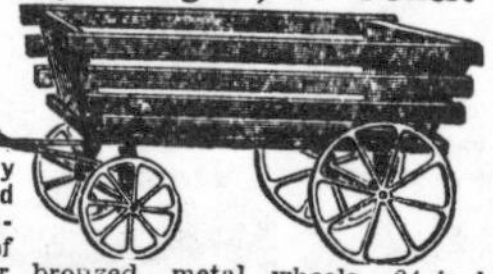

**Nicely painted red and varnished.** Body of wood, silver bronzed, metal wheels, 24-inch twisted wire handle. Size wagon, 9¾x5½x5¾ inches. 25 cents everywhere. Shipping weight, 24 ounces.
No. 49K1075 Price.............19c

## Wagon, 19c.

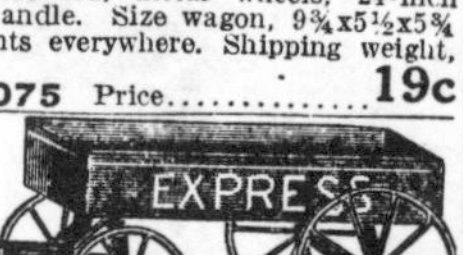


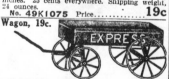

**Metal sides, nicely painted and varnished inside and out. With word "Express" on sides.** Metal bronzed wheels. Strong and durable. Size, 9½x5x4½ inches. A 25-cent wagon. Shipping weight, 20 ounces.
No. 49K1059 Price.............19c

## Trick Elephant.

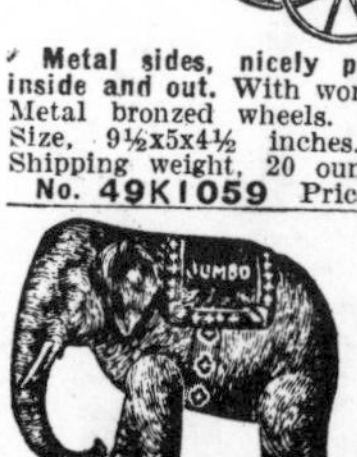


13c

**Nicely decorated in natural colors.** Very lifelike in appearance. Has friction jointed movable metal legs, with which it can be placed in many different comical and amusing positions. Strong and practically unbreakable. Size, 8¼x7½ inches. Shipping wt., 10 oz.
No. 49K1064 Price.............13c

# TOPS! TOPS! TOPS!

## Gyroscope Top, 15 Cents.

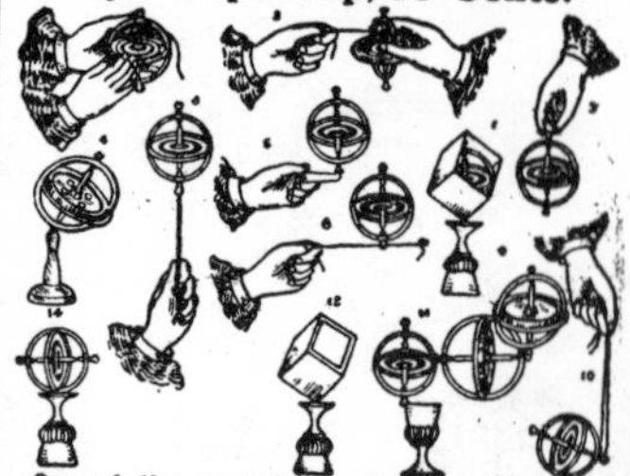

**One of the most instructive and interesting toys ever manufactured.** A wonder of science and perfection of mechanism. A great variety of experiments can be performed with this top, as shown in illustration above. An endless source of delight for the child. Put up one in box with pedestal and full directions. You will spend many enjoyable evenings with this top. Shipping weight, 8 ounces.
No. 49K441 Price.............15c

## Boys! Attention!

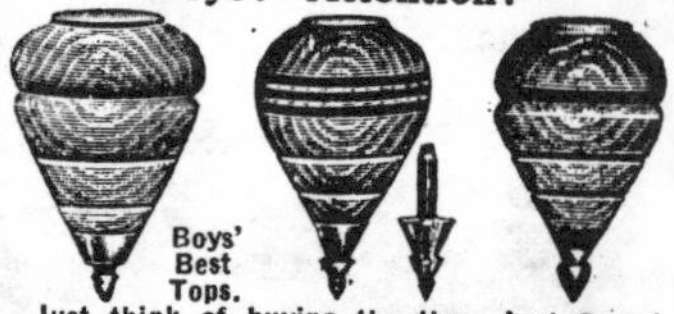


**Just think of buying the three best 5-cent tops complete with cords for only 10 cents.** Outfit consists of a **ball bearing top** (spins on a steel ball encased in a steel peg), one **Buster top** (spins on steel peg which rests on a rubber cushion, giving a high bounce when spun) and one **Ski-Hi top** (the high bouncing rubber cushion top). All these tops with spinning cords, complete in box. Regular value, 18 cents. Shipping weight, 1 pound.
No. 49K1099 Price, 3 for.........10c

## Our Best Musical Tops.

**The finest musical tops that can be purchased in Germany.** Made throughout of beautiful white celluloid, decorated in fancy colors. Has celluloid ring and fancy cord for winding. When spinning can be made to play several beautiful chords. This should not be confused with the cheaper tops, as it is classed by itself. Handsome in appearance. Each in box. Height, 8 inches. $1.50 value. Shipping weight, 8 oz.
No. 49K383 Price.............98c

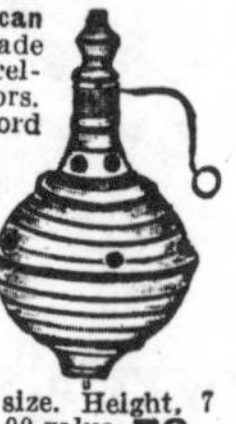

Same as above, but smaller size. Height, 7 inches. Shipping wt., 6 oz. $1.00 value.
No. 49K312 Price.............79c

## Nickel Plated Musical Top, 39 Cents.

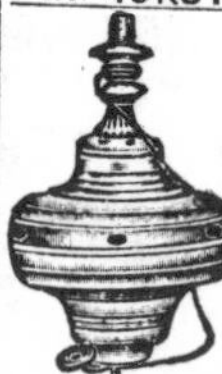

**A very handsome top,** nickel plated, and preferred by many boys, as its construction makes it a better street top. By tapping the top while spinning it gives several distinct chords. Shipping weight, 8 ounces.
No. 49K337 Price.........39c

## A Very Good Singing Top.

**Nickel Plated Metal Choral Top.** 8 inches high, and cord for spinning. By gently tapping top while top is in motion several distinct chords are produced. A big seller and wonderful value. Shipping weight, 6 ounces.
No. 49K313 Price.............21c

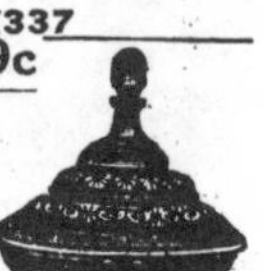

## Musical Top, 10 Cents.

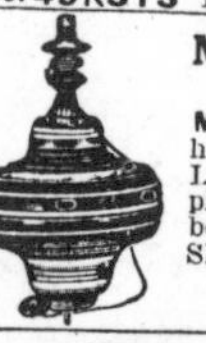

**Beautifully Lithographed Metal Musical Top,** 7 inches high, and cord for spinning. Loud musical tone, sure to please. A big seller and the best value known at the price. Shipping weight, 6 ounces.
No. 49K368 Price.............10c

## Encased Wizard Jumping Top.

**A mystifying and amusing trick top.** Defies gravitation. When spinning will jump out of case. About thirty other tricks can be performed with it. Complete with metal spinning top, wooden case, pedestal, jumping shell, wire walker, 20 feet wire for track, and full directions. Regular price, 50 cents. Shipping weight, 6 ounces.
No. 49K1223 Price.........39c

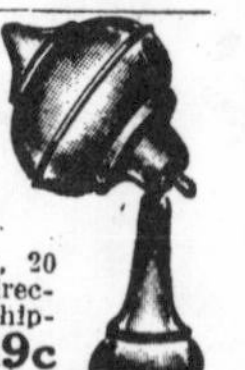

## Monorail Jumping Top.

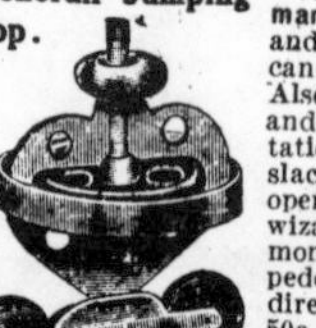

**A scientific mechanical marvel.** Amuses children and adults. Thirty tricks can be performed with it. Also rides on monorail and on wire; defies gravitation. Walks a tight or slack wire. A child can operate it. Complete with wizard top, jumping shell, monorail, wire track, pedestal, cord and full directions. Regular price, 50c. Shipping wt., 8 oz.
No. 49K1224 Price.............39c

## These Fine Wagons for Only 79c, 49c and 37c.

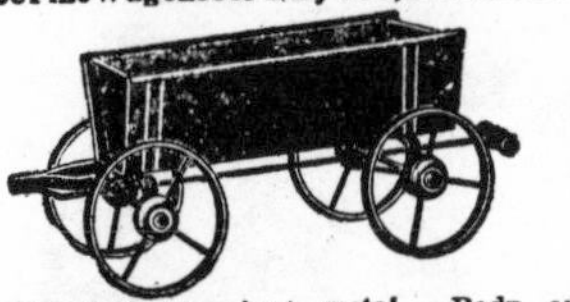

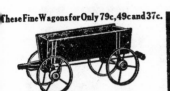

**Made of heavy sheet metal.** Body and wheels painted green, the bed red. Good heavy wheels. Metal tongue with wood handle at end. Hubs gilded. Very strongly made, will carry quite a load. Three sizes:

**Wagon.** Size body, 12½x7¼ inches. Shipping weight, 5 pounds.
**No. 49K1190** Price............**79c**

**Wagon.** Size body, 11x6 inches. Shipping weight, 4 pounds.
**No. 49K1181** Price............**49c**

**Wagon.** Size body, 10½x5½ inches. Shipping weight, 2½ pounds.
**No. 49K1177** Price............**37c**

## Rubber Tired Grocery Wagon.

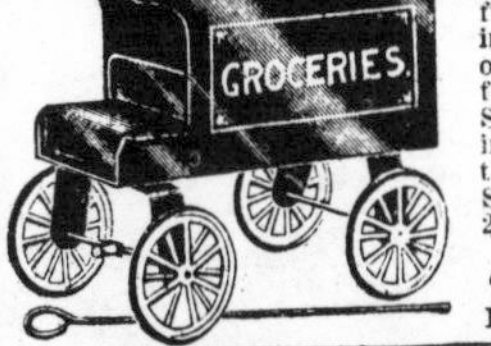


**Strongly made,** beautifully finished in bright colors. Movable front trucks. Size, 8x9x4 inches. Fine toy wagon. Shipping wt., 24 ounces.
**No. 49K1410** Price, **21c**

## Toy Milk Wagon, $1.39.

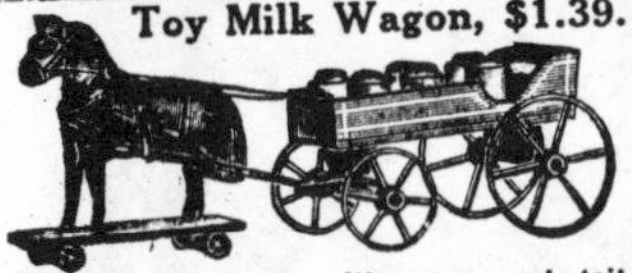

**Cloth covered horse with mane and tail.** Leather harness and attached to metal rim wood wheel milk wagon containing six milk cans. Movable tongue and horse on platform and rollers. Horse can be detached. Size of horse, 10½x11½ inches. Length over all, 28 inches. Shipping weight, 2½ pounds.
**No. 49K3062¼** Price............**$1.39**

## Horse and Truck, 95c.

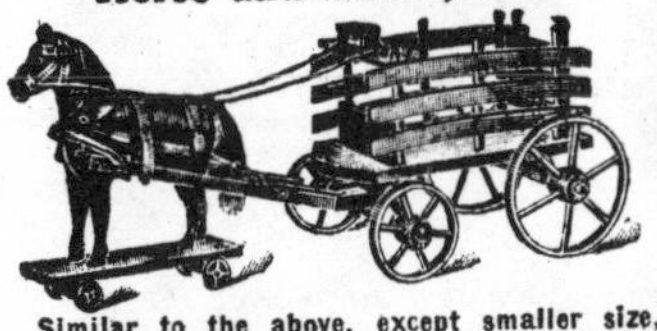

**Similar to the above, except smaller size,** and truck like illustration. Size of horse, 9x9 inches. Length over all, 24 inches. Shipping weight, 2¼ pounds.
**No. 49K3063¼** Price............**95c**

## Horses and Ice Wagon, 39c.

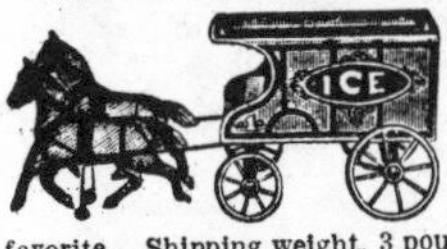


**Wagon of light steel.** The horses and wagon nicely painted and decorated. Size 17x8 inches. Very well made and a big favorite. Shipping weight, 3 pounds.
**No. 49K1078** Price............**39c**

## Horses and Delivery Wagon.

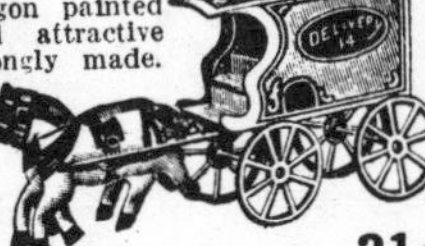


**Wagon of light steel,** the horses and wagon painted in bright and attractive colors and strongly made. Word "Delivery" painted on sides of wagon. Size, 14x6½ inches. Shipping wt., 2 pounds.
**No. 49K1079** Price............**21c**

## This Fine Leather Whip for 21c.

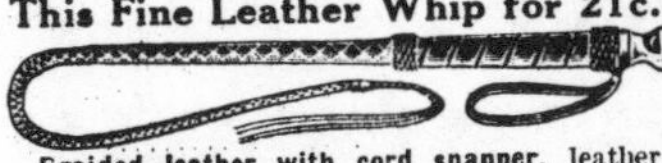

**Braided leather with cord snapper,** leather wound handle, wooden whistle. Length, 45 inches. Shipping weight, 4 ounces.
**No. 49K1291** Price............**21c**

## A Fine Toy Whip, 8c.

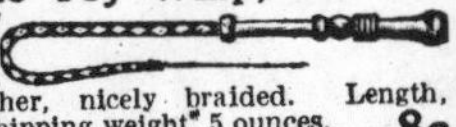

**Handle of white wood with whistle.** Imitation leather, nicely braided. Length, 30½ inches. Shipping weight, 5 ounces.
**No. 49K1144** Price............**8c**

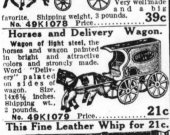

**Bing's All Metal Water Wagon,** finest sheet metal finished with thickly coated enamel in bright colors. Nothing about this toy to break. When filled with water the water can be sprinkled just as on a real water wagon. By moving a lever the water can be turned on or shut off as desired. Size of wagon, 7¼x11x5 in. Shipping wt., 2 lbs.

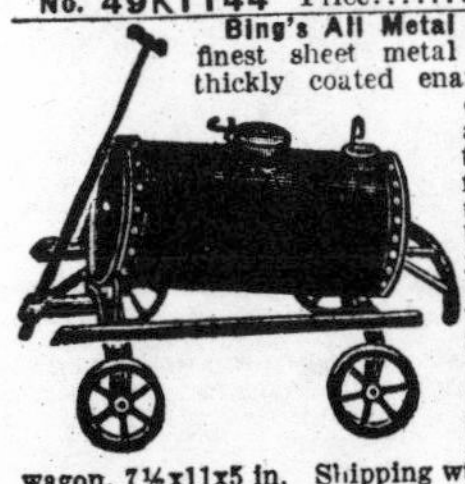

**No. 49K1260** Price............**98c**

## Buy This Horse for Your Boy.

**Ride and Steer It Like a Velocipede. Horse's Head Turns While Steering.**

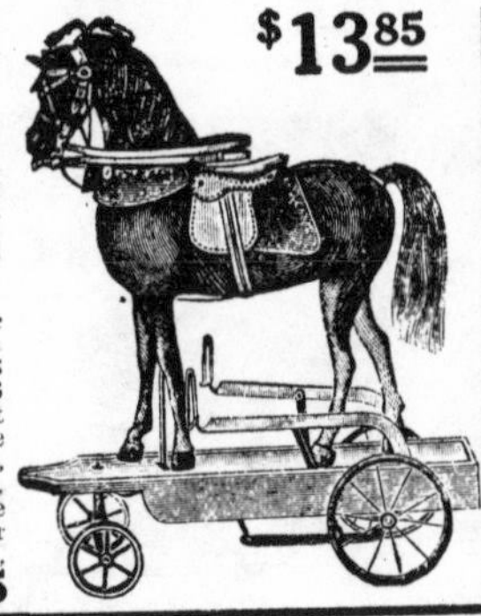

**$13.85**

**The highest quality toy possible to produce.** Real skin covered, long mane and tail, fine genuine leather double strap bridle, curb bit, genuine leather padded top saddle, with strong cinch straps. Handsome decorated blanket and collar. Removable bridle and saddle. Platform of heavy wood, nicely painted. Wheels are gilt decorated, strongly made, with heavy solid rubber tires, steering handle of ⅝-inch metal with wooden turned hand grips. Rod passes through horse's head and body, and is fastened to front wheels with bolt. Slight pressure on handle will turn horse's head and neck, giving the animal a strikingly lifelike appearance. Horse itself is 2 feet 3 inches high, 2 feet 2 inches long. Platform is 2 feet 6 inches long, 10 inches wide, 6¾ inches high. Sufficient room on rear for little child to stand while his playmate rides the horse. Propelling device is of lever principle, best made. This toy is absolutely safe, easy to propel, and far better than any velocipede. Last year we were unable to fill half our orders. We advise you to order early to avoid a chance of disappointment. Regular price, $20.00 to $25.00. Shipping weight, 40 pounds.
**No. 49K3064¼** Price............**$13.85**

## Genuine Skin Covered Horse, $14.25.

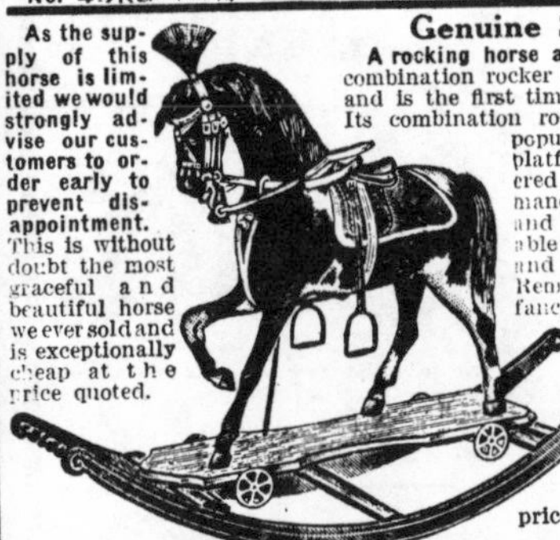

**As the supply of this horse is limited we would strongly advise our customers to order early to prevent disappointment.** This is without doubt the most graceful and beautiful horse we ever sold and is exceptionally cheap at the price quoted.

**A rocking horse and platform horse combined in one.** This great combination rocker has been imported by us direct from Germany and is the first time it has been offered for sale in this country. Its combination rocker and platform feature will make it very popular, as the child can have a rocking horse or platform horse at will. Black and white skin covered horse with real hair tail and long flowing mane, glass eyes and exceptionally graceful figure and well made. Fancy embossed red leather removable harness. All metal parts, such as bit, stirrups and buckles, are highly nickel plated and polished. Removable leather covered saddle, padded seat with fancy blanket and two-color fancy heavy plume on horse's head. Platform and rocker handsomely painted in red with black and gilt decorations; 4-inch metal wheels. Length of horse, 51 inches; height, 40 inches. Adjustable stirrups, 16 inches long. Suitable for boy from 2½ to 7 years of age. Platform can be removed from rocker by releasing two bolts. Easily changed. Regular price, $20.00 to $25.00. Ship. wt., 40 lbs.
**No. 49K3069¼** Price............**$14.25**

## SWINGING HOBBY HORSES.

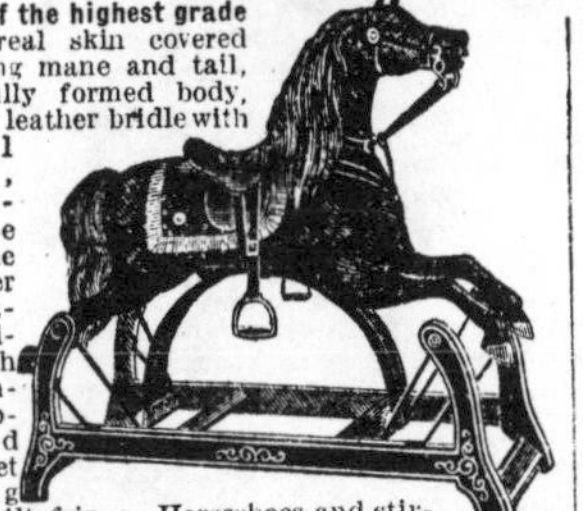

**One of the highest grade made,** real skin covered with long mane and tail, beautifully formed body, genuine leather bridle with metal bit, handsome genuine leather removable saddle with very fancy decorated blanket having heavy gilt fringe. Horseshoes and stirrups of metal gilded, the stirrup straps being adjustable in length to 15 inches from saddle. Glass eyes, lifelike appearance. Height over all, 33 inches; from hoof to hoof, 38½ inches. Shipping weight, 40 lbs.
**No. 49K3066¼** Price............**$10.50**

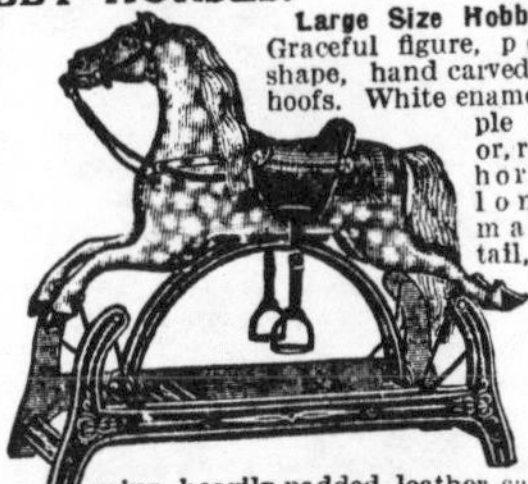

**Large Size Hobby Horse.** Graceful figure, perfect shape, hand carved legs and hoofs. White enameled dapple gray color, real metal horseshoes, long heavy mane and tail, glass eyes, leather bridle, metal gag bit, martingale, leather reins, heavily padded leather saddle with plush saddle skirt and gilt stirrups, and large fancy plush blanket with gilt fringe. Improved swinging attachment. Height of saddle from floor 26½ in; length bottom stirrup from top saddle adjustable to 15 in; length of horse over all, 40½ in.; height of horse from floor, 35½ in. Shipping wt., 30 lbs.
**No. 49K3032¼** Price............**$8.95**

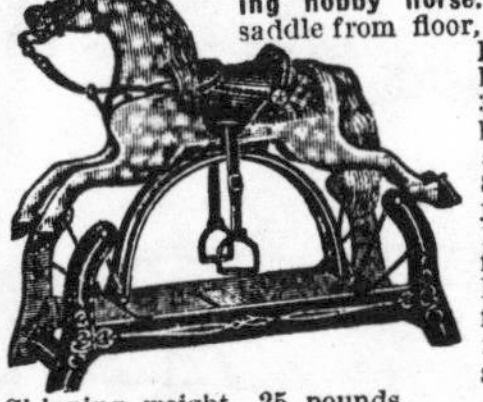

**Nice dapple gray finish swinging hobby horse.** Height of saddle from floor, 24½ inches; length of horse over all, 36½ inches; height over all, 32 inches. Stirrups adjustable to 12½ inches from saddle. Each carefully packed in crate for shipment. Shipping weight, 25 pounds.
**No. 49K3033¼** Price............**$6.85**

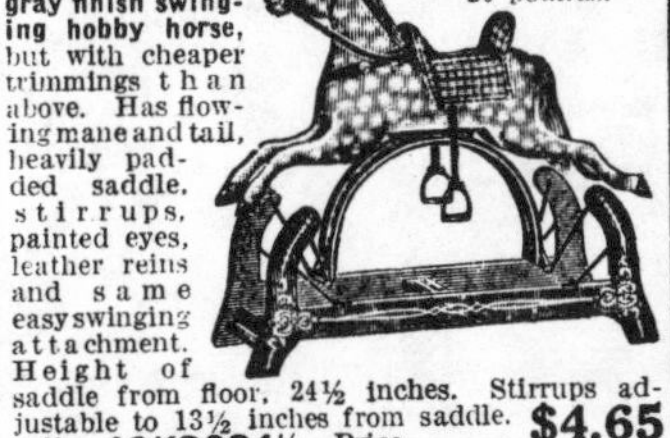

**Nice dapple gray finish swinging hobby horse,** but with cheaper trimmings than above. Has flowing mane and tail, heavily padded saddle, stirrups, painted eyes, leather reins and same easy swinging attachment. Height of saddle from floor, 24½ inches. Stirrups adjustable to 13½ inches from saddle. Shipping weight, 20 pounds.
**No. 49K3034¼** Price............**$4.65**

**Similar to the above, but smaller.** Height of saddle from floor, 23½ in.; stirrups adjustable to 13½ in. from saddle; length of horse over all, 34½ in.; ht. over all, 29½ in. Ship. wt., 20 lbs.
**No. 49K3035¼** Price............**$3.68**

## Swinging Horse, $2.25.

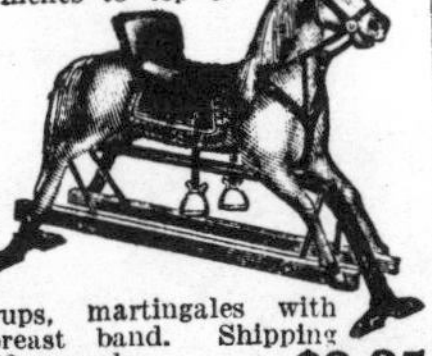

**Enameled air brush finish,** 42 inches long, 29 inches to top of head. Nicely red enameled and striped stand. English saddle in enamel cloth, enamel cloth saddle flaps trimmed with fancy colored fringe. Has hair mane and tail, stirrups, martingales with rings, heavy breast band. Shipping weight, about 22 pounds.
**No. 49K3078¼** Price............**$2.25**

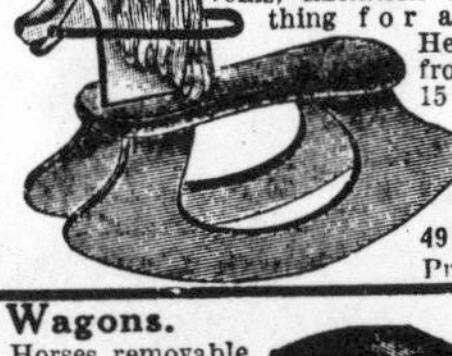

**Solid oak, nicely stained in natural colors;** hair mane, leather reins, imitation eyes. Just the thing for a young child. Height, 9 inches from floor; length, 15 inches. Regular $1.50 value. Shipping wt., 10 lbs.
**No. 49K3031¼** Price............**98c**

## Cloth Covered Horses With Wagons. 45c

**Excellent selection of toy horses and wagons.** Horses removable from shafts. Horse has cloth covered body, hair mane and tail. Mounted on platform with wheels.

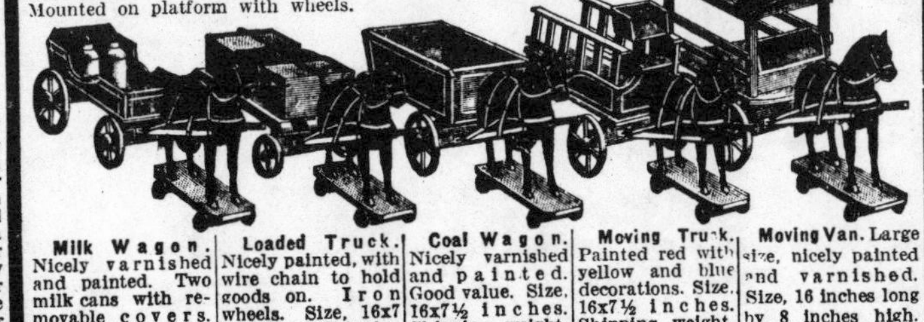

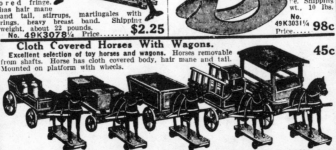

**Milk Wagon.** Nicely varnished and painted. Two milk cans with removable covers. Size, 16x7½ in. Shipping wt., 20 oz.
**No. 49K1299** Price............**45c**

**Loaded Truck.** Nicely painted, with wire chain to hold goods on. Iron wheels. Size, 16x7 inches. Shipping weight, 22 ounces.
**No. 49K1298** Price............**45c**

**Coal Wagon.** Nicely varnished and painted. Good value. Size, 16x7½ inches. Shipping weight, 20 ounces.
**No. 49K1297** Price............**45c**

**Moving Truck.** Painted red with yellow and blue decorations. Size, 16x7½ inches. Shipping weight, 28 ounces.
**No. 49K1296** Price............**45c**

**Moving Van.** Large size, nicely painted and varnished. Size, 16 inches long by 8 inches high. Shipping wt., 28 oz.
**No. 49K1295** Price............**45c**

## Shoo-Fly Rocking Horses.

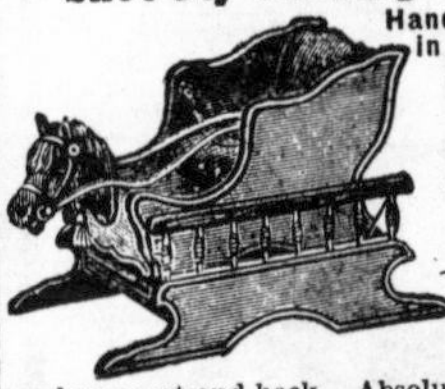

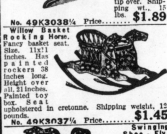

**Handsomely painted in red and gold and varnished.** Good strong construction; will last for years. Very natural horse head, real hair mane, glass eyes, leather harness, handsome cord reins. Heavily padded corduroy seat and back. Absolutely safe. Size, 35x20x16 in. Shipping wt., 22 lbs.
**No. 49K3075¼** Price............**$4.85**

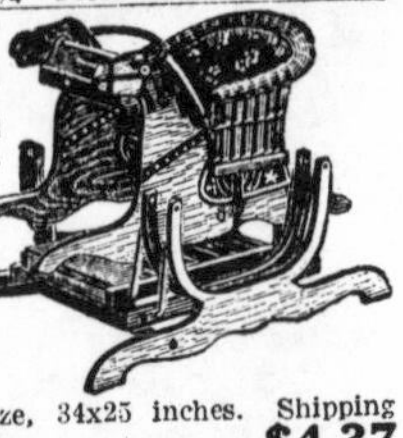

**Latest idea, two rockers in one.** Swings evenly and longer, runs easier. Finished in solid oak natural finish, varnished, painted harness and decorations, wicker basket seat with roll back. Heavily padded and covered with fancy pattern plush. Size, 34x25 inches. Shipping weight, 30 pounds.
**No. 49K3050¼** Price............**$4.37**

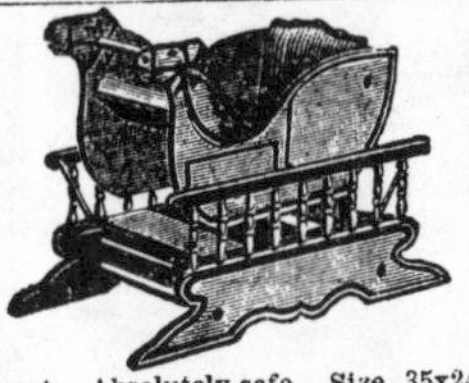

**Handsomely decorated in blue and white,** with gilt decorations and varnished. Painted harness and mane. Seat of good grade corduroy; heavily padded back and seat. Absolutely safe. Size, 35x24½x17 inches. Shipping weight, 23 pounds.
**No. 49K3076¼** Price............**$3.98**

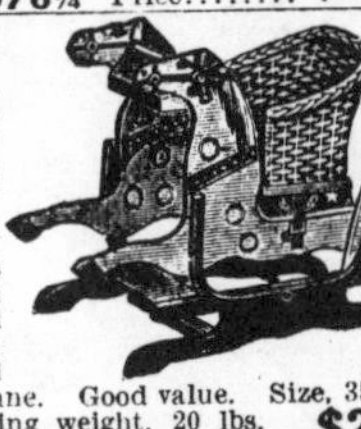

**Beautifully painted in natural colors.** Has swinging toy box, seat and back, fancy reed effect basket. Very strongly made. Has fancy plush cushion and back pad, imitation painted harness and mane. Good value. Size, 35x23½ inches. Shipping weight, 20 lbs.
**No. 49K3041¼** Price............**$2.79**

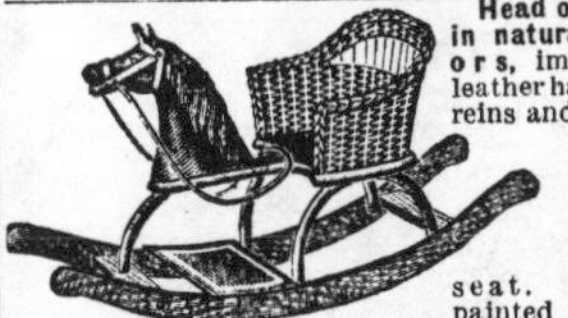

**Head of wood in natural colors,** imitation leather harness, reins and ears, real hair mane, reed basket seat. Nicely painted and decorated. Size, 43 x 24 inches. Shipping weight, 15 pounds.
**No. 49K3077¼** Price............**$2.95**

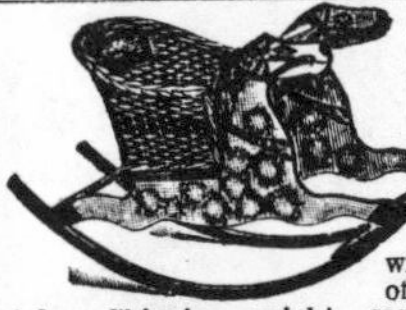

**Size, 21 x 38 inches.** The body is made of very fancy reed, best quality, strong and durable. Seat upholstered in fine velour, with back cushions of the same material. Shipping weight, carefully crated, 15 pounds.
**No. 49K3065¼** Price............**$2.25**

**Swinging Shoo-Fly Rocking Horse.** Size, 24 x 32 inches. Beautifully painted, has toy box, seat and back upholstered in cretonne, horses suspended on swinging frame. Not easy to tip over. Shipping wt., 15 lbs.

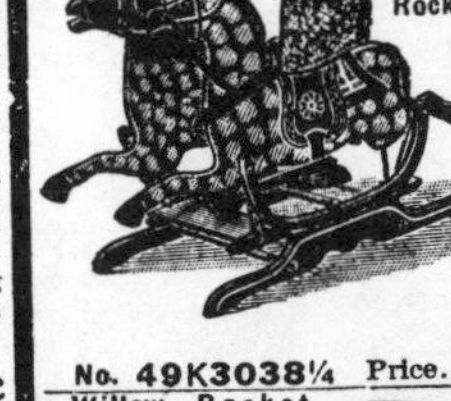

**No. 49K3038¼** Price............**$1.89**

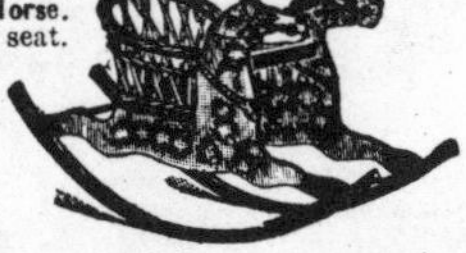

**Willow Basket Rocking Horse.** Fancy basket seat. Size, 11x11 inches. Has painted rockers 38 inches long. Height over all, 21 inches. Painted toy box. Seat upholstered in cretonne. Shipping weight, 12 pounds.
**No. 49K3037¼** Price............**$1.45**

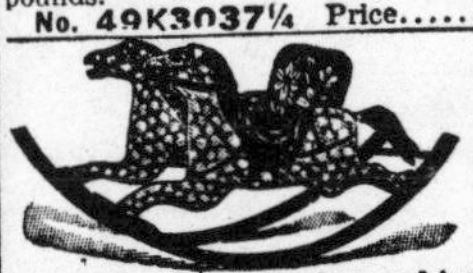

**Swinging Shoo-Fly, fancy cretonne padded upholstered back and seat. Height, 18 inches; rockers, 39 inches long.** Has toy box and is nicely finished throughout. Shipping wt., 12 lbs.
**No. 49K3036¼** Price............**$1.00**

147

*Sears Roebuck & Co.*

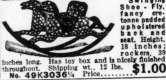

## FINEST TOY STOVES.

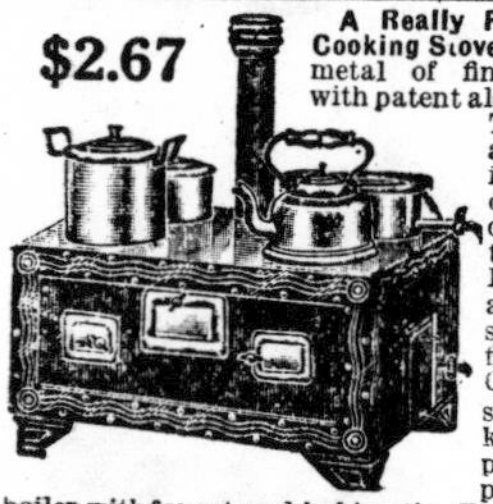

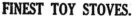

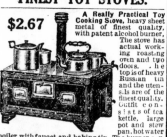

**$2.67** A Really Practical Toy Cooking Stove, heavy sheet metal of finest quality, with patent alcohol burner. The stove has actual working roasting oven and two doors. The top is of heavy Russian tin and the utensils are of the finest quality. Outfit consists of tea kettle, large pot and stew pan, hot water boiler, with faucet and baking tin. The burner can be regulated to the size of the flames. Size, 12 x 8½ x 10 inches, not including chimney. Shipping weight, 8 pounds.
**No. 49K742** Price .......... **$2.67**

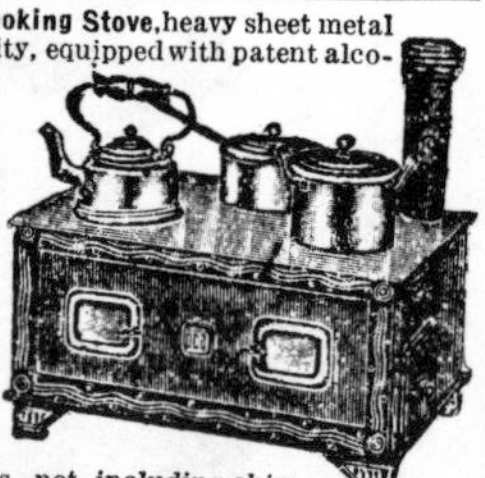

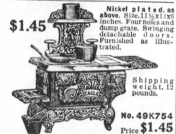

**Real Toy Cooking Stove,** heavy sheet metal of finest quality, equipped with patent alcohol burner, beautifully decorated with gilt lines, has two doors. The top is made of heavy Russian tin and the utensils consist of fine tea kettle, large pot and stewpan. Size, 8¾ x 6¾ x 3½ inches, not including chimney. Shipping weight, 5 pounds.
**No. 49K761** Price .......... **$1.39**

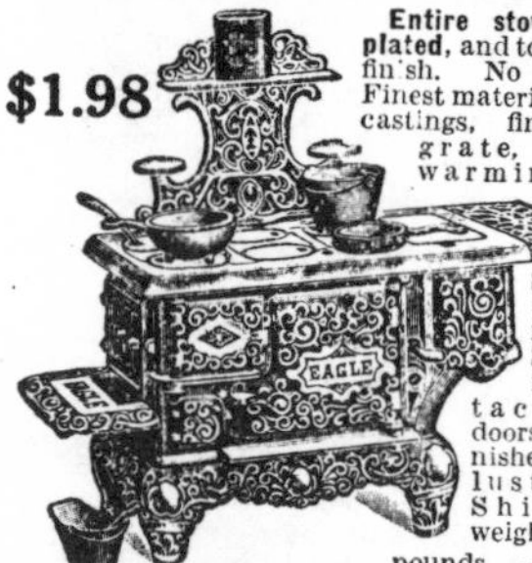

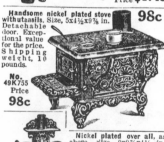

**$1.98** Entire stove nickel plated, and top in dull finish. No tarnish. Finest material, heavy castings, fine dump grate, large warming oven. Size, 13x16x6 inches. Swinging detachable doors. Furnished as illustrated. Shipping weight, 18 pounds.
**No. 49K3027¼** Price. ..... **$1.98**

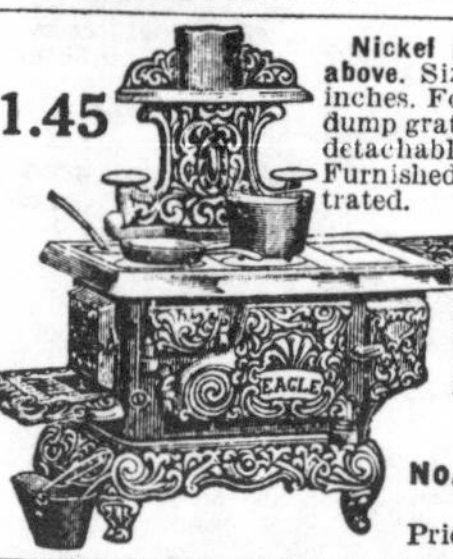

**$1.45** Nickel plated, as above. Size, 11½x11x6 inches. Four holes and dump grate. Swinging detachable doors. Furnished as illustrated. Shipping weight, 12 pounds.
**No. 49K754** Price **$1.45**

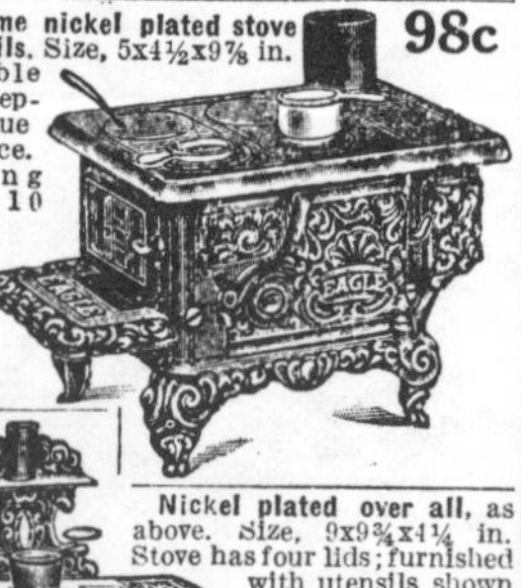

**Handsome nickel plated stove with utensils.** Size, 5x4½x9⅞ in. **98c** Detachable door. Exceptional value for the price. Shipping weight, 10 pounds.
**No. 49K755** Price **98c**

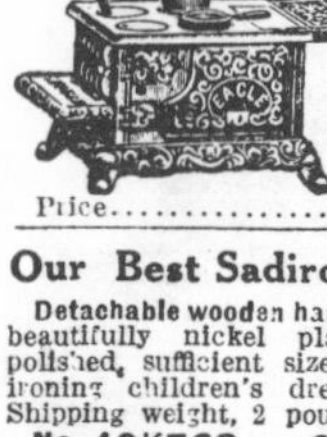

Nickel plated over all, as above. Size, 9x9¾x4¼ in. Stove has four lids; furnished with utensils shown in picture. Dump grate, swing detachable doors. Extra good value. Shipping weight, 5 lbs.
**No. 49K759**
Price .......... **49c**

### Our Best Sadirons.

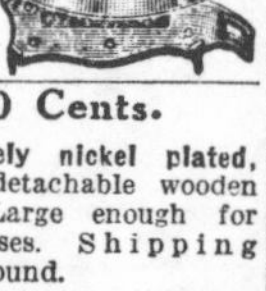

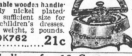

**Detachable wooden handle** beautifully nickel plated, polished, sufficient size for ironing children's dresses. Shipping weight, 2 pounds.
**No. 49K762** Price .......... **21c**

### Sadiron for 10 Cents.



Handsomely nickel plated, polished, detachable wooden handle. Large enough for dolly's dresses. Shipping weight, 1 pound.
**No. 49K763** Special price .......... **10c**

## BOYS' VERY BEST TOOL CHESTS.

### Compare Our Values With Those of Others.

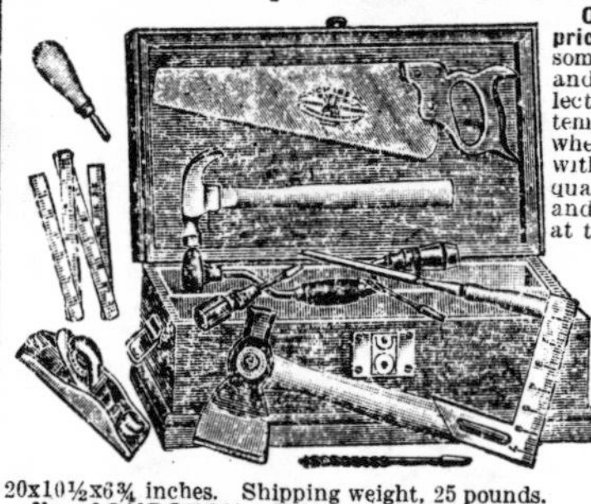

**One of the greatest values ever offered at the price.** Consists of regulation size tools in handsome stained mission chest with patent brass lock and handles. Each tool has been carefully selected and is of the best quality. All edged tools are tempered from forged steel and are ready to use when shipped. This outfit must not be compared with the average boys' set sold. Not quantity but quality. By putting in this outfit only practical and useful tools we are able to give the best grade at this low price.

**Our High Grade Twelve-Piece Set of practical tools** contains the following: 18-inch regulation saw, one 1½-inch tempered edge hatchet, one 13-inch forged steel hammer, one 1¼-inch regulation size brace with two tempered steel bits for same, one 12½-inch tempered steel chisel, one 10-inch screwdriver, one 6¾-inch adjustable metal plane, one 4¾-inch awl, 7½-inch square with ⅛-inch markings for measuring, and 24-inch folding rule. Box has 4½-inch sliding compartment. Size, 20x10½x6¾ inches. Shipping weight, 25 pounds.
**No. 49K3079¼** Price .......... **$4.85**

### Our $3.98 Value.

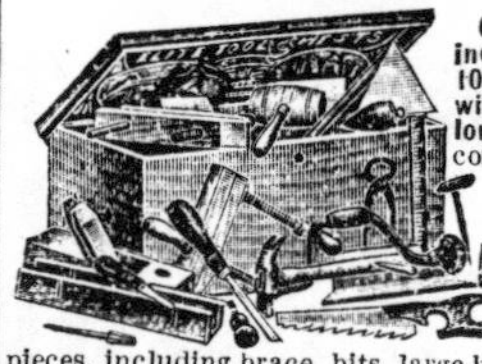

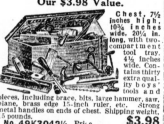

**Chest, 7½ inches high, 10¾ inches wide, 20¼ in. long,** with two-compartment tool tray, 4½ inches wide. Contains thirty extra quality boys' tools and pieces, including brace, bits, large hammer, saw, plane, brass edge 15-inch ruler, etc. Strong metal handles on ends of chest. Shipping weight, 15 pounds.
**No. 49K3042¼** Price .......... **$3.98**

### Our $2.35 Value.

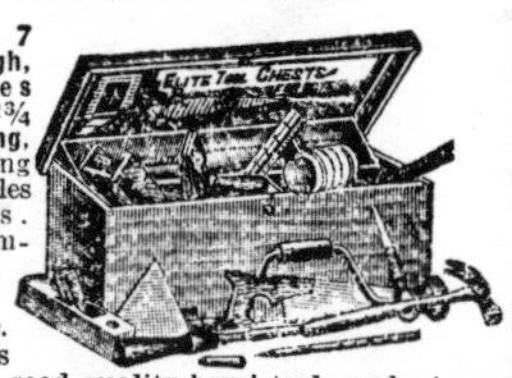

**Chest, 7 inches high, 10 inches wide, 17¾ inches long,** with strong metal handles on ends. Two-compartment tool tray, 4 inches wide. Contains twenty-five good quality boys' tools and pieces, including nickel head hammer, brace, bit, plane, saw, pincers, etc. An extra good value. Shipping weight, 12 pounds.
**No. 49K3043¼** Price .......... **$2.35**

### Our $1.68 Value.

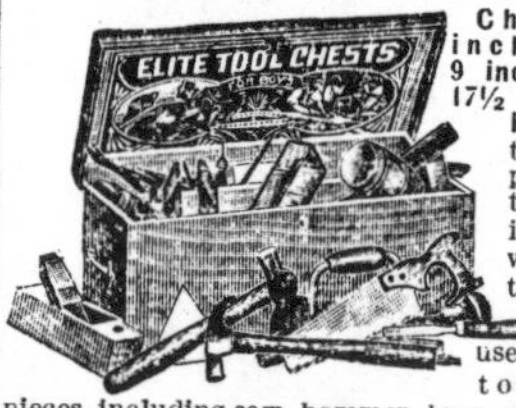

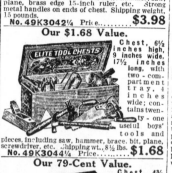

**Chest, 6½ inches high, 9 inches wide, 17½ inches long,** with two-compartment tray, 4 inches wide; contains twenty-one useful boys' tools and pieces, including saw, hammer, brace, bit, plane, screwdriver, etc. Shipping wt., 8½ lbs.
**No. 49K3044¼** Price .......... **$1.68**

### Our 98-Cent Value.

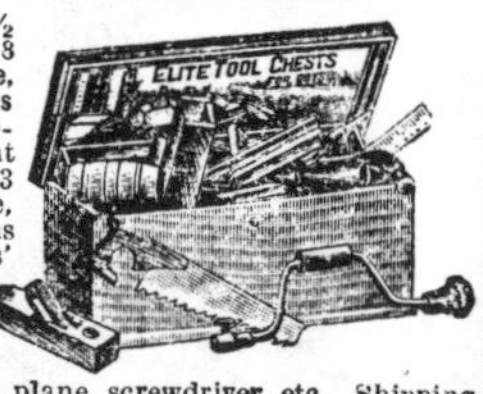

**Chest, 5½ inches high, 8 inches wide, 15¼ inches long,** with two-compartment tool tray 3 inches wide, and contains sixteen boys' tools and pieces, including brace, bit, hammer, saw, plane, screwdriver, etc. Shipping weight, 8 pounds.
**No. 49K1208** Price .......... **98c**

### Our 79-Cent Value.

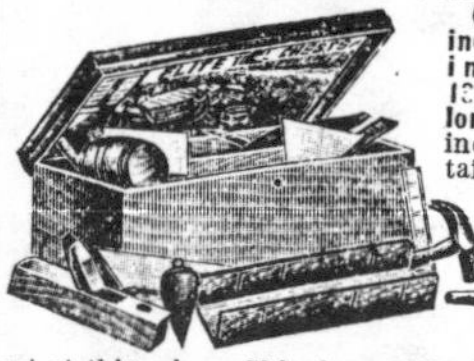

**Chest, 4¾ inches high, 6½ inches wide, 12¼ inches long,** with 2⅞-inch tray. Contains thirteen boys' tools and pieces, including hammer, plane, saw, ruler, etc. A very good set at this price. Shipping weight, 5 lbs.
**No. 49K1209** Price .......... **79c**

### Our Wonder 50-Cent Value.

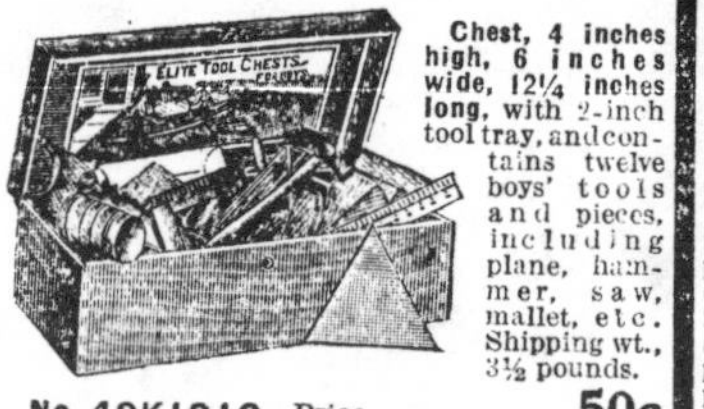

**Chest, 4 inches high, 6 inches wide, 12¼ inches long,** with 2-inch tool tray, and contains twelve boys' tools and pieces, including plane, hammer, saw, mallet, etc. Shipping wt., 3½ pounds.
**No. 49K1210** Price .......... **50c**

### Our 25-Cent Value.

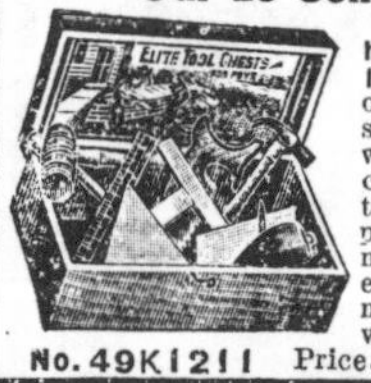

**Chest, 3½ inches high, 5¼ inches wide, 10¾ inches long,** without tray, but with same high polished, varnished, metal hinge chest, and contains ten boys' tools and pieces, including hammer, saw, ruler, top, etc. A beauty for the money. Shipping weight, 28 oz.
**No. 49K1211** Price .......... **25c**

### Our 8-Cent Value.

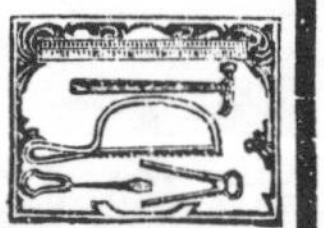

**A nice little set on card,** including hand saw, screwdriver, ruler, hammer and pincers. Shipping weight, 12 ounces.
**No. 49K1137** Price .......... **8c**

## FIRE ENGINES AND HOOK AND LADDER CARTS.

### Fire Engines.

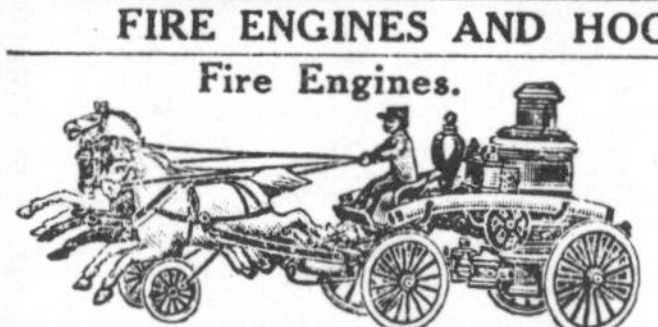

**Massive, 21x7x3¼ inches over all.** Beautifully enameled 9-inch galloping horses. Rubber tired wheels. Bell. Two 8½-inch lengths real hose. Shipping weight, 10 pounds.
**No. 49K3039¼** Price .......... **$2.85**

### Our Big $1.78 Value.

**Similar to above, but made of lighter weight metal, without hose, and with but two horses.** Rubber tired wheels. Size, 21x4½x7½ inches. Shipping weight, 8 pounds.
**No. 49K1115** Price .......... **$1.78**

### Strong Iron Fire Engine.

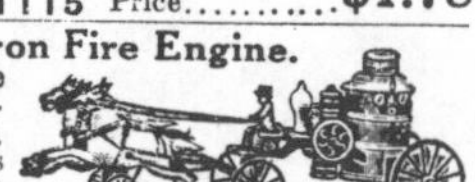

**Has three movable galloping horses.** Leather reins and chain traces enable horses to be removed from engine. Has continuously ringing bell. Size, 18x5x6½ inches. Shipping weight, 6 pounds.
**No. 49K1116** Price .......... **98c**

### A Big 39-Cent Value.

**Similar to above, but smaller.** Without reins and driver. Black enamel, with red and gilt trimmings. Size, 14½x3½x5 inches. Shipping weight, 5 pounds.
**No. 49K1117** Price .......... **39c**

### Hook and Ladder Carts.

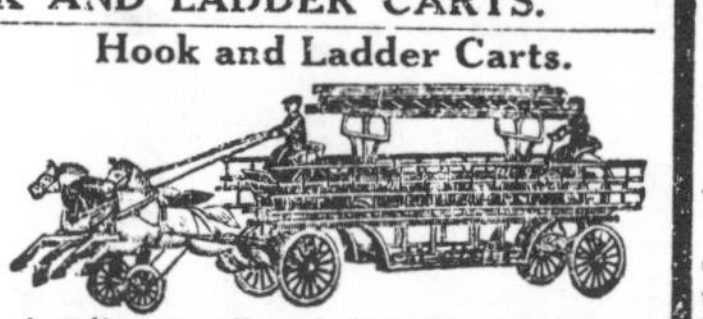

**Length over all, not including ladders, 30 inches.** Heavy enameled and decorated malleable iron. Rubber tired wheels. Six ladders. 9-inch galloping horses. Shipping weight, 9 pounds.
**No. 49K3040¼** Price .......... **$2.85**

### Examine This for $1.78.

**Similar to above, but smaller.** Three ladders, two galloping horses. Wheels rubber tired. Size, 27x4½x8 inches. Shipping weight, 6 pounds.
**No. 49K1179** Price .......... **$1.78**

### Our Big 98-Cent Value.

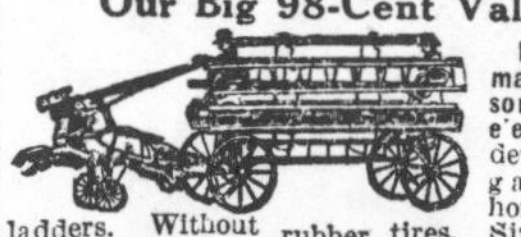

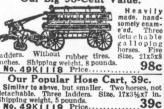

**Heavily made, handsomely enameled.** Three detachable galloping horses. Five ladders. Without rubber tires. Size, 21x5x8 inches. Shipping weight, 8 pounds.
**No. 49K1118** Price .......... **98c**

### Our Popular Hose Cart, 39c.

**Similar to above, but smaller.** Two horses, not detachable. Three ladders. Size, 17x3½x7 in. Shipping weight, 5 pounds.
**No. 49K1119** Price .......... **39c**

## POPULAR TOY BANKS

### Buster Brown and Tige Bank. 9c

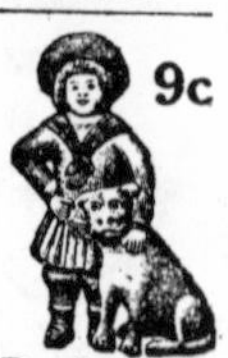

**One of the most popular banks ever manufactured.** Heavy metal, beautifully finished in gilt and color. Height, 5¼ inches. Shipping weight, 1½ pounds. (Unmailable).
**No. 49K1100** Price .......... **9c**

### Dime Savings Bank, 8c.

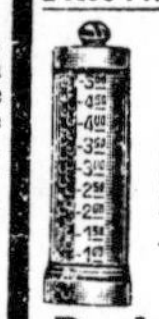

**Dime Savings Bank,** beautifully nickel plated. Holds up to $5.00 when bank opens. A novelty bank. A phenomenal seller. A very popular home item. Shipping weight, 3 ounces.
**No. 49K1114** Price .......... **8c**

### Donkey Bank, 8c.

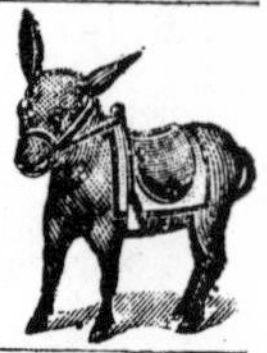

**All metal,** nicely painted, gilt bronze and saddle and bridle in colors. No lock to get out of order. Opens with screw. Very attractive. Size, 4¾x4½ inches. Shipping weight, 1 pound.
**No. 49K1103** Price .......... **8c**

### House Bank, 17c.

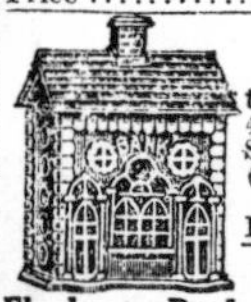

**Money bank, gilt and copper trimmed, nicely finished.** 5½x4x3 inches. Very popular. Shipping weight, 34 ounces. (Unmailable.)
**No. 49K1113** Price .......... **17c**

### Elephant Bank, 21c.

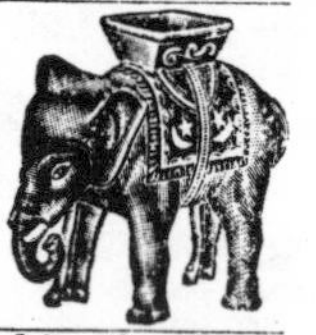

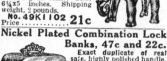

**Heavy, all metal,** nicely painted with gold bronze, with red painted strap around body. Very popular. A good seller. Size, 6¼x5 inches. Shipping weight, 2 pounds.
**No. 49K1102** **21c**

### Nickel Plated Combination Lock Banks, 47c and 22c.

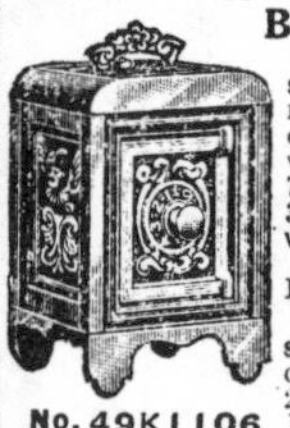

**Exact duplicate of real safe,** highly polished handle, real combination lock. Full directions how to open come with bank. No better made. 75-cent value. Size, 5½x3x3½ inches. Shipping weight, 2¾ pounds.
**No. 49K1105** **47c**

**Similar to above but smaller** size, 4½x2¾x3 inches. 50-cent value. Shipping wt., 2 pounds.
**No. 49K1106** Price .......... **22c**

### Home Savings Bank, 65 Cents.

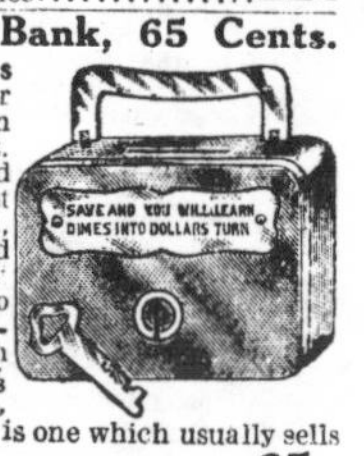


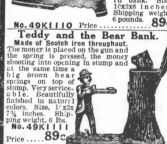

**The Home Savings Bank** is the most popular design that has ever been placed on the market. Made of the best cold rolled steel with the most perfect oxidized finish, durably constructed and is protected by means of a special patent device to prevent coins from dropping out. Key with each bank. Size, 4⅜x3¼x2⅜ inches. Shipping weight, 1¾ pounds. This bank is one which usually sells at $1.00.
**No. 49K1107** Price .......... **65c**

### The Kicking Mule Bank, 89c.

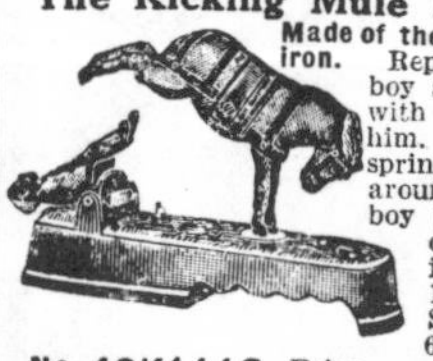

**Made of the very best Scotch iron.** Represents colored boy sitting on stump with mule in front of him. By pressing a spring, the mule whirls around, kicking the boy backwards and depositing money in bank. Size, 10x3x6 inches. Shipping weight, 6 pounds.
**No. 49K1110** Price .......... **89c**

### Teddy and the Bear Bank.

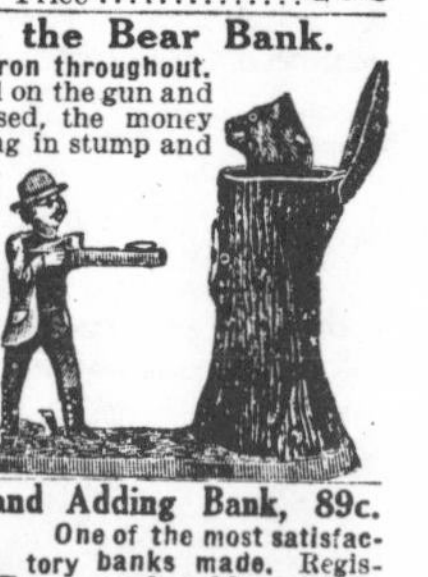

**Made of Scotch iron throughout.** The money is placed on the gun and the spring is pressed, the money shooting into opening in stump and at the same time a big brown bear springs on top of stump. Very serviceable. Beautifully finished in natural colors. Size, 10x3x7¾ inches. Shipping weight, 6 lbs.
**No. 49K1111**
Price .......... **89c**

### Self Registering and Adding Bank, 89c.

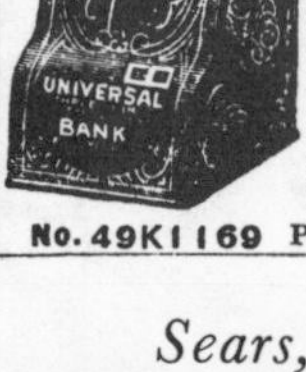


**One of the most satisfactory banks made.** Registers and adds nickels, dimes and quarters, showing the amount in the bank at all times. Made of strong sheet steel painted black with gilt decorations. A great seller. Creates a strong desire to save. Bank cannot be opened until $10.00 has been deposited. Size, 5¼x4¼ inches. Shipping weight, 2 pounds.
**No. 49K1169** Price .......... **89c**

### Toy Telephone, 21c.

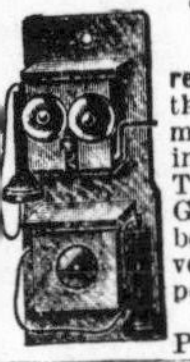

Made of wood to represent a regular wall telephone, without the mouthpiece. Two 1½-inch metal bells, which ring by turning handle. Size 11x5 inches. Two dummy receivers with cord. Great fun for child to ring the bell and hold a pretended conversation. Shipping weight, 1¼ pounds.
No. 49K1213 Price........ 21c

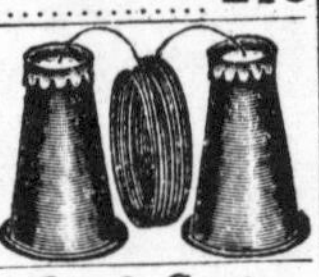

Black metal discs with sounding piece at the end. You can hear for a long distance. Packed in box. Shipping weight, 4 oz.
No. 49K1142 Price........ 8c

### Soap Bubble Outfit, 8 Cents.

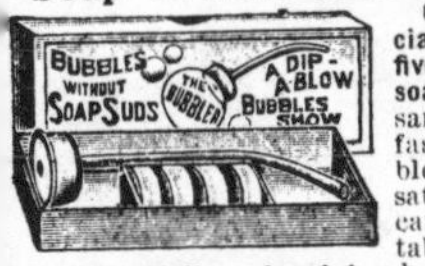


Consists of special blower and five round cakes of soap to fit. More sanitary than old fashioned pipe for blowing, and more satisfactory bubbles can be blown. One tablet makes over 500 beautifully colored bubbles. Shipping weight, 3 ounces.
No. 49K1035 Price........ 8c

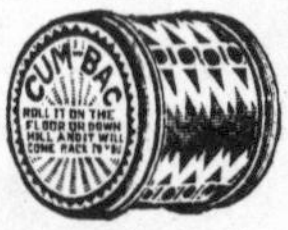


This is a most interesting and entertaining toy, made about the shape of a can, with round metal edges, decorated in gilt. Roll toy along the floor and it will "Cum-Bac" to you. It will even come back when rolled down hill. Well made, and no sharp edges. Size, 2¼ inches. Shipping weight, 5 ounces.
No. 49K1088 Price........ 8c

### The "Teddy R" Toy Pistol Belt, 9c

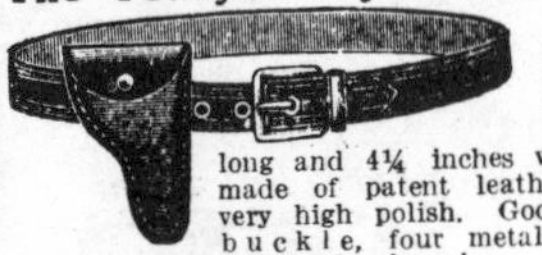

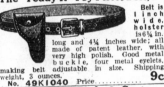

Belt is 1 inch wide, holster is 6¼ in. long and 4¼ inches wide; all made of patent leather, with very high polish. Good metal buckle, four metal eyelets, making belt adjustable in size. Shipping weight, 3 ounces.
No. 49K1040 Price........ 9c

### The Flying Bird, 8 Cents.

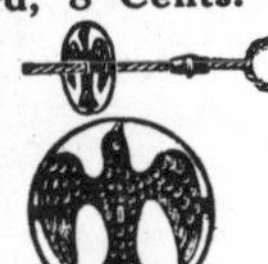

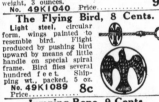

Light steel, circular form, wings painted to resemble bird. Flight produced by pushing bird upward by means of little handle on special spiral frame. Bird flies several hundred feet. Shipping wt., packed, 5 oz.
No. 49K1089 Price........ 8c

### Jumping Rope, 9 Cents.

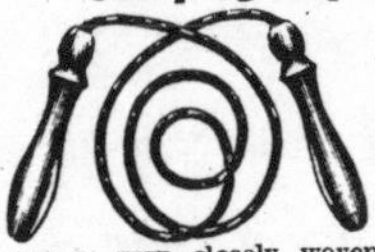

One of the best quality made. Very fancy black turned wood handles, 4⅛ inches in length. The rope is 5-16 inch in diameter, and exceptionally well made of strong, very closely woven colored cord, and is securely fastened into the handles. Shipping weight, 6 ounces.
No. 49K1095 Price........ 9c

### Doggy Muff, 98 Cents.

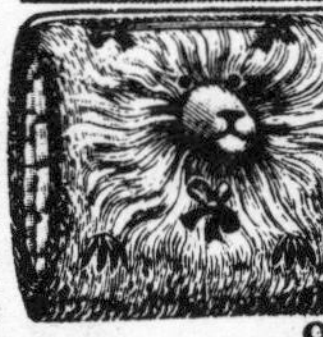

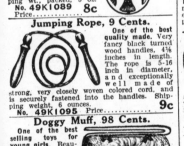

One of the best selling toys for young girls. Beautiful white mohair muff, white furry poodle dog's head. Heavy cord and blue ribbon trimmed. Muff, 8½x7 inches. A warm comfortable popular toy. Shipping weight, 1 pound.
No. 49K1029 Price........ 98c

### Teddy Bear Muff, 98 Cents.

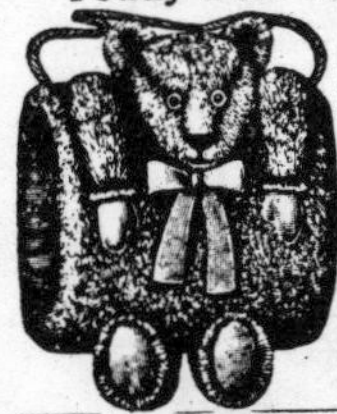

Every boy or girl loves their Teddy bear and this pretty white mohair muff with white bear head and paws and pink ribbon bow has been exceedingly popular. Size of muff, 8½x7 inches. Warm, and very sensible gift. Shipping weight, 1 pound.
No. 49K1044 Price........ 98c

### Toy Parasols, 17 and 25 Cents.

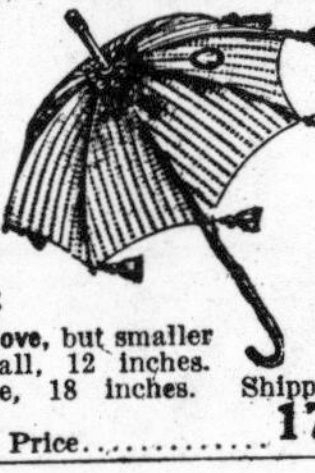

Fancy curved handle. Made of highly colored cloth, with silver tinsel and tassel decorations. Width, over all, 20 inches. Length, with handle, 26 inches. Shipping wt., 14 oz.
No. 49K1131 Price........ 25c

Parasol same as above, but smaller size. Width, over all, 12 inches. Length, with handle, 18 inches. Shipping weight, 10 ounces.
No. 49K1152 Price........ 17c

## High Grade Floor Trains.

Large 15½-inch engine and tender, and three 13½-inch red, white and blue Pullman cars, eight wheels to car. Entire length, 59 inches. Nicely finished in bright colors and gilt. Shipping weight, 7 pounds.
No. 49K970 Price........ $1.37

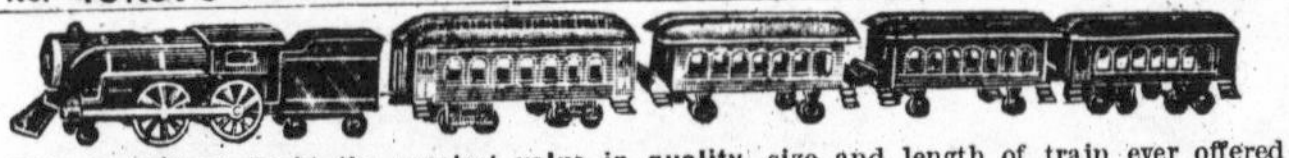

This is without doubt the greatest value in quality, size and length of train ever offered for 98 cents. 12-inch engine and tender, two 8½-inch red, white and blue enameled and gilt finished passenger cars, and two 9¼-inch eight-wheeled Pullmans. Entire length of train, 50 inches. Regular value, $1.50.
No. 49K930 Price........ 98c

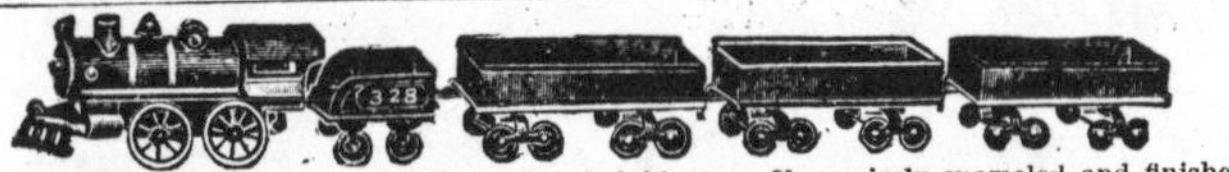

Heavy locomotive and three eight-wheeled freight cars. Very nicely enameled and finished. Length over all, 31 inches.
No. 49K925 Price........ 79c

Similar to above, but with four-wheeled cars. Length over all, 27 inches.
No. 49K927 Price........ 39c

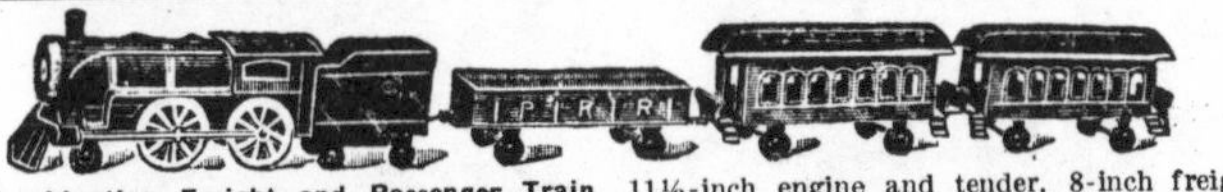

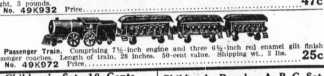

Combination Freight and Passenger Train, 11½-inch engine and tender, 8-inch freight car and two 8½-inch passenger cars. Train in red enamel and gilt finish. Entire length, 40 inches. Good $1.00 value. Shipping weight, 4 pounds.
No. 49K971 Price........ 69c

Just think of a train 29 inches in length, steel cars, 12-inch engine and tender for 47 cents. Comprises engine, freight car and passenger car. Good 75-cent value. Shipping weight, 3 pounds.
No. 49K932 Price........ 47c

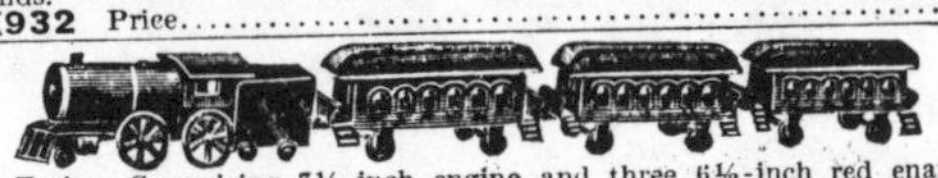

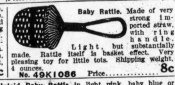

Passenger Train. Comprising 7½-inch engine and three 6½-inch red enamel gilt finish passenger coaches. Length of train, 28 inches. 50-cent value. Shipping wt., 2 lbs.
No. 49K972 Price........ 25c

### Children's Set, 18 Cents.

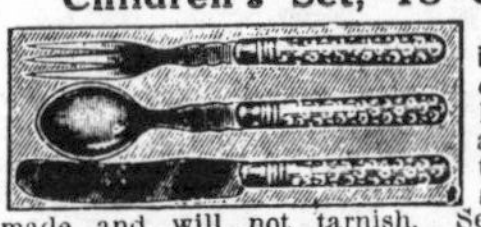

Very pretty imported set, colored china handles, balance in metal to imitate gold. Well made and will not tarnish. Securely fastened on card. Each set packed in box. Shipping weight, 5 ounces.
No. 49K758 Price........ 18c

### Children's Popular A B C Set.

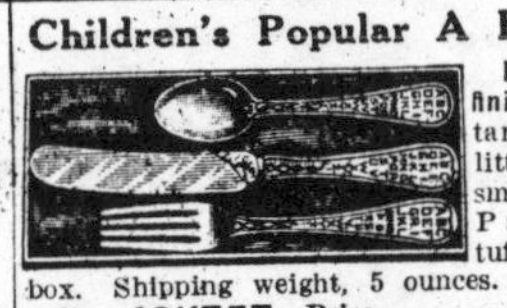

Bright metal finish. Will not tarnish. Nice little gift for small child. Packed in tufted lined box. Shipping weight, 5 ounces.
No. 49K757 Price........ 8c

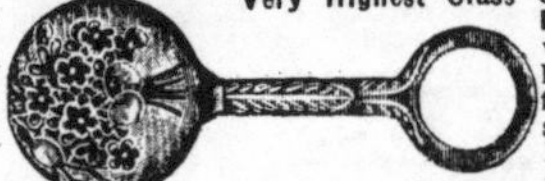

Very Highest Class Celluloid Rattle, with ring handle, fancy design. Rattle covered with very delicate white lines and on each side is a hand painted bunch of violets in natural colors, finely executed. Will not rub off. Length, 5½ inches. Well made. Shipping weight, 3 ounces.
No. 49K1082 Price........ 23c

### Red Rubber Rattle and Teething Ring, 29 Cents.

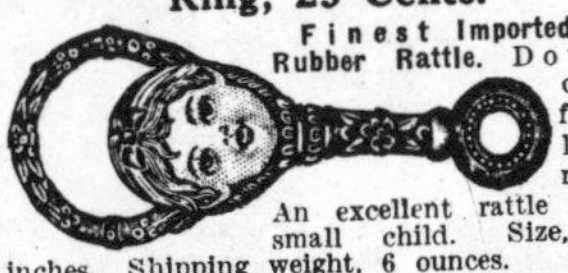

Finest Imported Red Rubber Rattle. Double child's face, large ring. An excellent rattle for a small child. Size, 7½ inches. Shipping weight, 6 ounces.
No. 49K1283 Price........ 29c

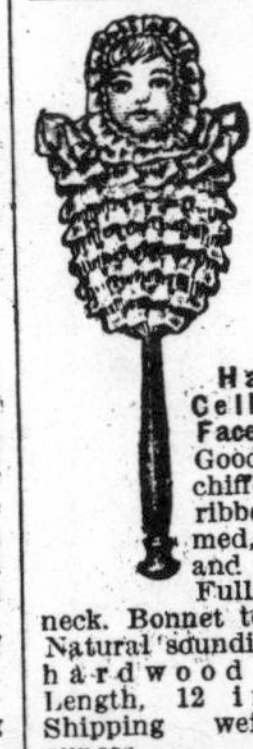

Handsome Celluloid Face Rattle. Good quality chiffon dress, ribbon trimmed, ruffled and shirred. Full around neck. Bonnet to match. Natural sounding voice, hardwood handle. Length, 12 inches. Shipping weight, 8 ounces.
No. 49K1026 Price........ 35c

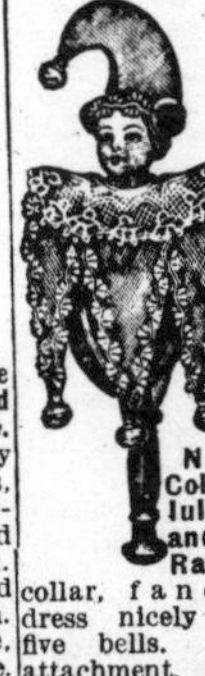

Natural Colored Celluloid Head and Face Rattle. Lace collar, fancy sateen dress nicely trimmed, five bells. Squeaking attachment. Hardwood handle. Length, 8¾ inches. Shipping weight, 6 ounces.
No. 49K1027 Price........ 23c

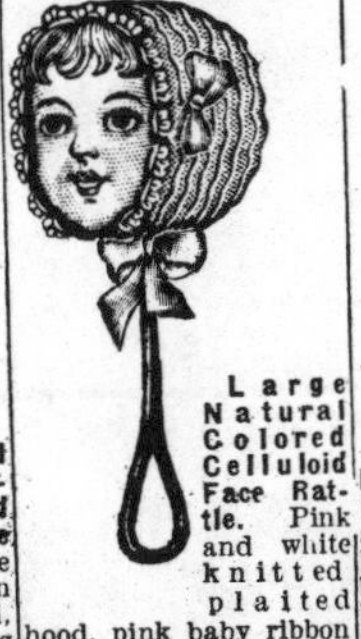

Large Natural Colored Celluloid Face Rattle. Pink and white knitted plaited hood, pink baby ribbon bows. A good strong rattle. Very pretty. Size, 8 inches. Shipping weight, 4 ounces.
No. 49K1004 Price........ 19c

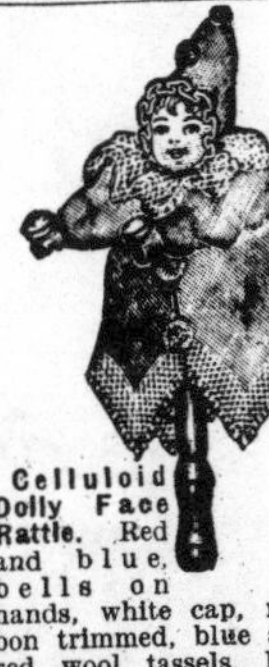

Celluloid Dolly Face Rattle. Red and blue, bells on hands, white cap, ribbon trimmed, blue and red wool tassels, lace trimmed dress and collar, whistle on handle. Length, 12 inches. Shipping weight, 8 oz.
No. 49K353 Price........ 19c

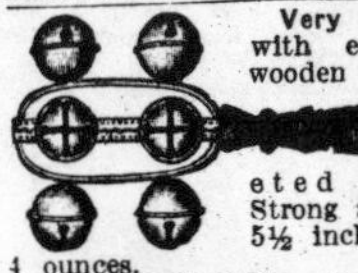

Very Popular Baby Rattle, with eight 1¼-inch bells, wooden handle. Very good for keeping child amused. Bells are riveted on heavy oilcloth. Strong and durable. Length, 5½ inches. Shipping weight, 4 ounces.
No. 49K1085 Price........ 8c

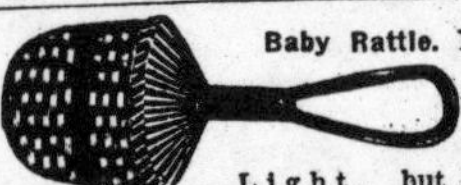

Baby Rattle. Made of very strong imported straw, with ring handle. Light, but substantially made. Rattle itself is basket effect. Very pleasing toy for little tots. Shipping weight, 4 ounces.
No. 49K1086 Price........ 8c

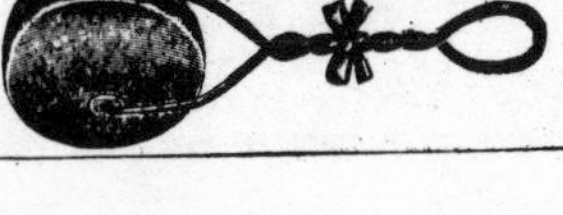

Celluloid Baby Rattle in light pink, baby blue or white. State color. One of the most popular rattles. Twisted handle, reinforced center and best grade celluloid. Shipping weight, 3 ounces.
No. 49K1083 Price........ 10c

### Boys' Box Kite, 21 Cents.

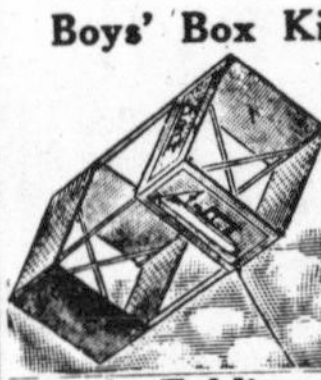

This is one of the best selling Box Kites made. Easy to adjust, flies easily, very light in weight, large in size and every boy's favorite. Carefully packed in box for shipment. Shipping weight, 1½ pounds.
No. 49K1028 Price........ 21c

### Eagle Folding Kite, 95 Cents.

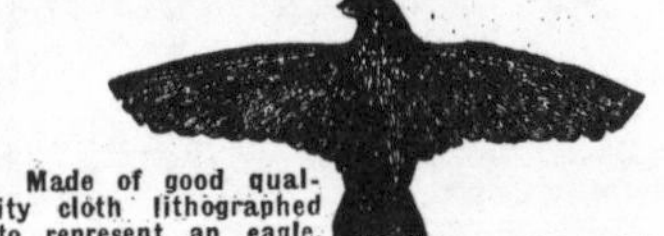

Made of good quality cloth lithographed to represent an eagle. Folds up like an umbrella; 5 feet from tip to tip. Very realistic. Just what the boy wants. Strongly made. Looks like a huge bird in the air. Flies easily. Shipping weight, 2 pounds.
No. 49K1109 Price........ 95c

### Boy Scouts' Camper's Ax, 12c.

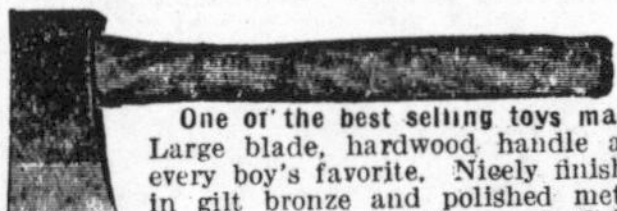

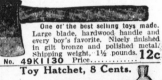

One of the best selling toys made. Large blade, hardwood handle and every boy's favorite. Nicely finished in gilt bronze and polished metal. Shipping weight, 1½ pounds.
No. 49K1130 Price........ 12c

### Toy Hatchet, 8 Cents.

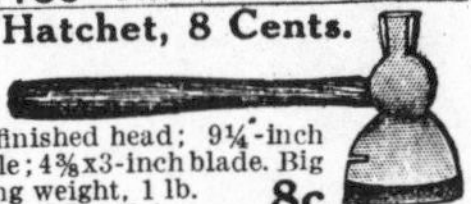

A High Grade Toy Hatchet, gilt finished head; 9¼-inch polished handle; 4⅜x3-inch blade. Big seller. Shipping weight, 1 lb.
No. 49K1128 Price........ 8c

### Toy Hammer, 8 Cents.

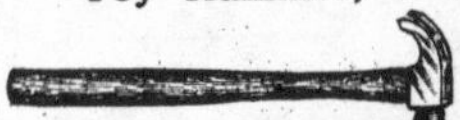

Very Fine Large Size Toy Hammer, with nickel plated head, polished handle. A boy's delight. Shipping wt., 14 oz.
No. 49K1129 Price........ 8c

### Our Large Size Kaleidoscope, 9c.

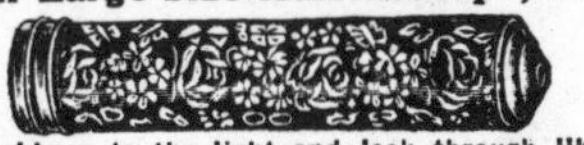

Hold up to the light and look through like telescope and see the pretty design. Length, 9 inches. Shipping weight, 16 ounces.
No. 49K1145 Price........ 9c

### Red Toy Lantern, 8 Cents.

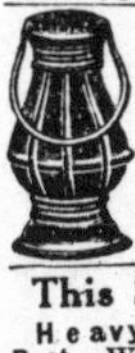

Very nicely nickeled top and bottom, and wire handle. Base has attachment for holding a candle. Length, without handle, 4½ inches. Shipping weight, 12 ounces.
No. 49K1138 Price........ 8c

### This Steamboat for Only 12c.

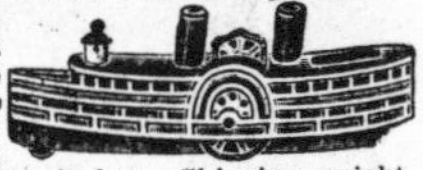

Heavy Metal Boat. Wheels at bottom turn so boat can be drawn over floor. Length, 7⅞ inches; height, 2½ inches. Shipping weight, packed, 1 pound.
No. 49K1206 Price........ 12c

### Food Chopper, 9c.

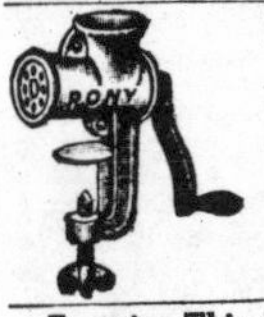


Represents large food chopper, except blades not detachable. Chops and pulverizes food. Screw fastener at bottom. Shipping weight, 20 ounces.
No. 49K1149 Price........ 9c

### Examine This Toy Automobile, 12c.

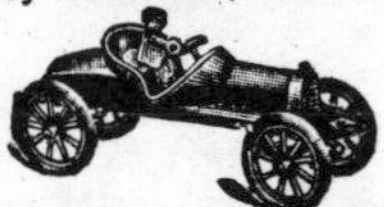

Very fine black enameled body, gilt wheels. Size, 8 inches long, 3½ inches high, 2⅞ inches wide. Driver painted in silver bronze. Shipping weight, 1 pound. Retails by many at 25 cents.
No. 49K1207 Price........ 12c

### This Fine Coffee Mill for 9c.

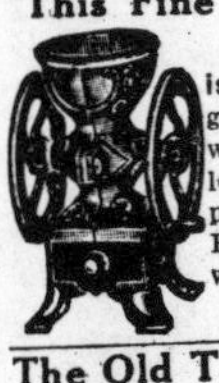

All metal, beautiful bronze finish with red trimmings. Real grinding surface. A toy with which a child can have an endless amount of pleasure. No playhouse complete without it. Height, 4 inches. Shipping weight, 1 pound.
No. 49K1093 Price........ 9c

### The Old Town Pump, 19c.

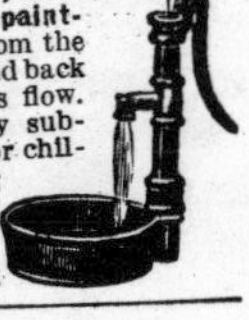

Made entirely of metal, nicely painted. It actually pumps water from the 4½-inch diameter metal tub and back into the tub with a continuous flow. Pump, 8¾ inches high. Very substantially made. Great sport for children, "water horses," playing "fireman," etc. Shipping weight, 30 ounces.
No. 49K1092 Price........ 19c

# MASKS, WIGS, CARNIVAL AND JOKE GOODS AND FAVORS

*Sears Roebuck & Co.*

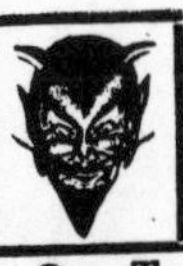

# AMATEUR MAGIC OUTFITS AND SEPARATE TRICKS AT POPULAR PRICES

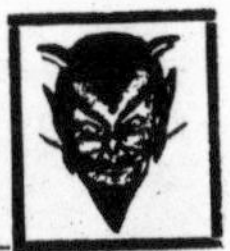

**The Improved Magic Outfits and Tricks shown below are high class** and have been carefully selected and represent the secrets of the world's best magicians. A most ingenious collection of very good tricks, put up in fancy boxes and are the best known today. By a little practice you can entertain your friends with these mystifying tricks, which are easy to perform and your friends will wonder how the tricks are possible. Full directions with each trick, making them very easy to learn. **The outfits represent the best values possible at the price,** but the magician should have a box as container and then buy separate tricks. For other trick decks of cards see page 628 and which should be included in your order.

## Our Ten-Trick Outfit for 45c.

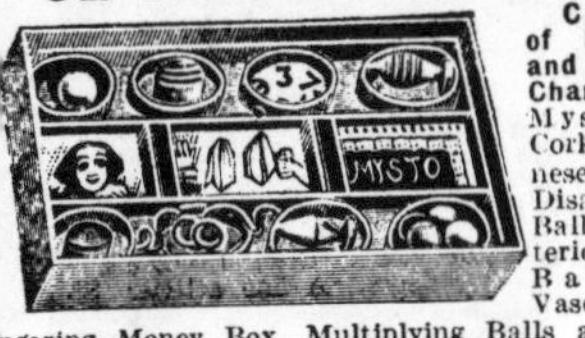

Consisting of Phantom and Wonder Change Card, Mysterious Corks, Chinese Rings, Disappearing Ball, Mysterious Discs, Ball and Vase, Disappearing Money Box, Multiplying Balls and celebrated Ball and Vase trick, with full directions. Apparently impossible tricks can be performed. No skill required. Handsome box, 13x9 inches. Shipping weight, 22 ounces.

No. 49K1301 Price........ **45c**

## Our Improved Mammoth Trick Outfit, 89 Cents.

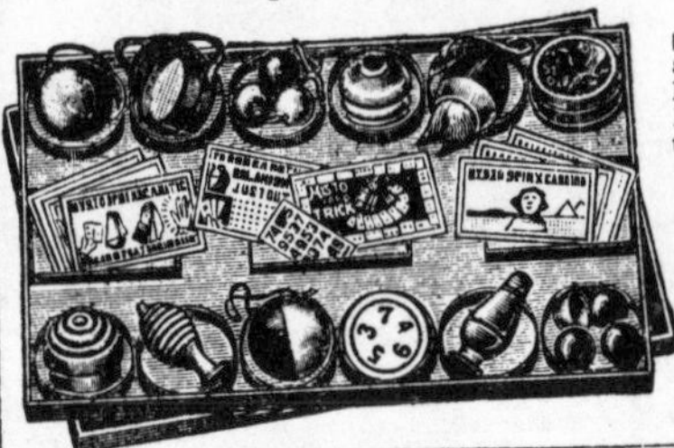

**The greatest and best outfit at the price ever offered.** Nineteen mysterious and multiplying tricks. Consisting of Multiplying Balls, Grandma's Necklace, Disappearing Money Box, Handkerchief trick with Miniature Silk Handkerchief, Ball and Vase, Disappearing Corks, Mysterious Discs, Vanishing Ball, Obedient Ball, Chinese Rings, Ring and Block, Marble and Vase, Money in Glass trick and six card tricks, with full directions. You can be a magician in your own home. Fool and astonish your friends. Exact duplicate of professional tricks. In handsome box, 16½x10½ inches. Shipping weight, 30 ounces.

No. 49K1300 Price........ **89c**

## Our Improved Outfit for 22c.

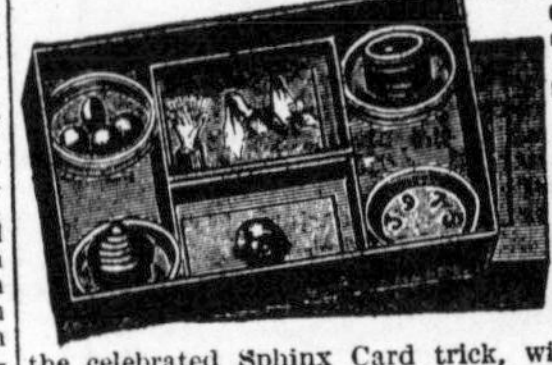

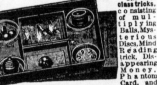

**Six first class tricks, consisting of multiplying Balls, Mysterious Discs, Mind Reading trick, Disappearing Money, Phantom Card,** and the celebrated Sphinx Card trick, with full directions. Easy to do but hard to detect. Packed in nice box, 9x6¼ inches. Shipping weight, 10 ounces.

No. 49K1302 Price........ **22c**

## Our Nine-Card Trick Outfit. 33c

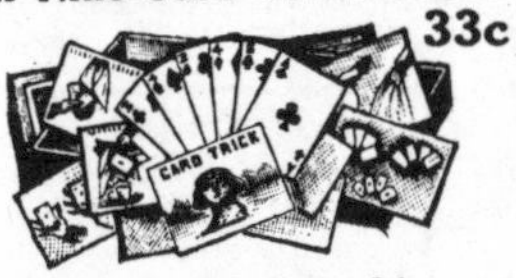

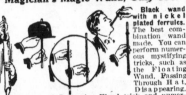

**Including Wonder Color Change Cards,** the Mysto Disappearing Spots, the Knock Out Card, The Sphinx Card, the Phantom Card, Pick It Out, the famous Fade Away, the Startling Card Tumbler trick, and the Spotter Cards. Full and simple directions. 4¾x8½ inches. Shipping weight, 9 oz.

No. 49K1306 Price........ **33c**

## Magician's Magic Wand, Only 89c.

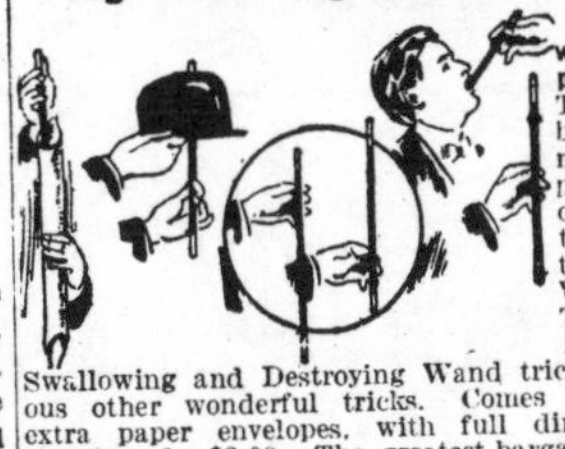

**Black wand with nickel plated ferrules.** The best combination wand made. You can perform numerous mystifying tricks, such as the Floating Wand, Passing Through Hat, Disappearing, Swallowing and Destroying Wand trick, and numerous other wonderful tricks. Comes complete with extra paper envelopes, with full directions. Sold elsewhere for $2.00. The greatest bargain ever offered, and the first time ever sold at this low price. Length, 14 inches. Shipping weight, 6 ounces.

No. 49K1344 Price for wand complete... **89c**

Extra envelopes, price, per dozen........ **60c**

## $1.00 Mammoth Combination Card Trick Outfit for 69 Cents.

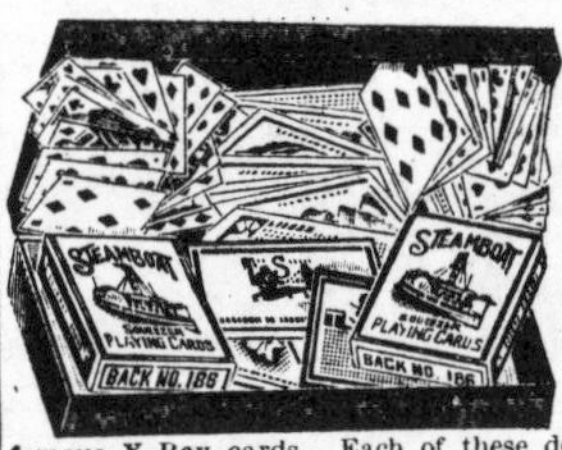

**Consists of nine carefully selected very best card tricks, as follows:** Disappearing Spots, Knock Out Card, Pick It Out, celebrated Fade Away Card, Phantom Card, Sphinx Card, Startling Card, Spotter and Wonder Change trick. Two regulation size decks (52 cards each) trick cards; consisting of the celebrated Stripper cards and the famous X-Ray cards. Each of these decks retail at from 25 to 50 cents each. Packed in fancy hinged box. Size, 5x8½ inches. Shipping weight, 13 ounces.

No. 49K1305 Price........ **69c**

## Our Six-Card Trick Outfit for Only 22 Cents.

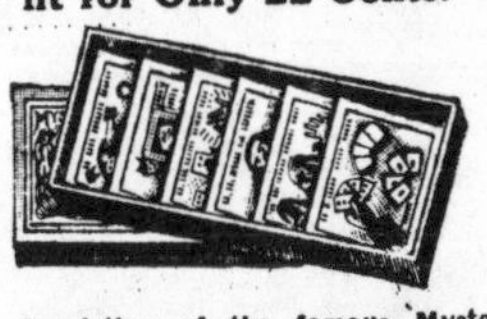

**Consisting of the famous Mysto Phantom Cards,** the Disappearing Card trick, the Vanishing Spot Cards, the Color Changing Cards, the Mysto Fade Away Cards, and the Mysto Sphinx Cards. All in fancy hinge cover box, 4x8¾ inches. Shipping weight, 6 ounces.

No. 49K1307 Price.... **22c**

## The Mysto Handkerchief Vanisher, 21c.

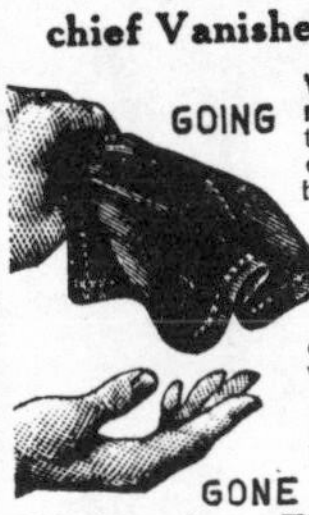


**With sleeves rolled back,** the performer takes a silk handkerchief, forces it into palm of hand until finally it entirely vanishes. No rapid movements required. Most mysterious. Easy to perform. Highly popular with magicians. Shipping weight, 5 ounces.

No. 49K1314 Price.... **21c**

## The Remarkable Spirit Slate, 45c.

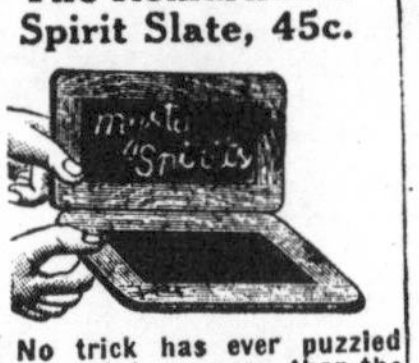

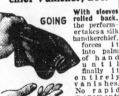

**No trick has ever puzzled the spectators more than the famous so called "spirit writings,"** which appear between sealed slates that have been carefully tied together, and given to a spectator to hold. Full simple directions; no chemicals required. Shipping weight, 22 ounces.

No. 49K1313 Price........ **45c**

## Magician's Rings, Now Only 47c.

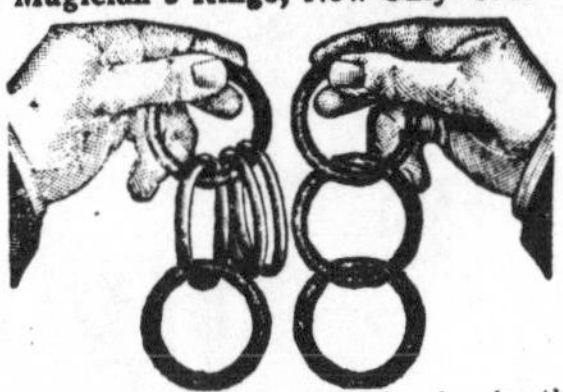

**The well known stage trick** whereby the performer passes apparently solid rings through each other at will. Same as performed by magicians on the stage, but smaller rings. Very mystifying and entertaining. Size of rings, 2 inches. With full directions. Packed in box. Shipping weight, 8 ounces.

No. 49K1341 Price, complete set........ **47c**

## Magic Coin Tray. 65c

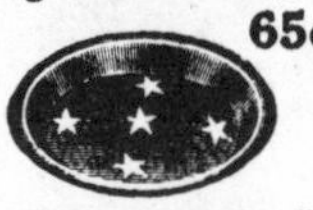

**A capital trick with the use of coins.** A number of coins are counted on a plate, and then visibly placed in the hands. A spectator is then requested to recount them and when he does so he finds they have marvelously increased in number. Used by magicians throughout the world. Shipping weight, 10 ounces.

No. 49K1322 Price........ **65c**

## Great Panel Trick. 19c

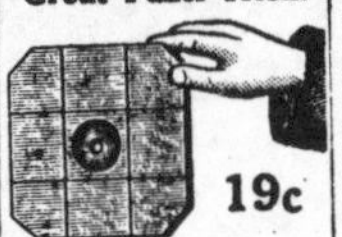

**Remarkable little trick that will astonish anyone.** Place a coin on center of panel, covered by a plain tin cover. On removing cover it has vanished. Can be made to reappear while the cover is held down by spectator. A well made, most popular trick. Shipping weight, 3 ounces.

No. 49K1312 Price........ **19c**

## Phantom Cards, 8c.

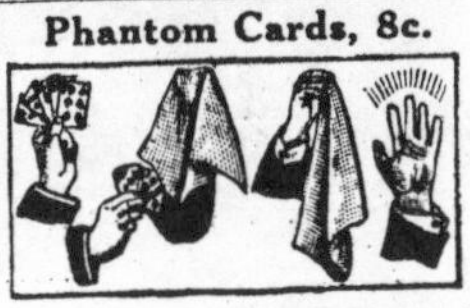

**A trick that will fascinate and bewilder any spectator.** From five cards three are mentally selected by spectator, placed under an ordinary handkerchief. Performer withdraws two cards, the ones not selected. The performer invites anyone to remove the others, and to the great astonishment of all, they have disappeared. No sleight of hand. One of the most ingenious card tricks invented. Shipping weight, 2 ounces.

No. 49K1315 Price.... **8c**

## Magic Coins, Only 12c.

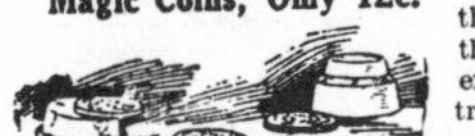

A mystifying and amusing trick. With this machine you can apparently make three bright new dimes from smooth, examined metal discs. A fine pocket trick. Shipping weight, 2 oz.

No. 49K1316 Price...... **12c**

## Mysto Cigarette Vanisher, Only 21c.

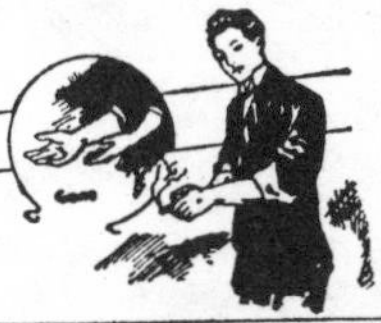

**The latest and unquestionably one of the cleverest new things in magic.** This interesting and astonishing trick consists in causing a lighted cigarette to vanish with the sleeves rolled to the elbows and hands outstretched away from the body. Harmless; easy to perform. Shipping weight, 2 ounces.

No. 49K1317 Price........ **21c**

## Magic Coin Wand, Only 89 Cents.

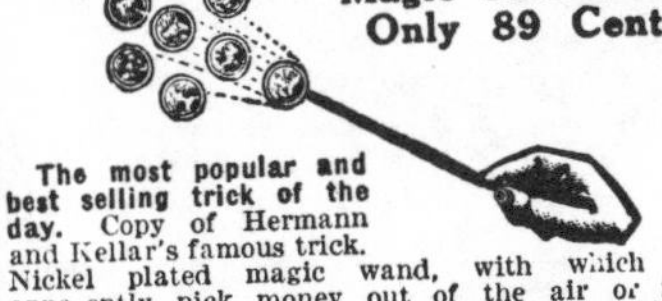

**The most popular and best selling trick of the day.** Copy of Hermann and Kellar's famous trick. Nickel plated magic wand, with which you apparently pick money out of the air or from another person's clothing anywhere. Very clever. Sure to please, and enjoyed alike by old and young. Size of wand, 18 inches, with five extra magic coins, and full directions. Shipping weight, 8 ounces.

No. 49K1345 Price, complete....... **89c**

## Vanishing Coins, Only 19 Cents.

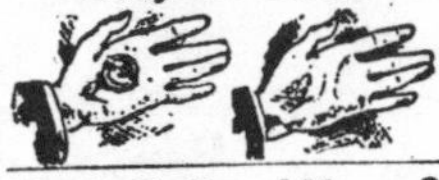

**A coin held in the palm of the hand is made to vanish when the hand is closed.** Only one hand used. No practice required. A very wonderful effect. Shipping weight, 2 ounces.

No. 49K1319 Price........ **19c**

## Magic Ball and Vase, 9c.

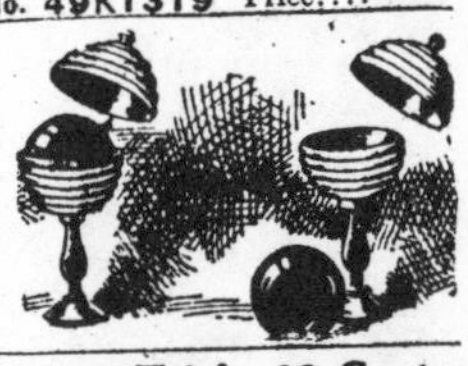

**A beautifully turned, painted and varnished vase containing a black ball** which can be made to appear and disappear right before one's eyes. A splendid low priced trick. Shipping weight, 2 ounces.

No. 49K1320 Price........ **9c**

## The Siberian Transport Chain. 65c

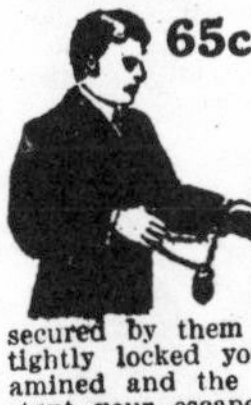

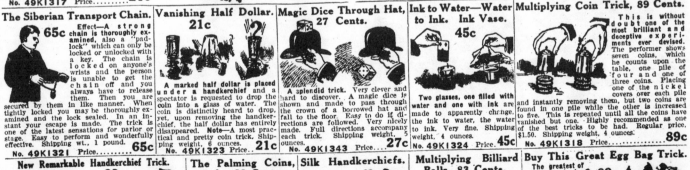

**Effect—A strong chain is thoroughly examined,** also a "padlock" which can only be locked or unlocked with a key. The chain is locked on anyone's wrists and the person is unable to get the chain off and you always have to release them. Then you are secured by them in like manner. When tightly locked you may be thoroughly examined and the lock sealed. In an instant your escape is made. The trick is one of the latest sensations for parlor or stage. Easy to perform and wonderfully effective. Shipping wt., 1 pound.

No. 49K1321 Price........ **65c**

## Vanishing Half Dollar. 21c

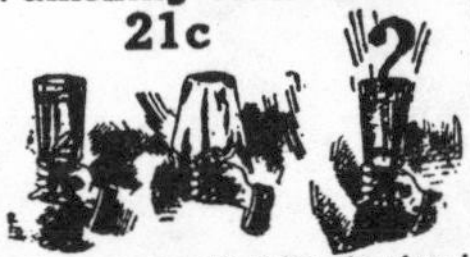

**A marked half dollar is placed under a handkerchief** and a spectator is requested to drop the coin into a glass of water. The coin is distinctly heard to drop, yet, upon removing the handkerchief, the half dollar has entirely disappeared. **Note**—A most practical and pretty coin trick. Shipping weight, 6 ounces.

No. 49K1323 Price... **21c**

## Magic Dice Through Hat, 27 Cents.

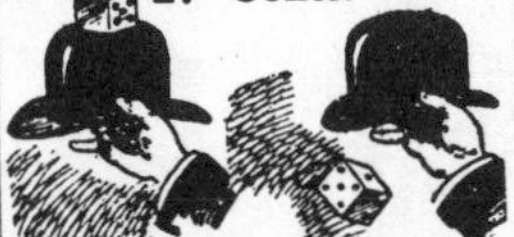

**A splendid trick.** Very clever and hard to discover. A magic dice is shown and made to pass through the crown of a borrowed hat and fall to the floor. Easy to do if directions are followed. Very nicely made. Full directions accompany each trick. Shipping weight, 5 ounces.

No. 49K1343 Price.... **27c**

## Ink to Water—Water to Ink. Ink Vase. 45c

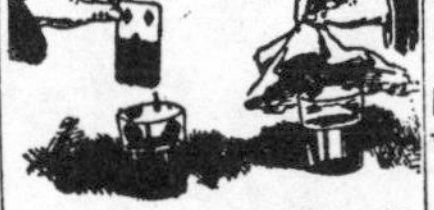

**Two glasses, one filled with water and one with ink** are made to apparently change, the ink to water, the water to ink. Very fine. Shipping weight, 4 ounces.

No. 49K1324 Price. **45c**

## Multiplying Coin Trick, 89 Cents.

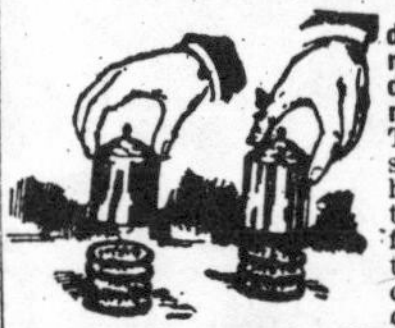

**This is without doubt one of the most brilliant and deceptive experiments ever devised.** The performer shows seven coins, which he counts upon the table, one pile of four and one of three coins. Placing one of the nickel covers over each pile and instantly removing them, but two coins are found in one pile while the other is increased to five. This is repeated until all the coins have vanished but one. Highly recommended as one of the best tricks to be had. Regular price, $1.50. Shipping weight, 4 ounces.

No. 49K1318 Price........ **89c**

## New Remarkable Handkerchief Trick. 89c

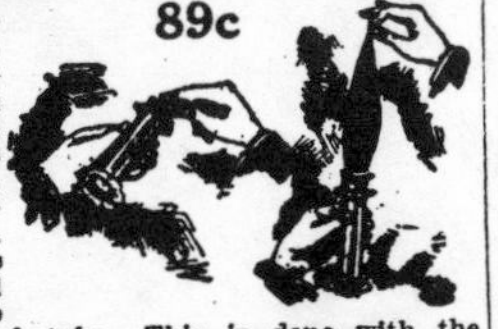

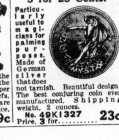

**This is the only practical tube in existence,** handsomely made, and can be worked under the eyes of the audience. Effect. — Everything examined, spectators make a drum head with paper on the end of the metal tube. This is done with the assistance of a metal ring, exactly fitting over the tube. With the tube still in their hands the paper is broken and two or more silk handkerchiefs, having been previously made to disappear, are withdrawn. Great for close work. Regular price, $2.00. Shipping weight, 8 ounces.

No. 49K1326 Price........ **89c**

## The Palming Coins, 3 for 23 Cents.

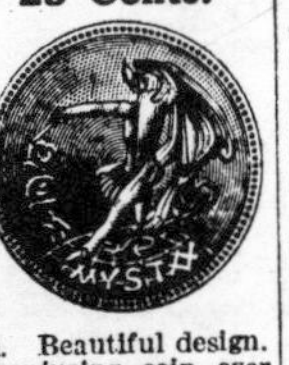


**Particularly useful to magicians for palming purposes.** Made of German silver that does not tarnish. Beautiful design. The best conjuring coin ever manufactured. Shipping weight, 2 ounces.

No. 49K1327 Price, 3 for........ **23c**

## Silk Handkerchiefs.

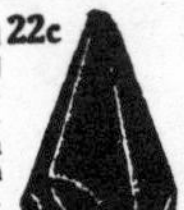

**We are pleased to offer special magicians' handkerchiefs** for conjuring work in connection with productions, etc. Compressed very fine. Striking colors. Recommended in connection with every magic act. Furnished in red or blue. Size, 12x12 inches. Shipping weight, 1 ounce.

22c

No. 49K1328 **Red silk.** Price........ **22c**

No. 49K1329 **Blue silk.** Price........ **22c**

## Multiplying Billiard Balls, 83 Cents.

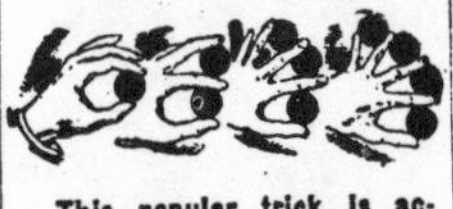

**This popular trick is accomplished with one hand only.** One of the best billiard ball tricks in existence. Four different balls. Can be made to appear or vanish. A trick we know will please you. Regular price, $1.00. Shipping weight, 6 ounces.

No. 49K1330 Price.... **83c**

## Buy This Great Egg Bag Trick. 89c

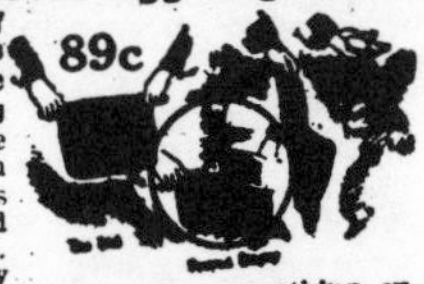

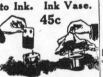

**The greatest of all egg tricks done with the acme of all egg bags.** Not to be compared with imitations of this excellent and wonderful trick. Almost every principle new. The bag, egg, everything examined, the performer either with coat removed or cuffs rolled back to the elbows, right in the midst of his audience causes the egg to vanish, reproducing it in the bag at will. The audience can actually feel in the bag or search the performer. **This trick is immense. Regular price, $2.50. Shipping weight, 1 pound.**

No. 49K1331 Price........ **89c**

151

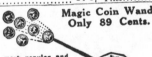

*Sears, Roebuck & Co.*

## Toy Dressers.

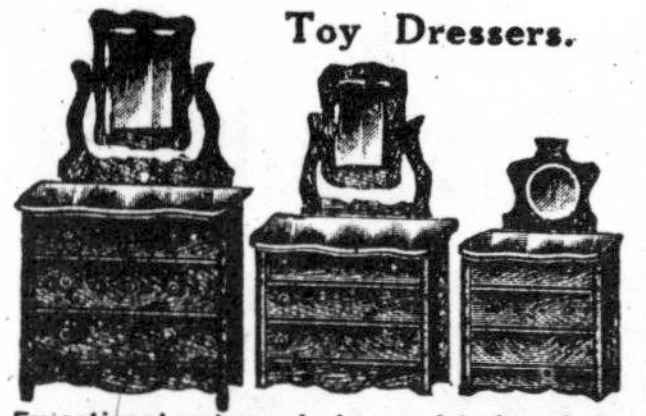

**Exceptional value, nicely varnished and finished in natural color wood, with drawers and mirror.** One of the nicest toys for a girl. A good substantial article. Carefully packed. Sizes as follows:

**Our largest size.** Dimensions, 27x16x7 inches over all; mirror, 7½x5½ inches. Shipping weight, 7 pounds.
**No. 49K3084¼** Price........ **$1.38**

**Our big 89-cent value. Similar to above,** but 21x13x6½ inches; mirror, 5½x4¼ inches. Same high grade finish. Shipping weight, 5 pounds.
**No. 49K3083¼** Price.......... **89c**

**Our 45-cent value. Similar to above,** but 13x11x5 inches, and has small round mirror, 2¾ inches. Same quality of workmanship. Great value. Shipping wt., 3½ lbs.
**No. 49K785** Price......... **45c**

## Toy China Closets.

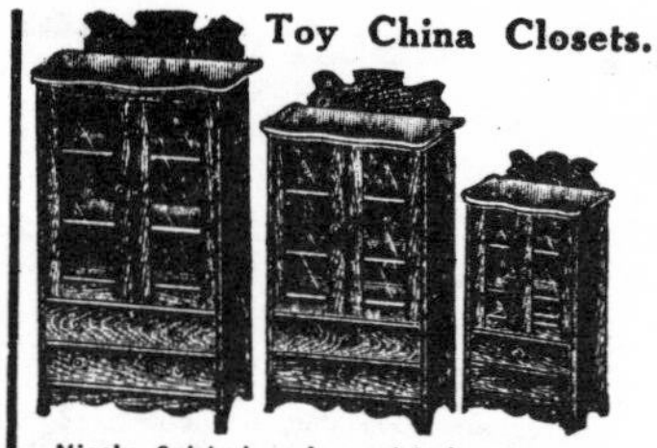

**Nicely finished and varnished natural color wood.** Has two drawers and two glass doors and wood shelves. All drawers and doors have metal pulls. A toy that fills a long felt want. Very popular everywhere. Sizes as follows:

**Our largest size.** Size, 24x13x7 inches. The best and most popular size. Carefully packed. Shipping weight, 6½ pounds.
**No. 49K3082¼** Price......... **$1.36**

**Our big 89-cent value. Similar to above,** but smaller size. Same high grade finish. Size, 21x11½x6½ inches. Shipping weight, 5½ pounds.
**No. 49K3081¼** Price........... **89c**

**Our 45-cent value. Similar to above,** but smaller size. Same high grade quality. Size, 16x8½x5 inches. Shipping wt., 2½ lbs.
**No. 49K784** Price............... **45c**

## Toy Kitchen Cabinets, 45c to $1.35

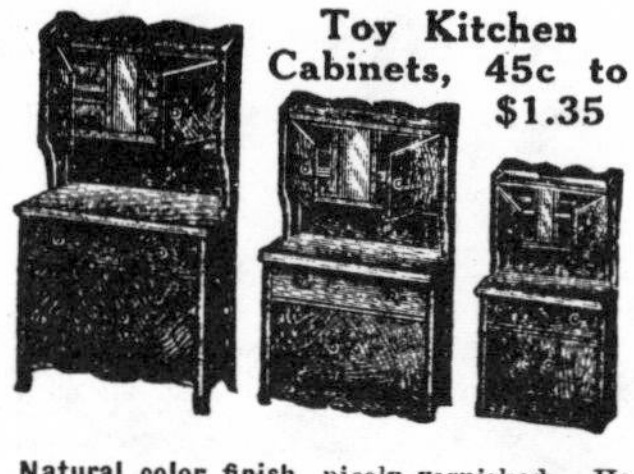

**Natural color finish,** nicely varnished. Has double doors and large drawer with metal pulls. Glass front flour bin with sliding outlet and two small shelves. Very strong and well made. Great value. Sizes as follows:

**Our best Cabinet.** Size, 22x12½x6½ inches. Carefully packed. Shipping weight, 5½ pounds.
**No. 49K3086¼** Price............. **$1.35**

**Our 89-cent value. Similar to above,** same high finish, but smaller size, 18x10½x5 inches. Shipping weight, 4¼ pounds.
**No. 49K3085¼** Price............. **89c**

**Our 45-cent value. Similar to above,** but smaller. Has no flour bin same finish. Size, 14x8x3¾ inches. Shipping wt., 3¼ lbs.
**No. 49K786** Price........... **45c**

## Toy Ice Chests.

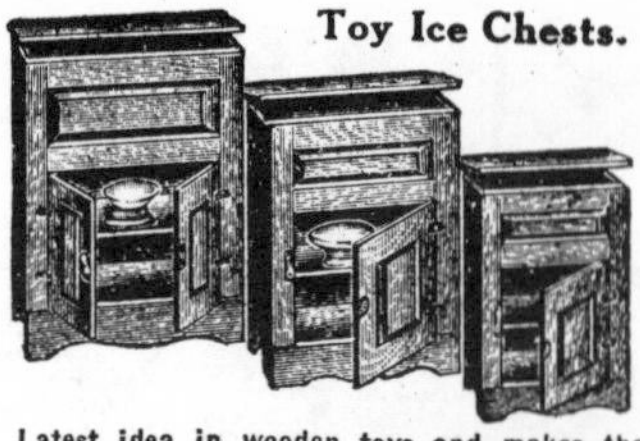

**Latest idea in wooden toys and makes the child's outfit complete.** Nicely finished and varnished in natural color wood, swing doors, tin shelves, raising lid top, tin tray and drip pan for ice. Three sizes as follows:

**Our largest chest.** Size, 16x12x6¾ inches, double swing doors. A fine article. Shipping weight, 5½ pounds.
**No. 49K3088¼** Price........ **$1.35**

**Our 89-cent value. Similar to above,** but smaller size. Has single door. Same high grade finish. Size, 14x10¼x6 inches. Shipping weight, 4¼ pounds.
**No. 49K3087¼** Price........... **89c**

**Our 45-cent value. Similar to above,** but small size. Single door. Same high grade finish. No drip pan to ice chest. Size, 11½x8x5 inches. Shipping weight, 2¼ lbs.
**No. 49K787** Price............. **45c**

## "Sandy Andy."

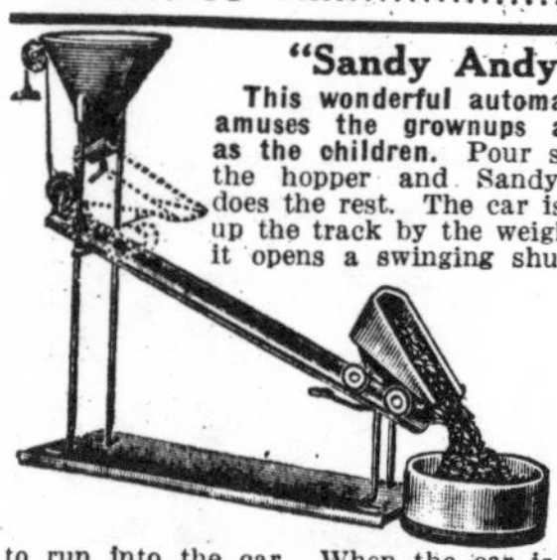

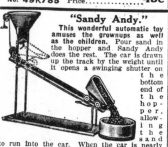

**This wonderful automatic toy amuses the grownups as well as the children.** Pour sand in the hopper and Sandy Andy does the rest. The car is drawn up the track by the weight until it opens a swinging shutter on the bottom end of the hopper, allowing the sand to run into the car. When the car is nearly full the added weight of the sand causes the car to run down the track and automatically dump the sand. The weight then again pulls the car up for another load and this operation is automatically continued as long as there is sand in the hopper. Great fun for the children. Size, 20½x18 inches. Shipping weight, 4½ pounds.
**No. 49K1409** Price............. **89c**

## Children's Dining Set, $3.85.

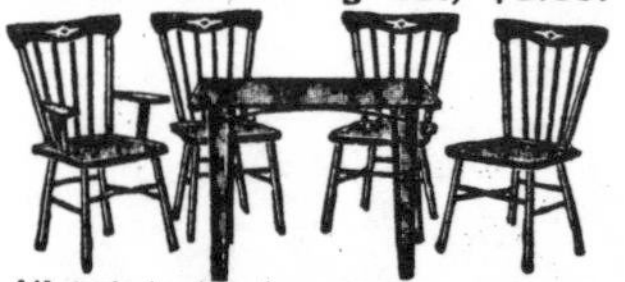

**All parts hardwood,** carefully and well made and varnished, with decorated panels. Consists of one arm chair, 12x12-inch seat and 24 inches high; three chairs, 12x12x24½ inches, and folding table, 18x26-inch top and 18½ inches high. Shipping weight, 40 lbs.
**No. 49K3020¼** Price......... **$3.85**

## The Finest We Carry.

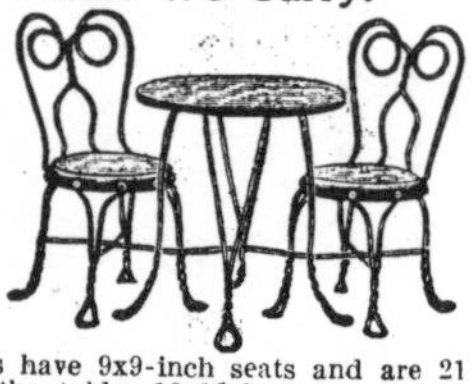

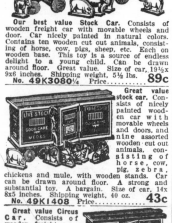

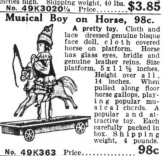

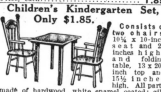

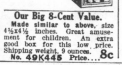

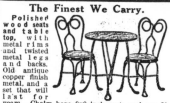

**Polished wood seats and table top,** with metal rims and twisted metal legs and backs. Old antique copper finish metal, and a set that will last for years. Chairs have 9x9-inch seats and are 21 inches high; the table, 16x16-inch top and is 17 inches high. Shipping weight, 40 pounds.
**No. 49K3023¼** Set, complete. Price................ **$4.49**
**No. 49K3024¼** Chair, separate. Price, each.......... **1.39**
**No. 49K3025¼** Table, separate. Price, each.......... **1.85**

## Children's Tea Furniture Set, $1.25.

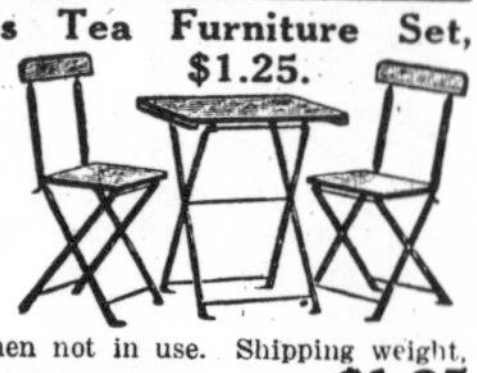

**Well made with metal frames** and red painted seats and top. Size, chairs, 9x7x19 inches. Table, 12½x14x15½ in. Folds up completely when not in use. Shipping weight, 6½ pounds.
**No. 49K3022¼** Price........ **$1.25**

## Children's Play Table, 98 Cents.

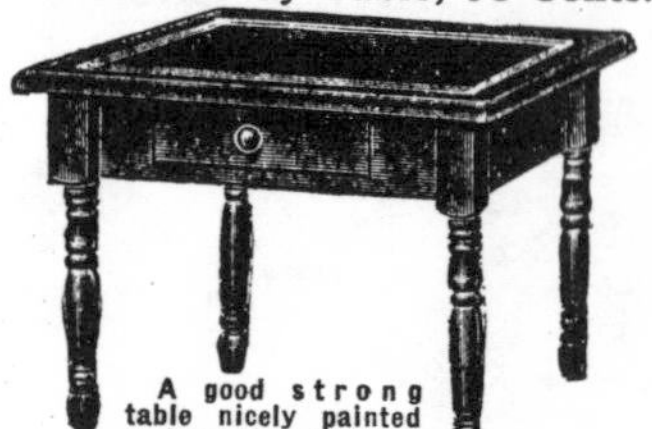

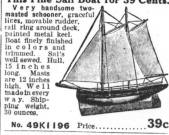

**A good strong table nicely painted and varnished.** Red, with yellow stripe in center of top. Has large drawer, 10x9¼ inches. Nicely turned legs. Top, 23½x19½ inches, 19 inches high. Shipping weight, 13 pounds.
**No. 49K3074¼** Price.............. **98c**

## Musical Boy on Horse, 98c.

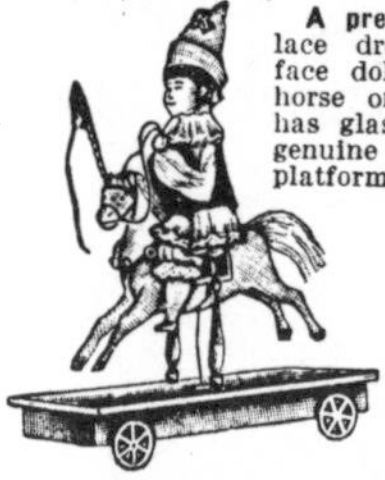

**A pretty toy.** Cloth and lace dressed genuine bisque face doll, cloth covered horse on platform. Horse has glass eyes, bridle and genuine leather reins. Size platform, 5x11½ inches. Height over all, 14 inches. When pulled along floor horse gallops, playing popular musical chords. A popular and attractive toy. Each carefully packed in box. Shipping weight, 4 pounds.
**No. 49K363** Price............. **98c**

## Children's Kindergarten Set, Only $1.85.

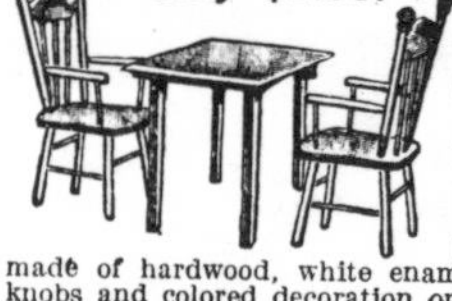

**Consists of two chairs,** 10¼ x 10-inch seat and 22 inches high, and folding table, 13 x 20-inch top and 15½ inches high. All parts made of hardwood, white enamel coated; gilt knobs and colored decoration on chairs. Shipping weight, 20 pounds.
**No. 49K3021¼** Price........ **$1.85**

## Stock Car and Animals.

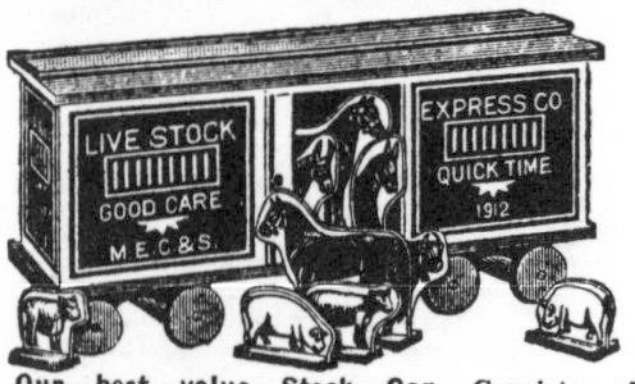


**Our best value Stock Car.** Consists of wooden freight car with movable wheels and door. Car nicely painted in natural colors. Contains ten wooden cut out animals, consisting of horse, cow, pigs, sheep, etc. Each on wooden base. This toy is a source of endless delight to a young child. Can be drawn around floor. Great value. Size of car, 19½x9x6 inches. Shipping weight, 5½ lbs.
**No. 49K3080¼** Price........... **89c**

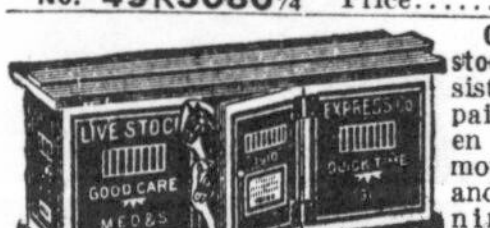

**Great value stock car.** Consists of nicely painted wooden car with movable wheels and doors, and nine assorted wooden cut out animals, consisting of horse, cow, pig, zebra, chickens and mule, with wooden stands. Car can be drawn around floor. A strong and substantial toy. A bargain. Size of car, 14x8x5 inches. Shipping weight, 40 oz.
**No. 49K1408** Price............. **43c**

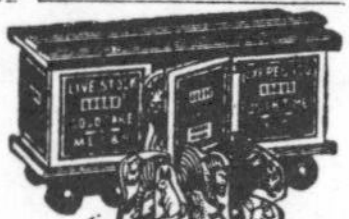

**Great value Circus Car.** Consists of wooden freight car nicely painted in colors. Size, 10½x5¼x4 inches. Movable wheels and doors. Contains six different wooden cut out animals, such as lion, bear, tiger, zebra, rabbit, squirrel, etc. Great fun for the children playing circus. Shipping weight, 24 ounces.
**No. 49K1407** Price.............. **19c**

## Boys' Good Grade Sword, 17c.

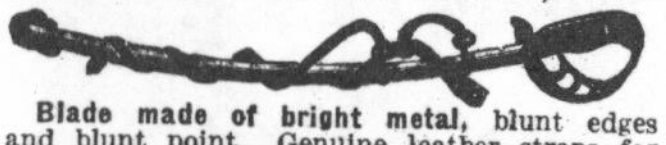

**Blade made of bright metal,** blunt edges and blunt point. Genuine leather straps for holding in proper position. Scabbard is of heavy tin. Length, 25 inches. 25-cent grade. Shipping weight, 12 ounces.
**No. 49K1164** Price.............. **17c**

## This Sword for Only 8 Cents.

**Blade of bright metal, dull edge and blunt point.** Imitation leather straps for holding in position. Length, 21 inches. Shipping wt., 10 oz.
**No. 49K1143** Price.............. **8c**

## Complete Mechanical Train and Station, $1.45.

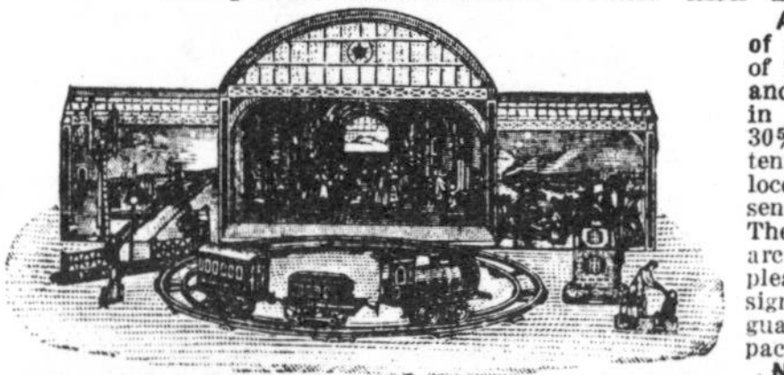

**A realistic miniature reproduction of a railway station.** Cover consists of two flaps which open to the side, and shows picturesque scenes of life in central railway station. Size, 30⅝x12 3-16x5⅞ inches. The contents consist of one complete train, locomotive with brake, tender, passenger car and circular set of rails. There is a ticket gate with imitation arc lamp and sign, "All tickets please." A watchman's house, a signal, and three cardboard figures, guard, porter and newsboy. Weight, packed, 3½ pounds.
**No. 49K935** Price.. **$1.45**

## Circus Puzzle Box, 43 Cents.

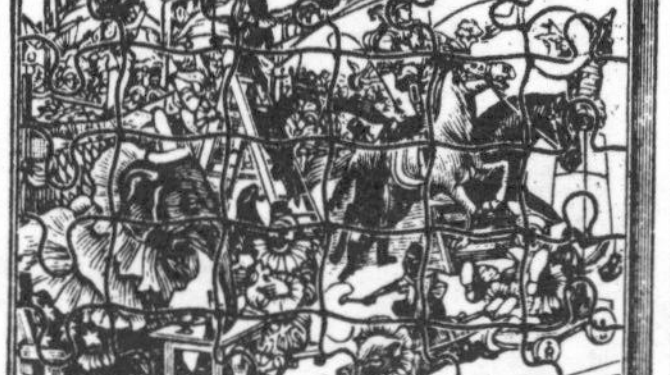

**The Children's Delight.** Consists of three assorted pictures of circus life, showing animals, performers, parade, etc. Lithographed on good strong strawboard, cut out in different shaped pieces. A source of endless amusement. Very high quality. Size of box, 18½x13 inches. Shipping weight, 3 pounds.
**No. 49K667** Price.............. **43c**

## Surprise Box, 17c.

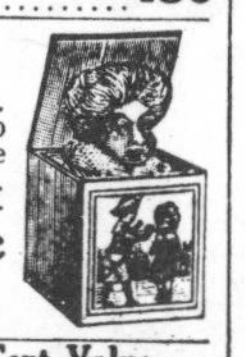

**Wooden box,** paper covered, with picture on front. Open top and figure inside with grotesque face pops out. Has strong spring. Size of box, 5x5 inches. Shipping wt., packed, 12 oz.
**No. 49K444** Price... **17c**

## Our Big 8-Cent Value.

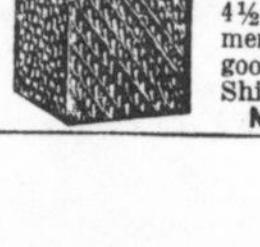

**Made similar to above,** size 4½x4½ inches. Great amusement for children. An extra good box for this low price. Shipping weight, 9 ounces.
**No. 49K445** Price.... **8c**

## Large Combination Puzzle Box.

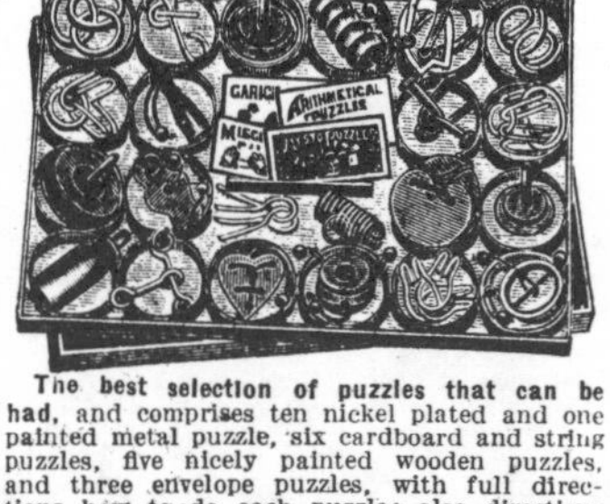


**The best selection of puzzles that can be had,** and comprises ten nickel plated and one painted metal puzzle, six cardboard and string puzzles, five nicely painted wooden puzzles, and three envelope puzzles, with full directions how to do each puzzle; also directions how to do many other puzzles; puzzles are a source of pleasure to both young and old. The best selection ever offered at this price. Handsome box, nicely packed. Size of box, 16½x10½ inches. Shipping weight, 35 oz.
**No. 49K1347** Price............ **89c**

## Twelve-Puzzle Assortment.

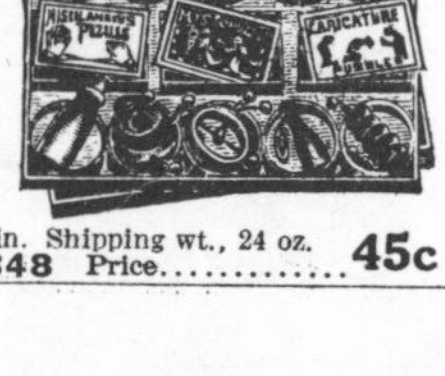

**Consisting of three metal puzzles,** two pasteboard puzzles, five wooden puzzles, two envelope puzzles. Nicely finished and full directions showing how each puzzle is done. Handsome box, 13x9 in. Shipping wt., 24 oz.
**No. 49K1348** Price.......... **45c**

## This Fine Sail Boat for 39 Cents.

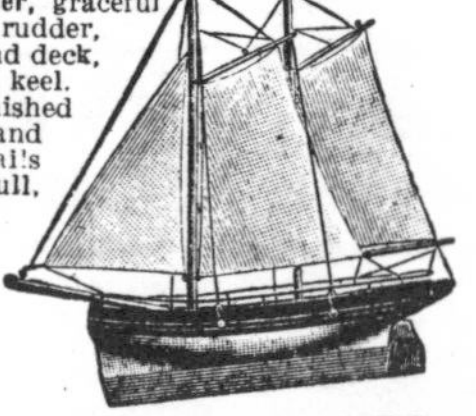

**Very handsome two-masted schooner,** graceful lines, movable rudder, rail ring around deck, painted metal keel. Boat finely finished in colors and trimmed. Sails well sewed. Hull, 15 inches long. Masts are 12 inches high. Well made in every way. Shipping weight, 30 ounces.
**No. 49K1196** Price............. **39c**

## A Very Good Boat, 19 Cents.

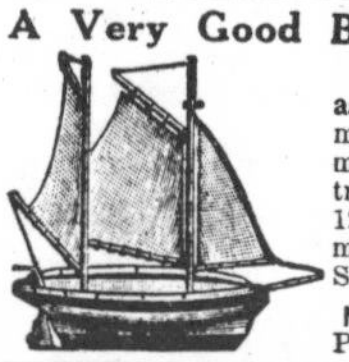

**Made in same manner as above,** same rigging, movable rudder, railing, metal keel, painted and trimmed. Length hull, 12 inches; height of masts, 10½ inches. Shipping wt., 20 oz.
**No. 49K1178** Price.......... **19c**

## Jumping Rabbit and Ball. 45c

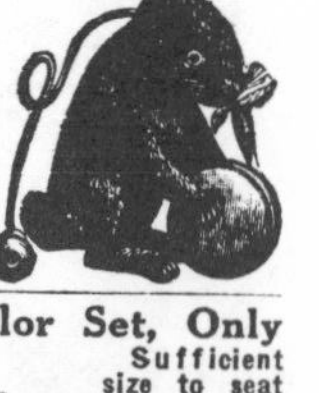

**A real fur covered rabbit with revolving ball between feet.** Has carrot in mouth; when rubber bulb is pressed the rabbit jumps forward, pushing ball along at the same time, moving his ears in a very comical manner. Very amusing. Size, 9x8 in. Shipping wt., 12 oz.
**No. 49K1264** Price.......... **45c**

## Princess Doll Parlor Set, Only 89 Cents.

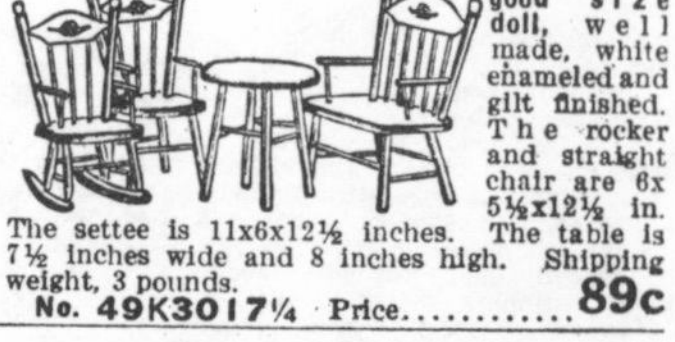

**Sufficient size to seat good size doll,** well made, white enameled and gilt finished. The rocker and straight chair are 6x5½x12½ in. The table is 7½ inches wide and 8 inches high. The settee is 11x6x12½ inches. Shipping weight, 3 pounds.
**No. 49K3017¼** Price.............. **89c**

# BIG VALUES IN HIGHEST GRADE IMPORTED KID BODY DOLLS, READY FOR DRESSING

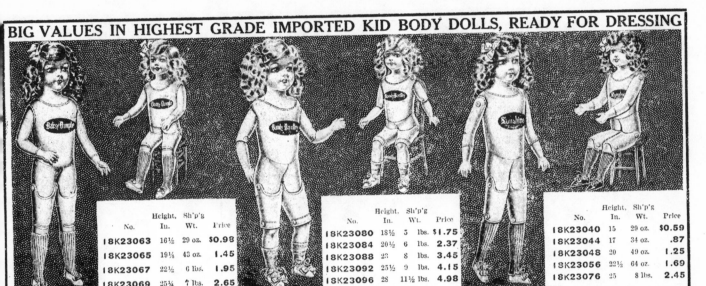

| No. | Height, In. | Sh'p'g Wt. | Price |
|---|---|---|---|
| 18K23063 | 16½ | 29 oz. | $0.98 |
| 18K23065 | 19¼ | 43 oz. | 1.45 |
| 18K23067 | 22½ | 6 lbs. | 1.95 |
| 18K23069 | 25¼ | 7 lbs. | 2.65 |

| No. | Height, In. | Sh'p'g Wt. | Price |
|---|---|---|---|
| 18K23080 | 18½ | 5 lbs. | $1.75 |
| 18K23084 | 20½ | 6 lbs. | 2.37 |
| 18K23088 | 23 | 8 lbs. | 3.45 |
| 18K23092 | 25½ | 9 lbs. | 4.15 |
| 18K23096 | 28 | 11½ lbs. | 4.98 |

| No. | Height, In. | Sh'p'g Wt. | Price |
|---|---|---|---|
| 18K23040 | 15 | 29 oz. | $0.59 |
| 18K23044 | 17 | 34 oz. | .87 |
| 18K23048 | 20 | 49 oz. | 1.25 |
| 18K23056 | 22½ | 64 oz. | 1.69 |
| 18K23076 | 25 | 8 lbs. | 2.45 |

### "Daisy Dimple" Talking Dolls.
Have automatic inside voice which imitates a child's cry for papa and mama by simply tilting the doll forward. No buttons to push, no strings to pull. Made with well proportioned, genuine kid body with riveted hip joints. Beautiful bisque heads of good quality. Sleeping eyes and natural looking eyelashes. Wigs of fine curled mohair, full sewed, ribbon tied and parted. Bisque forearms. Removable shoes and stockings. The larger the doll the better the proportions.

### "Dainty Dorothy" Kid Dolls.
Our very finest quality kid body dolls, ready for dressing, with most beautiful and perfect bisque heads. Finest possible quality hand curled mohair wigs, all sewed on net foundation, parted and ribbon tied. Bodies are beautifully proportioned and have perfect flesh tinted papier mache forearms and lower limbs. Riveted joints at elbows, hips and knees. Patented turning shoulder joints. Beautiful sleeping eyes with long lashes. Openwork lace half hose and fine slippers.

### Our "Sunshine" Kid Dolls.
We especially recommend this, our medium quality, to customers who want a good doll at a very moderate price. The bodies are well proportioned according to the height. Are made of good quality clean white kid leather. Riveted joints at hips and knees to allow the doll to assume a sitting position. The bisque heads are unusually attractive and have sleeping eyes and natural looking eyelashes. The daintily curled mohair wigs are sewed on a net foundation, have neat parting and are ribbon tied. Knee length openwork stockings. Medium quality sandals. At the prices offered these dolls are exceptional values for quality.

# FULL BALL JOINTED DOLLS WITH PERFECTLY FORMED BODIES, READY FOR DRESSING

| No. | H'g't, In. | Sh'p's Wt., | Price |
|---|---|---|---|
| 18K23130 | 7¾ | 13 | $0.25 |
| 18K23132 | 9 | 18 | .48 |
| 18K23133 | 9 | 25 | .75 |
| 18K23140 | 12¼ | 33 | .98 |
| 18K23141 | 14 | 35 | 1.39 |

| No. | H'g't, In. | Sh'p'g Lbs. | Price |
|---|---|---|---|
| 18K23010 | 17½ | 4½ | $1.75 |
| 18K23012 | 24½ | 8 | 2.98 |
| 18K23016 | 26¾ | 10½ | 3.89 |
| 18K23020 | 28 | 12 | 4.95 |

| No. | H'g't, In. | Sh'p'g Wt., Oz. | Price |
|---|---|---|---|
| 18K22994 | 10 | 15 | $0.25 |
| 18K22996 | 13½ | 26 | .50 |
| 18K22998 | 15 | 30 | .75 |
| 18K23000 | 18 | 33 | 1.19 |

### "Baby Ruth" Character Dolls.
Character dolls are so called because the model of both heads and bodies are copied after living children. The illustration cannot possibly do justice to the real beauty of these dainty dolls. Bodies are made of the very finest quality papier mache, molded in lifelike proportions. Jointed at hips and shoulders only. Childlike heads made of beautiful bisque, daintily tinted in flesh colors. All sizes except the smallest have bright baby eyes which fall asleep. Short bobbed hair. Lace trimmed chemise.

### "Maybelle" Jointed Dolls.
Our finest quality most beautifully proportioned full ball jointed dolls. All ready for dressing. Perfectly finished flesh tinted bodies with joints at hips, knees, shoulders, elbows and wrists. Finest quality bisque heads with hand curled wigs of best mohair, sewed on a net foundation, neatly parted and ribbon tied. These heads turn from side to side on the shoulders. Beautiful sleeping eyes with natural looking lashes. Good quality leather slippers. Handsome lace and ribbon trimmed chemise.

### "Little Cherub" Jointed Dolls.
Our bargain offer in medium quality full ball jointed dolls, with joints at hips, knees, shoulders, elbows and wrists. Good quality bisque heads with sleeping eyes. Curly mohair wigs are of good medium quality, neatly parted at side and tied with ribbon. Removable openwork half hose and tied slippers. Medium quality lace trimmed chemise. At the extremely low prices asked for this quality, these dolls are wonderful bargains. No. 18K23000 has natural looking eyelashes.

### Unbreakable Celluloid Dolls.

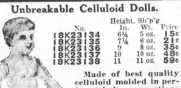

| No. | Height, In. | Wt. | Price |
|---|---|---|---|
| 18K23134 | 6¼ | 5 oz. | 15c |
| 18K23135 | 7¼ | 6 oz. | 21c |
| 18K23136 | 9 | 8 oz. | 35c |
| 18K23137 | 10 | 10 oz. | 48c |
| 18K23138 | 11 | 11 oz. | 59c |

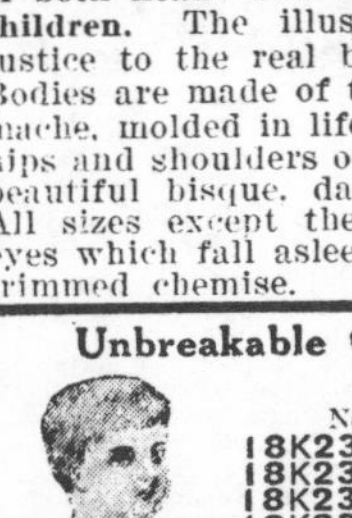

Made of best quality celluloid molded in perfect baby proportions with heads and bodies beautifully tinted with guaranteed fast colors. For these reasons as well as for their extreme lightness and durability they are ideal playthings for very young children. As bath tub toys they have no equal. The larger the doll the better the proportions and the facial features. Arms are movable.

### "Pansy" Kid Dolls.

| No. | Height, Inches | Sh'p'g Wt. | Price |
|---|---|---|---|
| 18K23024 | 12 | 18 oz. | 23c |
| 18K23028 | 16 | 29 oz. | 48c |
| 18K23032 | 18½ | 38 oz. | 69c |
| 18K23036 | 20½ | 48 oz. | 88c |

Our great special bargain dolls. Made of genuine white kid leather, well stuffed and beautifully proportioned. Have good quality bisque heads with sleeping eyes. Neatly curled mohair wigs, parted and ribbon tied. Medium quality bisque forearms. Knee length openwork stockings and slippers. Remarkable bargains at the prices asked.

### Character Dolls at Bargain Prices.

| No. | Height, In. | Sh'p'g Wt. | Price |
|---|---|---|---|
| 18K23143 | 10 | 16 oz. | 23c |
| 18K23144 | 11½ | 19 oz. | 38c |
| 18K23146 | 14 | 34 oz. | 89c |

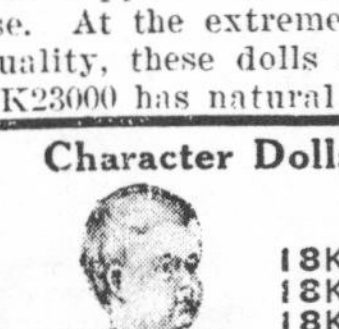

Have charming bisque heads which turn on the shoulders. Full jointed papier mache bodies of medium quality, finished in delicate flesh tints. Painted fast eyes and painted hair. Each doll in lace trimmed chemise. Extra special value at our very low price.

# FINEST QUALITY EXTRA LARGE SIZE DRESSED DOLLS—SELLING AT WHOLESALE PRICES

**$1.75**

No. 18K23198 This Bare Legged Baby Doll is one of our finest European novelties and at the price offered is a real bargain. The feature of the doll is the shapely full jointed body with long baby legs showing dimpled bare knees. Fine quality bisque head with sleeping eyes and natural looking eyelashes. Good quality full curled wig, parted and tied with ribbon bows.

**$1.75**

No. 18K23198 The dress is of light color flowered organdy trimmed with a combination of white Valenciennes lace and Valenciennes lace edging. Pretty ribbon sash with bow at side. Extra fine quality straw bonnet with ruffled edges of lace and silk ribbon trimming. Short socks and good quality shoes; extra well made lace edged underwear. Full height, including hat, 18 inches. Shipping weight, 52 ounces.

No. 18K23206

No. 18K23208   No. 18K23210   CHOICE $3.95

**Very High Grade Imported Dolls** with full jointed and beautifully proportioned bodies. Very lifelike handsome bisque heads with sleeping eyes and natural lashes. Open lips, showing teeth, and luxurious full sewed, parted and ribbon tied wigs of splendid quality. Good muslin underwear, lace edged; half hose and tied shoes. Full height, including hat, 24½ inches. Choice of two beautiful dolls as described below, both of which can be undressed. Dolls of this quality retail in the average store for not less than $7.50. Shipping weight, 8½ pounds.

No. 18K23208 Dress of extra fine quality light color satin with blouse and short overskirt effect of fine quality white allover lace. Dainty puff sleeves of combination lace and satin; silk ribbon sash and bow trimming at neck. Hat to match of satin and lace heavily trimmed with flowers. Good quality half hose and tied shoes. Price...........$3.95

No. 18K23210 Dress is made entirely of dainty white allover lace with deep lace flouncing over a slip of good quality light color mull which has wide edging of lace to match dress. Trimming of pretty light color silk braid used in combination with Valenciennes lace and silk ribbon. Hat of the allover lace to match. Trimming of hyacinths and ribbon. Double flounce petticoat. Price...........$3.95

## Our Best and Largest Dressed Dolls

**$4.95**

CHOICE $4.95

No. 18K23212    No. 18K23214

**Full 25 Inches High**, including hats. Dolls of this quality are sold in the average retail store at not less than $9.00 or $10.00. Beautiful lifelike full ball jointed bodies, wonderfully finished in flesh tints. Fine quality full bisque heads with parted lips showing teeth, moving eyes with natural eyelashes, extra quality full sewed curly wigs which are parted and tied with ribbon bows. Good quality neatly trimmed underwear. Choice of two styles as described below. Both can be undressed. Shipping wt., 11 lbs.

No. 18K23212 Dainty dress of good quality cashmere in box plaited Buster Brown style with black belt. Handsome coat with hat to match of good quality black velvetta trimmed with silk faced plush in splendid imitation of genuine ermine. High grade ribbed hose and genuine kid leather shoes. Price.......$4.95

No. 18K23214 Beautifully made Princess style dress with short waisted effect made of fine quality white net over silk slip. Trimming is of wide Valenciennes lace used in combination with imported bead insertion. Wide juby ribbon sash. Mushroom style mull hat with Tam o' Shanter crown. Good quality shoes and half hose. Price.........................$4.95

**Your Choice of Two Splendid Quality Beautifully Dressed Dolls.** Usually sell at $5.00 in the average retail store. Bodies are full ball jointed and perfectly finished in natural flesh tints. Heads of fine quality bisque with parted lips showing teeth, sleeping eyes with natural eyelashes. Good quality full sewed mohair wigs, nicely curled, parted and ribbon tied. Good quality lace trimmed muslin underwear. Pretty half hose and good quality tied shoes. Both styles can be easily undressed. Shipping weight, 10 pounds.

No. 18K23204 Extra well made dress of light color Japanese silk on foundation of heavier material, insuring good wear. Trimming of featherstitched silk braid, tiny buttons and silk juby ribbon. Unlined silk sleeves to match dress. Turban style hat of pretty straw braid. Trimming of flowers and silk ribbon. Full height, including hat, 22 inches. Price.......$2.88

No. 18K23206 20½-Inch Doll with dress of combined Valenciennes lace and white Nottingham allover lace. Very full underslip with extra white flouncings of light colored silk at bottom of skirt. Dress trimming of narrow black velvet ribbon. Cuffs of combined silk and Valenciennes lace. Pretty lace edged silk bonnet with long streamers to match dress. Price.......................$2.88

CHOICE $2.88    No. 18K23204

No. 18K23194    No. 18K23196    CHOICE $1.45

**At a very moderate price** we offer two really exceptional bargains in Beautifully Dressed Full Jointed Dolls. Dolls of this quality sell in the average retail store for not less than $2.50 to $3.00. Heads are of fine quality bisque with pretty baby faces, open lips showing teeth, sleeping eyes with natural eyelashes and full sewed nicely curled and parted wigs. Neat lace edged muslin underwear, openwork stockings and tied sandals. Both dolls can be undressed. Height, including hat, about 19 inches.

No. 18K23194 A beautifully made dress of fine quality French gingham. Trimming of pretty embroidered bands and wide Swiss embroidered edge. Silk ribbon bows at waist. Bonnet to match, trimmed with embroidery and ribbon. Shipping weight, 45 ounces. Price.........................$1.45

No. 18K23196 A good quality mercerized or silk finished cloth in light colors is used in this very stylish dress. Full box plaited skirt with bands of Valenciennes lace, plaited shawl collar of white mull edged with white Brussels net and drawn with white satin ribbon. Dainty straw bonnet, silk ribbon trimmed. Shipping weight, 53 ounces. Price..$1.45

### Unbreakable Dressed Doll.

No. 18K23346 A Very Durable Light Weight Doll with stuffed cloth body, having head, arms and legs of beautiful bisque finish celluloid. Open lips showing teeth, sleeping eyes and full curly wig. Extra well made dress of pin dotted light color material with full length overdress or apron neatly trimmed with narrow braid. Good quality underwear. A poke style bonnet with bow to match. Full size, including hat, 14 inches. Not large size, but fine quality. Shipping weight, 29 ounces. Price.........................98c

No. 18K23346    **98c**

No. 18K23242    **49c**

CHOICE $1.98

No. 18K23200    No. 18K23202

**These Wonder Value Dolls** are of splendid quality, well proportioned and full ball jointed. They have beautiful bisque heads with sleeping eyes and natural lashes, and full sewed and parted curly mohair wigs. Good quality lace trimmed underwear; half hose and tied shoes. Choice of two beautiful dolls as described below, both of which can be undressed. Full height, including hats, 19½ inches. Weight, packed for shipment, 6¼ pounds.

No. 18K23200 Dainty light color Japanese silk with Nottingham lace insertions ornamenting the waist and wide flounce of the same encircling the skirt, makes up the pretty dress shown on this doll. Sash of silk ribbon and ribbon drawn collar with double rosettes complete the trimming. Mushroom shape hat decorated with flowers. Price...........$1.98

No. 18K23202 An Unusually Attractive Doll, dressed in a coat of long nap plush in splendid imitation of ermine with collar edged in fluffy white marabou. Deep fitting hood to match trimmed with daisies caught with ribbon rosettes. Underneath the coat the doll wears a neatly made one-piece dress of good light color striped pique. Price...........$1.98

No. 18K23242 Absolutely unbreakable metal head with lifelike painted eyes and hair. Cloth body is extra well made. Neat polka dot sailor style dress with black trimming. Sailor hat to match dress. Removable long stockings and shoes. Full height, 14 inches. Shipping weight, 16 ounces. Price....49c

*Sears Roebuck & Co.*

# LATEST EUROPEAN NOVELTIES IN DRESSED DOLLS
## "SCHOENHUT'S" PERFORMING UNBREAKABLE ART DOLLS

### The "Romper Baby" With Crying Voice.

Practically unbreakable character doll with fat body of pink silesia. Curved baby legs and arms; jointed at hips and shoulders. Splendidly molded roguish face. The two smaller sizes have crying voices operated by pressing on the body. Largest size has automatic mama voice which cries when doll is tilted forward.

| No. | Ht. In. | Ship'g Wt. | Price |
|---|---|---|---|
| 18K23368 | 9 | 6 oz. | 19c |
| 18K23371 | 11 | 21 oz. | 44c |
| 18K23374 | 12½ | 25 oz. | 85c |

### "Funny Fritzie."

Very strong and durable character dolls with good stuffed bodies, jointed at hips and shoulders. Very large heads, having wonderful baby expression. Papier mache hands, neatly trimmed striped dress. Underwear and socks. Crying baby voice which operates by pressing the body.

| No. | Height Inches | Shipping Weight | Price |
|---|---|---|---|
| 18K23380 | 9¾ | 16 oz. | 25c |
| 18K23382 | 12¾ | 24 oz. | 85c |

### "Eskimo Girls."

Unbreakable dolls of beautiful silk faced plush. Well stuffed and having celluloid face. Hood of plush to match body covers the head. Jointed at the shoulders. Small doll has crying baby voice which operates by pressing on body. Larger doll automatically calls "mama" when it is laid to sleep. Suitable for the smallest children.

| No. | Height Inches | Shipping Weight | Price |
|---|---|---|---|
| 18K23268 | 11 | 14 oz. | 45c |
| 18K23269 | 14 | 26 oz. | 97c |

### Unbreakable Clown Doll.

Body of well stuffed plush, one side pink, the other blue, nicely painted full celluloid head with clown's cap and collar. Has rattle in head and a voice that sounds by pressing the chest. A wonderful doll and a great bargain at the prices asked.

| No. | Height Inches | Shipping Weight | Price |
|---|---|---|---|
| 18K23351 | 9 | 10 oz. | 25c |
| 18K23353 | 12½ | 16 oz. | 48c |

### Crying Character Babies.

This delightful character baby has a most lifelike tinted papier mache body, jointed at hips and shoulders. Head is of bisque with features of a baby and the two larger sizes have decorated bisque hoods tied under chin with ribbons. Crying voice which operates by pressing the shoulders down. Each one dressed in a neatly trimmed chemise. Great value for the money.

| No. | Height Inches | Shipping Weight | Price |
|---|---|---|---|
| 18K23292 | 6¾ | 14 oz. | 21c |
| 18K23294 | 8¾ | 17 oz. | 39c |
| 18K23296 | 10½ | 23 oz. | 65c |

### "We Can Cry for Papa and Mama."

**No. 18K23314 $1.95** — Full jointed finely finished and well formed papier mache body with large beautiful bisque head and a closely curled heavy full sewed wig. Has exceedingly lifelike voice sounded by push button concealed under dress. Dress of pretty cashmere, trimmed with silk and buttons, lace guimpe. Large mushroom shape hat to match dress. Lace half hose and tied sandals, good quality underwear. Easily undressed. Height, including hat, 20 inches. Shipping weight, 6 pounds.

**No. 18K23308 98c** — Extra good quality cloth body with papier mache forearms. Pretty bisque head with moving eyes and with wig of full curls. Light color dress of good material, nicely trimmed with lace. Mushroom hat of same material as dress, set off with silk ribbon rosettes. Openwork stockings and shoes. Lace edged underwear. Has clear mama and mama voice sounded by push button. Height, including hat, 18 inches. Shipping weight, 43 ounces.

**No. 18K23304 48c** — By pulling either one of the two cords doll will say papa or mama. Well stuffed cloth body with papier mache arms and bisque head. Head has sleeping eyes and good curly locks. Medium quality dress of allover lace, trimmed with Valenciennes edging and small bows. Bonnet to match dress. Height, including hat, 16½ inches. Shipping weight, 27 ounces.

**No. 18K23300 25c** — Exceptional value soft stuffed cloth body; nice bisque head, moving eyes and curly wig. Box plaited dress with lace trimming and dress to match. Papa and mama voice operated by pulling either one of two strings. Full height, including hat, 13 inches. Shipping weight, 20 ounces.

## "SCHOENHUT'S" ALL WOOD PERFECTION ART DOLLS

**No. 18K23470 $1.69** — 14-Inch Boy Doll with carved and painted wood hair. Fitted with union suit, shoes and stockings.

**No. 18K23472 $2.65** — 14-Inch Dressed Boy Doll, perfectly made. Overalls, shirt and straw hat. Carved and painted wood hair. Shoes and stockings.

**No. 18K23474 $2.98** — 14-Inch Girl Doll, beautiful dress and good underwear which can be removed. Fine quality genuine mohair curly wig. Shoes and stockings.

**No. 18K23476 $1.69** — 14-Inch Girl Doll with carved and painted wood hair. Lace trimmed union suit; shoes and stockings.

The latest wonderful product of the manufacturers who made the Humpty-Dumpty circus famous. Beautifully proportioned, wonderfully lifelike, unbreakable dolls made of hardwood and perfectly finished in flesh tints. Jointed at neck, shoulders, wrists, elbows, hips, knees and ankles with steel springs and hinges which allow these dolls to assume thousands of positions. Faces are perfectly childlike, with either painted hair or pretty mohair wigs. All dolls have beautifully made union suits, long stockings and real leather slippers. Metal posing stand furnished with each doll. Choice of boy or girl styles either dressed or undressed, as quoted above. Shipping weight, 30 ounces.

**No. 18K23216 23c** — Eskimo Doll dressed from head to foot in white fur. Has good bisque head and jointed arms and legs. A great bargain for a low price. Very pretty and popular. Height, 10 inches. Shipping weight, 12 ounces.

**No. 18K23153 17c** — Practically indestructible stuffed body, full celluloid head. Very neat sailor dress with hat to match. Rattle in the head. Height, including hat, 10½ inches. Shipping weight, 8 oz.

### The Little "Athlete" Dolls.

Wonderfully molded lifelike composition head which is practically unbreakable. Durable hair stuffed cotton flannel body, jointed at hips and shoulders. Dressed in a nicely knitted sweater, buttoned at shoulder. The large size is illustrated. Smaller size has smaller head and not so tall proportioned body. Has a mechanical voice, operated by pressing the body.

| No. | Ht. In. | Ship'g Wt. | Price |
|---|---|---|---|
| 18K23275 | 9½ | 15 oz. | 48c |
| 18K23280 | 13½ | 26 oz. | 89c |

### Delightful Character Dolls.

One of the cleverest character dolls made. Suitable for the smallest child. Pink silesia stuffed half jointed body with practically unbreakable childlike head. Has on a neat dress and stocking cap with tassel. Small size has a crying voice. (Press the body.) Large size has automatic mama voice. (Tilt the body forward.)

| No. | Ht. In. | Ship'g Wt. | Price |
|---|---|---|---|
| 18K23376 | 9 | 13 oz. | 44c |
| 18K23378 | 11¾ | 20 oz. | 85c |

### "Eskimo Boys."

Made of good quality well stuffed plush with lifelike painted celluloid face. Has jointed arms and legs. Has clear automatic voice which sounds when body is tilted. Unusually strong and durable. A great favorite with the children.

| No. | Ht. In. | Ship'g Wt. | Price |
|---|---|---|---|
| 18K23265 | 13½ | 21 oz. | 39c |
| 18K23266 | 18½ | 38 oz. | 73c |

### Rag Dolls With Celluloid Heads.

These so called "rag" dolls are beautifully made, with cloth body and pretty childlike full celluloid heads. Neat gingham dresses and bonnets. Absolutely unbreakable. Just the thing for small children. The larger size can be undressed.

| No. | Ht. In. | Ship'g Wt. | Price |
|---|---|---|---|
| 18K23340 | 11 | 12 oz. | 25c |
| 18K23343 | 13 | 16 oz. | 49c |

### Imported Novelty Character Dolls.

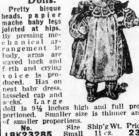

Pretty bisque heads, papier mache baby legs jointed at hips. By pressing mechanical arrangement in body, arms are waved back and forth and crying voice is produced. Has on neat baby dress, tasseled cap and socks. Large doll is 9½ inches high and full proportioned. Smaller size is thinner and of smaller proportions.

| No. | Size | Ship'g Wt. | Price |
|---|---|---|---|
| 18K23285 | Small | 11 oz. | 23c |
| 18K23290 | Large | 19 oz. | 48c |

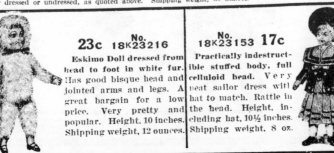
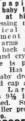
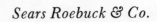

## SKIN AND HAIR DOGS.

Asstd. brown and black long hair, some white spotted, modeled faces, painted features.

**Standing** — 4 wheel red wood platform.

| | | | | Doz. |
|---|---|---|---|---|
| F3424— | 5 x5 | .1 doz. in box. | | $0 42 |
| F3425— | 6½x5½. | 1 " " " | | 75 |
| F3426— | 8 x7 . | 1 " " " | | 95 |
| F3428— | 10½x8 | ½ " " " | | 2 00 |

**Sitting** — 4 wheel red wood platform.

| | | | Doz. |
|---|---|---|---|
| F3430— | 7x6¼. | 1 doz. in box. | $0 90 |
| F3432— | 8x7½. | ½ " " " | 2 15 |

**On Casters**—Ribbon collar and string.

| | | | Doz. |
|---|---|---|---|
| F3434— | 8x7½. | ½ doz. in box. | $2 20 |
| F3435— | 10x9½. | ½ " " pkg. | 4 25 |
| F3436— | 13½ x 13, collar with bell, strong metal feet and rollers. ½ doz. in box.... | | 8 50 |

## WHITE ANGORA POODLE DOGS.

Well modeled, velvet bodies except F3469, long white silky fur manes and tails, glass eyes, ribbon bows.

| | | | Doz. |
|---|---|---|---|
| F3469— | 8x7½. | canton flannel body. ½ doz. in box. | $1 90 |
| F3471— | 9x9½. | ½ doz. in box .... | 4 00 |

*Following with blue or red felt blankets. ½ doz. in box.*

| | Doz. |
|---|---|
| F3475—13x11½. | $8 00 |
| F3477—13½x15. | 9 75 |

## TOY WATER SPANIEL.

**F3507**—10x9½, good model, flannel body fully covered with long **brown** silky Angora fur, glass eyes, ribbon neck bow. ½ doz. in box.
Doz. **$8.00**

## WHITE FRENCH POODLES.

Long white fleecy hair, painted features, bead eyes, red collar with bell and leash, metal rollers on feet. **barking voice.**

**F3422**—Ht. 7½ in., length 8 in. ¼ doz. in box.......... .....Doz. **$4.25**
**F3423**—Ht. 10 in., length 9 in. ⅙ doz. in box..........Doz. **$9.00**

## CLOTH COVERED DOGS.

Good models, strong wired feet, long ears, each with collar.

**F3465**—7x7, 2 styles, asstd. color astrakhan and felt. Asstd. ½ doz. in box. .......... .... ..Doz. **$2.00**
**F3467**—10x9½, asstd. color astrakhan. ¼ doz. in box.......Doz. **$4.50**

## ROVER DOGGIE.

**F3497**—14¾ in., sitting position, long brown Teddy bear plush, long ears, glass eyes, stitched nose and mouth, leather collar with brass buckle, strong wired front legs. 1 in box.
Each. **$1.10**

## ANGORA GOAT.

**F3478**—10½x14, white flannel covered well modeled body, glass eyes, flannel ears and horns, long curly Angora fur back and whiskers, ribbon collar. 1 in box......Each, **65c**

## FUR CAT WITH VOICE.

**F3437**—8x8, well modeled, natural fur covered, glass eyes, felt lined ears, when pressed on back raises head, opens mouth and mews. ½ doz. in box. ............Doz. **$9.00**

## HIGH GRADE FELT COVERED ANIMALS.

Fine molded pressed paper bodies, **on metal wheels.**

**Fox Terrier and Bulldog**—2 styles asstd., white felt covered, spotted black or tan heads, glass eyes, russet leather effect muzzles, collars and leash.

**F3504**—9 x 7¾. ½ doz. in box.
Doz. **$4.25**

**F3505**—16x10, nickel trim collar. ⅙ doz. in box..........Doz. **$9.60**

**F3511—Lion and Tiger.** 2 styles asstd., aver. 17x8½, natural color felt covered, lion with wool mane, tiger striped black, rings attached to necks, when pulled growl naturally. Excellent show pieces. ⅜ doz. in pkg.........Doz. **$9.75**

## IMPORTED STUFFED CATS.

Each with striped celluloid ball.

**F3452**—8x5½, spotted canton flannel, bead eyes, worsted collar. ½ doz. in box..................Doz. **$1.50**

**F3453**—12x6½, white velvet, painted and striped, glass eyes, ribbon collar. ½ doz. in box.....Doz. **$3.90**

**F3450**—15x7, long white wool plush, glass eyes, ribbon collar with bell. ½₂ doz. in box..............Doz. **$8.35**

## FELT AND PLUSH MONKEYS.

F3479      F3480

**F3479**—10 in., soft stuffed brown felt, free limbs, red flannel cap and collar with bell, elastic. 1 doz. in box.....................Doz. **89c**
**F3480**—10 in., soft stuffed brown plush, tinsel collar with bell, flannel cap. ½ doz. in box. Doz. **$1.75**

## GRAY FLANNEL ELEPHANTS.

Stuffed well modeled bodies, glass eyes, white felt tusks, red felt caparison, yellow embroidered borders.

| | | | Doz. |
|---|---|---|---|
| F3482—9¾x7. | ½ doz. in box.... | | $2 10 |
| F3483—10¾x8. | ½ doz. in box... | | 3 80 |
| F3485—13 x 11, circum. 18 in. | | | |
| 1 in pkg............ | ..... Doz. | | 8 00 |

## ASSORTED STUFFED ANIMA[LS]

**L9038**—Asstd. Cat and Dogs, sp[o]t 5 in. good model, heavy flannel [ ] stuffed sewed ears, dog with [ ] 2 doz. in box........... ....Doz.

**L9045**—5 in. dogs, cats, rabbits [ ] bears, movable legs. Asstd. 2 do[z.] box... .... ..............Doz.

**Six styles asstd.**—Cats, dogs an[d rab]bits, sitting positions, black, br[o] and grey spotted canton flan[nel] white underbodies, button eyes, n[ ] cords and pompons.
**F3443**—Aver. 6¼x4. 1 doz. in b[ox.] Doz.
**F3445**—About 10x7. ½ doz. in bo[x] Doz. $[ ]

**Riveted Jointed Felt** — 3 st[yles] asstd., brown dog, gray elepha[nt] maltese cat, glass eyes, col[lar] with bell, rivet joints, can place [in] any position.
**F3461**—7x7. ½ doz. in box. Doz. $1.[ ]

**Felt Covered**—4 styles asstd., d[on]key, horse, camel and dog, bead ey[es] wired legs, horse and donkey h[air] furry manes, leatherette or felt sa[d]dles and blankets, camel with f[elt] trappings, gilt harness.
**F3519**—Aver. 7x7. ¼ doz. in pk[g.] Doz. $2.[ ]

**F3520**—10x10. ½ doz. in pkg. Doz. $4.2[ ]

**Asstd. cats and dogs—with voice** finely modeled stuffed canton fla[n]nel, black and brown plush tails a[nd] ears, leatherette collars with met[al] buckles, ring for leash. ¼ doz. [in] box.
**F3449**—11x10½..........Doz. $4.0[ ]

---

## ELVET ANIMAL ASSTS.

Natural colors, painted and striped.
...ve for pin cushions as well as toys.

...4454—4 in., 3 styles asstd., dog, cat
...nd rabbit, sitting and standing,
...ead eyes, chenille collars. 1 doz.
...n box............ Doz. 94c

...3455—5½ in., 6 styles asstd., dogs,
...ats, rabbit and elephant, glass eyes,
...ribbon collars with bells. ½ doz. in
box.. ..........Doz. $1.75

...3457—7½x7½, 4 styles asstd., cat,
pug, dachshund and elephant, fine
models, glass eyes, ribbon collars
with bells. ½ doz. in box. Doz. $4.15

## ELVET COVERED
## QUACKING DUCKS.

Gray velvet bodies, asstd. bright
...olor heads, vari-color felt wings and
...ails, glass eyes, tape strings, quack
...hen pulled along floor.

...3500—7¾x7, metal wheels. ½ doz.
in box. ............ ........Doz. $4.00

F3502 — 10 x 8¼, invisible wheels,
...wings flap. ½ doz. in box.
..........Doz. $7.50

## WHITE WOOL SHEEP.

Splendid sellers. Smaller sizes used
...or tree ornaments.

...With Gilt Horns — Composition
heads, woolly fleece, painted wood
feet. 1 doz. in box.
F3523—2½ in.............Doz. $0 33
F3524—4½ in., bell at neck. " 72

...On Metal Wheel Red Platform—
Modeled faces, glass eyes, thick
wool covered, collars with bell,
painted wood feet, bleating voice.
Doz.
F3526—6x6⅜. ½ doz. in box..$2 15
F3528—9x9¼. ½ " " " ... 4 10
F3529—12x11. ⅓ " " " .. 8 75
F3530—14½x15. 1 in box.
EACH, $1.25

---

## POPULAR PRICED
## TEDDY BEARS.

F3491          F3492

F3491—7½ in., soft stuffed brown
cotton plush, jointed limbs, button
eyes, leatherette collar. 1 doz. in
box..........................Doz. 92c
F3492 — Turning Heads. 9 in.,
brown, with voice, soft stuffed, long
"Teddy Bear" plush, jointed limbs,
felt soles, glass eyes. ½ doz. in box.
..........................Doz. $2.15

F3493 — "Crying
Cub." 12 in.,
brown, ribbon
collar, double
bellows crying
voice. ½ doz. in
box....Doz. $4.20

F3495—17¾ in., ribbon collar, automatic deep growl. 2 brown,
1 white. ¼ doz. in pkg....Doz. $8.75

## CINNAMON PLUSH BEARS.

The pick of products of domestic
bear manufacturers.

Fine models, long pile brown plush
soft stuffed, turning head, glass eyes,
jointed limbs, chamois palms and
soles, voice. 1 in box.
F3600—14 in.......... ...Each, $0 55
F3601—16 "................ " 72
F3602—18 "................ " 84
F3603—20 "........ .. · " 95
F3604—22 "................ " 1 10

## BROWN PLUSH
## BEARS ON WHEELS.

Strongly made, fine models, brown
plush covered, nose rings with long
chain leash, wheels connected by
metal bars.

F3510—Length 8 in., ht. 5½. ½ doz.
in pkg. ......................Doz. $2.25

F3509—Length 10 in., ht. 7½, long
pile plush, metal muzzle. ½ doz. in
pkg.......................Doz. $4.50

---

## IMPORTED PAPIER
## MACHE HORSES.

Modeled dapple bodies, wood legs,
wooly manes and tails, bridles, colored
saddles or bands.

On 4-wheel Platforms—          Doz.
F3548—5¼x5. 1 doz. in box....$0 42
F3550—7x6¼. 1 " " " .... 82
F3552—10x10⅛. ½doz. in box. 2 20

On Rockers—                    Doz.
F3554—6x6. 1 doz. in box.....$0 45
F3555—7x7. 1 " " " .. 84
F3556—9¾x10. 1 doz. in box.. 2 20

## FELT COVERED ANIMALS
## —On 4-Wheel Platforms.

F3410—Ht. 5¾ in., asstd. color horses
and mules, tape bridles, fur tails.
5¼ in. red stained platforms. 1 doz.
in box.........................Doz. 90c

F3578—6x6¼, asstd. dapple gray,
black and bay horses, white fur
manes, hair tails, enameled bridles,
saddles, felt blankets, varnished
platforms. 1 doz. in box...Doz. 95c

## HOLLOW BODY
## METAL HORSES.

Good models, painted bodies,
bridles and saddles, 4 wheel wood
platforms painted green.
F3559 — 6½x6½, black, dapple and
bay. Asstd. 1 doz. in box... Doz. 92c
F3561—10¼x11¾, black and brown.
Asstd. ½ doz. in box...... Doz. $2.15

## IMPORTED
## PLUSH HORSES.

F3565—7x8. ½ doz. pkg..Doz. $2.20
F3568—11¼x9½. ½ dz. pkg.Dz. $4.15

---

## DAPPLE GRAY
## FELT HORSES.

Dapple felt covered well modeled
bodies, black leather ears, glass eyes,
white hair manes and tails, russet
saddles and bridles, red felt saddle
blankets, metal stirrups. 4-wheel
varnished 2-color wood platforms.

F3579—7½x7¾. ½ doz. in box.
Doz. $2.18

F3580—10¼ x 10¾, plush saddle.
½ doz. in box. ...........Doz. $4.10

F3581—13¾ x 13¾, plush saddle.
½ doz. in box.... Doz. $9.00

## LEATHER
## COVERED COWS.

Fine models, natural leather cov-
ered, glass eyes, collar with bell,
loud voice, on 4 wheel red painted
platforms.
F3539— 8  x6—½ doz. box. Doz. $4 25
F3541—11  x8—1 in box. EACH, 85
F3543—12  x9—1 "  " .. 1 10
F3544—15 x11—1 "  " .. 1 40

## IMPORTED PLUSH ROCKING HORSE.

Black plush covered, good models,
glass eyes, cropped manes, long tails,
removable plush saddles, embroidered felt blankets, leather reins,
metal stirrups, striped red wood
rockers.
F3583—Ht. 24½ in., 32 in. rockers.
1 in pkg., 5 lbs..........Each, $2.30

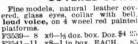

F3583

On Platform with Rockers.
Removable platforms with
4 iron wheels.
F3585—22 x 21½, rockers
36 in. 1 in pkg. 12 lbs.
Each, $3.40
F3587—25½ x 25, platform
28 in., rockers 40 in. 1 in
pkg., 15 lbs.....Each, $4.50

F3585-87

## IMPORTED PLUSH COVERED HORSES WITH WAGONS.

Removable harnessed plush horses on 4-wheel platforms, strongly made
wagons, painted and striped. A greatly improved line, better values than
ever.

F3592—3 styles, length 21¼ in., dapple horse 8½x8, 4-wheel hay wagon,
contractor's and truck, asstd. ¼ doz. in box.........DOZ. $4.50

F3593—Length 21¼ in., white
horse 8½x7, yellow milk wagon
with 6 cans. ½ doz. in box.
DOZ. $9.60

F3594—Length 27¼ in.,
dapple horse 9½x10¼, loaded truck, painted blue,
colored stripes, 3 sliding top
cases, 4 burlap bales, chain
fastener and tail slide. 1 in
box............ · Each, 90c

F3595—Length 26 in.,
white horse 9¼ x 10¼,
4-wheel truck with
high seat, painted blue,
yellow wheels. 1 in
box..........Each,$1.00

---

## PAPIER MACHE HORSES.
## With Carts and Wagons.

F3588—With Hay and Dump Carts.
9¾ in. varnished wood carts, dapple
gray horse, black oil cloth harness,
on 5x1½ metal wheel platform.
Asstd. ½ doz. in box......Doz. $1.05

F3591 — 3 styles, about 15⅛ in.,
4 wheel hay, sand and delivery wagons, dapple gray horse, wool mane
and tail, on 4 wheel platform. Asstd.
½ doz. in box.............Doz. $2.15

---

## IMPORTED PAPIER MACHE ANIMALS.
Practically indestructible.

**Farmyard Assts**—6 styles asstd., well modeled horses, donkeys, cows, sheep, etc., natural colors, felt finish. 1 doz. in box.
F3400—2¾ in....Doz. $0 27
F3401—3¾ "......." 45
F3402—5 "......." 84

**Wild and Domestic**—Glazed finish, 6 styles, asstd. horses, sheep, pigs, elephants, etc., painted in natural colors. 1 doz. in box.
F3406—Aver. 4½ in......Doz. $0 40
F3407—" 7 "......." 75

**Jungle Asst**—6 styles asstd., lion, elephant, camel, bear, tiger and hyena, felt finish, natural colors. 1 doz. in box.
F3403—Aver. 3½ in.........Doz. 45c

F3408—6 styles asstd., aver. 3¾ in., donkeys, horses, sheep, etc., painted glazed finish, 4 in. platforms, metal wheels. 1 doz. in box......Doz. 45c

**F3547 — Rocking Animals with Riders.** Full ht. 9 in., 3 styles, 6 in. felt finish goat, horse and donkey, leatherette bridles, horse and donkey with fur manes and tails, stained wood rockers, clown and jockey riders, lace trim costumes, painted composition heads. Asstd. ½ doz. in box...........Doz. $2.25

**F3203** — Box 5x5, litho front, Do Tige, Little Nemo, Hooligan, policeman, etc. Asstd. ½ doz. in pkg. ......Doz. $1.75

## NODDING HEAD ANIMALS.

**On 4 Wheel Platforms** — Asstd. horses, donkeys and cows in box, natural color felt finish, some with harness.
Doz
F3413—4⅝x4¾. 1 doz. in box..$0 42
F3414—5¼x5½. 1 " " " .79
F3415—6¼x6½. 1 " " " .95
F3416—8½x8, extra size.
½ doz. in box................ 2 10

**Elephants**—Natural color felt finish, cloth blankets, gold lace paper edge.
Doz
F3420—5x3½. 1 doz. in box... $0 87
F3421—8x5. ½ " " " .. 2 15

F3412—6x5½, 4 styles, asstd. bay horse, gray donkey, dapple goat and spotted cow, horse and donkey with paper saddles, nickeled wheels, **heads bob and tails switch.** 1 doz. in box.............. Doz. 95c

**F3405—Assortment.** Aver. 7 in., dog, cat, bear, rabbit and pig, felt finish, some glass eyes, long action. ½ doz. in box........ Doz. $1.95

**Nodding Donkeys with Riders**—Asstd. fancy dressed monkeys, clowns, dogs, etc., on felt finish donkeys, woolly manes, saddles and bridles, 4 wheel wood platforms.
F3418—About 8x9½. ½ doz. in box.
Doz. $2.15
F3419—About 9x12. ¼ doz. in box.
Doz. $4.10

### KINDERGARTEN TOY ASSTS—12 styles asstd. in box.

**F3196—Special 10 cent asst;** pop gun, 6 in. Punch and Judy show, 12 in. dressed clapping figure, 10 in. sail boat, horse with mane and tail and shaking head donkey on 4 wheel platform, wool sheep and horse with hay carts, 3¾x3¾ surprise box, dressed acrobat with chair, soldier boy in chair with clappers, litho performing horse and jockey. 1 doz. in box,........ Doz. 82c

## PERFORMING ANIMALS.

**F3514—Pneumatic.** 7 in., 2 styles, astrakhan covered jumping dog with voice, spotted fur jumping rabbit with moving ears; pressure on rubber bulb causes toy to perform. Asstd. ½ doz. in box.......Doz. $2.00

**F3216—Barking Dog.** 5 in. black fur dog, glass eyes, on red bellows platform which by pressing produces, voice and dog jumps. ½ doz. in box....................Doz. $2.25

**F3229—Jumping Fur Dog.** Black fur, painted features, 5x4¼ stained wood platform bellows handle, dog jumps and barks. ½ doz. in pkg.
Doz. $2.25

**F3217—Bear Acrobat.** 8 in. jointed brown fur on 9½ in. trapeze, 7¼x4¼ platform, performs by pressing attached spring. ½ doz. in box.
Doz. $3.95

**F3224 — Traveling Menagerie.** Ht. 6½ in., 13⅜x5½ four-wheel platform, 5-compartment cage, 3 hinged doors, papier mache lion, tiger, polar bear in center comes out and growls when door is opened. 1 in box.
EACH, 85c

**F3640 — Acrobatic Monkey.** 8¾ in., composition face, hands and feet, painted features, brown plush covered body, jointed limbs, long tail, on 10 ft. heavy cord, china ring one end, turned wood handles other, when handles are pulled alternately monkey climbs string. Each wrapped, ½ doz. in box.........Doz. $2.15

## PERFORMING FIGURES.

**F3230—Wood Toy.** 9x3, hand carved man and bear seesawing, hammers strike alternately. 2 doz. in box..........................Doz. 26c

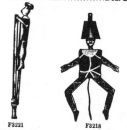

**F3221—Monkey on Stick.** 17 in. long, 6½ in. painted monkey. 2 doz. in pkg.........................Doz. 33c

**F3218—Jumping Jack.** 10½ in., double sided head and body, large cap, painted in gay colors. 1 doz. in pkg. ............Doz. 40c

**F2856—Boxers.** 3½ in. painted figures, movable arms, on 4¾x1 green platform; by working button men box naturally. 1 doz. in box. 72c

**F3226 — Gymnasts.** 8 in., well known characters, funny antics on double ladder, worked by wire. 1 doz. in box.................Doz. 75c

**F3227 — Jumping Figures.** 10 in., asstd. characters, painted composition heads, colored, cloth costumes, elastic and cord attached. Asstd. 1 doz. in box........Doz. 87c

Two styles F3227

**F2851—Punching Bag Toy.** 4¾ in. painted athlete, movable arms, on 6⅛x1¾ green wood platform, brown wood bag suspended on wire uprights; athlete punches bag when button is pressed. 1 doz. in box.
Doz. 80c

Two styles F3213

**F3213 — Clapping Figures.** 10½ in., Foxy Grandpa, Hooligan and policeman, painted composition heads, lace trim colored costumes, clap when chest is pressed. Asstd. 1 doz. in box. ...........Doz. 90c

**F3223 — Acrobat.** 14½ in., wood figure on wire pole, revo rapidly by pressing wood ha 1 doz. in box...............Doz.

### SHAKING HEAD FIGUR
Large heads which "wigwag" droll manner, painted features costumes, wood base.

F3208—6½ in., 6 styles asstd., F Grandpa, Happy Hooligan, L Nemo, etc. 1 doz. in box. Doz.
F3209—8¾ in., 6 styles asstd., c ical negro, dude, policeman, 1 doz. in box...............Doz.
F3210—6 styles asstd., extra la heads with wool mustaches, bea etc., short bodies. ½ doz. in box.
Doz. $

### IMPORTED
### BELLOW TOY

Asstd. styles, roosters, parro swans, birds in cages, cats, dogs, e painted in bright colors, some springs, bellows base produces vo 1 doz. in box.
F3189—About 4½ in.....Doz. $0
F3190—5¼ in............ "
F3191—7¼ "............. "
F3192—Aver. 8 in........... "

### IMPORTED
### SURPRISE BOXE

Fancy covered hinged boxes, co position head figures on springs p out when lid is unhooked, bello voice.

F3198
F3199
**F3198**—Box 2¾x2¾, figures attache to string. Asstd. 1 doz. in pkg.
Doz. 3
**F3199**—Box 3½x3, 6 styles. 1 doz. pkg............ .. Doz. 4

F3200
F3201
**F3200**—Box 4x4, litho front, 6 style Asstd. 1 doz. in box........Doz. 8
**F3201** — Box 4x4¼, litho front, styles, some with wool beard Asstd. 1 doz. in pkg........Doz.

F3195—5 cent asst; surprise box, dog, horses, sheep, shaking head donkey on 4 wheel platform, cricket rattle, wood trumpet, pop pistol, dressed figure on stick with voice, sheep with cart, figure wheel toy, clapping figure. 1 doz. in box.
Doz. 39c

F5751—11 Pc. Box 10x12¼. Set, 68c
F5752—17 Pc. Additional pigs, sheep and colt, box 12x14. Set, $1.25

## DECORATED TIN TRUMPETS.

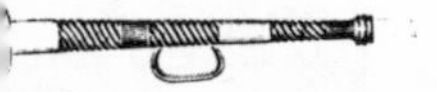

0—8½ in., embossed silver and brilliant stripes, china mouthpiece, good reed. Asstd. 2 doz. in ........ .. ............Doz. **20c**

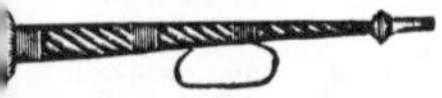

yles Asstd.—Gilt, silver and meled floral and picture designs, celain mouthpiece. Asstd. 2 doz. oox.
12—9¼ in . .............Doz. **28c**

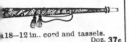

18—12 in.. cord and tassels. Doz. **37c**

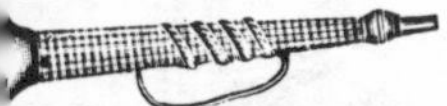

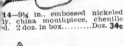

14—9¼ in., embossed nickeled ly, china mouthpiece, chenille d. 2 doz. in box..........Doz. **34c**

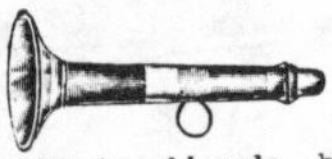

16—5½ in.. **bicycle,** brilliant nds, extra loud choral reed. 1 doz. box.....................Doz. **35c**

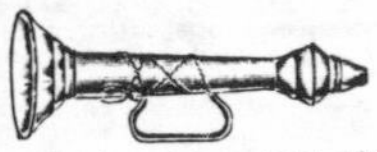

26—6¼ in., extra stout nickeled dy, painted funnel, choral reed, enille cord wound. 1 doz. in box. Doz. **40c**

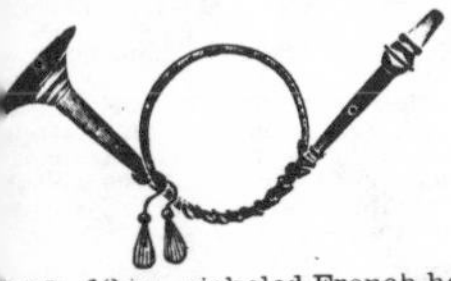

120—12 in., nickeled French horn, inted funnel, porcelain mouthiece, chenille cord wound. 2 doz. box...................Doz. **42c**

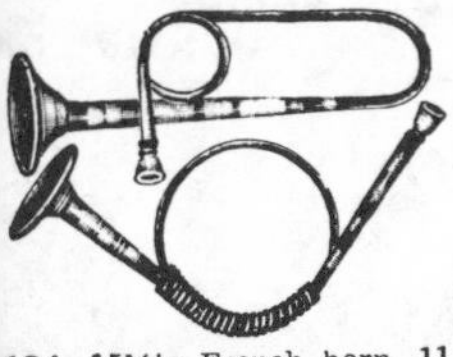

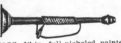

124—15⅛ in. French horn, 11 in. lto, gilt finish, colored stripes, ainted funnel, china cup mouthiece, trumpet reed, cord and tassel. ssstd. 1 doz. in box.........Doz. **45c**

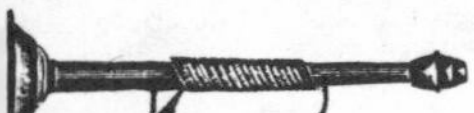

128—13 in., full nickeled, painted unnel, double reed, cord and tassel. doz. in box..... ..........Doz. **72c**

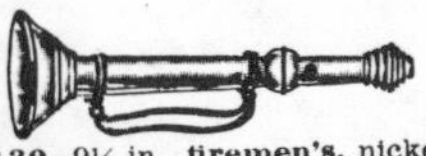

130—9½ in., **firemen's,** nickeled, bevel mouthpiece, double call, red cord wound. 1 doz. in box..Doz. **79c**

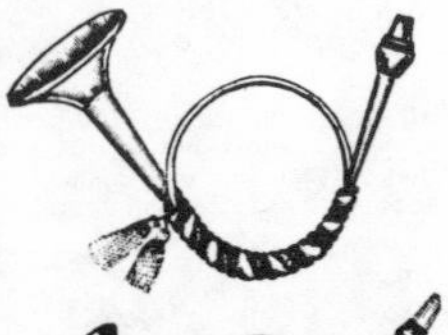

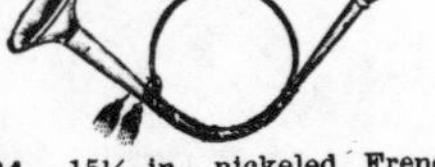

134—15½ in., nickeled French horn, metal mouthpiece, double reed, cord wound. 1 doz. in box. Doz. **82c**

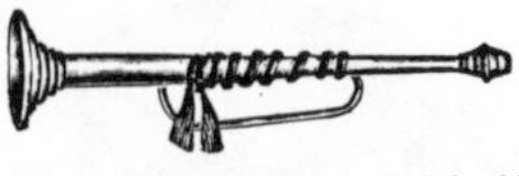

**F5138**—16¼ in., full nickeled, double call, chenille cord wound, heavy handle. 1 doz. in box. .... Doz. **87c**

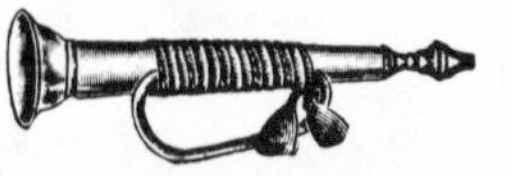

**F5140**—11¾ in., stout nickeled bugle double reed, extra heavy handle, cord and tassels. 1 doz. in box. Doz. **92c**

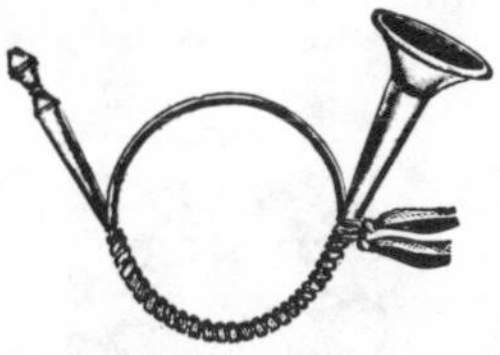

**F5142**—23 in. around, nickeled French horn, **extra size,** double reed, chenille cord and tassels. ⅙ doz. in box.............Doz. **$1.85**

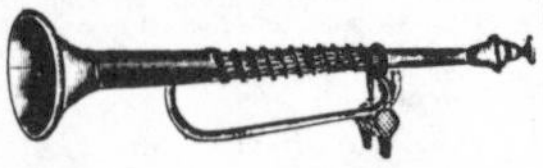

**F5145**—17¾ in., extra size, full nickeled, double reed, gilt tinsel & blue cord wound, tinsel tassels. ⅙ doz. in box.. ........ ....Doz. **$2.00**

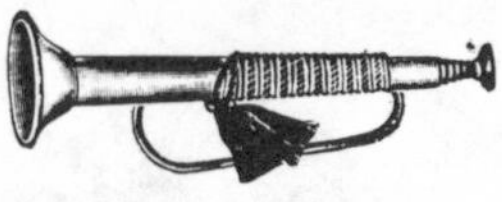

**F5148**—15⅛ in., heavy nickel plated, double reed, tinsel and cord wound, silk tassels. ⅙ doz. in box. Doz. **$2.10**

## TIN RATTLE TRUMPETS.

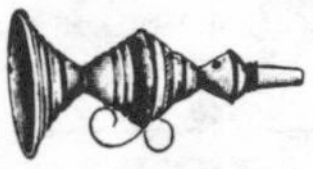

**F5067**—5½ in., asstd. nickeled and bright stripes, porcelain mouthpiece. 2 doz. in box........Doz. **40c**

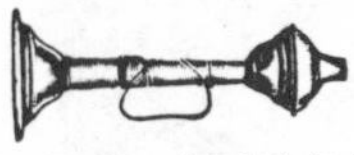

**F5069**—7½ in. nickeled body and mouthpiece, funnel painted blue, loud rattle, choral reed, wool cord wound. 2 doz. in box...... Doz. **45c**

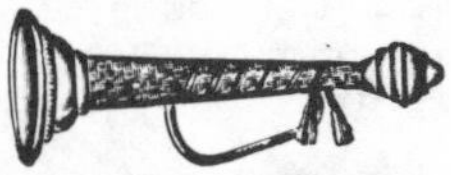

**F5071** — 11 in., embossed nickeled body, 3⅜ in. bell, loud rattle, choral reed, chenille wound, tassels. 1 doz. in box....... ..................Doz. **85c**

## ZYLONITE TRUMPETS.

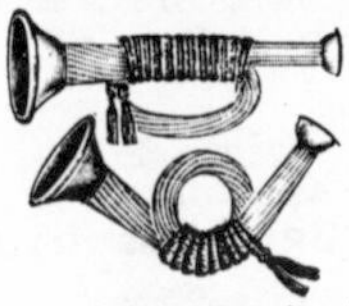

**F5159** — 6 in., asstd. color bodies, white mouthpiece, funnel and handle, chenille cord and tassel double call reed. 1 doz. in box. Doz. **85c**

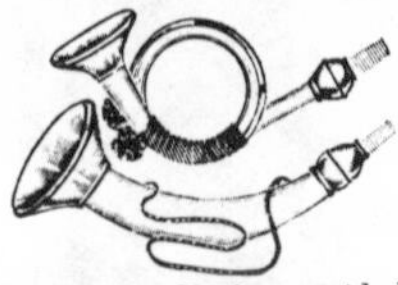

**F5164** — Aver. 9½ in., asstd. horn, bugle and trumpet, white zylonite, brass trim, double call, silk cords and tassels, 1 with chain. ⅙ doz. in box..........................Doz. **$1.95**

## NATURAL HORN TRUMPETS.

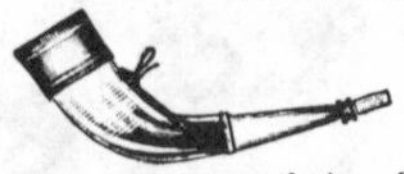

**F5151**—Porcelain mouthpiece, 9½ in. gilt metal trim. Good reeds, cord hangers. 2 doz. in box......Doz. **40c**

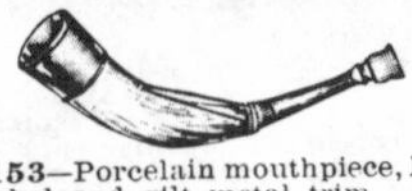

**F5153**—Porcelain mouthpiece, 12 in., nickel and gilt metal trim. Good reed, cord hanger. 1 doz. in box. Doz. **80c**

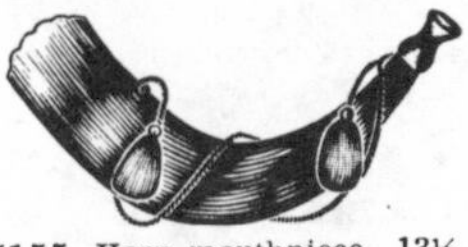

**F5155**—Horn mouthpiece, 13½ in. loud reed, silk cord hanger, 2 silk tassels. ⅙ doz. in box....Doz. **$2.25**

## "GABRIEL" AUTO HORNS.

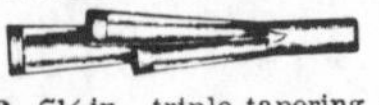

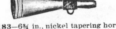

**F5182**—7⅛ in., triple tapering nickeled horns, **3 reeds,** choral call. 1 doz. in box ................Doz. **89c**

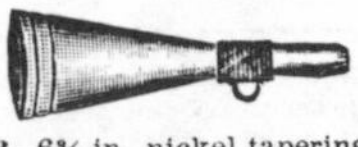

**F5183**—6¾ in., nickel tapering horn, wire ring, cord wound, melodious choral call. 1 doz. in box...Doz. **92c**

## NOVELTY TRUMPETS.

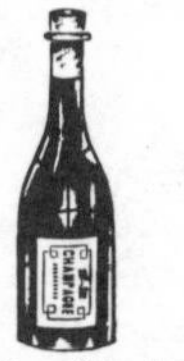

**F5184—Bottle.** 6 in. turned wood. enameled label, tinfoil top, loud double trumpet reed. 1 doz. in box. Doz. **40c**

## "PROFIT PAYERS" DECORATED TRUMPETS.

*Unmatchable values in these big selling Christmas staples.*

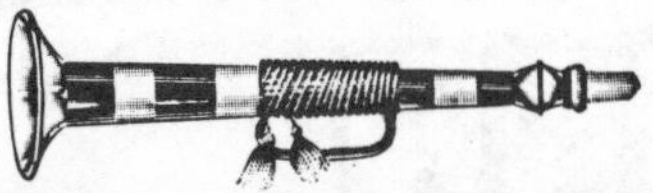

**F5122**—10¼ in., brilliant colors and gilt bands and stripes, cord wound handle, metal mouthpiece, loud reed. Asstd. 1 doz. in box. Doz. **45c**

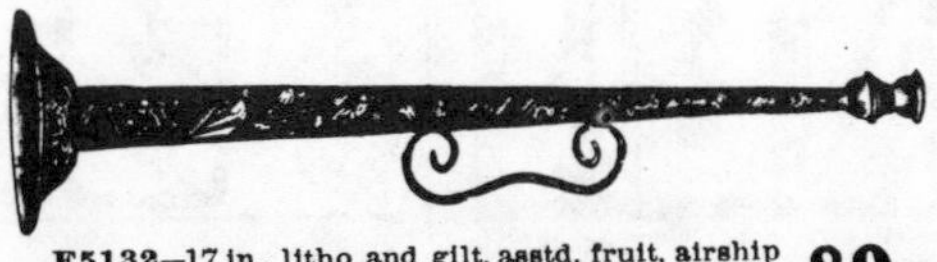

**F5132**—17 in., litho and gilt, asstd. fruit, airship and fancy designs, metal cup mouthpiece, **double reed,** cord and tassels. Asstd. 1 doz. in box. Doz. **89c**

## TAPERING TIN HORNS.

Turned wood mouthpieces, loud brass reeds, well finished. Asstd. brilliant red and blue.

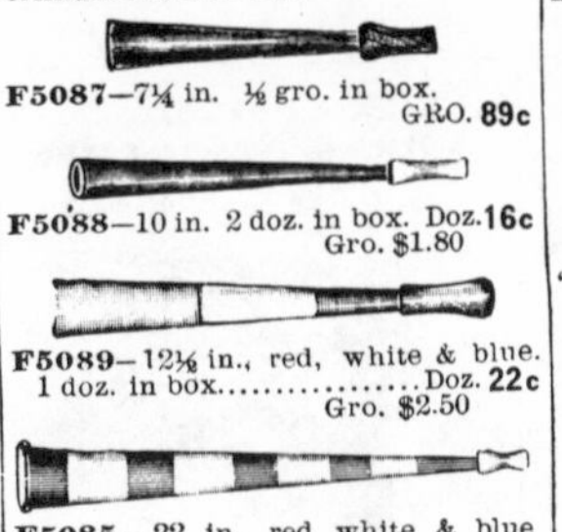

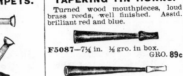

**F5087**—7¼ in. ⅙ gro. in box. GRO. **89c**

**F5088**—10 in. 2 doz. in box. Doz.**16c** Gro. **$1.80**

**F5089**—12⅛ in., red, white & blue. 1 doz. in box................Doz. **22c** Gro. **$2.50**

**F5085**—22 in., red white & blue enameled. 1 doz. in box....Doz. **69c** Gro. **$7.80**

## BELL BOTTOM TIN HORNS

Turned wood mouthpiece, loud brass reeds, well finished.

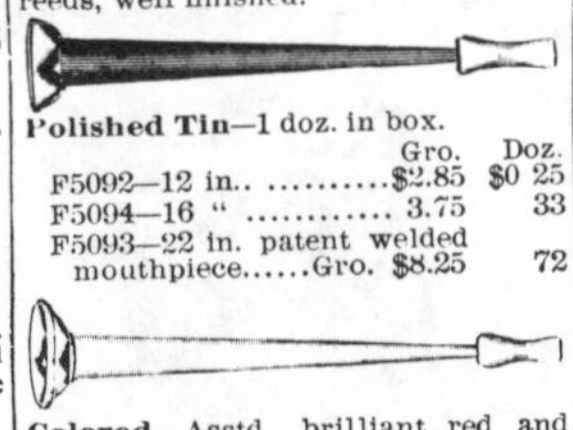

**Polished Tin**—1 doz. in box.

| | Gro. | Doz. |
|---|---|---|
| F5092—12 in.. .......... | $2.85 | $0 25 |
| F5094—16 " ............ | 3.75 | 33 |
| F5093—22 in. patent welded mouthpiece......Gro. | $8.25 | 72 |

**Colored**—Asstd. brilliant red and blue. 1 doz. in box.

| | | | |
|---|---|---|---|
| F5095—12 in..Gro. | $3.20 | Doz. | $0 28 |
| F5096—16 " | 4.00 | " | 35 |
| F5097—22 " | 8.40 | " | 73 |

## TIN HORNS—Extra Deep Tone.

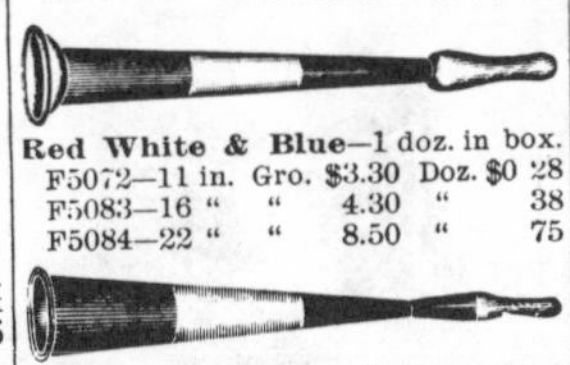

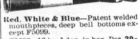

**Red White & Blue**—1 doz. in box.

| | | | |
|---|---|---|---|
| F5072—11 in. Gro. | $3.30 | Doz. | $0 28 |
| F5083—16 " " | 4.30 | " | 38 |
| F5084—22 " " | 8.50 | " | 75 |

**Red. White & Blue**—Patent welded mouthpieces, deep bell bottoms except F5099.

F5099—16 in. 1 doz. in box. Doz. **39c** Gro. $4.65

F5108—22 in. 1 doz. in box. Doz. **78c** Gro. $9.00.

F5109—30 in. ⅙ doz. in box. Doz. **$1.95**

## IMPORTED HORNS.

**Stars and Stripes**—Heavy strawboard, glazed paper covered, red & white stripes, white stars on blue band, **wood mouthpiece,** loud reeds. 1 doz. in box.

| | Gro. | Doz. |
|---|---|---|
| F5073—14⅛ in.......... | $2 10 | $0 19 |
| F5074—19¾ " .......... | 2 50 | 22 |
| F5075—23⅛ " ... .... | 3 30 | 29 |
| F5076—27½ " ... .... | 4 00 | 35 |

## NOVELTY TAPERING HORNS.

7 in., red, white and blue glazed paper covering, nickeled mouthpiece.

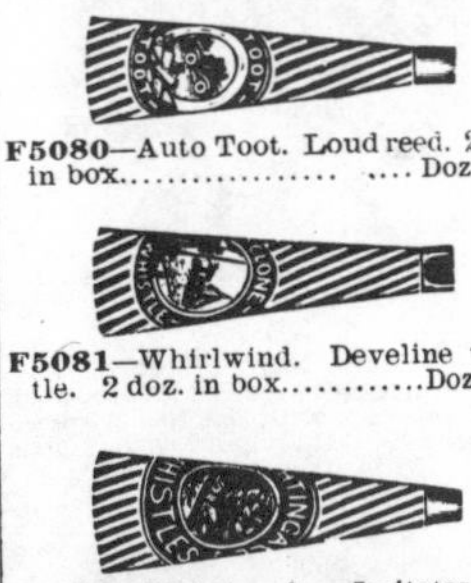

**F5080**—Auto Toot. Loud reed. 2 doz. in box.... ........ .... Doz. **25c**

**F5081**—Whirlwind. Develine whistle. 2 doz. in box..........Doz. **27c**

**F5082**—Nightingale. Imitates bird warbling. 2 doz. in box....Doz. **28c**

## TOY MEGAPHONES.

Strong brown fiber paper, polished wood mouthpieces.

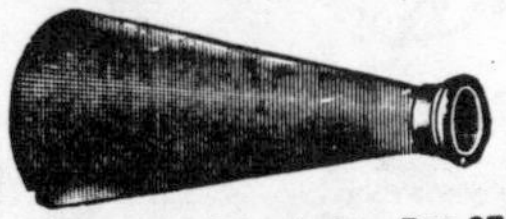

**F1975**—11 in., 2 doz. in box. Doz. **37c** Gro. $4.20

**F1976**—14 in., riveted sides, 1 doz. in box....... ......Gro. $8.40 Doz. **72c**

## COMBINATION CLAPPER HORNS.

Wood mouthpieces. **2-in-1 noise makers.**

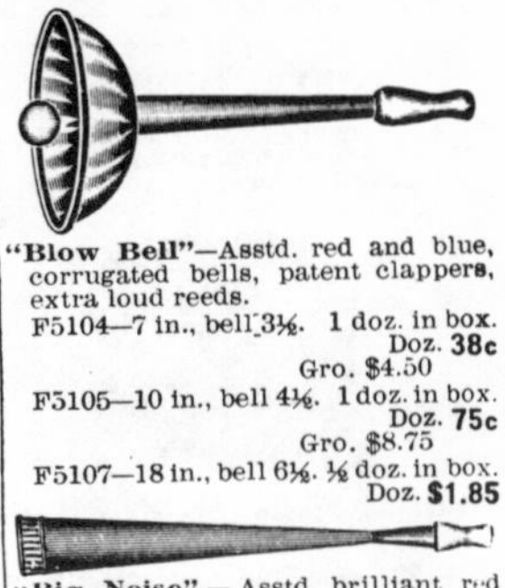

**"Blow Bell"**—Asstd. red and blue, corrugated bells, patent clappers, extra loud reeds.

F5104—7 in., bell 3⅛. 1 doz. in box. Doz. **38c** Gro. $4.50

F5105—10 in., bell 4⅛. 1 doz. in box. Doz. **75c** Gro. $8.75

F5107—18 in., bell 6⅛. ⅙ doz. in box. Doz. **$1.85**

**"Big Noise"** — Asstd. brilliant red and blue, patent mouthpieces, extra loud reeds, corrugated base, clapper.

F5100—20 in. 1 doz. in box. Doz. **75c** Gro. $8.65

F5101 — 27 in. ⅙ doz in box. Doz. **$1.65**

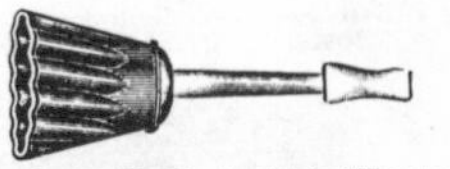

**"Lucky Strike"**—Asstd. brilliant red and blue, patent mouthpiece, loud reed, corrugated bell, clapper.

F5102—10 in. 1 doz. in box. Doz. **78c** Gro. $9.00

## CARNIVAL RATTLES.

Unrivaled noise-makers.

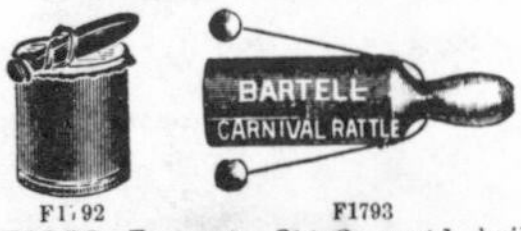


F1792 F1793

**F1792—Locust.** 2¼x2, asstd. brilliant color tin cups, white steel heads, wood handle with string. 1 doz. in box......... ........Doz. **25c**

**F1793—Clapper.** 6 in., slit hollow wood body, solid handle, colored ball clappers on steel springs. 1 doz. in box.. ........................Doz. **25c** Gro. $2.75

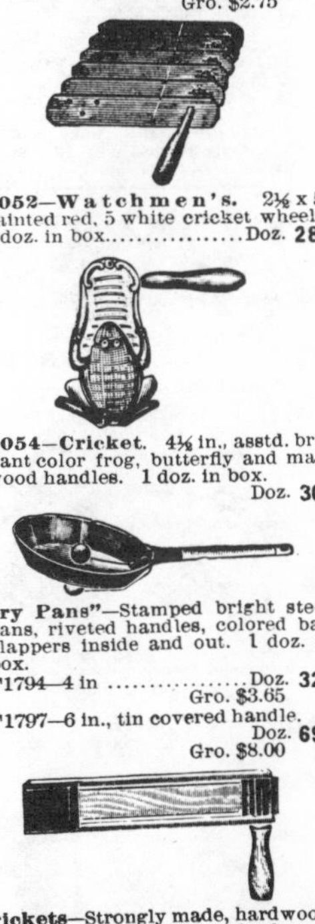

**F5052—Watchmen's.** 2⅛x5, painted red, 5 white cricket wheels. 1 doz. in box...................Doz. **28c**

**F5054—Cricket.** 4⅛ in., asstd. brilliant color frog, butterfly and man, wood handles. 1 doz. in box. Doz. **30c**

**"Fry Pans"**—Stamped bright steel pans, riveted handles, colored ball clappers inside and out. 1 doz. in box.

F1794—4 in ....................Doz. **32c** Gro. $3.65

F1797—6 in., tin covered handle. Doz. **69c** Gro. $8.00

**Crickets**—Strongly made, hardwood-turned wood handles, stained rachets, extra loud strong clappers 1 doz. in box.

F1978—Length 6⅜ in.....Doz. $0 36
F1979— " 9¼ "..... " 65

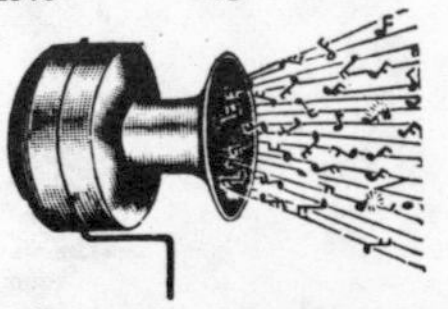

**F1795—Carnival Rooter.** Heavy IX polished stamped tin, metal crank, extra loud noise. Each in carton, 1 doz. in box..............Doz. **75c** Gro. $8.50

# DRUMS

**An improved showing.** Mostly put up in original case assortments insuring big variety, small investment and safe delivery. When you buy drums here, remember that you get not one, but from four to six styles assorted, the choice selection of the most popular sellers. In checking up prices be sure and *compare the goods* as well.

### METAL DRUMS.

White enameled steel heads and bottoms, each with 2 sticks, In heavy corrugated cartons.

**National**—Litho red, white & blue, steel hoops, colored cord.

F1338—6 in. 2 doz.in carton, 13½ lbs. Doz. **83c**
Gro. **$9.50**

F1339—7 in., 2 heights, 4⅞ and 3⅝ in. Asstd. 2 doz. in carton, 17½ lbs. Gro. **$11.25**

F1340—8½ in. 1 doz. in carton, 13 lbs...................Doz. **$1.75**

**F1341**—Extra quality. 8½ in., litho patriotic design body, black enameled steel hoops, red, white & blue cord, leather ears. 1 doz. in carton, 13½ lbs...........Doz. **$2.00**

**F1316**—Sheep Head, Fiber Bottom. Diam. 12 in., 2 hts., 6 and 8½ in., imit. ash metal bodies, gilt striped black wood hoops, heavy white cord, leather ears, red, white & blue web belt. ½ doz. in crate, 30 lbs.. ...................Doz. **$8.40**

### POPULAR PRICED DRUM ASSORTMENT.

In Heavy Fiber Cartons.

**F1312**—25c Asst. 6 styles, asstd., 7 in., plain and embossed metal bodies, litho designs and solid colors, wood hoops with cord, fiber heads and bottoms, sticks. 1 doz. in carton, 10 lbs...........Doz. **$1.98**

**F1314**—50c Asst. 6 styles, asstd., 8 in., plain and embossed metal bodies, litho designs and solid colors, embossed wood hoops with cord, with and without hooks, fiber heads and bottoms, web belts, sticks. ½ doz. in carton, 8 lbs....Doz. **$3.75**

**F1315**—$1.00 Asst. 6 styles, 12 in., embossed metal bodies, patriotic designs—eagle & flag, soldiers, flag & gilt star on colored band, etc., sheep heads, fiber bottoms, embossed wood hoops, hooks with cord, web belts, sticks. ½ doz. in case, 32 lbs.. ... .. ...Doz. **$8.25**

### METAL BODY DRUM ASSORTMENT.

**F1320** —Metal bodies, bright colored National, Boy Scout, circus, Colonial soldier, Indian and Teddy bear designs, silvered, gilt and colored bands, black hoops with cord, web belts, sticks; all fiber heads and bottoms except 12 in. which has sheep head. Case contains:

| | Retail at | Total Retail |
|---|---|---|
| ½ doz. 6½ in. | 25c............ | $1 50 |
| ½ " 8 " | 50c............ | 3 00 |
| ¼ " 10 " | 75c....... | 2 25 |
| ¼ " 12 " | $1.00...... | 3 00 |

Total 1½ doz. in case, 45 lbs. **$9 75**

Case, **$6.25**

See our 1914 line of attractive GAMES. A splendid showing.

### NICKEL PLATED SHELL MILITARY DRUM ASST.

**F1318**—Low military shape, nickel shells, sheep heads, fiber bottoms, ebonized hoops with colored cord and hooks, each with web belt and sticks. Case contains:

| | | | | |
|---|---|---|---|---|
| ½ doz. | 8 in. | @ $4.44 | $2 22 |
| ¼ " | 9 " | ......... " | 6.64 | 1 66 |
| ⅙ " | 10 " | ......... " | 8.04 | 1 34 |
| 1/12 " | 12 " | ......... " | 9.36 | 78 |

28 lbs., 1 doz. in case.....Doz. **$5.50**

### EMBOSSED WOOD SHELL DRUM ASST.

**F1317**—Embossed wood shells, natural finish, painted soldier and battleship designs, wood hoops with metal hooks and cord, sheep heads, fiber bottoms, web belts, sticks. Case contains:

½ doz. 8 in., asstd. 2 painted..$1 75
Doz. **$4.20**
⅓ doz. 9 in., 1 painted finish.. 2 00
Doz. **$6.00**
¼ doz. 11 in.,all natural finish. 2 25
Doz. **$9.00**

1 doz. in case 30 lbs.....Doz. **$5.94**

### "BOY SCOUT BAND" BASS DRU[M]

Nickel plated shells, black enam[eled] wood hoops, heavy white cord, leather ears for tightening, nicke[l] rules, sheep heads and bottom[, at]tached brass cymbals, solid r[...] head drum sticks, colored web sh[...] er straps, snap fasteners. 1 in ca[se] about 6 lbs.

F1332—12 in.................Each, "
F1333—14 " ................., "
F1323—16 " .. ...... ...... "

### CALF HEAD WOOD S[HELL] MILITARY DRUM A[SST.]

**F1319**—Low shape, cherry a[nd] finish wood shells, ebonize[d hoops] with hooks and colored cord, l[eather] ears, calf heads. sheep botto[ms] belts, sticks. Case contain[s:]
¼ doz. 10 in., ..... @ $ 8.75
½ " 11 " ....... 11.00
½ " 12 " ....... 13.25
½ " 13 " ....... 15.50
28 lbs. ½ doz. in case...Case, "

### HIGH GRADE CALF HEAD DRU[M]

**F1321**—Solid nickel shell, ste[el] bands, 13 in. calf head, sheep b[ottom] 6 in. high stays, hardwood s[ticks] 7 lbs. 1 in box.... .Each, "

**F1322**—Low orchestra[l fi]nished grained wood shell, enameled hoops, adjustable re[el] tightening, best calfskin head, bottom, heavy hook and sling[ed] ished hardwood sticks. 8 lbs. case ..............Each, "

---

# TOY WATCHES

With Neck Chains, Vest Chains, Fobs, etc. Note the many new designs and the numbers that come asstd. styles to the doz. Because we buy and sell so many of these little specialties for our several houses we can name such low prices. Choose *your* sellers from this showing.

### IMPORTED TOY WATCHES.

Printed dials, crystals, vest bars. 1 doz. on metal holder unless stated.

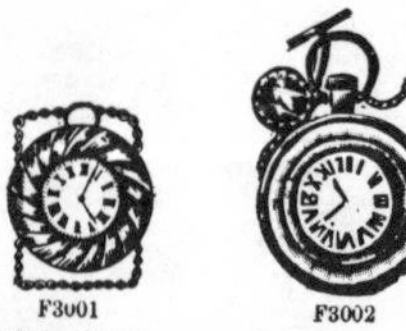

**F3001**—1¼ in., asstd. brilliant color embossed fronts, gilt backs. chain, vest hook. ¼ gro. in box..GRO. **87c**

### BOYS' WATCHES WITH FOBS.

Crystals, printed dials, moving hands.

**F3021**—1¾ in. embossed gilt case, bevel front, 4¼ in. gilt fob with clover charm. 1 doz. in box. Doz. **40c**

**F3023**—1¾ in. embossed gilt case, bevel front, gilt dial, satin ribbon fob, buckle, slide and charm. Each on card. 1 doz. in box... .Doz. **87c**

**F3010**—"Charter Oak" Asst. Asstd. sizes, plain and embossed silver and gilt finishes, white and fancy dials, some with panorama moving pictures, 7 in. chains with charms. On 15x14 litho oak card. 1 doz. in box.................. ...........Doz. **42c**

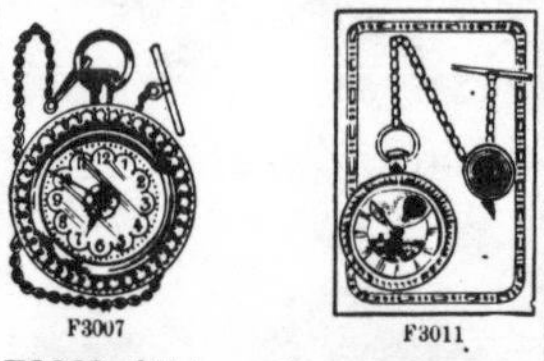

**F3007**—1¾ in., embossed gilt case, fancy dial, moving hands, 8 in. gilt chains. 1 doz. in box. ....Doz. **40c**

**F3011**—6 styles, asstd. sizes, gilt, silver and enamel faces, gilt, aluminum and fancy dials, moving hands, some with modern litho moving pictures of air ships, etc. Each with chain and charm. Each on card, asstd. 1 doz. in box......... .....Doz. **42c**

### GIRLS' TOY WATCHES.

Crystals and printed dials.

**F3026**—1⅜ in., asstd. gilt and silver finish embossed case, beveled fronts, moving hands, long chain. 1 doz. in box. ...............Doz. **35c**

**F3028**—1¼ in. gilt hunting case, embossed front and back, moving hands, 23 in. gilt chain, bead slide. 1 doz. in box..... .........Doz. **39c**

**F3030**— "Leader" Assortment. 6 styles, about 1¼ in., embossed gilt, floral enameled and plain backs, bevel fronts, printed, silvered and fancy brilliant dials, moving hands, crystals, 3 long chains, 3 assorted brooches, ¾ doz. on card. 1 doz. in box............ .............Doz. **42c**

### GIRLS' TOY WATCHES— Contd.

**F3031**—1¼ in. frosted gilt and silver cases, jeweled effect backs, beveled fronts, 27 in. chain with colored beads. Each in box. Asstd. 1 doz. in carton.....................Doz. **45c**

**F3034**—1⅜ in. gilt case, asstd. tinted medallion backs, moving hands. 46 in. bead jeweled chains. Each in box. 1 doz. in pkg...... ...Doz. **87c**

**F3014**—Up-to-Date Asst. 3 styles, 1¾ in. marathon design gilt and silver cases, shield embossed silver and silver & gilt bevel front, plain back; printed dials, moving hands, 8 in. chains with charms. ¼ doz. in card. 1 doz. in box...........Doz. **87c**

### BOYS' SPRING HUNTING CA[SE]

Moving hands, printed dials, metals, 8 in. chains with swivels.

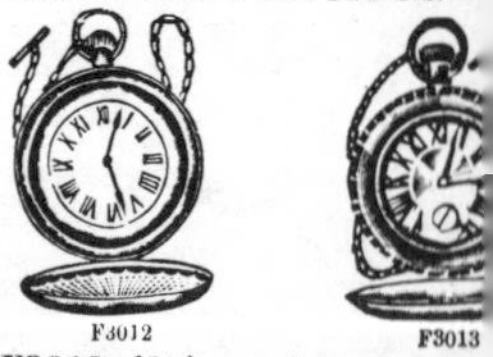

**F3012**—1⅝ in., embossed front [and] back, radium effect, silver [and] gilt finishes. 1 doz. in box..Doz. "

**F3013**—1⅝ in., plain silver an[d gilt] finishes. Fine model. 1 doz. in [box] Doz.

### MECHANICAL TICK WATCH[ES]

Crystals, printed dials, mov[ing] hands, 8 in. chains with vest bars [and] swivels. Tick when wound.

**F3015**—1¾ in. nickel and gilt be[vel] cases. Asstd.1 doz. in box. Doz. "

**F3017**—1¾ in. gun metal fin[ish] enameled case. 1 doz. in box. Doz. "

**F3018**—1¾ in. silvered case, be[vel] front. Each in litho box, 1 doz. [in] pkg. ...................Doz. "

## MPORTED RETURN BALLS.

owest prices for dependable goods.

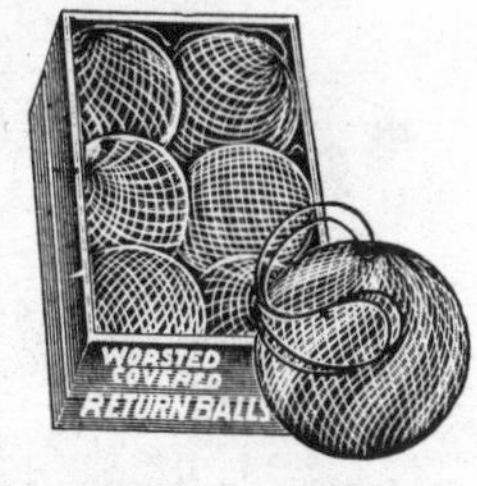


**Worsted Covered**—Openwork cover in asstd. colors over silver tinsel. Each with rattle and elastic cord.

| | Girth | In box | | |
|---|---|---|---|---|
| F3180— | 5¾ in. | .1 gro... | GRO. | $0 89 |
| F3181— | 8¾ " | ...1 doz.... | Doz. | 25 |
| F3182— | 10¾ " | ...1 " | ... " | 36 |
| F3183— | 13 " | ...1 " | ... " | 40 |

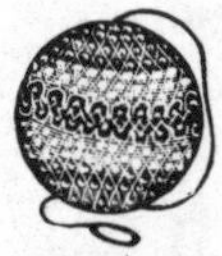

**F3184—Parlor Return Ball.** 10 in. girth, tufted knit rattle inside, elastic cord. Too soft to break window or hurt the baby, yet retains shape. 1 doz. in box........Doz. **85c**

## PAPIER MACHE RETURN BALLS.

Exceptional values at popular prices. Each with rattle and elastic cord.

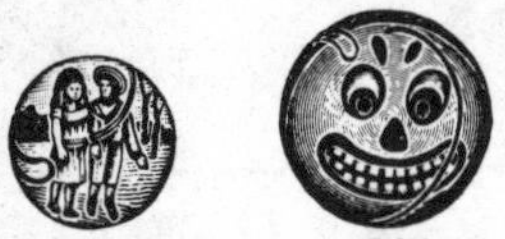
F3174 F3175

**F3174**—5¼ in. girth, asstd. color juvenile designs, gilt band. ½ gro. in box.........GRO. **89c**

**F3175**—8¼ in. girth, pumpkin face, natural color, painted features, gilt band, finger ring. 1 doz. in box. Doz. **28c**

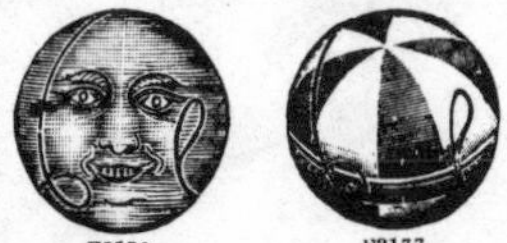
F3176 F3177

**F3176**—10½ in. girth Man-in-the-Moon, litho face both sides, glazed, finger ring. 1 doz. in box...Doz. **35c**

**F3177**—10½ in., combination red & white and blue & white, quartered jockey design, enameled gold band, finger ring. 1 doz. in box. Doz. **37c**

## ZYLONITE RETURN BALL.

Lighter and better bouncer than those made of other materials.

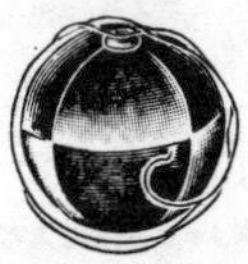

**F3185**—9¾ in. girth, heavy celluloid, asstd. red, blue, green, white, etc., quartered, reinforced top, 1 yd. elastic cord, cannot pull out. Asstd. 1 doz. in box.... ..Doz. **85c**

## HIGH BOUNCING SPONGE BALLS.

Filled with specially treated elastic sponge, will not rot, retain shape.

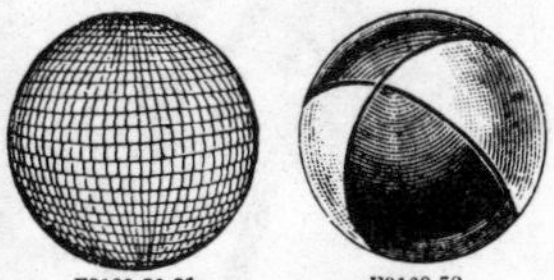
F3169-70-71 F3168-72

**Crocheted Cord Covered** — Asstd. bright colors.

| | Girth | In box | | |
|---|---|---|---|---|
| F3169— | 7½ in... | 1 doz.... | Doz. | $0 35 |
| F3170— | 10 " | ...1 " | ... " | 75 |
| F3171— | 14 " | ...1 " | ... " | 1 60 |

**Quartered Felt Covered** — Asstd. bright color combinations. 1 doz. in box

## ZYLONITE RATTLE BALLS.

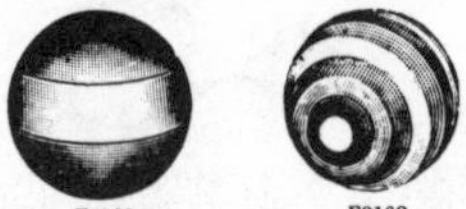
F3160 F3163

**National**—Red, white & blue bands.
F3160—3⅝ in., girth. ⅛ gro. in box. GRO. **89c**
F3161—5¼ in. girth. 3 doz. in box. Doz. **18c**

**Variegated**—3 styles, asstd. bright colors, heavy stock.
F3163—7⅝ in. girth. 1 doz. in box. Doz. **33c**

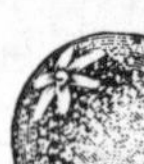

**Oranges**—Embossed, natural color, extra wt. stock. 1 doz. in box.
F3166—7¼ in. girth....... Doz. $0 42
F3167—8½ " " ....... " 80

**French Colorings**—Maroon and blue with pink and brown stripes, extra heavy stock.
F3164—9⅝ in. girth. 1 doz. in box. Doz. **75c**

## CRYING HEADS.

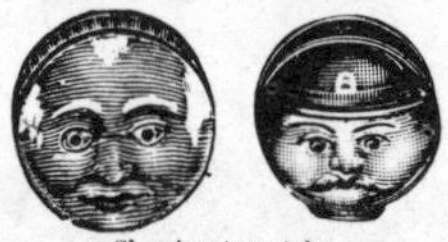
Showing two styles.

Composition double faces, asstd. Foxy Grandpa, Happy Hooligan and policeman, painted in colors, cloth covered bellows center. Asstd. 1 doz. in box. Doz.
F3186—7¼ in. girth.................. $0 39
F3188—9½ " " loud voice... 80

## RACKETS WITH RETURN BALLS.

Bent wood frame racket, string lacing

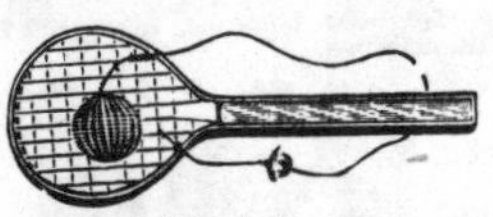

**F3157**—Racket. 12x4½, green knit covered ball on elastic cord with bell. 1 doz. in pkg. .........Doz. **37c**

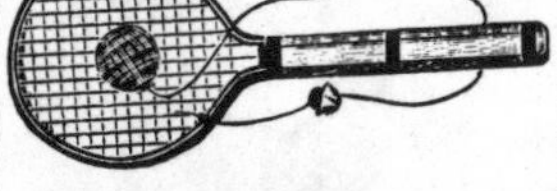

**F3158**—Racket 19⅛x6⅛, 2 color wood grip, rainbow knit foil covered ball on elastic cord, 2 bells. 1 doz. in pkg. .......................Doz. **82c**

## EXTRA VALUE SPRING ACTION TOP

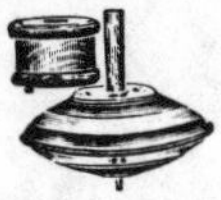

**F2329**—Girth 8 in., red, white & blue enamel striped metal body, hardwood automatic spring winder. 2 doz. in box.................Doz. **40c**

## TIRELESS SPINNER TOPS.

Turned edge heavy metal discs, red, white & blue enameled coil stripes, steel pin axle, spun by hand on stand, gives color illusion.

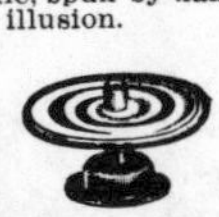

**F2300**—2 in. diam., metal stand. ⅛ gro. in box..... ......GRO. **82c**

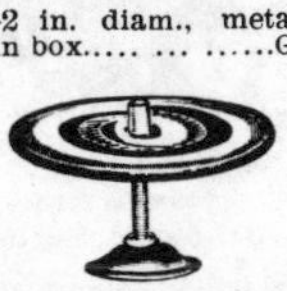

**F2302**—4 in. diam., metal capped wood stand. 2 doz. in box...Doz. **38c**

## WOOD TOPS.

Polished turned hardwood.

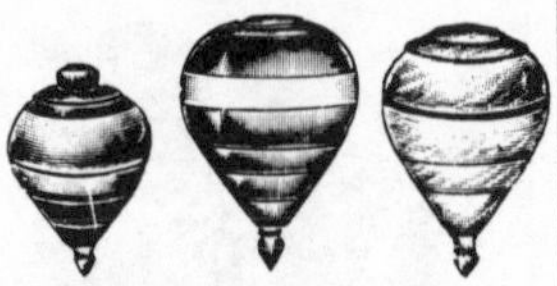
American F2334 Jersey Lily

**Stained American**—Well finished, asstd. colors. Best American manufacture. Sold by box only.
F2307—1⅝x2¾. ⅛ gro. in box. Gro. **73c**
F2312—1⅝x2¾, long cords with buttons. ½ gro. in box .....Gro. **85c**
F2311—1¾x2⅞. ⅓ gro. in box. Gro. **87c**
F2313—*Special 2c value.* 2x3, 3 doz. in box.................DOZ. **12c**

**Enameled Jersey Lily**—Red, blue, green, purple, yellow, etc., bright stripes.
F2334—1⅛x2⅛. ⅛ gro. in box. GRO. **92c**
F2335—1¾x2⅛. 4 doz. in box. Doz. **15c**
F2336—2x2¾. 3 doz. in box. Doz. **23c**

**Jersey Lily**—Varnished, red stripe.
F2315—1⅝x2⅜. ⅛ gro. in box. GRO. **$1.00**
F2316—1¾x2⅛. 4 doz. in box. Doz. **12c**
F2317—*Big 3c value.* 2x3. 3 doz. in box.........................Doz. **15c**

**Staple Varnished**—Selected red stripe.
F2319—1⅝x2⅝. ⅛ gro. in box. GRO. **$1.15**
F2320—*Big 3c value.* 1⅞x3. 3 doz. in box.......... ..........Doz. **18c**
F2321—2⅛x3⅛. 3 doz. in box. Doz. **20c**

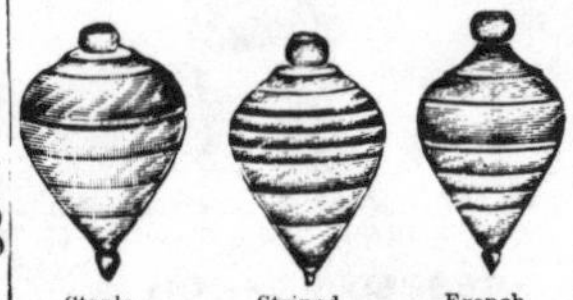
Staple Striped French

**Fancy Striped**—Varnished, wide red and black stripes, green knob. Doz.
F2323—1⅝x2⅝. 3 doz. in box..$0 12
F2324—2x3. 2 doz. in box...... 18
F2325—2⅛x3⅛. 2 doz. in box.. 20

**Fancy French**—Varnished, red knob, black and red stripes. Doz.
F2327—1¾x3⅛. 3 doz. in box. $0 18
F2328—2x3⅝. 2 doz. in box.... 21

## NOVELTY TOPS.

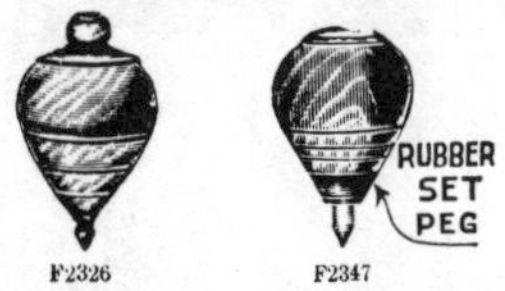

F2326 F2347

**F2326—Tri-color.** 1⅛ x 2⅜, red, green and natural hardwood. ⅛ gro. in box. GRO. **80c**

**F2347—Rubber Set Peg.** 1⅛x2⅛, stained asstd. colors. ⅛ gro. in box. GRO. **95c**

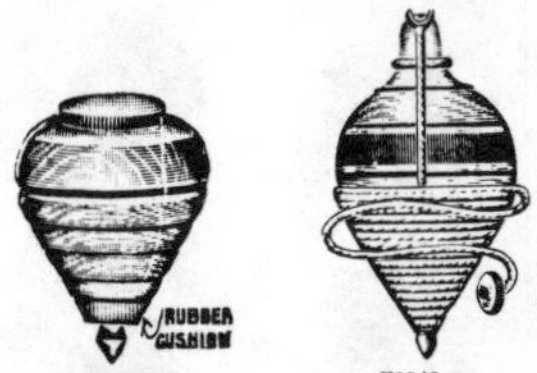

F2348 F2349

**F2348—Original Rubber Neck.** 1¾ x 2⅝, turned hardwood, painted asstd. colors and varnished, pat. rubber cushion causes rebound. 3 doz. in box..............Doz. **20c**

**F2349—Tip-Top.** 1¾x3⅛, varnished fancy turned hardwood, 3 bright wide stripes, cord with swivel and button. 2 doz. in box.......Doz. **24c**

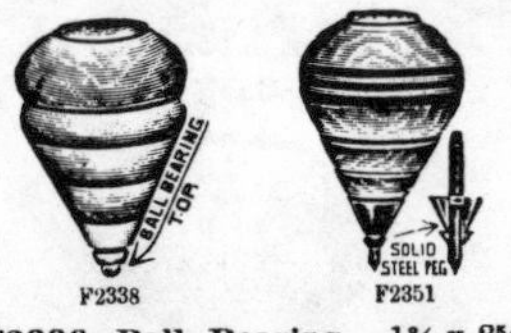

F2338 F2351

**F2338—Ball Bearing.** 1¾ x 2⅝, highly varnished hardwood, asstd. red, green and natural, spins on steel ball encased in steel peg. 2 doz. in box.......................Doz. **35c**

## NOVELTY TOP ASSORTMENT.

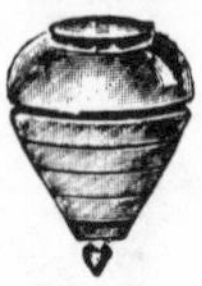

**F2357**—Turned hardwood, highly polished asstd. solid colors, some bright banded.
¾ doz. ball bearing.
¾ doz. "Bouncing Buster."
1½ doz. patent rubber cushion.
Asstd., 3 doz. in box.......Doz. **27c**

## MARBLES IN BAGS.

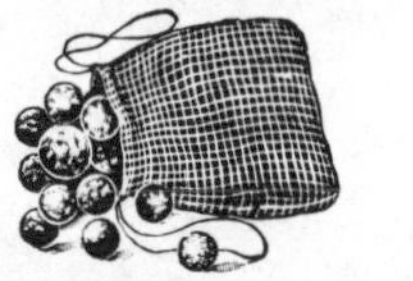

Polished, asstd. sizes and colors, 2 large shooters, and asst. of marbles in colored net bag.
F12—50 in bag. .......Doz. bags, $0 36
F13—75 " ......... " " 60

## AMERICAN MARBLES.

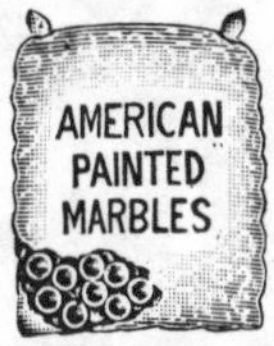


**F14**—Common gray. Compare size and weight with others. 1000 in bag. Per M, **21c**

**F15**—Common Painted. Asstd. colors. 1000 in bag. Cask of 50 M..Per M, **23c**

**F16**—Imported Polished Genuine Stone. Asstd. colors and sizes. 1000 in bag, full count......... Per M, **65c**

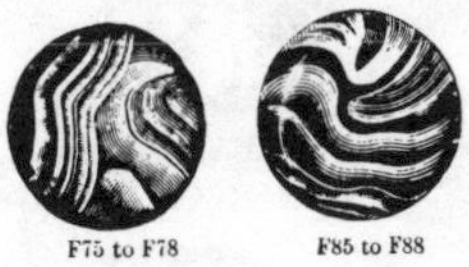
F75 to F78 F85 to F88

**American Onyx**—Every one perfect. A variety of colors. Per 100
F75—Size ⅝ in. 100 in box.......$0 45
F76— " 11/16 " 100 " " ...... 55
F77— " ¾ " 50 " " ...... 65
F78— " ⅞ " 50 " " ...... 85

**High Grade Cobalt Blue Onyx**—Selected smooth fire polished flint glass, first rich cobalt blue blended with snow white. Per 100
F85—Size ⅝ in. 100 in box.......$0 45
F86— " 11/16 " 100 " " ...... 55
F87— " ¾ " 50 " " ...... 65
F88— " ⅞ " 50 " " ...... 85

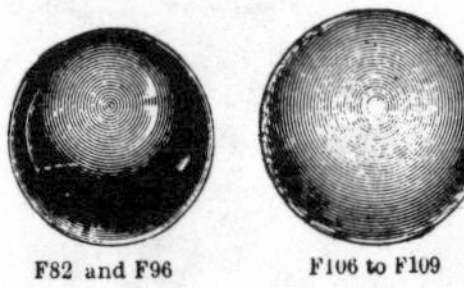
F82 and F96 F106 to F109

**F82 – American Steelie.** Size 1, hollow steel, asstd. colors, finely polished, will not rust, perfect shape, 100 in box...............Per 100, **50c**

**F96—Approximately Solid Steelie Marble.** ⅝ in., asstd. colors. 100 in box......................Per 100, **55c**

**Oriental Jade** — Rich dark green, high polished flint glass.
F106—Size ⅝ in. 25 in box. Box, $0 21
F107— " 11/16 " 25 " " " 23
F108— " ¾ " 25 " " " 25
F109— " 13/16 " 25 " " " 27

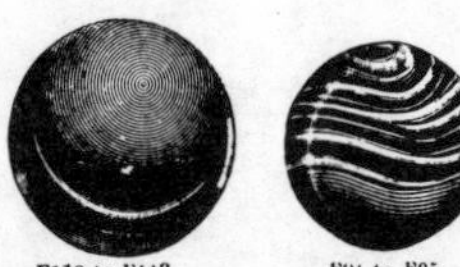
F110 to F113 F91 to F95

**Persian Turquoise** — Opaque rich azure, high polish.
F110—Size ⅝ in. 25 in box. Box, $0 22
F111— " 11/16 " 25 " " " 24
F112— " ¾ " 25 " " " 26
F113— " 13/16 " 25 " " " 29

**American Cornelians**—Nearest approach to genuine cornelian ever made, flint glass, machine polished, perfectly round, blended colors.

## IMPORTED MARBLES.

Approximate sizes: 00, 7/16 in.; 0, 9/16; 1, ⅝; 2, ¾; 3, ⅞; 4, 1; 5, 1 3/16; 6, 1 5/16; 7, 1⅜; 8, 1½; 9, 1¾; 10, 2.

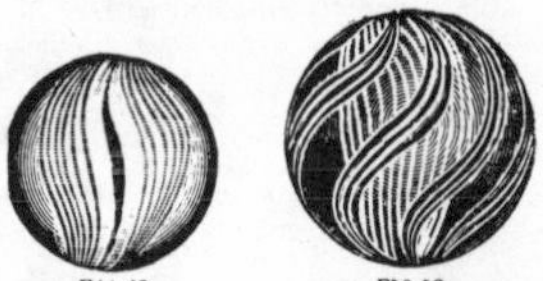
F44-49 F50-53

**Fine Glass** — Extra quality all threaded. Per 100
F44—Size, 0, 100 in box........$0 20
F45— " 1, 100 " " ..... 24
F46— " 2, 100 " " ..... 33
F47— " 3, 100 " " ..... 50
F48— " 4, 100 " " ..... 78
F49— " 6. Extra large. 1 doz. in box........................DOZ. **20c**

**Extra Size Fine Glass**—Asstd. fancy designs in colored threads. Doz.
F50—Size, 7, 1 doz. in box....$0 28
F51— " 8, 1 " " " .... 36
F52— " 9, 1 " " " .... 48
F53— " 10, 1 " " " .... 84

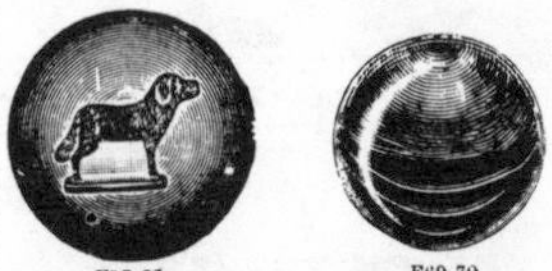
F57-61 F69-70

**Figured Glass**—Absolutely flawless —not clouded or specked. Silver birds, animals, etc. Doz.
F57—Size, 5, 1 doz. in box....$0 33
F58— " 6, " " " .... 39
F61— " 10, " " " .... 84

**Unselected Genuine Cornelians**—or reals, that the boys value so highly. Understood by the trade to run irregularly and no allowance is made for defective ones. BOX of 25
F69—Asstd. sizes 00, 0 and 1. $0 89
F70— " 1 and 2..... 1 60

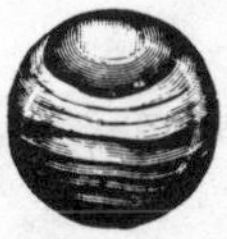

**Selected Genuine Cornelians or Agates** — Practically perfect but some may have slight defects and cannot be returned.
F72—Asstd. sizes, 00, 0 and 1. BOX of 25....**$2.10**
F73—Asstd. sizes, 1 and 2. BOX of 25....**$2.90**
F74—Asstd. sizes, 2 and 3. BOX of 12 ...**$2.35**

## IMPORTED FANCY GOLD BAND GLASS MARBLE ASST.

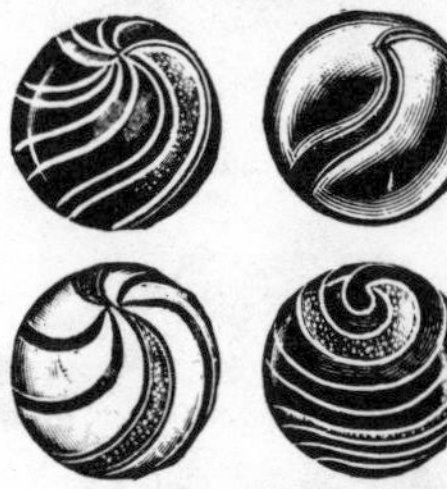

Asstd., 4 styles, all glass, each in 5 colors: (1) opal, fine colored stripes and gold bands; (2) transparent fine colored stripes and gold bands: (3) black opaque, asstd. color fine stripes and gold bands: (4) colored transparent with opaque spiral centers, stripes and gold bands. Per 100
F65—Size 0, 100 in box. asstd... $0 39
F66— " 1, 100 " " ... 50
F67— " 2, 100 " " ... 60
F68— " 3, 100 " " ... 95

## JACK STONES.

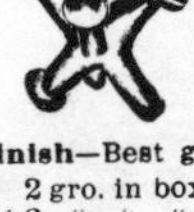

**Copper Finish**—Best goods.
F1737—0 2 gro. in box. Gro. $0 07
F1738—1½ 2 " " " 10
F1739—2 2 " " " 11
F1740—3 2 " " " 15

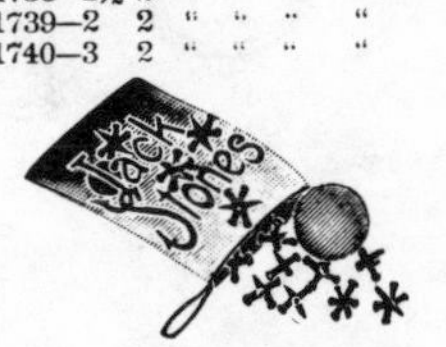

## "SURPRISE" NOVELTY TOYS.

Animal heads and figures made to appear and disappear at will.

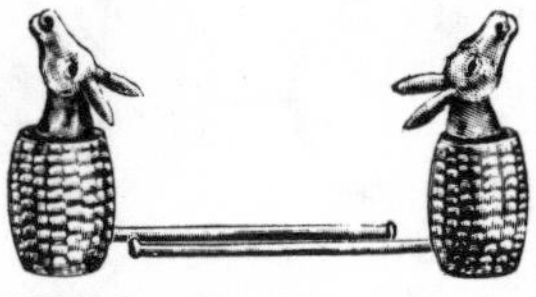

**F2588—Corn Cob Pipe.** Asstd. rubber elephants, horses, bears, chickens, etc. Blow through stem. Asstd. 1 doz. in box.............Doz. **39c**
Gro. $4.40

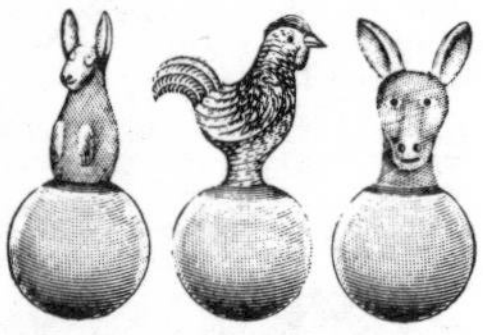

**F2561—Rubber Ball.** About 4 in., asstd. animals—cats, rabbits, donkeys, etc., squeeze ball. Asstd. 1 doz. in box........................Doz. **75c**
Gro. $8.75

## FRENCH RUBBER SPECIALTIES.

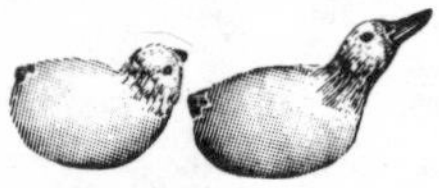

**F2412**—Chick and goose. Good quality, painted eyes and beaks, hollow bodies with voice. 1 doz. in box..........................Doz. **77c**

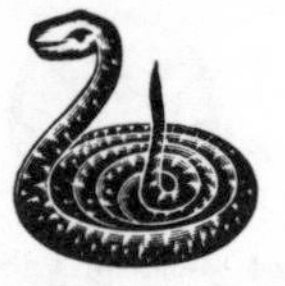

**Snakes**—Superior **hollow rubber**, painted and striped, very natural. 1 doz. in box.
F2414—8 in...................Doz. $0 89
F2415—14 in., stout......." 1 80

## WATER PISTOLS.

Exact models, nickel plated, all bulbs are guaranteed best material.

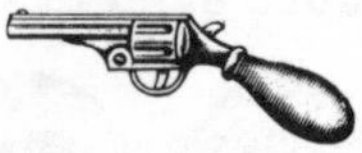

**Oval Bulbs**—Metal bodies.
F1895—4½in., bulb 1⅞. 2doz. in box. Doz. **38c**

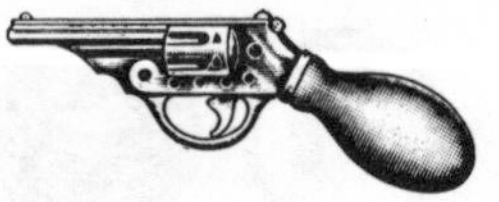

F1896—5⅜ in., bulb 2⅜. 1 doz. in box.......................Doz. **78c**

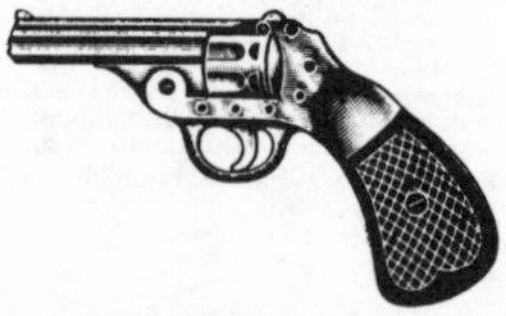

**F1897** – 5½ in., metal body, extra heavy corrugated rubber pistol grip. ½ doz. in box..............Doz. **$1.75**

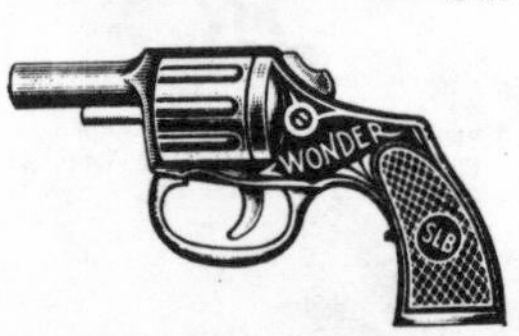


**F1898**—5½ in, nickeled steel, bulb concealed in cartridge chamber, water forced out by trigger action, imit. hammer, corrugated pistol grip. ½ doz. in box......Doz. **$1.85**

## RUBBER BABIES AND TOYS.

Painted features, each with **whistle voice.**

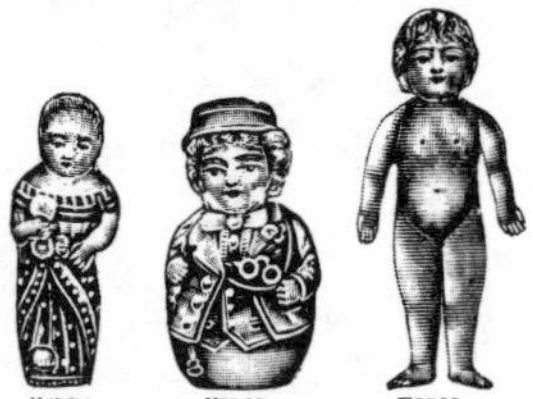

F2500 F2568 F2503

**F2500**—3¼ in., good stock, well finished. 1 doz. in box. ...Doz. **42c**
**F2568**—3½ in., asstd. babies on elastic cord. 1 doz. in box..Doz. **75c**
**F2503**—4¾ in., naked baby, free arms and legs. 1 doz. in box. ..Doz. **77c**

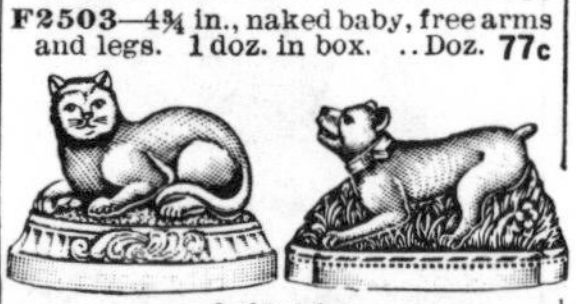

2 of 6 styles.

**F2504**—Aver. 3¼x2½, 6 styles, dogs cats, rabbits, chickens, etc. Asstd 1 doz. in box......................Doz. **77c**

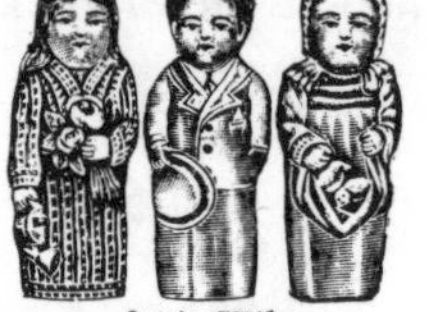

3 styles F2501

**F2501**—5¼ in., good stock, asstd. boys and girls. 1 doz. in box.....Doz. **79c**
Gro. $9.00

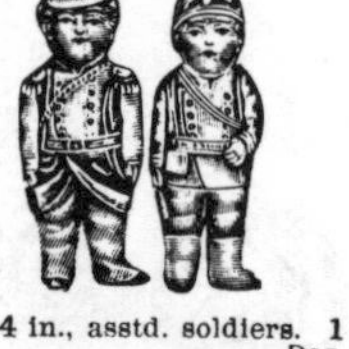

**F2502**—4 in., asstd. soldiers. 1 doz. in box............................Doz. **79c**
Gro. $9.00

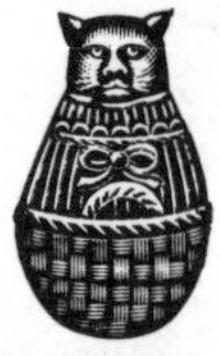

**F2505**—Ht. 4 in., babies and cats in baske*s ½ doz. in box.....Doz. **96c**

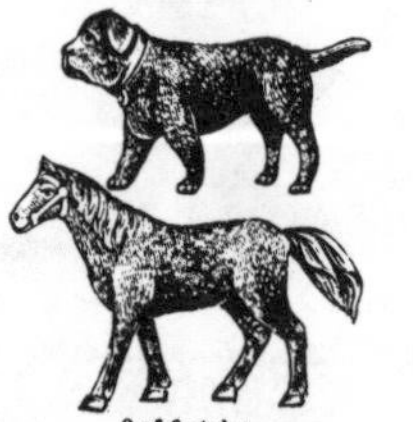

2 of 6 styles.

**F2508**—4x6, 6 styles, dog, horse, cow, sheep, etc., good models, natural rubber finish. Asstd. ½ doz. in box. Doz. **$1.75**

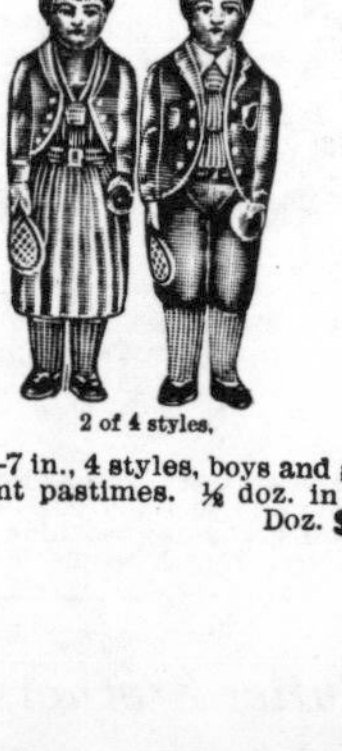

2 of 4 styles.

**F2497**—7 in., 4 styles, boys and girls, different pastimes. ½ doz. in box. Doz. **$1.80**

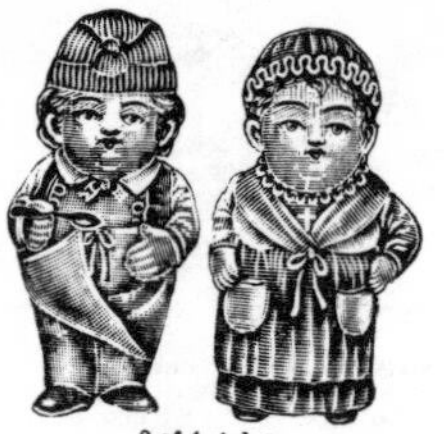

2 of 4 styles.

**F2498**—6 in., 4 styles, stout bodies Asstd. ½ doz. in box........Doz. **$1.98**

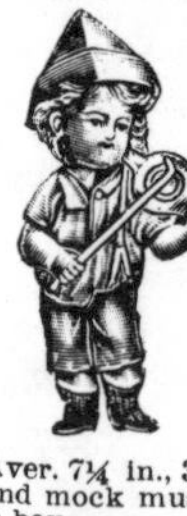

**F2499**—Aver. 7¼ in., 3 styles, clown fat boy and mock musician. Asstd. ½ doz. in box...............Doz. **$2.00**

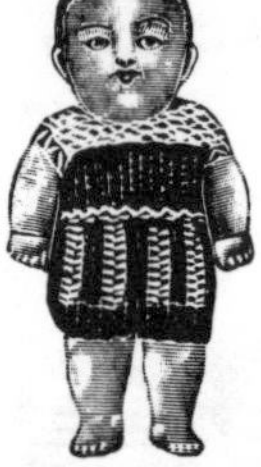

**F2509**—6½ in., asstd. girls and boys. ½ doz. in box.....................Doz. **$2.00**

## DRESSED FRENCH RUBBER DOLLS.

Painted features, embossed hair and feet, knitted worsted costumes, asstd. red & white and blue & white.

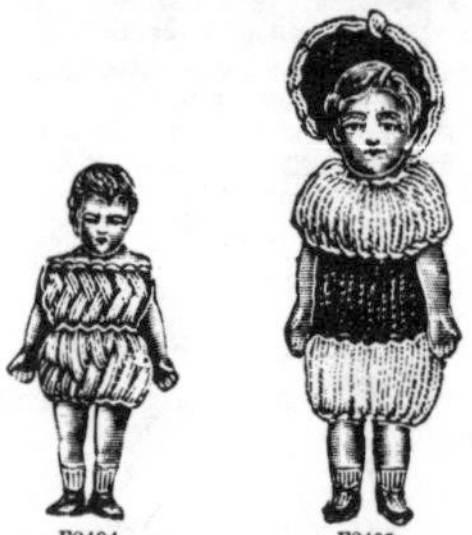

F2404 F2405

**F2404**—4½in. 1doz. in box...Doz. **84c**
**F2405**—7¼ in., voice. Asstd. ½ doz. in box......................Doz. **$2.00**

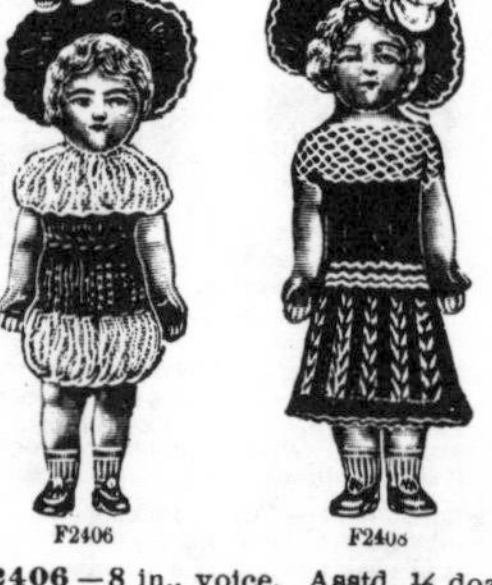

F2406 F2408

**F2406**—8 in., voice. Asstd. ½ doz. in box.......................Doz. **$2.50**
**F2408**—9½ in., voice, closely knit dress. ½ doz. in box.......Doz. **$4.10**

## TOY FOOTBALL.

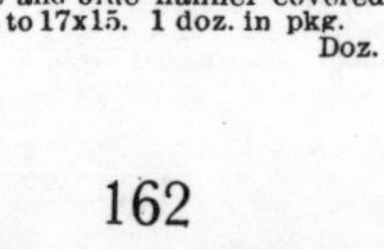

**F2567**—Heavy rubber balloon, red, white and blue flannel covered, inflates to 17x15. 1 doz. in pkg. Doz. **79c**

## RUBBER RATTLES.

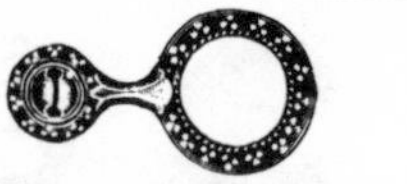

**F2566**—3¾ in., nickeled bell, large embossed rubber ring handle. 1 doz. in box........................Doz. **36c**

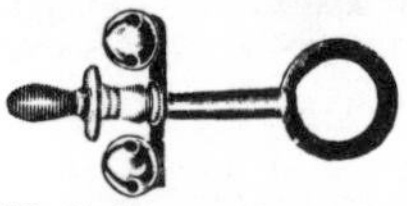

**F2562**—5 in. pacifier with bone shield, 2 bells on patent leather crosspiece, rubber teething ring. 1 doz. in box...............Doz. **39c**
Gro. $4.50

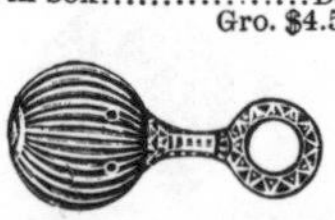

**F2564**—4½ in., large corrugated rubber ball rattle, embossed ring handle. 1 doz. in box..........Doz. **74c**

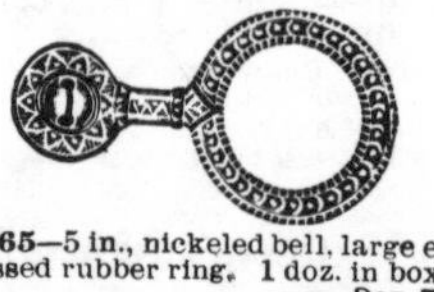

**F2565**—5 in., nickeled bell, large embossed rubber ring. 1 doz. in box. Doz. **74c**

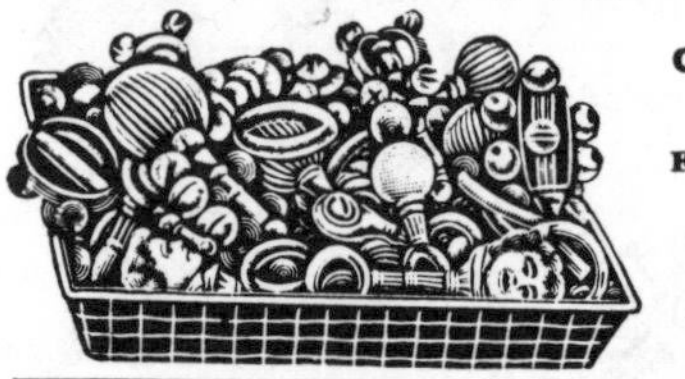

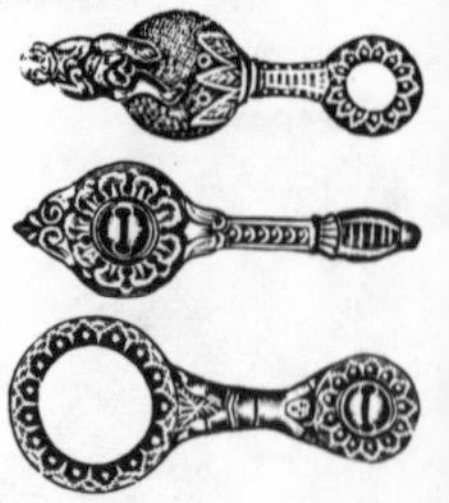

**F2563**—Aver. 4¾ in., 3 styles, ni eled bell and embossed figure ball, teething ring handles. 1 d in box....... ...........Doz.
Gro. $9.00

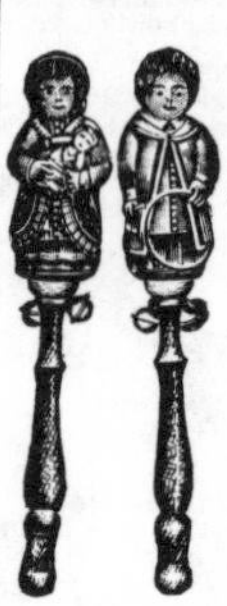

**F2413—Fren Rubber Ass** Length 9 in., 3¾ embossed baby ures, painted f tures, **whistle voi** polished turned wo handle with whis end, 2 nickeled bel 1 doz. in box.
Doz. 8

## COMBINATION RATTLE ASS

**F2569**—10 best selling styl rubber and bell rattles. As includes 3 large 25c rubb rattles. Wire basket inclu ed... ...............Doz. 85
3 doz. in basket, (Total $2.55)

# ZYLONITE TOY NOVELTIES

## ZYLONITE ROLLY-POLIES.

Weighted bottoms, always right themselves.

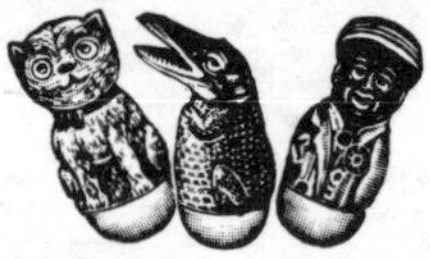

**F3140**—2¼ to 2½ in., 16 styles, figures with painted costumes, cats and dogs in natural colors. Asstd. 2 doz. in box...............Doz. **40c**

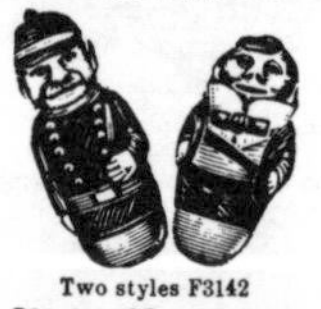

Two styles F3142

**F3142**—2¾ in., 12 styles, up to date characters, painted features and costumes. Asstd. 1 doz. box.Doz. **72c**

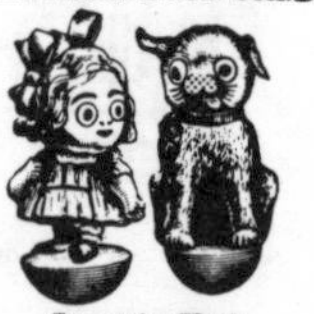

Two styles F3143

**F3143**—3½ in., 6 styles, chubby boys and girls with tinted costumes, natural color cats and dogs, painted features. Asstd. 1 doz. box.Doz. **95c**

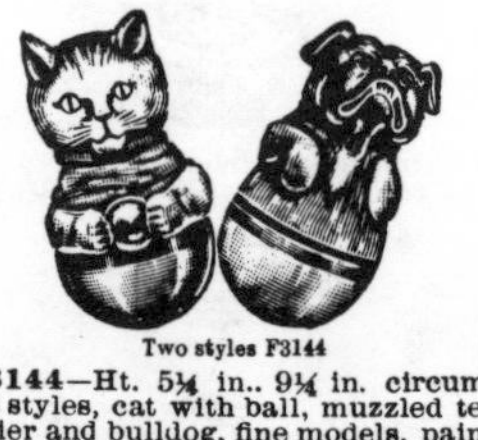

Two styles F3144

**F3144**—Ht. 5¼ in.. 9¼ in. circum.. 3 styles, cat with ball, muzzled terrier and bulldog, fine models, painted features and bodies. Asstd. ½ doz. in box. ... ........Doz. **$2.15**

## FLOATING ZYLONITE FIGURES

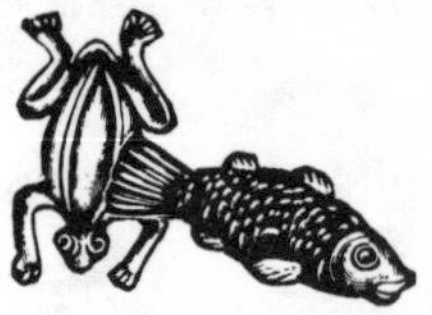

4 styles, asstd., swan, frog, fish an duck, natural colors, float in lifelik manner, for baby's bath, acquarium etc.
**F3148**—About 3½ in. 2 doz. in box Doz. 33
**F3149**—About 4½ in. 1 doz. in box Doz. 80

## RUNNING ZYLONITE MOUSE

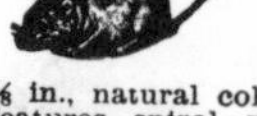

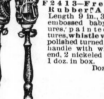

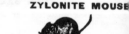

**F3132**—2⅝ in., natural color body painted features, spiral wire tai heavy metal roller on pivot, whe pushed runs in lifelike manne 1 doz. in box...............Doz. 45

## ZYLONITE BALANCING BIRDS

**Note**—By cutting beak card can b inserted, excellent favor or price tic ket holder.

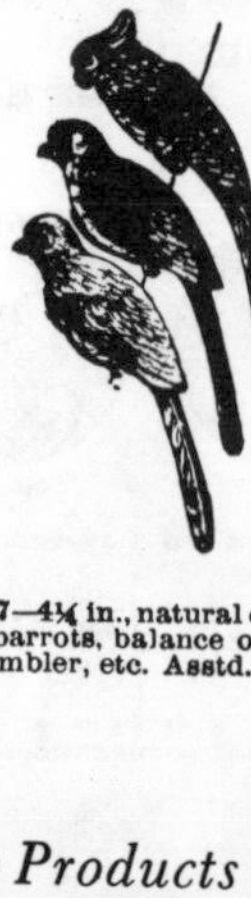

**F3147**—4½ in., natural color canarie and parrots, balance on string, edg of tumbler, etc. Asstd. 2 doz. in box Doz. 37

## CURTAIN MASKS.

air Quality—Cambric. 1 doz. pkg.
F3376—Black.............Doz. $0 18
F3377—White............. " 18
F3378—Pink............. " 18
F3379—Red............. " 18
F3380—Blue............. " 18
F3381—Green............. " 18
F3396—Asstd............. " 18
Above in gro. lots, $2.00

## IMPORTED TOY SAIL BOATS.

Truly balanced models of real
chts, enameled colors that will not
wash off.

3290—7½ in., varnished and striped hull, wire rail, steel keel. 1 mast,
2 sails. 1 doz. in box......Doz. 42c

3291—9½x8½, painted striped hull,
steel keel, wire rail, 2 masts, 3 sails.
1 doz. in box.................Doz. 87c

F3292—10 in., varnished and striped
hull, dug out, steel keel, 1 mast, 2
sails. 1 doz. in box........Doz. 89c

F2665—Steel. 13¼ in. (largest dime
seller) asstd. red and green hulls,
detachable steel mast, 1 large sail,
weighted center board, will not tip
in wind. 1 doz. in box.......Doz. 89c
Gro. $9.50

F1727—Steel Yacht. 12½ in., red
& white enameled hull, yellow
grained effect deck, rim edge,
weighted steel keel, 8¼ in. mast
with mainsail and ¹⁄₁b. 1 doz. in box.
Doz. 92c

F3293—12 in., oil painted gold striped wood hull, steel keel, dug out.
2 seats. 11¼ in. mast, 2 sails. ½ doz.
k. d. in box....... Doz. $1.95

## DOMINO MASKS.

"Lulops"—No curtains. 1 doz. in pkg.,
asstd. colors.
F3391—Sateen.............Doz. $0 33
F3392—Satin............. " 69

F5894—Horseshoe Magnet. 2 in.
heavy red painted body. ½ gro. in
pkg................Gro. 77c

## NOVELTY ZYLONITE SAIL BOAT.

For baby's bath, etc.

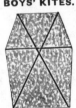

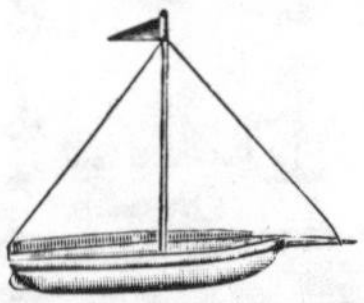

F1892—Length 6 in. ht. 5, full celluloid body mast, spar and flag, non-
sinkable, asstd. white, blue, etc.
1 doz. in box.........Doz. 80c

## BOYS' KITES.

Set up—Glazed heavy fiber paper in
asstd. colors, 3 pc. wood frame,
thread bound edge and ceuter, wide
turn pasted edge. Exceptionally
well made.
F1784—13x9⅝. Asstd. ½ gro. in pkg.
GRO. 89c
F1785—21¾ x 17¼. Asstd. 2 doz. in
pkg. .................Doz. 25c
F1786—27x20. Asstd. 2 doz. in
pkg. .................Doz. 39c

F1777—"High Flyer." Ht. 22½ in.,
steel wire frame, litho strong paper
covered. 2 doz. in box.... Doz. 42c

F1778—"Blue Hill" Box Kite.
14x14 in., 30 in. long, for all kinds of
wind. Each folded in pkg. with instructions. ½ doz. in bdl. Doz. $1.85

## SLING SHOTS.

F1753 F1754

F1753—Heavy steel, nki. finish, rubber strings and leather pocket.
1 doz. in bdl.............Doz. 40c

F1754—Japanned cast metal fork,
7¼ in. shaped rubber lined center.
1 doz. in box... .............Doz. 69c

## AMERICAN REAL HAIR MUSTACHES AND WIGS.

Asstd. Shades.

Mustaches—With fasteners.
F3370 — Penny seller. About 6 in,
1 gro. in box... ..........GRO. 87c
F3371—6 in., fine quality, curly ends.
1 doz. in pkg..........DOZ. 34c

F5892—Little Brown Jug. 1½ in.
1 gro. in box... .............Gro. 82c

## TOY REINS WITH BELLS.

White enameled oilcloth, red insert,
stitched edges, ⅞ in. nickeled bells.
1 doz. in box.

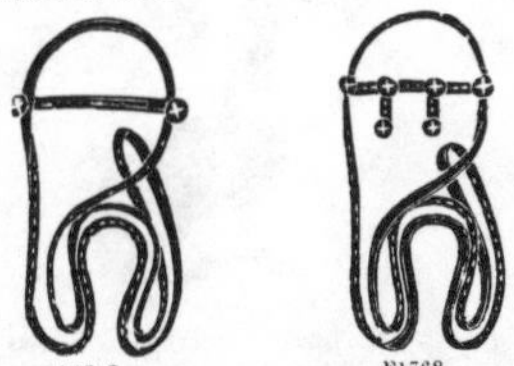

F1767 F1768

F1767—6 in. breast strap, 2 bells.
Gro. $4.25 Doz. 38c
F1768—8 in. breast strap, 6 bells.
Gro. $9.00 Doz. 79c

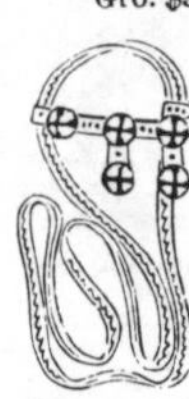

F1769—Exceptional 10c value. White
enameled oilcloth, pinked edges, red
or blue inserts, double stitched. six
1⅝ in. nickel bells. 1 doz. in box.
Doz. 87c
Gro. $10.00

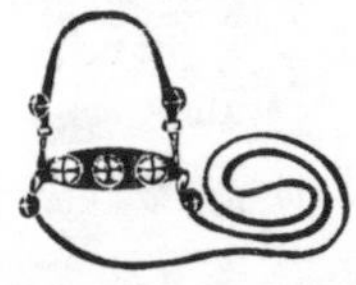

F1770—Length 52 in., tan leather,
6 in. breast strap, three 1¼ and four
⅞ in. nickeled bells, 2 metal snaps
and rings. ½ doz. in box.
Doz. $2.00

## JUMP ROPES.

Each with 4½ in. black enameled
wood handles. 1 doz. in bdl.

F1748—6 ft., heavy braided red &
white and blue & white rope.
Doz. 38c
F1749—7 ft., fine thread, heavy twist
white cotton rope....... ....Doz. 72c

F1756—"Loop The Loop Glider."
10x10¼ in., adjustable aeroplane,
fiber planes and rudder, wood frame,
steel wire sling shot, fine rubber
band flies 250 ft., loops the loop,
dips the dip, etc. ½ doz. in pkg.
Doz. $1.75

## ASSTD. MASK OUTFITS.

F3317—3 styles, consist of semi-wig,
mustache and beard, painted papier
mache nose with eyeglass rims, each
with attached elastic. Each set in
box. Asstd. 1 doz. sets in pkg.
Doz. sets, 79c

## SOAP BUBBLE OUTFITS.

F1772—6½ in., reed stem with tin
cone shape bowl containing soap.
½ gro. in pkg.. .........Gro. 82c

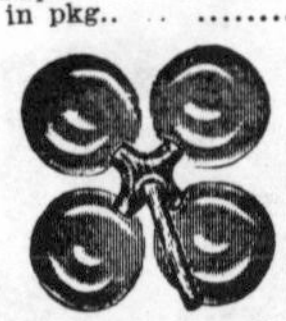

F1773—Quadruple clay pipe, bamboo
stem, pkg. of prepared soap, wire
ring and stem for tricks. 1 set in
env., 1 doz. in box.....Doz. sets, 37c

F1774—Makes bubbles without
soapsuds. 5 in. painted metal stem
with soap cup, 5 cakes prepared
soap. Each set in box with directions. 1 doz. sets in pkg.
Doz. sets, 72c

## TOY BEADS IN WOOD BOXES.

Asstd. shapes, sizes and colors in
box. Our boxes are full depth and full
measure. All except F1742 with label
tops designating contents.

F1742 — About 200 in round box.
diam. 1⅜ in., ht. ¾. ⅓ gro. boxes in
carton...............GRO. BOXS. 75c
F1743—Round box, 3¼x1¼. 3 styles
to doz. boxes. 1 doz. boxes in pkg.
Doz. bxs 32c

F1744—4½x3¾ box, sliding cover,
3 partitions. 3 styles to doz. box.
1 doz. boxes in pkg...Doz. boxes, 80c

## CHILD'S BEAD NECKLACE.

F3126—Length 14 in., 5 strand asstd.
bright beads, gilt clasp. 2 doz. in
pkg.....................Doz. 15c

## HORSESHOE MAGNETS.

Red painted top, polished
ends. 1 doz. in pkg.

Doz.
F3067—2½ in. long. $0 15
F3068—2¾ " " 22
F3069—3 " " 25
F3070—3½ " " 29
F3071—4¾ " " 60

## CHARACTER CARNIVAL HATS.

F3310—6 styles asstd., G. A. R., Pad-
dy, policeman, derby, U. S. Post and
Tyrolean with feather, matt finish,
glazed bands. 1 doz. in box. Doz. 89c

F5897 — Folding Pocket Knife.
Open 3 in. long, turned wood handle,
metal blade. ⅓ gro. in box..Gro. 89c

## BULLSEYE TOY DARK LANTERN.

F5267—Ht. 5 in., bronze lacquered
large bullseye, changeable to red,
white or green, removable oil fount,
open at top, attaches to bicycle.
Doz. 89c

## WHIRLING SPARKLER.

Wonderfully effective — absolutely
harmless.

F1983 — Fiber sandstone wheel on
shafting, pendan metal disc, strong
waxed cord with buttons. When
cord is twisted and pulled taut
wheel spins producing shower of
sparks. Each in box. 1 doz. in pkg.
Doz. 78c
Gro. $9.00

## IMPORTED TOY HAND SEWING MACHINES.

F2287—"Favorite." Ht. 5½ in., base
4x2, black enameled steel frame,
2 in. steel balance wheel, gilt decorated, spool thread, clamp fastening. Each in box. ¼ doz. in pkg.
Doz. $4.25

F2288—"Star." Ht. 7 in., base
6x3¾, steel frame, 2½ in. nkl. balance wheel, gilt decorated, nickel
trim, spool thread, clamp fastening.
1 in box.....................Each, 85c

F2290—"Elite." 8¼ x 7¾ x 4, heavy
metal frame, 2¾ in. nickel wheel,
gilt decorated, spool thread, clamp
fastening. Most practical hand machine made. 1 in box...Each, $1.50
Needles—1 doz. in pkg.
F2294—For F2287 machine. Doz. 17c
F2293—For F2288 and 2290 machines. Asstd.............Doz. 17c

## TRICK MIRRORS.

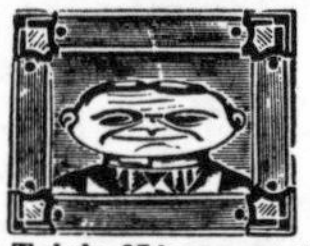

**F3127—Trick Mirror.** 3½ x 2¾, fancy frame, sure cure for leanness and fatness. 1 doz. in box. Doz. **28c**

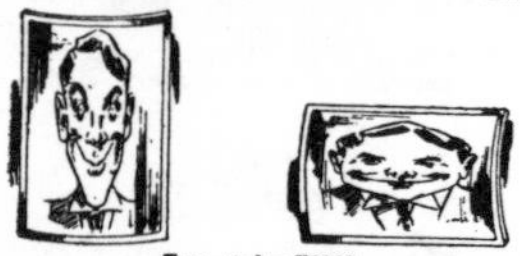

Two styles F3128

**F3128—"Look and Laugh" Mirror.** 3x2⅛ concave double mirror, covered edge, reflects lean or stout. 1 doz. in box.................Doz. **35c**

## TRICK NOVELTIES.

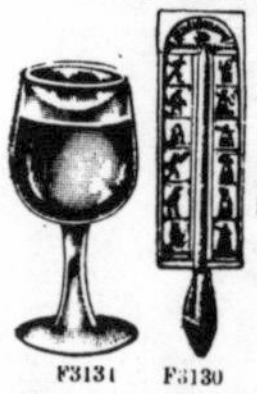

F3131 F3130

**F3131—Deception Wine Glass.** Ht. 3 in., regular blown wine glass filled with red liquor, thin glass top. 1 doz. box...Doz. **33c**

**F3130 — Matrimonial Thermometer,** 7 in. blown glass, red fluid, litho card indicating fury, anger, jealousy, etc. When held in hand fluid rises. Each in box. 1 doz. in pkg. Doz. **37c**

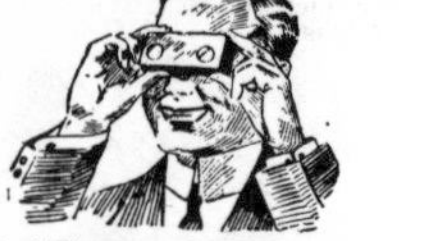

**F3137—"Funny Folks" Comic Cabinet.** 3½ in. double lens. 1 doz. in box.............. Doz. **89c**

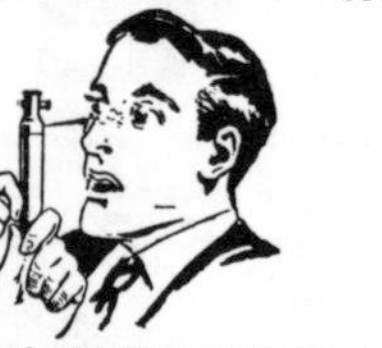

**F3139—Trick Kinematograph.** Metal magnifying lens top showing assorted views, side opening squirts water in face. 1 doz. in box. Doz. **$1.75**

## JAP. TRICK CAMERAS.

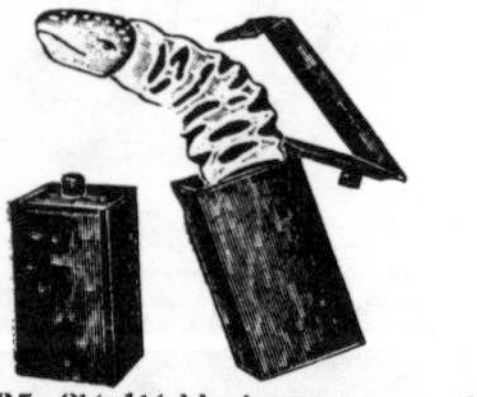

**L8835**—2¼x1⅛, black paper covered camera shape box, snap fastener, 9 in. cloth covered coiled wire snake springs out when opened. 2 doz. in box...........Gro. $3.00 Doz. **30c**

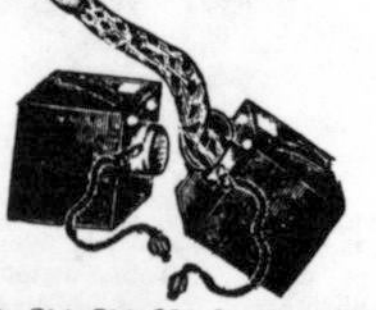

**L8838**—2¼x2¼x1¾, leatherette covered, handled box, glass lens, nickel barrel, bulb and cord, silver paper finders. When cord is pulled, shutter flies open and 7¼ in. paper covered wire snake springs out. 2 doz. in box. Gro. $4.00 Doz. **39c**

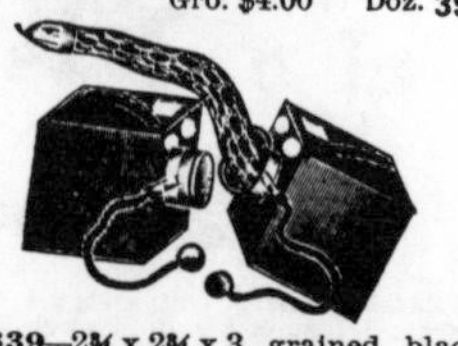

**L8839**—2¾ x 2¾ x 3 grained black leatherette handled box, 1¼ in. glass lens, nickel barrel, bulb & cord, glass finder. When cord is pulled shutter flies open and 12 in. mottled cotton covered snake springs out. 1 doz. in box . ............ Doz. **79c** Gro. $9.00

## JAPANESE TRICK FLASHLIGHT.

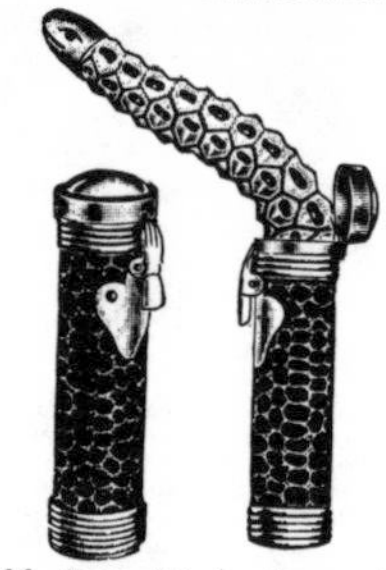

**L8841**—Case 4⅛ in. long, imit. leather, metal ends and catch, glass reflector, 12 in. cloth covered coiled wire snake, when flash spring is pressed snake flies out. 1 doz. in box. Doz. **72c**

## "SANTA CLAUS IN CHIMNEY" TRICK TOY.

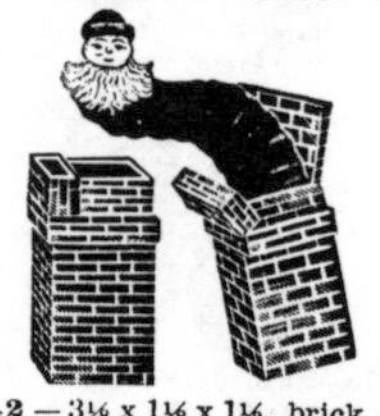

**L3142** — 3⅛ x 1⅛ x 1⅛, brick effect chimney. When top opens 12 in. Santa Claus figure with bell springs out. 1 doz. in box..........Doz. **75c**

## TRICK FANS.

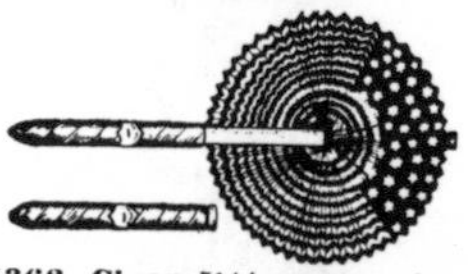

**L5368—Cigar.** 5⅛ in. square, closed, extended 13 in., red white and blue paper. 1 gro. in box....GRO. **$1.00**

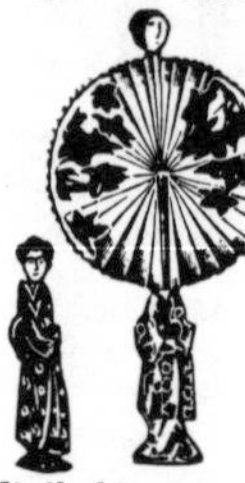

**L7292—Doll.** 6 in. extension, length 12⅛ in., bright color kimono floral decorated fan. 3 doz. in box. Doz. **15c** Gro. **$1.50**

## JAPANESE ANIMATED TOYS.

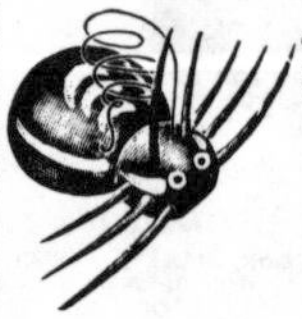

Least movement causes legs to vibrate.

**L3130 — Spider.** Length 2¼ in., black composition body, silver bead eyes, finely coiled wire spring 4 doz. in box.. Doz. **18c**

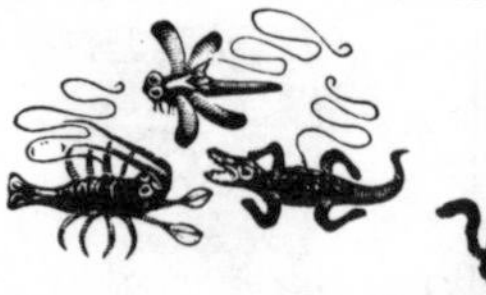

**L3131** — Aver. length 3⅛ in., asstd. alligators, spiders, lobsters, crabs and dragon-flies, finely coiled spring wire wings or legs. Asstd. 2 doz. in box......... ..............Doz. **30c**

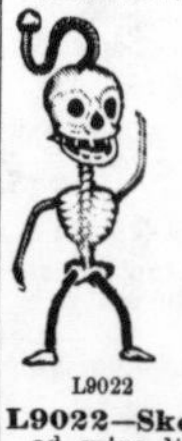

L9022

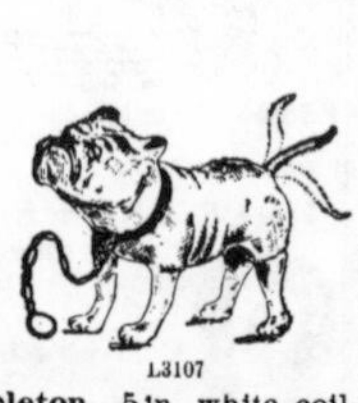

L3107

**L9022—Skeleton.** 5 in., white, coiled wire limbs, shaking skull with hinged wagging jaw. 2 doz. in box. Doz. **36c**

## MISCELLANEOUS JAPANESE TOYS.

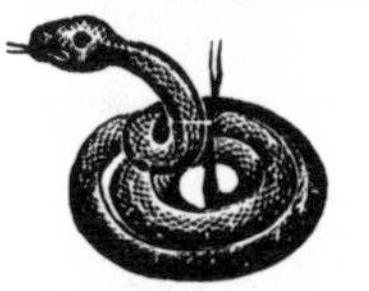

**L5361 — Woven Paper Snake.** Natural painted and spotted, 30 in. 2 doz. in box...............Doz. **25c**

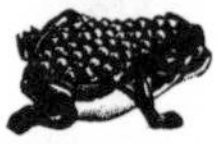

**L8568 — Frog.** 3 in., good model, natural color, tin. When squeezed opens mouth and croaks. 1 doz. in box..........................Doz. **30c**

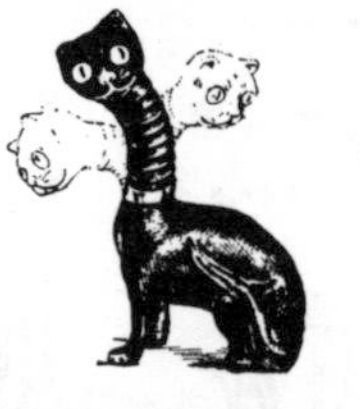

**L8402—Rubber Neck Cat Novelty.** 5 in., hollow body black cat, removable head, long jointed neck, can be placed in any position. Each in box, 1 doz. in carton.............Doz. **75c**

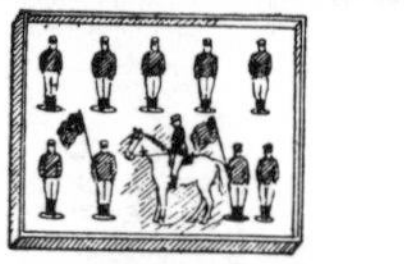

**L9030—10 Pc. Soldier and Sailor Set.** Aver. 2¼ in., papier mache soldiers and sailors in Japanese uniforms, 2 flag bearers, 1 mounted officer. 1 doz. sets in pkg. Doz. sets, **79c**

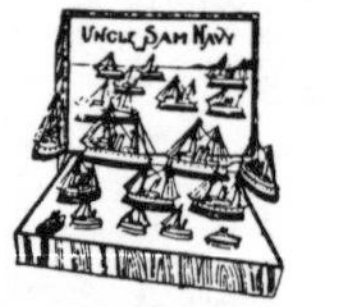


**L3106—Uncle Sam's Navy.** 12 pcs., 2⅛ to 3 in., light house, fort and 10 battleships, bright colors, cord rigging, American flags, gold names. Each set in box, 1 doz. sets in pkg. Doz. sets, **89c**

## JAPANESE NODDING HEAD TOYS.

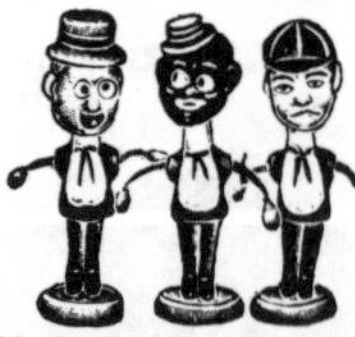

**L3122**—6 characters, 5 in. papier-mache body, wood base, coil wire arms, head moves on coil wire invisible spring. Asstd. 2 doz. in box. Doz. **33c**

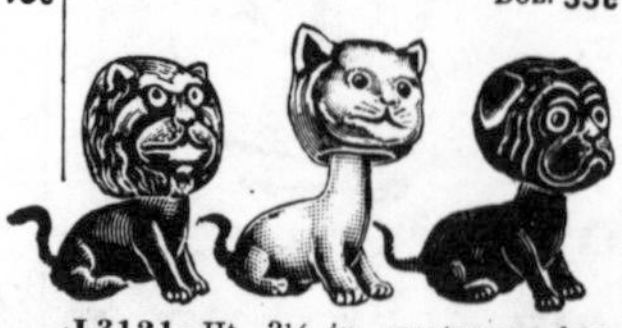

**L3121**—Ht. 3⅛ in., grotesque dog, cat and lion, sitting position, coil wire tail, head on invisible coil wire spring. Asstd. 2 doz. in box. Doz. **36c**

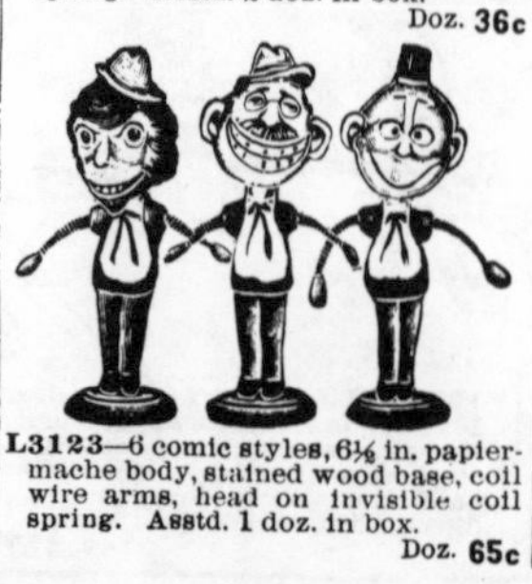

**L3123**—6 comic styles, 6⅛ in. papier-mache body, stained wood base, coil wire arms, head on invisible coil spring. Asstd. 1 doz. in box. Doz. **65c**

## PEWTER SOLDIERS.

2¼ in. soldiers, 2⅞ in. mounted officers, facsimile U. S. regular and sailors uniforms. Made of finest pewter, tinted faces, vari-color painted uniforms, large green base, folding white canvas tents on cardboard base, metal tent pole with flag. Each set elastic fastened to glazed card in flat box.

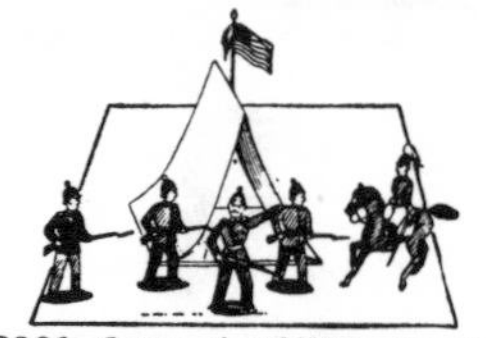

**F2201—6 pcs.,** 4 soldiers, mounted officer and tent. ⅙ doz. set in pkg. Doz. sets, **$2.15**

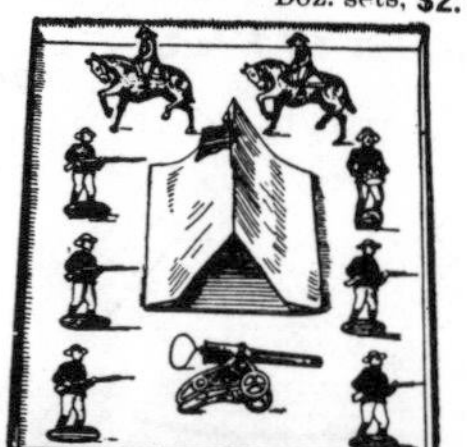

**F2204—10 pcs.,** 5 soldiers, captain, 2 mounted officers, brass finish mounted cannon, tent. ¼ doz. sets in pkg....... .......Doz. sets, **$4.10**

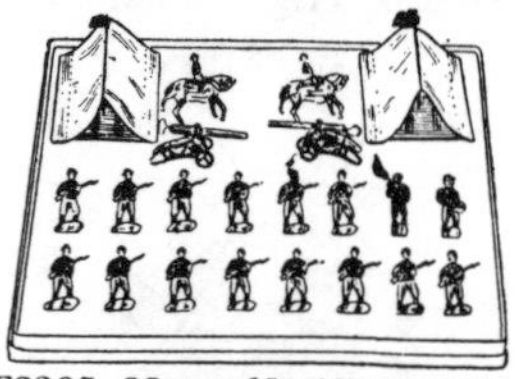

**F2205—22 pcs.,** 15 soldiers, captain, 2 mounted officers, 2 brass finish mounted cannons, 2 tents. 1/12 doz. sets in pkg...........Doz. sets, **$8.50**

**F2206 — Soldiers and Indians. 22 pcs.,** 7 soldiers, captain, 2 mounted officers, 7 Indians and Chief, 2 brass finish brass mounted cannons, 2 tents. 1/12 doz. sets in pkg Doz. sets, **$8.50**

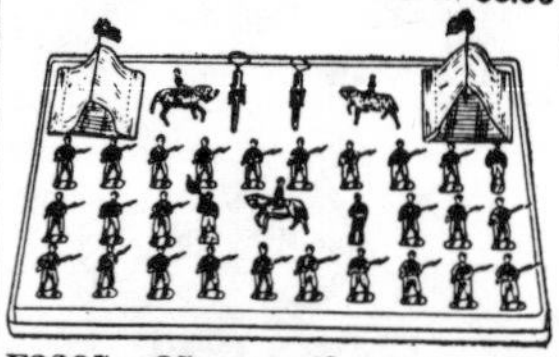

**F2207 — 35 pcs.,** 26 soldiers, flag bearer, captain, 3 mounted officers, 2 brass finish mounted cannons, 2 tents. 1 set in pkg.....SET, **$1.10**

## PEWTER TOY TEA SETS.

All bright silvered finish. Each set in spaced box.

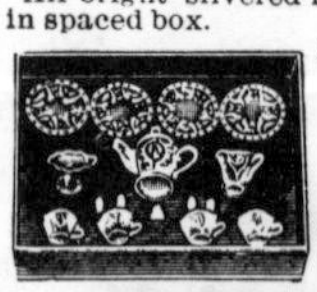

**F1842** — Embossed, 16 pcs., 4 cups and saucers, tea pot, creamer, sugar, 4 spoons. 5 x 6 box. 1 doz. sets in pkg. Doz. sets, **79c**

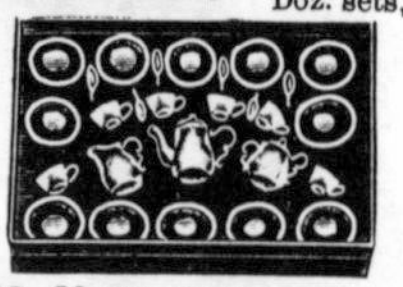

**F1843**—26 pcs., 6 cups and saucers, 6 plates, teapot, sugar, creamer, sugar tongs, spoons, embossed edge, 7x9⅛ box. ⅙ doz. sets in pkg. Doz. sets, **$1.90**

## PEWTER DOLL CARRIAGES.

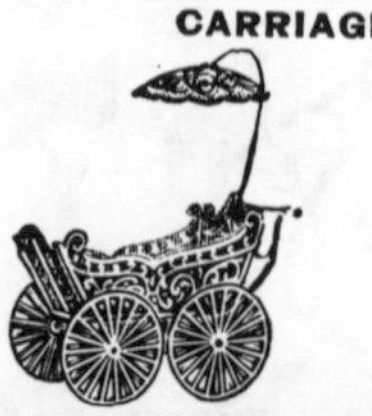

Filigree body and parasol, upholstered, moving wheels. Each in box, 1 doz. in pkg.

| | Doz. |
|---|---|
| F1844—3⅛x4.................................. | $0 42 |
| F1845—5¼x6, more elaborate.... | 87 |

## SOLDIER SETS.

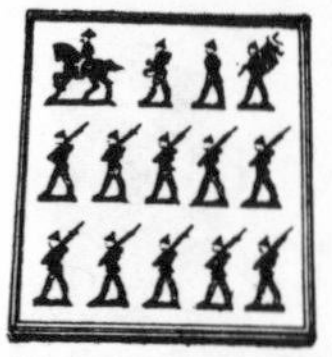

**F2202—Pewter. 14 pcs.,** c bearer, bugler, mounted officer 11 soldiers, painted U. S. dress forms. Each set in box, 1 doz. set pkg.............. ......Doz. sets,

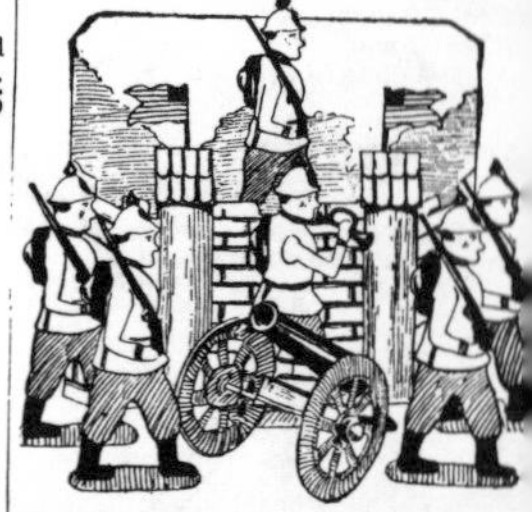

**F2203—Tin. 8 large pcs.,** 5¾ metal fort, 2 towers with U. S. fla mounted cannon shoots peas sticks, bugler and 5 soldiers, blue white painted uniforms. Each set box, ¼ doz. sets in pkg. Doz. sets, $4.

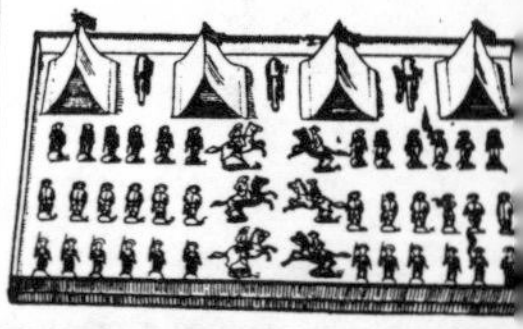

**F2208—Pewter Army & Na Outfit. 53 pcs.,** 14 in khaki col 14 in. dress uniform, 12 sailors cluding captain and drummer each, 6 mounted officers, 3 bra finish mounted cannons, 4 ten 1 set in box...............SET, $1.

## FLOATING WAX DUCKS

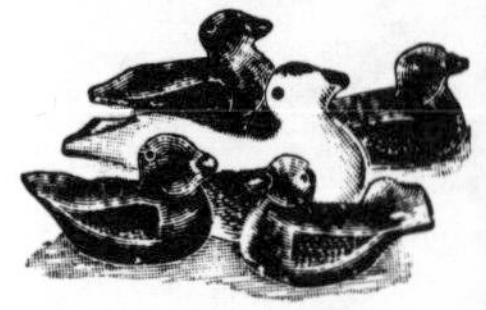

**F2829**—1 large and 4 small ducks set, natural tinted yellow compo tion wax, tested to 100° heat. Eac set in box, 1 doz. sets in pkg. Doz. sets, **85** Gro. sets, $9.75

## "CUM-BAC" TOY.

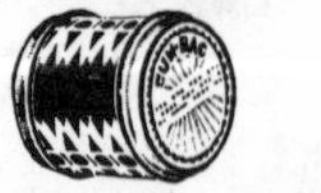

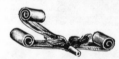

**F2375**—2¼x2¼, tin ends, litho car board body, when rolled on floor down incline returns. 1 doz. in bo Doz. **72**

## BLOW EXTENSION TOYS

Each with whistle mouthpiece.

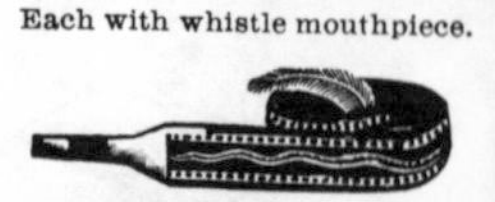

**F3151**—Extends 23⅛ in., asstd. colo parchment with snake design feather ends. 3 doz. in box. Doz. **15**

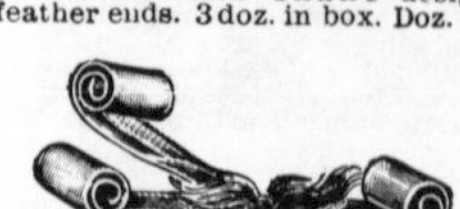

**F3152**—Extends 9¾ in., black hai mustache, 3 coils. 1 doz. in box. Doz. **28**

## BIRD TOY.

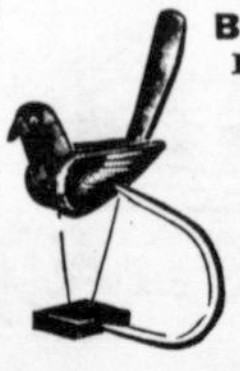

**L3161** — Decorated wooden bird, pivoted neck and tail attached to wood base by cords, bamboo loop spring for hand pressure. Asstd. colors, 2 doz. in box......Doz. **30c**

# TOY GUNS AIR RIFLES, PISTOLS, Etc.

Every boy wants them. Show a good line and the little fellows will bring their parents to your store. All selected well made goods.

### IMPORTED POP PISTOLS.

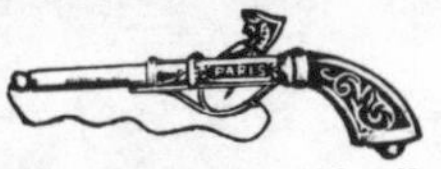

ll **Metal**—Embossed bronzed handle, trigger, hammer, suction rod, cork and string. 1 doz. in box.
F3236—About 7½ in.............Doz. $0 45
F3237— " 10½ "................ " 84

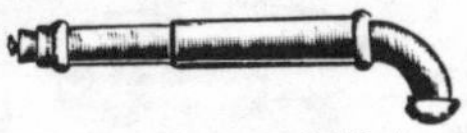

3239—10 in., mahogany finish, turned handle, rod attachment, cork on string. 1 doz. in box.......... ... ...............Doz. **45c**

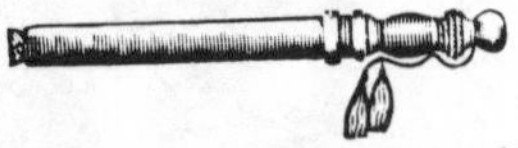

3240—Policeman's Club Pop-gun. 12 in., turned handles, varnished rosewood finish, cord and tassel, suction rod, cork attached to string. 1 doz. in box..... ... .... Doz. **82c**

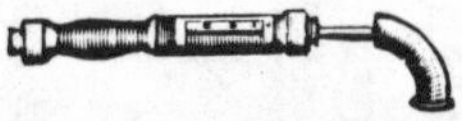

'3242 — 10¼ in., polished, turned wood, red and black striped, 3 harmonica reeds in silvered case, extra loud report, cork attached to wood rod. 1 doz. in box. Doz. **87c**

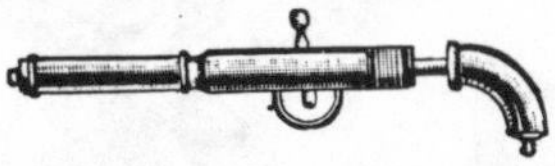

'3243—15¼ in., white enameled, bright color stripes, **extra loud,** trigger guard. ½ doz. in box............................Doz. **$2.00**

### ALL-METAL POP PISTOL.

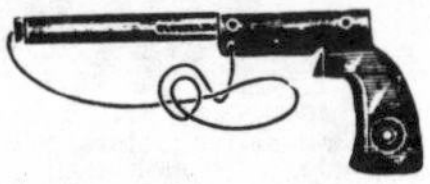

F2891—Length 7¾ in., nickel plated, heavy spring, perfect model of target pistol. Each in box. 1 doz. in pkg...............Doz. **75c**

**TOY GUNS—With Paper Ammunition.**

Harmless, extra loud report. Each with paper ammunition and directions.

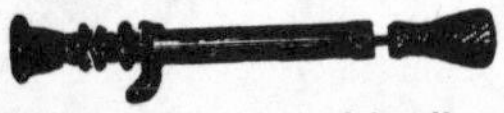

F2698—10 in. all steel wood handle pusher, metal, trigger cup end for loading. 1 doz. in box............ ...........................Doz. **85c**

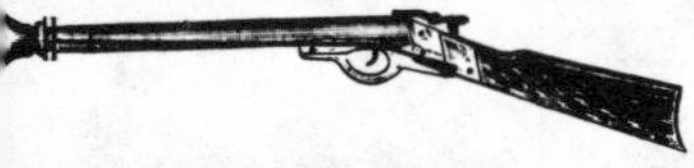

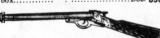

F2699—"Wizard," 18 in., stained wood stock, steel barrel and trigger, paper ammunition inserted by breaking down barrel. Each in box, ¼ doz. in pkg............Doz. **$1.90**

### JAPANESE POP PISTOLS AND GUNS.

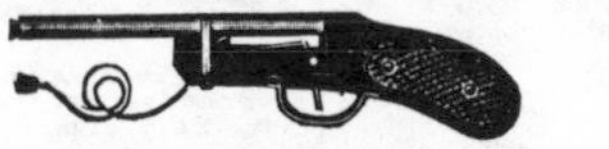

**L9034—Pistol.** 10¼ in., metal barrel, guard and sides, black wood stock, trigger string cork attachment. 2 doz. in box....Doz. **39c**

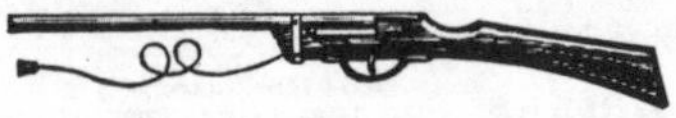

**Gun** — Brass lacquered barrel, stained wood stock, metal set trigger and guard, cork attachment. 2 doz. in box.
L5365—Length 15½ in... .........Doz. $0 42
L5366— " 21½ "....... ..... " 89

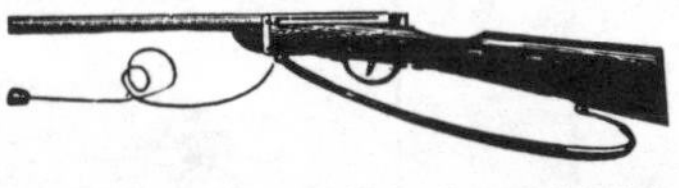

**L3105—Gun.** Length 24 in., heavy nickel tin barrel, polished walnut finish stock, nickel trim, leather sling. ¼ doz. in pkg. Doz. **$1.85**

### STEEL POP GUN AND CANNON.

**Attached Corks.**

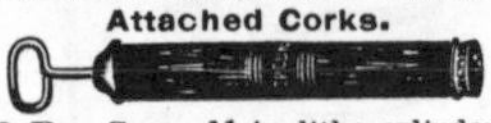

**F2183, Pop Gun.** 11 in. litho cylinder, handled copper suction rod, loud report. 1 doz. in box. .......... Doz. **80c**

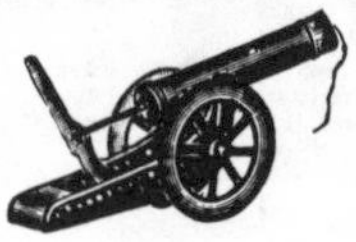

**Mounted Cannon.** Artillery models, polished steel cannon, lever compression, blue litho carriage, red open spoke wheels.
F2184—9½ in. 1 doz. in box.....Doz. **95c**

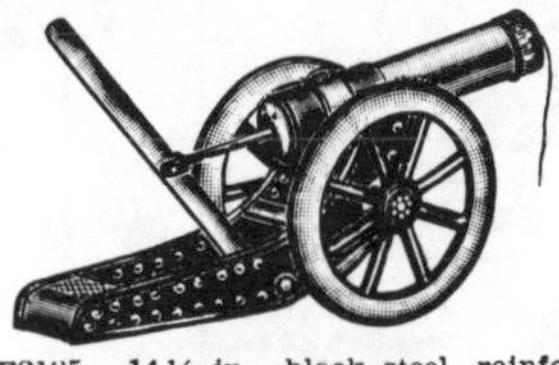

F2185 — 14½ in., black steel reinforced cannon, 6 in. wheels. ¼ doz. in box. Doz. **$1.90**

### "LITTLE DAISY" RIFLE MODEL POP GUNS.

Harmless and very popular. Shoots corks, etc.

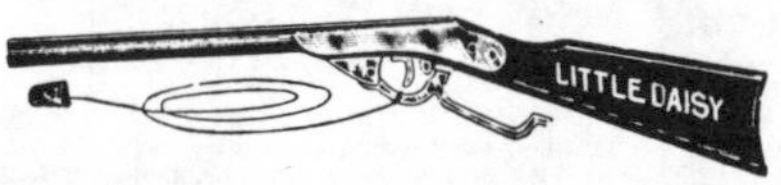


**F2040** — (*Mfrs. 10*), lever action. 17 in., modeled after big "Daisy" air rifles, polished nickel metal parts, walnut stock. Each with cork and string. 1/12 doz. in carton....... Doz. **$1.75**

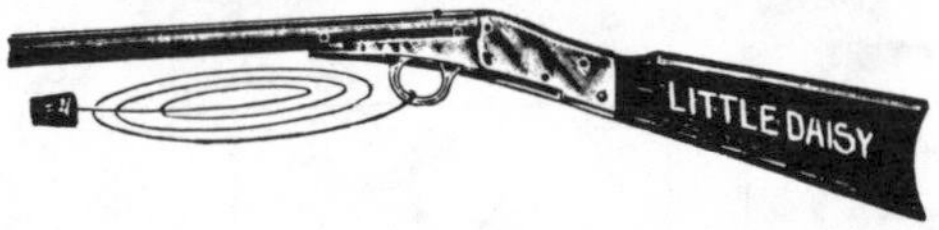


**F2041** — (*Mfrs. 14*), shoots cork or rubber ball, break action. 21 in. Each with rubber ball and cork. 1/12 doz. in carton............. .... ............ ...... ......Doz. **$4.00**

### "STERLING" RIFLETTE POP GUN.

*One of the leading all-year-round toys. Shoots corks, makes lots of noise— harmless.*

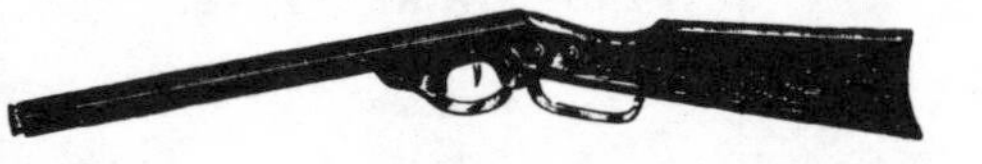

**F2020**—16½ in. over all, blued steel barrel and frame, lever action, stained walnut stock, complete with cork and string in carton. 1 doz. in pkg. Doz. ***95**

### "DIXIE" ALL METAL POP GUN.

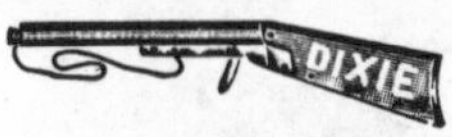


**F2893**—11 in., aluminum finish, break down action, cork attached to string. Each in box, 1 doz. in pkg. .... ..............Doz **92c**

### "IDEAL" TARGET OUTFITS.

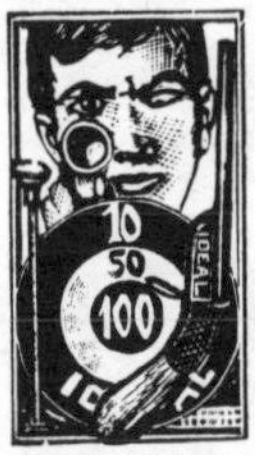

F3245

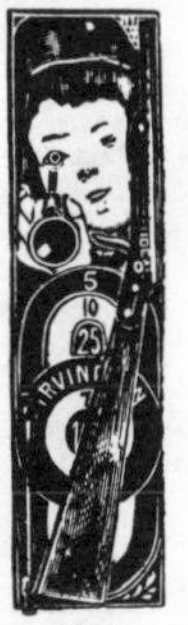

F3246

**F3245**—8½ in. black enameled metal pistol, wood butt, powerful spring, 5½ in. rubber suction end arrow, 9½x5 litho numbered target card. 1 doz. in box...... ...Doz. **84c**

**F3246**—18¼ in. gun, wood stock, black enameled metal barrel, 6 in. rubber suction end arrow, 19 x 4¾ litho numbered target card. 1 doz. in pkg....... ................Doz. **96c**

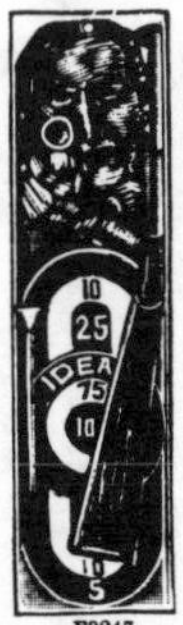

F3247

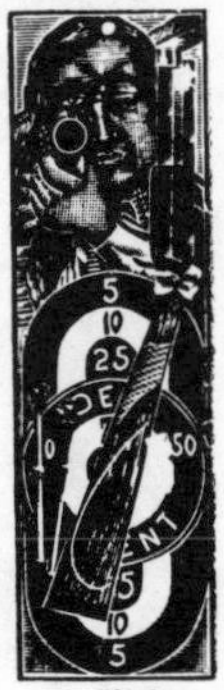

F3249

**F3247**—18¾ in., nkl. barrel gun, wood stock, 6 in. rubber suction end arrow in holder 21x5⅝, litho Indian target card. ½ doz. in box.... ............... Doz. **$1.75**

**F3249**—20 in. double barrel gun, wood stock, two 6 in. rubber suction end arrows, litho Indian numbered target card, 23x7. ⅛ doz. in box....... ......................Doz. **$4.00**

*"ERECTOR" STEEL TOYS*

*Finest toy a boy can have. Supplements manual training. Develops ingenuity. See our line in this book.*

## "STERLING" AIR RIFLES.

A line of mechanically perfect finely finished guns which are gaining in popularity each season.

Strong shooting springs, all working parts specially hardened, 1 pc. malleable levers, **blued barrels,** natural stained walnut stocks, barrel and frame stamped from 1 pc. sheet steel, accurately sighted peep rear and knife front. All models shoot air rifle shot or darts.

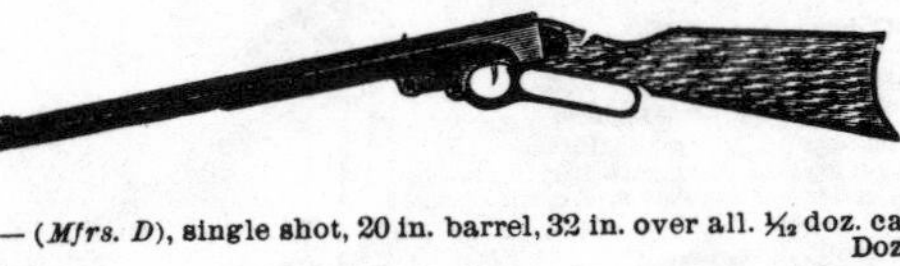

**F2021** — (*Mfrs. D*), single shot, 20 in. barrel, 32 in. over all. 1/12 doz. carton. Doz. **$6.50**

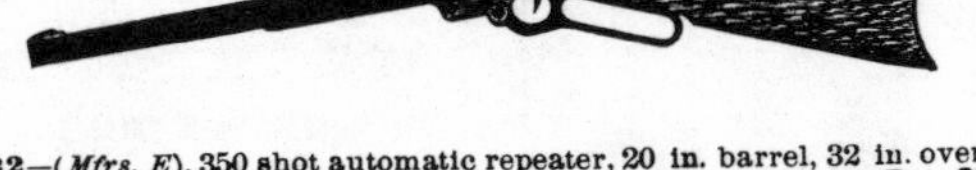

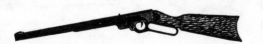

**F2022**—(*Mfrs. E*), 350 shot automatic repeater, 20 in. barrel, 32 in. over all. 1/12 doz. in carton......... .......... ...........................Doz. **$8.00**

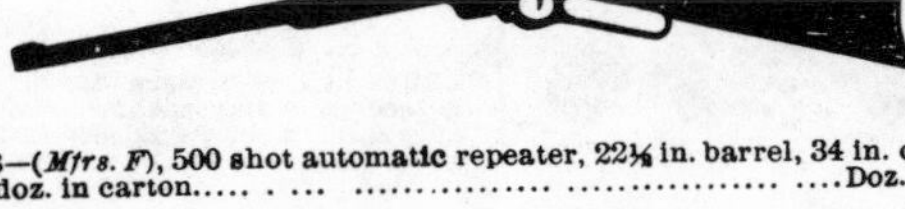

**F2023**—(*Mfrs. F*), 500 shot automatic repeater, 22¼ in. barrel, 34 in. over all. 1/12 doz. in carton..... . ... ................. ...................Doz. **$11.00**

### AIR RIFLE SHOT.

For use with any make of standard air rifles.

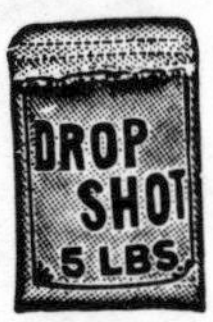


**F6110**—5c package, ¼ lb. shot in round wood box. 1 doz. boxes in carton.......................Doz. **42c**

**F2047**—5 lb. canvas bag. BAG (5 lbs.)....**55c**

**F2048**—25 lb. canvas bag. BAG (25 lbs )....**$2.25**

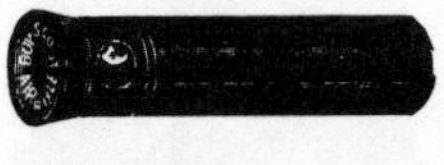

**F2049**—"Boy Scout." Shell tube with perforated side and sliding band to permit shot to be taken out. Shell or carton contains **6 doz. air rifle shot.** A big 5c seller. 1 doz. shells in box.......Doz. shells, **39c**
Case lots of 100 shells, $3.00

## FAMOUS "DAISY" AIR RIFLES.

This line to-day is one every dealer should handle—profits are good—merchandise easy to handle—investment small. The Famous "Daisy" Line has been greatly improved, all models are lever action, will shoot either air rifle shot or darts, except F2027. Polished and nickel plated barrels, walnut stocks, accurately sighted.

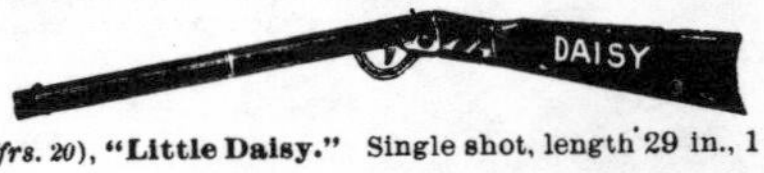


**F2027**—(*Mfrs. 20*), **"Little Daisy."** Single shot, length 29 in., 1 lb. 2 oz. Doz. **$4.00**

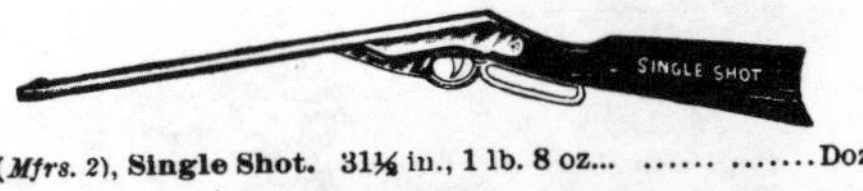


**F2028**—(*Mfrs. 2*), **Single Shot.** 31½ in., 1 lb. 8 oz... ...... .......Doz. **$6.50**

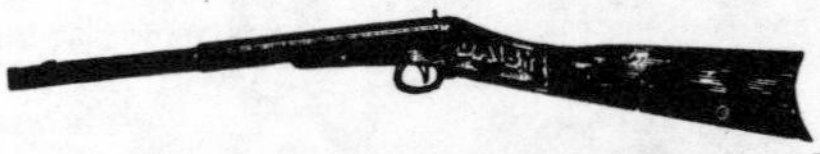

**F2032**—(*Mfrs. 1*), **350 Shot Repeater.** 31¼ in, 1 lb. 11 oz.......Doz. **$8.85**

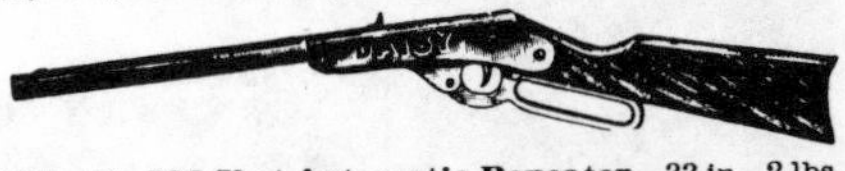

**F2036**—(*Mfrs. 30*), **500 Shot Automatic Repeater.** 33 in., 2 lbs. 7 oz. Doz. **$11.80**

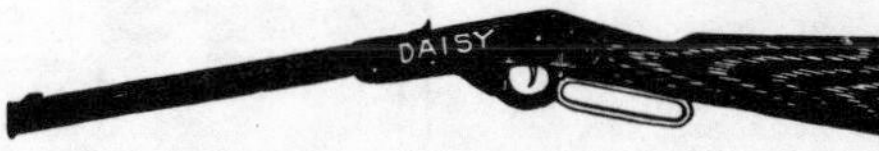


**F2037**—(*Mfrs. 3*), **1000 Shot Automatic Repeater.** 36 in., 2 lbs. 9 oz. Doz. **$13.20**

## DECORATED TIN STOVES.

Imit. brick, red and black bodies, black and blue trim.

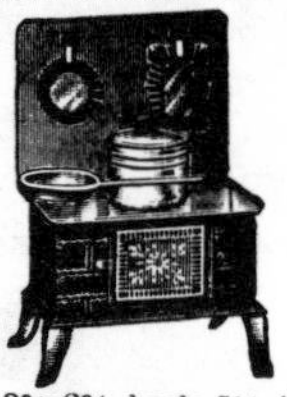

**F5362**—3⅜x2¾, back 5⅛ in., oven, 2 dishes, covered pan and fire dish, 2 hangers, asstd. colors. 1 doz. in box............ ..........Doz. **42c**

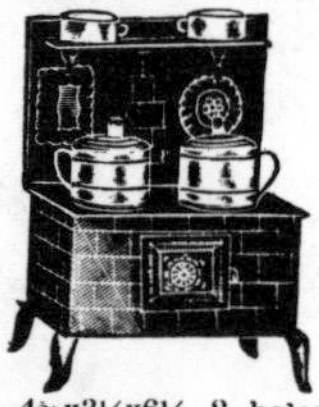

**F5364**—4⅝x3¼x6¼, 2 holes, oven, chimney, shelf with 2 cups, 2 hangers, 2 covered stew pans. 1 doz. in box.............................Doz. **84c**

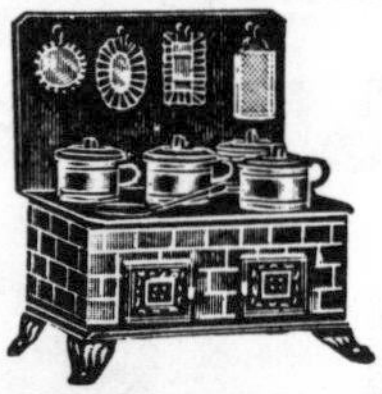

**F5366**—5⅛x3⅛, back 7⅛, 2 oven 4 stew pans, 5 dishes, 4 hangers, asstd. colors. 1 doz. in box. Doz. **89c**

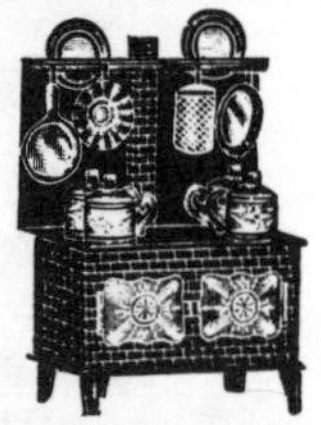

**F5369**—5¼x4⅛, ht. 9, chimney with rack, 2 hinged oven doors, 4 holes, 4 covered handled pots, 5 asstd. utensils. ⅓ doz. in box.. Doz. **$2.00**

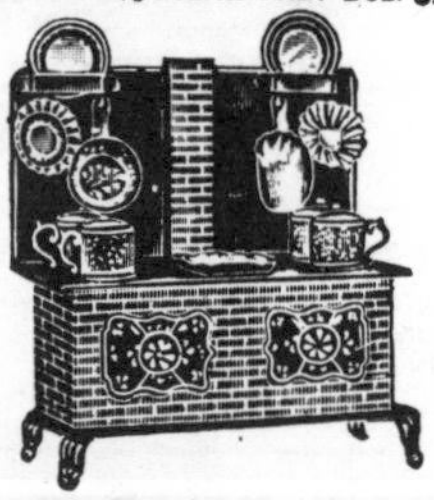

**F5370** — 9x4⅛, ht. 9⅛, 5 holes, 2 ovens, 11 utensils — 1 fry pan, 6 dishes, 4 covered stew pans. ⅙ doz. in box...................... Doz. **$2.25**

**F5371**—9¾x6¾, ht. 12, 5 holes, 2 ovens, 1 hot water faucet, 13 utensils—8 dishes, 2 large and 2 small covered stew pans, 1 coffee pot. ⅙ doz. in box............ Doz. **$4.10**

## CUPS AND SAUCERS, ETC.

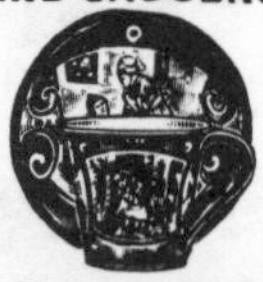

**F5314** — **Cup and Saucer.** Cup 2⅛x2⅛, saucer 4⅛, Red Riding Hood and Wolf designs in bright colors and gold. 1 doz. in box. Doz. **40c**

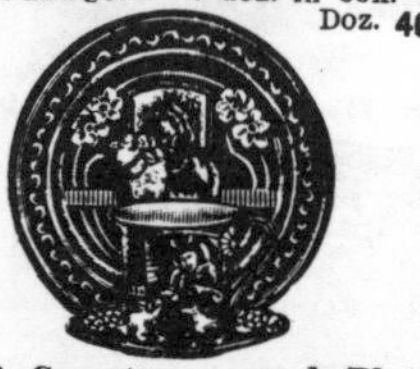

**F5316—Cup, Saucer and Plate.** 2⅛x2¼ cup, 4 in. saucer, 6¼ in. plate, gilt edge and decorated, asstd. menagerie and juvenile designs. 1 doz. sets in box......Doz. sets, **82c**

## LITTLE HOUSEKEEPERS' ENAMELED TOY SPECIALTIES.

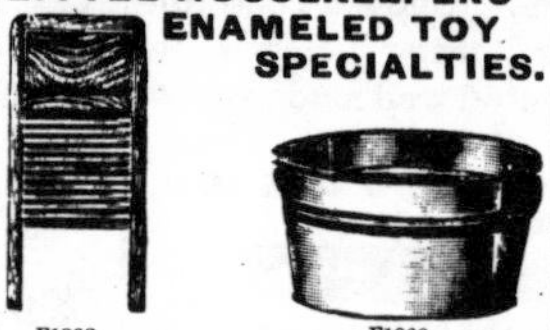

F1862 F1860

**F1862** — **Washboard.** 9¾x4⅛, all metal, asstd. red, green and blue enameled, corrugated surface both sides, turned edges. Asstd. 1 doz. in pkg...................Doz. **65c**

**F1860—Wash Tub.** 7⅛x3¼, asstd. red, blue and green enameled heavy tin hinged metal handles. 1 doz. in pkg.. ..........................Doz. **85c**

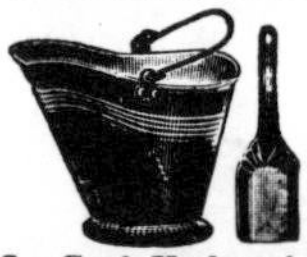

**F1863**—**Coal Hod and Shovel.** 6¼x4⅛, bail handle, 6 in. shovel, asstd. red, blue, green and black enameled. 1 doz. sets in box. Doz. sets, **84c**

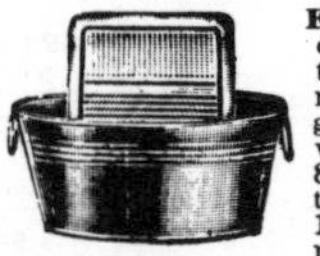

**F1858—Laundry Set. 2 pc.,** tin tub 7⅛x3¼, red, blue and green enameled, wire handles, 8⅛ in. bright tin washboard. 1 doz. sets in pkg. Dz.sets.**95c**

## TOY TIN WASH BOILER.

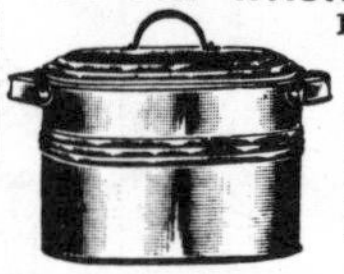

**F1856** — 5⅞ x 3⅛ x 5¼, bright tin, reinforced riveted handles, corrugated lid and body. 1 doz. in box. Doz. **75c**

## TOY FLOUR SIFTER.

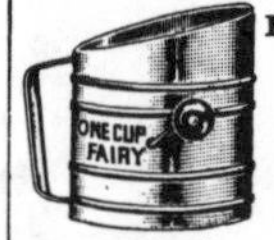

**F1855**—3x3⅛, heavy tin, bright finish, 3 strong agitators, enameled wood knob, 2 in. side handle, fine wire sieve. 1 doz. in box.....Doz. **72c**

## TOY DUST PANS.

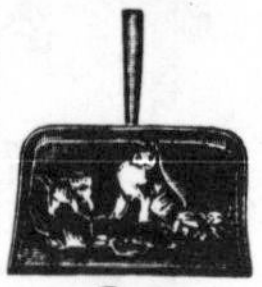

**F5375**—4¼ x 6⅛, litho, juvenile designs, handle with cord hanger. 2 doz. in pkg. Doz. **40c**

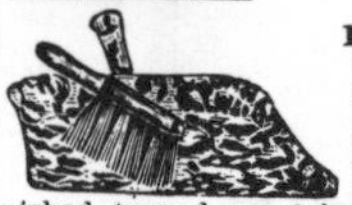

**F1864—2Pc. Set.** 6x9, red and blue brilliant embossed silverine tin, round handle, varnished turned wood handle brush. Asstd. 1 doz. box............Doz. **84c**

## WATERING POTS.

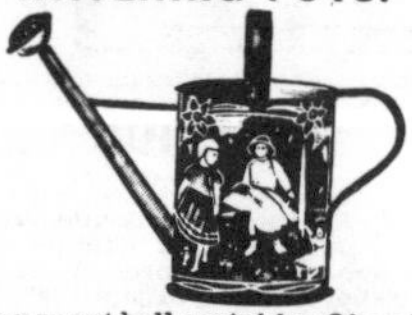

Long spout bell sprinkler, 2 handles, embossed cats, dogs and seashore designs in colors and gilt. Asstd. 1 doz. in box.

F5400—3¼ in.............. Doz. $0 42
F5402—5 " ............... " 87

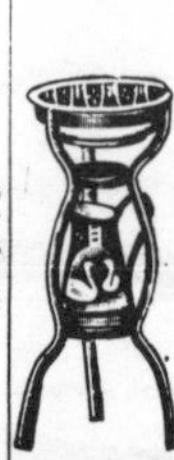

## 3 PIECE WATER STAND.

**F5377** — 7⅛ in. gilt lacquered stand, litho tin 2⅜ in. bowl and 3 in. handled pitcher. Each set in box. 1 doz. sets in pkg. Doz. sets, **89c**

## ENAMELED AND GILT TOY BED.

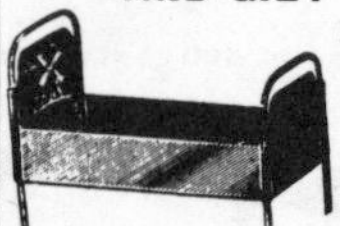

**F5378**—5⅛x4 finely enameled, gilt wire head and foot posts, litho medallion on head-post. 1 doz. in box. Doz. **42c**

## TIN TOY SPECIALTIES.

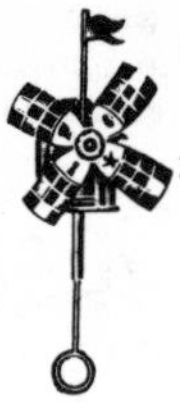

**F5294—Windmill.** Red and green painted house, bright litho mill wheel, 8 in. wire, pennant top, loop handle, wheel revolves when raised or lowered. 2 doz. in box. ........Doz. **30c**

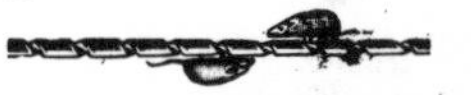

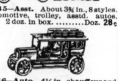

**F5292—Mice on 15 In. Pole.** 2 white mice, worsted tails, chase each other on pole. 2 doz. in box. Doz. **37c**

## TANGO TWIRLERS

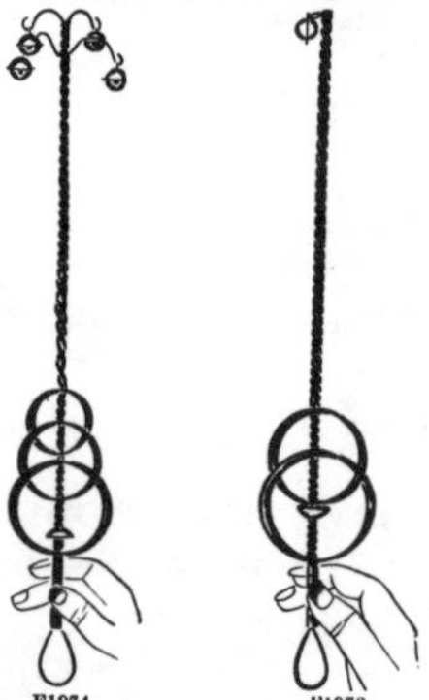

F1974 F1973

21 in. heavy twisted copper wire rods with slides, loop handles, brass bell ends, flat colored metal rings, give vari-colored bubble effects when slide is pushed. 1 doz. in box.

F1973—2 rings...............Doz $0 39
F1974—3 " 4 bells...... " 0 75

## MAGIC "RANE-BO" TOY.

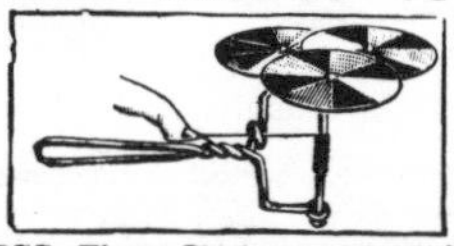

**F1877**—Three 2⅛ in. multi colored discs on heavy strawboard wheel, metal axle, 4½ in. twisted wire handle, kaleidoscopic colors produced by pulling string, continuous action. Each in env., with instructions. 1 doz. in box.........Doz. **75c** Gro. **$8.50**

## "MERRY WHIRL" TOYS.

**Whirl from end to end by reversing.**

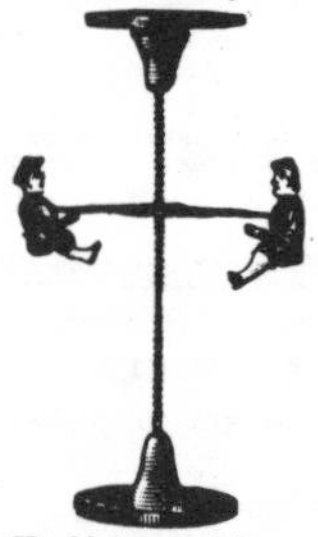

**F2142**—Ht. 11 in., bright, enameled in 6 colors, spiral rod, reversible figures on steel bar. 1 doz. in box. Doz. **89c**

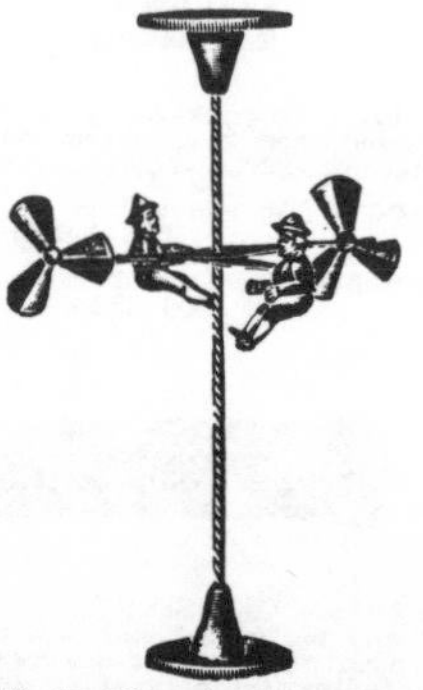

**F2144**—Ht. 16 in., 2 red & blue enameled steel crosspieces, reversible figures and colored pin-wheels. Each in box, ⅙ doz. in pkg......Doz. **$2.00**

## IMPORTED FRICTION TOYS.

Friction wheel, when turned sets toy in motion. Litho and striped in bright colors.

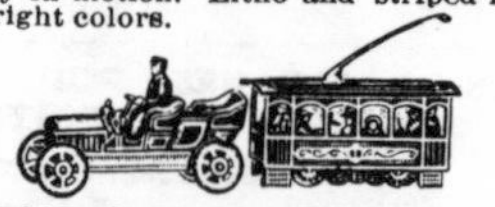

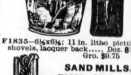

**F5445—Asst.** About 3¾ in., 8 styles. locomotive, trolley, asstd. autos, etc. 2 doz. in box. .........Doz. **28c**

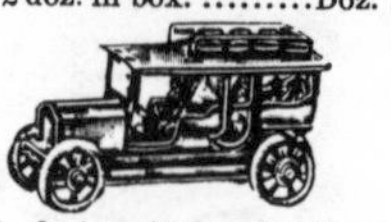

**F5446—Auto.** 4⅛ in., chauffeur and passengers, open spoke wheels, 1 doz. in box. ..............Doz. **40c**

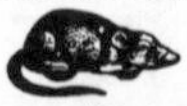

**F5450—Mouse.** 3 in., natural color, spiral wire tail, started by 2 or 3 pushes, runs long distance. 1 doz. in box.......................... Doz. **40c**

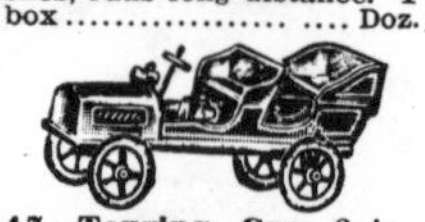

**F5447**—**Touring Car.** 6 in., red body, imit. rubber tire open spoke wheels. 1 doz. in box......Doz. **87c**

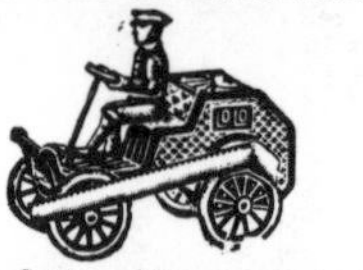

**F5448—Auto.** 4 in., green & white, imit. rubber tire wheels, chauffeur, rachet key, **Lehmann make.** 1 doz. in box................Doz. **89c**

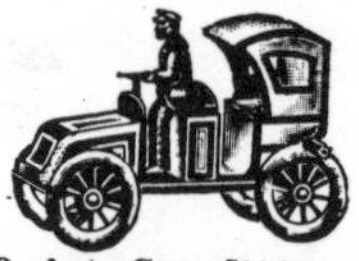

**F5449—Auto Car.** 5⅛ in., green & black, imit. rubber tire heavy metal wheels, chauffeur. 1 doz. in box. Doz. **95c**

## POPULAR HESSMOBILES.

Remarkable power, extra heavy friction wheel in hood, lever for starting and stopping, wound by crank, runs backward or forward by adjusting steering gear.

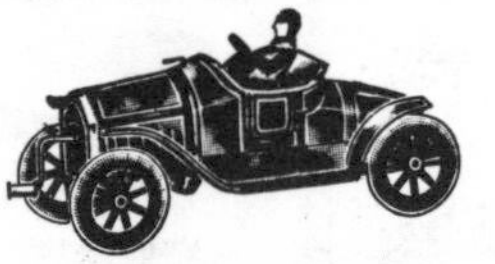

**F5454**—8¾ in., green body, red and gray stripes, black mud guards, open spoke yellow wheels, chauffeur. Each in box, ¼ doz. in pkg. Doz. **$4.00**

**F5456**—10 in., **racer,** red body, yellow & white stripes, black mud guards, open spoke wheels, chauffeur ½ doz. in box.... .........Doz. **$8.50**

## IMPORTED ROAMING TOYS.

Always moving, no winding, painted in bright colors, well made.

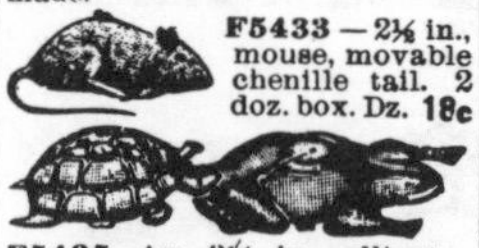

**F5433** — 2⅛ in., mouse, movable chenille tail. 2 doz. box. Dz. **19c**

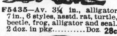

**F5435**—Av. 3¼ in., alligator 7 in., 6 styles, asstd. rat, turtle, beetle, frog, alligator and seal. 2 doz. in pkg...........Doz. **28c**

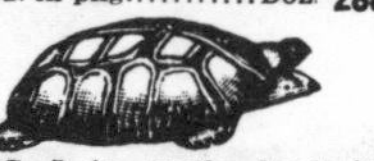

**F5437**—5 in. turtle, back in gilt and asstd. finishes. 1 doz. in box. ..........Doz. **35c**

## TIN TOYS ON WHEELS

German make, bright attractive colors.

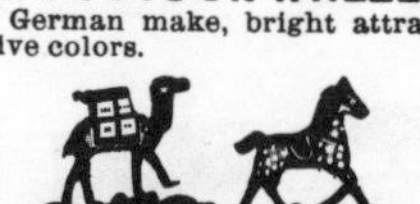

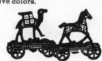

## LITHO SAND PAILS WITH SHOVEL

6 litho juvenile and seashore signs, lacquered gilt lined, wire ba turned wood handles; wood hand shovels. 1 doz. in carton.

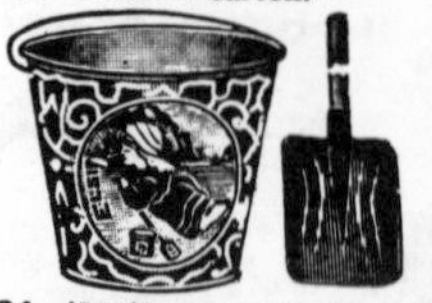

**F1834**—4⅞x4⅛; painted shove 8⅛ in......................Doz. 4

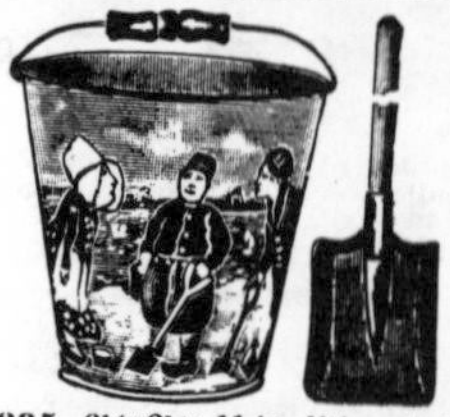

**F1835**—6⅛x6⅛; 11 in. litho pictu shovels, lacquer back..... Doz. 8 Gro. $9.75

## SAND MILLS

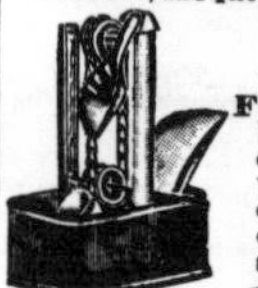

**F1828**—3¼x2¼ ba ht. 5in., painted colors and gilt, volving buckets chain, wire si crank, handl scoop. 1 doz. in b Doz. 7

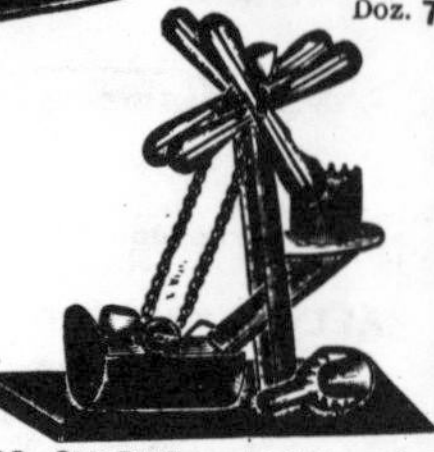

**F1829**—8⅛x3¼ base, ht. 9 in., paint in attractive colors, 2 buckets c chain, wire side crank, revolvi wind wheels, handled tin scoo ⅙ doz. in box..............Doz. **$1.9**

## "PANAMA" PILE DRIVER

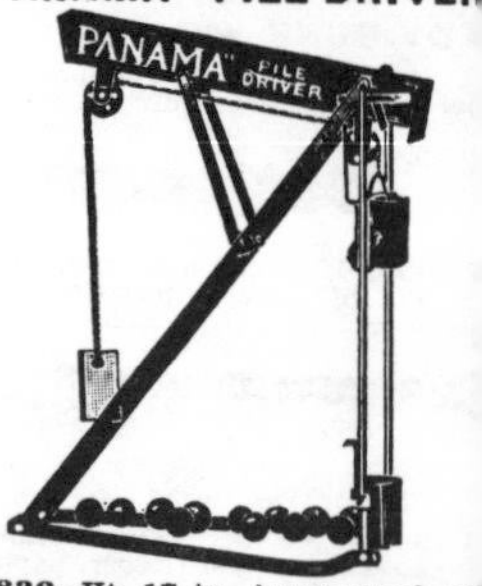


**F1838**—Ht. 17 in., heavy steel, re enameled incline runway, gilt lette ing, imitation weight automaticall operated by 12 large marbles, pil driving action. ½ doz. in box. Doz. **$8.5**

## AUTOMATIC SAND TOYS.

Car automatically fills from hopper takes incline, dumps and returns to top.

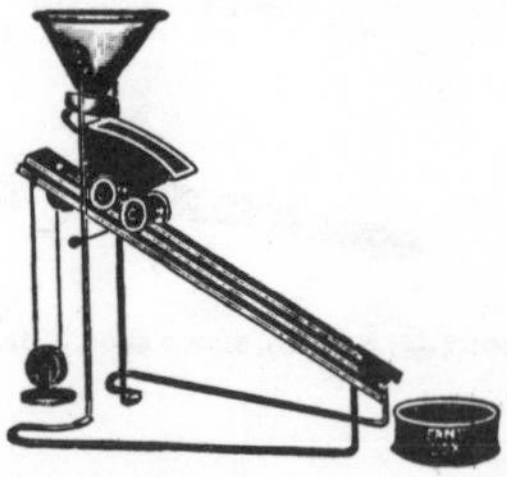

**F1832**—Ht. 13 in., heavy wire frame and uprights, lacquered 3⅛ in. hopper 14⅛ in. incline, 4 in. car, can of sand ½ doz. in box..................Doz. **$4.50**

## CHILDREN'S MUG.

Gilt inside, will not rust.

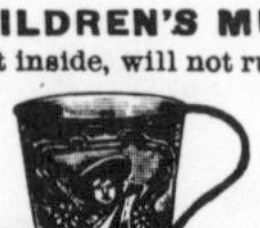

**F5306**—3x3, 2 designs asstd., embossed juvenile seashore pictures and asstd. animals in gilt frames 1 doz. in pkg...................Doz. **35c**

## IMPORTED MECHANICAL TOYS.

A selected line of the most reliable makes. Wound by attached keys less stated, good springs.

**Note**—All mechanical toys are perfect when they leave our house being sted in factory before packing. We cannot entertain claims for breakage.

**5489—Auto.** 4½x2x2¾, royal blue ody, white stripes, black mud guards, gray open spoke wheels, 2 passengers and chauffeur. 1 doz. in box.......................... Doz. **87c**

**5496—Beetle.** 5¾ in., red & black painted body, long feelers, runs in circle, stopping and starting automatically. 1 doz. in box....Doz. **89c**

**5490—Lehmann's Auto.** 4 in., green and blue litho., imit. rubber tires, chauffeur, spiral spring, runs in circle. 1 doz. in box.....Doz. **95c**

**5491—Asst.** 3 styles, aver. 5½ in., rooster, duck and goose, natural colors, gilt wheels, balance wheel, spiral springs. Asstd. 1 doz. in box. Doz. **95c**

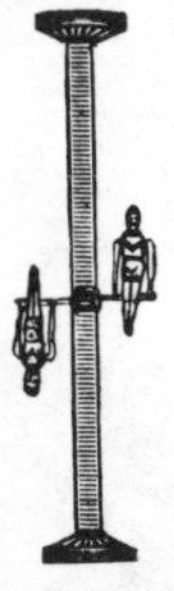

**F5494—Acrobats on Bar.** All metal, brightly painted, 11½ in. pole, acrobats turn somersaults from top to bottom, repeat when reversed. 1 doz. in pkg........... .... Doz. **96c**

**F5495—Performing Clown Asst.** Aver. 4½ in., 3 styles, harlequin painted, rolls hoop in circle, balances on horizontal bar between revolving hoops and rolls in hoop. Asstd. 1 doz. in box...................Doz. **96c**

**F5498—Billiard Player.** Length 6½ in., red & green painted table, figure with cue shoots balls automatically into numbered pockets, extra long action. Each in box. ¼ doz. in pkg.............Doz. **$1.80**

**F5500—Lehmann's "Naughty Boy and Chauffeur."** 5 in. blue striped white auto, imit. rubber tire red wheels, erratic action. Each in box, ⅙ doz. in pkg........ Doz. **$1.85**

2 styles F5503

**F5503—Tumbling Figures,** About 4½ in., brown bear, red, green and blue frog, brown Indian with red & yellow stripes, wound by turning forearms, turn lifelike somersaults. Each in box, asstd. ⅙ doz. in pkg. Doz. **$1.90**

**F5501—Beetle.** 6 legs, moving wings, all in motion at once, bright colors. Each in box, ⅙ doz. in pkg. Doz. **$1.95**

**F5506—Dancing Figures.** About 6¾ in., 3 styles, Frog, Newly-Wed Baby and Dude Negro, painted bright red, green and blue, vibrating dancing motion. Each in box, asstd. ⅙ doz. in pkg..............Doz. **$1.95**

**F5497—Auto Asst.** 3 styles, about 6¾ in., touring car, limousine and taxi, gray, blue and yellow bodies, black, white or red stripes, gray running gear, black mud guards, chauffeurs. Asstd. ⅙ doz. in pkg. Doz. **$2.00**

**F5505—Auto Dray.** 6¾ in., litho in red, yellow and white, imit. rubber tires, runs in circle. Each in box. ⅙ doz. in pkg...... ........Doz. **$2.00**

**F5507—Limousine.** 6½ in., red body, black and yellow stripes, mud guard, imit. rubber tires, chauffeur. Each in box, ⅙ doz. pkg..Doz. **$2.10**

F5509 F5510

**F5509—Climbing Miller Windmill.** Ht. 17 in., painted and lacquered, miller climbs and descends with bag on head, wheel revolves. Each in box, ⅙ doz. in pkg. Doz. **$2.00**

**F5510—Climbing Monkey.** 8½ in., yellow vest, green coat, red tasseled cap, climbs string. Each in box, ⅙ doz. in pkg.............Doz. **$2.00**

**F5520—Duck.** 6 in., painted natural colors, invisible wheels, swimming action. Each in box, ⅙ doz. in pkg. Doz. **$2.15**

**F5522—Auto Switchback.** 10¼x4⅞ double track enameled structure, 4 wheel racing auto with chauffeur, mechanical device raises auto to upper hinged incline, continuous action. Each in box, ⅙ doz. in pkg. Doz. **$2.15**

**F5516—Touring Auto.** 9½ in., spiral spring, red body, black & white striped, mud guard, wind shield, imit. rubber tires, chauffeur, runs ahead or circles. Each in box, ⅙ doz. in pkg..........Doz. **$2.15**

**F5729—Autos with Animal Chauffeurs.** Aver. 6 x 5½ in. 4 styles, cat, dog, polar and brown bears, felt, woolly and silk plush covered, button eyes, ribbon and patent leather collars; red racing autos, open spoke imit. rubber tire wheels, run straight or in circle. Each in box, asstd. ⅙ doz. in pkg. Doz. **$22.5**

**F5513—Hand Car, Bicycle and Auto Delivery.** Aver. 5½ in., painted bright colors, good action, figures operate machines with natural motion, strong **spiral spring.** Each in box, asstd. ⅙ doz. in pkg. Doz. **$2.25**

**F5519—Circus Asst.** About 8 in., 3 styles, clowns with galloping horse and donkey, circus rider in donkey cart, good action, new spiral springs. Each in box, asstd. ⅙ doz. in pkg. Doz. **$2.25**

**F5515—Fowl Asst.** 7 in., parrot, goose and chicken, run and flap wings, painted in colors, 2 wheels. Each in box, asstd. ⅙ doz. inpkg. Doz. **$2.25**

**F5521—Taxicab.** 7 in., white and black striped body, hinged doors, imit. rubber tires, mud guard, chauffeur, runs ahead or in circles. Each in box, ⅙ doz. in pkg.....Doz. **$2.25**

**F5511—Galloping Horses With Riders.** 5 in., hunter and Arab painted in bright colors, dapple and black horses, gallop and rear, erratic natural action. Each in box, asstd. ⅙ doz. in pkg........ .....Doz. **$2.25**

**F5529—Clown, Stubborn Donkey and Cart.** About 8 in. long, patented, donkey goes forward, backs, kicks, decorated cart. Each in box, ¼ doz. in pkg. ............Doz. **$3.60**

**F5525—Grotesque Asst.** 3 styles, aver. ht. 7 in., clown at telephone, barber with customer and nurse bathing baby, amusing action, enameled bright colors. Each in box, asstd. ¼ doz. in pkg.......Doz. **$3.60**

**F5533—Scissors Grinder.** 6½x5¾, litho figure at bench, black enameled metal vise, 2⅜ in. drive wheel with tread, grinder holds scissors against revolving emery wheel which produces sparks, natural action. Each in box, ¼ doz. in pkg. Doz. **$3.90**

**F5754—Road Roller.** 5½x9, black body, yellow and red stripes, 2 open spoke wheels, heavy adjustable roller, runs straight or in circle. Each in box, ¼ doz. in pkg......Doz. **$3.95**

**F5535—Limousine.** 9 in. red body, black & gilt stripes, black mudguards, hinged doors with catch, 2 adjustable lamps, luggage carrier top, imit. rubber tire wheels, spiral spring, chauffeur, runs straight or in circle. Each in box, ¼ doz. in pkg......................Doz. **$4.00**

**F5728—Playful Animals.** Aver. 6¼ in., white woolly plush cat with ball between paw, brown felt covered dachshund with large decorated red ball, run in circles. Each in box, asstd. ⅙ doz. in pkg. Doz. **$4.10**

**F5538—Lehmann's "Zigzag."** Car with two 5 in. wheels, passenger at wheel, 1 at brake, erratic action. Each in box, ¼ doz. in pkg. Doz **$4.15**

## EDUCATED ANIMALS.

*The two most life like and amusing mechanical toys 1914 has produced. Bring quick sales and good profits.*

F5523

F5530

**F5523—Trick Dog.** 6¼ in., black & white bull terrior, turns somersault, extra strong spring. Each in box, ¼ doz. in pkg. Doz. **$3.50**

**F5530—Educated Duck.** 8½ in., enameled in 8 colors, extra strong spring, long action, special device, when placed on table finds its way around edges without falling off. Each in box, ¼ doz. in pkg. Doz. **$3.75**

## IMPORTED MECHANICAL TOYS—

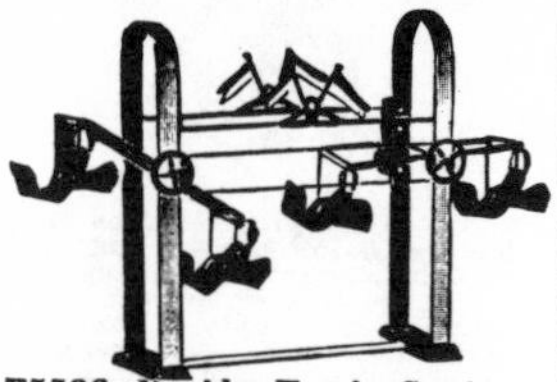

**F5536—Double Ferris Swing.** 13⅛x8½, bright colors, double revolving swings with passengers. Each in box, ¼ doz. in pkg. Doz. **$4.25**

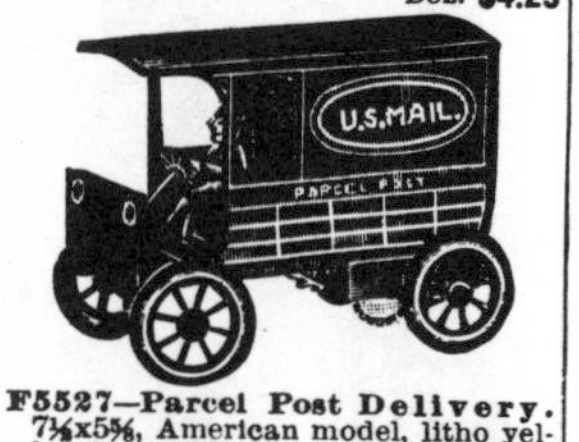

**F5527—Parcel Post Delivery.** 7⅛x5⅝, American model, litho yellow body, black top, double hinged doors with lock at back, open spoke wheels, heavy spiral springs, chauffeur. Each in box, ¼ doz. in pkg. Doz. **$4.25**

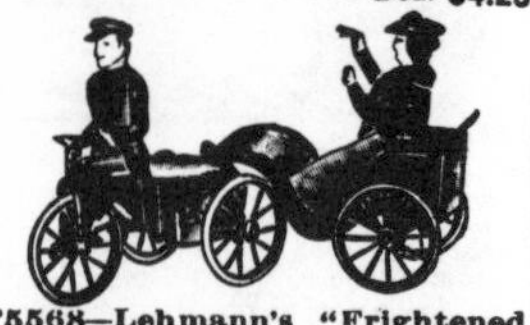

**F5568—Lehmann's "Frightened Bride."** Length 9 in., groom on motor cycle, bride in basket trailer, eccentric action, bride jumps up and down waving handkerchief. Each in box, ¼ doz. in pkg. Doz. **$4.25**

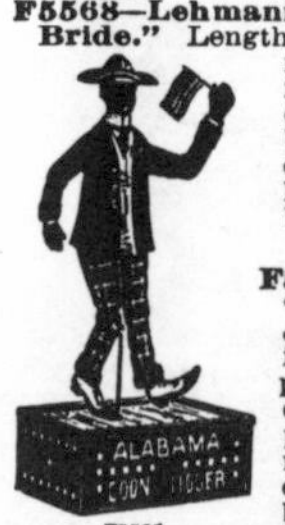

F5531

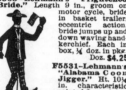

**F5531-Lehmann's "Alabama Coon Jigger."** Ht. 10¼ in. characteristic painted figure, jointed limbs, 4⅝x3¾ platform, lever for regulating speed dances, plantation breakdown. Each in box, ¼ doz. in pkg...... Doz. **$4.25**

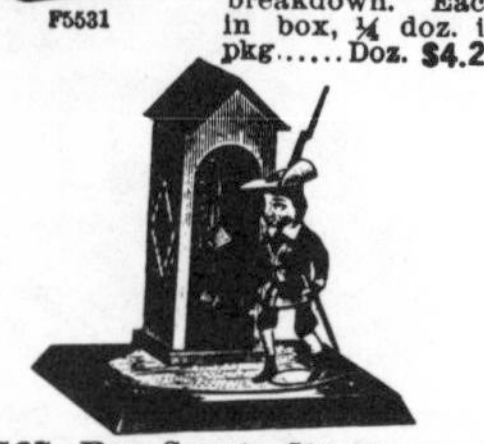

**F5567—Boy Scout.** 5⅜x4¾ guard house, beveled grass effect base, scout with gun and sword marches back and forth continually, bright colors. Each in box, ¼ doz. in pkg. Doz. **$4.25**

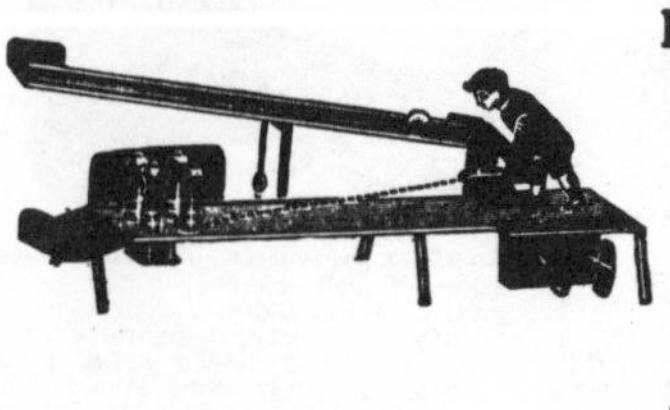

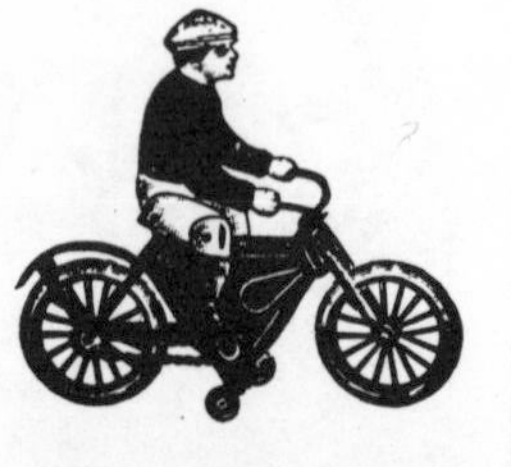

**F5524—Motorcycle with rider.** 8½ in., exact copy of motor cycle, chain gear, imit. rubber tires, brightly painted, extra strong spring, wound by attached key, rider pedals, **long action**, rides in large and small circles, figure "8" etc. Each in box, ¼ doz. in pkg. Doz. **$4.00**

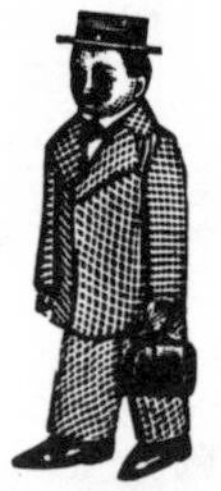

**F3636—Dude Salesman.** 8¾ in., gray and black cloth suit, soft collar, shirt and vest, with suit case, when wound struts around comically. Each in box, ¼ doz. in pkg. Doz. **$4.40**

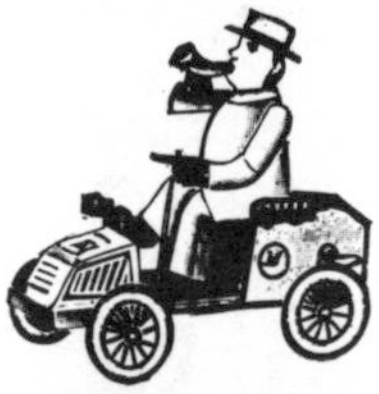

**F5542—Lehmann's Auto.** 6⅝x6¾, white with red trim, imit. rubber tire wheels, 2 gilt metal dashboard lanterns, chauffeur blows gilt horn, steers and changes course. Each in box, ¼ doz. in pkg. ....... Doz. **$4.50**

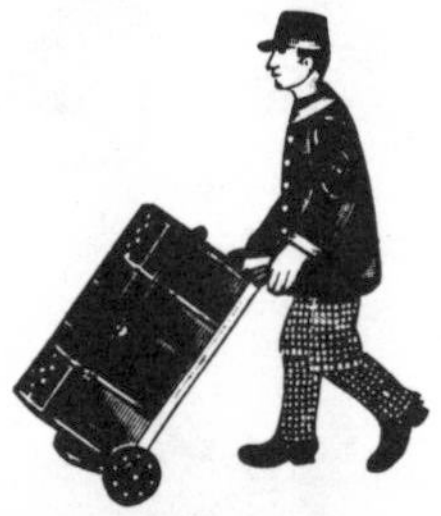

**F5543—Lehmann's "Adams' Expressman."** 8 in., expressman with hand truck and removable hinged trunk, brightly painted, walks naturally pushing truck. Each in box, ¼ doz. in pkg........ Doz. **$4.50**

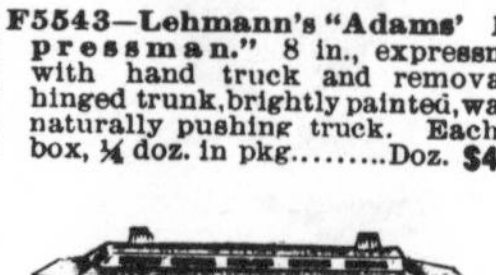

**F5566—Lehmann's "Vineta" Monorail Car.** Easily operated, nothing to get out of order. 9⅜x5, blue & red litho, glass effect windows, 2 red ventilators, 2 wheels, long action. Each in box, ¼ doz. in pkg........................ Doz. **$4.50**

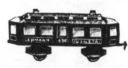

**F5546—"Bowling Boy."** *Runs 5 minutes.* 13¼ in. footed alley, 4 turned wood pins which automatically right themselves, ball rolls into 10¼ in. runway returning to player, fine action. Each in box. ⅙ doz. in pkg. Doz. **$8.25**

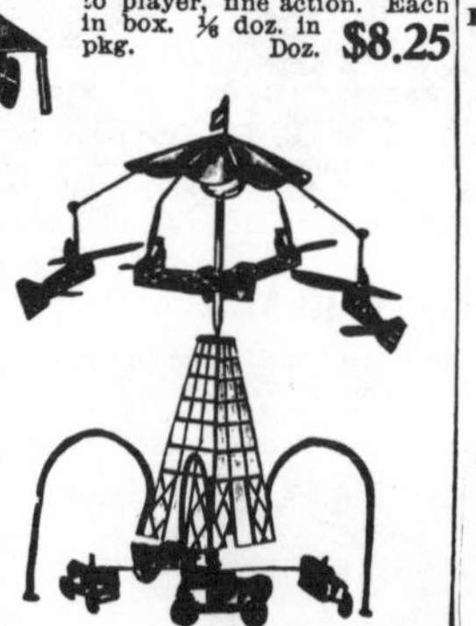

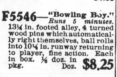

**F5547—County Fair Tower.** Ht. 15⅛ in., 4 autos run in circle through gilt arches, revolving canopy top with 4 pendent airships, enameled in bright colors and gilt, extra heavy spring. ⅙ doz. in box. Doz. **$8.40**

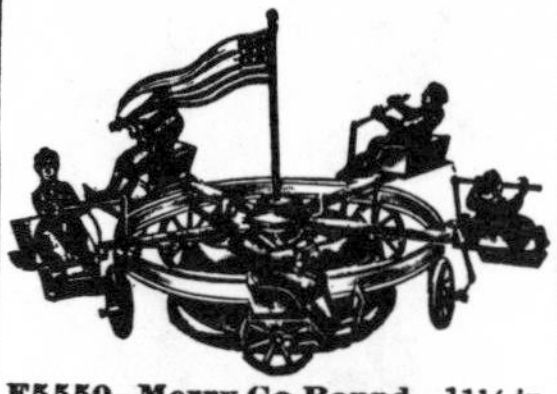

**F5550—Merry Go Round.** 11⅛ in. circum., ht. 6⅛ in., painted bright colors, metal base, 5 figures in cars work back and forth, operating levers. ⅙ doz. in box.... Doz. **$9.00**

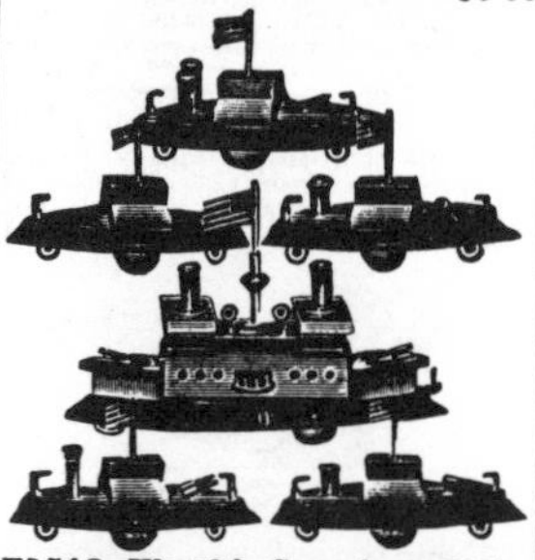

**F5548—Warship Squadron.** 8¾ in. large warship with powerful spring, five 5⅛ in. gun boats, litho in colors, 7 asstd. wire attachments for connecting, run straight or in circle. ⅙ doz. in spaced box with diagrams. Doz. **$9.50**

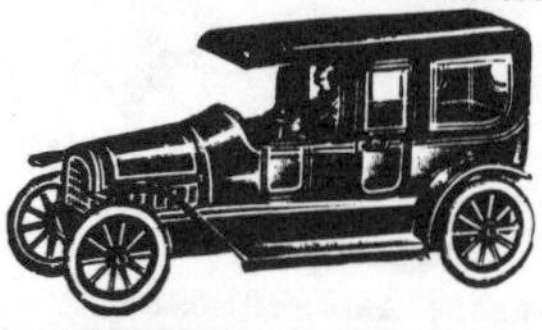

**F5551—Touring Car.** 13¾ in., maroon enameled body, black stripes, top and mud guard, handled hinged doors, open spoke imit. rubber tire wheels, chauffeur, ¾ in. heavy clock spring, runs straight or in circle. 1 in box.................. EACH, **80c**

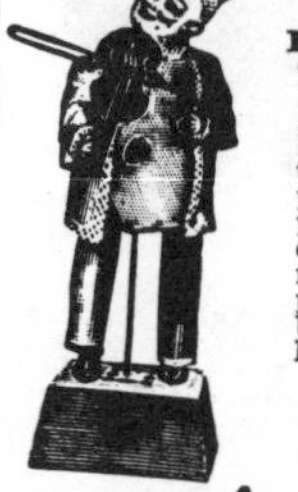

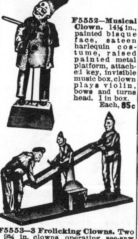

**F5552—Musical Clown.** 14⅛ in., painted bisque face, sateen harlequin costume, raised painted metal platform, attached key, invisible music box, clown plays violin, bows and turns head. 1 in box. Each, **85c**

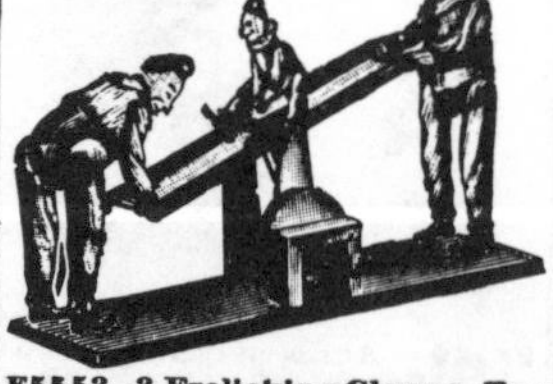

**F5553—3 Frolicking Clowns.** Two 9⅝ in. clowns operating see-saw with juvenile clown on 4-wheel wagon, continuous music, 15⅝x4⅝ bevel platform, bright enameled. 1 in box.................... Each, **95c**

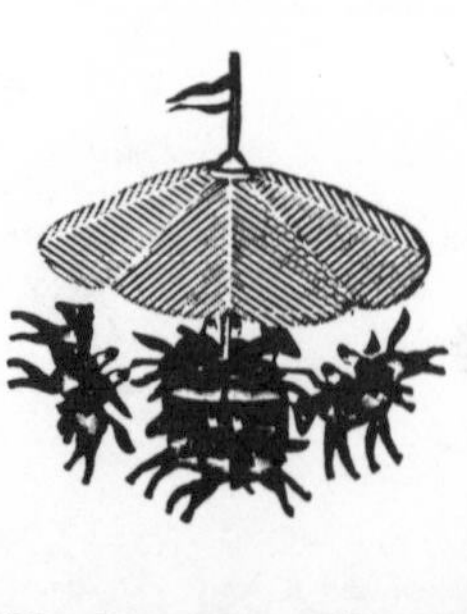

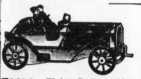

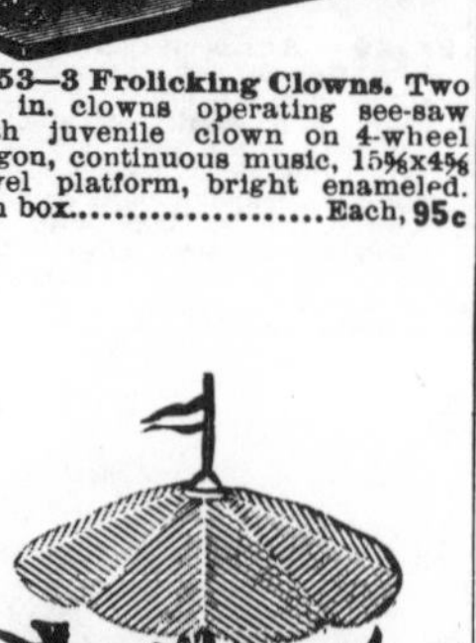

**F5554—American Merry-Go-Round.** Ht. 13¾ in., eight 5⅛ in. brown and white galloping horses with boy riders, red & white striped cloth canopy with American flag, continuous music, excellent action. 1 in box....... ......... Each, **$1.50**

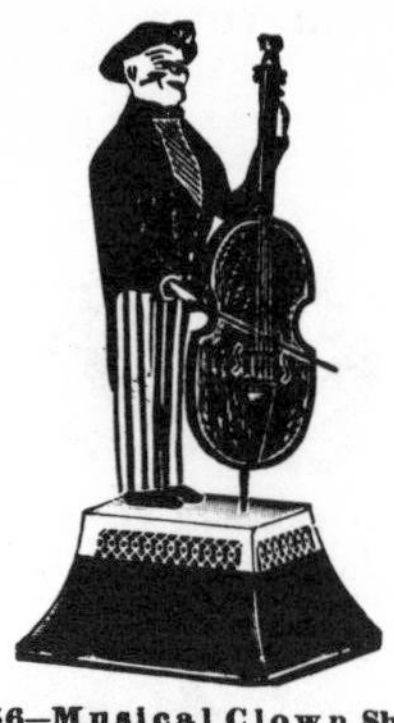

**F5556—Musical Clown Showpiece.** Ht. 17⅛ in., painted features, blue & white striped trousers, 4 button green satin vest, red felt coat and hat with pompons, 11⅛ in. bass viol, on gilt striped red & white platform, extra heavy spring, when wound plays viol, 16 note musical attachment. 1 in box. Each, **$1.85**

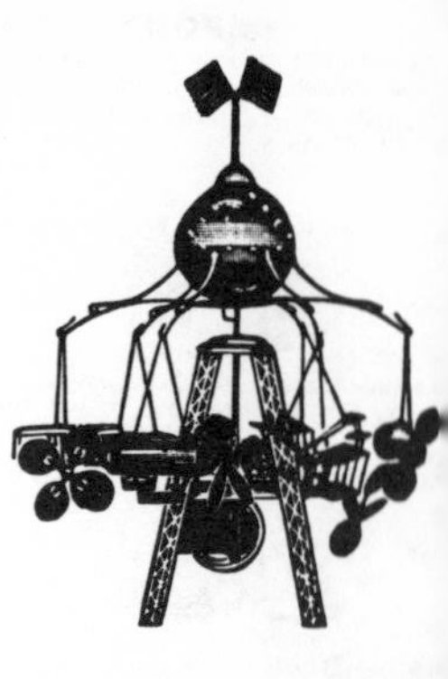

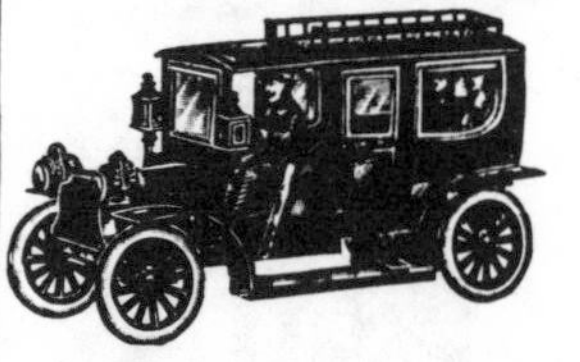

**F5557—Mechanical Airship Sho[w]piece.** Runs an hour, ht. 20 [...] colored metal tower, large revolvi[ng] red, white and blue ball, 3 dir[ig]ibles and aeroplanes, each with p[ro]peller and passenger, ball revolv[es] balloons and airships fly arou[nd] tower. 1 in box........ Each, **$2.**

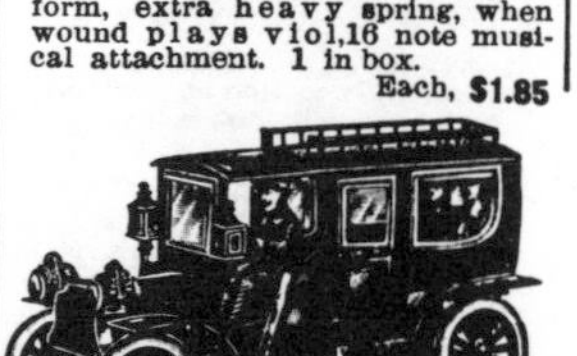

**F5559—Palace Touring Ca[r].** Length 16 in., ht. 9, limousine bod[y] dk. green with black, maroon & lig[ht] stripes, bevel glass windows, hing[ed] doors, 3 nkld. lamps, 3 passenge[rs] and chauffeur, rubber tire whee[ls] runs straight or in circle, brake a[nd] reversing levers, extra stro[ng] spring. 1 in box...... ..Each, **$2.**

## GUARANTEED DOMESTIC MECHANICAL TOYS.

Fine enameled steel, guaranteed springs, wound by cranks or attached keys, extra long speedy action, front wheels turn, run straight or in circle, each with chauffeur.

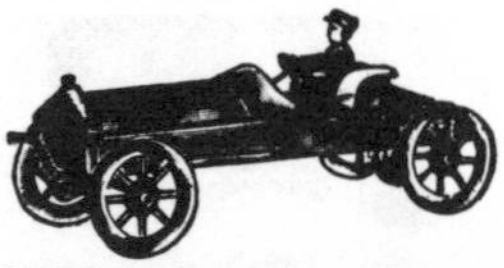

**F2053—Racing Auto.** 9¼ in., red body, yellow wheels, gilt trim, spiral spring. Each in box, ¼ doz. in pkg. Doz. **$4.10**

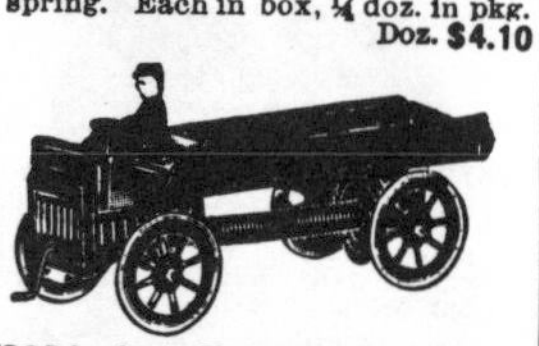

**F2054—Auto Express.** 9½ in., blue body, yellow wheels, gilt trim, spiral spring. Each in box, ¼ doz. in pkg. Doz. **$4 10**

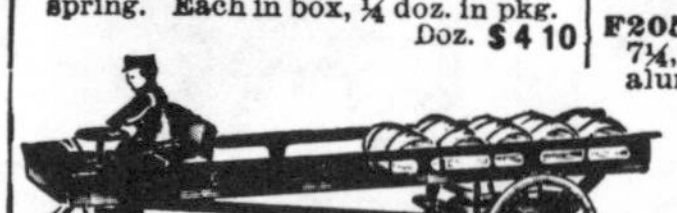

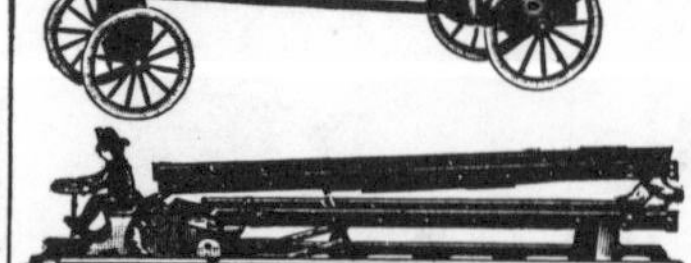

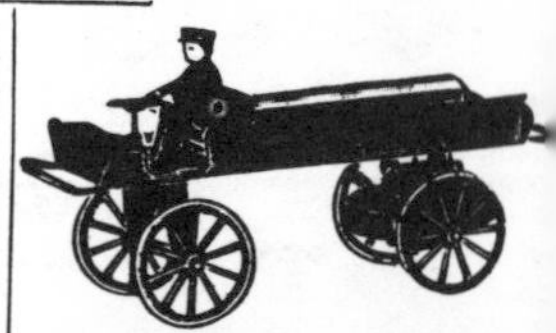

**F2056—Reversible Auto Truc[k].** 11⅛ in., red body, **rubber tire** ye[l]low wheels, rubber covered bump[ers], rear wheels on pivot, reverse[s] automatically on bumping into a[n] object, clock spring. ⅙ doz. in bo[x]. Doz. **$8.9**

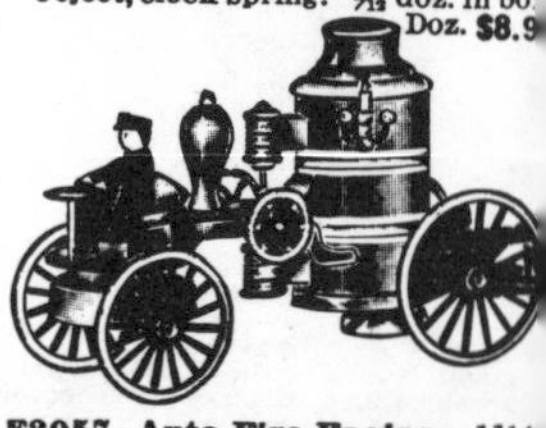

**F2057—Auto Fire Engine.** 11¼ 7¼, yellow body, gilt boiler and trim aluminum stripes, **rubber tire** re[d] wheels, automatic gong, clock spring. 1 in box. EACH, **$1.15**

**F2055—Loaded Auto Dray.** 15 in., blue enameled, red an[d] gilt trim, **rubber tire wheel[s]**, clock spring, lever actio[n] brake to rear wheels, 5 turn[ed] wood barrels. ⅙ doz. i[n] box. ..................Doz. **$8.7**

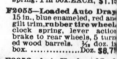

**F2058—Auto Hook and Ladder.** 18⅛ in., white body, re[d] stripes and **rubber tire** wheels, rubber covered bum[per]. Two 9 in. ladders, 27¼ in. extension ladder automat[ic]ally raises when aut[o] bumps into any object, cloc[k] spring. 1 in box. EACH, **$1.25**

## EXTRA LONG ACTION Guaranteed Domestic Mechanical Toys.

Run on entirely new principle, guaranteed spiral springs on steel shaft adjusted to series of cogs, run 150 ft. with 1 winding. Fine enameled steel, each with chauffeur, front wheels turn.

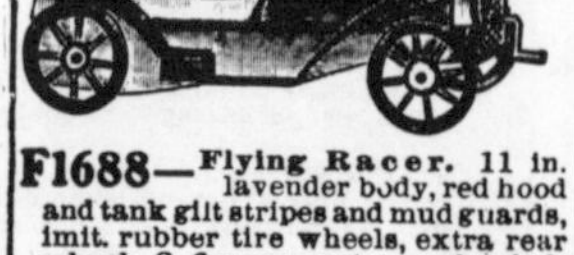

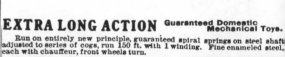

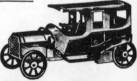

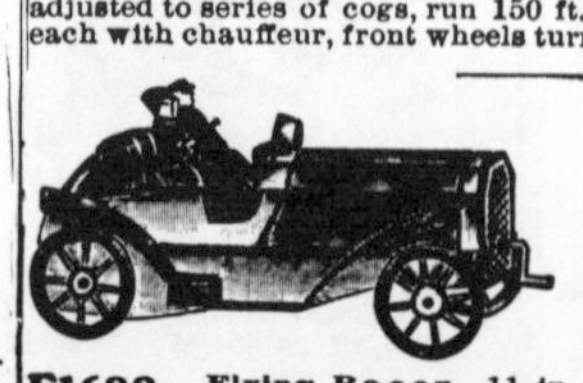

**F1688—Flying Racer.** 11 in. lavender body, red hood and tank gilt stripes and mud guards, imit. rubber tire wheels, extra rear wheel, 2 figures, auto crank winding. ⅙ doz. in box. Doz. **$8.00**

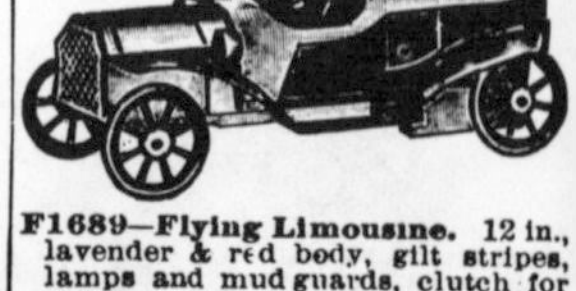

**F1689—Flying Limousine.** 12 in., lavender & red body, gilt stripes, lamps and mud guards, clutch for starting and stopping, wound by pushing along floor. 1 in box. Each, **89c**

## MECHANICAL LOCOMOTIVES.

Good models, attached keys, clock springs, cog wheels.

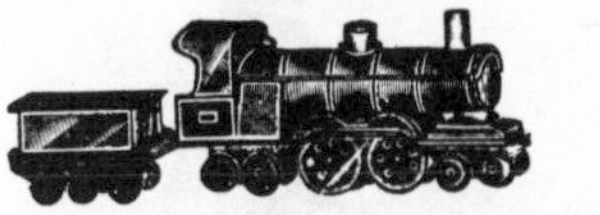

**F5575**—10 in., green litho, striped, 8 wheel double truck, foot rail, hand bar. ½ doz. in box. .................. Doz. **$2.25**

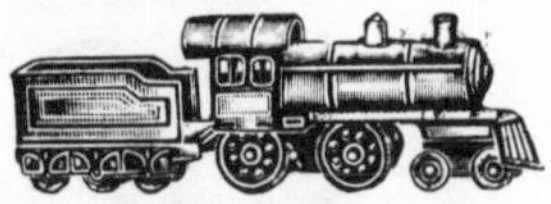

**F5576**—13 in., litho red & black, 8 wheel double truck, foot rail, hand bar, nickeled dome. Each in box, ¼ doz. in pkg. Doz. **$4.50**

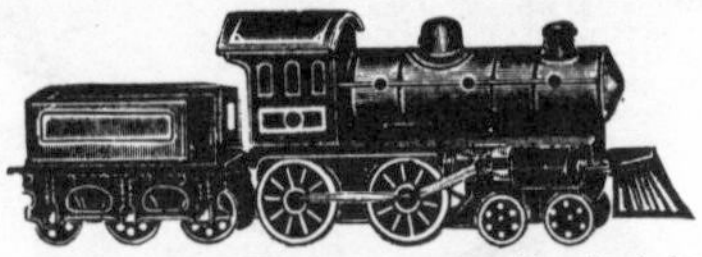

**F5577**—22 in., red & black litho, black & gilt stripes, 10 wheel locomotive, triple drive, brassed hand rail, bell, 6 wheel tender with imit. coal. Will not unwind until placed on floor. 1/12 doz. in box. ................................................ Doz. **$8.40**

**F5578**—19½ in., litho green & black, 10 wheel double truck, foot rail, hand bar, nickeled dome, gong and piston rod, extension platform, cow-catcher, **automatic stop.** 1 in box. EACH, **98c**

## BRIDGES.

Papier mache on wood frame, realistic molded scenic effect, sanded roadbed. Each in box.

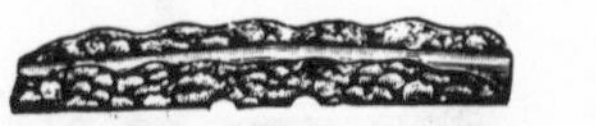

**F1813**—Length 21 in., width 4⅛. For mechanical or small imported electric trains. ½ doz. in pkg. .................. Doz. **$1.75**

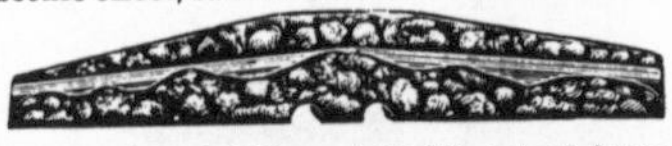

**F1814**—Length 28 in., width 6¾, raised fancy sides and rail. For Nos. F1652, F1653, F1656, F1657 and F1674, electrical trains and F1651 and F1680 trolleys.....Doz. **$6.25**

## TUNNELS.

Papier mache, realistic molded scenic effect. Each in box.

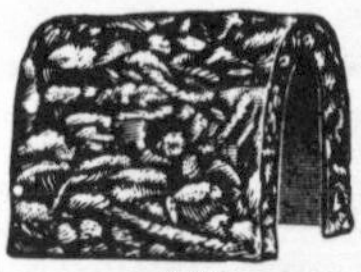

F1815

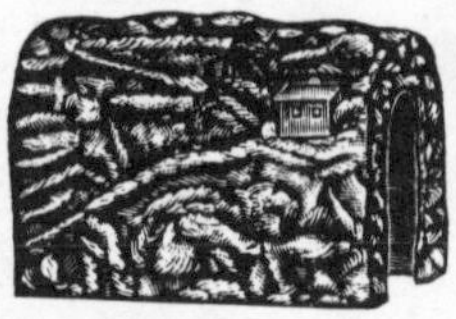

F1810

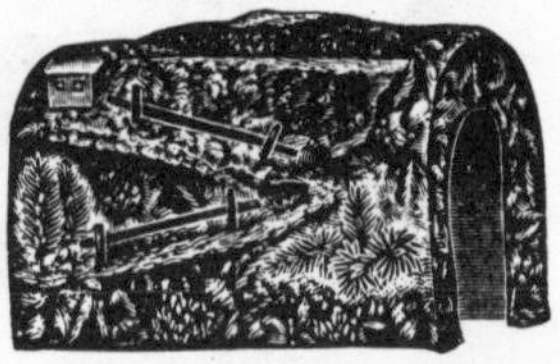

F1811

**F1815**—Length 8¾ in., width 7¾, ht. 7. For small imported and domestic mechanical and electrical trains. ½ doz. in pkg. .................................... Doz. **$1.75**

**F1810**—Length 12 in., width 8⅛, ht. 8, mountain effect, pathway and house. For mechanical, imported electric and Nos. F1652, F1653, and F1656. Large size Electrical trains. ¼ doz. in pkg. ............................................ Doz. **$3.25**

**F1811**—Length 14⅛ in., width 10, ht. 9, moss covered, fenced path and trees one side, house on each side. For Nos. F1657 and F1674 Electrical trains, and F1651 and F1680 trolleys. Doz. **$6.50**

## MECHANICAL TRAINS—With Tracks

Brightly litho and striped unless stated, passenger coaches with sliding tops, good springs, attached keys, all with speed regulators except F5580. **Each in spaced box.**

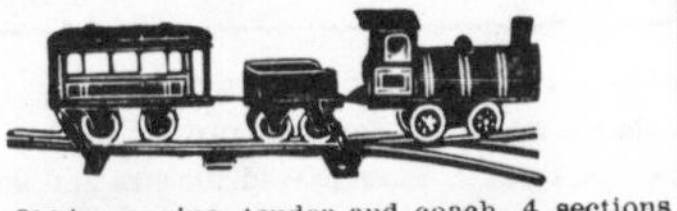

**F5580**—9¼ in., engine, tender and coach, 4 sections track 36 in. circum. ½ doz. in pkg....... Doz. **$1.95**

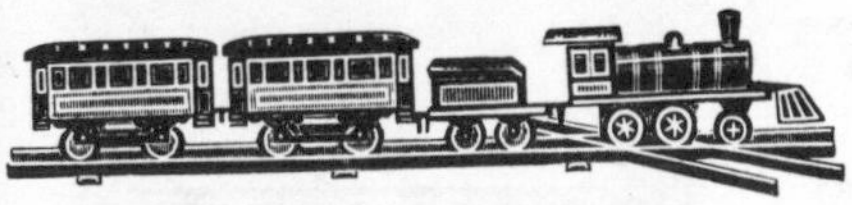

**F5581**—21¾ in., engine with lever stop, tender and 2 coaches; 4 sections track with automatic stop forming circle 60 in. circum. ¼ doz. in pkg... Doz. **$4.50**

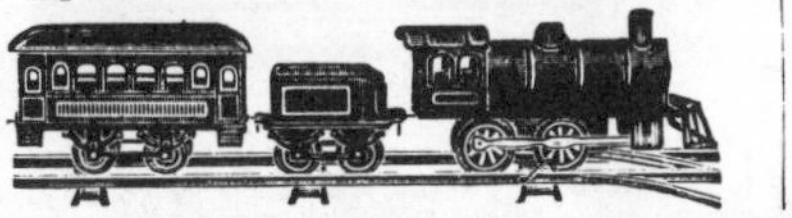

**F5582**—18 in., engine with piston rod, automatic brake, continuous whistle, tender and coach, 4 sections track with automatic stop forming circle 54 in. circum. ⅙ doz. in pkg. .................. Doz. **$7.00**

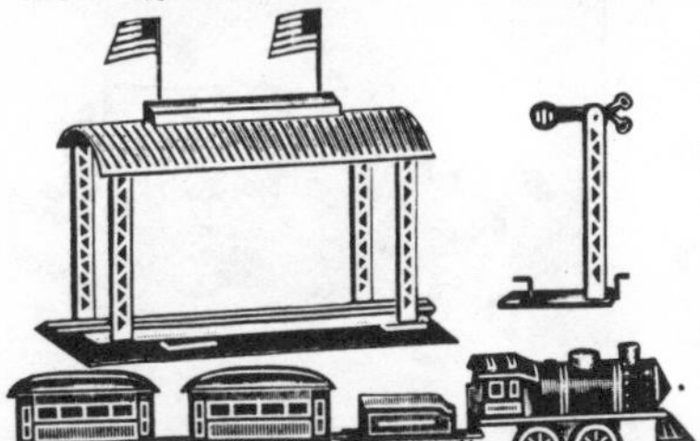

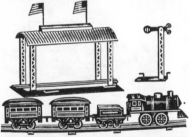

**F5585—Outfit.** 18 in. 4 piece train, locomotive, tender and 2 open window coaches, 5 sections track, 10x6¾ litho metal shed with 2 flags, block system signal with automatic stops............ Doz. **$8.50**

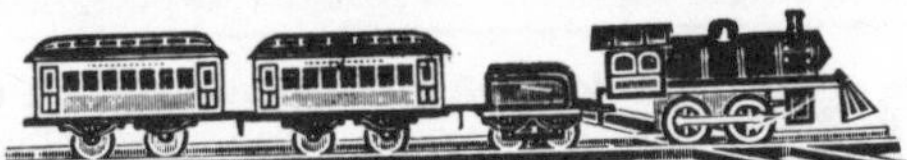

**F5583**—24 in., engine with piston rod and brake, tender and 2 open window coaches, 8 sections track and crosspiece, forms figure eight. Doz. **$9.00**

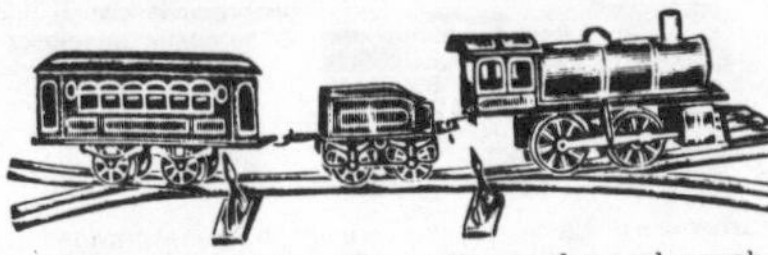

**F5586**—19⅛ in., locomotive with brake, tender and coach, 5 sections track, 2 switches, forms circle 18 in. diam. inside 25 in. oval, train runs in circle and oval.... .............................. EACH, **85c**

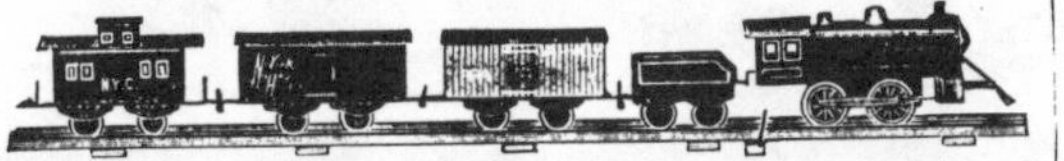

**F5589**—31¾ in. American model 5 piece train, engine with piston rod, automatic brake and rail guard, tender, 2 sliding door freight cars and caboose, black, maroon and gray enameled, yellow stripes; 8 sections oval track with spring button auto matic stop............ EACH, **$1.40**

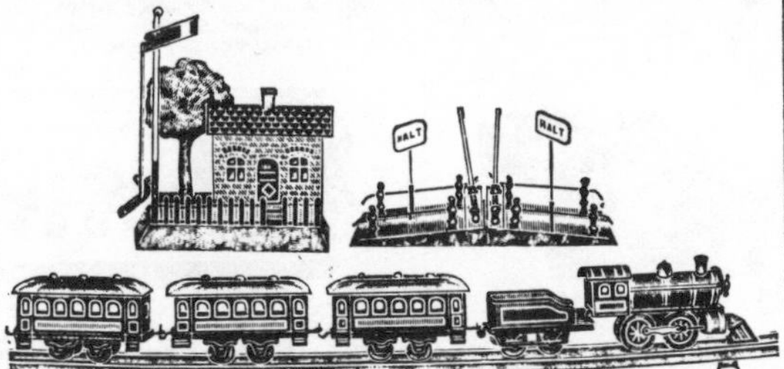

**F5590**—32 in. 5 piece train, locomotive with piston rod, tender and 3 coaches, bright enameled and striped; 8 sections track with automatic stop, hinged door metal station on base with fence and tree, danger signal, 2 road crossings with guards and warning posts...EACH, **$1.80**

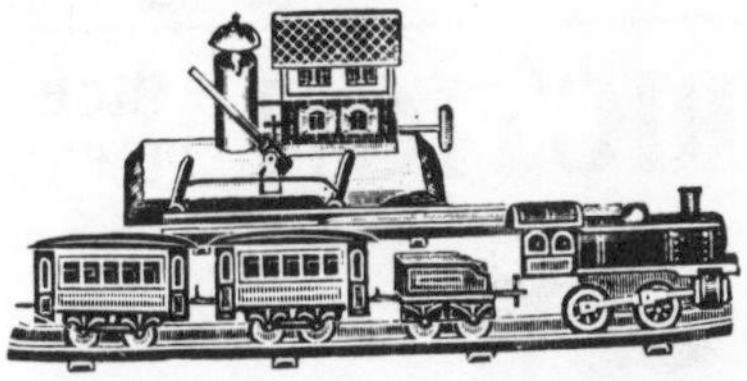

**F5592**—17 in. 4 piece train, engine, tender and 2 coaches, 10 sections track oval 44½ in. diam., litho station, bell tower and road gate on raised platform, station with spring and attached key, bell rings, gate closes and automatic switch is set which stops train and releases it............ EACH, **$2.00**

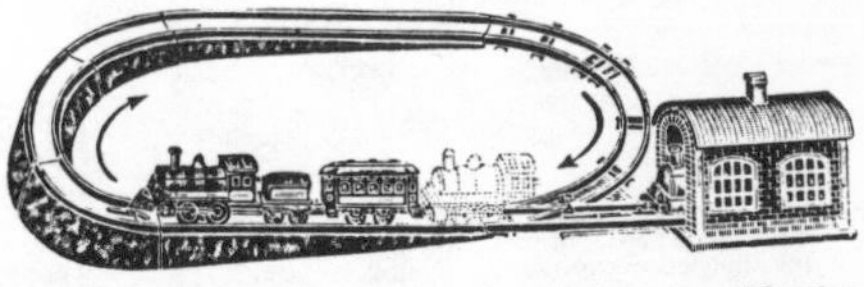

**F5594—Incline Railway.** 17½ in. train, engine with piston rod, tender and coach, 62 in. inclined track, painted metal embankment and shed, **extra engine** is automatically released from shed and pushes train up incline, returns and repeats action............................ EACH, **$3.60**

### SEPARATE TRACKS.

Length 10½ in., each with pin, standard "O" gauge, for all mechanical trains except F5580.

F5617—Straight. 1 doz. pcs. in pkg. ............ Doz. pcs. $0 40
F5618—Curved. 1 " " " " ............ " " 40

"ERECTOR" STEEL CONSTRUCTION TOY

Every boy likes to make things. Here's the ideal toy for young builders. Sells on sight to parents. See the index.

## "OVERLAND FLYER" MECHANICAL TRAINS

**With Tracks.** Best reproduction of the large trains ever made. Improved locomotive with brass gears and bearings. All steel coaches, facsimile of leading flyers with names. Latest track improvements. Absolutely the best in the American market. **Each in spaced box with guarantee.** Latest model black enamel castiron engines, gold painted stripes, heavy open spoke steel driving wheels, black enamel tender with imitation coal except F1800, facsimile litho steel coaches with ventilator tops, adjustable couplings, tracks graded so trains will not jump or turn over.

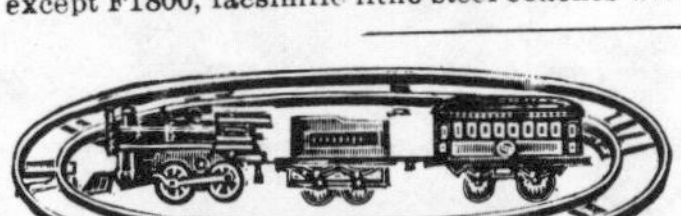

F1800

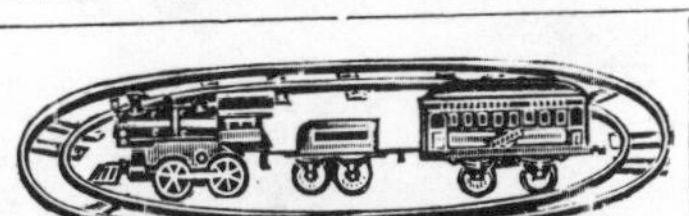

F1801

**F1800—3 pc.** 6¾ in. locomotive, tender and coach, full length 17 in., 8 sections of track form circle, 83 in. circum. ¼ doz. in pkg. .............................. Doz. **$8.00**

**F1801—3 pc.** 5¾ in. locomotive with spring action brake and driving rods, large tender, full length 17¾ in., 10 sections of track form oval, circum. 104 in.... .... ..........Each, **95c**

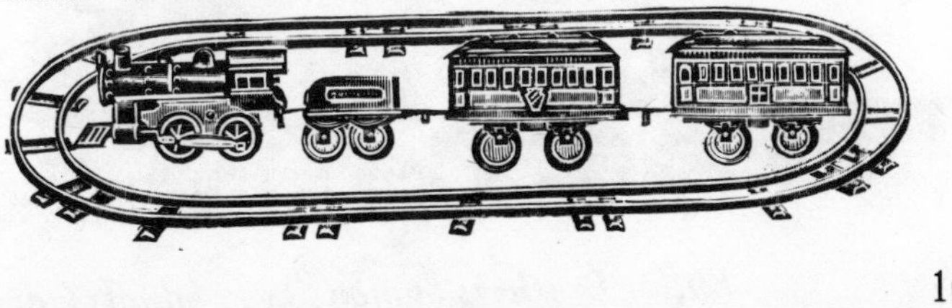

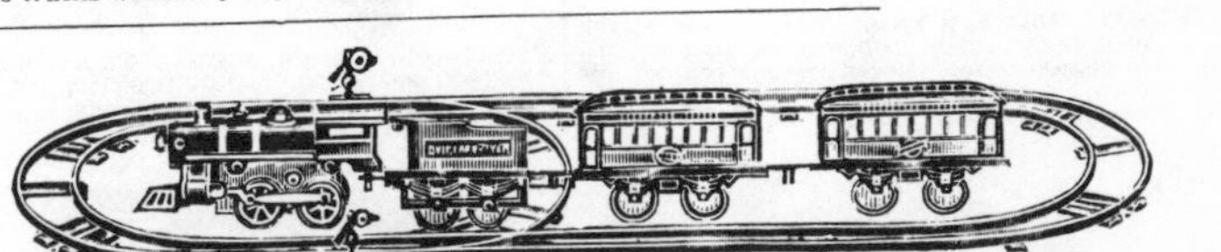

**F1804—4 pc.** 7¼ in. locomotive with spring action and driving rods, large tender, two 6½ in. coaches, full length 27½ in., 14 sections track and 2 double switches form circle within oval, trains run in circle and oval, controlled by switches, complete length of track 14¾ ft. Each, **$1.85**

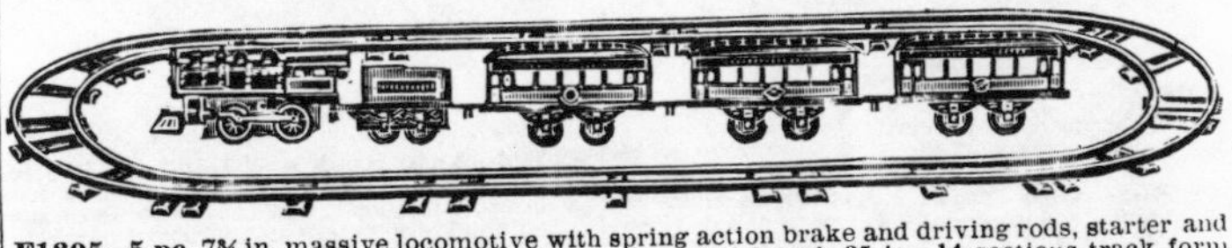

**F1805—5 pc.** 7¾ in. massive locomotive with spring action brake and driving rods, starter and automatic stopper, tender, three 6½ in. coaches, full length 35 in., 14 sections track form oval 145 in. circum. automatic red & white signal stop, train started by releasing brake. Each, **$2.10**

## MECHANICAL BOATS.

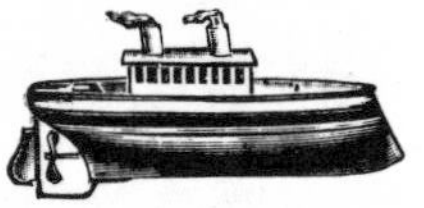

**F5562—Revenue Cutter.** 7¼ in., red body, black and white stripes, open window cabin, 2 smoke stacks, imit. rapid fire gun, single screw propeller, adjustable rudder, imit. smoke, key. ⅙ doz. in pkg.........Doz. **$2.25**

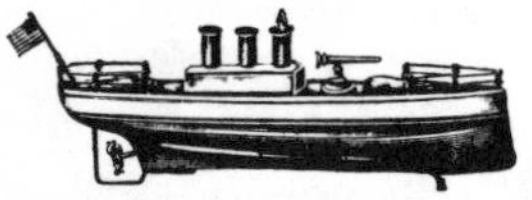

**F5563—Pleasure Yacht.** 10 in., red and white, 3 gilt smoke stacks, cannon, rails, single screw, rudder, flag. Each in box, ¼ doz. in pkg....................Doz. **$4.50**

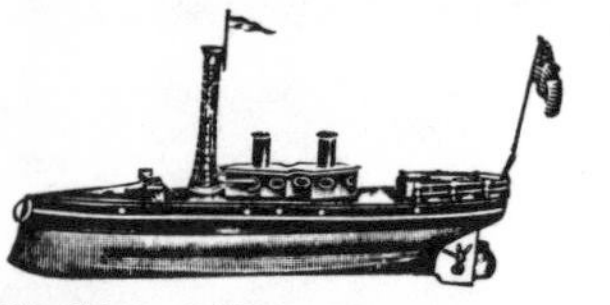

**F5564—Man o' War.** 17¼ in., brown and black body, maroon stripes, gray deck, bridge, fighting tower, 4 guns, 2 in turret, 2 funnels, silvered rail, flag, single screw propeller, adjustable rudder. 1/12 doz. in box. Doz. **$8.40**

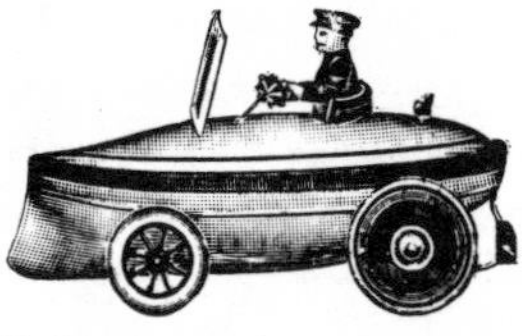

**F5565—Combination Floor or Water Auto Boat.** 9⅛ in., cream and green body, gilt and colored stripes, on 4 wheels, 2 with paddles, runs on floor or in water. 1 in box.......................EACH, **85c**

## MECHANICAL BOAT OUTFIT.

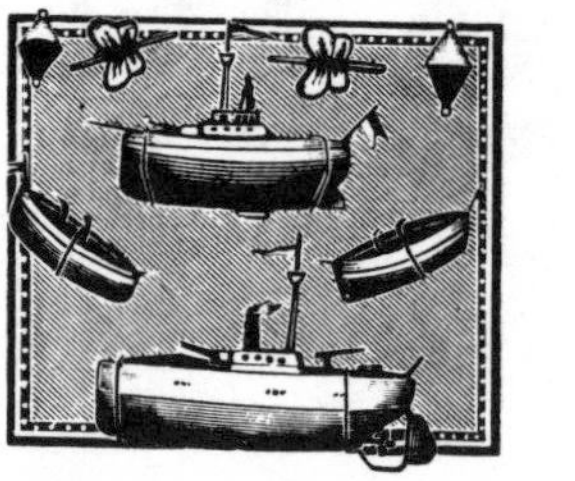

**F5560—8 pcs.,** 7¼ in. gunboat, single screw and rudder, 5¼ in. gunboat, two 3 in. launches, magnetic bows, 2 butterfly magnets, bright colors. 1 set in 11x9⅛ box..Doz. sets, **$8.40**

## BING'S CELEBRATED MECHANICAL TOYS

Guaranteed springs, excellent action.

*Extra strong guaranteed springs, with keys.*

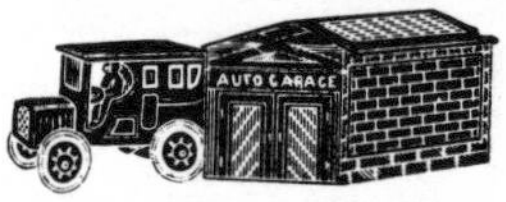


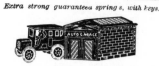

**F5748—Garage with Auto.** 5⅛x3⅜, limousine model, litho bright colors, open spoke imit. rubber tire metal wheels, adjustable front wheels, runs straight or in circle, with chauffeur; 6¼x3¾ extension roof litho cardboard garage, hinged front with knob. Each set in box, ⅙ doz. sets in pkg. Doz. sets, **$2.25**

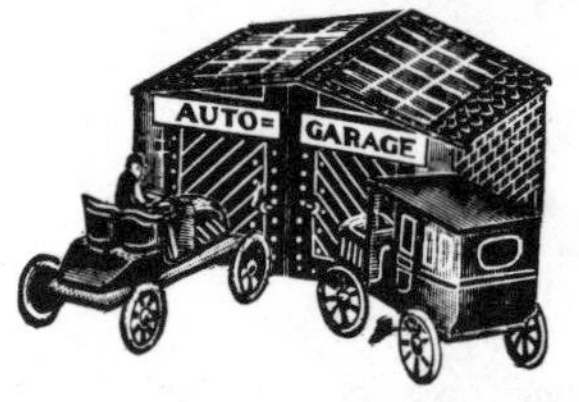


**F5750—Garage with 2 Autos.** 5⅛x3⅜, limousine, 5⅛x3⅜ racer, bright litho and striped, imit rubber tire open spoke metal wheels, adjustable front wheels, run straight or in circle, with chauffeurs; 6⅛x7⅛ double litho cardboard garage, extension roof, 2 metal pull hinged doors. Each set in box, ¼ doz. sets in pkg. ........Doz. sets, **$4.25**

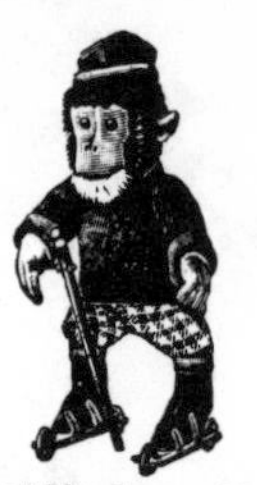

**F5724—Dressed Monkey.** 8 in.. soft plush head and jointed limbs, button eyes, felt hands and feet, colored felt costume, 2 wheel metal skates, backward, forward and military motions, regulated by stick. 1 in box.............. .. ...... ......Each. **75c**

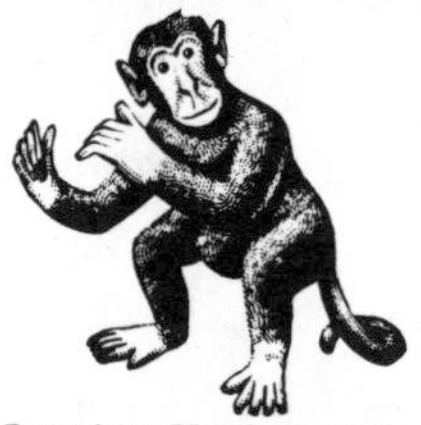

**F5726—Jumping Monkey.** 8 in., brown plush covered, jointed limbs, felt hands and feet, turning head, modeled face, glass eyes, jumps in grotesque manner. 1 in box. Each, **80c**

# FRICTION HIGH POWER TOYS

**Better than ever!** Embodying all the latest improvements, patent double friction power, heavy cast iron fly-wheel, guaranteed against getting out of order, easily operated, baked brilliant enamel finish, will not peel or rub off, unsurpassed for **size** and **durability.**

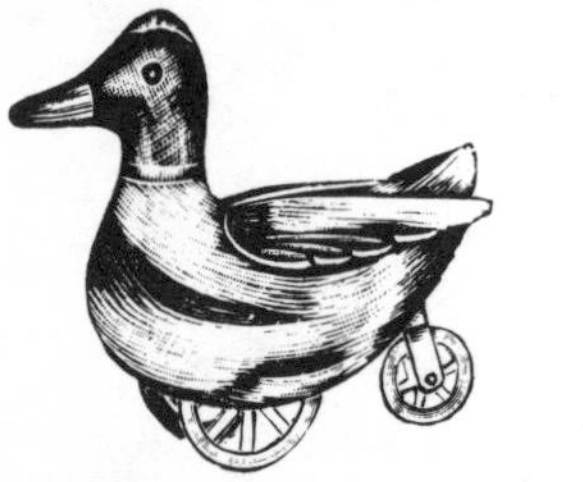

**F1693—Tricky Duck.** 9x7¾, natural colors, steering wheel, runs straight or in circle, unexpected maneuvers. 1/12 doz. in box. Doz. **$3.95**

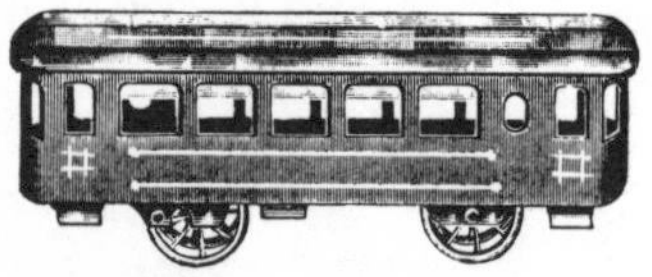

**F1698—Pullman Car.** For F1704 locomotive, **without power,** green enameled, red roof and steps, gilt stripes and wheels. 1 in box. ⅙ doz. in pkg...............Doz. **$4.00**

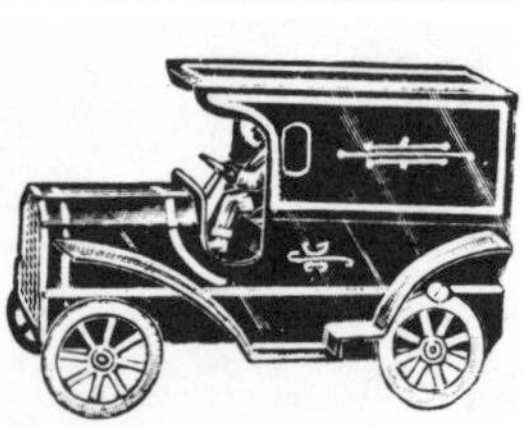

**F1692—Delivery Van.** 7x11, yellow enameled body, green top, white stripes, gilt mud-guards and wheels, driver; front wheels turn, runs straight or in circle. 1/12 doz. in box..........................................Doz. **$4.25**

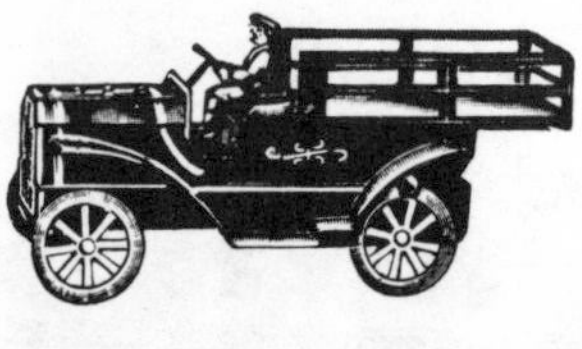

**F1695—Auto Truck.** 13¾x6, green enameled body, red open-side carrier, gilt stripes, wheels and mud-guard, driver; front wheels turn, runs straight or in circle. 1/12 doz. in box.................................................Doz. **$4.25**

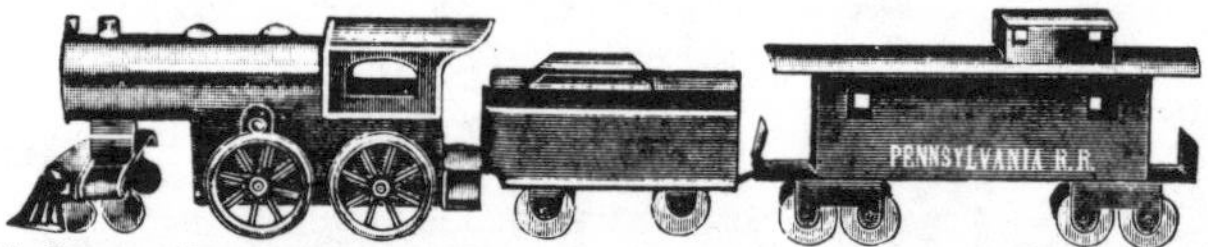


**F1687—Locomotive, Tender and Caboose.** Length 30 in., red enameled engine and tender, gilt trim, white striped, red caboose blue roof. 1/12 doz. in box......................Doz. **$7.50**

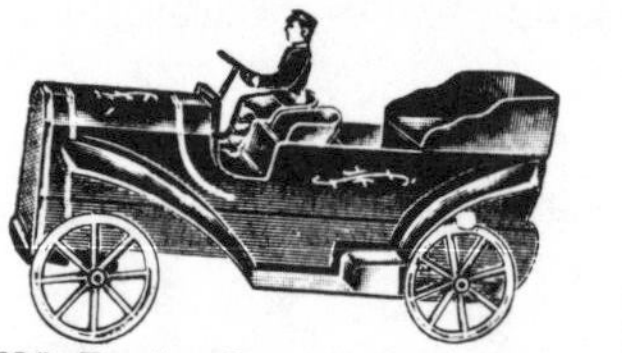

**F1696—Touring Car.** 11 in., lavender enameled body, gilt wheels, mud-guards and stripes, imit. rubber tires, chauffeur, front wheels turn, runs straight or in circle. 1/12 doz. in box. ....... ... .......Doz. **$4.25**

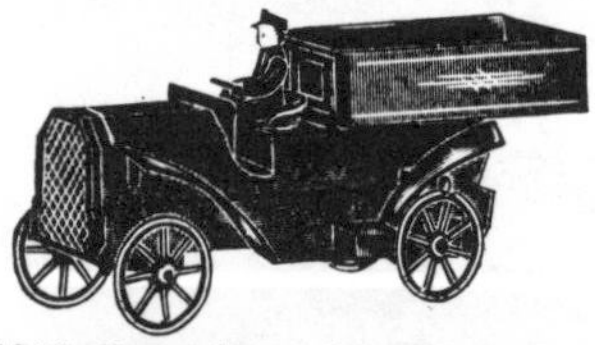

**F1700—Dump-Auto.** 13⅛x6, bright red & green enameled body, gilt wheels, mudguards and stripes, driver; weighted carrier dumps when released by lever. 1/12 doz. in box..............................Doz. **$4.25**

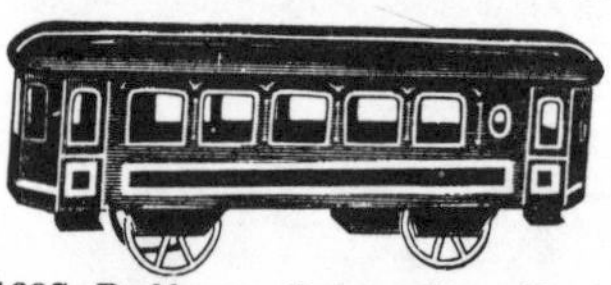

**F1697—Pullman Palace Car.** 15¼ in., green enameled, yellow interior, red roof and steps, gilt stripes and wheels, coupling for attaching to locomotive. 1/12 doz. in box. Doz. **$4.25**

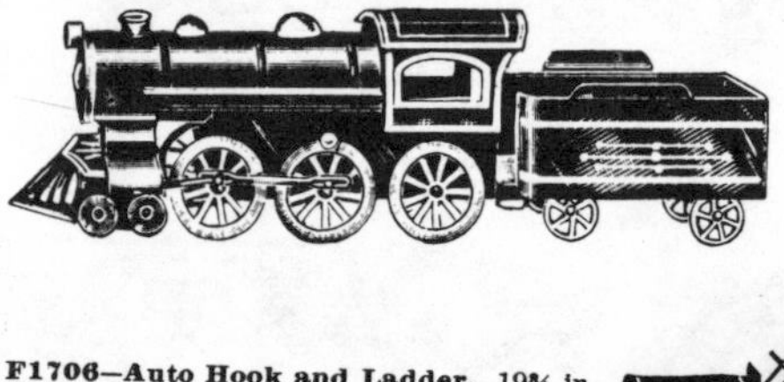

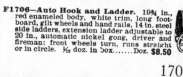

**F1706—Auto Hook and Ladder.** 19¾ in., red enameled body, white trim, long footboard, gilt wheels and hand rails, 14 in. steel side ladders, extension ladder adjustable to 20 in., automatic nickel gong, driver and fireman; front wheels turn, runs straight or in circle. 1/12 doz. in box.......Doz. **$8.50**

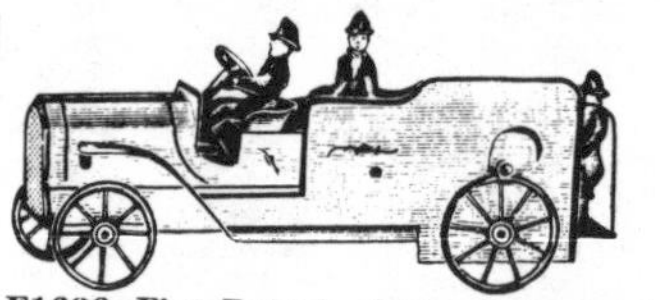

**F1686—Fire Patrol.** 15 in., red enameled green running board, white stripes, gilt wheels and hand rails, imit. chemical tank, 2 firemen and driver; front wheels turn, runs straight or in circle. 1/12 doz. in box. Doz. **$7.75**

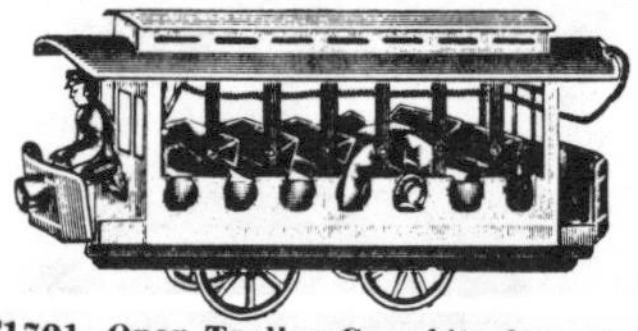

**F1701—Open Trolley Car.** 14¼x6¾, yellow & green enameled body and roof, green footboards, reversible seats, gilt wheels and hand-rails, **bell and cord,** motorman. 1/12 doz. in box........................Doz. **$7.75**

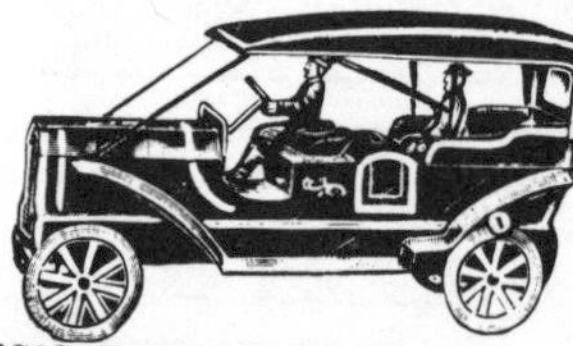

**F1707—Touring Car.** 13¾x7⅛, lavender enameled, top with **steel** supports, gilt stripes, wheels and mud-guards, chauffeur and passenger riveted to seats; front wheels turn, runs straight or in circle. 1/12 doz. in box..........Doz. **$8.50**

**F1704—Locomotive and Tender.** 24 in., red enameled, green cab, gilt trim and stripes, moving piston rods, **all gilt movable wheels.** 1/12 doz. in box. Doz. **$8.50**

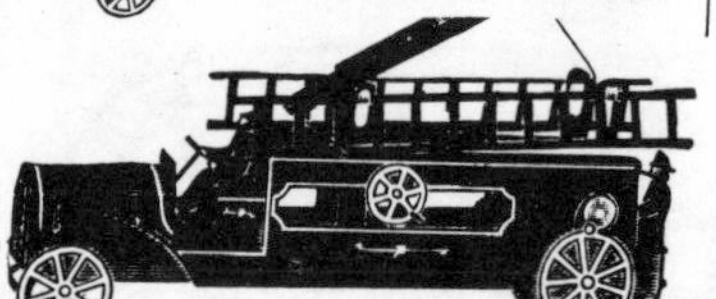

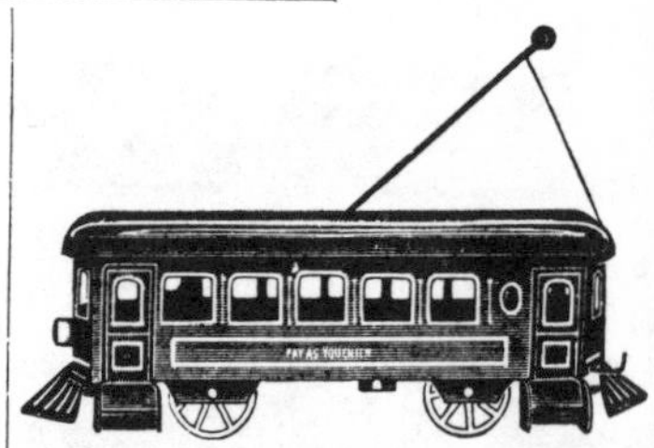


**F1703—"Pay-as-you-enter" Trolley.** 18 in., yellow enameled, green roof, green & white stripes, gilt wheels, lever rings bell and opens doors. 1/12 doz. in box. Doz. **$8.50**

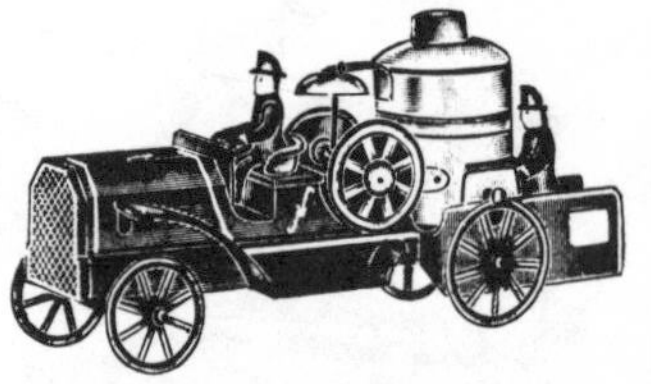

**F1710—Auto Fire Engine.** 14¾x7½, red enameled truck, green mud-guards, white stripes, aluminum boiler and revolving pump wheels, **automatic bell,** driver and fireman; front wheels turn, runs straight or in circle. 1/12 doz. in box.......Doz **$8.50**

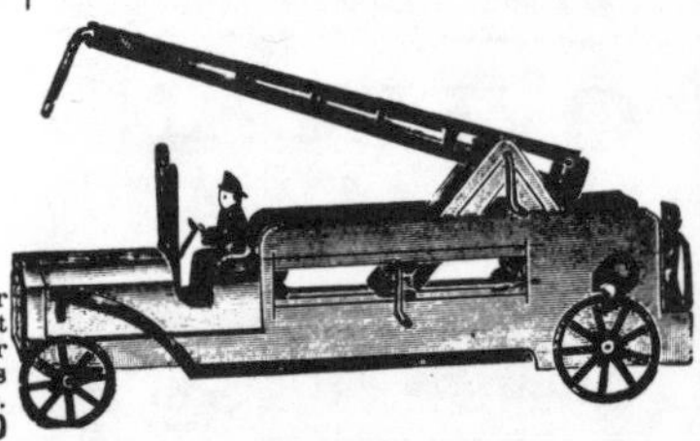

**F1702—Auto Water Tower.** 19⅛ in., green & yellow body, running board, gilt wheels and hand rails, red water tower raised by 2 levers to 28⅛ in., driver and fireman; front wheels turn, runs straight or in circle. 1/12 doz. in box...... .. ... .. .......Doz. **$8.50**

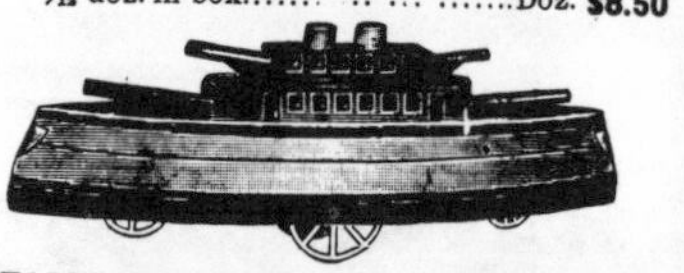

**F1694—Battle-ship.** 15⅛x5⅛, red & gilt striped white enameled hull, orange deck, 4 gilt cannon, on wheels. 1/12 doz. in box. Doz. **$4.25**

## ELECTRICAL ENGINES.

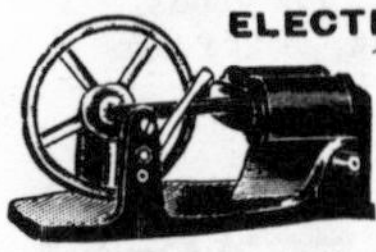

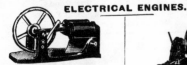

**Horizontal**—Lever controlling forward and reverse speeds, heavy grooved driving wheel, black enameled cast iron base. Each in box. ¼ doz. in pkg.
F1661—4x3 in..........Doz. $4 25
F1662—5½x3½ in.......... " 8 50
F1663—7x4¼ " Extra heavy driving wheels..EACH, 86

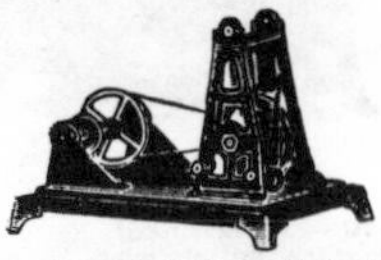

**F1664—Upright.** Base 4x4, ht. 5¾, full nkl. plated steel maroon coils and center of platform yellow striped; reversible, operates with 1 dry battery. 1-12 doz. in box. DOZ. **$8.40**

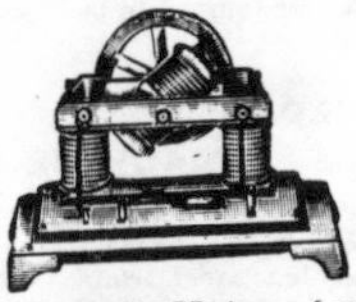

**F1666—Electric Motor.** Laminated armature and fields, hard drawn brass commutator properly insulated, self adjusting brushes, minimum friction, 2¼ in. balance wheel nkl. face, steel shaft with set screw, groove pulley for belting to engine or any light toy, all parts of electrified nickeled steel, maroon enamel iron base with screws, 300 to 2000 revolutions per minute, runs on dry battery. 1 in box..........Each, **75c**

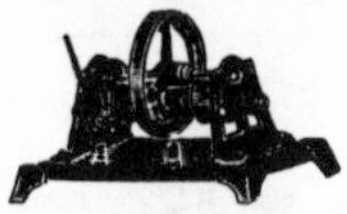

**F1665—Horizontal.** 4½ x 6½, cast iron base and frame, red enamel and gilt finish, reversible, high speed, runs on dry battery. 1 in box. Each, **75c**

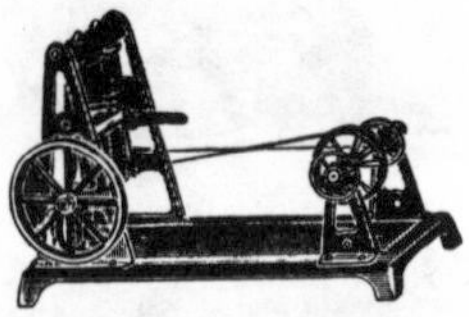

**F1667—Upright.** Base 4x8⅜, ht. 5½, nkl. plated steel, maroon coils and center of platform, yellow striped, reversible, counter shafting, with 3 fly wheels, runs on dry battery. 1 in box..........Each, **98c**

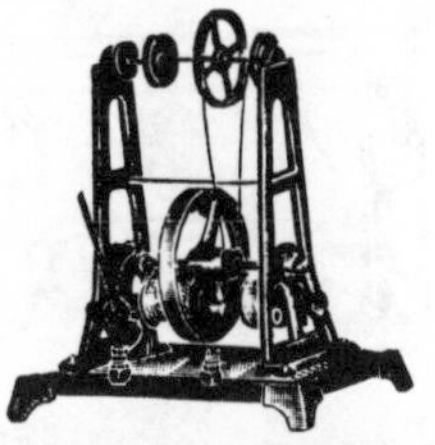

**F1668—Upright.** 4½x6½, cast, iron base and frame, ht. 8½ in., red enamel and gilt finish, reversible shafting with 4 pulleys to connect to toys. 1 in box.......... Each, **$1.35**

## ELECTRICAL SPECIALTIES.

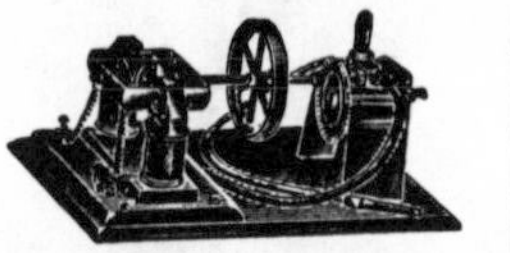

**F1669—Water Pump.** 6x8½, steel base and frame, ht. 3½ in., red enamel and nkl. plated, fly wheel and gearing, 20 in. rubber hose. Perfect in every respect..........Each, **$1.35**

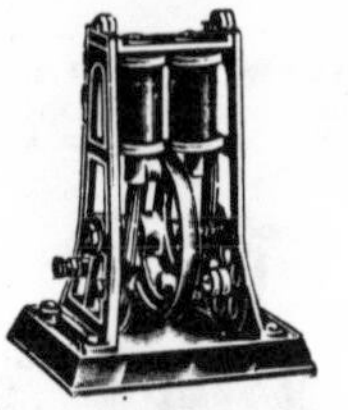

**F1670—Double Upright.** Extra size, cast iron base and frame, aluminum and gold finish base 4x5, ht. 7 in., perfect model, very powerful, 2 speeds forward and reverse. Each, **$1.35**

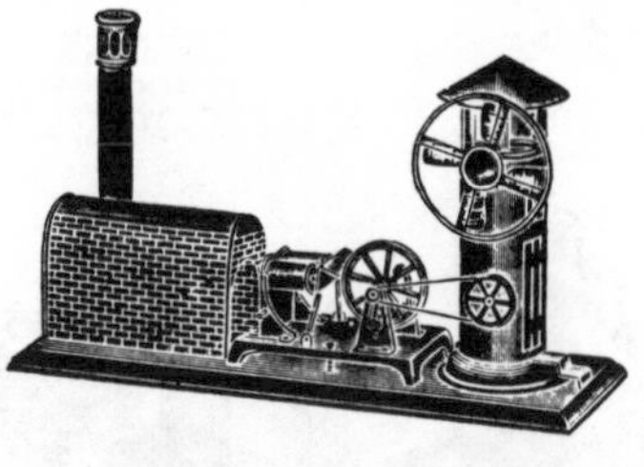

**F1650—Mill Outfit.** Base 18x6½, wood base, ht. 10 in., enameled in colors, metal tower windmill, full nkld. steel engine, red enameled platform, reversible, pulley attachment to mill, metal battery container, gun metal smokestack, runs on 1 dry battery..........Each, **$1.90**

## CURRENT REDUCERS.

**Guaranteed.** For reducing alternating or direct current for the purpose of running electrical trains and toys. 6 ft. mercerized covered insulated flexible cord, swivel connecting plug.

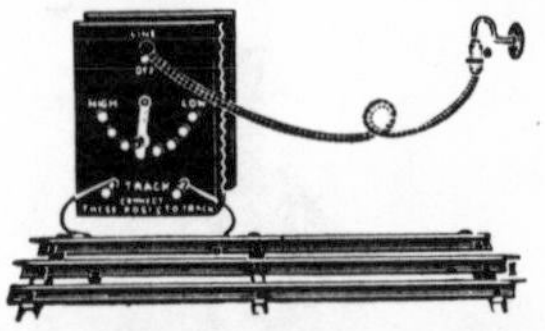

**F1655—Alternating current,** heavy black enameled casting, nickel plated binding posts, copper reducing plates and wire winding. Each, **$3.00**

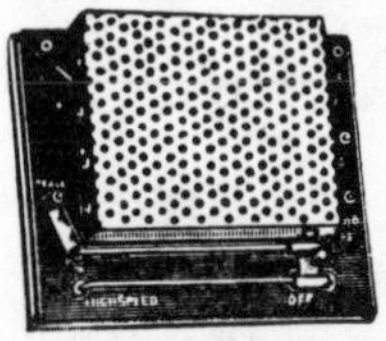

**F1654—Direct current,** 4 porcelain tubes wound with fine resistance wire on slate base 8x8x¾, covered with perforated Russian iron, sliding lever regulates voltage. Each, **$4.00**

PUT ONE OF THESE ELECTRICAL TOYS IN YOUR WINDOW

Nothing will draw a crowd quicker than an electric train or some other electric toy in action.

## IMPORTED ELECTRICAL TRAINS.

Third rail system, run on alternating or direct current, also storage and dry batteries. (For batteries see index). All regulation steam model engines, sliding top cars.

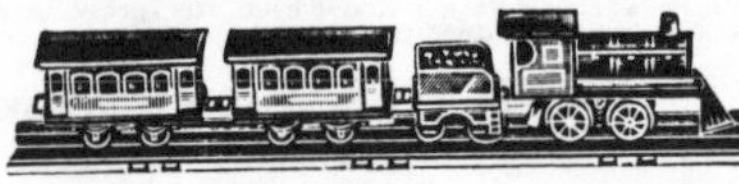

**F5700**—16 in. bright litho engine, tender and two coaches, 53 in. of circular track. 1 in spaced box..........Each **85c**

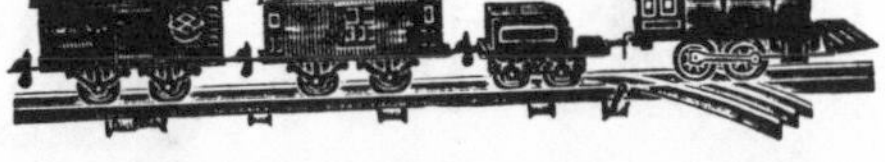

**F5702**—24 in., bright enameled, sheet iron engine with piston rod, **electric headlight**, tender. American model mail and freight cars with sliding doors, patent couplings, 8 sections 3rd rail track, 1 with 2 brass binding posts. 1 in spaced box..........Each, **$2.00**

**American models**—Black enameled cast iron engines, nickeled trimmings and bells, **electric headlights,** piston rods, extra heavy open spoke steamer wheels, powerful tested comb geared motors, fine enameled cars with sliding doors, double truck wheels, patent couplings, track with binding posts and insulated automatic reverse switch. 1 in spaced box.

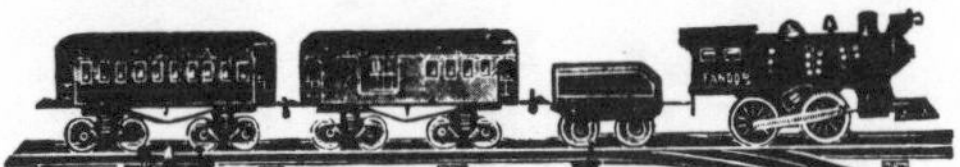

F5704—26¾ in., engine, tender coach and baggage car, 8 sections track..........Each, **$3.50**

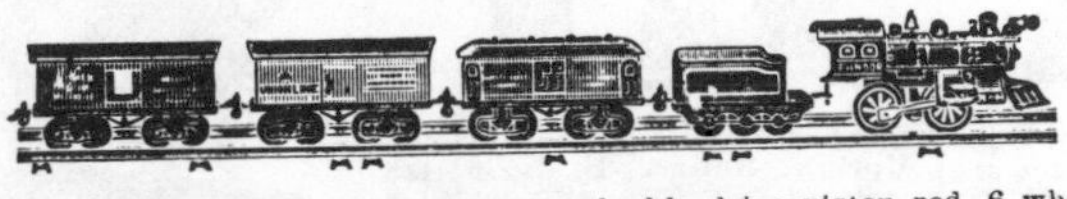

F5706—36 in., engine with automatic reverse, double drive piston rod, 6 wheel tender, baggage and 2 box cars, 12 sections track..........Each, **$4.75**

## SEPARATE TRACK.

**F5619—3rd Rail Straight.** 10½ in. for electric trains F5700, F5702, F5704 and F5706. ½ doz. pcs. in box..........Doz. pcs. **80c**

## ELECTRICAL TROLLEYS—With Wired Headlights.

12x6 in. up-to-date vestibule cars, red enamel body, yellow window frames, hinged doors and ventilator tops, transparent imit. glass windows, black steps, nickeled trucks, run on 3 dry batteries or reduced alternate or direct currents.

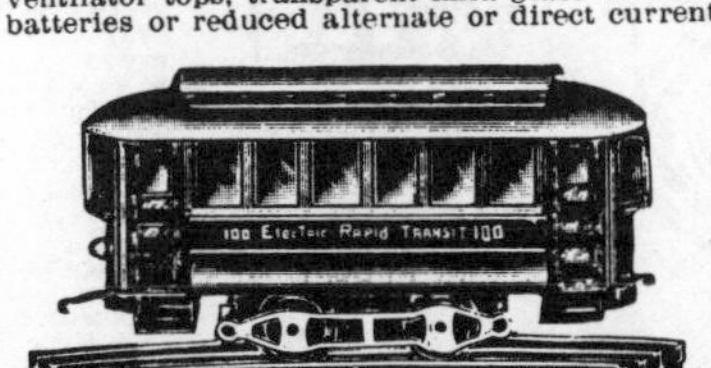


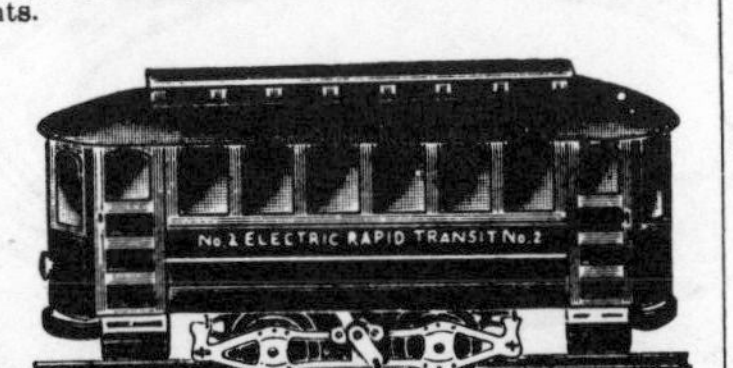


**F1651**—10½ ft. circular track.... Each, **$3.50** | **F1680 — With lever switches,** 14¼ ft.

## LARGE SIZE AMERICAN ELECTRICAL TRAINS.

Finest goods manufactured. Every one guaranteed. Perfect reproductions of the large electric railway trains.

Heavy steel throughout, baked enameled, massive locomotives with bells and electric headlights, nickel trim, powerful motors, cars with free turning, heavy steel double trucks, patent couplings, brass contact points.

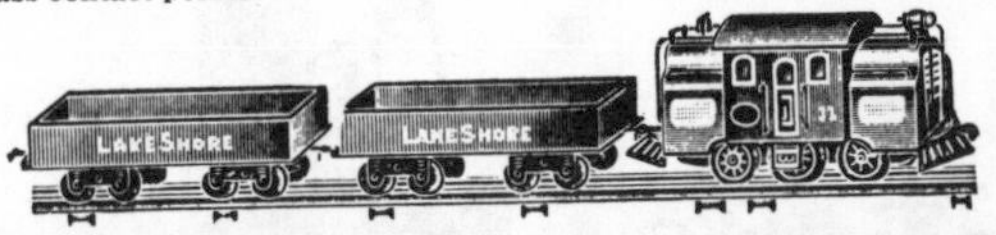


**F1652—Freight.** 11x3¾ in. locomotive, gilt hand rails and steps, green enameled body, red trim, 2 red enamel stenciled 9x3½ in. gondola cars, full length 31 in. circular track 138 in. circum. 1 in spaced box..........Each, **$5.00**

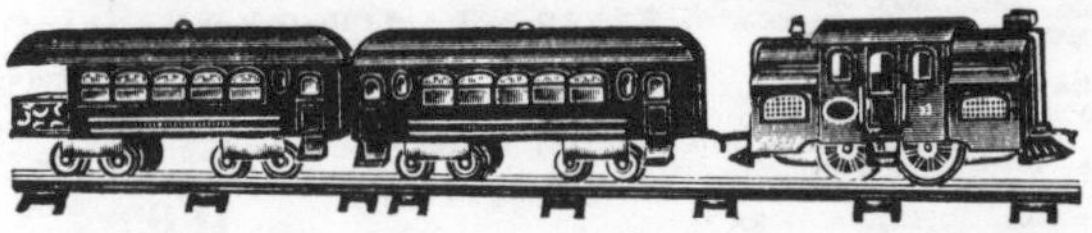

**F1653** "Leader." 12 in. locomotive, gilt perforated ventilators, hand rails and steps, nickeled bell and **electric headlight,** royal blue enameled. two 11 in. Pullman cars with seats, removable tops, imit. stained glass windows, gilt hand rails, steps and observation platform, nickeled free turning double trucks, patent couplings, full length 34½, circular track 10½ ft. circum. **A De Luxe outfit** in spaced box. Each, **$6.50**

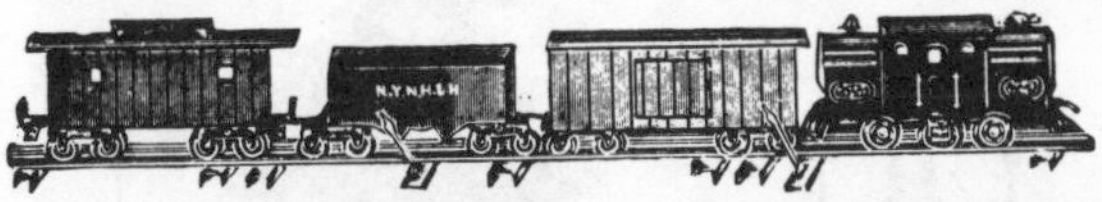

**F1656—Freight.** 11x3¾ in. locomotive, green enamel body, red trim, hand rails and steps, 9 in. maroon enameled dump ballast car, 9½ in. yellow box car, with sliding door, 10 in. red caboose, full length 42½ in. oval track 16 ft. circum. 1 in spaced box..........Each, **$7.00**

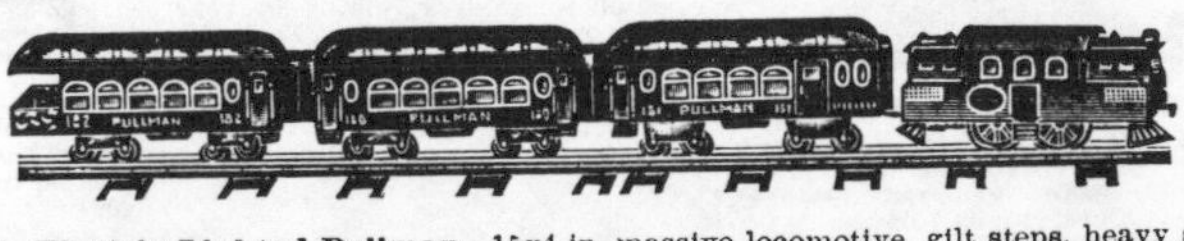

**F1657—Electric Lighted Pullman.** 15x4 in. massive locomotive, gilt steps, heavy spoked drivers, cow catcher, **reversing lever,** maroon enameled combination Pullman and baggage, Pullman and observation cars, air tanks, imit. stained glass ventilators and window tops, sliding doors, red enamel seats, gilt steps, observation platform and trim, **each car electric lighted,** full length 55½ in., oval track circum. 16 ft. 1 in spaced box..........Each, **$14.00**

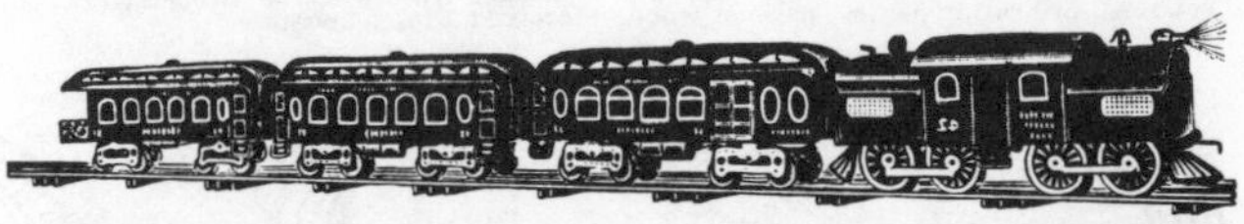

**F1674—"Perfection."** 15½x5 in. massive black enamel locomotive, spoked driving wheels with connecting rods, sliding door, red enamel trim and cow catcher, 16¼ in. yellow enameled Pullman, Pullman & baggage and observation cars with seats, imit. stained glass windows and ventilators, swinging doors, gilt hand rails, steps and observation platform, **each car electric lighted,** full length 68 in., oval track, circum. about 21 ft..........Each, **$20.00**

## EXTRA TRACKS FOR LARGE SIZE ELECTRICAL TRAINS.

14 in. lengths.

**F1646**—Straight. ½ doz. in box.......... Doz. **$1.44**
**F1647**—Curved. ½ " " " .......... " **1.44**

# STEAM TOYS

### "WEEDENS" AMERICAN

We save you money on these big selling goods. Exact imitations of the big engines. All fitted with genuine brass boilers and
Russian fire boxes. Mechanically perfect and easy to operate.

## FAMOUS "WEEDEN" STEAM ENGINES.

Exact models of the big engines, mechanically perfect, easily operated.
Russia steel fire boxes, **brass boilers** each with alcohol lamp, wrench and
extra washers.

**F1938—Upright.** Ht. 9 in., 1¾ in. wheel, base 3¼x3¼. Nickel plated boilers, balance wheels with 2 color molded edges, steel bases. ¼ doz. in pkg............Doz. **$2.10**

**F1941—Up-right.** Ht. 12 in., sheet iron fire box, black enameled stairs and railing, water gauge, whistle, 8x5 hardwood base. ½ doz. in box. Doz. **$9.00**

**F1939—Upright.** Ht. 11 in., 2¼ in. wheel, base 4½x4½, whistle, water gauge. Nickel plated boilers, balance wheels with 2 color molded edges, steel bases. ¼ doz. in pkg. Doz. **$3.98**

**F1944—Steam Engine and Force Pump.** Ht. 8¾ in., safety valves, whistle and water gauge, red enameled nickel trim single action pump, suction and nozzled leading hose, 6x8½ steel base. 1 in box. EACH, **$1.00**

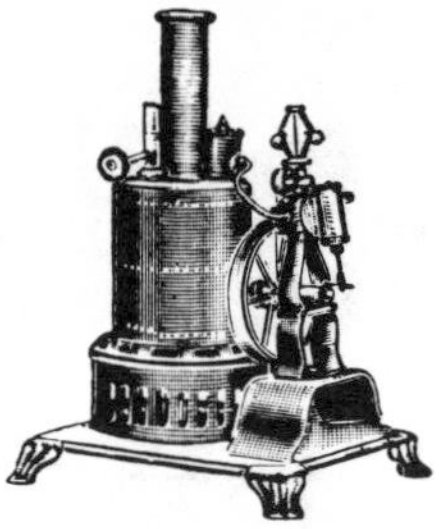

**F1945 — Reversible.** Ht. 8½ in., nickel plated boiler, throttle stops or reverses action, whistle, water glass, governor balls, 4½x6 red enameled & nickeled base. 1 in box. Each, **$1.25**

**F1946— Horizontal.** 6 in. boiler, cylinder steam chest and slide rest cast in one pc., eccentric slide and safety valves, water gauge, whistle, nickel trim, 3-burner lamp, 6x6 red enameled cast iron base. 1 in box. Each, **$2.10**

**F1948—Horizontal Engine with Upright Boiler.** Ht. 12 in., extra large nickel plated boiler, whistle, safety valve, water gauge, eccentric valve engine, 1 pc. cylinder and steam chest, shut-off valve, governor balls, 2 heavy fly-wheels and pulleys, nickel and red enamel trim, 2-burner lamp, 7x10 cast iron base. 1 in box............ Each, **$3.50**

**F1950 — Horizontal.** 10x8x3, 4½ in. brass boiler with blued steel jacket, nickeled engine, 1-pc. cast cylinder head, steam chest and eccentric box, brass steam and water pipes with valve shut-off, safety valve, whistle, water glass, extra heavy fly-wheel, nickel trim, 3-burner lamp. 1 in box. Each.**$4.00**

### "WEEDEN" MACHINE SHOP.

**F1960**—Ht. 7¼, 5x11½, red & white enameled, steel frame, heavy cast base, 3 machines—saw, emery wheel and drill, with shafting and pulleys. 1 in box....................Each, **75c**

### STEAM LAUNCH.

**F1951**—Length 15½ in., red & black enameled hull, gray inside, 3¼ in. brass boiler, spring action cylinder head, steel propeller and shaft, alcohol tank and burner. ½ doz. in box....................Doz. **$8.50**

### SEPARATE MECHANICAL DEVICES.

Attach to any toy steam engine.

**F1957**—3¾x2½, 12 styles, agricultural and mechanical, painted metal, on platforms, attaching wheels. Asstd. 1 doz. in box........Doz. **69c**

**F1958**—4½x3½, 6 styles, drill, grindstone, buzz saw, churn, kneader and mill on platforms, bright colors. Asstd. ¼ doz. in box......Doz. **$1.65**

**F1940—Beam Engine.** Ht. 10¼ in., nickel plated boiler, safety valve, whistle, walking beam with iron supports, turned fly-wheel, shaft with pulley. 9¾ in. hardwood base. ½ doz. in box............Doz. **$8.75**

**F1943—Steam Pile Driver.** *Sold exclusively by us.* Ht. 13 in., safety valve, filler, whistle, water glass, double balance wheel and winding drum, shipper lever, gallows frame. hammer on pulley cord, polished nickel working parts base 6x8½. 1 in box.......Each, **$1.00**

**F1947—Horizontal.** Ht. 8¼ in., nickel plated boiler, 1 pc. cast cylinder and steam chest, eccentric and safety valves, governor balls, whistle, steam pipe with shut-off valve, heavy fly-wheel with 2 pulleys, red enameled and nickel trim, 2 burner lamp. 8¾ x6½ polished cast iron base. 1 in box....................Each, **$2.50**

## ELECTRICAL TOYS.

**F5710—Walking Beam.** 9x6½ bevel base, platform with steps, walking beam, grooved flywheel, bright colors, run by 1 battery. 1 in box....................Each, **85c**

**F5708—Mill.** Ht. 5 in., base 7x6½, litho house, revolving wheel connected to stamper, motor in rear. Runs on 1 battery. 1 in box. Each, **75c**

**F5709—Airship Carousal.** 4½x8 wood base, 7½ in. tower, 3 litho airships, passenger baskets, side propellers, with electric motor, runs on 1 dry battery. 1 in box...Each, **98c**

**F1962—Horizontal Engine with Upright Boiler.** Ht. 7½ in., 4x8 polished steel base with invisible alcohol tank, Russia steel boiler, drawn brass cylinder head and eccentric, extra heavy fly wheel with pulley. 1 in box.......EACH, **$1.25**

**F5571**—9¼x6 metal platform, horizontal boiler, painted and enameled in colors, gilt striped, heavy fly wheel, extra good action. ½ doz. in box..............Doz. **$8.40**

**F5569 — 3** styles, aver. 6½x5½, horizontal with governor, vertical with trip hammers and walking beam engines, metal platforms, painted bright colors, good springs, each with attached winding key. Each in box. Asstd. 3 in pkg. Doz. **$4.50**

## ELECTRICAL AUTOMOBILE RACE.

8 in. enameled all steel up-to-date racing cars, nickel trim, genuine rubber tires, on back, chauffeur and mechanic, finest motors, green enameled steel roadbed, 3rd rail in center, painted wood "Start and Finish" posts.

**F1711**—1 auto, single roadbed, circum. 16 ft............Each, **$5.50**

**F1712**—2 autos, double roadbed, outer bed circum. 16 ft., inner bed 14½ ft., patent clamps prevent separating, turned screw end binding post. Each, **$10.75**

# "ERECTOR" FAMOUS STEEL BUILDING TOYS

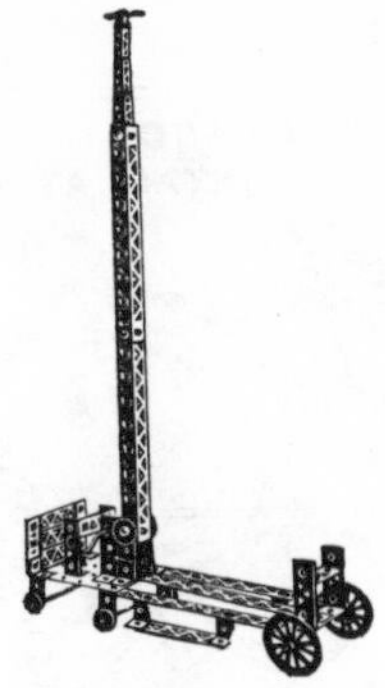

Practical engineering ideas worked out in miniature form. Will supplement manual training now used in schools. Bound to please any boy who is mechanically inclined. The only toy embodying the real structural steel building features.

Note the remarkable number of toys that can be made with each set.

**F1963—61 models.** 50 parts, asstd. pcs. pierced steel, nuts, bolts, wheels and angles. Each set in litho box with illustrated folder. 1 doz. in pkg.
Doz. sets, 82c

*Following each set in leatherette covered partition box, litho top, instruction book with large illustrations of each model. Each with screw driver and large supply of nuts, screws and bolts.*

**F1964—69 models.** 98 parts, asstd. size girders, ends, bushings, pulley and cog wheels, etc. Builds small bridge, flag tower, swing, signals, etc. ¼ doz. sets in pkg............ Doz. sets, $3.85

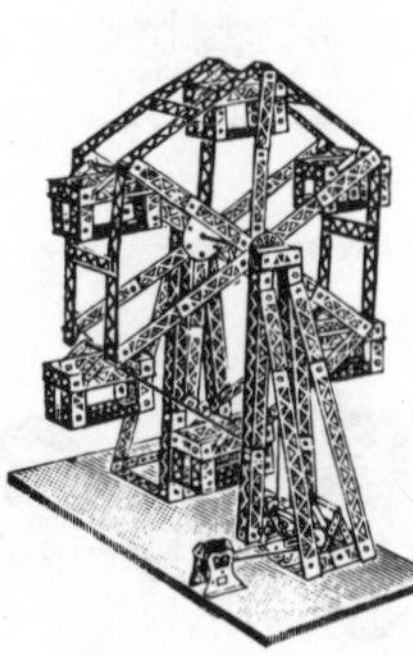

**F1965—88 models.** 140 parts, 24 large girders, ends and bushings, large base plate, 4 pulley wheels, 5 steel rods, crank, etc. Builds elevator, windmill, derrick, etc. ⅛ doz. sets in pkg............ Doz. sets, $8.00

**F1966—120 models.** 205 parts, 34 asstd. size girders, large base plate, 21 single and double angles, builder strips, complete set of washers and small angles, 6 steel rods, crank and shaft, 4 double spoke red enameled wheels, 4 pulley wheels, red cord. Builds bridges, towers, fire dept. toys, autos, steam shovel, etc.......................... Set, $1.35

**F1967—176 models.** 345 parts, 60 large and small girders, 2 base plates, 42 large angles, crosspieces and ends, large supply of small angles and washers, 4 pulley wheels, 4 brass gears, worm gear, speed regulating plate, 8 steel rods, crank and shaft, 4 double spoke red enameled wheels, red cord. Builds large towers, bridges, elevator, derricks, etc.......................... Set, $2.00

*Following with nickel plated motor, on hardwood base, ready for use.*

**F1968—207 models.** 571 parts, partition tray box, 90 large and small girders, 4 large base plates, speed-regulating plate, large supply asstd. angles, crosspieces, beam ends, 5 adjustable pulley or trolley wheels, 5 asstd. brass gear and gear wheels, worm gear, 8 asstd. steel rods, crank and shaft, 4 double spoke red enameled wheels, 2 bdls. red cord. **Very complete,** builds carrier railway, extension bridge, mechanical engine, etc.............. ..Set, $3.25

**F1969—229 models.** 679 parts, partition tray box, 90 asstd. girders, 32 crosspieces, 8 pulley wheels, 8 asstd. size brass gear and gear wheels, worm gear, 4 base plates, 2 speed regulating plates, large supply asstd. size angles and beam ends, 10 rods, crank and shaft, 4 red enameled open spoke wheels, 2 red enameled propeller blades, 2 bdls. red cord. Builds extra large aero plane, incline railway, electric trolley and trailer, drawbridge, machine shop, etc................. ........Set, $4.75

*Following each set in oil finished hardwood box, partition wood tray.*

**F1970—264 models.** 1000 parts, 69 large and 67 medium and small girders, 40 crosspieces, 5 base plates, 2 speed regulating plates, large supply beam ends, washers and asstd. angles. 10 pulley wheels, 7 brass gear and gear wheels, worm gear, brass rod connecters. 1 box each nuts and 2 sizes of screws, 15 asstd. steel rods, crank and shaft, 4 duoble spoke red enameled wheels and 3 belting pulleys, 4 propeller blades. 3 bdls. red cord. Box 10 x 15 x 4, Builds suspension bridge, drawbridge, dirigible balloons, aeroplane, Ferris wheel, etc.............Set, $6.50

**F1971—278 models.** 1291 parts, 85 large, 100 medium and small girders, 48 crosspieces, 3 large base plates, 2 speed regulating plates, 8 triangles, large supply beam ends, nuts and asstd. angles, 14 pulleys, 7 brass gear and gear wheels, worm gear, 1 box each of nuts and 2 sizes screws, 4 red enameled double spoke wheels and 3 belting pulleys, 18 asstd. steel rods, crank and shaft. 4 propeller blades. Constructs almost any model. Box 12½x 20½x4¼, lock and key......Set, $9.75

**F1972 — Perfection outfit, 304 models.** 1843 parts, 180 large, 140 medium and 50 short girders, 4 steel base plates, 2 speed regulating plates. 40 crosspieces large supply beam ends, steel rods, asstd. angles, screw eyes and washers, 2 boxes nuts, 2 boxes large screws, 1 box small screws, shafting joiners, 2 cranks, 1 crank shafting, 3 brass gears, 5 interchangeable gear wheels, 16 pulleys, 5 red enameled belting pulleys, 4 large double spoke red enameled wheels, 32 triangles, 2 bdls. red cord, 4 propeller blades. Makes practically anything. Box 12½x20½x5, 2 partition trays, lock and key...... .........Set, $16.75

## "ERECTOR" ACCESSORY SETS.

Anyone desiring to increase size of set already purchased can obtain extra parts without buying a complete new set.

**F1980**—Additional pieces for F1964 to make it like F1965. 1 set in box.
Set, 32c

**F1981**—Additional pieces for F1965 to make it like F1966. 1 set box. Set, 65c

**F1989**—Additional pieces for F1966 to make it like F1967. 1 set box. Set, 65c

**F1990**—Additional pieces for F1967 to make it like F1968. 1 set box. Set, $1.30

**F1991**—Additional pieces for F1968 to make it like F1969. 1 set box. Set, $1.60

---

# TOY STOVES AND RANGES

## NICKELED STEEL TOY RANGES.

Made just like the big ranges and a fire can be built in them. Hinged doors, removable lids except F2240.

F2240                    F2241

**F2240**—3x4, shelf back. 1 doz. in box........................ Doz. 69c

**F2241**—5x4¼x3½, skillet, stew pan and lifter. ¼ doz. in box..Doz. $1.75

**F2242**—6¼ x 5x3¼, extension front, lower shelf; fry pan, kettle and lifter. ¼ doz. box. Doz. $1.90

**F2249**—*Exceptional $1.05 value.* 11½x10½x5, burnished edges and ornaments, high back, extension front, lower and side shelves, 4 lids, water tank with cover, **movable grate,** 4 large utensils. $8.00
⅒ doz. in box.

**F2243**—8½x5½x5, burnished edges, ornaments and legs, extension front, lower shelf. 4 lids, water tank with cover; skillet and lifter. 1 in box.
⅙ doz. in pkg.............Doz. $3.90

**F2244**—8½x9x5½, burnished edges and ornaments, extension front, high top shelf, 4 lids, water tank with cover; fry pan and kettle. 1 in box. ⅛ doz. in pkg........Doz. $4.25

"**Eagle**" **Range**—Burnished ornaments and legs, side and lower shelves, hot water tank with cover, moveable grate, loose damper. 1 in box.

**F2246**—13x13x6¼. 4 lids, 5 large utensils.... .......EACH, $1.10

**F2247**—17x13½x7, 6 lids. 6 large utensils....... ..... .EACH, $1.65

**F2248**—20 x 16½ x 8¼, burnished edges and ornaments, large back with 2 hinged warming ovens, lower and side shelves, movable grate and damper, 6 lids, water tank with cover, 6 large utensils. 1 in box, EACH, $2.25

### NICKELED STEEL TOY RANGES—Contd.

**F2250—Massive design.** 23x19x8½, highly burnished sides, ornaments and legs, embossed back with 2 hinged door warming ovens, lower and side shelves, 6 large lids, large water tank, hinged front and side doors, open grate effect, damper; large burnished copper tea kettle, coal hod with shovel, lifter, handled stew pot, skillet and footed kettle, some white enameled lined. 1 in box...... ....... EACH, $3.50

### NICKEL TRIM BLACK STEEL RANGES.

Black steel bodies and chimneys, nickeled tops, hinged doors and base, burnished edges and embossings.

**F2118**—4¼ x 3½ x 6½, 2 lids, oven door, copper skillet, kettle and lifter. ½ doz. in box. Doz. $1.95

**F2119**—8½x4½x8½, oven door, side shelf, 4 lids, grate, coppered skillet, kettle and lifter. Each in box, ⅙ doz. in pkg. Doz. $4.15

F2118                    F2119

**F2120**—8½x6½x12¼, adjustable grate, 3 hinged doors, 4 lids, coppered skillet, kettle, coal hod and shovel, aluminum finish lifter. ½ doz. in box.
Doz. $8.25

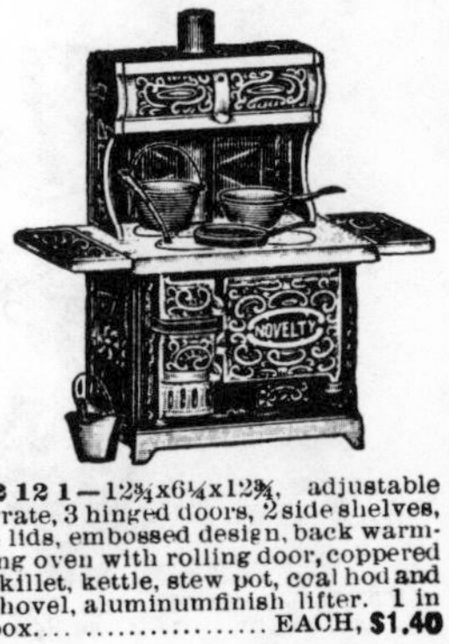

**F2121**—12¾x6¼x12¾, adjustable grate, 3 hinged doors, 2 side shelves, 4 lids, embossed design, back warming oven with rolling door, coppered skillet, kettle, stew pot, coal hod and shovel, aluminum finish lifter. 1 in box.... ...............EACH, $1.40

## POPULAR PRICED IRON TOYS.

Improved line. Painted in bright colors. Note that we assort 3 and 4 styles to most numbers. Compare prices and you will be more than satisfied to give us your Iron Toy business.

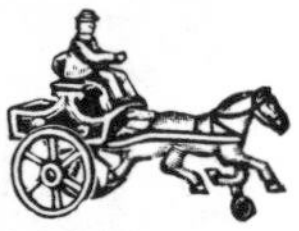

**F2000**—4¼x2¾, aluminum pony cart, horse and driver, red wheels. 1 doz. in box. Doz. **36c** Gro. $4.20

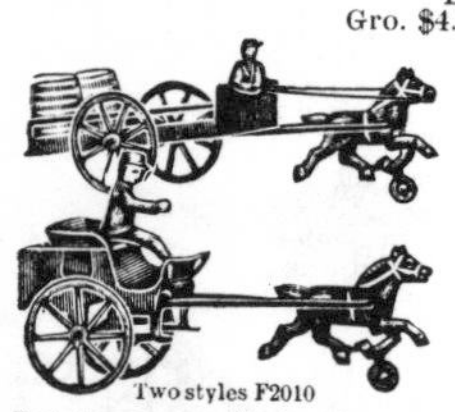

Two styles F2010

**F2010**—3 styles, aver. 7½ in., dump cart, dray with 2 barrels, trap, drivers. Asstd. 1 doz. in box... Doz. **75c** Gro. $8.60

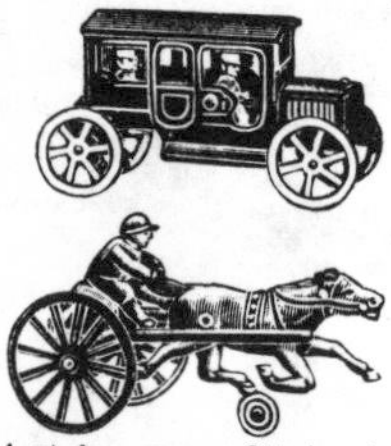

**F2006** — 4 styles, aver. 6½ in., locomotive, sulky, goat cart and taxi, some with drivers Asstd. 1 doz. in box... Doz. **77c** Gro. $9.00

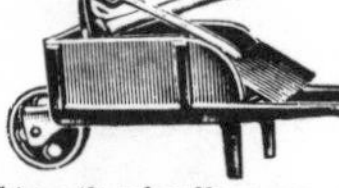

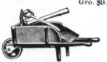

**F2002**—7 in. gilt wheelbarrow, red trim, shovel and pick. **1 set in box**, 1 doz. sets in pkg. Doz. sets, **78c** Gro. sets, $9.00

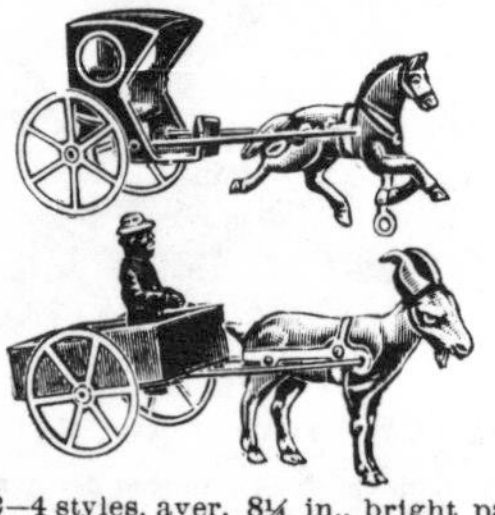

**F2012**—4 styles, aver. 8¼ in., bright painted hansom, wagon and dump cart with aluminum wheels and horse, goat and donkey, aluminum road cart with red wheels and black horse; drivers. Asstd. 1 doz. in pkg. Doz. **78c** Gro. $9.00

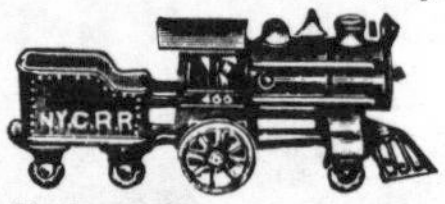


**F2004**—7¼ in., black locomotive, gilt wheels and trim. 1 doz. in box... Doz. **84c** Gro. $9.60

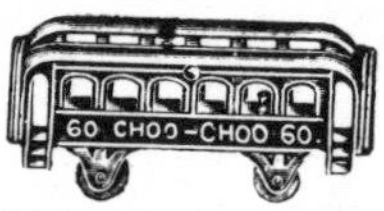


**F2007** —6½ in., aluminum coach movable wheels. 1 doz. in box... Doz. **84c** Gro. $9.60

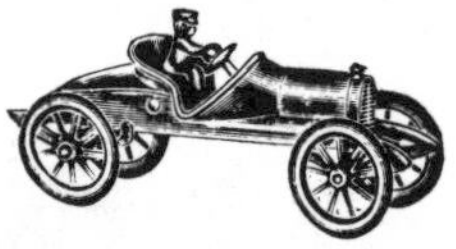

**F2013**—7¾x3, yellow racing auto, red wheels, gilt driver. ½ doz.. in box... Doz. **94c**

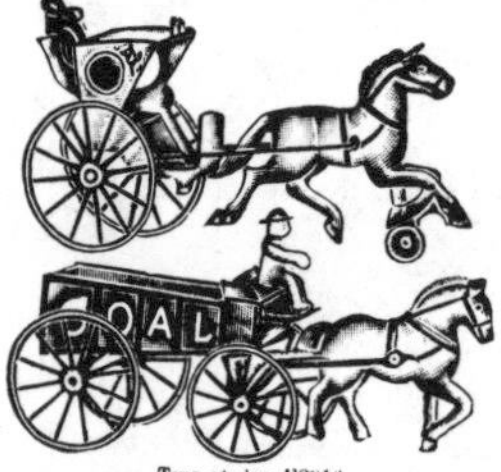


Two styles F2016

**F2016**— 4 styles, aver. 9 in., yellow hansom and dump cart, green coal wagon, large aluminum sulky with red & blue painted jockey; black and aluminum horses. Asstd. ⅓ doz. in box... Doz. **$1.70**

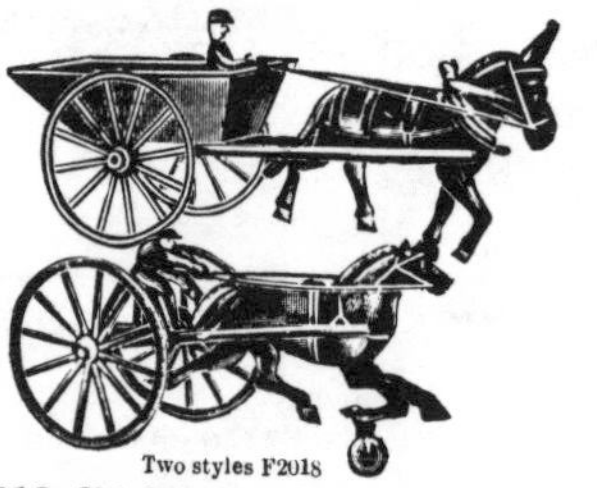

Two styles F2018

**F2018**—3 styles, aver. 9 in., aluminum sulky, red auto and plantation cart, yellow wheels horses painted black, gilt harness. Asstd. ½ doz in box... Doz. **$1.79**

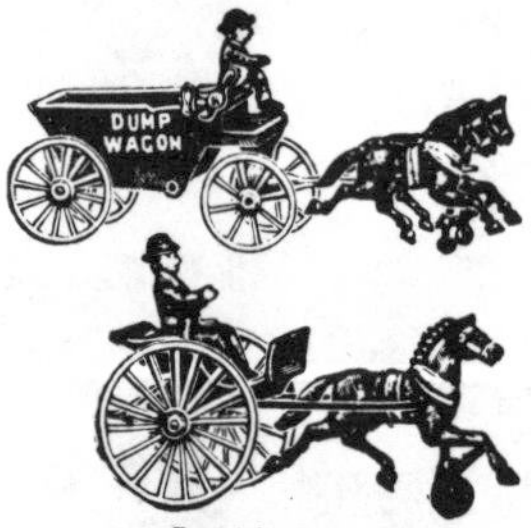


Two styles F2029

**F2029** — 4 styles, aver. 11 in., red dump wagon with drop bottom and gilt lettered ice wagon, yellow wheels, with team; red road car aluminum wheels, and removable seat; green delivery wagon, red wheels, large horse, drivers. Asstd ⅓ doz. in box. Doz. **$1.95**

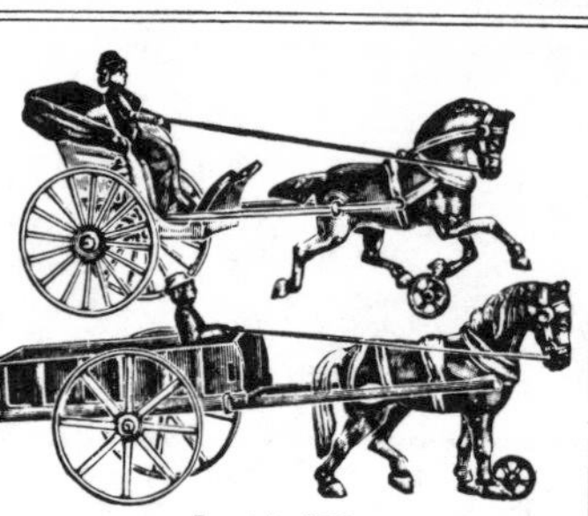

Two styles F2042

**F2042**—4 styles, aver. 13⅛ in. yellow surrey, aluminum wheels; red dump cart, yellow wheels; yellow dray, red wheels; green express, red wheels, large black horses, gilt harness, drivers. Each in box, asstd. ⅓ doz. in pkg... Doz. **$3.75**

## ASSTD. IRON TOYS TO RETAIL AT 50c.

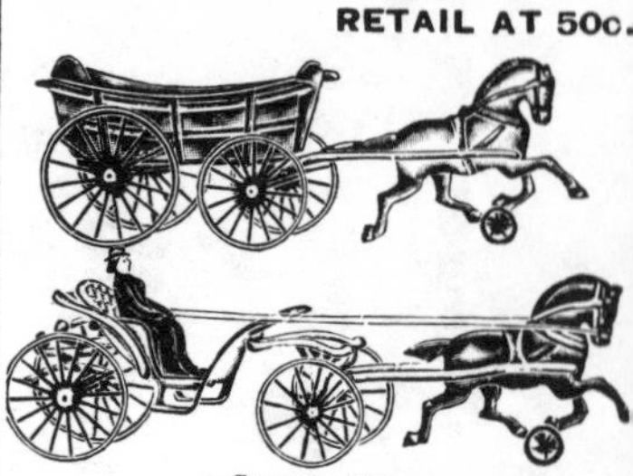

Two styles F2045

**F2045**—3 styles, aver. 16 in., blue hay wagon, yellow wheels; gilt striped black cab, yellow wheels; yellow & blue phaeton, aluminum wheels, large horses, gilt harness, drivers. Each in box, asstd. ¼ doz. in pkg. Doz. **$4.20**

## IRON TOYS TO RETAIL AT 50c, 75c AND $1.00

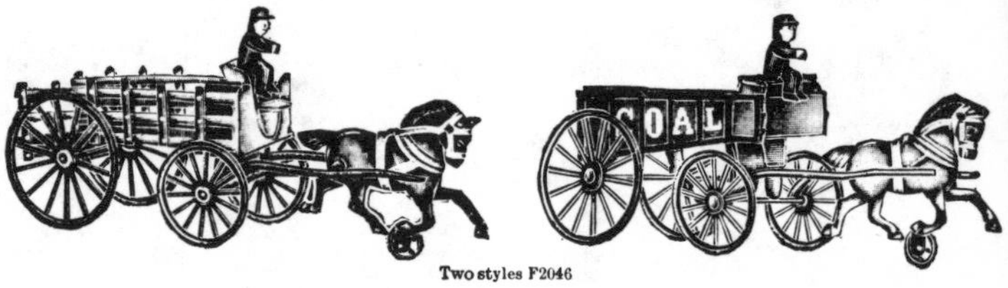


Two styles F2046

**F2046**—3 styles, aver. 15 in., yellow dray, red wheels; black horse; green coal wagon with chute, yellow wheels, brown horse; red road wagon, yellow wheels, removable seat, black and white horses with chain traces, gilt trim, large drivers. Each in box, asstd. ¼ doz. in pkg... Doz. **$4.25**

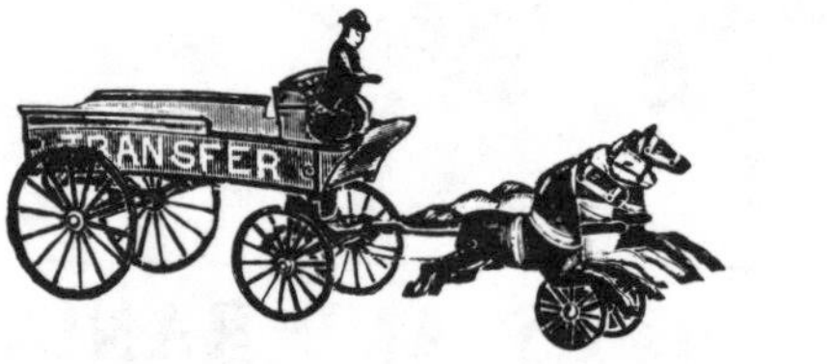


**F2050**—18½ in., yellow transfer wagon, red and blue letters, three 6¾ in. black and white horses, gilt harness, chain traces, driver. $\frac{1}{12}$ doz. in box... Doz. **$7.80**

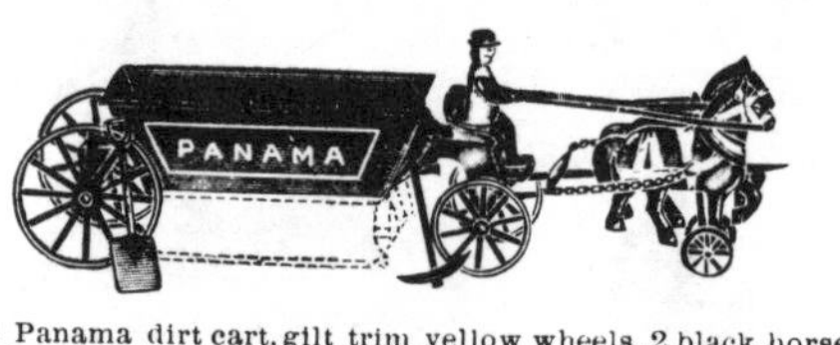


**F2051**—19½ in. red Panama dirt cart, gilt trim yellow wheels, 2 black horses, driver, leather reigns, pick and shovel, patent drop bottom, lever attachment. $\frac{1}{12}$ doz. in box... Doz. **$8.25**

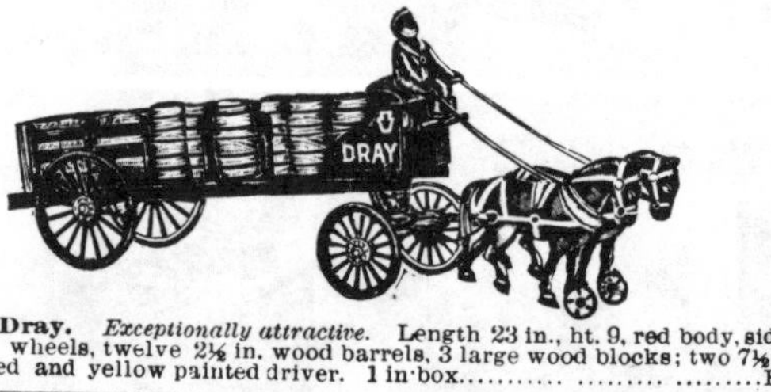


**F2052—Loaded Dray.** *Exceptionally attractive.* Length 23 in., ht. 9, red body, side and rear chains, yellow wheels, twelve 2⅛ in. wood barrels, 3 large wood blocks; two 7½ in. horses, gilt harness, red and yellow painted driver. 1 in box... EACH, **90c**

## SPECIAL ASSORTMENT OF SIX STYLES.

*Dandy value for the money.*

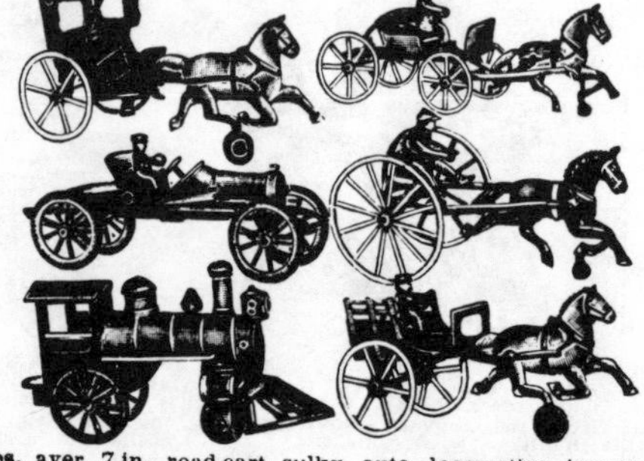

**F2014 – 6 styles**, aver. 7 in., road cart, sulky, auto, locomotive, hansom and surry; bright colors, drivers. Asstd. ⅛ doz. in box... Doz. **92c** Gro. $10.50

## SPECIAL ASSORTMEN OF THREE STYLES.

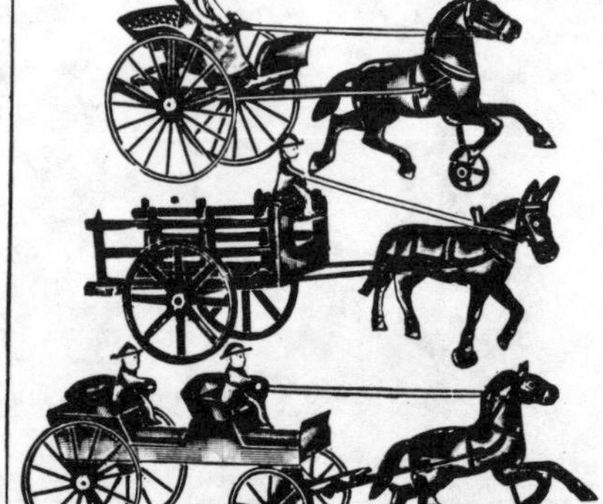

*Be sure you order this one.*

**F2019**—3 styles, aver. 11 in., yellow road wagon, 2 seats, red wheels, brown horse; red road cart, aluminum wheels black horse; yellow farm cart, red wheels, black donkey; drivers. Asstd. ¼ doz. in box... Doz. **$1.98** Gro. $22.00

# FIRE DEPARTMENT IRON TOYS

**F2067—Engine.** 7x3½, aluminum finish, red wheels, driver. 1 doz. in box. ........Doz. 72c
Gro. $8.35

**F2068—Hook and Ladder.** 9x3½, aluminum finish, red wheels, 4¾ in. iron ladder, driver and steersman. 1 doz. in box. ......... Doz. 72c
Gro. $8.35

**F2065—Engine.** 9¾x3½, aluminum body, red wheels, driver. 1 doz. in box ........ ....Doz. 89c
Gro. $10.25

**F2066—Hook and Ladder.** 9½x3¾, aluminum finish, red wheels, 4¾ in. ladder, driver. 1 doz. in box....... Doz. 89c
Gro. $10.25

**F2078—Engine.** 11x4½, gilt trim black body, yellow wheels, 3 large horses. driver. ¼ doz. in box............Doz. $1.92

**F2079—Hook and Ladder.** 15x5, gilt trim blue body, yellow wheels, 3 large horses, two 6½ in. yellow ladders, driver and steersman. ¼ doz. in box. ...........Doz. $1.92

**F2082—Engine.** 15½x6, gilt trim white enameled body, red wheels, three 6 in. black and white horses, driver and fireman. Each in box, ½ doz. in pkg...................Doz. $3.90

**F2083—Hook and Ladder.** 20x7, white body, blue uprights red stripes and wheels, two 12 in. wood ladders, three 6 in. black and white horses, driver and steersman. Each in box ½ doz. in pkg..................Doz. $3.90

**F2073—Engine.** 22x5¾, gilt trim black body, yellow wheels, four 6 in. black and white horses, driver and steersman. Each in box, ½ doz. in pkg. ........ .......Doz. $4.20

**F2091—Hose Cart.** 18x7½, gilt trim white enameled body, red wheels and hose reel, two 7 in. black and white horses, chain traces, nickel gong, driver and fireman. ½ doz. in box. .... ..............Doz. $7.40

**F2086—Engine.** 19x7¼. gilt trim black enameled body, yellow wheels, three 7 in. **galloping** horses, chain traces, nickel gong, driver and fireman. ½ doz. in box..Doz. $8.00

**F2088—Hook and Ladder.** 22½x9, silver trim blue enameled body and uprights, yellow wheels, one 12 in. and two 14 in. wood ladders, three 7 in. **galloping** horses, chain traces, driver and steersman. ½ doz. in box.....Doz. $8.00

**F2084—Engine.** 25x7½, black enameled, gilt striped dome, yellow wheels, four 7 in. brown horses, driver and steersman. ½ doz. in box................. ..... Doz. $8.10

**F2085—Hook and Ladder.** 30x9, gilt trim dk. red enameled body, blue uprights, yellow wheels, one 12 in. and two 14 in. wood ladders, four 7 in. brown horses, driver and steersman. ½ doz. in box..................... ..........Doz. $8.10

**F2092—Water Tower.** 26½ in., gilt trim blue enameled body, yellow wheels, red uprights, 16 in. white & gilt adjustable tower and pipe, three 6½ in. black and white galloping horses, chain traces, nickel gong, driver. ½ doz. in box. Doz. $8.10

---

## "4 STYLES" FIRE DEPARTMENT TOY ASSORTMENT.

*Surprisingly big sellers. Almost every boy will want the complete set.*

**F2031—4 styles,** 12 in. hose cart, large horse, hose with nozzle; 12¼ in. chief's wagon; 12 in. engine, 3 horses, 2 iron ladders; 16 in. hook and ladder, 3 horses, two 6¼ in. steel ladders, drivers painted bright colors, gilt trim. Asstd. ½ doz. in box.
Doz. *1.68

---

## EXTRA SIZE FIRE DEPARTMENT TOYS.

**F2093—Water Tower.** 28 in., gilt trim red body, yellow uprights and wheels, 16 in. white & gilt adjustable tower and pipe, three 9½ in. black & white galloping horses, chain traces, nickel gong, large driver. 1 in box........ Each, 92c

**F2081—Hook and Ladder.** 28¾x9½, yellow body, red frame and wheels, blue upwrights, three 14 in. red ladders, three 9½ in. galloping horses, gilt harness, chain traces, nickel gong, driver and steersman. 1 in box.... ..........Each, 95c

**F2080—Engine.** 21½x7½, black enameled boiler, gilt top and and trim, yellow wheels, three 9 in. galloping horses, gilt harness, chain traces, nickel gong, hose, driver and fireman. 1 in box....... ..............Each, 95c

**F2089—Engine.** 22x8½, nickel plated boiler, polished air chamber, gilt trim red frame and wheels, imit. rubber tires, 2 extra large galloping horses, rubber hose, nickel gong, driver and fireman. 1 in box.....................Each, $1.50

*Butler Brothers (now City Products Corp.)*

# POPULAR IRON TRAINS

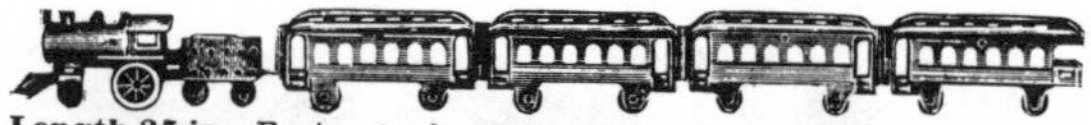

**Length 25 in.**—Engine, tender and 4 coaches. ½ doz. in box.
F2104—Nickel .......................................................Doz. **$2.18**

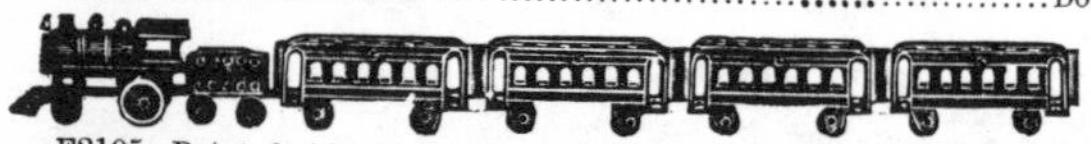

F2105—Painted, black engine and tender, red coaches...........Doz. **$2.18**

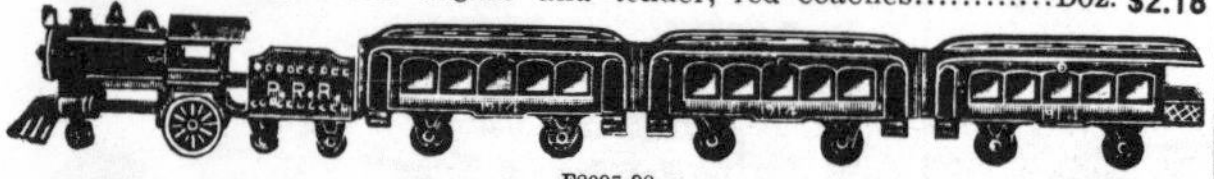

F2097-98

**Copper Finish, Burnished Tops**—Locomotive, tender and 3 coaches. 1/12 doz. in box.
F2097—26⅛ in. ¼ doz. in pkg. ........................................Doz. $3 98
F2098—33 in., separate tender. ........................................ " 6 25

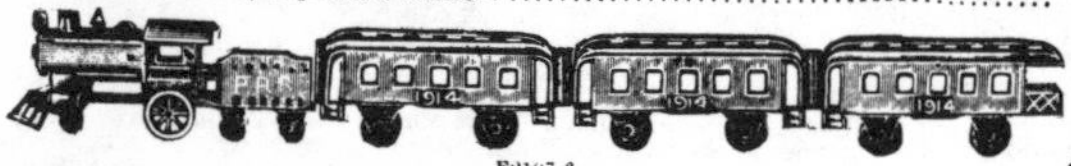

F2107-6

**Length 26 in.**—Engine, tender, 2 coaches and observation car. ¼ doz. in box.
F2107—Nickel, polished cab.............................................Doz. **$3.60**
**F2106** — Painted, black enameled engine, red, white and blue coaches, gilt trim Doz. **$3.60**

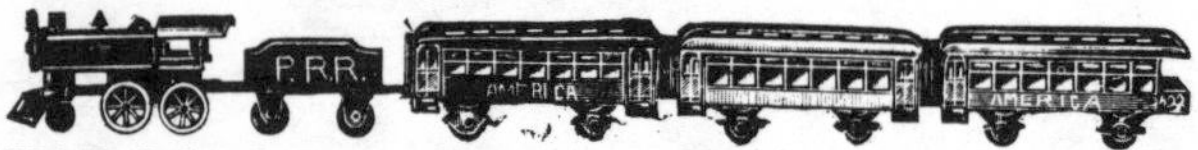

**F2108—Painted,** 32½ in., black enameled engine and separate tender, red and white coaches, blue observation car, gilt trim. Each in box, ¼ doz. in pkg. Doz. **$4.25**

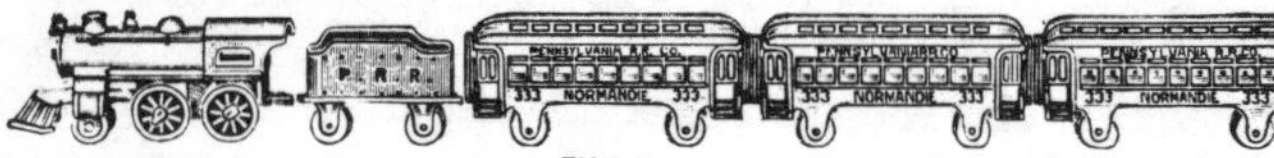

F2111-15

**Lenght 38 in.**—Large engine and separate tender, 2 coaches and observation car. 1/12 doz. in box.
F2111—Nickel, burnished roofs.........................................Doz. **$7.80**
F2115—Painted, black enamel engine and tender, red and white coaches, blue observation car, gilt trim .........................................Doz. **$7.80**

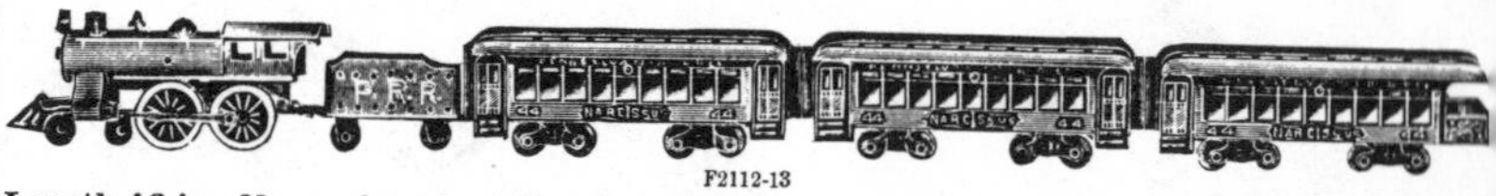

F2112-13

**Length 46 in.**—Mammoth engine with piston rod, separate tender, 2 double truck coaches and observation car. 1 in box.
F2112—Nickel, burnished roofs .........................................Each, **90c**
F2113—Painted, black enameled engine and tender, red and white coaches, blue observation car, gilt trim Each, **90c**

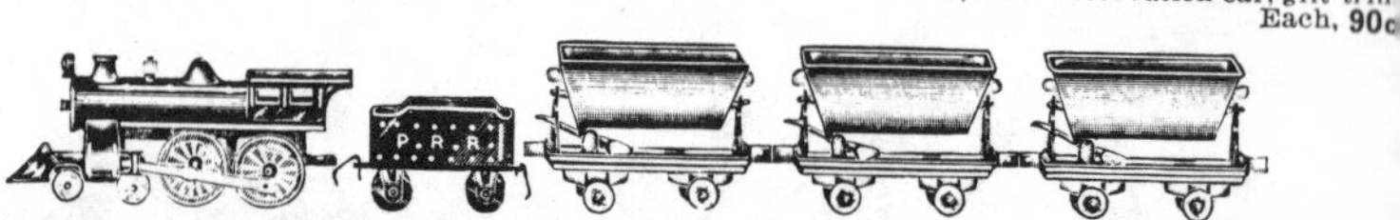

**F2114—Contractors' dump train.** 35 in., large black enameled engine with piston rod, separate tender 3 yellow dirt cars levers for dumping. 1 in box.........................................Each, **90c**

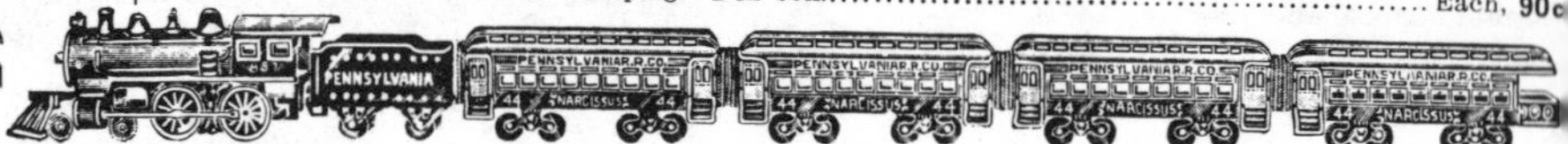

**F2117—Painted,** 58 in., extra large black enameled engine with piston rod, separate tender, 3 large rep coaches and observation car, gilt trim. 1 in box.........................................Each, **$1.60**

## ALL STEEL TRAINS.

Well modeled massive black enameled engines, attached tenders, red enameled cars, gilt trim, ventilator tops.

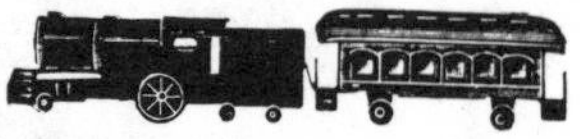

**F2124—12 in., engine and car.** 1 doz. sets in box.........................................Doz. sets, **75c**

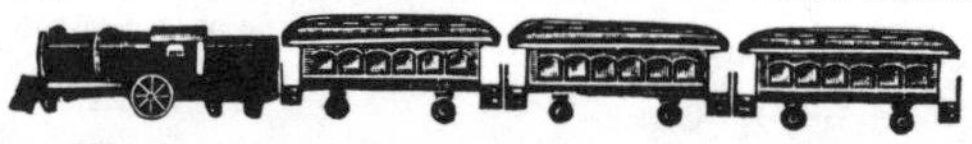

**F2125**—24 in., engine, 3 cars. ½ doz. sets in box.........................................Doz. sets, **$1.75**

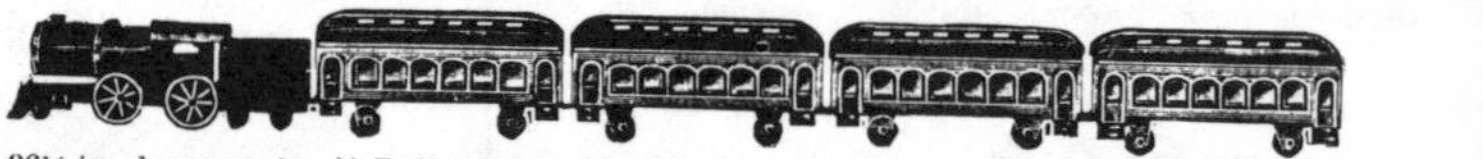

**F2127**—36½ in., large engine, 4 Pullman coaches. Each set in box, ⅙ doz. in pkg.........Doz. sets, **$3.80**

## EXTRA LARGE ALL STEEL TRAINS.

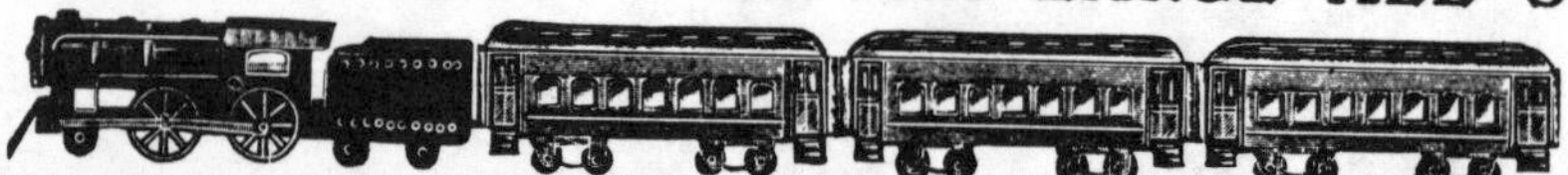

**F2128**—48 in., large engine with piston rod, red enameled iron wheels and running board, hand rails, 3 double truck effect Pullman coaches. 1/12 doz. sets in box.........................................Doz. sets, **$7.80**

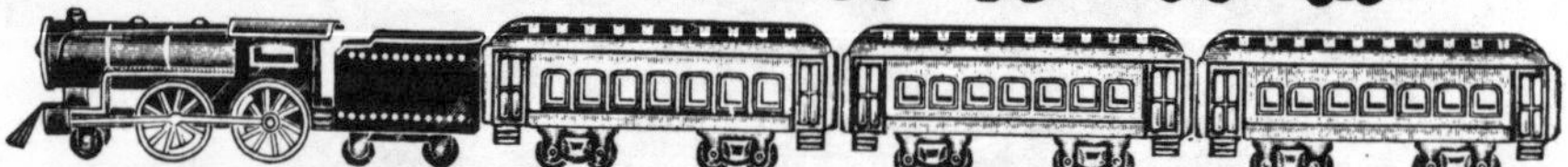

**F2129**—*Exceptional $1.00 value.* 59 in., large engine with piston rod, red enameled iron wheels and running board hand rails 4 double truck effect Pullman coaches. 1/12 doz. sets in box..........Doz sets, **$9.00**

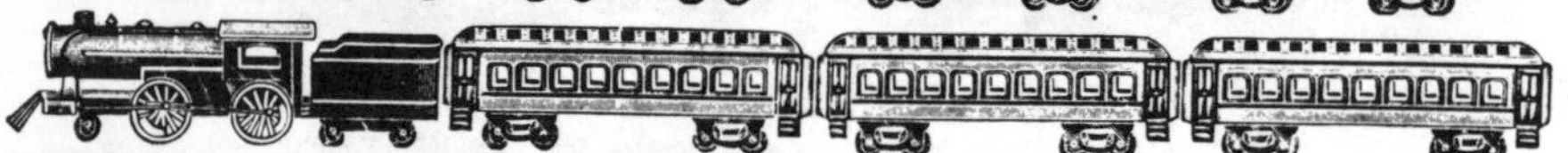

**F2130**—62 in., mammoth engine with piston rod, red enameled iron wheels and tender, running board, 3 large double truck effect Pullman coaches. 1 set in box.........................................Set, **$1.00**

# TOY SADS AND OTHER KITCHEN TOYS

Little housekeepers must have them. Note our extra good values.

### TOY SAD IRONS.

All double pointed, some large enough for light ironing. Each with stand.

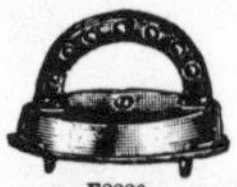

F2220

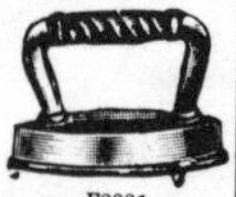

F2221

**F2220**—2⅜ in., solid, smooth sides and bottom, gilt top and handle. 1 doz. in box.................Doz. **35c**
**F2221**—3 in., solid, smooth sides and bottom, gilt top, aluminum handle. 1 doz. in box.................Doz. **36c** Gro. $4.10

*Following with heavy nickeled bottoms and sides.*

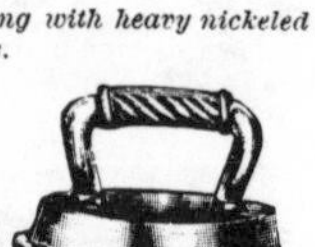

**F2222**—3½ in., solid, gilt top, aluminum handle. 1 doz. in box. Doz. **75c** Gro. $8.75

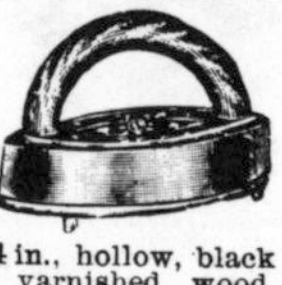

**F2223**—4 in., hollow, black enameled top, varnished wood handle. 1 doz. in box.................Doz. **78c** Gro. $9.00

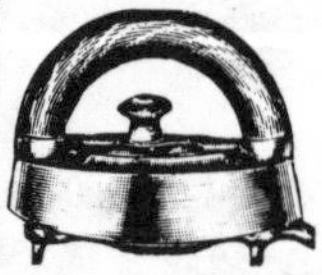

### TOY SAD IRONS—Contd.

**F2227**—4¾ in., solid, gilt top, patent detachable varnished wood handle. Used for laces, etc. Each in box, ½ doz. in pkg.................Doz. **$1.95**

### "DOVER" ASBESTOS SAD IRONS.

Heavy polished nickeled bottoms and removable covers with turned wood enameled handles, lever catch. Dead air space guarantees cold handle. Each with stand.

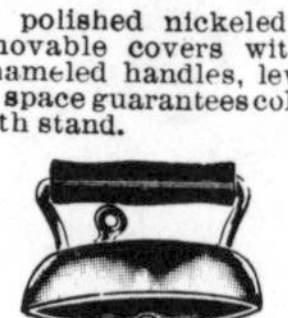

**F2232**—3⅛ in. 1 doz. in box. Doz. **82c** Gro. $9.60

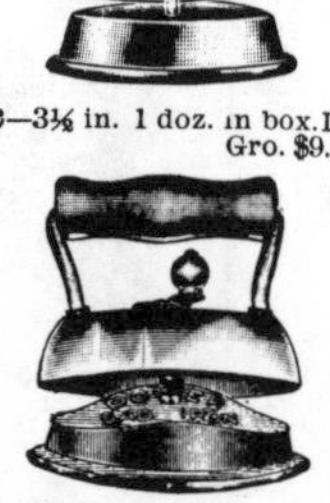

**F2234**—4¾ in., extra heavy, asbestos lined stand. Large enough for practical use. ½ doz. in box..Doz. **$1.95**

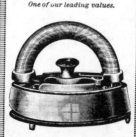

### TOY SAD IRON.

*One of our leading values.*

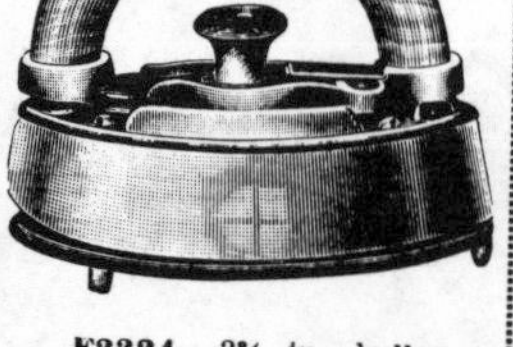

**F2224** — 3¾ in., hollow aluminum top, heavy nickeled bottom and sides, patent detachable varnished handle. 1 doz. in box. Doz. **82c** Gro. $9.65

### TOY COFFEE MILLS.

Except F1781 each with removable drawer, will actually grind coffee.

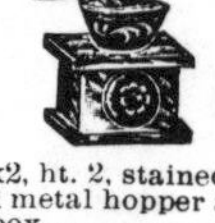

**F1781**—2x2, ht. 2, stained wood box, lacquered metal hopper and handle. 1 doz. in box.................Doz. **36c**

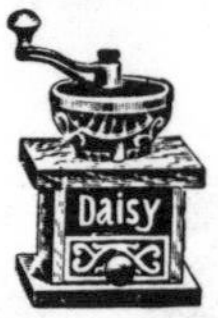


**F1782**—2⅛x2⅛, ht. 3¾, varnished stained wood box, gilt metal drawer front, hopper and handle. 1 doz. in box.................Doz. **75c**

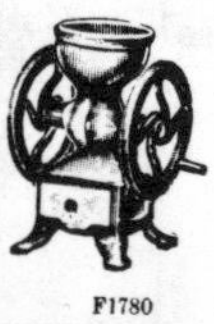

F1780

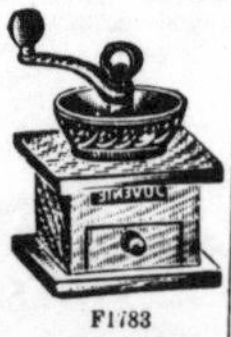

F1783

**F1780**—Grocer's style, solid iron, ht. 4 in., 2¼x2¼ footed base, asstd. red and gilt finishes. 1 doz. in box. Doz. **84c**
**F1783**—4x4, ht. 6, varnished oak box, gilt metal hopper, wood knob lacquered handle. Each in box. ⅙ doz. in pkg.................Doz. **$1.90**

### "BABY" TOY FOOD CHOPPER.

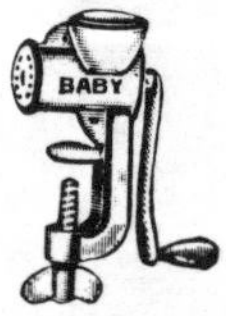


**F1997**—5x2¾, aluminum finish, adjustable table clamp. 1 doz. in box. Doz. **72c**

### TOY IRON SCALES

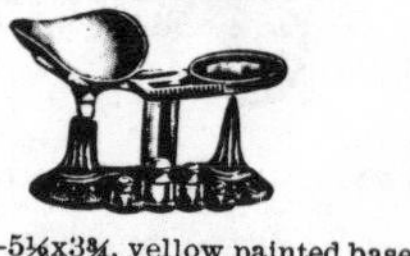

**F1994**—5⅛x3¾, yellow painted base, aluminum beam and weight adjustor, tin scoop, 4 weights. 1 doz. in box.................Doz. **89c**

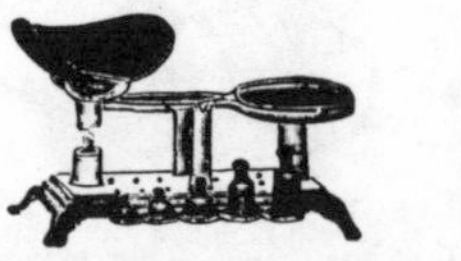

**F1999** — 6⅛ x 3, footed base, full aluminum, large tin scoop, 5 iron weights. Each in box, ⅙ doz. in pkg. Doz. **$1.75**

# STEEL TOYS

Strong and durable, attractively painted in colors and neatly finished. Not as heavy as iron toys, but equally substantial and save you on freight. *Note our line.*

## STEEL CARTS.

Strong and durable, neatly painted and finished. Deep bodies, turned edges, except F2235 attractive litho sides, red open spoke wheels, green hub caps, twisted wire loop handles, patent holders.

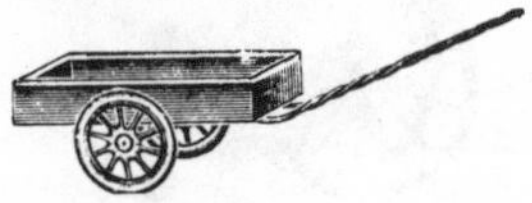

**F2235**—5x2 green body, red inside. 2 doz. in box........................................Doz. **40c**

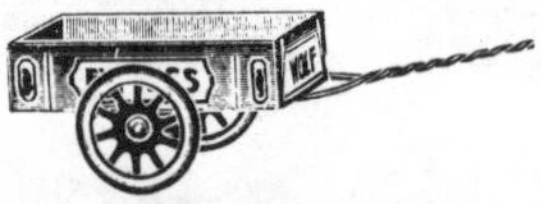

**F2236**—6⅜ x 3⅝, yellow & white litho body, red inside. 1 doz. in box..... .....Doz **75c**

## STEEL WAGONS.

Strong and durable, neatly painted and finished. Deep bodies, turned edges, attractive litho sides, red open spoke wheels, green hub caps, twisted wire loop handles, patent holders. Front wheels turn.

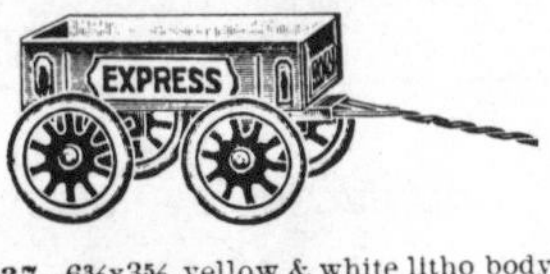


**F2237**—6⅜x3⅝, yellow & white litho body, red inside. 1 doz. in box...............Doz. **87c**

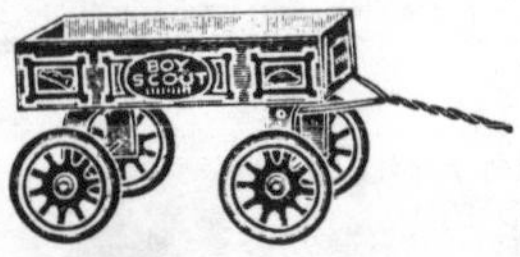


**F1720**—7¾x4½, green & red litho body, red inside. 1 doz. in box................Doz. **94c**

## STEEL CARTS AND WAGONS—With Horses.

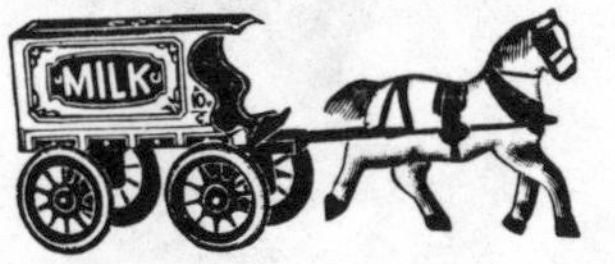


**Delivery Wagons**—Litho in bright colors and asstd. stencils, imit. rubber tire metal wheels.
F1715—Length 11⅛ in., ht. 4⅛. 1 doz. in box.......... ... ................Doz. **80c**
Gro. $9.00

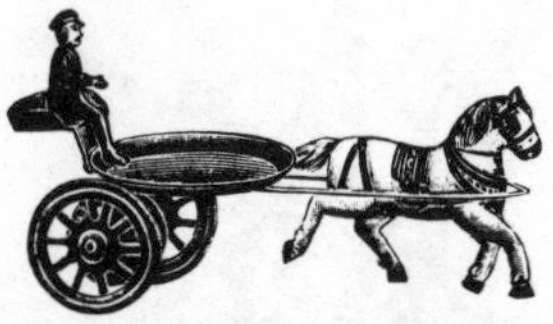

**F1716—Gong Sulky.** Length 11¾ in., large horse, litho driver fastened to seat, when drawn across floor gong rings loudly. 1 doz. in box........................Doz. **85c**
Gro. $9.50

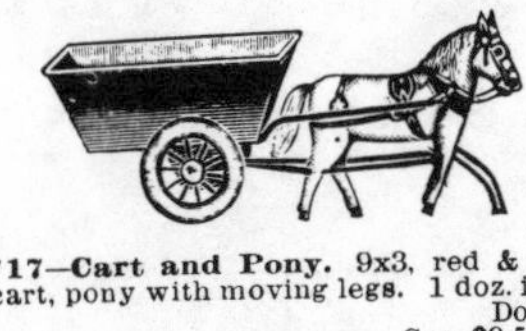

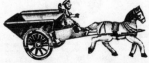

**F1717—Cart and Pony.** 9x3, red & green cart, pony with moving legs. 1 doz. in box. Doz. **84c**
Gro. $9.50

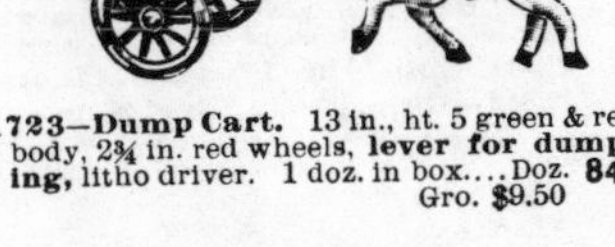

**F1723—Dump Cart.** 13 in., ht. 5 green & red body, 2¾ in. red wheels, **lever for dumping,** litho driver. 1 doz. in box....Doz. **84c**
Gro. $9.50

## STEEL CARTS AND WAGONS -With Horses—Contd.

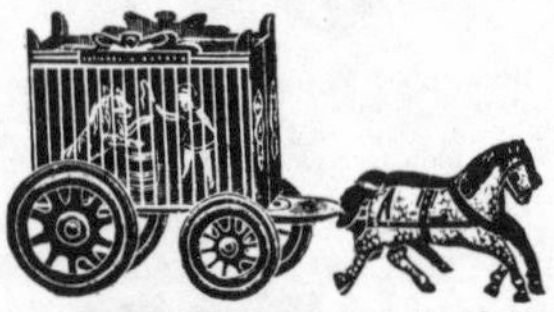

**F1719—Circus Wagon.** Length 11 in., ht. 5½, bright circus litho, 2 horses. 1 doz. in box..........................................Doz. **94c**

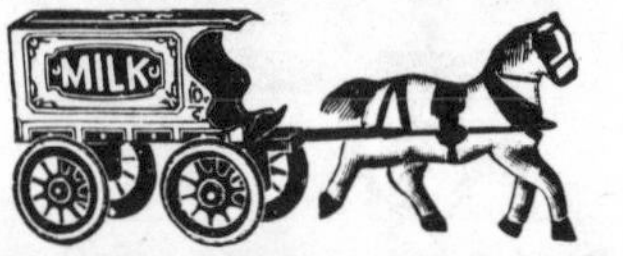


**Delivery Wagons**—Litho in bright colors and asstd. stencils, imit. rubber tire metal wheels.
F1721—Length 12 in., ht. 5⅛. 1 doz. in box. Doz. **95c**

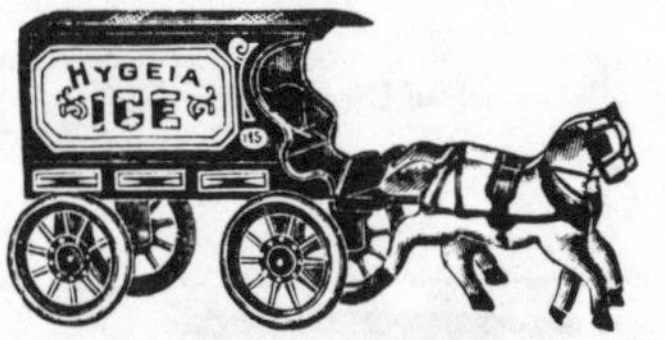


F1726—Length 13 in., ht. 6, 2 horses. ½ doz. in box.............................Doz. **$1.75**

## TOY WATER WAGONS.

All steel red and gray litho lettered tanks, hinged opening for filling, yellow sprinkler, green enameled truck, red open spoke wheels, long handles, patent holders.

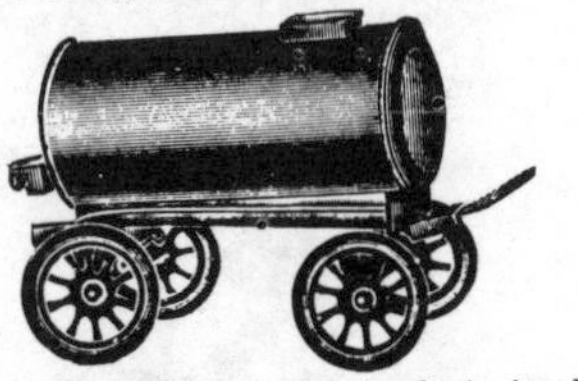

**F1728**—Length 7 in., ht. 6, twisted wire handle. 1 doz. in box...............................Doz. **95c**
**F1729**—Length 9½ in., ht. 6¾, sprinkler with lever stop, throws fine spray, long coppered wire handle. ½ doz. in box.... ..Doz. **$1.80**

## STEEL SPECIALTIES.

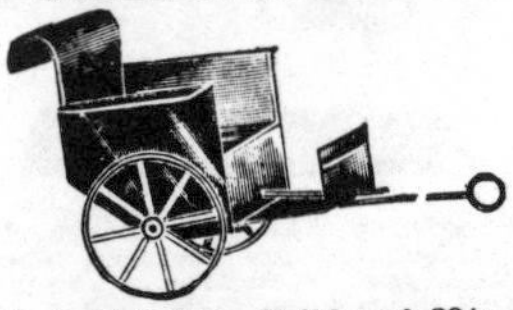

**F2259—Doll Sulky.** Full length 29 in., width 6¾, asstd. red and blue enameled, aluminum finish open spoke wheels, long copper wire handle. 1 doz. in box...............Doz. **84c**

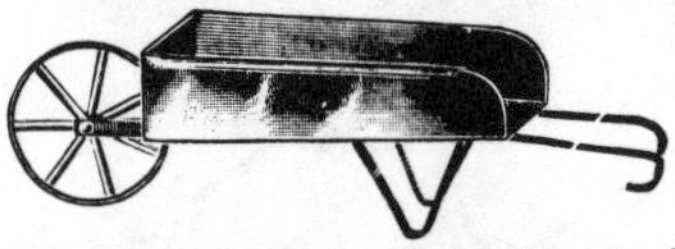

**F2275—Wheelbarrow.** 22x5, asstd. red and blue enameled, 3¾ in. aluminum finish wheel. 1 doz. in pkg...... ...... Doz. **95c**

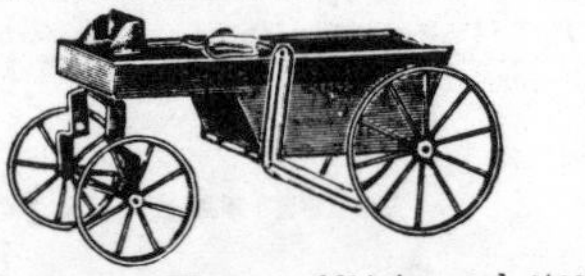

**F1733—Dump Wagon.** 10¼ in., red steel body and seat, wood sides, open spoke cast iron wheels, front wheels turn on steel axle, lever for dumping, long twisted wire handle. ⅙ doz. in pkg.......................Doz. **$1.75**

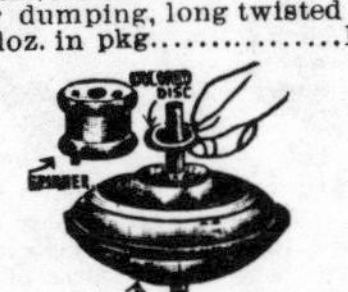

**F2333—"Rainbow Never-Stop" Hummer.** Girth 10 in., bright enameled steel, 5 colored paper discs produce rainbow effects. 1 doz. in box..........................Doz. **78c**

## STEEL RAILROAD TOYS.

All with **double truck wheels.** Wonderful values, not cheap flimsy make. To be sold separately or made up in trains.

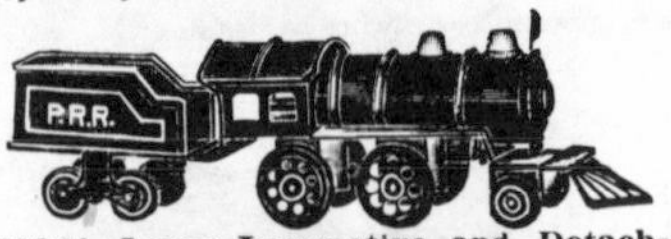


**F1984—Large Locomotive and Detachable Tender.** 14 in., black enameled, red wheels. ½ doz. in box. .............Doz. **95c**

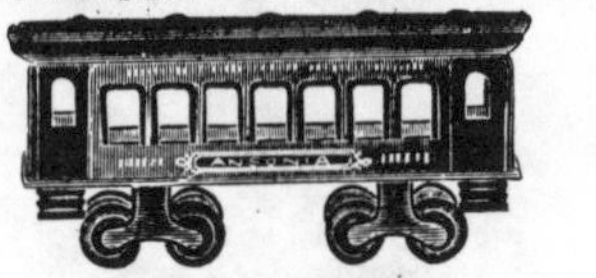

**F1985—Passenger Car.** 10 in., enameled bright colors. ⅙ doz. in box.........Doz. **95c**

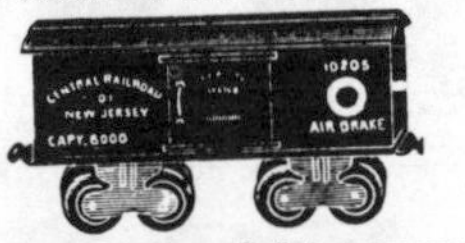

**F1987—Freight Car.** 7x3½, gray enameled black lettering, sliding doors. 1 doz. in box. Doz. **95c**

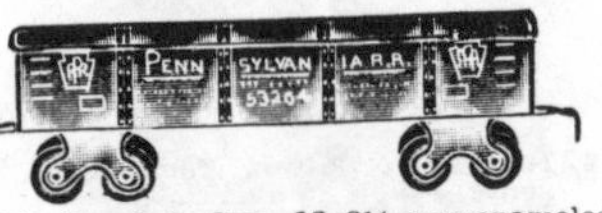


**F1986—Gondola Car** 12x3½, gray enameled stamped steel. 1 doz. in box........Doz. **95c**

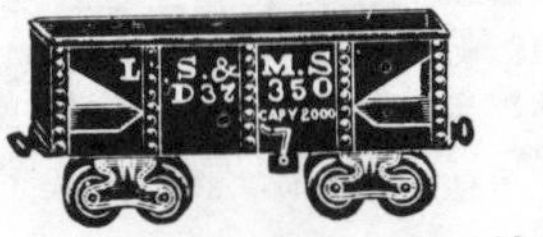

**F1993—Coal Car.** 7x3½, gray enameled, black lettering, automatic drops. 1 doz. in box. Doz. **95c**

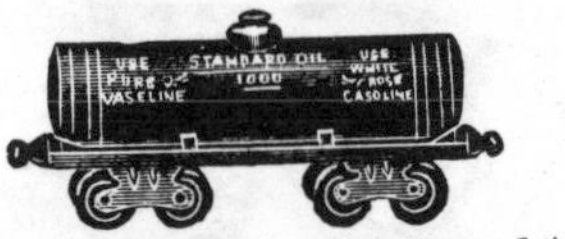

**F1988—Oil Tank Car.** 9 in., steel gray finish complete in every detail. 1 doz. in box. Doz. **95c**

## STEEL PUSH TOYS.

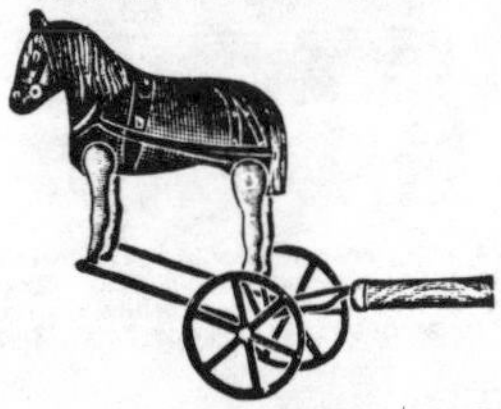

**Galloping Pony**—Double litho wood horse, metal legs, painted steel wheels, heavy wire frame, 19¼ in. wood handle.
F2855—1 doz. in box............ ....Doz. **85c**

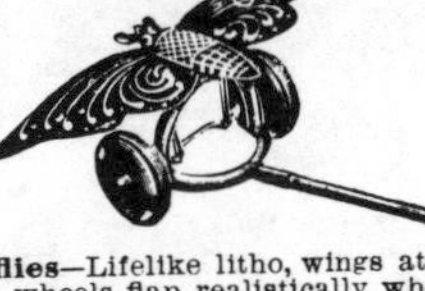

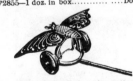

**Butterflies**—Lifelike litho, wings attached to steel wheels flap realistically when drawn across floor. Turned wood handles. 1 doz. in box.
F1730—Width 9 in..................Doz. **82c**
Gro. $9.50

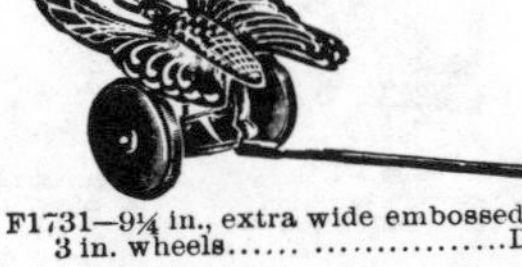

F1731—9¼ in., extra wide embossed wings, 3 in. wheels...... ...............Doz. **95c**

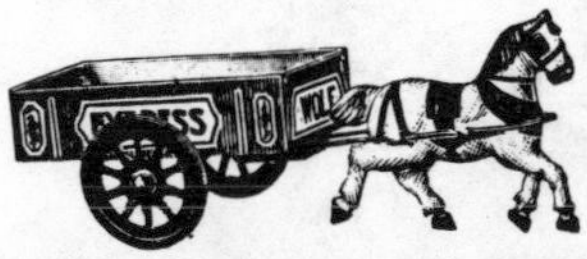

**F1722—Delivery Cart.** 12x3⅝, yellow & white litho body, red inside, large horse. 1 doz. in box.........................Doz. **94c**

## MISCELLANEOUS STEEL TOYS.

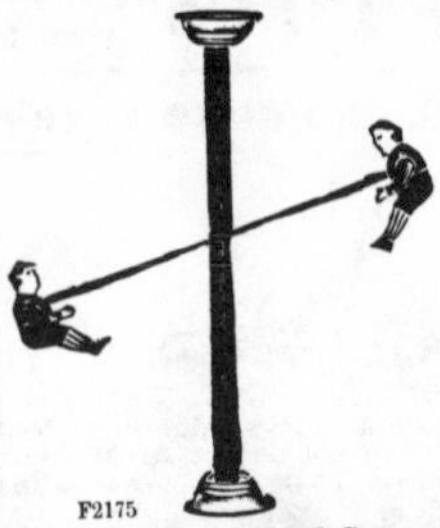

F2175

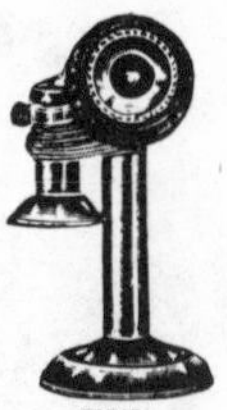

F1747

**F2175—Mechanical See-saw.** Ht. 12½ in., brightly enameled, 11 in. crosspiece with two 3 in. figures see-saws from end to end when reversed. 1 doz. in box......Doz. **92c**
Gro. $10.80

**F1747—Telephone Set.** (2 phones to set) Ht. 7 in., red & black enameled, adjustable mouthpiece, 2½ in. receivers, long string, enameled hooks. 1 doz. sets in box.
Doz. sets, **95c**

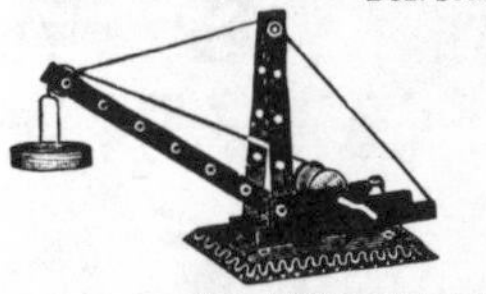

**F1998—"Panama Canal" Derrick.** Ht. 5½ in., 4x5 red & black enameled base, pierced steel derrick, wire supports, swings to any position, metal bucket on cord attached to pulley and crank, steel brake. 1 doz. in box.
Doz. **95c**

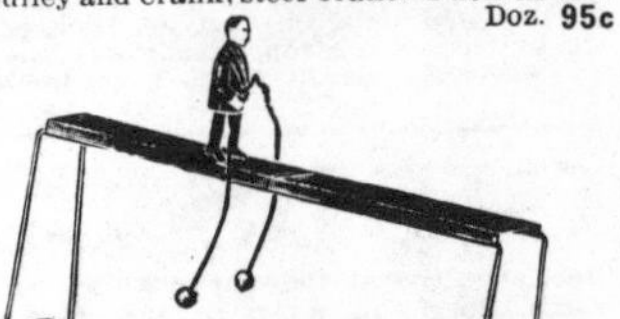

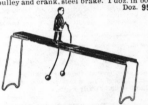

**F1878—"Gravity Jim."** *Nothing to get out of order.* 14 in. green litho steel slanting platform, folding nickeled supports, 3½ in. litho figure, movable legs with weighted balance rod, when placed at top of platform walks to lower end. Each in box, ½ doz. in pkg.
Doz. **$2.00**

## TOY HATCHETS.

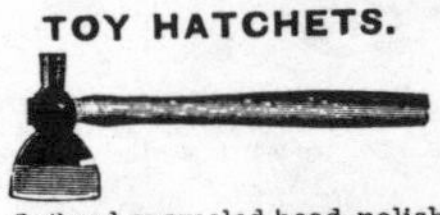

**F1995**—2x3 red enameled head, polished edge, 8¾ in. turned wood handle. 1 doz. in box.
Gro. $3.90 Doz. **34c**

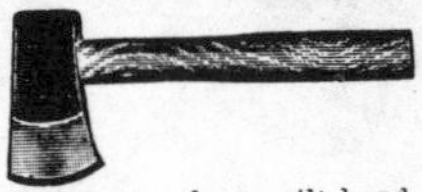

**F1996**—4¾ in., axe shape, gilt head, polished ground blade, 12½ in. hickory handle. ½ doz. in box...........................Doz. **84c**

## 3 PIECE TOY GARDEN SETS.

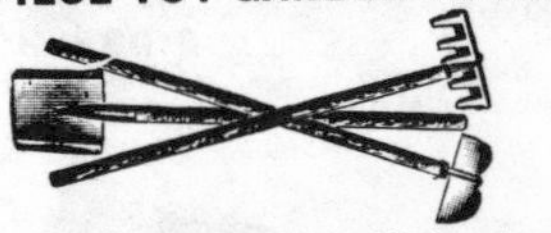

**F2723** — Galvanized steel, 18 in., turned handles, steel ferrules, spade 3¼x2¾, 5 tooth rake, hoe 3x1⅛. 1 doz. sets in pkg.
Doz. sets, **42c**

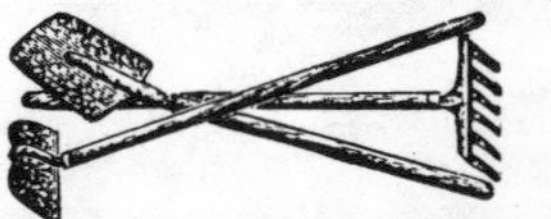

**F2724**—Heavy galvanized steel shank spade 4¼x3½, 4½ in., 6 tooth rake, hoe 3¾x2¼, nickel ferrules, 18 in. turned handles. 1 doz. sets in pkg....................Doz. sets, **84c**

## TOY LAWN MOWER.

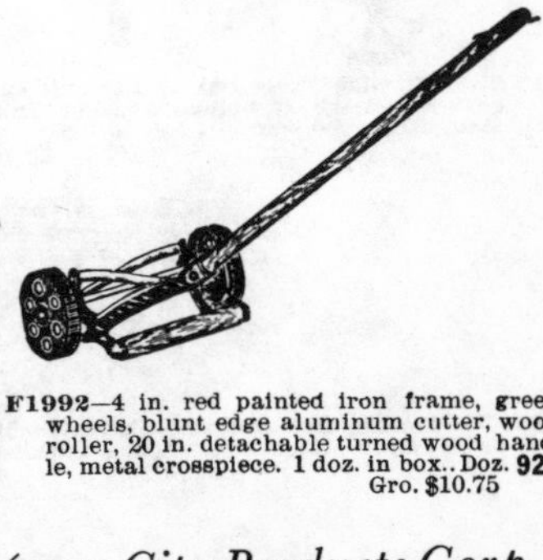

**F1992**—4 in. red painted iron frame, green wheels, blunt edge aluminum cutter, wood roller, 20 in. detachable turned wood handle, metal crosspiece. 1 doz. in box..Doz. **92c**
Gro. $10.75

# GONG TOYS

The cream sellers in this line. Do not fail to show them, for the little folks MUST have them.

## BELL AND GONG TOYS—Set in motion by drawing across floor.

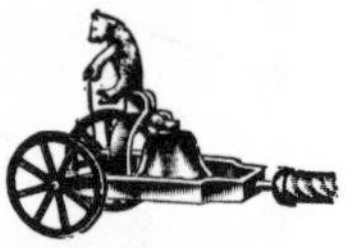

**F2154**—2 styles dbl. gongs, aluminum bear on nickeled bell, wood handle. Asstd. 1 doz. in box. .......... .......... .......Doz. **78c**

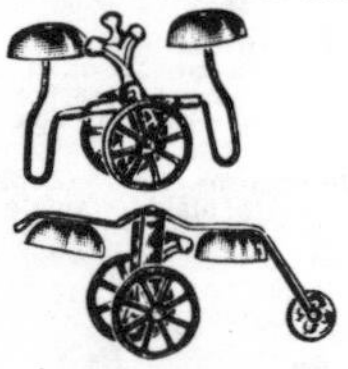

**F2156**—Aver. 6¼ in., 2 styles, double nickeled gongs, coppered steel frames, lever hammers strike gongs. Asstd. 1 doz. in box. Doz. **79c**

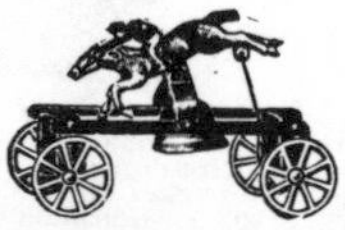

**F2160**—Aver. 6½ in., 3 styles, bear, possum and jockey on coppered frames, nickeled bells and wheels. Asstd. ½ doz. in pkg. Doz. **$1.90**

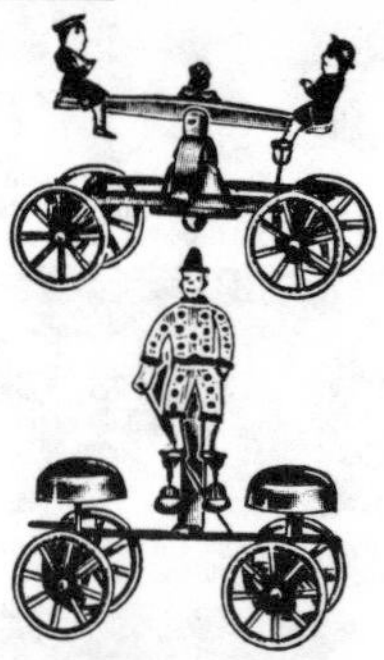

**F2161**—6½ in., 3 styles, darkey and clown on seesaw, bear and clown between 2 bells, figures in colors and aluminum, nickeled frames. Asstd. ¼ doz. in box....Doz. **$1.95**

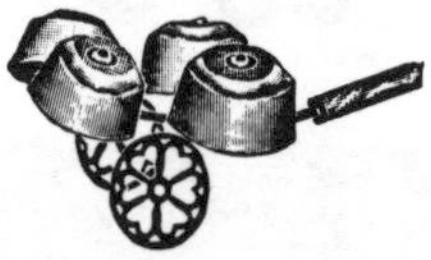

**F2164—Swiss Chime.** Four 2¼ in. nickel gongs, double ratchet hammers, nickeled frame and wheels, 23½ in. colored wood handle. ½ doz. in box............Doz. **$1.95**

## BELL AND GONG TOYS—Contd.

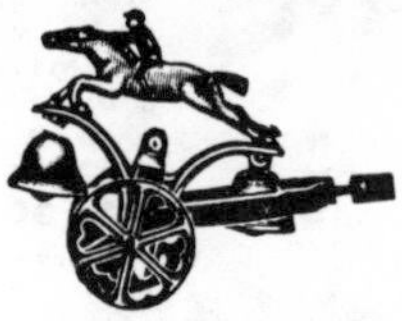

**F2162**—7 in., 3 styles, 2 with horse and rider, other galloping horse, nickel bells and wheels, coppered frames, 18 in. turned wood handles. Asstd. ½ doz. in box. Doz. **$1.98**

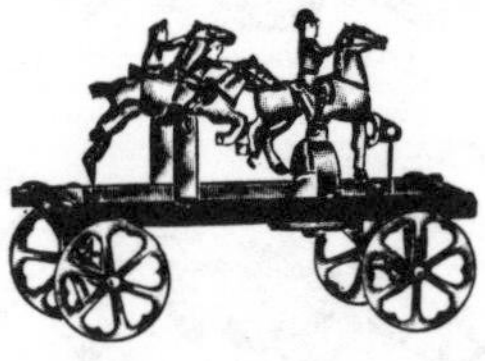

**F2168**—3 styles, rough riders, clowns and jockeys on galloping horses, aver. 9½x3½ coppered platforms, nickel bells and wheels. Asstd. ¼ doz. in pkg......... ... Doz. **$3.85**

Our line of Dressed Dolls this season is especially attractive.

## IMPORTED WHEEL GONG TOY

Each with leatherette leader.

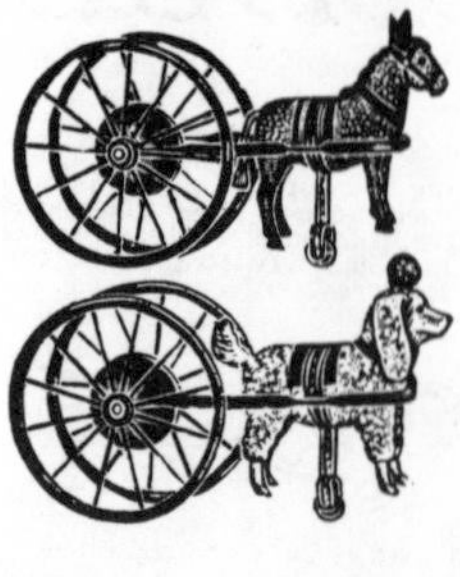

**F2167**—10¾ in., 4 styles, bear, donkey, hors and sheep, natural color felt and plus covered, some with harness, gilt and bro zed traces, 5½ in. red and gray enamele wheels, large double nickel plated gong Each in box, asstd. ½ doz. in pkg.Doz. **$4.2**

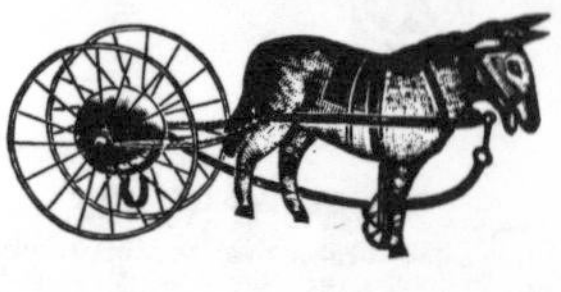

**F2171**—16¾ in., 2 styles, brown felt covere horse and gray felt covered mule, blac manes, leatherette harness, gilt traces, 6 in. double spoke blue enameled wheels, 3 in double nickel plated gongs. Each in box asstd. 6 doz. in pkg..............Doz. **$8.4**

# GIBBS WELL KNOWN AMERICAN MADE TOYS

Very attractive all-the-year round sellers. Toys that "take" wherever displayed. Order a few sample dozens and make the most of the excellent profit possibilities. All are carefully finished and substantially made.

## GIBBS' STEEL CARTS.

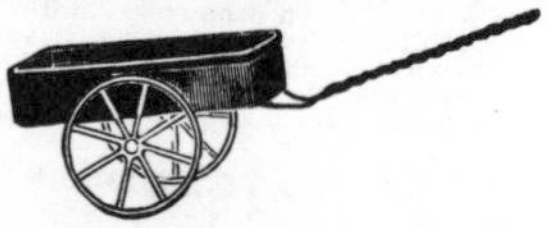

**F2273—Daisy Cart.** 5¼x3, red steel body, yellow wood bottom, aluminum steel wheels, 24 in. wire handle. 1 doz. in box. Doz. **72c**

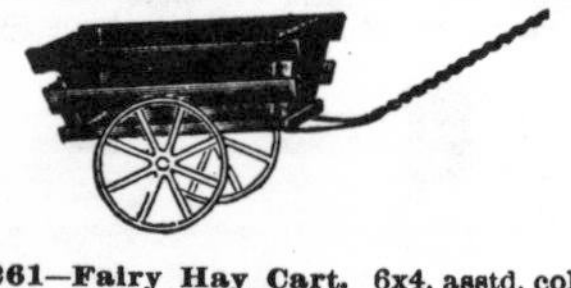

**F2261—Fairy Hay Cart.** 6x4, asstd. colors enameled wood body, aluminum steel wheels, 21 in. wire handle. 1 doz. in box. Doz. **77c**

## GIBBS' STEEL WAGONS.

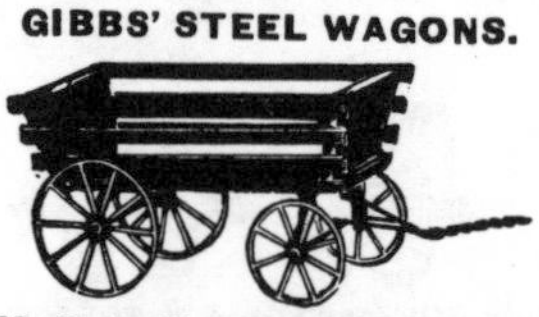

**F2267—Fairy Hay Wagon.** 10¾x5¾, asstd. colors enameled wood body, steel gear, large aluminum steel wheels, front wheels turn under, 24 in. wire handle. ½ doz. in box. Doz. **$1.85**

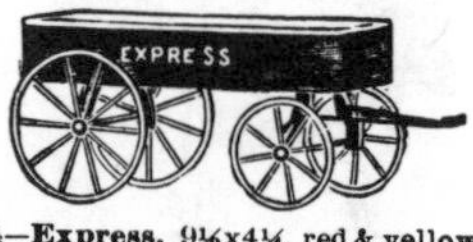

**F2274—Express.** 9½x4¼, red & yellow enameled, black stencil, steel gear, large aluminum steel wheels front wheels, turn under, 23 in. steel handle. ½ doz. box...Doz. **$1.85**

## GIBBS' HORSES AND WAGONS.

Litho wood horses, movable steel legs attached by wire to wagon wheels giving natural walking motion. All wheels aluminum steel unless stated.

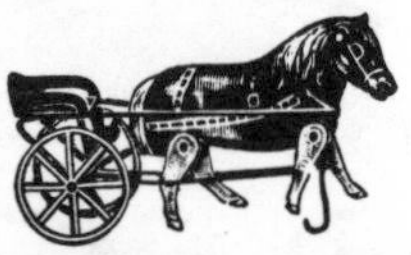

**F2272—Pony pacer.** 7¼ in., red steel surrey. 1 doz. in box...................... . Doz. **79c**

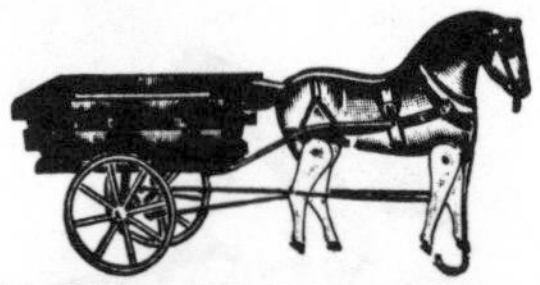

**F2268—Pacing Bob Horse.** 13½ in., asstd. colors enameled wood cart. ½ doz. in box. Doz. **$1.85**

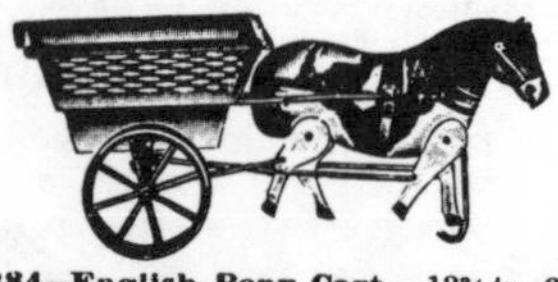

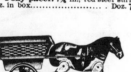

**F2284—English Pony Cart.** 13⅜ in., 6½x5 enameled steel body, embossed basket effect, stout litho wood pony. ½ doz. in box. Doz. **$2.00**

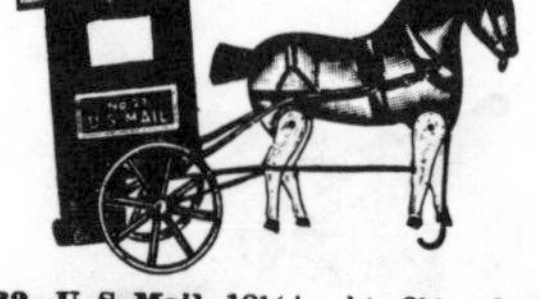

**F2282—U. S. Mail.** 12½ in., ht. 6½, red enameled steel wagon, black roof, open back, front and side windows. ½ doz. in box. Doz. **$2.00**

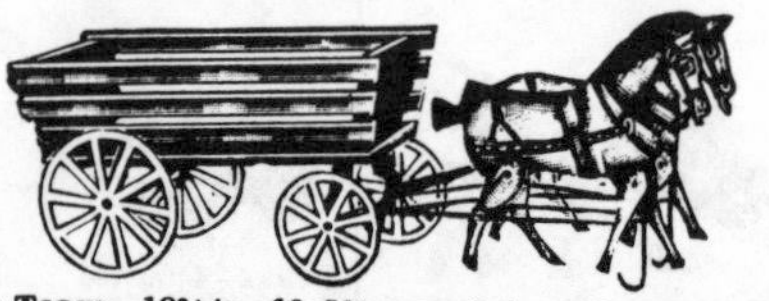

**F2271—Pacing Bob Team.** 18¾ in., 10x5¾ enameled wood wagon, front wheels turn under, 2 horses. Each in box, ½ doz. in pkg.......................... .....Doz. **$3.80**

## GIBBS' "GIPSY" WAGON.

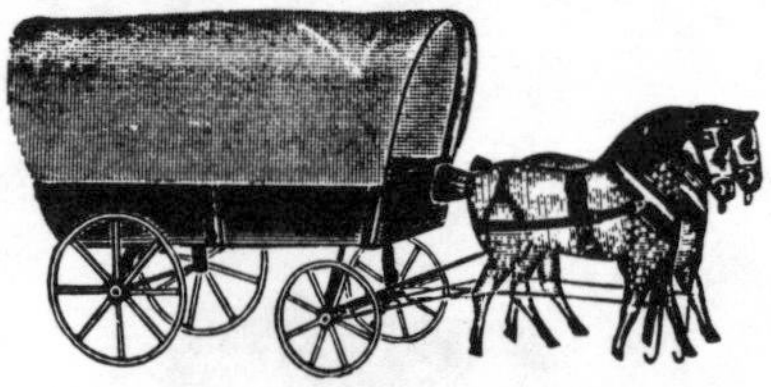

**F2285—"Gipsy."** 18½ in., 9¾x4¾ re enameled wood & steel body, yellow wheels, front wheels turn under, can vas covered, drawstrings at back 2 horses. ½ doz. in box.... Doz. **$3.8**

## GIBBS' PERFORMING ANIMALS.

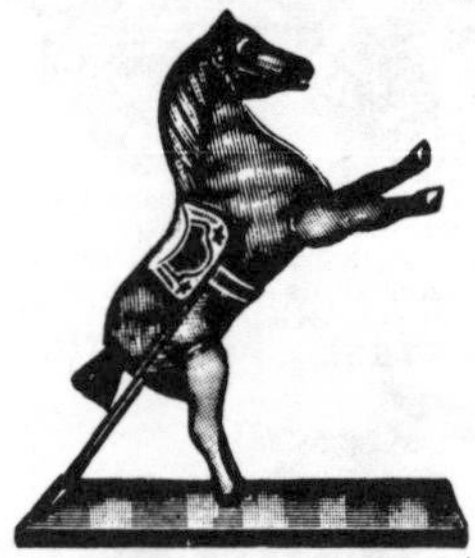

**F2263—Horse.** Length 8 in., ht. 6¾, litho wood body, movable steel legs, attached by wire to green wood base, can be placed in many circus poses. 1 doz. in box. Doz. **78c**

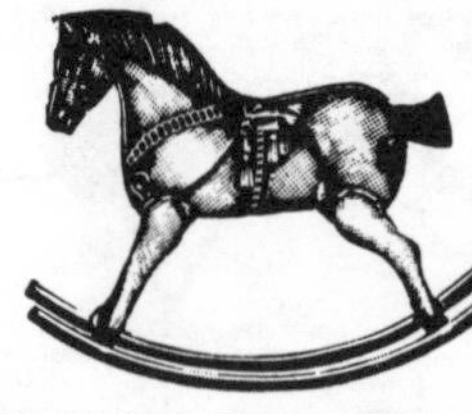

**F2281—Rocking Horse.** 9x6½, litho wood horse, steel legs, red painted wood rockers. 1 doz. in box....................Doz. **82c**

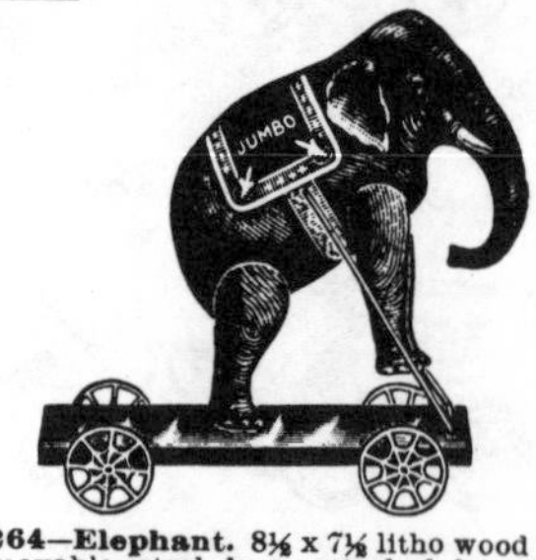

**F2264—Elephant.** 8½ x 7½ litho wood body, movable steel legs, attached by wire to 10x4 green wood platform, aluminum steel wheels, adjustable to many circus poses. ½ doz. in box ......................Doz. **$1.88**

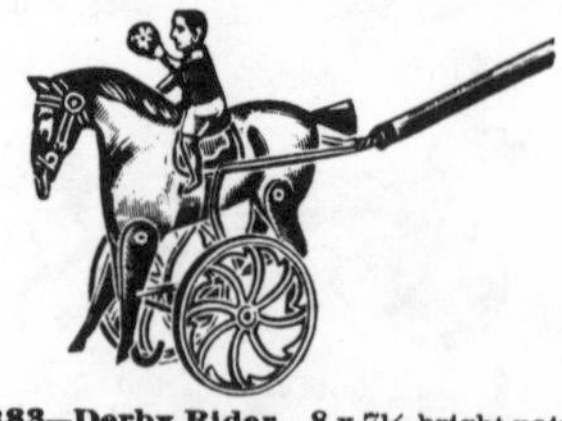

**F2283—Derby Rider.** 8 x 7¼, bright painted metal jockey on litho wood horse, movable steel legs attached by wire to fancy aluminum wheels, 24 in. handle. ½ doz. in box. Doz. **$1.88**

## GIBBS' FAMOUS TOPS—With Automatic Spring Winders.

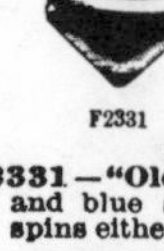

F2331

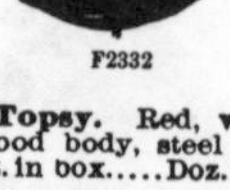

F2332

**F2331—"Old Glory" Topsy.** Red, white and blue striped wood body, steel peg, spins either end. 2 doz. in box.....Doz. **38c**

**F2332—"Never Stop."** Girth 10 in., bright enameled steel, whistles when spun. 1 doz. in box. .... ...... .... ............ .Doz. **75c**

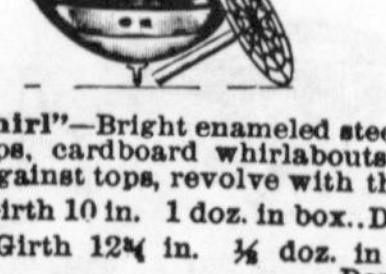

**"Merry Whirl"**—Bright enameled steel humming tops, cardboard whirlabouts which, placed against tops, revolve with them.

**F2341**—Girth 10 in. 1 doz. in box..Doz. **78c**

**F2342**—Girth 12¾ in. ½ doz. in spaced box... ....... ....... ......... Doz. **$1.75**

## "GEM" POCKET SAVINGS BANKS.

Nickeled, registers contents.

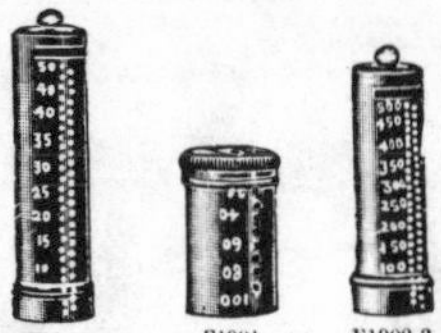

F1900 F1901 F1902-3

**F1900** — For 50 pennies. Open by screw at top. 1 doz. in box. Doz. **57c** Gro. $6.60

**F1901** — For 20 nickels, when full top springs open. 1 doz. in box. Doz. **57c** Gro. $6.60

**F1902** — For 50 dimes. Screw top. 1 doz. in box................Doz. **57c** Gro. $6.60

**F1903** — For 50 dimes. Spring top. 1 doz. in box................Doz. **57c** Gro. $6.60

## VEST POCKET DIME REGISTER BANK.

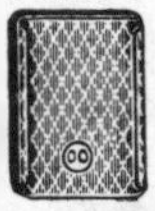

**F1904**—2⅜x1¾, embossed nickeled steel, locks and opens automatically, registers to $1.00. 1 doz. in box........Doz. **85c**

## POCKET COIN HOLDER.

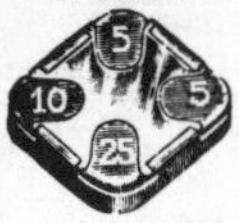

**F1905**—Nickel case, 1⅞ x 1⅞, 4 spring compartments for 5, 10 and 25c pieces. 1 doz. in box.....Doz. **75c**

## TIN BANKS—Lock and Key.

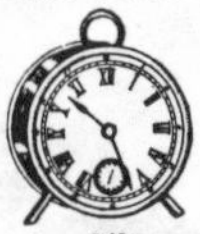

**F5278—Clock.** Gilt metal, printed dial, moving hands, ring top, door and money slot in back. 2 doz. in pkg.........................Doz. **36c**

**F5280—Asst.** 3x2x2. 2 styles, black enameled trunk, embossed straps, binding etc.; antique silver finish chest, embossed and beaded art design; hinged covers. 1 doz. in box. Doz. **42c**

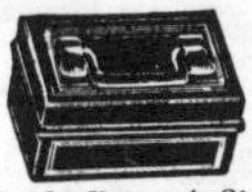

**F5276—Cash Box.** 4x2½x2, asst., fancy litho and black with gilt stripes, top handle. 1 doz. in pkg. Doz. **90c**

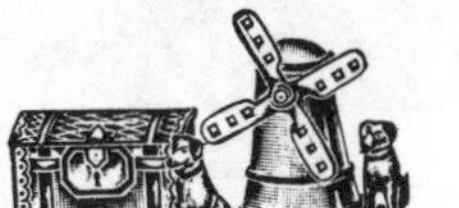

**F5282** — **Asstd.** Nickeled clock, windmill, doghouse, chest, etc., coin opening hinged door bottom, each with black and white enameled metal dog attached. 1 doz. in box. Doz. **95c**

## POPULAR TOY BANKS.

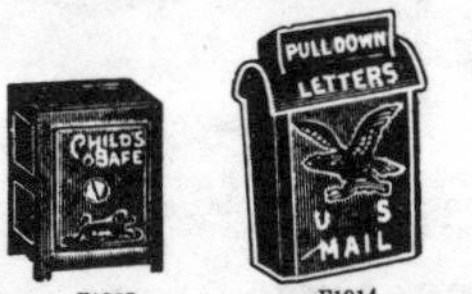


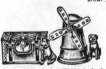

F1907 F1914

**F1907—Fire-proof Safe.** 3x2, red sheet steel, green hinged door, lock and key. 1 doz. in box.....Doz. **36c** Gro. $4.20

**F1914 — Mail Box.** 4x2½x1, aluminum finish iron, red letters. 1 doz. in box..................Doz. **72c** Gro. $8.35

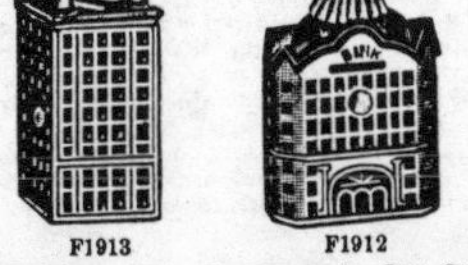

F1913 F1912

**F1913 — "Sky Scraper."** 2¼x2¼x4½, aluminum finish iron, gilt top. 1 doz. in box..................Doz. **82c**

## BRONZED IRON BANKS.

Gilt decorated.

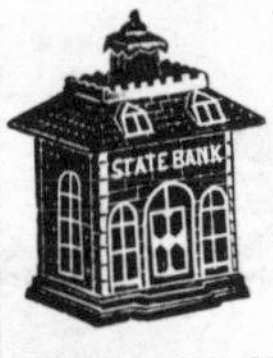


**F1909**—2 x 1¾ x 3 in. 1 doz. in box. Doz. **40c** Gro. $4.60

**F1910**—3x2⅜x4⅛ in. 1 doz. in box. Doz. **82c** Gro. $9.50

**F1911** — 4 x 3⅛-x5¾, lock and key, hinged door. ⅓ doz. in box. Doz. **$1.92**

## LOCK AND KEY IRON BANK.

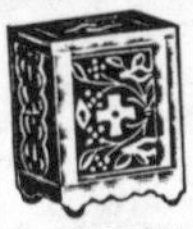

**F1906**—2⅝x3⅛, ht. 4⅛. polished edges and embossed designs sides and top, lock and key. ¼ doz. in box...Doz. **$1.95**

## COMBINATION NICKELED IRON SAFES.

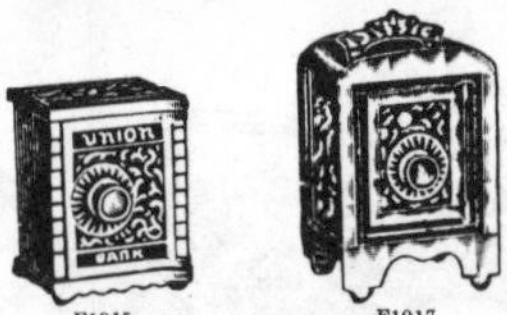


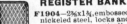

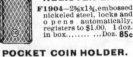

F1915 F1917

**F1915** — 2¼x2⅛x3⅛. Embossed designs sides and tops, steel sides and back. 1 doz. in box..........Doz. **79c** Gro. $9.25

**F1917**—5x3x2⅛, as above, polished edges, handle top. ⅙ doz. in box. Doz. **$1.95**

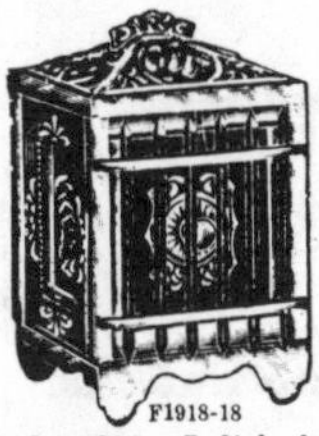

F1918-18

**F1918**—6x4x3⅛. Polished designs and edges, handle tops. Each in box. ⅙ doz. in pkg...................Doz. **$4.10**

**F1919**—8x5x5, as above. ½ doz. in box.............................Doz. **$8.95**

## STEEL COMBINATION SAFES—On Wheels.

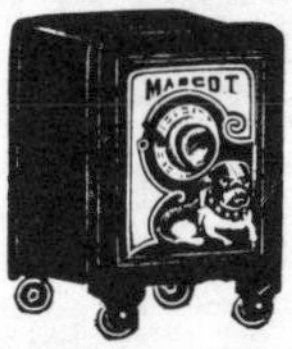


Black japanned, litho doors, combination locks with numbered dials. Each with combination.

F1952—3⅝x3, ht. 5⅛. 1 doz. in box. Doz. **89c** Gro. $10.50

F1953—4¾x3⅛, ht. 6. ⅙ doz. in box. Doz. **$1.75**

## "KODAK" NICKELED IRON BANK.

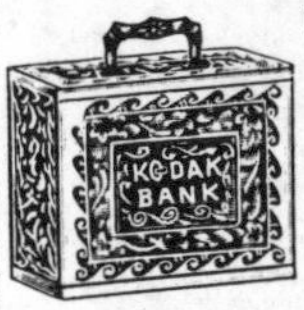


**F1916** — 5 x 2¾, ht. 4¼, floral embossed all sides and top, burnished edges and adjustable handle, lock and key. Each in box, ¼ doz. in pkg. Doz. **$3.95**

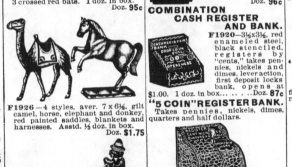

## NOVELTY BANKS.

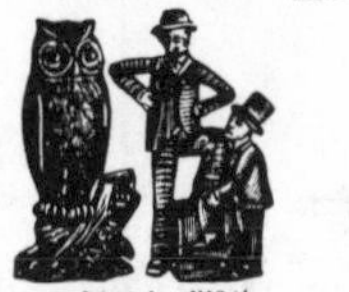

2 of 3 styles F1924

**F1924** — 3 styles, aver. 4½ in., gilt Campbell Kids, Mutt & Jeff and wise owl. Asstd. 1 doz. in box.. Doz. **78c** Gro. $9.00

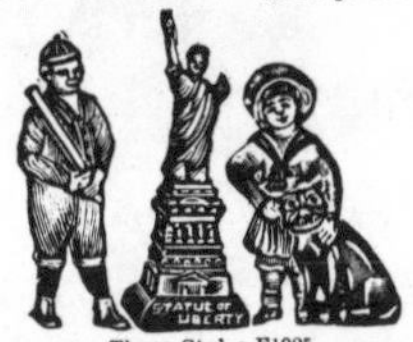


Three Styles F1925

**F1925** — 3 styles, aver. 6 in., gilt Statue of Liberty, Buster & Tige and elk, painted features. Asstd. 1 doz. in box.......... ...........Doz. **85c** Gro. $9.75

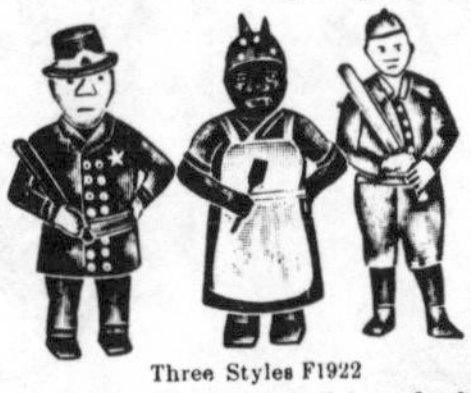

Three Styles F1922

**F1922—6 styles,** aver. 6 in., darkey with gilt hat and shirt, black pants; gilt clown, baseball player and bear; mammy with blue dress, aluminum apron, red bandana; blue uniform policeman; painted features. Asstd. 1 doz. in box..... ...........Doz. **85c** Gro. $9.75

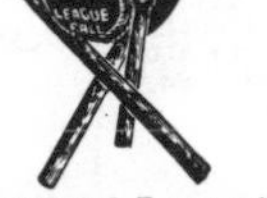


**F1931**—**"Official League" Base-ball Bank.** Ht. 5¼ in., aluminum finish iron baseball with slot, on 3 crossed red bats. 1 doz. in box. Doz. **95c**

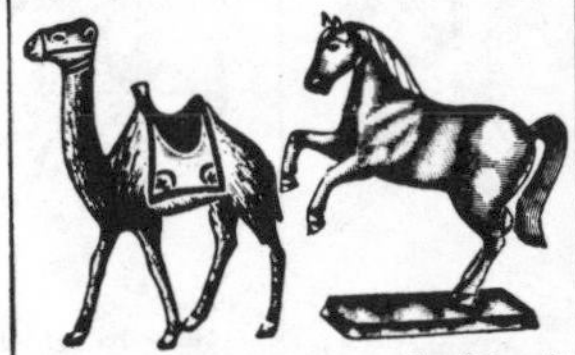

**F1926** — 4 styles, aver. 7 x 6⅛, gilt camel, horse, elephant and donkey, red painted saddles, blankets and harnesses. Asstd. ⅓ doz. in box. Doz. **$1.75**

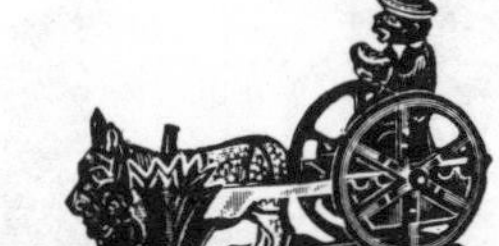

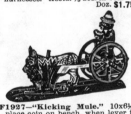

**F1927**—**"Kicking Mule."** 10x6⅛, place coin on bench, when lever is pressed mule turns quickly and upsets darkey, depositing coin. ½ doz. in box.......... ............Doz. **$7.80**

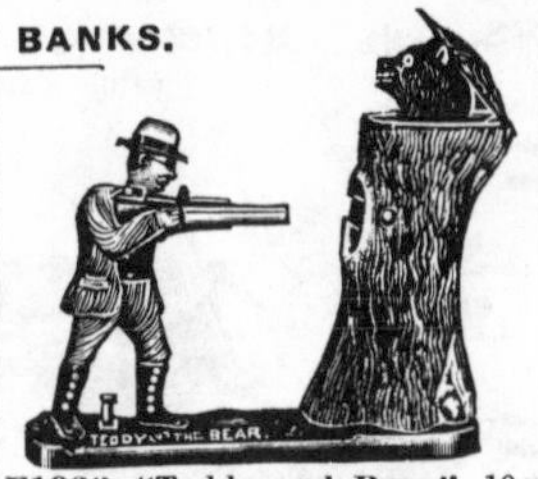


**F1928**—**"Teddy and Bear."** 10 x 7⅛, painted hunting costume, bear concealed in tree, place coin on gun, when lever is pressed coin shoots in tree and bear appears. ½ doz. in box........... ............Doz. **$8.00**

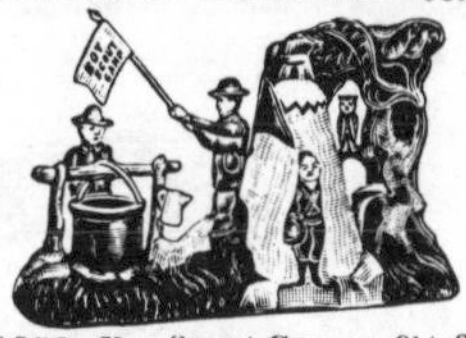

**F1929**—**Boy Scout Camp.** 9⅛x3⅛, green bronze finish base tent, camp, fire with kettle, 3 figures, when coin is deposited one figure raises flag. ½ doz. in box.......Doz. **$8.00**

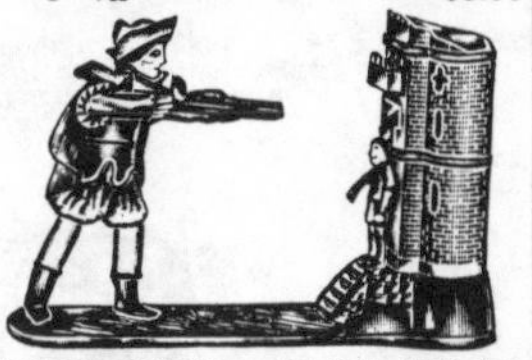

**F1930**—**"William Tell."** 10⅛x6¼, castle and figure in colors, place coin on gun, when lever is pressed apple falls from child's head and money is deposited. ½ doz. in box. Doz. **$8.00**

## STEEL "TELEPHONE" BANK.

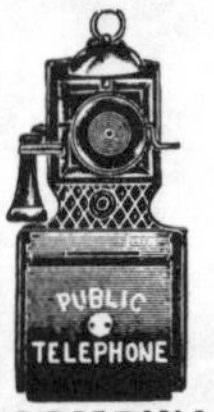


**F1745**—7⅛ x 3⅝ in. black japanned steel, nickeled bell with crank, turned edge transmitter, receiver on long cord, polished steel hook, slotted telephone box for coins. 1 doz. in box. Doz. **96c**

## COMBINATION CASH REGISTER AND BANK.

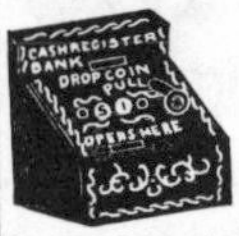


**F1920**—3⅛x3⅛, red enameled steel, black stenciled, registers by "cents," takes pennies, nickels and dimes. lever action, first deposit locks bank, opens at $1.00. 1 doz. in box..........Doz. **87c**

## "5 COIN" REGISTER BANK.

Takes pennies, nickels, dimes, quarters and half dollars.

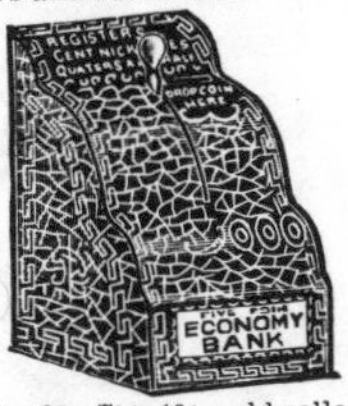


**F1889**—6¾x7¼x4¾, cold rolled steel in hammered brass effect, gold stencil nickeled lever, when drawn down registers amount and bell rings, first deposit locks bank, registers to $10.00. ½ doz. in box. Doz. **$9.00**

## REGISTER BANKS.

Cold rolled steel, gilt decorated, when lever is pressed amount is automatically registered. With directions.

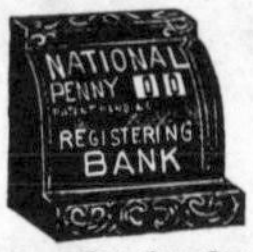


**Small Size** — 3⅛x3¼x3⅛, black japanned. Each in box, ⅙ doz. in pkg.

| | Registers to | |
|---|---|---|
| F1879—Penny. | $1.00....Doz. | $1 90 |
| F1908—Nickel. | 10.00.... " | 1 90 |
| F1880—Dime. | 10.00.... " | 1 90 |

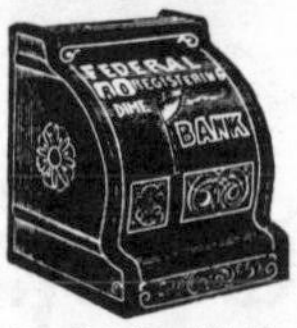


**"Federal"**—4⅞x4⅛x4¼, black japanned, red & gilt lettering, celluloid covered register dial, bell rings when coin is deposited. Each in box, ¼ doz. in pkg.

| | |
|---|---|
| F1891—Penny.............Doz. | $4 25 |
| F1949—Nickel .............. " | 4 25 |
| F1893—Dime .................. " | 4 25 |

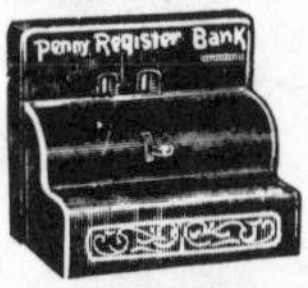


**Cash Register Model**—4¾ x 4 x 3. High grade, baked black enameled heavy steel, bell rings when coin is deposited. 1 in box.

| | Registers to | |
|---|---|---|
| F1933—Penny. | $1.00.....Doz. | $5 50 |
| F1934—Dime. | 10.00..... " | 5 50 |

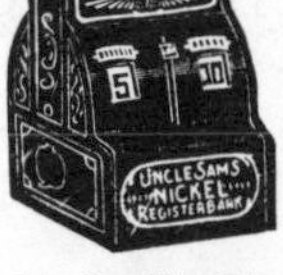


**"Uncle Sam"** — 4⅛ x 3⅛ x 4⅛, high grade, black enameled heavy steel, gun metal & brass plates, bell rings when coin is deposited. 1 in box.

| | Registers to | |
|---|---|---|
| F1935—Nickel. | $10.00.....Doz. | $8 50 |
| F1936—Dime. | 20.00.... " | 8 50 |
| F1937—Quarter. | 20.00..... " | 8 50 |

## "3 COIN" REGISTER BANKS.

**For 5, 10 and 25c.** Locks with first coin — unlocks at $10.00. Bell rings with each deposit.

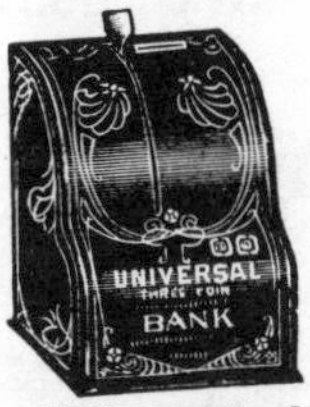


**F1887** — **"Universal."** 5 x 4 x 5⅛, heavy black baked enameled steel, gilt ornamented, coin slot with lever. ½ doz. in box..... ........Doz. **$9.00**

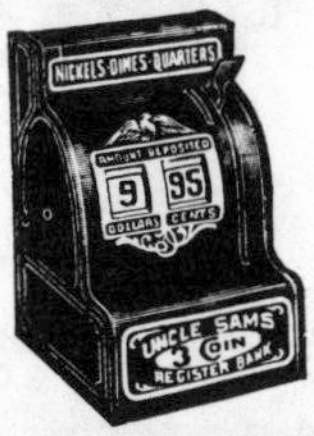


**F1888**—**"Uncle Sam."** 8x4x5⅛, extra heavy black enameled sheet steel, brass trim, nickel register and bell, coin slot with lever. ½ doz. in box..........................Doz. **$12.00**

## TOY CASH REGISTER.

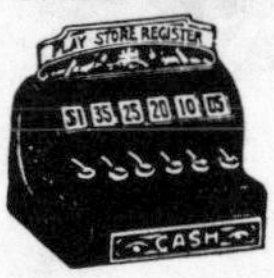


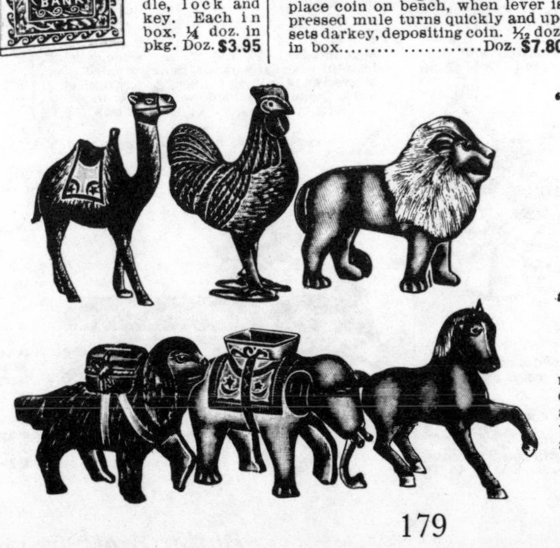

## "6 STYLES" IRON BANK ASSORTMENT.

*Wonderfully big sellers. Models that will please the wee customer.*

**F1921—6 styles,** 5x3¾, gilt rooster, camel, lion and bull-dog, gray elephant with blanket and saddle, black horse, red, silver and gilt decorated. Asstd. 1 doz. in box. Doz. **85c** Gro. $9.75

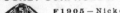

## WOOD WHEELBARROWS.

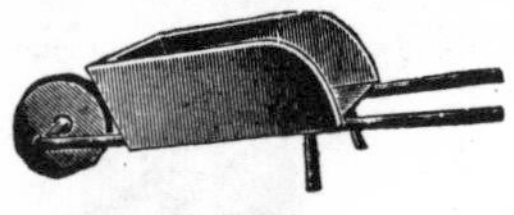

**F1359**—About 24x8, stained red, solid wheel. 1 doz. in crate, 12 lbs................ Doz. **89c**

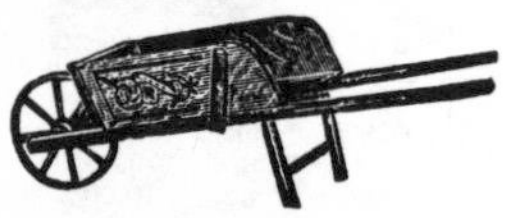

**F1363**—Length 24 in., varnished and stenciled, 6 in. spoke wheel, tin tire. ½ doz. in crate, 17 lbs.............. ................Doz. **$1.95**

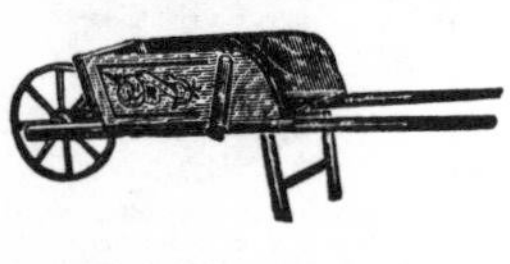

**F1364**—Length 35 in., varnished and stenciled, 8 in. spoke wheel, iron tire. ⅓ doz. in crate, 28 lbs ........................ ..Doz. **$3.98**

## STEEL WHEELBARROWS.

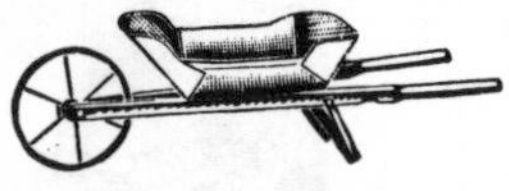

**F1366**—**"Panama."** Length 24½ in., 9x11¾x 6½ red enameled sheet steel body, 6½ in. single spoke black enameled wheel, red end handles, steel legs. 1 doz. in crate, 20 lbs. Doz. **$2.25**

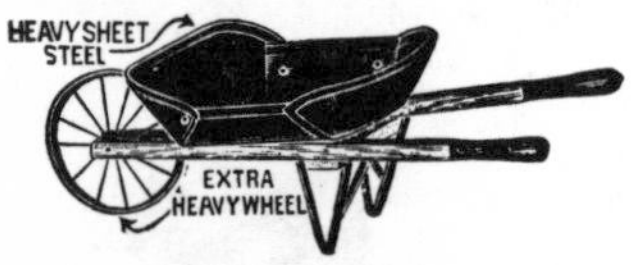


**F1367**—**"Panama."** Length 34 in. 12x 14x3½ maroon enameled heavy sheet steel body, 8 in. tangent spoke heavy tinned wheel. ½ doz. in crate, 18 lbs. Doz. **$3.95**

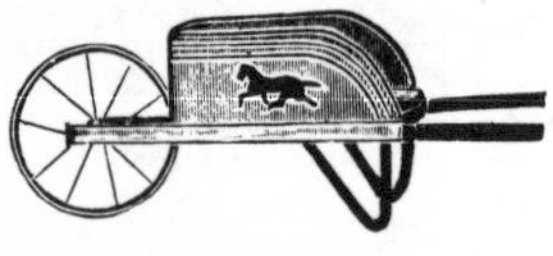

**F1369**—**Extra Large.** Length 50 in., 18x15x 6½ bright red body, gilt stripes, 14 in. double spoke steel wheel, iron foot rests. ⅓ doz. in crate, 16 lbs.............Doz. **$8.10**

## BOYS' WOOD CARTS.

**Long Handles.**

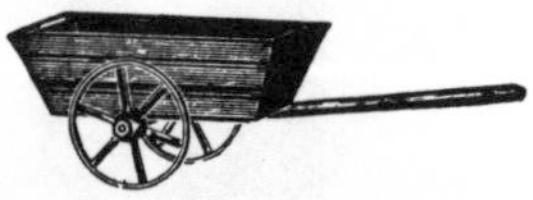

**F1434**—**Hay cart.** 13½ x 7, stained body, 3 slat open sides, tin capped wheels. 2 doz. in crate, 26 lbs........................Doz. **75c**

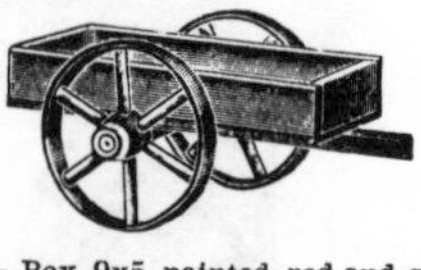

**F1435**— Box 9x5, painted red and stenciled, 6 in. tin tire wheels. 2 doz. in crate, 25 lbs. Doz. **75c**

## EXTRA LARGE SIZE STEEL CARTS.

Baked red enameled heavy steel bodies, black enameled steel wheels, wood axles and long handles.

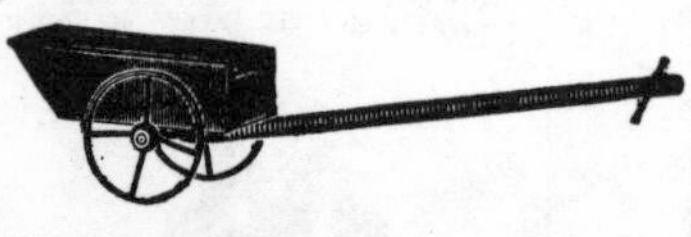

**F1484**—9¾x6¾, 3 in. deep, 5 in. single spoke wheels. 1 doz. in crate, 25 lbs..... Doz. **$2.25**
**F1485**—12¾ x 9¼, 3¾ in. deep, 7¼ in. double spoke wheels. ⅓ doz. in crate, 20 lbs. Doz. **$3.90**

## BOYS' WOOD WAGONS.

**Long Handles.**

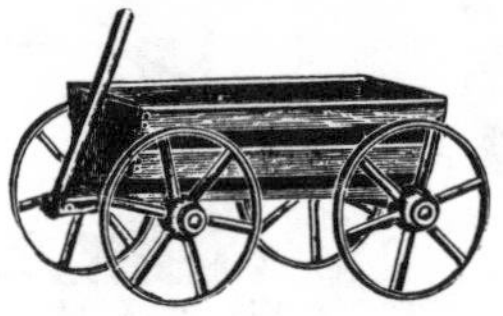

**F1436**—**Hay wagon,** 11x5½, ht. 4 red stained body, 6 in. wheels, tin tires and caps. 2 doz. in crate, 26 lbs.......................Doz. **89c**

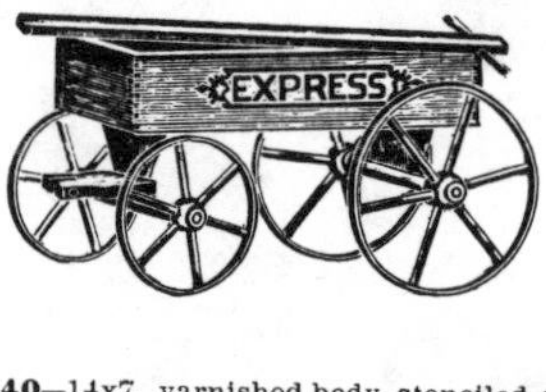


**F1440**—14x7, varnished body, stenciled, solid tail board, 6 & 8 in. wheels, steel tires. 1 doz. crate, 30 lbs.................Doz. **$1.95**

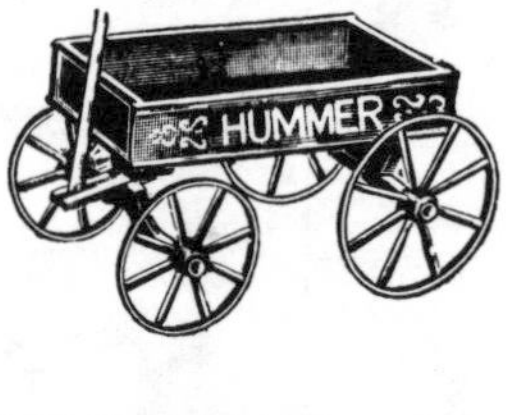


**F1444**—20x10½, painted body, stenciled sides, maple finish molding, 8 and 12 in. metal tire wheels. ⅓ doz. in crate, 47 lbs Doz....**$4.25**

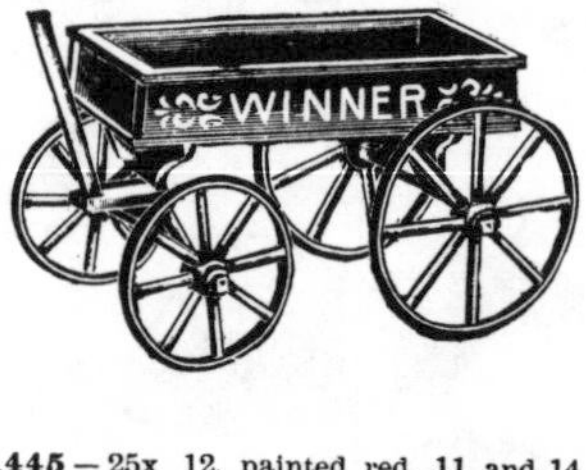


**F1445** — 25x 12, painted red, 11 and 14 in. wheels, iron axles, right and left nuts. ⅓ doz. in crate, 63 lbs.......... ........Doz. **$8.75**

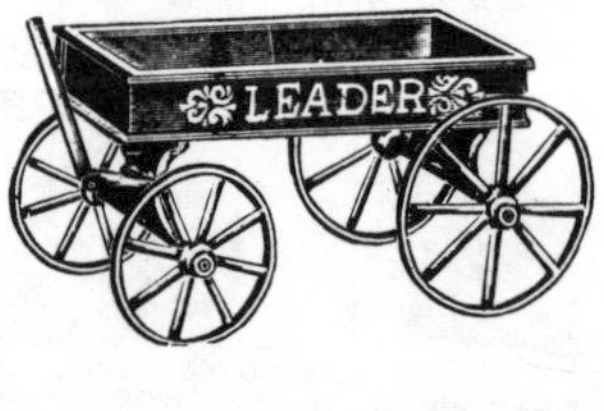


**F1446**—28x13, stenciled natural finish hardwood body, 11 and 14 in. wheels, heavy iron axles in iron thimble skeins, wood braces, malleable iron tongue fastening and fifth wheel. ⅓ doz. in crate, 62 lbs....Doz. **$9.50**

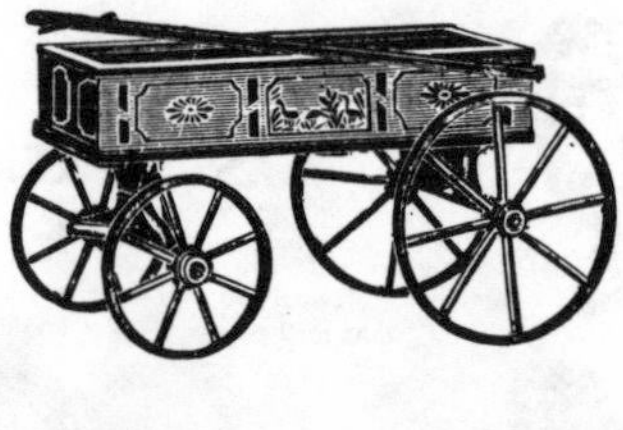

**Extra Quality** — Varnished and stenciled hardwood bodies, dovetail corners, oval tires, hub caps, steel axles.
**F1499**—29x15, 11 and 16 in. wheels. 4 in crate, 97 lbs. ......... ........ ..........EACH, **$1.35**
**F1500**—32x16, 13 and 18 in. wheels. 2 in crate, 60 lbs............................EACH, **$1.75**

## BOYS' WOOD WAGONS—Contd.

**Long Handles.**

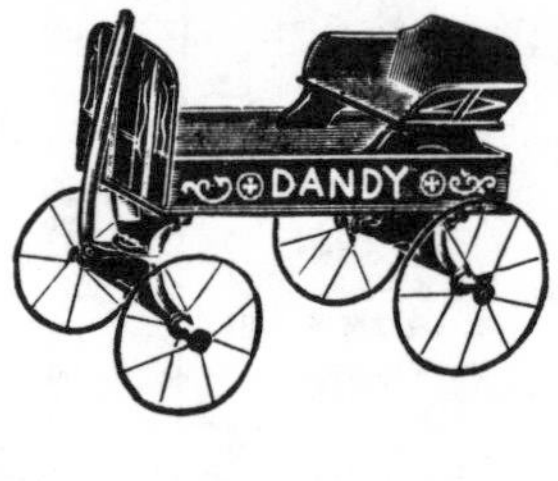


**F1447** — **Buggy** — 26x13, natural varnished seat and stenciled body, 12 and 16 in. wheels, iron axles, iron tongue draw and fifth wheel, hub caps. 2 in crate, 52 lbs.......Each. **$1.00**

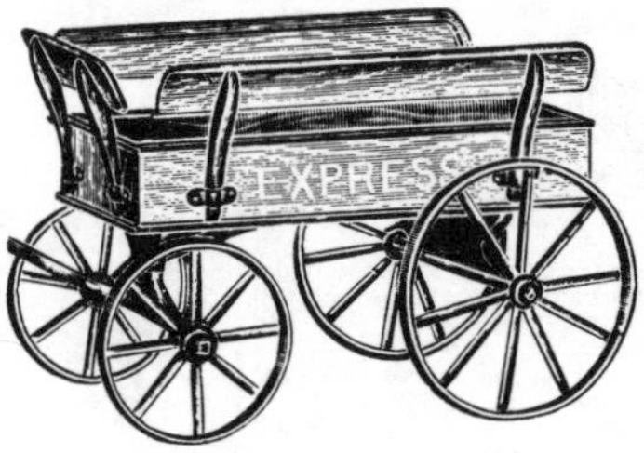


**Removable Sideboards and Dash.** Varnished natural hardwood, heavy welded tires, shaved spokes, strong striped handle, steel grip. 1 in crate.

| | Wheels | | Each |
|---|---|---|---|
| F1449—31x15, | 12 and 16 in., | wt. 36 lbs. | $2 00 |
| F1450—34x17, | 14 and 18 in., | wt. 46 " | 2 25 |

## HIGH GRADE WOOD WAGONS.

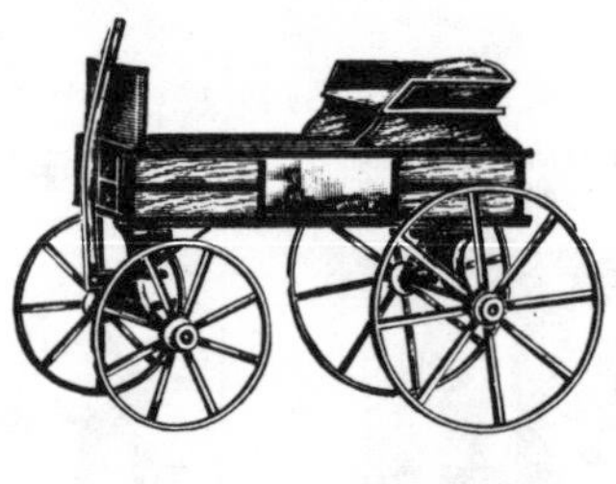

**F1473** — 28x14, bright red, landscape panel sides, painted seat and dash, 12 and 16 in. wood wheels, hub caps, iron braces, iron tongue draw, fifth wheel. 2 in crate, 52 lbs. Each, **$1.40**

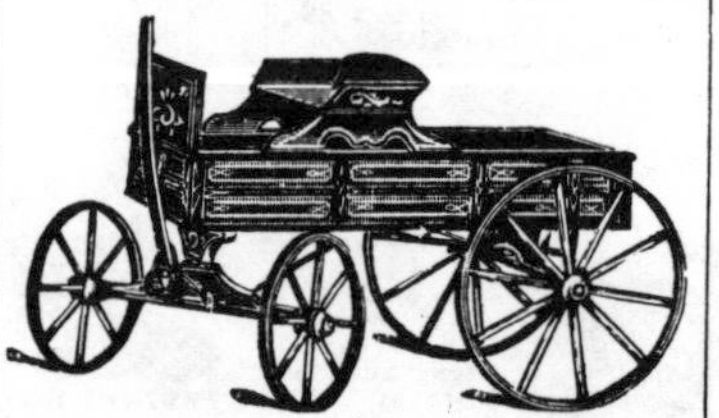

**F1458** — 38 x 18, painted, paneled sides, high seat and dash, 14 and 20 in. wood wheels, iron hub caps and bands, heavy welded tires, shaved spokes, iron braces, ⅝ in. round steel axle, removable sideboards. 1 in crate, 50 lbs..............................Each, **$3.75**

## "MARATHON" COASTER WAGONS

Hardwood body and gearing, varnished, decorated, bright red wheels, welded shrunk ¾x⅛ in. tires, malleable iron caps and band heavy round steel axles, extra heavy improved malleable iron steering gear, brake, removable bed.

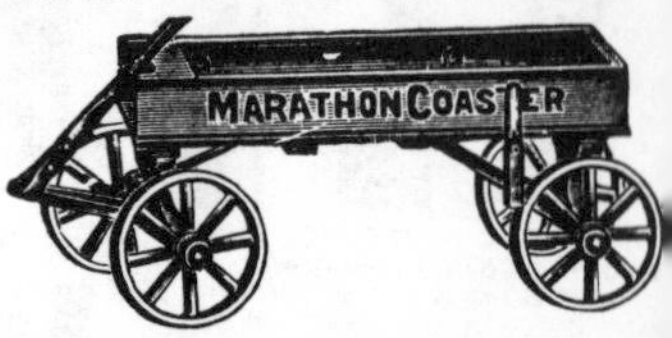


**F1501**—Body 13x28, wheels 8¼ in., 2 in crate 40 lbs........................ .........Each, **$1.3**

*Following with extra malleable iron hubs.*

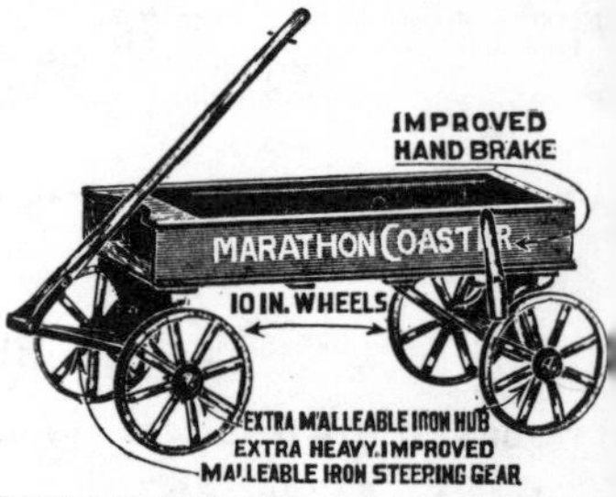


**F1502**—Body 14x32., wheels 10 in. 1 in crate 34 lbs................. ......... .Each, **$2.1**
**F1503**—Body 16x36, heavier and more substantial. 1 in crate, 40 lbs......Each, **$2.7**

## MINIATURE FARM WAGONS.

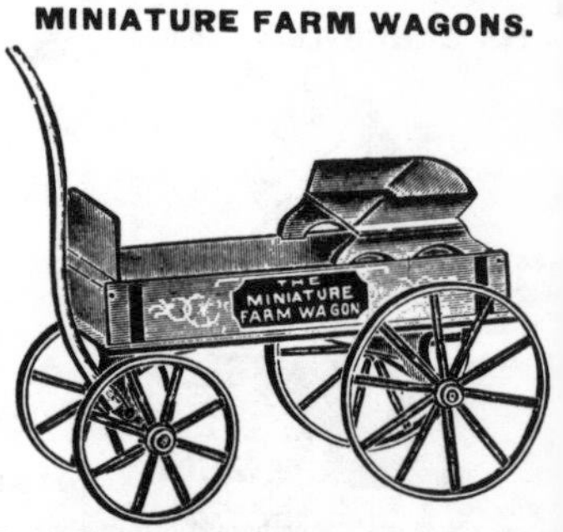


**F1455**—31x14½, varnished green hardwood body, dashboard and removable seat, yellow striped stenciled sides, varnished inside, removable sides and ends, 16 and 12 in. shaved spoke welded iron rim wheels, hub caps, strong wood axles, iron brace, heavy shaped iron-grip varnished wood handle. 1 in crate, 36 lbs.................... ..........Each, **$2.40**

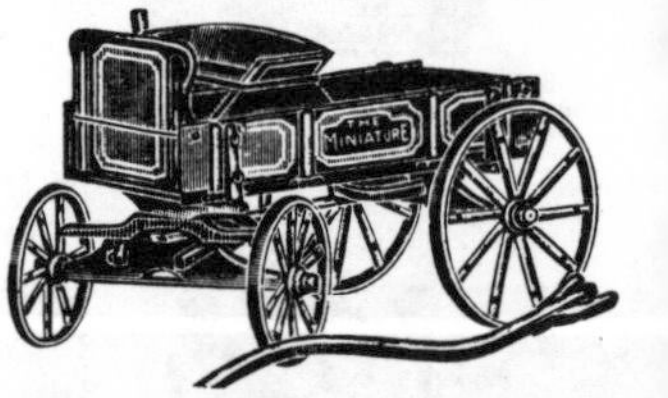

**F1457**—Body 18x36 in., hardwood frame, seat and dashboard, removable sides and ends, painted and ornamented, wheels 14 and 20 in., shaved spokes, heavy welded tires, malleable iron hub caps and bands, strongly ironed and braced, ⁹⁄₁₆ in. round steel axle, heavy handle. 1 in crate. 57 lbs.......Each, **$4.25**

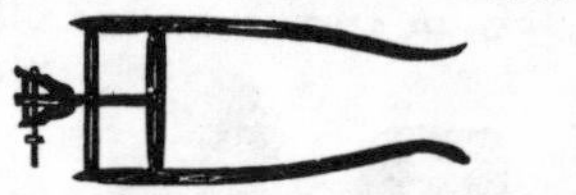

**F1471**—**Goat or Dog Shafts.** For F1457 farm wagon, length 42 in., width 17, painted red, black striped, 5 lbs...............Each, **65c**

## ROLLER BEARING AUTO WHEEL COASTER WAGON.

**With Quick Detachable Box.**

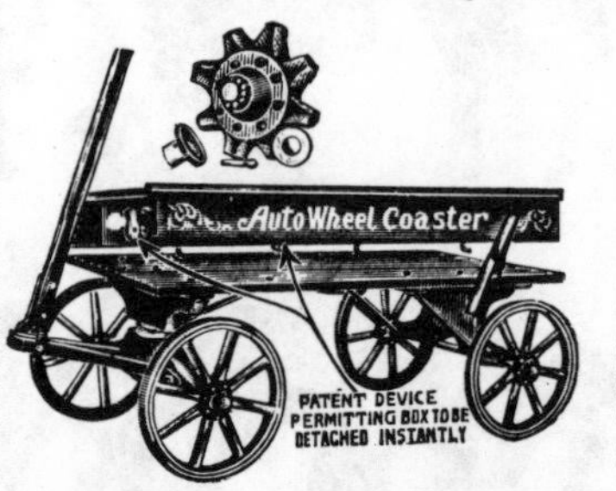


Extra high grade, built for strength and speed. Easiest running, and most durable wagon on the market.

Standard automobile type wheels, seasoned ash spokes, ovaled, mitred and machine riveted in hub, felloes ⅞x¾ in., with ⅛ in. flat steel tire, welded and shrunk on by hydraulic pressure, hard drawn Bessemer steel roller bearings running on cold drawn polished steel axles, steel cap and washer protecting hub and bearings from dirt; wagon bed of well seasoned white ash, natural finish, well varnished; bolsters of hard maple, thoroughly steel braced; wheels, edge of bed and top rim painted bright red, all metal parts black japanned and baked; patent locking device allows box to be removed instantly.

**F1504**—Body 14x34 in., wheels 10 in. 1 in carton, 30 lbs...... ...... ...... **Each, $3.00**

# "MARATHON" STEEL EXPRESS WAGONS

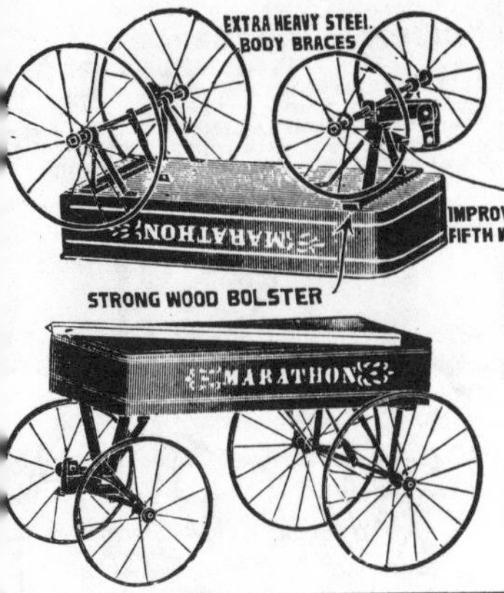


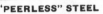

Heavy steel sides, corrugated band, **extra heavy steel braces and bolsters** attached to body by bolts (not screws), improved 5th wheel, heavy iron axles, extra heavy enameled wheels, body painted bright red, gilt name and stripe, inside green, varnished inside and out. **Nos. F1463** to **F1468** have extra braces attached to body and rear axle. All have patent handles that will not fall to ground.

F1469—Body 8¼ x 16 ⅛, wheels 8 and 6. ⅙ doz. in crate, 30 lbs..........Doz. **$4.25**

F1460—Body 8x18, wheels 9 and 6, ⅙ doz. in crate, 36 lbs..................Doz. ★**4.50**

*The following put up ⅙ doz. in crate.*

| | Body | Wheels | | | |
|---|---|---|---|---|---|
| F1461 | 10x20 | 10 " 7 | 14 " | .... " | $ 6 50 |
| F1462 | 11x22 | 11 " 8 | 17 " | .... " | 7 25 |
| F1463 | 12x24 | 12 " 8 | 22 " | .... " | 8 90 |
| F1464 | 13x26 | 13 " 10 | 30 " | .... " | 10 75 |
| F1465 | 14x28 | 14 " 11 | 32 " | .... " | 11 85 |
| F1466 | 15x30 | 15 " 12 | 36 " | .... " | 13 75 |
| F1467 | 16x32 | 16 " 13 | 40 " | .... " | 15 40 |

*Following Each in Crate.*

F1468—18x36 18 and 14 32 lbs....Doz. 22 50

**F1470—"Marathon" Steel Wagon Asst.** *6 of our best sellers.* 1/12 doz. each of above numbers F1461 to F1466 inclusive. ⅙ doz. crate, 80 lbs..........CRATE of 6...**$5.00**

# "PEERLESS" STEEL EXPRESS WAGONS.

Extra high quality, guaranteed the finest on the market. Heavy steel sides, corrugated bands, extra heavy steel braces and bolsters attached to body by bolts, improved 5th wheel and steel axles, baked black enameled double spoke wheels, heavy nickel plated caps on extra large hubs; body blue enameled outside, red inside, gold stenciled, extra braces attached to body and rear axles, strong patent painted handle, steel grip. 1 in crate.

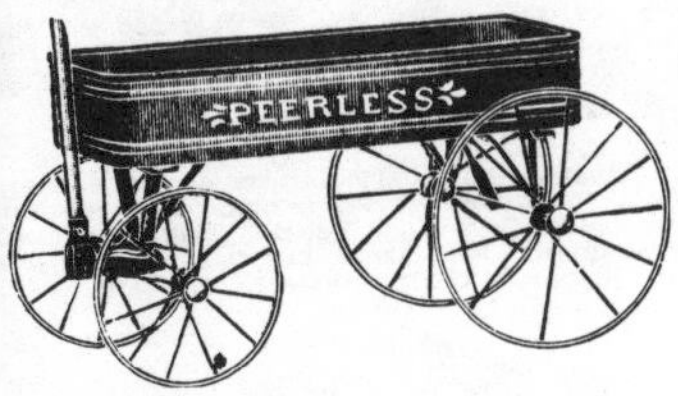


| | Body | Wheels | | | |
|---|---|---|---|---|---|
| F1474 | 12x24 | 8 and 12 | 16 lbs. | ....Doz. | $11 75 |
| F1475 | 13x26 | 10 " 13 | 17 " | .... " | 13 75 |
| F1476 | 14x28 | 11 " 14 | 19 " | .... " | 15 00 |
| F1477 | 15x30 | 12 " 15 | 20 " | .... " | 16 25 |

*As above with ½ in. rubber cushion tires.*

| | Body | Wheels | | | |
|---|---|---|---|---|---|
| F1479 | 12x24 | 8 and 12 | 16 lbs... | EACH, | $1 35 |
| F1480 | 13x26 | 10 " 13 | 17 " | .... " | 1 50 |
| F1481 | 14x28 | 11 " 14 | 19 " | .... " | 1 70 |
| F1482 | 15x30 | 12 " 15 | 20 " | .... " | 1 85 |

# STEEL BODY EXPRESS WAGON.

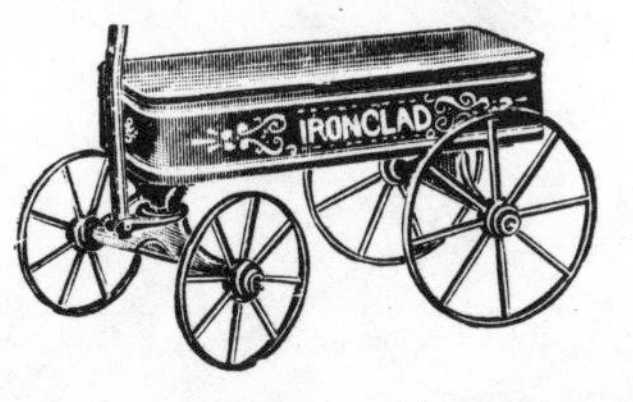


**F1443**—Body 10x20, bright red, gold striped, wood axle, hardwood gear, 8 and 10 in. wood wheels. ⅙ doz. in crate, 44 lbs. Doz. **$4.50**

# PATROL WAGON.

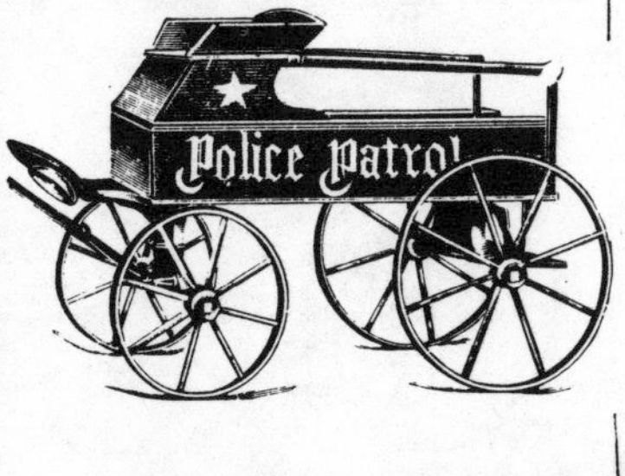


**F1459**—41x17, painted blue, stenciled sides, front and 2 side seats, wood rail, foot pressure gong, 12 and 16 in. wheels, oval tires. 1 in crate, 45 lbs..................Each, **$3.00**

# "MASCOT" HAND CAR.

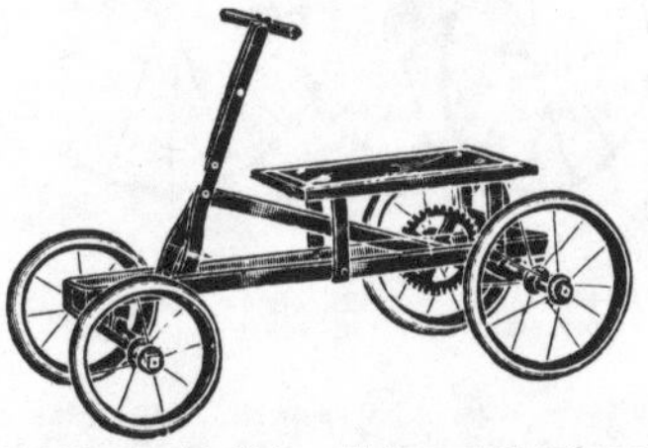

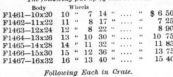

**F1047**—Length 26 in., gilt decorated red seat, black enameled steel frame and grip handle, 6⅛ and 8 in. black double spoke wheels, ⅜ in. rubber tires. 1 in crate, 20 lbs. Each, **$2.00**

# "INVINCIBLE" HAND CAR.

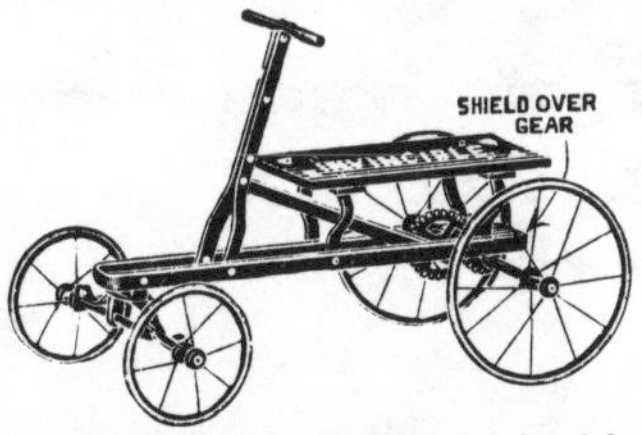


**F1048**—Length 32 in., 7⅛x16 painted and decorated seat, solid steel frame, steel handle and grip, black enameled heavy steel axles, 8 and 12 in. double spoke wheels, ⅜ in. rubber tires, shield over gear. 1 in crate, 30 lbs. Each, **$2.40**

# YANKEE FLYER HAND CAR.

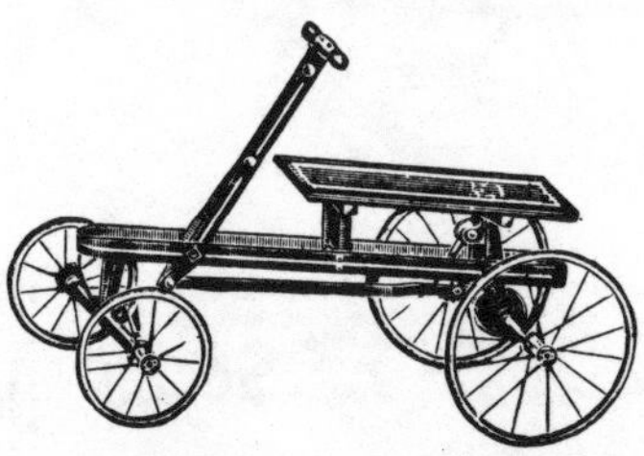

**F1057**—Length 35 in., 17¾x8¾ red enameled hardwood seat, black & gold decorated, green enameled heavy steel frame and handle, white stripes, varnished wood grip, 8 and 12 in. double spoke wheels, ⅜ in. rubber tires. 1 in crate, 50 lbs.....Each, **$3.25**

*"ERECTOR" STEEL TOYS*

*Finest toy a boy can have. Supplements manual training. Develops ingenuity. See our line in this book.*

# "MARATHON" STEEL HAND CARS

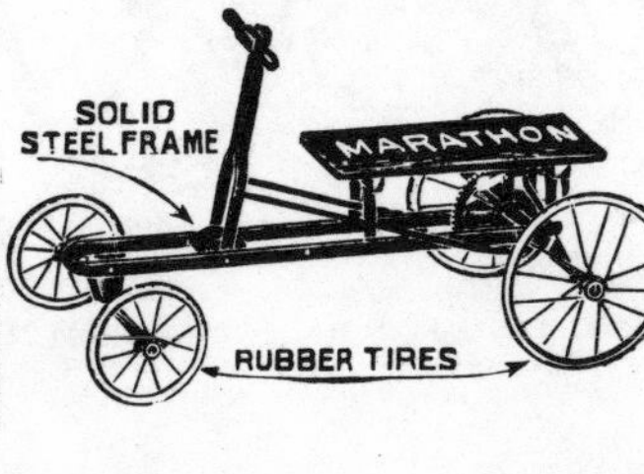


Bright painted and decorated seats, baked black enameled solid steel frames, improved gearing, double spoke wheels, ⅜ in. rubber tires.

**F1053**—**"Junior Special."** Length 30 in., wood grip steel handle, 8 and 10 in. wheels. For ages 3 to 7 yrs. 1 in crate, 22 lbs. Each, **$2.50**

**F1049**—**"Senior."** 39 in., wood grip steel handle, 8 and 12 in. tinned steel wheels. 1 in crate, 30 lbs, Each, **$3.00**

# "BEN HUR" HAND CAR.

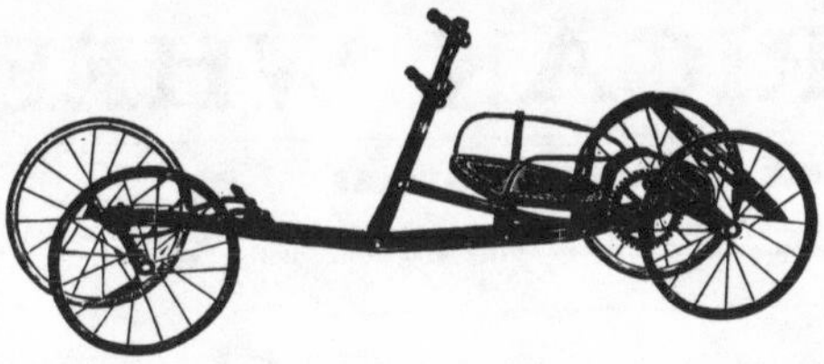

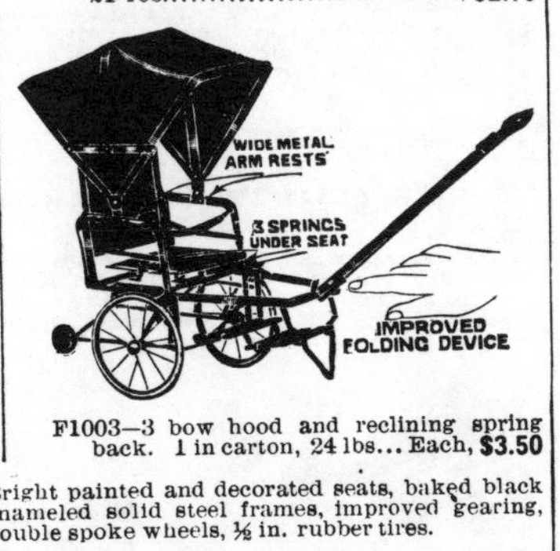

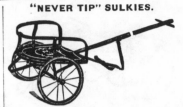

**F1068**—Length 60 in., 11 x 14¼ green enameled hardwood seat, steel back, extra heavy red steel frame, yellow stripes, 14⅛ in. foot rest, adjustable double grip enameled handle, 14 in. green enameled double spoke wheels, brass hub caps, **⅝ in. rubber tires**, extra rear wheel, shield covered gear. 1 in crate, 50 lbs. Each, **$6.00**

# "IRISH MAIL" HAND CAR.

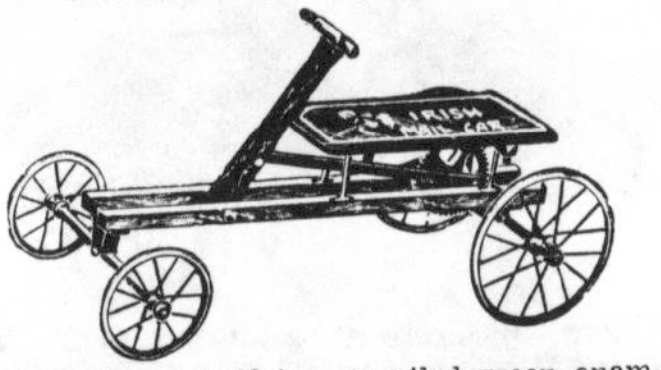


**F1050**—Length 40 in., stenciled green enameled seat, automobile gear, smooth sanded finish solid hickory frame, has greater tension than steel, 8 and 12 in. tinned steel wheels, extra heavy spokes and hubs, ⅜ in. rubber tires. 1 in crate 30 lbs..Each, **$2.98**

# "OUTING" ONE MOTION FLAT FOLDING SULKIES.

New 1914 line with many improvements, adding to comfort and convenience in their use. *Sulkies stand alone when folded.*

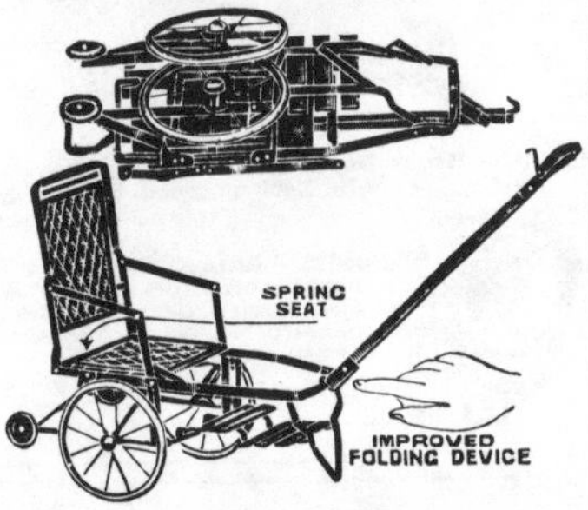


**F1000**—10 in. double spoke wheels with hub caps, ⅜ in. rubber tires, reinforced Bessemer steel frame, extra high tufted style fiber back and spring seat, extended folding foot rest, rear anti-tip and shock absorbing device with rubber tire wheels, baked black enamel finish. 3 in case, 50 lbs..Each, **$1.95**

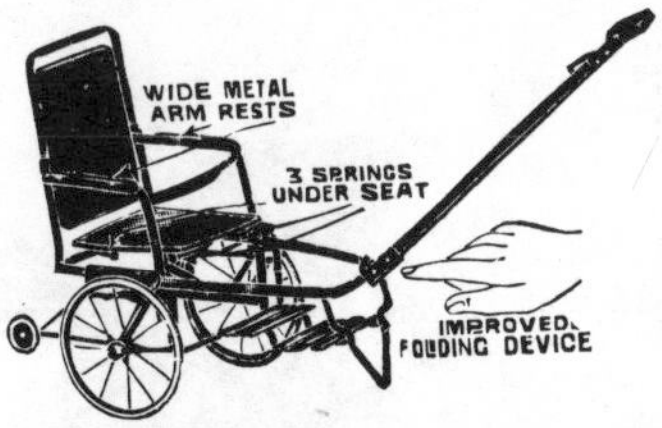


**Padded Seat and Back**—Similar to F1000 with padded imitation leather seat and back, 3 springs under seat, **wide metal arm rests,** mud guards, ⅜ in. rubber tires.

F1001—1 in carton, 18 lbs.......Each, **$2.50**

F1002—Reclining spring back. 1 in carton, 21 lbs...........................Each, **$2.75**

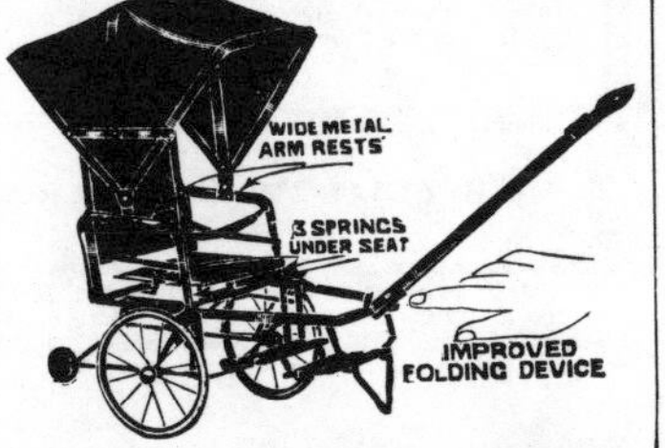


F1003—3 bow hood and reclining spring back. 1 in carton, 24 lbs...Each, **$3.50**

# "NEVER TIP" SULKIES.

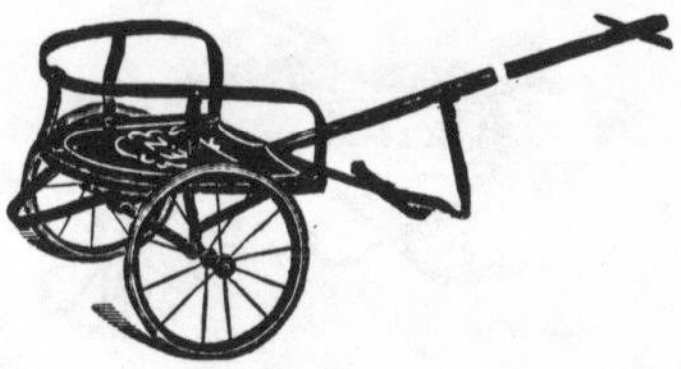

**F1008—Dandy.** Easily carries 150 lbs., seat 11x14, length 56 in., ht. 15 in., heavy 10 in. retinned rubber tire wheels, extra heavy handle and braces, asstd. bright red and green enamel painted striped seats and poles, baked black enameled gear, braces and adjustable foot rest. Asstd. ⅙ doz. in crate, 17 lbs.........................DOZ. **$8.75**

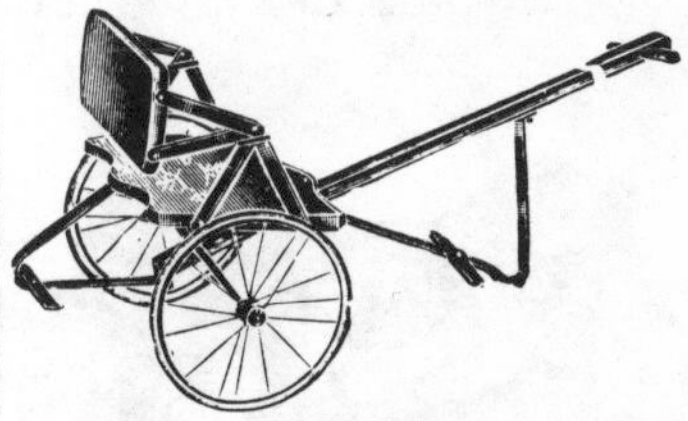

**F1009—Reversible.** Heavy wood seat 14x10, red painted, green stenciled, reinforced brace for reversing, adjustable front and back foot rests, 10 in. japanned double spoke wheels, ⅜ in. **rubber tires,** 48 in. heavy wood handle. 2 in crate, 24 lbs...Each, **89c**

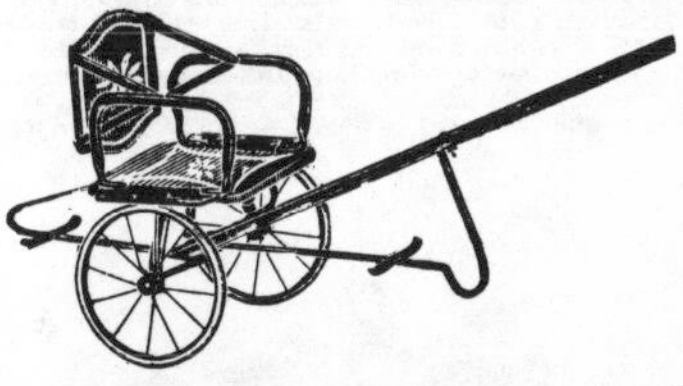

**Reversible**—Seat 10½x14, side bars and mud fenders, black enameled double action braces, adjustable front and back foot rests, 10 in. double spoke black enameled wheels, ⅜ in. rubber tires, nickeled hub caps, 52 in. striped enameled handles.

F1012—Heavy wood seat, painted bright red, yellow stripes. 2 in crate, 24 lbs. Each, **$1.15**

F1013—Padded leatherette seat and back. 2 in crate, 28 lbs..............Each, **$1.30**

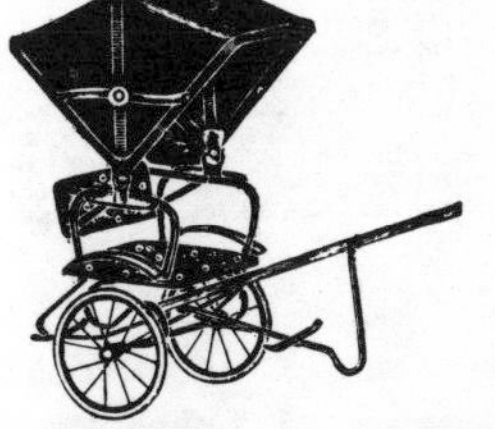

**Reversible, upholstered**—Seat 11x14, enameled red, green handles, striped in gold, 10 in. steel wheels, ½ in. rubber tires, nickeled hub caps, mud guard, 7/16 in. square iron axle with spring seat and back upholstered in leatherette, loop hand hold. 1 in crate.

F1018—Without hood. 19 lbs....Each, $1 75

F1019—With hood. 23 lbs...... " 2 50

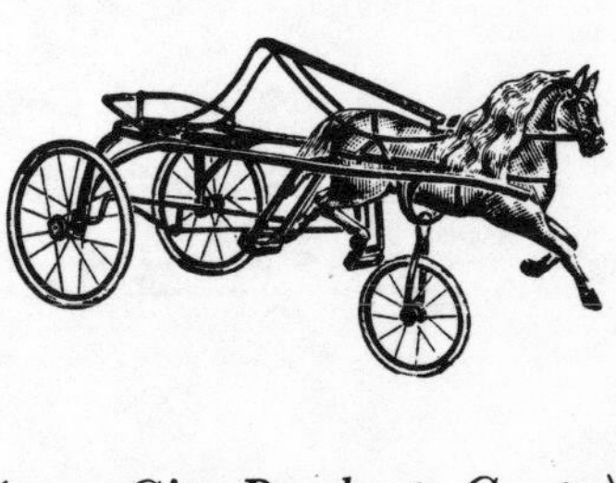

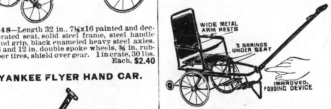

# AMERICAN WHEEL TOYS

## JUVENILE STEEL AUTOMOBILES.

The strongest line of juvenile autos on the market. All up-to-date models, handsomely finished, sheet steel bodies, auto steering gear, open bottoms, strong double spoke wheels. **Each in crate.**

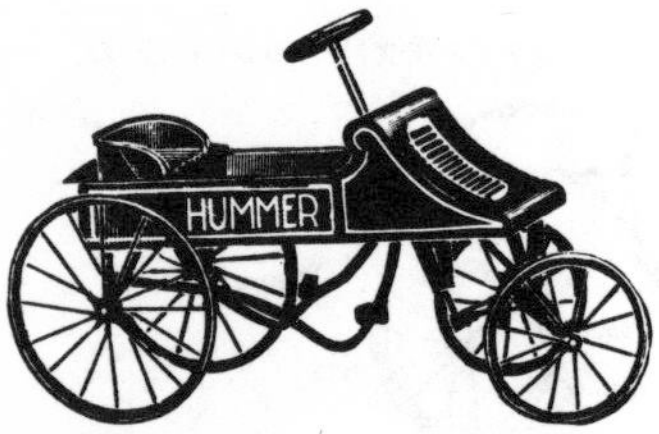


**"Hummer"**—30 x 14, bright red bodies and adjustable steel-back seats, gilt stenciled and striped, green inside, imit. ventilators, rachet cranks, malleable iron steering wheels, baked black enameled gear, 10 and 16 in. wheels. 1 in crate, 34 lbs.

F1042—Steel rim wheels ..... .Each, $2.75

F1035—⅜ in. **rubber tires**...... " 3.15

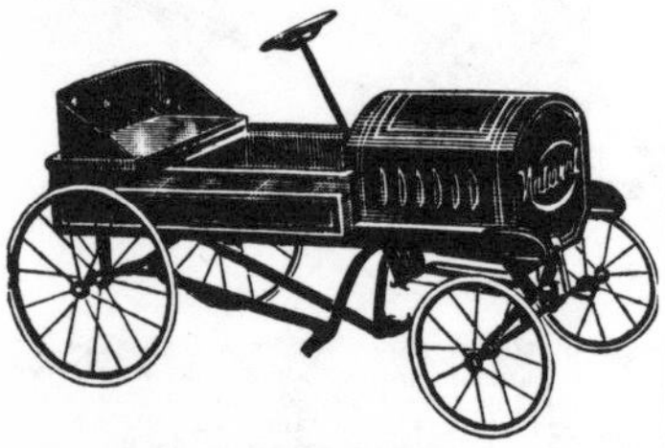

**F1036—"National."** 41x15, baked blue enameled steel body, gilt stripes, 11 in. wood seat, round steel back, rachet crank, black enameled gear pedals and steering wheel. 10 and 14 in. red enameled wheels, ½ in. rubber tires. 1 in crate, 44 lbs..Each, **$4.10**

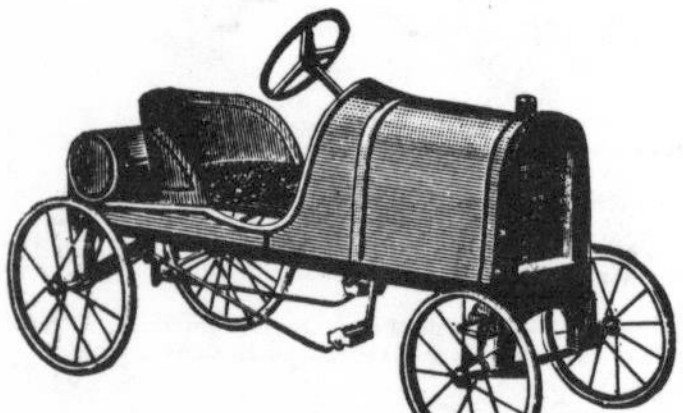

**F1041—"Pedalmobile" Ball Bearing.** 38x15⅛, red enameled body, black stripes, cowel dash, radiator front, water plug, gasoline tank, black leatherette upholstered seat, genuine auto steering gear, wood rim, 8 and 10 in. wheels, ½ in. rubber tires. Exceptionally easy running, for the small child. 1 in crate, 38 lbs.........Each, **$5.25**

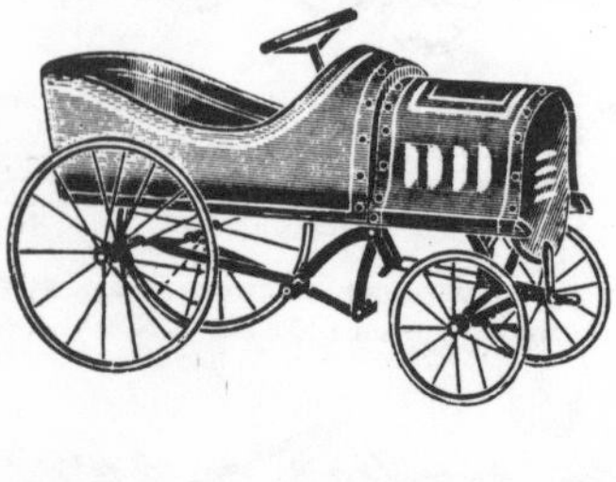

**F1037—"Wizard."** 37½x13½, red enameled body, blue & yellow stripes, brass studded, padded leatherette seat, gilt rachet crank, black gear and pedals, 10 and 16 in. red enameled wheels, ½ in. rubber tires. 1 in crate, 50 lbs.......................Each, **$5.40**

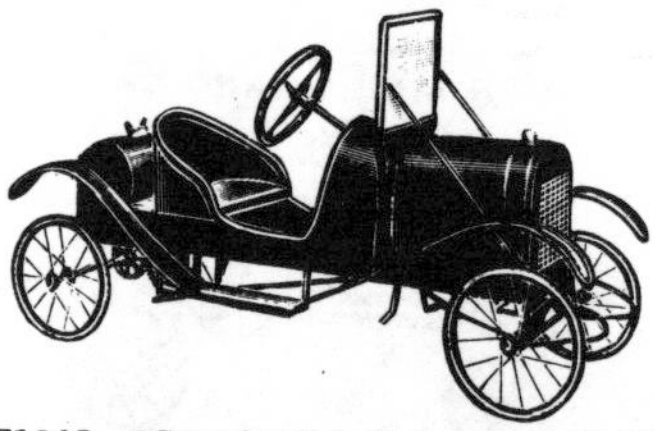

**F1043—"Scorcher" ball bearing,** 51x22, baked yellow enameled body and gasoline tank, black stripes, attachment for extra wheel, water plug, wire radiator, extension springs. 15x11 braced glass wind shield, mahogany finish wood rim steel steering wheel, large padded leatherette seat, extra high steel back, gilt striped black enameled continuous mud guards, extra heavy solid steel pedals, black steel gear, smooth cog-wheel action, 16 in. black enameled wheels, ½ in. rubber tires. 1 in crate, —— lbs. Each, **$9.50**

## JUVENILE AUTO SUPPLIES.

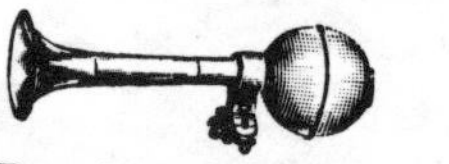

**F2890—Brass horn,** length 7 in., protected reed, rubber bulb. Each wrapped. Each, **38c**

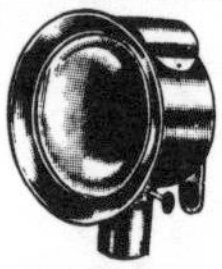

**F2892—Lamp,** 4⅛ in., removable brass oil fount with wick, large bullseye, polished nickeled reflector, bracket for attaching. 1 in box. Each, **42c**

## "CLIPPER" STEEL TIRE VELOCIPEDES.

Adjustable heavy leather seat on pat. saddle spring, extra heavy red enam. steel wheels, baked black enameled frame and brass ferrule grips. 1 pc. fork with adjustable catch, doing away with screws and bolts for setting up.

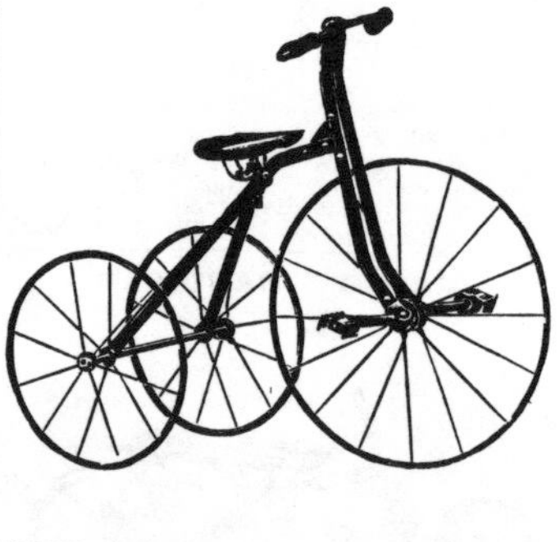

**F1248**—(Mfrs. 0). Wheels 14 and 10 in., for very small children, 3 in crate, 40 lbs. Each, **$1.05**

**F1249**—(Mfrs. 1). Wheels 16 and 12 in., 3 to 7 yrs. 3 in crate, 44 lbs..........Each, **$1.15**

**F1250**—(Mfrs. 2). Wheels 20 and 14 in., 5 to 9 yrs. 3 in crate, 52 lbs..... .....Each, **$1.35**

**F1251**—(Mfrs. 3). Wheels 24 and 16 in., 7 to 11 yrs. 3 in crate, 60 lbs..........Each, **$1.65**

**F1252—Asst.** Contains 2 only F1249, 1 only F1250 and F1251. 4 in case, 60 lbs. Asst. **$5.25**

## "SPEEDWELL" AUTO.

**Will delight any boy.**

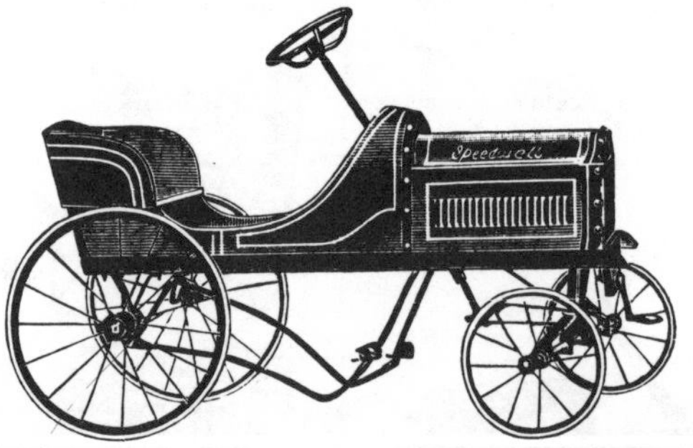


**F1038**—43½x15, gray enameled hardwood panels, steel frame, sides and seat white striped, black enameled, gold stencil, pierced brassed radiator, brass studded hood bands, massive effect, rachet crank, iron grip steering wheel, green enameled gear and pedals, 10 and 16 in. wheels, ½ in. rubber tires, license tag. 1 in crate, 70 lbs. Each, **$6.25**

## SPECIAL "CLIPPER" RUBBER TIRE VELOCIPEDES.

Red enameled steel frame and wheels, extra strong rear axle supports, padded leather bicycle saddle with nickel plated **double springs,** nickel plated adjustable handle bar with leather wound grips.

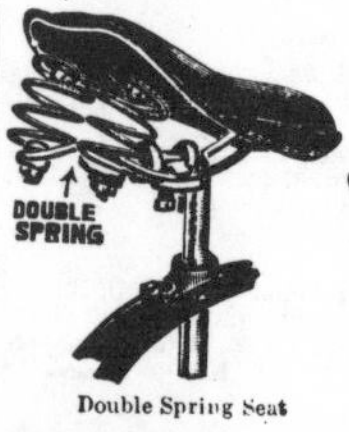


Double Spring Seat

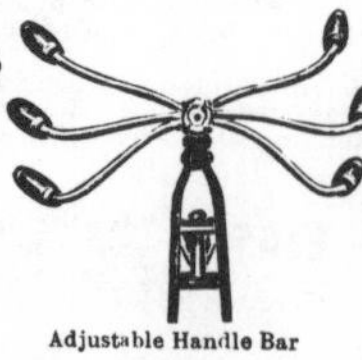

Adjustable Handle Bar

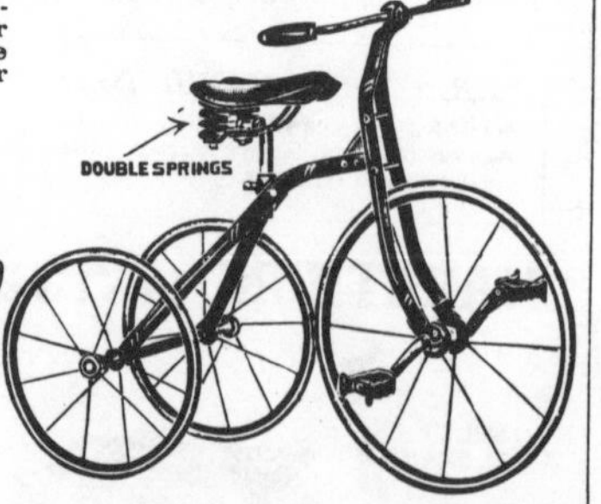


**F1254**—Wheels 16 and 12 in., ⅝ in. tires, 3 to 7 yrs. 1 in crate, 20 lbs.......... .Each, **$3.50**

**F1255**—Wheels 20 and 14 in., rear ½, front ⅝ in. tires. 5 to 9 yrs. 1 in crate, 25 lbs. Each, **$3.90**

**F1256**—Wheels 24 and 16 in. ⅝ in. tires. 7 to 11 yrs. 1 in crate, 23 lbs... ...... Each, **$4.25**

## "CLIPPER" RUBBER TIRE VELOCIPEDES

Adjustable heavy leather seat on pat. sadd spring, **extra heavy red enam. steel wheel** baked black enameled frame and brass ferru grips. 1 pc. fork with adjustable catch, doin away with screws and bolts for setting up.

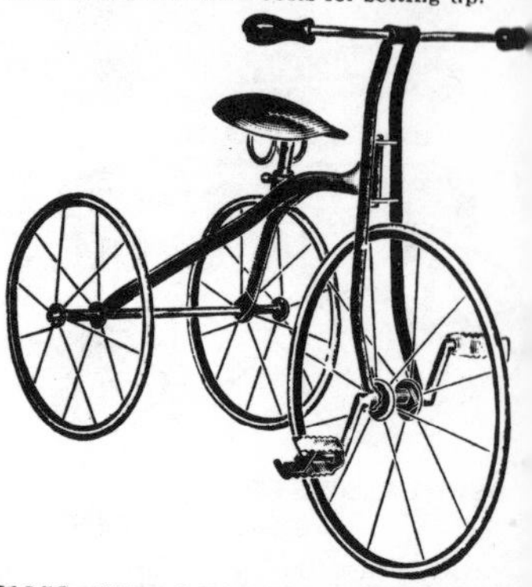

**F1253**—(Mfrs. O.R.). Weeels 14 and 10 in. for very small children. 1 in crate, 15 lbs Each, **$1.89**

**F1260**—(Mfrs. 1R). Wheels 16 and 12 in., ⅜ in. rubber tires, 3 to 7 yrs. 1 in crate 17 lbs.........................Each, **$2.08**

**F1261**—(Mfrs. 2R). Wheels 20 and 14 in., rear ⅜, front ½ in. tires. 5 to 9 yrs. 1 in crate 21 lbs..... ....................Each, **$2.40**

**F1262**—(Mfrs. 3R). Wheels 24 and 16 in., rear ⅜, front ½ in. tires. 7 to 11 yrs. 1 in crate. 25 lbs...........................Each, **$2.65**

## "CLIPPER" TRICYCLES.

Mechanically perfect in construction, finely finished, easiest propelled make on the market, enameled frame and gearing, bright retinned seat support and arms, heavy tinned wheels and pedals, plush upholstered seat and back. Each in crate.

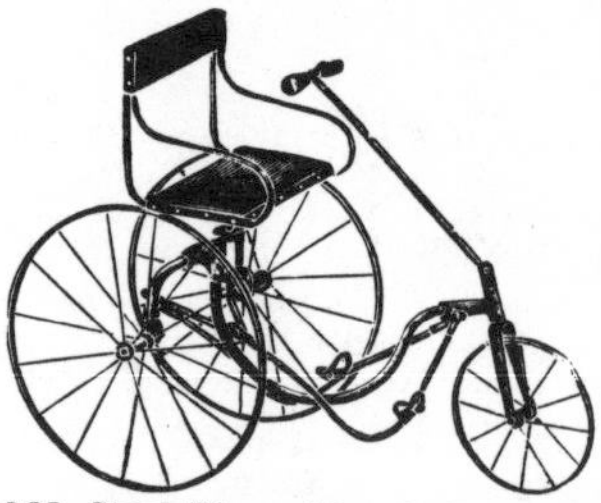

**F1263—Steel Tires.** 18 and 10 in. wheels. ages 2 to 6 yrs, 30 lbs.. ..........Each, **$2.75**

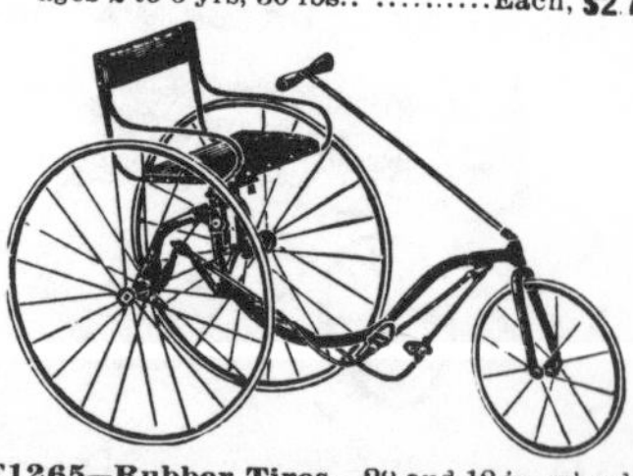

**F1265—Rubber Tires.** 20 and 12 in. wheels. rear ½, front ⅜ in. tires. 3 to 8 yrs. 30 lbs. Each, **$5.25**

## HIGH GRADE "CLIPPER" RUBBER TIRE TRICYCLES.

Rear wheels ⅝ in. tires, front ½.

Red baked enamel steel frame, gear and mud guards, gilt striped and decorated, perfectly constructed and finished, easily propelled, retinned steel wheels, red padded leatherette spring seat and back, nickel plated arms and steering rod, leather wound grips.

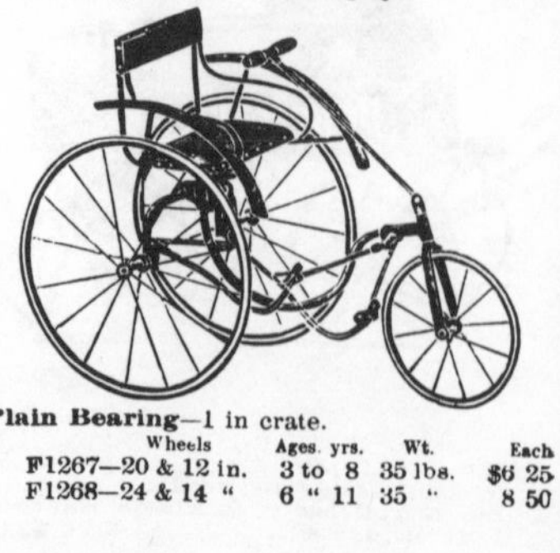

**Plain Bearing**—1 in crate.

| | Wheels | Ages yrs. | Wt. | Each |
|---|---|---|---|---|
| F1267 | 20 & 12 in. | 3 to 8 | 35 lbs. | $6.25 |
| F1268 | 24 & 14 " | 6 " 11 | 35 " | 8.50 |

## REED GO-CARTS.

Fancy reed bodies, turned wood posts and nobs.

*1224—Folding, ht. 21 in., large body, low dasher, 7 in. rear and 5 in. front wheels. 1 doz. in crate, 23 lbs.............Doz. **$2.00**

F1227—Ht. 21 in., large body, high dasher, 7 in. rear and 5 in. front wheels, enameled metal tires. 1 doz. in crate, 23 lbs. Doz. **$2.15**

F1225—Folding, ht. 23 in., oil cloth covered seat, reed back, 5 and 7 in. wood spoke metal tire wheels, green enameled handle and gear. ⅓ doz. in crate, 25 lbs.Doz. **$3.90**

F1226—Ht. 23 in., 7½x7½ oil cloth covered seat, metal springs, 5 and 9 in. wheels, green metal tires. ¼ doz. in crate, 18 lbs. Doz. **$3.95**

F1228—Ht. 26 in., 8x8½ varnished oilcloth covered seat, metal springs, 6 and 12 in. green enameled solid tire metal wheels. ¼ doz. in crate. 7 lbs.............Doz. **$9.00**

## SIDWAY'S "ALLWIN" SEMI-COLLAPSIBLE GO-CARTS.

F1200—Ht. 23 in., 14x7¾ maroon leatherette body, blued finish steel frame, 1 pc. handle, 5½ in. double spoke wheels. ⅙ doz. in crate, 17 lbs...........................DOZ. **$3.98**

F1203—Ht. 25 in., 25½x8½ double stitched leatherette body, full adjustable back, wood grip handle, black enameled steel frame and gearing, 6 in. double spoke wheels, asstd. black and green. ⅙ doz. in crate, 27 lbs. DOZ. **$8.00**

*Following have leatherette bodies, folding auto hoods and side curtains, adjustable backs, black enameled pushers and frames, wood grip handles.*

F1204—Ht. 23 in., body 18x9¾, 7 in. black steel rim wheels. Asstd. maroon and dk. green. 4 in crate, 35 lbs........ ..Each, **89c**
F1206—Ht. 23 in., body 18x9¾, 7 in. double spoke wheels, ⅜ in. rubber tires, nickel hub caps. Asstd. maroon and brown. 4 in crate, 36 lbs.......................Each, ★**89**
F1209—Ht. 25 in., body 20½x11, extra reinforced side gearing and axle braces, 9 in. double spoke wheels, ⅜ in. rubber tires, nickel hub caps. Asstd. maroon and brown. 2 in crate, 29 lbs ...................Each, **$1.75**

F1211 — Ht. 25½ in., body 22x11, nickel plated tubular pusher, heavy wood grip, full brown leatherette auto hood, retinned locker arms, brown enameled 3 ply veneer sides, gilt striped, black frame and gear, 9 in. retinned double spoke wheels, nickel hub caps, ⅜ in. rubber tires. 1 in crate, 16 lbs.Each, **$2.50**

F1210—Ht. 25 in., 21 x 11 brown leatherette body and folding hood, side curtains, adjustable back, black tubular pusher, wood grip, 9 in. double spoke wheels, ⅜ in. **rubber tires**, nickel hub caps. 1 in crate, 14 lbs.    Each, **$2.10**

## STEEL FOLDING GO-CARTS.

Full ht. 24½ in., canvas seat and back, long bent handle, bright enameled steel frame, 5½ in. double spoke steel wheels. ⅙ doz. in crate.

F1199—Without hood. 18 lbs......Doz. **$4.00**

F1198—With hood. 20 lbs.........Doz. **$4.40**

## WIRE GO-CARTS.

Strong and durable, light weight. Asstd. blue and cherry lacquered woven wire, turned fronts and backs, scroll sides, double spoke retinned steel wheels, removable handles and folding axles permit packing in small pkg. Each securely wrapped.

F1237—Ht. 16½ in., length 15, 3¾ in. front and 5½ in. rear wheels. ¼ doz. in case, 17 lbs. Doz. **$4.20**

F1238—Ht. 23 in., length 16, 5½ in. front and 8¼ in. rear wheels. ⅓ doz. in case, 16 lbs. Doz. **$8.00**

## WIRE DOLL CARRIAGES.

Strong and durable, light weight, asstd. blue and cherry lacquered woven wire, turned fronts and backs, scroll sides, spoke retinned steel wheels, removable handles and folding axles permit packing in small pkg. Each securely wrapped.

F1241—Ht. 17½ in., length 14¼, 5¾ in. wheels. ½ doz. in case, 15 lbs... .......Doz. **$4.20**

F1242—Ht. 23½ in., length 16, 8¼ in. wheels. ⅓ doz. in case, 17 lbs. ............Doz. **$8.00**

## REED DOLL CARRIAGES.

F1230—Ht. 19 in., body 15x7½, 5 in. wheels. 1 doz. in crate, 25 lbs.... ..........Doz. **$2.00**

F1232—Ht. 21 in., body 19x9, covered removable seat, 7 in. wheels, blocks between body and axles. ½ doz. in crate, 18 lbs.Doz. **$4.00**

F1233—Ht. 26 in., body 20x10, covered removable seat, 8 in. wheels, green enameled metal tires, blocks between body and axles strengthening rod; folding parasol with metal holder. ⅓ doz. in crate, 25 lbs..Doz. **$6.75**

# SHOO FLYS ROCKING HORSES, Etc.

## "SHOO FLY" ROCKING HORSES.

Except F1488 all painted and dappled horses, red rockers. Best values in America.

**F1488** — 12x34, oil finished natural wood, striped and ornamented, painted mane, hair tail. ½ doz. in crate, 57 lbs..... Doz. **$4.40**

**F1490** — 17 x 34, cretonne upholstered seat and back, painted mane, hair tail. ½ doz. in crate, 53 lbs..... Doz. **$7.25**

**F1491** — 21x38, in cretonne upholstered seat and back, play box, hair tail. ½ doz. in crate, 70 lbs..... Doz. **$8 60**

**F1492** — 21 x 38, cretonne upholstered seat, willow back, play box, tape reins. 4 in crate, 72 lbs..... EACH, **89 c**

## ASST. "SHOO FLY" ROCKING HORSES.

To Retail at 50c and $1.00.

**F1487** — Asst. comprises —
1 only 12x34, natural finish varnished.
2 " 16x36, white, dappled, painted seat.
2 " 17x34, cretonne padded seat.;
1 " 21x38, padded cretonne seat and back with play box, etc., 6 in asst. 70 lbs..... Each, **55c**

## HIGH GRADE SHOO FLYS.

Extra fine quality and finish, knocked down, easily set up.

Varnished mahogany finish hardwood horses, hand decorated bridles, saddles, harness, footboards and play boxes, hair manes and tails, extra high back corduroy upholstered seats, red rockers.

**F1429** — 21x39. 2 in crate, — lbs... Each, $1 50
**F1430** — 22x44. 2 in crate, — lbs... " 1 85
**F1431** — 25 x44, **extra fine finish** 1 in crate, — lbs..... Each, 2 25
**F1432** — 19½x35, solid wood sides, highly varnished natural finish, hand decorated saddles, manes and tails, bright red play box and footboard, white and gilt decorated, gimp trim green corduroy upholstered seat and back, tape reins. Set up with nickeled washers and screws. 1 in crate, — lbs..... Each, **$2.75**

## "SHOO FLY" SWINGING HORSES.

Painted and dappled horses, red rockers.

**F1498** — 22x27, cretonne upholstered seat and back, play box, hair tails, striped red rockers. 2 in crate, 40 lbs..... Each, **$1.15**

**24x38** — Upholstered seats and backs, play boxes, hair tails, striped red rockers. 2 in crate, 40 lbs.
**F1493** — Cretonne upholstered.. Each, $1 25
**F1494** — Plush upholstered..... " 1 50

**F1495** — 22x36x16, Dapple white enameled, varnished play box, velour upholstered seat, closely woven rattan back. 2 in crate, 50 lbs..... Each, **$2.10**

**F1497** — 22x36x16, dapple white enameled, varnished play box, velour upholstered seat, heavy rattan roll top back. 1 in crate, 35 lbs..... Each, **$ 3.10**

## HORSE HEAD SHOO FLY.

**F1496** — 42 in. long, ht. 23, 12x9 hardwood seat, woven wicker back, bent wood braces, solid wood bay horse head, perfect model, horse hair mane, leather bridle and reins, heavy red enameled rockers with foot rest. 1 in crate, 30 lbs..... Each, **$2.10**

## ROCKING HORSES.

Dapple white enameled, leatherette bridles, gimp trim English saddles, hair manes and tails, turned legs, bright red stenciled hardwood rockers.

**F1159** — 4 in crate, 53 lbs..... Each, $1.00
**F1160** — Stirrups. 4 in crate, 56 lbs.
Each, **$1.25**

**F1157** — Ht. 29 in., 6 in. block, leatherette martingales, corduroy saddle, stirrups. 3 in crate, 00 lbs..... Each, **$1.90**

## STICK HORSE.

**F1186** — 42 in. long, painted and dappled horse head, with reins, 6 in. solid wheels. 1 doz. in crate. 18 lbs..... Doz. **95c**

> **WHEEL TOYS** Offer splendid profit getting and trade winning opportunities. Ours is a line of BIG VALUES.
> *SEE INDEX*

## SWINGING HORSES.

*Made by the best manufacturer in America.*

## HORSE BENCH ROCKERS.

Big sellers for the smaller children.

**F1176** — 21 in. long, seat 9 in. high, dapple gr enameled. ½ doz. in crate, 22 lbs. Doz. $4.

**F1177** — Folding. 30½x22½, dapple horse, 17 6½ flat top, gold striped red enameled saddle, modeled head, button eyes, leather reins and bridle, black metal stirrups, leather straps, heavy shaped legs, black enameled collapsible braces, red painted stron wood folding rockers. 2 in crate, 22 lbs.
EACH, **$1.**

## IMPROVED SWINGING AND GALLOPING HORSES.

Well painted, carved legs, long hair mane and tails, swing on iron rods, red painted and striped stands. Each in crate.

**Dapple Gray** — Bridles with web reins, stirrups, upholstered saddles; stands 35½x12¾.
**F1182** — Horse 34½x26, 5 in. block. Crated 26 lbs..... Each, $2.9
**F1183** — Horse 37 x 28, 6 in. block. Crated 27 lbs..... Each, $3.4

**Bay Color** — Extra fine models, glass eyes, curb bits, leather bridles with buckles and reins, padded leather saddles, gilt fringe trim silk plush skirt, tinned stirrups, real horseshoes on hind feet.
**F1184** — Horse 37 x 30, 6 in. block, stand..... $5.50

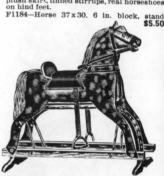

**F1169** — Comprising only staple numbers and best sellers.
2 only F1159 rocking horse.
1 " F1160 " "
2 " F1157 " "
1 " F1162, swinging horse.
Total 6 in case. 85 lbs., no charge for case. Asst. **$8.70**

## NPORTED TOY FURNITURE.

Each piece in box.

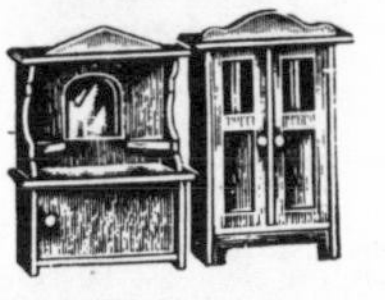

2645—6 styles asstd., aver. ht. 4½ in., sideboard, wardrobe, desk, etc., varnished oak finish, hinged doors, 3 with mirrors. 1 doz. in pkg. Doz. 42c

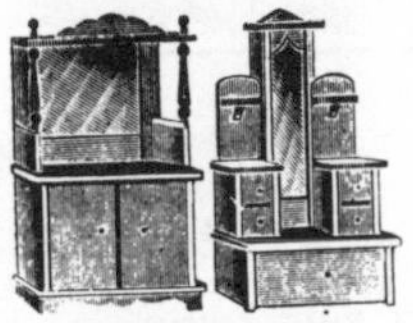

2646—6 styles asstd., aver. ht. 6 in., varnished oak finish, bureau with mirrors and removable drawers, closets with hinged doors, 1 with mirror, sideboards with mirrors and hinged doors. ⅙ doz. in pkg. Doz. 75c

## OY WOOD FOLDING BEDS.

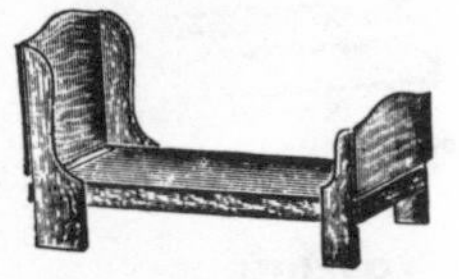

1136—14½x7x8½, varnished hardwood, kindergarten pattern silkaline covered fiber bottom, folds flat. 2 doz. in crate..............Doz. 95c

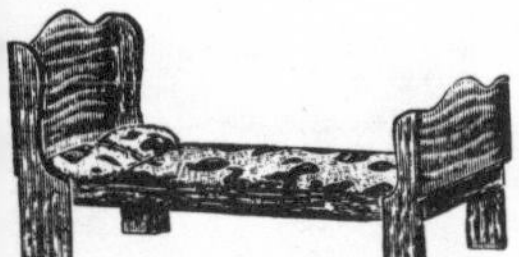

olden Oak Finish—Wood slat bottom, kindergarten pattern quilted silkaline mattresses and pillows.
F2775—17x9x10. ⅓ doz. in pkg. Doz. $1.95
F2776—20½x11x12. ⅙ doz. in pkg. Doz. $3.95

## TOY FURNITURE SET.

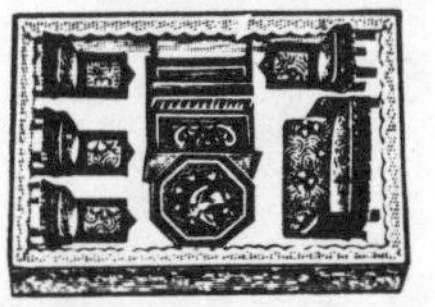

F2647—6 and 7 pc. sets, 3 styles, music room, bedroom and parlor, upholstered chairs and sofas, decorated tables. Each set in box, asstd. ⅙ doz. sets in pkg....Doz. sets, $1.80

## TOY FURNITURE ASSTS.

Varnished light maple finish.

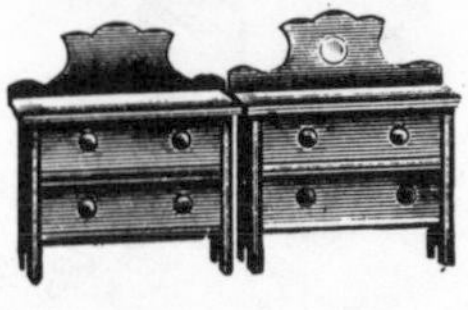

F1837—5x6x7, 2 styles, sideboard and dresser, 2 drawers. Asstd. 1 doz. in pkg.................Doz. 85c Gro. $9.80

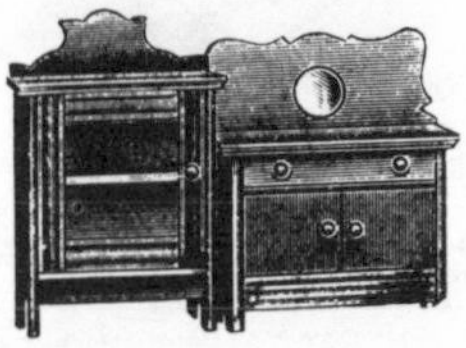

F1289—4 styles, aver. 10x8¾ dresser and wash stands with mirrors and drawers, 11x7½ china closet, 11½x7¾ chiffonier. Asstd. 1 doz. in case, 40 lbs. ....................Doz. $1.85 Gro. $21.50

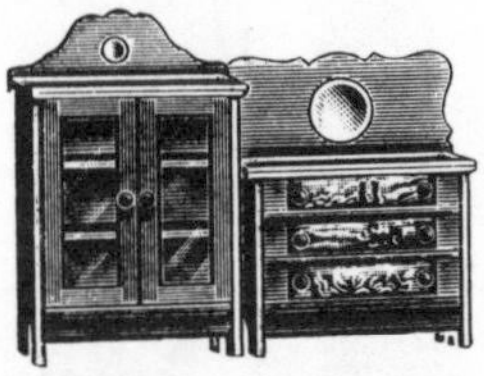

F1290—4 styles, 12½x9 glass door china closet and chiffonier with 4 drawers, 11½x9 bureau and sideboard with mirror backs. Asstd. 1 doz. in crate, 40 lbs.....Doz. $2.00

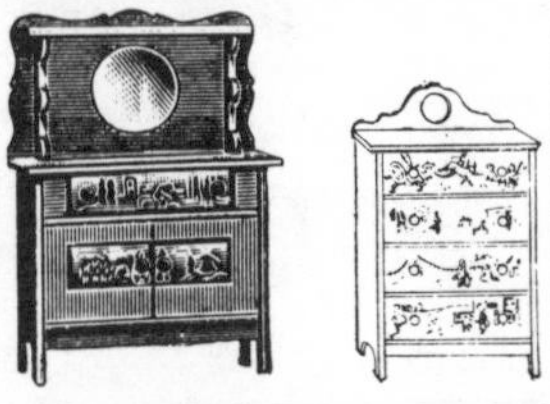

F1291—4 styles, 9x15 bureau and sideboard, 9x15¼ china closet and chiffonier, some with mirror backs. Asstd., ⅙ doz. in crate, 35 lbs. Doz. $4.10

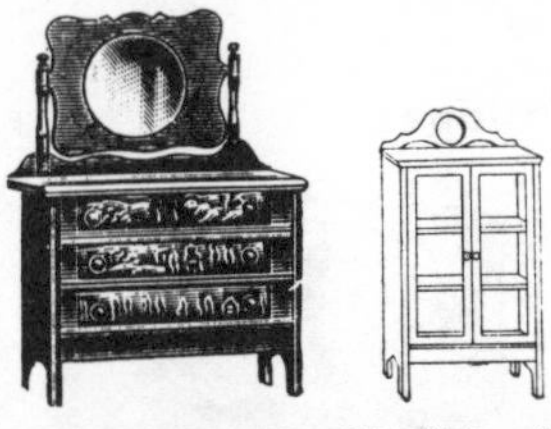

F1292—4 styles, 12¾x18½ sideboard and bureau, 21¾x11 three-shelf china closet and 5 drawer chiffonier, mirror backs. Asstd. ⅓ doz. in crate. Doz. $8.50

## HIGH GRADE WHITE ENAMELED TOY FURNITURE.

Large pieces, brilliant finish, hand painted pink flower decorations washable.

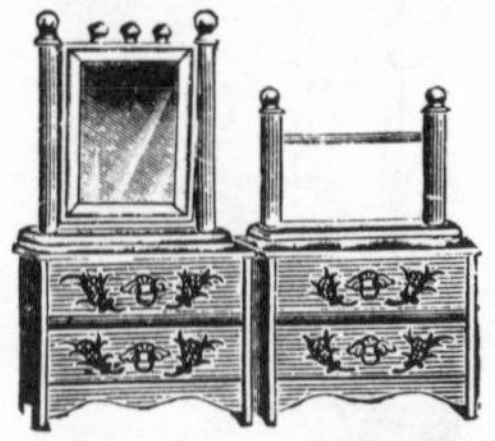

F1297—5 styles: 1 washstand 15½x10x6½, 1 dresser 15½x10x6¼ in. with 4x5 mirror, 2 dressers 19 x 10 x 6¼ with 5x7 mirror, 1 dresser 18x12x6¾. All with 2 drawers, brass pulls. 6 in case. 30 lbs...... .....Each, 89c

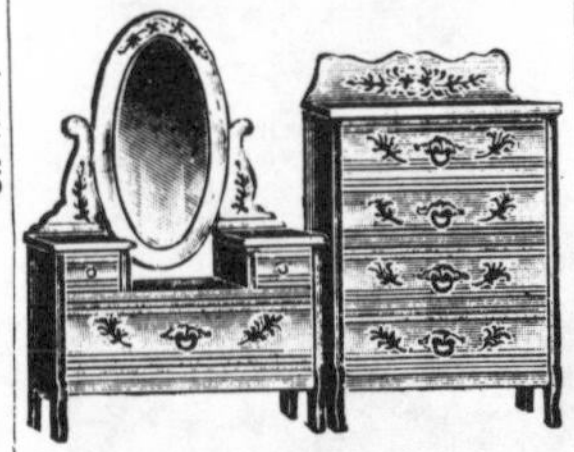

F1300—4 styles, 17x11¼ four-drawer chiffonier, 19x11½ bureau with large mirror and 3 shelf china closet, 19x13¾ dresser, large oval mirror, brass pulls and hinges. Asstd. 4 in crate, — lbs...... Each, $1.10

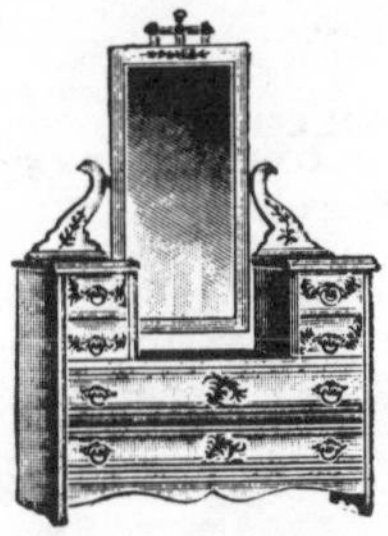

F1303—Dresser. 32 x 20¾ x 5¼, 2 large and 4 small drawers, fancy pulls, 9¼ x8 in. swinging mirror, fancy top, 1 in case. 23 lbs. Each $2.85

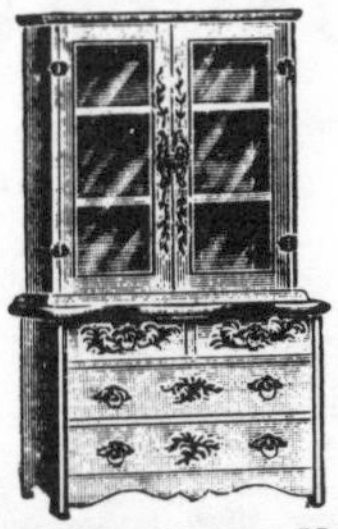

F1302—China Closet. 32x18½x9, glass doors, 2 shelves, 4 drawers, brass hinges and pulls. 1 in box. 28 lbs.......................Each, $3.00

## FOLDING WHITE ENAMELED CRADLES.

Selected turned stock, finely finished.

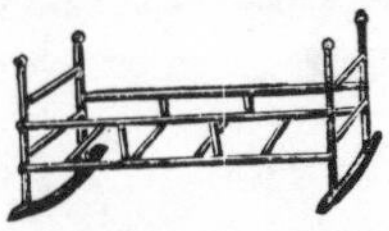

F2849—12x9, 1 doz. in pkg. Doz. 89c

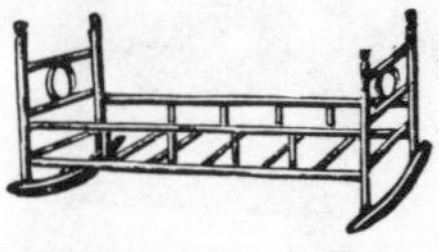

F1135—18x10, gold knobs. 1 doz. in crate.....................Doz. $1.95

F2888—16x9¼x14, rockers. 1 doz. in pkg ...................Doz. 89c
F2889—12x6½x7, striped cardboard mattress. 1 doz. in box.... Doz. 89c

## CANOPIED BRASS BEDS—

Silkaline Trimmed.

Collapsible round gilt metal frames, flat sides, white muslin covered mattresses and pillows, asstd. flowered silkaline, turn-down hemmed covers and lace trim canopies and pillow slips.

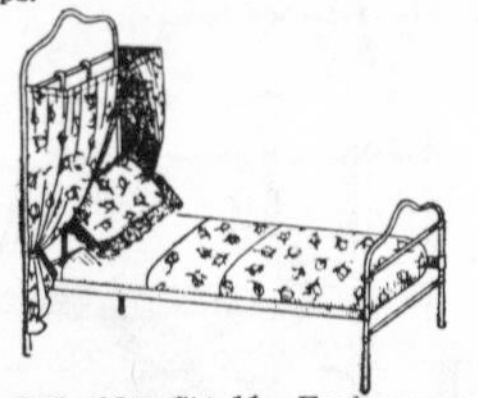

F2883—12¾x7½x11. Each wrapped and tied. ½ doz. in pkg...Doz. $2.00

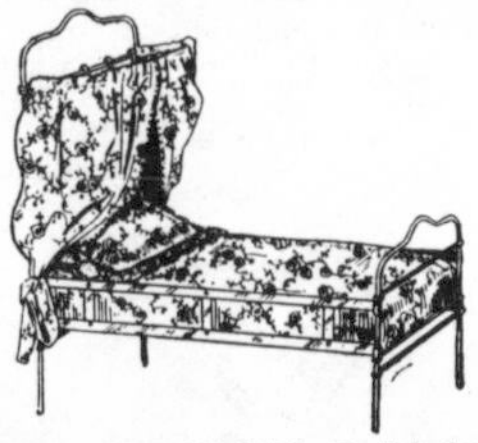

F2884—14¼x9¼x14¼. Each in box. ¼ doz. in pkg............Doz. $3.98

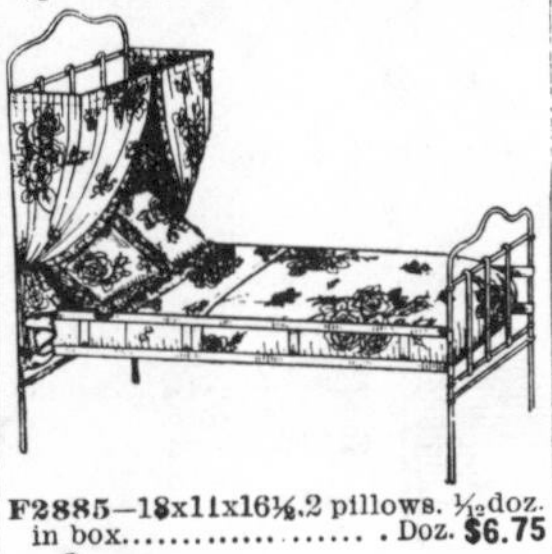

F2885—18x11x16½, 2 pillows. ½ doz. in box................Doz. $6.75

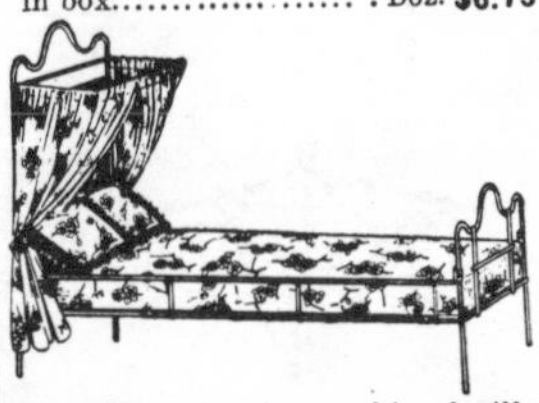

Extra Size—As above, shirred silkaline backs ribbon tied canopies, 2 pillows.
F2886—24½x12¼x17. ½ doz. in box. Doz. $8.65
F2887—30x15¼x19¾. 1 in box. EACH, 98c

## TUBULAR BRASS BED.

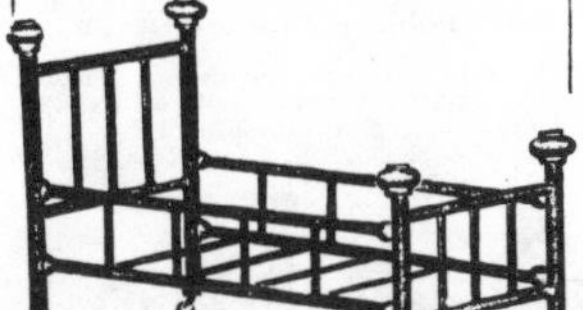

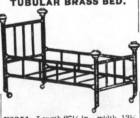

F2251—Length 27½ in., width 13½, ht. 16¾, massive design, acid-proof polished brass tubing, will not tarnish, 1½ in. posts, heavy knob tops, ⅝ in. sides and crosspieces, ⅜ in. filling rods, steel casters. 1 in box. Each, $2.00

## SOLID BRASS DOLL BEDS.

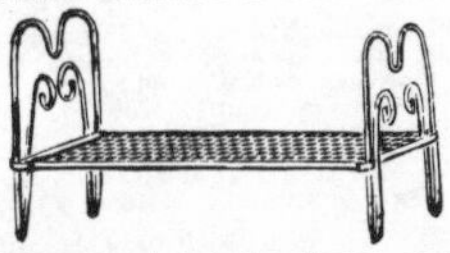

Fancy bent tubular brass, scroll trim, woven wire mattresses, can be taken apart. ½ doz in box.
F2252—20½x10x11½.....DOZ. $8.90
*Following with rubber knob feet.*

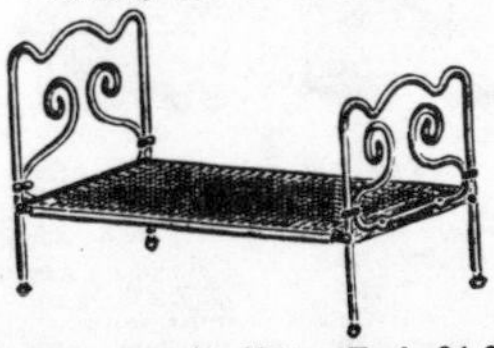

F2253—23¼x13x13⅝....Each, $1.00

## CANOPIED TOY BASSINETS.

Folding fancy gilt metal frames, asstd. flowered silkaline hanging baskets, removable mattresses and lace trim pillows and canopies.

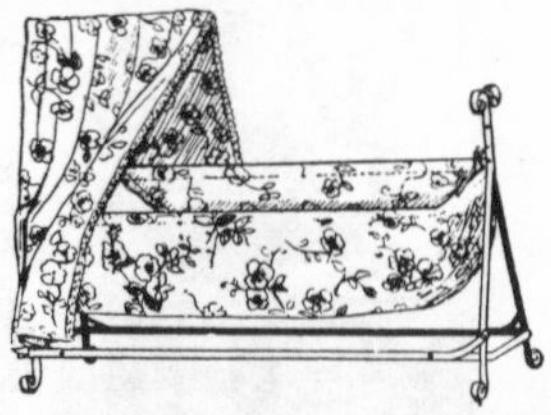

F2880—15x9½x14½. Each in box. ¼ doz. in pkg................Doz. $3 95
F2881—23¾x13¼x22. ½ doz. in box. Doz. $8.50

## DOLLS' FOLDING LAWN SWINGS.

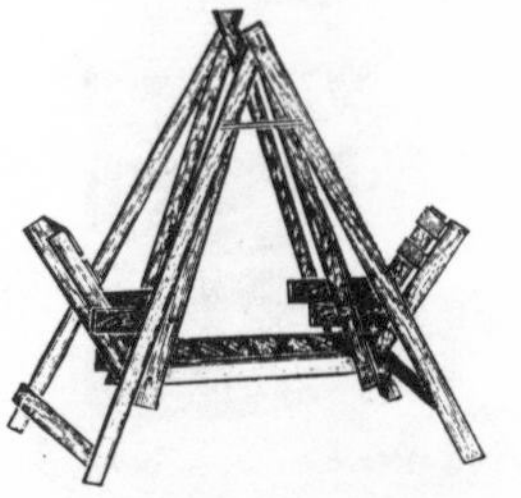

F1515—17½x17½x11½, braced natural wood frame, 2 stained seats, slat foot rest, full folding. 2 doz. in crate, 95 lbs................. Doz. 95c

Striped Cloth Canopies—Strongly braced natural wood frames, 2 stained wood seats, slat foot-rests. Each wrapped.

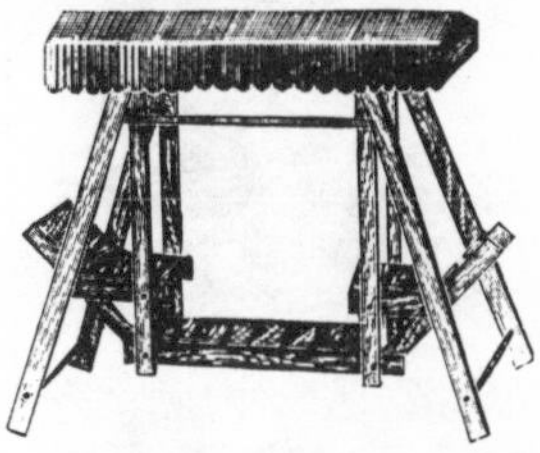

F2763—22½x9¾x16. ⅙ doz. in pkg. Doz. $1.90
F2777—24x12x19. ¼ doz. in pkg. Doz. $3.95
F2778—29x15½x22. ⅙ doz. in carton.... ..... ...........Doz. $7.90

## CHILD'S FOLDING SWING.

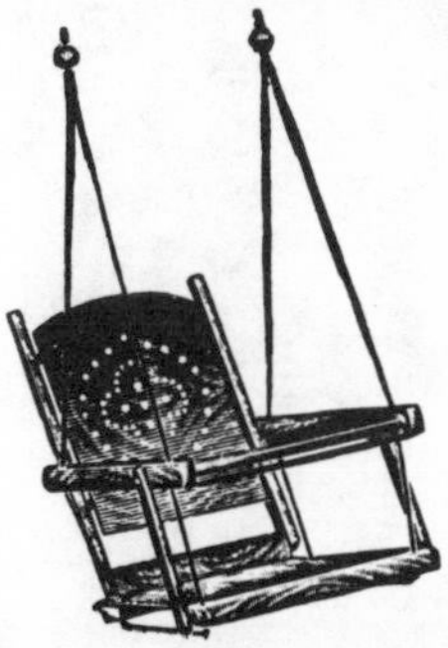

F1894—Natural wood frame and play, tray, 12x12 three ply veneer perforated seat and 15 in. back, wood armsmooth waxed rope, 2 heavy screw hooks. Folded flat. ½ doz. pkg. Doz. $8.00

## COLLAPSIBLE TOY HAMMOCK.

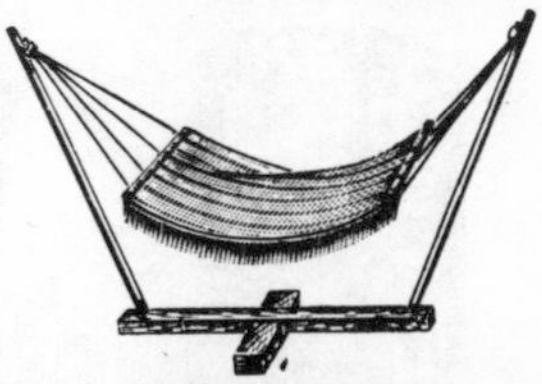

F2784—35½ in. wood frame with crosspiece, 18 in. asstd. color woven hammock, fringed sides, spreader top, cord ends with rings. 1 doz. in pkg...........................Doz. 87c

## "DOLLAR LEADER" TOY FURNITURE ASST.

Dark Oak Finish.

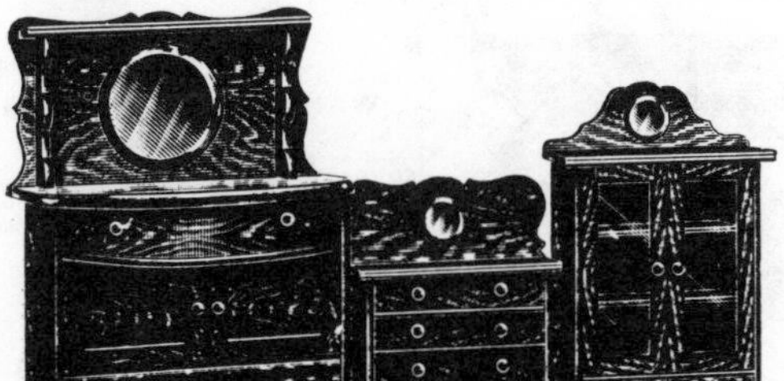

**F1294**—4 styles, dresser, sideboard, chiffonier and china closet, some with mirror backs. Asst. contains:

| | | | | | |
|---|---|---|---|---|---|
| 1 doz. aver. | 8x11 to retail at 25c each | ..... | Retail value, | | $3.00 |
| ¼ " | " 7½x14 " " " 50c " | ...... | " | " | 3.00 |
| ⅓ " | " 10x20 " " " $1.00 " | ...... | " | " | 4.00 |

Total retail value, $10.00

1⅓ doz. in crate, 90 lbs. ASST. (1⅓ doz.)....**$7.25**

## TOY KITCHEN CABINETS WITH GROCERIES.

Varnished hardwood, well finished; large supply facsimile pkgs. groceries, some filled.

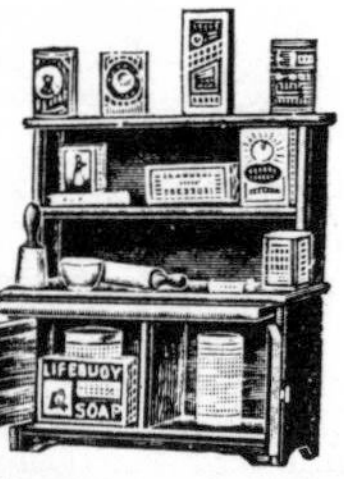

**F1308**—12½x5¼, ht. 14, shelf top, 2 hinged doors, rolling pin, bake board, potato masher. ½ doz. in crate, 24 lbs........... ...Doz. **$3.98**

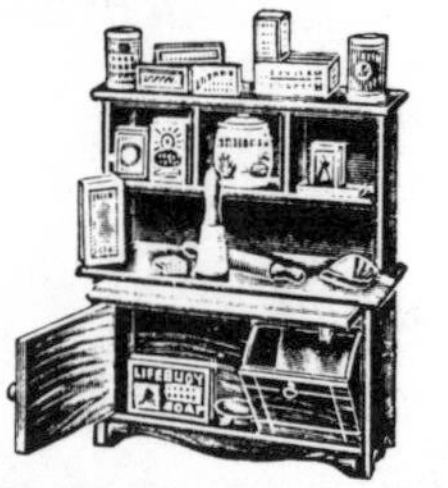

**F1309**—13½x6, ht. 16, partition shelf top, china spice jar, rolling pin, bake board, potato masher, flour bin with scoop, hinged door. ⅓ doz. in crate, 25 lbs........... .........Doz. **$8.40**

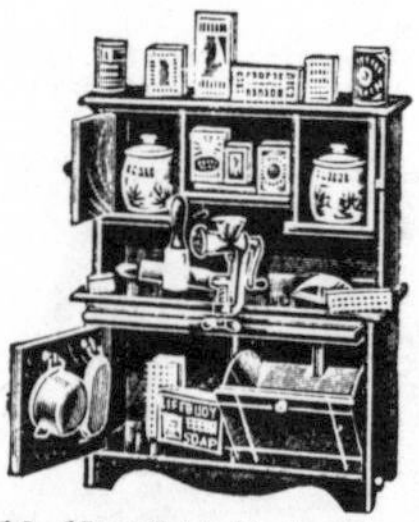

**F1310**—15¼ x 7, ht. 19, double closet top with hinged doors, shelf between 2 china spice jars, food chopper, rolling pin, bake board, potato masher, flour bin with scoop, lower closet with 4 tin cooking utensils. 1 in carton, 10 lbs......EACH, **$1.15**

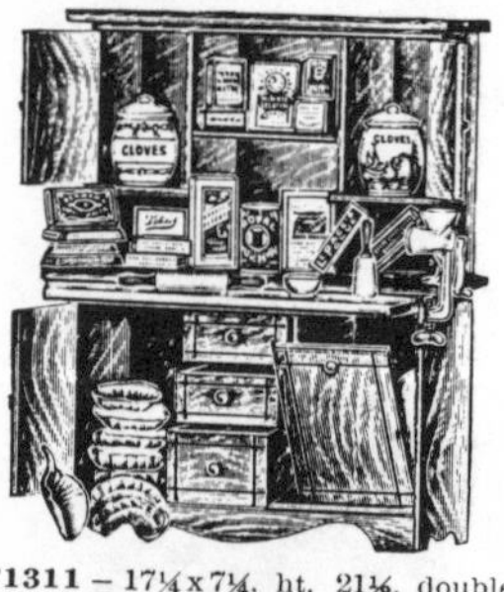

**F1311** — 17¼ x 7¼, ht. 21½, double closet top with hinged doors, shelf between, 2 china spice jars, food chopper, rolling pin, potato masher, bake board, flour bin with 2 scoops 3 drawrs, lower closet with 6 tin cooking utensils. 1 in carton. 13 lbs ..................EACH, **$1.50**

## TOY GROCERY STORES.

Each with facsimile pkgs. groceries, some filled, guaranteed under Pure Food law.

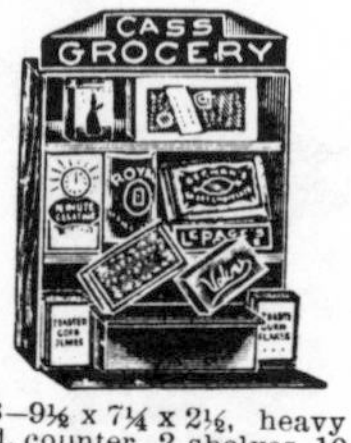


**F2928**—9½ x 7¼ x 2½, heavy card-board, counter, 2 shelves, 10 pkgs. 1 doz. in pkg..................Doz. **1.00**

## LAUNDRY TOYS.

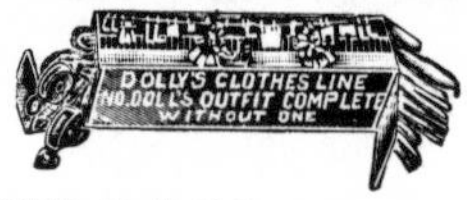


**F2843—Dolly's Clothesline.** 20 ft. woven white cord, 2 pulleys, 6 clothes pins. Each set in litho box, 1 doz. sets in pkg......Doz. sets, **72c**

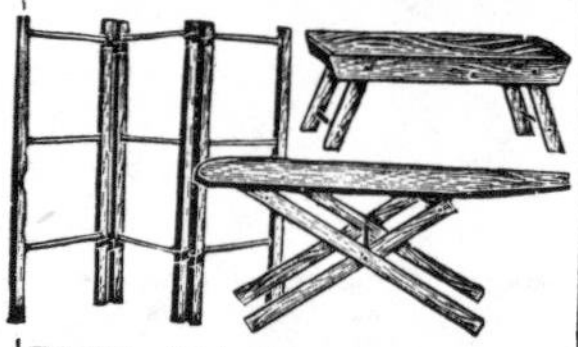

**F1129—Asst.** Natural wood, clothes horse 9x16 folded, extends to 28½ in., ironing board 6x20x13, wood slatted wash bench 5x14x5½. Asstd. 3 doz. pcs. in crate, 49 lbs.
Doz. pcs. **60c**
Gro. pcs. $9.25

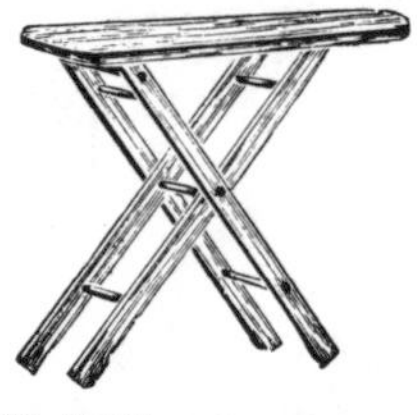

**F1128—Folding Ironing Board.** 18x6x13, katural wood. 2 doz. in crate, —lbs..................Doz. **80c**
Gro. $9.25

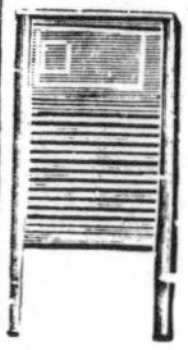

**Washboards**—Smooth wood frames, corrugated tin fronts, soap boxes. 1 doz. in pkg. Doz.
F2846—9½x4½....$0 35
Gro. $4.00
F1132—15x7. 10 lbs. 69
Gro. $7.80
F1133 — 17 x 8. ⅞ in. heavy wood frame, coated steel rubbing surface, **will not rust.** 10 lbs. Doz. **82c**
Gro. $9.50

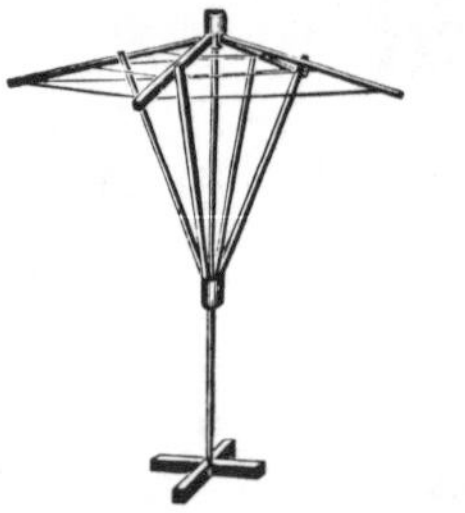

**F2842—Folding Clothes Dryer**—Perfect model, turned wood frame, ht. 18 in., four 12 in. hinged arms with sliding braces, 3 lines each 4 sides, heavy wood stand. 1 doz. in bdl..............................Doz. **85c**

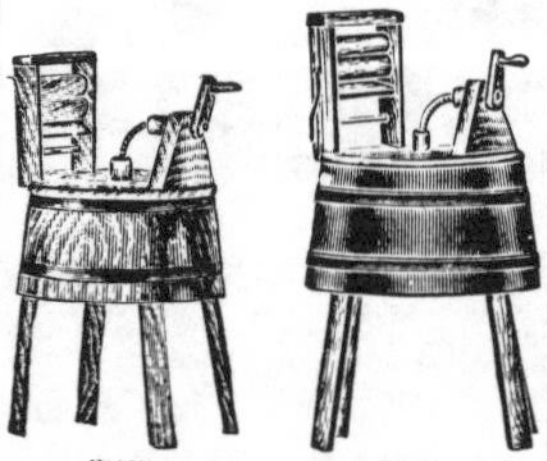

F1125 F1126

**Washing Machines** — Red painted wood tub, black steel hoops, removable legs, oak stained top, wood crank turns 4-spindle washer, detachable wringer. Each in carton.
F1125—Ht. 16½ in., tub 10 in. ⅓ doz. in pkg.,—lbs........... Doz. **$3.85**
F1126 — Ht. 19½ in., tub 11¼ in. ⅙ doz. in pkg., —lbs.....Doz. **$8.20**

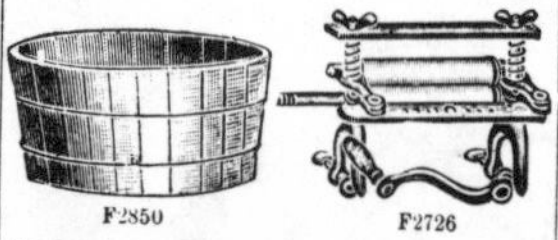

F2850 F2726

**F2850—Tub.** 9½x4½, heavy natural wood, welded wire bands. 2 doz. in crate............................Doz. **87c**

**F2726**—Toy Wringer. Made by American Wringer Co., 7 x 6, wood frame, galvanized clamps, solid rubber rolls, strong spring, detachable handle. 1/12 doz. in box...Doz. **$4.50**

## TOY LAUNDRY SETS.

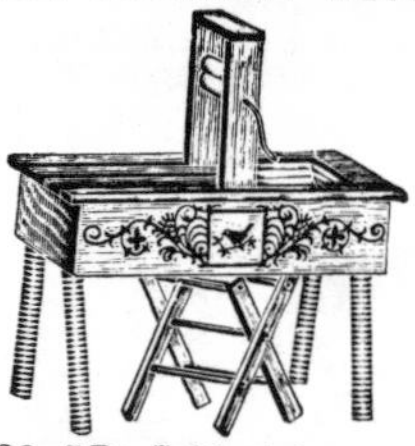

**F1120—5 Pc.** 7x12 red slat top table, 5 in. wringer, 6 in. clothes rack, basket, tin lined stationary tub. 1 doz. sets in crate, 24 lbs..Doz. sets, **$1.85**

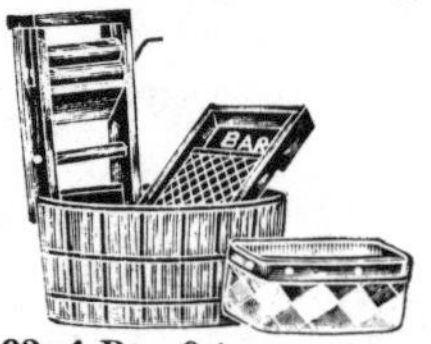

**F1102—4 Pc.** 9 in. natural wood tub, galvanized wire hoops, 7 in. wringer, 8¼ in. wood back washboard, basket. ⅓ doz. sets in carton, —lbs..........Doz. sets, **$3.85**

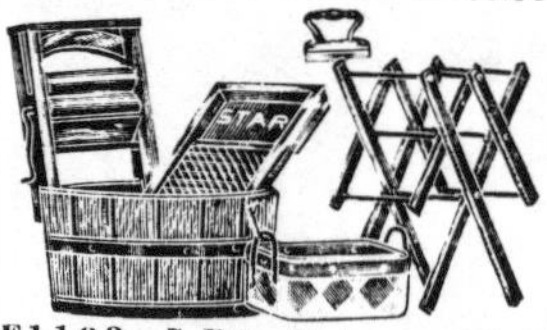

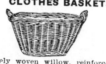

**F1103—7 Pc.** 11 in. varnished grained wood tub, red steel hoops, 9 in. wringer, 12¾ in. wood back washboard, large handled basket, iron with stand, clothes line on spool. ⅙ doz. sets in cartoon, lbs.
Doz. sets, **$8.25**

## TOY WILLOW CLOTHES BASKETS.

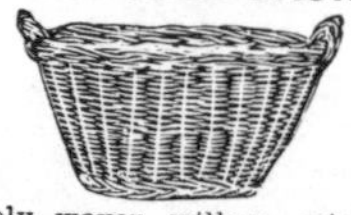

Closely woven willow, reinforced tops and handles.
F5409 — 8½x6½, 4½ in. deep. 1 doz. in bdl.........................Doz. **85c**
F5410 — 11 x 8½, 5 in. deep. ½ doz. in bdl......... ..................Doz. **$1.75**

## TOY CLOTHES PINS.

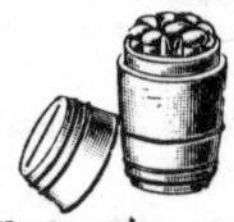

**F2844—Clothes Pins.** Twelve 2⅜ in. pins in 2x3⅛ turned wood bbl., slotted removable top. 1 doz. in box.
Doz. **35c**
Gro $4.00

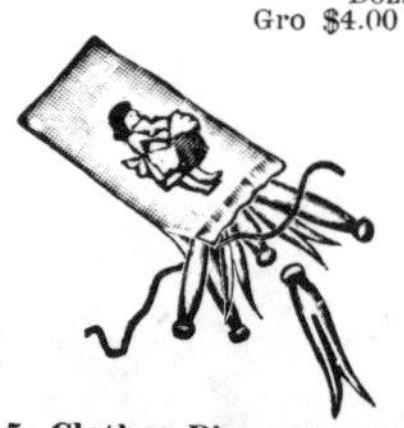

**F2845—Clothes Pins.** Nine 2⅜ in. pins in muslin drawstring bag, stencilled for embroidering. 1 doz. in pkg...........................Doz. **36c**

## WOOD PASTRY SETS.

All handles stained red. 1 set in box

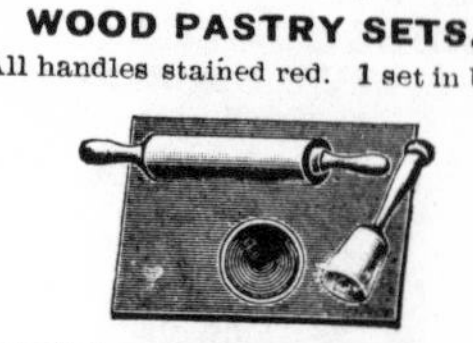

**F2852**—Board 4x6, bowl 1½ in masher 3¼, rolling pin 6⅛. 1 doz sets in pkg............Doz. sets, **33**
Gro. sets, $3.75

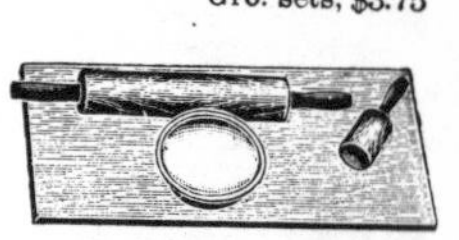

**F2853**—Board 6½x11¾, bowl 2½ in. masher 4¼, rolling pin 10¼. ½ doz sets in pkg......... ....Doz. sets, **72c**
Gro. sets, $8.25

**F2854** — Board 6½x13⅛ in., bowl 3⅜ in., masher 4⅜, rolling pin 11⅞. ⅙ doz. sets in pkg. Doz. sets, **$1.60**

## BISSELL'S TOY CARPET SWEEPERS.

Miniature sweepers that do actual work. Varnished natural hardwood 2 color gilt and black, stenciled lettering, red stained wheels, genuine bristle brush, double spring dust catchers, 24 in. turned wood handles.

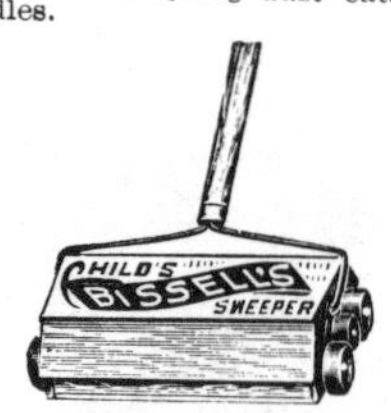


**F1788**—"Child's Delight." 8 x 4¾ in. ½ doz. in pkg.............Doz. **$2.05**

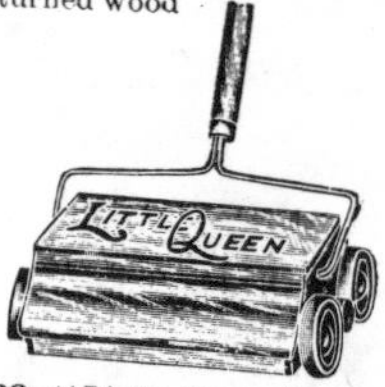


**F1789**—"Little Queen." 8⅜ x 5½, extra high, rubber tired wheels, varnished handle. ⅓ doz. in pkg.
Doz. **$3.75**

## CHILDREN'S TOY BROOM.

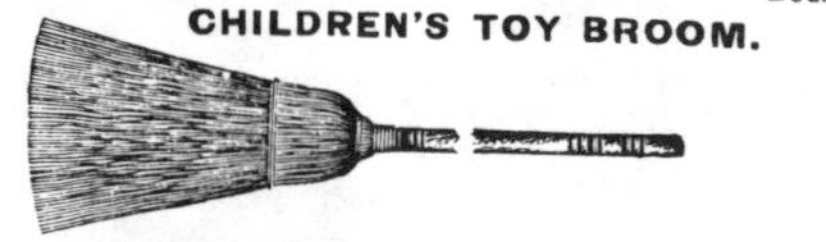

**F1519**—30 in., good grade green corn, double sewed, natural finish, striped handle. 1 doz. in bdl..................................................
Doz. **89c**

## TOY SNOW SHOVELS.

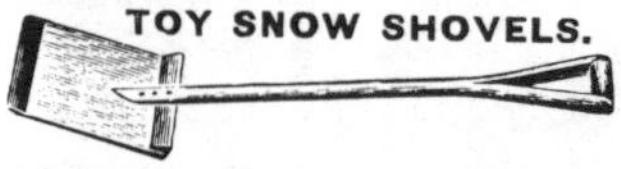

**F1130**—7x10, metal tipped wood scoop, extra long reinforced handle. 1 doz. in pkg. 10 lbs...... .... ...... ..... ........ ........................Doz. **79c**

# TOY TRUNKS

**Latest sellers,** with up-to-date finishings and steel trimmings. Mostly put up assorted styles in crate, carefully selected and priced to leave the retailer a good margin of profit.

## CHILDREN'S TRUNKS.

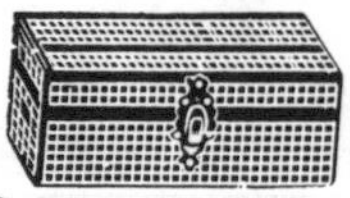

**F2797**—8x4½x3¼ wood frame imit. linen plaid covered, 3 stained slats, leather handles, card board tray, fancy paper lined, brassed clasp. Asstd. colors. 1 doz. in pkg..Doz. **89c**

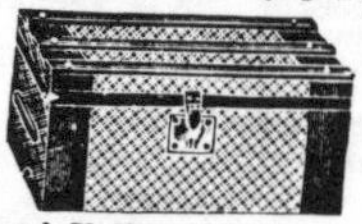

**Red and Yellow Plaid.** Red valance and binding, wood slat top, leather grips, brass lock, green paper lined tray.
F1109—11 in. 1 doz. in crate, 20 lbs.
Doz. **$1.75**
F1110—13 in. ⅙ doz. in case, 20 lbs.
Doz. **$3.60**

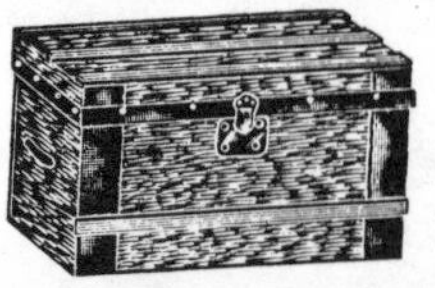

**Brown Wood Grain Covered**—black bound, natural varnished wood slats, brass lock, leather handles, paper lined, tray.
F1113—11 in. 1 doz. in crate, 20 lbs.
Doz. **$1.75**
F1114—13 in. ⅙ doz. in crate, 20 lbs.
Doz. **$3.60**
F1115—18 in., metal valance, wood tray with hat box. ¼ doz. in crate, 20 lbs .......... .......Doz. **$7.80**

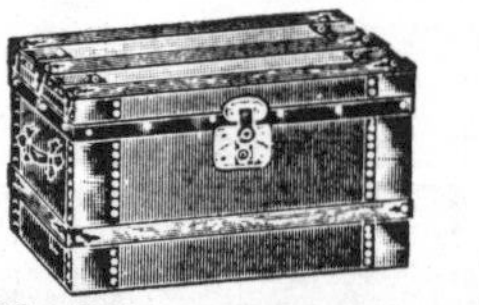

**F1099** — Baked red enameled steel, brass bindings, **Yale lock,** leather, grips, varnished oak slats, wood tray paper lined, 16 and 18 in., hat box in tray. Asst. comprises.

| | | | Total |
|---|---|---|---|
| 1/12 doz., 12 in........@ | $ 7.50 | | $0 63 |
| 1/12 " 14 "........ " | 10.40 | | 87 |
| 1/12 " 16 "........ " | 13.20 | | 1 10 |
| 1/12 " 18 "........ " | 15.00 | | 1 25 |

⅓ doz. in case, 25 lbs. Case, **$3.85**

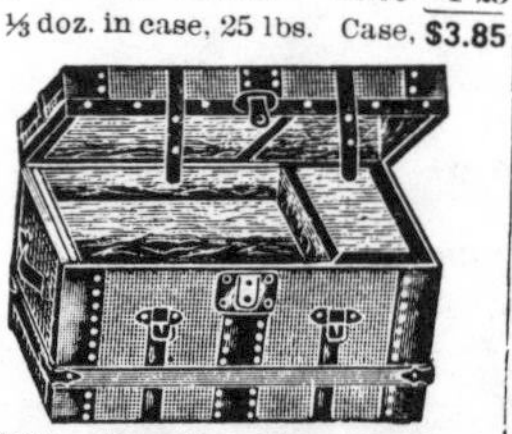

**F1105 — Asstd. red, green and brown burlap,** guaranteed not to fade, part brass, partblack japanned steel binding, Yale locks, varnished hard wood slats, 2 leather straps to match, moire linen lined, trays, 3 with hat compartments. Assortment comprises:

| | | Total |
|---|---|---|
| 1/12 doz. 12 in........@ | $ 9.00 | $0 75 |
| 1/12 " 14 "........ " | 12.00 | 1 00 |
| 1/12 " 16 "........ " | 15.00 | 1 25 |
| 1/12 " 18 "........ " | 18.00 | 1 50 |

⅓ doz.crate.asstd.37lbs. Crate, **$4.50**

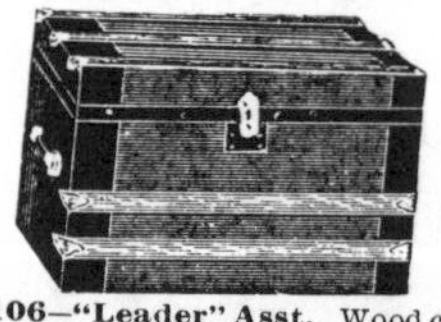

**F1106—"Leader" Asst.** Wood covered with imit. red and yellow plaid and shepherd check leather or canvas, all except 8 in. have natural finish oak slats and metal protectors, wood frame tray, fancy paper lined, leather side handles, locks and clasps.

| | |
|---|---|
| 1 doz. 8 in. to retail.........@ | $0 10 |
| ½ " 11 " " " ........ " | 25 |
| ⅓ " 13 " " " ........ " | 50 |
| ⅙ " 18 " " " ........ " | 1 00 |
| 2 doz. in Total retail value, | $6 70 |

crate, 43 lbs. Crate, **$4.25**

## WARDROBE TRUNKS.

Rawhide finish leatherette, metal bound, sole leather corners and straps, Yale lock, moire linen lined throughout, brass pull drawers, extension hanger with 4 coat hooks. Each wrapped.

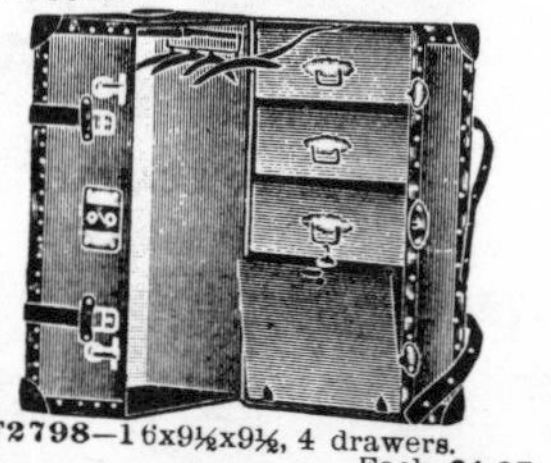

**F2798**—16x9½x9½, 4 drawers.
Each, **$1.25**
**F2799**—18x10½x10½ 3 drawers and hat box, 2 metal clasps. Each, **$1.50**



*Butler Brothers (now City Products Corp.)*

## WOOD NOAH'S ARKS.

Bright colors, hinged roofs, painted [car]ved wood animals.

3205—7¼ x 3¼, about 8 animals.
1 doz. in box..............Doz. 43c
3206—9¾ x 4, about 16 animals.
1 doz. in pkg................Doz. 82c

3207—13¼x5¾ x 3⅝, about 32 animals. ⅙ doz. in pkg.....Doz. $1.95

## WOOD STOCK FARMS.

Brick effect barn with shingle roof, 3 stalls, feed boxes, circular windows. Each with 6 litho wood animals—horse, mule, pig, cow, sheep and rooster.
F2825—8¾x8x5¼. 1 doz. in pkg................Doz. 95c
F2826—10¼x10x6, ¼ doz. in pkg..............Doz. $1.80

## FARMYARD SETS.

3 styles, well made bright color cardboard houses, green trees, barnyard animals, sheep or chickens, with farmer. 1 set in box.

F3211—11 Pc. 2 houses, 2 trees, 6 animals. 1 doz. sets in pkg.
Doz. sets. 92c

F3212—20 Pc. 3 houses, 12 animals, 2 trees, 2 sections fence. ⅙ doz. sets in pkg............Doz. sets. $2.50

## CIRCUS STOCK CARS WITH ANIMALS.

Litho wood cars, stained tops, hinged doors, on wheels; double litho animals on wood, stained bases.
F2830—9x4½, 4 animals. 1 doz. in pkg........................Doz. 95c
F2831—11¼x6, 6 animals. ½ doz. in pkg........................Doz. $1.80
F2832—14x7, 8 animals. ⅓ doz. in pkg........................Doz. $3.75

## TOY BATTLESHIPS— On Wheels.

F2734—20½x2¾, stained wood deck and bottom, litho cardboard sides, upper deck with turret, wood smokestacks and 3 mounted cannon, 3 poles with litho flags. ¼ doz. in pkg........................Doz. $1.95

# TOY TOOLS

These toys always sell out clean, because the boys MUST have them.

## TOOL CHESTS WITH TOOLS.

The best made merchandise on the market at the price. Varnished golden oak finish chestnut, beveled edges, dovetail corners, litho labels inside hinged covers, metal clasps.

Note particularly in comparing price the completeness of our sets.

F2339—8¾x4, sliding cover, buck-saw, pinchers, hammer, plane and steel square. 1 doz. in pkg. Doz. 92c
Following each wrapped, contain wood mallet, saw, hammer, T and try squares, triangle, rule, sand paper, chalk, tacks and nails. Larger sizes with additional tools as stated.

F2954—11¼ x 5⅝ x 3, 9 fittings. ⅙ doz. in pkg.............Doz. $1.95
F2955—12¼x6x4, removable tray, 12 fittings, including sawing angle, plane, tape, etc. ⅙ doz. in pkg. Doz. $3.95
F2956—14⅜x7¼x4, removable tray, 15 fittings, including plane, chisel, screw driver, sawing angle, tape, etc. ¼ doz. in pkg.......Doz. $6.00
F2957—15¾ x 7¾ x 5¼, removable tray, 18 fittings, including vise, mitre box, sawing angle, screw driver, sawing angle, etc. ⅓ doz. in pkg......... ....Doz. $8.75

Following with removable partition trays, coppered handles.

F2958—21 fittings, 18x9x6½, including brace and bit, vice, plane, mitre box, marking gauge, hatchet, etc.............................Each, 89c
F2959—25 large fittings, 19½x9½x7, including spirit level, awl, pincers, tack claw, vice. brace and bit, etc........................Each, $1.50
F2960—29 large fittings, 20½x-10½x7¾, including brace and bit, scroll saw, spirit level, compass. miter box, oil can, chalk line on spool, etc................Each, $2.25
F2961—27 practical tools, 21½x-10⅝x8¾, large and small vises, saw-planes, brace and bits, chisel, pliers, spirit level, mitre box, etc.
Each, $2.75

## WOOD BUNGALOWS.

Painted brick effect sides and chimneys, tile roofs, printed curtained windows and doors, hinged veranda fronts with pillars, decorated inside. All except F2770 with imit. stone foundations. **Each in carton.**

F2770—9½x7, ht. 9½. ⅛ doz. in pkg.... Doz. $1.95
F2771—11¼x9¼, ht. 12¼. ⅛ doz. in pkg..Doz. $3.90
F2772 — 13 x 12, ht. 14, with steps. ½ doz. in pkg............Doz. $8.20
F2773—15x13¾, ht. 14¾, gabled roof, 2 chimneys, railed balcony, bay window, veranda with steps. EACH, 95c
F2774—18x12¼, ht. 16½, extension roof, 2 chimneys, large balcony, front and side veranda and steps. EACH, $1.25

## THREE BIGGEST SPECIALTIES IN CARDBOARD TOYS.

Made exclusively for BUTLER BROTHERS.

Bright litho heavy cardboard, miniature fac-similes. Each in envelope, 1 doz. in pkg.

F2950—Cottage. 18¼ in. x 12½, ht. 16¼, asstd. red and green litho. imit. weather-board sides, green and red litho, shingled gable roof and brick chimney, bay and dormer windows, swinging doors and shutters, moire and net effect curtains, put together without rivets..............Doz. 95c

F2951—Windmill. 14¾ x 15¼ in., ht. 19¾, asstd. red and green brick effect base, green and red imit. shingle roof and sides, wood effect doors and steps, cobweb waxed paper windows, 15 in. revolving wheel attached to turning roof, catches wind from any angle. Each with env. of brass rivets....Doz. 95c

F2952—Doll's Rocking Horse. 19½x7¼, ht. 14¼, extra heavy cardboard, dapple gray horse, red litho saddle, harness, rockers and seat, black stripes, reinforced base and crosspiece, holds large doll. Each with env. brass rivets......Doz. 92c

## MISSION TOOL CHESTS.

Waxed mission finish, oiled natural finish inside, dovetailed corners, beveled edges and molding, brass hinges, handles and locks with keys, removable trays. Steel tools — forged hatchet, cast saw, screw driver, awl, pliers, brace and bit, 2 ft. folding rule, etc. 1 in pkg.

F1954 — 7 fittings, 17¾ x 7¾ x 5¾. Each, $2.25

F1955—8 fittings, 17¾ x 9¼ x 6⅝, including large chisel and steel square............. ......Each, $3.00

F1956 — 10 fittings, 20x10½x6⅝, partition tray, including large hammer, steel plane, chisel, T-square, etc......................Each, $4.25

## WORK BENCHES WITH TOOLS.

So popular last season that we could not get enough to supply the demand. This year we offer a larger and improved line. Each wrapped.

Clean stock, alternating natural and walnut finish tops, backs and dovetail corner drawers, braced square legs, knocked down, easily put together with nuts and bolts—not screws, joints reinforced with steel staples. Each with tool rack and drawer containing hammer, mallet, plane, saw, T square, screw driver, rule, pencil, sand paper, chalk, nails, screws, etc. All with attached vise except F2943.

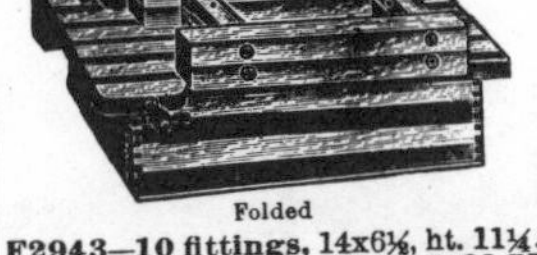

Folded

F2943—10 fittings, 14x6¼, ht. 11¾. ⅙ doz. in pkg ...........DOZ. $8.75
F2944—12 fittings, 16x7¾, ht. 11¾. 1 in pkg......................Each, $1.00
F2945—15 fittings, 18x7½ ht. 12¾, including brace and bit, pincers, etc. 1 in pkg........................Each, $1.40
F2947—16 large fittings, 22x8¾, ht. 16. 1 in pkg........Each, $2.25
Following put together with nuts, screws and washers, tops 1¼ in. thick.
F2948—15 fittings, 26½x11¾, ht. 11¾, including brace and bit, spirit level, chisel, marking gauge, etc. 1 in crate........................Each, $3.00
F2949—16 large fittings, 30x12¾, ht. 22½, steel pincers, hatchet, brace and bit, chisel, extra large screw driver, etc. 1 in crate. Each, $3.75

## COMPLETE DRAWING SET.

F2701—Consists of T square, brass protractor, steel right and obtuse angle scales, compass, 2 tubes of glue, ruler, box of crayons, pen, pencil, eraser, 1 doz. thumb tacks, tracing paper, enlargement tracer, drawing board and large pad of drawing paper, 21¾x17¼ glazed box. 1 set in box....................Set, 98c

## LITTLE CARPENTERS' SETS.

Each set on card.

F2146—Card 9x6, 5 pcs., metal hammer, awl and chisel with stained wood handles, metal pliers, 6¼ in. rule. 1 doz. sets in pkg. Doz. sets, 39c

## LATEST NOVELTY GAMES.

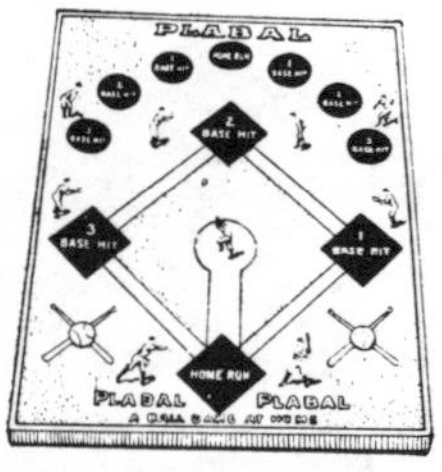


**F2379—Target and Baseball.** *2 Games in 1.* 12¼x15 heavy cardboard box, litho baseball diamond cover and inside, 3 wood darts, spinner and men. 1 doz. in pkg. Doz. **78c**
Gro. $9.00

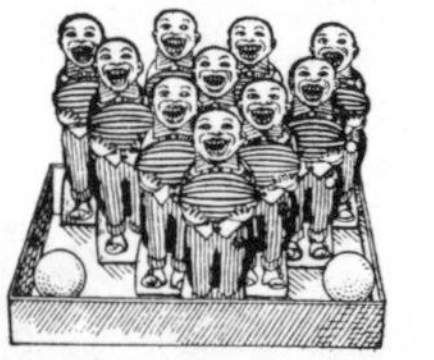

**F2381—Darkey Ten Pins.** Ten 6½ in. heavy cardboard litho coons on wood bases. 2 stained wood balls. litho box 7¼ x 10¼. 1 doz. sets in pkg..........DOZ. SETS, **83c**

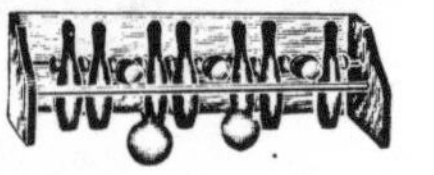

**Box Bowling**—Varnished natural wood frame, 10 varnished numbered pins separated by red beads on heavy copper rod, 3 varnished hardwood balls, when pins are struck swing on wire showing numbers. 1 in box with score cards.

F2210—8x4¼: 2½ in. pins. ⅓ doz. in pkg.................... Doz. **$1.75**

F2211—11x5¼. red striped top. 3¼ in. pins. larger balls. ⅙ doz. in pkg....... ... ....Doz. **$3.85**

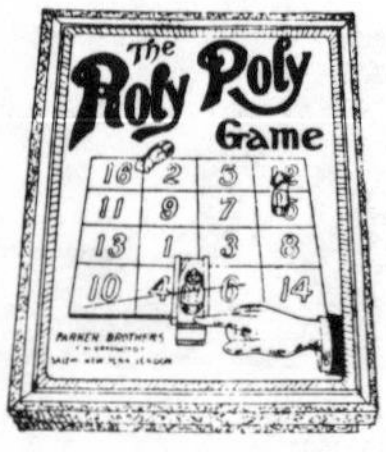


**F2706—2 styles** Roly-Poly and Tops, (1) 2 weighted figures, jump from spring lever to numbered squares: (2) 4 colored tops, numbered squares, box 13x10¼. Asstd. ⅓ doz. in pkg..............Doz. **$1.80**

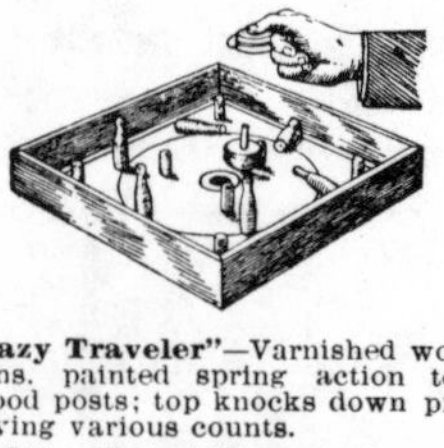

**"Crazy Traveler"**—Varnished wood pins. painted spring action top. wood posts; top knocks down pins giving various counts.

F2768—12¼ x 12¼ stained wood frame box, printed cardboard bottom, 6 pins, 7 posts. ⅓ doz. in pkg. Doz. **$1.80**

F2761—14x14 varnished hardwood box, red markings, 8 pins, 8 posts, ⅙ doz. in pkg..........Doz. **$4.15**

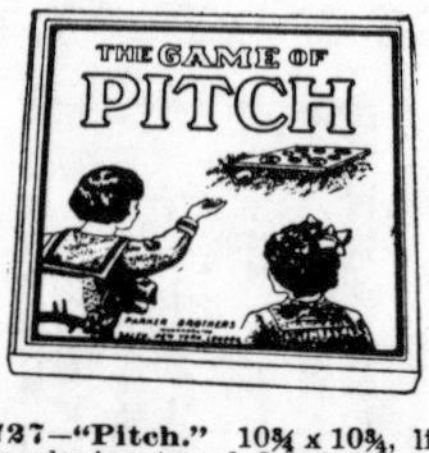


**F2727—"Pitch."** 10¾ x 10¾, litho top playing board, 9 colored numbered holes, five 1½ in. rubber discs, when thrown in hole registers count. ⅓ doz. in pkg.....Doz. **$1.80**

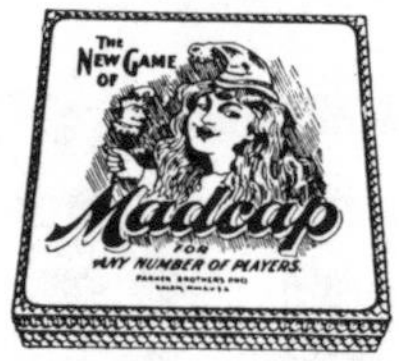


**F2707—3 styles,** 50 Up, Madcap and Twirly-Gig, litho boxes, aver. 11x11. ¼ doz. in pkg...............Doz. **$1.85**

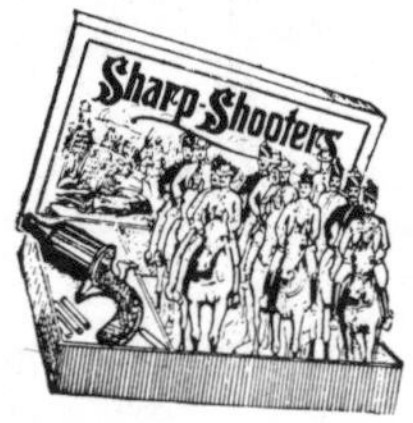


**Sharp Shooters**—6½ in. litho soldiers on wood bases, repeating pistol, 12 slugs. Excellent war game.

F2712—12 soldiers, box 10¼x7¼. ⅓ doz. in pkg........... Doz. **$1.85**

F2713—20 soldiers, box 20¼ x 14¼. ⅙ doz. in pkg. ..........Doz. **$3.85**

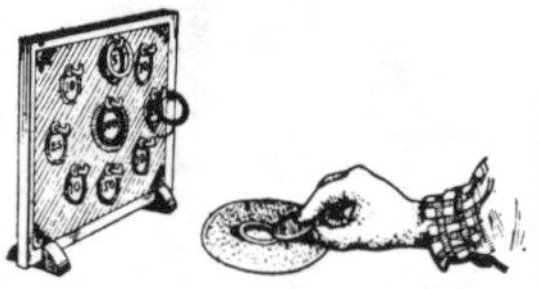

**F2416—Ring the Pin.** 6¼ x 6¼ numbered litho wood target. wood base, 9 hooks, 6 vari-colored bone rings. 3 shooters, felt mat. 1 set in box. ⅓ doz. in pkg.
DOZ. SETS, **$1.90**

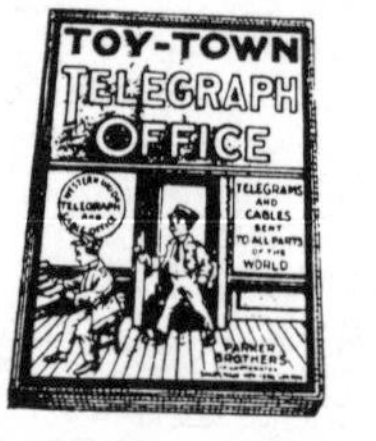


**F2709—"Toy Town Telegraph Office."** Telegraph key, stamp and pad. imitation money, pencil, telegraph blanks, envelopes, messenger boy cap and mask, litho spaced box 8x10¾. ¼ doz. in pkg....Doz. **$1.90**

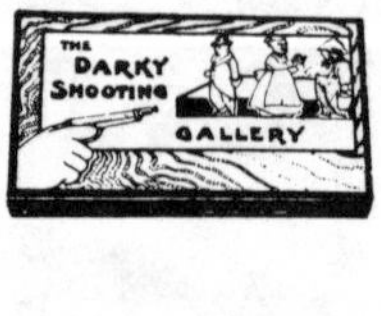


**F2474—"Little Darkey"** Shooting Gallery. 3 comic cardboard targets, spring gun and vacuum rubber tipped arrow. Each set in box, ⅙ doz. in pkg. .......................Doz. **$1.95**

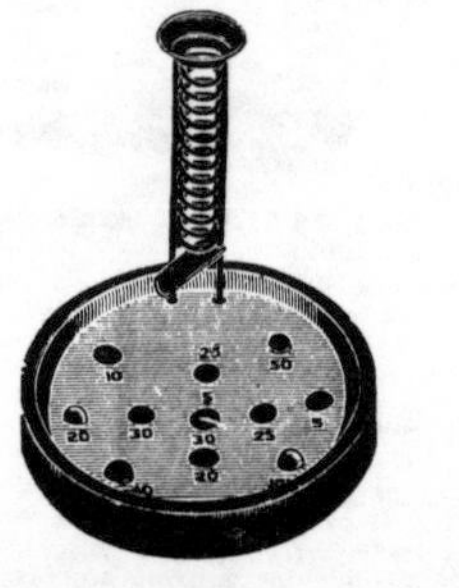

**F2714—"Down and Out" Marble Game.** 6¾ in. tray, ivory and red enameled, numbered colored pockets, 7 in. spiral chute, 4 marbles, roll down chute registering in pockets. 1 in carton, ⅙ doz. in pkg.
Doz. **$3.75**

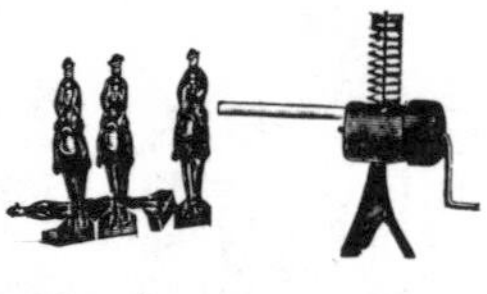

**Rapid Fire Cannon Games**—Each with 9½x9 brass cannon, black wood magazine with metal crank, steel base, envelope of wood projectiles. 1 set in heavy cardboard box.

F2731—Four 6½ in. litho cardboard mounted soldiers on wood bases. ¼ doz. sets in pkg. Doz. sets, **$3.85**

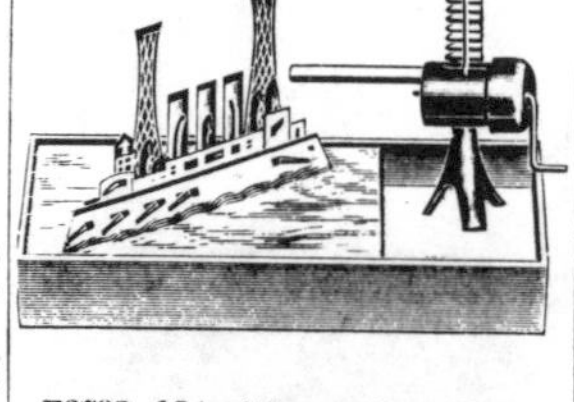

F2732—12 in. litho cardboard battleship in 7 pieces, each on wood base, falls in sections when hit. raised litho marine scenic platform. ⅙ doz. sets in pkg.
Doz. sets, **$8.00**

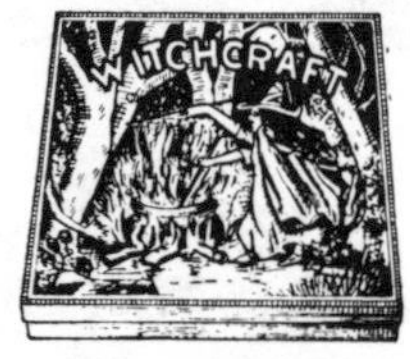


**F2382—Witch Fortune Teller.** Cardboard circles with 56 questions and answers, litho witch with stick on magnetized base, when changed from one circle to other answers question asked, 10¾x10¾ litho box. ¼ doz. in pkg..............Doz. **$3.90**

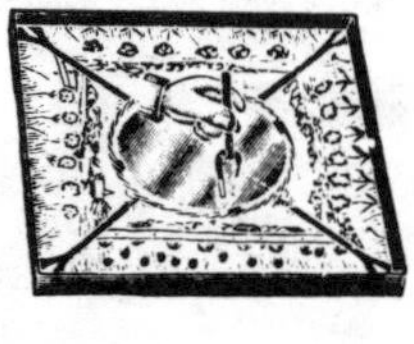

**F2380—Magnetic "Honey Bee,"** 12½x12½ box, board with 4 colors litho flowers, removable polished steel disc with 4 exits covering 24 colored "bee" counters, drawn out with handled magnet to cover corresponding color flowers. ¼ doz. in pkg...... ...............Doz. **$3.30**

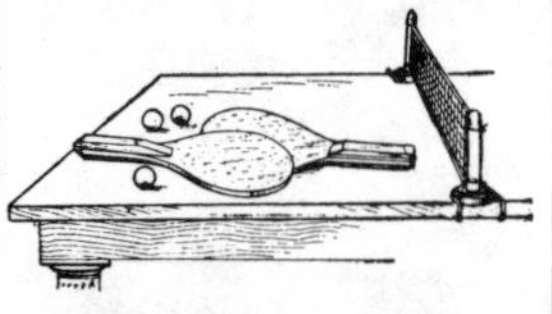

**Ping Pong**—Two 11¾ in. bats, white tape bound cord nets, 2 varnished posts and felt lined table clamps, white celluloid balls. 1 set in strong litho box.

F2384—Varnished hardwood bats, shaped handles, 4 balls, 42 x 6 white net........DOZ. SETS, **$8.75**

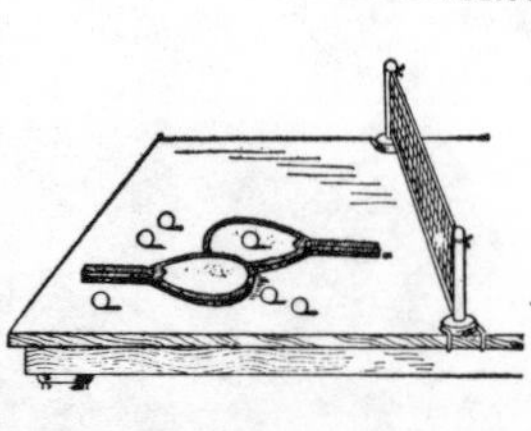

F2386—Tan leather covered bats, maroon leather bound and handles, 6 balls, 47x6 green net.
SET, **$1.30**

## IMPORTED GAMES.

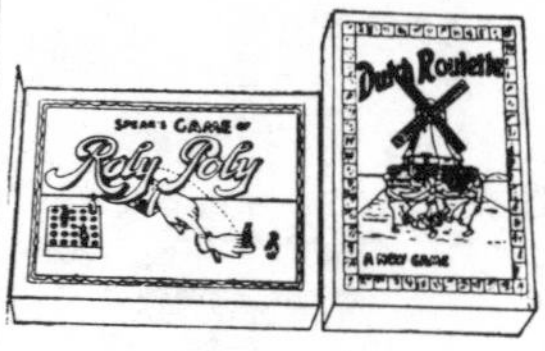


**F2378—3 styles.** Dutch Roulette Magnetic fish pond, Rolly-poly. box aver. 5½x4¾ bright litho tops. Asstd. 1 doz. in pkg................Doz. **40c**

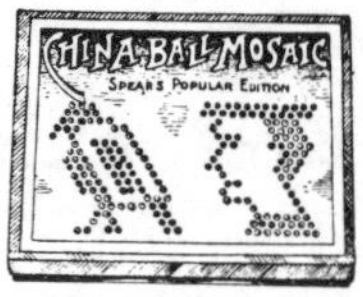


**F2487—China Ball Mosaic.** 5½x7¼ heavy cardboard box, raised perforated board, large number asstd. color balls, placed in holes make various designs. 1 doz. in pkg.
Doz. **87c**

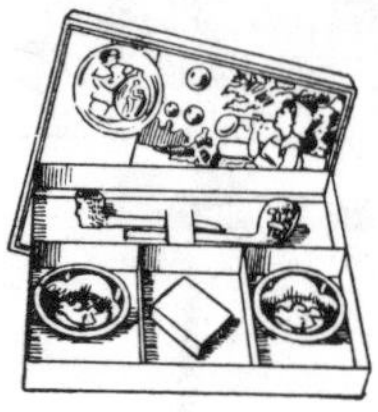

**F2480—Bubble Outfit.** 2 clay, pipes, cups and soap, 8¾x6½ spaced box. 1 doz. in pkg..........Doz. **89c**

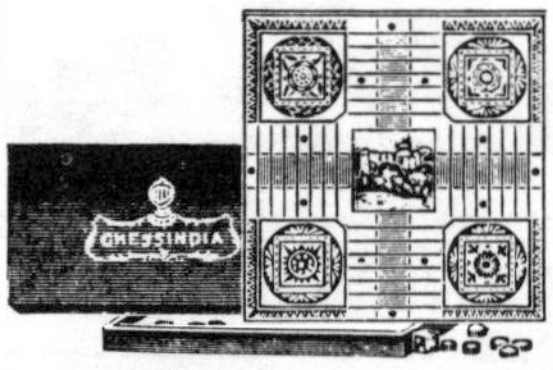


**F2486—Chessindia.** 5¾x11, embossed cover box, folding board and 16 men 2 dice, instructions. 1 doz. in pkg.......................Doz. **92c**

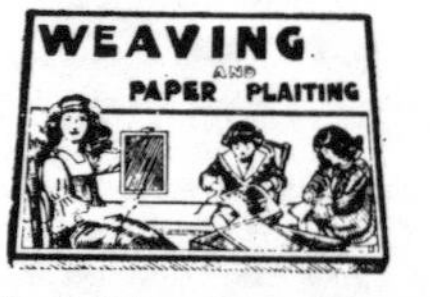


**F2481**—3 styles. **Paper Weaving.** asstd. color paper strips and patterns; **Art Needlework,** cards for sewing, thimble, scissors, needles, colored silks, etc.; **Basket Work,** card board basket frames. thin varilength sticks for weaving, 10¼x6½ litho boxes. Asstd. 1 doz. in pkg.
Doz. **95c**

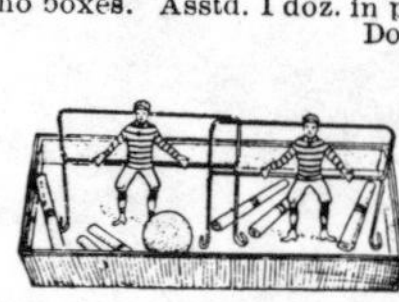

**F2488—"Blow Football" Game.** 6 tubes, celluloid balls, 2 goal posts, played on table by as many as 6 persons. Each in box 5x10½, with instructions. 1 doz. in pkg...Doz. **95c**

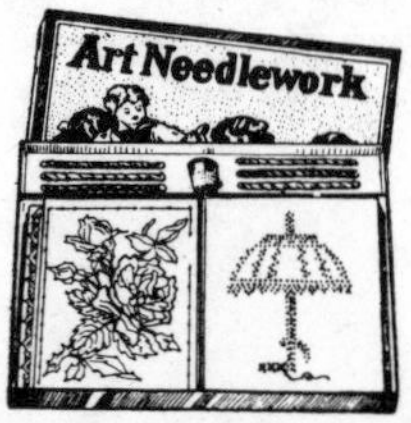


**F2483—Kindergarten Games.** 6 styles, wood mosaic, paper weaving, art needlework, drawing and painting, basketwork or stickbuilding and "familiar objects." 1 in box, 8¾ x 10¼, bright litho covers. ¼ doz. in pkg............. Doz. **$2.00**

## IMPORTED GAMES--

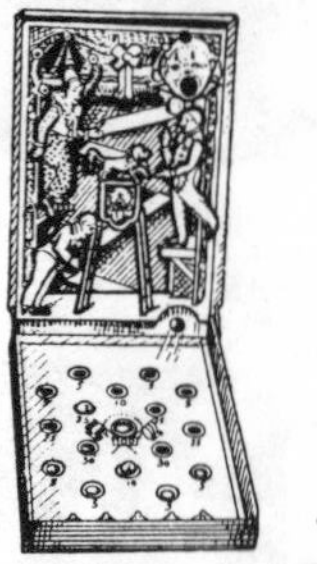

**F2385—"Tivoli."** Box 11x7¼, hin cover with cut-out clowns and way, numbered perforations in b when marbles roll down runw clowns perform. ½ doz. in pkg.
Doz. **$2.**

## POPULAR GAME OF INDI

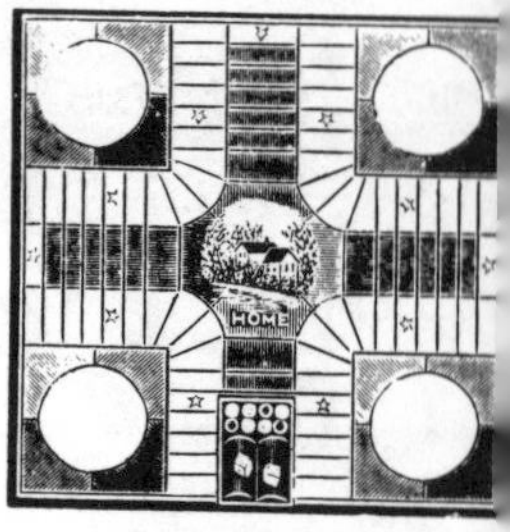


**F2472**—Open 19 x 19, extra hea binders' board, black imit. leathe dice, dice cups and men. ½ doz. pkg..............................Doz. **$1.**

## CHESSINDIA.

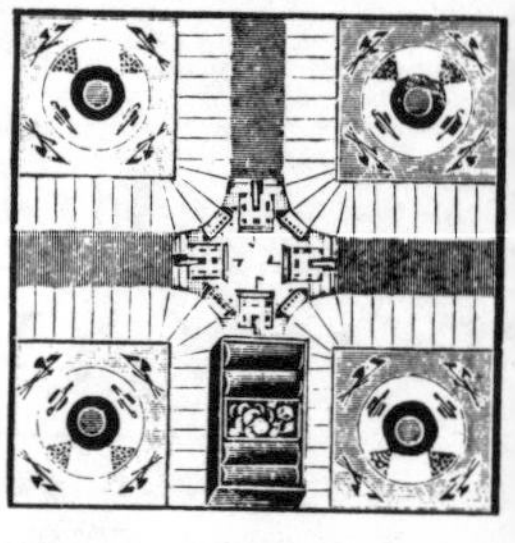

**F2447**—15¾x16. flat board size, con plete. ½ doz. in pkg......Doz. **$1.8**

**F2448**—18½x18¾ folding imit. leath er board, 4 sets of dice, dice cup and men. ¼ doz. in pkg..Doz. **$3.8**

## GAME OF PARCHESI.

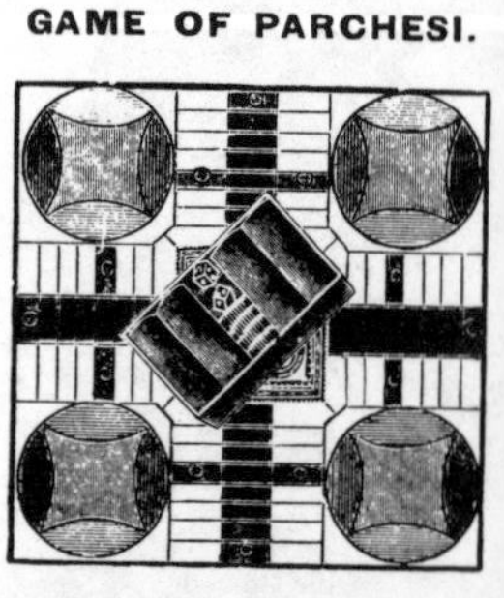

**F2449**—So well known only the price is needed to tell the story. 3 in pkg. ..... ..................Each, **50c**
In lots of 1 doz., $5.50

## DONKEY PARTY GAME.

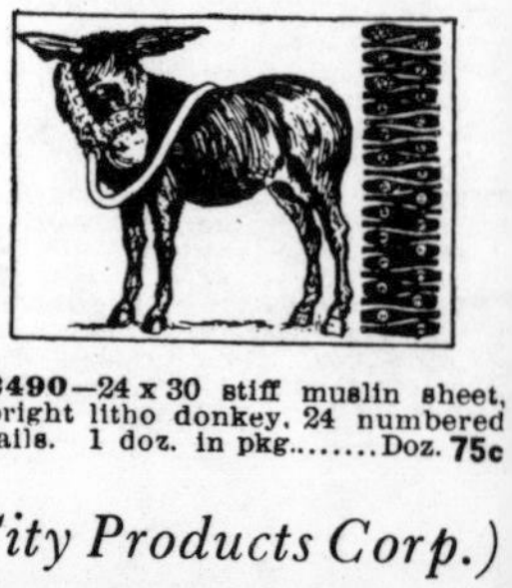

**F2490**—24 x 30 stiff muslin sheet, bright litho donkey. 24 numbered tails. 1 doz. in pkg........Doz. **75c**

## SORTED CARD GAMES.

F2422 — 6 styles. Authors, Peter Coddle, Stars and Stripes, Wild Flowers, Old Maid and Races; box 4x4¼. Asstd. 1 doz.in pkg. Doz. 25c
Gro. $2.85

F2423 — 12 styles. Authors. Old Maid, little Red Men, Mother Goose, Lotto, etc.. box 4x5, gold and colored labels. Asstd. 1 doz. in pkg........ Doz. 32c
Gro. $3.65

F2424 — 12 styles. Jack and Jill. Golden Locks, Puss-In-Boots, Peter Coddle, Authors, etc., box 5x6, gold graced litho labels. Asstd. 1 doz. in pkg........ Doz. 44c
Gro. $5.00

F2426 — 12 styles, Merry-Go-Round, Peter Coddle, Cinderella, Doctor Busby, etc.. box 5½ x 6¾. Asstd. 1 doz. in pkg............... Doz. 68c
Gro. $7.75

F2425 — 4 styles, Trolley Came Off, Letters, Historical and My Wife and I, litho box 5x6½. Asstd. 1 doz. in pkg........ ..... Doz. 68c
Gro. $7.75

F2427 — 6 styles, colored cards, heavy stock, The House that Jack Built, Ten Little Niggers, Mother Goose, Peter Coddle, Authors, etc., litho box 6x4¾. Asstd. 1 doz. in pkg. Doz. 72c
Gro. $8.20

F2429 — 6 titles, Authors, Jack Straws, Doctor Busby, Old Maid, Snap, Peter Coddle, very complete, some with large colored cards, litho box 6⅝x8¾. Asstd. 1 doz. in pkg. Doz. 82c
Gro. $9.35

F2435 — 6 titles, Venetian Fortune Teller, Great Detective, Snap, Peter Coddle, Quit and Old Maid, some with animal, comic and numeral cards; 5½x7½ gilt lettered leatherette covered box. Asstd. ½ doz. in pkg............... Doz. $1.75

## POPULAR GAMES.

Heavy enameled finish cards, fancy backs. Each set in attractive box, full directions.

F2492 — Domino Cards. Fifty-five 1⅞x2⅜ cards, gilt edges, round corners, fly backs, black dots and numerals; telescope box. Plays 8 games. ½ doz. in pkg............... Doz. $1.70

F2743 — Rumme. 52 numbered cards, litho partition box. To be played by 2 or more. ½ doz. in pkg. Doz. $1.75

F2478 — Flinch. 150 numbered cards. ¼ doz. in pkg..... Doz. $3.60

F2491 — Roodles. 4 sets of 12 extra quality red & black litho cards, leatherette covered partition box. ¼ doz. in pkg............... Doz. $3.60

F2471 — Rook. 4 sets cards, red, black, green and yellow printing; leatherette covered partition box. Played similar to auction pinochle. ¼ doz. in pkg............... Doz. $3.60

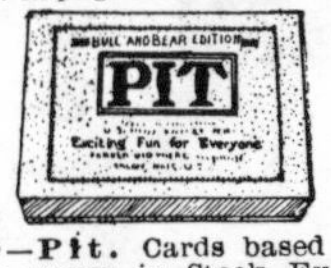

F2469 — Pit. Cards based on exciting scenes in Stock Exchange, leatherette covered partition box. Played by 3 or more. ¼ doz. in pkg. Doz. $3.60

F2475 — Boy Scouts. 50 cards, 5 patrols of 10 cards each, printed in colors. Scout picture backs; litho partition box. ¼ doz. in pkg. Dz. $3.60

F2479 — Plaza. 5 sets of 12 cards each, colored numbers, leatherette covered partition box. Latest building game. ¼ doz. in pkg.. Doz. $3.60

## OLD MAID.

F2417 — 39 colored cards, up-to-date pictures, box 4x5. 1 doz. in pkg. Doz. 30c
Gro. $3.40

## AUTHORS.

F2419 — 24 cards, well known authors in colors, box 4x5. 1 doz. in pkg. Doz. 30c

F2420 — 32 high grade cards, tinted backs, fine photo fronts, box 4¼x5¾. 1 doz. in pkg.... Doz. 68c
Gro. $7.75

F2421 — 56 finely enameled flexible cards, modern authors — Jack London, Booth Tarkington, Winston Churchill, James Barrie, etc., litho box 7x5½. ½ doz. in pkg. Doz. $1.80

## FISH PONDS.

F2450 — 12¼x12¼ litho box, 8 fish, 2 rods. 1 doz. in pkg........ Doz. 75c
Gro. $8.75

F2451 — 10¼x19¾ litho box, raised pond, slots for placing fish in swiming position, 22 litho fish, 2 rods. ¼ doz. in pkg. ..... Doz. $1.85

F2452 — Magnetic. 12 litho cardboard fish with metal rings, 2 poles with horseshoe magnets, 11¼x11¼x 8¼ folding litho aquarium; box 10x 22⅛. ½ doz. in pkg ......Doz. $1.90

## POPULAR PLAYING CARDS.

S999 — "Steamboat." Asstd. backs. 1 doz. in box. ............... Doz. 70c
Gro. $8.25

S808 — "Bicycle." Ivory finish, red or blue back. 1 doz. in box. Doz. $1.85

## "MOTHER GOOSE" RHYME ASST.

F2442 — 10¼x 17¾, 6 styles, Mother Hubbard, Frog-Who-Wuld-A-Wooing Go, Curly-Locks, Mistress Mary, Sailor Boy, and Little Soldier. Asstd. 1 doz. in pkg.
Gro. $9.50     Doz. 90c

## ASSTD. CARDBOARD GAMES.

Up-to-date titles.  Attractive litho labels.

F2433 — 5¼x5¼, 6 styles, Foot Race, Babes in the Woods, Buffalo Hunt, Fox and Hounds, Taking the Fort, Going to the Fire. Asstd. 1 doz. in pkg............... Doz. 32c
Gro. $3.65

F2434 — 7¼x7¼, 6 styles, Race for the Cup, Circus, Three Little Kittens, Bicycle Race, Mother Goose, Round the World. Asstd. 1 doz. in pkg. Doz. 38c
Gro. $4.25

F2436 — 9x9, 12 styles, gilt titles and decorated, Little Nemo, Wild West, Sailor Boy, The Victor, Beauty and the Beast, India, etc. Asstd. 1 doz. in pkg............... Doz. 42c
Gro. $4.75

F2437 — 8x14, 6 subjects, Peter Pumpkin Eater, Little Bo-Peep, Crooked Man, Old Maid, Jack Spratt, etc. Asstd. 1 doz. in pkg... Doz. 68c
Gro. $7.80

F2438 — 6¾ x 15¾, litho covers, 6 styles, Jack and Jill, Jack Horner, Robinson Crusoe, Fire Fighters, Steeple Chase, Miss Muffet. Asstd. 1 doz. in pkg...... Doz. 72c
Gro. $8.20

F2440 — 11¼ x 11¼, 6 subjects, Enchanted Forest, Cabin Boy, Frog School, Cock-a-Doodle-Doo, etc. Asstd. ½ doz. in pkg... Doz. 74c

## CARDBOARD GAMES.

F2442 — 10¼x 17¾, 6 styles, Mother Hubbard, Frog-Who-Wuld-A-Wooing Go, Curly-Locks, Mistress Mary, Sailor Boy, and Little Soldier. Asstd. 1 doz. in pkg.
Gro. $9.50     Doz. 90c

F2443 — 10x20, 6 styles, Mother Goose, Fast Mail, U. S. Postman, Messenger Boy, Drummer Boy, Little Red Riding Hood. Asstd. 1 doz. in pkg............... Doz. 95c
Gro. $11.00

F2445 — 15x16½, 6 titles, Messenger Boy, Puss, U. S. Mail, Mother Hubbard, Across the Sea, Checkered Life, 2 dice cups, dice and men. Asstd. ½ doz. in pkg...... Doz. $1.75

F2444 — Crokinole. 15¼ in. square, crokinole and checker board, wood frame, litho numbered circles in cardboard bottom, set of wood checkers. ½ doz. in pkg.. Doz. $1.80

F2446 — 14x21, 6 styles, Soldier Boy, Fast mail, Round the World, India, North Pole, Fortune Teller; 2 dice cups, dice and men. Asstd. ½ doz. in pkg. ......... Doz. $1.85

F2460 — 14 x 23, 3 styles, Steeple Chase, Dreamland, Merry-Go-Round; raised litho boards, 2 dice cups, dice and men. Asstd. ¼ doz. in pkg............... Doz. $2.00

## GAME BOARDS.

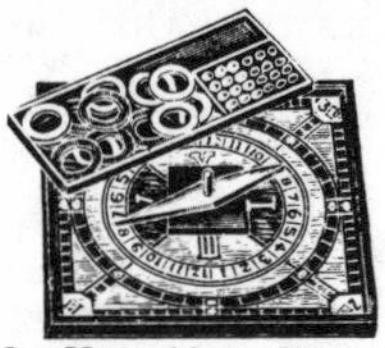

**F1679 — Marveldex.** 16x16, wood frame, grained wood effect surface. 25 interesting games can be played —Baseball, Checker Polo, Ring Toss, etc., complete with checkers, rings and spinner, instructions inside cover. 1/12 doz. in carton. DOZ. **$7.80**

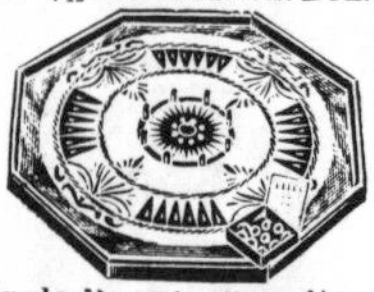

**Crokinole Board**—29 in. diam., mahogany finish, complete with 24 hardwood rings and book of rules.
F1324—3 in crate.........Each, $1 05
F1325—Felt lined, 2 in crate " 1 35

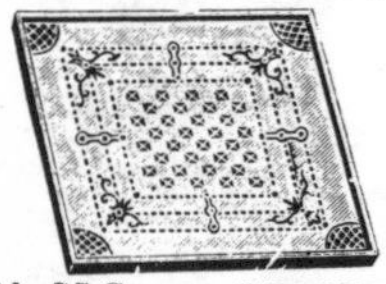

**F1334—75 Games.** 28½x28½, hardwood rims, 3 ply veneer center, select stock, diagram both sides in 2 colors stencil work, reversible net pockets, strong and deep, 75 games, 60 pieces of equipment: 29 rings, 2 cues, 10 pins, back stop, rule book, Crokinole, Nine Pins, Chess, Fortune Telling, etc. 1 in crate, 12 lbs.
Each, **$1.80**

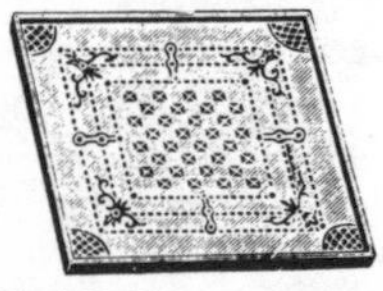

**F1335—100 Games.** As F1334, diagrams in 3 color stencil work. 100 games can be played, 109 pieces of equipment; 4 colors, 15 numbered discs, 2 dice boxes, 4 dice, 38 pawns, 2 boxes for men. Each with revolving stand. 1 in crate, 11 lbs.
Each, **$2.25**

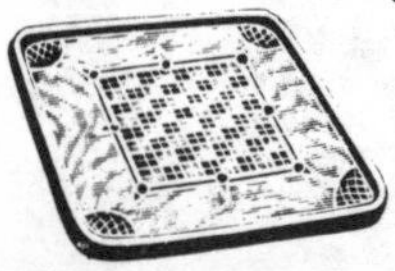

**F1328—Combination Carrom and Checker Board.** 29 in. square, reversible pocket, center ply, entire board white maple, natural finish, green felt cushions, 50 games, 57 pc. equipment, 1 in crate...Each, **$2.25**

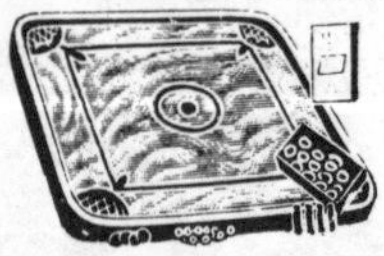

**F1329—Combination Carrom and Crokinole Board.** 29 in. square, white maple crokinole panel, in imit. mahogany, felt cushions, reversible net pockets, 50 games, 54 pc. equipment. 1 in crate.
Each, **$2.60**

## GAME BOARDS—Contd.

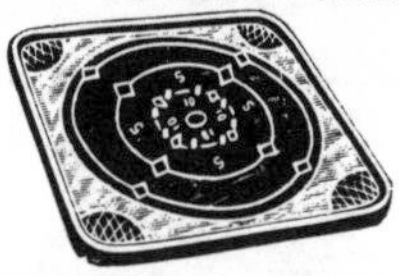

**F1330—65 Games.** "Crown" 65 gameboard, white birch center veneer, rims hard maple, polished, reversible, net pockets, 29x29. Cues, discs and rules, Spider and the Fly, Crokinole, Ten Pins, 3 Ring Glance, Traveling Carroms, Rotation Cue Pocket Backgammon, etc. 1 in crate.
Each, **$2.60**

## "ARCHARENA" COMBINATION GAME BOARD.

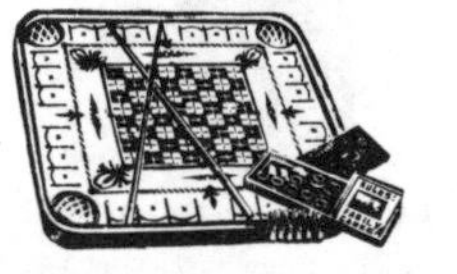

**F1326**—58 games, 29 in. square, round corners, white maple carrom rim, 3 ply white maple veneer panel, select stock, natural finish, red and green diagrams. Equipped with 29 hardwood rings, 10 ten pins, 2 spinners, 1 combination backstop and score tab, 3 spinning tops and 1 book of rules. 1 in pkg.
Each, **$2.00**

## CROKINOLE RINGS AND TEN PINS FOR GAME BOARDS.

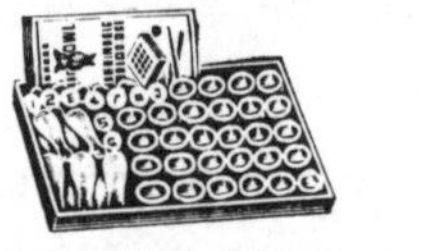

**F2489**—20 maple rings, asstd. colors and ten 2 in. ten pins. Each set in box. ½ doz. in pkg.......Doz. **$2.10**

## FOLDING GAME BOARD STAND.

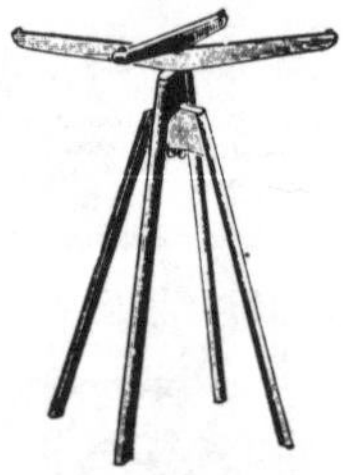

**F2377** — Hardwood, varnished, revolves freely and stands rigidly, folds compactly, board rests on rubber tips which prevent it sliding or being marred........... Doz. **$4.50**

*DOLLS. Ours is a complete line of the best sellers in every range of price. The choicest values from American and European factories. SEE INDEX.*

## "INDOOR" BASEBALL GAME.

*The only game on which four plays are registered at one time, giving the action of a real baseball game.*

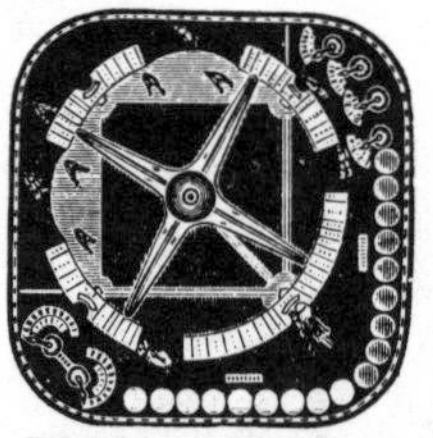

**F2496**—13¼ x 13¼, all steel, green litho. field and raised diamond, buff base paths and infield positions, litho players in places, 1 in. side fence and stand, nickel plated 4 point dial on oiled bearing pointing to various plays, 6 small tally dials, 22 metal discs, white enameled faced with name of players in each team. 1/12 doz. in box.
Doz. **$8.50**

## RING TOSS.

Varnished oak crosspiece, 5 turned varnished and striped posts, 3 rings. Each set in litho box.

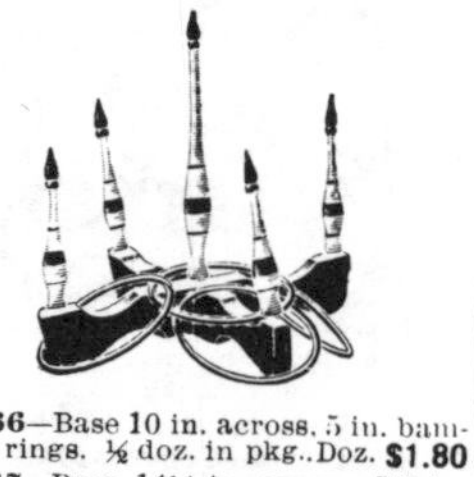

**F2766**—Base 10 in. across, 5 in. bamboo rings. ½ doz. in pkg..Doz. **$1.80**
**F2767**—Base 14½ in. across, 5¾ in. colored felt wound rings. ⅓ doz in pkg. .....................Doz. **$3.85**

## TABLE CROQUET.

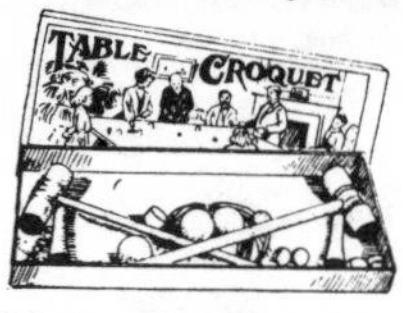


**F2296**—Four 7¾ in. turned mallets, 3 painted balls, wire wickets with wood bases, 2 stakes; 5x11¼ litho box. ½ doz. sets in pkg.
Gro. sets, $8.50 Doz. sets, **75c**

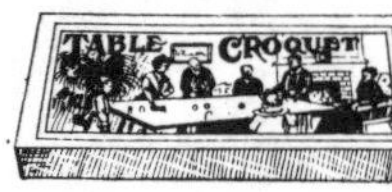


**F2297**—Four 8 in. turned mallets, 4 asstd. color balls, copper wire wickets with wood stands, 2 home stakes, tape with coppered wire fixtures: 5¼x11¾ litho box. ½ doz. sets in pkg. .... ...... Doz. sets, **95c**

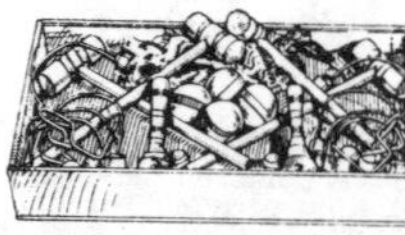

**F2298**—Four 9 in. varnished striped mallets and balls, 2 striped home stakes, wood base copper wickets, tape with copper wire fixtures. 6⅛x12⅛ wood box. ⅓ doz. sets in pkg..... ........... Doz. sets, **$1.85**

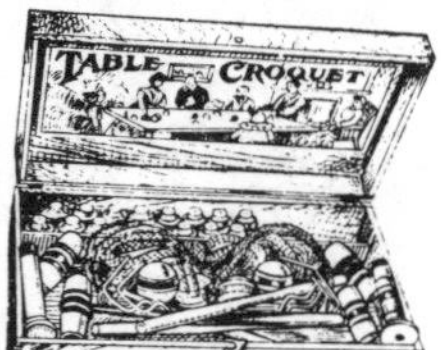


**F2299**—Four 10¼ in. heavy varnished striped wood mallets and balls, striped home stake, wood base twisted wire wickets, tape and copper brackets: 7⅛ x 11¾ green painted hinged wood box. ⅙ doz. sets in pkg...... ..........Doz. sets, **$3.85**

## STEAMER QUOITS.

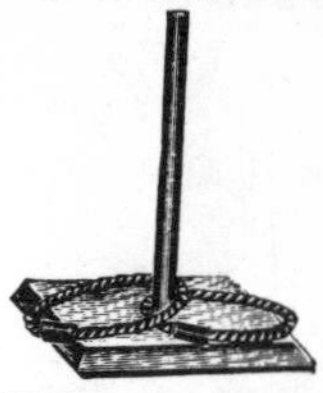

**F2765W**—6x6 mission finish be[se], 8 in. stained wood post, 2 r[ope] rings with wood grips. Each se[t in] holly box. 1 doz. sets in pkg.
Doz. sets.

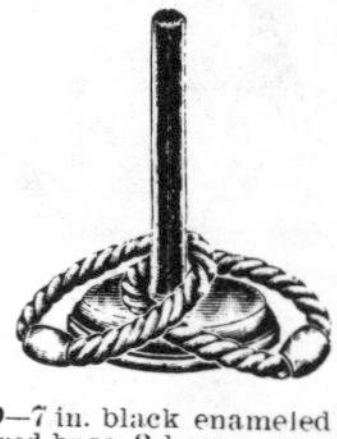

**F2769**—7 in. black enameled post 5 in. red base, 2 heavy rope quo[its], colored wood grip. Each set in b[ox]. ⅓ doz. sets in pkg...Doz. sets, **$1**

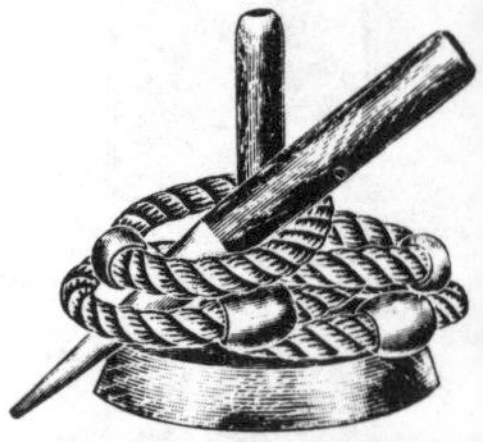

**F2833**—6½ in. polished mahoga[ny] finish bevel base, 6½ in. black e[n]amel post, 4 heavy variegated ro[pe] quoits, colored wood grips, r[ed] enamel stake for playing out doo[rs]. Each set in box. ¼ doz. sets in pk[g].
Doz. sets, **$3.**

## FAMOUS "OUIJA" TALKING BOARD

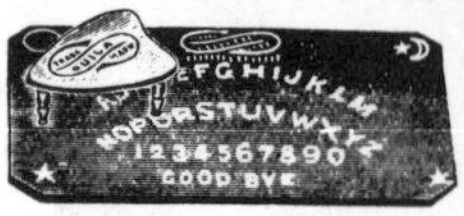


**F2189**—12½x18 board, 3 ply vene[er], full alphabet, numbers, etc., to[o] well known to need descriptio[n]. 1 in pkg.... ...........Doz. **$7.0**

## NUMERAL FRAMES.

Varnished hardwood frames, turned wood handles, rows vari-colored woo[d] counters on copper wires.

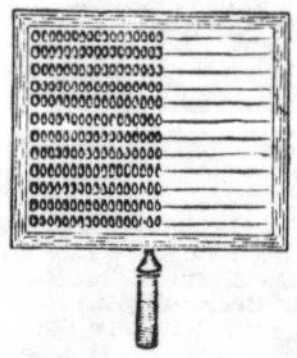

**F2468**—8½x6½, 5 rows of counter[s]. 1 doz. in box. .......... ...Doz. **85**
**F2428**—9¾x10¾, 10 rows of coun[t]ers. ½ doz. in box.......Doz. **$1.9**

## BAGATELLE BOARDS.

With strong spring shooters.

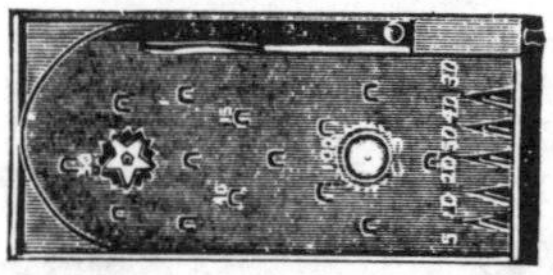

**F2343**—6¼x12, red stained wood frame, 1¼ in. bell brass star. ½ doz. in pkg. Doz. **75c**
Gro. $8.75

**F2344**—8x18, heavy varnished, wood frame, 2 bells, brass star. ½ doz. in pkg... ............Doz. **$1.85**

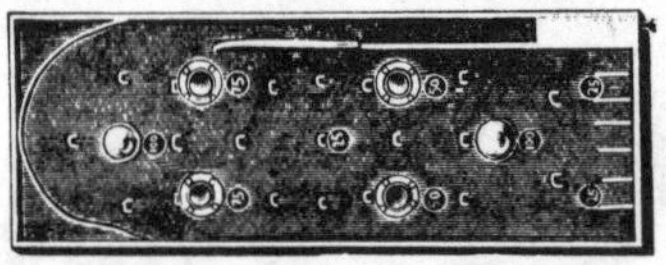

**F2345**—9 x 24, varnished hardwood frame, glazed red lined, 2 nickeled bells, 4 brass pockets. ⅙ doz. in pkg... ...........Doz. **$3.75**

## TOY BOWLING ALLEY.

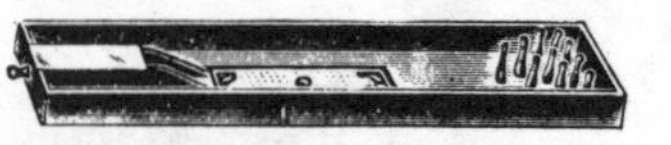

**F2717**—21½x4¼ varnished wood alley, heavy cardboard sides, reinforced wood end, ten 1¾ in. turned pins, 2 marbles, adjustable stained wood runways: litho cover. 1 doz. in pkg.............. ...............Doz. **92c**

## WOOD BOWLING ALLEYS.

Varnished hardwood frames and alleys, reinforced backs, adjustable spring action shooter, ten turned pins. Same shots can be made as on full size alley.

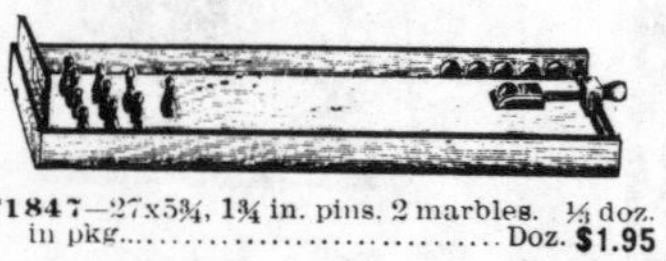

**F1847**—27x5¾, 1¾ in. pins, 2 marbles. ½ doz. in pkg.............................Doz. **$1.95**

## WOOD ALLEY GAMES.

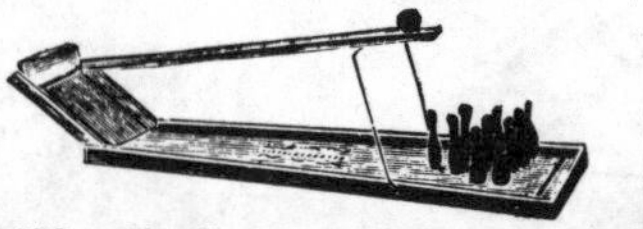

**F1678 — "Bowlingola."** 40x9, red striped varnished hardwood, ten 3⅜ in. red stained pins, balls roll down adjustable incline, making any hit possible. 1/12 doz. in carton.
Doz. **$8.00**

## WALLIE DORR FAMOUS BILLIARD AND POOL TABLES

New construction, removable cushions which by reversing convert table for pool or billiards. Heavy mahogany finish frames, brass trim, high grade green English felt covered, knit cord pockets, larger sizes with absolutely accurate placement dots, perfect turned cues. Each with set of 16 solid color balls, inlaid numbers.

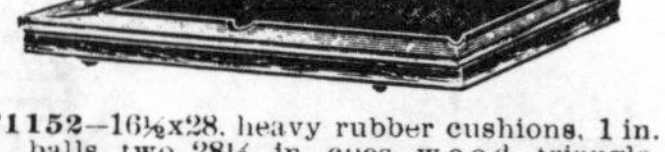

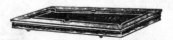

**F1152**—16½x28, heavy rubber cushions, 1 in. balls, two 28¼ in. cues, wood triangle, chalk. 1 in carton, 7 lbs........Each, **$2.85**

**F1153—As F1152**, 21x36, 36½ in. cues, heavier cushions, 1⅛ in. balls. 1 in carton, 15 lbs.
Each, **$4.55**

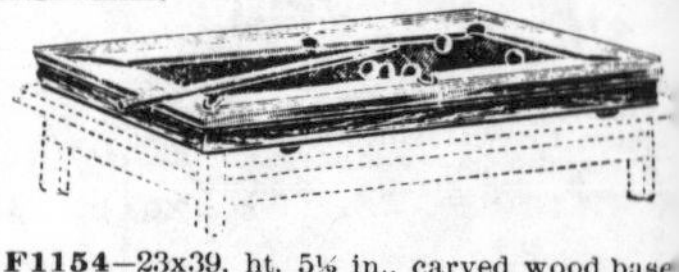

**F1154**—23x39, ht. 5½ in., carved wood base, heavy slate bed, regulation cushions, dee[p] pockets, 1¼ in. balls, varnished angle, tw[o] 36½ in. cues. 1 in crate, 40 lbs. Each, **$6.7**

**F1155** — As F1154, 24¾x41¾, 1¾ in. balls, 42 in. cues, leather trim pockets. 1 in crate, 70 lbs.... ..........................Each, **$10.6**

**F1156**—28x48½, ht. 6½, massive frame, turned legs, extra fast table for accurate playing, heavy slate bed, regulation rubber cushions, red leather trim deep pockets, large polished angle, 1¾ in. balls, two 50½ oil finished hardwood cues. 1 in crate, 95 lbs.
Each, **$18.5**

# PECIALTY DOLLS

**Active quick selling novelties.** The latest and most attractive products of American makers, representative of the wonderful ancement made in this line. Of those to retail at 25c, 50c, $1.00 and up we have the market's cest selection. Generous and reliable profit payers for the merchant who gives them due prominence.

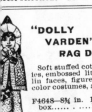

## "DOLLY VARDEN" RAG DOLLS.

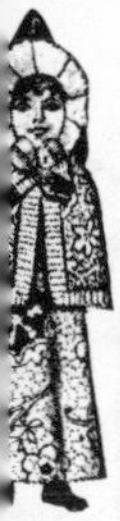

Soft stuffed cotton bodies, embossed litho muslin faces, figured bright color costumes, asstd.

F4648—8¾ in. 1 doz. in box.......... Doz. **35 c**

F4650—13 in. 1 doz. in box............. Doz. **45 c**

## DESTRUCTIBLE CELLULOID HEAD DOLLS.

ll celluloid heads, each with le, painted features, eyes and hair, stuffed bodies, attached shoes, ssed in colored fancy worsted, felt fur effect costumes.

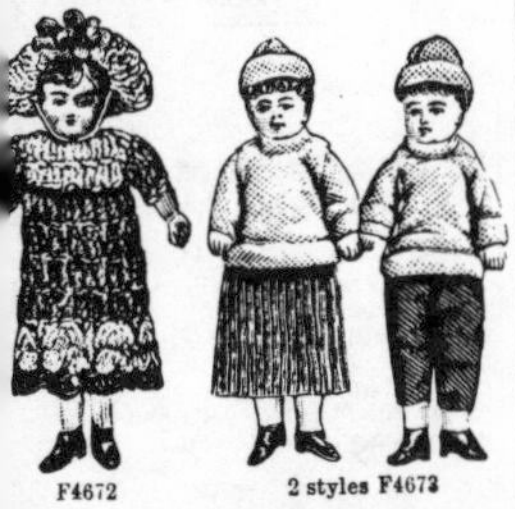

F4672 2 styles F4673

672—7½ in., 2 styles, colored wor-ed dresses and hats. Asstd. 1 doz. box.................Doz. **87c** Gro. $10.20

673—7½ in., boy and girl, asstd. ed, blue, green and purple trousers nd skirts, white sweaters and caps. sstd. 1 doz. in box.........Doz. **92c** Gro. $10.75

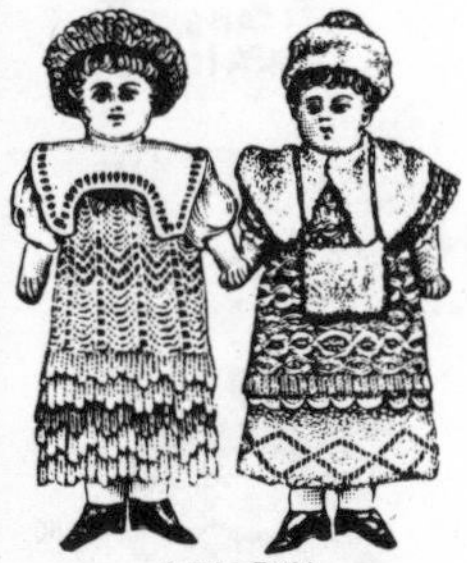

2 styles F4674

4674—10 in., 3 styles and colors worsted dresses, empire, crochet am o'shanter; Russian blouse, fur effect muff, collar and cap; flounced dress with mushroom hat. Red, blue and pink, combined with white. Asstd. ½ doz. in box..... Doz. **$2.00**

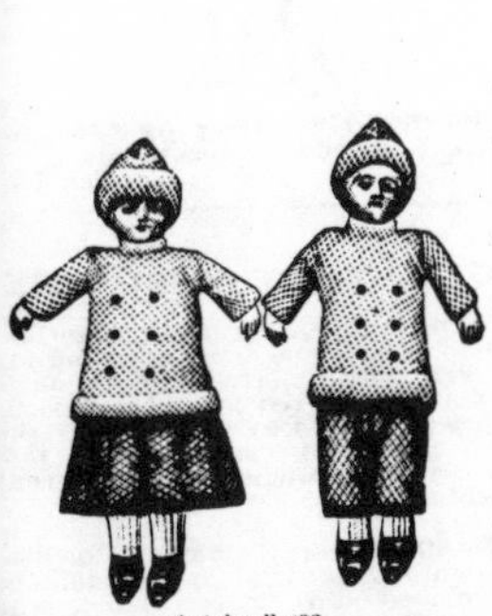

2 styles F4682

4682—9½ in., boy and girl, asstd. red and blue trousers and skirts, white sweaters and caps. ½ doz in box...........................Doz. **$2.10**

## WORSTED DRESSED DOLLS.

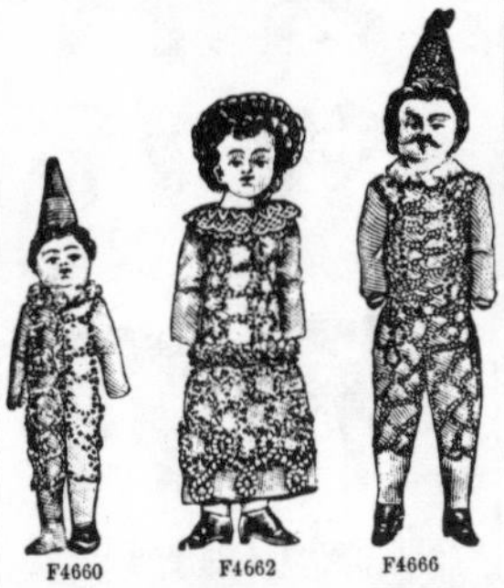

F4660 F4662 F4666

Flesh tinted stockinette faces, bead eyes, worsted features and hair, soft stuffed bodies, worsted figured 3-color costumes (red, blue and yellow), lace or worsted ruffs, knit or peaked muslin caps, colored sewed-on shoe feet. All but first number asstd. boys and girls, and with bells. Doz.

F4660—7½ in. 2 doz. in box.....$0 42

F4662—9½ and 8¼ in. 1 doz. box. **87**

F4666—14 and 12½ in. ½ dz. box. **2.10**

## ACCORDION VOICE DOLLS.

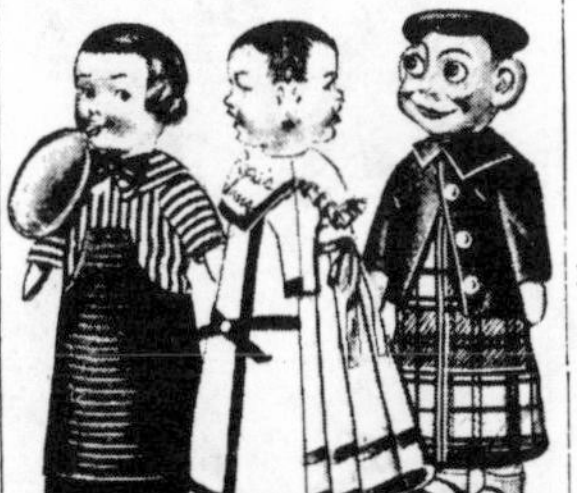

**F4975**—3 styles, aver. 10½ in., boy with rubber balloon which inflates, overall costume; laughing & crying double face baby, ribbon trim white slip; comic boy with large glass goggle eyes, flannel jacket and cap, plaid kilts, painted footwear; painted composition heads, bodies with accordion folds, when pressed down rise slowly with crying voice. Each in box., asstd. ¼ doz. in pkg. Doz. **$5.00**

## "ESKIMO" FUR CLAD DOLLS.

Soft and warm for the baby.

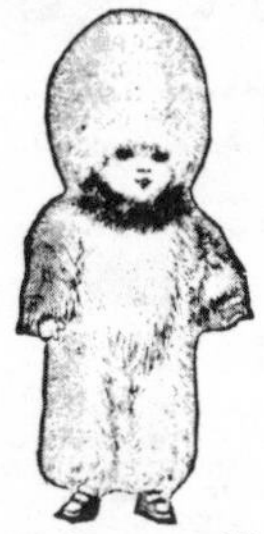

Bisque heads, composition bodies, jointed limbs, white and asstd. color fur, painted shoes.

F4644—6 in., painted features. Asstd. 1 doz. in box,.................Doz. **92c**

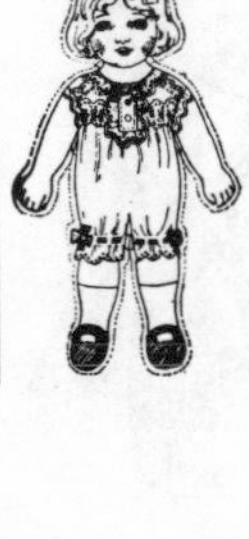

**F2193—Dolls & Animals.** Sheet 18 x18, 15 in. made up. Dottie Dimple, Pussy Mew, Dog Tray, Red Riding Hood, Japanese & Greenaway. Asstd. 1 doz. in pkg. Doz. **79c**

## DOLL SPECIALTIES.

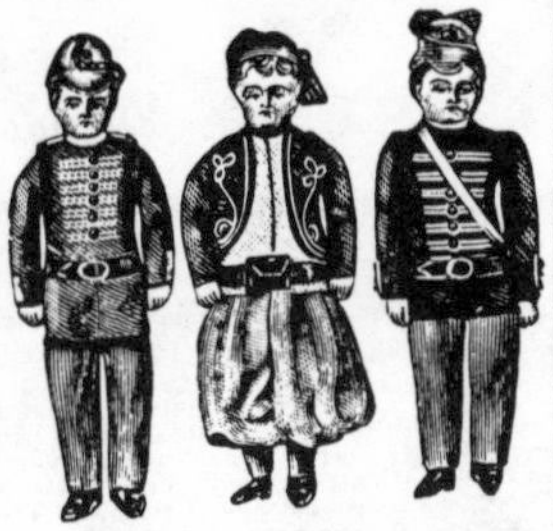

**F4678—Felt Soldiers.** About 6½ in., celluloid heads, painted features and embossed hair, bright color felt military costumes of different nations, worsted, patent leather and buckle trimmings. Asstd. 1 doz. in box.............................Doz. **92c**

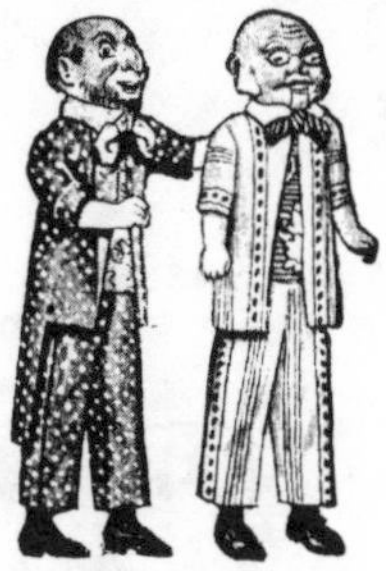

**F4638—"Character."** 11½ in., 6 styles, Happy Hooligan, clown, policeman, Sunny Jim, etc., composition heads, stuffed bodies, asstd. color fabric costumes, opens mouth with voice when bellows are pressed. ½ doz. in box.........Doz. **$2.20**

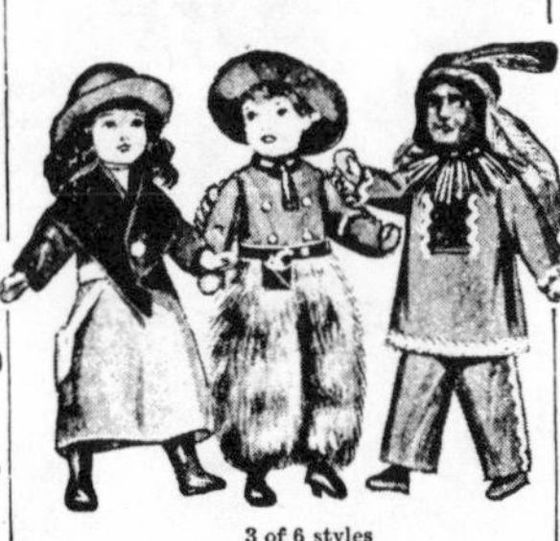

3 of 6 styles

**F4635—Asstd.** 8½ in., 6 styles, bisque heads, glass eyes, mohair wigs, cowboy and girl, Indians, aviator and school boy, solid and combination felt and fur costumes, felt hats, feather headdress and leather cap, painted footwear. Asstd. ½ doz. in box.......Doz. **$2.30**

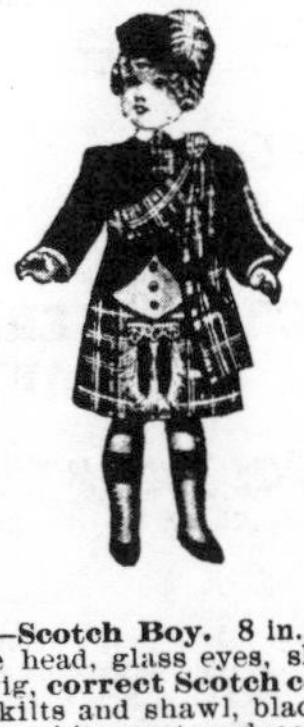

**F4629—Scotch Boy.** 8 in., turning bisque head, glass eyes, short mohair wig, **correct Scotch costume,** plaid kilts and shawl, black velvet jacket, white vest and collar, red flannel tights, black velvet Scotch cap with feather, painted shoes and stockings. ½ doz. in box...Doz. **$2.80**

## CELLULOID HEAD FELT BODY CHARACTER DRESSED DOLLS.

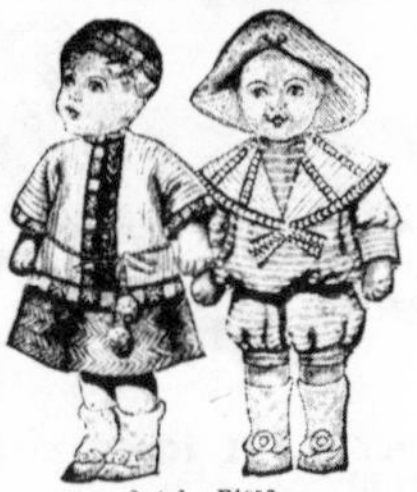

2 styles F4657

Unbreakable celluloid heads, natural expressions, painted features and hair, good models, soft flesh tinted felt bodies, dressed to represent different nations, white socks and shoes, lace trim underwear. Each in box.

**F4657**—9¼ in., jointed shoulder, hip and knee, turning composition hands, **American** boy and girl, white pique collars on striped blue madras; **Chinese** boy and girl, red and braid trim white pique mandarin coats. Asstd. ½ doz. in pkg.................Doz. **$5.75**

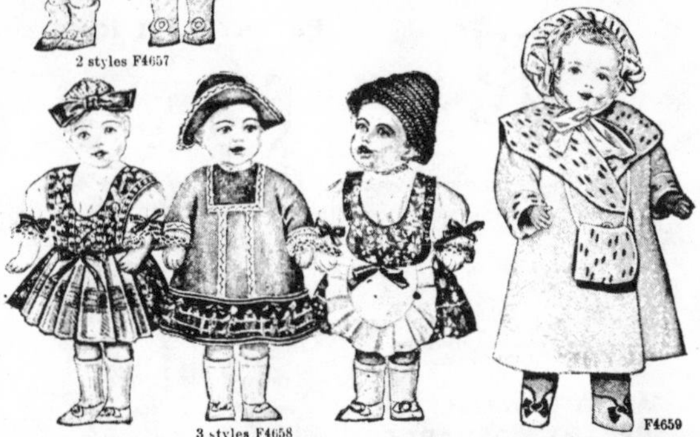

3 styles F4658 F4659

**F4658**—11½ in., jointed shoulder and hip, **Holland** and **German** peasant costumes, figured borders and braid on plain frock or flowered dress, colored aprons, white guimpes; straw, satin and linen hats and caps. Asstd. ¼ doz. in pkg.......................................Doz. **10.00**

**F4659**—15½ in., jointed shoulder and hip, Alaskan costume, ermine effect eiderdown double breasted coat, hat and muff, pink madras dress, white footwear..........................................EACH. **$1.40**

## HARLEQUIN DOLLS ON STICKS.

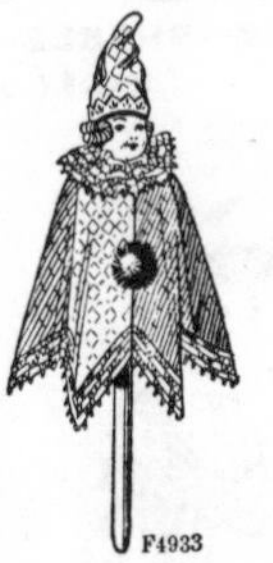

F4933

With **bellows voice,** polished turned wood handles.

**F4933**—Full length 13½ in., bisque head, painted features, curly hair, 3-color dress, lace collar and trim, pointed cap, gilt lace band. 1 doz. in bdl.........................Doz. **89c**

**F4934**—Full length 15½ in., celluloid face, painted features, cap with bell, 4-color lace, braid and pompon trim outfit, lace points with bells, handle with whistle end. Asstd. ½ doz. in box..........................Doz. **$2.00**

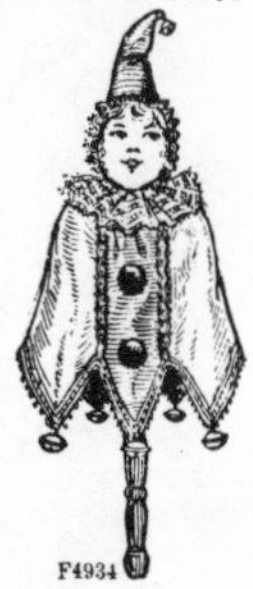

F4934

## MUSICAL DOLLS.

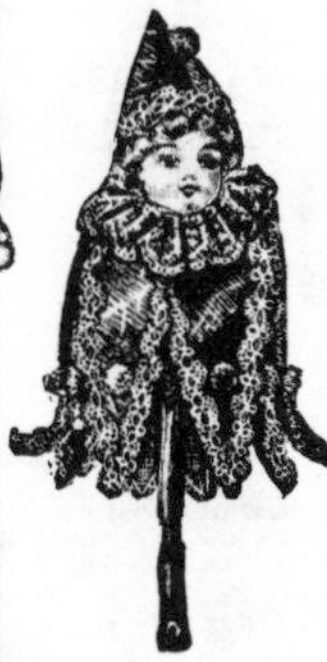

F4937

Bisque heads, natural glass eyes, open mouths, mohair ringlet wigs, pointed satin caps with pompons, lace ruche necks.

**F4937—Swinging.** Extreme 15 in., satin harlequin collar, braid and chenille pompon trim, polished turned wood handle, whistle end; when revolved concealed music box plays. 1-12 doz. in box. Doz. **$10.80**

**F4935—On Cord.** 15 in., composition hands, 2-color satin harlequin costume, lace, braid and pompon trim, white slippers and stockings, music box played by pressing bellows in chest or dancing on cord, ring end. 1 in box. Each, **95c**

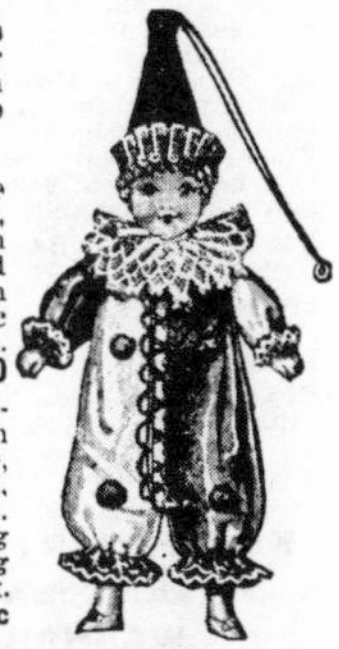

F4935

## CLOTH DOLLS AND ANIMALS.

**To be cut out and stuffed.** Litho in bright oil colors on strong cloth. Simple to make up, parts fit accurately, practically indestructible. Each doll or animal on separate sheet with instructions.

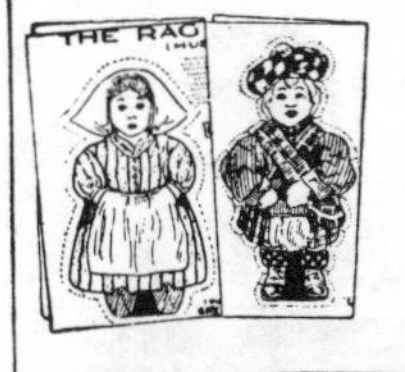

**F2192—"Rag Family" and Asstd. Animals.** 12 styles, from 8 to 17½ in., costume dolls of all nations and dog, cat, elephant, camel, pony, etc. Asstd. 1 doz. in pkg.......Doz. **34c**

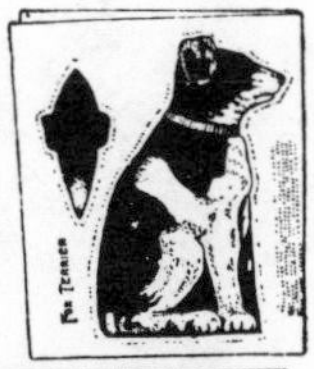

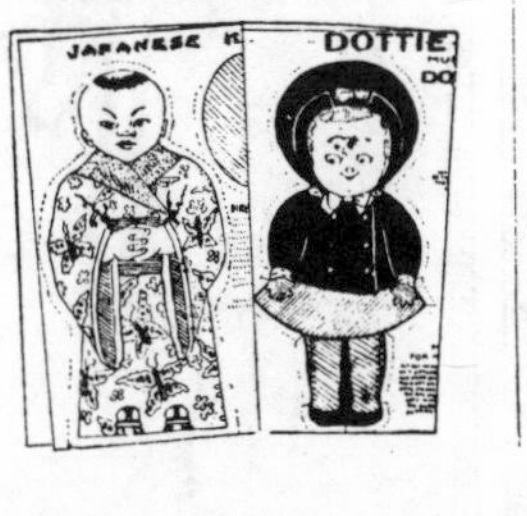

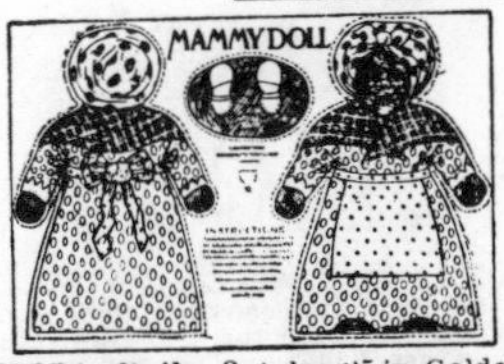


**F2194—Dolls.** 3 styles, 25 in. Golden Locks with 2 dollies, 23 in. Mammy, 17 in. Topsy Turvy, sheets about 35x24. Asstd. ½ doz. pkg..Doz. **$1.25**

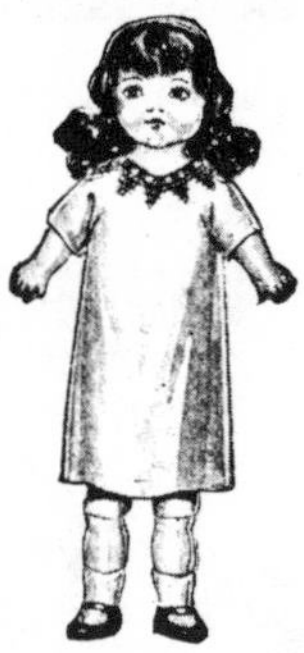

Patent washable head, asstd. long blonde, tosca and brunette hair, painted features, black glass eyes, composition hands and feet, stout stuffed bodies, color trimmed slips, printed footwear. Doz.

F4210—8¾ in. 1 doz. in box.....$0 45
F4214—14 " 1 " " " .... 89
F4216—14 in., natural glass eyes. 1 doz. in box. .... ............ 1 10
F4220—17 in., natural glass eyes. 1 doz. in box..................... 1 60

## "FAVORITE NAME" PATENT WASHABLE DOLLS.

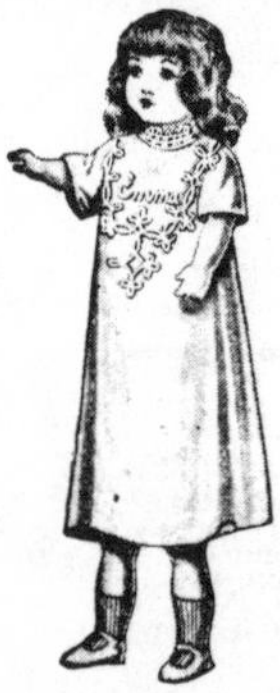

Specially made for us. Patent washable heads and limbs, natural glass eyes, painted eyebrows and lashes, blonde, tosca and brunette Rembrandt hair, painted footwear, embroidered name on muslin slip—Mary, Emma, Edith, Ruth, Mabel and Pauline, lace trim necks, scroll bib effect fronts in asstd. blue, red and pink. Doz.

F4222—18½ in. 1 doz. in box.....$2 25
F4224—20 " ½ " " " .... 2 50
F4226—24¾ " ⅓ " " " .... 4 10
F4228—26 " ⅓ " " " .... 4 90
F4230—30 " ⅙ " " " .... 7 20
F4232—Length 34 in. girth 16¾, extra large body and head. ⅙ doz. in box........................ 9 00

## "KINDERGARTEN" PATENT MATLOCK WASHABLE DOLLS.

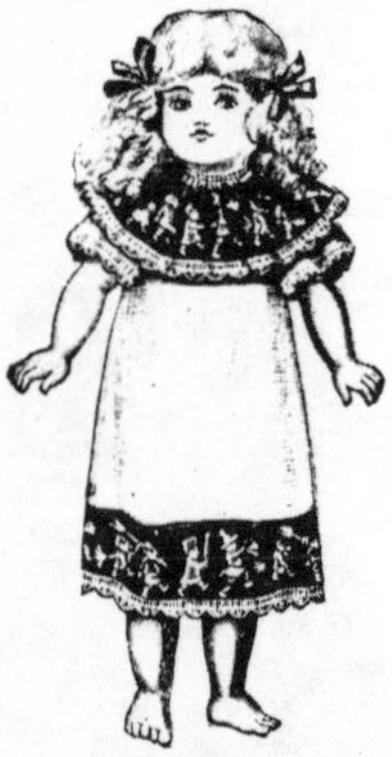

Composition heads and limbs, painted expressive features, natural glass eyes, asstd. blonde, tosca and brunette side part curly wigs, larger sizes with ribbon bows, sitting bodies, movable arms, white chemises, colored kindergarten picture borders and collars.

F4256—11 in. 1 doz. box..Doz$ 1 10
F4257—13 " ½ " " " 2 25
F4258—18½" ⅓ " " " 5 25
F4259—25¾" ⅙ " " " 10 25

Patent washable heads and limbs, blonde, tosca and brunette Rembrandt hair, natural glass eyes, painted footwear, insertion color chemise on first number, and mull dress with lace collar and ribbon effect on 3 highest priced numbers.

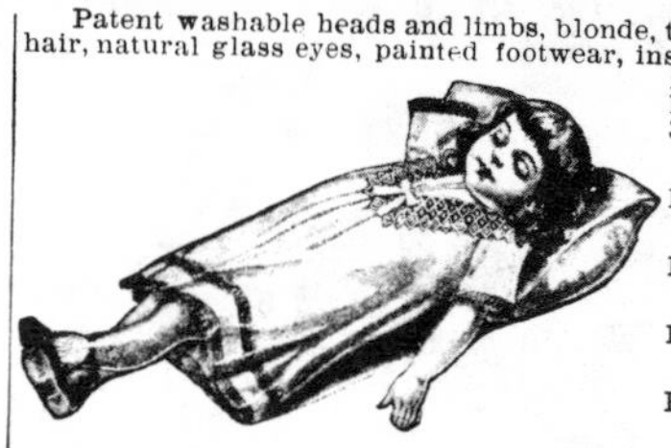

F4234—18½ in. ½ doz. in box. Doz. **$2.25**
F4236—23 in. ⅓ doz. in box. Doz. **$4.65**
F4238—26 in. ⅓ doz. in box. Doz. **$7.50**
F4240—31 in. ⅙ doz. in box. Doz. **$10.00**

## PATENT MATLOCK WASHABLE CHARACTER DOLLS.

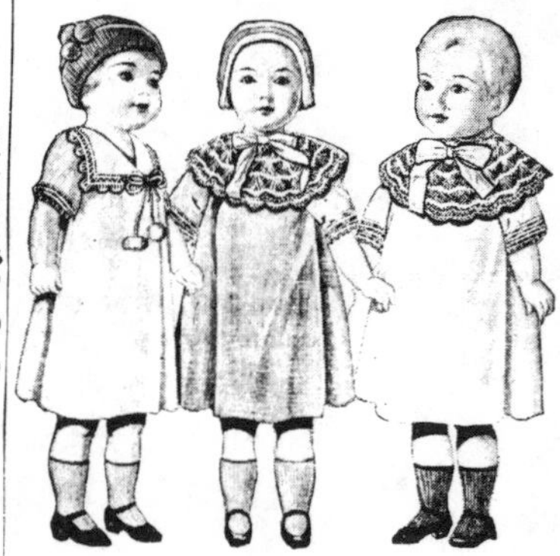

Patent washable bisque finish heads and limbs, extra large muslin covered sitting bodies, natural glass eyes, painted eyebrows and hair, 3 styles asstd., American and Holland girls and boys, hatless and with painted Holland hood or cap, painted footwear.

F4282—13½ in. Asstd. ½ doz. in box. Doz. **$2.25**
F4283—15¾ in. Asstd. ⅓ doz. in box. Doz. **$4.50**

## COTTON STUFFED PATENT WASHABLE DOLLS.

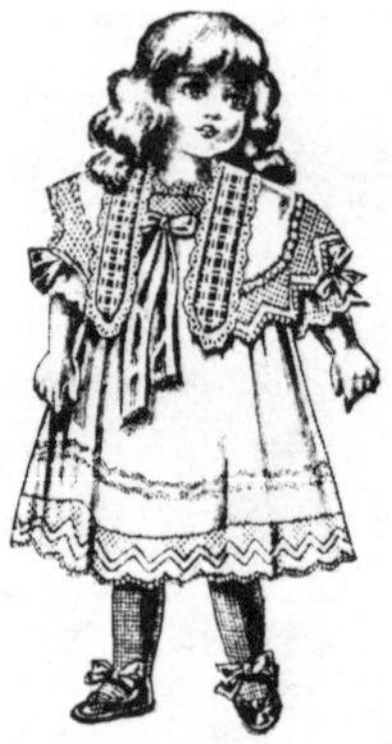

Flesh tint patent washable heads and hands, long wavy blonde, tosca and brunette hair, painted features, natural glass eyes, white muslin body, shaped hands, legs and feet, lace and ribbon trim slip, real shoes and stockings. Doz

F4268—13½ in. ½ doz. in box...$4 50
F4270—17¼ in. ⅟₂ " " " .. 8 00

*Following good for show purposes.*

F4272—21¾ in. 1 in box. Each, $1 15
F4274—24½ " 1 " " " 1 35
F4276—26½ " 1 " " " 1 75

## PATENT WASHABLE SHOW DOLL.

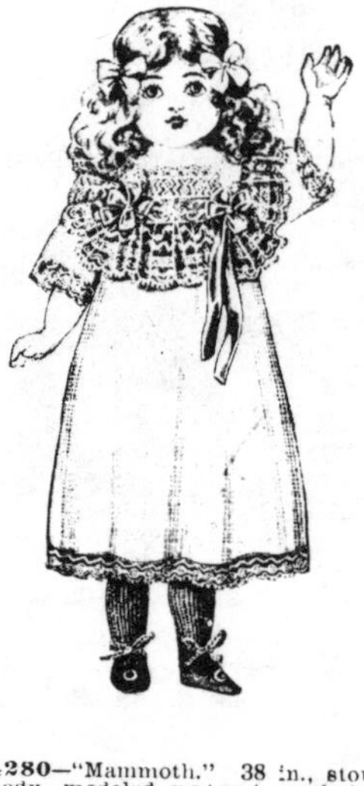

**F4280**—"Mammoth." 38 in., stout body, modeled patent washable head and limbs, center part blonde, tosca or brunette wig, side curls ribbon tied, natural glass eyes, painted eyebrows and lashes, exposed teeth, muslin chemise, lace trim bolero, neck and sleeves, ribbon and braid front, real shoes and stockings. 1 in wood case. Each, **$3.25**

## PATENT WASHABLE "CRYING" CHARACTER BABY.

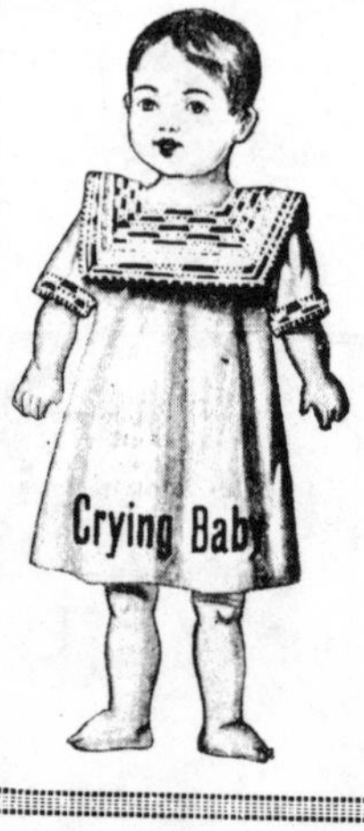


*When rocked from side to side it has a crying v ice which gives a very human illusion to the little mother.*

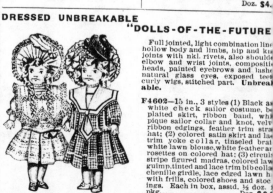

**F4265**—12⅜ in., well modeled sitting body, patent washable head and limbs, movable arms, character baby face, painted features and hair, invisible, double bellows, lace and braid trim square neck excellent quality slip, "Crying Baby" inscription. ½ doz. in box. Doz. **$2.25**

## DRESSED PATENT WASHABLES.

**In Display Boxes.**

Patent washable heads and limbs, stuffed bodies, blonde or brunette wigs, natural glass eyes, painted footwear.

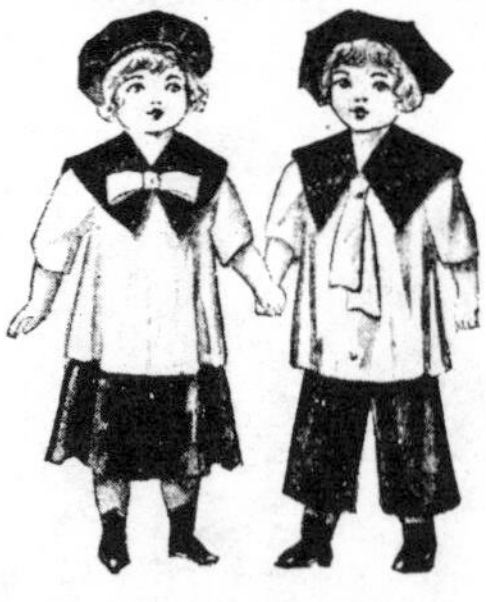

**F4293—Sailor Boy and Girl.** 11 in., short hair, dark blue, light blue and white costumes. Asstd. 1 doz. in box........................Doz. **89c**

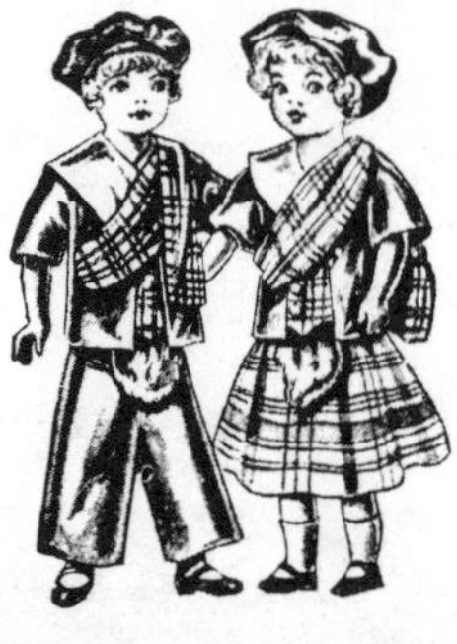

**F4295—Scotch Lads and Lassies.** 13 in., curly hair, plaid and blue Highland costumes. Asstd. ½ doz. in box........................Doz. **$2.20**

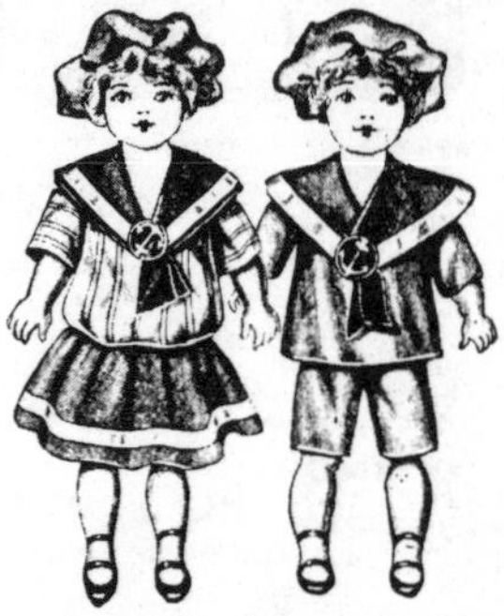

**F4299—Sailor Boy and Girl.** 14½ in., curly hair, 2-color flannel costumes. Asstd. ½ doz. in box. Doz. **$2.25**

VERY IMPORTANT

Sizes given on dolls in this book are ACTUAL NOT INCLUDING HAT OR BONNET. In comparing with others, demand the same standard of measurement—in justice to us and to yourself.

## NOVELTY PLUSH DO

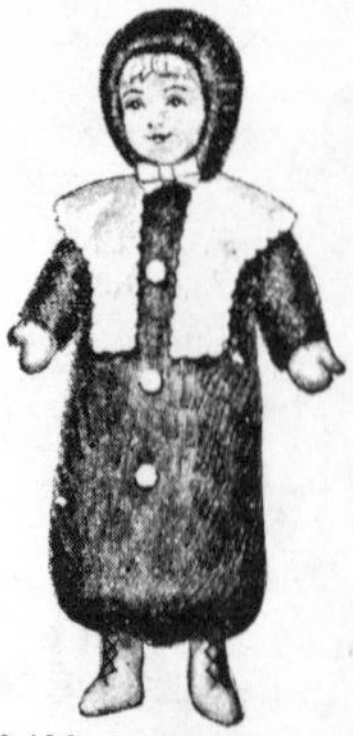

Celluloid faces, painted feature embossed hair, soft stuffed bo jointed arms, asstd. color wool p coat effect and hood, white felt lars, silk buttons, white felt h and feet, red cord lacing. **With v**

F4949—19 in. ⅓ doz. in box. Doz. $

## "PAPA, MAMMA" PATENT WASHABL DOL

Patent washable heads and li natural glass eyes, asstd. blo tosca, and brunette Rembrandt 2 cords attached to bellows w pulled one saying "Papa," "Mamma," gilt lettered slips, collars and trim caps.

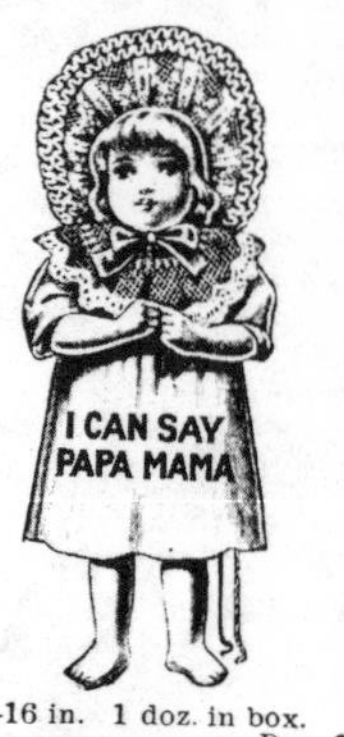


**F4260**—16 in. 1 doz. in box. Doz. $2

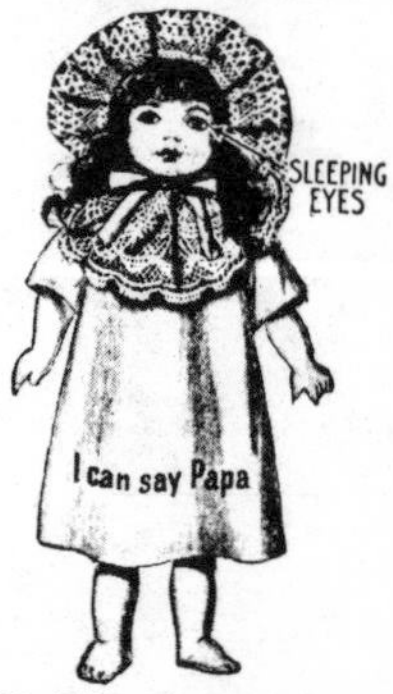


**F4262**—17 in., **sleeping eyes,** st sitting body. ⅓ doz. in box. Doz. $4.

## DRESSED UNBREAKABLE "DOLLS-OF-THE-FUTURE

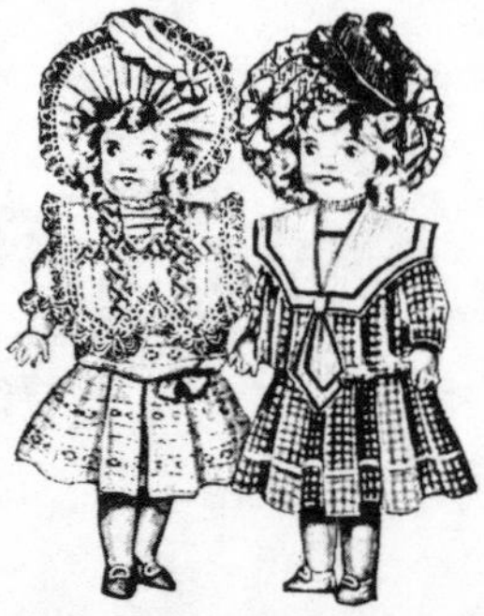

Full jointed, light combination line hollow body and limbs, hip and kn joints with nkl. rivets, also shoulde elbow and wrist joints, compositi heads, painted eyebrows and lashe natural glass eyes, exposed tee curly wigs, stitched part. **Unbreak able.**

**F4602**—15 in., 3 styles (1) Black a white check sailor costume, b plaited skirt, ribbon band, wh pique sailor collar and knot, velv ribbon edgings, feather trim stra hat; (2) colored satin skirt and la trim yoke collar, tinseled bra white lawn blouse, white feather a rosettes on colored hat; (3) circul stripe figured madras, colored la guimp, tinted and lace trim bib coll chenille girdle, lace edged lawn h with frills, colored shoes and stoc ings. Each in box, asstd. ⅓ doz. i pkg....... .... ....... ......Doz. $9.

## "POPULAR" DRESSED JOINTED BISQUE DOLLS.

Turning bisque heads, blonde, tosca and brunette flowing and curly wigs, jointed shoulders and hips, dresses and hats in asstd. colors, painted shoes and stockings unless stated. Measurements do not include hats.

### To Retail at 5c and 10c.

*Following with glass eyes and exposed teeth.*

4697—5 in., painted eyes, 3 styles. pink, blue and red tarlatan slips. ruffle yokes. Asstd. 1 doz. in box. Doz. 45c

4699—5¾ in., painted eyes, red, blue and pink asstd. slips, lace trim fronts, plaited white caps. Asstd. 1 doz. in box............ Doz. 48c

*Following with glass eyes and exposed teeth.*

2 styles F4701

4701—8 in., black glass eyes, pink, blue and red tarlatan dresses, lace trim, colored and gold figured front panels, pinked edge white revers, asstd. 1 doz. in box. ......Doz. 84c

2 of 3 styles

4705—5¼ in., 3 styles (1) cambric dress, lace apron and revers; (2) coat costume, braid and button trim; (3) nurse maid, lace trim apron, 3 styles caps, asstd. pink, blue and red. 1 doz. in box.Doz. 87c

2 styles F4703

4703—7½ in., black glass eyes, pink, blue and red dresses, white braid trim yokes and bretelles. Asstd. 1 doz. in box....... Doz. 89c

### VERY IMPORTANT!

Sizes given on dolls in this book are ACTUAL, NOT INCLUDING HAT OR BONNET. In comparing with others, demand the same standard of measurement—in justice to us and to yourself.

---

F4707—8 in., pink, blue and red figured fabric, lace and braid trim collars, white caps. Each in box, asstd. 1 doz. in pkg........ Doz. 89c

2 of 3 styles

F4715—6¼ in., 3 styles, lacy white frocks or red, pink and blue dresses with lace, braid and bow trimmings, color trim white lingerie hats. Asstd. 1 doz. in box.............. Doz. 95c

### Special 15c Values.

2 of 6 styles

F4711—"All-Nations" Asst. 6¼ in., 6 styles, blue, red, khaki and combination colors, braid, gilt buttons, belt and buckle trimmings, national hats. Asstd. 1 doz. in box........................ Doz. 95c

2 of 3 styles

F4717—7½ in., 3 styles, sailor boy and girl, Red Riding Hood and American costumes, flannel, tarlatan and percale, solid and asstd. colors, hats to match. Asstd. 1 doz. in box.................... Doz. $1.08

---

### Special 15c Values—Continued.

3 of 4 styles

F4712—4 styles. 9½ in., turning bisque heads, natural glass eyes, jointed shoulders and hips, accordion plaited mull and self jacquard figured fabrics in solid blue, pink and red, round and "V" collars, lace and braid trim, some with rosettes, fluted picture hats, painted footwear. *Usual 25c values.* Each in lace trim box, asstd. 1 dz. in pkg. **$1.10**

2 of 3 styles

F4713—8½ in., 3 styles, pink, blue and red novelty fabrics, round revers and bretelle collars of percale and lace, braid and plaited lace, colored hats to match. Each in box, asstd. 1 doz. in pkg....... ...... ...Doz. 95c

F4721—7¾ in., Scottish costumes, bright color plaid kilts and sashes, red jackets, white collars. Asstd. 1 doz. in box................. Doz. 98c

2 styles F4719

F4719—8 in., automobilists, navy blue flannel knickerbocker and skirt costumes, long tan auto coats and caps, gilt buttons, goggles. 1 doz. in box.. ................... Doz. $1.00

---

2 styles F4723

F4723—7¾ in., 2 styles: (1) Pink, red or blue flannel coat costume, gilt buttons, cape collar, tam o'shanters: (2) White bretelle aprons over pink, blue or red slips, plaited caps. Asstd. 1 doz. in box.................Doz. 1.10

2 styles F4728

F4728—9 in., sailor boy and girl in pairs, each pair in 3 solid colors, white with blue trimmings, navy with white, Alice blue with white, gilt buttons, shoes and stockings. Two (1 pr.) in box, asstd. ½ doz. in pkg........................ Doz. $1.50

2 of 4 styles

F4730—10¼ in., 4 styles, stripe, self figure and check fabric dresses, lacy yokes, lace edged necks, square, ruffle and revers collars, ribbon and buckle trim; white straw hats and fabric bonnets, white footwear. Each in box, asstd. ½ doz. in pkg. Doz. $1.85

### "LITTLE PLAYMATES" DRESSED DOLL ASSORTMENT.

*Three dainty styles, very attractively dressed.*

F4738 — 11½ in., moving eyes, blonde, tosca or brunette curly wigs, jointed shoulders and hips, 3 styles, white pique and self figured solid color fabric with contrasting color pipings, silk button trim; white accordion plaited lawn, lace trim round collar, cord and pompon belt; felt and lawn roll brim hats, white footwear. Each in lace trim box, asstd. ¼ doz. in pkg. Doz. **$2.25**

---

### "SPECIAL VALUE" BISQUE TURNING HEAD DOLLS.

Turning bisque heads, natural glass eyes, exposed teeth, long blonde, tosca and brunette hair, side curls, shoulder and hip joints, underwear, shoes and stockings.

2 of 3 styles

F4732—11½ in., 3 styles, solid red, blue and lavender lawn and self figured dresses, button trim French plaited blouse, plain slip with lace trim apron, and white pique sweater with colored skirt; straw hat. Normandy cap and pique toque, black footwear. Each in box, asstd. ½ doz. in pkg........Doz. $2.15

2 of 6 styles

F4736 — 10½ in., moving eyes, 6 styles and colors, point, square, surplice, empire and blouse effect figured or plain lawn yokes and collars, braid, lace, ribbon and tinsel trim, solid and combination colors, hats to match, self color, black and white shoes and stockings. Each in box, asstd. ½ doz. in pkg......... .......Doz. $2.20

F4748—10 in., moving eyes, mohair curls, sailor boys and girls, navy blue and white flannel suits, stitched collars, braid trim, caps, shoes and stockings. Two (1 pr.) in box, asstd 1 doz. in pkg......Doz. $2.25

*Following with REGISTERED "BABY BETTY" heads. A new model which is especially dainty.*

2 of 3 styles

F4742—"Sunshine Girl." Asst. 11 in., 3 styles, striped jumper with plain bands, plain lawn with striped bands and lawn Russian blouse, lace, braid and gilt button trim, caps of straw and dress materials, artificial flower and chiffon bow trim, shoes and stockings. Each in box, asstd. colors ½ doz. in pkg. Doz. $2.2

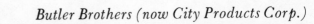

*Following have moving eyes, full jointed shoulder, elbow, hip and knee, be dressed and undressed, fastenings are buttons and hooks & eyes.*

**F4811**—12½ in., **moving eyes,** 3 American styles, 6 popular shades linene, coatee, long blouse and Russian models, revers collars and plaited lawn yoke effects, lace and novelty braid trim, 2 with crush girdles, rosettes and buckles; roll brim and lingerie hats, ruche and bow trim, white footwear. Each in lace trim box. Asstd. ⅙ doz. in pkg. **Doz. $4.00**

**F4827**—13¾ in. **moving eyes,** sewed wig, jointed shoulder, elbow, hip and knee, **4 styles,** flowered dimity cotton serge and Roman stripe fabrics, self and embroidery yokes, Empire, French and box coat styles, flower, ribbon, lace, embroidery and novelty braid trimmings; straw, flare brim felt and combination straw and fabric hats, colored footwear. Each in lace trim box. Asstd. ⅓ doz. in pkg. **Doz. $5.20**

**F4825**—"**Summer Girls.**" 16 in., stitched side part wig, **3 dainty styles,** flowered lawn, solid color silk crepe and moire dresses, round and pointed lace collars, lace trim lawn revers, ribbon girdles and rosettes, one style with deep lace flounce; straw and combination straw and silk hats, lace and ribbon trim, white footwear. Each in lace trim box. Asstd. ¼ doz. in pkg. **Doz. 10.00**

**F4858**—18½ in., stitched center p[art] wigs, 3 styles, full blouse flower[ed] dimity, Russian blouse poplin m[odel], allover white embroidery ba[nd] model, crossbar and ribbon r[un] yoke, shirred ribbon, rosette a[nd] embroidery band trim; straw, c[om]bination straw & poplin and linge[rie] hats, colored footwear. Each in l[ace] trim box, asstd. ¼ doz. in pkg. **Doz. 10**

**F4813**—13 in., **moving eyes,** 3 styles and color combinations, modish 1 pc. dresses, contrasting girdles and stitched bands, white lace "V" neck, novelty braid, button and lace trimmings, lingerie hats, ruche or bow trim, white footwear. Each in pkg. Asstd. ½ doz. in pkg..... **Doz. $4.40**

**F4833**—13½ in., **moving eyes,** jointed shoulder, elbow, hip and knee, **4 styles,** linen and lawn empire and Russian blouse models, 1 coat style with lacy guimpe "V" and square yokes, lace and braid trim collars, full accordion plaited skirts, braid, button and ribbon trim, Normandy flare brim and puff crown hats, colored socks, white slippers. Each in lace trim box. Asstd. ⅓ doz. in pkg. **Doz. $5.25**

**F4845**—"**The Travelers.**" 15½ in., side part pompadour wigs, 3 coat-and-skirt costumes, 2 linene and shepherd plaid fabric coats over white crossbar and solid color lawn dresses, also sateen suit with box plait skirt, frill lawn vest front, linene hand bag, braid, button and combination color trim, silk tam o' shanter, straw and puff crown straw front bonnets, ribbon rosette trim, black footwear. Each in lace trim box. Asstd. ¼ doz. in pkg. **Doz. 10.00**

**F4860**—"**Society Buds.**" 17 i[n], stitched side part pompadour wi[gs] **3 styles,** lace inserted fine color[ed] lawn, lace trim surplice; allove[r] two-tone shadow lace over wh[ite] lawn dress; white lace bordered c[ol]ored lawn, empire style, Dresd[en] silk and lace yokes, plaited brete[lle] and square collars, ribbon a[nd] sequin braid trim; 3 styles fril[led] picture hats, white footwear. Each [in] lace trim box. Asstd. ¼ doz. in p[kg] **Doz. 11.**

**F4815**—"**The 3 Rosebuds.**" 13 in., **moving eyes,** 3 rose satin costumes, white lace, black & white shepherd check and tan linene revers collars, lace, velvet, oriental and Roman stripe braid trim, combination Normandy bonnets to match, white footwear. Each in lace trim box. Asstd. ¼ doz. in pkg...... **Doz. $4.60**

**F4829**—"**Normandy Girls.**" 13¾ in., **moving eyes,** 3 styles, solid color linene, colored embroidery edged revers collar, belted lawn Russian model; white crossbar muslin with blue apron, all with oriental band trim, 3 style Normandy caps, 2 lace and bow trim, white and colored footwear. Each in lace trim box. Asstd. ¼ doz. in pkg..... **Doz. $4.35**

**F4837**—15 in., stitched side part wig, **moving eyes,** 3 styles, chic Frenchy models, red, pink or blue satin and cashmere, lacy and self collars, oriental band, black velvet ribbon and cord braid trim, crush and ribbon girdles, 1 with black satin hdkf. bag; Normandy, felt and black satin poke hats, oriental band, rosette and feather trim, black footwear. Each in lace trim box. Asstd. ¼ doz. in pkg.. **Doz. $7.50**

**F4848**—15¾ in., **eyelashes,** stitched side part waved curly wigs, 3 styles, asstd. colors linen, lawn and mull dresses, embroidered bands on apron over lawn dress, tucked yoke, red & blue embroidered white dress, braid trim linen with puff yoke and sleeves, ribbon beading and rosette trims, puff crown straw front 3 style bonnets, one cherry trim, white slippers, white and colored openwork socks. Each in lace trim box. Asstd. ¼ doz. in pkg. ......... **Doz. 10.25**

**F4853**—"**American Girl**" Asst. 17 in., **eyelashes,** side part ext[ra] curly wigs, 3 American model[s] plain and novelty linenes, orien[tal] embroidered band trim front a[nd] sleeves, button trim lapel collar a[nd] box plait fronts, 2 with stitche[d] belts and box plaited skirts, 1 wit[h] red piping; 3 style straw hat[s], feather, rosette and band & buck[le] trim, white footwear. Each in lac[e] trim box. Asstd. ¼ doz. in pkg. **Doz. 11.0[0]**

**F4824**—"**Little Fairy**" Asst. 14¼ in., **moving eyes,** 4 styles, albatros, round oriental lace collar, ribbon rosettes; flowered dotted swiss, lace ruffle square yoke, ribbon run beading, lace edge ruffle skirt, jacquard figured fabric, full blouse, braid and lace trim lacy coat; silk crepe, ribbon run beading and lace trim blouse, lace banded skirt; straw and lingerie hats and bonnet, rosette and lace ruche trim, white footwear. Each in lace trim box. Asstd. ½ doz. in pkg...... **Doz. $5.10**

**F4835**—16 in.. 3 styles, novelty plaid and check fabrics, lace edged self collar and embroidery revers; 1 solid color lawn coat style, Persian rever collar, braid trim, white lawn dress with embroidery yoke; straw, puff white lawn and flare brim felt hats, colored footwear. Each in lace trim box. Asstd. ¼ doz. in pkg. **Doz. $4.40**

**REMEMBER**
*Sizes are ACTUAL, not including hat or bonnet*

*Following have moving eyes, full jointed shoulder, elbow, hip and knee, can be dressed and undressed, fastenings are buttons and hooks & eyes.*

**F4839**—15½ in., 3 Parisian styles, sateen surplice, colored sateen and silk stripe box plaited dresses, lace panels or bands on plaited or kilted skirts, ribbon run insertions, on surplice, round or point collars, grenadine ribbon rosettes, Dresden figured or white lingerie hats with grenadine ribbon bows. Each in box. Asstd. ¼ doz. in pkg. **Doz. $9.75**

**F4852**—"**Debutantes.**" 17 in., eye[lashes], side part curly wigs, [?] styles, 2 china silk asstd. colors an[d] one white dotted swiss, shadow lac[e] effect square and full round collar[s] shirred ribbon edged or met[al] buckle & rosette trim, corded, shi[r]red or ribbon girdled waists, lace o[r] braid panel and insertion trim skirts, straw and puff crown hat[s] flower and ribbon trim, white foot[wear]. Each in lace trim box. Asst[d] ¼ doz. in pkg............ **Doz. 11.2[?]**

# Beautiful Character Dolls

LONG CURLS REAL HAIR

MOVING EYES

## Full Jointed Doll

### $9.45  Our Largest and Finest.

**18T3006**—This great big doll looks like a real young lady with her handsome parted hand sewed wig of real hair with long curls. She has moving eyes and eyelashes, too. Open mouth shows pretty teeth. Her body is beautifully molded of strong composition, tinted a natural flesh pink and finished with a lustrous glaze coating. Jointed at neck, shoulders, elbows, wrists, hips and knees, held together by strong elastic cord. Fine quality white lawn dress and underslip trimmed with lace. Fancy slippers and hose. A high grade doll and a big value. Height, about 24 inches. Shipping wt., 6 lbs.

## Dressed Character Babies.

### With Mohair Wigs.

| Catalog No. | Height, Inches | Shipping Wt., Lbs. | Price |
|---|---|---|---|
| 18T3008 | 20¾ | 4 | $3.75 |
| 18T3011 | 18½ | 3¼ | 2.98 |
| 18T3014 | 15½ | 2¼ | 1.98 |

This special value doll has a neatly made dress of good firm quality cotton chambray with bonnet to match, both trimmed with fancy embroidered braid. Plump stuffed body and bent baby legs. Lace trimmed underwear. Becoming mohair wig in popular bobbed style. Composition arms and head with painted eyes and features. Each doll fitted with fine mercerized bootees.

MOHAIR WIG

MOVING EYES

## Our Finest Eskimo Baby

### $9.25  A Real High Class Doll.

**18T3018**—Has a very fine quality soft, fuzzy, knitted white wool suit with large hood to match. Jacket has buttonholes and fastens with white pearl buttons. Baby shaped body stuffed nice and plump with cork. Lifelike moving eyes. Composition head with handsome bobbed style sewed mohair wig. Finely shaped composition arms and hands. Eskimo baby is dressed to withstand the coldest weather. Height, about 23½ inches. Shipping weight, 5½ pounds.

### $1.29

**18T3022** — Peterkin—the winsome doll. Made entirely of strong composition, with a plump, rigid body and movable arms. Beautifully tinted. Painted hair and features. Popular for Christmas gifts, favors and home decorating. Will stand up. Peterkin is furnished bare. The small illustration merely shows a cute dressing effect obtained by using 1 yard of 4-inch ribbon as a sash around the waist. Height, about 12½ inches. Shipping weight, 2 pounds.

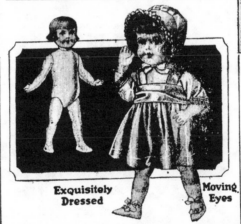

**Exquisitely Dressed**

**Moving Eyes**

| Catalog No. | Height, Inches | Shipping Wt., Lbs. | Price |
|---|---|---|---|
| 18T3024 | 16¾ | 3 | $4.98 |
| 18T3026 | 14¼ | 2 | 3.98 |

Charming Moving Eye Doll with fine quality dainty silk crepe de chine dress made in a pretty suspender style. Sheer white lawn vestee underneath is edged with lace. The dress and vestee are finished in back with buttonholes and white pearl buttons. Lace trimmed undergarments. Doll made entirely of strong composition fiber and has a beautiful bisquelike finish. Jointed at neck, shoulders and hips. Bobbed style mohair wig. Crepe de chine bonnet to match dress. Fancy hose and slippers.

### $2.45

**18T3023** — Little Orphan Annie—ready for some nice little girl to adopt her. She is very clean and sweet and her mohair wig is parted and put up in two pretty braids tied with ribbon. Dress is of checked material and covered with a white lawn apron having two pockets. Stuffed body is jointed at hips and shoulders. Finely tinted composition head and pretty molded composition arms. Painted eyes and features. Underwear, socks and slippers. Height, about 14½ inches. Shipping weight, 1½ pounds.

### $1.98

**18T3027**—This doll is cunningly dressed and right in style, too, with her fashionable cape and hood of colored flannelette. The sweet dress of sheer lawn matches the cape and hood, has a lace trimmed collar and is finished with real buttons and buttonholes in the back. Natural looking curly ringlet wig of soft mohair. Finely tinted composition arms and head, with painted eyes. Strong cloth covered body, well stuffed and jointed at shoulders and hips. Good underwear, socks and slippers. Height, about 11½ inches. Shipping weight, 1½ pounds.

### $1.98

**18T3028**—This Doll is just as sweet as her picture and feels very proud in her neat dress of lawn and bonnet to match. The dress is also trimmed with lace and has insertion around the waist with ribbon beading. Her head is of durable composition and her eyes and mouth are finely painted. A curly mohair ringlet wig makes her look just like a real little girl. Stuffed body is jointed at shoulders and hips. Underwear, socks and shoes. Height, about 11½ inches. Shipping weight, 1½ pounds.

# KEWPIES

$1.33  18T3036

$1.98  18T3038

$1.98  18T3040

Aren't they sweet? See their plump bodies, roguish eyes and smiling faces! Everybody loves a Kewpie. Made of light but durable composition beautifully tinted. Movable arms, rigid body. Splendid for Christmas gifts, favors and home decorating. Will stand up. 18T3030 is furnished bare like illustration; 18T3032 is fitted with neat apron and bonnet; 18T3034 has flowered pattern dress and bonnet to match; 18T3036 is furnished with cute knitted sweater and cap; 18T3038 has splendidly made dress and fancy hat; 18T3040 has charming dress and hat of point d'esprit net with large silk ribbon sash. Height, about 8½ inches. Av. shpg. wt., 12 oz. Order by catalog number.

98¢  18T3030

$1.15  18T3032

$1.29  18T3034

# Dolls *for* Dressing

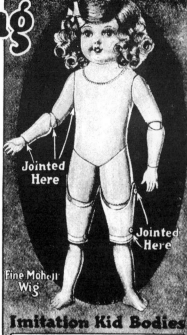

## Jointed Bodies Pretty Mohair Wigs

| | Height, Inches | Shpg. Wt. Lbs. | Price |
|---|---|---|---|
| 18T3166 | 16¼ | 3½ | $4.98 |
| 18T3168 | 13¾ | 2¾ | 3.95 |

## Character Babies with Moving Eyes

High grade baby with lifelike moving eyes and sewed mohair wig. Jointed at neck, shoulders and hips. Looks like bisque, but far more durable, being made of a strong composition fiber. Fitted with fine lawn dress and underslip, both lace trimmed. Illustration was made with dress off to show how beautifully the body is molded.

### Fine Mohair Wig

### Jointed Here

### Jointed Here

## Sleeping Eyes Fine Wig

| | Height, Inches | Shpg. Wt., Lbs. | Price |
|---|---|---|---|
| 18T3156 | 22½ | 5½ | $4.98 |
| 18T3158 | 20½ | 4 | 4.39 |
| 18T3160 | 17½ | 2¾ | 3.48 |
| 18T3162 | 14½ | 2 | 2.39 |
| 18T3164 | 11¾ | 1½ | 1.98 |

Mothers! If you want a doll to dress for your little girl, we highly recommend this quality. She has a full mohair sewed wig that you can easily care for, and she can be put to sleep because she has moving eyes. Beautiful head of composition, finely colored. Baby formed body, stuffed plump and covered with strong cloth. Fitted with good quality close fitting union suit, also socks and fancy bootees. A splendid foundation for charming dressing effects.

## Fine Celluloid Babies

### Ready to Dress.

| | Height, Inches | Shpg. Wt., Oz. | Price |
|---|---|---|---|
| 18T3186 | 5 | 5 | $0.33 |
| 18T3188 | 6½ | 6 | .43 |
| 18T3190 | 9 | 8 | .95 |
| 18T3192 | 12 | 14 | 1.85 |

You can have lots of fun dressing this little celluloid baby. She will look cute in almost any clothes you make for her, or will amuse baby in the bathtub. Jointed at the hips and shoulders. Light weight. Unbreakable. Natural flesh tinted. Color will not come off. Perfectly safe in hands of smallest child.

## Imitation Kid Bodies

| | Height, Inches | Shpg. Wt., Lbs. | Price |
|---|---|---|---|
| 18T3180 | 22½ | 4½ | $6.95 |
| 18T3182 | 19 | 3¼ | 5.65 |
| 18T3184 | 15 | 2¾ | 3.98 |

We highly recommend this fine doll for dressing. Has lifelike moving eyes and a fine grade sewed and parted mohair wig made on a net foundation with lovely curly ringlets. Jointed at shoulders, elbows, wrists, hips and knees. Finely formed white imitation kid body stuffed very plump. Durable composition head and hands. Hollow wooden arms joined to shoulders with strong elastic cord. Composition legs finished in a natural flesh pink shade. High class doll in every respect.

## Low Prices on Moving Eye Dolls.

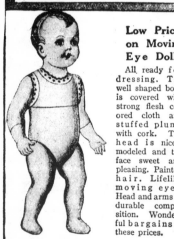

All ready for dressing. The well shaped body is covered with strong flesh colored cloth and stuffed plump with cork. The head is nicely modeled and the face sweet and pleasing. Painted hair. Lifelike moving eyes. Head and arms of durable composition. Wonderful bargains at these prices.

| | Height, Inches | Shpg. Wt. Lbs. | Price |
|---|---|---|---|
| 18T3196 | 16 | 2¼ | $1.95 |
| 18T3194 | 14 | 1¾ | 1.69 |

## DOLL HEADS
### With Moving Eyes and Fine Wigs

Beautifully Modeled Doll Heads fitted with moving eyes and high grade mohair parted wigs with ringlets and ribbon bows. Tinted in natural flesh pink color with rosy colored cheeks. Made of strong composition fiber. See instructions below "How to Order Heads."

| | Height, Inches | Across Shoulders, In. | Shpg. Wt., Lbs. | Price |
|---|---|---|---|---|
| 18T3547 | 4⅞ | 2¾ | 1 | $1.19 |
| 18T3545 | 6 | 3¼ | 1¼ | 1.48 |
| 18T3543 | 6¾ | 3½ | 1½ | 1.98 |
| 18T3541 | 7½ | 4⅜ | 1¾ | 2.48 |

## All Composition Doll for Dressing.

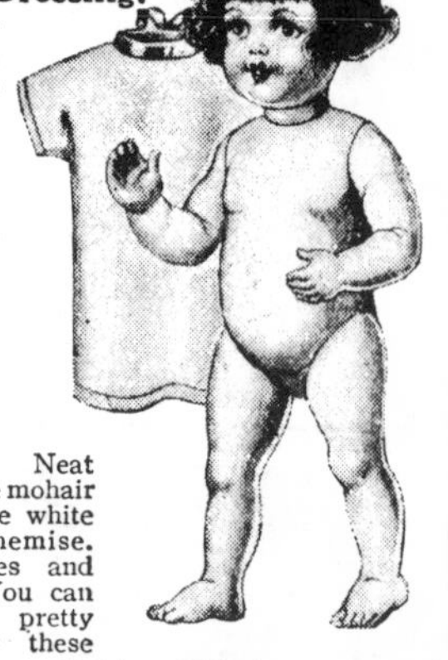

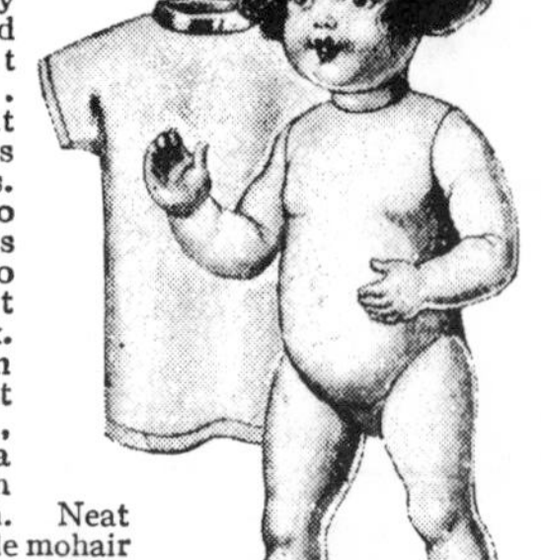

Nicely shaped straight legs. Jointed at shoulders and hips. The two largest dolls are also jointed at the neck. Light in weight, but durable, and have a pretty flesh pink finish. Neat bobbed style mohair wig and fine white lawn chemise. Painted eyes and features. You can plan many pretty dresses for these dolls.

| | Height, Inches | Shipping Wt., Lbs. | Price |
|---|---|---|---|
| 18T3198 | 17 | 2¼ | $2.48 |
| 18T3200 | 14½ | 1¾ | 1.98 |
| 18T3202 | 12 | 1¼ | 1.48 |
| 18T3204 | 10¼ | 1 | .98 |

## How to Order Heads

To fit a doll be sure to measure the body from shoulder to shoulder across the top, allowing for the curve of the shoulders. The sizes of our doll heads are measured across the shoulders in this manner. After you have this measurement it is very easy for you to determine what number to order by simply referring to the sizes and numbers given.

## With Wigs

Beautiful Doll Heads with pretty bobbed style wigs of good quality mohair. Made of an almost unbreakable composition which is light in weight yet very durable. Heads are finely tinted and have artistically painted eyes. They have a hole in each corner of the breastplate so you can easily sew them to a doll body, or you can glue them on if you prefer.

| | Height, Inches | Across Shoulders, In. | Shpg. Wt., Lbs. | Price |
|---|---|---|---|---|
| 18T3521 | 4¾ | 2¾ | ¾ | $0.79 |
| 18T3509 | 5½ | 3⅜ | 1 | .98 |
| 18T3505 | 6¼ | | 1¼ | 1.39 |
| 18T3503 | 7¼ | 4½ | 1½ | 1.98 |

## With Painted Hair

Low Priced Doll Heads. Very good values. Well made of an almost unbreakable composition which is light in weight but very durable. Natural looking flesh colorings with artistically painted hair and features. They have a hole in each corner of the breastplate so you can easily sew them to a doll body, or you can glue them on if you prefer.

| | Height, Inches | Across Shoulders, In. | Shpg. Wt., Lbs. | Price |
|---|---|---|---|---|
| 18T3537 | 4¾ | 2¾ | ¾ | $0.45 |
| 18T3533 | 5½ | 3⅜ | 1 | .59 |
| 18T3529 | 6¼ | 4 | 1¼ | .75 |
| 18T3525 | 7¼ | 4½ | 1½ | 1.25 |

# Moving Eye Dolls
## Remarkable Values    Fine Mohair Wigs

**The seven lovely dolls** at the top of this page have wonderfully lifelike sleeping eyes. All have natural looking wigs of fine mohair arranged charmingly. The costumes are most cleverly designed and neatly made of very good materials. 18T3047 has an all composition character body and will stand. The others have strong cloth bodies stuffed plump. Light, almost unbreakable composition heads and hands nicely tinted. 18T3043 is 17 inches high; others photographed in proportion. The prices vary with the size and costume. Order by catalog number. Average shipping weight, 2½ pounds.

**$3⁴⁸**
18T3043

**$2⁴⁸**
18T3051

**$3²⁵**
18T3046

**$2⁹⁸**
18T3047

**$2⁸⁹**
18T3050

**$2¹⁹**
18T3052

**$2²⁹**
18T3054

## Beautiful Long Curls
**MOVING EYES**    **REAL HAIR**

**FINE DRESSES**

### Handsome Coats

| | Height, Inches | Shipping Wt., Lbs. | Price |
|---|---|---|---|
| 18T3055 | 20¾ | 4¼ | $6.45 |
| 18T3059 | 18¼ | 3½ | 4.48 |
| 18T3067 | 16¾ | 3 | 3.48 |
| 18T3068 | 14½ | 1¾ | 2.79 |

Very high quality character baby with lifelike moving eyes and bobbed style mohair wig. Fine white lawn lace trimmed dress, cut low at the top to show the pretty neck and chest. Handsome lace edged pink coat fastened in front with a little beauty pin. Lawn bonnet elaborately trimmed with lace, dainty embroidery and lustrous ribbon rosettes. Neat underwear. Splendidly shaped cloth covered body with bent baby legs. The two largest dolls have knitted bootees; the others have felt bootees.

| | Height, In. | Shpg. Wt., Lbs. | Price |
|---|---|---|---|
| 18T3070 | 24 | | $6.95 |
| 18T3072 | 20 | 3½ | 5.25 |
| 18T3074 | 18 | 2½ | 2.98 |
| 18T3076 | 16 | 1¾ | 2.95 |
| 18T3078 | 14 | 1½ | 2.48 |

Our wonderful new line of long curl dolls, much finer and lovelier than those we sold in previous catalogs and which we strongly recommend. The sleeping eyes are very lifelike. The charming style dress is made of fine quality printed lawn. The pretty ruffle on skirt and the panel over each shoulder are lace trimmed. A lustrous satin ribbon sash tied in a neat bow around waist matches ribbon in hair. Fine quality long curled, hand sewed, parted wig of real human hair frames a lovely face with a sweet childlike expression. Underskirt and drawers of good quality. Heads and hands of light, almost unbreakable composition finely tinted. Body covered with strong flesh colored cloth and stuffed plump.

### When I Awake I Cry *Ma Ma!*

**$3⁷⁵**

**18T3079**—This pretty dolly cries when it is being raised from sleep to an upright position. Then you can give her the charming little covered nursing bottle pictured. She has a lovely two-tone knitted wool jacket and bonnet to match, lifelike moving eyes and neat mohair wig. Her natural baby body and bent legs are stuffed very plump and her white lawn dress is most becoming, being trimmed with lace edging and insertion. Good underwear, socks and slippers. Lightweight composition head, arms and hands, almost unbreakable. A splendid doll for any girl to own. Height, 16½ inches. Shipping weight, packed in strong box, 2¾ pounds.

# Novelty Dolls

**Cute Novelty Doll With Wig.**
Represents bathing girl seated in a shell shaped beach seat; attractively decorated. It is artistically made of a so called unbreakable composition. Has brunette hair wig. About 7½ inches high. Shipping wt., 1¾ lbs.
**69T7219....$2.47**

**The Popular "Tiss-Me" Doll With Wig.**
Everybody loves this doll with her lips all puckered up. Has neatly dressed real hair, auburn shade, with net. Mantel or dresser decoration. Made of plaster, 7 inches high. Carefully packed. Shipping weight, 1¾ lbs.
**69T7216....$2.79**

**"Splash-Me" Bathing Suit Girl.**
Now popular all over the country. Made of plaster. About 6 in. high. Head painted, imitating hair, bathing suit and slippers. Complete with removable cloth bathing cap. Shpg. wt., 1¼ lbs.
**69T7214....$1.19**

**Sweetie Kid Is Very Popular.**
Made of so called unbreakable composition. Painted to resemble a girl in a bathing outfit. About 6½ inches high. Comes complete with a removable rubberized cloth bathing cap. Shipping wt., 1⅛ pounds.
**69T7215....$1.00**

**Fat Bathing Doll.**
Made of so called unbreakable composition. 7 in. high. Has movable arms, cute painted face, removable yellow mercerized suit, cotton cloth cap. Shipping wt., 1½ pounds.
**69T7213....98c**

**This Is a Winner.**
Attractive babylike expression. Painted in attractive colors. Made of plaster and measures about 7 inches in height. Has a cotton cloth hood. Shipping weight, 1¼ pounds.
**69T7217.....98c**

**One of Our Cutest Novelty Dolls.**
Cute dolly nicely made and painted in attractive colors. Made of so called unbreakable composition. Clever expression and ribbon headdress. About 7½ inches high. Shipping weight, 1⅛ pounds.
**69T7218....$1.67**

**Tom Tinker —The Ball Man.**
**45c**

The doll made for hard usage. Made of round wooden balls. Finished and painted with harmless colors, held together by a strong cord, making the doll both flexible and durable. Practically unbreakable. Shipping weight, 10 ounces.
**69T7223—Price..45c**

**Large Size Rubber Doll.**

Popular, unbreakable, large size, good grade gray rubber doll. About 8½ in. high, with whistle. Assorted designs. Shipping weight, 10 ounces.
**49T4409..47c**

**Makes a Rag Doll About 2 Feet High.**

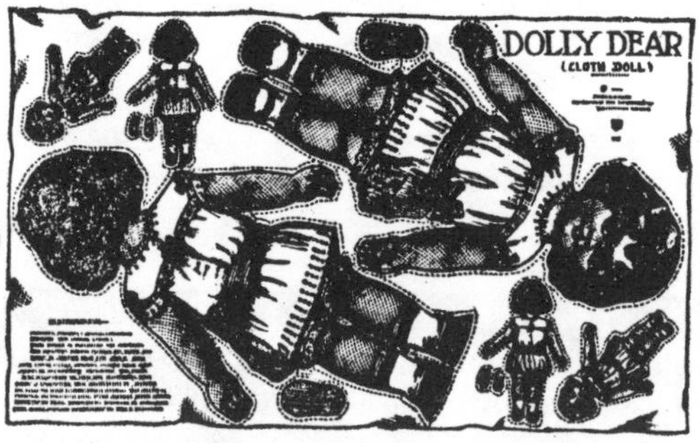

Large enough to wear a real baby's own clothes. The big doll and two little dolls are lithographed in colors on cloth to cut out and stuff. An extra large cut-out doll at this price. Height of doll, about 25 inches; height of two little dolls, about 7 inches each. **This is one of our most popular items in the Toy Department.** The dolls are lithographed upon a sheet, about 21x36 inches. Simply cut out, sew and stuff and you have idea! unbreakable rag dolls for the youngsters. Shpg. wt., 4 oz.
**69T7212—Price........ ........................25c**

**"Toodles" Novelty Dolls.**

A cute baby doll of so called unbreakable composition, intended either for ornamentation or as a play doll. Painted hair. Measures about 10⅛ inches high. Shipping weight, 1½ lbs.
**69T7221—Price. 98c**
**With Wig.**
Same as above, but with wig instead of ribbon.
**69T7220**
Price ............**$1.47**

**Stuffed Rag Doll.**

Stuffed with light weight material. About 10¾ inches high. A serviceable doll for the youngsters. Shipping weight, 4 ounces.
**69T7201**
Price ..... **1.00**

## Roly Poly Toys

**Popular Floor Toys for Babies. Cannot Be Tipped Over. Always Stand Upright.**

| | | | |
|---|---|---|---|
| About 12 in. high. Assorted designs. Each in box. Shipping weight, 1¼ lbs. | About 9¾ in. high. Assorted designs. Shipping weight, 1½ lbs. | About 8¼ in. high. Assorted designs. Shipping weight, 1¾ lbs. | About 4¼ in. high. Assorted designs. Shipping weight, 10 oz. |
| **69T7008** | **69T7009** | **69T7007** | **69T7010** |
| Price ....**$1.39** | Price ......**89c** | Price ......**47c** | Price ...... **19c** |

**The Squawking Baby.**
Press head down and as it comes up makes so called crying noise. Squawker inside of doll. Head made of so called unbreakable composition; dress and arms of cotton cloth. Lace around neck. Cute expression and features on dolly. About 8¼ inches high. Can be thrown around and no danger of breaking. Shipping weight, 1¼ lbs.
**69T7200—Price ..........47c**

## Rubber Dolls

**Girl**
Good grade red rubber girl with whistle. Height, about 5 inches. Shpg. wt., 3 oz.
**49T4435**
Price ......**25c**

**Baby**
Red rubber baby. Height, about 4⅝ inches. With whistle. Shpg. wt., 2 oz.
**49T4439**
Price ......**25c**

**Boy**
Height, about 4⅞ inches. Complete with whistle. Shipping weight, 4 ounces.
**49T4440**
Price ......**25c**

**Cute Clown.**
Good grade red rubber with whistle. Height, about 6½ inches. Shpg. wt., 6 oz.
**49T4438**
Price ......**47c**

**Baby Face Rubber Rattle.**

About 4¾ in. long. Good grade gray rubber. Assorted designs. Round rubber handle on end used as teething ring. Small bells inside of head tinkle when rattle is shaken to attract baby. Shipping wt., 2 ounces.
**49T4408**
Price ............**15c**

**Gray Rubber Roly Poly Shaped Doll.**

Made of gray rubber. Roly Poly shaped doll measuring about 5 inches in height and 3 in. in diameter at the widest point. Shipping weight, 6 ounces.
**49T4412—Price..25c**

**Paper Doll and Three Paper Costumes.**

Twelve-inch prettily colored paper doll with three separate assorted design costumes. Cut-out hats to match. All in envelope. Shpg. wt., 5 ounces.
**69T7202—Price ..........12c**

**Cute Boy**
Made of good grade gray rubber with whistle. Assorted designs. Height, about 6¾ inches. Shipping weight, 6 oz.
**49T4429**
Price ......**25c**

**Sailor Boy**
Good grade rubber Sailor Boy with whistle. About 4⅞ in. high. Shipping weight, 6 ounces.
**49T4407**
Price ......**15c**

**Pretty Maid**
Made of good grade gray rubber with whistle. Assorted designs. Height, about 6½ inches. Shipping weight, 6 ounces.
**49T4430**
Price ......**25c**

**Dressed Doll**
Gray rubber doll with yarn dress and hat. Height, about 6¾ inches. Shipping weight, 5 ounces.
**49T4411**
Price ..... **25c**

# Dolly's Supplies

**Human Hair Doll Wigs With Curls.**

Long pretty curls. Come in five sizes to fit heads 10 to 14 inches in circumference. **In ordering give measurement in inches around head at forehead.** Doll head not included. Comes in two shades. Average shipping weight, 6 ounces.

69T7145—Blond, wig only. Price.......... **97c**
69T7146—Brunette, wig only. Price .................. **97c**

**Our Best Doll Wigs.**

Made of human hair. Curls kept in position by ribbon ending in two pretty bows, one on each side. Comes in sizes to fit doll heads 9 to 16 inches in circumference. **Be sure to give measurement in inches around head at forehead.** Doll head not included. Average shipping weight, 10 ounces.

69T7170—Brunette, wig only. Price .................. **$1.69**
69T7171—Blond, wig only. Price.......... **1.69**

**Kewpie Style Wigs for Kewpies or Other Dolls.**

**(Enclosed in Hair Net.)**

Many children prefer the high Kewpie style wig. Looks good on any doll. Comes in sizes 9 to 16 inches. **Be sure to give measurement in inches around head at forehead.** Doll head not included. Average shipping weight, 5 ounces.

69T7125—Brunette, wig only. Price.......... **$1.47**
69T7126—Blond, wig only. Price.......... **1.47**

**Big Value Medium Priced Wig.**

Made from human hair. Has long curls. Two bows, one on each side. Sizes from 9 to 16 inches. **Give measurement in inches around head at forehead.** Doll head not included. Average shpg. wt., 10 oz.

69T7121—Brunette, wig only. Price.............. **$1.39**
69T7122—Blond, wig only. Price.............. **1.39**

**Put a Wig on Your Character Doll.**

Cute little bobbed wigs, made from human hair, which are particularly adapted for character dolls. Come in eight sizes, 9 to 16 inches, according to circumference of doll's head. **Give measurement in inches around head at forehead.** Doll head not included. Av. shpg. wt., 6 oz.

69T7123—Brunette, wig only. Price.............. **97c**
69T7124—Blond, wig only. Price.............. **97c**

**How to Measure for Wig.**

Measure around doll's head, as shown in illustration. Send us size in inches.

**Five-Piece Bedroom Set.**

This set consists of dresser, about 5⅛x5⅝x2⅛ inches over all; two chairs, about 4¼ inches over all; table top measures about 2¾x3¾ inches over all and dressed bed about 6x4¾x4 inches over all. Good value for the money. Made of light weight stained wood. Shipping weight, 1½ pounds.

69T8502—Price, per set........ **25c**

**Doll White Slippers.**

**29c**

Made of white imitation leather. Have bow and buckle. **In ordering give length of doll's foot in inches from heel to toe.** Can furnish up to 3¾ in. in length. Shipping wt., 2 oz.

69T7141—Price, per pair..... **29c**

**Doll White Slippers.**

**19c**

With pretty buckle and bow. Made of white imitation leather. **In ordering give length of doll's foot in inches from heel to toe.** Shipping weight, 2 ounces.

69T7142 Price, per pair.......... **19c**

**Complete 7-Piece Parlor Set.**

**25c**

Baby grand piano, 4½-in. piano bench, 5½-in. settee, 3¾-in. table, picture, 4¼-in. chair and 7½-in. hall clock. Measurements are over all. Made of light weight stained wood. Shpg. wt., 1¾ lbs. **25c**

69T8562—Price, per set ....

**39c**

**Dolly's White Button Shoes.**

With heels. Made of white imitation leather. Well shaped. **Give length of foot in inches from heel to toe.** Sizes up to 3¼ inches in length. Shpg. wt., 3 oz.

69T7140 Per pair...... **39c**

**Cotton Stockings for Dolly.**

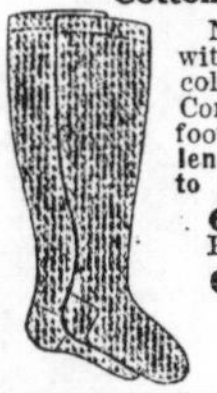

No dolly's wardrobe is complete without an assortment of different colored stockings. Well made. Come in sizes up to 3¼ inches foot length. **In ordering give length of foot in inches from heel to toe.** Shipping weight, 2 oz.

69T7135—White. Price, per pair .......... **17c**
69T71 6—Pink. Price, per pair ..... **17c**
69T7137—Blue. Price, per pair ..... **17c**

**Quality Laundry Set.**

**$1.98**

Metal tub, nicely painted, 10½ inches in diameter at the top. Washboard, 5¼x11¼ inches over all, has a heavy glass rubbing surface. A practical toy. Metal wringer with 4-inch rubber rollers. Clothes rack is collapsible and when set up measures about 13x19 inches over all. About a dozen small clothespins in a fancy bag and a good grade wash basket. Shpg. wt., 7 lbs.

79T1701¼—Price, per set. **$1.98**

**39c**

**Toy Ironing Board and Iron.**

Board made of wood smoothly finished and stands about 15¼ inches high. Ironing surface measures, over all, about 5½x21½ inches. Iron nicely nickel plated. Stands about 2¼ inches high and base measures 3½x1⅝ inches. Has a removable handle. Shipping weight, 2¼ pounds.

49T1781—Price.......... **39c**

**$2.87** **A Toy Sewing Machine That Will Sew.**

One of the popular little girls' toys. Make dresses for dolly. Enjoyment for the little girl making dresses out of the scrap cloth around the house. Well made of sheet steel, cast iron wheel, and has a mechanism which will really sew. It is nicely finished and can easily be fastened to table or quickly removed. Packed in box with clamp to fasten to table. Ready to use. No cloth, thread or extra needles furnished. Size over all, about 7¾x6½x4½ in. Shpg. wt., 2½ lbs.

69T5826—Price .......................... **$2.87**

**Brightly Polished Aluminum Toy Kettle.**

1½-pint capacity. Measures about 6 inches high, including handle, and about 6½ inches wide, including spout. A toy that every girl will appreciate. Shipping wt., 1¼ lbs.

49T1850 Price. **98c**

**69c**

**Tin Wash Set.**

Consists of 6⅜-inch tub, 7-inch washboard, 5½x3¼-inch wash boiler and 3½x4½-inch water kettle. All utensils for dolly's washing. Shipping weight, 1¼ pounds.

49T1791 Price, per set.................. **69c**

**This Laundry Outfit Makes a Dandy Present for a Little Girl.**

Made of wood. Ironing board about 5¾x12¾x19¾ inches over all, 16x25-inch clothes rack and 5x13x4½-inch bench. Included are 10¾-inch long clothes basket, clothes line and clothespins, 6½x13½-inch washboard, washtub, wringer and 3½x1⅝x2¼-inch sadiron. The wringer is very well made, has rubber rolls, metal uprights, and alone would make an ideal present. The outfit makes a big appearance and one your little girl will surely enjoy. Packed complete in box. Shipping weight, 9 pounds.

79T1787¼—Price .......................... **$1.98**

**Good Toy Wringer.**

Rubber rollers, 4 inches long. Looks and works just like mother's. Width, not including handle, about 7½ in. Springs at top regulating pressure. Adjustable screws for fastening on tubs, pails, etc. Each in box. Shpg. wt., 1½ lbs. **98c**

49T1793—Price ..........

**Quality Toy Wash Set.**

Consists of metal tub, 10 inches in diameter, nicely painted. Washboard of good grade wood, measuring, over all, 11¼x5¼ inches, with a heavy glass rubbing surface measuring 5¾x4 inches. Clothes rack is collapsible, stand and upper part of metal and center support of wood. Size, over all, about 15 inches high and 18 inches wide. Clothes line for rack and clothespins in bag included. Shipping weight, 2½ pounds.

79T1700¼—Price ............ **98c**

**15c**

**Our Small Nickel Plated Sadiron.**

Removable handle. Size of base, 3½x1⅝ inches. Height over all, about 2¼ inches. Shipping weight, 1 pound.

69T9125—Price **15c**

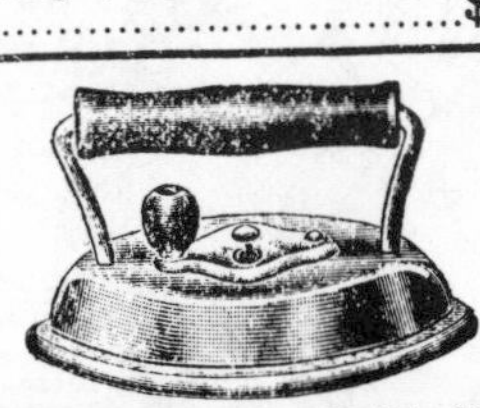

**25c**

**Nicely Nickel Plated and Polished Sadiron.**

Size of base, 4⅛x1⅝⁄16 inches, and stands about 2½ inches high over all. Removable handle. Shipping weight, 1¼ pounds.

69T9124—Price .............. **25c**

**Toy Washing Machine With Wringer.**

Made of wood. Tub has two iron hoops. Height over all, 15 in.; width, 10 inches. Tub at top, 7 in. in diameter. Outside painted. Stands on four wooden legs. Wooden wringer. Turn the crank and machine will wash the dolly's clothes. Shipping weight, 4 lbs.

49T1777 Price .... **69c**

# Doll Carriages

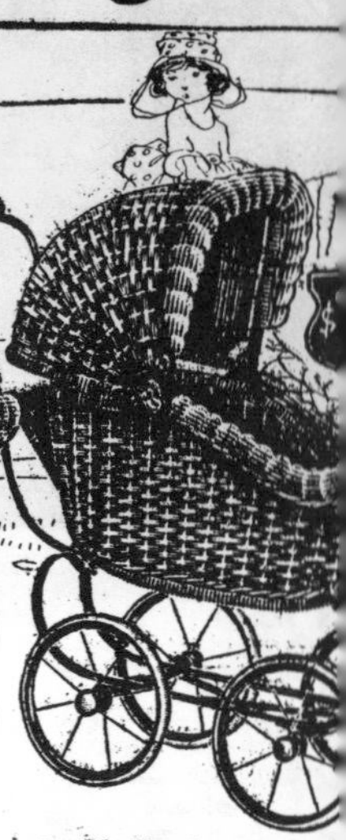

**Our Highest Quality Imitation Reed Doll Buggy.**
Made of round imitation reed closely woven, with full rounded shape throughout. Hood, bottom inside and both sides of body lined with high grade corduroy. Seat and back of seat padded. Will hold up to about 25-inch doll. Has a footwell also. Body finished in white enamel. Running gear in a dark color. Has reclining back and adjustable hood. Height of handle from floor, 26 inches. Height, over all, 37 inches. Inside measurement of body, 9x20 inches. Metal 10-inch wheels, ⅜-inch rubber tires. Polished hub caps. Unmailable. Shipping weight, 32 pounds.
79T8292¼
Price .............. $14.87

**Our Best Genuine Reed Doll Buggy.**
Genuine reed, finished in cream color enamel. Will hold up to about 24-inch doll. Hood, seat proper, sides and back of seat and bottom of body lined with corduroy. Inside measurement of body, 9½x21 inches. Height of handle from floor, 26 inches. Height, over all, about 35 inches. Adjustable hood, reclining back, leather hold-in strap. Polished hub caps. 10-inch metal wheels with ⅜-inch rubber tires. Unmailable. Shipping weight, 24¼ pounds.
79T8290¼—Price .............. $10.98

**Pretty Imitation Reed Doll Buggy.**
Cream color enamel. Holds 22-inch doll. Handle, 23½ inches above floor. Height, over all, 30 inches. Hood, seat proper, sides and back of seat lined with printed cloth. Body, 8x18½ inches. Adjustable hood. Reclining back, hold-in strap and hub caps. 9-inch metal wheels, ⅜-inch rubber tires. Unmailable. Shipping weight, 16½ lbs.
79T8281¼—Price..... $8.98

**Our Medium Priced Genuine Reed Do**
Gray enamel finish. Ho
doll. Hood, seat proper,
seat and back corduroy lin
24 inches above floor. Heigh
about 28 inches. Body, 8
Equipped with adjustable
clining back and hub ca
metal wheels with ⅜-inch r
Unmailable. Shpg. wt., 15 lb
79T8280¼—Price....

**Our Best and Largest Folding Doll Go-Cart.**
Nicely enamel finished metal collapsible sides, painted and striped; reclining back, four-bow hood; bottom of body lined with imitation leather; 8-inch wheels, 5/16-inch rubber tires. Holds up to about a 28-inch doll. Height of handle from floor, about 28 inches. Doll not included. Shipping weight, 16¼ pounds.
79T8263¼—Price .............. $5.50

**Our Leader Imitation Reed Doll Buggy, $4.98.**
Imitation reed, with back, bottom and sides of seat cloth lined. Metal gear. Will hold up to about 20-inch doll. Height of handle from floor, 25 in. Height, over all, 28⅛ in. Inside measurement of body, 7½x16 in. 7¼-inch wheels with ⅜inch rubber tires. Adjustable hood; polished hub caps. Unmailable. Doll not included. Shipping weight, 12½ pounds.
79T8266¼—Gray enamel finish. Price... $4.98
79T8267¼—Cream enamel finish. Price. 4.98

**Our $2.79 Value With Reclining Back**
Nice enamel finish. Folding imitation leath
7-inch wheels, ¼-inch rubber tires. Reclini
Holds up to about a 22-inch doll. Height o
from floor, about 24½ inches. Doll not i
Shipping weight, 7 pounds.
79T8259¼—Price....................

**Medium Priced Folding Doll Go-Cart.**
Has three-bow hood, reclining back, 8-inch wheels, 5/16-inch rubber tires. Metal parts enameled. Cart is semi-collapsible. Polished hub caps. Will hold up to about a 26-inch doll. Height of handle from floor, about 28 inches. Shpg. wt., 13 lbs.
79T8262¼—Price.............. $4.79

**A Big Value for $3.87.**
This cart is made of metal, nicely enameled. Three-bow collapsible hood, covered with imitation leather. Reclining back. 7-inch metal wheels with 5/16-inch rubber tires. Semi-collapsible. Cart holds up to about a 24-inch doll. Height of handle from floor, about 24½ inches. Shipping weight, 9¼ pounds.
79T8261¼
Price .......... $3.87

**Our $2.39 Special.**
Semi-collapsible. Has imitation leather three-bow folding hood, 6-inch rubber tired metal wheels. Metal nicely enameled. Holds doll up to about 20 inches. Height of handle from floor, about 24½ inches. Shipping weight, 6¼ pounds.
79T8260¼
Price............ $2.39

**Good Value in Low Priced Folding Cart, $1.87.**
Made of steel with imitation leather trimming and three-bow hood. Has 6-inch metal wheels with ¼-inch rubber tires. All metal parts nicely enameled. Height of handle above floor, about 25 inches. Will hold doll up to about 20 inches. Shipping weight, 6 pounds.
79T8254¼—Price $1.87

**Semi-Collapsible**
Enameled ste
Trimmed with
leather. 6-inch
wheels, ¼-inc
tires. Holds up
18-inch doll.
about 22 inch
floor. Shpg. w
79T8253¼
Price.........

# And Go-Carts

**$6.45**

**$7.98**

**$9.98**

**$12.45**

**A Large Size Fine Quality Imitation Reed Doll Buggy With Wooden Wheels.**
Flat and round imitation reed, gray enamel finish. Hood, seat proper, sides and back of seat and bottom of body lined with corduroy. Leather strap to hold dolly in. Has 10-inch wooden wheels, ⅜-inch rubber tires. Will hold up to about a 24-inch doll. Running gear and wheels painted in a dark color; hub caps are polished. Adjustable hood and reclining back. Height of handle from floor, 29½ inches. Height, over all, 35 inches. Inside measurement of body, 9½x21 inches. Unmailable. Shpg. wt., 17½ lbs.
**79T8291¼—Price........ $12.45**

**Our Most Popular Imitation Reed Buggies.**
cream enamel finish. Has ad-hood and reclining back. Seat sides and back of seat are lined ted cloth. Height of handle from inches. Height, over all, about 28 Inside measurement of body, 8x s. Polished hub caps on 8-inch eels with ⅜-inch rubber tires. d up to about a 20-inch doll. weight, 15 pounds.
**8279¼—Price.... $6.45**

**Imitation Reed Gondola Style Doll Buggy.**
Gray enamel finish, hood and body lined with corduroy. Bottom of body padded. Will hold up to about a 22-inch doll. Height of handle from floor, 26 inches. Height, over all, about 32 in. Inside measurement of body, 9x19½ in. Adjustable hood and hub caps polished. 9-in. metal wheels with ⅜-inch rubber tires. Unmailable. Shpg. wt., 18 lbs. **$7.98**
**79T8271¼—Price....... $7.98**

**Genuine Reed Doll Buggy, Dark Blue Finish.**
Genuine reed, in dark blue enamel finish and running gear in light color. Will hold up to about a 22-in. doll. Hood, seat proper, sides and back of seat lined with corduroy. Height of handle from floor, 28½ in. Height, over all, about 31 in. Has 9-in. metal wheels with ⅜-in. rubber tires. Inside measurement of body, 8x18 in. Reclining back, adjustable hood, leather hold-in strap and polished hub caps. Unmailable. Shipping weight, 17½ pounds. **$9.98**
**79T8282¼—Price........... $9.98**

**$2.67**

**$2.19**

**$4.35**

**g Value Doll Cart With Rubber Tires, $2.67.**
s cart is made with nice dark color painted body and is just the cart for the youngsters. ped with imitation leather folding hood. Has 6-inch wheels with ¼-inch rubber tires. Will up to about a 16-inch doll. Size of body, 7¼x16½ s. Height of handle from floor, about 22 inches. Doll ated not included. Shipping wt., 5½ lbs.
**T8213¼—Price.................... $2.67**

**Our $2.19 Leader Doll Buggy.**
Exceptional value in low priced perambulator. Metal body finished in dark color and striped. Three-bow folding hood covered with imitation leather. Has 6-inch metal wheels. Holds up to about a 16-inch doll. Inside measurement of body, 7¼x16½ inches. Height of handle from floor, 21½ inches. Doll illustrated not included. Shipping weight, 5¼ pounds. **$2.19**
**79T8212¼—Price......... $2.19**

**Medium Size Imitation Reed Doll Buggy, $4.35.**
Made of imitation reed, cream enamel finish. Has metal gear. Will hold up to about an 18-inch doll. Bottom and back of seat lined with printed cloth. Height of handle from floor, about 22½ inches. Height, over all, about 25 inches. Inside measurement of body, 15x7¼ inches. Has 6¾-inch metal wheels with ¼-inch rubber tires. Doll illustrated not included. Shpg. wt., 9½ lbs. **$4.35**
**79T8269¼—Price....... $4.35**

**97¢**

**$3.45**

**$3.47**

**$3.98**

**Collapsible Doll Carriage With Top.**
constructed, trimmed with on leather. Steel frame, d. 5-inch, single spoked, wheels. Large enough to oll up to about 18 inches. t of handle from floor 21 inches. Shipping wt., nds.
**T8252¼—Price.. 97c**

**Small Size Imitation Reed Doll Buggy.**
Gray enamel finish. Metal gear. Will hold up to about 16-inch doll. Height of handle from floor, 21 inches. Height, over all, 24 inches. Inside measurement of body, 5½x14 inches. Back and seat lined with printed cloth. 7-inch metal wheels with ¼-inch rubber tires. Adjustable hood. Shpg. wt., 8¼ lbs.
**79T8278¼—Price.. $3.45**

**Dolly's Buggy Robes.**
Light color, assorted sheep's wool and goat's hair, flannelette lined. Center of each cut as illustrated. Doll not included.
Size, about 17x25 in. Ribbon bow. Shipping weight, 1 pound.
**69T8275**
**Price ...........$1.00**
Size, about 16x22 in. Shipping weight, 14 oz.
**69T8276**
**Price ..............87c**
Size, about 12x16 in. Shipping weight, 5 oz.
**69T8277**
**Price ..............67c**

**Our Medium Priced Doll Perambulator.**
Wood body enameled in dark color. Striped. Has folding three-bow imitation leather hood. 7-inch metal wheels with ¼-inch rubber tires. Will hold up to about a 16-inch doll. Size of body inside, 7x17 inches. Height of handle from floor, about 24 inches. Shpg. wt., 8 lbs.
**79T8214¼—Price..$3.47**

**Our Largest Wood Perambulator.**
Three-bow imitation leather hood. Body is nicely painted and striped. Equipped with 7-inch metal wheels, ¼-inch rubber tires. Holds up to about an 18-inch doll. Size wood body, inside measurement, 7x17 inches. Height of handle from floor, about 24 in. Shpg. wt., 8¼ lbs.
**79T8215¼—Price............... $3.98**

# Gifts for Little Girls

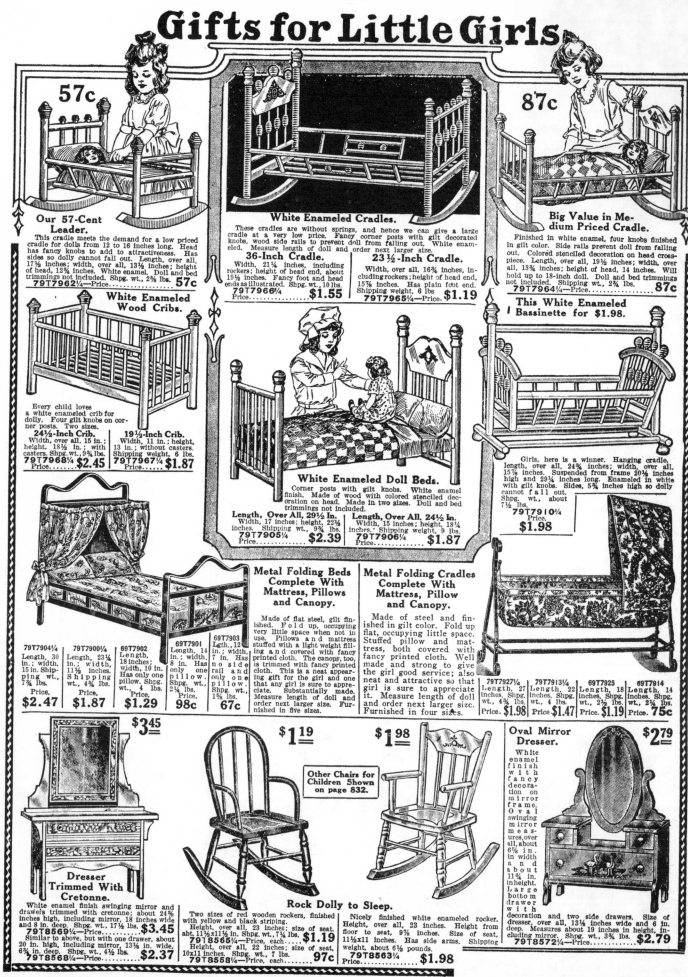

57c

## Our 57-Cent Leader.

This cradle meets the demand for a low priced cradle for dolls from 12 to 16 inches long. Head has fancy knobs to add to attractiveness. Has sides so dolly cannot fall out. Length, over all, 17½ inches; width, over all, 13½ inches; height of head, 12¾ inches. White enamel. Doll and bed trimmings not included. Shpg. wt., 2⅝ lbs.
79T7962¼—Price **57c**

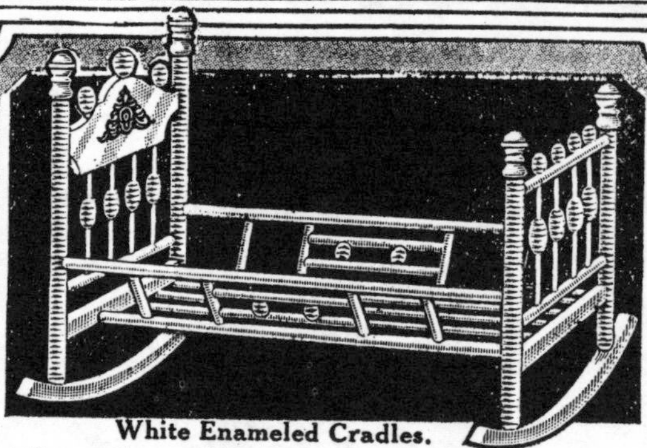

## White Enameled Cradles.

These cradles are without springs, and hence we can give a large cradle at a very low price. Fancy corner posts with gilt decorated knobs, wood side rails to prevent doll from falling out. White enameled. Measure length of doll and order next larger size.

**36-Inch Cradle.** Width, 21¼ inches, including rockers; height of head end, about 19½ inches. Fancy foot and head ends as illustrated. Shpg. wt., 10 lbs.
79T7966¼ Price **$1.55**

**23½-Inch Cradle.** Width, over all, 16¾ inches, including rockers; height of head end, 15⅞ inches. Has plain foot end. Shipping weight, 6 lbs.
79T7965¼—Price **$1.19**

87c

## Big Value in Medium Priced Cradle.

Finished in white enamel, four knobs finished in gilt color. Side rails prevent doll from falling out. Colored stenciled decoration on head crosspiece. Length, over all, 19½ inches; width, over all, 13¾ inches; height of head, 14 inches. Will hold up to 18-inch doll. Doll and bed trimmings not included. Shipping wt., 2¾ lbs.
79T7964¼—Price **87c**

## White Enameled Wood Cribs.

Every child loves a white enameled crib for dolly. Four gilt knobs on corner posts. Two sizes.

**24½-Inch Crib.** Width, over all, 15 in.; height, 18½ in.; with casters. Shpg. wt., 9¾ lbs.
79T7968¼ Price **$2.45**

**19½-Inch Crib.** Width, 11 in.; height, 13 in.; without casters. Shipping weight, 6 lbs.
79T7967¼ Price **$1.87**

## White Enameled Doll Beds.

Corner posts with gilt knobs. White enamel finish. Made of wood with colored stenciled decoration on head. Made in two sizes. Doll and bed trimmings not included.

**Length, Over All, 29½ In.** Width, 17 inches; height, 22½ inches. Shipping wt., 9¾ lbs.
79T7905¼ Price **$2.39**

**Length, Over All, 24½ In.** Width, 15 inches; height, 18¼ inches. Shipping weight, 9 lbs.
79T7906¼ Price **$1.87**

## This White Enameled Bassinette for $1.98.

Girls, here is a winner. Hanging cradle, length, over all, 24¾ inches; width, over all, 15⅞ inches. Suspended from frame 20½ inches high and 29¼ inches long. Enameled in white with gilt knobs. Sides, 5¾ inches high so dolly cannot fall out. Shpg. wt., about 7½ lbs.
79T7910¼ Price **$1.98**

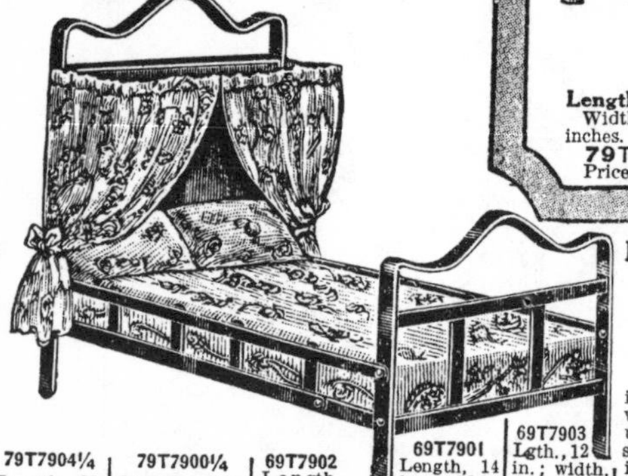

## Metal Folding Beds Complete With Mattress, Pillows and Canopy.

Made of flat steel, gilt finished. Fold up, occupying very little space when not in use. Pillows and mattress stuffed with a light weight filling and covered with fancy printed cloth. The canopy, too, is trimmed with fancy printed cloth. This is a neat appearing gift for the girl and one that any girl is sure to appreciate. Substantially made. Measure length of doll and order next larger size. Furnished in five sizes.

| 79T7904¼ | 79T7900¼ | 69T7902 | 69T7901 | 69T7903 |
|---|---|---|---|---|
| Length, 30 in.; width, 15 in. Shipping wt., 7¾ lbs. | Length, 23¼ in.; width, 11½ inches. Shipping wt., 4¾ lbs. | Length, 18 inches; width, 10 in. Has only one pillow. Shpg. wt., 4 lbs. | Length, 14 in.; width, 8 in. Has only one pillow. Shpg. wt., 2¼ lbs. | Lgth., 12 in.; width, 7 in. Has no side rail and only one pillow. Shpg. wt., 1⅝ lbs. |
| Price, **$2.47** | Price, **$1.87** | Price, **$1.29** | Price, **98c** | **67c** |

## Metal Folding Cradles Complete With Mattress, Pillow and Canopy.

Made of steel and finished in gilt color. Fold up flat, occupying little space. Stuffed pillow and mattress, both covered with fancy printed cloth. Well made and strong to give the girl good service; also neat and attractive so that girl is sure to appreciate it. Measure length of doll and order next larger size. Furnished in four sizes.

| 79T7927¼ | 79T7913¼ | 69T7925 | 69T7914 |
|---|---|---|---|
| Length, 27 inches. Shpg. wt., 4¾ lbs. | Length, 22 inches. Shpg. wt., 4 lbs. | Length, 18 inches. Shpg. wt., 2½ lbs. | Length, 14 inches. Shpg. wt., 2¼ lbs. |
| Price **$1.98** | Price **$1.47** | Price **$1.19** | Price **75c** |

$3.45

## Dresser Trimmed With Cretonne.

White enamel finish swinging mirror and drawers trimmed with cretonne; about 24⅜ inches high, including mirror, 18 inches wide and 8 in. deep. Shpg. wt., 17½ lbs.
79T8569¼—Price **$3.45**

Similar to above, but with one drawer, about 20 in. high, including mirror, 13⅜ in. wide, 6¾ in. deep. Shpg. wt., 4½ lbs.
79T8568¼—Price **$2.37**

$1.19

Other Chairs for Children Shown on page 832.

$1.98

## Rock Dolly to Sleep.

Two sizes of red wooden rockers, finished with yellow and black striping.

Height, over all, 23 inches; size of seat, abt. 11½x11½ in. Shpg. wt., 7¼ lbs.
79T8565¼—Price, each **$1.19**

Height, over all, 22 inches; size of seat, 10x11 inches. Shpg. wt., 7 lbs.
79T8558¼—Price, each **97c**

Nicely finished white enameled rocker. Height, over all, 23 inches. Height from floor to seat, 9⅞ inches. Size of seat, 11½x11 inches. Has side arms. Shipping weight, about 6½ pounds.
79T8563¼ Price **$1.98**

## Oval Mirror Dresser.

$2.79

White enamel finish with fancy decoration on mirror frame. Oval swinging mirror measures, over all, about 6⅝ in. in width and about 11¾ in. in height. Large bottom drawer with decoration and two side drawers. Size of dresser, over all, 13⅛ inches wide and 6 in. deep. Measures about 19 inches in height, including mirror. Shpg. wt., 3¾ lbs.
79T8572¼—Price **$2.79**

# Girls' Miscellaneous Toys

**Beautiful Nickel Plated Toy Stoves.**
These toy stoves are big favorites with little girls. Made like mother's cook stove. Nicely nickel plated and smooth parts brightly polished. Small fire can be built with paper or wood in the larger size stoves if mother is willing. Prices include metal cooking utensils. Made in seven sizes.

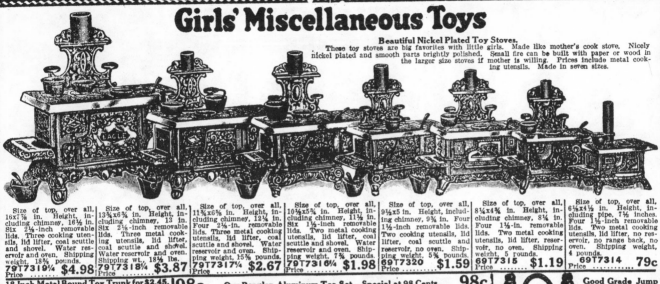

Size of top, over all, 16x7⅞ in. Height, including chimney, 16½ in. Six 2⅛-inch removable lids. Three cooking utensils, lid lifter, coal scuttle and shovel. Water reservoir and oven. Shipping weight, 18¾ pounds.
79T7319¼ Price **$4.98**

Size of top, over all, 13¾x6¾ in. Height, including chimney, 13 in. Six 2⅛-inch removable lids. Three metal cooking utensils, lid lifter, coal scuttle and shovel. Water reservoir and oven. Shipping wt., 18¼ lbs.
79T7318¼ Price **$3.87**

Size of top, over all, 11¾x6⅝ in. Height, including chimney, 12¼ in. Four 2⅛-in. removable lids. Three metal cooking utensils, lid lifter, coal scuttle and shovel. Water reservoir and oven. Shipping weight, 15⅝ pounds.
79T7317¼ Price **$2.67**

Size of top, over all, 10⅛x5¾ in. Height, including chimney, 11½ in. Six 1½-inch removable lids. Two metal cooking utensils, lid lifter, coal scuttle and shovel. Water reservoir and oven. Shipping weight, 7¾ pounds.
79T7316¼ Price **$1.98**

Size of top, over all, 9½x5 in. Height, including chimney, 9¾ in. Four 1½-inch removable lids. Two cooking utensils, lid lifter, coal scuttle and reservoir, no oven. Shipping weight, 5¾ pounds.
69T7320 Price **$1.59**

Size of top, over all, 8¼x4¾ in. Height, including chimney, 8¼ in. Four 1½-in. removable lids. Two metal cooking utensils, lid lifter, reservoir, no oven. Shipping weight, 5 pounds.
69T7315 **$1.19**

Size of top, over all, 6⅛x4½ in. Height, including pipe, 7½ inches. Four 1½-inch removable lids. Two metal cooking utensils, lid lifter, no reservoir, no range back, no oven. Shipping weight, 4 pounds.
69T7314 Price **79c**

**18-Inch Metal Bound Toy Trunk for $2.45.**

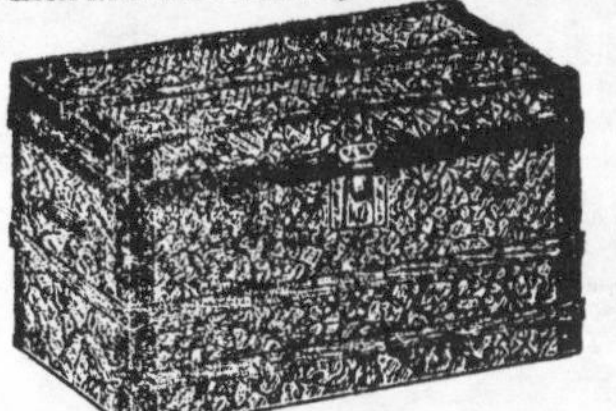

Made of wood covered with mottled colored paper. Reinforced with three wooden slats on top and two on the front. Bound with enameled metal and metal corners. Has a removable inside tray with compartment for dolly's hat. Metal lock and key. Size, 18x10½x10½ inches. Shipping weight, 7 pounds. See trunk on page 839.
79T8400¼—Price .......... **$2.45**

**13-Inch Trunk.**

A 13-inch trunk that will hold dolly's wardrobe. Wood, covered with fancy paper, hinged cover, removable inside tray, metal lock, slat protectors on top. Size over all, about 13x6x7½ inches. Shipping weight, 2½ pounds.
69T8408—Price .......... **79c**
See trunk on page 839.

**A Toy Sewing Machine That Will Sew.**

**Make Dresses for Dolly.**

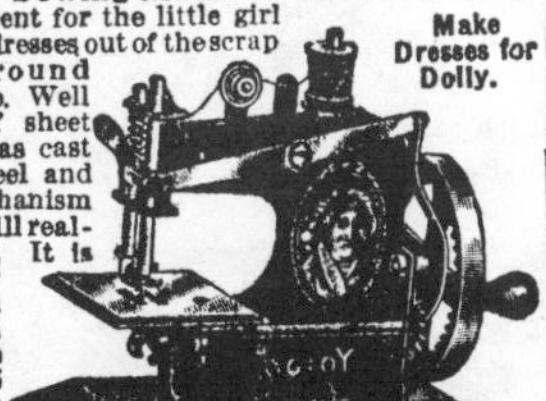

Enjoyment for the little girl making dresses out of the scrap cloth around the house. Well made of sheet steel. Has cast iron wheel and a mechanism which will really sew. It is nicely finished and can easily be fastened to table and quickly removed. Packed in box. Size, over all, 7¾x6½x4½ inches. Shipping weight, 2½ pounds.
69T5826—Price **$2.87**

**Toy Nurse Outfit for Girls.**

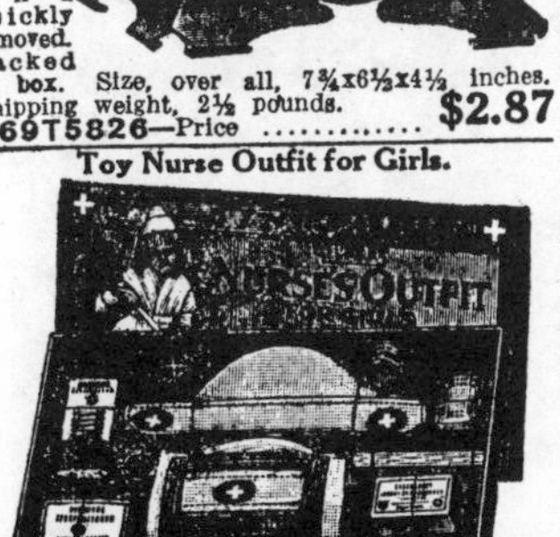

Consists of toy scissors, about 4 inches long, and white cotton cloth apron, hat and arm band. With outfit comes a small supply of pins, court plaster, adhesive plaster, gauze, cotton, wooden splints, etc. Sure to interest and amuse the girl. Shpg. wt., 1¾ lbs.
69T9111—Price .......... **$1.79**

**98c** **Our Popular Aluminum Tea Set. Special at 98 Cents.** **98c**

This set consists of four 3½-inch plates, four cups, 2¼ inches wide, four 3¼-inch saucers, teapot and cover, 5¾x3¼ inches over all; four 3¼-inch spoons; sugar bowl, 1⅞ inches wide; creamer, 1½ inches high. Dandy set packed in box. Shpg. wt., 2¼ lbs. **98c**
49T1862—Special price, per set..........

**Aluminum Domestic Science Set. Special at $1.00.**
Large enough to be of use to the little girl. Convex kettle, 3½ inches wide, with cover and bail, one lipped skillet, one plain saucepan, deep bread pan, preserving kettle, stew pan, dish pan and one pudding pan. Shipping weight, 2⅛ lbs.
49T1860
Special price, per set.. **$1.00**

**Toy Kitchen Cabinets.**
A complete outfit, consisting of kitchen cabinet and dummy packages of popular household commodities. Each has two or more compartments and bread board. Backs are cardboard and the balance of cabinet wood. Five sizes.

Our Largest Kitchen Cabinet. Four compartments with doors and five drawers. Height, 23½ inches; width, 18⅞ inches; depth, 7 inches. Shipping weight, 13½ lbs.
79T8521¼—Price .......... **$3.69**

Sizes, 21x17x7 inches. Three drawers, four compartments with doors. Shipping weight, 11¼ lbs.
79T8517¼—Price ... **$2.98**

Size, 18¼x15½x6¾ inches. Four compartments with doors. Shipping weight, 9¼ pounds.
79T8518¼—Price ... **$2.59**

Size, 15½x13½x6 inches. Three compartments with doors; four open shelves. Shpg. wt., 6¾ lbs.
79T8519¼—Price ... **$1.98**

Size, 13¾x11⅞x4¾ inches. Two closed compartments with doors; three open shelves. Shpg. wt., 4 lbs.
79T8520¼—Price ... **$1.00**

**Toy Kitchen Set, 79 Cents.**

Household outfit for the little girl. Consists of flour sifter, 3¾x3⅛ inches; all metal coffee grinder, 3¾ inches high; aluminum finish metal food chopper with screw to fasten to table, size, over all, 3x5 inches; large rolling pin; wood potato masher, 4⅜ inches; 1⅞-inch wood mixing bowl; metal scale, nicely finished, complete with scoop and weights. Shipping weight, 4 pounds.
69T9153 Price.......... **79c**

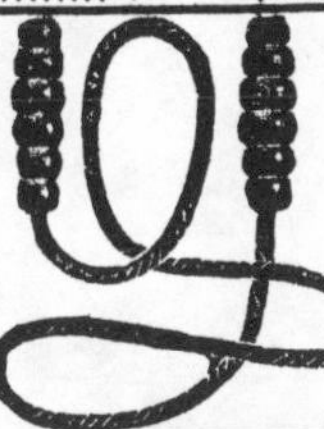

**Good Grade Jump Rope.**
Wood handles and a generous length good quality rope. Shipping weight, 3 oz.
69T9132 Price ... **25c**

**Ten Jacks and Ball.**

Set of ten metal jacks and a solid rubber ball, about 1½ inches in diameter. Shipping weight, 8 ounces.
69T9109—Price.......... **10c**

**Complete Embroidery Set for 33 Cents.**

Every girl should have one. Consists of 5-inch hoop, needle, thimble, three skeins of cotton, four small transfer designs, stamping paddle to transfer designs on to doilies, and three cloth doilies. Complete with instructions. Shipping weight, 10 ounces.
49T3818—Price .......... **33c**

**Big Value in Paints, 79 Cents.**

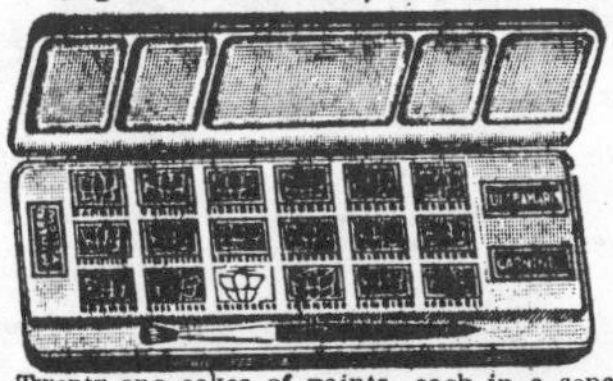

Twenty-one cakes of paints, each in a separate metal compartment. Size, 3⅛x8 inches. Shipping weight, 10 ounces.
49T3885—Price .......... **79c**

**Dandy 12-Piece Tea Set for 47 Cents.**

This set of twelve pieces consists of 2½-inch teapot, four cups and saucers and 6⅛x4⅛-inch tray, lithographed. Made of tin plate. Shipping weight, 10 ounces.
49T1812—Price, per set.......... **47c**

**Wood Beads for Stringing.**

Consists of about 95 assorted colored wooden beads and colored cords. Children enjoy stringing beads. Child can learn the different colors while playing. Shipping weight, 8 ounces.
49T3831 Per set..... **25c**

# CHILDREN'S DISHES

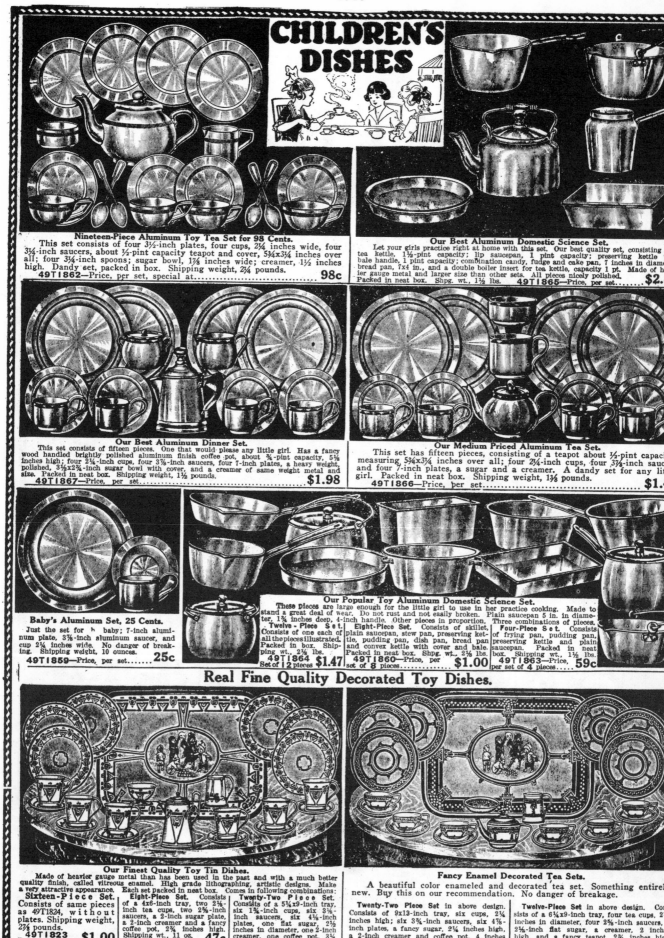

**Nineteen-Piece Aluminum Toy Tea Set for 98 Cents.**
This set consists of four $3\frac{1}{2}$-inch plates, four cups, $2\frac{1}{4}$ inches wide, four $3\frac{1}{4}$-inch saucers, about $\frac{1}{2}$-pint capacity teapot and cover, $5\frac{3}{4}$x$3\frac{1}{4}$ inches over all; four $3\frac{1}{4}$-inch spoons; sugar bowl, $1\frac{7}{8}$ inches wide; creamer, $1\frac{1}{2}$ inches high. Dandy set, packed in box. Shipping weight, $2\frac{1}{4}$ pounds.
49T1862—Price, per set, special at........................ **98c**

**Our Best Aluminum Domestic Science Set.**
Let your girls practice right at home with this set. Our best quality set, consisting of a tea kettle, $1\frac{1}{2}$-pint capacity; lip saucepan, 1 pint capacity; preserving kettle with bale handle, 1 pint capacity; combination candy, fudge and cake pan, 7 inches in diameter; bread pan, 7x4 in., and a double boiler insert for tea kettle, capacity 1 pt. Made of heavier gauge metal and larger size than other sets. All pieces nicely polished. Packed in neat box. Shpg. wt., $1\frac{1}{2}$ lbs. 49T1865—Price, per set........ **$2.87**

**Our Best Aluminum Dinner Set.**
This set consists of fifteen pieces. One that would please any little girl. Has a fancy wood handled brightly polished aluminum finish coffee pot, about $\frac{3}{4}$-pint capacity, $5\frac{1}{8}$ inches high; four $2\frac{1}{4}$-inch cups, four $3\frac{7}{8}$-inch saucers, four 7-inch plates, a heavy weight, polished, $3\frac{1}{2}$x$2\frac{3}{4}$-inch sugar bowl with cover, and a creamer of same weight metal and size. Packed in neat box. Shipping weight, $1\frac{1}{2}$ pounds.
49T1867—Price, per set........ **$1.98**

**Our Medium Priced Aluminum Tea Set.**
This set has fifteen pieces, consisting of a teapot about $\frac{1}{2}$-pint capacity, measuring $5\frac{3}{4}$x$3\frac{1}{4}$ inches over all; four $2\frac{1}{4}$-inch cups, four $3\frac{7}{8}$-inch saucers and four 7-inch plates, a sugar and a creamer. A dandy set for any little girl. Packed in neat box. Shipping weight, $1\frac{3}{8}$ pounds.
49T1866—Price, per set........ **$1.47**

**Baby's Aluminum Set, 25 Cents.**
Just the set for the baby; 7-inch aluminum plate, $3\frac{7}{8}$-inch aluminum saucer, and cup $2\frac{1}{4}$ inches wide. No danger of breaking. Shipping weight, 10 ounces.
49T1859—Price, per set....... **25c**

**Our Popular Toy Aluminum Domestic Science Set.**
These pieces are large enough for the little girl to use in her practice cooking. Made to stand a great deal of wear. Do not rust and not easily broken. Plain saucepan 5 in. in diameter, $1\frac{3}{4}$ inches deep, 4-inch handle. Other pieces in proportion. Three combinations of pieces.

**Twelve-Piece Set.** Consists of one each of all the pieces illustrated. Packed in box. Shipping wt., $2\frac{1}{4}$ lbs.
49T1864 Set of 12 pieces **$1.47**

**Eight-Piece Set.** Consists of skillet, plain saucepan, stew pan, preserving kettle, pudding pan, dish pan, bread pan and convex kettle with cover and bale. Packed in neat box. Shpg. wt., $2\frac{1}{8}$ lbs.
49T1860—Price, per set of 8 pieces........ **$1.00**

**Four-Piece Set.** Consists of frying pan, pudding pan, preserving kettle and plain saucepan. Packed in neat box. Shipping wt., $1\frac{1}{2}$ lbs.
49T1863—Price, per set of 4 pieces..... **59c**

## Real Fine Quality Decorated Toy Dishes.

**Our Finest Quality Toy Tin Dishes.**
Made of heavier gauge metal than has been used in the past and with a much better quality finish, called vitreous enamel. High grade lithographing, artistic designs. Make a very attractive appearance. Each set packed in neat box. Comes in following combinations:

**Sixteen-Piece Set.** Consists of same pieces as 49T1824, without plates. Shipping weight, $2\frac{7}{8}$ pounds.
49T1823 Price, per set.... **$1.00**

**Eight-Piece Set.** Consists of a 4x6-inch tray, two $2\frac{1}{8}$-inch tea cups, two $2\frac{5}{8}$-inch saucers, a 2-inch sugar plate, a 2-inch creamer and a fancy coffee pot, $2\frac{3}{4}$ inches high. Shipping wt., 11 oz.
49T1821—Per set. **47c**

**Twenty-Two Piece Set.** Consists of a $5\frac{1}{4}$x9-inch tray, six $1\frac{3}{4}$-inch cups, six $3\frac{1}{8}$-inch saucers, six $4\frac{1}{8}$-inch plates, one flat sugar, $2\frac{1}{2}$ inches in diameter, one 2-inch creamer, one coffee pot, $3\frac{1}{4}$ inches high over all. Shipping weight, $2\frac{7}{8}$ pounds.
49T1824 Price, per set.... **$1.47**

**Fancy Enamel Decorated Tea Sets.**
A beautiful color enameled and decorated tea set. Something entirely new. Buy this on our recommendation. No danger of breakage.

**Twenty-Two Piece Set** in above design. Consists of 9x13-inch tray, six cups, $2\frac{1}{4}$ inches high; six $3\frac{3}{4}$-inch saucers, six $4\frac{7}{8}$-inch plates, a fancy sugar, $2\frac{1}{4}$ inches high, a 2-inch creamer and coffee pot, 4 inches high over all. A very attractive set. Shipping weight, $2\frac{7}{8}$ pounds.
49T1825—Price, per set.... **$1.87**

**Twelve-Piece Set** in above design. Consists of a $6\frac{1}{4}$x9-inch tray, four tea cups, $2\frac{1}{8}$ inches in diameter, four $2\frac{5}{8}$-inch saucers, a $2\frac{1}{2}$-inch flat sugar, a creamer, 2 inches high, and a fancy teapot, $2\frac{3}{4}$ inches high over all. A dandy set. Shipping weight, 11 ounces.
49T1822—Price, per set....... **79c**

# Toy Chairs, Tables and Banks

For Higher Grade Children's Furniture see pages 1103 and 1104.

For Other Furniture for Children see page 811.

### Small Size Red Rocker and Chair.

These chairs are made of good grade wood and are substantially built for chairs of this size. Painted in red, with yellow stripe. Just the chair for the little tots. Height over all, about 18 inches. Height from floor to seat, 8½ inches. Seat, 8½x8½ inches. Shipping weight, 3 pounds.

69T8560 Red Chair. Price .... 50c

69T8561 Red Rocker. Price .... 63c

### Medium Priced Chairs.

These chairs are made of good grade wood. Painted in red, with black and yellow stripes. Height over all, 22 inches. Height from floor to seat is 10 inches. Seat is 10x11 inches.

79T8558¼ Red Rocker. Shipping weight, 7 lbs. Price ........ 97c

79T8559¼ Red Chair. Shipping weight, 6½ lbs. Price........ 87c

### Red Wooden Tables.

Painted and varnished in red, with yellow striping. Drawer, 6½x8⅞ in.

79T8536¼—Top, 22½x17 in. Height, 19 inches. Shipping weight, 11½ pounds. Price ................ $1.79

79T8537¼—Similar to above. Top, 20¾x14¾ inches. Height, 17 in. Shpg. wt., 7½ lbs. Price ................ $1.47

69T8576—Small Table. Plain top; no drawer. Size, about 18x12¾x13 in. Shpg. wt., 3¼ lbs. Price ................ 79c

### Large Size Red Rocker and Chair.

These are our largest red toy chairs and rockers. The children will be greatly pleased with them. They are strongly constructed to stand the everyday use which will be given them. Finished in red, with yellow and black striping. Height over all, 22½ inches. Height of seat from floor, 10½ inches. Size of seat, 11⅜x11⅜ inches.

79T8565¼ Red Rocker. Shipping wt., 7¼ lbs. Price $1.19

79T8566¼ Red Chair. Shipping wt., 6¾ lbs. Price $1.10

### Children's Red Tea Set for $1.79.

Nicely red finished wood tea set, consisting of two chairs, height, 18 inches over all; seats, 8½x8½ inches, with yellow striping, and a table, top measuring 18x12¾ inches; height, about 13 inches. Big favorite with children. Shipping weight, about 8¾ pounds.

79T8528¼ Price, per set................ $1.79

### Children's Furniture.

Veneered and varnished wood seats and table top, with twisted metal legs and backs. Oxidized finished metal. Chairs are 20 inches high. Height from floor to seat, 10 inches. Table top is 16 inches in diameter and is 17½ inches high.

79T8544¼—Set, two chairs and table. Shipping wt., 24 lbs. Per set.... $4.87

79T8545¼—Chair. Shipping wt., 4½ pounds. Price, each.... 1.39

79T8546¼—Table. Shipping wt., 6¾ pounds. Price, each.... 2.39

### A Well Made Children's Furniture Set.

Made of good wood, finished in mahogany color. Table top thick veneered wood about 20½x15¼ inches, oval shape. Height, about 16 inches. Has fancy legs. Chairs measure about 18½ inches high over all. Seat size over all, about 8½x11 inches. Height from floor to seat, 9¾ inches. Scroll shape back strip. Shipping weight, 15 pounds.

79T8529¼—Table and two chairs. Price, per set....... $2.47

### Folding Tables.

These tables are made, finished and varnished in natural wood colors. Favorites with children. Each table folds up flat and occupies little space.

79T8532¼—Size top, 18x28 in. Height, 19 inches. Shipping weight, 12¼ pounds. Price. $1.47

79T8533¼—Size top, about 16x24 inches. Height, 17 in. Shpg. wt., 8¼ lbs. Price.. $1.19

79T8530¼—Size top, about 14x22 inches. Height, 14 inches. Shpg. wt., 4¾ lbs. Price....... 98c

### Our Best Five-Coin Registering Bank.

Registers pennies, nickels, dimes, quarters and halves. Opens automatically when a total of $10.00 is deposited. Made of sheet steel, embossed and lithographed in gilt and several colors. Well made and attractive bank. Size, 7¼x7½x5⅛ inches. Shipping weight, 3½ pounds.

69T8703—Price, each.... $2.39

### The Home Five-Coin Bank.

Opens automatically when a total of $10.00 is deposited. Registers pennies, nickels, dimes, quarters and halves. Made of sheet steel, lithographed in several colors. Size over all, 7x6⅞x4¾ inches. Shipping wt., 3 lbs.

69T8701—Price, each.... $1.89

### Provident Four-Coin Bank.

A four-coin registering bank. Opens automatically when a total of $10.00 is deposited. Registers pennies, nickels, dimes and quarters. Made of sheet steel, lithographed. Size over all, 5x4¼x4¾ inches. Shipping weight, 2⅛ pounds.

69T8702 Price, each........ $1.39

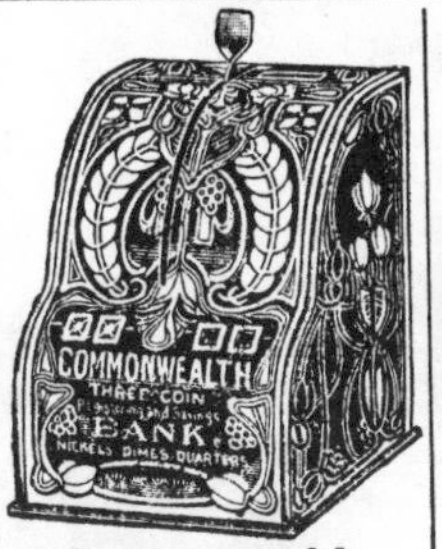


### Commonwealth Three-Coin Bank.

This three-coin registering bank is made of sheet steel, lithographed. Registers nickels, dimes and quarters. Opens automatically when a total of $10.00 is deposited. Size, 5x5¼x4 in. Shpg. wt., 2¼ lbs.

69T8700 Price, each........ $1.19

### Household Savings Bank.

Cold rolled steel, oxidized finish. Durably constructed and protected by special patent device to prevent coins from dropping out. Key with each bank. Size, 4⅛x3x2¼ inches. Shipping weight, 1½ pounds.

69T8707 Price, each........ $1.19

### The Wise Pig Encourages Thrift.

The wise pig's broad smile induces the child to want to place a coin in his head to please him. Made of plaster. Height, 6 in. Securely packed. Shipping weight, 14 ounces.

69T8714—Each ... 25c

### Cutie Pup Bank.

Cute puppy. Popular with kiddies. Made of iron, nicely painted and finished. Size over all, 4x2½ inches. Shipping weight, 1½ pounds.

69T8715 Price, each........ 21c

### Telephone Bank.

When crank is turned bell rings. Light sheet steel. Size over all, 7¼x3½ inches. Shipping weight, 1¼ lbs.

69T8730 Price, each....... 21c

### Toy Cash Register.

Made of metal, nicely lithographed. Size over all, 3½x3½x3½ inches. Shipping weight, 15 ounces.

69T8712 Price, each............ 22c

### Indian Bank.

Iron Indian bank, nicely painted and finished. Height, about 6¼ inches. Shipping weight, 1½ lbs.

69T8716 Price, each. 19c

### Bunny Bank.

All children like bunnies. Nicely painted and finished iron bank. Size over all, 4¾x4¼ inches. Shipping wt., 1½ pounds.

69T8717 Price, each....... 17c

### Scout Bank.

Made of iron, nicely finished and painted. Height, about 5¾ in. Shpg. wt., 1¼ lbs.

69T8718 Price, each ..... 18c

# Fine Long Racing Sleds

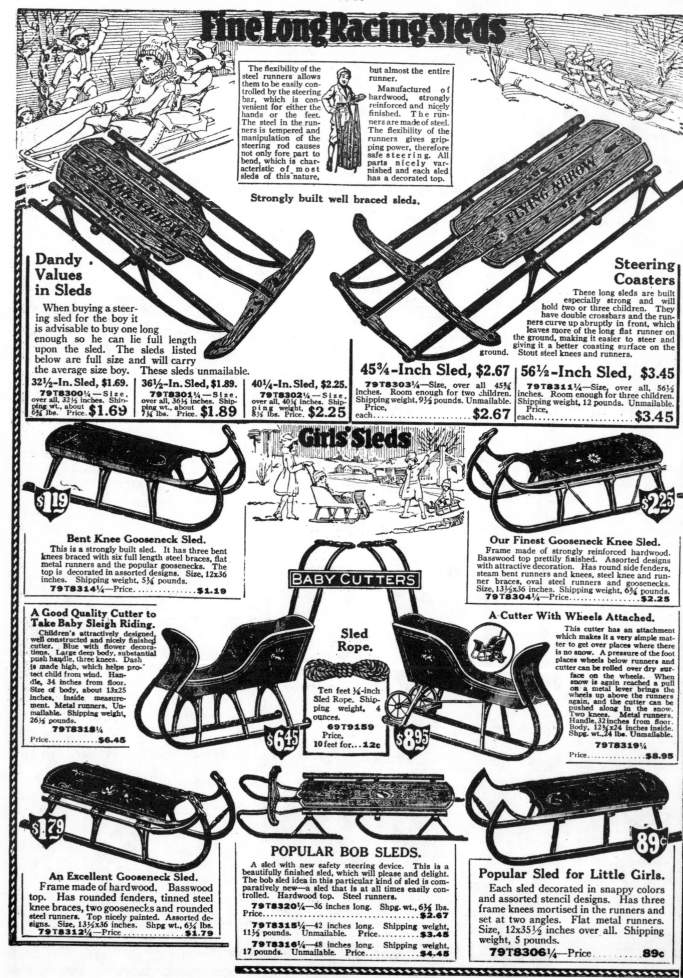

The flexibility of the steel runners allows them to be easily controlled by the steering bar, which is convenient for either the hands or the feet. The steel in the runners is tempered and manipulation of the steering rod causes not only fore part to bend, which is characteristic of most sleds of this nature, but almost the entire runner.

Manufactured of hardwood, strongly reinforced and nicely finished. The runners are made of steel. The flexibility of the runners gives gripping power, therefore safe steering. All parts nicely varnished and each sled has a decorated top.

**Strongly built well braced sleds.**

## Dandy Values in Sleds

When buying a steering sled for the boy it is advisable to buy one long enough so he can lie full length upon the sled. The sleds listed below are full size and will carry the average size boy. These sleds unmailable.

**32½-In. Sled, $1.69**
79T8300¼—Size, over all, 32½ inches. Shipping wt., about 6¾ lbs. Price. **$1.69**

**36½-In. Sled, $1.89**
79T8301¼—Size, over all, 36½ inches. Shipping wt., about 7¼ lbs. Price. **$1.89**

**40¼-In. Sled, $2.25.**
79T8302¼—Size, over all, 40¼ inches. Shipping weight, 8¼ lbs. Price. **$2.25**

## Steering Coasters

These long sleds are built especially strong and will hold two or three children. They have double crossbars and the runners curve up abruptly in front, which leaves more of the long flat runner on the ground, making it easier to steer and giving it a better coasting surface on the ground. Stout steel knees and runners.

**45¾-Inch Sled, $2.67**
79T8303¼—Size, over all 45¾ inches. Room enough for two children. Shipping weight, 9½ pounds. Unmailable. Price, each. **$2.67**

**56½-Inch Sled, $3.45**
79T8311¼—Size, over all, 56½ inches. Room enough for three children. Shipping weight, 12 pounds. Unmailable. Price, each. **$3.45**

## Girls' Sleds

**$1.19**

### Bent Knee Gooseneck Sled.

This is a strongly built sled. It has three bent knees braced with six full length steel braces, flat metal runners and the popular goosenecks. The top is decorated in assorted designs. Size, 12x36 inches. Shipping weight, 5¼ pounds.
79T8314¼—Price. **$1.19**

**$2.25**

### Our Finest Gooseneck Knee Sled.

Frame made of strongly reinforced hardwood. Basswood top prettily finished. Assorted designs with attractive decoration. Has round side fenders, steam bent runners and knees, steel knee and runner braces, oval steel runners and goosenecks. Size, 13½x36 inches. Shipping weight, 6¾ pounds.
79T8304¼—Price. **$2.25**

## BABY CUTTERS

### A Good Quality Cutter to Take Baby Sleigh Riding.

Children's attractively designed, well constructed and nicely finished cutter. Blue with flower decorations. Large deep body, substantial push handle, three knees. Dash is made high, which helps protect child from wind. Handle, 34 inches from floor. Size of body, about 13x25 inches, inside measurement. Metal runners. Unmailable. Shipping weight, 26½ pounds.
79T8318¼
Price. **$6.45**

**$6.45**

### Sled Rope.

Ten feet ¼-inch Sled Rope. Shipping weight, 4 ounces.
69T9159
Price, 10 feet for. **12c**

**$8.95**

### A Cutter With Wheels Attached.

This cutter has an attachment which makes it a very simple matter to get over places where there is no snow. A pressure of the foot places wheels below runners and cutter can be rolled over dry surface on the wheels. When snow is again reached a pull on a metal lever brings the wheels up above the runners again, and the cutter can be pushed along in the snow. Two knees. Metal runners. Handle, 32 inches from floor. Body, 12¾x24 inches inside. Shpg. wt., 24 lbs. Unmailable.
79T8319¼
Price. **$8.95**

**$1.79**

### An Excellent Gooseneck Sled.

Frame made of hardwood. Basswood top. Has rounded fenders, tinned steel knee braces, two goosenecks and rounded steel runners. Top nicely painted. Assorted designs. Size, 13½x36 inches. Shpg wt., 6¾ lbs.
79T8312¼—Price. **$1.79**

### POPULAR BOB SLEDS.

A sled with new safety steering device. This is a beautifully finished sled, which will please and delight. The bob sled idea in this particular kind of sled is comparatively new—a sled that is at all times easily controlled. Hardwood top. Steel runners.
79T8320¼—36 inches long. Shpg. wt., 6½ lbs. Price. **$2.67**
79T8315¼—42 inches long. Shipping weight, 11½ pounds. Unmailable. Price. **$3.45**
79T8316¼—48 inches long. Shipping weight, 17 pounds. Unmailable. Price. **$4.45**

**89c**

### Popular Sled for Little Girls.

Each sled decorated in snappy colors and assorted stencil designs. Has three frame knees mortised in the runners and set at two angles. Flat metal runners. Size, 12x35½ inches over all. Shipping weight, 5 pounds.
79T8306¼—Price. **89c**

# Toy Guns and Targets

## Schoenhut's Rubber Ball Shooting Gallery.

Made of light wood with cloth back. Front part of gallery covered with nicely lithographed paper. Contains figures and target, representing comical figures and animals, which fall down when hit. Comes with popgun, 15 in. long over all, and a rubber ball and cork. Size of target over all, 13x13¼x4¼ inches. Shipping weight, 3 pounds.
**69T5631**—Price **$1.39**

## Real Toy Machine Gun.

### The Gilbert Machine Gun.
One of the best toy machine guns on the market. The 16-inch barrel is sheet steel, painted black. Length of barrel, over all, about 20 inches. Has wooden base reinforcing barrel. Will shoot at any angle and is also revolving. Tripod stand. Complete with wooden bullet ammunition. A dandy gun. Shipping weight, 3¾ pounds.
**69T5604**—Price **$2.98**
**69T5605**—Extra Wooden Bullets. Shpg. wt., 2 oz. Pkg. of 12... **12c**

## Rapid Fire Cannon.

Just think of it! A rapid fire gun. Repeats automatically as crank is turned. Set consists of cannon, about 7¼x5⅝ inches, with wood body and iron supporting stand, also wooden ammunition and four colored cardboard soldiers or cavalrymen, about 6¼ inches high, on wood base. Shipping weight, 1⅜ pounds.
**69T5656**—Price... **67c**

## Toy Pistol and Belt With Wooden Bullets.

Boys' ideal outfit, consisting of toy pistol about 11½ inches long, 26-inch belt, with eight wooden bullets. Belt for carrying cartridges included with this set. Shipping weight, 12 oz.
**69T5629**—Price... **45c**

## The "Three-In-One" Toy Air Rifle, Only 89c.

One of our best combination air rifles, popguns and small rubber ball shooters. Just the rifle for the boy at this time. Very interesting, and will give him some good training in marksmanship, especially if he is a Boy Scout. No changing of parts. Simply change ammunition. Small rubber ball and cork on string included with gun. Nickel plated steel barrel and wood stock. Shoots air-gun shot with accuracy. Length, about 29 in. Shpg. wt., 1¾ lbs.
**69T5614**—Price... **89c**

## 8¾-Inch Pistol.

Well made popgun with wood pistol shaped handle, lever action. Sheet steel barrel. Complete with cork. Shipping weight, 8 ounces. **25c**
**69T5603**—Price...
Same pistol as above, 8¾ inches over all, with fringed holster with belt made of imitation patent leather. Shipping wt., 12 oz. **45c**
**69T5608**—Price, per set...

## 11-Inch Popgun for 19c.

Big value in 11-inch lever action popgun, complete with cork. Has sheet steel barrel and wood stock. Our cheapest popgun and one we are proud to offer at this price. Shipping weight, 8 ounces.
**69T5644**—Price... **19c**

## This Fine 21-Inch Popgun for Only 59 Cents.

Shoots large cork or rubber ball. Use cork for noise and rubber ball for sport. Nickel plated steel barrel and wood stock. Has good steel spring and does not get out of order quickly. Just the thing for the youngsters. Length over all, about 21 inches. Shipping weight, 1¼ pounds.
**69T5600**—Price... **59c**

## Shoots Automatically and Is Harmless.

A rapid fire popgun. One of the most popular guns yet introduced. No ammunition needed. Cork inside of barrel does all the popping. In order to obtain rapid fire, trigger must be pulled and released quickly and repeatedly. Made of good grade sheet steel. Size over all, 6½x3¼ inches. Shipping weight, 9 ounces.
**69T5619**—Price... **29c**

## Mechanical Armored Car.

Made of wood, painted a fighting gray. Good spring. Will run straight or in circle, and at the same time imitate gunfire and will puff talcum powder out of the imitation cannon to resemble smoke. A popular car for small boys. Harmless. Size over all, 9x4½x5 inches. Shipping weight, 2 pounds 3 ounces.
**69T5749**—Price... **$1.37**

## The Popular Toy Pump Gun.

Pump action reminds one of a large repeating rifle. Finished to imitate a big gun. Shoots ten times without reloading. Shaped dark finish stock. Barrel made of sheet steel. Included with gun are twenty-five wooden balls for ammunition. Length over all, about 24½ inches. Shipping weight, 1¼ pounds.
**69T5618**—Price... **69c**
**69T5617**—Extra Ammunition, 25 balls to package. Shpg. wt., 1 oz. Price... **5c**

## Combination Military and Shooting Gallery Outfit.

Consists of six 6½-inch infantry and cavalrymen, assorted, a 13¼-inch good spring gun, with steel barrel and wood stock and a 16¾-inch novelty wooden shooting gallery. The whole outfit is nicely colored and well made and will afford lots of amusement for the youngsters. A gun is particularly appealing to boys and with this target and gun they have lots of fun. Shipping weight, 1 pound.
**69T5665**—Price... **69c**

## A New Pump Popgun.

A dandy noisemaker and a harmless one. Pulling and pushing pump mechanism back and forth makes gun pop. Barrel made of nickel plated steel and stock of wood. Measures about 27 inches long. Shipping weight, 1 pound.
**69T5648**—Price... **98c**

## Metal Water Pistol.

This 5-in. water pistol affords lots of fun for the children. Works by pressing trigger. Will shoot water a fairly good distance. Shipping weight, 8 ounces. **14c**
**69T5667**—Price...

## Big Value Soldier Outfit.

Set consists of four 2⅞-inch metal soldiers, one 3¼-inch cavalryman and 9¼-inch popgun. Shipping weight, 9 ounces.
**69T5601**—Price, per set... **25c**

## Lever Action Toy Gun.

Has lever action, like illustration. Length over all, about 16¾ inches. Shoots cork only. Barrel made of sheet steel, wood stock. A good seller. Popping report. Shipping weight, 11 ounces.
**69T5647**—Price... **25c**

## Noisy Paper Ammunition Toy Gun.

Has patent attachment whereby ordinary newspaper is inserted at end of barrel. When gun is fired causes loud report. About 18 inches long. Paper ammunition with each gun. Barrel made of sheet steel. Stock of gun is wood. One of our best sellers and a good bargain at this price. Shipping weight, 13 ounces.
**69T5630**—Price... **39c**

## Our 39c Soldier Outfit.

Set consists of six 6½-inch nicely colored assorted design soldiers. Made of stout cardboard. Gun about 9¼ inches long, wood stock, with ammunition. Shipping weight, 13 ounces.
**69T5602**—Price, per set... **39c**

## Eighteen Soldiers and Gun for 69c.

Boys, here is a dandy, just what you want. Consists of sixteen 3x1⅛-inch lithographed metal (not lead) soldiers on foot, two soldiers on horseback, 3x3 inches, and 13¾-inch popgun. Assorted design soldiers. Good value for the money. Laid out neatly in strong box. Shipping weight, about 2 pounds.
**69T5650**—Price... **69c**

## Wooden Soldiers With 16¼-Inch Gun.

Outfit consists of four cavalrymen and four infantrymen, made of wood, about ¼ inch thick and standing about 1¾ inches high, supported by a wooden base. They are printed in several colors. Gun is about 16¼ inches long, with a sheet steel barrel, wood stock and shoots a cork which is tied to the gun by a spring. Shipping weight, 3 lbs.
**69T5666**—Price... **$1.25**

## Gilbert Mechanical Tank.

The battle tank is a very popular toy this year. We have in this Gilbert Mechanical Sheet Steel Tank one propelled by a mechanical motor, which runs equally well on either its top or bottom. Has chain caterpillars. If in its path it encounters an obstacle which will turn it over on its back it will come right back in the same direction on its back. Size, 14x6½x5 in. Shpg. wt., 3 lbs.
**69T5764**—Price, each... **$4.47**

## Archery Games.

Archery games. Just the thing to train the eye. Interesting to adults as well as children. Target made of wood, fiber bristle center, three supports, four darts with fiber bristle ends and two bows. Target, 10½ inches in diameter, and two bows, about 22 inches long. Shipping weight, 4 pounds.
**69T5653**—Price... **98c**
Target, 5¾ inches in diameter, 4 darts and two bows, about 15 inches long. Shipping weight, 1¼ pounds.
**69T5652**—Price... **47c**

## On Guard.

Consists of eight 9½-inch cardboard infantrymen and a toy pistol with wooden ammunition. Packed in attractive box, 13½x10½ inches. Shipping weight, 2 lbs.
**69T5625**—Price... **47c**

## Shoot the Wild Animals.

Hitting the target automatically makes hunter pop up. Target, over all, 9x9¼ inches. 9¼-inch metal barrel gun and wooden ammunition. Shipping wt., 1 lb.
**69T5640**—Price, each set... **39c**

## Blow Up the Battleship.

Here is great sport for the boys. A gunboat, made in sections, and painted a "fighting gray." Boat can be blown up and then put together and is ready to be "shot" again. Boat, 2½x11½ inches. Torpedo, 3¼ inches long. Shipping wt., 14 ounces.
**69T5649**—Price... **25c**

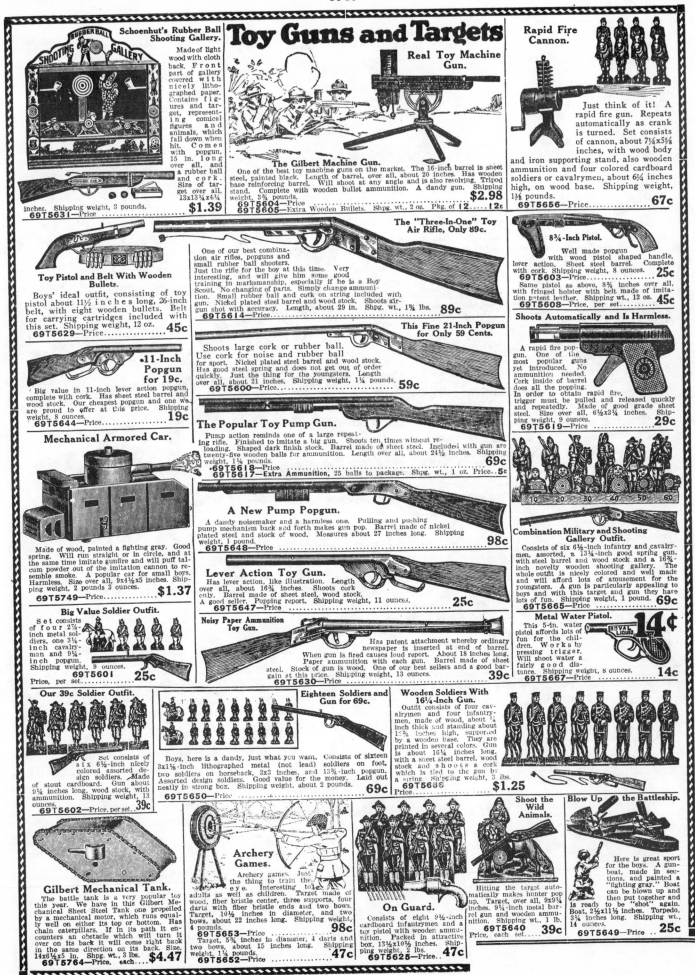

# Mechanical Toys

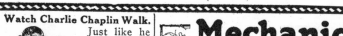

### Watch Charlie Chaplin Walk.

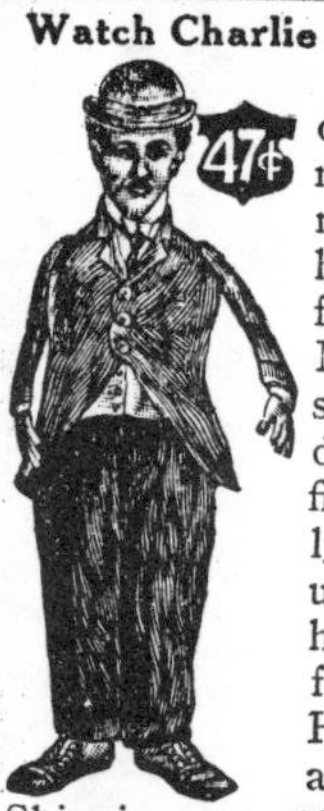


Just like he does in the movies. Very realistic. See him move his funny feet. Made of sheet steel, nicely decorated and finished. Merely wind him up and see how he walks. Fun for the kiddies. Height over all, 8½ inches.
Shipping wt., 1⅜ lbs.
69T5729—Price....... **47c**

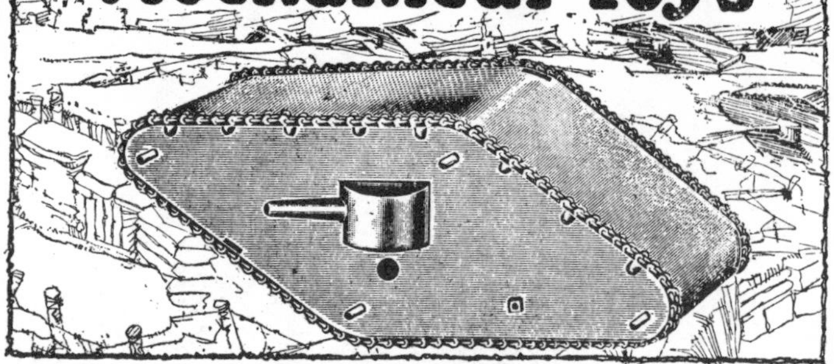

### A Big Mechanical Tank With Chain Caterpillars.

Made of sheet steel finished in battleship gray. Chain caterpillars. Has strong clockwork, which, when wound up, makes the tank crawl along. Runs equally well on either top or bottom. If incline is steep enough to turn tank over on its back, it will start right ahead again toward incline. Size, 14x6½x5 inches. Shipping weight, 3 pounds.
69T5764—Price **$4.47**

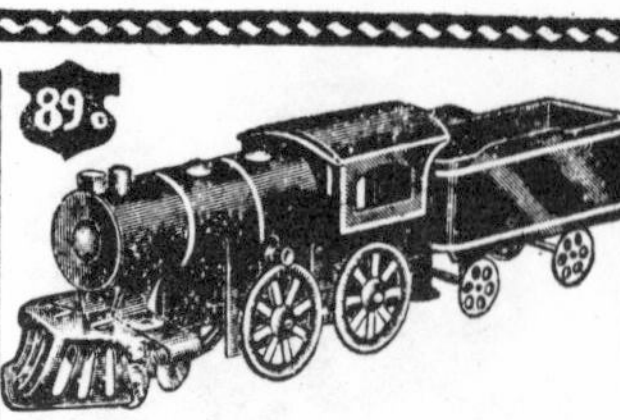


### Friction Locomotive and Tender.

**No springs to break. Propelled by friction.**

Put toy on floor, push forward three or four times, putting pressure directly above friction motor, and it will go ahead when released. Made of sheet steel, brightly enameled and decorated. Has four real wheels and measures, in length, 19 inches over all. Shipping weight, 3 pounds.
69T5719—Price.............. **89c**

### Long Running Automobile Mechanical Toy.

**Forward on upper incline, backward on lower incline, automatically lifted up and starts over again.**

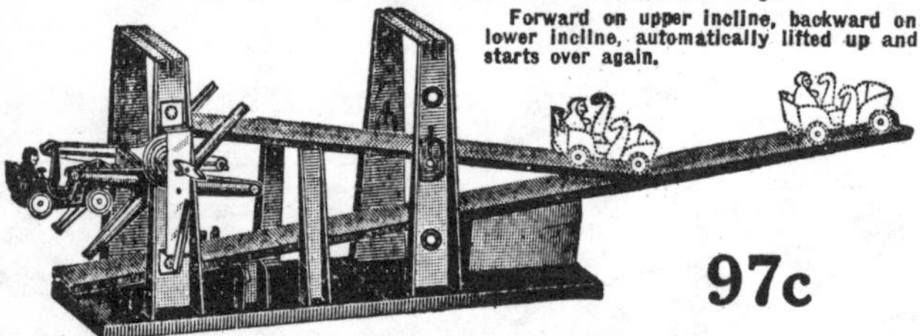

**97c**

Made of sheet steel, nicely decorated. Wind up motor, then place 2¼-inch metal auto on upper track and it will run down incline due to its own weight. After the auto reaches lower end of bottom track the motor will automatically start and, by means of the carrier, will pick the auto up and carry it to upper track. This will be repeated until motor runs down. Size over all, 19½x5¾x3½ inches. Shipping wt., 2⅛ lbs.
69T5765—Price.................................... **97c**

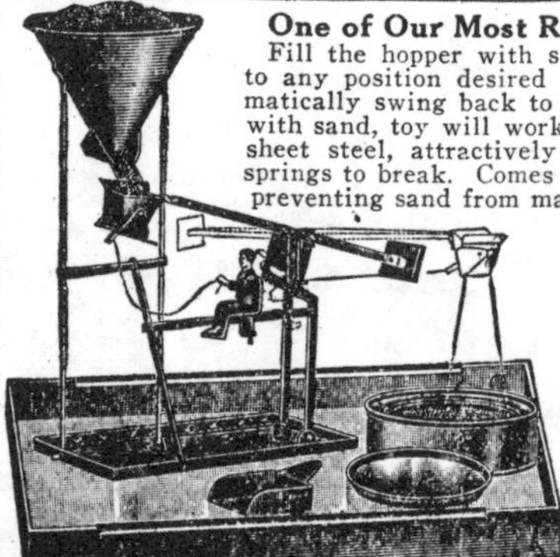

### One of Our Most Remarkable Mechanical Toys.

Fill the hopper with sand, watch the man guide the load to any position desired and see the empty receptacle automatically swing back to be refilled. If hopper is kept filled with sand, toy will work continuously. Made of light gauge sheet steel, attractively painted. Exceedingly simple. No springs to break. Comes in carton which has high sides, thus preventing sand from making a mess. Size, 13¾ inches high, 12 inches wide over all. Shipping weight, 3⅛ pounds.
69T5782—Price........ **$1.19**

### Dumping Sandy.

Interesting toy. Similar in principle to the above, without man and connection. Sand conveyed automatically from hopper to pan in box by means of little dumper. Complete in box with sand, all ready for use. Made of light gauge sheet steel, attractively painted. Simply constructed, not easily gotten out of order. Height, 12¼ inches. Shipping weight, 1¾ pounds.
69T5761—Price............ **69c**

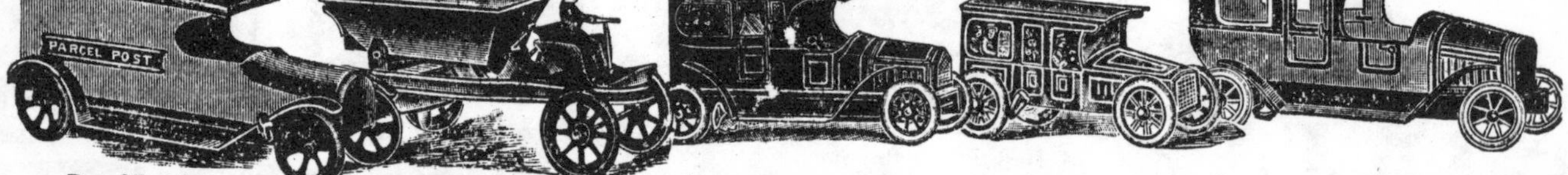


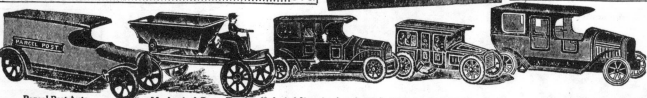

### Parcel Post Auto.

Has good mechanism. Made of light gauge sheet steel, finished in attractive colors. Substantially made. Door in rear opens. Length over all, 12½ inches. Shipping weight, 1¾ pounds.
49T5046—Price ... **$1.00**

### Mechanical Dump Truck.

Made of sheet steel, nicely painted and finished. Has key to wind spring underneath. Has dumping device alongside of seat. Back end piece of dump is removable. Has driver. Size over all, 9x4x3½ in. Shpg. wt., 1½ lbs.
49T5006—Price ..... **89c**

### Mechanical Limousine Auto for 47c.

Made of light weight metal. Size over all, 7¾x3x3¾ inches. Lithographed in several colors. Can be adjusted to run in circle or straight line. Key is fastened to spring, lessening liability of being lost. Shpg. wt., 13 oz.
49T5004—Price ..... **47c**

### Big Value—Mechanical Auto for 23c.

Made of light weight metal, nicely lithographed in several colors. Limousine body with good grade spring. Can be made to run in circle or in straight line. Size over all, 5¾x3¼x2¾ inches. Shipping weight, 13 ounces.
49T5000—Price ..... **23c**

### Our Largest Mechanical Limousine.

Made of light weight metal, lithographed in attractive colors. Size over all, 10½x4x4¾ inches. Has door on each side that can be opened. Will run in circle or straight. Key fastened to spring. Shipping weight, 1¼ pounds.
49T5005—Price ....... **97c**

### Structo Auto Builder.

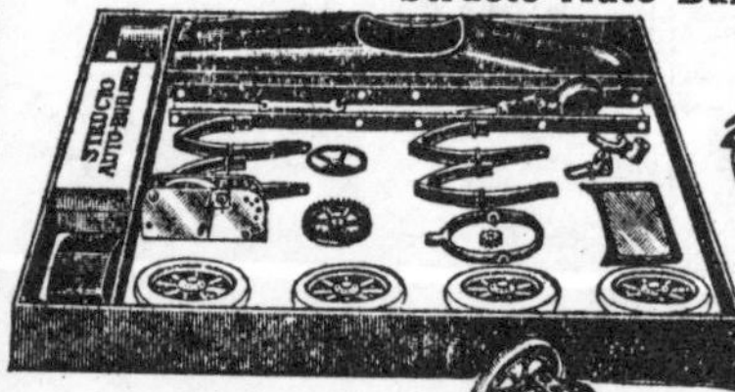


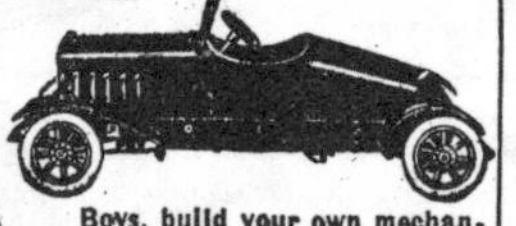

**Boys, build your own mechanical auto!**

A valuable educational toy for the boy. A mechanically accurate toy automobile can be made from this outfit. Outfit consists of necessary parts to build a real toy mechanical automobile. Body made of medium grade sheet steel. Nicely finished. All other parts are made of metal and fit perfectly when they are assembled. Strong wheels 2½ inches in diameter and a strong clockwork motor to run auto. Fender and running board for each side about 1 inch wide. Instructive and very interesting for boys. Something new in the line of construction toys. Complete with small wrench, screwdriver and booklet of instructions for building. Packed in box. 15½x15½x3 inches. Shipping weight, 6¾ pounds.
79T5766¼—Price **$5.98**

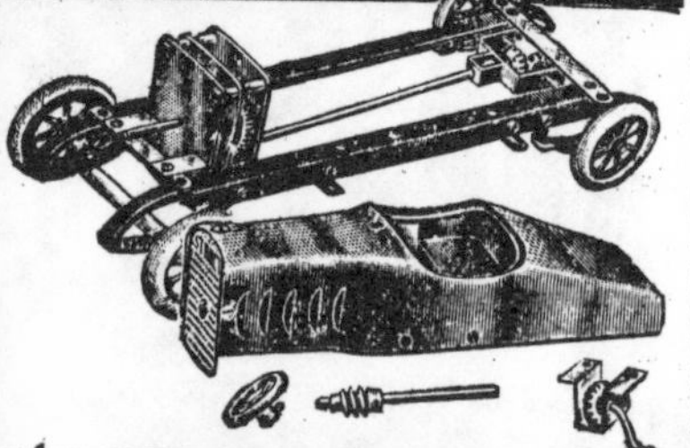

### Sandy Andies. Price, $1.19 and 69 Cents.

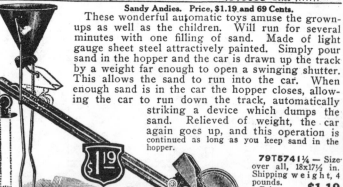

These wonderful automatic toys amuse the grown-ups as well as the children. Will run for several minutes with one filling of sand. Made of light gauge sheet steel attractively painted. Simply pour sand in the hopper and the car is drawn up the track by a weight far enough to open a swinging shutter. This allows the sand to run into the car. When enough sand is in the car the hopper closes, allowing the car to run down the track, automatically striking a device which dumps the sand. Relieved of weight, the car again goes up, and this operation is continued as long as you keep sand in the hopper.

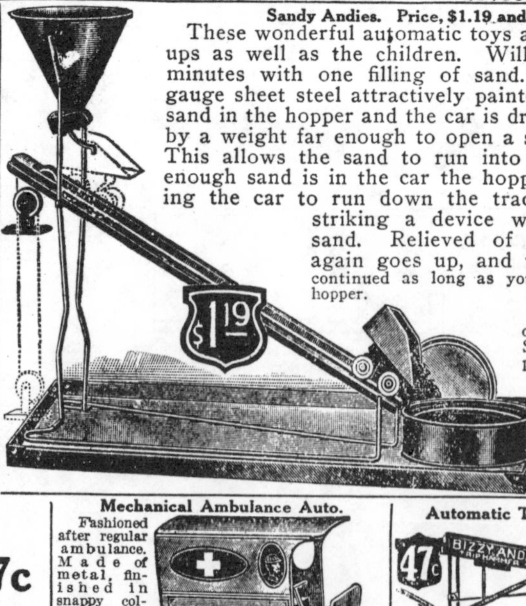


79T5741¼ — Size over all, 18x17½ in. Shipping weight, 4 pounds.
Price....... **$1.19**

69T5742 Size over all, 9¼x10¾ inches. Shipping weight 1¾ lbs.
Price..... **69c**

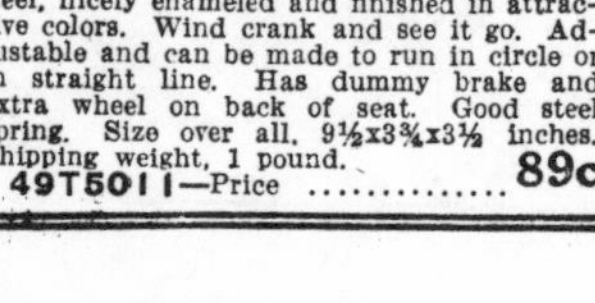

### Real Cranking Roadster.

Mechanical racing roadster, made of sheet steel, nicely enameled and finished in attractive colors. Wind crank and see it go. Adjustable and can be made to run in circle or in straight line. Has dummy brake and extra wheel on back of seat. Good steel spring. Size over all, 9½x3¾x3½ inches. Shipping weight, 1 pound.
49T5011—Price ............. **89c**

### See-Saw.

Small child can operate it. Very simple construction; requires no winding. Figures "teeter-totter" down the pedestal, then turn toy upside down and figures again assume upright position and repeat the performance. Made entirely of metal, nicely painted in bright colors. Height, 14½ in. Shpg. weight, 1 pound.

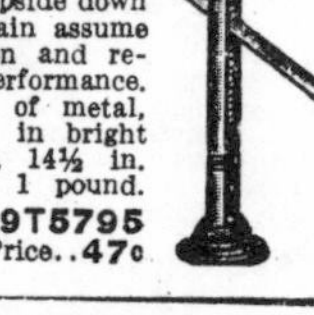

**47c**

69T5795
Price..47c

### Mechanical Ambulance Auto.

Fashioned after regular ambulance. Made of metal, finished in snappy colors. Has crank in front, which winds up spring, which when released drives machine forward.

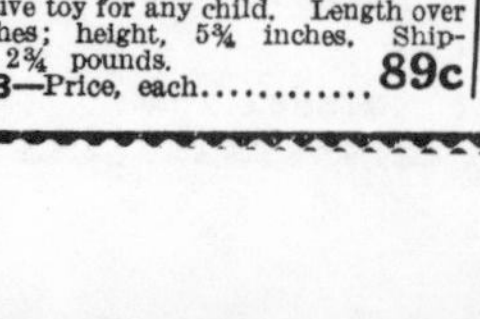


A very attractive toy for any child. Length over all, 8⅝ inches; height, 5¾ inches. Shipping weight, 2¾ pounds.
49T5003—Price, each............ **89c**

### Automatic Toy Triphammer.

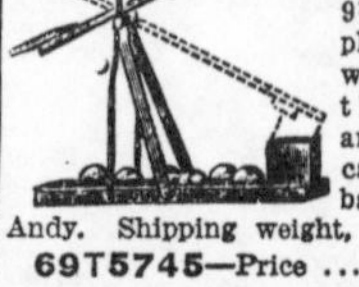


Made of light gauge sheet steel, finished nicely in attractive colors. Size over all, 10¾x9⅛x3¼ in. Complete with marbles, which are put in the upper hopper and are automatically transferred to base of the Bizzy Andy. Shipping weight, 1¼ lbs.
69T5745—Price .............. **47c**

# Mechanical Toys

79c

**See Him Eat.**

This brightly colored metal rooster pecks away at the basin with pecking noise, as though he were eating. Made of metal. Nicely decorated. Clockwork spring. Size over all, 7⅛x2⅜x4⅝. Shpg. wt., 12 oz. 79c
69T5772—Price .............. 

79c

**Long Running Mechanical Toy.**

Runs nearly ten minutes with one winding. Boys teetering back and forth and in circle, passing a celluloid ball from one to the other. A fine toy to keep baby amused. Made of metal. Nicely decorated. Length, 8¼ inches; height, about 5 inches. Shipping weight, 14 ounces.
69T5753—Price .............. 79c

67c

**Polly, the Bareback Rider.**

Rides galloping horse around, as clown imitates cracking the whip. Brightly colored. Made of metal. Height over all, 6 inches; width, 6 inches. Shipping weight, 11 ounces.
69T5754—Price .............. 67c

$1.37

**Bowler Andy Mill.**

Made of sheet steel, nicely painted. Fill upper hopper with large marbles, that are included, and watch the marbles automatically pass down to the bottom. Windmill turns during performance. Height over all, about 21 inches; width, about 9½ inches. Easily set up. Packed in box. Shipping weight, 2¼ pounds.
69T5743—Price .. $1.37

89c

**Cyclone Windmill Pump.**

Fill hopper with sand that is furnished with outfit and then operate pump handle. Sand will run out of spout of pump, imitating flowing water. Has pulley attachment that can be used in connection with a toy motor which will work mill and pump at the same time. Shipping weight, 2⅛ lbs.
69T5744 89c
Price..............

**Panama Pile Driver.**

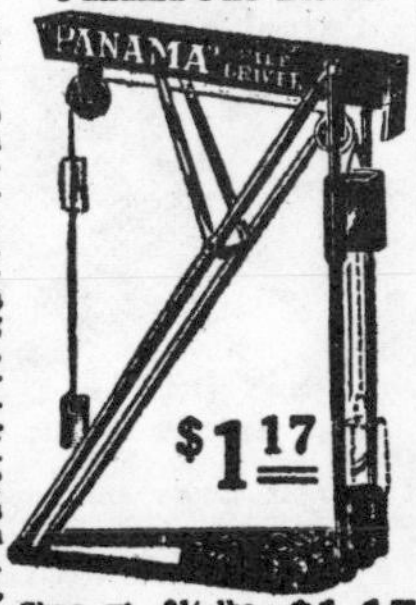


$1.17

When marbles are placed in chute they automatically fall into pile driver which drops and automatically releases marble. The weight, which is attached to a cord running over pulleys, causes it to return and allows another to enter hammer. Made of metal. Comes complete with twelve marbles. Size, set up, 17x12½ inches. Shpg. wt., 2½ lbs.
69T5822—Price.............. $1.17

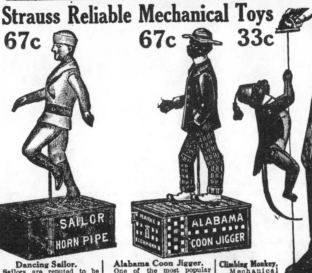

## Strauss Reliable Mechanical Toys

67c

**Dancing Sailor.**

Sailors are reputed to be hornpipe dancers. This sailor, rigged out like a regular navy boy, dances when spring is wound up and then released. Made of metal. It has a device with which the mechanism can be stopped and started again. Shipping weight, 13 ounces.
69T5746
Price.............. 67c

67c

**Alabama Coon Jigger.**

One of the most popular and largest selling mechanical toys. A realistic dancing negro who goes through the movements of a dancer. Very amusing and fascinating. Decorated in natural colors. A good spring. Stops or dances at will. Height, 11 inches. Shipping wt., 13 oz.
69T5730
Price.............. 67c

33c

**Climbing Monkey.**

Mechanical monkey which moves up and down cord. Easy to work. Movable arms and legs. Can be made to stop at any point on cord. Made of metal and finished in natural color. Size of monkey, about 7¾ inches long. Shipping wt., 8 oz.
69T5706—Price.. 33c

67c

**Mechanical Fighters.**

Wind them up and then see them box. Can be started and stopped at will. Fighters made of wood and paper nicely painted. Wooden platform on metal base. Good spring. Size over all, 5½x4x6 inches. Shipping weight, 12 ounces.
69T5760—Price.............. 67c

45c

**Popular Balking Mule.**

One of the best mechanical toys made. With one winding the mule runs forward, backward and in circles. A very clever mechanical toy and one which always pleases a child. Made of sheet steel, attractively painted. Size, 9 inches long. Shpg. wt., 12 oz.
69T5747—Price.............. 45c

45c

**Trick Auto.**

A dandy toy. Clever mechanical auto. With one winding this auto runs forward, backward and in circles. Surely a trick automobile. Made of sheet steel, painted in attractive colors. Size, 7¾ inches long. Shipping weight, 12 ounces.
69T5748—Price.............. 45c

$1.37

**Mechanical Armored Car.**

Made of wood, painted a fighting gray. Good spring. Will run straight or in circles and at the same time imitate gunfire and smoke by puffing talcum powder out of imitation cannon. Size over all, 9x3⅞x5 inches. Shipping weight, 2¼ pounds.
69T5749—Price.............. $1.37

23c

**Kan-U-Katch Game.**

This is not a mechanical toy but another of the famous Strauss toys. Place featherweight transparent ball furnished in wire receiver, release spring at side of handle and see if you can catch it. Great sport for either youngsters or grownups. Develops skill and quickness. Receiver, 12 inches long over all. Shipping weight, 8 ounces.
69T9105—Price.............. 23c

**Walking Man With Cart.**

45c

This is a dandy mechanical toy for the child. Wind it up and see the porter push cart ahead of him. Movable legs. Made of metal, nicely lithographed in attractive colors. Size over all, 6¼x5¾x2¼ inches. Shipping weight, 10 ounces.
69T5759
Price.............. 45c

**Watch Charlie Chaplin Dance.**

33c

Wind up the toy and he will dance. Jointed legs to make dancing more natural. Made of metal. Nicely decorated. Width, 5⅝ in.; height, 7 in.; depth, 1¼ in. Winds with spring. Shpg. wt., 13 ounces.
69T5701
Price, 33c

**Show Clown Beating Drum.**

Standing on a platform cart drawn by horse, a show clown keeps beating a colored metal drum and clapping cymbals, when drawn along floor. Made of metal. Nicely decorated. Come in assorted colors. Measures over all, 10 in. high; 13½ in. long. Shipping weight, 2⅛ pounds.
69T5758 59c
Price..............

59c

**These Clowns Dance.**

59c

One full winding of the spring and these brightly decorated clowns perform a lively dance. Made of metal. Nicely decorated. Size over all: Height, 8¾ in.; width, 7½ in.; depth, 2 in. Shipping weight, 1 lb.
69T5780
Price,
59c

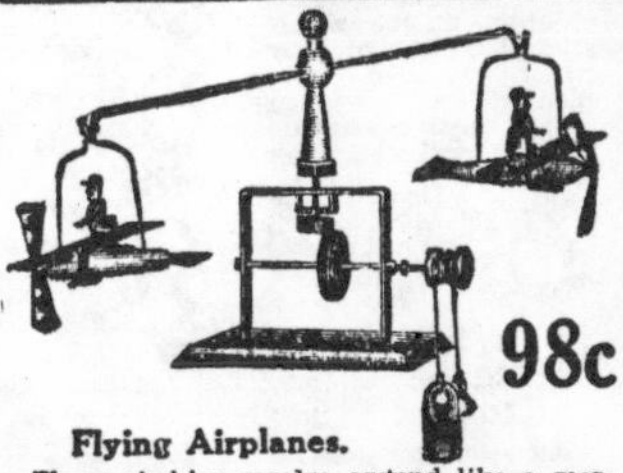

98c

**Flying Airplanes.**

These airships revolve around like a merry-go-round with propellers whirling. Motion caused by slow action of weights over wheel. When heavier weight has gone down as far as it can go, simply raise it. Release it and airplane will go around again. Made of wood and metal. Nicely decorated. Nothing to get out of order. A dandy action toy. Shipping weight, 1¾ pounds.
69T5762
Price.............. 98c

**Boy on Delivery Mechanical Motorcycle.**

47c

Wind the spring and watch him go. Made of metal. Brightly colored. Size, over all: Length, 7 inches; width, 2 inches; height, 4½ inches. Shipping weight, 10 ounces.
69T5755
Price.............. 47c

89c

**A Dandy Roadster for 89 Cents.**

Made of sheet steel, nicely painted. Equipped with good grade mechanism. Winding key under rear of car provides mechanical power. Length over all, 9⅛ inches. Shipping weight, 2⅜ pounds.
69T5713
Price, each.............. 89c

# Floor Toys

## GIBBS' AMERICAN TOYS

### Pacing Bob With Movable Legs.

Horse has lifelike movement when drawn along, legs moving back and forth. A popular and large seller. Horse and two-wheel wagon. Wheels, legs and all moving parts made of metal, balance of wood. Size over all, 13½ inches long, 6½ inches high. Shipping weight, 1⅜ pounds.
49T5455—Price .................... 39c

### The Gray Beauty Pacers.

One of our most popular toys. Horses are lifelike, legs moving back and forth. This toy is well made and durable; will not readily get out of order. Wheels, legs and all moving parts are made of metal, balance of toy is wood. Size over all, 18½x5½ in. Shpg. wt., packed, 2¼ lbs.
79T5454¼—Price .................... 69c

### Jumbo on Platform.

Elephant mounted on platform so it can be drawn around the room. Movable legs and can be made to assume various positions. Wheels, legs and all moving parts made of metal, balance of wood. Size over all, natural position on platform, 10x9¼ inches. Shipping weight, 1¼ pounds.
49T5463—Price .................... 35c

Elephant without platform. Has jointed, movable metal legs. Size over all, natural position, 8¼x7½ inches. Shipping wt., 10 oz.
49T5462—Price .................... 19c

### Galloping Pony in Wheel.

Wheel measures about 12¼ inches in diameter; rim made of wood, painted. Wire spokes. Horse, 7½x5½ inches, and made of wood, nicely colored. When drawn along floor has a galloping motion. Complete with nicely colored metal rider; also a twisted wire handle about 21 inches long. Shipping wt., 1¾ lbs.
49T5456—Price .... 50c

### Metal Butterfly on Wheels.

Made of light sheet steel, lithographed in attractive colors. Wheels of metal, aluminum color. When drawn along floor, wings of butterfly move up and down. With wings expanded butterfly is 9 inches wide. Will please any child. Complete with twisted wire handle about 20 inches long. Shpg. wt., 1⅛ lbs.
49T5459—Price .................... 39c

### Derby Rider.

Nicely colored wooden horse, size, 7½x6¾ inches. Metal wheels, aluminum color. Has colored metal rider attached to horse. When toy is drawn along floor, horse's legs move back and forth in lifelike way. Complete with twisted wire handle, about 22 inches long. Shipping weight, 1¾ pounds.
49T5453—Price .................... 39c

### Fairy Hay Wagon.

Nicely painted. Body of wood, finished in bright color. Metal wheels finished in aluminum color; 24-inch twisted wire handle. Size of wagon over all, 10¼x5½x5¾ inches. Shipping weight, 1¾ pounds.
49T5458—Price .... 39c

## OTHER POPULAR FLOOR TOYS

### This Big Stick Horse Only 47 Cents.

What child does not want a stick horse? We all like horses, so why shouldn't the children have a toy stick horse to play with? Wooden 5½-inch wheels on wooden axle. Horse has handle through head. Size over all, 37½ inches. Shpg. wt., 1¾ lbs.
79T9171¼ Price........ 47c

### Our Popular Horse Line.

$3.45 $2.45 $1.59

The two large horses made of wood, finished in dapple gray color. Strong and substantial. The smallest one made of papier mache, finished in dapple effect. Natural looking eyes, manes and tails, bridle and saddle of imitation leather. Cast iron wheels on two smaller ones; wood wheels on the large one.

79T7617¼ — Size over all, 20x20½ inches. Shipping weight, 9 pounds. Price .... $3.45

79T7618¼—Size over all, 16x16 inches. Shipping weight, 5 pounds. Price .... $2.45

69T7616—Size over all, 11x11¾ inches. Shipping weight, 1⅛ pounds. Price .... $1.59

### Buy Baby a Waddling Goose.

Made entirely of wood, painted to represent a goose. Mounted on wheeled platform. Wheels slightly off center, thereby producing waddling effect. Size over all, 10x10½ in. Shipping weight, 14 ounces.
69T9102 Price.. 25c

### The Popular Cum-Bac Toy.

Cylinder shape, with round metal edges. Roll toy along the floor and it will "Cum Bac" to you. Shipping weight, 6 oz.
Price 69T9123 9c

### Dog on Wheels.

An attractive push or pull toy for small children. Made of steel and good grade wood. Dog is white and spotted. It stands with front feet on revolving wheel in center of the axle and with its hind feet on swinging steel wire fastened to steel frame. Well made and substantial. Length over all, about 46 in. Size of dog over all, 10x15 in. Wheels, 6 in. in diameter. Shpg. wt., 4½ lbs.

79T9172¼—Price .................... $1.19

### Dandy Set for 29 Cents.

Consists of one 8⅛-inch wooden express auto and one two-wheel coal cart with horse. Size over all, about 10 inches. Made of wood with metal wheels. Shipping weight, per set, 14 ounces.
69T7606—Price, per set .... 29c

### Donkey and Real Dump Cart for 35 Cents.

Donkey on wheeled platform attached to dump cart. Length over all, 14 inches. Shipping weight, 1¼ pounds.
69T7609—Price .................... 35c

### Buy These Crawling Bugs.

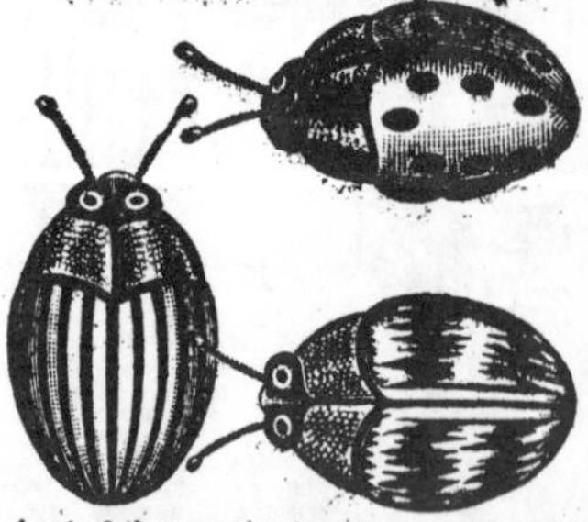

A set of three moving bugs in assorted colors. Made of metal and measure about 2 inches long. Look like real bugs. Press and move backward 2 feet and release. Lots of fun for little money. Shipping wt., 4 oz.
69T9107—Price for 3 bugs...... 39c

### 7⅞-Inch Cast Iron Racer, 21 Cents.

This is a very substantially built car. Attractively finished in colors. Iron man included. Good pull toy, 7⅞ inches long. Shpg. wt., 1¼ lbs.
49T5001—Price .................... 21c

### Milk Wagon With Moving Leg Horses.

Printed in colors. Wheels and horses' legs metal. Length over all, 18¾ in. Complete, with metal milk cans and driver. Shipping weight, 3½ pounds.
79T7620¼—Price .................... $1.39

### Parcel Post Delivery Truck.

15½ Inches Long.

Large size truck. Big value at price. Made of sheet steel, nicely painted. Two rear doors that open. Makes a dandy floor toy. Size over all, 15½x7x7¼ in. Shipping weight, 3¾ pounds.
69T9108—Price .................... $1.19

### Imitation Armored Tanks—Two Sizes.

Men Bob Up and Down—Noisy.

Made of stained wood and light weight sheet metal. Has two wooden imitation cannon on each side and one on the top between the two men. Size over all, 12x6¾x5⅛ in. Shipping weight, 1⅞ pounds.
69T5611—Price .......... $1.19

Similar to above, only has one man. Size over all, 9x5x4⅛ inches. Shipping weight 1 pound.
69T5612—Price .......... 59c

### Dandy See-Saw.

Draw toy along the floor and the animals "teeter-totter" up and down. Made of wood with wire wheels. Attractive to any child. Size over all, 14⅛x9¾x4 inches. Shipping weight, 1¾ lbs.
69T9104—Price .................... 50c

### Milk Wagon and Team for 69 Cents.

Pull toy. Horses and wagon made of wood, painted metal wheels. Size over all, 16½x5⅜x6⅛ inches. Shpg. wt., 2 lbs.
79T7621¼—Price .... 69c

# FRICTION TOYS

These new friction toys are an American invention and very popular. No springs to break. Merely put the toy on the floor, push forward three or four times, putting pressure directly above friction motor, and see it go ahead.

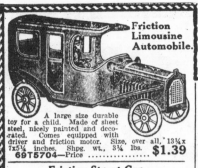

**Friction Limousine Automobile.**

A large size durable toy for a child. Made of sheet steel, nicely painted and decorated. Comes equipped with driver and friction motor. Size, over all, 13¾x7x5¼ inches. Shpg. wt., 3¼ lbs.
69T5704—Price .................. $1.39

**Big Red Engine and Tender.**

Made of sheet steel, brightly enameled, with gilt decorations. Equipped with friction motor. Engine is of the large camel back type, with eight wheels, while tender has four wheels. This is a very fine present for the little boy and one that he will appreciate. Length, over all, about 24 in. Shpg. wt., 6¼ lbs.
79T5708¼—Price, complete .................. $1.39
Similar to above, only engine has four wheels instead of eight and size is smaller. Length, over all, 19 inches. Shipping weight, 3 pounds.
69T5719—Price .................. 89c

**Auto Delivery Wagon.**

Made of sheet steel, nicely painted, finished and decorated. Equipped with friction motor. Has driver at steering wheel. Wagon will run either straight or in a circle. Length, over all, 10½ in. Shpg. wt., 3¼ lbs.
69T5734—Price .................. 89c

**Friction Street Car.**

Doors open and close by lever.

Made of sheet steel, nicely painted and decorated. Equipped with friction motor. A good, substantial toy. Size, over all, 18⅞x6½x4½ inches. Shipping weight, 4¾ pounds.
79T5736¼ Price .................. $1.39

**Friction Power Metal Airplane.** $1.39

Runs along floor. Will not fly. Made of sheet steel attractively painted and decorated. Equipped with friction motor. Can also be used as a pull toy. Length, 17 in.; width, 10¾ in.; height, 6 in. Propeller at the front of machine turns when toy is in motion. Shipping weight, 4¼ pounds.
69T5700—Price .................. $1.39

**Friction Armored Auto.** 59c

Fashioned after a real armored car. Made of sheet steel nicely decorated. Has side fenders, dummy gun and a good friction motor. Size, over all, 7x4½x3½ in. Shpg. wt., 2½ lbs.
69T5710—Price .................. 59c

**Girl and Goose Friction Toy.** 69c

Made of sheet steel, nicely painted, finished and decorated in several colors. When toy is set in motion girl on platform has the appearance of running after the goose. Length, over all, 10½ inches. Shipping weight, 1¾ pounds.
69T5726—Price .................. 69c

89c

**Friction Battleship.**

Every child likes to have a battleship. Attractively decorated and trimmed sheet metal warship. Has four dummy guns. Equipped with a good friction motor. Size, over all, 13x7¼x3⅝ inches. Shipping wt., 2¾ lbs.
69T5739—Price .................. 89c

**Armored Tank With Friction Motor.** $1.39

Made of sheet steel, nicely decorated and trimmed. Has five dummy cannon and imitation caterpillars. Guns can be moved in different directions. Size, over all, 12¼x4¾x6½ inches. Shipping weight, 3½ pounds.
69T5705—Price .................. $1.39

**Auto Delivery Truck.** 89c

Made of sheet steel, nicely painted, decorated and trimmed. Equipped with friction motor. Comes complete with driver and three barrels. Will run either straight or in a circle. Length, over all, 13¼ inches. Shipping weight, 3¼ pounds.
69T5723—Price .................. 89c

**Fire Engine in Bright Colors.** $1.39

Made of sheet steel, nicely painted and decorated. A good friction motor. Complete with two 7-inch sheet steel ladders and two men. Has a dummy bell. Size, over all, 14½x4¾x7 inches. Shipping wt., 4¾ pounds.
69T5711—Price .................. $1.39

**Friction Hook and Ladder Truck.** $1.39

Made of sheet steel, nicely painted in bright colors with gilt and green trimmings. Equipped with friction motor and has two men, two detachable ladders and one attached to form extension ladder. Will run in a circle or straight. Size, over all, 19½x4⅝x7⅞ inches. Shipping wt., 5⅝ pounds.
79T5715¼—Price .................. $1.39

**Roadster With Friction Motor.** 59c

Attractively colored sheet steel friction power roadster. Gilt trimmings. Length, over all, 7 inches. Substantial and well made. Complete with rider. Shipping weight, 3¼ lbs.
69T5709—Price .................. 59c

**Mechanical Delivery Wagon.** 89c

Nicely lithographed delivery wagon. Made of sheet steel and has a good spring which is wound by cranking. Will run straight or in circle. Complete with driver. Size, over all, 7½x4¼x5¾ inches. Shipping weight, 2¾ pounds.
49T5007—Price .................. 89c

## NEW FLOOR TOYS.

**A Dandy Miniature Farm Tractor Outfit.** $4.67

A mechanical miniature tractor which resembles a real farm tractor. Rear wheels are 5 inches in diameter and front are 2⅞ inches. Made of sheet steel and iron, nicely painted. A good clockwork motor with a lever attached to start and stop it at will. Complete with three miniature farm implements—wooden roller, 4¾ inches long, with two metal strips for attaching to tractor; a 5-inch metal disc harrow, and a double plow, size over all, 10x4½ inches, including metal strips for attaching. Size of tractor by itself, over all, 9½ in. long, 5¼ in. wide, 5⅛ in. high. Shpg. wt., 4¼ lbs.
79T5008¼—Price, complete .................. $4.67

**Large Wooden Auto Truck.** 69c

A dandy floor toy. This truck is well made of wood, nicely painted in attractive colors. Has dummy steering wheel. Length, over all, 14 inches; width, 6 inches; height, 6¼ inches. Shipping weight, 1½ lbs.
49T5002—Price .................. 69c

**Our Best Toy Milk Wagon.** Over 2 feet long.

This wagon is made of wood and is nicely painted. Horse is made of papier mache and stands on a wooden platform with cast iron wheels. Horse also has imitation leather harness. Three metal milk cans included. Length, over all, about 26½ inches. Shipping weight, 3¾ pounds.
79T7622¼—Price, complete .................. $2.47

**A Mechanical Truck for 69c.**

Made of sheet steel, nicely finished in attractive colors. Has crank in front which winds spring, making it run. Size, over all, 9x4x3½ inches. Shipping weight, 1¾ pounds.
49T5012—Price .................. 69c

**Large Size Metal Dump Truck.**

About 1½ feet long.

A big value in a floor toy. Also substantially made. Nicely painted in attractive colors. Made of sheet steel. Has a dumping device. Size, over all, 17¾x7x7¼ inches. Well made and finished floor toy. Shipping weight, 5⅝ pounds.
49T5009—Price .................. $1.19

**A Novel Mechanical Limousine Motor Car.**

The mechanism is so constructed that by throwing lever backward and running toy forward a short distance, thus winding the spring, and then drawing lever forward, the toy will run forward a considerable distance. Made of sheet steel, nicely painted and decorated. Size, over all, 13¼x7x5 in. Complete with driver. Shpg. wt., 4¾ lbs.
69T5718—Price .................. $1.39

# Toy

$3.98
For Velocipedes, Hand Cars, Wagons, Automobiles, Etc., See Pages 846 to 850.

**This Complete Outfit Only $3.98.**

Picture the delight of the kiddies over this 32-inch train, beautifully lithographed in colors. Has 7-inch black enamel locomotive, driven by clockwork, with a key, 3⅞-inch tender with imitation coal and three 5⅜-inch cars. Many formations are possible with the eighteen sections of track and cro Tunnel, semaphore and bridge included. Runs forward only. Engine equipped with start and stop device. Shipping weight, about 6⅛ pounds. Engine equipped with start and stop device. Shipping weight, about 6⅛ pounds.
79T5129¼—Price, complete.......... $

$2.98

**This 31-Inch Length Mechanical Train for $2.98.**

Clockwork motor. Three 5⅜-inch cars made of sheet steel, nicely lithographed in colors. Has 7-inch locomotive, made of metal, painted black, and 3⅞-inch tender. Train is about 31 inches long. Has fourteen sections of track and crossover. Engine c stopped and started by device on engine. Train runs forward only. Shipping weight, 5½ pounds.
79T5106¼—Price, complete.......... $

$1.97

**A Fine Quality Strong Spring Train for $1.97.**

Has 6½-inch iron locomotive with clockwork. Engine equipped with piston rod and start and stop device. Has 3⅞-inch tender and two 5⅝-inch Pullman style cars, nicely graphed in colors. Length of train, about 23½ inches. Includes 10 sections of track. Train runs forward only. Shipping weight, 4 pounds.
79T5127¼—Price, complete.......... $

**Straight.**

Length, each, about 10¼ inches. Shipping weight, box, 1 pound.
49T5202—Box of 6 sections.......... 45c

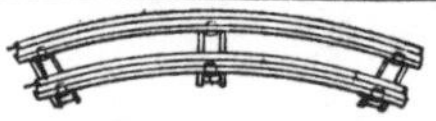

**Curved.**

Length, each, about 10¼ inches. Shipping weight, box, 1 pound.
49T5201—Box of 6 sections.......... 45c

**Crossover.**

Length, 10¼ inches. Shipping weight, 14 ounces.
49T5203—Price, each.. 50c

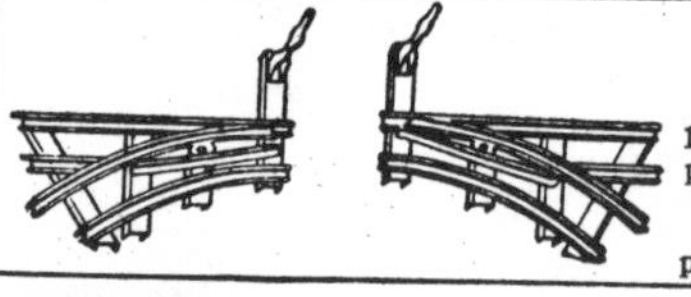

**A Two-Piec versible Sw**

Size, over al 10¼x5½ inches. ping weight, 1 p
49T520
Price, complete.......... $

# Floor Trains

$1.98

**Our Largest Size Pull Train.**

Measures, over all, about 40 inches in length. Has large engine and tender, measuring, over all, about 23½ inches long, 6½ inches high, and a car about 15¼ inches and about 5¾ inches high, with four large size movable wheels. Made of sheet steel painted in attractive colors and trimmed in gilt. The large size, bright red and green trimmed engine has six large movable wheels. Tender large enough to haul small blocks. While of large size, can be easily drawn by small child. Shipping wt., 6¾ lbs.
79T5277¼—Price, complete.......... $1

$1.67

PRR
PRR

**Buy the Boy a Dump Car Train for $1.67.**

This train is made of cast iron, nicely painted in black, with gilt trimmings. Each of two dump cars has an attachment with which contents of cars can be dumped out th bottom. Child can have lots of fun with this train. It measures, over all, about 32 inches in length and will average about 3 inches in height. Easily pulled on floor or side Shipping weight, 7⅛ pounds.
49T5282—Price, complete.......... $1

$1.00

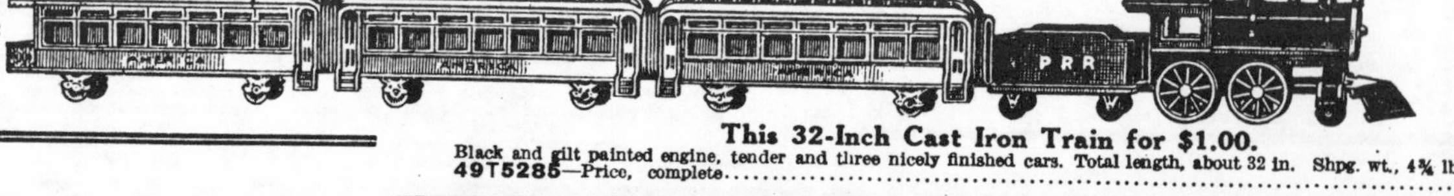
PRR

**This 32-Inch Cast Iron Train for $1.00.**

Black and gilt painted engine, tender and three nicely finished cars. Total length, about 32 in. Shpg. wt., 4¾ lbs.
49T5285—Price, complete.......... $

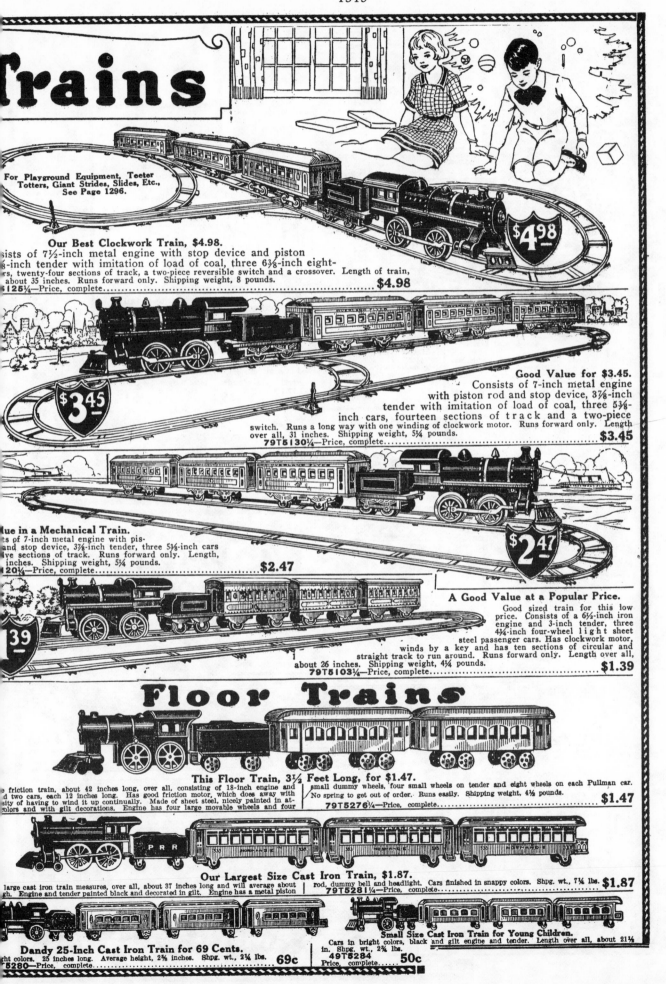

# Trains

**Our Best Clockwork Train, $4.98**

...sists of 7½-inch metal engine with stop device and piston ...8-inch tender with imitation of load of coal, three 6⅜-inch eight- ...rs, twenty-four sections of track, a two-piece reversible switch and a crossover. Length of train, about 35 inches. Runs forward only. Shipping weight, 8 pounds. ...125¼—Price, complete.............................**$4.98**

**Good Value for $3.45.**
Consists of 7-inch metal engine with piston rod and stop device, 3⅞-inch tender with imitation of load of coal, three 5⅜-inch cars, fourteen sections of t r a c k and a two-piece switch. Runs a long way with one winding of clockwork motor. Runs forward only. Length over all, 31 inches. Shipping weight, 5¼ pounds. 79T5130¼—Price, complete.............................**$3.45**

**...lue in a Mechanical Train.**
...s of 7-inch metal engine with pis- ...and stop device, 3⅞-inch tender, three 5⅜-inch cars ...ve sections of track. Runs forward only. Length, ...inches. Shipping weight, 5¼ pounds. ...20¼—Price, complete.............................**$2.47**

**A Good Value at a Popular Price.**
Good sized train for this low price. Consists of a 6½-inch iron engine and 3-inch tender, three 4¼-inch four-wheel light sheet steel passenger cars. Has clockwork motor, winds by a key and has ten sections of circular and straight track to run around. Runs forward only. Length over all, about 26 inches. Shipping weight, 4¼ pounds. 79T5103¼—Price, complete.............................**$1.39**

# Floor Trains

**This Floor Train, 3½ Feet Long, for $1.47.**
...e friction train, about 42 inches long, over all, consisting of 18-inch engine and ...d two cars, each 12 inches long. Has good friction motor, which does away with ...ity of having to wind it up continually. Made of sheet steel, nicely painted in at- ...olors and with gilt decorations. Engine has four large movable wheels and four small dummy wheels, four small wheels on tender and eight wheels on each Pullman car. No spring to get out of order. Runs easily. Shipping weight, 4½ pounds. 79T5276¼—Price, complete.............................**$1.47**

**Our Largest Size Cast Iron Train, $1.87.**
...large cast iron train measures, over all, about 37 inches long and will average about ...gh. Engine and tender painted black and decorated in gilt. Engine has a metal piston rod, dummy bell and headlight. Cars finished in snappy colors. Shpg. wt., 7¼ lbs. 79T5281¼—Price, complete.............................**$1.87**

**Dandy 25-Inch Cast Iron Train for 69 Cents.**
...ght colors. 25 inches long. Average height, 2⅝ inches. Shpg. wt., 2¼ lbs. ...5280—Price, complete.............................**69c**

**Small Size Cast Iron Train for Young Children.**
Cars in bright colors, black and gilt engine and tender. Length over all, about 21½ in. Shpg. wt., 2¾ lbs. 49T5284—Price, complete.............................**50c**

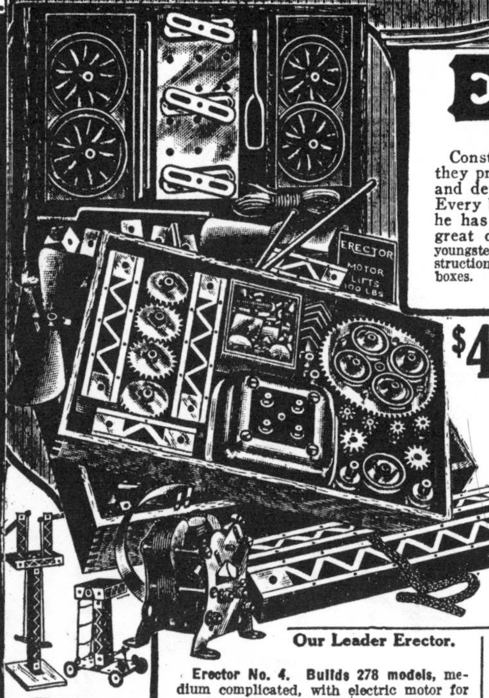

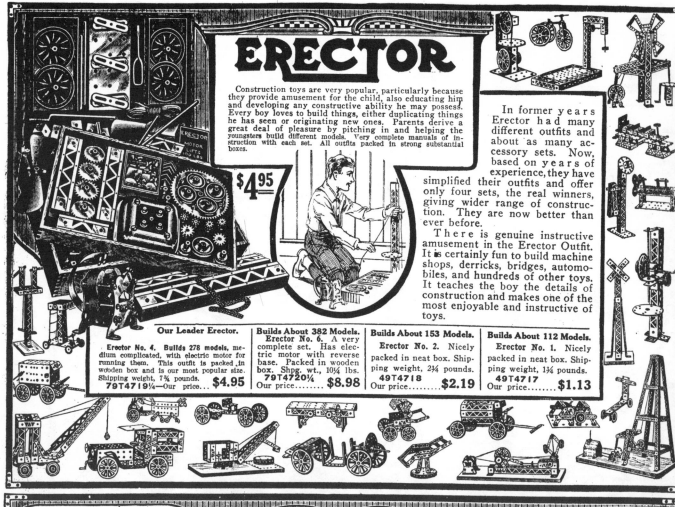

# ERECTOR

Construction toys are very popular, particularly because they provide amusement for the child, also educating him and developing any constructive ability he may possess. Every boy loves to build things, either duplicating things he has seen or originating new ones. Parents derive a great deal of pleasure by pitching in and helping the youngsters build different models. Very complete manuals of instruction with each set. All outfits packed in strong substantial boxes.

$4.95

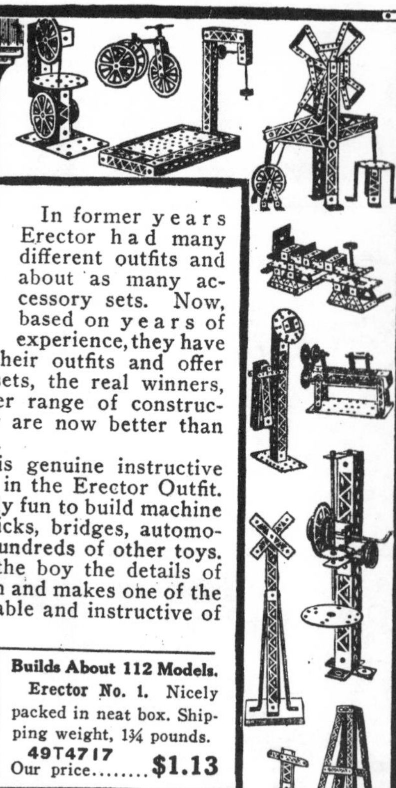

In former years Erector had many different outfits and about as many accessory sets. Now, based on years of experience, they have simplified their outfits and offer only four sets, the real winners, giving wider range of construction. They are now better than ever before.

There is genuine instructive amusement in the Erector Outfit. It is certainly fun to build machine shops, derricks, bridges, automobiles, and hundreds of other toys. It teaches the boy the details of construction and makes one of the most enjoyable and instructive of toys.

**Our Leader Erector.**
Erector No. 4. Builds 278 models, medium complicated, with electric motor for running them. This outfit is packed in wooden box and is our most popular size. Shipping weight, 7¾ pounds.
79T4719¼—Our price... $4.95

**Builds About 382 Models.**
Erector No. 6. A very complete set. Has electric motor with reverse base. Packed in wooden box. Shpg. wt., 10¼ lbs.
79T4720¼
Our price........ $8.98

**Builds About 153 Models.**
Erector No. 2. Nicely packed in neat box. Shipping weight, 2¾ pounds.
49T4718
Our price.........$2.19

**Builds About 112 Models.**
Erector No. 1. Nicely packed in neat box. Shipping weight, 1¾ pounds.
49T4717
Our price........$1.13

# MECCANO

## Toy Engineering for Boys.

You can build hundreds of models like those shown in this picture. They are instructive as well as entertaining, and will produce no end of enjoyment for old and young alike.

Meccano outfits include perforated strips, girders, plates, nuts, bolts, wheels, gears and scores of other parts made of steel or brass.

If you have a small Meccano set you can buy accessory parts to make the set you have equal to a larger one. There is also a set called the "Inventors'" outfit, which contains parts which are desirable no matter what the number of the outfit is that you own.

$4.00

**Meccano No. 00.** Consists of sufficient parts, including perforated strips, wheels, nuts, bolts, etc., to make about 60 simple models. Packed in box 7⅜x11½ inches. Shipping wt., 1½ lbs.
49T4724
Price ........89c

**Meccano No. 0.** Contains enough parts, including rectangular and sector plates to make about 78 models, including bridges, monoplanes, turntables and gangway. Packed in box 13⅝x9½ inches. Shipping weight, 2⅛ lbs.
49T4725
Price ........$1.34

**Meccano No. 1.** Consists of enough parts to build about 105 models. Instruction manual included. Box size, 15⅞x10¾ inches. Shpg. wt., 3½ lbs.
49T4726
Price ...$2.69

**Meccano No. 2.** Will build about 145 models, including rotating cranes, tower wagons, bridges, etc. Packed in box, size 13½x10 in. Shipping wt., 5⅛ pounds.
49T4727
Price...$5.39

**Our Leader Outfit.**
Good set with electric motor. Size of box, 12⅞x9¾ in. Sufficient parts for building about 105 medium complicated models. Motor for running. Shpg. wt., 4⅝ lbs.
49T4721—No. 1X, with motor. Price..............................$4.00

**Meccano No. 2 X, With Motor.**
Contains enough parts to build about 145 interesting models. A set for the child more advanced. Complete with motor, in box size 10x13 in. Shpg. wt., 6½ lbs.
49T4722
Price .........$6.75

**Meccano No. 3 X, With Motor.**
Will build about 190 models, such as shown on edge of this page. Complete with motor in strong box size 13⅜x10⅜ inches. Shpg. wt., 7¾ lbs.
79T4723¼
Price ......$10.79

**Meccano No. 4, With $2.00 Motor.**
Builds about 247 models. The best Meccano we list. Will build any model shown here and many more, depending on the inventive genius of the boy. Comes packed in strong box. Shpg. wt., 10 lbs.
79T4738¼
Price ..............$13.79

## ACCESSORY OUTFITS.

49T4735—No. 00A. Converts a No. 00 into a No. 0 outfit. Shipping weight, 12 ounces. Price........................................45c

49T4731—No. 0A. Converts a No. 0 into a No. 1 outfit. Shipping weight, 1¾ pounds. Price........................................$1.35

49T4732—No. 1A. Converts a No. 1 into a No. 2 outfit. Shipping weight, 2½ pounds. Price........................................$2.70

49T4733—No. 2A. Converts a No. 2 into a No. 3 outfit. Shipping weight, 2½ pounds. Price........................................$2.70

49T4734—No. 3A. Converts a No. 3 into a No. 4 outfit. Shipping weight, 2½ pounds. Price........................................$5.40

49T4736—Inventors' Accessory Outfit. Shipping weight, 2⅛ pounds. Price........................................$2.70

# Gilbert Educational Toys *for the* Older Boy

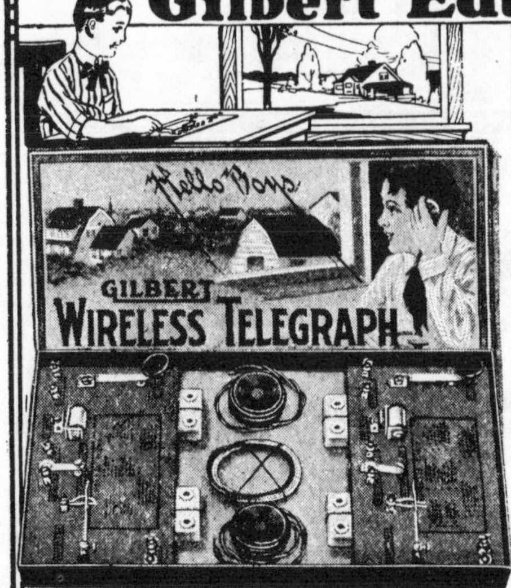


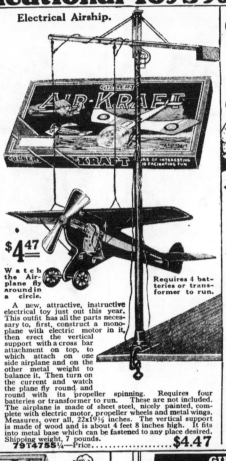

## Wireless Telegraph Outfit, $4.47.

Nearly every boy is interested in the workings of that wonderful invention—wireless telegraphy. We offer here a complete practical working toy set of two stations so that two boys may work together, each having a sending and receiving station in his house. Together they can learn the code and receive education as well as pleasure out of the outfit. Each outfit includes instructions containing complete information concerning the theory of wireless telegraphy, correct wireless apparatus, operation of the Gilbert wireless set and regulations governing wireless. Each station board measures 9¾x5½ inches and has detector, receiving and sending connections, also a wireless code printed right on it. Outfit packed in neat box, 18x10x1¼ in. Shpg. wt., 3¼ lbs.

**79T4751¼**—Price, each........... **$4.47**

## Electrical Airship.

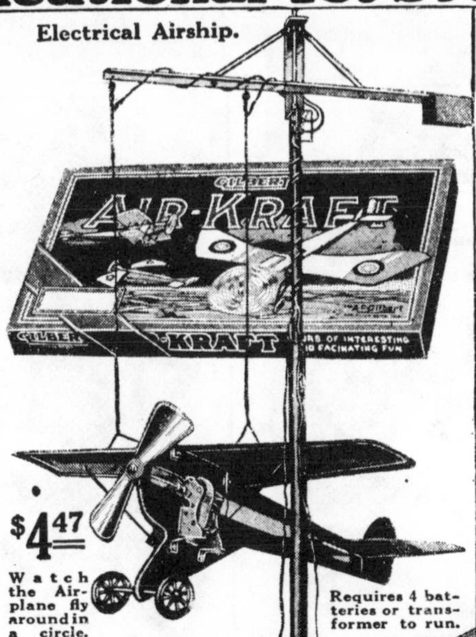


**$4.47**

**Watch the Airplane fly around in a circle.**

**Requires 4 batteries or transformer to run.**

A new, attractive, instructive electrical toy just out this year. This outfit has all the parts necessary to, first, construct a monoplane with electric motor in it, then erect the vertical support with a cross bar attachment on top, to which attach on one side airplane and on the other metal weight to balance it. Then turn on the current and watch the plane fly round and round with its propeller spinning. Requires four batteries or transformer to run. These are not included. The airplane is made of sheet steel, nicely painted, complete with electric motor, propeller wheels and metal wings. Measures, over all, 22x19½ inches. The vertical support is made of wood and is about 4 feet 8 inches high. It fits into metal base which can be fastened to any place desired. Shipping weight, 7 pounds.

**79T4755¼**—Price.............................. **$4.47**

## GILBERT Chemistry Outfits

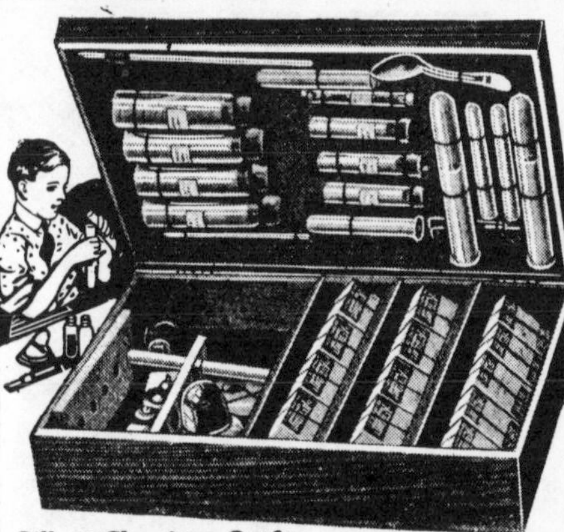

**Gilbert Chemistry Outfits.**

We offer here three chemistry outfits so put up that the elements of chemistry are made plain. An effort is made in the instructions to explain by experiment things a boy or girl sees and uses in everyday life. Many of the experiments are mystifying and startling because of the reactions between chemicals. A program of chemical magic is included among the instructions, the experiments in which are a great source of entertainment at parties or gatherings. No chemicals are used in these sets which are classed as poisonous, neither is there any likelihood of poisonous gases or substances being formed from the mixing of two or more of any of these chemicals. Pleasure here for either child or adult. Instructions are complete and simply compiled, having also many illustrations. Each set includes a copper and zinc plate, also carbon rod to make wet cell.

**Our Largest Set, $4.47.** Consists of 13 boxes and 8 bottles of chemicals, 6 test tubes, 1 rack and other accessories. Packed in wooden box, 13x8¼x3¼ inches. Shpg. wt., 3¾ lbs.
**79T4752¼**
Price. **$4.47**

**Our Medium Priced Set, $3.19.** Consists of 12 boxes and 7 bottles of chemicals, 5 test tubes and other accessories. Packed in cardboard box, 18x10x1¼ in. Shpg. wt., 2⅞ lbs.
**79T4753¼**
Price. **$3.19**

**Our Lowest Priced Set, $1.79.** Consists of 6 boxes and 4 bottles of chemicals, 3 test tubes and other accessories. Packed in cardboard box, 12¼x8¾x1¼ in. Shpg. wt., 1¾ lbs.
**49T4754**
Price. **$1.79**

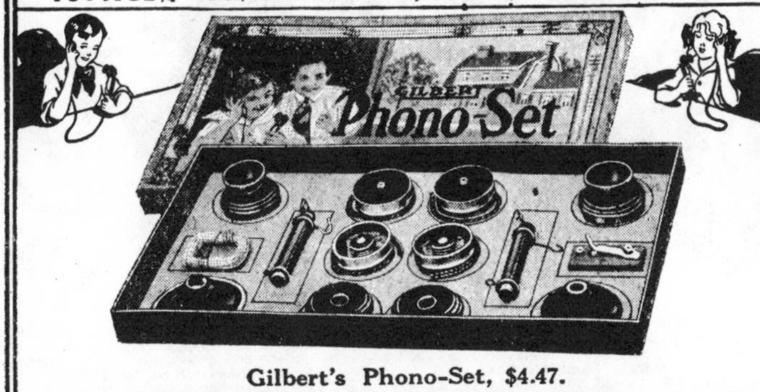


## Gilbert's Phono-Set, $4.47.

A miniature telephone outfit, yet practical for operation at distance covered by wire included and even greater distances if properly relayed. This set consists of all the parts necessary to assemble two complete working model desk telephones, together with about 50 feet of wire for a short line and a switch for shutting off the battery current when the outfit is not in use. It is fashioned after regular phones, and after absorbing the theoretical and practical explanations given in the simply worded instructions, a boy has a good idea of just how the telephone system is built up and how it operates. A special effort has been made to make the entire instructions simple enough for a boy to easily understand. The outfit is packed in box 18x10x1¼ inches. Shpg. wt., 2½ lbs.

**79T4756¼**—Price.............................. **$4.47**

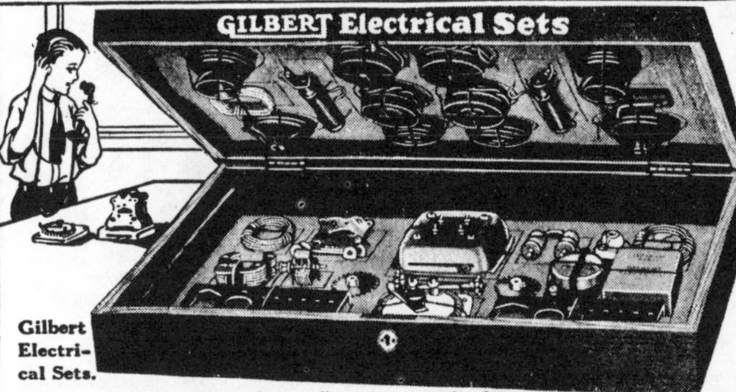


**Gilbert Electrical Sets.**

These electrical experimental sets offer an opportunity for a boy to learn elementary electricity. Book of instructions gives experiments to try.

**Our Largest Set for $8.98.** In strong wooden box, 20¼x12⅛x3¼ inches. Consists of parts to construct two desk telephones and an electric motor with reverse base. Has a galvanometer, rheostat and complete gear box. Reverse base, 4x4 inches. Shipping weight, 9¼ lbs.
**79T4758¼**—Price, each... **$8.98**

**Our Medium Priced Set for $4.47.** Consists of all parts necessary to construct an electric motor with reverse base. Has a rheostat, galvanometer and gear box. Packed in neat cardboard box. Reverse base is 4x4 inches. Gear box sides are 5¾ inches high. Shpg. wt., 3¼ lbs.
**79T4757¼**—Price, each... **$4.47**

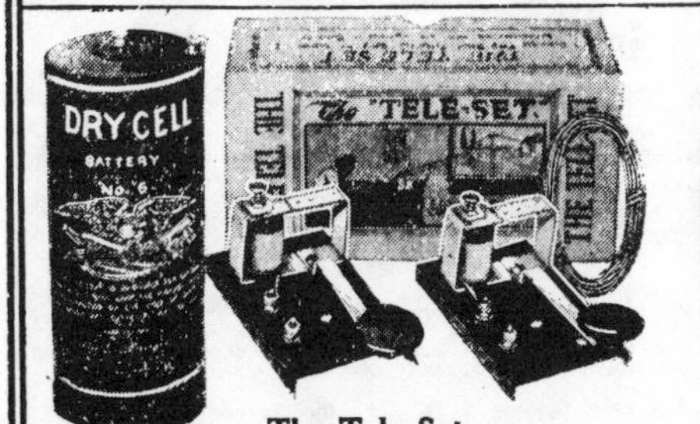


## The Tele-Set.

Boys, you surely want one of these outfits. All boys like to send messages to their friends.

**Complete Two-Station Telegraph Outfit for the Learner.** Outfit consists of two complete telegraph sets with two telegraph instruments, about 50 feet of wire, one dry cell battery, code chart and miniature telegraph blanks. The instruments are well made, have nicely polished sounding levers mounted on a metal base, 3½x2¼ inches. The stations may be set up in different houses or wherever desired. Complete instructions, clear and easy to follow, are included with each set. A fine gift for a boy. Shpg wt., about 3¾ lbs.

Complete Two-Station Telegraph Set with 1 dry cell and about 50 feet insulated copper wire and full directions.
**49T4762**
Price, with battery......................... **$1.50**

## GILBERT ERECTOR

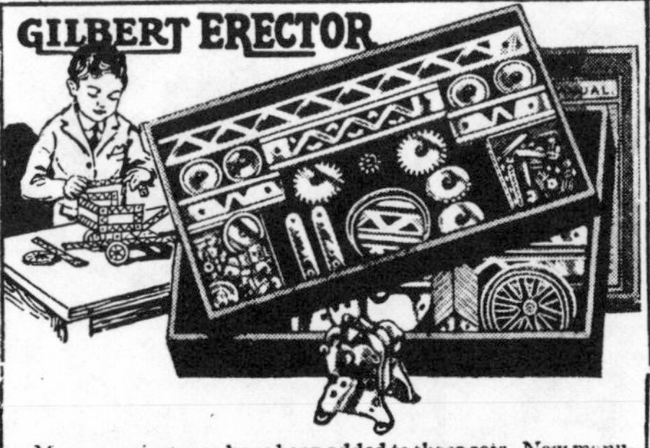

Many new features have been added to these sets. New manuals have been built up. Different new parts have been added.

**No. 4 Erector.** Builds about 278 models. Has electric motor and packed in wooden box, 13x9x3 inches. Shipping weight, 7¾ lbs.
**79T4719¼**
Price............ **$4.95**

**No. 2 Erector.** Builds 153 models. Shpg. wt., 2¾ lbs.
**49T4718**
Price........... **$2.19**

**No. 1 Erector.** Builds abt. 112 models. Shpg. wt., about 1⅞ pounds.
**49T4717**
Price............ **$1.13**

**No. 6 Erector.** Includes reversible motor. Builds abt. 382 models. Shpg. wt., 10¼ lbs.
**79T4720¼**
Price........... **$8.98**

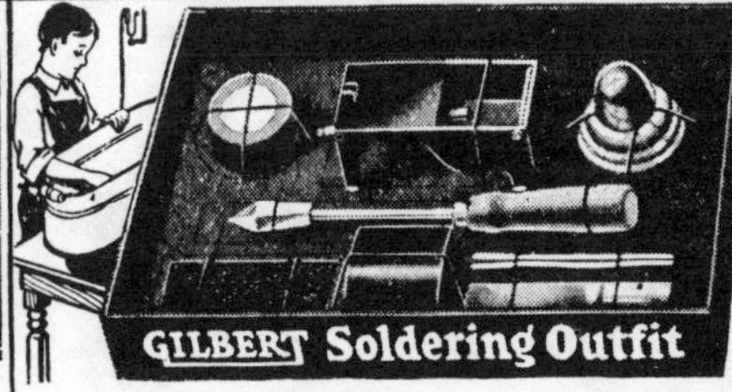


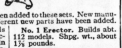

## Gilbert Soldering Outfit, $2.19.

This is a practical outfit for the handy boy about the home. Every boy likes to tinker and mend as well as to construct new things. Everything necessary to mend pots, kettles, pans, etc., included in the set, such as furnace which can be attached to gas, solder, solder paste, sandpaper, oil burner and 8½-inch soldering iron. Complete instructions come with each set. Packed in neat carton. Shipping weight, 2⅜ pounds.

**49T4763**—Price.............................. **$2.19**

# Every Boy Wants a Toy Tool Chest

These are medium grade tools, especially suitable for the boy, as they are the right size to fit his hand and his strength. Every schoolboy will be pleased with one of these sets, to have as his own to work with as he pleases. Their use aids in broadening his mind and teaches him the value of doing things for himself. He can make small pieces of furniture, such as book racks, stools, tables, etc. Buy your boy one and see how delighted he will be. Remember, these are not men's size high grade tools, but a lower priced quality in smaller sizes suitable for boys.

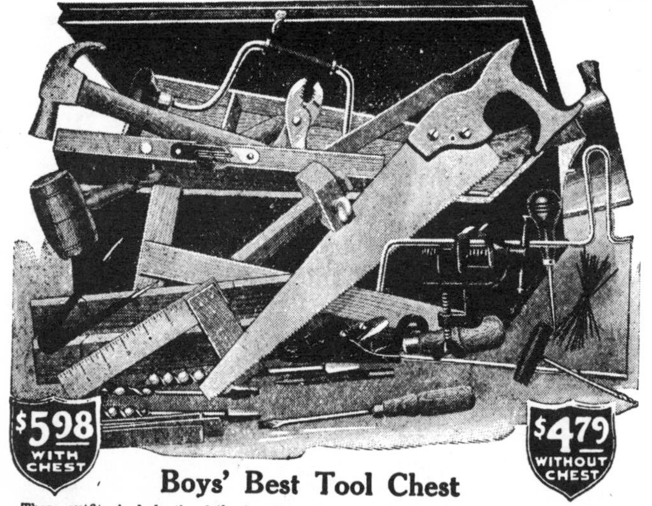


## Boys' Best Tool Chest

These outfits include the following 25 tools: 15-inch steel blade tempered saw, 6⅛-inch metal plane, 2-ft. folding rule, 10-oz. hammer, good grade try square, good grade wooden mallet, brace, three good grade assorted size steel bits, chisel, screwdriver, 12-in. plumb and level, 8½-in. wood gauge, nail punch, good grade 10-in. wood miter box, gimlet, coping saw with 13 blades, iron vise, nickel plated hatchet, awl, metal divider, pliers, 14¼-in. good grade T square and file

**Above Tools in Chest for $5.98.**

**79T7425¼**—25 tools and 12 coping saw blades in good mission finished hinged covered hardwood chest; size, over all, 21½x9¼x6⅛ inches. Shipping weight, 15¼ lbs. Price........ **$5.98**

**Above Tools Without Chest for $4.79.**

**79T7426¼**—25 tools and 12 coping saw blades without chest so boy can build his own chest. Packed in good shipping box. Shipping weight, 9¾ pounds. Price........ **$4.79**

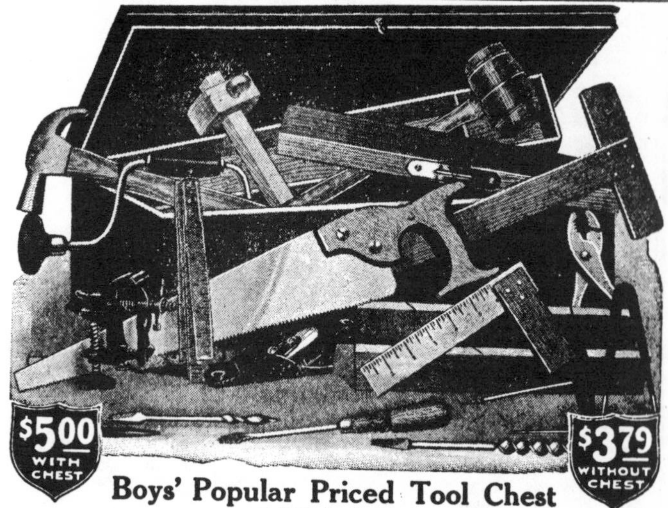


## Boys' Popular Priced Tool Chest

**21 Tools for the Boy.**

Tools include 15-inch blade tempered saw, 10-oz. hammer, 6⅛-inch metal plane, handled screwdriver, brace, 2 good grade bits, 2-foot folding rule, chisel, nail punch, gimlet, good grade wooden mallet, good grade try square, 8½-in. wood gauge, 11⅞-in. level, metal divider, good grade 10-inch miter box, pliers, awl, good grade 14¼-inch T square and metal vise.

**Tools in Chest for $5.00.**

**79T7427¼**—21 tools above in mission finished hinged covered hardwood chest; size, over all, about 21½x9¼x6⅛ inches. Shipping weight, 13 pounds. Price, special at........ **$5.00**

**Tools Without Chest for $3.79.**

**79T7428¼**—21 tools above without chest. Packed for shipment. Shipping weight, 7¾ pounds. Price........ **$3.79**

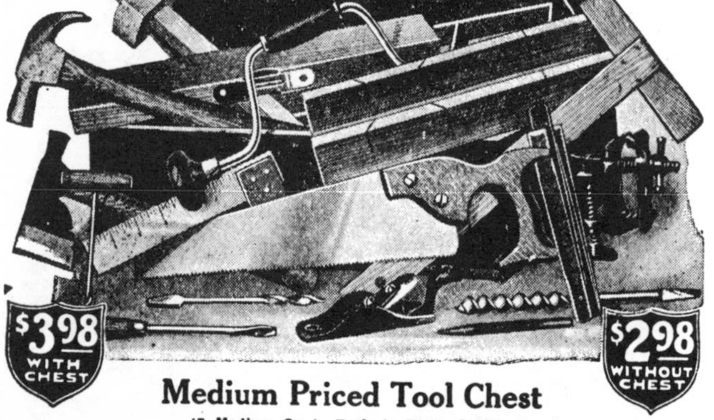


## Medium Priced Tool Chest

**17 Medium Grade Tools in These Outfits.**

Tools include 12-inch blade tempered saw, 10-oz. hammer, 6⅛-inch metal plane, brace, two good grade bits, screwdriver, 2-foot folding rule, good grade 14¼-inch T square, 8½-inch wood gauge, 11⅞-inch level, 2⅞-inch blade hatchet, nail punch, gimlet, good grade try square, good grade 10-inch wood miter box and metal vise.

**Tools in Chest for $3.98.**

**79T7429¼**—17 tools above in mission finish hinged cover hardwood chest, size, over all, about 16½x8⅞x6 inches. Shipping weight, 10½ pounds. Price........ **$3.98**

**Tools Without Chest for $2.98.**

**79T7430¼**—Same 17 tools as above, without chest. Carefully packed for shipment. Shipping weight, 6 pounds. Price........ **$2.98**

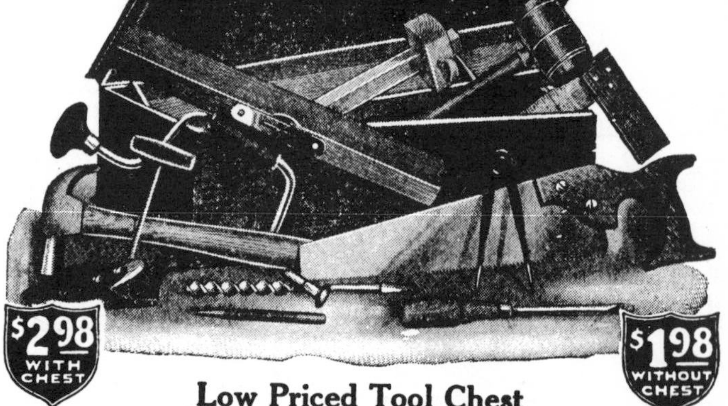


## Low Priced Tool Chest

**13 Tools for the Boy to Make Things.**

A big value in tool chests. Tools include 12-inch blade tempered saw, 10-oz. hammer, 6⅛-inch metal plane, screwdriver, brace, good grade bit, 8½-in. wood gauge, 11⅞-in. wood level, gimlet, nail punch, metal divider, good grade try square and good grade wooden mallet.

**Tools in Chest for $2.98.**

**79T7431¼**—13 tools above in mission finish hardwood chest, size, over all, 16½x8⅞x6 inches. Shipping wt., 9¼ lbs. Price........ **$2.98**

**Tools Without Chest for $1.98.**

**79T7432¼**—Same 13 tools above, without chest. Carefully packed for shipment. Shipping weight, 4½ pounds. Price........ **$1.98**

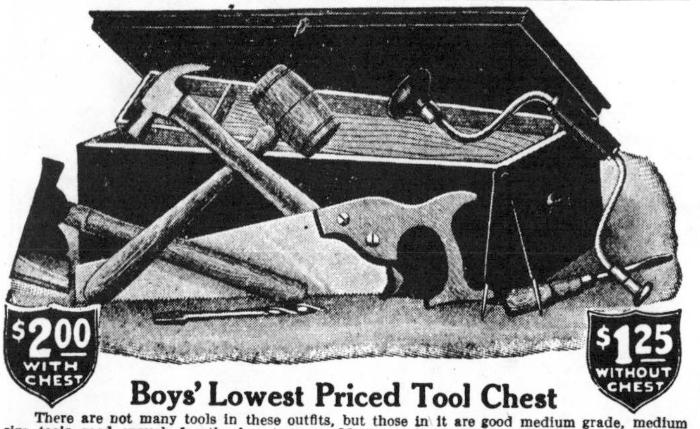


## Boys' Lowest Priced Tool Chest

There are not many tools in these outfits, but those in it are good medium grade, medium size tools good enough for the boy to use. Must not be confused with the very small size tools sometimes sold in cheap toy tool chests. Includes 12-inch blade medium grade steel saw, 7-oz hammer, 8-in. screwdriver, good brace, good grade bit, hatchet 10⅝ inches long over all, metal divider and good grade wood mallet.

**Tools in Chest for $2.00.**

**79T7433¼**—8 tools above, in mission finish hardwood chest. Size, over all, about 16½x8⅞x6 inches. Shipping weight, 7¾ lbs. Price........ **$2.00**

**Tools Without Chest for $1.25.**

**79T7434¼**—Same 8 tools above without a chest. Carefully packed for shipment. Shipping weight, 3¼ pounds. Price........ **$1.25**

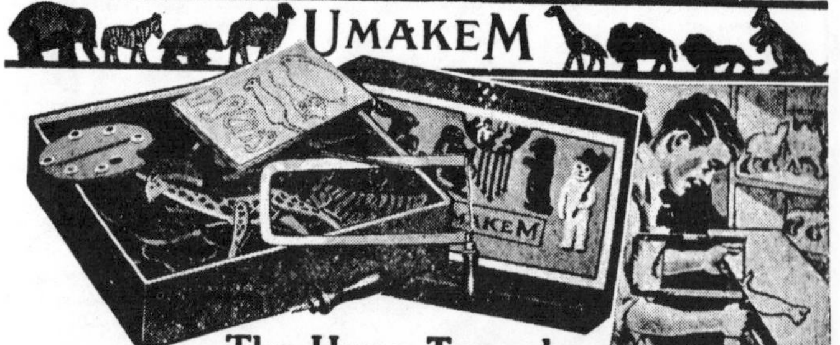


## The Home Toymaker

Make toys for yourself, for brother and sister. Umakem presents a simple, complete and ready means of producing many toys, quickly cut out, easily assembled, strong and substantial. We list three sets.

**Our 87-Cent Set.**

Steel scroll saw frame, 10x3⅜ inches, seven 5-inch saw blades, design sheets, cotter pins, crayons and three-ply veneer boards for making eighteen toys. Packed in box. Makers set No. 2. Shipping wt., 4¼ pounds.

**49T3841** Price........ **87c**

**Advanced Set for $1.79.**

Steel saw frame 10x3⅜ inches, thirteen saw blades, 5-inch awl, 24 cotter pins and a large number of washers. Palette about 7 inches long with six water colors and brush. Three-ply veneer boards and design sheets for making about twelve jointed animals. Packed in box. Makers set No 4. Shipping wt., 5 lbs.

**49T3842**—Price **$1.79**

**Our Largest Set for $2.79.**

Steel scrool saw frame, 10x3⅜ inches, thirteen saw blades, 5-inch awl, design sheets, 7-inch palette, six water colors, brush, sandpaper, 24 cotter pins, washers, brads, and necessary tools and wood to make a great number of jointed animals and figures. Makers set No. 6. Shipping weight, 6 lbs.

**79T3843¼** Price........ **$2.79**

# Balls, Tops, Marbles and Kites

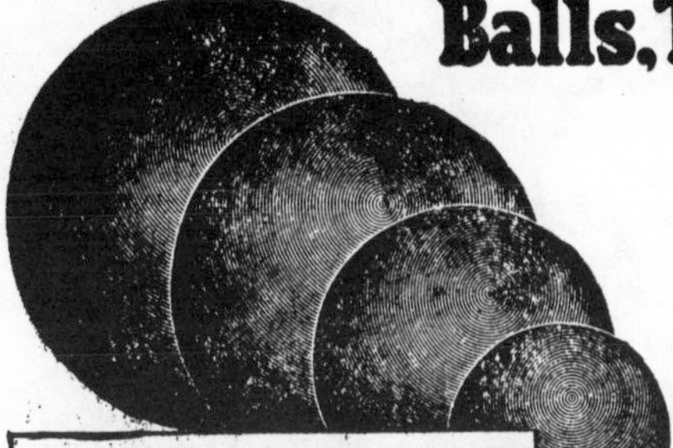

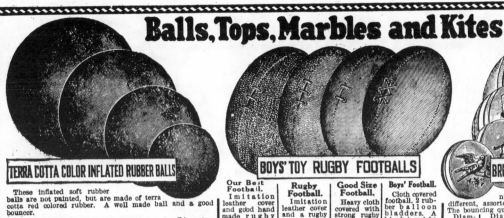

## TERRA COTTA COLOR INFLATED RUBBER BALLS

These inflated soft rubber balls are not painted, but are made of terra cotta red colored rubber. A well made ball and a good bouncer.

- Diameter, 5 inches. Shpg. wt., 1 lb. 69T7702 Price...57c
- Diameter, 4¼ in. Shpg. wt., 14 oz. 69T7703 Price...35c
- Diameter, 3½ in. Shpg. wt., 13 oz. 69T7707 Price...25c
- Diameter, 2½ in. Shpg. wt., 7 oz. 69T7713 Price...15c

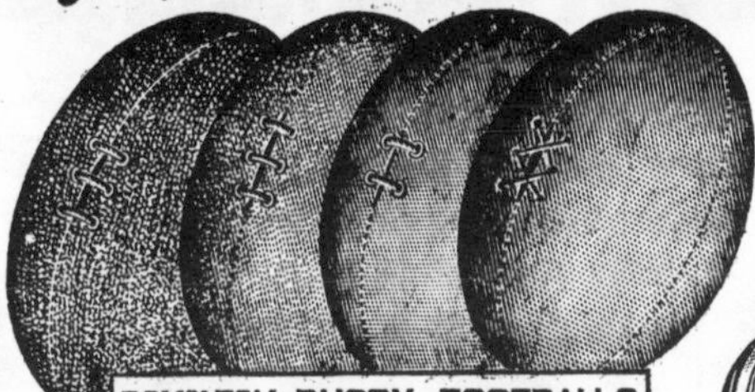

## BOYS' TOY RUGBY FOOTBALLS

**Our Best Football.** Imitation leather cover and good hand made rugby shaped rubber bladder. Size, inflated, about 19x24 inches in circumference. It pays to buy the best. Shpg. wt., 6 ounces. 69T7717 Price ....97c

**Rugby Football.** Imitation leather cover and a rugby shaped rubber bladder. Size, inflated, about 22x17 inches in circumference. Shpg. wt., each, 4 oz. 69T7709 Price....75c

**Good Size Football.** Heavy cloth covered with strong rugby shape rubber bladder. Size, inflated, about 20x16 inches in circumference. Shpg. wt., 4 ounces. 69T7718 Price....47c

**Boys' Football.** Cloth covered football. 2 rubber balloon bladders. A light weight ball for the small child. Size, inflated, about 20x16 in. in circumference. Shipping weight, 3 oz. 69T7710 Price......25c

For Regulation Footballs See Page 1292.

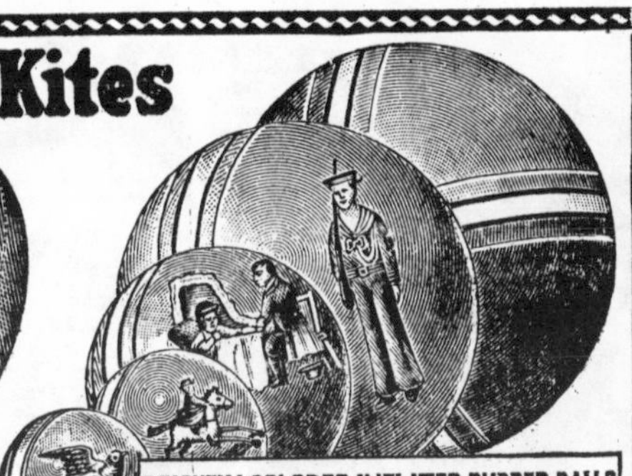

## BRIGHTLY COLORED INFLATED RUBBER BALLS

These soft, hollow rubber balls are nicely colored in assorted designs. Every ball different, assorted decorations. The colors will not rub off. The bouncing qualities are all that could be asked.

- Diameter, 2¼ in. Shpg. wt., 2 oz. 69T7704 Price, 13c
- Diameter, 3½ in. Shpg. wt., 7 oz. 69T7705 Price, 25c
- Diameter, 4½ inches. Shpg. wt., 8 ounces. 69T7706 Price.45c
- Diameter, 5 inches. Shpg. weight, 1 lb. 69T7731 Price...59c
- Diameter, 5½ in. Shpg. wt., 1 lb. 69T7730 Price...79c

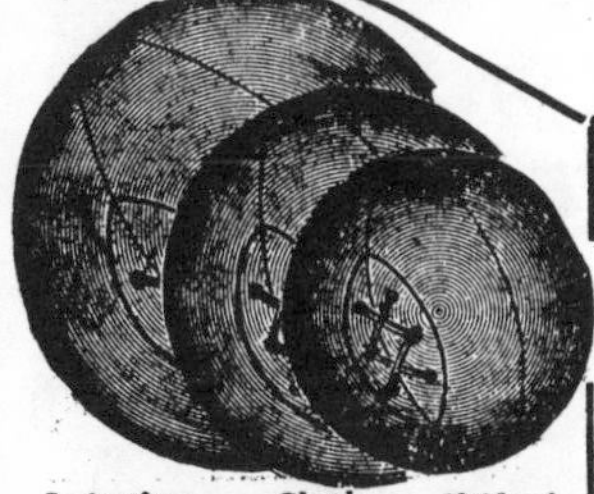

**Imitation Leather Play Ball.** Good quality imitation leather cover with strong rubber bladder. Size, inflated, about 8 in. in diameter. Shpg. wt., 6 oz. 69T7738 Price ...97c

**Cloth Covered Play Ball.** Strong, cloth cover with shaped rubber bladder. 7 inches in diameter. Shpg. wt., 4 oz. 69T7737 Price.47c

**Children's Play Ball.** Cloth covered rubber balloon bladder. Size, inflated, abt. 6 in. diameter. Shpg. wt., 3 oz. 69T7735 Price.25c

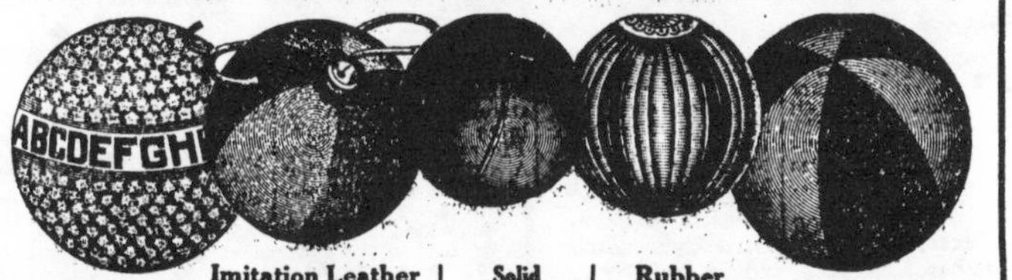


**3½-Inch Rubber ABC Ball.** Gray inflated rubber. Alphabet in raised nicely painted letters around center. Diameter, 3½ inches. Shipping wt., 5 oz. 69T7714 Price ........22c

**Imitation Leather Return Ball.** Diameter, 3 inches. Lots of fun for the kiddies. When the ball is thrown into the air, rubber elastic should be fastened on finger, which will make it return to thrower. Shpg. wt., 2 ounces. 69T7701 Price ................13c

**Solid Rubber Ball.** Every child will enjoy this 2-inch diameter solid rubber ball. A good bouncer. Shpg. wt., 5 ounces. 69T7708 Price...13c

**Rubber Whistle Ball.** Corrugated rubber ball. Decorated in several colors. Well made and finished. Whistle in end. Diameter, 2¼ in. Shpg. wt., 4 oz. 69T7724 Price.....13c

**Felt Covered Cork Filled Ball.** Specially adapted for indoors. Ball is cork filled, with felt covering, making it very light in weight. Well made and finished. 3½ in. in diameter. Shpg. wt., 6 oz. 69T7721 Price ..............15c

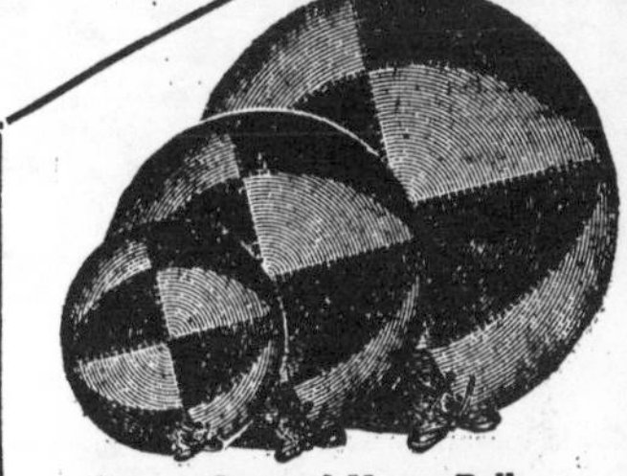

**Sateen Covered House Balls.** Cover made of assorted colors of sateen. Rubber balloon bladder. Light and strong. Just the thing for indoor play. Ball is well made and sewing on cover neat. Average shipping wt., 2 oz.

- 69T7711—Diameter, 9 inches. Price ................ 29c
- 69T7712—Diameter, 7 inches. Price ................ 23c
- 69T7700—Diameter, 5 inches. Price ................ 17c

**A Leader Novelty Top.** 25c

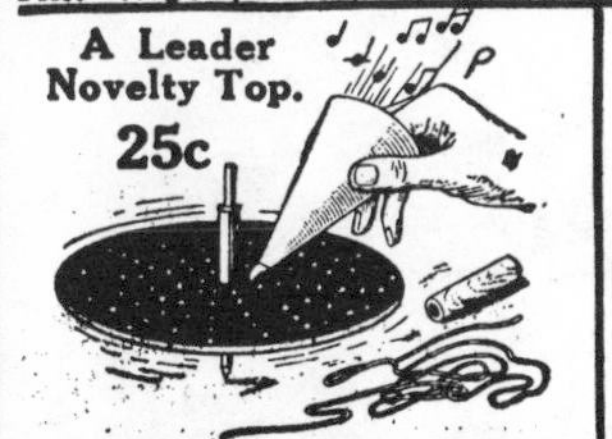

A musical spinning top. Upper surface of top has a series of notes, the lowest note being nearest spindle. Hold flat surface of tip of paper cone against the projections on the top, keeping the cone at an angle so the small end points in direction of rotation of top. Extra cones can be made from any fairly stiff paper. Diameter, 3½ inches. Packed in box, complete with directions and paper cone, together with paint and colored discs for rainbow effects. Shpg. wt., 8 oz. 69T7762—Price ................25c

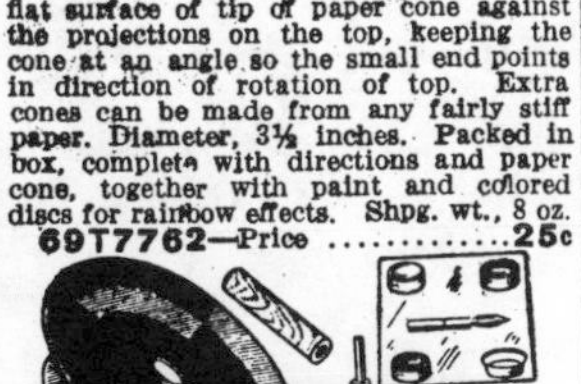

## THE WONDERFUL GYROSCOPE TOP.

**The So Called Trick Top Because It Spins in So Many Different Ways and Assumes Such Wonderful Positions Impossible With Any Other Style Top.**

19c

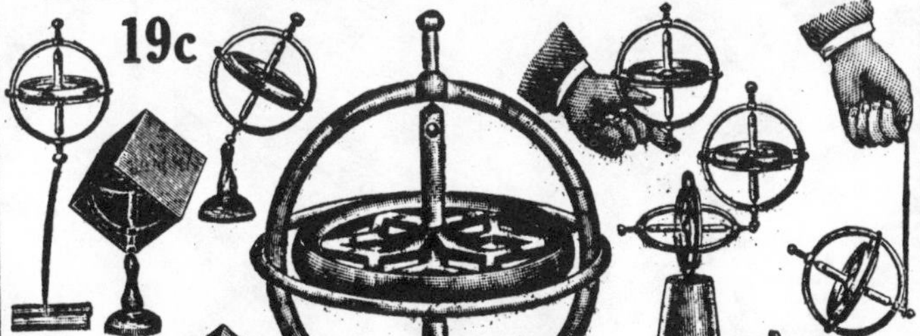

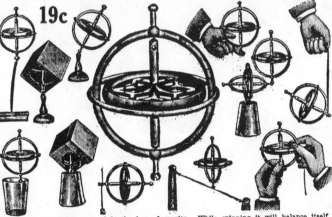

A top that appears to defy the law of gravity. While spinning it will balance itself upon one end and surprise you by standing in that position until it runs down. The bearings on either end of the axis are well made and the top, when properly spun with the string as furnished, runs at least six minutes without stopping. The above illustration shows a few of the experiments that can be performed with one or more of these tops. Full directions with each top. Shipping weight, 8 ounces. 19c

69T7760—Price ................

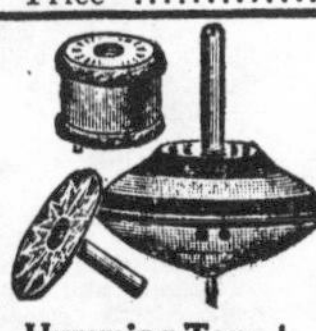

**Humming Top.** Has whirlabout and colored discs. Made of metal, nicely painted. Automatic spinner. Diameter, 3 inches. Shipping wt., 4 oz. 69T7766 Price ........14c

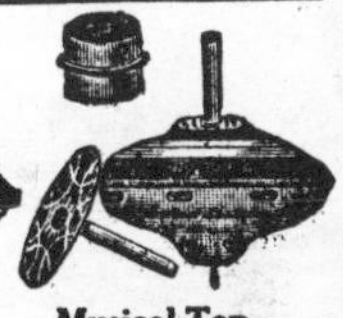

**Musical Top.** Large size top with paper whirlabout attachments and colored discs. Automatic spinner. Nicely decorated in light colors. Makes humming sound when spinning. Diameter, 4 inches. Shpg. wt., 9 oz. 69T7768 Price ................35c

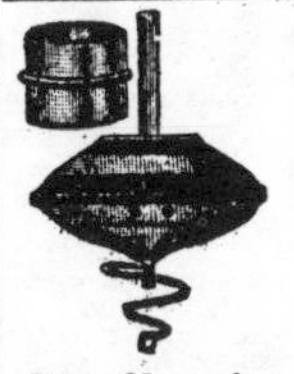

**Dixie Humming and Jumping Top.** Made of metal. Diameter, 3 inches. Shipping wt., 7 oz. 69T7769 Price ........14c

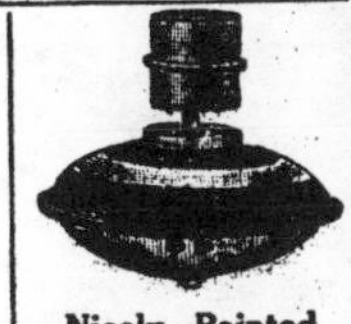

**Nicely Painted Humming Top.** Made of metal. Hums while spinning. Diameter, 3½ inches. Ball point. Shpg. wt., 5 oz. 69T7774 Price ........14c

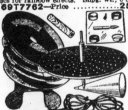

## KITES.

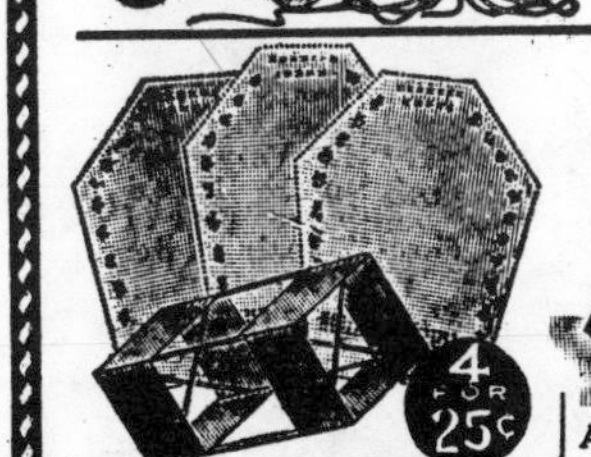


**Four Kites for 25 Cents.** Boys, make your own kites. Enough material to make one box kite, size 10x10x21 in., and three three-stick high flyer kites, size 18x16 in. Colored paper, cord and sticks for making. Full directions enclosed. Shpg. wt., 1½ lbs. 69T7797 Price, 4 kites for.......... 25c

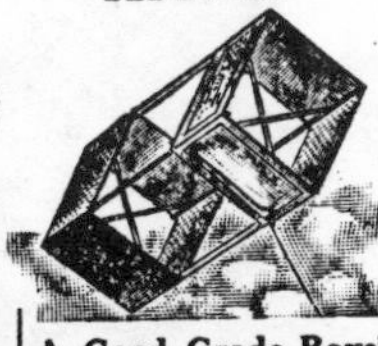

**A Good Grade Boys' Folding Box Kite.** This is one of the most popular made box kites. Easy to adjust, flies easily, light in weight, and a favorite with boys. Shipping weight, 12 oz. 69T7790 25c Price ..........

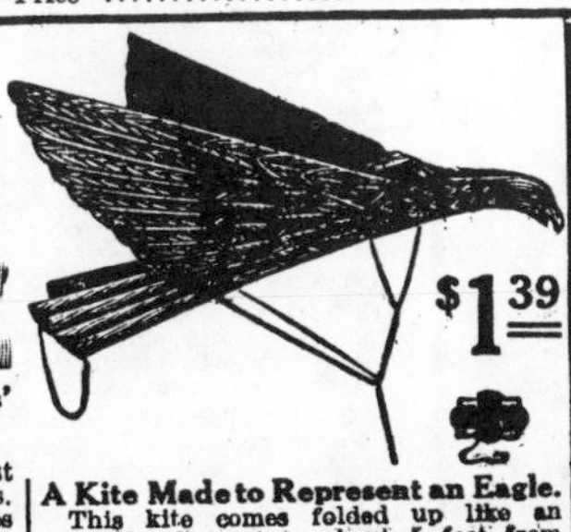

$1.39

**A Kite Made to Represent an Eagle.** This kite comes folded up like an umbrella, but opens about 5 feet from tip to tip. It is made of cloth and paper, printed in colors to represent an eagle, and when it gets up in the air looks like a huge bird. Shpg. wt., 1¾ lbs. 69T7791—Price ................$1.39

## MARBLES.

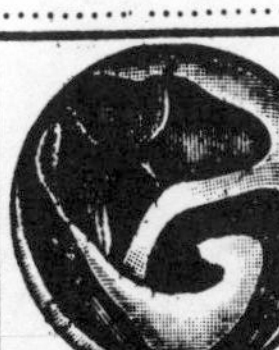

**Glass Imitation Onyx Marbles.** Six large glass marbles, exact size of illustration. Green, brown and blue imitation onyx. Shipping weight, 5 ounces. 69T7746 Price, 6 for 17c

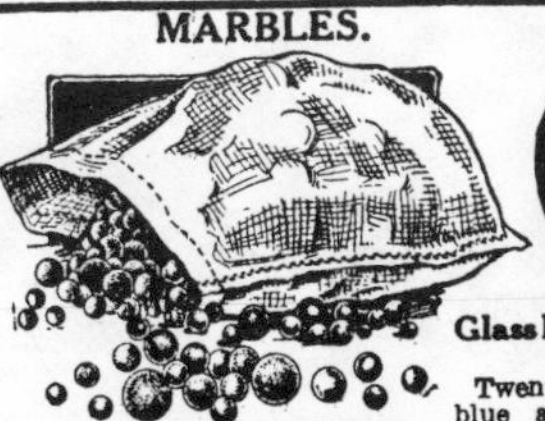

**About 175 Clay Marbles in Strong Bag.** Some shooters, some medium size and balance in smaller marbles. Shipping weight, 1⅝ pounds. 69T7741—Price.. 13c

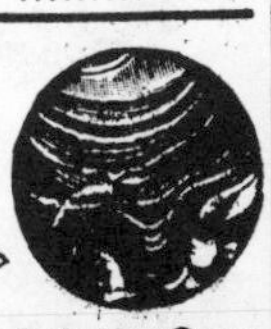

**Glass Imitation Onyx Marbles.** Twenty assorted green, blue and brown glass imitation onyx marbles. Exact size of illustration. Made of colored glass. Shipping weight, 8 ounces. 69T7740 Price, 20 for.. 25c

# Alphabet and Building Blocks

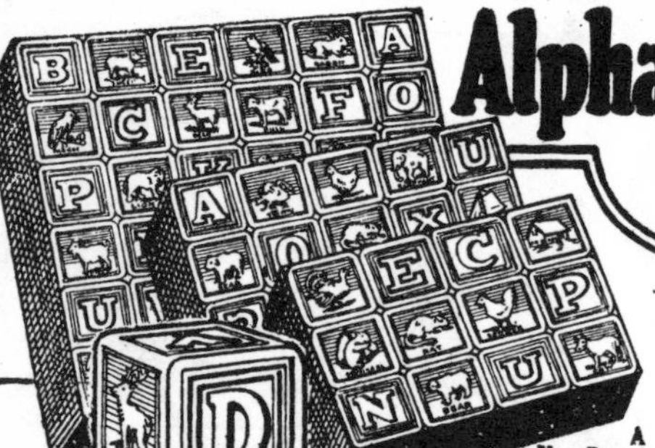

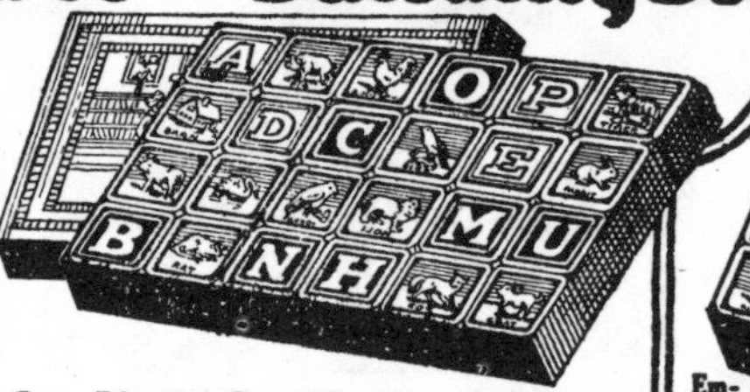

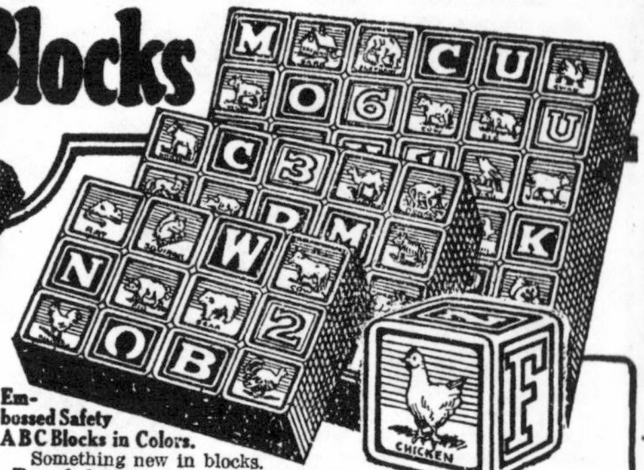

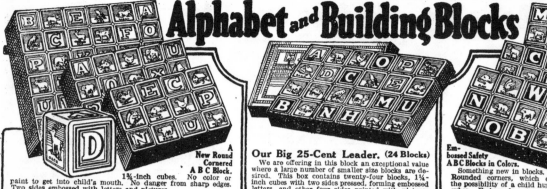

**A New Round Cornered A B C Block.** 1¾-inch cubes. No color or paint to get into child's mouth. No danger from sharp edges. Two sides embossed with letters and pictures.

| Thirty-six Block Set. | Twenty Block Set. | Twelve Block Set. |
|---|---|---|
| Box, 11x11 in. Shpg. wt., 3½ lbs. | Box, 9 x 7¼ inches. Shipping wt., 2 lbs. | Box, 7¼ x 5¼ in. Shpg. wt., 1¾ lbs. |
| 49T3656 Price........98c | 49T3655 Price........69c | 49T3654 Price........45c |

**Our Big 25-Cent Leader. (24 Blocks)**
We are offering in this block an exceptional value where a large number of smaller size blocks are desired. This box contains twenty-four blocks, 1¼-inch cubes with two sides pressed, forming embossed letters, and other four sides printed with pictures and letters in colors. These blocks have all corners rounded, eliminating sharp edges. Size of box, 8x5½ inches. Shipping wt., 1⅛ lbs.
49T3651—Price, per set....... **25c**

**Embossed Safety A B C Blocks in Colors.**
Something new in blocks. Rounded corners, which eliminate the possibility of a child hurting itself on sharp edges. 1¾-inch cubes. Embossed on two sides. Four sides printed in animals, letters and numbers.

| Thirty-six Block Set. | Twenty Block Set. | Twelve Block Set. |
|---|---|---|
| Box, 11x11 in. Wt., 3¼ lbs. | Box, 9 x 7¼ inches. Wt., 1¾ lbs. | Box, 7¼ x 5¼ in. Wt., 1¼ lbs. |
| 49T3657 98c | 49T3653 69c | 49T3652 45c |

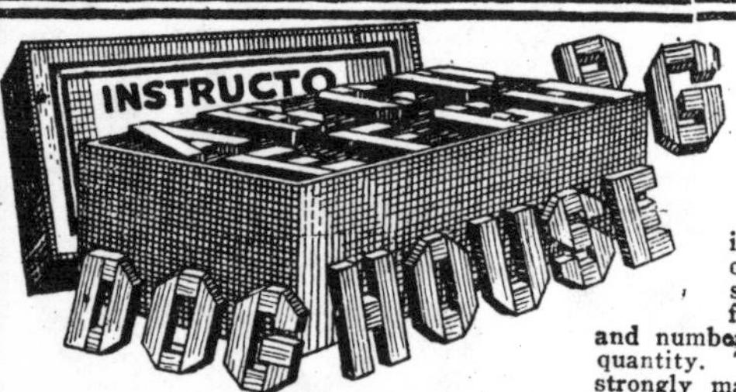

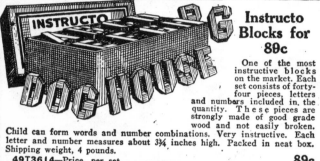

## Instructo Blocks for 89c

One of the most instructive blocks on the market. Each set consists of forty-four pieces, letters and numbers included in the quantity. These pieces are strongly made of good grade wood and not easily broken. Child can form words and number combinations. Very instructive. Each letter and number measures about 3¾ inches high. Packed in neat box. Shipping weight, 4 pounds.
49T3614—Price, per set....................... **89c**

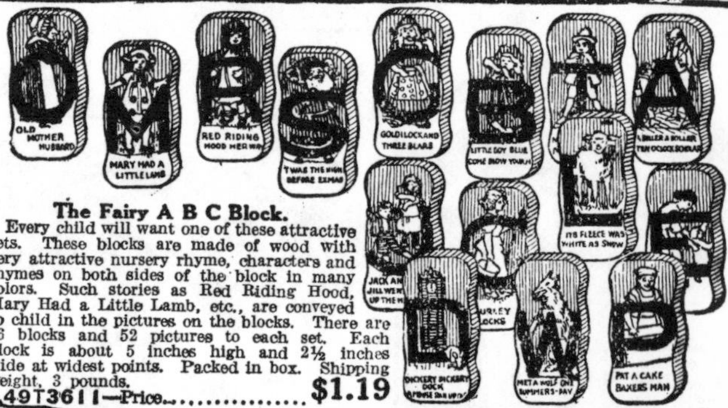

**The Fairy A B C Block.**
Every child will want one of these attractive sets. These blocks are made of wood with very attractive nursery rhyme, characters and rhymes on both sides of the block in many colors. Such stories as Red Riding Hood, Mary Had a Little Lamb, etc., are conveyed to child in the pictures on the blocks. There are 26 blocks and 52 pictures to each set. Each block is about 5 inches high and 2½ inches wide at widest points. Packed in box. Shipping weight, 3 pounds.
49T3611—Price... **$1.19**

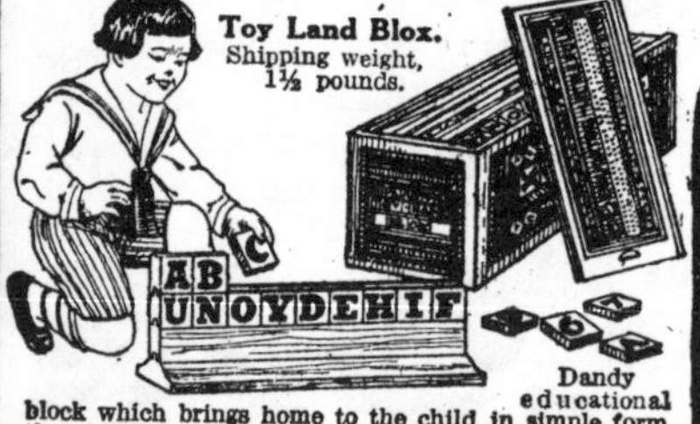

**Toy Land Blox.** Shipping weight, 1½ pounds.

Dandy educational block which brings home to the child in simple form the fundamentals of word forming and sentence building. Consists of thirty-six blocks representing two complete alphabets and two sets of numerals which can be arranged on bases to spell words and sentences. Parts included so that rows of different heights can be arranged. Packed in attractive wood box with sliding cover, 9x3½x3½ inches.
49T3619—Price, per set....... **45c**

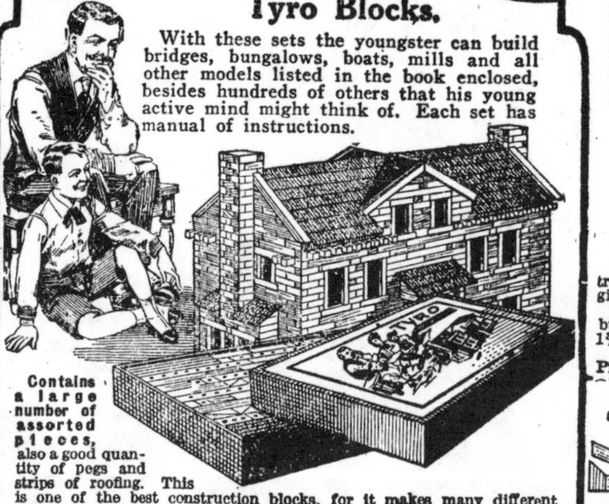

## Tyro Blocks.

With these sets the youngster can build bridges, bungalows, boats, mills and all other models listed in the book enclosed, besides hundreds of others that his young active mind might think of. Each set has manual of instructions.

Contains a large number of assorted pieces, also a good quantity of pegs and strips of roofing. This is one of the best construction blocks, for it makes many different attractive models which will really hold together well because of the connecting principle used, and which will be appreciated by every child receiving them.

| Our Best Set | Our $2.47 Set | Our 97c Set |
|---|---|---|
| contains about 575 pieces. Size box, 15x10¼ inches. Shipping wt., 10 pounds. | contains about 245 pieces. For building toy furniture, pianos, etc. Size box, 14½x10 in. Shpg. wt., 5½ lbs. | contains about 115 pieces. For building bird house, etc. Size box, 8½x5¾ inches. Shpg. wt., 2¼ lbs. |
| 79T4747¼ Price........$4.47 | 49T4746 Price........$2.47 | 49T4745 Price........97c |

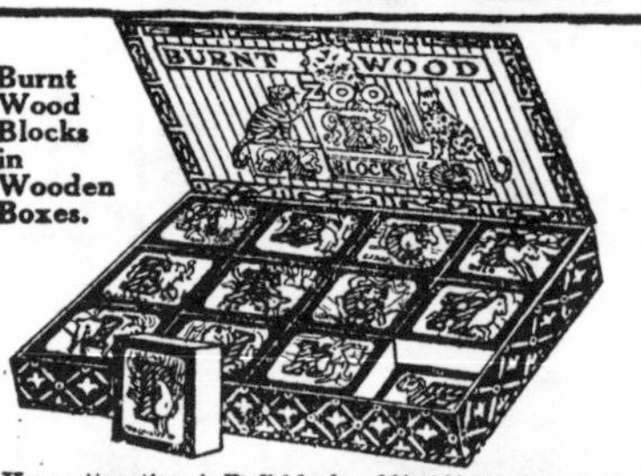

**Burnt Wood Blocks in Wooden Boxes.**

Very attractive A B C blocks, 2¼x2¼x¼-in. in attractive burnt wood hinge boxes. Makes a dandy gift. Comes in two sizes.

| Twenty-four Block Set | Twelve Block Set |
|---|---|
| in burnt wood box, 9½x7¼x 1⅝ in. Shpg. wt., 1½ lbs. | in burnt wood box, 9½x7¼x ⅞ in. Shpg. wt., 1⅛ lbs. |
| 49T3609 Price, per set..... 67c | 49T3606 Price, per set..... 39c |

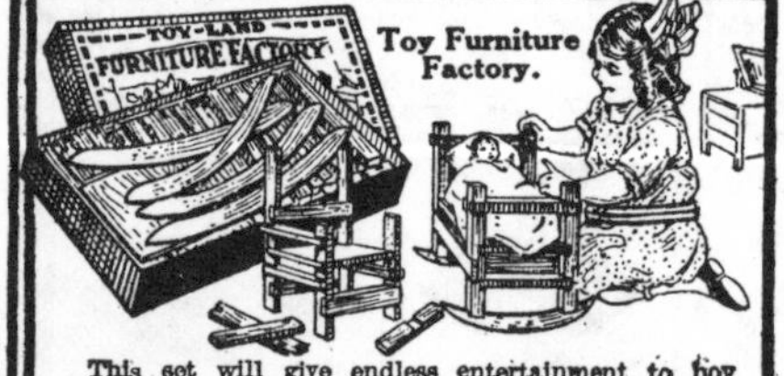

**Toy Furniture Factory.**

This set will give endless entertainment to boy or girl. There are enough parts to build two pieces of furniture at a time. Such pieces of furniture as a chair, table, rocker, cradle or bed can be built with this set. Chair, for instance, made up, measures 10 inches high and 5½ inches wide. Packed in box. Shipping weight, 1½ pounds.
49T3620—Price, per set....... **45c**

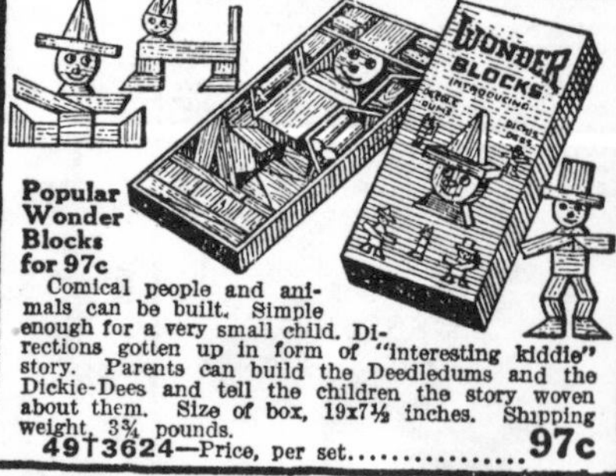

**Popular Wonder Blocks for 97c**
Comical people and animals can be built. Simple enough for a very small child. Directions gotten up in form of "interesting kiddie" story. Parents can build the Deedledums and the Dickie-Dees and tell the children the story woven about them. Size of box, 19x7½ inches. Shipping weight, 3¾ pounds.
49T3624—Price, per set.............. **97c**

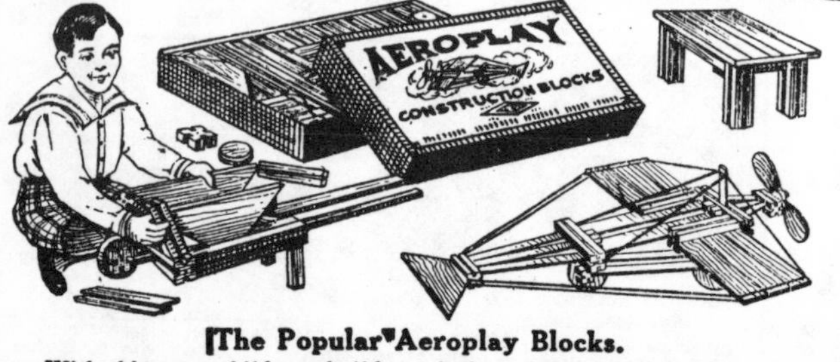

**The Popular Aeroplay Blocks.**
With this set a child can build an airplane, houses, bridges, towers, etc. Possibilities of this set give child plenty of opportunity to exercise ability to build things. Makes an attractive airplane with a revolving propeller. Every child is interested in airplanes, particularly in building them. Packed in nice box, 12⅞x8⅛ inches. Shipping weight, 3 pounds.
49T4748—Price, per set....................... **89c**

**"Two-In-One" Wagon Blocks.**
These building blocks are made of good grade woods, and the box they are packed in can be used as a toy wagon.

**About 100 pieces.** Wagon size, 10½x16½ inches. Has tongue and movable front axle so wheels can turn under wagon. Shipping weight, 11 lbs.
79T3632¼ Price.............. **$1.47**

**About Ninety-four Blocks.** Wagon, 10½x16¾ in. Wheels only, tongue and axle not included. Shpg. wt., 8 lbs.
79T3647¼—Price.... **98c**

**About Thirty-four Blocks.** Makes wagon 7½x13¼ inches. Wheels only. Shipping weight, 3½ pounds.
49T3648—Price..... **47c**

**About Sixteen Blocks.** Makes wagon 6x9 inches. Wheels only. Shpg. wt., 2 lbs.
49T3649—Price.... **23c**

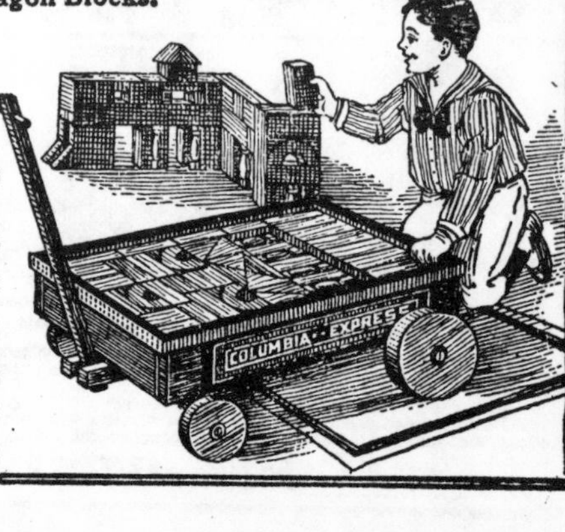

# Paints and Educational Toys

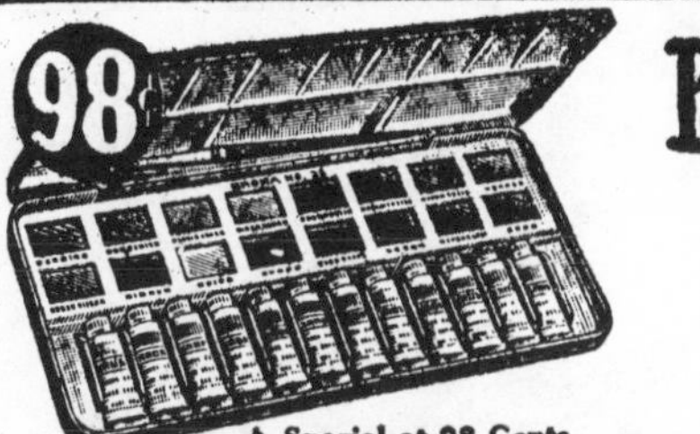


**A Special at 98 Cents.**
A popular size box, contains sixteen dry colors, twelve tube colors, paint brush. Size of metal box, 8½x3½ inches. A practical set. Shipping wt., 12 oz.
49T3856—Price .................... 98c

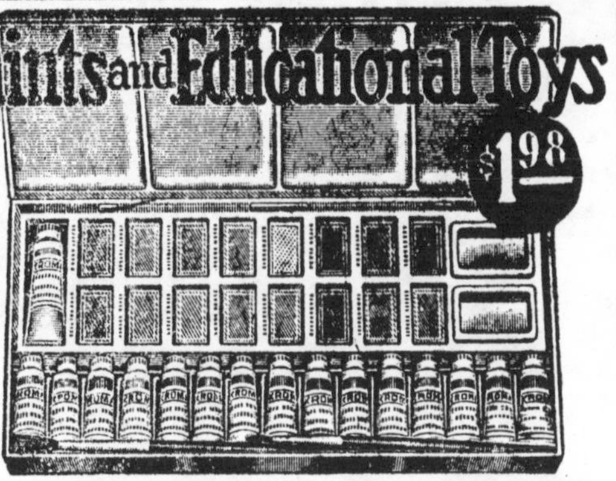


**The Well Known Prang Kroma Colors in Metal Boxes.**
Consisting of sixteen dry colors, sixteen tube colors, two brushes and two compartments for mixing. A practical set of colors. Metal hinged cover box, 9x4½ inches. The best set to buy if quality is desired. Shpg. wt., 1¼ lbs.
49T3858—Price .................... $1.98

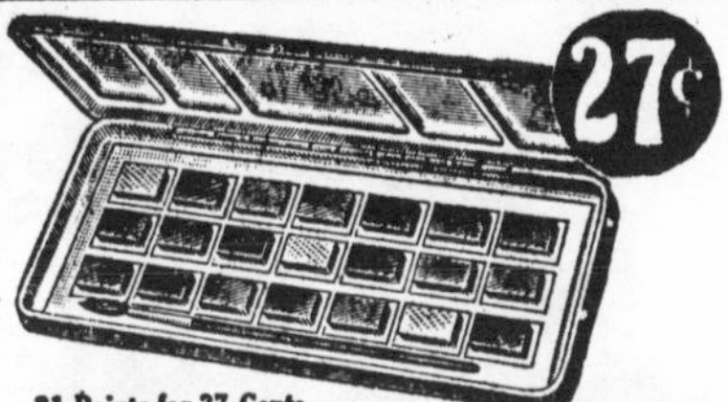


**21 Paints for 27 Cents.**
Metal box, 3x8 inches. Contains twenty-one colors and a quill brush. Shipping weight, 8 ounces. 27c
49T3854—Price....................

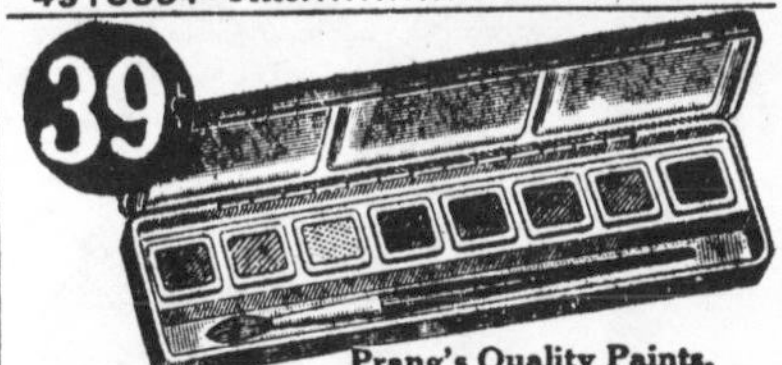


**Prang's Quality Paints.**
Eight-color paint box and paint brush. Hinged cover metal box, 8½x2 inches. Shipping wt., 8 oz.
49T3877—Price.............. 39c

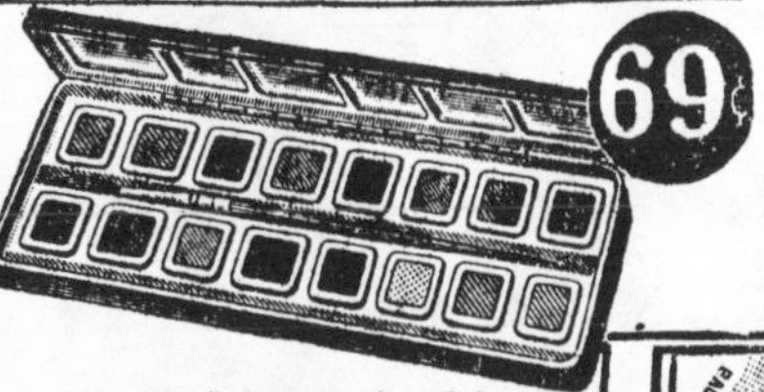


**Prang's Kroma Quality Colors.**
Sixteen paints and two brushes. Metal box, 8⅛x3¼ in. Shpg. wt., 10 oz.
49T3878—Price ............ 69c

## CUT-OUT MAPS OF THE UNITED STATES.

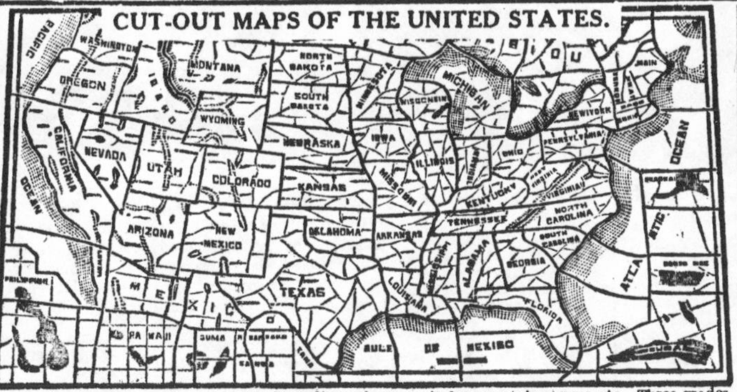


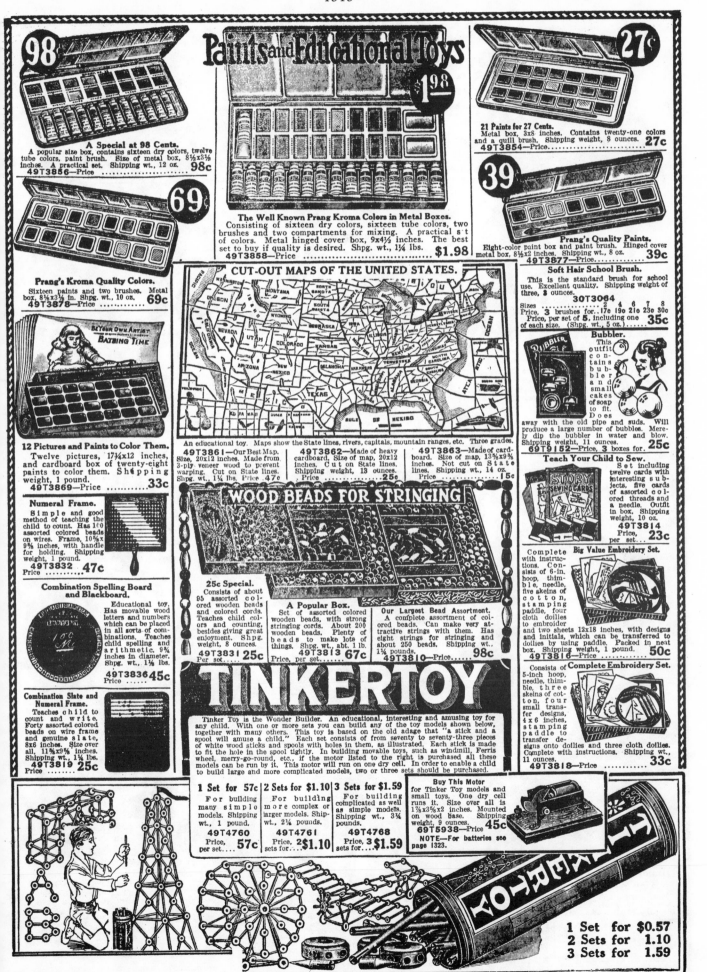

An educational toy. Maps show the State lines, rivers, capitals, mountain ranges, etc. Three grades.

49T3861—Our Best Map. Size, 20x12 inches. Made from 3-ply veneer wood to prevent warping. Cut on State lines. Shpg. wt., 1¼ lbs. Price 47c

49T3862—Made of heavy cardboard. Size of map, 20x12 inches. Cut on State lines. Shipping weight, 13 ounces. Price .................... 25c

49T3863—Made of cardboard. Size of map, 13⅝x9⅝ inches. Not cut on State lines. Shipping wt., 14 oz. Price .................... 15c

**Soft Hair School Brush.**
This is the standard brush for school use. Excellent quality. Shipping weight of three, 3 ounces.
30T3064

| Sizes .................... | 2 | 4 | 6 | 7 | 8 |
|---|---|---|---|---|---|
| Price, 3 brushes for.. | 17c | 19c | 21c | 23c | 30c |

Price, per set of 5, including one of each size. (Shpg. wt., 5 oz.)........ 35c

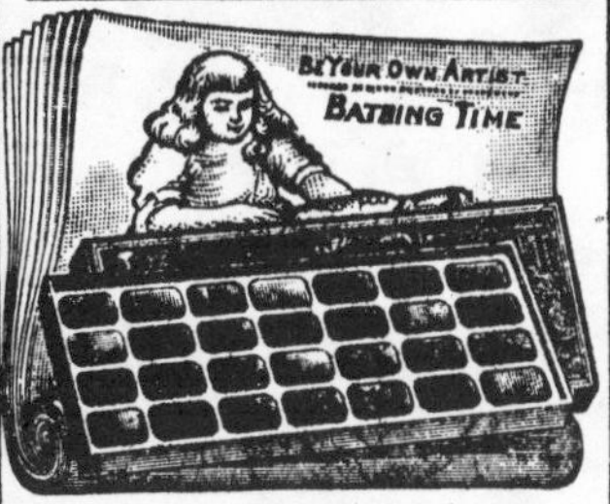


**12 Pictures and Paints to Color Them.**
Twelve pictures, 17¾x12 inches, and cardboard box of twenty-eight paints to color them. Shipping weight, 1 pound.
49T3869—Price ............ 33c

**Bubbler.**

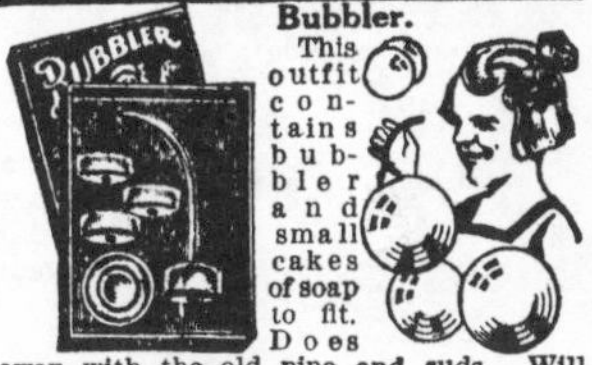


This outfit contains bubbler and small cakes of soap to fit. Does away with the old pipe and suds. Will produce a large number of bubbles. Merely dip the bubbler in water and blow. Shipping weight, 11 ounces.
69T9152—Price, 3 boxes for. 25c

**Teach Your Child to Sew.**

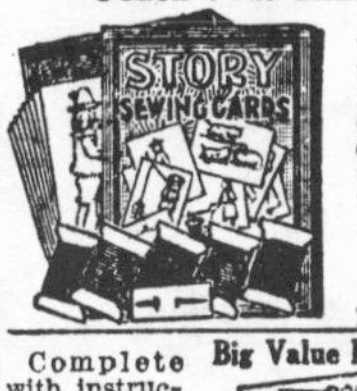


Set including twelve cards with interesting subjects, five cards of assorted colored threads and a needle. Outfit in box. Shipping weight, 10 oz.
49T3814
Price, per set... 23c

**Numeral Frame.**

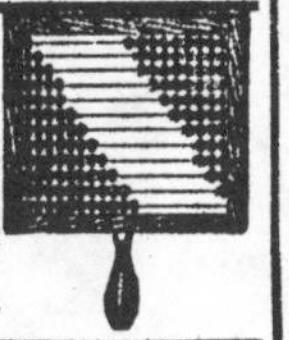

Simple and good method of teaching the child to count. Has 100 assorted colored beads on wires. Frame, 10⅝x9⅝ inches, with handle for holding. Shipping weight, 1 pound.
49T3832
Price .......... 47c

## WOOD BEADS FOR STRINGING

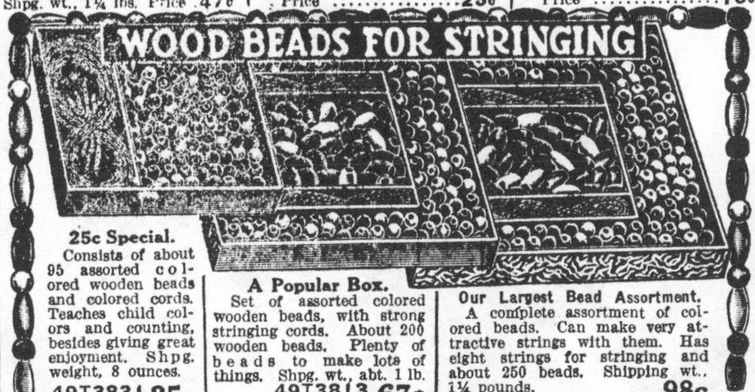

**25c Special.**
Consists of about 95 assorted colored wooden beads and colored cords. Teaches child colors and counting, besides giving great enjoyment. Shpg. weight, 8 ounces.
49T3831 Per set.... 25c

**A Popular Box.**
Set of assorted colored wooden beads, with strong stringing cords. About 200 wooden beads. Plenty of beads to make lots of things. Shpg. wt., abt. 1 lb.
49T3813 Price, per set.... 67c

**Our Largest Bead Assortment.**
A complete assortment of colored beads. Can make very attractive strings with them. Has eight strings for stringing and about 250 beads. Shipping wt., 1¼ pounds.
49T3810—Price...... 98c

**Big Value Embroidery Set.**

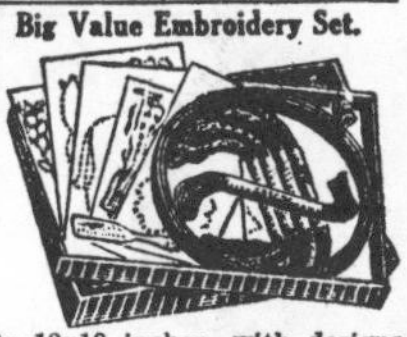

Complete with instructions. Consists of 6-in. hoop, thimble, needle, five skeins of cotton, stamping paddle, four cloth doilies to embroider and two sheets 12x18 inches, with designs and initials, which can be transferred to doilies by using paddle. Packed in neat box. Shipping weight, 1 pound.
49T3816—Price .................... 50c

**Combination Spelling Board and Blackboard.**

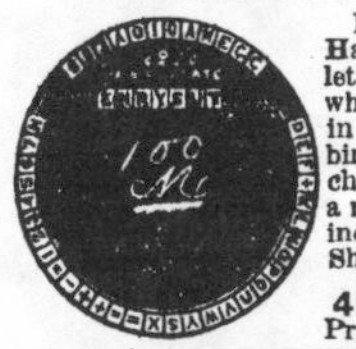

Educational toy. Has movable wood letters and numbers which can be placed in all sorts of combinations. Teaches child spelling and arithmetic. 9¾ inches in diameter. Shpg. wt., 1⅛ lbs.
49T3836
Price ...... 45c

**Combination Slate and Numeral Frame.**

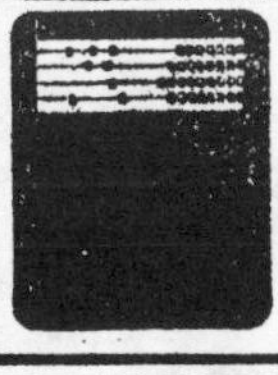

Teaches child to count and write. Forty assorted colored beads on wire frame and genuine slate, 8x6 inches. Size over all, 11⅝x9⅝ inches. Shipping wt., 1¼ lbs.
49T3819
Price ........ 25c

# TINKERTOY

Tinker Toy is the Wonder Builder. An educational, interesting and amusing toy for any child. With one or more sets you can build any of the toy models shown below, together with many others. This toy is based on the old adage that "a stick and a spool will amuse a child." Each set consists of from seventy to seventy-three pieces of white wood sticks and spools with holes in them, as illustrated. Each stick is made to fit the hole in the spool tightly. In building movable toys, such as windmill, Ferris wheel, merry-go-round, etc., if the motor listed to the right is purchased all these models can be run by it. This motor will run on one dry cell. In order to enable a child to build large and more complicated models, two or three sets should be purchased.

**Complete Embroidery Set.**

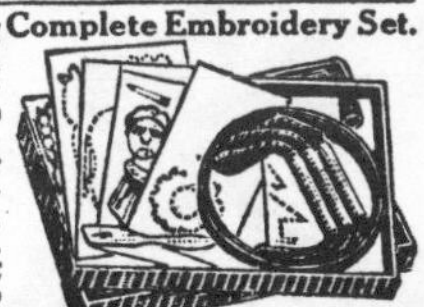

Consists of 5-inch hoop, needle, thimble, three skeins of cotton, four small transfer designs, 4x6 inches, stamping paddle to transfer designs onto doilies and three cloth doilies. Complete with instructions. Shipping wt., 11 ounces.
49T3818—Price .............. 33c

**1 Set for 57c**
For building many simple models. Shipping wt., 1 pound.
49T4760
Price, per set... 57c

**2 Sets for $1.10**
For building more complex or larger models. Shipping wt., 2¼ pounds.
49T4761
Price, 2 sets for... $1.10

**3 Sets for $1.59**
For building complicated as well as simple models. Shipping wt., 3¼ pounds.
49T4768
Price, 3 sets for... $1.59

**Buy This Motor**
for Tinker Toy models and small toys. One dry cell runs it. Size over all is 1⅞x3⅝x2 inches. Mounted on wood base. Shipping weight, 9 ounces.
69T5938—Price 45c

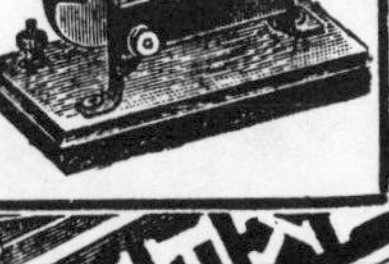

NOTE—For batteries see page 1323.

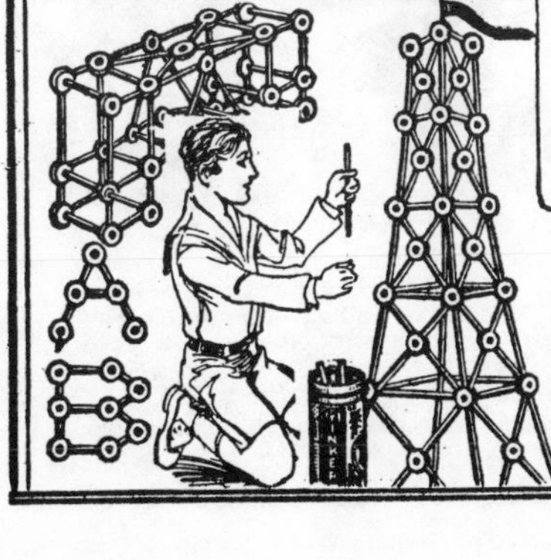

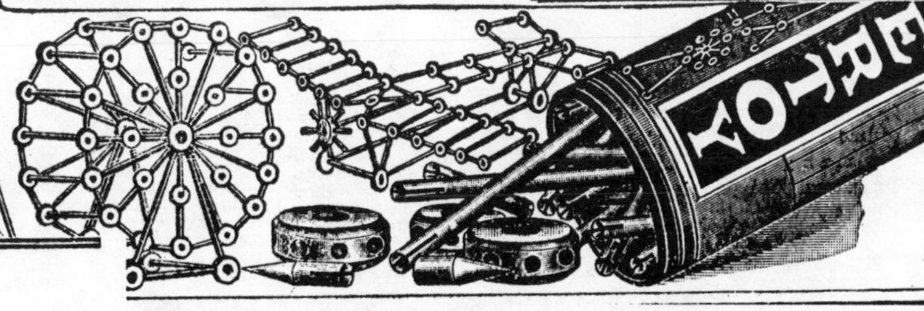


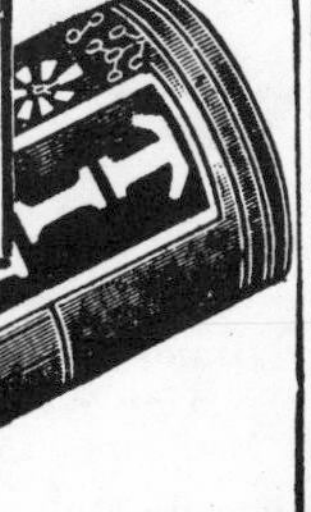


**1 Set for $0.57**
**2 Sets for 1.10**
**3 Sets for 1.59**

# Every child loves a Teddy Bear
## Our Highest Quality Bears

### Our Finest Quality Bears.

This bear represents a very high quality in Teddy Bears. Finely shaped and stuffed with a soft cottonlike material, which makes the bear light for the child and very pliable in its joints. Soft to the touch; fine for baby. Made of long pile plush and has movable head, arms and legs, also glass eyes. Shpg. wt., 2¾ lbs.

49T4328—About 17 in. high.
Price.............$2.98

49T4329—About 15 in. high.
Price.............$2.39

### Just as Cute as He Can Be.

A fine baby bear. Good grade. Has long plush hair. Has movable head, arms and legs. Glass eyes. Height, about 10 inches. Shipping weight, 14 ounces.

49T4324
Price...............98c

### Old Shaggy Tom.

Besides making an attractive appearance, this bear will give long and satisfactory service. He is made of long plush. Has glass eyes. Head, arms and legs movable. About 17 inches high. Shipping weight, 2¾ pounds.

49T4325
Price..........$2.87

### Little Lost Brother.

The plush of this Teddy Bear is long. Well formed and jointed body. Measures about 15 inches high. A remarkable value. Has glass eyes. Head, arms and legs are movable. Shipping weight, 1¼ lbs.

49T4327
Price...........$2.25

### My Fur Is Nice and Soft.

It is made of long plush with glass eyes. Stands about 13 inches high. The arms, legs and head are all movable and can be turned into many comical and amusing positions. Shipping weight, 1¼ pounds.

49T4320
Price...............$1.67

### Electric Eye Bears.

We do not sell electric eye bears as, up to the present, we have not found one that will give entire satisfaction. The batteries soon wear out and the small bulb glass eyes break easily. We recommend the plain bears.

## Our popular priced Teddy Bears

### Little Tots Love This Tiny Wee Bear.

Head, arms and legs are movable. A small bear for the baby. It is made of fair grade short plush, has natural looking glass eyes and is about 10 inches high. Shipping weight, 11 ounces.

49T4318
Price..............69c

### The Middle Size Bear.

Head, arms and legs are movable and most comical positions are possible. It is made of short plush, is about 16 inches high and has glass eyes. Shipping weight, 1½ pounds.

49T4323
Price..............$1.59

### A Great Big Companionable Bear.

It is about 19 inches high, made of short plush and has natural looking glass eyes. Fairly well proportioned and while not such good quality as the long plush bears, it is the largest satisfactory bear that we are able to offer at this price. Shipping weight, 3 lbs.

49T4321
Price..........$1.98

### The Wee-Wee Bear.

An intermediate size bear, about 12-inch size, will be most acceptable to the smaller children. This bear is made of short plush, has movable arms and legs and natural looking glass eyes. Shipping weight, 14 ounces.

49T4322
Price. $1.00

### The Big Brother Bear.

A popular size. Although the plush is short, it is of fair quality and well made and the body is nicely formed. Natural looking glass eyes, movable head, arms and legs. Height, about 14 in. Shpg. wt., 1½ lbs.

49T4319
Price....................$1.25

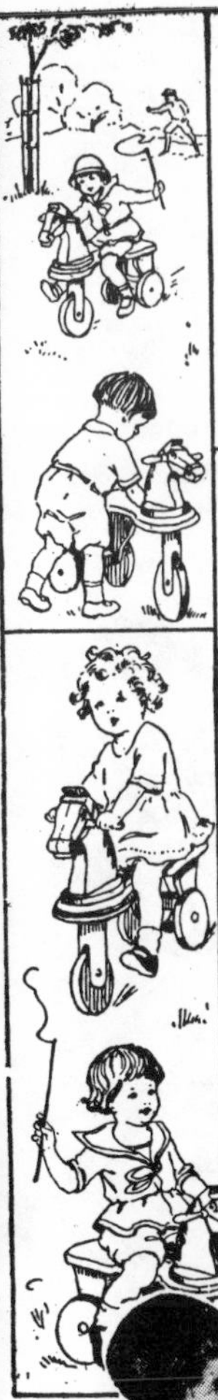

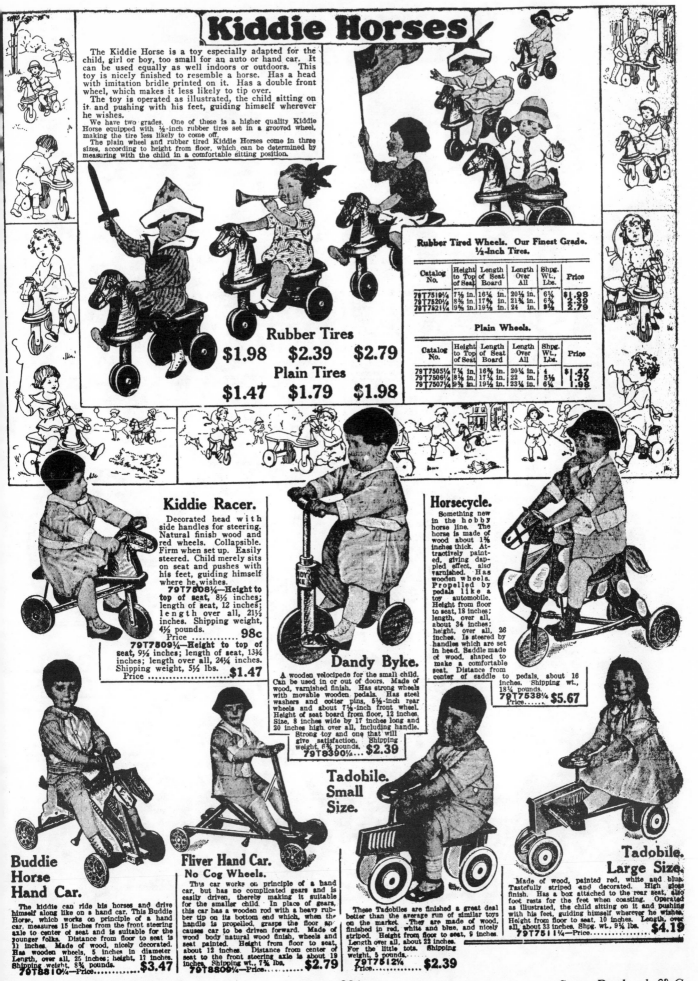

# Kiddie Horses

The Kiddie Horse is a toy especially adapted for the child, girl or boy, too small for an auto or hand car. It can be used equally as well indoors or outdoors. This toy is nicely finished to resemble a horse. Has a head with imitation bridle printed on it. Has a double front wheel, which makes it less likely to tip over.

The toy is operated as illustrated, the child sitting on it and pushing with his feet, guiding himself wherever he wishes.

We have two grades. One of these is a higher quality Kiddie Horse equipped with ½-inch rubber tires set in a grooved wheel, making the tire less likely to come off.

The plain wheel and rubber tired Kiddie Horses come in three sizes, according to height from floor, which can be determined by measuring with the child in a comfortable sitting position.

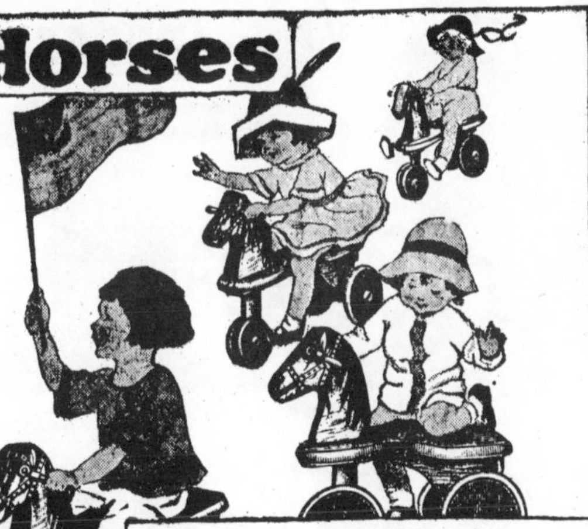

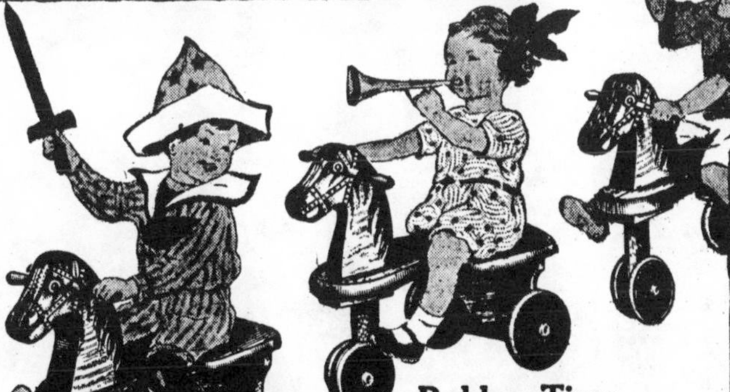

**Rubber Tires**
**\$1.98 \$2.39 \$2.79**
**Plain Tires**
**\$1.47 \$1.79 \$1.98**

**Rubber Tired Wheels. Our Finest Grade. ½-Inch Tires.**

| Catalog No. | Height to Top of Seat | Length of Seat Board | Length Over All | Shpg. Wt., Lbs. | Price |
|---|---|---|---|---|---|
| 79T7519¼ | 7½ in. | 16¼ in. | 20½ in. | 6¼ | \$1.98 |
| 79T7520¼ | 8⅜ in. | 17⅝ in. | 21¾ in. | 6¾ | 2.39 |
| 79T7521¼ | 9⅝ in. | 19½ in. | 24 in. | 9½ | 2.79 |

**Plain Wheels.**

| Catalog No. | Height to Top of Seat | Length of Seat Board | Length Over All | Shpg. Wt., Lbs. | Price |
|---|---|---|---|---|---|
| 79T7505¼ | 7¼ in. | 16⅜ in. | 20¼ in. | 4 | \$1.47 |
| 79T7506¼ | 8⅛ in. | 17¼ in. | 22 in. | 5⅛ | 1.79 |
| 79T7507¼ | 9⅜ in. | 19½ in. | 23¼ in. | 6¼ | 1.98 |

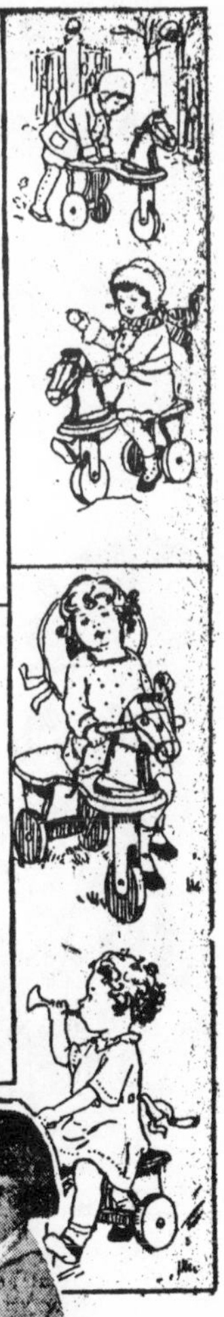

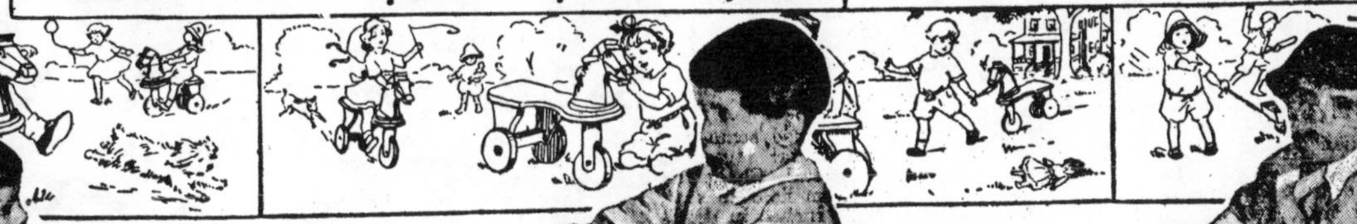

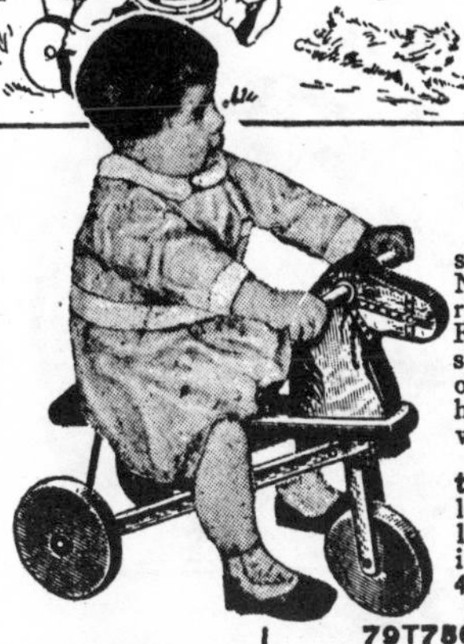

## Kiddie Racer.

Decorated head with side handles for steering. Natural finish wood and red wheels. Collapsible. Firm when set up. Easily steered. Child merely sits on seat and pushes with his feet, guiding himself where he wishes.

**79T7508¼—Height to top of seat**, 8½ inches; length of seat, 12 inches; length over all, 21½ inches. Shipping weight, 4½ pounds.
Price ............ **98c**

**79T7509¼—Height to top of seat**, 9½ inches; length of seat, 13¼ inches; length over all, 24¼ inches. Shipping weight, 5½ lbs.
Price ...................... **\$1.47**

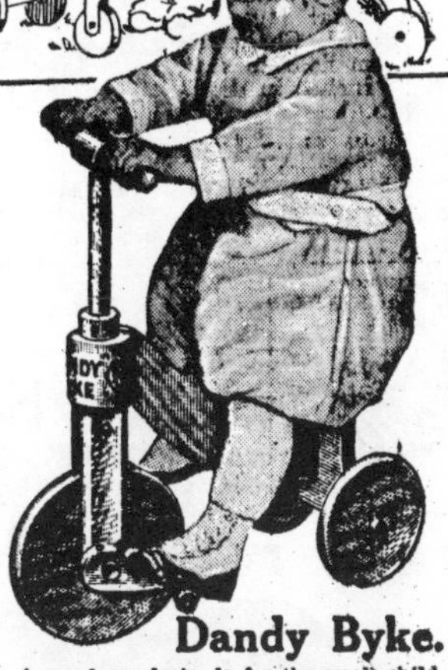

## Dandy Byke.

A wooden velocipede for the small child. Can be used in or out of doors. Made of wood, varnished finish. Has strong wheels with movable wooden pedals. Has steel washers and cotter pins, 5½-inch rear wheels and about 7½-inch front wheel. Height of seat board from floor, 12 inches. Size, 8 inches wide by 17 inches long and 20 inches high over all, including handle. Strong toy and one that will give satisfaction. Shipping weight, 6¾ pounds.
**79T8390¼... \$2.39**

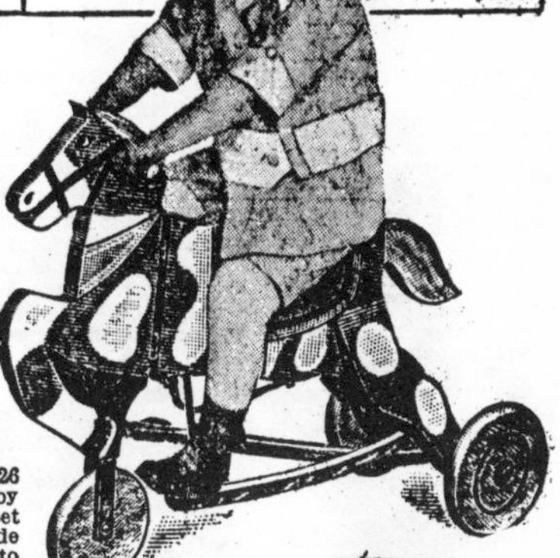

## Horsecycle.

Something new in the hobby horse line. The horse is made of wood about 1⅝ inches thick. Attractively painted, giving dappled effect, also varnished. Has wooden wheels. Propelled by pedals like a toy automobile. Height from floor to seat, 18 inches; length, over all, about 34 inches; height, over all, 26 inches. Is steered by handles which are set in head. Saddle made of wood, shaped to make a comfortable seat. Distance from center of saddle to pedals, about 16 inches. Shipping wt., 18¼ pounds.
**79T7538¼**
Price...... **\$5.67**

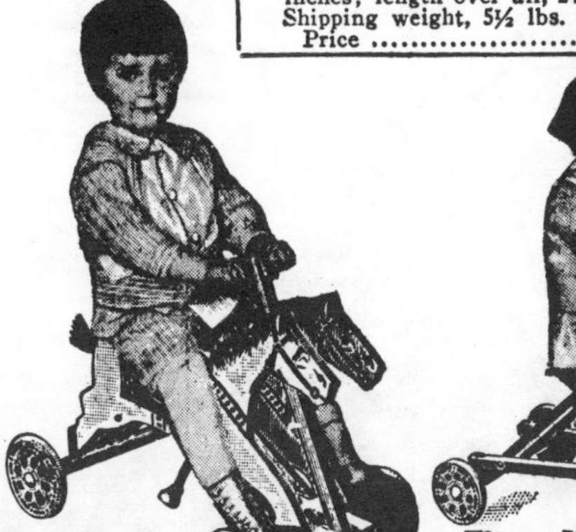

## Buddie Horse Hand Car.

The kiddie can ride his horses and drive himself along like on a hand car. This Buddie Horse, which works on principle of a hand car, measures 15 inches from the front steering axle to center of seat and is suitable for the younger folks. Distance from floor to seat is 11 inches. Made of wood, nicely decorated. Has wooden wheels, 5 inches in diameter Length, over all, 25 inches; height, 17 inches. Shipping weight, 8¾ pounds.
**79T8810¼**—Price............ **\$3.47**

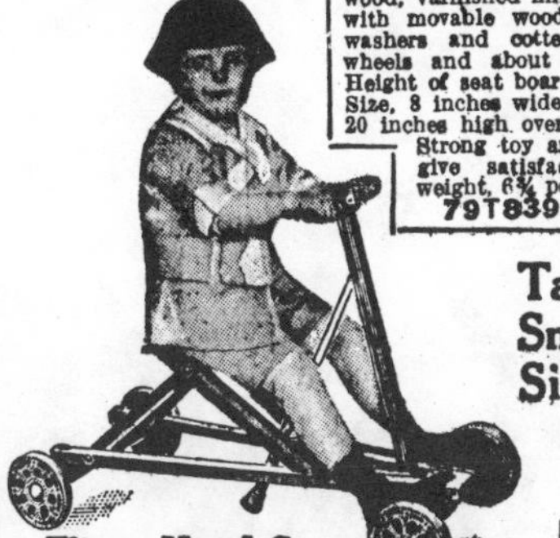

## Fliver Hand Car.
### No Cog Wheels.

This car works on principle of a hand car, but has no complicated gears and is easily driven, thereby making it suitable for the smaller child. In place of gears, this car has a wooden rod with a heavy rubber tip on its bottom end which, when the handle is propelled, grasps the floor and causes car to be driven forward. Made of wood body natural wood finish, wheels and seat painted. Height from floor to seat, about 12 inches. Distance from center of seat to the front steering axle is about 19 inches. Shipping wt., 7¾ lbs.
**79T8809¼**—Price.......... **\$2.79**

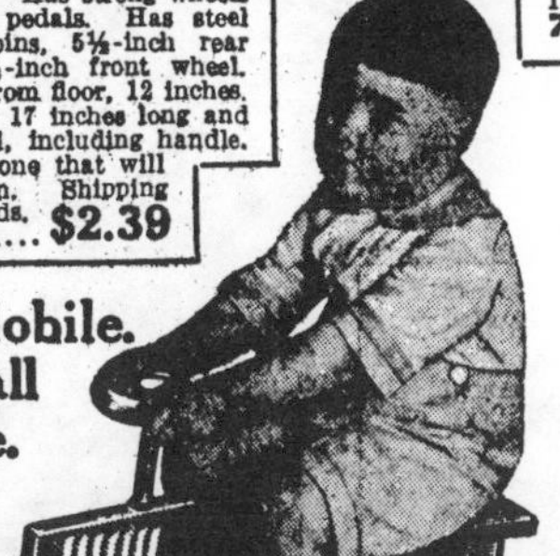

## Tadobile. Small Size.

These Tadobiles are finished a great deal better than the average run of similar toys on the market. They are made of wood, finished in red, white and blue, and nicely striped. Height from floor to seat, 9 inches. Length over all, about 22 inches. For the little tots. Shipping weight, 5 pounds.
**79T7512¼**
Price.............. **\$2.39**

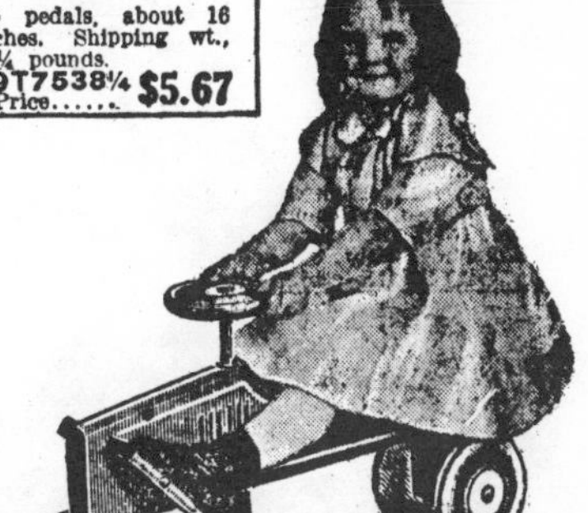

## Tadobile. Large Size.

Made of wood, painted red, white and blue. Tastefully striped and decorated. High gloss finish. Has a box attached to the rear seat, also foot rests for the feet when coasting. Operated as illustrated, the child sitting on it and pushing with his feet, guiding himself wherever he wishes. Height from floor to seat, 10 inches. Length, over all, about 33 inches. Shpg. wt., 9¼ lbs.
**79T7511¼**—Price................ **\$4.19**

# Velocipedes and Playcars

For Playground Equipment, Teeter Totters, Slides, Giant Strides, Etc., see page 1296.

**$3⁶⁷ And Up.**

**$8⁹⁸ And Up.**

## Velocipedes.

SPRING SEAT

STRONG HEAD

**Low Priced, but a Good Velocipede for the Money.**

These numbers represent the lowest priced dependable velocipedes we have been able to find. Each of our velocipedes is equipped with rigid handle bars with wood grips, adjustable spring seat and steel wheels. The front fork is made of good quality steel, one-piece crank. The whole frame is painted. Take leg measurement from crotch to heel and state measurement on your order. Measurements given below are with seat as low as it will go, and careful comparison of these with leg measurement should be made before selection. Adjustment of about 2½ in. more in length can be made by raising seat as child grows.

**Bicycle Features on Velocipedes.**

As the boy on a bicycle tries to imitate the motorcycle rider with his long handle bars and low seat, so the little fellow enjoys a velocipede that imitates a bicycle in its makeup. Has strong seat and leather wound wood grips. The handle bars are adjustable. The seat can be raised or lowered, allowing for the growth of the child. The frame is nicely painted, striped and strongly reinforced with bicycle style head. Strong wheels, ⅝-inch rubber tires. To order right size take measurement from crotch to heel. Measurements given below are with seat as low as it will go, and careful comparison of these with leg measurement should be made before selection. Adjustment of about 2½ inches more in length can be made by raising seat as child grows. Unmailable.

**Bicycle Features:**
Adjustable Handle Bars.
Leather Wound Grips.
Padded Seat.
Coil Springs.
Rubber Tires.

Note the Bicycle Style Front Fork.

79T8354¼, 79T8355¼, 79T8357¼ and 79T8358¼ are unmailable.

| Catalog No. | Wheels, In. Front | Rear Wheels, Inches | Center of Seat to Lower Pedal | Shpg. Wt., Lbs. | Price | Catalog No. | Front Wheels, In. | Rear Wheels, Inches | Center of Seat to Lower Pedal | Shpg. Wt., Lbs. | Price |
|---|---|---|---|---|---|---|---|---|---|---|---|
| | WITHOUT RUBBER TIRES. | | | | | | WITH ½-INCH RUBBER TIRES. | | | | |
| 79T8352¼ | 16 | 12 | 19 in. | 16 | $3.67 | 79T8356¼ | 16 | 12 | 19 in. | 17 | $5.27 |
| 79T8353¼ | 20 | 14 | 21 in. | 20 | 4.35 | 79T8357¼ | 20 | 14 | 21 in. | 22 | 5.73 |
| 79T8354¼ | 24 | 16 | 23 in. | 21 | 4.87 | 79T8358¼ | 23½ | 16 | 23 in. | 23 | 6.18 |
| 79T8355¼ | 26 | 16 | 24 in. | 23 | 5.27 | | | | | | |

| Catalog No. | Wheels, Inches Front | Rear | Measurement From Center of Saddle to Pedal at Extreme Length | Shipping Weight | Price |
|---|---|---|---|---|---|
| 79T8364¼ | 16 | 12 | About 20½ inches | 28 lbs. | $8.98 |
| 79T8365¼ | 20 | 14 | About 23 inches | 33 lbs. | 9.45 |
| 79T8366¼ | 23½ | 16 | About 25 inches | 38 lbs. | 9.98 |

## GIRLS TRICYCLES $11⁹⁵

We list below the size which has proved to be one which will fit most girls using tricycles. Made of metal with upholstered seat in imitation leather. Adjustable spring seat, wooden handles, easy working pedals. Front wheel, 12 inches; rear wheels, 20 inches; rubber tired. Frame is painted black. Equipped with ½-inch tires. Measurement from center of seat to pedal, about 18¾ inches. Adjustable to about 20½ inches. Shipping weight, about 36½ pounds.
**79T8371¼—Price, each..................$11.95**

## Ball Bearing $11⁹⁵ And Up.

Well constructed of good quality materials. Bicycle head and arched fork frame; heavy front fork; rear wheels fitted with ball bearings placed in the hubs so they cannot become lost; adjustable handle bars; leather wound wood grips; good quality saddle with adjustable saddle post and spring seat, and has rat trap ball bearing bicycle pedals. Frame attractively painted and striped. Handle bars, cranks and pedals nickel plated. All wheels have ¾-inch rubber tires. Unmailable.

| Catalog No. | Wheels, Inches Front | Rear | Measurement From Center of Seat to Pedal at Extreme Length | Shpg. Wt. About | Price |
|---|---|---|---|---|---|
| 79T8380¼ | 16 | 12 | 21½ inches | 32 lbs. | $11.95 |
| 79T8381¼ | 20 | 14 | 23½ inches | 34 lbs. | 12.98 |
| 79T8382¼ | 23½ | 16 | 25½ inches | 40 lbs. | 13.98 |

# Hand Cars and Irish Mails

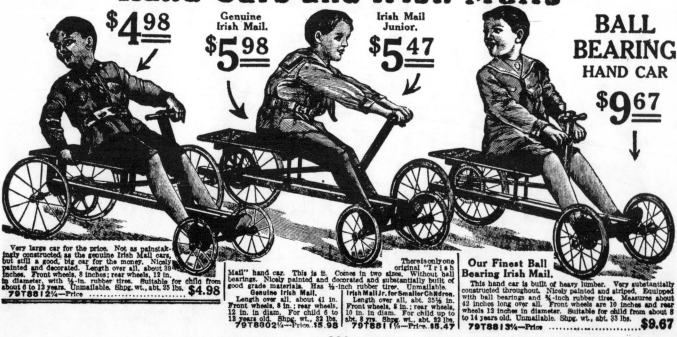

**$4⁹⁸**

**Genuine Irish Mail. $5⁹⁸**

**Irish Mail Junior. $5⁴⁷**

**BALL BEARING HAND CAR $9⁶⁷**

Very large car for the price. Not as painstakingly constructed as the genuine Irish Mail cars, but still a good, big car for the money. Nicely painted and decorated. Length over all, about 39 inches. Front wheels, 8 inches; rear wheels, 12 in. in diameter, with ½-in. rubber tires. Suitable for child from about 6 to 12 years. Unmailable. Shpg. wt., abt. 25 lbs.
**79T8812¼—Price...................$4.98**

There is only one original "Irish Mail" hand car. This is it. Comes in two sizes. Without ball bearings. Nicely painted and decorated and substantially built of good grade materials. Has ½-inch rubber tires. Unmailable.
**Genuine Irish Mail.**
Length over all, about 41 in. Front wheels, 8 in.; rear wheels, 12 in. in diam. For child 6 to 12 years old. Shpg. wt., 32 lbs.
**79T8802¼—Price..$5.98**

**Irish Mail Jr. for Smaller Children.**
Length over all, about 35½ in. Front wheels, 8 in.; rear wheels, 10 in. in diam. For child up to abt. 8 yrs. Shpg. wt., abt. 22 lbs.
**79T8811¼—Price..$5.47**

**Our Finest Ball Bearing Irish Mail.**
This hand car is built of heavy lumber. Very substantially constructed throughout. Nicely painted and striped. Equipped with ball bearings and ¾-inch rubber tires. Measures about 42 inches long over all. Front wheels are 10 inches and rear wheels 12 inches in diameter. Suitable for child from about 8 to 14 years old. Unmailable. Shpg. wt., abt. 33 lbs.
**79T8813¼—Price...................$9.67**

# Toy Automobiles

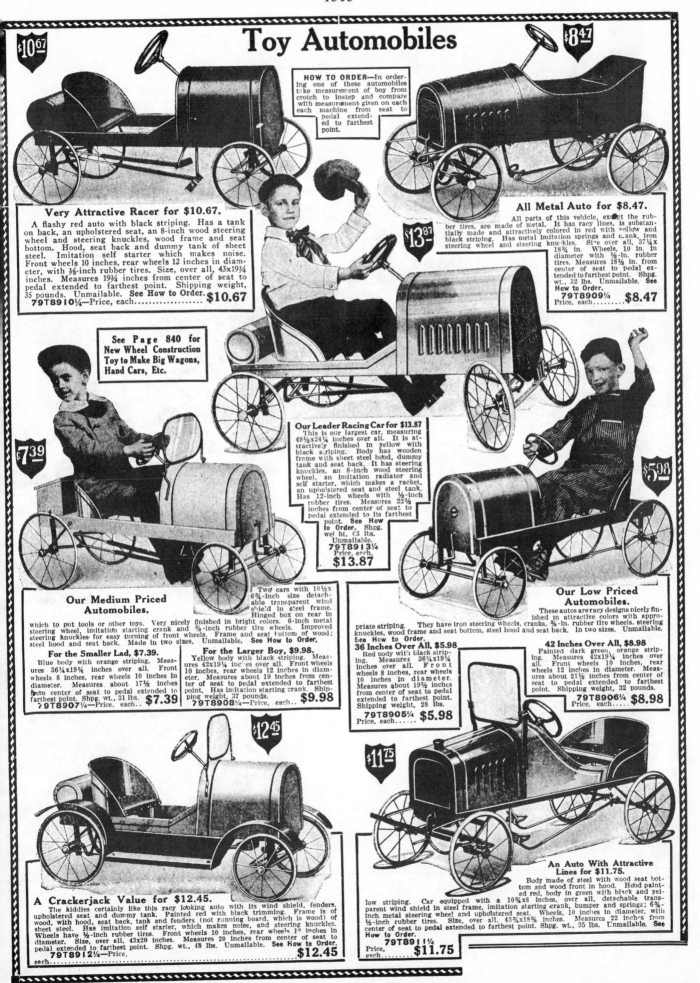

**HOW TO ORDER**—In ordering one of these automobiles take measurement of boy from crotch to instep and compare with measurement given on each machine from seat to pedal extended to farthest point.

## Very Attractive Racer for $10.67.

A flashy red auto with black striping. Has a tank on back, an upholstered seat, an 8-inch wood steering wheel and steering knuckles, wood frame and seat bottom. Hood, seat back and dummy tank of sheet steel. Imitation self starter which makes noise. Front wheels 10 inches, rear wheels 12 inches in diameter, with 3/8-inch rubber tires. Size, over all, 43x19¾ inches. Measures 19¾ inches from center of seat to pedal extended to farthest point. Shipping weight, 35 pounds. Unmailable. **See How to Order.**

**79T8910¼**—Price, each.................. **$10.67**

## All Metal Auto for $8.47.

All parts of this vehicle, except the rubber tires, are made of metal. It has racy lines, is substantially made and attractively colored in red with yellow and black striping. Has metal imitation springs and crank, iron steering wheel and steering knuckles. Size over all, 37¼x18¾ in. Wheels, 10 in. in diameter with ½-in. rubber tires. Measures 18½ in. from center of seat to pedal extended to farthest point. Shpg. wt., 32 lbs. Unmailable. **See How to Order.**

**79T8909¼**

Price, each......... **$8.47**

**See Page 840 for New Wheel Construction Toy to Make Big Wagons, Hand Cars, Etc.**

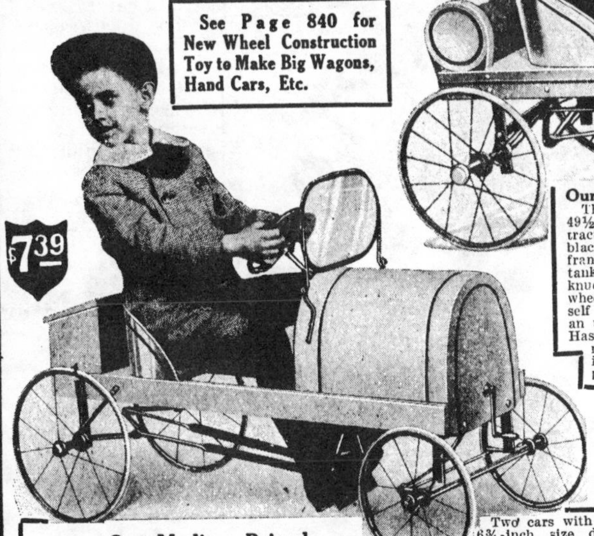


## Our Leader Racing Car for $13.87

This is our largest car, measuring 49½x24¼ inches over all. It is attractively finished in yellow with black striping. Body has wooden frame with sheet steel hood, dummy tank and seat back. It has steering knuckles, an 8-inch wood steering wheel, an imitation radiator and self starter, which makes a racket, an upholstered seat and steel tank. Has 12-inch wheels with ½-inch rubber tires. Measures 22½ inches from center of seat to pedal extended to its farthest point. **See How to Order.** Shpg. weight, 63 lbs. Unmailable.

**79T8913¼**

Price, each.

**$13.87**

## Our Medium Priced Automobiles.

Two cars with 10½x6¾-inch size detachable transparent wind shield in steel frame. Hinged box on rear in which to put tools or other toys. Very nicely finished in bright colors. 6-inch metal steering wheel, imitation starting crank and 3/8-inch rubber tire wheels. Improved steering knuckles for easy turning of front wheels. Frame and seat bottom of wood; steel hood and seat back. Made in two sizes. Unmailable. **See How to Order.**

**For the Smaller Lad, $7.39.**

Blue body with orange striping. Measures 36¼x19¾ inches over all. Front wheels 8 inches, rear wheels 10 inches in diameter. Measures about 17½ inches from center of seat to pedal extended to farthest point. Shpg. wt., 31 lbs.

**79T8907¼**—Price, each.. **$7.39**

**For the Larger Boy, $9.98.**

Yellow body with black striping. Measures 42x19¼ inches over all. Front wheels 10 inches, rear wheels 12 inches in diameter. Measures about 19 inches from center of seat to pedal extended to farthest point. Has imitation starting crank. Shipping weight, 37 pounds.

**79T8908¼**—Price, each.. **$9.98**

## Our Low Priced Automobiles.

These autos are racy designs nicely finished in attractive colors with appropriate striping. They have iron steering wheels, cranks, 3/8-in. rubber tire wheels, steering knuckles, wood frame and seat bottom, steel hood and seat back. In two sizes. Unmailable. **See How to Order.**

**36 Inches Over All, $5.98**

Red body with black striping. Measures 36¼x19¼ inches over all. Front wheels 8 inches, rear wheels 10 inches in diameter. Measures about 19½ inches from center of seat to pedal extended to farthest point. Shipping weight, 28 lbs.

**79T8905¼**

Price, each...... **$5.98**

**42 Inches Over All, $8.98**

Painted dark green, orange striping. Measures 42x19¼ inches over all. Front wheels 10 inches, rear wheels 12 inches in diameter. Measures about 21½ inches from center of seat to pedal extended to farthest point. Shipping weight, 32 pounds.

**79T8906¼**

Price, each..... **$8.98**

## A Crackerjack Value for $12.45.

The kiddies certainly like this racy looking auto with its wind shield, fenders, upholstered seat and dummy tank. Painted red with black trimming. Frame is of wood, with hood, seat back, tank and fenders (not running board, which is wood) of sheet steel. Has imitation self starter, which makes noise, and steering knuckles. Wheels have ½-inch rubber tires. Front wheels 10 inches, rear wheels 12 inches in diameter. Size, over all, 43x20 inches. Measures 20 inches from center of seat to pedal extended to farthest point. Shpg. wt., 48 lbs. Unmailable. **See How to Order.**

**79T8912¼**—Price, each........................................ **$12.45**

## An Auto With Attractive Lines for $11.75.

Body made of steel with wood seat bottom and wood front in hood. Hood painted red, body in green with black and yellow striping. Car equipped with a 10¾x8 inches, over all, detachable transparent wind shield in steel frame, imitation starting crank, bumper and springs; 6¾-inch metal steering wheel and upholstered seat. Wheels, 10 inches in diameter, with ½-inch rubber tires. Size, over all, 43¾x18¾ inches. Measures 22 inches from center of seat to pedal extended to farthest point. Shpg. wt., 35 lbs. Unmailable. **See How to Order.**

**79T8911¼**

Price, each......... **$11.75**

$4.67

# BOYS' WAGONS

$3.67

See Page 840 for new construction toy to build wagons, handcars, etc.

## This Play Wagon, $4.67.

Wood body is nicely painted and stenciled with neat design. Has removable seat and dashboard. The wheels are 12 and 18 inches in diameter with welded metal tires. Wheels are painted to match body. Body, wheels, seat and dashboard are painted and striped. Size of body, over all, 15x30 inches. Unmailable. Shipping weight, 30¼ pounds.

79T7648¼
Price .................. $4.67

## Boys' Medium Priced Wagon, $3.67.

Front wheels are 11 inches and back wheels about 14½ in. in diameter. Made of wood with steel tires. Size of body, over all, 14x28 inches. Wood parts finished in natural wood color, varnished. Body, seat and dashboard nicely striped. Just the wagon for the young children. Removable seat and dashboard. Shipping weight, 25 pounds.

79T7630¼
Price .........$3.67

## Every Child Likes His Own Wheelbarrow.

These wheelbarrows have sheet steel sides with wooden bottom. Body painted in bright colors and stenciled in assorted designs. All iron parts finished in a dark color. Easily set up.

| Catalog No. | Size of Body, Over All, About, Inches | Size of Wheel In. | Lgth., Over All, Including Handle, About, In. | Shpg. Wt., Lbs. | Price |
|---|---|---|---|---|---|
| 79T7625¼ | 6¼ x 9¼ x 3¾ | 6 | 26 | 3¼ | $0.89 |
| 79T7626¼ | 8½x11 x 4½ | 8 | 30 | 4½ | 1.19 |
| 79T7627¼ | 10 x12¾x 4¾ | 10 | 34½ | 5½ | 1.33 |
| 79T7628¼ | 11½x14½x 5 | 11 | 39 | 7¼ | 1.50 |

## Our Peerless Ball Bearing Coaster Wagons $6.45 and $5.98

The feature of this wagon is the ball bearings, which are set in the wheels, producing an easy running wagon. Has hardwood sides, heavy wheels and hand brake, while hubs, bands and tires are made of metal. Tires welded. Finished in natural wood color with red trimming. Made in two sizes.

79T7653¼—Size of body, over all, about 17x36 inches. Size of wheels, 10 inches. Shpg. wt., 31 lbs. Price....... $6.45

79T7654¼—Size of body, over all, about 15x32 inches. Size of wheels, 10 in. Shpg. wt., 28 pounds. Price..... $5.98

## Standard Coaster

Made of strong wood. Wheels have heavy spokes, painted. Each wagon is equipped with brake. The hub bands and tires are metal. Tires are welded. Removable sides and ends on all except small size. Smaller sizes have no metal grips. Made in four sizes.

| Catalog No. | Size of Body, Over All, About, Inches | Size of Wheels, Inches | Shpg. Wt., Lbs. | Price |
|---|---|---|---|---|
| 79T7679¼ | 17 x36 | 10 | 32 | $5.98 |
| 79T7674¼ | 15 x32 | 10 | 34 | 5.45 |
| 79T7680¼ | 13¾x30 | 9 | 27 | 4.47 |
| 79T7672¼ | 12¾x28 | 8 | 20¼ | 3.25 |

For Playground Equipment, Teeter-Totters, Slides, Giant Strides, Etc., see page 1296.

## Low Priced Steel Wagons.

Made of good grade steel and painted in attractive colors. Bottom of wood, painted. The tongue is of hardwood and fitted so as to be adaptable for coasting.

| Catalog No. | Size of Body, Over All, About, Inches | Size of Wheels, Inches | Shpg. Wt., Lbs. | Price |
|---|---|---|---|---|
| 79T7623¼ | 8 x18 | 6 | 6 | $1.39 |
| 79T7624¼ | 10½x22 | 8 | 7¾ | 1.67 |
| 79T7631¼ | 11¾x24½ | 10 | 12 | 1.98 |
| 79T7632¼ | 12½x26 | 10 | 13½ | 2.37 |
| 79T7633¼ | 13½x28⅝ | 11 | 16 | 2.67 |
| 79T7634¼ | 14⅝x30½ | 11 | 16½ | 2.98 |

## Our Finest Steel Exprcss Coaster Wagons.

Good grade steel wagon. The body is deep and has heavy sheet steel sides with beading around the top to insure strength. Hardwood handle, adaptable for coasting. The gears and wheels are substantially made and nicely painted in black. Body nicely finished in durable colors. These wagons are equipped with polished hub caps. Wood bottom. 79T7645¼ cannot be shipped by parcel post.

| Catalog No. | Size of Body, Over All, About, Inches | Size of Wheels, Inches | Shpg. Wt., Lbs. | Price |
|---|---|---|---|---|
| 79T7641¼ | 13 x26 | 10 | 18½ | $2.98 |
| 79T7643¼ | 14½x30 | 11 | 21½ | 3.98 |
| 79T7645¼ | 16½x36½ | 12 | 27¼ | 4.98 |

# The Harvard $9.98
# The Harvard $8.98 (Junior)

## THE BOYS' DELIGHT

**There Is More Pleasure to the Dollar in a Harvard Wagon Than in Most Things a Boy Can Have.**

—it is pretty hard to show all the various combinations that may be made from this wagon—the sketches around this page give some idea of its possibilities. Remember, the seat, sides, front, back and bottom are removable and that our price includes an extra reach. With a Harvard a boy can coast, haul wood or give his playmates a ride; and, by purchasing pole and doubletrees or shafts (listed extra below), he may hitch up dogs or goats, singly or in teams; also with a set of runners (listed separately below) a dandy coasting sled is produced.

—the Harvard Wagon is built to withstand the hard knocks it is certain to receive—the tires are metal, about 3/32 inch thick; hub bands are metal; wheels have staggered spokes, and wagon is built with solid steel axle, 9/16 inch in diameter. All of these features make for sturdiness and long life.

—materials used are good quality—the lumber is of good quality, and the entire wagon is painted and finished similar to a full size farm wagon. Front wheels are 14-inch, rear 20-inch. The Harvard Wagon is made in two sizes, as listed below. The larger of the two has a longer reach, heavier wheels, wider metal tires and larger body.

**Harvard Wagon.**

**79T7676¼**—Body over all, 18x40 inches, complete with handle and one extra extension reach. Shipping wt., crated, about 64 lbs. Unmailable. Price........ **$9.98**

**Harvard Junior Wagon.**

**79T7675¼**—Body over all, 18x36 inches. Complete with handle and one extra extension reach. Shpg. wt., crated, abt. 64 lbs. Unmailable. Price........ **$8.98**

### EXTRA WHEELS.

**79T7660¼**—Front Wheels for large wagon. Price, each.................$1.08
**79T7661¼**—Front Wheels for small wagon. Price, each....................98c
**79T7662¼**—Rear Wheels for large wagon. Price, each.................$1.19
**79T7663¼**—Rear Wheels for small wagon. Price, each..................$1.10
Average shipping weight, 3¾ pounds.

### SHAFT, POLE, RUNNERS (EXTRA).

**79T7677¼**—Set of four Sled Runners to put on in place of wheels. Shipping weight, 7½ pounds. (See illustration below.) Price ......................$2.19
**79T7678¼**—Pole and Doubletree for team of dogs or goats. Length, 63 inches over all. Shipping weight, 3½ pounds. Unmailable. (See illustration below.) Price...............$1.79
**79T7664¼**—Shafts to put on in place of handle, 51 inches long over all. Shipping weight, 3¾ pounds. Unmailable. (See illustration below.) Price...................98c

# GILBERT
# New Wheel Toy

Makes hand car 47 inches long; height of seat from floor, 8 inches.

## The Only Construction Toy That Builds Practical Outdoor Toys

### FOR THE BOY 8 TO 16 YEARS OF AGE.

**Boys, Make Your Own Hand Cars, Wagons, and Many Other Similar Articles.**

Called Gilbert's New Toy because it has not as yet been actually named. With the material in the flat wooden boxes shown on this page you can make such articles as you see illustrated. These represent only a few possibilities. Boys, think of making a wheelbarrow, a truck, a sled, a hand truck, a real·hand car with cog wheels, or an endless number of other things. The limit of the possibilities of construction with these outfits is not known.

The beauty of it all is that what you make is not a toy model, but one just as strong as you would buy in a store as a regulation article. All you need is one of these sets and a screwdriver and wrench. The outfits contain everything else, such as painted steel plates, angle irons, gears, axles, nuts, bolts, bars and boards of tough hardwood, nicely finished, and four strong round edge steel wheels. When you get tired of a wagon, take it apart and build a wheelbarrow or a hand car. You can make a sled for Wintertime also. This toy is made up in two sets, one with gears and pinions to make a real hand car, which we sell for $8.98, and a smaller set with fewer pieces and which has no gears or pinions, and consequently will not build a hand car with gears.

Makes wagon 11 inches high, 14 inches wide and 41 inches long, including handle.

Makes wheelbarrow 31 inches long and 10 inches wide.

### This Size for $5.47

Packed in strong wood box, 10x18x2¾ inches. Will build any one of the models shown, except hand car with cog wheels and wagon box sled. Shipping weight, 15 pounds.

79T4765¼
Price, complete,

**$5.47**

Makes glider 29 inches long and 22 inches high.

### The One We Recommend.

Complete with gears and pinions. Packed in strong wood box, 12¼x20¼x3½ inches. Will build any one of the models shown on this page. Shipping weight, 29¼ pounds.
79T4764¼—Price, complete... **$8.98**

Baby Sulky. Large enough to take baby out riding.

# QUALITY Converse TOYS

**MADE IN TOY-TOWN (WINCHENDON) MASS.**

## Our Leader Musical Chimes.

**Buy the Baby a Floor Chime.**

Nicely varnished wooden wheels and snappily decorated metal body. Good clear musical tones and a source of much enjoyment for the little tots, both in and out of doors. See page 823 for other sizes of floor chimes.

**Our Best Chime, $1.39.**

Fine clear tones. Metal sides in attractive colors. Nicely finished wooden wheels. Long ferrule wooden handle, about 22 inches long, for pushing or pulling. Size over all, about 7⅛x7¾ inches. Shipping weight, 3½ lbs.

**49T2306**
Price, each....... **$1.39**

**Chime for 69c.**

Same construction as 49T2306, but smaller. Handle, about 18 inches long. Size over all, about 5½x6¼ inches. Shipping weight, 1¾ pounds.

**49T2317**
Price, each....... **69c**

**Stock Farms—The Popular Toy.**

Substantially made of wood and printed in bright colors. Endless enjoyment for the child. Both barns are equipped with two sliding doors.

**Largest Size Stock Farm.**

The best selling size. Large enough for the child to really enjoy. Includes nine cut-out animals on standards. Length, 13¼ in.; height, 11⅜ in.; width, 9¼ in. Shpg. wt., 7 lbs.

**79T8120¼**—Price....... **98c**

**Medium Size Stock Farm.**

Finished same as 79T8120¼, but smaller size. Includes five cut-out animals on standards. Length, 10⅝ in.; height, 8⅛ in.; width, 6⅝ in. Shpg. wt., about 3 lbs.

**79T8121¼**—Price....... **50c**

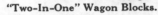

## "Two-In-One" Wagon Blocks.

These building blocks are made of good grade wood, finished in different colors and the box they are packed in can be used as a toy wagon. The wheels and handle are included on the large wagon, but the wheels only on the smaller size.

About 100 pieces. Wagon size, 10½x16½ inches. Has movable front axle, so wheels can turn under wagon. Shipping weight, 11 pounds.

**79T3632¼**—Price.............. **$1.47**

About ninety pieces. Wagon size, 10½x16¼ inches. Shipping weight, 8 pounds.

**79T3647¼**—Price.................. **98c**

**Our Leader Mahogany Finish Furniture Set, $2.47.**

Made of good grade wood, finished in mahogany color. Table top of thick veneered wood and measures about 20½x15¼ inches, oval shape. Height, about 16 inches. Has fancy legs. Chairs measure about 18½ inches high over all. Height of seat above floor, 9¾ inches. Size of seat over all, about 8¼x11 inches. Scroll shape back. Shpg. wt., 15 lbs.

**79T8529¼**—Table and Two Chairs.
Price.............................. **$2.47**

**Kiddie Racer.**

This toy is a very popular one for the tots too small to handle an automobile or velocipede. Good exercise for any child in paddling itself along the floor, sidewalk or street. Wood in natural finish with steel supports in rear. Head shaped and decorated to represent a horse's head. Wood handles so that child can steer very easily. No mechanism to handle, simply propelled by the child sitting on seat board and pushing it along with his feet and guiding it wherever he wishes. Comes in two sizes.

| | Height, Inches | Length, Seat, Inches | Length, Over All, Inches | Shipping Wt., Lbs. | Price |
|---|---|---|---|---|---|
| **79T7516¼** | 8½ | 12 | 21½ | 4½ | **$0.98** |
| **79T7517¼** | 9½ | 13¾ | 24¼ | 5½ | **1.47** |

**Dapple Gray Hobby Horses.**

These horses are wood finished in dapple gray and mounted with swinging metal rods. The bridle and saddle are made of oilcloth and imitation leather.

Our 38-inch horse. Length from center of saddle to bottom of stirrup, about 16 inches; height of saddle from floor, about 24 inches. Unmailable. Shipping wt., 34 lbs.

**79T7528¼**
Price......... **$6.47**

Our 34-inch horse. Length from center of saddle to bottom of stirrup, about 15 inches; height of saddle from floor, about 23 inches. Unmailable. Shpg. wt., 30 lbs.

**79T7529¼**
Price....... **$5.67**

**For Other Size Hobby Horses, see page 830.**

**Good Grade Toy Drum With Calfskin Head.**

Every boy likes to have a drum to play with. This is a good grade calf head drum. Has wooden hoops and good grade wood side, nicely painted and finished. Its hooks are iron and its ears are made of leather. Has good cord tighteners and cloth shoulder sling. Genuine calfskin top and sheepskin bottom, giving it a very nice, snappy sound. Comes complete with good grade drum sticks. Shpg. wt., average, 2½ lbs.

**79T2441¼**—Diameter, about 14 inches.
Price.................................. **$3.67**
**79T2442¼**—Diameter, about 12 inches.
Price.................................. **$2.98**
**79T2443¼**—Diameter, about 10 inches.
Price.................................. **$2.37**

**Big Value. 16-Inch Doll Trunk, $1.19.**

It is made of wood, covered with good grade colored paper. Has wooden slats on top and front. Cover is metal bound. Has removable inside tray. Has leather handholds and metal suit case lock and key. Size, over all, about 16x9x9 inches. Doll clothes not included. Exceptional value at the price. Shpg. wt., 15 pounds.

**79T8406¼**—Price......................... **$1.19**

**A brand new floor toy.**

**Whirligig Floor Toy.**

This is a toy with action and flash of colors. Made of wood, nicely painted in red, white and blue. Has 5-inch wooden wheels, two towers about 6¼ inches high and a windmill shaped wheel. When toy is pushed or pulled along the floor, the windmill wheel and towers will revolve. Very interesting and amusing for the child. Complete with ferruled wooden handle. Shipping weight, 1¾ pounds.

**69T9127**—Price......................... **47c**

# Baby Needs

**Baby's Play Swing.**

2-In-1 Baby Bed and Play Swing. A combination bed and play swing, 10 inches deep, made of good weight duck, with holes for baby's legs. Baby cannot fall out. Frame is made of flat steel. Has four duck straps on sides, which are riveted together at top and fastened by a hook. Seams reinforced with tape. Baby can sit on one side and have toys in front of him on the other. Rod can be pushed back, thus making the swing into a bed. Has cloth strings which can be tied together over top of bed to prevent child from falling out. Size over all, 13x30 in.; height, 40 inches. Toys not included. Shipping weight, 4¾ lbs.
**79T9175¼—Price.....$1.98**

**Baby's Adjustable Walker.**

Ideal for teaching the child to walk. Can be hung in the house or outdoors and gives baby first lessons in walking. Made of strong duck, with strong seat and four duck straps on sides riveted at top and fastened by metal hook. Furnished with spring to allow baby to teeter up and down with feet on floor. Frame is of good quality steel wire and edges are reinforced with tape. Is adjustable in length from 4 to 5 feet. Size of seat, 9½x10¾ inches. Shipping weight, 2½ pounds.
**69T9174 $1.79**

**The Perfection Baby Walker.**

Adjustable. Can be folded up when not in use. A soft comfortable seat for baby while learning to walk. Frame made of flat steel, enameled. Edges rounded and smooth; wide base prevents tipping over. Seat and play box made of duck, with holes for baby's legs. Ball bearing swivel casters. Has straps on side, making seat adjustable to length of baby's legs. Folds up as illustrated, small enough to be put behind door. Toys not included. Diameter, about 26 inches; stands about 15 inches high. Shipping wt., 9 pounds 8 ounces.
**79T9176¼—Price.........$3.98**

**"Rock-a-Bye" Swing.**

Duck seat, with holes for baby's legs. Complete with hook to attach to doorway or ceiling. Reinforced with steel in the canvas hemmed edges. Has four strong duck straps on sides which converge together at top and are riveted together and fastened by iron metal hook. Has strong supports. Size of seat, 13x13 inches; height, 40 inches. Shipping wt., 1½ pounds.
**69T9140 Price 98c**

**"Rock-a-Bye" Swing With Back Rest.**

Made of strong duck. Holes for baby's legs. Bound with tape. Frame made of steel wire, painted. Four strong duck straps, riveted together at top and fastened by metal hook. Has duck back rest with steel wire frame which makes it more comfortable for the infant. Size of seat, 13x13 inches; height, 48 in. Complete with screw eye. Can be folded flat when not in use. Shpg. wt., 2 lbs.
**69T9139 Price $1.79**

**This Natural Looking Bulldog Barks.**

Bulldog has large glass eyes. Cloth covered frame and painted in natural colors. One of the most attractive animal toys now on the market. Pressure on the head makes dog bark. Height, 6¾ in. Shipping wt., 1 lb.
**49T4087 Price 25c**

**Velveteen Duck on Wheels.**

Velveteen duck with good quality colored head, colored cloth feathers and bill. Squeaking noise produced when duck is drawn along floor. Has metal wheels. Size, over all, 8x6½ inches. Shipping wt., 1¼ lbs.
**49T4100—Price 98c**

**Large Sitting Bunny.**

One of our biggest values in stuffed animals. Made of good grade plush, have glass eyes and ribbon around neck. Length, 8 inches; height, 6 inches. Shipping weight, 1½ pounds.
**49T4024 Price 97c**

**These Dogs Bark!**

These white cloth covered little dogs represent one of our best animal values. Although small and light, they are well made, and the addition of a noise imitating a "bow-wow" appeals to the children. Have colored glass eyes. Brown spots on back and head. When head is slightly hit on top with the hand the mouth opens and the dog barks. Made in two sizes.

| | |
|---|---|
| **49T4088** Large dog. Size over all, 6½x6½ in. Shpg. wt., 1¼ lbs. Price.... **25c** | **49T4013** Small dog. Size over all, about 5½x5¼ in. Shpg. wt., 5 ounces.) Price.......**17c** |

## Floating Toys for Baby's Bath.

**Six Celluloid Floating Toys for 67c.**

Fine assortment of floating toys to keep baby amused while bathing. Assortment consists of fine grade celluloid toys, consisting of two 2¾-inch ducks, two 2¾-inch swans and two 3¾-in. fish. Shpg. wt., 8 oz.
**69T7852—Price, per box of 6... 67c**

**Swany and Her Family**

Floats in water; fine for baby's bath. Consists of a floating toy swan 2¾ inches long, and her five little ones, each 1⅜ inches long. Nicely finished. An attractive little set for the baby. Packed in box. Shpg. wt., 6 oz.
**69T7853—Price, per set.........39c**

**Buy Baby a Kitty With Voice.**

This pussy makes a noise when head is pressed. Has large glass eyes. Cloth covered frame and painted to represent striping on real kitty. Admired by all children. Height, 6¾ in. Shipping weight, 7 oz.
**49T4089 Price 25c**

**St. Bernard Dog.**

Good quality long pile plush, white and brown colors, glass eyes. Collar around neck. Nicely shaped and formed. Height, 7½ inches; length, 9 inches, including tail. Shpg. wt., 1¼ lbs.
**49T4026—Price $1.25**

**Sitting Cat.**

Made of plush. Well formed and finished throughout. Has glass eyes, ribbon around neck, and colored yarn ball between front paws. Length, 10 inches; height, 7½ in.
**49T4035—Price $1.25**

## White and Red Rubber Animals.

**Just the Thing for the Baby.**

Assorted white rubber animals of good grade rubber, with whistles. Average size, 4¼x2¾ inches. Shipping weight, 5 ounces.
**49T4406 Price, each 15c**

**White Rubber Cat in Basket.**

Made of good grade rubber. Has whistle. Height, about 4 inches. Shipping wt., 4 oz.
**49T4404 15c**

**Real Looking White Rubber Animals.**

Assorted animals, complete with whistles. Average size, 3½x5 in. Shipping weight, 7 oz.
**49T4428 Price, each 25c**

**Red Rubber Cat.**

Heavy red rubber. Complete with whistle. Size over all, 4½x2 inches. Shpg. wt., 7 oz.
**49T4433 Price 25c**

**Sitting Rabbit.**

Made of good grade red rubber, complete with whistle. Height, 5 inches. Shipping wt., 6 oz.
**49T4434 Price 25c**

**Peter Rabbit.**

Made of good grade red rubber, with whistle. Height, 5¾ inches. Shipping wt., 6 ounces.
**49T4432 Price 25c**

**Cute Rubber Dog.**

Red rubber dog with whistle. Size, over all, 5x4¼ in. Shpg. wt., 5 oz.
**49T4436 47c**

**Red Rubber Horse.**

Heavy red rubber. Complete with whistle. Size, over all, 5x4¾ inches. Shipping weight, 6 oz.
**49T4437 Price 47c**

# Shoo flies

**Medium Priced Rocker Shoofly.**

Ponies are painted white with imitation harness decorations and red rockers. Wooden seat and back painted red. Has a swinging play box. Length, 37 inches; height, 17½ in.; width, 12 in. Shipping weight, 10¾ lbs. Unmailable.
**79T7584¼**
Price..$1.79

Similar to 79T7584¼, only made of a thinner grade of wood and smaller in size. Size, over all, length, 32 inches; height, 16 in.; width, 11½ in. Shpg. wt., 7½ lbs. Unmailable.
**79T7581¼**
Price. $1.50

**Horse Head Rocker.**

Good grade wood. Horse's head nicely made and finished. Baby sits with horse's head between legs, which insures it against falling out of rocker. Size, over all, height, 19 in.; length, about 56 in. Shpg. wt., 10½ lbs. Unmailable.
**79T7589¼**—Finished in white enamel, trimmed in gilt.
Price..$4.39
**79T7582¼**—Natural wood finish, varnished and striped.
Price......$3.98

**Good Quality Shoofly.**

Made of heavy wood, nicely enameled in white, gilt decorations. Large wooden play box for baby's toys. Seat is padded and upholstered in corduroy. Has foot rest and braces under and behind seat. In two designs. Unmailable.
**79T7590¼**—Swan design. Lgth. over all, abt. 35½ in.; ht., 21½ in. Shpg. wt., 23 lbs. Price.....$5.47
**79T7591¼**—Horse design. Length over all, abt. 35 in.; ht., abt. 19 in. Shpg. wt., 21 lbs.....$5.47

**This Rocker Shoofly Only $1.98.**

Seat and back of seat upholstered. Rockers painted red and ponies in white with colored designs of imitation harness. Complete with a play box for small toys. Size, over all, length, about 37 inches; height, 17 inches. Shipping weight, 13 pounds. Unmailable.
**79T7585¼**—Price .....................$1.98

**Our Highest Grade Convertible Auto and Shoofly.**
**Pull Auto for Outdoors. Rocking Shoofly for Home.**

Made of heavy good grade wood, enameled white with blue and gilt decorations. Has large wooden play box in front, strong wooden seat. When auto is lifted off rockers it rests on four good wooden wheels and can be pulled around. Length, 37½ in.; height, 17¾ in. Shipping weight, 28 pounds. Unmailable.
**79T7592¼**
Price......$6.98

Good grade wood, enameled in white with gilt and black decorations. Seat upholstered in corduroy. Play box and foot rest. Length, 35 in.; height, 23 in.; width, 15½ in. Shipping weight, 20 pounds. Unmailable.
**79T7593¼**
Price .........$6.98

**Our Best Swan Design Swinging Shoofly.**

Swings on iron rods. Strongly braced.

**Medium Priced Rocker.**

Strong 36-inch rockers. Painted ponies, basket of imitation reed. Seat upholstered in cloth with back cushion of same material. Size, about 12x22x36 in. Shpg. wt., 15 lbs. Unmailable.
**79T7580¼**—Price.$3.67

**Low Price Is the Feature Here.**

Painted rockers, 36 inches long, with upholstered seat and willow basket. Size, about 12x19x36 in. Shpg. wt., 15 lbs. Unmailable.
**79T7576¼**
Price .............$2.67

**Baby's First rthday**
**Good Grade Swinging Shoofly.**

Horses painted white and decorated. Swinging frame is made of hardwood, nicely painted. Seat and back of seat upholstered in printed cloth. Complete with play box. Size, about 31x20x17 in. Shpg. wt., 15¾ lbs. Unmailable.
**79T7577¼**—Price .............$3.19

**Our Best Double Swing Shoofly.**

Reed and willow basket seat. Double swing frame is hardwood, varnished. Horses painted white, with red decorations. Size, over all, 20x 26x34 in. Shpg. wt., 37 lbs. Unmailable.
**79T7579¼**—Price ......$5.98

**Upholstered Seat Cushion on This One.**

Imitation reed basket seat; painted imitation harness. Size, over all, 12x36x34 inches. Shipping weight, 30 pounds. Unmailable.
**79T7578¼**—Price ..$4.98

# HOBBY HORSES

They have glass eyes, stationary imitation leather saddle and blanket, mane and tail. Made of wood, dapple gray finish, in three sizes, each a good reproduction of a pony for a boy.

**Our Best Horses**

These horses are about 3 feet high and built on strong, substantial frames.

**For the Little Tots.**

A good value for a low price. Some of the other ponies are too big for the little folks. This dapple gray has mane and tail, with rockers about 35¼ inches in length. The little rider sits on the saddle with his feet almost to the floor (the pony's ears are only a little over 1½ feet from the floor.) Made of wood, dapple gray finish. Shpg. wt., 10 lbs.
**79T7536¼**—Price .............$2.98

Lgth. abt. 44 in.; ht. abt. 38 in. Stirrups adjustable from 16 in. to 22 in. Shpg. wt., 54 lbs. Unmailable.
**79T7531¼**
Price ......$13.69

Length, 39 in.; height, about 35 in. Stirrups adjustable from 13 to 17 in. Shipping weight, 45 lbs. Unmailable.
**79T7526¼**
Price ......$11.45

Length, about 37 in.; ht., abt. 32 in. Stirrups adjustable from 13 to 17 in. Shpg. wt., 45 lbs. Unmailable.
**79T7527¼**—$9.98

**A Fine Christmas Present.**

Imitation hair mane and tail, strong bridle; is about 27½ inches high over all. Shipping wt., carefully packed, 18½ lbs. Unmailable.
**79T2535¼**—Price .............$4.45

# Indoor Games

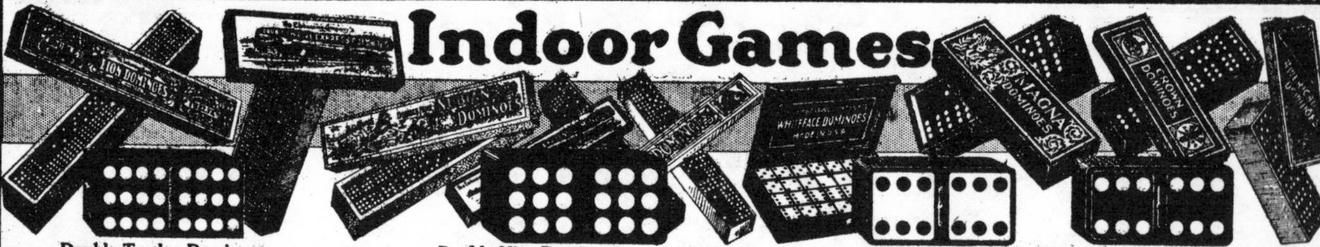

## Double-Twelve Dominoes.

Made of good quality wood. Double-Twelve. Embossed. Each domino 1¾x⅞x⅜ inch. Each set in box. Shpg. wt., 2¼ lbs.
49T166
Per set.....$1.19

Set of 1⅝x¾x¼-inch Double-Twelve Dominoes in box. Made of embossed wood. Shipping weight, 1½ lbs.
49T165
Per set.....50c

## Double-Nine Dominoes.

Made of wood, embossed. Double-Nine. Each domino 1³⁄₁₆x1⅝x⁵⁄₁₆ inch. Shipping weight, 1¼ pounds.
49T162
Per set.....48c

Set of Double-Nine Dominoes, each one measuring 1⅝x¾x¼ in., embossed. Shipping weight, 1 lb.
49T123
Per set.....33c

Made of wood, embossed. Double-Nine. Each domino 1⁷⁄₁₆x¾x¼ inches. Shipping weight, 12 ounces.
49T232
Per set.......25c

## Double-Six Dominoes.

White Face Double-Six Dominoes. Size, 2x1x⁷⁄₁₆ in. Embossed wood. Complete in imitation leather case. Shpg. wt., 1¼ lbs.
49T164
Per set.........$1.19

Embossed wood Double-Six Dominoes. Size, 2⅛x1¹⁄₁₆x½ inch. In box. Shipping weight, 1¼ lbs.
49T161
Per set.....69c

Double-Six. Size, 2x1x⅜ in. In paper covered box. Shpg. wt., 1 lb.
49T124
Per set...35c

Embossed wood. Double-Six Dominoes, measuring 1⅝x¾x⁵⁄₁₆ inch. In paper box. Shipping wt., 9 oz.
49T233
Per set.......19c

## Toy Pool Table, $1.67.

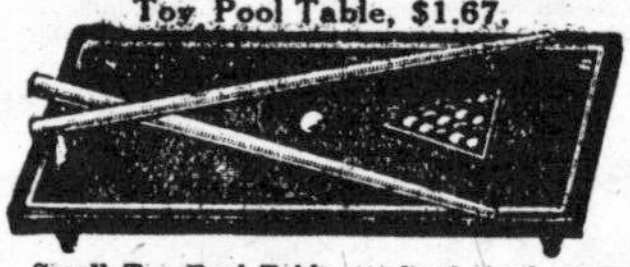

Small Toy Pool Table, made of wood, complete with two 20-inch cues, a triangle, fifteen 1¹⁄₁₆-inch numbered composition balls and a cue ball. Table measures 21x12 inches. It is small but complete, and a delight to the kiddies. Not suitable for real game, but for toy purposes only. Shipping weight, 3¼ pounds.
49T208
Price, complete.....$1.67

## Jack Straws.

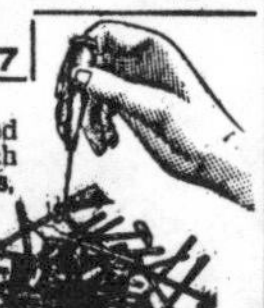

Regular old fashioned game of Jack Straws, with numbered wooden shovels, hoes, guns and other pieces. Box, size, 7⅝x5⅝ in. Shpg. wt., 6 oz.
49T142
Price ..........29c

## Lotto Game.

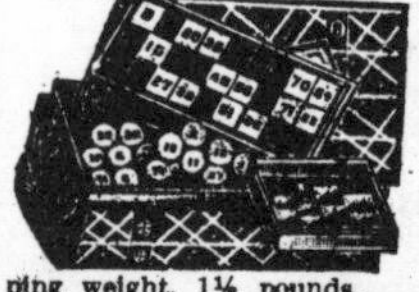

Nicely colored and printed cardboard box to resemble trunk. Size, 6¾x4⅛x2⅝ in. Complete with numbered wooden discs and glass counters. Shipping weight, 1⅛ pounds.
49T114—Price ..........................35c

## Ring My Nose.

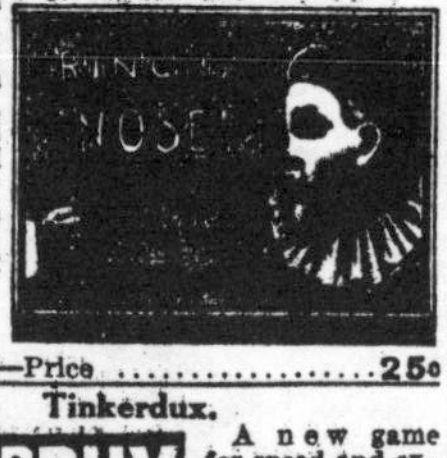

Printed in several colors. Clown target with curved nose, six colored rings and different valuations on pegs on face. Box, 10¾x7⅝ in. Shipping weight, 11 ounces.
49T136—Price ..........................25c

## Tinkerdux.

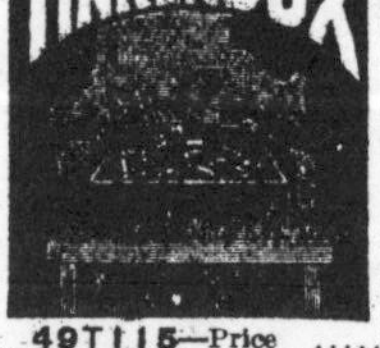


A new game for speed and excitement. Consists of two hammers that are used to catch colored cylindrical wooden pegs. Simple to learn, but requires skill to be consistent winner. A winner with the kiddies. Shipping wt., 1 lb.
49T115—Price ..................45c

## Three Games for 39 Cents.

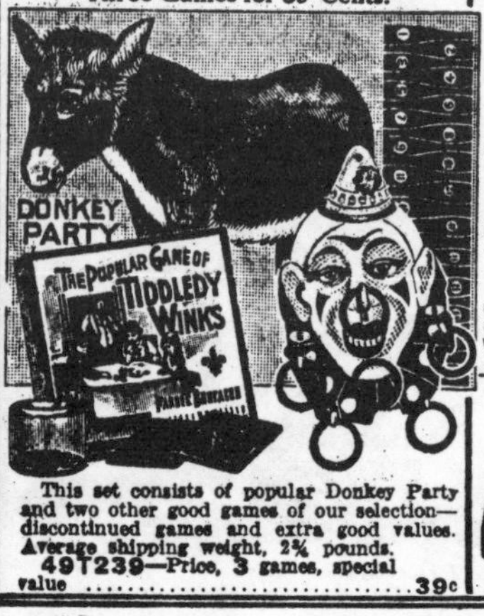


This set consists of popular Donkey Party and two other good games of our selection—discontinued games and extra good values. Average shipping weight, 2⅜ pounds.
49T239—Price, 3 games, special value ..................39c

## Tiddledy Winks.

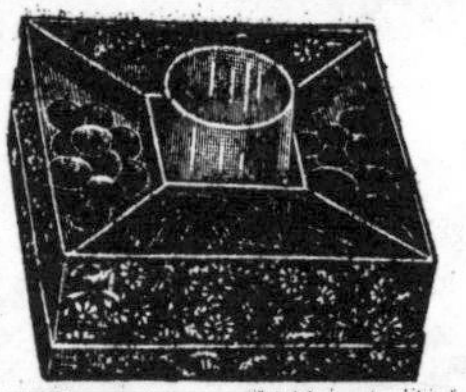

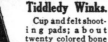

Cup and felt shooting pads; about twenty colored bone discs and four bone shooting discs. Shipping weight, 12 oz.
49T147
Price complete.......25c

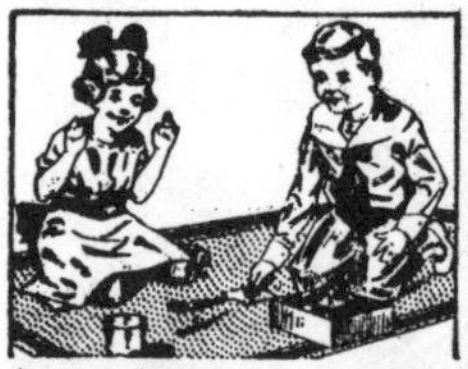

## Checker and Backgammon Boards.

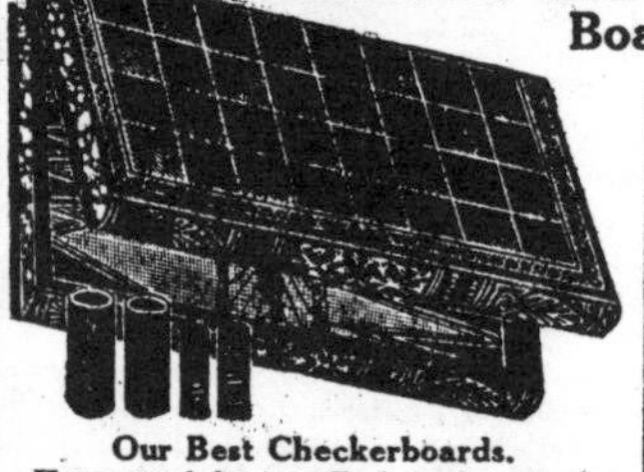

### Our Best Checkerboards.

Heavy wood frame. Book back and edge effect. Fancy heavy paper covered. Printed in red, black and gilt. Gloss finish. Glazed paper inside. Extension edge. Complete with checkers, dice cup and dice. Made in two sizes.

Size, 18½x17⅛ inches. Has 1¾-inch squares. Shipping weight, 2¼ pounds.
49T137—Price .................$1.19

Size, 16x14¼ inches. Has 1½-inch squares. Shipping weight, 1¾ pounds.
49T116—Price ......................79c

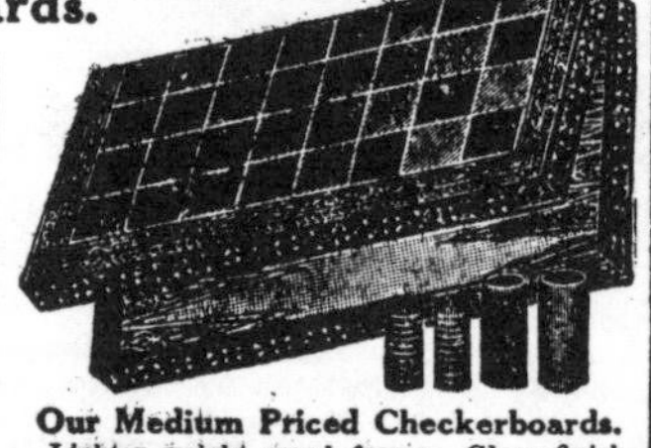

### Our Medium Priced Checkerboards.

Lighter weight wood frame. Gloss finish. Complete with checkers, dice cup and dice. Made in three sizes.

Size, 18x17¾ inches. Has 1¹¹⁄₁₆-inch squares. Shipping weight, 2 pounds.
49T119—Price ....................50c

Size, 16x15¾ inches. Has 1½-inch squares. Shipping weight, 1⅝ pounds.
49T117—Price ....................39c

Size, 15x15 inches. Not as well finished. Shipping weight, 1½ pounds.
49T118—Price ....................25c

## A High Grade Line of Ten Pins.

Every child likes to bowl down the ten pins. Very easy to play, and ten pins are practically indestructible. Smoothly turned wood. Varnished and striped in red. Each outfit includes three balls. Complete in box. A superior line to that previously sold.

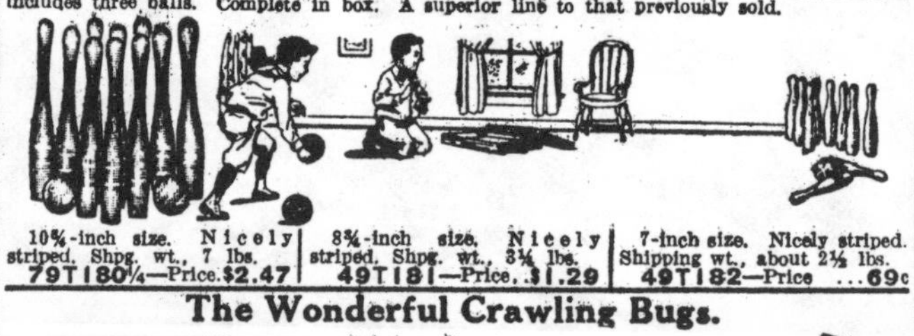

10¾-inch size. Nicely striped. Shpg. wt., 7 lbs.
79T180¼—Price.$2.47

8¾-inch size. Nicely striped. Shpg. wt., 3¼ lbs.
49T181—Price. $1.29

7-inch size. Nicely striped. Shipping wt., about 2½ lbs.
49T182—Price ...69c

## The Wonderful Crawling Bugs.

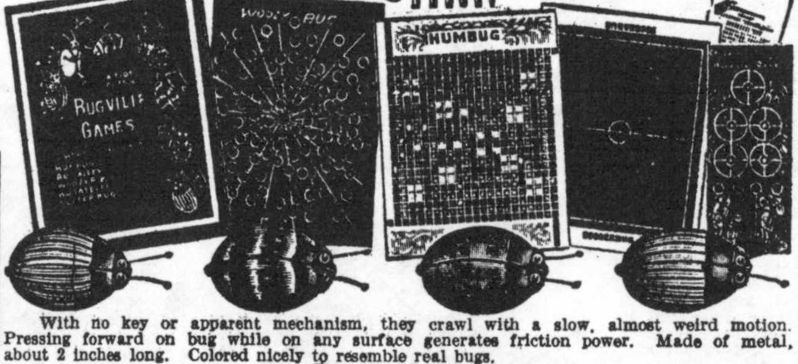


With no key or apparent mechanism, they crawl with a slow, almost weird motion. Pressing forward on bug while on any surface generates friction power. Made of metal, about 2 inches long. Colored nicely to resemble real bugs.

### Bugville Games.

With this outfit five interesting and amusing games can be played: Bugatelle, bugalley, soccerbug, humbug, woozybug, etc. Outfit has four assorted colored bugs which move around as if they were alive. They can also be used to do all sorts of tricks. Shipping weight, 1¾ pounds.
49T105—Price ..................................$1.39

## Game of Shufflebug.

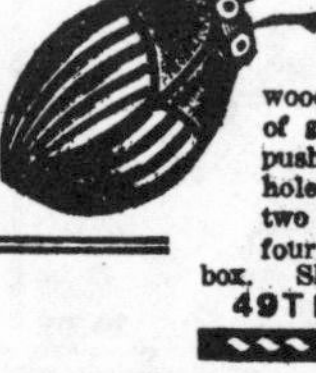

A new and interesting game played with one bug and eight wooden discs. The object of game is to have the bug push the wooden discs into holes. To be played by two persons, each using four discs. Packed in neat box. Shipping weight, 6 oz.
49T108—Price .... 39c

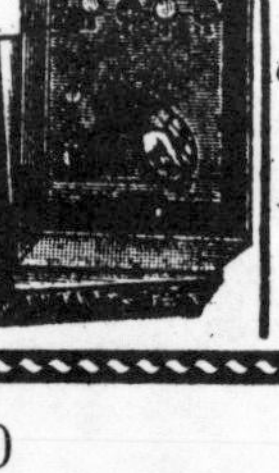

## Extra Bugs.

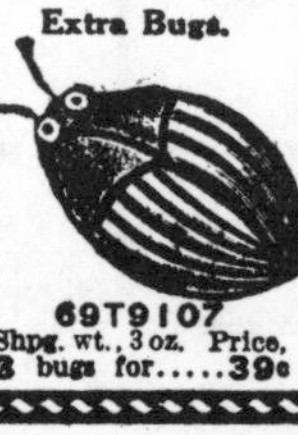

69T9107
Shpg. wt., 3 oz. Price, 3 bugs for.....39c

## Cortella Game.

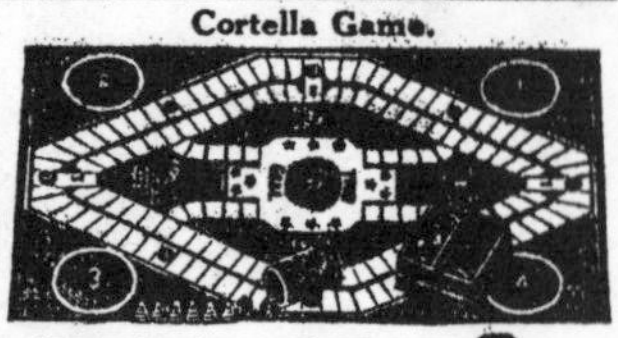

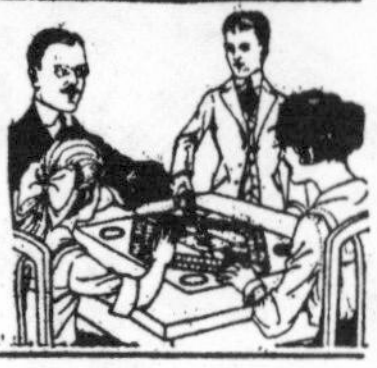

A race for two or four. Complete with dice box, dice and men. Size of board, 23¾x15 inches. One of our most popular board games. Shpg. wt., 2 lbs.
49T289
Price ......67c

## Chessmen.

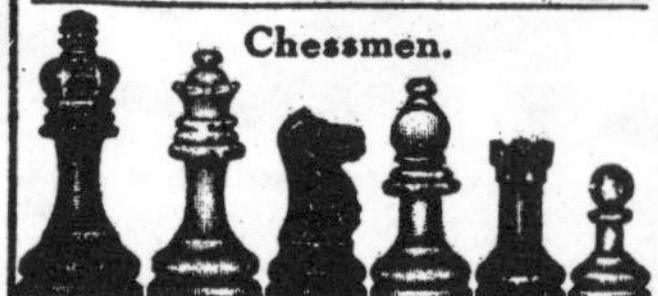

We have three grades of chessmen.

49T198—Staunton pattern, loaded bottoms with felt pads. Shpg. wt., 1½ pounds. Price ..............................$2.79

49T199—Same as above, only bottoms not loaded and no felt pads. Shipping weight, 11 ounces. Price.............$1.47

49T194—Our lowest price set. Not as fancy as the other two. Shipping weight, 10 ounces. Price..........................67c

## Pollyanna.

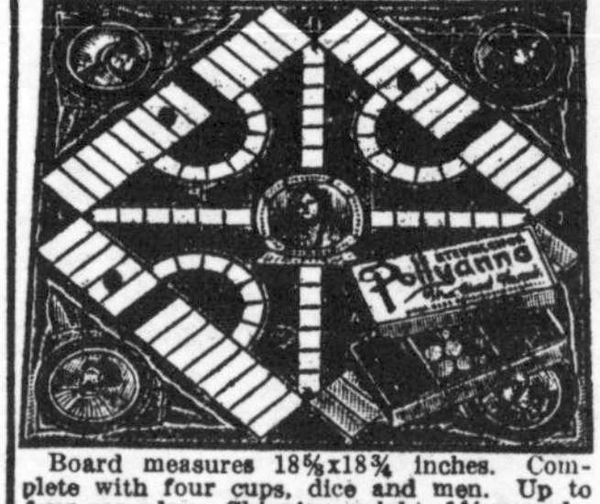


Board measures 18⅝x18¾ inches. Complete with four cups, dice and men. Up to four can play. Shipping weight, 1½ pounds.
49T120—Price ........................98c

## Table Croquet.

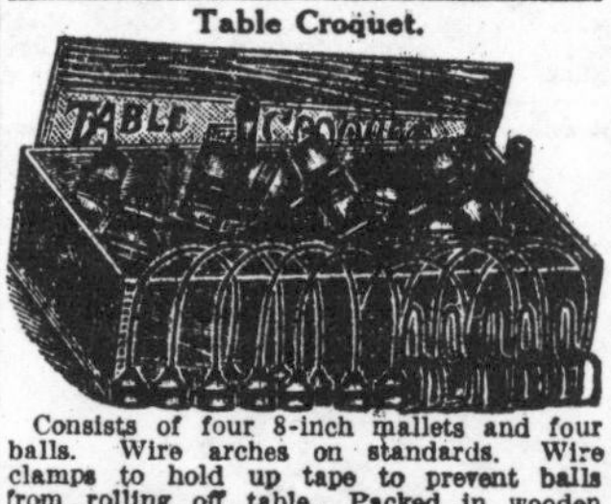


Consists of four 8-inch mallets and four balls. Wire arches on standards. Wire clamps to hold up tape to prevent balls from rolling off table. Packed in wooden box. Size, 11⅝x7¼x2⅞ inches. Shipping weight, 1¾ pounds.
49T111—Price, complete....... 79c

## Attack, Up to Date War Game.

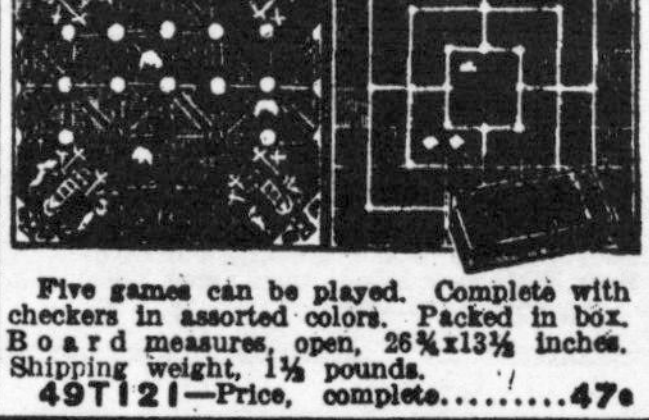

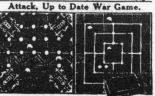

Five games can be played. Complete with checkers in assorted colors. Packed in box. Board measures, open, 26¾x13⅜ inches. Shipping weight, 1½ pounds.
49T121—Price, complete..........47c

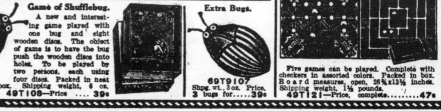

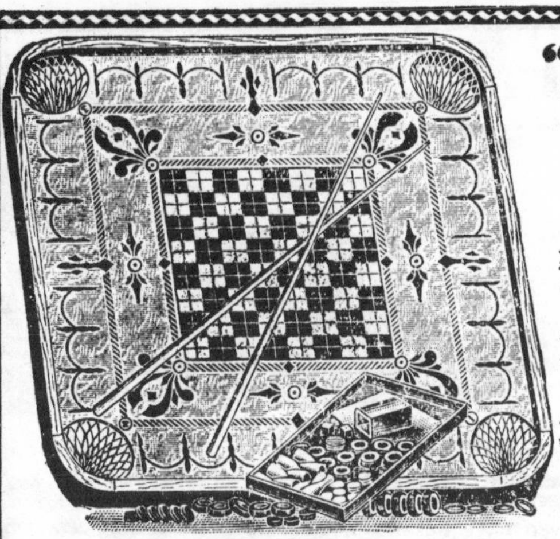

# "I'll Play You A Game"

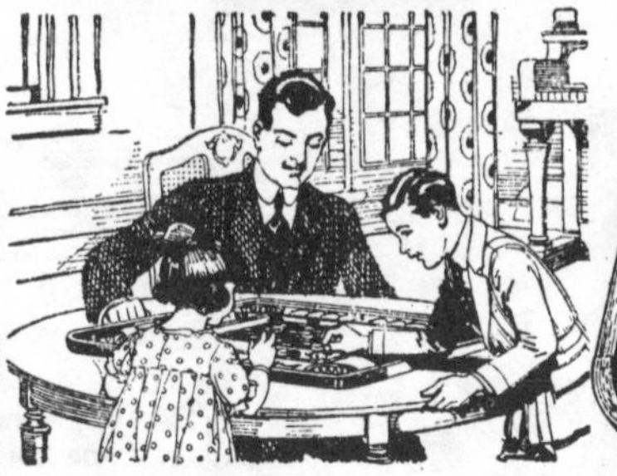

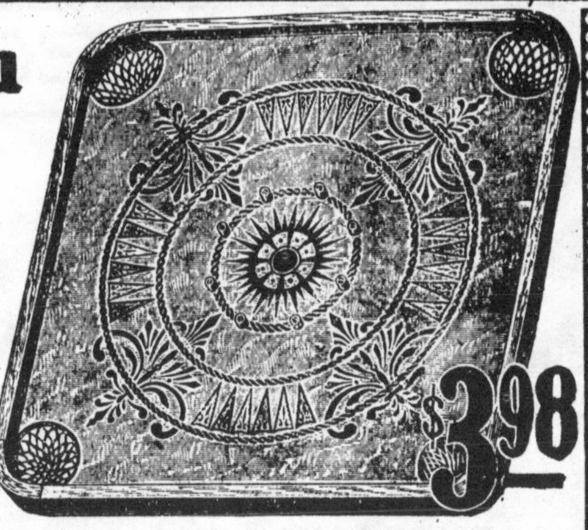


## Fifty-Seven Interesting Games Can Be Played on This Moderate Priced Game Board

Very well made, moderate priced game board. It is one of our most popular boards and will furnish amusement for the entire family, young and old. Makes a very acceptable present which will be used at all times. Equipped with reversible net pockets. Complete with full set of equipment to play fifty-seven games. The panel is made of three-ply maple veneer, natural wood finish. Crokinole and checker sections are artistically stenciled on the polished surface of the wood, producing a pleasing effect. Size, 29 inches square. Shipping weight, 11½ pounds. On account of size, this board cannot be shipped by parcel post.

79T489¼—Price .......................................... $3.98

### $2.98 Complete.

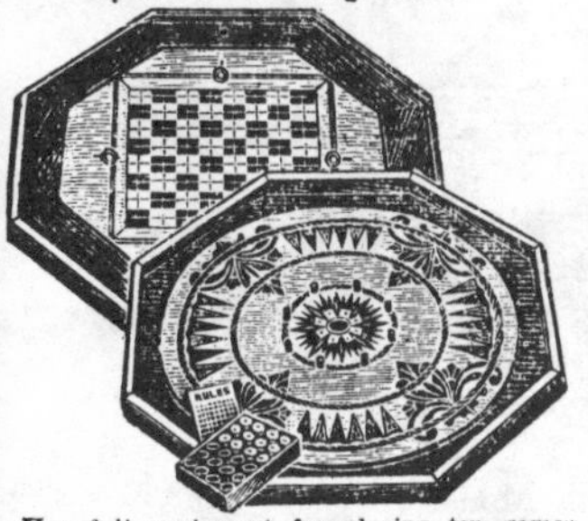

Has full equipment for playing ten games. Crokinole, checkers and caroms are the games featured. Made of good grade wood, smoothly finished. Colored transferred designs. Complete equipment and directions. Diameter, 28 inches. Shipping weight, 11¼ pounds. On account of size, board cannot be shipped by parcel post.

79T490¼—Price .............. $2.98

### A Medium Priced Combination Game Board.

**Forty-Six Different Kinds of Games and Twenty-One Variations Can Be Played on This Board.**

A big favorite and a great source of amusement. The crokinole panel has imitation mahogany finish and the remainder of the board is white maple, polished, natural wood finish. Center is made of three-ply veneer, thereby giving strength, but still maintaining lightness of weight. Equipped with reversible net pockets. The entire edge or cushion of one side of the board is lined with green felt. The cues and other pieces of equipment are smoothly finished and are packed in cardboard carton. Score boards and full directions for forty-six different kinds of games and twenty-one variations are included. Entire board has rubbed finish, making very good shooting surface. Size, 28½x28½ inches. Shipping weight, 13¼ pounds. On account of size board cannot be shipped by parcel post.

79T487¼ Price ............ $5.47

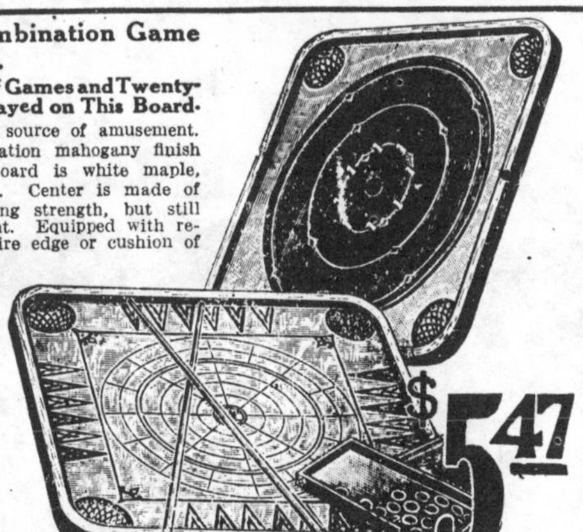


### Crokinole Rings.

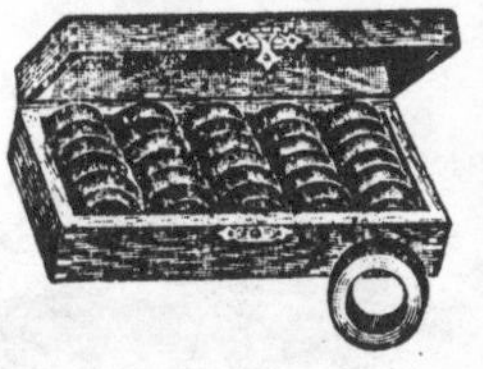

Complete set of rings, made of hardwood, for use on crokinole boards. Same rings in two style boxes.

49T481—In nicely finished wooden case (as illustrated). Case protects the rings. Shipping wt., 14 ounces.
Price .......................... 69c

49T480—In plain cardboard box, same rings as above. Shipping weight, 8 ounces.
Price .......................... 35c

### Tuff Luck Board.

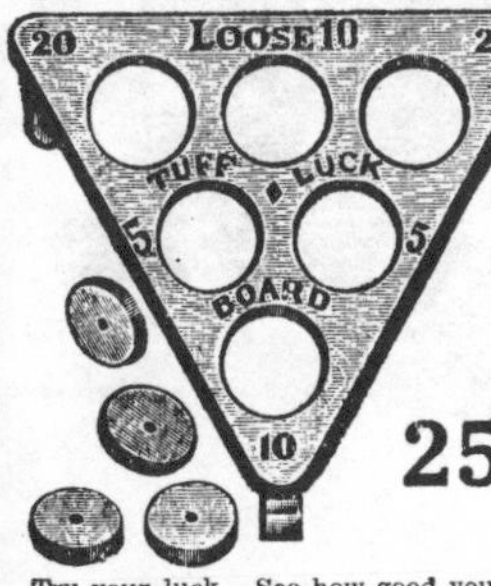


25c

Try your luck. See how good your eye is in tossing. This 13-inch triangle shaped board is made of three-ply veneer, nicely finished. Six round holes, about 2½ inches in diameter, each numbered, are cut out in board. Four assorted colored discs, about 1¼ inches in diameter, are furnished to be used for tossing. Interesting and amusing for young and old. Shipping weight, 1 lb.

49T107—Price .............. 25c

### Original Ouija Board—The Magic Game

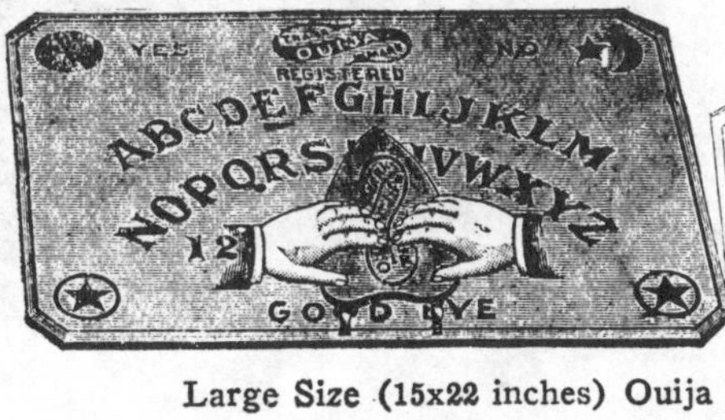


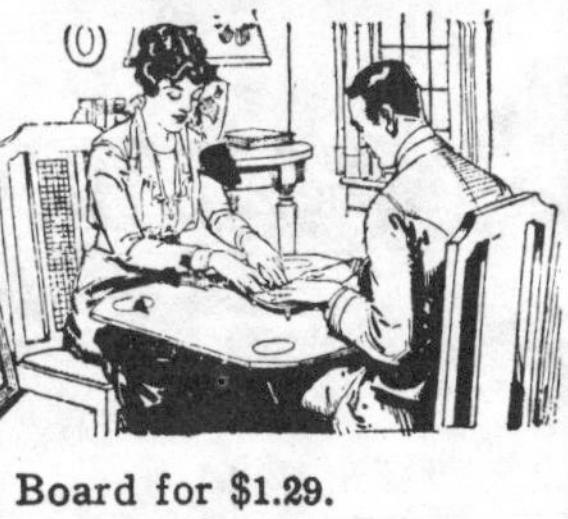

**Large Size (15x22 inches) Ouija Board for $1.29.**

Interesting and mystifying game. Great mirth making game for parties. Apparently answers questions concerning past, present and future. Full directions accompany each package. Nicely finished board, with felt tipped table on which you place your hands. Size, 15x22 inches. Shipping weight, 3¼ pounds.

79T112¼—Price ........................................ $1.29

### Jack Board.

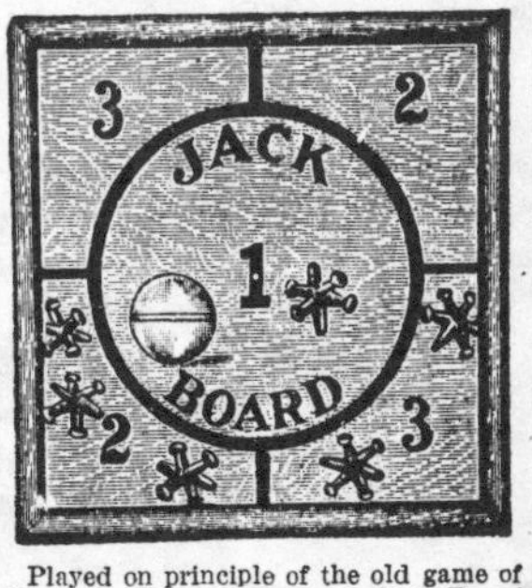


Played on principle of the old game of "Jacks." Two or more can play. Board measures 12x12 inches, nicely finished in natural wood color. Amusing and interesting for young folks. A set of metal jacks and a small size rubber ball furnished with board. Shipping weight, 1¾ pounds.

49T109—Price ............ 47c

### Grasshopper Tennis.

**A Very Exciting Game.**

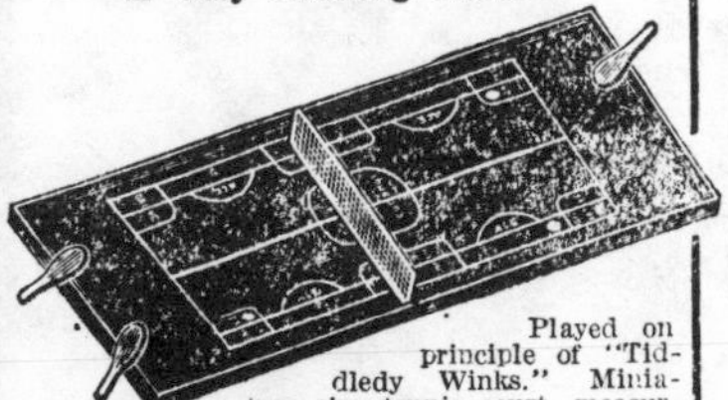

Played on principle of "Tiddledy Winks." Miniature size tennis court, measuring 12x26 inches. Made of heavy cardboard. Made to close same as box, size, 12x13 inches. Bottom of court covered with heavy cloth. Netting measures 11x2 inches. Rackets made of wood, about 3 inches long. In place of balls, little round bone discs, about ⅝ inch in diameter, are furnished. Complete with four rackets and four discs. Shipping weight, 1¾ pounds.

49T101—Price .............. 97c

### Parcheesi

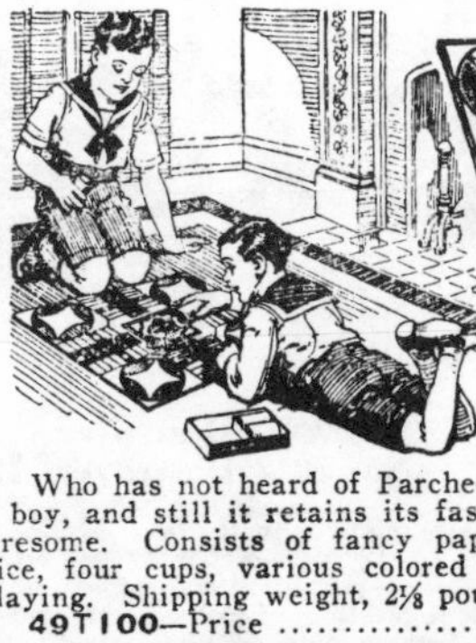

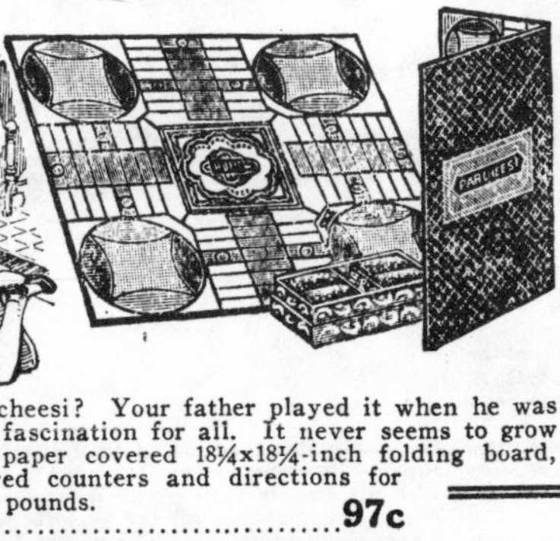

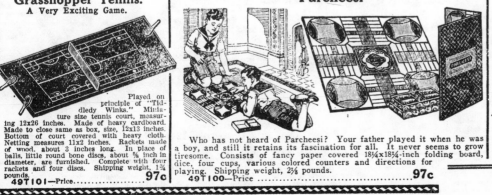

Who has not heard of Parcheesi? Your father played it when he was a boy, and still it retains its fascination for all. It never seems to grow tiresome. Consists of fancy paper covered 18¼x18¼-inch folding board, dice, four cups, various colored counters and directions for playing. Shipping weight, 2⅛ pounds.

49T100—Price .............................. 97c

### Grande Auto Race.

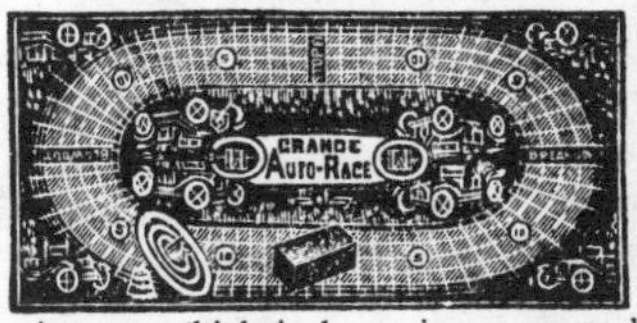


A game which is becoming more and more popular each year. It is especially fascinating because of the spirit developed and will be enjoyed by all. Board in colors to represent an automobile track. Complete with cup and dice and four metal autos. Two to four can play. Size, 23¾x15 inches. Shipping weight, 1¾ pounds.

49T288—Price ................ 67c

# IVES MECHANICAL BOATS

## DIVING SUBMARINE

This Ives Submarine is a wonder. When wound up with its key it shoots along the surface and dives again and again, just like a real submarine. You can have no end of fun with it attacking wooden ships that you make for your war game.

**No. 1009 Diving Submarine, 10½-inch Model.**

## IVES MOTOR BOAT or HARBOR PATROL

See this trim motor boat, equipped with ventilators, windshield, seats and flag. It is long, low and speedy. Built of steel, beautifully painted and equipped with Ives clockwork. Made in two sizes.

**No. 4009 Motor Boat,  9-inch Model.**
**No. 4012 Motor Boat, 12-inch Model.**

**No. 6009 Merchant Marine,  9-inch Model.**
**No. 6012 Merchant Marine, 12-inch Model.**

**No. 2009 Tug Boat, 9-inch Model.**

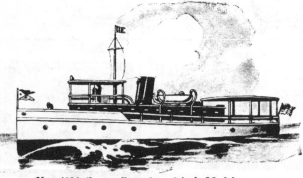

**No. 4010 Scout Patrol,  9-inch Model.**
**No. 4013 Scout Patrol, 12-inch Model.**

**No. 5009 Ocean Liner,  9-inch Model.**
**No. 5012 Ocean Liner, 12-inch Model.**

## The Ives Merchant Marine

The ships of the Ives Merchant Marine and the ships of the Ives Navy are built like real ships and include the famous Hog Island type of steamship as well as tugs, steam launches, yachts, torpedo boat destroyers, submarines that dive, scout patrols, etc. They are strongly made of real steel and beautifully painted and equipped to look like the real ships which were used as designs.

### RUN BY IVES CLOCKWORK

These ships are run by Ives clockwork, installed in the hull in such a way that water cannot get to it and injure it. They wind up with a key and will glide through the water under the power of their real propellers, for a long while. They can be steered in any direction by means of their rudders. The Ives submarine will glide along the surface then dive automatically, rise to the surface and dive again, just like a real submarine.

### WHAT IVES SHIPS MEAN TO AMERICAN BOYS

With one of the boats of the Ives fleets a boy can have fun outdoors all summer long, while in the winter he can sail it in the bath tub. But better still, he can get thoroughly interested in the great game of commerce and the big Merchant Marine of his country. He can talk it, play it and interest his chums in it. Together they can get a number of "Ives" ships and play the whole game of sea transportation. Who knows but what it may lead them into the big business of transportation by sea that is going to play such a wonderful part in the future world trade of the United States?

Of course, all of you boys cannot follow the sea, no matter how attractive it may seem to you and how much bigger and better paid a profession it is going to be in the future. For some of you will have to be the big merchants who will handle the cargoes from foreign ports and some of you will have to fill the important positions of looking after the tremendous shipments leaving this country. In fact, the building of the great United States Merchant Marine will mean a new phase of American business and will open up many avenues and opportunities to the American boy of to-day. The more you know about ships and shipping, ports of call, navigation and all the things pertaining to the sea, the better fitted you will be to enter this new branch of service of our glorious country.

**No. 3009 Destroyer,  9-inch Model**
**No. 3012 Destroyer, 12-inch Model**

Ives

### No. 4570. AUTOMOBILE

A perfect reproduction in miniature of the well known "Flivver." Undoubtedly one of the best selling small toys on the market and gaining in popularity each day. Body finished in enamels of different colors; windshield bronzed; steering gear black and movable wheels bronze finish. Packed one dozen to the box.

### No. 4610. TRUCK

Companion piece to our famous No. 4570 Automobile. Finished and packed exactly the same as the above number.

### No. 4620. ENGINE

We herewith present to you our newest numbers in those shown on this and the next page. First the engine, of the latest model. Body and movable wheels in black enamel. Packed one dozen to the box.

### No. 4623. PULLMAN COACH

This article as well as all those shown on this page, has movable and easily running wheels. Finished in colored enamels and packed one dozen to the box.

### No. 4621. TENDER

Coupling device enables it to be securely attached to the engine and the cars following. Movable wheels and body finished in black enamel, and packed one dozen to the box.

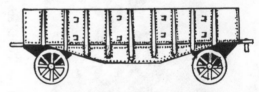

### No. 4624. FLAT CAR

Finished in colored enamels and packed one dozen to the box.

### No. 4622. BAGGAGE CAR

Finished in colored enamels and packed one dozen to the box. Also has movable wheels.

NOTE—These articles we are not packing in sets but are selling in individual packing so that the child buying same can make up any kind of train he or she wishes.

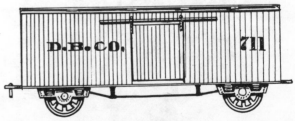

### No. 4625. BOX CAR

Finished in colored enamels and packed one dozen to the box.

NOTE—It is our intention to follow this line with the production of other models of the approved and most generally known types of railway equipment. These we expect to have ready for presentation in the very near future.

# Tootsietoy Doll House

This house is a reproduction of a fine brick Colonial home, and is the most complete ever shown at a popular price.

Made of container board (same as used in shipping cases.) Very substantial and no breakage.

Painted in seven colors, with oil paint; washable.

Inside is fully decorated with curtains, rugs, pictures, tile in bath room, and linoleum in kitchen. Six rooms, living, dining, kitchen, two bed rooms and bath.

Size when set up 18" long, 12" wide, 16" high.

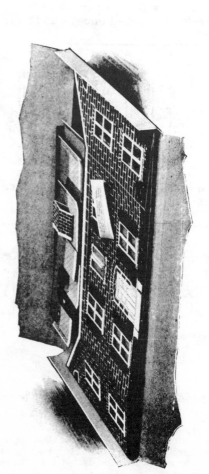

The above illustration shows the packing of the Tootsietoy Doll House.

The complete house folds into a sturdy carton only ½ inch high.

Size 30"x18½" x½".

Weight 5½ lbs. each.

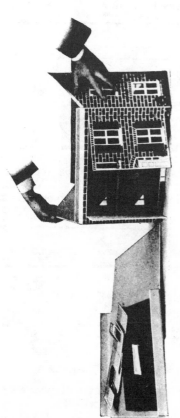

Showing how the house is set up, by merely pressing on the ends and inserting a few metal fasteners.

# Individual Numbers of
# DOLL HOUSE FURNITURE

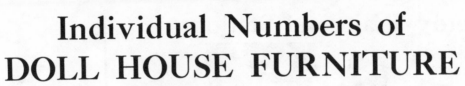

**No. 114. ROCKING CHAIR**

An exceptionally attractive piece that makes an instant appeal because "it rocks." Finished in assorted colors. Packed one dozen in a box.

**No. 107. FLOOR LAMP**

Assorted colors with gilt finish shade. Very popular. One dozen in a box.

**No. 120. TEA CART**

A doll tea cart with wheels that really move. A fine reproduction of the real thing. Assorted colors. One dozen to a box.

**No. 113. CHAIR**

A staple item of doll house furniture — securely made. In assorted colors. One dozen in a box.

**No. 105. VICTROLA**

Ideal for the doll house or as a favor. Exact shape and style of late model Victrola. Cover lifts up. Assorted colors. One dozen to a box.

**No. 121. KITCHEN RANGE**

Realistic and clever reproduction of a gas range. A wonderful novelty as well as a toy. Children go wild over this. One dozen in a box.

**No. 104. LIBRARY TABLE**

Miniature of a large library table—for the doll house or as a single toy. In assorted colors. One dozen to a box.

**No. 4402. DESK**

The right size for the doll house and with front opening lid. Finished in bright bronze. One dozen in a box.

# CANDELABRAS

**No. 4623. FOUR LIGHT**

**No. 4521. TWO LIGHT**

**No. 4629. ONE LIGHT**

Beautiful reproduction of real candelabras. Finished in a brilliant gold bronze. Packed two dozen to the box.

**No. 4522. THREE LIGHT CANDELABRA**

Gold bronze finish. Two dozen to the box.

**No. 4524. FIVE LIGHT CANDELABRA**

Gold bronze finish. Two dozen to the box.

**No. 4446. CANDLEHOLDER**

Brightly finished in silver—a reproduction of the old fashioned "night light." Holds a size 00 candle. A staple seller. One gross to the box.

**No. 4465. CLERMONT**

The first steamboat in a faithful, clever reproduction. Paddle wheel turns around. Attractively finished in bronze. One gross to the box.

**No. 4437. LIBERTY STATUE**

A handsome reproduction of the original statue, 2¼ in. high, finished in durable gilt bronze. A splendid souvenir and novelty. One dozen to a box.

**No. 203. WATER PISTOL**

The "boys' delight," will throw a stream of water ten to twelve feet. Always a good seller. Good quality rubber bulb. Every pistol perfect. One gross to the box.

*Tootsietoy*

# Tootsietoy Train and Station

Packed in the famous
Tootsietoy Box

No. 11

A train set that is good for steady all-year round sales. Consists of Engine, Tender and three Pullman Coaches and Folding Station in handsome colors. Boys never tire of playing with trains and every boy is a prospect for this complete set. Movable wheels and coupling devices. In black and colored enamels.

# Tootsietoy Auto and Garage

Packed in the famous
Tootsietoy Box

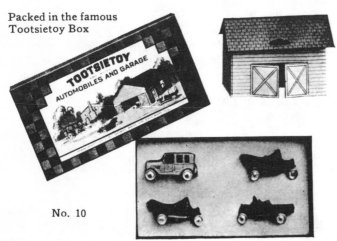

No. 10

A very fine set of four automobiles with a folding garage. The set includes a Sedan, Truck, Roadster and Touring Car. Each automobile is about 3¼ in. long, of late design and with movable wheels. The colors are realistic.

## Metal Animals

**No. 4601. HORSE**

Miniature horse on movable wheels. Realistic, natural colors and a spirited pose. Wheels bronze finish. Fine either as toy or a favor.

One Dozen to the Box

**No. 4602. DOG**

A husky St. Bernard on wheels that move. He's finished in black, dark and light brown. Be sure you have plenty.

One Dozen to the Box

**No. 4603. LION**

Faithful reproduction of a lion. He's the favorite animal of most children. On movable wheels. In dark and light brown.

---

### No. 4482. AEROPLANE

Packed 2 dozen to the box

Any boy will understand the fine points of this reproduction of a well-known make of monoplane. Propeller and wheels turn. Bright gilt finish with colored wheels. A sure sale to any boy who sees it.

### No. 4341. TELEPHONE

Miniature Desk Phone that measures only 2¼ inches high, yet has movable head and receiver. Mouthpiece and base are of black enamel, movable head in silver plate. Wonderful as a novelty or a toy.

Packed 1 dozen to the box

### No. 4400. FOLDING GO-CART

Packed 2 dozen to the box

Miniature Folding Go-Cart in brilliant bronze finish. Folds like a real go-cart. Movable wheels.

### No. 4528. LIMOUSINE

Simply can't be surpassed as a quick seller. Lines are perfect and everything about it stamps it as a high-class small toy. Colored enamel finishes and silver plated smooth running wheels.
Packed 1 dozen to the box.

*Tootsietoy*

# TOOTSIETOY
## Mansion

The addition of the new furniture to the TOOTSIETOY line made the addition of a new house to accommodate the furniture not only desirable, but necessary. We present the TOOTSIETOY MANSION, designed by one of America's greatest architects who specializes in the Spanish type of architecture. True to type and with every detail carefully worked out to make it not only strong but easy of assembly, we offer what we consider is the finest house five dollars can buy. Made of heavy book-board and colored in oil colors (washable) in nine colors, easy access to every room and the whole packed in an attractive carton with full directions for the assembly, we consider it a fitting s e t t i n g for TOOTSIETOY furniture.

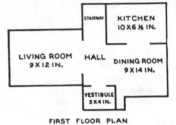

FIRST FLOOR PLAN

SECOND FLOOR PLAN

# TOOTSIETOY
## Furnished
## Mansion

The set that will be featured in our 1930 National Advertising Campaign. You know now what our campaign brought you in past years. Prepare for it now. Five rooms of furniture and the Mansion, all packed in an attractive shipping carton measuring 24x20x4 inches will be in great demand d u r i n g the coming Christmas season. The make-up of the sets is pictured here; the mansion is pictured above.

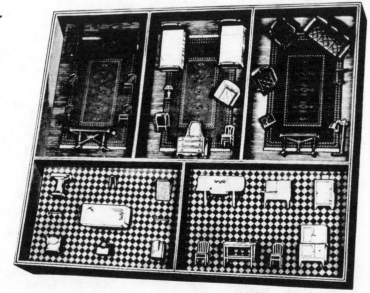

### No. 4680—Overland Bus

Improvements in design which include modern top ventilators, observation platform and fenders, radiator and lamps of a new type feature the Overland Bus. The toys are 3¾ inches long and are packed one dozen to the box.

### No. 4629—Sedan

This special sedan may be had in enamel colors of yellow, red, green and blue combined with gilt disc wheels. It is three inches long and comes in boxes of a dozen.

### No. 4636—Coupe

Other combinations of colors feature this toy which comes in yellow, red, green and blue with gilt disc wheels. Length, 3 inches. Packed one dozen to the box.

### No. 23—Racer

A driver in khaki pilots each of the various colored racing cars with gilt disc wheels. Weight, 20 pounds to the gross. Packed one dozen to the box.

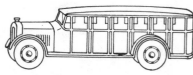

### No. 4651—Safety Coach

An accurate duplication of the heavy duty type of transcontinental bus, this toy is finished in four colors, yellow, red, green and blue. All have gold wheels. Length, 3⅝ inches. Packed one dozen to the box. Weight, 35 pounds to the gross.

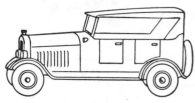

### No. 4641—Touring Car

Always one of the TOOTSIETOY best sellers, the touring car now comes in brilliant shades of yellow, red, green and blue. All have gold disc wheels. Length, 3⅛ inches; weight, 20 pounds to the gross. Packed four of each color to the box.

### No. 4630—Delivery Van

This TOOTSIETOY is always included in every selection made. It is finished in solid colors, red, green, yellow and blue. Length, 3 inches; weight, 25 pounds to the gross. Packed three of each color to the box.

### No. 4685
### TOOTSIETOY Whistle

Twelve 2½-inch shrill whistles, assorted in four sparkling colors ready for display. Every boy will want one.

## FINISHED IN SPARKLING COLORS

*Tootsietoy*

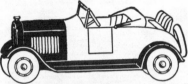

### 6-01 Roadster

This colorful assortment of popular Roadsters immediately recommends this package of twelve pieces, consisting of three Buicks, with blue chassis and yellow body; three Cadillacs, with grey chassis and blue body; three Oldsmobiles, with red chassis and grey body; three Chevrolets with yellow chassis and red body.

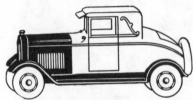

### 6-02 Coupe

Stylish and substantial Coupes are truly portrayed in this package of twelve. It is made up of three Cadillacs, three Buicks, three Chevrolets, and three Oldsmobiles. (See Roadster for color combinations.)

### 6-03 Brougham

See how perfectly the pleasing contours of the Brougham are reproduced in this package of twelve. The assortment has three Buicks, three Cadillacs, three Oldsmobiles, and three Chevrolets. (See Roadster for color combinations.)

### 6-04 Sedan

The baby Sedan with all its fine appointments is displayed in this mixed box of three Buicks, three Cadillacs, three Oldsmobiles, and three Chevrolets. (See Roadster for color combinations.)

### 6-05 Touring Car

A box of surprising brilliance is this package of twelve Touring Cars with three Buicks, three Cadillacs, three Oldsmobiles, and three Chevrolets. (See Roadster for color combinations.)

### 6-06 Delivery Truck

A pleasure and a study are the details of harmony and perfect reproduction combined in this box of twelve Delivery Trucks. Three Buicks, three Cadillacs, three Chevrolets, three Oldsmobiles. (See Roadster for color combinations.)

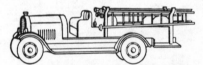

### No. 4652—Hook and Ladder

Three detachable gilt ladders are set on a blue body, which in turn is mounted on a red chassis with gilt disc wheels. Weight, 25 pounds to the gross. Packed one dozen to the box.

### No. 4653—Water Tower

This attractive toy is completed with yellow body, red adjustable tower mounted on red chassis with gilt disc wheels. Length, three and seven-eighths inches; weight, twenty-seven pounds to the gross. Packed one dozen to the box.

## FINISHED IN SPARKLING COLORS

# WANTED: A Mama to Dress Me! WE PAY POSTAGE

$1.55 And Up
4 Sizes
Bisque Head
Sleeping Eyes
Kidiline Body

I Sleep

Water-Proof Body
*Easily Cleaned*

The most inexperienced little seamstress will find this pretty Dolly easy to dress. Four sizes—everyone nice to sew for and she's sure to look charming in whatever she wears. Beautiful bisque head; sleeping eyes; two tiny teeth showing and long soft curls of good quality mohair.

Her body is covered with a fine grade white imitation kid which is waterproof and easily cleaned. It's loads of fun to put her clothes on because she is jointed securely at knees, hips, elbows and shoulders, and moves very easily. Her arms are hard-to-break composition. She wears removable buckled shoes and socks. Your order shipped Same Day it is received.

| Article No. | Height | Each | |
|---|---|---|---|
| 48 E 2640 | 16⅛ in. | $1.55 | We Pay The Postage |
| 48 E 2641 | 18⅛ in. | 1.89 | |
| 448 E 2642 | 20 in. | 2.25 | |
| 448 E 2643 | 23¼ in. | 2.75 | |

I Sleep

**Baby Doll With Layette** $1.00

One pretty little Baby Doll just 7½ inches tall. Bisque head; go-to-sleep eyes. Composition arms and legs jointed at shoulders and hips. The three pictures show her different dresses. Wears a white slip and has two outfits besides. A cap, sacque, panties and bootees of downy white flannelette, blue trimmed. A white ruffled frock with matching cap, blue ribbon trim. Pacifier. We Pay Postage.$1.00
48 E 2897—Complete 9-piece set.......$1.00

Water-Proof Finish
13 Inches Tall

Head and hands of hard-to-break composition. Stuffed body and legs. We Pay Postage.
48 E 2679 ... 39¢

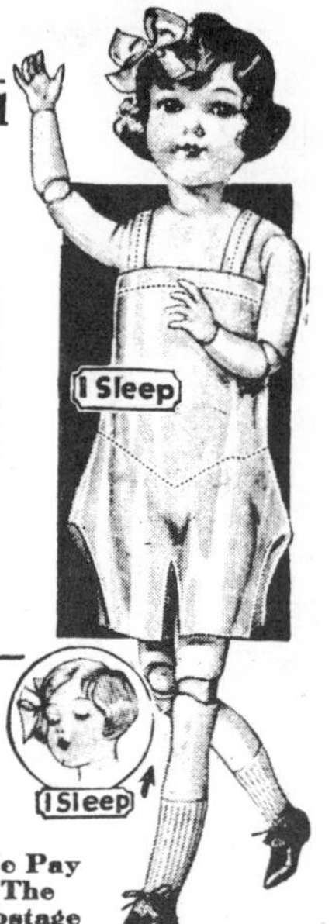
I Sleep

**Imported Jointed Doll Girlish Type**
**A Dolly That's Easy to Dress**
**Bisque Head—Slender Ball and Socket Joints**
**"I Wear Dainty Undies"**

The manager of Ward's Toy Department searched the factories throughout Europe to find these slender little Girl Dolls so much in demand. They are really beautiful! Extremely strong, molded composition bodies, shaped exactly like a real child's.

Shaped wooden arms jointed at shoulder, elbow and wrist. Composition hands. Well formed composition legs jointed at hips and knees. Fine quality enamels used throughout. Bisque head, sleeping eyes with real eyelashes. Sewed mohair wig on cloth foundation. Dressed in dainty hemstitched rayon chemise; neat slippers and socks.

48 E 2854—Height about 14¼ inches. We Pay Postage.......... $1.44
48 E 2855—Height 17⅞ inches. We Pay Postage.......... 1.98
448 E 2856—Height 21 inches. We Pay Postage.......... 2.29
448 E 2857—Height 24¼ inches. We Pay Postage.......... 2.69

We Pay The Postage

We Sit Alone

29¢ Each

**"Topsy and Eva" Babies**

An adorable pair—a mischievous pickaninny and a dear little white baby—both the same size, 9½ inches tall. All composition; painted eyes; hair and features. They're cunning together if you want both. Often sell for 50¢ each. We Pay Postage.
48 E 2503—White doll.......... 29¢
48 E 2502—Pickaninny doll.... 29¢

I SLEEP
I SIT ALONE

$1.00 And Up
5 Sizes

WE PAY POSTAGE

*Lovable Baby* **"Sally"**

Happy little Sally just knows that a loving mother is waiting for her somewhere. So her big eyes with their absurdly long lashes smile happily and hopefully. Sally's rosebud mouth shows two tiny white teeth.

Baby head of fine bisque with sleeping eyes and fluffy bobbed mohair wig on sewed cloth foundation. Hard-to-break composition body, beautifully modeled and tinted like a real baby's; jointed at hips and shoulders. Chubby legs are half bent at knees. She comes to you in a white lace trimmed slip ready to dress. Pretty bead necklace. Five sizes listed below are exactly alike except for size.

| Article No. | Height | Each | |
|---|---|---|---|
| 48 E 2648 | 12½ in. | $1.00 | Postage Prepaid |
| 48 E 2649 | 14 in. | 1.59 | |
| 448 E 2650 | 15½ in. | 2.19 | |
| 448 E 2651 | 17 in. | 2.63 | |
| 448 E 2652 | 22 in. | 3.45 | |

12½ In. Tall

This Is "Mary Ann" Dressed 79¢ "Mary Ann" Undressed

New slender type American made Doll—exactly like a real little American girl. Almost unbreakable molded composition body; slim, graceful legs and arms jointed at shoulders and hips. Finely modeled composition head—a real child expression on the serious little face. Radiant coloring of a healthy, sturdy youngster. Mary Ann wears a gaily printed frock—sleeveless and modishly short. Half socks and slippers. White muslin combination. Height 12½ inches. We Pay Postage.
48 E 2510.......... 79¢

**19-Inch Dolly** 83¢
*We Pay The Postage*

A great big, nineteen-inch Dolly with a beautiful composition head—not the ordinary type but made especially for us according to our strict specifications. Hair molded in latest wind-blown bob and very naturally tinted. Wide blue eyes and babyish features are carefully painted. Composition arms jointed at shoulder. Cotton stuffed legs. Well shaped stuffed body. Black cloth feet give effect of shoes. Colorfully printed romper suit; pretty bonnet. One of our best doll values! We Pay Postage.
48 E 2511.......... 83¢

Ward's Pays The Postage

I SLEEP

$1.00 Doll in Cradle

**"Rock-A-Bye Baby"**
*In Swinging Basket*

A 6½-inch new baby—rocks gently to sleep in her dainty basket-cradle. Sleeping eyes. Basket is 5½ by 8 inches long. Swing has wood base with wicker arch. Baby nestles cozily between coverlet and pillow of lace trimmed rayon. We Pay Postage. Complete outfit at one low price!
48 E 2853 .... $1.00

**Lithographed Metal Tea Sets**

Each set has 6¼-in. tray; 1½-in. cups; 2-in. teapot; 4¼-in. plates; 2¾-in. saucers. We Pay Postage.

48 E 972—Service for 6. 20 Pieces..... 57¢
48 E 971—Service for 4. 14 Pieces..... 45¢
48 E 970—Service for 2. 8 Pieces...... 33¢

**Large Aluminum Set** *With Teapot or Percolator* **23 Pieces $1.39**

Heavy, highly polished aluminum in handsome paneled design. Includes 4 napkin rings; four 5¾-inch plates; four 2¾-inch cups; four 4-inch saucers; 4 spoons; urn shaped creamer and sugar bowl, each 2¼-in. high. Postpaid.

**With Real Teapot**
48 E 931—Above Set with real 4-inch teapot; teaball hanging inside from lid... $1.39

**With Real Coffee Percolator**
48 E 945—Above Set with real 4¾-inch percolator. Wood handle; glass top. Hinged cover. $1.39

Only $1.00

**Aluminum Percolator Set**

Real Percolator 4¼ inches high, with wood handle and glass top. Sugar bowl; creamer; 4 cups; 4 plates; 4 saucers; 4 spoons. Other pieces same size as pieces in set 48 E 950 below at left. We Pay Postage.
48 E 946—Complete 19-piece set. $1.00

33¢

Speedy Shipping Service

**Toy Cutlery in Drainer**

Four each of knives, forks and spoons, in miniature wire netting drainer. Stiff metal frame, three compartments. Size of drainer 3 by 3¾ inches. The knives are 3⅛ inches long, other pieces in proportion. We Pay Postage.
48 E 942.......... 33¢

50¢ **19-Piece Toy Aluminum Tableware Set**

Will not tarnish. Six knives, 3¾ inches long; 6 spoons and 6 forks; serving ladle. Grooved box 5¾ by 4⅛ inches. We Pay Postage.
48 E 940—19 pieces.... 50¢

**Paneled Aluminum** 73¢ 23 Pieces

Paneled Teapot with wood knob on top; height 3⅛ inches. Four 2-inch cups; four 3½-inch saucers; four 4½-in. plates; creamer 1⅞ in. high; sugar bowl 1⅝ in. high. Paneled design. Four spoons and four napkin rings. All pieces well made. We Pay Postage.
48 E 950—23-piece set.... 73¢

69¢

Swedish Enamel

**Baby Plate and Mug**

Sanitary baby plate with wide base; almost impossible to upset. Inside bowl is rounded, easily cleaned. Has picture bottom. Mug to match. Plate 7⅛ in. diam., 1 in. deep. Mug 2¾ in. high. We Pay Postage.
48 E 2717—Two pieces.......... 69¢

42¢

For Baby

Embossed ABC design on 7½-inch aluminum plate. Deep sides. Patented clamps to fasten to high chair or table. Keeps baby from spilling food. We Pay Postage.
48 E 2722—Per set .... 42¢

**Real Electric Toy Iron**
97¢

Separate Stand.

Length 5¼ inches. Nickel-plated. Wood handle enameled in color. Tip-up stand. 5-foot rayon cord; 2-piece plug fits any socket. Separate stand.
48 E 904—We Pay Postage.......... 97¢

**These Actually Iron!**

59¢ Large Size

Exactly like the famous Mrs. Potts' irons that mother uses—but not too heavy for baby hands. Detachable handles of polished wood. Polished nickel-plated irons, with tiny tapered ends. Metal stand included. We Pay Postage.
48 E 939—Length 4⅜ inches. Each....... 59¢
48 E 938—Length 3⁵⁄₁₆ inches. Each....... 35¢

**Every Little Girl Wants an Ironing Board**

Selected smooth white wood (no splinters). Adjusts 19¼ to 22½ inches high; board 36 by 10½ inches. We Pay Postage.
448 E 937... 97¢

97¢ Large Size

Smooth Finish Sturdy

**Smaller Size Ironing Board**
48 E 936—21 by 5½ in. Adjusts 14½ to 16 in. high. We Pay Postage.......... 47¢

**Happy Monday Laundry Set**

Glass washboard 11 by 5⅛ inches with wood frame. Non-leak laundry tub 10 in. diameter. Collapsible clothes dryer 12¾ in. square at top, 14 in. high. Clothespins in bag. Metal wringer with 3¾-in. rubber rollers. Wash basket 7 by 11⅛ in. We Pay Postage.
448 E 721—Complete...... $2.29

**Small Set**
Everything listed above, except basket and wringer. We Pay Postage. $1.00
448 E 947.....

# I AM BUBBLES! EFFanBEE

I Cry
I Sit Alone
I Sleep

## WE PAY POSTAGE!

There goes that dimpled little finger again—straight into her rosebud mouth! Preciously like a real one-year-old baby with her twinkling blue eyes, face just puckering into an April smile, and chubby little active hands. **The widely advertised EFFanBEE BUBBLES.** No other doll so exactly reproduces a real baby's expression. Blue eyes that go to sleep. Open mouth with two little teeth. Composition arms, cotton stuffed body. Dainty white organdie dress trimmed in lace. Underskirt and real rubber diaper. Almost unbreakable composition head, arms and legs jointed at shoulders and hips. Legs are curved just like a baby's. Every doll has EFFanBEE locket and chain and **six** photographs which the little mother can give to her friends. The two large sizes have "mama" voices and real leather booties. The small sizes have crying voices and imitation white leather booties. Five sizes. **We Pay Postage.**

| | | |
|---|---|---|
| 48 E 2890 | Height 16 inches.... | $4.19 |
| 48 E 2891 | Height 17½ inches.. | 5.00 |
| 448 E 2892 | Height 20 inches.... | 6.59 |
| 448 E 2893 | Height 22 inches.... | 8.39 |
| 448 E 2894 | Height 24 inches.... | 9.98 |

## Childlike Composition Bodies · WE PAY POSTAGE

Make
Dresses
for
Them

### EFFanBEE PATSY $2.75

**WARD'S *Is The Only Mail Order Distributor***

American babyhood is personified in this dainty three-year-old child. Nationally advertised "Patsy" is the nation's most imitated doll. But the roguish expression of the famous patented tilting head, unconscious baby grace of arms and legs, are the work of an artist and cannot be duplicated. Entirely of finest American composition—exquisite child body is easy to dress. Painted features, molded composition hair. Jointed at neck, shoulders, hips—she sits or stands alone. Smart red print pantie frock. Scarlet satin hair ribbon. Red and white rayon socks; red slippers. Height 13½ inches **We Pay Postage.**
48 E 2694......$2.75

### $1.47 → BOOTS—*Like A Real Little American Girl*

Modeled entirely from fine quality composition—radiant, sunbrowned coloring. Well shaped head, jointed at neck. Arms and legs are jointed at shoulders and hips. Childlike body of hard composition extremely easy to sew for. Boots stands firmly alone in almost any pose. Crisp pink organdie frock. Pink combination. Ribbon headband. Slippers and socks. Ht. 13½ in. **We Pay Postage.**
48 E 2684
..$1.47

I Walk
I Cry
I Sleep
21 Inch
"Mary Lee"
$5.00

### Doll With Wind-blown Bob *Newest* EFFanBEE CREATION...... "Mary Lee"

Tousled, wind-blown hair, ruddy cheeks, bright laughing eyes — another miniature of perfect childhood created by EFFanBEE—famous manufacturers of fine dolls.

Head of almost unbreakable composition with new patented style, fine quality mohair wig firmly sewed on cloth foundation. Sleeping eyes fringed with real lashes. Smiling lips disclose row of tiny teeth. Shaped cotton stuffed body. Crying voice. Composition beautifully modeled limbs jointed at shoulders and hips. Rose pink organdie frock; gay flower-print dimity trim. Matching bonnet. Organdie ruffled slip. Combination cuffed at knees with pink organdie. Socks; pink slippers. Height 21 in. **We Pay Postage.**

448 E 2668—Golden hair......$5.00
448 E 2828—Brown hair...... 5.00

*Prompt Shipment*

### $1.00 Baby Fleur

An accurate reproduction of the French Type Dolls. Composition head; curly bobbed wig of mohair, jointed arms and legs. Two-tone felt frock. Ruffled skirt finished with flowers of contrasting felt. Large picture hat. Felt shoes; white socks. Height 12 inches. **Postpaid.**
48 E 2673—.....$1.00

Oh,
How
We
Can
Dance

SQUEEZE
VOICE

### Dutch Dolls

Little Dutch Boy and Girl, each 11¼ inches tall, with papier-mache heads; painted features. Composition hands and legs. **Real wooden shoes!** Dressed in character of Dutch peasants. Squeeze voices. **We Pay Postage.**

69¢ Each

48 E 2843—Dutch boy.69¢
48 E 2880—Dutch girl.69¢

### Two Separate Dolls They Dance Together $2.48

A cunning Flapper and her Sheik "strut their stuff" to the latest jazz rhythm. A new patented feature—these dolls clasp hands and by means of an attached cord can be made to dance together, keeping time to radio or phonograph. Boy is 13½ inches tall and wears "sheik" suit with eton jacket, brass buttoned vest and checked trousers. Girl 13 inches tall, wears colorful print pantie frock. Both have childish composition heads; painted features. Mohair wigs. **We Pay Postage.**

48 E 2667—Per pair.....$2.48

## Our Finest Doll Buggy

*Holds 28-Inch Doll or Baby*

*Sells in Many Stores Up to $25*

APPROVAL
Fine Nickel-Plated Bumper

*Compartment Under Seat for Dolly's Bottle*

**$13.98**

**Reversible Body**

**Showing Storm Curtain in Use**

**Other features are footbrake, sliding hood fixtures, hood windows, reversing body, reclining back, tubular pushbar, nickel plated bumper, corduroy lining and heavy wood wheels.**

### Luxurious Fittings

Large enough for any 28-inch doll—or even a small baby. Body and hood of finest quality round fiber reed with **beauty rolls** on body and hood. Transparent windows in hood with nickel-plated frames. The entire body and hood are upholstered in genuine velvet corduroy, with cushioned seat and back. **Corduroy wind curtain included.**

English type artillery wood wheels 12¼ inches in diameter with **1-inch balloon type rubber tires.** Reversing gear permits body to be swung around so that baby faces the little mother. Extra strong frame and footbrake. Hood is mounted on rod with sliding attachment to allow full adjustment. Full tubular underslung gear with full tubular pusher. Nickel-plated handle bumper and hub caps. Reclining back. **Beautiful Scroll Springs.** Leather hold-in strap.

Length of body 27 inches; height to top of hood 37 inches; height to top of handle 28 inches. Width 13 inches. Ship. wt. 47 lbs. **Not mailable.**

148 E 3504—Two-tone ivory and green; dark green diamonds. Ivory undergear; beaver upholstery..........$13.98
148 E 3509—Two-tone blue and gold. Gray undergear and upholstery.......... 13.98

## A Quality Buggy

*Note Superior Construction*
*Pushbar Attaches to Rear Axle*
*Artillery Wheels*

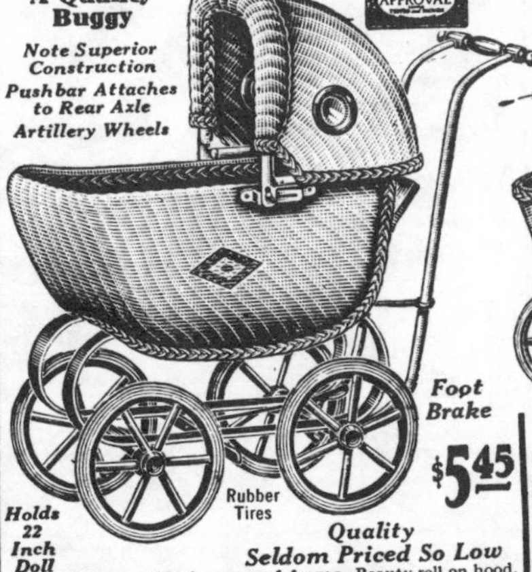
APPROVAL
Foot Brake
Rubber Tires

*Holds 22 Inch Doll*

**$5.45**

### *Quality Seldom Priced So Low*

Round fiber reed body **on wood frame.** Beauty roll on hood, transparent windows in nickel-plated frame. Sliding adjustable hood fixtures. Reclining back. Foot brake. Pushbar braced to body and riveted to rear axle. Rigid and permanent. Has 8½-inch artillery wood wheels with ½-inch rubber tires. Body 20½ inches long; width 10 inches; depth 9½ inches. Height to top of hood 30 inches, to handlebars 25 inches. Ship. wt. 16 lbs. **Not mailable.**

148 E 3506—Ivory with blue diamond design.....$5.45
148 E 3511—Pastel green; dark green diamonds.. 5.45

### $4.00 Rigid Construction

***Reclining Back***

Often Sells for $5.00
Hood Lights
Foot Brake

For dolls up to 20 inches. Fine, round fiber reed, with a cuff on **body and hood.**

Even this small Buggy has a strong built-in wood frame—much sturdier than many $5 buggies!

Transparent **hood windows,** nickel-plated frame. **Foot brake.** Full sliding adjustment of hood. Pushbar **bolted to rear axle. Reclining back.** 7-inch wheels with ⅜-inch tires. Length of body 19 inches; width 9 inches; depth 7½ inches. Height to top of hood 24 in., to handlebars 21 in. **We Pay Postage.**

448 E 3507—Ivory.........$4.00
448 E 3512—Pastel green.... 4.00

$1.87 $1.73

### Fiber Reed Strollers

Extremely low priced for such good quality. Perfect Stroller for dolly's morning or afternoon ride. Fine, round reed—cafe au lait (coffee cream) color trimmed with blue braid. Seat 7 by 8½ inches. Height 12½ inches. 6-inch rubber tired wheels; length including tongue, 26½ inches. Tape hold-in strap. **We Pay Postage.**
448 E 3494.$1.87

A gift any little girl will love—and a wonderful value at this low price! Just like a real baby's stroller. Handsomely woven of flat fiber reed and Royal Blue color. Seat 7 by 8½ inches; height 12½ inches. 6-inch rubber tired wheels. Length, including tongue, 26½ inches. Tape hold-in strap. **We Pay Postage.**
448 E 3495..$1.73

### Baby's First Doll Buggy

**$2.59 Priced Low**

*Holds 16 Inch Doll*

*Nickel-Plated Hub Caps*

Steel frame; wood bottom. Loom woven fiber reed body and hood. Size 17 inches long; 7½ inches wide. To top of hood, 21 inches; to handle, 22½ inches. Six-inch double spoke rubber tired wheels. **We Pay Postage.**
448 E 3501—Cream color.$2.59
448 E 3502—Royal blue..$2.59

# UNBREAKABLE DOLLS WITH METAL HEADS

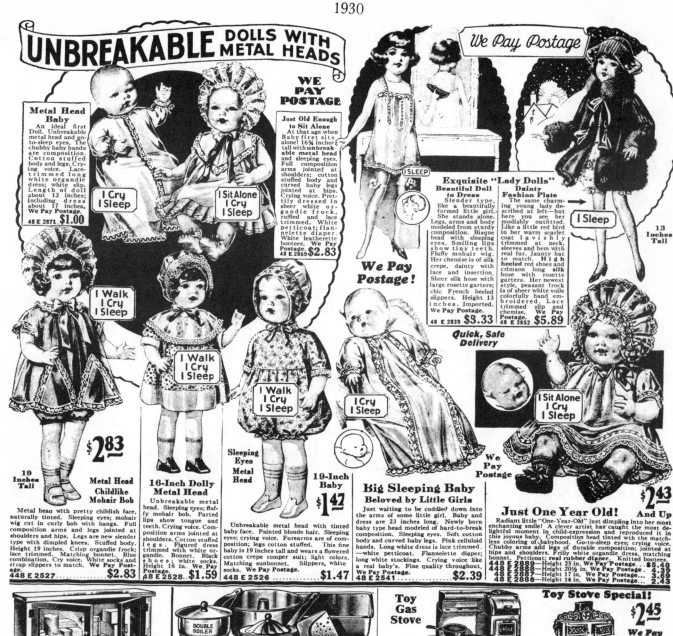

**WE PAY POSTAGE**

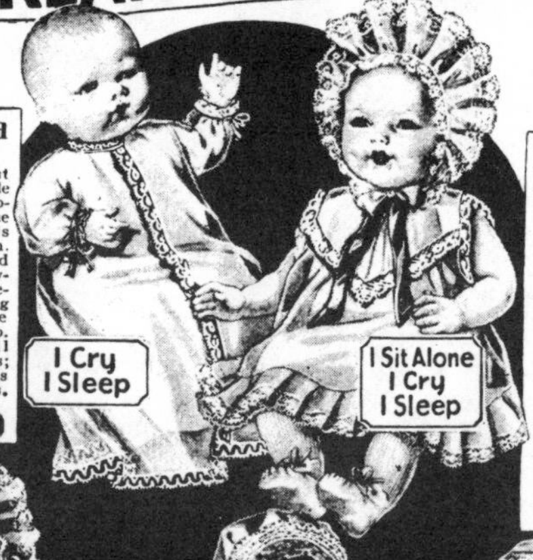
I Cry
I Sleep
I Sit Alone
I Cry
I Sleep

**Metal Head Baby**

An ideal first Doll. Unbreakable metal head and go-to-sleep eyes. The chubby baby hands are composition. Cotton stuffed body and legs. Crying voice. Lace-trimmed long white organdie dress; white slip. Length of doll about 13 inches; including dress about 17 inches. **We Pay Postage.**
48 E 2871..**$1.00**

**Just Old Enough to Sit Alone**

At that age when Baby first sits alone! 16¾ inches tall with **unbreakable metal head** and sleeping eyes. Full composition arms jointed at shoulders; cotton stuffed body and curved baby legs jointed at hips. Crying voice. Prettily dressed in sheer white organdie frock, ruffled and lace trimmed. White petticoat; flannelette diaper. White leatherette bootees. **We Pay Postage.**
48 E 2869 **$2.83**

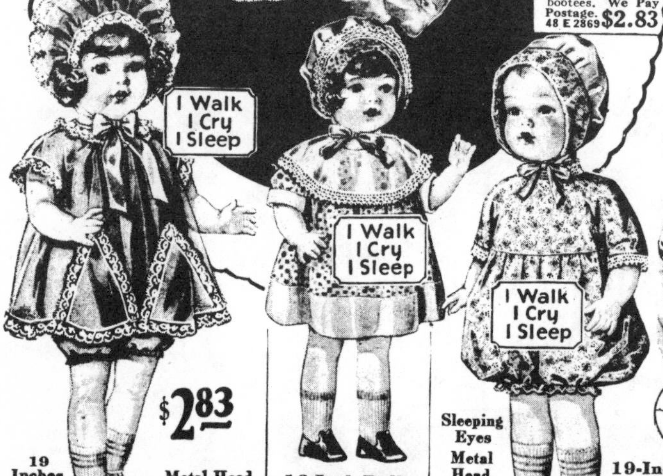
I Walk
I Cry
I Sleep
I Walk
I Cry
I Sleep
I Walk
I Cry
I Sleep

$2.83

19 Inches Tall

**Metal Head Childlike Mohair Bob**

Metal head with pretty childish face, naturally tinted. Sleeping eyes; mohair wig cut in curly bob with bangs. Full composition arms and legs jointed at shoulders and hips. Legs are new slender type with dimpled knees. Stuffed body. Height 19 inches. Crisp organdie frock; lace trimmed. Matching bonnet. Blue combination. Cry voice. White socks and strap slippers to match. **We Pay Postage.**
448 E 2527.............. **$2.83**

**16-Inch Dolly Metal Head**

Unbreakable metal head. Sleeping eyes; fluffy mohair bob. Parted lips show tongue and teeth. Crying voice. Composition arms jointed at shoulders. Cotton stuffed legs. Figured dress trimmed with white organdie. Bonnet. Black shoes; white socks. Height 16 in. **We Pay Postage.**
48 E 2528.. **$1.59**

**Sleeping Eyes Metal Head**

**19-Inch Baby**

$1.47

Unbreakable metal head with tinted baby face. Painted blonde hair. Sleeping eyes; crying voice. Forearms are of composition; legs cotton stuffed. This fine baby is 19 inches tall and wears a flowered cotton crepe romper suit; light colors. Matching sunbonnet. Slippers, white socks. **We Pay Postage.**
448 E 2526 ............ **$1.47**

*We Pay Postage*

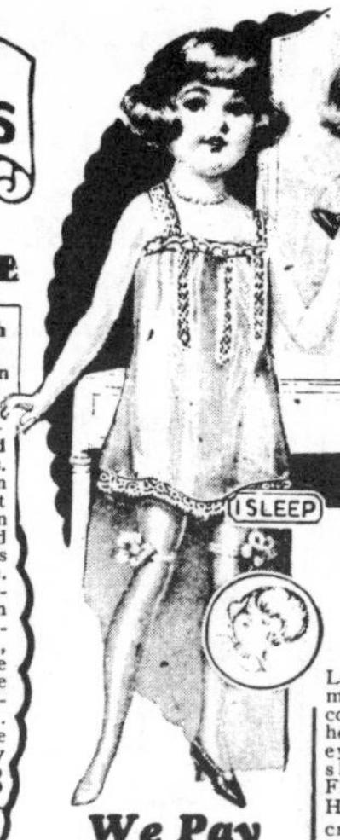
I SLEEP

*We Pay Postage!*

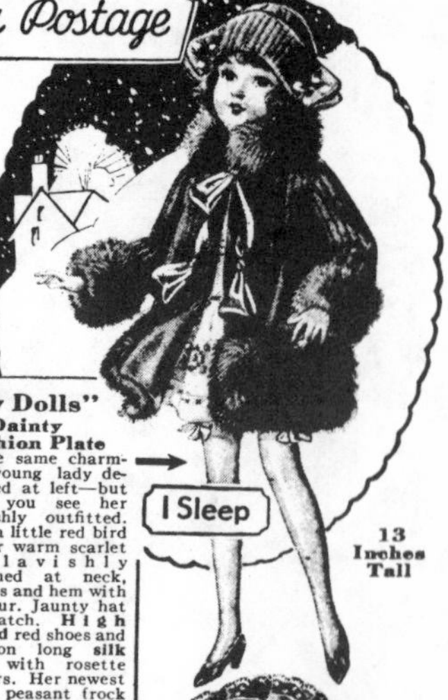
I Sleep

13 Inches Tall

## Exquisite "Lady Dolls"

**Beautiful Doll to Dress**

Slender type, like a beautifully formed little girl. She stands alone. Legs, arms and body modeled from sturdy composition. Bisque head with sleeping eyes. Smiling lips show tiny teeth. Fluffy mohair wig. Her chemise is of silk crepe, dainty with lace and insertion. Sheer silk hose with large rosette garters; chic French heeled slippers. Height 13 inches. Imported. **We Pay Postage.**
48 E 2839 **$3.33**

**Dainty Fashion Plate**

The same charming young lady described at left—but here you see her modishly outfitted. Like a little red bird in her warm scarlet coat lavishly trimmed at neck, sleeves and hem with real fur. Jaunty hat to match. **High heeled** red shoes and crimson long **silk** hose with rosette garters. Her newest style, peasant frock is of sheer white voile colorfully hand embroidered. Lace trimmed slip and chemise. **We Pay Postage.**
48 E 2852. **$5.89**

***Quick, Safe Delivery***

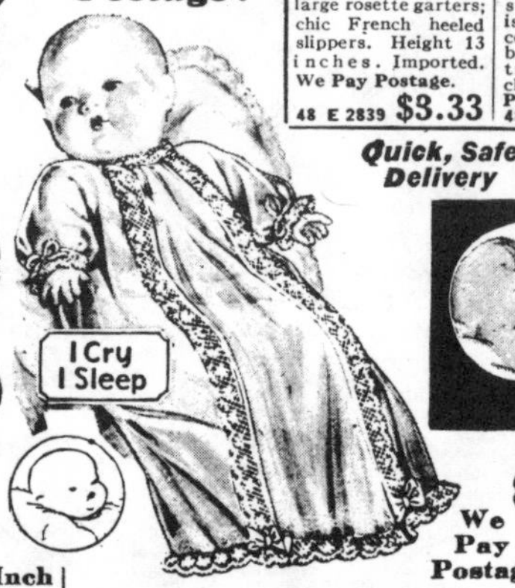
I Cry
I Sleep

**We Pay Postage**

## Big Sleeping Baby

**Beloved by Little Girls**

Just waiting to be cuddled down into the arms of some little girl. Baby and dress are 23 inches long. Newly born baby type head modeled of hard-to-break composition. Sleeping eyes. Soft cotton body and curved baby legs. Pink celluloid hands. Long white dress is lace trimmed. —white petticoat. Flannelette diaper; long white stockings. Crying voice like a real baby's. Fine quality throughout. **We Pay Postage.**
48 E 2541 ............... **$2.39**

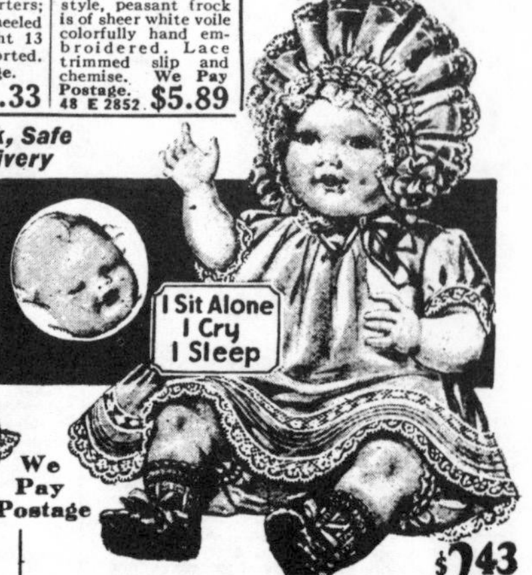
I Sit Alone
I Cry
I Sleep

$2.43 And Up

## Just One Year Old!

Radiant little "One-Year-Old" just dimpling into her most enchanting smile! A clever artist has caught the most delightful moment in child-expression and reproduced it in this joyous baby. Composition head tinted wth the matchless coloring of babyhood. Go-to-sleep eyes; crying voice. Chubby arms and legs of durable composition; jointed at hips and shoulders. Frilly white organdie dress, matching bonnet. Petticoat; **real rubber diaper.** Knitted bootees.
448 E 2889—Height 25 in. We Pay Postage... **$5.48**
448 E 2888—Height 20½ in. We Pay Postage. **4.39**
48 E 2887—Height 17 in. We Pay Postage... **3.69**
48 E 2886—Height 14 in. We Pay Postage... **2.43**

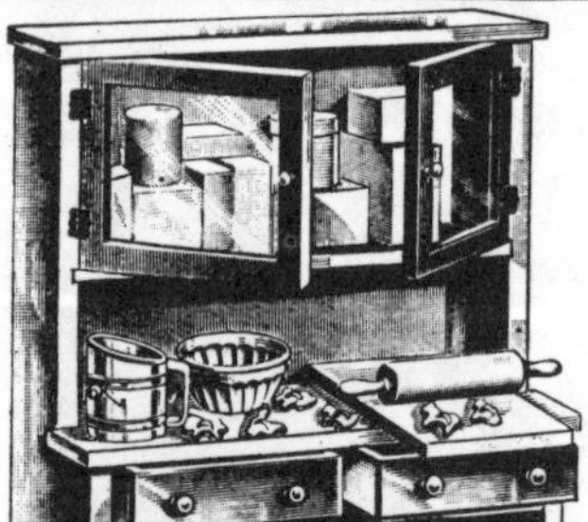

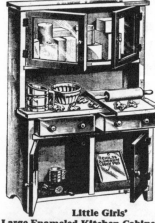

## Little Girls' Large Enameled Kitchen Cabinet

$7.50 value! Sturdy cabinet, ivory with green trim. Sides ¾-inch thick. Mortised shelving. Two well fitting, easy sliding drawers. Glass doors above; wood paneled ones below. Strong frames, with regular furniture snap-locks. Metal hinges. Miniature groceries included. Height of cabinet 26 inches. Width 16⅛ inches. Depth 8½ inches. We supply this cabinet **with** or **without** pastry outfit 48 E 728 described below Ship. weights 20 and 18 pounds. **Not mailable and not prepaid.**
148 E 3410—Cabinet and pastry set... **$6.28**
148 E 3408—Cabinet only............ **5.89**

## For Little Pastry Cooks

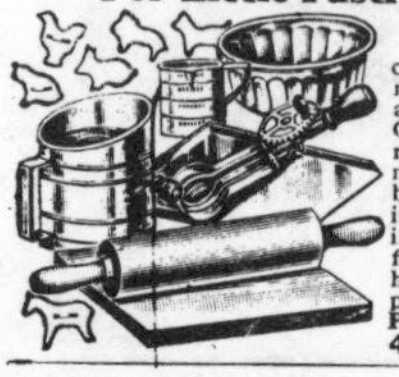

Six aluminum cookie cutters, aluminum baking pan and mixing bowl. One-cup flour sifter, real egg beater, measuring cup, bread board and rolling pin. Egg beater is 5½ inches long, flour sifter 3½ in. high. Other pieces in proportion. **We Pay Postage.**
48 E 728... **69¢**

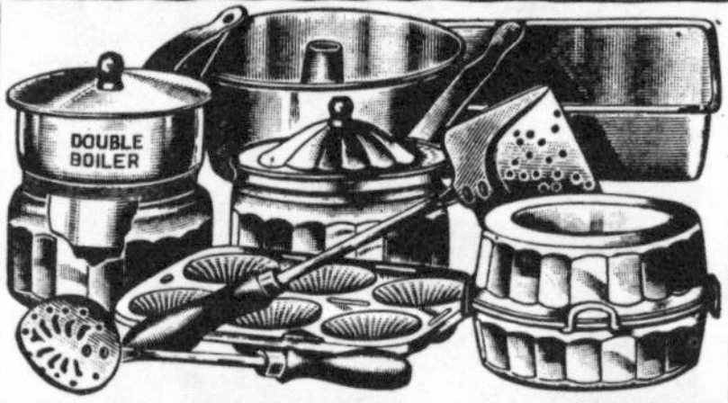
DOUBLE
BOILER

## For First Cooking Lessons
### *Aluminum Set*

Seal of APPROVAL

Highly polished 8-piece aluminum assortment. All handles and wooden knobs are enameled bright red. Convex sauce pan with cover 3½-inch diameter. Bread pan 2¾ by 4⅞ inches. Double boiler or rice cooker, 3¼ inch diameter with cover which fits both top and bottom, allowing them to be used separately. Tube cake pan for angel food, 4¾ inches diameter. Two-piece double roaster, 4-inch diameter, can be used separately; 6-cup muffin pan 3⅞ by 5¾ inches. Also 7½-inch mixing spoon and 8½-inch pancake turner with redwood handles. **We Pay Postage.**
48 E 722—8 pieces large enough for beginners....... **$1.00**

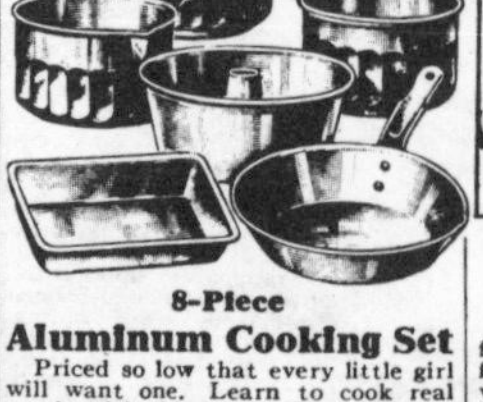

**8-Piece**

## Aluminum Cooking Set

Priced so low that every little girl will want one. Learn to cook real meals with this set. Contains convex kettle, saucepan, stewpan, mixing bowl, pudding pan, frying pan, tube cake pan and ordinary cake pan. Tube cake pan is 3¾ inches diameter. Other pieces in proportion. Speedy shipping service assured at Ward's! **We Pay Postage.**
48 E 724—
Complete 8-piece set....... **67¢**

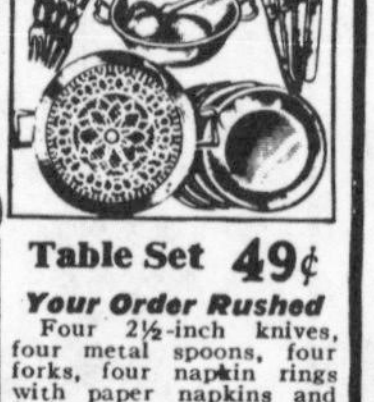

## Table Set 49¢

***Your Order Rushed***

Four 2½-inch knives, four metal spoons, four forks, four napkin rings with paper napkins and four metal plates. Serving bowl with a serving ladle and a 2¾-inch glass covered cake tray with metal rim. Complete in hinged, lace trimmed box. Size of box 8⅝ by 6¾ inches. **We Pay Postage.**
48 E 700—
23-piece set....... **49¢**

## Toy Gas Stove

**Imitation Fire**

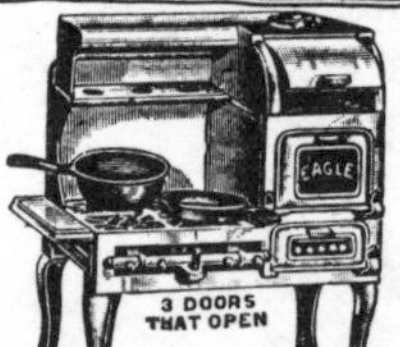
EAGLE
3 DOORS
THAT OPEN

$2.45

Turn lever and you'll see playlike tongues of flame rise up! Cast iron, enameled white; blue trimmed. Real doors on the oven, warming closet and broiler compartments. Shelf for heating plates under the canopy. Height 9½ in. Depth 5 in. Width 8¾ in. Skillet and frying pan included. **Postpaid.**
48 E 912.................... **$2.45**

## Another Bargain!

***Nickel Plated Cast Iron***

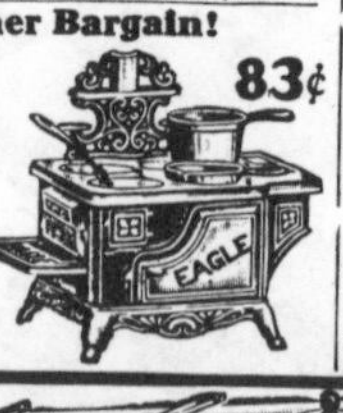
EAGLE

83¢

Extra fine Stove. Oven door opens. Four eyes with removable covers. Make-believe reservoir and firebox. Size 5¼ by 6 by 4 inches. **We Pay Postage.**
48 E 910.. **83¢**

## Toy Stove Special!

$2.45 ***We Pay Postage!***

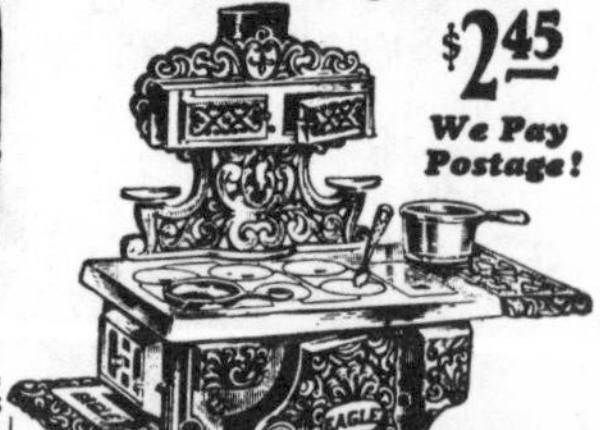
EAGLE

***Usually Sold for $3.00***

A remarkable purchase permits our offering you this extra large cast iron nickel-plated Stove at this price. A regular $3 stove. Height 11¾ inches: length 12⅜ inches; depth front to back 5½ inches. Doors of warming closet and oven door really open. Six lids, reservoir cover, and front and back aprons are removable. Nickel-plated with all raised parts highly polished. With stove are included lid lifter, fry pan, pot, coal scuttle and shovel. Speedy shipping service guaranteed. **We Pay Postage.**
48 E 903.................... **$2.45**

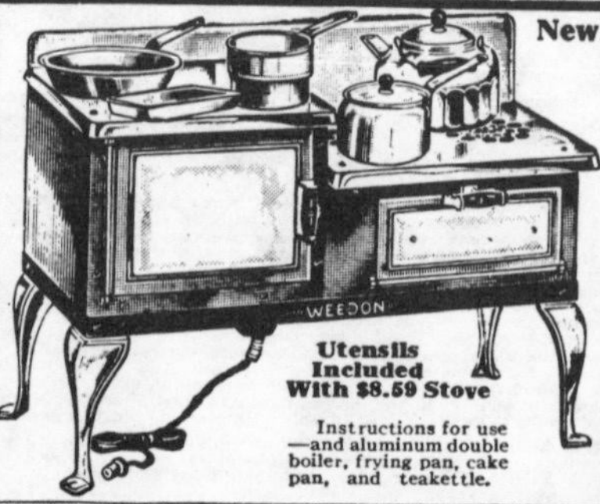
WEEDON

**Utensils Included With $8.59 Stove**

Instructions for use —and aluminum double boiler, frying pan, cake pan, and teakettle.

## New! Safe Electric Stoves

SAFE Electric Range—all walls insulated. Gray and blue enamel with nickel trim; 14 by 6¼ by 11½ inches high. Oven bakes small cakes, apples and other dainties (recipe book included tells you how). Also two burners for frying and boiling water. Hot closet space below. Six-foot cord fits any 110-volt standard light socket, direct or alternating. **We Pay Postage.**
448 E 913...... **$8.59**

**Low Priced Electric Stove**

Good quality standard Electric Stove. Size 12½ by 5½ by 13 inches high. Black enameled steel, white porcelain panels and nickel trim. Large burner and oven. Heavily tinned muffin, pie and bread pans; 6-foot cord. For 110-volt, direct or alternating. **We Pay Postage.**
448 E 909...... **$4.00**

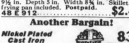

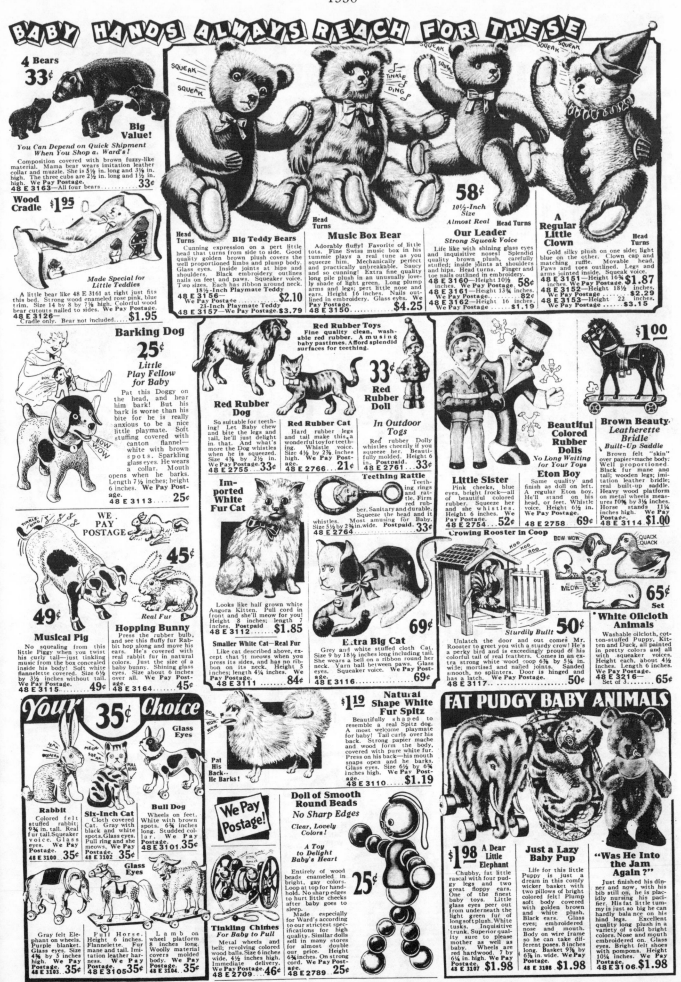

# BABY HANDS ALWAYS REACH FOR THESE

**4 Bears 33¢**

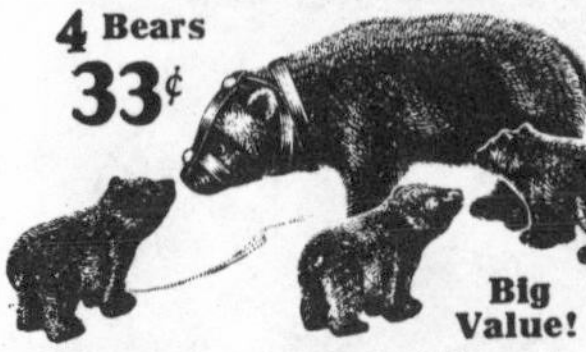

**Big Value!**

*You Can Depend on Quick Shipment When You Shop at Ward's!*

Composition covered with brown fuzzy-like material. Mama bear wears imitation leather collar and muzzle. She is 5½ in. long and 3⅛ in. high. The three cubs are 2½ in. long and 1½ in. high. We Pay Postage. 33¢
48 E 3163—All four bears.......... 33¢

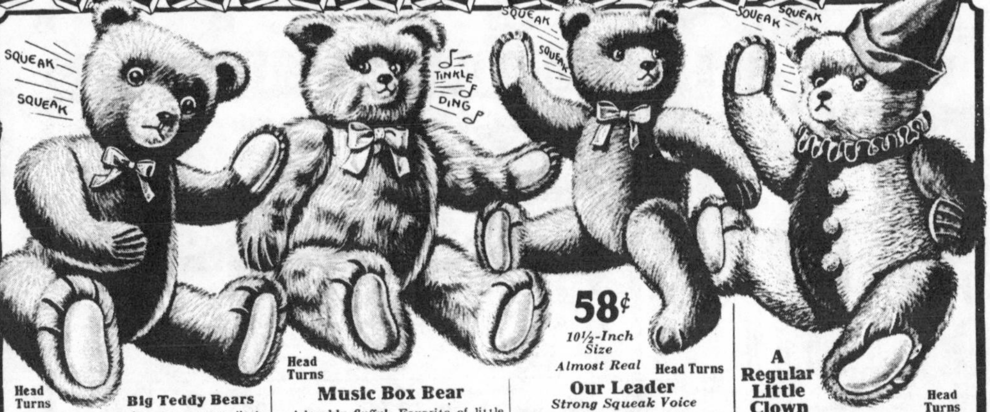


**Big Teddy Bears**

Head Turns

Cunning expression on a pert little head that turns from side to side. Good quality golden brown plush covers the well proportioned limbs and plump body. Glass eyes. Inside joints at hips and shoulders. Black embroidery outlines nails on feet and paws. Squeaker voice. Two sizes. Each has ribbon around neck.
*18½-Inch Playmate Teddy*
48 E 3156—We Pay Postage............ $2.10
*23-Inch Playmate Teddy*
48 E 3157—We Pay Postage.$3.79

**Music Box Bear**

Head Turns

Adorably fluffy! Favorite of little tots. Fine Swiss music box in his tummie plays a real tune as you squeeze him. Mechanically perfect and practically unbreakable. Saucy and so cunning! Extra fine quality long pile plush in an unusually lovely shade of light green. Long plump arms and legs; pert little nose and ears. Height 16 inches. Nails outlined in embroidery. Glass eyes. We Pay Postage.
48 E 3150............ $4.25

**58¢** *10½-Inch Size* *Almost Real*

**Our Leader**

Head Turns

*Strong Squeak Voice*

Life like with shining glass eyes and inquisitive noses! Splendid quality brown plush, carefully stuffed; inside joints at shoulders and hips. Head turns. Finger and toe nails outlined in embroidery.
48 E 3160—Height 10½ inches. We Pay Postage. 58¢
48 E 3161—Height 13¾ inches. We Pay Postage........ 82¢
48 E 3162—Height 16 inches. We Pay Postage........ $1.19

**A Regular Little Clown**

Head Turns

Gold silky plush on one side; light blue on the other. Clown cap and matching ruffle. Movable head. Paws and toes outlined. Legs and arms jointed inside. Squeak voice.
48 E 3151—Height 16¾ inches. We Pay Postage. $1.87
48 E 3152—Height 18½ inches. We Pay Postage........ $2.29
48 E 3153—Height 22 inches. We Pay Postage........ $3.15

**Wood Cradle $1.95**

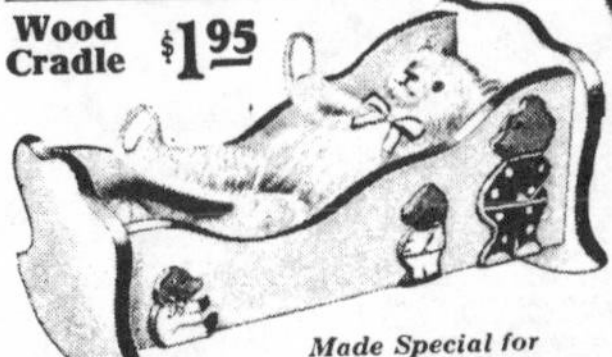

*Made Special for Little Teddies*

A little bear like 48 E 3161 at right just fits this bed. Strong wood enameled rose pink, blue trim. Size 14 by 8 by 7⅛ high. Colorful wood bear cutouts nailed to sides. We Pay Postage.
48 E 3126—Cradle only. Bear not included..... $1.95

## Barking Dog

**25¢**

*Little Play Fellow for Baby*

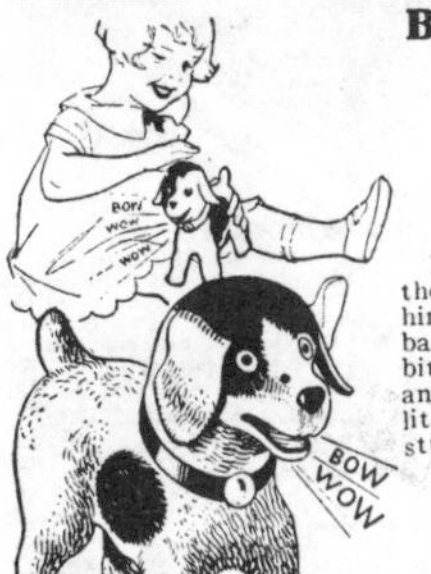


Pat this Doggy on the head, and hear him bark! But his bark is worse than his bite for he is really anxious to be a nice little playmate. Soft stuffing covered with canton flannel—white with brown spots. Sparkling glass eyes. He wears a collar. Mouth opens when he barks. Length 7½ inches; height 6 inches. We Pay Postage.
48 E 3113..... 25¢

**Red Rubber Toys**

Fine quality clean, washable red rubber. Amusing baby pastimes. Afford splendid surfaces for teething.

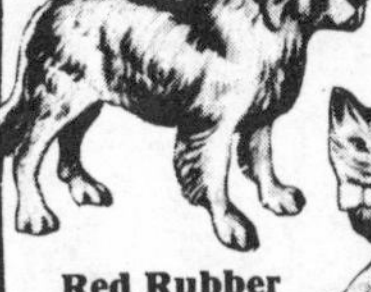

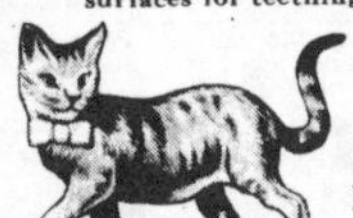

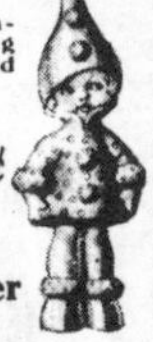

**33¢ Red Rubber Doll**

**Red Rubber Dog**

So suitable for teething! Let Baby chew and bite the legs and tail, he'll just delight in that. And what's more the Dog whistles when he is squeezed. Size 4⅞ by 2½ in. We Pay Postage.
48 E 2755...33¢

**Red Rubber Cat**

Hard rubber legs and tail make this a wonderful toy for teething. Whistle voice. Size 4½ by 2⅞ inches high. We Pay Postage.
48 E 2766...21¢

*In Outdoor Togs*

Red rubber Dolly whistles cheerily if you squeeze her. Beautifully molded. Height 6 in. Postpaid.
48 E 2761...33¢

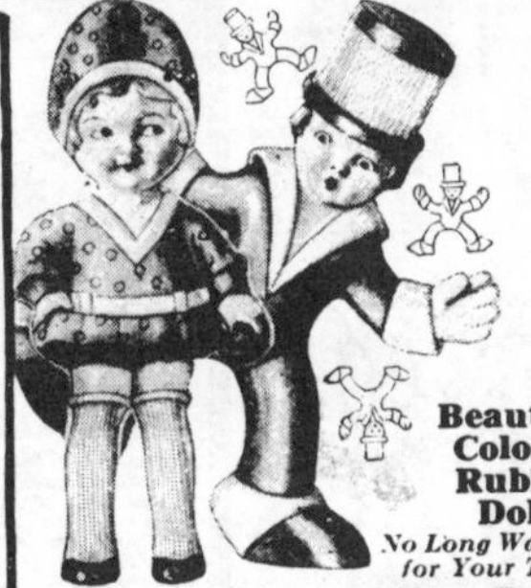

**Beautiful Colored Rubber Dolls**

*No Long Waiting for Your Toys*

**Little Sister**

Pink cheeks, blue eyes, bright frock—all of beautiful colored rubber. Squeeze her and she whistles. Height 6 inches. We Pay Postage.
48 E 2754...52¢

**Eton Boy**

Same quality and finish as doll on left. A regular Eton boy. He'll stand on his head, or feet. Whistle voice. Height 6½ in. We Pay Postage.
48 E 2758...69¢

**$1.00**

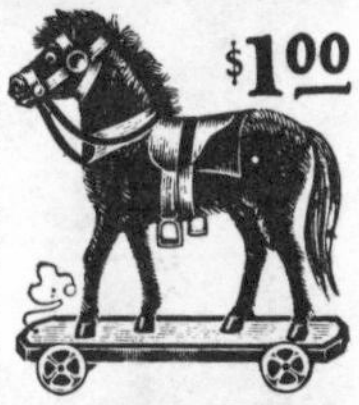

**Brown Beauty**

*Leatherette Bridle*

*Built-Up Saddle*

Brown felt "skin" over papier-mache body. Well proportioned. Black fur mane and tail; wooden legs; imitation leather bridle; real built-up saddle. Heavy wood platform on metal wheels measures 10⅝ by 3⅛ inches. Horse stands 11¼ inches high. We Pay Postage.
48 E 3114...$1.00

**WE PAY POSTAGE**

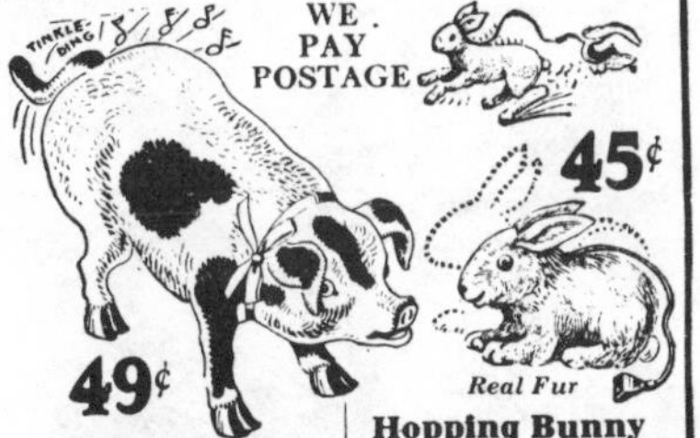


**49¢**

**Musical Pig**

No squealing from this little Piggy when you twist his curly tail—just tinkling music from the box concealed inside his body! Soft white flannelette covered. Size 6½ by 3½ inches without tail. We Pay Postage.
48 E 3115...49¢

**45¢**

*Real Fur*

**Hopping Bunny**

Press the rubber bulb, and see this fluffy fur Rabbit hop along and move his ears. He's covered with real rabbit fur in natural colors. Just the size of a baby bunny. Shining glass eyes. Size about 6 inches over all. We Pay Postage.
48 E 3164.....45¢

**Imported White Fur Cat**

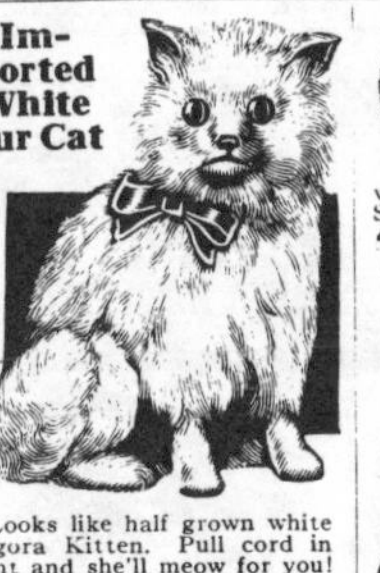

Looks like half grown white Angora Kitten. Pull cord in front and she'll meow for you! Height 8 inches; length 7 inches. Postpaid
48 E 3112.......$1.85

**Smaller White Cat—Real Fur**

Like cat described above, except that it meows when you press its sides, and has no ribbon on its neck. Height 5 inches; length 4¼ inches. We Pay Postage.
48 E 3111.......84¢

**Teething Rattle**

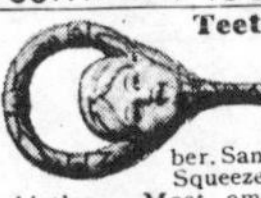

Teething rings and rattle. Firm red rubber. Sanitary and durable. Squeeze the head and it whistles. Most amusing for Baby. Size 5½ by 2⅜ in. wide. Postpaid.
48 E 2764.......33¢

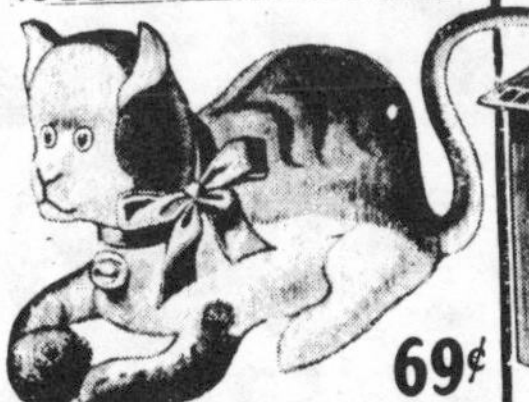

**69¢**

**Extra Big Cat**

Grey and white stuffed cloth Cat. Size 9 by 18½ inches long including tail. She wears a bell on a ribbon round her neck. Yarn ball between paws. Glass eyes. Squeaker voice. We Pay Postage.
48 E 3116.......69¢

**Crowing Rooster in Coop**

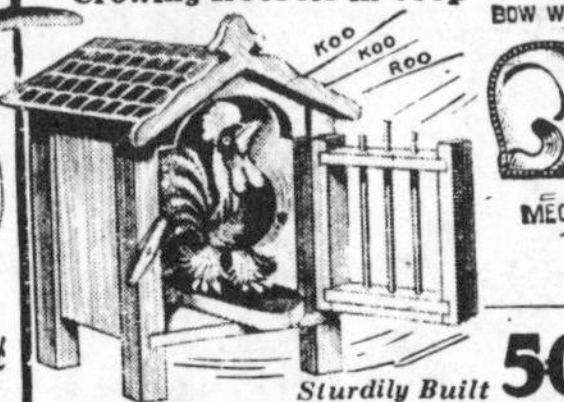


*Sturdily Built* **50¢**

Unlatch the door and out comes Mr. Rooster to greet you with a sturdy crow! He's a perky bird and is exceedingly proud of his colorful tail of real feathers. Comes in an extra strong white wood coop 6⅞ by 5¼ in. wide; mortised and nailed joints. Sanded smooth, no splinters. Door is hinged and has a latch. We Pay Postage.
48 E 3117.......50¢

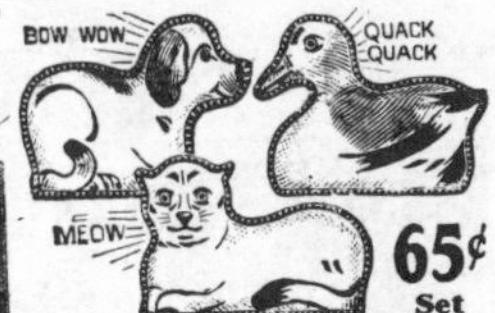


**65¢ Set**

**White Oilcloth Animals**

Washable oilcloth, cotton-stuffed Puppy, Kitten and Duck, all painted in pretty colors and all with squeaker voices. Height each, about 4½ inches. Length 6 inches. We Pay Postage.
48 E 3216—Set of 3.......65¢

## Your 35¢ Choice

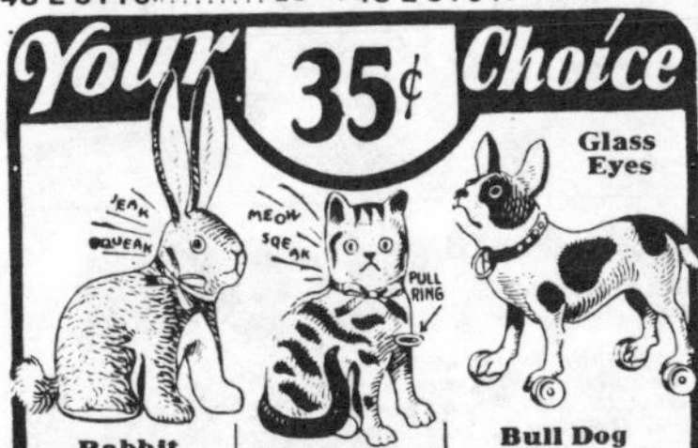


Glass Eyes

**Rabbit**

Colored felt stuffed rabbit; 9¾ in. tall. Real fur tail. Squeaker voice. Glass eyes. We Pay Postage.
48 E 3100...35¢

**Six-Inch Cat**

Cloth covered Cat. Gray with black and white spots. Glass eyes. Pull ring and she meows. We Pay Postage.
48 E 3102...35¢

**Bull Dog**

Wheels on feet. White with brown spots. 6¾ inches long. Studded collar. We Pay Postage.
48 E 3101...35¢

Glass Eyes

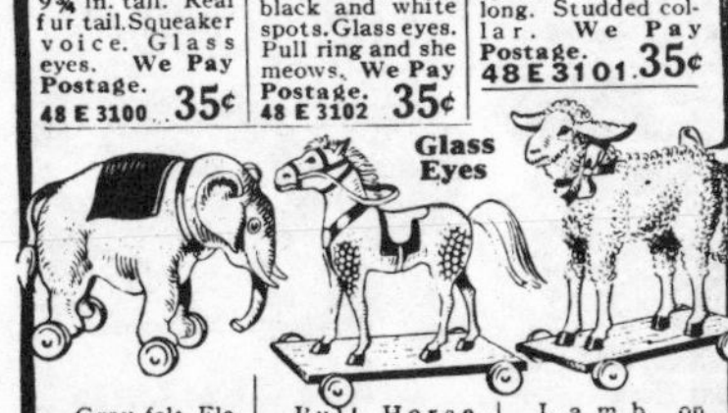

Gray felt Elephant on wheels. Purple blanket. Glass eyes. Size 4¾ by 5 inches high. We Pay Postage.
48 E 3103...35¢

Pull Horse. Height 6 inches. Flannelette. Fur mane and tail. Imitation leather harness. We Pay Postage.
48 E 3105...35¢

Lamb on wheel platform 8 inches long. Woolly material covers molded body. We Pay Postage.
48 E 3104...35¢

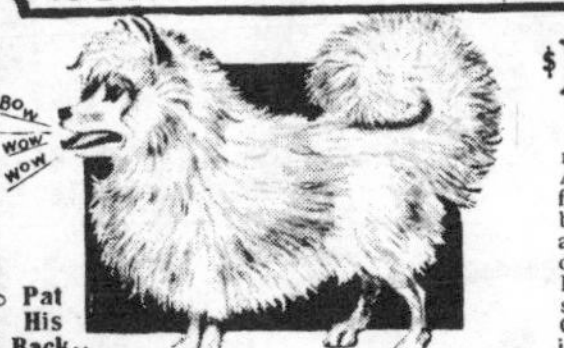


*Pat His Back.. He Barks!*

**$1.19 Natural Shape White Fur Spitz**

Beautifully shaped to resemble a real Spitz dog. A most welcome playmate for baby! Tail curls over his back. Strong papier mache and wood form the body, covered with pure white fur. Press on his back—his mouth snaps open and he barks. Glass eyes. Size 6½ by 6¾ inches high. We Pay Postage.
48 E 3110.....$1.19

**We Pay Postage!**

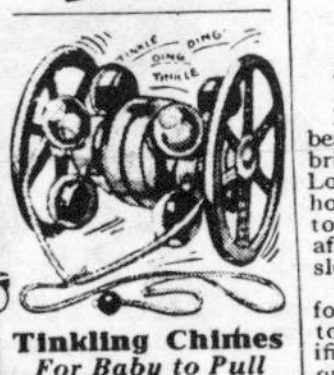


**Tinkling Chimes**

*For Baby to Pull*

Metal wheels and bell; revolving colored wood balls. Size 6 inches wide, 4½ inches high. Immediate delivery. We Pay Postage.
48 E 2709.....46¢

**Doll of Smooth Round Beads**

*No Sharp Edges*

*Clear, Lovely Colors!*

*A Toy to Delight Baby's Heart*

Entirely of wood beads enameled in bright, gay colors. Loop at top for hand-hold. No sharp edges to hurt little cheeks after baby goes to sleep.

Made especially for Ward's according to our strictest specifications for high quality. Similar dolls sell in many stores for almost double our price. Height 6¾ inches. On strong cord. We Pay Postage.
48 E 2789.....25¢

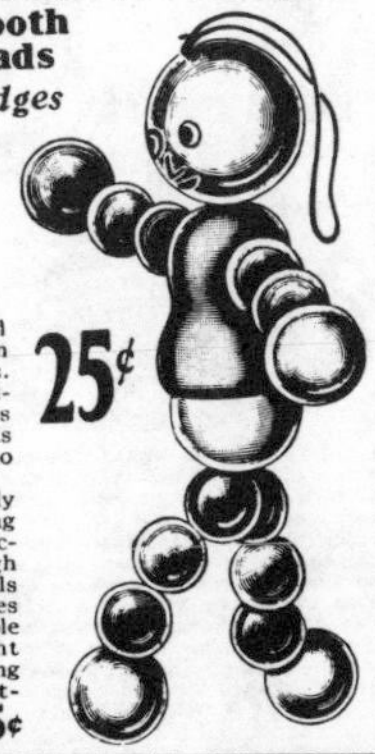

**25¢**

## FAT PUDGY BABY ANIMALS

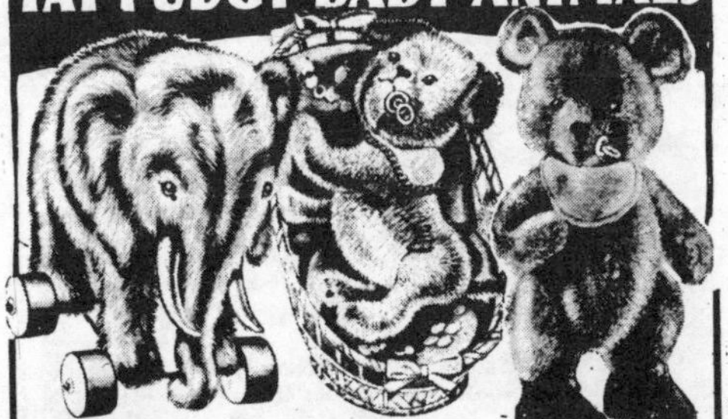

**$1.98 A Dear Little Elephant**

Chubby, fat little rascal with four pudgy legs and two great floppy ears. One of the finest baby toys. Little glass eyes peer out from underneath the light green fur of long soft plush. White tusks. Inquisitive trunk. Superior quality sure to please mother as well as baby. Wheels are red hardwood. 7 by 6¼ in. high. We Pay Postage.
48 E 3107 $1.98

**Just a Lazy Baby Pup**

Life for this little Puppy is just a dream in this comfy wicker basket with two pillows of bright colored felt! Plump soft body covered with golden brown and white plush. Black ears. Glass eyes; embroidered nose and mouth. Body on wire frame so he can take different poses. 8 inches long. Basket 9⅞ by 6⅞ in. wide. We Pay Postage.
48 E 3108 $1.98

**"Was He Into the Jam Again?"**

Just finished his dinner and now, with his bib still on, he is placidly nursing his pacifier. His fat little tummy is just so big he can hardly balance on his hind legs. Excellent quality long plush in a variety of solid bright colors. Nose and mouth embroidered on. Glass eyes. Bright felt shoes with pompons. Height 10¼ inches. We Pay Postage.
48 E 3106.$1.98

# GAMES ·· We Pay Postage

## Popular Card Games at Lower Prices

### Juvenile Pool Tables

---

### $1.00 — Enameled Military Tenpins

Ten imported wood soldiers in brilliant red hats and coats, blue pants and black shoes. Beautifully enameled and varnished. Height 8 inches. Three 1¾-inch round wood balls, enameled red, white and blue. Set comes in pretty box suitable for gift. A $1.50 value. We Pay Postage.
48 E 2208......$1.00

### 50¢

Nicely enameled wood soldier Tenpins. Blue and crimson uniforms with black shako hats. Height 5¼ inches. Three 1¼-inch colored wood balls.
48 E 2209—We Pay Postage............50¢

### Uncle Wiggily

Boys and girls find great enjoyment in playing this popular game. Depicts Uncle Wiggily's mishaps on the way to Doctor Possum's. The first to get Uncle Wiggily to the doctor wins. Board 16 by 16 inches. Cloth hinges. Four Uncle Wiggily men and 140 cards. We Pay Postage.
48 E 2132............63¢

### Fun for All

Painstakingly made in Europe. About fifty wood Jack-raws and two wooden-handled lifters. Shaped like saws, ladders, hoes, rakes and other miniature implements. The labor alone in making this set is worth more than our selling price. We Pay Postage............25¢
48 E 2115

### Twelve Imported Wire Puzzles

Fascinating pastime for every member of the family. Twelve of the best puzzles ever devised in Europe. Made by master craftsmen—many have been handed down from generation to generation. Of heavy gauge steel wire, highly polished. Complete instructions for working each puzzle in case you can't figure them out. We Pay Postage............47¢
48 E 2139

### Touring—A Popular Game 63¢

One of the liveliest games for a progressive party, and a world of fun to brighten evenings at home. Proves that the safe driver beats the fast driver to town. Punctures, blowouts, empty gas tank, and various other hazards may delay you. 100 highly glossed cards. Instructions so simply written that small children can understand them.
48 E 2114—Complete. We Pay Postage............63¢

### Three Well Known Games

Funny Old Maid game with 31 nice round corner cards printed in colors; Doctor Quack and that very instructive game of Authors. Each game has 32 fine finish cards. Dr. Quack is a funny game that keeps everyone laughing. Each in a neat box 6½ by 5 inches. We Pay Postage.
48 E 2120—Three games............29¢

### IT?

Funniest new card game of the year! Forty-five fine quality cards with the most amusing captions and pictures. Be sure to add it to your collection—Ward's sells IT for less. We Pay Postage............95¢
48 E 2137

### Game of Rook

Play 12 different games with this Rook deck; 9 games for adults and 3 games for children. 56 handsome enameled cards. Instructions included. We Pay Postage.
48 E 2100............63¢

### Wings

Ninety-nine fine quality enameled playing cards; 72 red back mail cards; 27 blue back delay and release cards. Based on air-mail landings at 12 leading cities. 2, 3 or 4 can play. Instructions. We Pay Postage.
48 E 2172............63¢

### "Lindy" Air Mail Game

A race between two contending aviators over a 3200-mile course. Ninety-nine high-grade cards, 12 different kinds. For two, three, four or six players. We Pay Postage.
48 E 2103............47¢

### Flinch Cards for 2 to 8 Players

Hilarity—excitement! Flinch is a card game you simply can't be without. Contains 150 gloss enameled cards—excellent quality. Complete playing instructions.
48 E 2135—We Pay Postage............63¢

### Parlor Pool Tables $5.99

Mahogany finished wood frame tables. Composition bottoms reinforced with steel girders. Green cloth covered beds. Steel corner plates. Solid rubber cushions. Cloth pockets. Firmly braced legs. Not mailable.

**Large Size $8.59** — Length 54 inches; width 28 inches; height 29 inches. Two 36-inch tapered wood cues with leather tips. Wood triangle. 15 numbered and 1 white cue ball, 1⅞ in. diameter. Ship. wt. 40 pounds.
148 E 2213............$8.59

**Small Size $5.99** — Length 42½ inches; width 22½ inches; height 25¼ inches. Two 33-inch tapered wood cues with leather tips. Wood triangle. 15 numbered and 1 white cue ball, diam. 1⅜ in. Ship. wt. 21 lbs.
148 E 2220............$5.99

### $1.50 — Real Pool Balls — Miniature Pool Table

Convenient size pool table—11¾ by 18 inches—that can be used anywhere. Made of steel; enameled grain mahogany finish. Green felt surface. Six pockets; automatic ball return. Live rubber cushions. Complete with triangle rack and sixteen ¾-inch colored and numbered pool balls (not marbles). Two 8-inch spring cues. We Pay Postage.
48 E 2212—Complete............$1.50

### $1.15 — Machine Gun Nest

Shooting game with real action! The wood machine gun has a metal clip on top that holds six wood bullets. The gun can be fired out at any desired speed. Swivel attachment for aiming up, down, or sideways. Height 8 in.; barrel 7 in. long. Lots of fun shooting at the six cardboard soldiers which are 5⅝ in. tall. All pieces finished in attractive colors. Twelve wood bullets included.
48 E 859—We Pay Postage............$1.15
48 E 857—36 extra bullets. Postpaid............21¢

---

### Junior Combination Board — Bradley's Famous Set

Hinged board 16 by 16½ inches. Colored glazed playing surface on each side. Plays 12 games—India, Checkers, Yacht Race, Fortune Telling, Bicycle Race, Hop, Pussy in the Corner, American Corners, Railroad Game, Cornering the Pig, Johnny Jumps and Steeplechase. 55 playing pieces; spinner and book of rules. Complete set in handsome box. We Pay Postage.
48 E 2195—Complete............98¢

### Big Value Tenpins 33¢

Usually Sells for 50¢

A tremendous order enables us to sell this well-made set of imported Tenpins at an amazingly low price! Ten turned wood pins, 7 inches high, with colored stripes. Two 1¾-inch balls also of white wood, colorfully striped. Develops skill in judging aim and distances. We Pay Postage.
48 E 2199............33¢

### 53¢ — Spinning Top Puts Marbles In Holes

Spin the top and count your score from the value of the holes into which it puts the marbles. The red and yellow enameled steel plate is 8¼ inches in diameter. Will not warp or crack like wood. Five brightly colored balls and a top. Instructions for playing included. Depend on Ward's for fast same day shipment. We Pay Postage.
48 E 2143—Complete............53¢

### 47¢ — Checker Sets and Men

Varnished black and red playing surface—wood frame; cloth hinges. 1-inch wooden checkers—30 in all; two dice. Backgammon board on inside. We Pay Postage.
48 E 2205—Size of board 14 by 13½ in............47¢
48 E 2206—Size of board 16½ by 17¼ in............59¢

### Shoot the Ducks 50¢

Duck pond with 9 ducks, each about 1½ inches high, on metal stands. Each covers a number—shoot them with the 12½-inch gun. Box 6½ by 13¼ inches. Extra bullets included in the box. We Pay Postage.
48 E 840—Complete............50¢

### Crows in the Corn 87¢

Four laughable crows cut out of cardboard are perched on the wooden fence. Realistic cornfield background in colors (12¼ by 8¼ inches). Try to hit the crows with the 17-inch cork shooting pop gun; break action. Complete in colorful box—12¾ by 13 in. 3 corks included. Harmless. We Pay Postage.
48 E 853............87¢

---

### "WE"—Parkers' Magnetic Flying Game

Colored boards representing six of the leading flying fields of the U. S. are placed on furniture about the room. Contesting players or "flyers" lift planes with magnets on strings and endeavor to carry them and "land" from one field to another. Lifting magnets can carry planes only when exceeding care is used. Poles with strings and magnets attached and 16 planes, 4 for each player; 6 colored cardboard flying fields, each 6½ by 6½ inches. Complete with instructions in lithographed box. We Pay Postage.
48 E 2112—Complete set............99¢

### Four Board Games

Fine combination of games. Two boards 12 inches square, each hinged in center with game playing surface on either side, making a total of four games. Games are: India Home, played for centuries; Army and Navy, a war game; Big Game Hunt and Auto Race. Lithographed in bright colors; varnished. We Pay Postage. All necessary pieces included. Boards printed in bright colors; varnished. We Pay Postage.
48 E 2164—Complete............47¢

### Rubber Horseshoes 83¢

Complete Set For Fun Indoors and Outdoors

Speedy Shipment

Play Horseshoes anywhere in the house, any time you want to, with this fine set—and you will have as much fun as you would out of doors. Full size horseshoes of live, resilient rubber, reinforced inside with steel wire. They make very little noise and will not mar the furniture. The pegs are fastened to round steel plates that cling snugly to the floor. These plates are lithographed in black and gold rings—it's no trouble to decide which shoe is nearest the post. You can make ringers and leaners, and best of all, two of the shoes are black and two are red so that there will be no argument as to whom the winning shoes belong. Complete instructions included. We Pay Postage.
48 E 2118—Complete set............83¢

### Electric Magic Board 94¢

Never Makes a Mistake
We Pay the Postage

Answers 144 questions electrically and with magical accuracy. Plug in the question you want to ask. When the correct answer is found the electric bulb lights. Fine fiberboard figure 10 inches high by 8½ inches wide, printed in vivid colors. Electric battery included. Twelve series; 12 questions to a set. Usually sells for $1.50.
48 E 2201—We Pay Postage............94¢

### Little Tots' Croquet Set In Wood Box

Four hardwood mallets, each 18½ in. long. Four hardwood balls striped to match; varnished. Set, including wickets and varnished posts in wood box 22½ by 5½ by 4½ inches; hinged cover. Suitable for lawn or parlor floor. We Pay Postage.
448 E 2197—Complete............$1.00

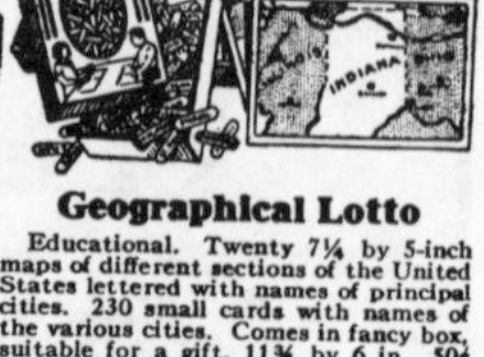

### Geographical Lotto

Educational. Twenty 7¼ by 5-inch maps of different sections of the United States lettered with names of principal cities. 230 small cards with names of the various cities. Comes in fancy box, suitable for a gift. 11¾ by 6 in. 50¢ value. We Pay Postage.
48 E 2176............35¢

*Montgomery Ward & Co.*

# For Grownups—Enjoyed by Little Folks, Too

**We Pay Postage!**

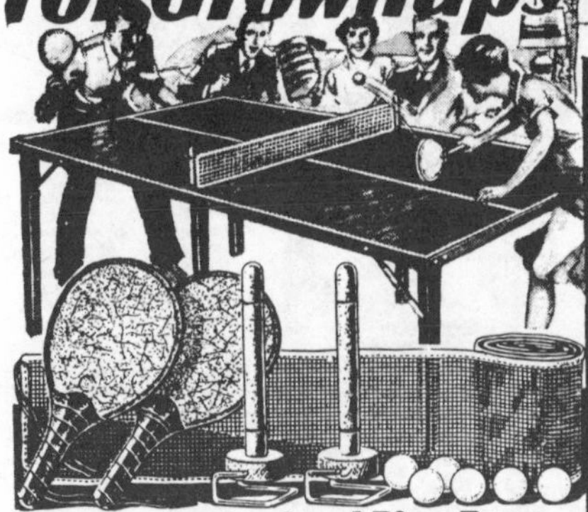

## Parkers' Professional Ping-Pong

Our finest! Contains two handsome Newport rackets, leather bound and covered; 6 match Ping-Pong balls; one 54-inch green net; two posts with rigid table clamps. 68-page Ping-Pong book with introduction by "Big Bill" Tilden included. **Postpaid.**
48 E 2216—Complete set in box............**$5.95**

**Parkers' Lower Priced Ping-Pong Set in Box**
Consists of two professional size plywood rackets sanded to give backspin. Four regulation Ping-Pong balls, table clamps and net. Association rules. **We Pay Postage.**
48 E 2191—Complete set............**$2.42**

**Imported Table Tennis**
Two smooth unvarnished hardwood rackets 11 by 5½ inches; two regulation size balls; table posts with clamps and net. Boxed. We Pay Postage.
48 E 2151—Complete set............**98¢**

**Table for Ping-Pong**
Professional Tournament Size. Plywood top painted green with white markings. Thick 1⅛-inch wood frame. Slide lock on steel leg braces. ⅞-inch wood girders under table. 5 by 9 ft.; 30¾ in. high. Folds flat. **Shipped from Ludington, Mich.**
248 E 2217—Shipping weight 130 pounds............**$31.50**

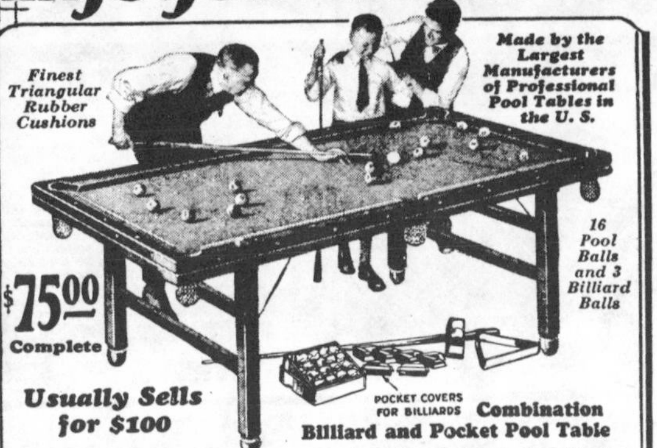
Finest Triangular Rubber Cushions
Made by the Largest Manufacturers of Professional Pool Tables in the U. S.
16 Pool Balls and 3 Billiard Balls
$75.00 Complete
POCKET COVERS FOR BILLIARDS

**Usually Sells for $100**

## Combination Billiard and Pocket Pool Table

Almost regulation size—3½ by 7 feet long; height 32 inches. Seasoned wood frame, mahogany finish. Folds flat.

**Note These Features**

(1) Specially constructed bed covered with fine quality regulation green wool cloth. (2) Resilient rubber, triangular cushions, covered with strong wool cushion cloth. (3) Rail sights, wood pocket nets, genuine leather trim. (4) Necessary rigidity; leveling device on each leg. (5) Convenient folding legs. (6) Easily convertible into billiard table; plugs for each pocket furnished. Supplies include fifteen 2-inch numbered agate balls, 1 white cue ball; 1 maple triangle; 4 51-inch maple cues; 1 wood bridge 51 inches long; 6 pocket plugs; three 2-inch Ivorylene billiard (one red) balls; cue chalk, and book of rules. Ship. wt. 206 lbs. **Not mailable. Shipped from nearby warehouse.**
248 E 2140—Complete outfit............**$75.00**
448 E 2141—Extra 51-inch cue; We Pay Postage............**$1.79**

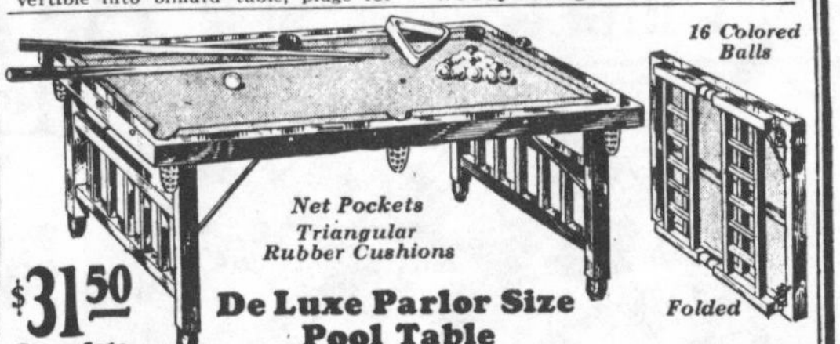
16 Colored Balls
Net Pockets
Triangular Rubber Cushions
Folded

**$31.50 Complete**

## De Luxe Parlor Size Pool Table

Fine seasoned wood frame with mahogany finish. Green felt covered bed and cushions. Folding legs are rigidly braced and quickly leveled by special adjusting feet. Size 70 by 38 inches at outside rail and 32 inches high. 15 colored, numbered, 1⅞-inch pool balls; 1 white cue ball; two 48-inch regulation, cushion tipped cues; triangle; piece of cue chalk and book of rules. Shipping weight 85 pounds. **Not mailable.**
148 E 2147—Complete outfit............**$31.50**
448 E 2141—Extra 51-inch cue. We Pay Postage............**$1.79**

**Nationally Known Made by PARKER BROS.**

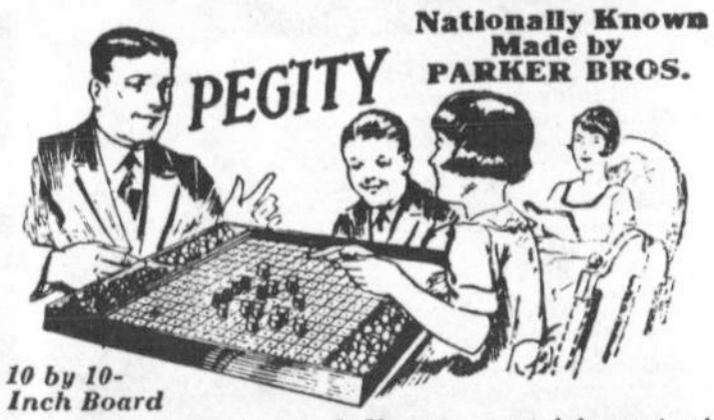
PEGITY

10 by 10-Inch Board

Are you a Pegity fan, too? If not you certainly must get one of these popular, nationally advertised games. For two, three or four people. Big playing board has holes in which you put the turned colored wooden pegs. Get five of your color in a row before your opponent blocks you. Instructions. We Pay Postage.
48 E 2165—Parkers' Pegity Game............**$1.19**

**WE PAY POSTAGE**

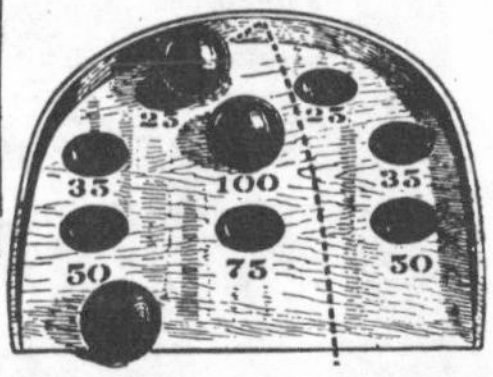
25
35
100
35
75
50
50

## Bollo Ball 97¢

Improved Bollo Ball board is built with a curving surface in back to return ball in case you do not score. Place board, measuring 12¼ inches wide by 11½ inches from front to back, on table or floor and allow each player to have a chance to score by rolling the three 1¾-inch colored balls at the numbered pockets. Similar to bowling. Possible, with the three balls, to score 225 points. We Pay Postage.
48 E 2186—Board and balls complete............**97¢**

## Horse Race $2.29

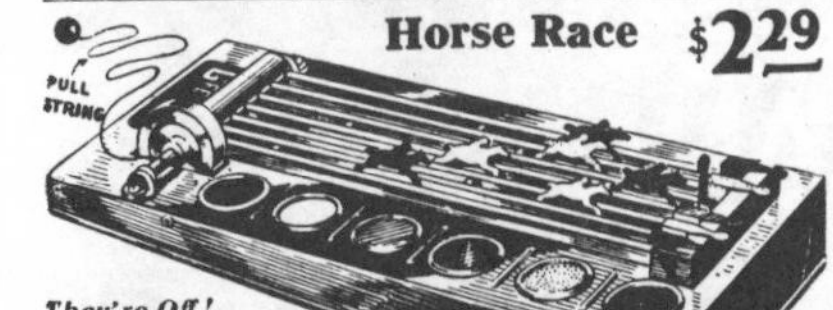
PULL STRING

*They're Off!* Sensationally realistic Horse Race Game. A different horse may win each time. Six horses leave the barrier on the split-second and the race is on! Which horse will reach the goal post first? Entirely of 24-gauge steel, lithographed in bright colors; practically indestructible. Six differently colored horses, each in separate track. When horse reaches post a flag of matching color is automatically raised. Place your bets on cups at side corresponding in color to horses. Large fly wheel set in motion by pulling string is connected to a square axle. In each track is a ball bearing which is speeded on its way as it hits the square axle. Ball bearings in turn push horse down the track. Exciting for children as well as grownups. Size of game 5½ by 15 inches long. We Pay Postage.
48 E 2214—Complete............**$2.29**

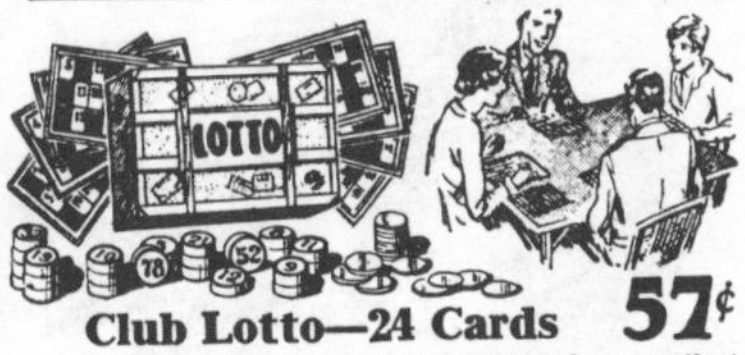
LOTTO

## Club Lotto—24 Cards 57¢

Big enough for a large party—twenty-four excellent quality heavy cards about 4 by 7 inches long, printed in black and green. Ninety-nine numbered discs ⅝-inch in diameter are made of pure white hardwood heavily embossed and printed on the face in red. Numbers show distinctly. Ample allowance of steel discs to put over numbers on cards as they are called off. Instructions included. Packed in partitioned box 8½ by 5¾ inches. We Pay Postage.
48 E 2223—Complete set............**57¢**

## Bridge Keno—New! Exciting! Sensation Everywhere!

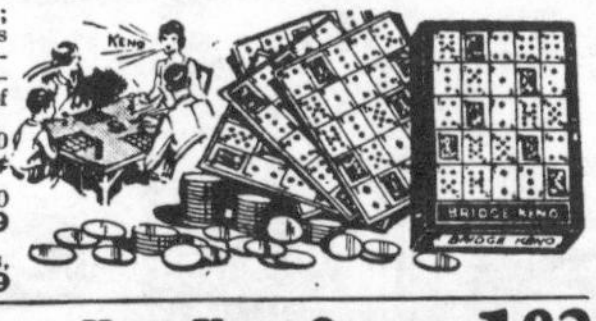
BRIDGE KENO

Bridge Keno cards are 8 by 6 inches; colored discs and simple instructions for playing. Used with any deck of playing cards (not included). Boards reproduce in colors the faces of entire deck of cards. We Pay Postage.
48 E 2224—For 4 players: 4 cards, 100 discs. We Pay Postage............**95¢**
48 E 2227—For 8 players: 8 cards, 200 discs. We Pay Postage............**$1.89**
48 E 2228—For 12 players: 12 cards, 300 discs. We Pay Postage. **$2.79**

**$2.19**

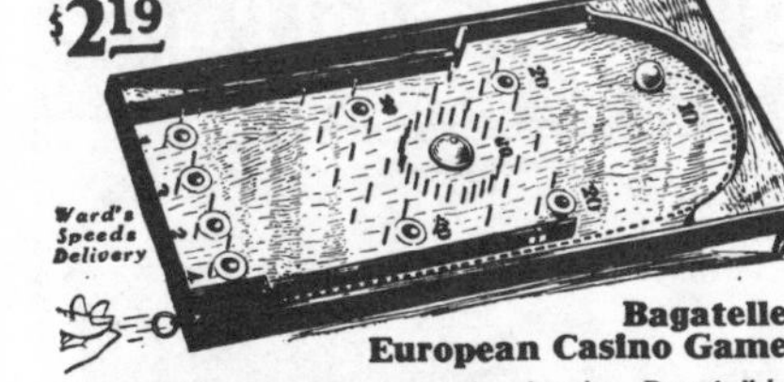

*Ward's Speeds Delivery*

## Bagatelle European Casino Game

Imported from Europe, where it is a favorite. Drop ball in alley, pull back ring and spring shoots ball around circle dropping it into one of the numbered pockets. Striking bell in center scores 60 points. Any number can play. Highly polished smooth wood board, stained green and finished with coat of transparent, highly lustrous varnish. 11¼ by 23¾ inches long; 1½ inches high. We Pay Postage.
48 E 2153—Complete. Everything including, ball. **$2.19**

*We Pay Postage*

## Have Your Own Home Bowling Alley $1.83

*Fun for the Whole Family*
*Automatic Pin Setter*

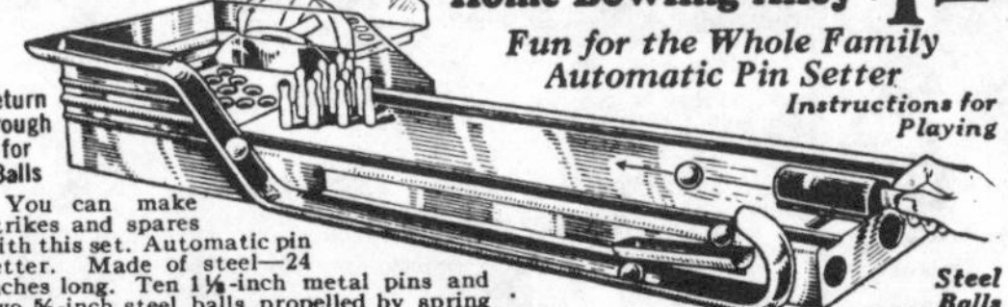
Instructions for Playing
Return Trough for Balls
Steel Balls

You can make strikes and spares with this set. Automatic pin setter. Made of steel—24 inches long. Ten 1⅛-inch metal pins and two ⅝-inch steel balls propelled by spring gun on swivel. Return trough for balls. Finished in bright colors. We Pay Postage.
448 E 2196—Complete outfit............**$1.83**

## Thrilling Baseball Game $1.19

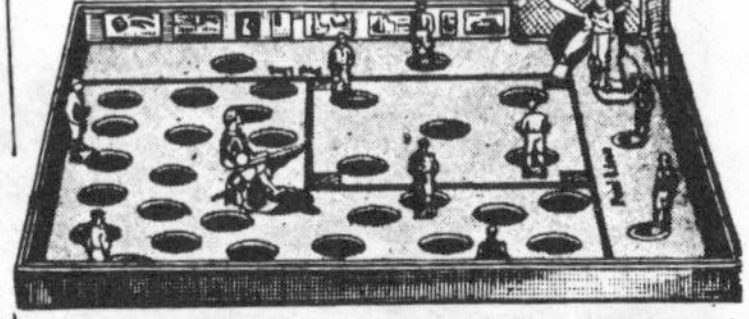

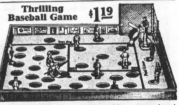

Works automatically. Batter and base runners in uniform of one color; catcher, pitcher and field men in uniform of another color. All plays that happen on a real diamond are represented on this board by the 40 depressions clearly printed with name of play and action that takes place. Diamond surrounded by imitation fence printed with bill-boards. Playing field 17 inches square. Thirteen players described above are of metal; 2 inches tall. One solid rubber ball ⅝ inch in diameter. Your skill in actually pitching or batting the ball decides the outcome of the game. Instructions on back of cover. We Pay Postage.
48 E 2126—Complete............**$1.19**

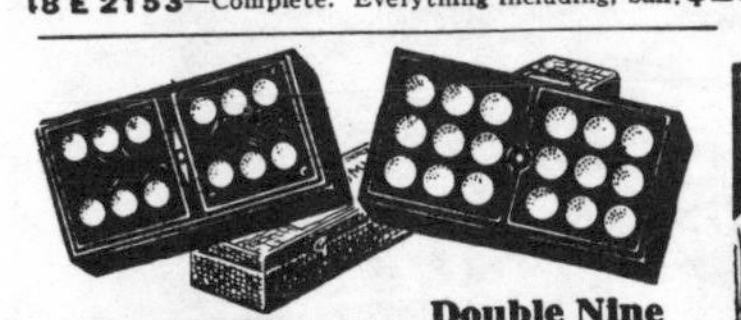

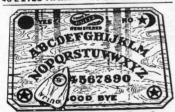

## Double Six

Twenty-eight ebonized hardwood dominoes. Sunken, white enameled dots. Size 1⅞ inches by 1 5/16 inch by ¼ inch. Plain box. Imported. We Pay Postage.
48 E 2123—Per set **25¢**

## Double Nine
*In Wood Box*

White dots on black. Fifty-six, ebonized hardwood dominoes, each 2 inches by 1 inch by ⅜ inch. Packed in hinged covered wood box which closes with latch. Postpaid.
48 E 2129—Per set **83¢**

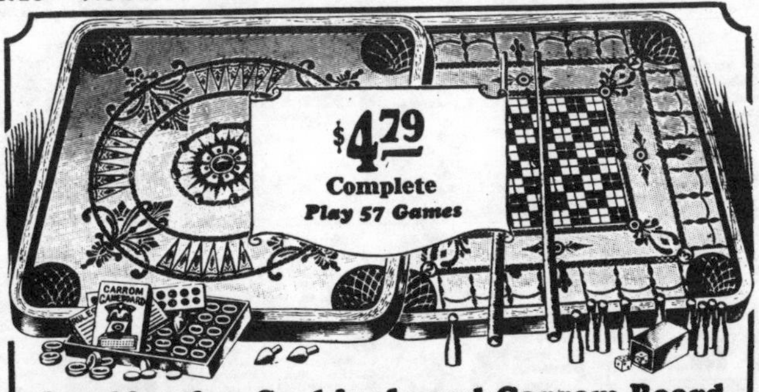
$4.79
Complete
Play 57 Games
CARROM

## Baseball or Football

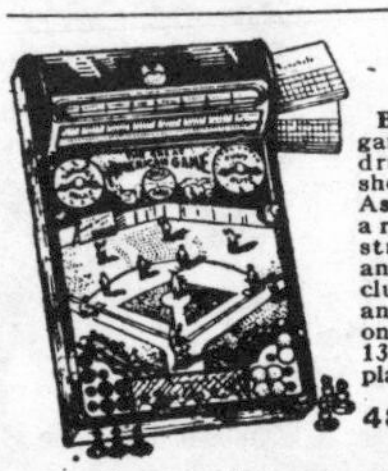

**Baseball Game.** To start game press the button. The drum revolves and stops, showing result of the play. As interesting as watching a real ball game. Dials show strikes, balls, innings, runs, and outs. Scorecards included. Metal playing field and revolving drum cover on dovetailed wood frame 13½ by 9 by 3¼ inches; 18 players. We Pay Postage.
48 E 2131............**$1.79**

**Football Game.** Constructed as above, but arranged for football. Players can use judgment. Ball advances as in real game. Endorsed by college coaches. We Pay Postage.
48 E 2130............**$1.79**

YES
NO
REGISTERED
ABCDEFGHIJKLM
NOPQRSTUVWXYZ
1234567890
GOOD BYE

## Fuld's Ouija Mystery Board
*Used for Psychic Research*

Many people believe you can communicate with the spirit world through the Genuine Fuld's Ouija Board. Made of hardwood, varnished. Equipped with Fuld's new patented transparent indicator. Ouija is mentioned in all books on psychic research. We Pay Postage.
48 E 2124—Size 15 by 22 inches............**$1.19**
48 E 2125—Size 12 by 18 inches............**.89**

## Combination Crokinole and Carrom Board
### You Can Play 57 Games—Every Home Needs One!

Many fascinating games can be played on either side of this Combination Board. Entertainment for the whole family during long winter evenings—never a boring moment! There are crokinole, carroms and more than fifty other games; every one a popular pastime. The carrom and bank shots and parlor pool will give you wonderful practice for real pool or billiards and they are bound to improve your aim in the other sports, too.

Fine, natural varnish finish, three-ply veneer wood, 28½ inches square with heavy frame. Pockets are of strongest net. Twenty-nine rings, two 26-inch cues thirty-nine other pieces and complete instruction book for playing fifty-seven games. Remember our new speedy shipment—mail order's fastest delivery. Shipping weight 13 pounds. **Not mailable.**
148 E 2144—Complete outfit............**$4.79**

**33¢**

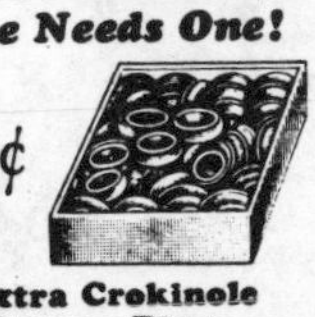

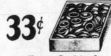

**29 Extra Crokinole or Carrom Rings**

Smooth, fine hardwood. This set includes twelve red, twelve green and four white shooter rings and a black center ring. Specially priced. We Pay Postage.
48 E 2145—Per set............**33¢**

**89¢**

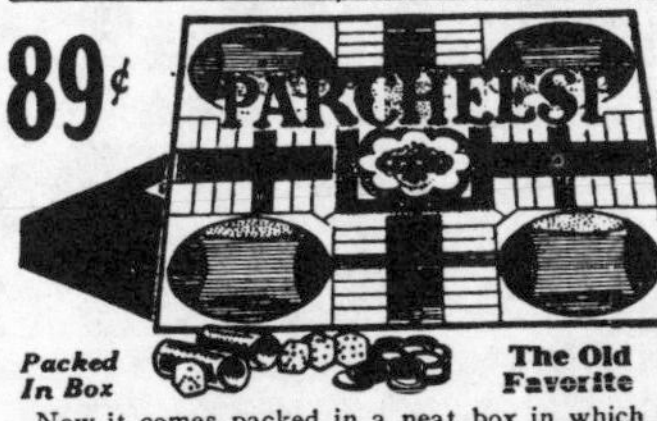
PARCHEESI

*Packed In Box*

**The Old Favorite**

Now it comes packed in a neat box in which to keep it. The original Parcheesi with the complete equipment of playing pieces. Two cardboard dice cups, 4 dice, 16 brassbound counters (4 of each color). Good quality linen board, hinged in the middle, 15¾ inches by 15¾ inches. Printed in the regulation colors. We Pay Postage.
48 E 2099—Complete set............**89¢**

# Toys That Teach

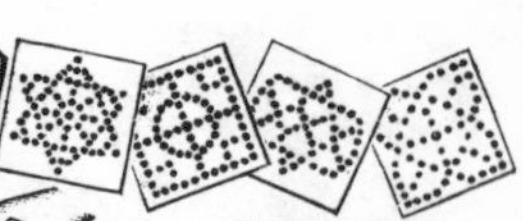

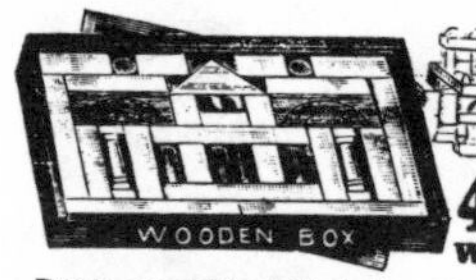


**47¢ Wood Blocks**

Dandy set of Wood Blocks in a strong wood box. Build bridges, churches and other buildings. Round pillars, square beams and oval archways of clear grained, smooth wood. Some pieces are white, others are stained blue, green or red. Box 10½ by 7 inches. We Pay Postage.
48 E 521—Complete with model.........**47¢**

**Blocks With New Building Features**

Wood Building Blocks. Artistic and well proportioned from pillars to plainest pieces. Smooth, clear grained wood. Artistic tall French windows with transparent green and red panes and arch tops to harmonize with doorway design. Assorted shapes, combinations of dark and light wood, some with scrolls and colors. Comes in heavy wood box 17½ by 10 inches. We Pay Postage.
48 E 522—Complete with model.........**$1.59**

## Toy Typewriter

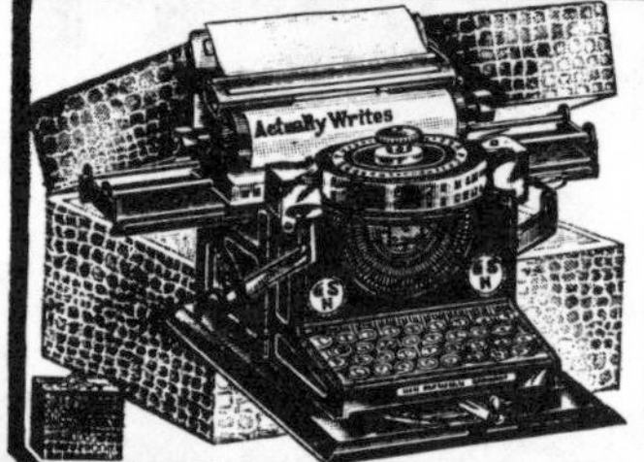


**In Wood Carrying Case**

A Toy Typewriter that really writes! Turn the cylinder on top and press the levers either at the right or left. That's all you have to do to write. The carriage moves from side to side as you type. Takes paper up to 3½ inches wide. Writes capitals and small letters, numerals, punctuation marks as well as plus and minus signs. Package of paper and envelopes to fit included. Typewriter of metal, shaped and finished in black to resemble a real typewriter. Size $7\frac{1}{16}$ by 8 by 4¾ inches high. Comes in substantial wood carrying case size 9 by 8 inches with nickel-plated handle. Full instructions and tube of ink for rollers included. We Pay Postage.
48 E 2226..............**$2.59**

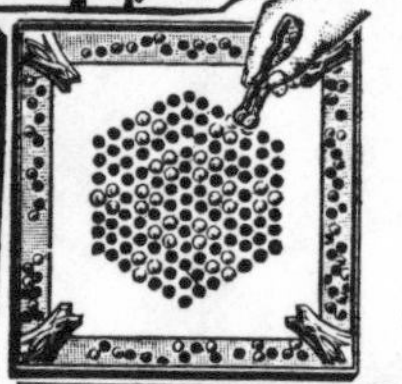

**Imported Glass Pearl Mosaic**

Beautiful! Translucent, solid glass—yellow, orange, light blue and red. Arrange the 100 pearl-like balls in the two design plates (square and hexagonal). 40 colored designs for the child to work out and metal tweezers included. Fascinating pastime. We Pay Postage.
48 E 2215..........**48¢**

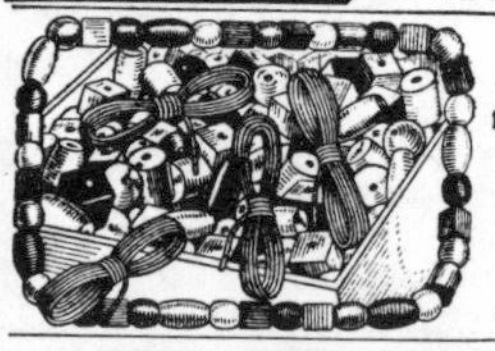

**225 Wood Beads for Stringing 45¢**

Bright colored ½-inch cubes, cylinders, balls and ⅞-inch ovals. Four cords with metal tips. We Pay Postage.
48 E 568—Beads and cords..........**45¢**

**Historical Lead Soldiers**

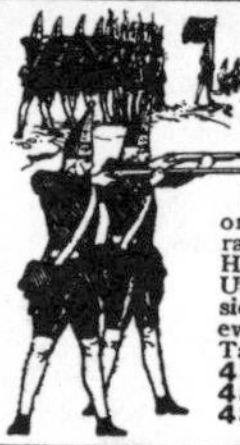

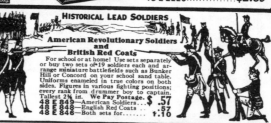

**American Revolutionary Soldiers and British Red Coats**

For school or at home! Use sets separately or buy two sets of 19 soldiers each and arrange miniature battlefields such as Bunker Hill or Concord on your school sand table. Uniforms enameled in true colors on both sides. Figures in various fighting positions; every rank from drummer boy to captain. Tallest 2¾ in. We Pay Postage.
48 E 849—American Soldiers.........**$ .57**
48 E 848—English Red Coats.........**.57**
48 E 846—Both sets for.........**1.10**

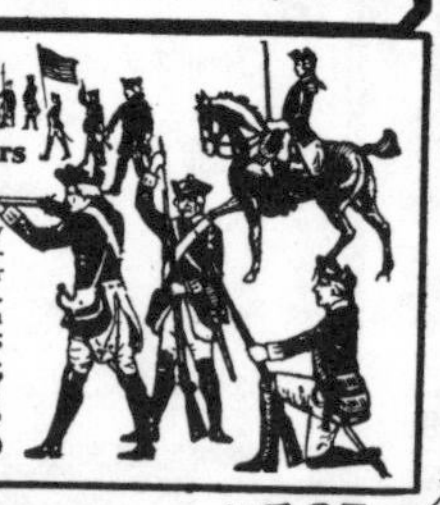

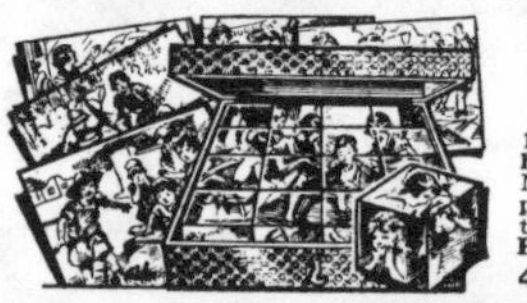

**Picture Puzzle Blocks 59¢**

Twenty solid wood, 1¾-inch cubes in hinged wood case. Makes six colored pictures. Key pictures included. We Pay Postage.
48 E 525—Per set.....**59¢**

*Our Prize Building Block Set And a Wagon to Carry It*

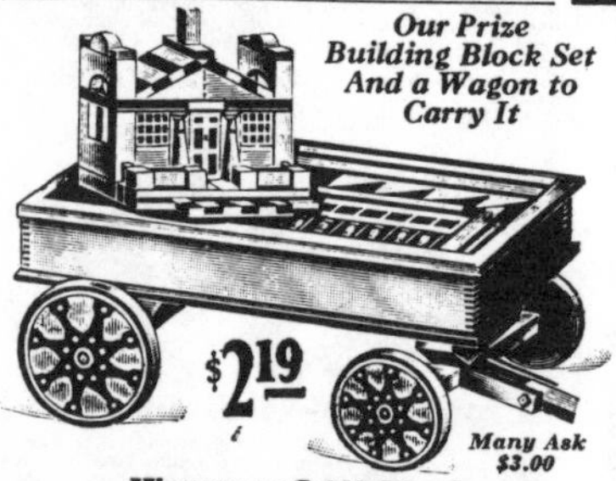

**$2.19** *Many Ask $3.00*

**Wagon and 188 Blocks**

Build houses, barns, sheds, garages! Different sized colored wood in a Wagon of purple and orange wood, size 17½ by 10¾ inches. Well made and ready to put together. Wood disc wheels. Front wheels will turn under the wagon. Book containing 38 building ideas is included. We Pay Postage.
448 E 536—Wagon and blocks..........**$2.19**

*We Pay the Postage*

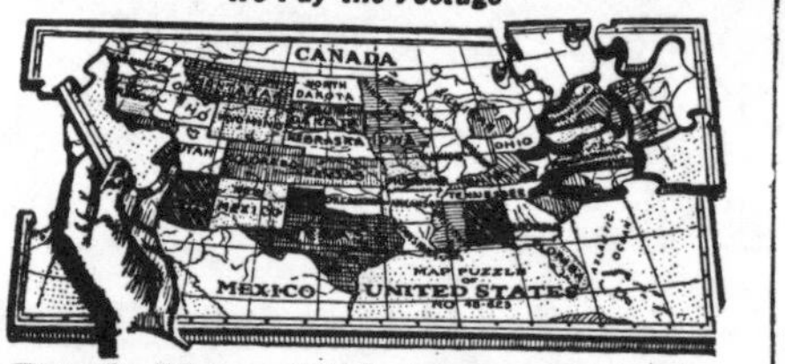


**Puzzle Maps—U. S., Europe, World**

All three Maps listed here are of quality seldom offered for less than $1.50. Up-to-date maps, beautifully printed in colors, glued to fine quality 3-ply non-warping basswood panels and jig-sawed (not die-cut, leaving splinters) along boundary lines. Children learn arrangements and shapes of states quicker with these puzzles. Complete in detail showing rivers, mountain ranges, cities, etc. Each map in box suitable for gift.

**Large Map of U. S.** 48 E 625—Size 12 by 20 inches. We Pay Postage. Complete......**95¢**

**Map of World** 48 E 628—Size 13½ by 20½ inches. We Pay Postage. Complete......**97¢**

**Map of Europe** 48 E 630—Size 15½ by 11¼ inches. We Pay Postage. Complete......**85¢**

**$1.87**

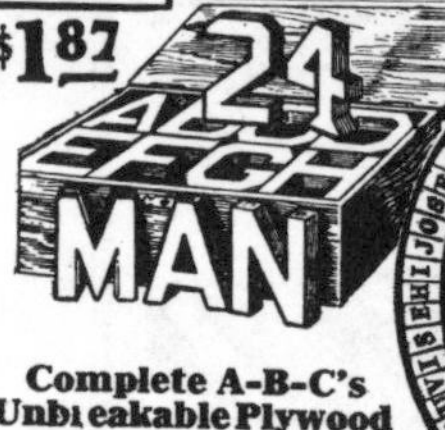


**Complete A-B-C's Unbreakable Plywood**

Set of A-B-C's and numerals 1 to 9 made of 5-ply pure white wood. So strong a man may stand on the letter L upside down without breaking it. Height of letters 3¾ inches. In hinged wood box 12½ by 8¼ by 3½ in. We Pay Postage.
48 E 547..............**$1.87**

**Same set as above, without numerals.**
48 E 545—In cardboard box. We Pay Postage..........**$1.00**

**Twenty-Six Three-Ply Letters**
Unbreakable. Size 2¾ by 2¼ in. Cardboard box. We Pay Postage.
48 E 546..........**50¢**

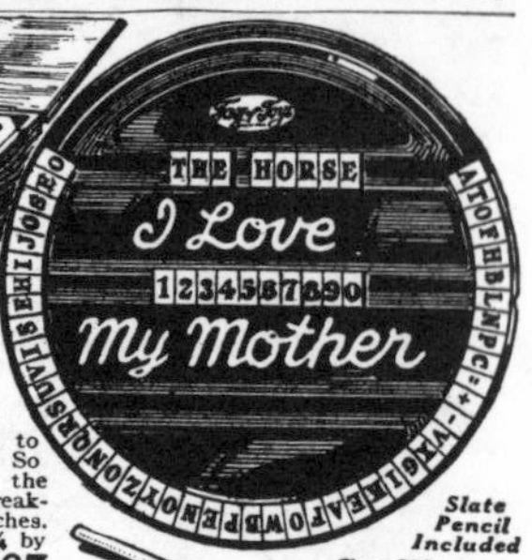


*Slate Pencil Included*

**Spelling Slate**

Three grooves. 48 numerals and letters. Both sides slate surfaced.
48 E 571—Diameter 9¾ in. We Pay Postage..........**42¢**
48 E 570—Diameter 13 inches. 65 letters and numerals. We Pay Postage..........**83¢**

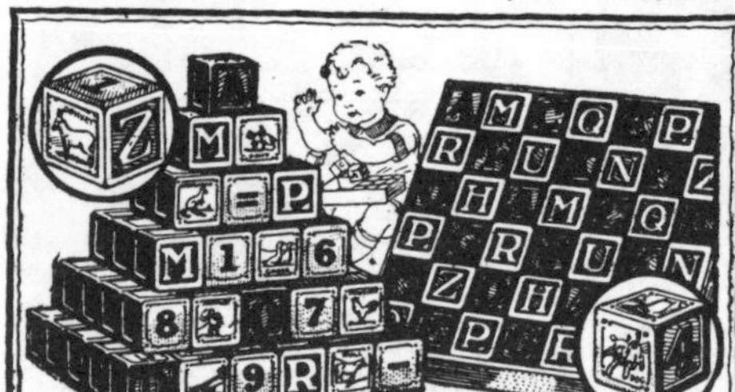

**29¢ 24 Blocks**

**Ward's Is Exclusive Mail Order Distributor of Round Cornered Rainbow Blocks**

Red and blue enameled A-B-C embossed letters on the colorful RAINBOW BACKGROUND are sure to please baby! The blocks have safe, rounded corners with alphabet letters on two sides and numbers and colored pictures of animals on the other sides. They are splendid for building houses. Only clear grain wood used. Packed in colored boxes with gay pictured labels. Two sizes offered below.

**1¾-Inch Round Corner Blocks**

42 Blocks **95¢** 48 E 540—We Pay Postage.
36 Blocks **82¢** 48 E 541—We Pay Postage.

**$1\frac{5}{16}$-Inch Round Corner Blocks**

**72 Blocks** $1\frac{5}{16}$ inches. Packed two layers deep. We Pay Postage. 48 E 539...**79¢**

**42 Blocks** 42 round cornered $1\frac{5}{16}$-inch A-B-C blocks. We Pay Postage. 48 E 542...**49¢**

**24 Blocks** 24 round cornered $1\frac{5}{16}$-inch A-B-C blocks. We Pay Postage. 48 E 543...**29¢**

**Perfected Modeling Clay**

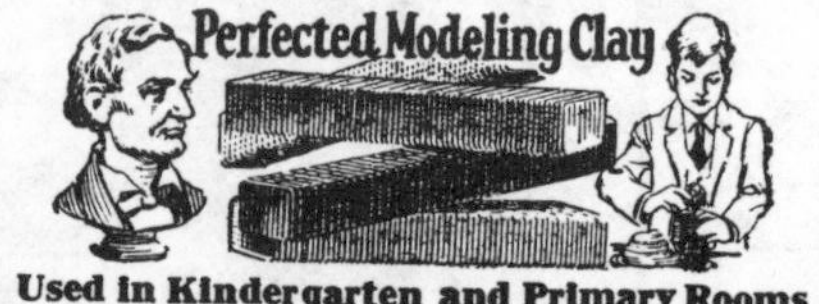

**Used in Kindergarten and Primary Rooms**

For school or home modeling. Teach little hands to work. Co-ordinates mind, hand and eye. Something of interest for idle hours indoors. Perfected clay in one-quarter pound tissue wrapped bars, each a different color. Will not harden when exposed to air. Quality seldom offered for less than 50¢ per pound. We Pay Postage.
48 E 560—One-pound assortment (four bars)..........**39¢**
48 E 524—Three pounds (all gray)..........**88¢**

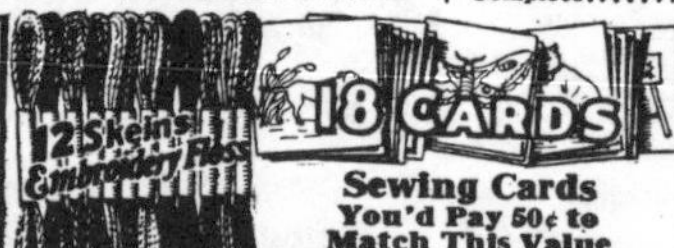


**Sewing Cards You'd Pay 50¢ to Match This Value**

Eighteen sewing cards, nine of them colored. Each 5½ inches square. Printed designs to outline with colored thread; 12 skeins of colorful floss. Needle and thimble. Splendid value! We Pay Postage.
48 E 558—Complete..........**33¢**

**Rubber Stamp Outfits for Schoolwork**

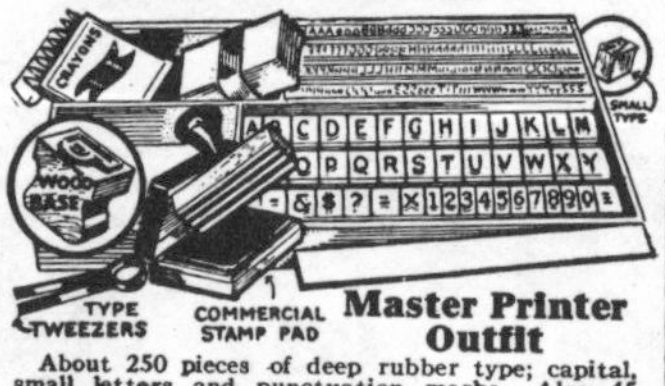


**Master Printer Outfit**

About 250 pieces of deep rubber type; capital, small letters and punctuation marks. Also 45 letters for sign printing mounted on wood blocks. Type holder tweezers. Stamp pad, crayons and blank cards. Used in many schools. We Pay Postage.
48 E 582—Complete outfit..........**95¢**

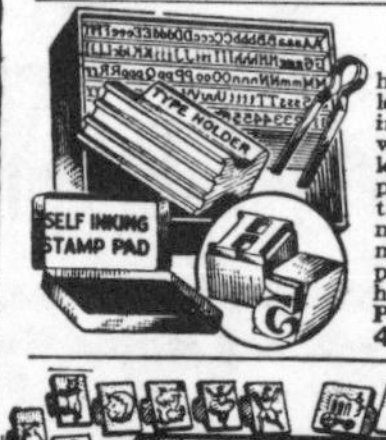


**Rubber Type Set**

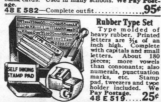

Type molded of heavy rubber. Printed letters are $\frac{3}{16}$ of an inch high. Complete with capitals and small letters. About 180 pieces; more vowels than consonants; also numerals, punctuation marks, etc. Stamp pad, tweezers and type holder included. We Pay Postage.
48 E 519.....**25¢**

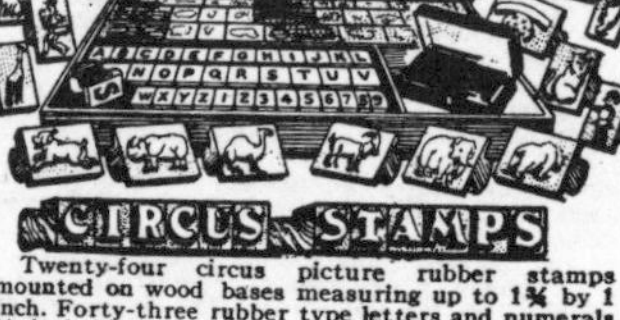


Twenty-four circus picture rubber stamps mounted on wood bases measuring up to 1⅜ by 1 inch. Forty-three rubber type letters and numerals ½ inch high. Inked stamp pad; ruler. We Pay Postage.
48 E 584—Complete set..........**83¢**

## Fine Quality School Paints

**Our Paints are finest ground true colors, easily soluble in water. Suitable for water color sketching, hence they more than fill requirements of the schools. Tested by actual artistic water color work!**

**Artists' Water Colors**

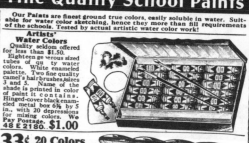

Quality seldom offered for less than $1.50. Eighteen generous sized tubes of quality water colors. White enameled palette. Two fine quality camel's hair brushes, sizes 3 and 5. Name of the shade is printed in color of paint it contains. Hinged-cover black enameled metal box 6⅞ by 5 in., with 20 depressions for mixing colors. We Pay Postage.
48 E 2180..**$1.00**

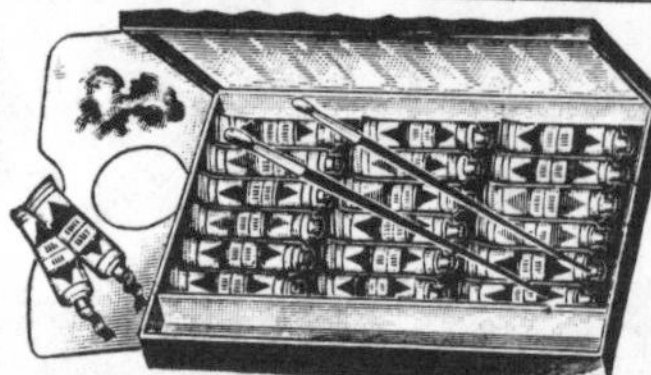

**33¢ 20 Colors**
**2 Fine Brushes**

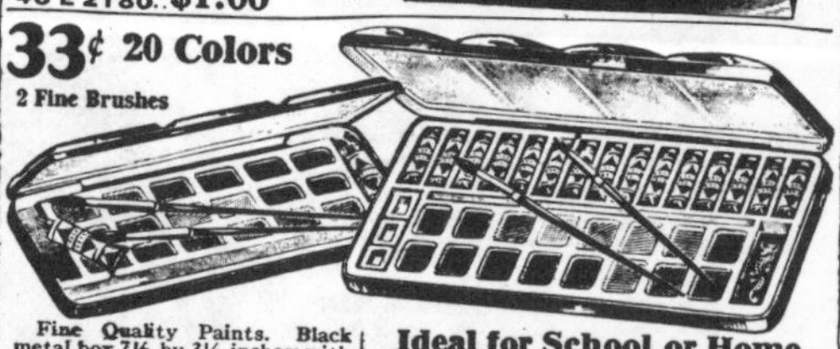

Fine Quality Paints. Black metal box 7½ by 3¼ inches; with three mixing pans. 18 cakes; 2 tubes of semi-moist colors; 2 brushes. We Pay Postage.
48 E 2184—Per set....**33¢**

**Ideal for School or Home**

Black metal box 9½ by 5 inches. Has 17 cakes of paint, 15 tubes of water colors, 2 camel's hair brushes. Seven mixing compartments. We Pay Postage.
48 E 2190—Complete..........**95¢**

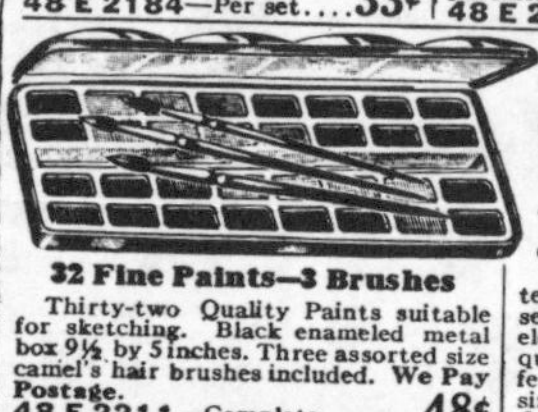

**32 Fine Paints—3 Brushes**

Thirty-two Quality Paints suitable for sketching. Black enameled metal box 9½ by 5 inches. Three assorted size camel's hair brushes included. We Pay Postage.
48 E 2211—Complete.......**48¢**

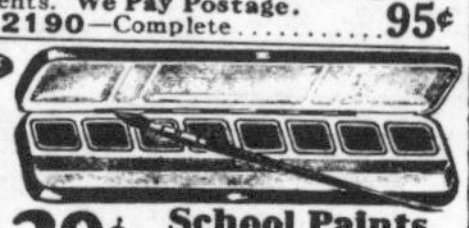

**39¢ School Paints New Low Price**

Handy—useful in school. Guaranteed Quality Paints. Eight pure, semi-moist primary colors, in enameled metal box 8 by 2 inches. Good quality camel's hair brush, metal ferrule, black wood handle, medium size. We Pay Postage.
48 E 2210—Complete.....**39¢**

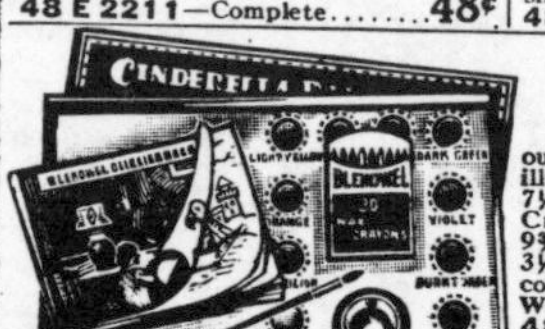


**Child's Coloring Set**
**Paints, Crayons and Pictures to Color**

Youngsters will love to paint the outlined figures in the attractively illustrated 32-page book. Page size 7¼ by 5⅝ inches. Practical Paint and Crayon Set in handsome box 14¾ by 9¾ inches. Eight non-melting crayons 3½ inches long. Ten cakes of water color paints. Camel's hair brush. We Pay Postage.
48 E 532—Complete.......**33¢**



*Montgomery Ward & Co.*

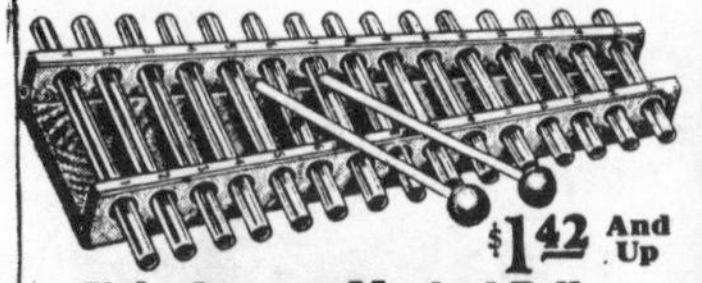

$1.42 And Up

## Xylophone or Musical Bells

Mellow toned seamless brass tubing carefully sized for faultless pitch. Even the smallest size tube on this instrument gives a clear silvery note—much superior to the cheap wood xylophone. Three sizes, each with 15 keys—almost two complete octaves. Play real melodies with the two wood hammers included. The bells or tubes are swung from wood frames with wool or cotton cords which have no effect on the vibrations of the metal. Larger tubes give fuller tone.

| 48 E 3655— | 48 E 3656— | 48 E 3657— |
|---|---|---|
| ⅝-inch tubing. Length 23½ in. Extreme width 6½ in. We Pay Postage. | ½-inch tubing. Length 21 in. Extreme width 5¾ in. We Pay Postage. | ⅜-inch tubing. Length 19 in. Extreme width 4¼ in. We Pay Postage. |
| $1.98 | $1.69 | $1.42 |

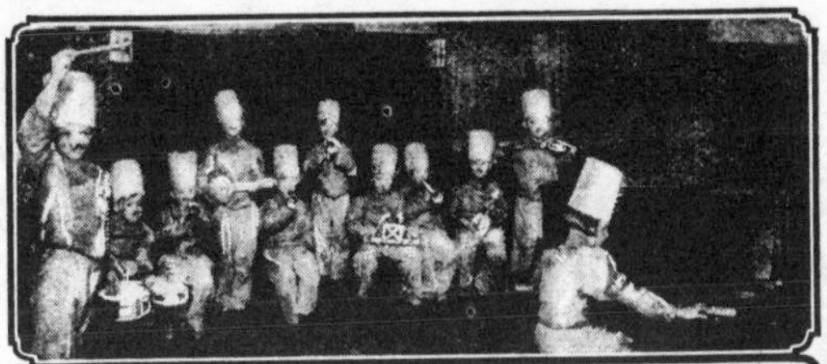

**Primary Rhythm Band Scores Hit With Ward's Toy Instruments**

*"I was more than pleased with the MUSICAL TOY INSTRUMENTS from WARD'S," writes Miss Rose Bolton, who trained this band of little second graders from the Irving School, Maywood, Illinois. "These musical toys were far superior in quality to any I have seen for the same prices."*

## Jazz King Clarinet and Saxophone . . .

$4.98 For Combination

***Only Toy Saxophone Made With Half Notes***

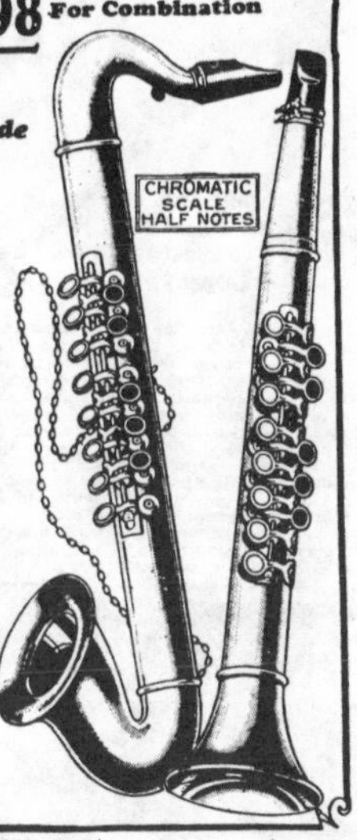


Want to join your school Jazz Orchestra? Here's just the outfit for a beginner! Simplified—easy to learn—and you can play many popular melodies. Imported from manufacturers of real band instruments. Made in Paris, France.

With this outfit you have, at will, a chromatic Saxophone or a chromatic Clarinet. **Mid-section with the 13 notes (8 full notes, 5 half notes) is interchangeable.** A clarinet mouthpiece and bell and a saxophone mouthpiece and bell are included. Parts all fitted with friction joints, easily changed. Clarinet measures 22 inches in length, almost full size; hard clarinet type ebonized composition mouthpiece. Diameter of bell 3⅜ in. Saxophone 18 inches in length, exclusive of bell and mouthpiece. Bell is 3¼ inches in diameter; goose neck with saxophone type mouthpiece of ebonized composition. Padded airtight keys. Fine quality brass reeds. All metal parts are highly polished brass. We Pay Postage.

**48 E 3693—Saxophone and clarinet with interchangeable parts.** ...... $4.98

**48 E 3689—Saxophone only.** We Pay Postage...... $3.98

**48 E 3694—Clarinet only.** We Pay Postage...... $3.59

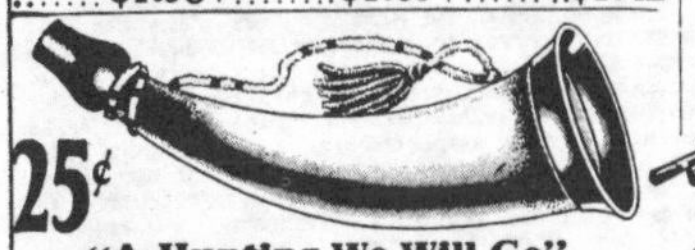

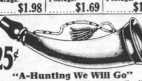

25¢

## "A-Hunting We Will Go"

Shaped exactly like the old time, resounding Hunting Horn which was made of a cow's horn. Strong metal, colored ivory white with dark splotches; practically unbreakable. Clear brass reed tone. Length 10½ in. Colored hanging cord. 25¢

**48 E 3663**—We Pay Postage............

*Kiln-Dried Wood*

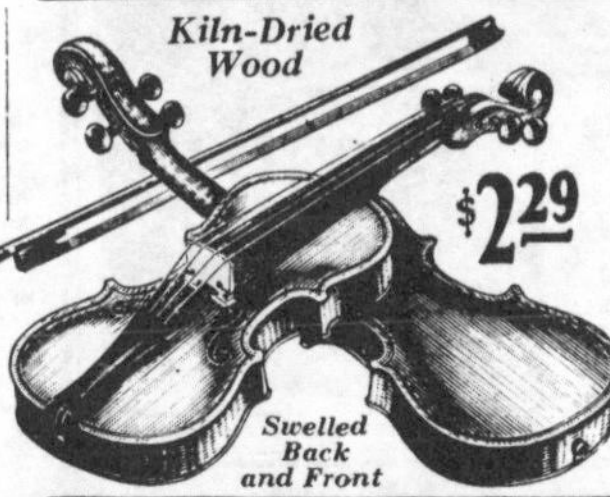

$2.29

*Swelled Back and Front*

## Imported Toy Violins

Exact in color and general detail and only slightly smaller than a full size Violin. Of kiln-dried wood with swelled front and back; curved neckpiece. Ebonized wood fingerboard, keys and tailpiece; 3 catgut and 1 metal G string. Horsehair bow with tension screw; rosin. Choice of two sizes and qualities.

**20-Inch Violin**

Our better quality; hand rubbed, varnished finish. 17½-in. bow. **We Pay Postage.**

**48 E 3675**........ $2.29

**19-Inch Violin**

High gloss varnished finish—not hand rubbed. 16-in. bow. **We Pay Postage.**

**48 E 3676**........ $1.63

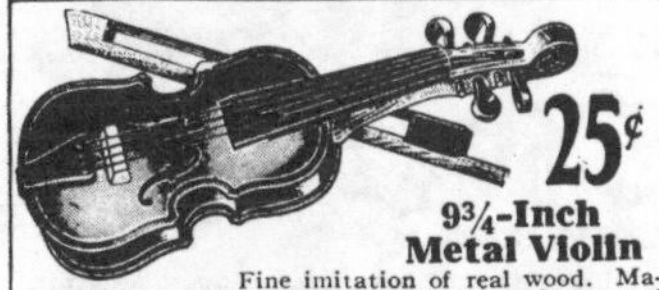

25¢

## 9¾-Inch Metal Violin

Fine imitation of real wood. Mahogany finish. Swelled front and back. Wood neck; ebonized keys; four catgut strings; horsehair bow. Rosin included. Metal bridge. 25¢

**48 E 3672**—We Pay Postage..............

*Calfskin Heads*

*Wood Shell*

$2.19

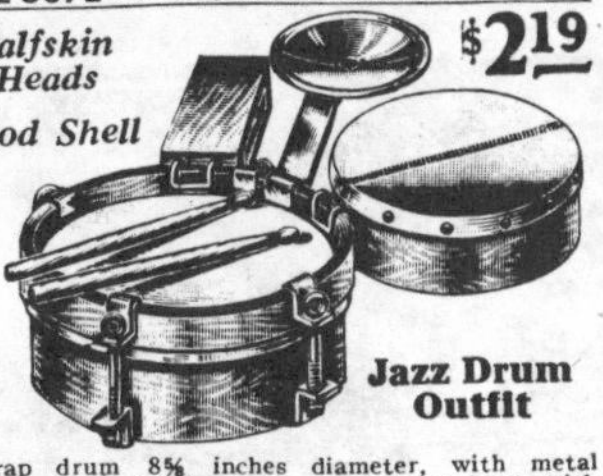

## Jazz Drum Outfit

Trap drum 8⅝ inches diameter, with metal tension keys; 6-inch treble tambourine-drum with wood shell and spring snare. Both have good quality **calfskin heads.** Deep resonant tone—not a noise. 4½-inch metal cymbal and hollowed wood horse trotter. Lacquered Chinese red. Two hardwood drumsticks. **Used in Primary Band above.** We Pay Postage.

**48 E 3684**—Outfit.............. $2.19

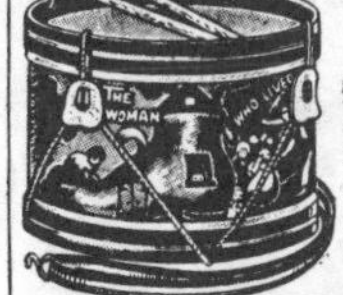

## Leather Head Drum

Ten-inch Drum with genuine sheepskin head and tough fiber bottom. Two snares and khaki webbing shoulder tape; leather ears. Two hardwood drumsticks. Metal side, colorfully lithographed with fairy tale design. Height 7⅛ in. We Pay Postage.

**48 E 3679**.... $1.29

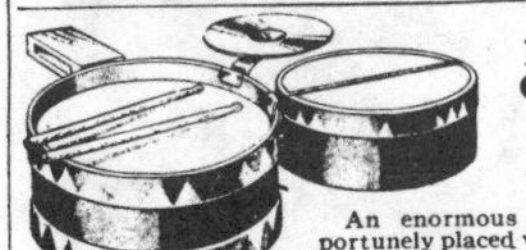

## Jazz Drum Outfit

59¢

An enormous order, opportunely placed with a European manufacturer, cuts the price on this Jazz Drum Outfit and brings you a notable saving! Large drum, 7⅛ inches in diameter has heavy parchment head; attached to edge is smaller 5½-inch drum. Has one wire snare. 4¾-inch cymbal fastens on other side of large drum. Hollow wood horse trotter. Two shaped drumsticks 6⅜ inches long. **We Pay Postage.**

**48 E 3685**—Outfit........................ 59¢

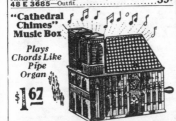

## "Cathedral Chimes" Music Box

*Plays Chords Like Pipe Organ*

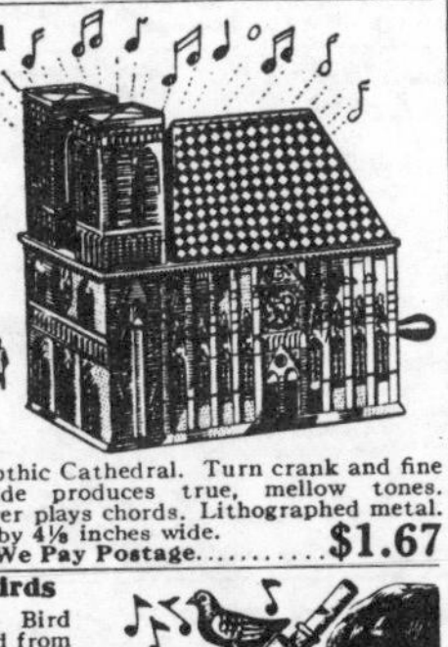

$1.67

Like an old Gothic Cathedral. Turn crank and fine mechanism inside produces true, mellow tones. Geared fan blower plays chords. Lithographed metal. Size 6⅝ by 6⅝ by 4⅛ inches wide. $1.67

**48 E 3609**—We Pay Postage.

## 3 Musical Birds

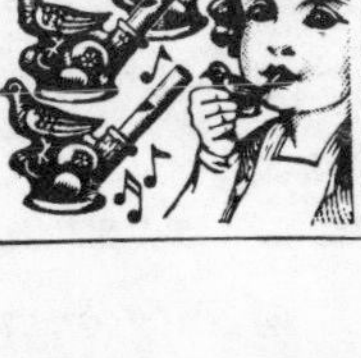

Set of three Bird Whistles, molded from metal. Partly fill them with water, then by blowing you can imitate the trilling song of a canary. A durable, inexpensive toy that affords hours of amusement. Length each, 3 in. Exceptional value! **We Pay Postage.**

**48 E 3664**—Set of 3...... 25¢

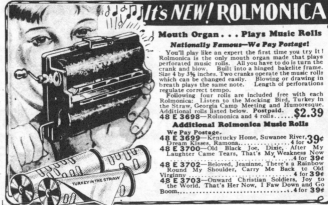

## It's NEW! ROLMONICA

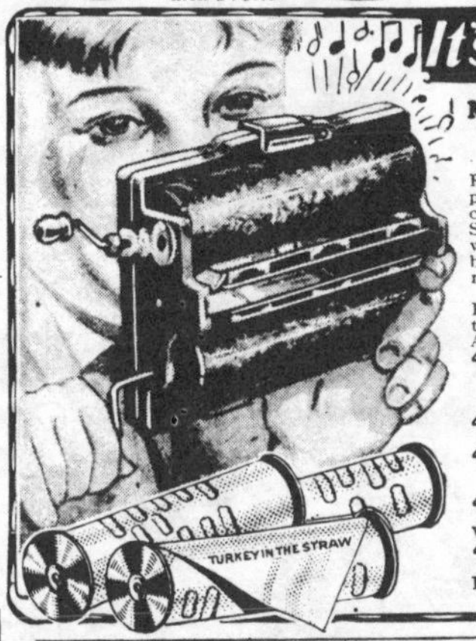


**Mouth Organ . . . Plays Music Rolls**

***Nationally Famous—We Pay Postage!***

You'll play like an expert the first time you try it! Rolmonica is the only mouth organ made that plays perforated music rolls. All you have to do is turn the crank and blow. Built into a hinged bakelite frame. Size 4 by 3⅝ inches. Two cranks operate the music rolls which can be changed easily. Blowing or drawing in breath plays the same note. Length of perforations regulate correct tempo.

Following four rolls are included free with each Rolmonica: Listen to the Mocking Bird, Turkey in the Straw, Georgia Camp Meeting and Humoresque. Additional rolls listed below. **Postpaid.**

**48 E 3698**—Rolmonica and 4 rolls...... $2.39

**Additional Rolmonica Music Rolls**

**We Pay Postage.**

**48 E 3699**—Kentucky Home, Suwanee River, Dream Kisses, Ramona.................4 for 39¢

**48 E 3700**—Old Black Joe, Dixie, After My Laughter Came Tears, That's My Weakness Now ......4 for 39¢

**48 E 3702**—Beloved, Jeannine, There's a Rainbow Round My Shoulder, Carry Me Back to Old Virginny.......4 for 39¢

**48 E 3703**—Onward Christian Soldiers, Joy to the World, That's Her Now, I Faw Down and Go Boom...............4 for 39¢

## Schoenhut's Fine Toy Pianos

**WE PAY POSTAGE**

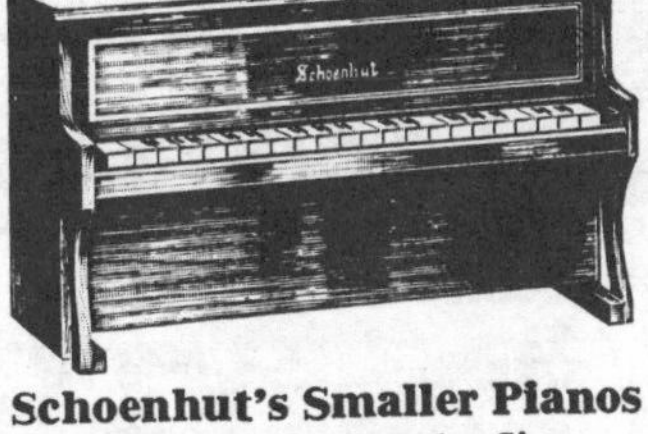


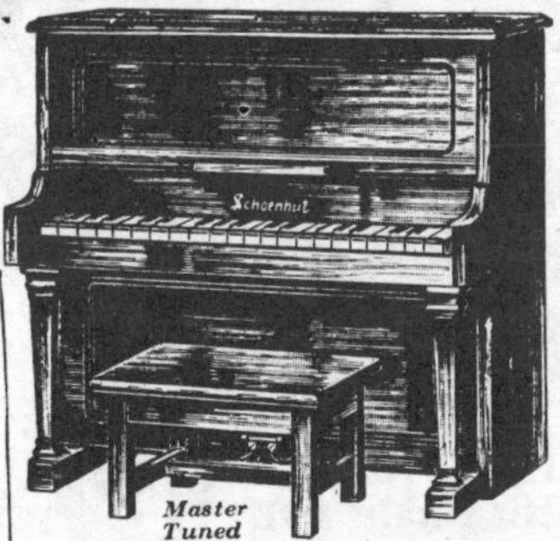


*Master Tuned*

### Schoenhut's Smaller Pianos

*Choice of Five Popular Sizes*

Splendid, low priced Pianos—the dependable Schoenhut quality. A delightful toy and a useful one, for the steel notes are **master tuned.** Varnished in beautiful mahogany finish with gold line stripe trimming. White keys correctly spaced as on large pianos. Excellent for finger exercises and actual preparation for real playing. Book of easy music and instructions included. We lower the price on every size of these nationally advertised toy pianos. **We Pay Postage.**

| Article Number | No. of Keys | Width In. | Height In. | Depth In. | | Each |
|---|---|---|---|---|---|---|
| 448 E 3631 | 22 | 22⅞ | 13½ | 9½ | We Pay Postage | $5.25 |
| 448 E 3634 | 18 | 19⅜ | 12½ | 8⅜ | | 4.25 |
| 448 E 3630 | 16 | 16¾ | 11 | 8 | | 3.25 |
| 48 E 3629 | 11 | 12 | 8¼ | 6½ | | 1.69 |
| 48 E 3628 | 7 | 8½ | 6½ | 5 | | .85 |

Mother will like these beautiful master tuned pianos. Mahogany finish; highly polished. White keys are same size and spaced same as on large piano, therefore useful for real finger exercises. The lid lifts, and the front can be taken out to see the mechanism. The wooden hammers strike upwards on the music steel keys and fall back on felt pads. Imitation pedals. Music rack. Book of simple musical selections with each piano. **Only small size is mailable.** Weight 25 pounds.

| Article No. | Keys | Width | Height | Depth | Each |
|---|---|---|---|---|---|
| 148 E 3707 | 22 | 23⅜ in. | 21⅛ in. | 11⅛ in. | $10.98 |
| 448 E 3708 | 18 | 19⅜ in. | 16⅜ in. | 8¾ in. | 5.48 |

**48 E 3721**—PIANO BENCH. Same finish as pianos. Size 12¼ by 7 by 7½ in. high. **We Pay Postage**.................. $1.53

## "Tiny Tot" Phonograph

*For Little Folks*

$1.00

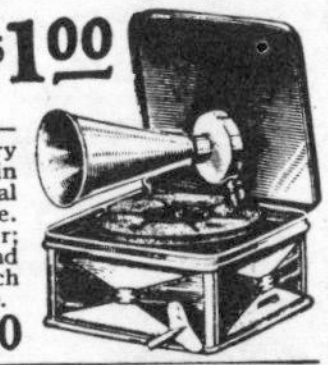

A most remarkable value and just the thing for smaller children. Light convenient weight—easily handled by the very youngest. All is contained in the grained wood effect metal case only 5¾ inches square. Substantial reproducer; splendid motor. Stop and start device. Plays 6-inch records. **We Pay Postage.**

**48 E 3638**..... $1.00

## Phonograph Records

Double-faced 10 or 6-inch records—two selections each. Records in each set are different. **We Pay Postage.**

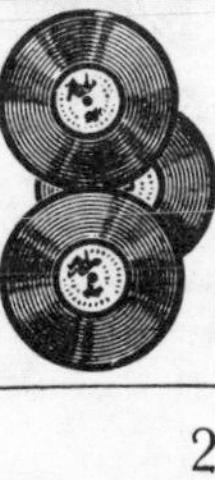

**10-Inch Double Faced — Set of 3**

**48 E 3718**—6 selections... 93¢

**48 E 3719**—6 selections... 93¢

**48 E 3720**—6 selections... 93¢

**6-Inch Double Faced — Set of 3**

**48 E 3715**—6 selections... 49¢

**48 E 3716**—6 selections... 49¢

**48 E 3717**—6 selections... 49¢

## The "Valora"

*Child's Enclosed Horn Phonograph*

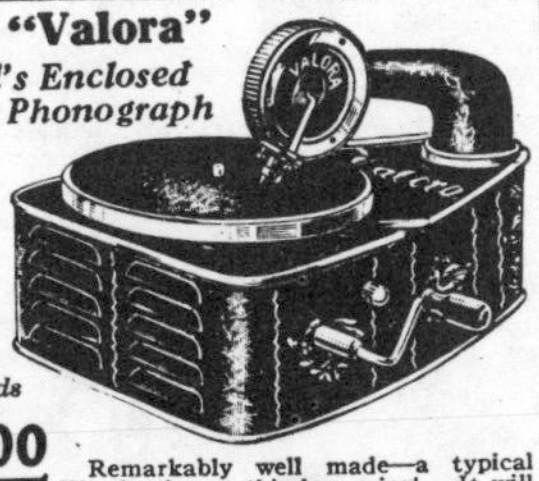


*Plays 10-Inch Records*

$5.00

Remarkably well made—a typical Ward value at this low price! It will delight older boys and girls who are long past the age for toys. Plays 10-inch records.

Full size reproducer; mica diaphragm. Concealed horn, steel cabinet. Brown crackle finish. Size 10½ by 6 inches; 6-inch velvet padded turntable. Speed control; stop and start lever; crank wind. Guaranteed motor. **We Pay Postage.**

**48 E 3640**........................ $5.00

Style as above. White enamel finish, with 5⅜-inch turntable. Size 9 by 6 by 5½ inches. Plays records up to 8 inches. Not as fine a reproducer, but a wonderful toy. **We Pay Postage.**

**48 E 3614**........................ $2.19

**We Pay Postage**

$1.37 Large Size

*Fine Toy Saxophone Values!*

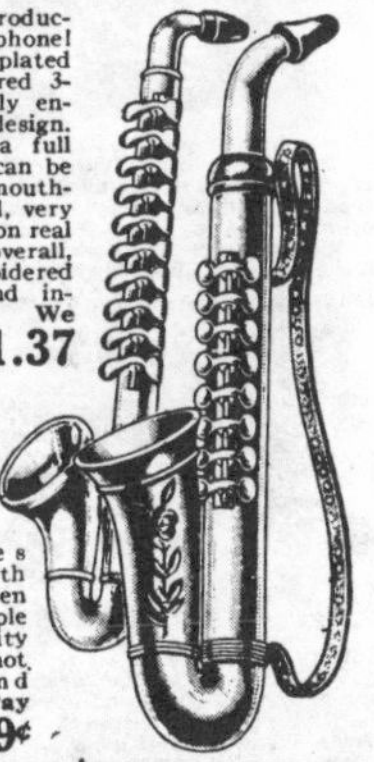

A fine miniature reproduction of a real saxophone! Highly polished, nickel-plated metal. Gracefully flared 3-inch bell is artistically engraved with floral design. Eight padded keys—a full octave; simple tunes can be played. Duck-bill type mouthpiece of ebonized wood, very similar to those found on real saxophones. Height overall, 17½ inches. Embroidered neckband. Music and instructions included. We Pay Postage.

**48 E 3687**..... $1.37

**Ten-Key Nickel-Plated Saxophone**

Not as good quality as the toy saxophone above. 15¼ inches long, all metal with nickel-plated finish. Ten keys; will play simple melodies. Good quality reed notes. Bell not engraved. Music and instructions. We Pay Postage.

**48 E 3686**..... 89¢

$1.98

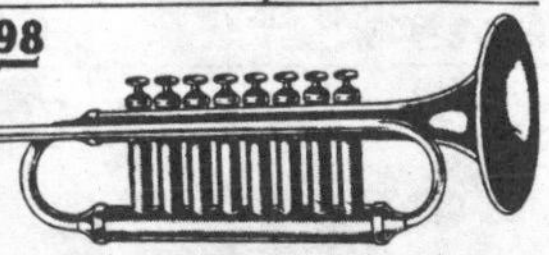

## Large French Tremolo Cornet

*Heavy Brass Seamless Tubing*

A larger, finer quality with a beautiful **tremolo** tone. Keys are set into the instrument just like a real band cornet. Can be removed for cleaning. Very fine workmanship. Made in France, of seamless solid brass tubing, highly polished; extra heavy throughout. Length 11½ inches. Bell 3 inches diameter. An unusual value at our price! **We Pay Postage.**

**48 E 3647**—With 8 keys............. $1.98

Same as above except not such heavy quality. Not tremolo. Removable keys for cleaning instrument. Flared bell 2½ inches diameter. Either will blow all bugle calls. **We Pay Postage.**

| 48 E 3648—Length 7⅝ inches. With 4 keys...... 67¢ | 48 E 3649—Length 10½ inches. With 8 keys...... $1.19 |
|---|---|

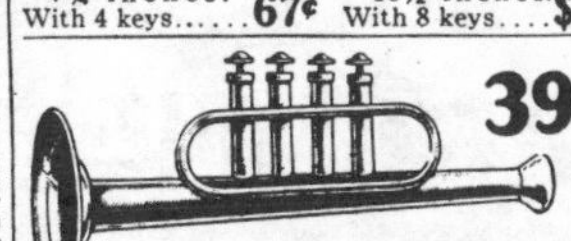

39¢

## Four-Key Cornet

Clear, sweet tones—fine for playing bugle calls. Well made of nickel-plated metal with high polish; four push-button keys; fine quality brass reed notes. Mouthpiece and 3-inch bell are extra strong metal that will not dent easily. Full 9 inches long. This is a wonderful value at our price! **We Pay Postage.**

**48 E 3646**............................. 39¢

*Real Skin Head*

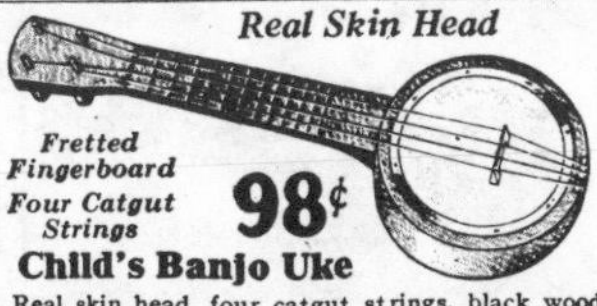

*Fretted Fingerboard*

*Four Catgut Strings*

98¢

## Child's Banjo Uke

Real skin head, four catgut strings, black wood keys. Wooden neck with carefully fretted fingerboard. Diameter of head 5½ inches. Length 16½ inches. Just the right size for children. Instructions for playing included. Easy to learn. **We Pay Postage.**

**48 E 3658**............................. 98¢

Same shape as above with thin wood head. Well made, complete in detail. Length 14¼ in. Diameter 5 inches. **We Pay Postage.**

**48 E 3653**............................. 49¢

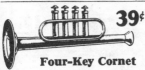

# NEWEST MECHANICAL MARVELS

**WE PAY POSTAGE**

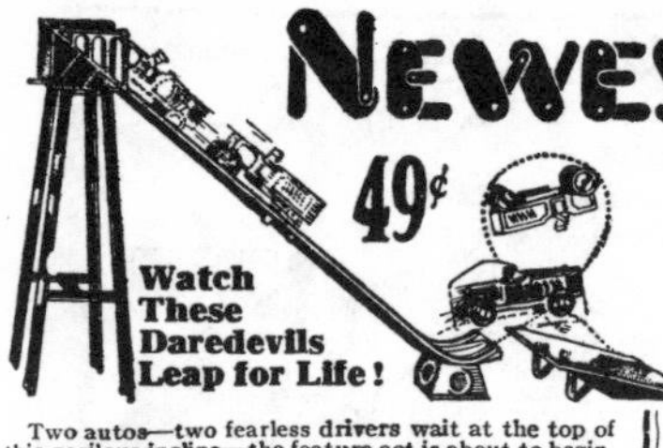

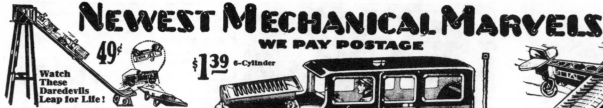

**49¢ Watch These Daredevils Leap for Life!**

Two autos—two fearless drivers wait at the top of this perilous incline—the feature act is about to begin. Pull the starting release and the first automobile rushes down at break-neck speed—reaches the gap and at that breath-taking, crucial moment leaps high into the air, turning a complete backward somersault landing on board on opposite side of gap. Second auto starts its thrilling descent upon the instant of the first car's takeoff—so skillfully timed that while the first auto is upside down in mid-air the second car takes the gap in one death-defying leap. Metal brightly lithographed. Height 16 in. Length 27 in. Platform 9¾ inches long. Two autos, each 3¼ in. long. We Pay Postage.
48 E 3969—Complete.......................49¢

**$1.39 6-Cylinder**

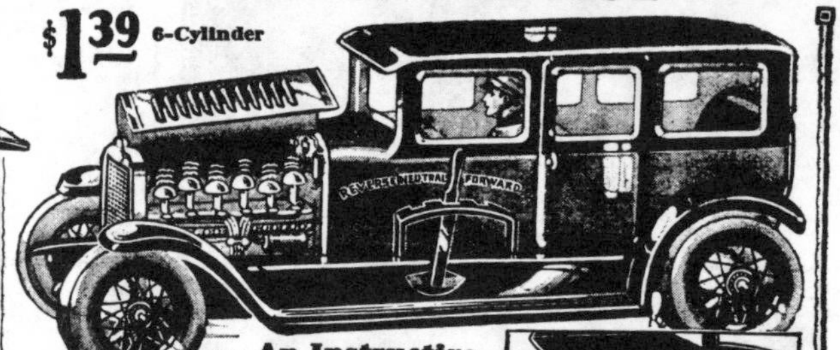

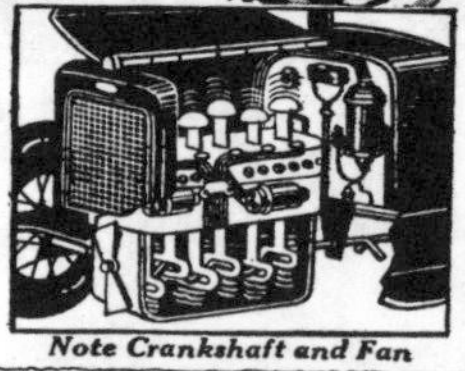

Note Crankshaft and Fan

## An Instructive Toy

*See the Engine in Motion*

Wind the strong spring, lift either side of hood and see this remarkable Engine in motion. Valves work automatically, fan revolves, crankshaft spins. Real gearshift.

**6-Cylinder Size**, 9⅜ by 4 inches. Chauffeur. Doors open. Three speeds. We Pay Postage. 48 E 4016....$1.39

**4-Cylinder Size**, 8 by 3⁷⁄₁₆ inches. Chauffeur. Doors do not open. Two speeds. Postpaid. 48 E 4015.......95¢

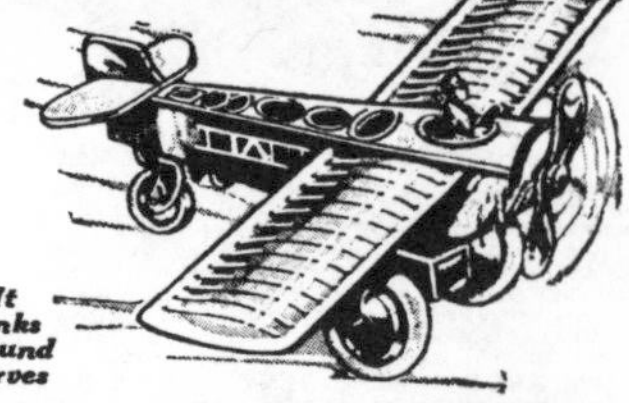

*It Banks Around Curves*

## 79¢ Imported Airplane

*Safe, Quick Delivery*

See how this metal Airplane rolls along the floor in graceful curves to right and left. Its body and wings slant from side to side like a great airplane banks in making curves in the clouds. The propeller revolves as it rolls. Strong spring motor. A $1 feature airplane imported and sold exclusively by us this year at almost half price. Wing spread 9½ inches. Length 7¼ inches. Sturdily constructed, all metal—built to stand a lot of abuse. Finished in attractive light tan. Blue trim. Imitation cabin windows. We Pay Postage.
48 E 3940.......................79¢

**We Pay Postage!**

## "Sandy Andy" A Willing Worker 67¢

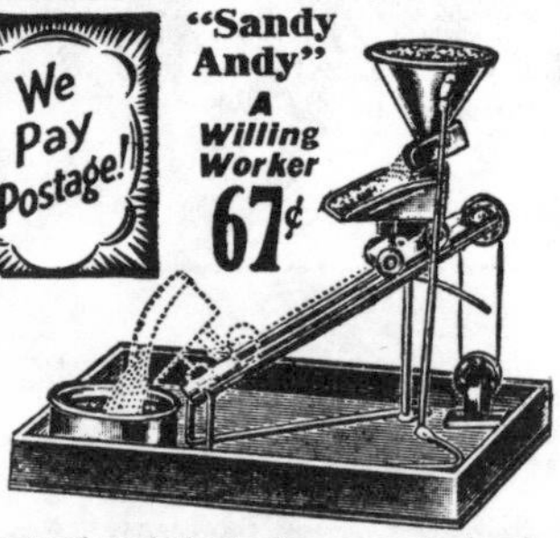

Car travels up inclined railway, opens the trap in sand hopper. When car is filled with sand, hopper closes, car descends and dumps sand in can at bottom of track. Repeats operation as long as there is sand in hopper. Size set up, 10¾ by 9¼ inches. Sand included. Use box as tray.
48 E 3974—We Pay Postage.........67¢

## FELIX...The Movie Cat

*See How He Gets Away*

Designed by Pat Sullivan—originator of famous Felix of the movies. Similar high quality seldom found at our low price. Wind scooter and see impudent Felix whisk away, waving his tail behind him. Never in a cartoon did he seem more anxious to get somewhere else mighty quick. Felix is made entirely of metal lithographed in real colors. An exact reproduction of the trouble-making cartoon cat. Size 6¾ inches long by 6½ inches tall. We Pay Postage.
48 E 3961.......................63¢

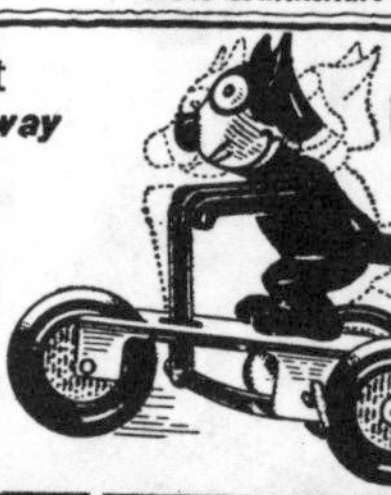


**63¢**

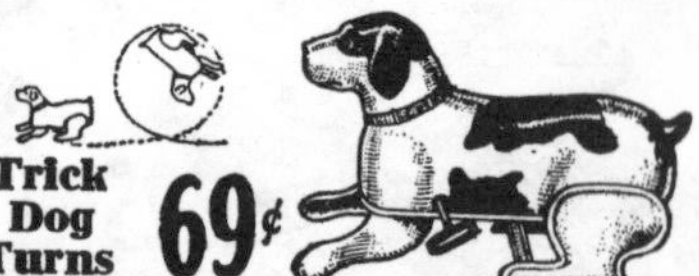

## Trick Dog Turns Back Somersaults 69¢

Like a trick circus dog. Lithographed metal—realistic shape and coloring. Fitted with strong spring motor. When wound up, Doggie will turn backward somersaults one after another. Size 4¾ inches by 4 inches high. We Pay Postage.
48 E 3976.......................69¢

**$1.00 A Toy to Pull**

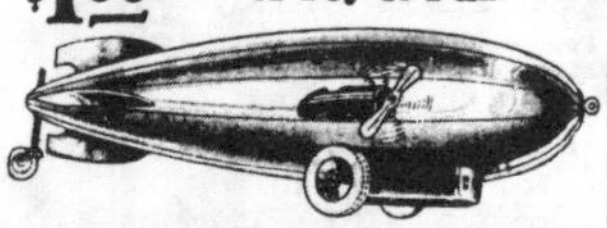

## 28½-Inch Giant Zeppelin

A fine miniature reproduction—measures 28 in. long, 13 in. wide. All metal, lithographed silver and bright red. Two gondolas on sides and propeller that is operated through connection with the three 3½-inch steel wheels. Famous Marx construction. No spring motor but loop in front for attaching string and pulling.
48 E 4019—We Pay Postage..........$1.00

# MARX Guaranteed Toys

**WE PAY POSTAGE**

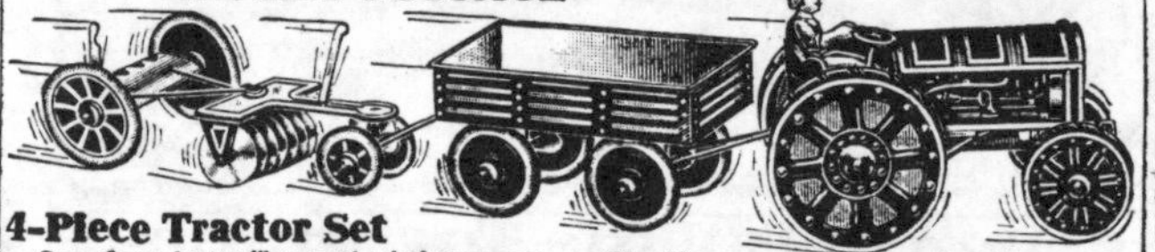

## 4-Piece Tractor Set

One of our best selling mechanical toys—certainly a splendid value at our low price! Equipped with guaranteed unbreakable Marx spring. See how carefully the driver guides the tractor, pulling the three pieces of machinery. Wagon is well made, with disc wheels. Is large enough to carry your small supply of grain ready to seed.

Disc Harrow and Rake have imitation levers. Length over all 25½ inches; height 6 inches; width 4 inches. All pieces beautifully lithographed in natural colors. All or only one of trailers can be used at a time. We Pay Postage.
48 E 3936—Complete..............$1.00

## Joy Riders Elope 49¢

**We Pay Postage**

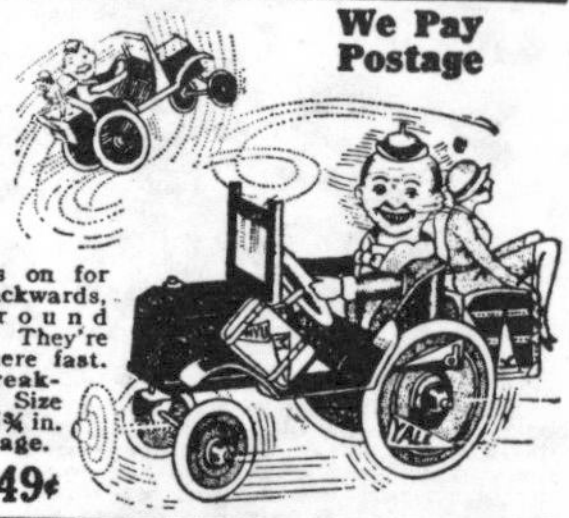

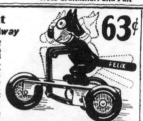

His head's in a whirl—and his "girl friend" holds on for dear life! Backwards, forwards, around and around. They're getting nowhere fast. Marx unbreakable spring. Size 7¾ by 2¾ by 5¾ in. We Pay Postage.
48 E 4006 49¢

**25½ Inches Wing Spread**

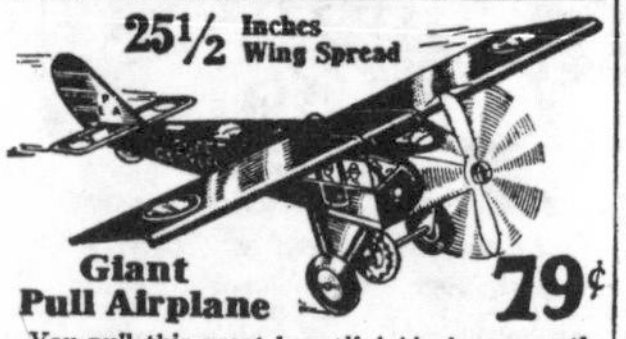

## Giant Pull Airplane 79¢

You pull this great beautiful Airplane over the floor. 25½ in. from tip to tip of wings, and is 24 in. long. Remember, we pay the postage anywhere in the United States. Beautifully finished in bright yellow and red. Cabin showing passengers at windows. Colored target on wings. Revolving propeller makes a motor-like noise.
48 E 4020—We Pay Postage.........79¢

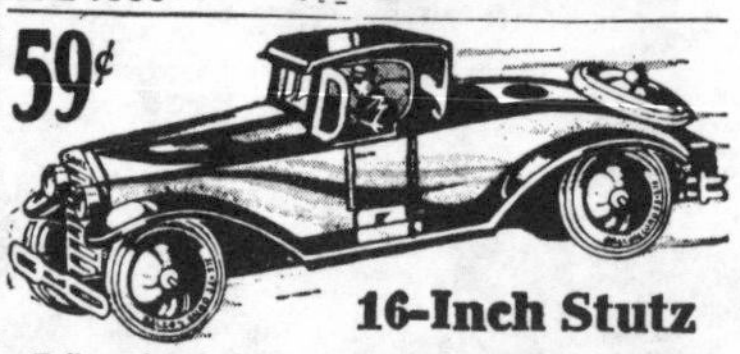

## 59¢ 16-Inch Stutz

Fully equipped with bumpers, play headlights, motometer, gas tank. Extra wheel in rear. Lithographed in brilliant colors. Marx unbreakable spring. Size 16 inches long. Big toy for the price. We Pay Postage.
48 E 4018.......................59¢

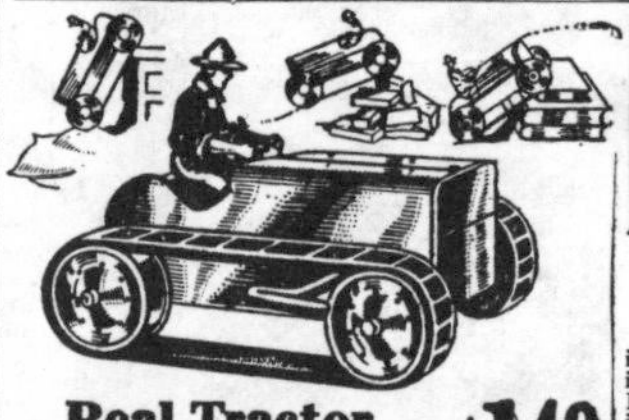

## Real Tractor With Chain Pull $1.49

Constructed on the same mechanical principle as the steel tanks used during the war. This Tractor will climb almost anything that is not at complete right angles with the floor. Make piles of books or dig holes in the sand and watch her go over the top!

### Sturdy Construction

Fitted with guaranteed Marx unbreakable spring. All metal parts are aluminum except driver at the wheel. Stop and start lever gives you opportunity of stopping tractor though spring is not completely unwound. About 7½ inches long, 3¾ inches wide and 6 inches high over driver's head. Chains that run over wheels are of heavy black rubber with suction cups that hold tractor to its course in steep ascents. Runs slowly with strong pulling power for quite a distance. We Pay Postage.
48 E 4021—Aluminum tractor...$1.49

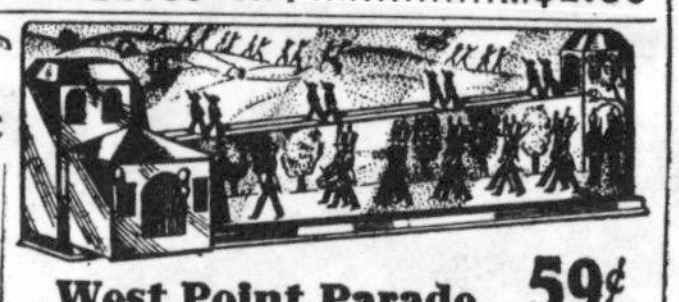

## West Point Parade 59¢

Thrillingly realistic! West Point cadets march in never ending parade. Up an incline they go marching two abreast. Wind the guaranteed unbreakable Marx spring in the guard house beneath to see them in action. At a distance it is quite impossible to tell what causes this perpetual procession. Made entirely of metal lithographed in realistic colors showing cadets, trees and shrubbery. Height over all 5¼ inches. Length 14½ inches.
48 E 4022—We Pay Postage...........59¢

## Miniature Regulation Army Truck 59¢

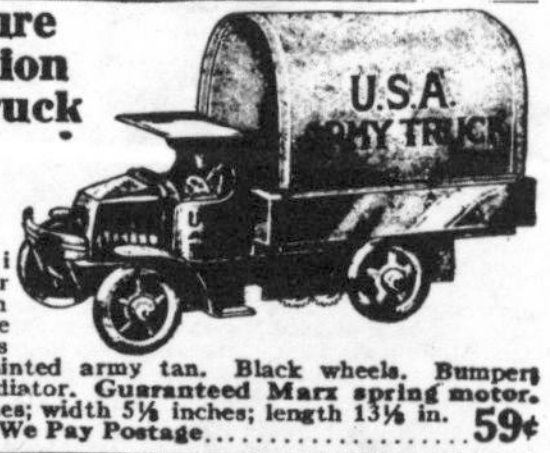


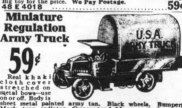

Real khaki cloth cover stretched on metal bows—use on or off. Body is sheet metal painted army tan. Black wheels. Bumpers. Mack type radiator. Guaranteed Marx spring motor. Height 7¼ inches; width 5¼ inches; length 13½ in.
48 E 3948—We Pay Postage.........59¢

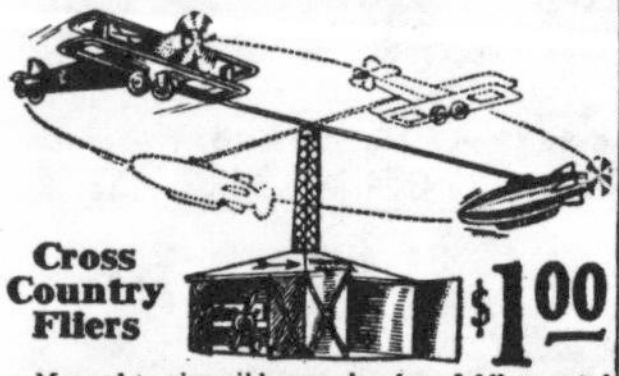

## Cross Country Fliers $1.00

Moored to airmail hangar is a long folding metal arm that balances weighted zeppelin and airplane. Equipped with Marx motor. When wound up it revolves propeller causing airplane to fly around, and carrying arm with zeppelin. Force of air thus created revolves zeppelin's propeller. Metal lithographed in colors. Over all measurement set up: 20 in. by 39 in. wide.
48 E 3944—We Pay Postage......$1.00

## Walking—Laughing

*Marx Spring*

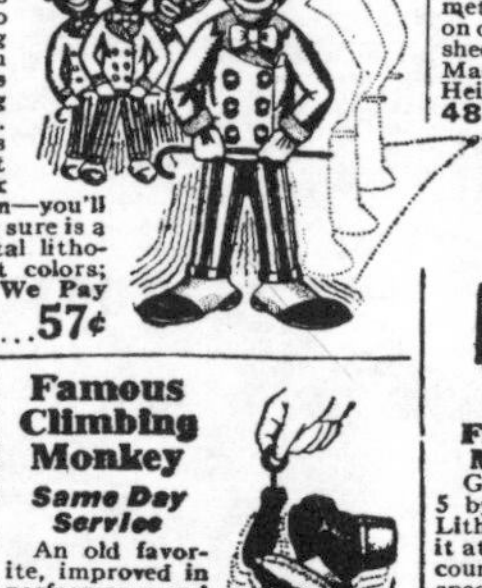

Mammy's black-faced boy is up to something! He laughs—he's gloomy only to burst out laughing again. See him wiggle his ears as he shuffles along from side to side. What tricks he's planning — what thoughts are back of his silly grin—you'll never know but he sure is a funny feller! Metal lithographed in bright colors; 11 inches tall. We Pay Postage.
48 E 3988.........57¢

## Gas Station 2 Autos

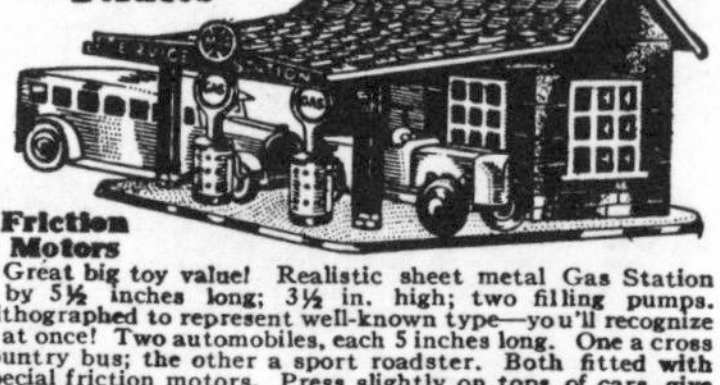

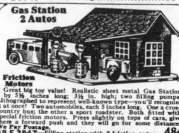

**Friction Motors**

Great big toy value! Realistic sheet metal Gas Station 5 by 5½ inches long; 3½ in. high; two filling pumps. Lithographed to represent well-known type—you'll recognize it at once! Two automobiles, each 5 inches long. One a cross country bus; the other a sport roadster. Both fitted with special friction motors. Press slightly on tops of cars, give them a forward push and they will go for some distance. We Pay Postage.
48 E 3947—Filling station with 2 friction autos...48¢

## Airplane With Parachute 98¢

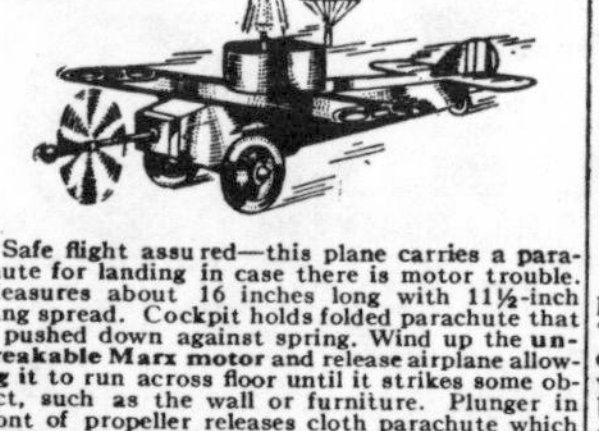

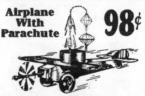

Safe flight assured—this plane carries a parachute for landing in case there is motor trouble. Measures about 16 inches long with 11½-inch wing spread. Cockpit holds folded parachute that is pushed down against spring. Wind up the unbreakable Marx motor and release airplane allowing it to run across floor until it strikes some object, such as the wall or furniture. Plunger in front of propeller releases cloth parachute which is shot up, almost to ceiling. It then opens and floats to floor. All metal plane lithographed in colors. We Pay Postage.
48 E 3945—Complete.......................98¢

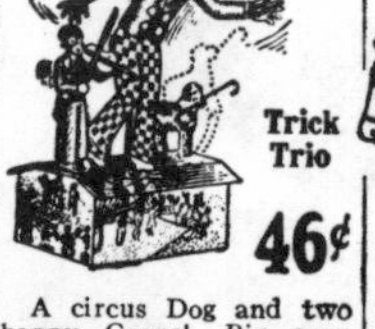

## Trick Trio 46¢

A circus Dog and two happy Coons! Big coon "Charlestons" as the little one fiddles, and dog acts with cane. Size 9 by 4¾ by 3½ inches. Lithographed in bright colors. Genuine Marx spring. We Pay Postage.
48 E 4008.......46¢

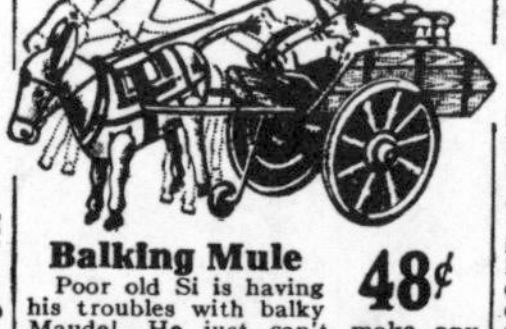

## Balking Mule 48¢

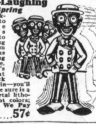

Poor old Si is having his troubles with balky Maude! He just can't make any headway with the stubborn critter. She goes backwards, rears up on her hind legs, sideways and stops and balks. Made of metal lithographed in bright colors that make a big appeal to little folks. Marx guaranteed unbreakable spring. Length over all 10½ inches. Height 5¼ inches. We Pay Postage.
48 E 3983.......................48¢

## Famous Climbing Monkey

*Same Day Service*

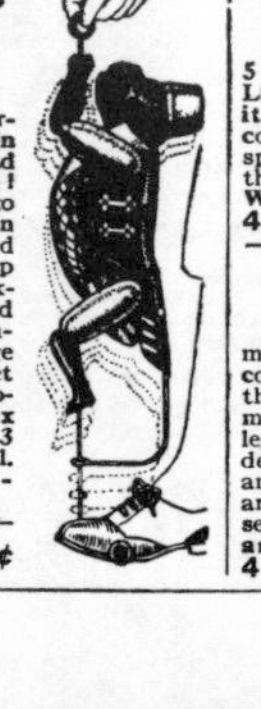

An old favorite, improved in performance and appearance! Watch Jocko climb. Step on the string—hold it taut and up he comes. Slacken your hold and down he scampers. Extra large size made of sheet metal lithographed in six bright colors; 3 in. by 10 in. tall. We Pay Postage.
48 E 3946—
Each.....21¢

## Limping Lizzie

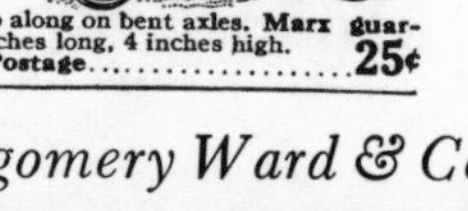

Battered old Lizzie has most certainly had a college education. All the "wise crack" sayings most popular with college and high school students are painted on her ancient sides. Looks and acts like a "flivver" sedan. Rear wheels bump along on bent axles. Marx guaranteed spring. Size 7 inches long, 4 inches high.
48 E 3966—We Pay Postage.................25¢

248 Montgomery Ward & Co.

# Keystone ··· Toys That Last— We Pay Postage

$5.69 Keystone's Best Many Ask $7.50

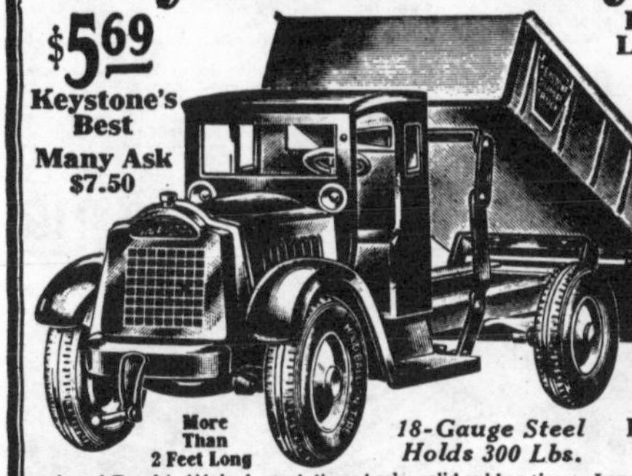

More Than 2 Feet Long

18-Gauge Steel Holds 300 Lbs.

Solid Rubber Tires

A real Truck! 4½-inch steel disc wheels; solid rubber tires. Length over all 26½ inches; height 10½ inches. Truck body is 15¼ by 8¼ inches. Dump lifts 6½ inches from chassis. Black enameled with red chassis and wheels. Turning crank in front lifts bed. We Pay Postage.
448 E 1212.................................................$5.69

Patent Locking Gate

$7.67

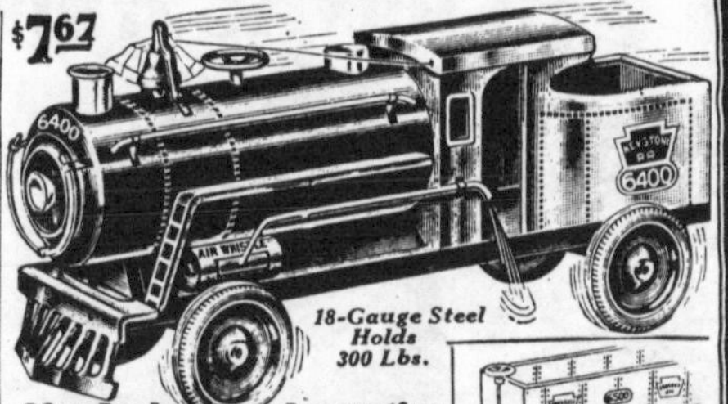


18-Gauge Steel Holds 300 Lbs.

**26½-Inch Locomotive**

Tested to carry 300 lbs. Is 28 inches long and 12 inches high; 4½-inch wheels, solid rubber tires. You can sit on cab and ride down hill. Hand wheel on top guides front wheels. Glossy black and red baked-on enamel finish. Polished brass bell and rails. Real whistle. Coupling pin connects with freight car 448 E 1211 at right. A very handsome toy. We Pay Postage.
448 E 1210..................$7.67

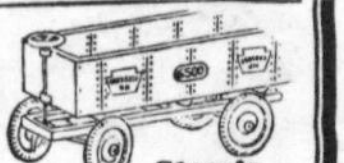

**Steer's Freight Car for Above**

Matches above engine; 18-gauge steel. 20¾ by 9¾ inches high. Rubber tires. We Pay Postage.
448 E 1211 $4.19

We Pay Postage

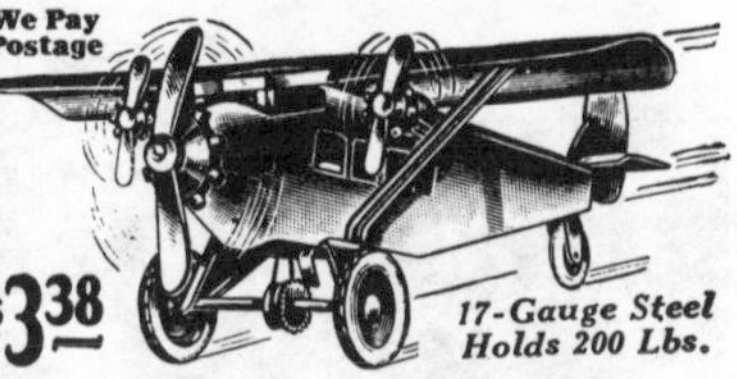

$3.38

17-Gauge Steel Holds 200 Lbs.

## Heavy Steel Airplane

**Proved Carrying Strength 200 Pounds**
**Lasting Enameled Finish**
**In Bright Beautiful Colors**

Extra heavy gauge auto body steel. A man can really **sit on it** and coast down hill. Passenger space has 4 windows on each side and pilot's cockpit above. Curved steel wings. Steel disc wheels with rubber tires. Size: 26½ in. long; 23¾ in. wing spread and 9 in. high. Front wheels 3¾ inch diam.; center propeller 8 in. long. Enamel baked on. Cream body, red wheels and wings and black whirlwind motors. Ratchet on front axle revolves propellers and makes noise like motor. Your choice of two types. As pictured with 3 propellers; or one only, in center.

448 E 1213—Triple motors. We Pay Postage..........$3.38 | 448 E 1217—Single motor. We Pay Postage..........$2.39

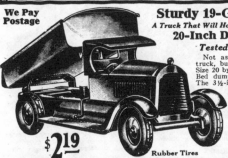

We Pay Postage

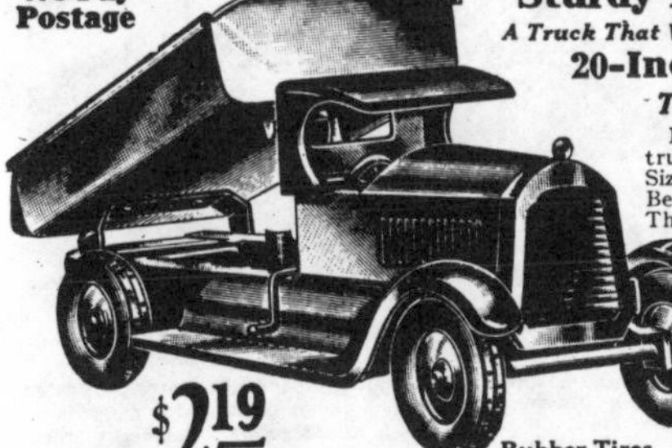

$2.19

Rubber Tires

## Sturdy 19-Gauge Steel

*A Truck That Will Hold a 200-Pound Man*

**20-Inch Dump Truck**

*Tested Quality!*

Not as fine as our Keystone truck, but a tremendous value! Size 20 by 7 inches by 8¼ high. Bed dumps with crank at side. The 3½-inch wheels have rubber tires molded on steel base. Blue enamel with red fenders, wheels and cab. Trimmed with stripings of gold. Made entirely of automobile steel. No sharp edges.

We Pay Postage.

448 E 1221..$2.19

Priced Low $1.39

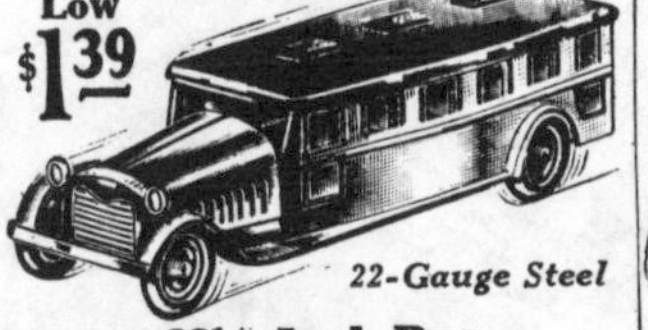

22-Gauge Steel

## 23½-Inch Bus

***Strongly Constructed***

Just like big busses you see along highways! Length 23½ inches; 6 inches high, 6¼ inches wide. Attractively finished in baked-on blue enamel with red stripes; 3⅛-inch disc wheels with steel tires. A small child can sit on it. We Pay Postage.
448 E 1216.................................$1.39

$1.10

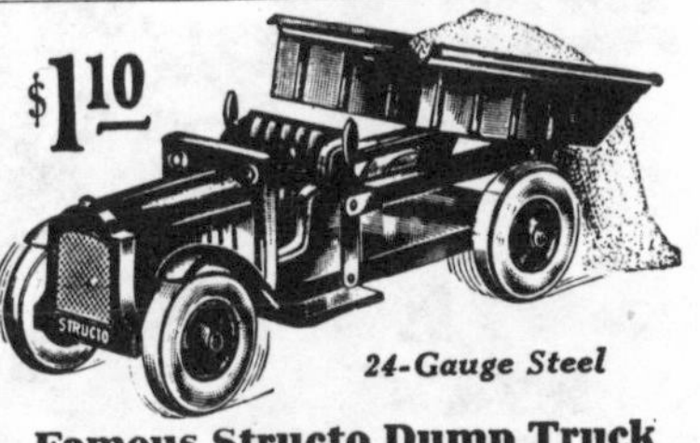


24-Gauge Steel

## Famous Structo Dump Truck

Splendidly constructed. Beautifully finished baked-on enamel, red with black dumping frame and seat. Pulling levers throw dump. Length 18 in.; width 5¾ in.; height 6 in. Bed is 6 by 9¼ in. Smooth, no rough edges. We Pay Postage.
48 E 1230..............................$1.10

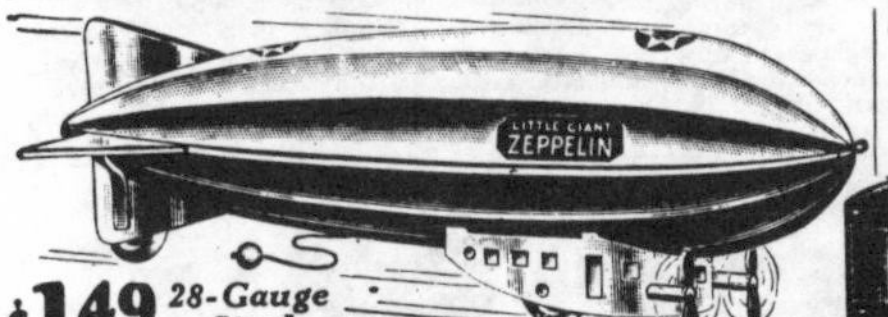


$1.49 28-Gauge Steel

*Supports 100 Lbs. Over 2 Feet Long*

## Heavy Steel Zeppelin

Plenty of thrill and satisfaction in owning this toy! It is so impressive it will appeal to any child. Shaped to correct proportions and made of heavy gauge steel. Strong enough for a small boy to ride, as it will support 100 pounds. Modeled after the Graf Zeppelin, with passenger gondola beneath. Supported on three wheels. Length 26 inches; width 5¾ inches; height 7 inches. Aluminum finish with red, white and blue trim. Two propellers on front of gondola revolve when Zeppelin is pulled along the floor, making a noise like a motor. We Pay Postage.
448 E 1224..........................$1.49

*24-Gauge Steel*

***Structo***

*Nationally Known*

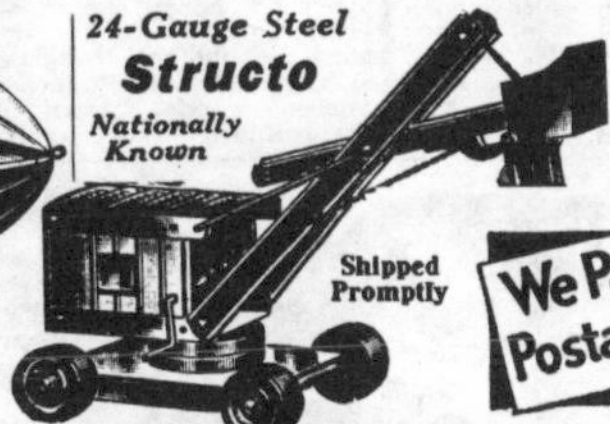

Shipped Promptly

We Pay Postage!

$1.00 **Steam Shovel**

*Digs Dirt Like a Real Steam Shovel*

Scoop bites in and picks up dirt. House on revolving drum carries it around and pulling trip drops it. Raise and lower bucket arm with chain on wood drum. Automatic lock on bottom of bucket. Riveted together. Size 16¼ by 5¾ by 13⅛ inches high. We Pay Postage.
48 E 1219..................$1.00

*26-Gauge Steel Body 24-Gauge Wing*

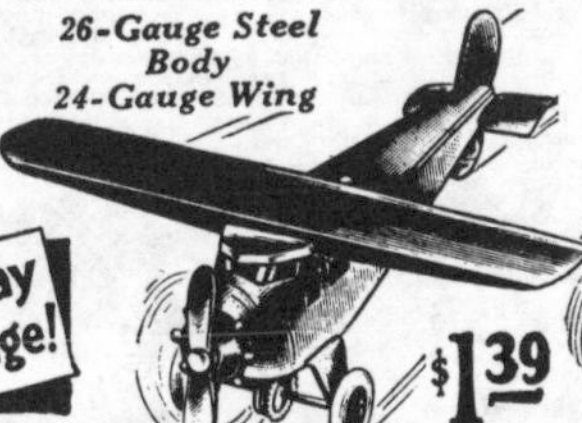

$1.39

## Heavy Steel Airplane

***Practically Indestructible***

Same heavy gauge steel as much higher priced toys. Length 21¼ inches; wing spread 20 inches; height 7¼ inches. High gloss enamel finish. Cream cabin, red wings, tail and disc wheels. Black whirlwind motor. Propeller turns as plane is pulled along floor, making a motor-like noise. Note gauge of steel used. We Pay Postage.
448 E 1229..........................$1.39

Tested Quality $1.87

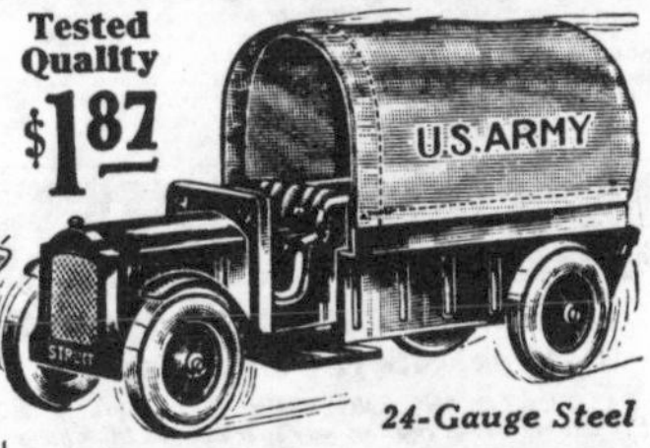


24-Gauge Steel

## Famous Structo Army Truck

Every child is happy with a great truck like this to pull over the floors! Large roomy body made by Structo of 24-gauge steel. Detachable steel bows in the back over which you can stretch the khaki tent-like cover just like real army trucks. Body finished in olive green baked-on enamel. Red disc wheels; tires painted on in white. Size: 17 by 5½ by 9 inches high. Bed 9¾ by 5½ inches. We Pay Postage.
448 E 1231..........................$1.87

$3.48

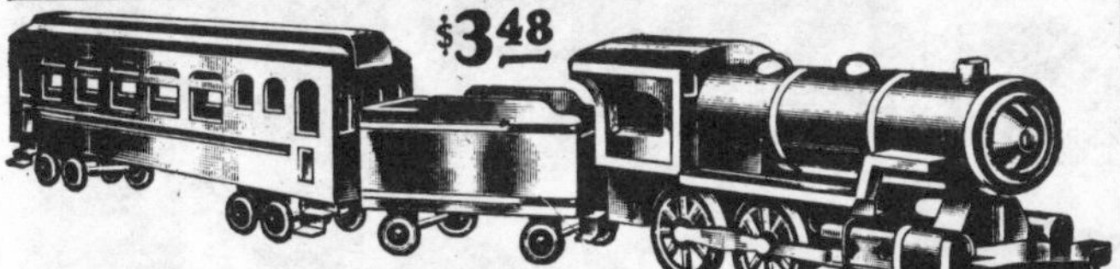

## Pull Train—Length 4½ Feet

***Strong Auto Body Steel Supports the Weight of a Child***

A child can sit on engine or car and ride down hill or scoot along without breaking it. Engine and tender is 30 by 4½ inches by 8 inches high. Car is 24 by 4¼ by 8 inches; eight steel wheels. The massive boiler, roomy cab and tender are all made of heavy gauge sheet steel. Red, gold and orange finish. We Pay Postage. Fast shipping service at Ward's!
448 E 1036......................$3.48

We Pay Postage!

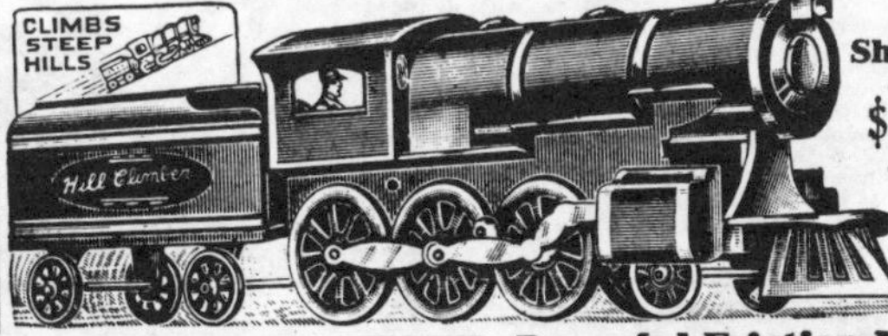


Fast Shipment $1.59

## Powerful Friction Motor Engine and Tender

***Length 27¾ Inches***

A bright red Locomotive with powerful friction motor which propels the 6 big drivewheels. Length 27¾ inches; height 6¾ inches; width, 5¼ inches. Friction motor will easily carry engine and tender up an incline. Steel engine is enameled bright red with gilt trim. We Pay Postage. No long delays at Ward's!
448 E 1032—Complete........$1.59

## Famous Structo

*Tractor Wagon Harrow Rake*

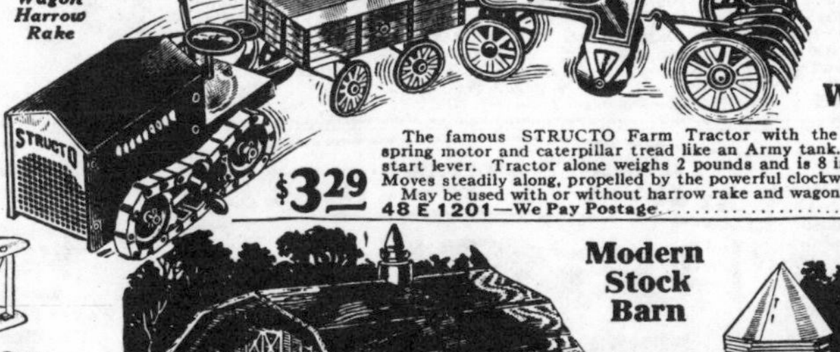


This Set Sold Only at Ward's

$3.29

The famous STRUCTO Farm Tractor with the wonderful spring motor and caterpillar tread like an Army tank. Stop and start lever. Tractor alone weighs 2 pounds and is 8 inches long. Moves steadily along, propelled by the powerful clockwork motor. May be used with or without harrow rake and wagon.
48 E 1201—We Pay Postage..................$3.29

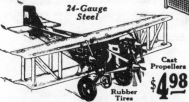

*24-Gauge Steel*

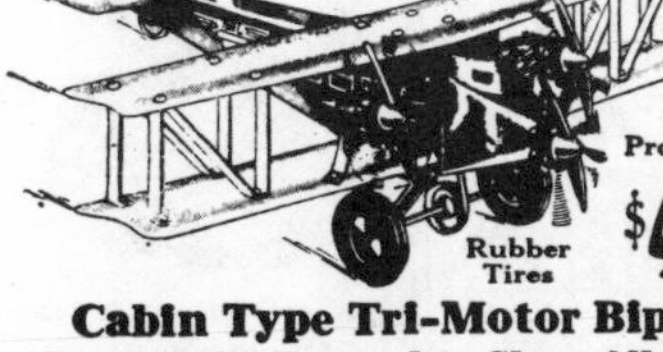

Cast Propellers

Rubber Tires

$4.98

## Cabin Type Tri-Motor Biplane

**Beautifully Formed to Show All Details**

The well made toy-gift that will more than delight every child. Wonderful minature model Plane made of heavy gauge pressed steel. Beautifully finished. Blue passenger cabin has brass doors and windows, pilot's cabin above. Silver aluminum color wings. Gilt braces and red, white and blue rudder. Red disc wheels with black rubber tires. The three propellers revolve when plane is pulled along the floor. Rudder is adjustable to three positions.

By removing top wing you can turn this model into a monoplane. Or by removing the two side propellers a single drive motor can be made. Size 21½ inches long; wing spread 23½ in.; height 7¾ in. One of our most beautiful toys. We Pay Postage.
448 E 1225..........................$4.98

## Modern Stock Barn

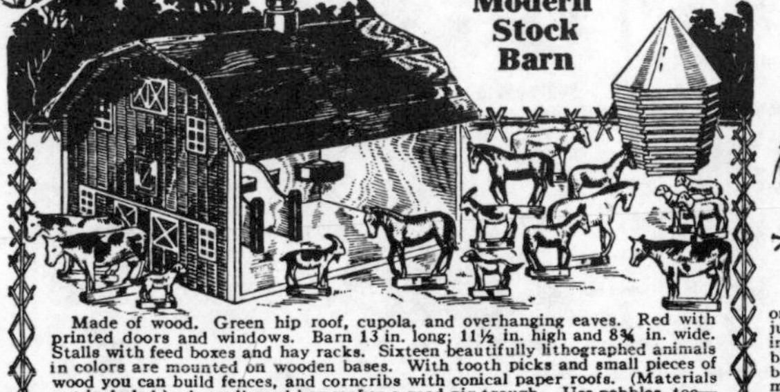

Made of wood. Green hip roof, cupola, and overhanging eaves. Red with printed doors and windows. Barn 13 in. long; 11½ in. high and 8¾ in. wide. Stalls with feed boxes and hay racks. Sixteen beautifully lithographed animals in colors are mounted on wooden bases. With tooth picks and small pieces of wood you can build fences, and corncribs with conical paper roofs. (Materials not included.) A cardboard box makes a good pig trough. Use pebbles too—it will look so real! Hours of entertainment are thus afforded. We Pay Postage.
448 E 3125—Barn and 16 animals..............................$1.29

## Police Set

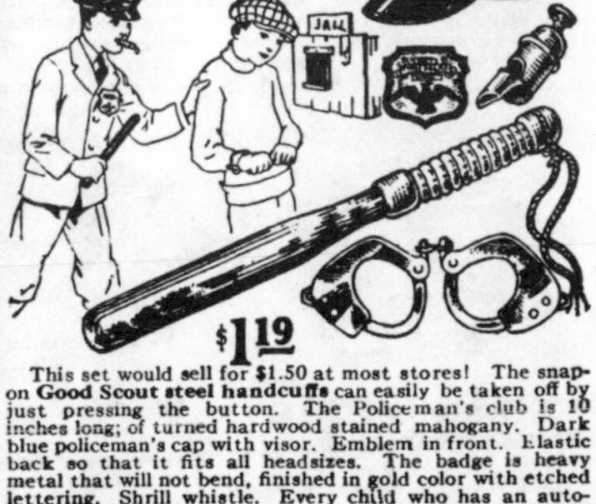


$1.19

This set would sell for $1.50 at most stores! The snap-on **Good Scout steel handcuffs** can easily be taken off by just pressing the button. The Policeman's club is 10 inches long; of turned hardwood stained mahogany. Dark blue policeman's cap with visor. Emblem in front. Elastic back so that it fits all headsizes. The badge is heavy metal that will not bend, finished in gold color with etched lettering. Shrill whistle. Every child who has an automobile will love having this set to play traffic cop with. We Pay Postage.
48 E 1398—Complete set..................$1.19

For Stop and Go Signal see Page 434.

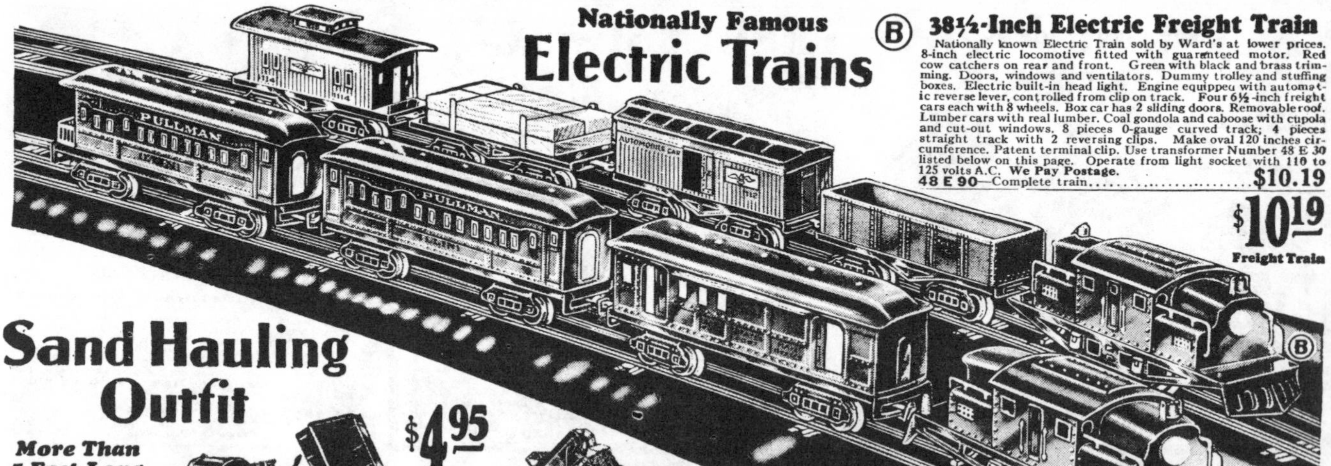

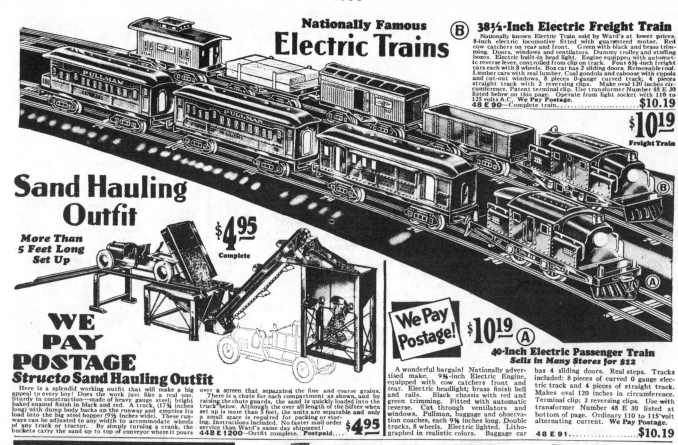

# Nationally Famous Electric Trains

## (B) 38½-Inch Electric Freight Train

Nationally known Electric Train sold by Ward's at lower prices. 8-inch electric locomotive fitted with guaranteed motor. Red cow catchers on rear and front. Green with black and brass trimming. Doors, windows and ventilators. Dummy trolley and stuffing boxes. Electric built-in head light. Engine equipped with automatic reverse lever, controlled from clip on track. Four 6½-inch freight cars each with 8 wheels. Box car has 2 sliding doors. Removable roof. Lumber cars with real lumber. Coal gondola and caboose with cupola and cut-out windows. 8 pieces 0-gauge curved track; 4 pieces straight track with 2 reversing clips. Make oval 120 inches circumference. Patent terminal clip. Use transformer Number 48 E 30 listed below on this page. Operate from light socket with 110 to 125 volts A.C. **We Pay Postage.**

**48 E 90**—Complete train.......................... **$10.19**

**$10.19** Freight Train

# Sand Hauling Outfit

*More Than 5 Feet Long Set Up*

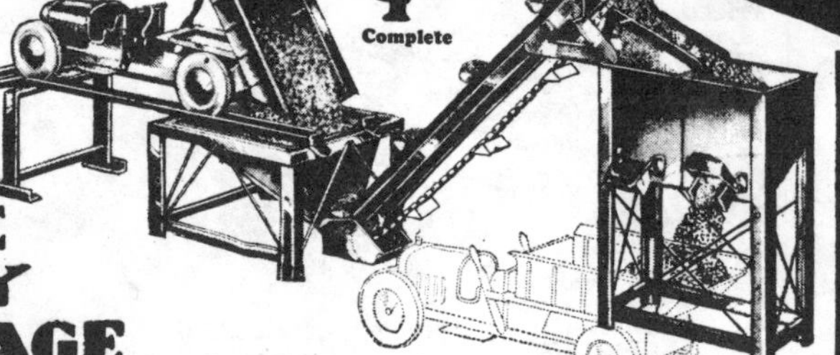

**$4.95** Complete

**WE PAY POSTAGE**

## *Structo* Sand Hauling Outfit

Here is a splendid working outfit that will make a big appeal to every boy! Does the work just like a real one. Sturdy in construction—made of heavy gauge steel; bright baked enamel finish in black and red. A truck, (17¾ inches long) with dump body backs up the runway and empties its load into the big steel hopper (9½ inches wide). These runways can be adjusted to any width to accommodate wheels of any truck or tractor. By simply turning a crank, the buckets carry the sand up to top of conveyor where it pours over a screen that separates the fine and coarse grains.

There is a chute for each compartment as shown, and by raising the chute guards, the sand is quickly loaded into the truck below. Although the over all length of the Sifter when set up is more than 5 feet, the units are separable and only a small space is required for packing or storing. Instructions included. No faster mail order service than Ward's same day shipment!

**448 E 1200**—Outfit complete. **Postpaid**.... **$4.95**

**We Pay Postage!** **$10.19** (A)

## 40-Inch Electric Passenger Train

***Sells in Many Stores for $12***

A wonderful bargain! Nationally advertised make. 9⅜-inch Electric Engine, equipped with cow catchers front and rear. Electric headlight; brass finish bell and rails. Black chassis with red and green trimming. Fitted with automatic reverse. Cut through ventilators and windows. Pullman, baggage and observation coaches, each 9⅜ inches long. Double trucks, 8 wheels. Electric lighted. Lithographed in realistic colors. Baggage car has 4 sliding doors. Real steps. Tracks included: 8 pieces of curved 0 gauge electric track and 4 pieces of straight track. Makes oval 120 inches in circumference. Terminal clip; 2 reversing clips. Use with transformer Number 48 E 30 listed at bottom of page. Ordinary 110 to 115 volt alternating current. **We Pay Postage.**

**48 E 91**......................... **$10.19**

# Mechanical Trains

## Complete Railroad System $7.59

***Most Stores ask $10.00***

*ORDERS TO THE ENGINEER: "Switch through freight on siding at junction, giving right-of-way to Midnight Flier passenger train."*

**More Equipment Than Any Outfit Sold at This Price**

Two complete trains—a 31½-inch passenger train and a 38-inch freight train. 204 inches of 0-gauge track including 3 switches, a bridge and a turntable on which engines can be reversed without removing them from track. A crossing watchtower with stairs to second floor and signal arm. Realistic 10-inch semaphore with ladder—in fact, all equipment necessary for **really playing Train.** Each train has 6½-inch heavy cast iron locomotive, both fitted with **brake, piston rods and guaranteed clock-spring motor,** keys for winding attached. Tenders loaded with imitation coal.

**Passenger Train** consists of baggage car with sliding door, pullman passenger car and one observation car with rear platform.

**Freight Train** has 4 cars, each 5½ inches long—stock car with slatted sides; one coal or gravel gondola; one box car and the caboose at the end with cupola for brakemen.

**Track** has ten pieces of curved track; 3 switches; 4 pieces of straight track. With arrangement of tracks shown, freight or passenger trains may be switched to inside track allowing other train to pass at full speed on outer oval. Trains can be run in opposite directions on the same track by using switches.

**We Pay Postage.**

**448 E 101**—Complete Railroad System.......... **$7.59**

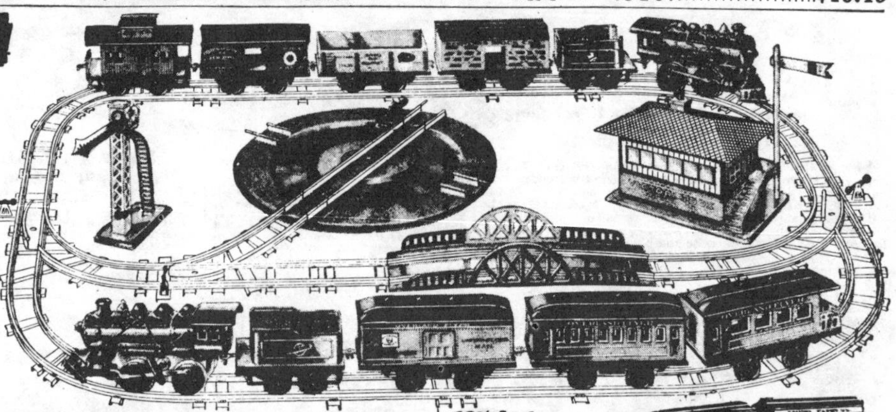

## 38-Inch Freight Train $2.99

***Shown Above at Right***

Same freight train shown above in the big combination set can be bought separately with a 123-inch oval 0-gauge track. 6½-inch cast iron engine is fitted with piston rods and brake and guaranteed motor; key for winding; coal tender half filled with imitation coal. Consists of stock car with slatted sides, one coal or gravel gondola; one box car and the caboose with cupola for brakemen. Four cars each 5½ inches long lithographed with markings of real freight cars. Track has 8 curved pieces and 4 straight pieces. **We Pay Postage.**

**48 E 102**—Freight Train and Track............... **$2.99**

## 31½-Inch Passenger Train $5.19

***Shown Above***

A small complete railway system with passenger train. 162-inch 0-gauge track makes small double oval. Includes ten curved pieces, two straight pieces **and two switches.** Realistic semaphore with ladder; 31½-inch train, bridge and crossing watchtower with signal are the same as those illustrated above in big combination. 6½-inch cast iron engine fitted with brake, and piston rods and guaranteed clock-work motor; attached key for winding. Four cars; baggage car, pullman passenger car and observation car with real platform, each 5½ inches long and lithographed to exactly resemble a real train. See additional track and accessories listed at bottom of page. **We Pay Postage.**

**448 E 103**—Passenger Train Outfit.................. **$5.19**

## 19½-Inch 2-Car Train

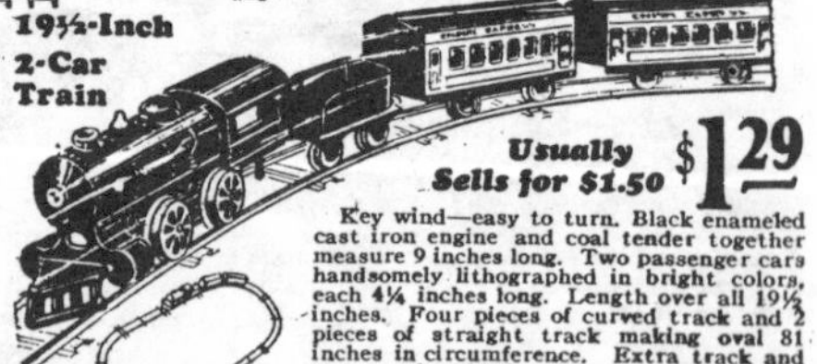

***Usually Sells for $1.50*** **$1.29**

Key wind—easy to turn. Black enameled cast iron engine and coal tender together measure 9 inches long. Two passenger cars handsomely lithographed in bright colors, each 4¼ inches long. Length over all 19½ inches. Four pieces of curved track and 2 pieces of straight track making oval 81 inches in circumference. Extra track and cars may be added as this train takes standard 0-gauge track. **Postpaid.**

**48 E 15**—Complete.......... **$1.29**

## Designed for Use With Trains

**You can buy cheaper transformers, but none better or safer for the use of children. Reduces house lighting current to the right voltage for operating electrical trains, toys, small motors and electric doorbells. Regulates the voltage, thus eliminating rheostats for speed control. Replaces batteries. Conforms to Underwriters' Laboratory requirements. With 6-foot cord and two-piece plug. For 105 to 120-volt 60-cycle alternating current only. Will stand 25 per cent overload without harm.**

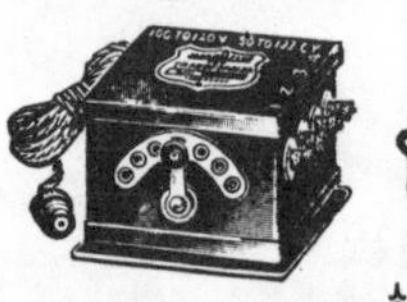

### 75-Watt Transformer $3.19

Produces 5½ to 11½ volts in 1-volt steps. Gives 18 secondary and 2 permanent voltage steps or speeds. Size 3⅛ by 3⅞ by 4 inches long. **We Pay Postage.**

**48 E 30**.............. **$3.19**

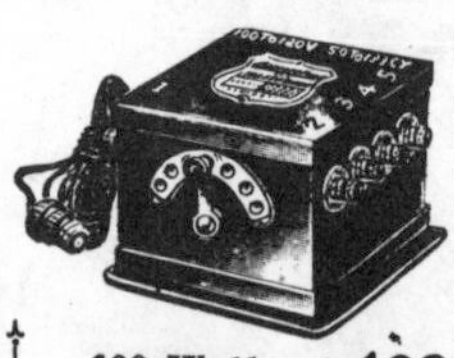

### 100-Watt Transformer $4.98

Produces 5½ to 23 volts in ¾-volt steps. Gives 25 secondary and 3 permanent voltage steps or speeds. Large enough to add electric accessories. Size 3⅜ by 4 by 4 inches long. **We Pay Postage.**

**48 E 21**.............. **$4.98**

# Train Accessories

**$1.49**

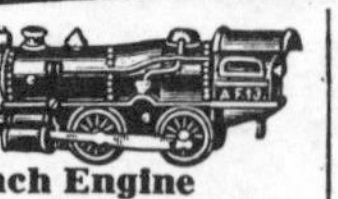

### 7-Inch Engine

For use with mechanical trains. Guaranteed spring motor. Cast iron. Black; gold and yellow trim. Red spoke drive wheels, nickel-plated piston rods. **We Pay Postage.**

**48 E 71**................. **$1.49**

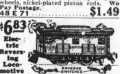

**$6.83** **Electric Reversing Locomotive**

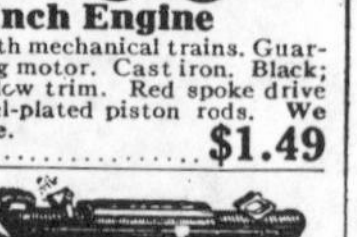


Reversing Electric Locomotive. Length 8 inches; height 4¼ inches. Fits 0-gauge track. Enameled orange; black chassis and brass trim. Real headlight; automatic reverse. Reverse trips for attaching to track. **We Pay Postage.**

**48 E 72**................. **$6.83**

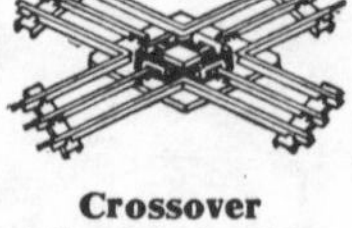

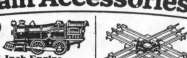

### Crossover

Make a figure 8 track from your present track with this crossover.

**For Electric Trains**

**48 E 54**—0-gauge (1⅜ inches wide). Size 10 by 5¼ in. **Postpaid.** Each crossover.... **$1.37**

**48 E 80**—Standard gauge (2¼ inches wide). Size 12 by 12 inches. **We Pay Postage.** Each crossover.... **$1.43**

**For Mechanical Trains**

**48 E 27**—0-gauge (1⅜ in. wide). Size 10 by 5¼ inches **We Pay Postage.** Each crossover....... **44¢**

## Extra Track at Low Prices

**All 0-gauge track is 1⅜ inches from center to center of outside rails. Standard wide gauge is 2¼ inches from center to center of outside rails.**

### Straight Track

**We Pay Postage.**

**For Electric Trains**

**48 E 24**—0-gauge (1⅜ inches wide). 10 in. long. **4 pieces**.. **64¢**

**48 E 82**—Standard wide gauge (2¼ inches wide). 14 inches long. **2 pieces**.............. **79¢**

**For Mechanical Trains**

**48 E 22**—0-gauge (1⅜ in. wide) 10 inches long. **4 pieces**.. **27¢**

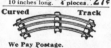

### Curved Track

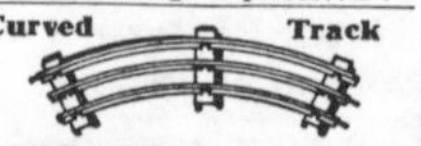

**We Pay Postage.**

**For Electric Trains**

**48 E 25**—0-gauge (1⅜ in. wide). 10 in. long. **4 pieces** **64¢**

**48 E 81**—Standard gauge (2¼ in. wide). 14 in. long. **2 pieces.** **79¢**

**For Mechanical Trains**

**48 E 23**—0-gauge (1⅜ in. wide) 10 inches long. **4 pieces**... **27¢**

### Switches for Trains Right and Left

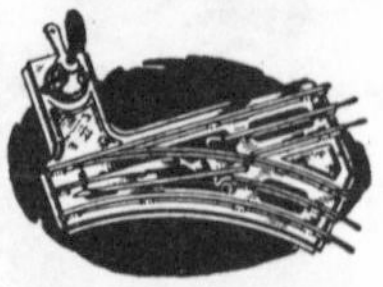

**For Electric Trains**

**48 E 53**—0-gauge (1⅜ in. wide). Size 10 by 5½ inches. **We Pay Postage.** Per pair........... **$2.63**

**48 E 83** — Standard gauge (2¼ inches wide). Size 14 by 8 inches. **We Pay Postage.** Per pair.. **$4.89**

**For Mechanical Trains**

**48 E 26**—0-gauge (1⅜ inches wide). Size 10 by 5½ inches. **We Pay Postage.** Per pair............... **98¢**

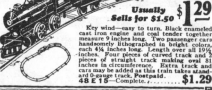

## Magic Lantern Outfit

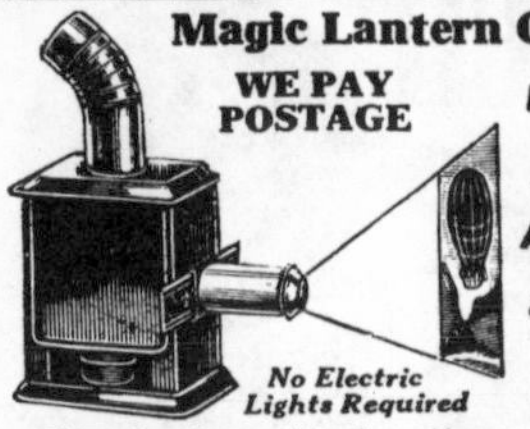

WE PAY POSTAGE

75¢

*A Good Buy at Our Low Price*

*No Electric Lights Required*

Oil-burning lamp with glass chimney, wick and burner. Size 9 inches high and 7½ inches long without extending focusing lenses. Width 3¼ inches. Black enamel lamp house with hinged door. Nickel-plated reflector. Magnifying, focusing lenses. Three colored 1-inch slides included. **We Pay Postage.**
48 E 1325—Each..........75¢

**Extra Lantern Slides. We Pay Postage.**
48 E 1331—12 Assorted..........45¢
48 E 1334—12 Comic..........45¢

## The Mysterious Diver 55¢

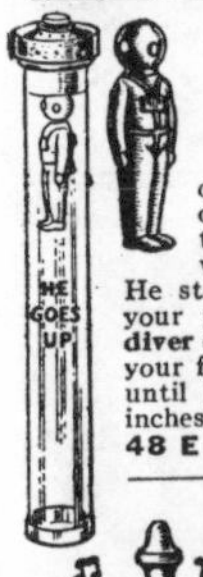


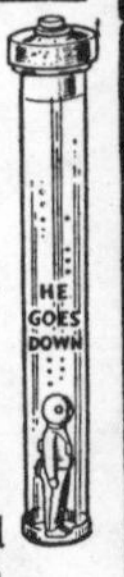


See him at the top of the tube of water. Speak to him and down he goes clear to the bottom. But if you tell him to, he will come up and stop half way. He stops anywhere in the tube at your pleasure. **What makes the diver dive?** That's the secret. Fool your friends. They will never learn until you tell them. Tube is 5½ inches long. **We Pay Postage.**
48 E 894..........55¢

## Three-Chord Musical Top

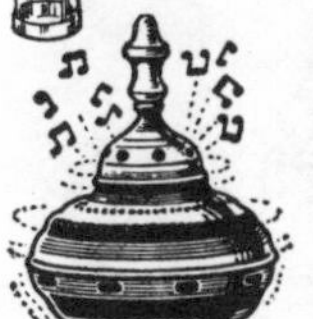

Beautiful metal Top decorated in gay colors. Plays three chords on 12 metal reels. Wood handle which you tap when you want to change the chord. Lgth. 8 inches; diameter 5½ inches. **We Pay Postage.**
48 E 2058..........57¢

**Two-Chord Musical Top**

Height 7 inches; diameter 4½ inches. Plays two chords on 8 reeds. **We Pay Postage.** 38¢
48 E 2059

## 49¢ Whistling Top

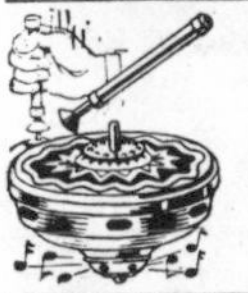

Complete with 4¾-inch spinning rod to give the Top momentum and make it spin for a longer time. While spinning the highly colored top gives a beautiful rainbow effect . . . at the same time it whistles musically. Diam. 3¾ inches. Illustrated instructions. Shipped promptly. **We Pay Postage.**
48 E 2056..........49¢

## Rainbow Top

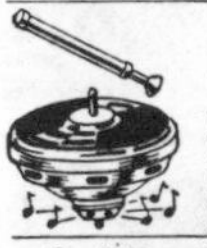

59¢

Ever-changing color! An inner disc of gorgeous colors revolves at a slower speed giving off a rainbow effect. Diam. 3¾ in. Spinning stick 4¾ inches. Illustrated instruction sheet. Whistles. Extremely well made. **We Pay Postage.**
48 E 2057..........59¢

## Musical Prohibition Camel

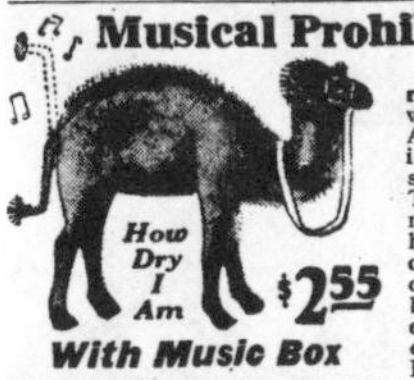


$2.55

*With Music Box*

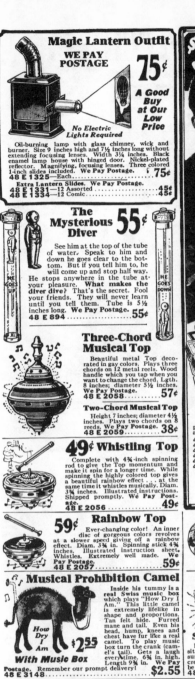

Inside his tummy is a **real Swiss music box** which plays "How Dry I Am." This little camel is extremely lifelike in shape and proportions. Tan felt hide. Furred mane and tail. Even his head, hump, knees and chest have fur like a real camel. To play music box turn the crank (camel's tail). Gets a laugh every time. 6¾ in. high. Length 9¾ in. **We Pay Postage.** Remember our prompt delivery!
48 E 3148..........$2.55

# $5 ELECTRIC MOVIE

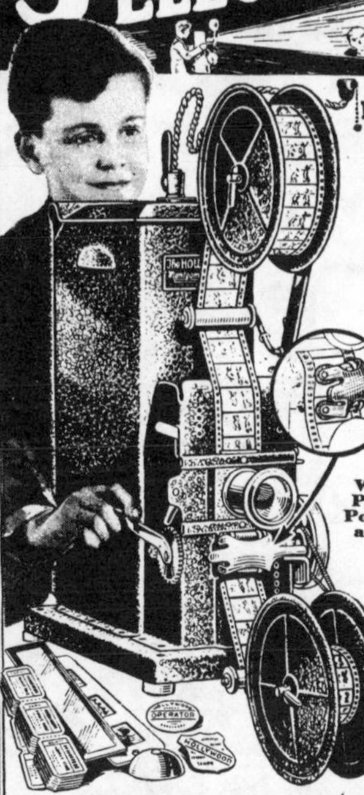

## Hollywood Improved!

New! Bigger! BETTER THAN EVER—The equal of $10 projectors sold at most stores. Extra powerful lens. Two 200-ft. capacity reels; **spring tension alligator holds film securely on spools.** Geneva movement—same principle as professional machines, automatic rewind. New large housing, ventilated. 17½ inches high. **Green crackle finish similar to $100 movie machines.** Heavy steel base. Rubber feet.

Can be operated on house current with 32-volt or 105 to 120-volt A.C. or D.C. with 75 or 100-watt bulb. Tickets and badges for operating small theater included. Complete with 6-foot cord. Bulb and film not included. **We Pay Postage.**

448 E 1330—Improved Hollywood...$5.00

448 E 1323—Standard Hollywood. Same as listed in previous years for $5. Black crackle finish; 16½ inches high; rubber feet. No alligator on this cut price model. **We Pay Postage..$4.67**

**We Pay Postage**

### Join Our Film Exchange

Order 200-foot film. Use it as long as you wish; return in good condition with 50¢ and we will send another. Exchange as often as you wish for one year. Then keep film you have. For Hollywood owners only. Join when you buy machine. Inflammable film.
**We Pay Postage.**
48 E 1354—Action..........$2.85
48 E 1355—Comedy..........2.85
48 E 1356—Western..........2.85

### Non-Inflammable Films

Open flame will cause them to melt but not to flame. Inspected and listed by National Board of Fire Underwriters. **We Pay Postage.**

**Charlie Chaplin Films**
48 E 1370—10-ft. Balky Mule..........$ .83
48 E 1371—25-ft. In Bad Again..........1.87
48 E 1372—50-ft. Window Washer..........3.85

**Our Gang Comedy Films**
48 E 1385—10-ft. Spooks..........$ .83
48 E 1379—25-ft. Pirate Ship..........1.79
48 E 1386—50-ft. Haunted House..........3.69

**Felix—the Cartoon Cat**
48 E 1387—10-ft. Felix & Lion..........$ .85
48 E 1388—25-ft. Musical Felix..........1.95

**Miscellaneous**
48 E 1374—25-ft. Mutt and Jeff..........$1.98
48 E 1341—25-ft. Our Presidents..........1.87
48 E 1375—25-ft. Ben Turpin..........1.89
48 E 1344—25-ft. Tom Mix..........1.89
48 E 1345—10-ft. Lindy..........89
48 E 1346—25-ft. Lindy to Mexico..........1.89
48 E 1347—50-ft. Lindy N.Y. to Paris..........3.89

### Used Theater Films Highly Inflammable

Cut from selected comedies and western pictures. Good condition. Long title footage eliminated. **We Pay Postage.**
48 E 1360—50-ft. Comedy..........$ .93
48 E 1361—50-ft. Western..........93
48 E 1362—100-ft. Comedy..........1.54
48 E 1363—100-ft. Western..........1.54
48 E 1364—200-ft. Comedy..........2.98
48 E 1365—200-ft. Western..........2.98

***Send for Our Special Film Catalogue***

## Powerful Electric Postcard Projector

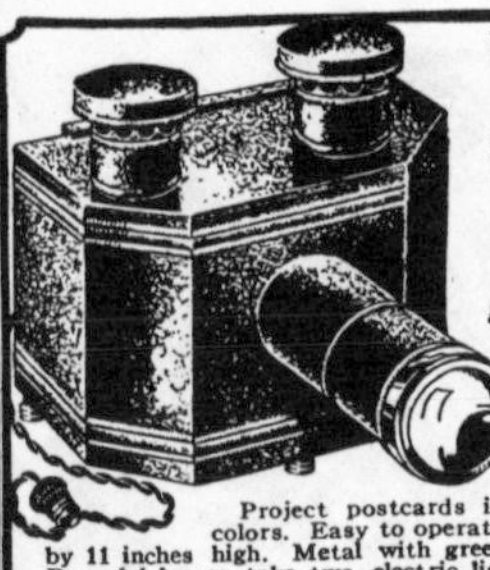

$4.48

*Educational and Amusing*

*Fun the Year Round!*

Project postcards in their natural colors. Easy to operate. Size 9½ by 9 by 11 inches high. Metal with green crackle finish. Powerful lenses take two electric light bulbs (bulbs not included); two bright reflectors, two cooling chimneys. Wood knob on sliding panel at the back. Complete with five-foot cord and plug. Use any ordinary electric current. **We Pay Postage.**
448 E 1339..........$4.48

## WE PAY POSTAGE!

## War Periscope

***Sold Exclusively by Ward's***

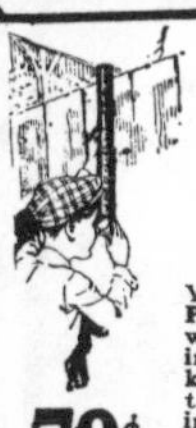

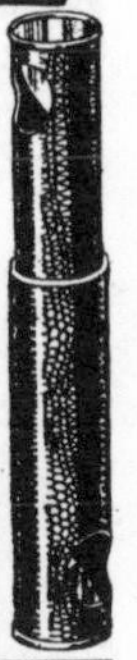

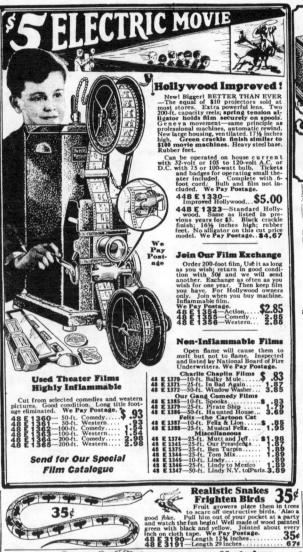

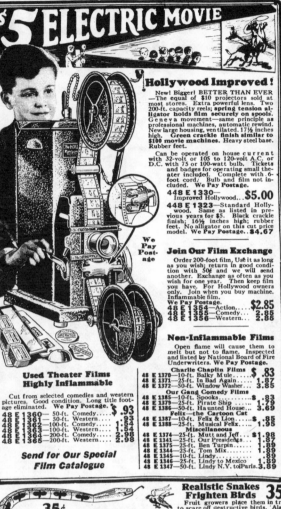

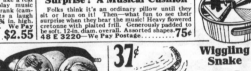

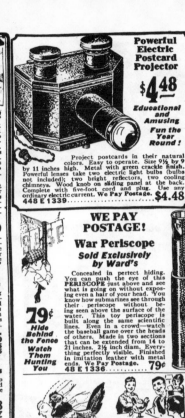

79¢

*Hide Behind the Fence*

*Watch Them Hunting You*

Concealed in perfect hiding. You can push the eye of this **PERISCOPE** just above and see what is going on without exposing even a hair of your head. You know how submarines see through their periscope without being seen above the surface of the water. This toy periscope is built along the same scientific lines. Even in a crowd—watch the baseball game over the heads of others. Made in two sections that can be extended from 14 to 21 inches. 2½ inch diam. Everything perfectly visible. Finished in imitation leather with metal ends. **We Pay Postage.**
48 E 1336..........79¢

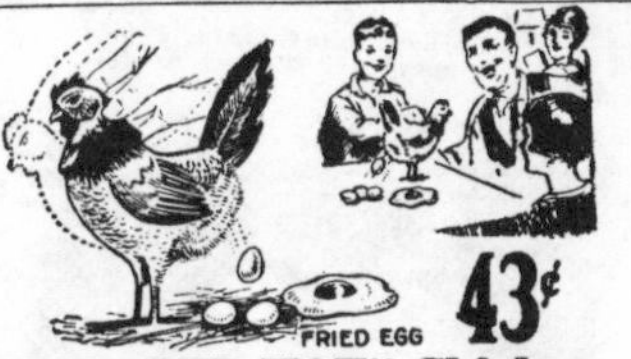


43¢

## THE "RED HOT" Chicken

***SHE LAYS FRIED EGGS***

Did you ever hear of a trick chicken before? By patting her gently on the head you can induce her to lay several wooden eggs and finally, to cap the climax, she lays a little fried egg! For the laugh getter of the year this is the best bet! Papier-mache constructed body covered with felt feathers in colors and real feather tail. A clever little toy carefully carried out in detail—even the imitation fried egg shows yellow on both sides, so no matter which side falls uppermost it looks real. Height 6½ inches. **We Pay Postage.**
48 E 3182..........43¢

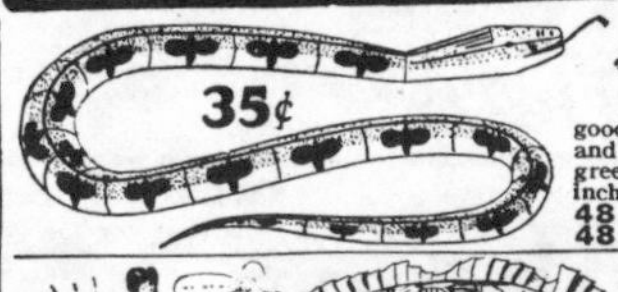


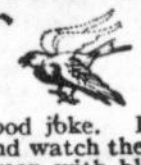

## Realistic Snakes Frighten Birds 35¢

Fruit growers place them in trees to scare off destructive birds. Also a good joke. Pull him out of your pocket at a party and watch the fun begin! Well made of wood painted green with black and yellow. Jointed about every inch on cloth tape. **We Pay Postage.** 35¢
48 E 3190—Length 12¾ inches..........35¢
48 E 3191—Length 29 inches..........67¢

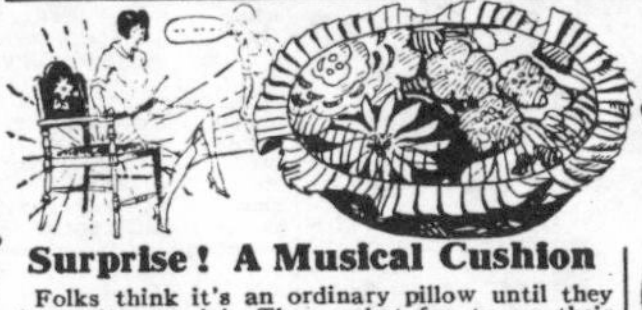

## Surprise! A Musical Cushion

Folks think it's an ordinary pillow until they sit or lean on it! Then—what fun to see their surprise when they hear the music! Heavy flowered cretonne with plaited frill. Generously padded to be soft. 12-in. diam. overall. Assorted shapes.
48 E 3220—We Pay Postage..........75¢

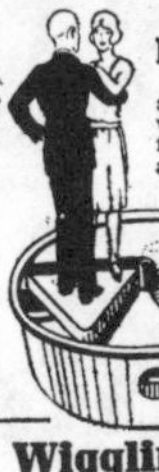

## Mysterious Endurance Dancers 63¢

What makes them dance? No one seems to know! This tireless couple waltz on and on over the mirrorlike floor. Both the man and the woman are in evening dress. They turn round and round as they move about the platform. May be lifted from floor. No visible connection. Just keep your friends guessing—it affords lots of entertainment.
48 E 3222—We Pay Postage..........63¢

## Wood Chicken House

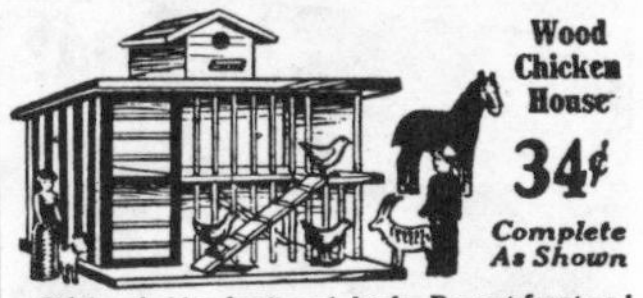

34¢

*Complete As Shown*

Chicken ladder front and back. Bars at front and sliding wall at back. This little chicken-farm set complete with 3 chickens, 3 small farm yard animals and a small man and woman. Size of house 4⅜ by 4 inches high. Pigeon house on top. **We Pay Postage.**
48 E 3118—Complete 9 pieces..........34¢

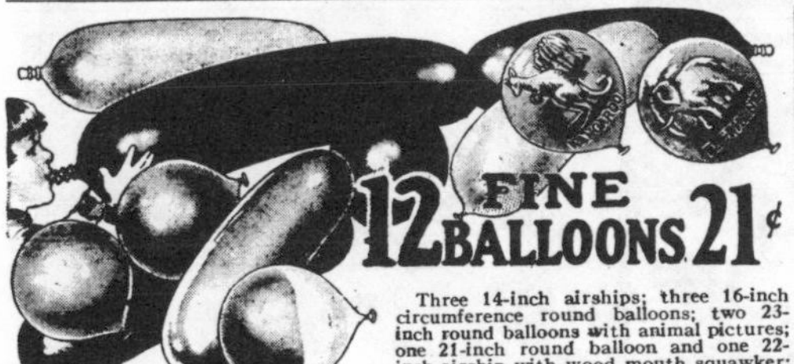

## 12 FINE BALLOONS 21¢

Three 14-inch airships; three 16-inch circumference round balloons; two 23-inch round balloons with animal pictures; one 21-inch round balloon and one 22-inch airship with wood mouth squawker; two 10-inch airship squawkers. **We Pay Postage.**
48 E 3121—12 balloons..........21¢

37¢

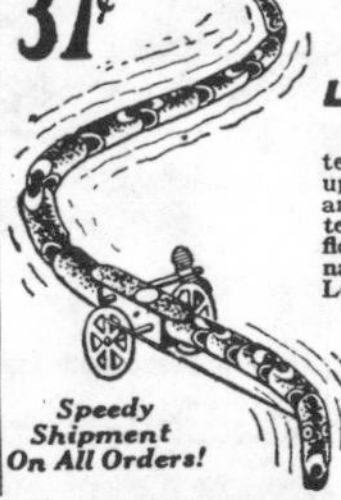

*Speedy Shipment On All Orders!*

## Wiggling Snake

***Looks So Real!***

Wiggly, green spotted Snake—wind him up, put him on the floor and see the folks scatter. Runs along the floor in an extraordinary life-like manner. Length 17¼ inches; has 12 joints. **We Pay Postage.**
48 E 3200..........37¢

***We Pay Postage!***

# WE PAY POSTAGE

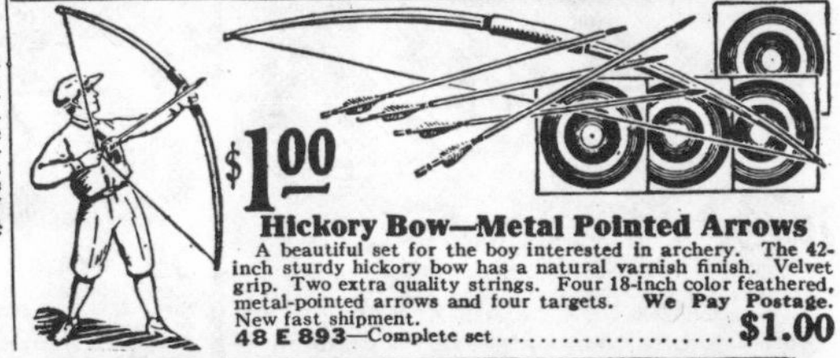

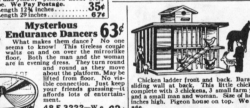

$1.00

## Hickory Bow—Metal Pointed Arrows

A beautiful set for the boy interested in archery. The 42-inch sturdy hickory bow has a natural varnish finish. Velvet grip. Two extra quality strings. Four 18-inch color feathered, metal-pointed arrows and four targets. **We Pay Postage.** New fast shipment.
48 E 893—Complete set..........$1.00

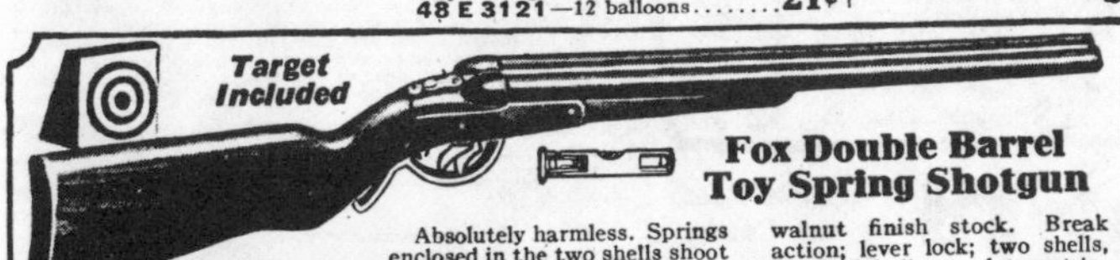

*Target Included*

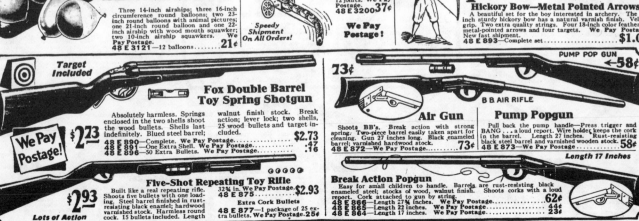

## Fox Double Barrel Toy Spring Shotgun

*We Pay Postage!*

$2.73

Absolutely harmless. Springs enclosed in the two shells shoot the wood bullets. Shells last indefinitely. Blued steel barrel; walnut finish stock. Break action; lever lock; two shells, 25 wood bullets and target included.
48 E 890—Complete. We Pay Postage..........$2.73
48 E 891—One Extra Shell. We Pay Postage..........47
48 E 896—50 Extra Bullets. We Pay Postage..........16

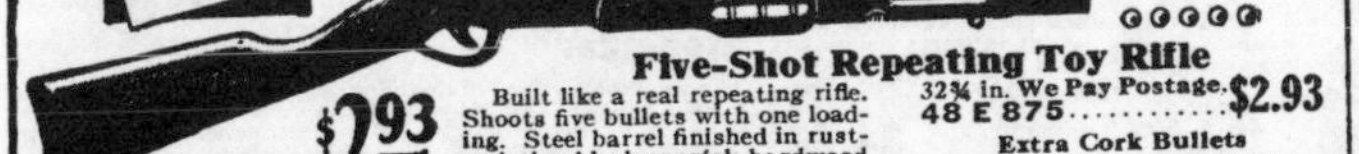

## Five-Shot Repeating Toy Rifle

$2.93

*Lots of Action*

Built like a real repeating rifle. Shoots five bullets with one loading. Steel barrel finished in rust-resisting black enamel; hardwood varnished stock. 15 bullets included. Length 32¾ in. **We Pay Postage.**
48 E 875..........$2.93

**Extra Cork Bullets**
48 E 877—1 package of 25 extra bullets. **We Pay Postage.** 25¢

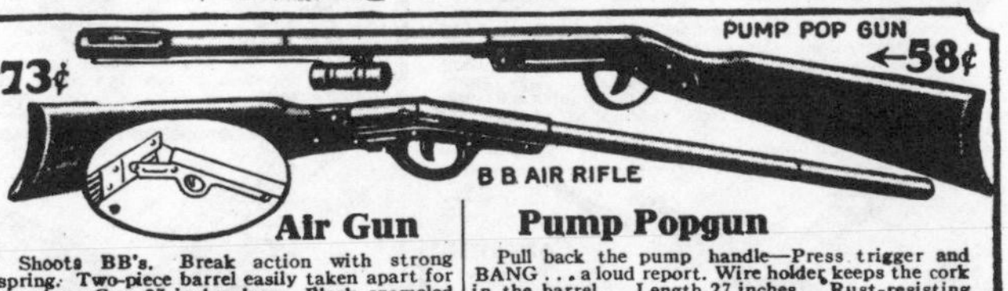


73¢

←58¢

## Air Gun

Shoots BB's. Break action with strong spring. Two-piece barrel easily taken apart for cleaning. Gun 27 inches long. Black enameled barrel; varnished hardwood stock.
48 E 872—We Pay Postage..........73¢

## Pump Popgun

Pull back the pump handle—Press trigger and BANG . . . a loud report. Wire holder keeps the cork in the barrel. Length 27 inches. Rust-resisting black steel barrel and varnished wooden stock.
48 E 873—We Pay Postage..........58¢

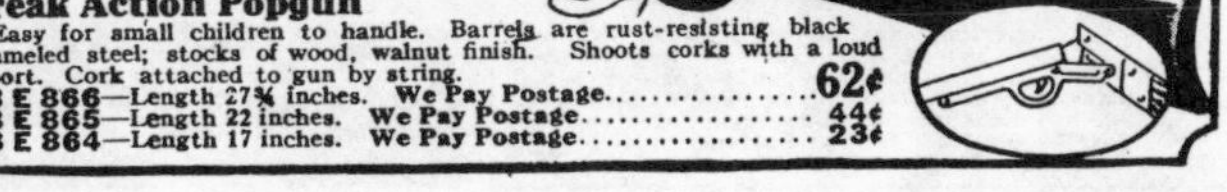

*Length 17 Inches*

## Break Action Popgun

Easy for small children to handle. Barrels are rust-resisting black enameled steel; stocks of wood, walnut finish. Shoots corks with a loud report. Cork attached to gun by string.
48 E 866—Length 27¾ inches. We Pay Postage..........62¢
48 E 865—Length 22 inches. We Pay Postage..........44¢
48 E 864—Length 17 inches. We Pay Postage..........23¢

251 *Montgomery Ward & Co.*

# *Famous* WEEDEN Reversing Steam Engine

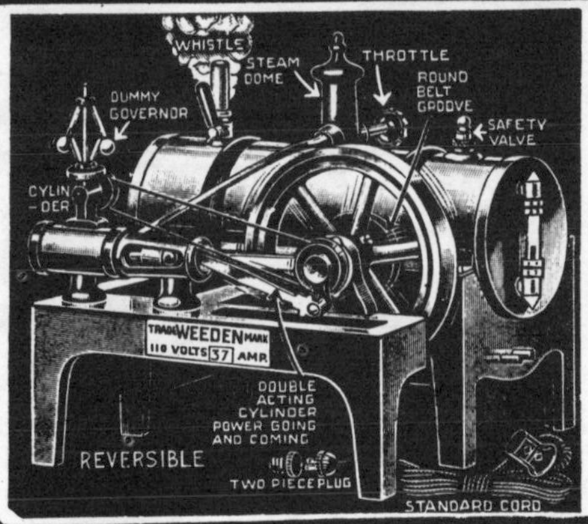


$3.98 With Alcohol Burner

## American Style

***Electric or Alcohol Heat***

America's most popular Toy Steam Engine has now been fitted with a built-in electric heating unit like mother's electric iron. We are still selling thousands with alcohol heat.

The double-action cylinder pushes and pulls like a locomotive, giving greater power. **Will run backward or forward.** Polished brass boiler equipped as in picture. Real water gauge. Cast iron flywheel about 3¼ inches diameter. Pulley to run small toys attached. Steam chest has revolving dummy governor. Cast iron base 5⅞ by 5¾ inches. Height over all 6¾ inches. Small wrench, funnel for filling boiler and directions for operating included. Either electric or alcohol heating unit as listed below.

**Enclosed Electric Heating Element**

48 E 20—Has standard cord and two-piece plug for screwing into 110 to 120-volt light socket. No flame required. Heats very rapidly. Absolutely safe! **We Pay Postage.** ........ **$6.93**

**Above Engine Equipped for Alcohol Heat**

48 E 38—Has a 3-burner alcohol stove, also a container for burning canned heat. Only small flame necessary. Absolutely safe! **We Pay Postage.** ........ **$3.98**

## Weeden Electric Steam Engine

### Guaranteed Electric Heating Element

$5.19

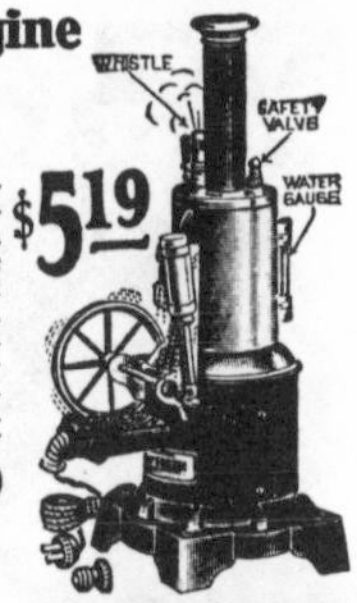


Made by Weeden! The world's foremost manufacturer of Toy Steam Engines. First to produce a guaranteed Electric Engine to sell at a price so low! Polished brass boiler; cast iron base 4¼ inches square, painted red. Black firebox and smoke stack. Equipped with whistle, safety valve, water glass, nickel-plated piston flywheel. Height 11¾ inches. Enclosed electric heating element—6-foot cord; plug can be attached to ordinary light socket supplying alternating or direct current from 110 to 115 volts. Absolutely safe! **We Pay Postage.**
48 E 60 ........ **$5.19**

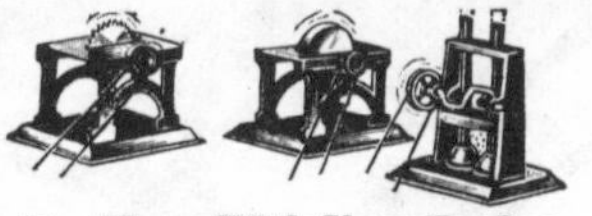

### Use These With Your Engine

Three necessary accessories for your Steam engine at one astonishingly low price! Stamping Mill, 3 inches high; Grindstone and Saw each 2⅜ by 2½ by 2¾ inches high. All equipped with pulleys to attach to engine or shafting. **We Pay Postage.**
48 E 69—All 3 pieces ........ **53¢**

### Pulley Shaft

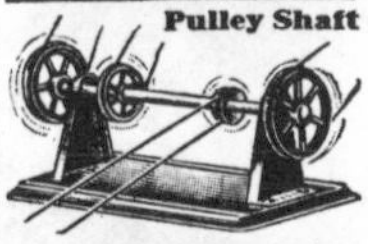

4 Pulleys of different sizes; steel shaft. 6⅞ by 3⅛ inches. **We Pay Postage.**
48 E 46 ........ **29¢**

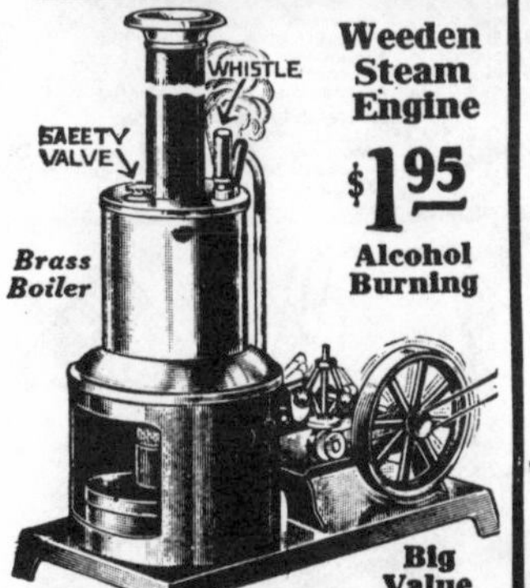


## Weeden Steam Engine

$1.95

**Alcohol Burning**

***Brass Boiler***

**Big Value**

Polished brass boiler equipped with safety valve and whistle. Steel base size 8 by 4 inches. Polished 2⅝-inch flywheel. Dummy governor. Entire height 10⅛ inches. Small steel alcohol stove. Pulley on flywheel to operate small toys. **We Pay Postage.**
48 E 62—Weeden Steam Engine ........ **$1.95**

## Mighty-Mite

***Speedy Shipment!***

$1.47

***Sold in U. S. Only by Ward's***

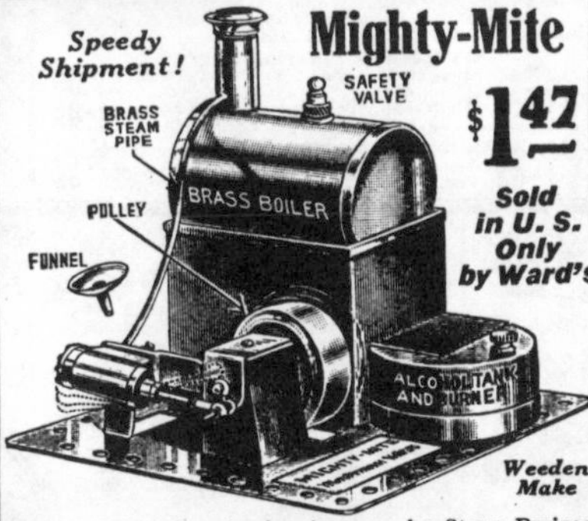


***Weeden Make***

Another gigantic order for these popular Steam Engines brings them to you at the same low price. Small, safe—easy to handle. Steel plate base 5 inches square, perforated for attaching to Steel-Tech, Erector and Meccano models or may be screwed to block of wood. Polished brass boiler 2¾ inches long; steam dome and safety valve. Entire height 6 inches. Gracefully curved steam pipe carries steam from boiler to engine. Piston carries brass-plated heavy flywheel at a high rate of speed. Heated by alcohol stove. **We Pay Postage.**
48 E 100—Mighty-Mite Steam Engine ........ **$1.47**

## Real Electric Steam Engine

### Upright Type

$5.48

***Genuine Weeden Brass Boiler***

***6-Foot Cord***

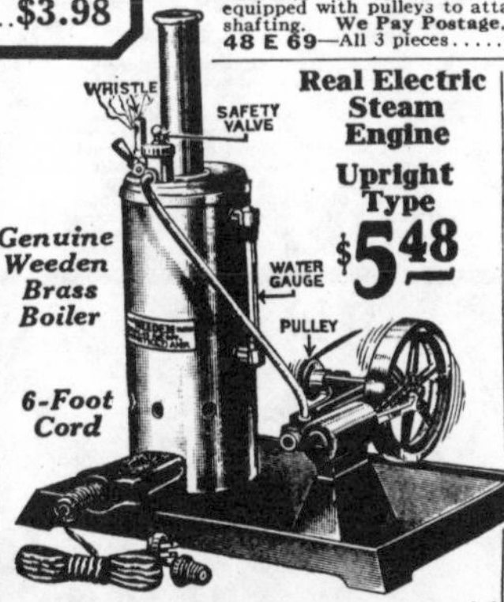


Broad 9½ by 6½-inch base of cast iron enameled red. Fine quality spun brass boiler; nickeled finish. Whistle with wood handle; safety valve; water glass. Red flywheel, 3 inches diameter, has nickel-plated rim. Smokestack also nickel plated. Red enameled cast iron frame. Guaranteed tested electric heating element, enclosed. Fits any light socket supplying 110 to 115 volts A.C. or D.C. Height 11 inches. **We Pay Postage.**
48 E 63—Electric Steam Engine ........ **$5.48**

$5.00 **Electric**

## WEEDEN Upright Reversing Engine

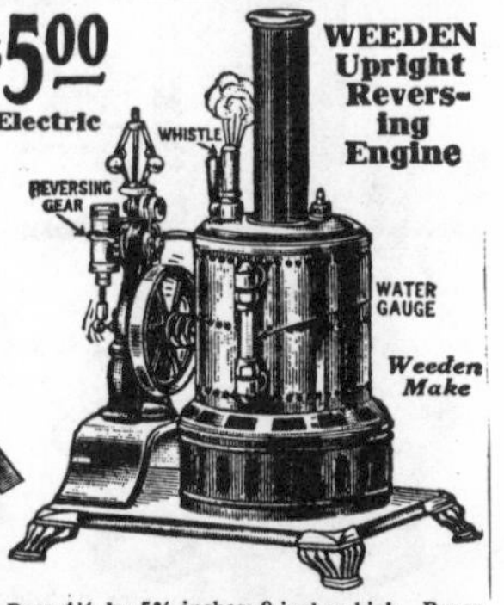


***Weeden Make***

Base 4½ by 5⅜ inches; 9 inches high. Brass boiler with shrill whistle, water gauge and safety valve. 2-inch flywheel with two pulleys. Fitted with 2-burner alcohol stove or electric heating unit operating from any 110 to 120-volt, A. C. or D. C. light socket. **We Pay Postage.**
48 E 37—Alcohol burner ........ **$3.19**
48 E 36—Electric heater ........ **5.00**

$6.19

**We Pay Postage!**

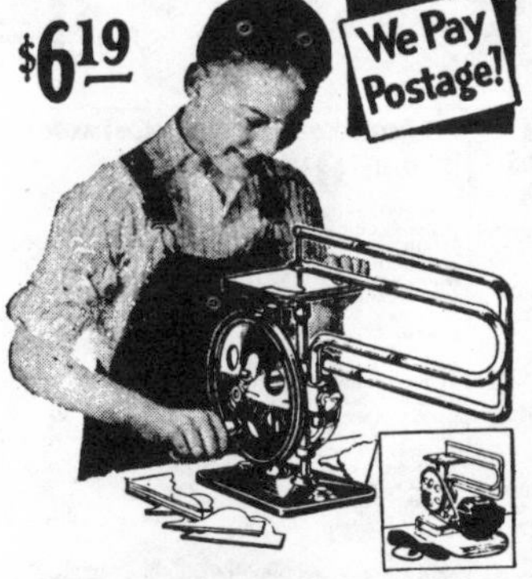

## American Scroll Saw

There is no end to the number of fancy things a boy can make with this Scroll Saw. Hanging book shelves with attractive curved sides for mother, toy animals, soldiers and dolls for little sisters and brothers, open work panels for the home-built radio, or a dandy bird house.

Real expression for a boy's creative ability. Cuts wood up to 1 inch thick, bakelite fiber, thin brass and aluminum. Strong cast iron base. Height 11½ inches; length 11 inches; width 4½ inches. 8-inch clearance from blade to throat of frame. Grooved flywheel. Nickel-plated work table and frame. Two saw blades included. Extra blades listed below. **We Pay Postage.**
448 E 1168—Complete ........ **$6.19**
448 E 1169—Twelve extra saw blades for cutting wood or metal. Ship. wt. 3 oz. ........ **53¢**

# GILBERT "Big Boy" Tool Chests

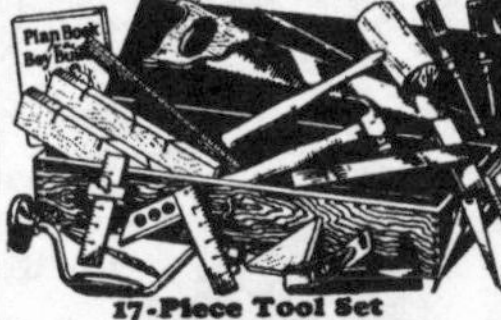

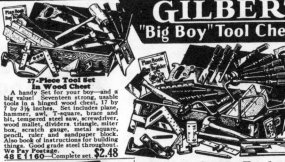

**17-Piece Tool Set in Wood Chest**

A handy Set for your boy—and a big value! Seventeen strong, usable tools in a hinged wood chest, 17 by 7 by 3½ inches. Set includes plane, hammer, awl, T-square, brace and bit, tempered steel saw, screwdriver, wood mallet, dividers, triangle, miter box, scratch gauge, metal square, pencil, ruler and sandpaper block. Also book of instructions for building things. Good grade steel throughout. **We Pay Postage.**
48 E 1160—Complete set ........ **$2.48**

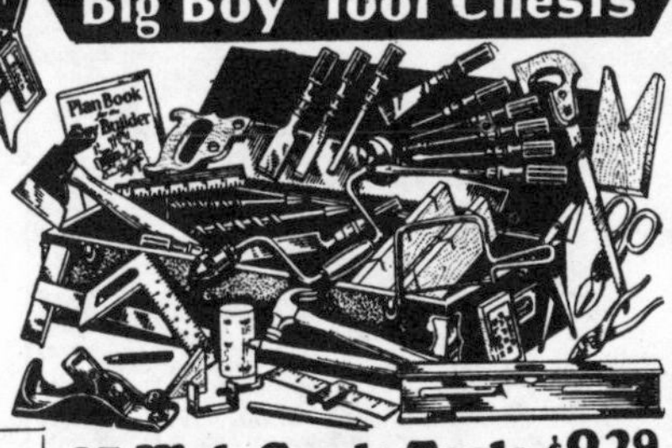

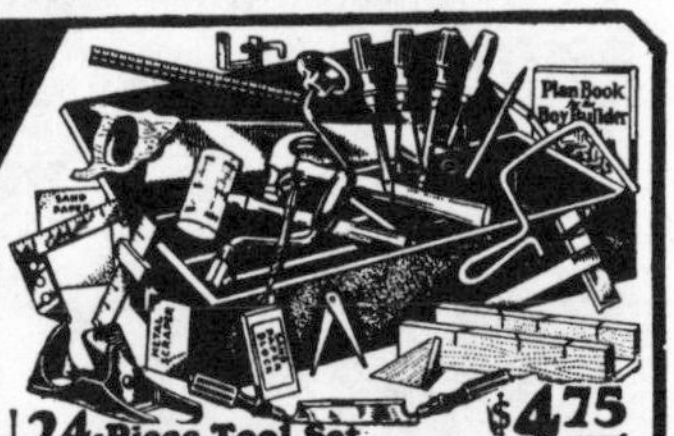

**24-Piece Tool Set** $4.75

***In Chinese Red Lacquered Chest***

Popular choice of boys who want to build and dads who like to tinker. A value that's hard to match! Set includes a 17½-inch tempered steel saw, screwdriver, plane, awl, brace, bit, metal scratch gauge, hammer, wood scraper, draw knife, ¼-inch chisel, mallet, miter box, T square, dividers, pencil, clamp, metal square, rule, scroll saw and blade, sandpaper block, sandpaper, putty knife, wood triangle and book on carpentry. Chest of ⅜-inch wood, finished Chinese red; brass finish hinges, hasps and grip ends; three nail compartments. Size 21⅜ by 4⅜ by 8¼ inches. **We Pay Postage.**
448 E 1158—Complete set ........ **$4.75**

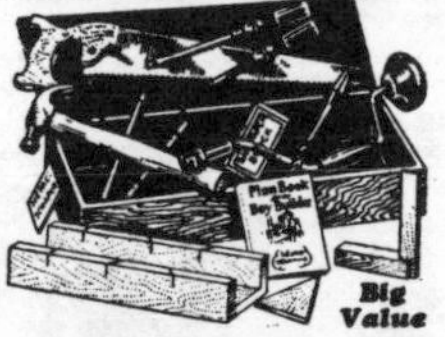

***Big Value***

**13-Piece Tool Set in Chest**

Tools for the boy's first carpentry. Wood tool chest, 14⅜ by 6 by 3 inches. Thirteen tools: 14½-inch tempered steel saw, good grade hammer, brace and bit, awl, screwdriver, metal scraper, pencil, sandpaper block, miter box, square, triangle and ruler. Book of plans for easy building. **We Pay Postage.**
48 E 1167—Complete set ........ **$1.19**

## 37 High-Grade Tools $8.29

**Walnut Stained Metal Bound Chest**

***Usual $10.00 Value***

Includes **Gilbert's** 14-page instruction book, practical steel spirit level, carpenter's brace, full size hatchet and hammer, metal plane, 19½-in. hand saw made of tempered steel, 17-in. keyhole saw, wood mallet, triangle, large screw-driver, small screw-driver, wood-handled file, 1-inch chisel, ½-inch chisel, ¼-inch chisel. Dividers, steel scratch gauge, saw-block miter box, soldering copper with wood handle, stick of solder, work board. Scroll saw and blade, sandpaper block, carpenter's 2-foot folding rule, tinner's snips, metal tri-square, steel pliers, draw knife. Awl, nail set, large auger bit, small auger bit, putty knife, pencil, metal clamp, T square—37 tools in all, and one manual. Heavy wood chest, finished in Chinese red. Dovetailed corners, metal bound. Brass hinges, countersunk end-grips and clasps. **We Pay Postage.**
448 E 1157—Complete outfit ........ **$8.29**

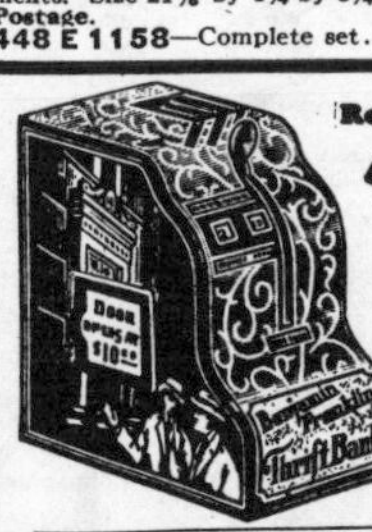

**3-Coin Registering Bank**

49¢

Registers nickels, dimes and quarters. Opens when $10.00 has been deposited. Drop in a nickel and it rings once; a dime and it rings twice. Drop in 25¢ and hear 5 rings. Sturdy steel, lithographed in colors. 2¼ by 4 in. **We Pay Postage.**
48 E 3862 ........ **49¢**

***Lively Quality***

***Pure White Rubber***

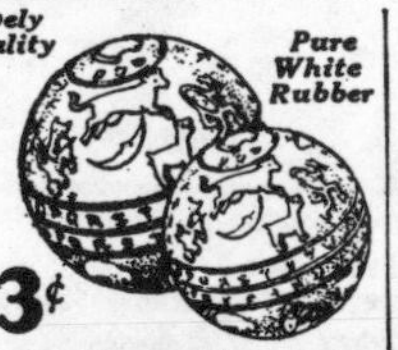

53¢

## 6-Inch Size Educational Balls

Keep baby happy with this gleaming white Ball! Heavy, selected quality rubber with nursery rhyme characters, animals and A-B-C's embossed on surface. We guarantee each ball to be live, resilient and fully inflated. The larger the ball, the deeper the embossed designs.
48 E 3133—Diameter 6 inches. **We Pay Postage.** ........ **53¢**
48 E 3134—Diameter 5 inches. **We Pay Postage** ........ **39¢**

29¢

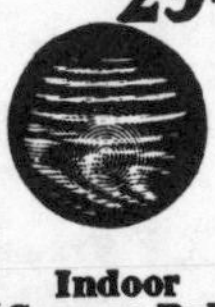

## Indoor Sponge Ball

***Multi-Colored***

Gaily colored, soft sponge rubber. Hollow with ½-inch walls. Puncture-proof. A real indoor ball! Can throw it against window or mirror. Diameter 3½ inches. **We Pay Postage.**
48 E 3140 ........ **29¢**

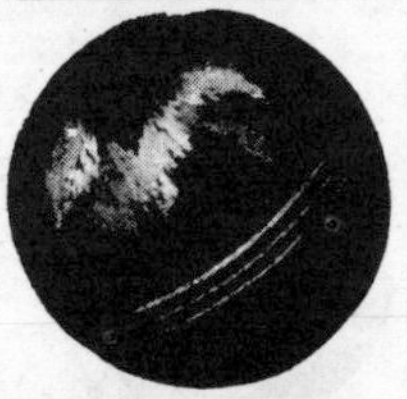

## Famous Weaver Non-Burst Health Balls

Live tire rubber. Stands one-ton test without bursting. In bright blending colors—that will fascinate little tots. **We Pay Postage.**

| Article No. | Diameter | Each |
|---|---|---|
| 48 E 3158 | 10 in. | $1.75 |
| 48 E 3145 | 8 in. | .89 |
| 48 E 3144 | 6 in. | .47 |

## 42-Inch Reinforced Beach Ball

**Gum Bladder**

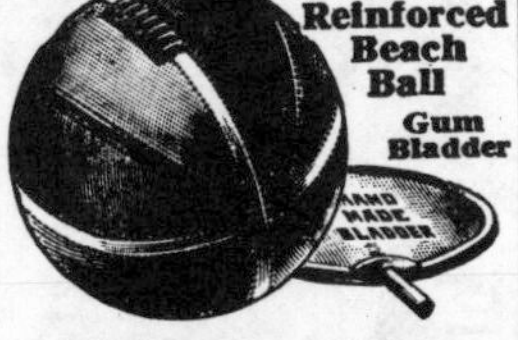


## 87¢ Bright Colors

Water-proof cloth cover of this big 42-inch Beach Ball is paneled in clear, bright colors. A gay, pretty plaything for big and little folks. Double flaps at opening. Metal eyelets. All seams are strongly reinforced with tape. Two-piece bladder is hand made from pure gum rubber and guaranteed. **We Pay Postage.**
48 E 3141—Ball and bladder ........ **87¢**
48 E 3147—Extra gum rubber bladder. We Pay Postage ........ **37¢**

## Lighthouse Bank

A beautiful imported miniature steel lighthouse design Bank. Height 7⅜ in.; diameter of base 2⅝ in. Enameled white with green trimming. Does not really light up. **We Pay Postage.**
48 E 3864 ........ **39¢**

39¢

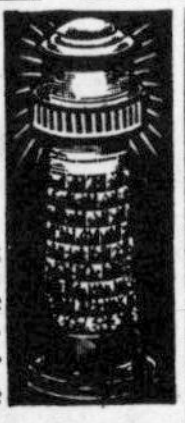

## Large Size Registering and Adding Bank

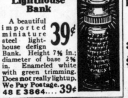

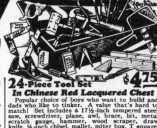

**3-Coin**

$1.83

**Rings at Each Deposit**

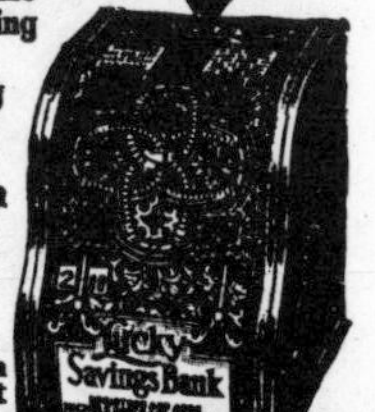


It's fun to save in a Bank like this! Pull lever down slowly and this bank rings once for a nickel, twice for a dime and five times when you drop a quarter in. Registers total amount and opens when you have saved $10.00. Of beautiful etched metal decorated in gold, red, green and blue. Size 5 by 3⅞ by 5 inches. A splendid savings bank—it keeps up the child's interest and is a real incentive to save. **We Pay Postage.**
48 E 3860—Lucky Savings Bank ........ **$1.83**

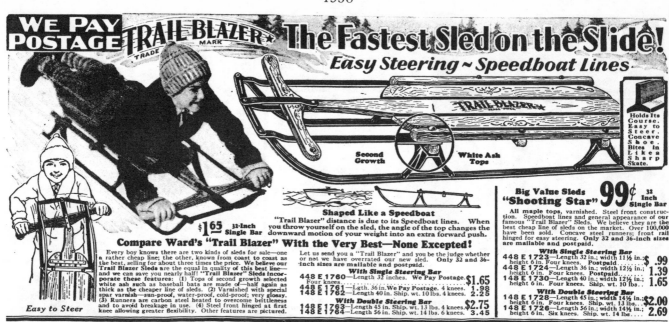

# WE PAY POSTAGE TRAIL BLAZER The Fastest Sled on the Slide!

## Easy Steering ~ Speedboat Lines

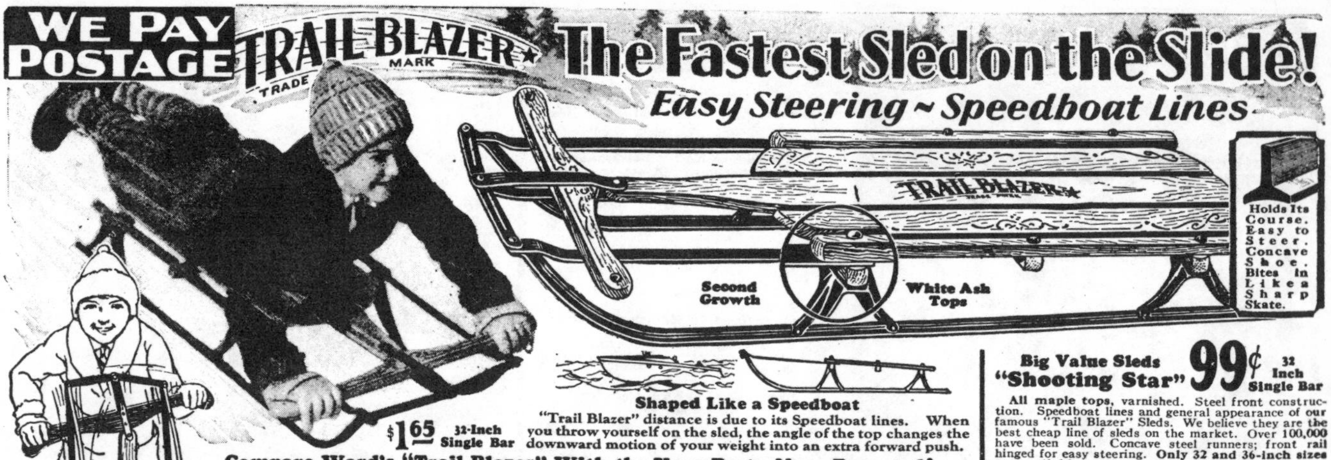
TRAIL BLAZER
TRADE MARK
Second Growth
White Ash Tops
Holds Its Course. Easy to Steer. Concave Shoe. Bites in Like a Sharp Skate.
Easy to Steer

**Shaped Like a Speedboat**

"Trail Blazer" distance is due to its Speedboat lines. When you throw yourself on the sled, the angle of the top changes the downward motion of your weight into an extra forward push.

$1.65 32-Inch Single Bar

## Compare Ward's "Trail Blazer" With the Very Best—None Excepted!

Every boy knows there are two kinds of sleds for sale—one a rather cheap line; the other, known from coast to coast as the best, selling for about three times the price. We believe our **Trail Blazer Sleds** are the equal in quality of this best line—and we can save you nearly half! **"Trail Blazer" Sleds incorporate these features:** (1) Tops of second growth selected white ash such as baseball bats are made of—half again as thick as the cheaper line of sleds. (2) Varnished with special spar varnish—sun-proof, water-proof, cold-proof; very glossy. (3) Runners are carbon steel heated to overcome brittleness and to avoid breakage in use. (4) Steel front hinged at first knee allowing greater flexibility. Other features are pictured.

Let us send you a "Trail Blazer" and you be the judge whether or not we have overrated our new sled. **Only 32 and 36-inch sizes are mailable and postpaid.**

***With Single Steering Bar***

448 E 1760—Length 32 inches. We Pay Postage. Four knees. . . . . . $1.65
448 E 1761—Lgth. 36 in. We Pay Postage. 4 knees. 1.98
148 E 1762—Length 40 in. Ship. wt. 10 lbs. 4 knees. 2.25

***With Double Steering Bar***

148 E 1763—Length 45 in. Ship. wt. 13 lbs. 4 knees. $2.75
148 E 1764—Length 56 in. Ship. wt. 14 lbs. 6 knees. 3.45

**Big Value Sleds "Shooting Star" 99¢ 32 Inch Single Bar**

All maple tops, varnished. Steel front construction. Speedboat lines and general appearance of our famous "Trail Blazer" Sleds. We believe they are the best cheap line of sleds on the market. Over 100,000 have been sold. Concave steel runners; front rail hinged for easy steering. **Only 32 and 36-inch sizes are mailable and postpaid.**

***With Single Steering Bar***

448 E 1723—Length 32 in.; width 11½ in.; height 6 in. Four knees. **Postpaid** . . . . . . $ .99
448 E 1724—Length 36 in.; width 12½ in.; height 6 in. Four knees. **Postpaid** . . . . . . 1.39
148 E 1730—Length 40 in.; width 12½ in.; height 6 in. Four knees. Ship. wt. 10 lbs. . 1.65

***With Double Steering Bar***

148 E 1728—Length 45 in.; width 14½ in.; height 6 in. Four knees. Ship. wt. 13 lbs. . . $2.00
148 E 1726—Length 56 in.; width 14½ in.; height 6 in. Six knees. Ship. wt. 14 lbs. . . . 2.69

$2.58

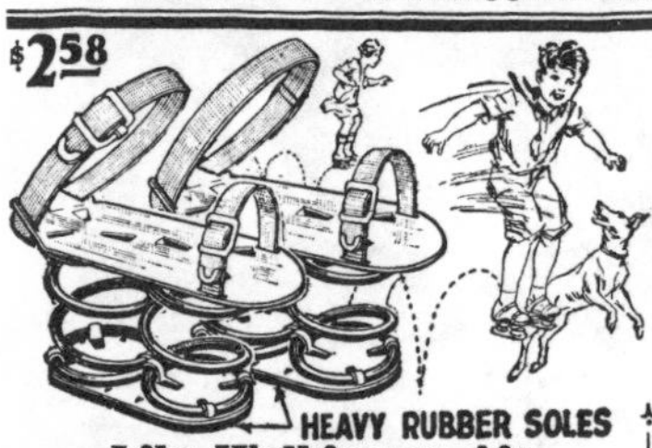
HEAVY RUBBER SOLES

## Like Walking on Air

***When You Wear Spring-Shus***

You'll feel like a slow motion movie with a pair of Spring-Shus on your feet! An athletic coach has said: "They bring stomach and leg muscles into healthful, active use." For running, dancing, jumping around and taking long steps like a giant. Perfectly safe. All steel with webbing straps. **Rubber** soles. Nickel trimmings. **We Pay Postage.**

48 E 1705—For child 6 to 8 yrs. of 45 to 60 lbs.
48 E 1706—For child 9 to 11 yrs. of 60 to 75 lbs.
48 E 1707—For child 12 to 15 yrs. of 75 to 100 lbs. Per pair, any size. . . . . . . . $2.58

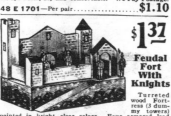

$1.10

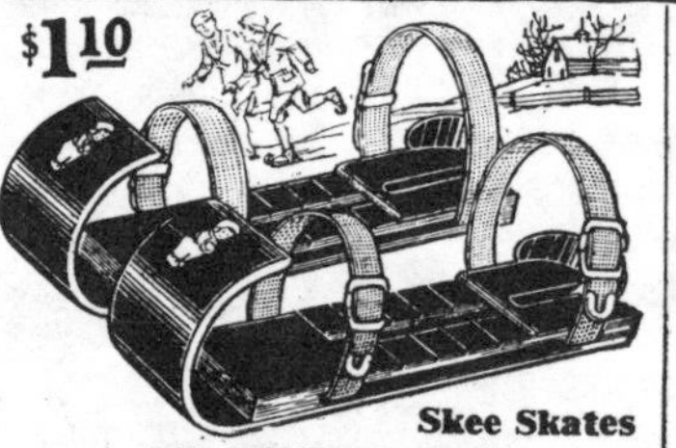

## Skee Skates

***Jolly Cold Weather Sport!***

Over the snow's crusted top you skim—down the hill in a long glorious slide! Rosy cheeks, bounding health—wholesome fun for the crisp days of winter! Designed for positive safety—constructed to withstand wear and weather. Skee Skates strengthen the ankles. Hardwood, steam bent at the front and grooved at the bottom, just like real skis for grown-ups. The foot-rest has web strap over toes and adjustable heel plate with six positions to fit firmly on shoes from 6 to 10 inches long, including sole. Web strap underneath heel plate holds foot firm. Can be worn with overshoes. Feet are always warm, dry and comfortable. **We Pay Postage.**

48 E 1701—Per pair. . . . . . . . . . . . . . . . . $1.10

## Snow Skates

***For Boys and Girls***

From the first real snowfall of winter until the last ice is melting from the sidewalks, you can use your Snow Skates! Invigorating sport for little folks—the smallest can skate with them. No ankle strain—marvelous exercise for leg muscles. A child can easily put them on or take them off. Light in weight and low set. Just the thing for skating on the slippery, snowy sidewalks when going to school. One size suitable for all.

### Use on Snow or Ice

Selected hardwood, with concave **steel shoe** nearly one inch wide fastened to heavy wood runner. The two edges of the steel shoe are fine on the ice and snow, the width and concave surface causes the snow to pack underneath runner, making them almost like skis. Hold up equally well on soft snow. Just tie them on with the rawhide thongs over leggings and overshoes. A rubber pad on the skates prevents foot slipping. Wonderful for teaching young children to skate. Ward's new shipping service speeds your order—no long delay! **We Pay Postage.**

48 E 1704—Per pair. . . . . $1.67

WE PAY POSTAGE

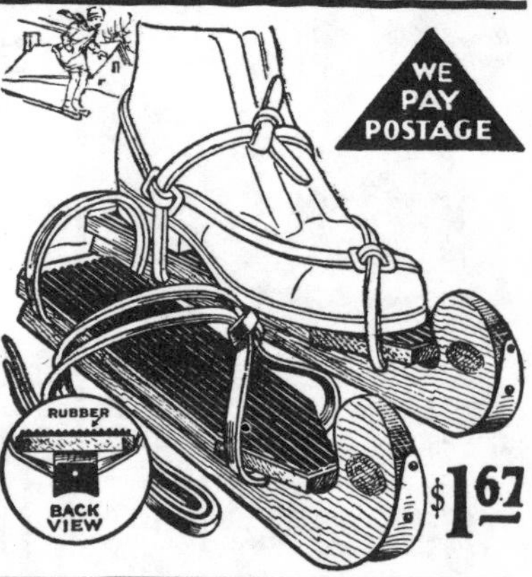
RUBBER
BACK VIEW

$1.67

## Children's Snowshoes

WE PAY POSTAGE

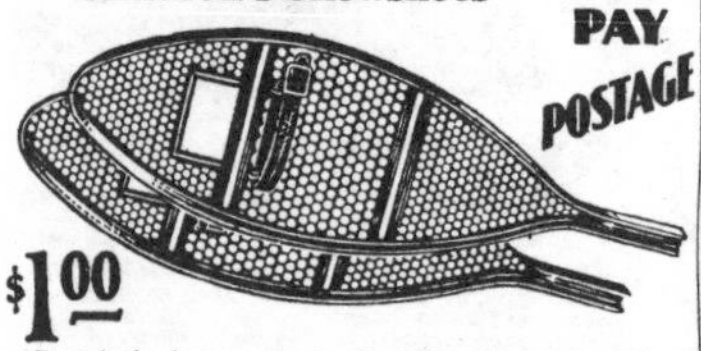

$1.00

Practical, low priced Snowshoes! An ingenious manufacturer conceived the idea of making them from light weight metal—sharply cutting the price on this ordinarily expensive toy. Perforations in soles of snow shoes make them almost as light as the wooden frame woven shoe. Loads of fun—they easily hold weight of child on top of very soft snow. Very easy to put on and take off. Enameled bright red; web straps for attaching. Length 22¼ inches; width 7⅞ inches. Large enough for children 6 to 13 years. **We Pay Postage.**

48 E 1711—Per pair. . . . . . . . . . . . . . . . $1.00

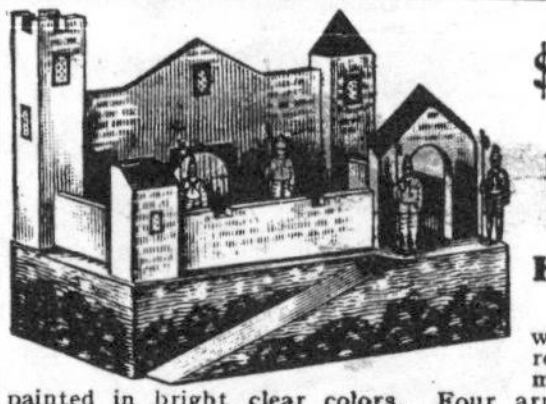

$1.37

## Feudal Fort With Knights

Turreted wood Fortress (3 dummy towers) painted in bright clear colors. Four armored lead knights. Movable arms carry long pointed lances. Size of Fort set up; length 10½ in.; height 8 inches; width 7½ inches. Easily assembled or taken apart when fort is put away. Knights with lances, each 3 inches high. Additional knights listed below.

48 E 827—Fort and 4 knights. **We Pay Postage** . . . . . . . . . . $1.37
48 E 829—**Extra knights**; five in all; 4 foot-soldiers as above, and one on horseback (height 3¼ inches.) **We Pay Postage** . . . . . . . . . . 59¢

***Wood Bullets***

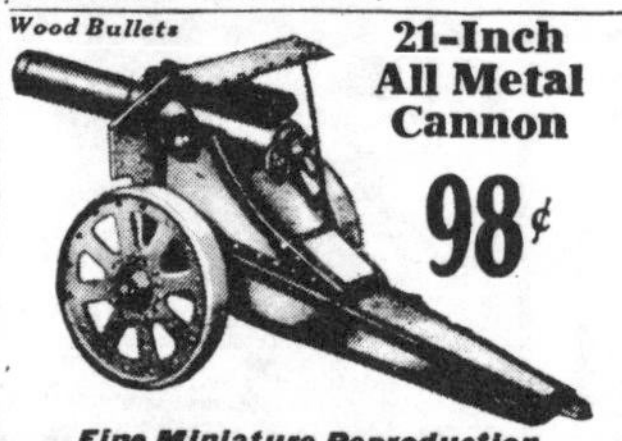

## 21-Inch All Metal Cannon

98¢

***Fine Miniature Reproduction***

Joint bolt heads and rivets embossed on sides. Realistic coloring. Bullet shield in front; spring mechanism. Pull back plunger, drop wooden bullet in muzzle, release plunger and bullet is propelled 6 or 8 feet. 21 in. long; 8 in. high; 8 in. wide. About 12 wood bullets. **We Pay Postage.**

48 E 836. . . . . . . . . . . . . . . . . . . . 98¢

## Miniature Army—Complete

**Only $1.00**

Metal Army complete—ammunition and kitchen wagons; cannon; ambulance and lead soldiers; 5 infantrymen each 1⅝ in. high; 3 soldiers on horseback, each 1⅞ by 1½ in. Riding driver on each wagon; ambulance and kitchen each 5 in. long; 3½-inch gun carriage—all drawn by teams of horses; 3¼-inch cannon; spring trigger; shoots peas or wads of paper. All vehicles green with gray wheels. **We Pay Postage.**

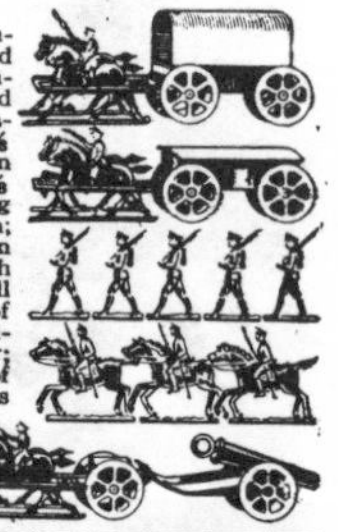

48 E 856 Set. . . $1.00

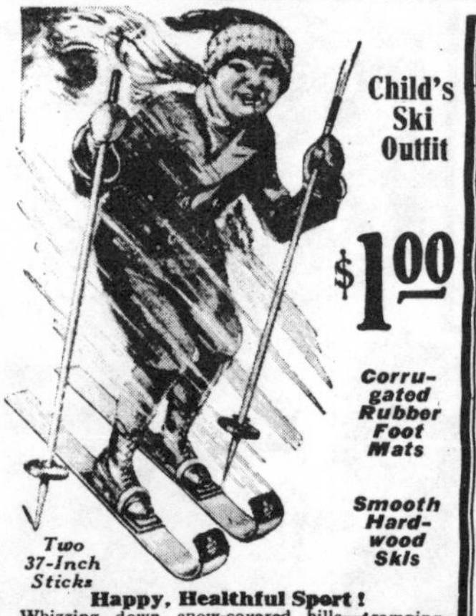
Two 37-Inch Sticks

## Child's Ski Outfit

$1.00

***Corrugated Rubber Foot Mats***

***Smooth Hardwood Skis***

**Happy, Healthful Sport!**

Whizzing down snow-covered hills—tramping back with aid of the two supporting sticks. This outfit is scaled down in size to make skiing easy for youthful amateurs. Skis are of smooth finished, varnished hardwood, 21¼ by 2⅜ inches wide. Corrugated rubber mat for foot on slightly built-up platform. Web harness strap for holding ski firmly to shoe. Two poles, each 37 inches long. Supporting movable ring at bottom is 3 inches in diam. Each pole finished with wrist strap at top. A set that means healthful outdoor exercise for little folks during cold, invigorating winter weather. Our great buying power brings you a substantial saving. **We Pay Postage.**

448 E 1702—Set of 2 skis and 2 poles . $1.00

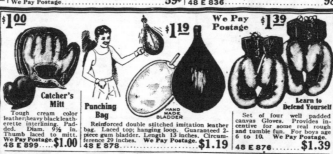

We Pay Postage

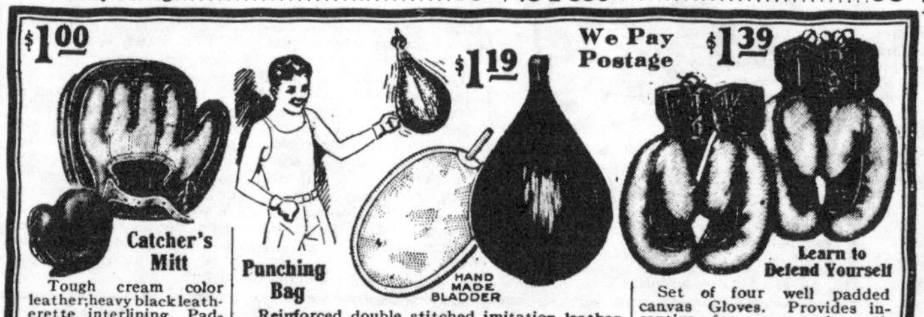
HAND MADE BLADDER

$1.00 **Catcher's Mitt**

Tough cream color leather; heavy black leatherette interlining. Padded. Diam. 9½ in. Thumb laced to mitt. **We Pay Postage.**

48 E 899. . . . $1.00

$1.19 **Punching Bag**

Reinforced double stitched imitation leather bag. Laced top; hanging loop. Guaranteed 2-piece gum bladder. Length 13 inches. Circumference 29 inches. **We Pay Postage.**

48 E 878. . . . . . . . . . . . . . . . . . . . $1.19

$1.39 **Learn to Defend Yourself**

Set of four well padded canvas Gloves. Provides incentive for some real rough and tumble fun. For boys age 6 to 10. **We Pay Postage.**

48 E 876. . . . . . . $1.39

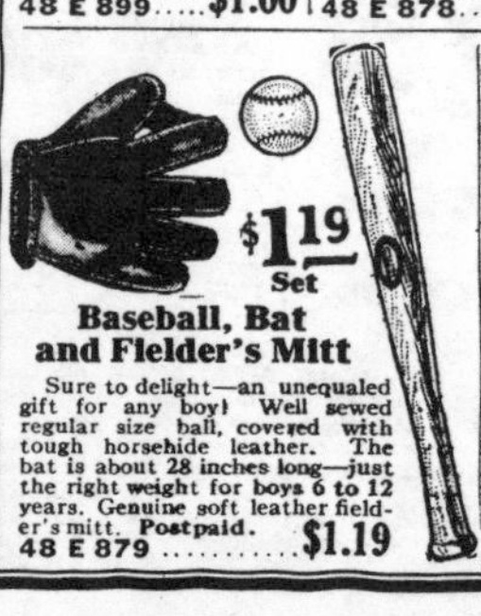

$1.19 Set

### Baseball, Bat and Fielder's Mitt

Sure to delight—an unequaled gift for any boy! Well sewed regular size ball, covered with tough horsehide leather. The bat is about 28 inches long—just the right weight for boys 6 to 12 years. Genuine soft leather fielder's mitt. **Postpaid.**

48 E 879 . . . . . . . . . . $1.19

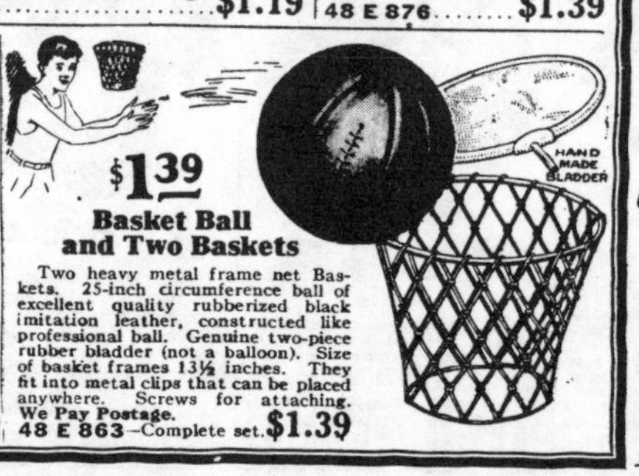
HAND MADE BLADDER

$1.39

### Basket Ball and Two Baskets

Two heavy metal frame net Baskets. 25-inch circumference ball of excellent quality rubberized black imitation leather, constructed like professional ball. Genuine two-piece rubber bladder (not a balloon). Size of basket frames 13½ inches. They fit into metal clips that can be placed anywhere. Screws for attaching. **We Pay Postage.**

48 E 863—Complete set. $1.39

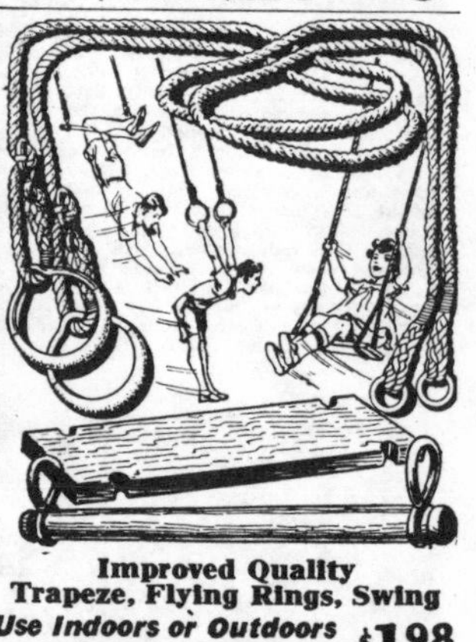

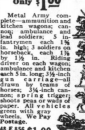

### Improved Quality Trapeze, Flying Rings, Swing

***Use Indoors or Outdoors***

**3-Piece Set** $1.98

Made to capture the child's interest—designed for absolute safety—a constant source of healthful fun! Fine pure white imported manila rope with ends woven in. Length 8 feet. (Two feet longer than others). Swinging rings are made of ⅜-inch polished steel; padded grips covered with selected leather (not scraps). Smoothly sanded white hardwood trapeze bar 1¼-inch diameter; heavy steel attaching rings sunk in to prevent slipping. Swing board 18¾ by 4⅝ inches; 11/16 inch thick. Amply strong for 200-pound man. **We Pay Postage.**

48 E 4050—Complete set. . . . . . . . . $1.98

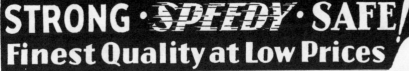

# STRONG · SPEEDY · SAFE!
## Finest Quality at Low Prices

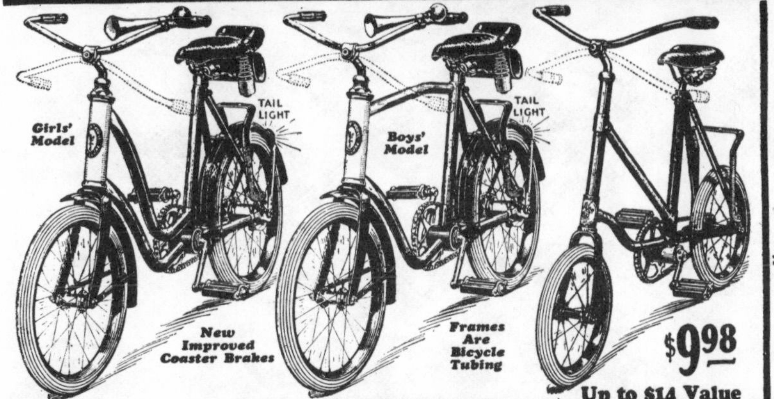
Girls' Model
Tail Light
Boys' Model
Tail Light
New Improved Coaster Brakes
Frames Are Bicycle Tubing

$19.89 Each

**For Boys or Girls**

**Order Parkcycles and Velocipedes according to measurement of child from crotch to ball of foot.**

### De Luxe "Hawthorne" Sidewalk Bikes

Fnest quality. Very safe even for the smaller children because of the 14-inch wheels which keep the feet close to the ground. Strongly constructed. Frame is of the regular bicycle type, 1-inch tubing. Easy riding leather bicycle saddle with double coil nickel-plated springs—can be adjusted to increase the leg length from 23 to 26 inches. Leather tool kit. Mudguards front and rear. Imported motorcycle horn. 14½-inch wheels with brightly nickeled spokes and hubs. New Departure Coaster Brake.

Extra heavy 1⅛-inch rubber tires. ¾-inch nickel-plated handlebars can be adjusted to suit. Ball-bearing rubber pedals. Nickel-plated, ball-bearing crank hangers and sprocket wheel. "Take-up" bicycle chain. Bikes geared low for perfect safety. Beautifully finished in red and white with handsome nickel-plated fittings. Shipped with handlebars, pedals and saddle detached. Ship. wt. 37 lbs. **Not mailable.**

**148 E 1846**—For Boys. Bar runs from steering post straight to saddle.......... **$19.89**

**148 E 1847**—For Girls. Brace runs from top of steering post to bottom of seat post.......... **$19.89**

$9.98

**Up to $14 Value**
***Note Strong Brace!***

Neither strength nor quality have been sacrificed to make this low price. Most stores ask $14 for equal quality. Large enough for children from 5 to 9 years of age. Handlebars adjustable from 31 to 33 inches; saddle from 26½ to 28½ inches from lowest pedal. Double brace backbone same as the higher priced Parkcycles. Tubular frame enameled red. Nickel-plated tubular handlebars diameter ¾ inch; rubber grips; ball-bearing crank; rubber pedals. The 11½-inch wheels have 1-inch rubber tires. Real leather saddle; coil springs. Entire length 42 inches. Ship. wt. 30 pounds. **Not mailable.**

**148 E 1835**...... **$9.98**

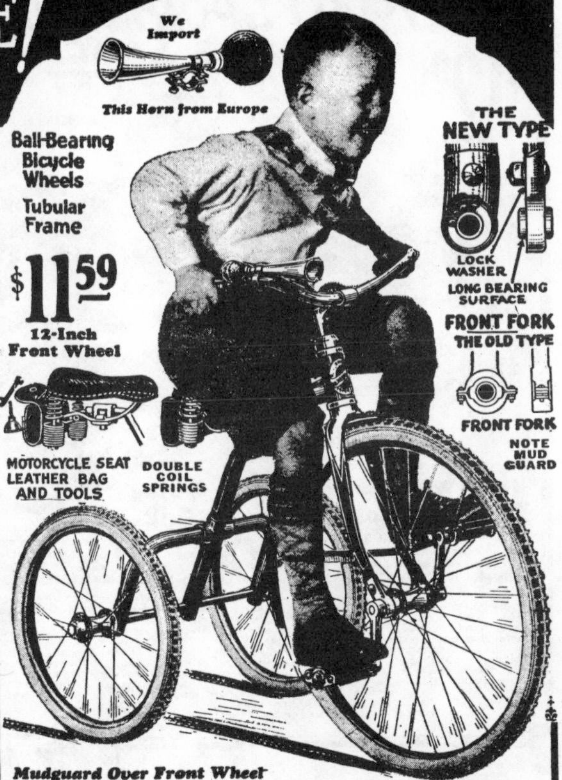
We Import
This Horn from Europe
Ball-Bearing Bicycle Wheels
Tubular Frame
$11.59
12-Inch Front Wheel
THE NEW TYPE
LOCK WASHER
LONG BEARING SURFACE
FRONT FORK
THE OLD TYPE
FRONT FORK
NOTE MUD GUARD
MOTORCYCLE SEAT
LEATHER BAG AND TOOLS
DOUBLE COIL SPRINGS
Mudguard Over Front Wheel

### Finest Velocipede We've Ever Seen

***See This Velocipede in Colors on Page 2***

STRONG! So strong its frame will carry 500 pounds weight—its wheels bear up 200 pounds before bowing and then spring back to true! Same sturdy strength at every point—a Velocipede built to stand the wear a husky youngster gives the toy he loves best and uses most. For nearly twelve years we have sold it. This manufacturer because he insisted on QUALITY first, today leads the world in fine velocipede production devoting three huge modern factories to production of children's wheel toys. He sells to no other retail mail order house. This same velocipede, his finest, costs at least $5 more at most other stores. This velocipede is featured in the finest department stores.

### It Pays to Buy Quality!

Frame of 1-inch seamless tubing, hand-brazed joints. Joints are malleable castings, ground smooth as steel with shanks ¼ to ½ inch longer than on most velocipedes. Three arms to rear axle add strength. Handlebar post with sharp angle of real bicycle. Handlebars, nickel-plated over copper, are ¾-inch tubing and are fitted with motor-cycle rubber grips. Imported nickel-plated motorcycle horn included. Heavily padded bicycle Troxel saddle with double coil, nickel-plated springs; leather tool bag and tools. Rust-proof spokes; 1¼-inch selected quality corrugated rubber tires with new molded auto type treads. Heavily nickel-plated ball-bearing crank hangers with ball-bearing rubber pedals. Nickel spearpoints on fork crown.

The new type curved front fork is a malleable casting, and will never break. The ball-bearing retainers in the shapely concave hubs have the same long inner sleeves as found on bicycles and prevent "wobbly" wheels. Ball-bearings in front wheel are held fast by special construction—won't lose off because of some nut dropping off. Heavy steel mudguard on front wheel. Beautifully finished in Nile green baked-on enamel, with tangerine head. Measurements taken with saddle at lowest point. Measure child from crotch to instep. When comparing prices be sure to notice wheel sizes—Ours Are Larger. Two smallest sizes are mailable. We Pay Postage.

| Article Number | Diameter Front Wheel | Diameter Rear Wheel | Saddle to Lowest Pedal | Ship. Wt. Lbs. | Each |
|---|---|---|---|---|---|
| 448 E 1900 | 12 inches | 10 inches | 17 to 19 in. | Post | $11.59 |
| 448 E 1901 | 16 inches | 12 inches | 18 to 20 in. | Paid | 12.85 |
| 148 E 1902 | 20 inches | 14 inches | 19 to 21 in. | 32 | 13.98 |
| 148 E 1903 | 24 inches | 16 inches | 21½ to 23½ in. | 39 | 15.65 |

***We Pay Postage!***

### High Quality Scooters—We Pay Postage
*Immediate Shipment*

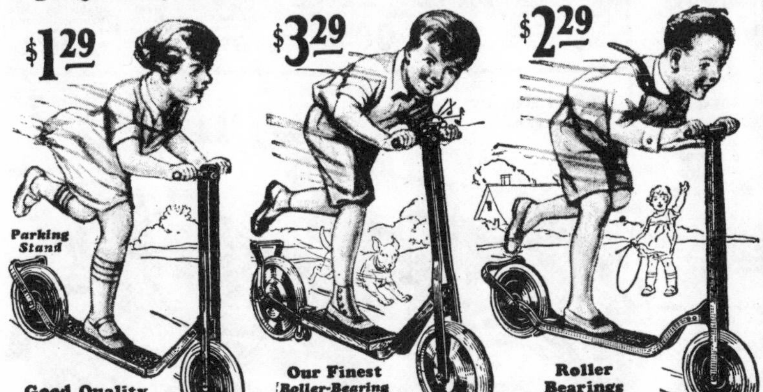
$1.29
Parking Stand
$3.29
$2.29

**Good Quality**
***Steel Wheels Rubber Tires and Tread***

Large enough for a 9-year-old child. Steel frame with underslung bridge construction supporting steel platform. Rubber non-skid step mat. Height of adjustable handlebars up to 26 in.; length 31½ in. Steel wheels 7¾ in. in diameter with ½-in. rubber tires. Parking stand. Red frame; yellow wheels. **We Pay Postage.**

448 E 1864.............. **$1.29**

**Our Finest**
***Roller-Bearing Wheels***
***1-Inch Tires***

Same wheels as on Road Test Wagon, on Page 436. Heavy underslung steel frame. Hardwood platform 5 by 12½ inches with non-skid rubber mat. Safety brake; convenient parking stand. Adjustable handle. Bicycle bell. Black frame; red wheels. Entire length 38 in.; height 31½ in. **We Pay Postage.**

448 E 1876.............. **$3.29**

**Roller Bearings**
***Parking Stand and Brake***

Steel frame with underslung bridge construction. Height 29¾ inches; length 33¾ inches (not including the sturdy parking stand). Roller bearing 8-inch wheels with 11/16-inch rubber tires. Rubber mat on foot platform. Practical footbrake. **We Pay Postage.**

448 E 1862.............. **$2.29**

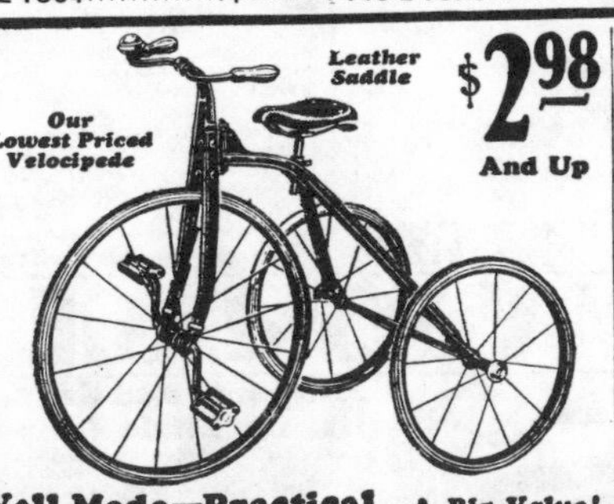
Our Lowest Priced Velocipede
Leather Saddle

$2.98 And Up

### Well Made—Practical *A Big Value!*

Concentrated value. Real leather saddle; strong double spoke wire wheels with **½-inch front and rear rubber tires.** Nickel-plated hub caps and bell. Handlebars with wood grips. Frame of heavy half oval steel, ⅞ inch wide. Malleable cast head. Beautifully finished in black enamel. Bright red wheels. Only two smallest sizes mailable. Shipped taken apart to save freight. Easy to assemble. Measurements taken with saddle at lowest point; can be raised 2 inches. Measure child from crotch to instep. **Two smallest sizes are mailable. We Pay Postage.**

| Article Number | Diam. Front Wheel | Diam. Back Wheel | Saddle to Lowest Pedal | Ship. Wt. | Each |
|---|---|---|---|---|---|
| 448 E 1866 | 14 in. | 9 in. | 15 to 17 in. | Post- | $2.98 |
| 448 E 1867 | 16 in. | 12 in. | 16 to 18 in. | paid | 3.59 |
| 148 E 1868 | 20 in. | 14 in. | 17 to 19 in. | 22 lbs. | 4.48 |
| 148 E 1869 | 24 in. | 16 in. | 20 to 22 in. | 27 lbs. | 5.48 |

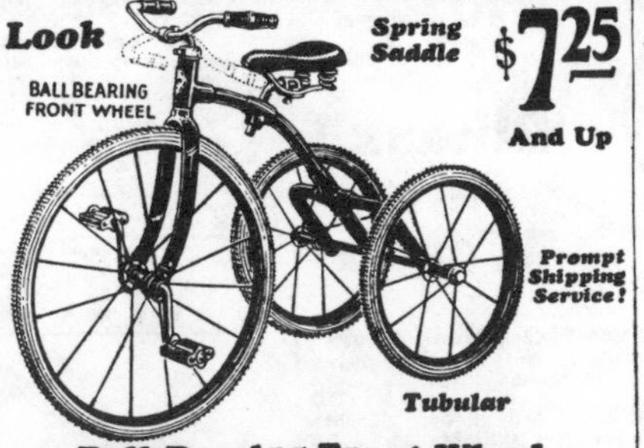
Look
Spring Saddle
BALLBEARING FRONT WHEEL
Prompt Shipping Service!
Tubular

$7.25 And Up

### Ball-Bearing Front Wheel

**The front wheel has fine bicycle ball bearings.** Rear wheels are plain bearing. **Seamless tubular frame;** hand-brazed joints with malleable castings at all junctions. Long shanks hold brazings permanently fast. One-inch rubber tires with new cut thread tread. Beautifully finished in Yale blue enamel. Nickel-plated handlebars, coil springs and hub caps. Spokes and tire rims new bright rust-proof finish. Coil spring saddle and handlebars adjustable about 2½ inches, allowing for growth of child. Rubber hand grips and pedals. **Two smallest sizes are mailable. We Pay Postage.**

| Article Number | Diameter Front Wheel | Saddle to Lowest Pedal | Shipping Weight | Each |
|---|---|---|---|---|
| 448 E 1916 | 12 in. | 17 to 19 in. | Post- | $ 7.25 |
| 448 E 1917 | 16 in. | 18 to 20 in. | paid | 8.75 |
| 148 E 1918 | 20 in. | 19 to 21 in. | 31 lbs. | 9.98 |
| 148 E 1919 | 24 in. | 21½ to 23½ in. | 34 lbs. | 11.45 |

$8.95 And Up

***De Luxe Equipment***

**Standard Quality Everywhere**

***Our Prices Deserve Your Order***

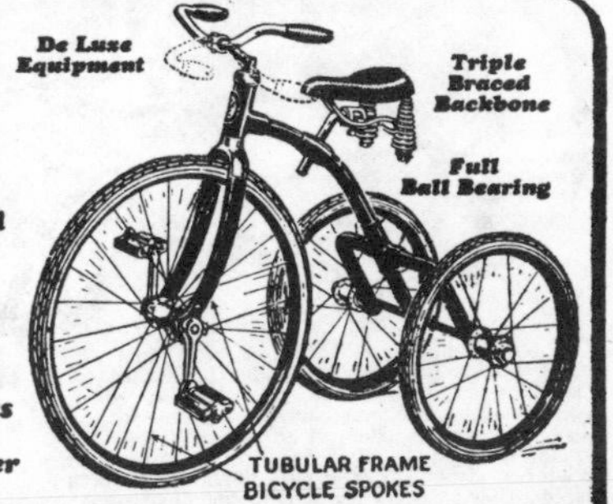
Triple Braced Backbone
Full Ball Bearing
TUBULAR FRAME
BICYCLE SPOKES

This is the tubular, full ball-bearing Velocipede many merchants call best. Sells under a nationally famous name at much higher prices. Seamless bicycle tubing. Drop-forged cranks. Ball-bearing pedals. Curved fork; nickel-crowned. Nickel-plated hub caps; black hard rubber hand grips and a fine quality double coil spring bicycle saddle. Adjustable nickel-plated handlebars ⅝ inch in diameter. Enameled blue with yellow striping. Sturdy wire wheels have bicycle type rust-proof spokes with screw tension nipples and are equipped with **1¼-inch auto tread rubber tires. Two smallest sizes are mailable. We Pay Postage.**

| Article Number | Diameter Front Wheel | Saddle to Lowest Pedal | Shipping Weight | Each |
|---|---|---|---|---|
| 448 E 1910 | 14 inches | 17 to 19 in. | Post- | $ 8.95 |
| 448 E 1911 | 16 inches | 18 to 20 in. | paid | 10.29 |
| 148 E 1912 | 20 inches | 19 to 21 in. | 32 lbs. | 11.25 |
| 148 E 1913 | 24 inches | 21½ to 23½ in. | 35 lbs. | 12.98 |

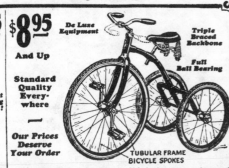

# 1930 Sport Model
## Long Snappy Lines

**$19.98** Most Stores Ask $22.50 to $25.00

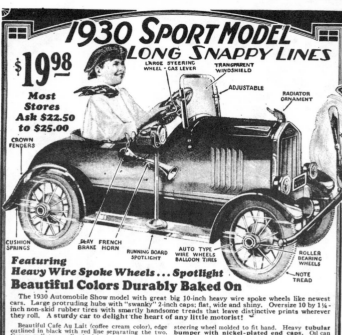

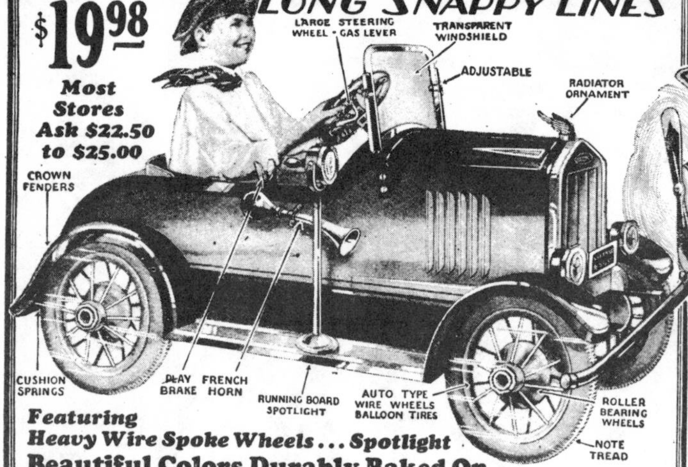
LARGE STEERING WHEEL - GAS LEVER
TRANSPARENT WINDSHIELD
ADJUSTABLE
RADIATOR ORNAMENT
CROWN FENDERS
CUSHION SPRINGS
PLAY BRAKE
FRENCH HORN
RUNNING BOARD SPOTLIGHT
AUTO TYPE WIRE WHEELS BALLOON TIRES
ROLLER BEARING WHEELS
NOTE TREAD

***Featuring Heavy Wire Spoke Wheels . . . Spotlight***

### Beautiful Colors Durably Baked On

The 1930 Automobile Show model with great big 10-inch heavy wire spoke wheels like newest cars. Large protruding hubs with "swanky" 2-inch caps; flat, wide and shiny. Oversize 10 by 1¼-inch non-skid rubber tires with smartly handsome treads that leave distinctive prints wherever they roll. **A sturdy car to delight the heart of any little motorist!**

Beautiful Cafe Au Lait (coffee cream color), edge outlined in black with red line separating the two. Cream radiator outlined with aluminum band. Yellow spokes in wheels. Finish BAKED on all metal parts. Black die pressed steel crown fenders. Wood running board with nickel-plated metal binding. Red leatherette upholstery. Strikingly distinctive running board; nickel-plated spotlight. Hexagonal drum headlights, real glass lenses. Adjustable windshield. Aluminum motometer. Speedometer with revolving dial. Play brake. Loud, rubber bulb imported horn. Nine-inch rubberized composition steering wheel molded to fit hand. Heavy **tubular bumper with nickel-plated end caps.** Oil can clipped inside hood. Easy riding cushion springs. Heavy gauge auto body steel tonneau. FULL ROLLER BEARING WHEELS. Length about 45 inches; height to top of windshield 26¾ inches. Center of seat to pedal at lowest point 19¼ inches—this measurement corresponds to child's inseam from crotch to instep. For children 6 to 11 years old. Shipping weight 65 pounds. **Not mailable.**

**148 E 1828** .......................... **$19.98**

# "Spirit of St. Louis" Improved Design

**Your Choice $10.98**

## "Air Pilot" New Model Monoplane

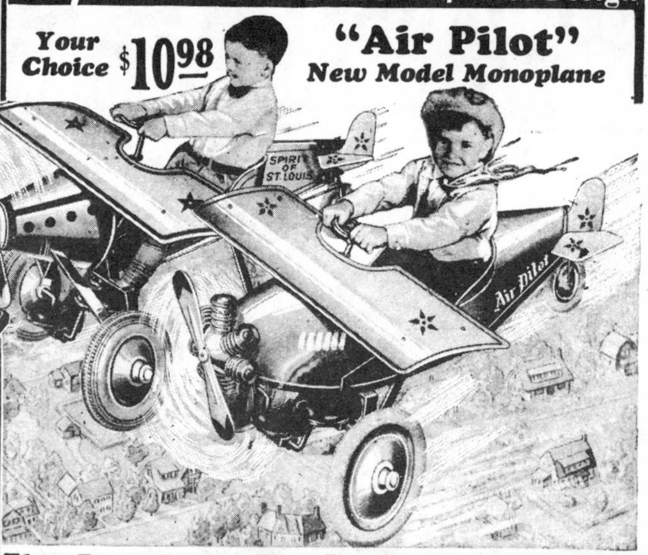
SPIRIT OF ST. LOUIS
Air Pilot

## They Don't Really Fly...But Oh, How They Go!

An improved model of the famous **"Spirit of St. Louis"** Riding Airplane. Built like a beautiful monoplane. Real airplane type balloon front wheels. Sides of the 10½-inch auto steel disc wheels are die pressed to look like heavy 2-inch balloon tires; 1-inch heavy tread rubber tires. Nickel-plated hub caps. 7¾-inch rear wheel has ⅝-inch tire. Built to ride straddle—no bumping of shins at high speed.

**Front drive axle floats in ball bearings** for smooth, easy riding. Has 29¼-inch wing spread; 52 inches long over all; 27 in. to top of steering wheel. Body is cut from lumber 1 inch thick and 13 inches wide. Tapering in long graceful lines—exceptionally strong. Elevators, rudder wings and radiator front are auto body steel. Steel propeller turns freely. Rubber pedals. Play gas lever. Beautiful aluminum finish trimmed in red; aluminum elevators, rudder and wings. Red and blue star on each wing. Oil can and oil. Suitable size for children with 20 to 24-inch inseam. Shipping weight 45 pounds.

**148 E 1823**—**Not mailable** .... **$10.98**

**Latest model "Air Pilot"** built with rotary type motor in front. This big plane with inclosed type body is roomy enough for a large boy. 18 inches from center of seat to pedal at lowest point; 50½ inches long overall; 29½-inch wing spread. Heavy gauge auto body steel. Wings strongly reinforced underneath—will bear weight of child without bending. Guide this plane through the rear wheel which turns from side to side as controlled by the steering wheel. Wing on tail also moves with steering wheel. Metal propeller is not large enough to hurt a child. Moves freely, but not geared to wheels.

Airplane is fitted with 3 double disc steel wheels. Two in front are 10 inches in diameter; ⅝-inch cushion rubber tires. Rear wheel has ½-inch cushion rubber tire. Finished in bright red enamel, baked on. Green wings and trim; yellow propeller. Rotary cylinders on motor are black. Steering wheel fitted with gas lever. Operate plane by using pedals which are on front axle and give direct control. Suitable for child with inseam measuring 18 to 24 inches. Shipped partly taken apart to save you freight. Shipping weight 45 pounds.

**148 E 1827**—**Not mailable** ... **$10.98**

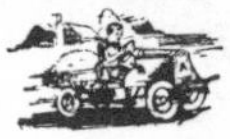

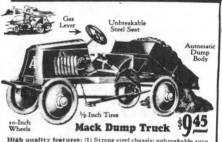

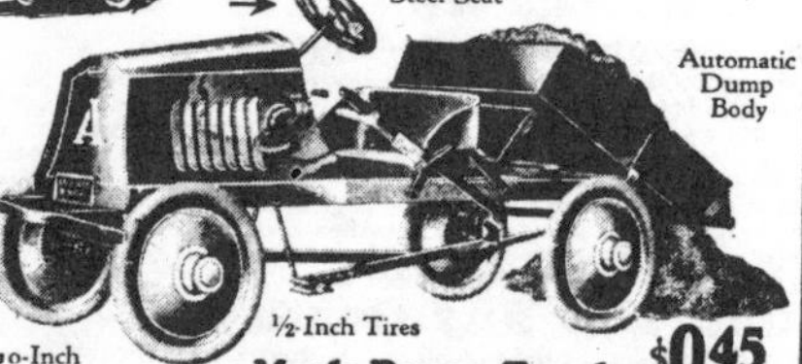
Gas Lever
Unbreakable Steel Seat
Automatic Dump Body
½-Inch Tires
10-Inch Wheels

## Mack Dump Truck $9.45

**High quality features:** (1) Strong steel chassis; unbreakable auto body steel seat and dump box. (2) **10-inch** double disc steel wheels; ½-inch rubber tires; nickel-plated hub caps. (3) Equipped with real bumper, loud horn, gas lever, license plate, radiator name plate, rubber pedals. Enameled bright red with yellow striping. Black dump box. Size over all 20 by 43 inches. Length center of seat to pedal 18 inches. Dump box 13½ by 13½ inches. Shipped taken apart to save freight. Ship. wt. 80 lbs. **Not mailable.**

**148 E 1824** .............................. **$9.45**

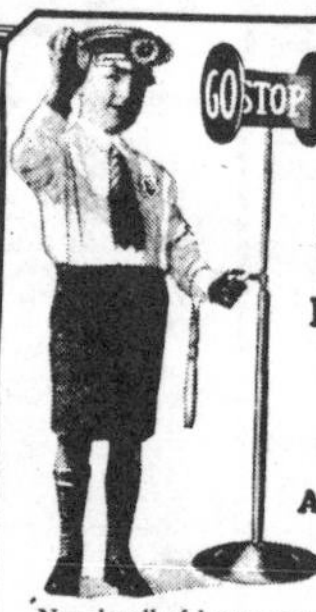
GO STOP

## Toy Traffic Signal $1.19 Postpaid

**Turn Handle and Signal Automatically Changes**

Nearly all of heavy steel, enameled bright green and red with yellow lettering. 9¼-inch metal base enameled black. Width at top 8¾ in.; height 34½ in. Policeman's outfit on Page 428. **We Pay Postage.**

**448 E 1844** ........... **$1.19**

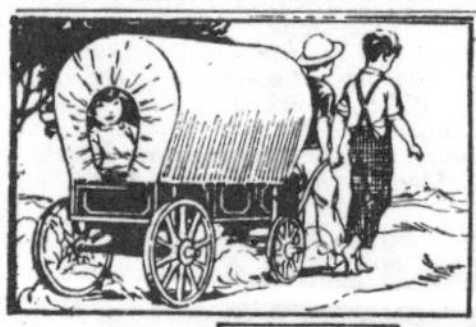

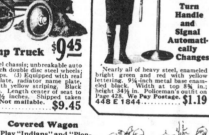

## Covered Wagon

**Play "Indians" and "Pioneers." Buy the wagon with weather-proof khaki cover and detachable steel bows—quickly transformed into a regular covered wagon like those used in pioneer days.**

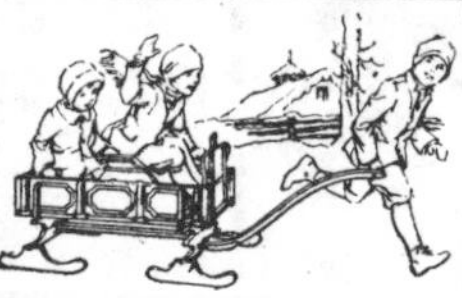

*With Sled Runners*

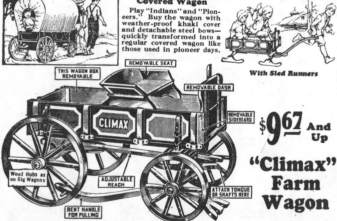

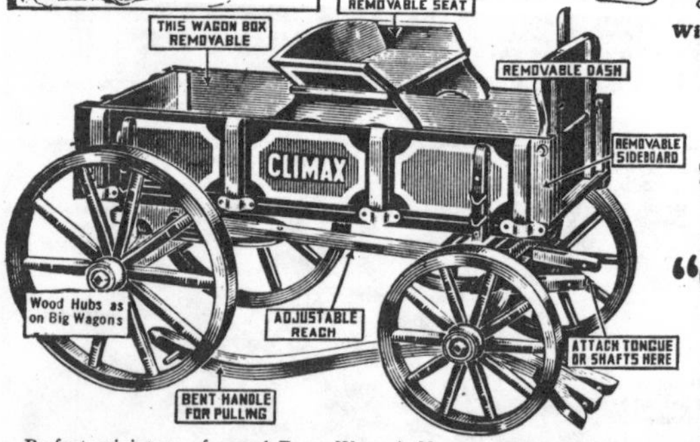
THIS WAGON BOX REMOVABLE
REMOVABLE SEAT
REMOVABLE DASH
REMOVABLE SIDEBOARD
CLIMAX
Wood Hubs as on Big Wagons
ADJUSTABLE REACH
ATTACH TONGUE OR SHAFTS HERE
BENT HANDLE FOR PULLING

## $9.67 And Up "Climax" Farm Wagon

Perfect miniature of a real Farm Wagon! No detail to make it an exact reproduction is omitted. Chores magically become play—hauling wood, doing errands—each one a different game with the aid of this wagon. Best of all you can use it the whole year 'round. With the first good snowfall of winter, attach the steel-shod hardwood runners listed below. Shafts for harnessing dog or goat can also be bought separately. Enormous purchases year after year enable us to offer the **Climax** Farm Wagon at rock bottom prices!

***Enameled in Bright, Lasting Colors***

Kiln dried hardwood, lastingly enameled red and green. Seat, sides, endgate and bottom are removable at will. Gearing with bent hounds and adjustable reach. All parts strongly ironed and braced. Electrically welded heavy steel tires shrunk on to the wood by hydraulic pressure. Steel bushings; wood hubs; staggered spokes. ½-inch steel axles. 14-inch front wheels; 20-inch rear wheels.

**With Bows and Water-Proof Covers**

**148 E 1641**—Size of bed 18 by 36 inches. Shipping weight 53 pounds. **Not mailable** ........ **$11.55**

**148 E 1643**—Size of bed 18 by 40 inches. Ship. weight 56 lbs. **Not mailable** .. **$12.55**

**Without Bows or Covers**

**148 E 1651**—Size of bed 18 by 36 inches. Shipping weight 52 pounds. **Not mailable** ........ **$9.67**

**148 E 1653**—Size of bed 18 by 40 inches. Ship. wt. 53 lbs. **Not mailable** ..... **$10.67**

**Hardwood Shafts for Goat or Dog**

For any of these wagons. **We Pay Postage.**

**448 E 1655** ................ **$1.62**

**Hardwood Steel-Shod Sled Runners**

To fit these wagons. **We Pay Postage.**

**448 E 1673**—Set of 4 ........... **$2.95**

**Dog or Goat Harness on Page 436**

***With Roller Bearings***

**$12.50**

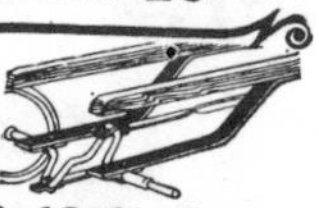

***Real Cushion Springs In Rear***

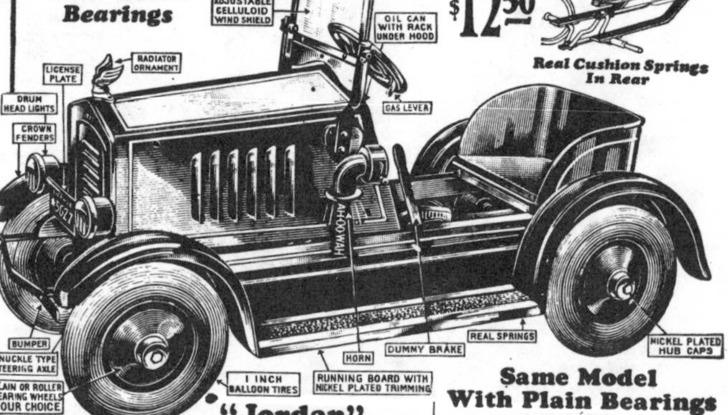
ADJUSTABLE CELLULOID WIND SHIELD
OIL CAN WITH RACK UNDER HOOD
RADIATOR ORNAMENT
LICENSE PLATE
DRUM HEAD LIGHTS
CROWN FENDERS
GAS LEVER
BUMPER
KNUCKLE TYPE STEERING AXLE
PLAIN OR ROLLER BEARING WHEELS YOUR CHOICE
1 INCH BALLOON TIRES
RUNNING BOARD WITH NICKEL PLATED TRIMMING
HORN
DUMMY BRAKE
REAL SPRINGS
NICKEL PLATED HUB CAPS

## "Jordan"

Off for a spin—and oh boy! how she "holds the road." Finished in every detail to delight a boy. New balloon type 10¼-inch steel wheels; 1-inch rubber tires. Steel sides of wheels shaped to look like 2-inch tires. Roller bearings. Sheet steel body and wheels are Yale blue with sky blue panels and yellow trim. Fenders, horn, headlights, steering wheel, undergearing and springs are enameled lustrous black. Cushion springs.

***Fine Construction Features***

Supported throughout with steel braces. Drum headlights, license plates, bumper, aluminum motometer. Steel radiator front; Jordan nameplate. Adjustable, transparent windshield. Dummy brake; shelf with clip and oil can inside hood. Front wheels on knuckle type steering axles. To top of windshield 26 inches; length overall 40½ inches. Rubber pedals with 2-inch adjustment to fit growing children with inseam of 20 to 22½ inches. Shipped taken apart to save you freight; easily assembled. Shipping weight 56 pounds. **Not mailable.**

**148 E 1808** ........................... **$12.50**

## Same Model With Plain Bearings

Another up-to-the-minute model sure to make a big hit with every youngster. Similar in practically every detail to the car pictured above. Has all of the special features except that it has regular (not balloon type) 10-inch double disc steel wheels with plain bearings; ½-inch corrugated rubber tires. Only auto body sheet steel is used, (no scraps) and best workmanship throughout. Guaranteed to stand close inspection and to run perfectly. Shipped taken apart to save you freight. Ship. wt. 50 pounds. **Not mailable.**

**148 E 1815** .......... **$11.45**

***Ward's Speeds Delivery!***

# WE PAY POSTAGE

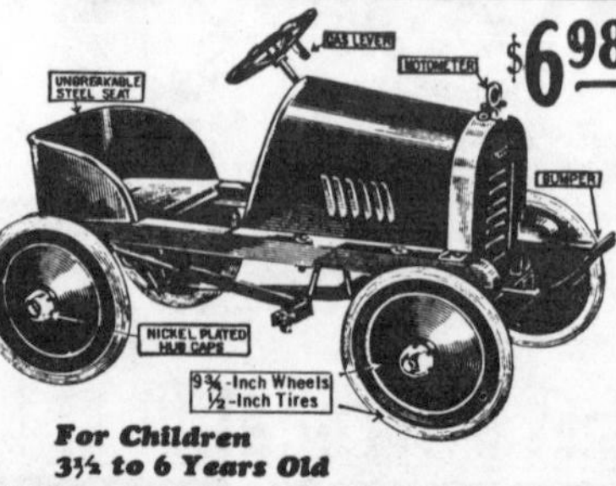
GAS LEVER
MOTOMETER
UNBREAKABLE STEEL SEAT
BUMPER
NICKEL PLATED HUB CAPS
9¾-Inch Wheels ½-Inch Tires

***For Children 3½ to 6 Years Old***

**$6.98**

## Sporty Red Roadster for Little Fellows

Light sturdy construction. Enameled brilliant red, trimmed in yellow. Steel radiator, hood, seat and running gear. Front wheels are on knuckle type steering axle. Dummy gas lever. Steel bumper; nickel-plated hub caps. Height to top of steering wheel 22 inches. Length over all 34½ inches. Shipped partly taken apart to save you freight. Length from center of seat to pedal at farthest point 16½ inches.

**Disc Wheel Model**

Has 9¾-inch steel disc wheels; ½-inch corrugated rubber tires. Ship. wt. 36 lbs. **Not mailable.**

**148 E 1831** .............. **$6.98**

**Spoke Wheel Model**

Has 9¾-inch double spoke steel wheels; ⅝-inch corrugated rubber tires. Ship. wt. 33 lbs. **Not mailable.**

**148 E 1832** .............. **$5.75**